Present and Future of Gravitational Wave Astronomy

Present and Future of Gravitational Wave Astronomy

Editor

Gabriele Vajente

MDPI • Basel • Beijing • Wuhan • Barcelona • Belgrade • Manchester • Tokyo • Cluj • Tianjin

Editor
Gabriele Vajente
California Institute of Technology
USA

Editorial Office
MDPI
St. Alban-Anlage 66
4052 Basel, Switzerland

This is a reprint of articles from the Special Issue published online in the open access journal *Galaxies* (ISSN 2075-4434) (available at: https://www.mdpi.com/journal/galaxies/special_issues/pfgwa).

For citation purposes, cite each article independently as indicated on the article page online and as indicated below:

LastName, A.A.; LastName, B.B.; LastName, C.C. Article Title. *Journal Name* **Year**, *Volume Number*, Page Range.

ISBN 978-3-0365-5225-5 (Hbk)
ISBN 978-3-0365-5226-2 (PDF)

Cover image courtesy of Gabriele Vajente

© 2022 by the authors. Articles in this book are Open Access and distributed under the Creative Commons Attribution (CC BY) license, which allows users to download, copy and build upon published articles, as long as the author and publisher are properly credited, which ensures maximum dissemination and a wider impact of our publications.

The book as a whole is distributed by MDPI under the terms and conditions of the Creative Commons license CC BY-NC-ND.

Contents

Gabriele Vajente
Present and Future of Gravitational Wave Astronomy
Reprinted from: *Galaxies* 2022, 10, 91, doi:10.3390/galaxies10040091 1

Homare Abe, Tomotada Akutsu, Masaki Ando, Akito Araya, Naoki Aritomi, Hideki Asada, Yoichi Aso, Sangwook Bae, Rishabh Bajpai, Kipp Cannon, Zhoujian Cao, Eleonora Capocasa, Man Leong Chan, Dan Chen, Yi-Ru Chen, Marc Eisenmann, Raffaele Flaminio, Heather K. Fong, Yuta Fujikawa, Yuya Fujimoto, I. Putu Wira Hadiputrawan, Sadakazu Haino, Wenbiao Han, Kazuhiro Hayama, Yoshiaki Himemoto, Naoatsu Hirata, Chiaki Hirose, Tsung-Chieh Ho, Bin-Hua Hsieh, He-Feng Hsieh, Chia-Hsuan Hsiung, Hsiang-Yu Huang, Panwei Huang, Yao-Chin Huang, Yun-Jing Huang, David C. Y. Hui, Kohei Inayoshi, Yuki Inoue, Yousuke Itoh, Pil-Jong Jung, Takaaki Kajita, Masahiro Kamiizumi, Nobuyuki Kanda, Takashi Kato, Chunglee Kim, Jaewan Kim, Young-Min Kim, Yuichiro Kobayashi, Kazunori Kohri, Keiko Kokeyama, Albert K. H. Kong, Naoki Koyama, Chihiro Kozakai, Jun'ya Kume, Sachiko Kuroyanagi, Kyujin Kwak, Eunsub Lee, Hyung Won Lee, Ray-Kuang Lee, Matteo Leonardi, Kwan-Lok Li, Pengbo Li, Lupin Chun-Che Lin, Chun-Yu Lin, En-Tzu Lin, Hong-Lin Lin, Guo-Chin Liu, Ling-Wei Luo, Miftahul Ma'arif, Yuta Michimura, Norikatsu Mio, Osamu Miyakawa, Kouseki Miyo, Shinji Miyoki, Nozomi Morisue, Kouji Nakamura, Hiroyuki Nakano, Masayuki Nakano, Tatsuya Narikawa, Lan Nguyen Quynh, Takumi Nishimoto, Atsushi Nishizawa, Yoshihisa Obayashi, Kwangmin Oh, Masatake Ohashi, Tomoya Ohashi, Masashi Ohkawa, Yoshihiro Okutani, Ken-ichi Oohara, Shoichi Oshino, Kuo-Chuan Pan, Alessandro Parisi, June Gyu Park, Fabián E. Pe na Arellano, Surojit Saha, Kazuki Sakai, Takahiro Sawada, Yuichiro Sekiguchi, Lijing Shao, Yutaka Shikano, Hirotaka Shimizu, Katsuhiko Shimode, Hisaaki Shinkai, Ayaka Shoda, Kentaro Somiya, Inhyeok Song, Ryosuke Sugimoto, Jishnu Suresh, Takamasa Suzuki, Takanori Suzuki, Toshikazu Suzuki, Hideyuki Tagoshi, Hirotaka Takahashi, Ryutaro Takahashi, Hiroki Takeda, Mei Takeda, Atsushi Taruya, Takayuki Tomaru, Tomonobu Tomura, Lucia Trozzo, Terrence T. L. Tsang, Satoshi Tsuchida, Takuya Tsutsui, Darkhan Tuyenbayev, Nami Uchikata, Takashi Uchiyama, Tomoyuki Uehara, Koh Ueno, Takafumi Ushiba, Maurice H. P. M. van Putten, Tatsuki Washimi, Chien-Ming Wu, Hsun-Chung Wu, Tomohiro Yamada, Kazuhiro Yamamoto, Takahiro Yamamoto, Ryo Yamazaki, Shu-Wei Yeh, Jun'ichi Yokoyama, Takaaki Yokozawa, Hirotaka Yuzurihara, Simon Zeidler and Yuhang Zhao
The Current Status and Future Prospects of KAGRA, the Large-Scale Cryogenic Gravitational Wave Telescope Built in the Kamioka Underground
Reprinted from: *Galaxies* 2022, 10, 63, doi:10.3390/galaxies10030063 7

Craig Cahillane and Georgia Mansell
Review of the Advanced LIGO Gravitational Wave Observatories Leading to Observing Run Four
Reprinted from: *Galaxies* 2022, 10, 36, doi:10.3390/galaxies10010036 33

Ilaria Nardecchia
Detecting Gravitational Waves with Advanced Virgo
Reprinted from: *Galaxies* 2022, 10, 28, doi:10.3390/galaxies10010028 63

Sibilla Di Pace, Valentina Mangano, Lorenzo Pierini, Amirsajjad Rezaei, Jan-Simon Hennig, Margot Hennig, Daniela Pascucci, Annalisa Allocca, Iara Tosta e Melo, Vishnu G. Nair, Philippe Orban, Ameer Sider, Shahar Shani-Kadmiel and Joris van Heijningen
Research Facilities for Europe's Next Generation Gravitational-Wave Detector Einstein Telescope
Reprinted from: *Galaxies* 2022, 10, 65, doi:10.3390/galaxies10030065 91

Evan D. Hall
Cosmic Explorer: A Next-Generation Ground-Based Gravitational-Wave Observatory
Reprinted from: *Galaxies* **2022**, *10*, 90, doi:10.3390/galaxies10040090 . . . . **127**

Yuki Kawasaki, Ryuma Shimizu, Tomohiro Ishikawa, Koji Nagano, Shoki Iwaguchi, Izumi Watanabe, Bin Wu, Shuichiro Yokoyama and Seiji Kawamura
Optimization of Design Parameters for Gravitational Wave Detector DECIGO Including Fundamental Noises
Reprinted from: *Galaxies* **2022**, *10*, 25, doi:10.3390/galaxies10010025 . . . . **149**

Sudarshan Karki, Dripta Bhattacharjee and Richard L. Savage
Toward Calibration of the Global Network of Gravitational Wave Detectors with Sub-Percent Absolute and Relative Accuracy
Reprinted from: *Galaxies* **2022**, *10*, 42, doi:10.3390/galaxies10020042 . . . . **165**

Lucia Trozzo and Francesca Badaracco
Seismic and Newtonian Noise in the GW Detectors
Reprinted from: *Galaxies* **2022**, *10*, 20, doi:10.3390/galaxies10010020 . . . . **179**

Sheila E. Dwyer, Georgia L. Mansell and Lee McCuller
Squeezing in Gravitational Wave Detectors
Reprinted from: *Galaxies* **2022**, *10*, 46, doi:10.3390/galaxies10020046 . . . . **199**

Derek Davis and Marissa Walker
Detector Characterization and Mitigation of Noise in Ground-Based Gravitational-Wave Interferometers
Reprinted from: *Galaxies* **2022**, *10*, 12, doi:10.3390/galaxies10010012 . . . . **215**

Marek Szczepańczyk and Michele Zanolin
Gravitational Waves from a Core-Collapse Supernova: Perspectives with Detectors in the Late 2020s and Early 2030s
Reprinted from: *Galaxies* **2022**, *10*, 70, doi:10.3390/galaxies10030070 . . . . **247**

Mario Spera, Alessandro Alberto Trani and Mattia Mencagli
Compact Binary Coalescences: Astrophysical Processes and Lessons Learned
Reprinted from: *Galaxies* **2022**, *10*, 76, doi:10.3390/galaxies10040076 . . . . **257**

Ornella Juliana Piccinni
Status and Perspectives of Continuous Gravitational Wave Searches
Reprinted from: *Galaxies* **2022**, *10*, 72, doi:10.3390/galaxies10030072 . . . . **321**

Arianna I. Renzini, Boris Goncharov, Alexander C. Jenkins and Patrick M. Meyers
Stochastic Gravitational-Wave Backgrounds: Current Detection Efforts and Future Prospects
Reprinted from: *Galaxies* **2022**, *10*, 34, doi:10.3390/galaxies10010034 . . . . **357**

Editorial

Present and Future of Gravitational Wave Astronomy

Gabriele Vajente

LIGO Laboratory, California Institute of Technology, Pasadena, CA 91125, USA; vajente@caltech.edu

Citation: Vajente, G. Present and Future of Gravitational Wave Astronomy. *Galaxies* **2022**, *10*, 91. https://doi.org/10.3390/galaxies10040091

Received: 27 May 2022
Accepted: 30 May 2022
Published: 19 August 2022

Publisher's Note: MDPI stays neutral with regard to jurisdictional claims in published maps and institutional affiliations.

Copyright: © 2022 by the author. Licensee MDPI, Basel, Switzerland. This article is an open access article distributed under the terms and conditions of the Creative Commons Attribution (CC BY) license (https://creativecommons.org/licenses/by/4.0/).

Gravitational waves (GW) are propagating perturbations of the space-time metric, generated by time-varying mass distributions. Their existence was predicted more than 100 years ago, in 1916, as a consequence of the General Relativity theory of gravitation [1]. The most intense sources of gravitational waves are astrophysical objects such as neutron stars and black holes. Despite the large amount of energy emitted in the form of gravitational waves by the coalescence of compact binary systems, the radiation has to travel tens or thousands of Mpc before reaching earth, where it can be detected. This, and the weakness of the coupling to matter, are the reasons why the direct observation of gravitational waves has been such a challenging scientific endeavor, and why the signal from the first binary black hole coalescence, detected in 2015, produced a relative change in the local earth space-time metric of only about 10^{-21} [2], see Figure 1. Many sources of noises had to be understood and overcome [3], so that the two Advanced LIGO observatories [4,5] were sensitive enough to detect this event with high signal-to-noise ratio, opening the era of gravitational-wave astronomy and astrophysics. This event was the first demonstration of the existence of binary black holes, and the first confirmation that General Relativity is still valid in the intense-field regime involved in the collision of two compact objects such as black holes.

The first detection, dubbed GW150914, was only the first step of the newly-born gravitational-wave astronomy. The second major milestone was the detection of the first binary neutron star merger, GW170817 [6], only two years after the first event, see Figure 2. By then, the LIGO and Virgo [7,8] detectors had joined forces, and had already detected several more binary black hole events. However, the importance of the detection of two neutron stars colliding was on par with the first discovery. Not only we could detect gravitational waves from the two objects, proving without a doubt that they had masses compatible with neutron stars, but we also observed a short gamma-ray burst in coincidence with the event, proving the connection between the two phenomena. The sky localization provided by the gravitational wave observation by multiple detectors, LIGO and Virgo, allowed optical telescopes to identify the aftermath of the collision, and subsequently follow up in the entire electromagnetic spectrum. The promise of multi-messenger astronomy was indeed fulfilled.

The network of instruments actively observing the gravitational-wave universe is going to grow with the KAGRA detector [9,10]. As a first step, KAGRA operated in conjunction with the GEO 600 observatory [11] after the LIGO and Virgo O3 run ended [12]. In the three main observing runs carried out so far, the LIGO and Virgo collaborations have reported a total of 90 events with high probability of being of astrophysical origin [13], see Figure 3, an average of one event every five days in the last run.

Signals from coalescing binary systems [14] are just the beginning of the discoveries that gravitational-wave detectors will bring. Short-duration signals are expected to be produced by other sources, the most important being core-collapse supernovae [15]: both modeled and unmodeled searches are ongoing for such signals. Additionally, continuous-wave signals are expected to be produced by rotating pulsars [16]. Although they have not been detected yet, the upper limits obtained so far are already more stringent that the spin-down limits for many systems. With improved sensitivities, ground-based gravitational-wave observatories might be finally able to detect stochastic backgrounds [17] either from the confusion noise of coalescing binary systems, of from a cosmological origin.

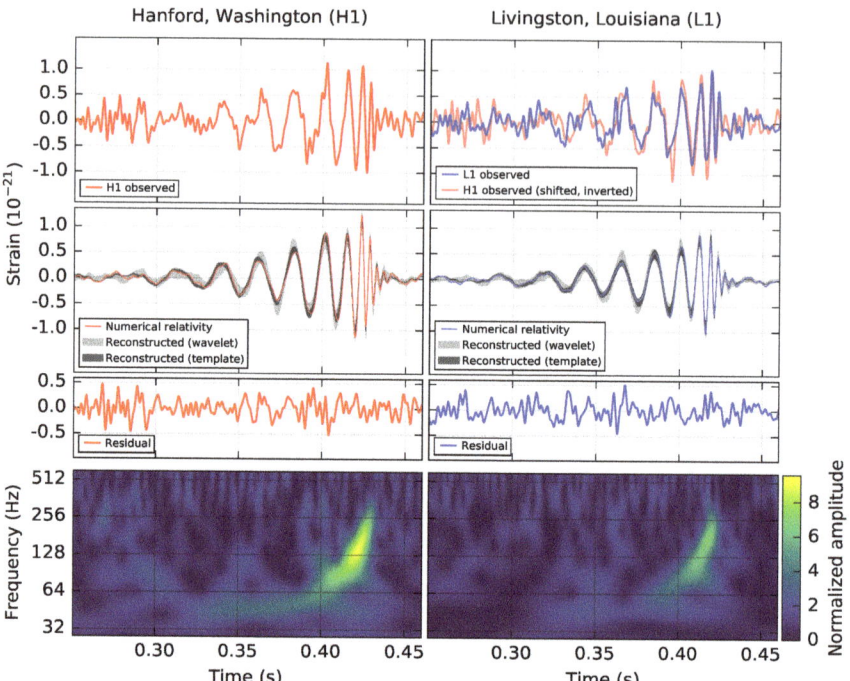

Figure 1. Strain data for the gravitational-wave event GW150914, produced by the collision of two black holes, and observed by the LIGO Hanford and LIGO Livingston detectors. The top row shows the band-passed strain output of the two detectors. In the right panel the LIGO Hanford signal is superimposed to the LIGO Livingston signal, with a time shift, to show the agreement between the two waveforms. The second row shows the comparison between the numerical relativity model of the event and the reconstructed signals. The residual difference between model and measurement in the third row shows the good agreement between theory and experiment. Finally, the bottom row shows time-frequency representations of the signals, where the characteristic chirp waveform is evident. Graphics reproduced from [2] under Creative Commons License.

The increasingly large number of gravitational wave detections made it possible to study the astrophysics of the sources [18] and the behavior of gravity in the intense field regime [19]. To be able to infer precise information on those fundamental topics, it is crucial to continuously increase the detector sensitivity, to improve the signal-to-noise ratio of the events, but it is also of the utmost importance to calibrate the detector output with high precision [20] and to remove any additional spurious disturbance that might mimic astrophysical signals [21].

The instruments that allowed all those scientific discoveries are laser Michelson interferometers [22]. The phase of two coherent laser beams propagating along orthogonal directions is changed by the passage of gravitational waves, modifying the interference condition at the beam recombination. The phase change is proportional to the differential fluctuation in the length of the two arms, due to the strain induced by gravitational-wave signals. Therefore, the detector sensitivity is directly proportional to the baseline length of the Michelson interferometer: this is the main reason to build km-scale detectors. Even with such large scale Michelson interferometers, the fundamental limitation due to laser quantum noise would not have allowed the sensitivity needed to detect gravitational waves. Over the years, the initial design of the detectors evolved to include more and more complex techniques aimed at increasing the sensitivity. The Michelson interferometer arms were replaced by resonant Fabry–Perot cavities to increase the phase accumulation by the laser beam in response to gravitational-wave signals. Power-recycling cavities were added to increase the circulating laser power. Signal-recycling cavities were added to shape the detector bandwidth. Quantum-measurement techniques such as squeezed vacuum injections were implemented [23] to beat the laser shot-noise limit. Sophisticated seismic isolation and suspension systems were developed to reduce noise from ground motion [24]. Cryogenic operation of the interferometer test masses was implemented [10] to reduce thermal noise. The result of all those efforts are the currently operating Advanced Virgo [8], Advanced LIGO [5] and KAGRA observatories [10].

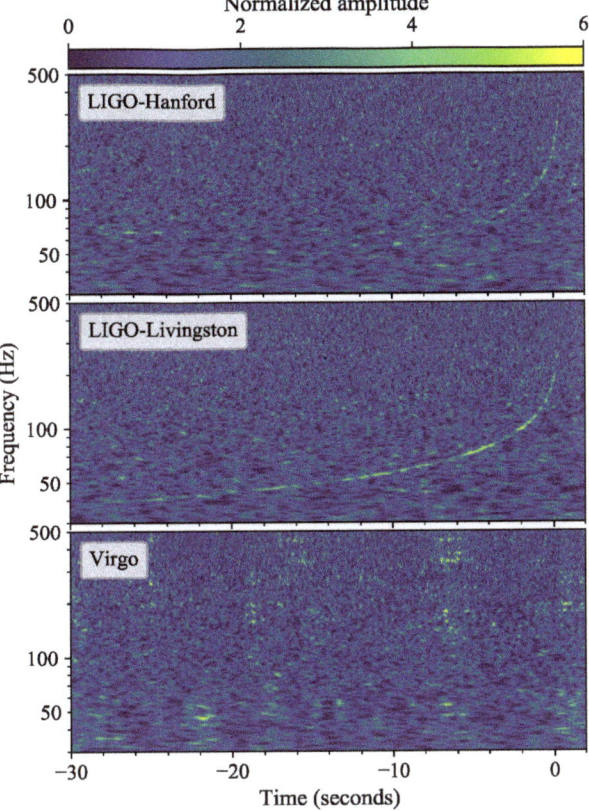

Figure 2. Time-frequency maps of the LIGO and Virgo detector outputs during the gravitational-wave event GW170817, created by the collision of two neutron stars. The signal stayed in the detector bandwidth for several tens of seconds, increasing in frequency following a characteristic chirp-like pattern. Graphics reproduced from [6] under Creative Commons License.

At the time this special issue is being published, the major ground-based detectors are undergoing an upgrade period. They are expected to be back in observation in 2023, with improved sensitivity to all kind of gravitational-wave sources. Further improvements are planned in the coming years for those detectors [25], and design studies are well underway for the next generation observatories. The next decades will see the European project Einstein Telescope [26] and the US project Cosmic Explorer [27] move from the drawing board to construction and operation. The currently existing detector will undergo upgrades, to move to silicon test masses operated at cryogenic temperatures [25], providing not only a significant improvement in sensitivity, but also serving as a crucial research and development platform for Einstein Telescope and Cosmic Explorer. Together with the planned space-borne gravitational-wave detectors LISA [28] and DECIGO [29], they hold the promise of detecting signals from the coalescence of compact binary systems from the entire observable universe, many of those events with very large signal-to-noise ratio, opening the era of high precision gravitational-wave physics, astrophyisics and cosmology.

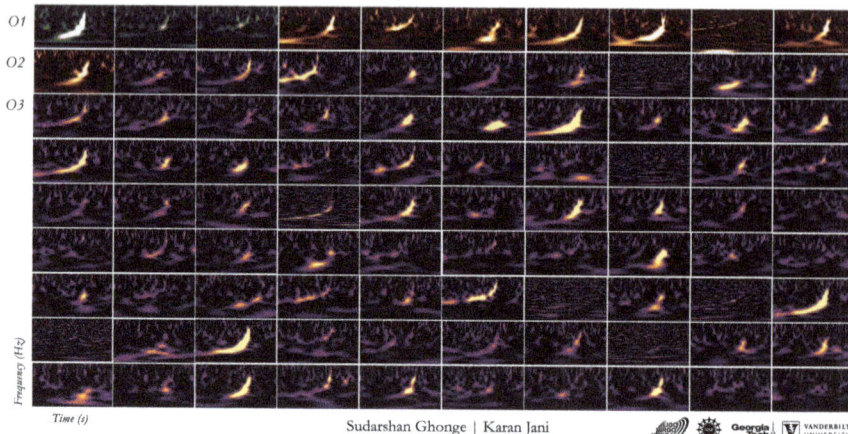

Figure 3. Collection of time-frequency maps of all the LIGO and Virgo detections in the first three observation runs. Graphics reproduced from [30].

Funding: LIGO was constructed by the California Institute of Technology and Massachusetts Institute of Technology with funding from the National Science Foundation, and operates under cooperative agreement PHY-1764464. Advanced LIGO was built under award PHY-0823459.

Acknowledgments: This material is based upon work supported by NSF's LIGO Laboratory, which is a major facility fully funded by the National Science Foundation. The authors gratefully acknowledge the support of the United States National Science Foundation (NSF) for the construction and operation of the LIGO Laboratory and Advanced LIGO, as well as the Science and Technology Facilities Council (STFC) of the United Kingdom, and the Max-Planck-Society (MPS) for support of the construction of Advanced LIGO. Additional support for Advanced LIGO was provided by the Australian Research Council.

Conflicts of Interest: The authors declare no conflict of interest.

References

1. Einstein, A. Naeherungsweise Integration der Feldgleichungen der Gravitation. *Sitzungsber. Preuss. Akad. Wiss.* **1916**, *1*, 688.
2. Abbott, B.P.; Abbott, R.; Abbott, T.D.; Abernathy, M.R.; Acernese, F.; Ackley, K.; Adams, C.; Adams, T.; Addesso, P.; Adhikari, R.X.; et al. Observation of Gravitational Waves from a Binary Black Hole Merger. *Phys. Rev. Lett.* **2016**, *116*, 061102. [CrossRef] [PubMed]
3. Whitcomb, S. Making LIGO Possible: A Technical History. In Proceedings of the APS April Meeting 2019, Denver, Colorado, 13–16 April 2019. Available online: https://dcc.ligo.org/public/0157/G1802281/001/G1802281-v1.pdf (accessed on 1 June 2022).
4. Aasi, J.; Abbott, B.P.; Abbott, R.; Abbott, T.; Abernathy, M.R.; Ackley, K.; Adams, C.; Adams, T.; Addesso, P.; Adhikari, R.X.; et al. Advanced LIGO. *Class. Quantum Grav.* **2015**, *32*, 074001.
5. Cahillane, C.; Mansell, G. Review of the Advanced LIGO Gravitational Wave Observatories Leading to Observing Run Four. *Galaxies* **2022**, *10*, 36. [CrossRef]
6. Abbott, B.P.; Abbott, R.; Abbott, T.D.; Acernese, F.; Ackley, K.; Adams, C.; Adams, T.; Addesso, P.; Adhikari, R.X.; Adya, V.B.; et al. GW170817: Observation of Gravitational Waves from a Binary Neutron Star Inspiral. *Phys. Rev. Lett.* **2017**, *119*, 161101. [CrossRef]
7. Acernese, F.A.; Agathos, M.; Agatsuma, K.; Aisa, D.; Allemandou, N.; Allocca, A.; Amarni, J.; Astone, P.; Balestri, G.; Ballardin, G.; et al. Advanced Virgo: A second-generation interferometric gravitational wave detector. *Class. Quantum Grav.* **2015**, *32*, 024001. [CrossRef]
8. Nardecchia, I. Detecting Gravitational Waves with Advanced Virgo. *Galaxies* **2022**, *10*, 28. [CrossRef]

9. Akutsu, T.; Ando, M.; Arai, K.; Arai, Y.; Araki, S.; Araya, A.; Aritomi, N.; Aso, Y.; Bae, S.; Bae, Y.; et al. Overview of KAGRA: Detector design and construction history. *Prog. Theor. Exp. Phys.* **2021**, *2021*, 05A101. [CrossRef]
10. Abe, H.; Akutsu, T.; Ando, M.; Araya, A.; Aritomi, N.; Asada, H.; Aso, Y.; Bae, S.; Bajpai, R.; Cannon, K.; et al. The Current Status and Future Prospects of KAGRA, the Large-Scale Cryogenic Gravitational Wave Telescope Built in the Kamioka Underground. *Galaxies* **2022**, *10*, 63. [CrossRef]
11. Dooley, K.L.; Leong, J.R.; Adams, T.; Affeldt, C.; Bisht, A.; Bogan, C.; Degallaix, J.; Gräf, C.; Hild, S.; Hough, J.; et al. GEO 600 and the GEO-HF upgrade program: successes and challenges. *Class. Quantum Grav.* **2016**, *33*, 075009. [CrossRef]
12. Abbott, R.; Abe, H.; Acernese, F.; Ackley, K.; Adhikari, N.; Adhikari, R.X.; Adkins, V.K.; Adya, V.B.; Affeldt, C.; Agarwal, D.; et al. First joint observation by the underground gravitational-wave detector, KAGRA, with GEO600. *arXiv* **2022**, arXiv:2203.01270.
13. Abbott, R.; Abbott, T.D.; Acernese, F.; Ackley, K.; Adams, C.; Adhikari, N.; Adhikari, R.X.; Adya, V.B.; Affeldt, C.; Agarwal, D.; et al. GWTC-3: Compact Binary Coalescences Observed by LIGO and Virgo During the Second Part of the Third Observing Run. *arXiv* **2021**, arXiv:2111.03606.
14. Spera, M. Compact Binary Coalescences: Astrophysical Processes and Lessons Learned, *Galaxies* **2022**, *10*, 76. [CrossRef]
15. Szczepańczyk, M.; Zanolin, M. Gravitational Waves from a Core-Collapse Supernova: Perspectives with detectors in the late 2020s and early 2030s. *Galaxies* **2022**, *10*, 70. [CrossRef]
16. Piccinni, O.J. Status and perspectives of Continuous Gravitational Wave searches. *Galaxies* **2022**, *10*, 72. [CrossRef]
17. Renzini, A.I.; Goncharov, B.; Jenkins, A.C.; Meyers, P.M. Stochastic Gravitational-Wave Backgrounds: Current Detection Efforts and Future Prospects. *Galaxies* **2022**, *10*, 34. [CrossRef]
18. Abbott, R.; Abbott, T.D.; Acernese, F.; Ackley, K.; Adams, C.; Adhikari, N.; Adhikari, R.X.; Adya, V.B.; Affeldt, C.; Agarwal, D.; et al. The population of merging compact binaries inferred using gravitational waves through GWTC-3. *arXiv* **2021**, arXiv:2111.03634. [CrossRef]
19. Abbott, R.; Abe, H.; Acernese, F.; Ackley, K.; Adhikari, N.; Adhikari, R.X.; Adkins, V.K.; Adya, V.B.; Affeldt, C.; Agarwal, D.; et al. Tests of General Relativity with GWTC-3. *arXiv* **2021**, arXiv:2112.06861. [CrossRef]
20. Karki, S.; Bhattacharjee, D.; Savage, R.L. Toward Calibration of the Global Network of Gravitational Wave Detectors with Sub-Percent Absolute and Relative Accuracy. *Galaxies* **2022**, *10*, 42. [CrossRef]
21. Davis, D.; Walker, M. Detector Characterization and Mitigation of Noise in Ground-Based Gravitational-Wave Interferometers. *Galaxies* **2022**, *10*, 12. [CrossRef]
22. Vajente, G.; Gustafson, E.K.; Reitze, D.H. Precision interferometry for gravitational wave detection: Current status and future trends. In *Advances in Atomic, Molecular, and Optical Physics*; Academic Press: Cambridge, MA, USA, 2019; Chapter 3, Volume 68, pp. 75–148.
23. Dwyer, S.E.; Mansell, G.L.; McCuller, L. Squeezing in Gravitational Wave Detectors. *Galaxies* **2022**, *10*, 46. [CrossRef]
24. Trozzo, L.; Badaracco, F. Seismic and Newtonian Noise in the GW Detectors. *Galaxies* **2022**, *10*, 20. [CrossRef]
25. Adhikari, R.X.; Arai, K.; Brooks, A.F.; Wipf, C.; Aguiar, O.; Altin, P.; Barr, B.; Barsotti, L.; Bassiri, R.; Bell, A.; et al. A Cryogenic Silicon Interferometer for Gravitational-wave Detection. *arXiv* **2020**, arXiv:2001.11173. [CrossRef]
26. Di Pace, S.; Mangano, V.; Pierini, L.; Rezaei, A.; Hennig, J.S.; Hennig, M.; Pascucci, D.; Allocca, A.; Tosta, e Melo, I.; Nair, V.G.; et al. Research Facilities for Europe?s Next Generation Gravitational-Wave Detector Einstein Telescope. *Galaxies* **2022**, *10*, 65. [CrossRef]
27. Hall, E. Cosmic Explorer: A next-generation ground-based gravitational-wave observatory, *Galaxies* **2022**, *10*, 90. [CrossRef]
28. Danzmann, K.; LISA Study Team. LISA: Laser interferometer space antenna for gravitational wave measurements. *Class. Quantum Grav.* **1996**, *13*, A247. [CrossRef]
29. Kawasaki, Y.; Shimizu, R.; Ishikawa, T.; Nagano, K.; Iwaguchi, S.; Watanabe, I.; Wu, B.; Yokoyama, S.; Kawamura, S. Optimization of Design Parameters for Gravitational Wave Detector DECIGO Including Fundamental Noises. *Galaxies* **2022**, *10*, 25. [CrossRef]
30. GWTC-3 Poster. Available online: https://dcc.ligo.org/LIGO-G2102338/public (accessed on 1 June 2022).

Article

The Current Status and Future Prospects of KAGRA, the Large-Scale Cryogenic Gravitational Wave Telescope Built in the Kamioka Underground

Homare Abe [1], Tomotada Akutsu [2], Masaki Ando [3], Akito Araya [4], Naoki Aritomi [3], Hideki Asada [5], Yoichi Aso [6], Sangwook Bae [7], Rishabh Bajpai [8], Kipp Cannon [9], Zhoujian Cao [10], Eleonora Capocasa [2], Man Leong Chan [11], Dan Chen [6], Yi-Ru Chen [12], Marc Eisenmann [2], Raffaele Flaminio [13], Heather K. Fong [9], Yuta Fujikawa [14], Yuya Fujimoto [15], I. Putu Wira Hadiputrawan [16], Sadakazu Haino [17], Wenbiao Han [18], Kazuhiro Hayama [11], Yoshiaki Himemoto [19], Naoatsu Hirata [2], Chiaki Hirose [14], Tsung-Chieh Ho [16], Bin-Hua Hsieh [20], He-Feng Hsieh [21], Chia-Hsuan Hsiung [22], Hsiang-Yu Huang [17], Panwei Huang [23], Yao-Chin Huang [12], Yun-Jing Huang [17], David C. Y. Hui [24], Kohei Inayoshi [25], Yuki Inoue [16], Yousuke Itoh [15], Pil-Jong Jung [26], Takaaki Kajita [20], Masahiro Kamiizumi [20], Nobuyuki Kanda [15], Takashi Kato [20], Chunglee Kim [27], Jaewan Kim [28], Young-Min Kim [29], Yuichiro Kobayashi [15], Kazunori Kohri [30], Keiko Kokeyama [31], Albert K. H. Kong [21], Naoki Koyama [14], Chihiro Kozakai [6], Jun'ya Kume [9], Sachiko Kuroyanagi [32], Kyujin Kwak [29], Eunsub Lee [20], Hyung Won Lee [33], Ray-Kuang Lee [12], Matteo Leonardi [2], Kwan-Lok Li [34], Pengbo Li [35], Lupin Chun-Che Lin [29], Chun-Yu Lin [36], En-Tzu Lin [21], Hong-Lin Lin [16], Guo-Chin Liu [22], Ling-Wei Luo [17], Miftahul Ma'arif [16], Yuta Michimura [3], Norikatsu Mio [37], Osamu Miyakawa [20], Kouseki Miyo [20], Shinji Miyoki [20], Nozomi Morisue [15], Kouji Nakamura [2], Hiroyuki Nakano [38], Masayuki Nakano [39,*,†], Tatsuya Narikawa [20], Lan Nguyen Quynh [40], Takumi Nishimoto [20], Atsushi Nishizawa [9], Yoshihisa Obayashi [20], Kwangmin Oh [24], Masatake Ohashi [20], Tomoya Ohashi [15], Masashi Ohkawa [14], Yoshihiro Okutani [41], Ken-ichi Oohara [20], Shoichi Oshino [20], Kuo-Chuan Pan [12], Alessandro Parisi [22], June Gyu Park [42], Fabián E. Peña Arellano [20], Surojit Saha [21], Kazuki Sakai [43], Takahiro Sawada [15], Yuichiro Sekiguchi [44], Lijing Shao [25], Yutaka Shikano [45], Hirotaka Shimizu [46], Katsuhiko Shimode [20], Hisaaki Shinkai [47], Ayaka Shoda [2], Kentaro Somiya [1], Inhyeok Song [21], Ryosuke Sugimoto [48], Jishnu Suresh [20], Takamasa Suzuki [1], Takanori Suzuki [14], Toshikazu Suzuki [20], Hideyuki Tagoshi [20], Hirotaka Takahashi [49], Ryutaro Takahashi [2], Hiroki Takeda [3], Mei Takeda [15], Atsushi Taruya [50], Takayuki Tomaru [2], Tomonobu Tomura [20], Lucia Trozzo [20], Terrence T. L. Tsang [51], Satoshi Tsuchida [15], Takuya Tsutsui [9], Darkhan Tuyenbayev [15], Nami Uchikata [20], Takashi Uchiyama [20], Tomoyuki Uehara [52], Koh Ueno [9], Takafumi Ushiba [20,*,†], Maurice H. P. M. van Putten [53], Tatsuki Washimi [6,*,†], Chien-Ming Wu [12], Hsun-Chung Wu [12], Tomohiro Yamada [46], Kazuhiro Yamamoto [54], Takahiro Yamamoto [20], Ryo Yamazaki [41], Shu-Wei Yeh [12], Jun'ichi Yokoyama [9], Takaaki Yokozawa [20], Hirotaka Yuzurihara [20], Simon Zeidler [55] and Yuhang Zhao [20]

Citation: Abe, H.; Akutsu, T.; Ando, M.; Araya, A.; Aritomi N.; Asada, H.; Aso, Y.; Bae, S.; Bajpai R.; Cannon K.; et. al. The Current Status and Future Prospects of KAGRA, the Large-Scale Cryogenic Gravitational Wave Telescope Built in the Kamioka Underground. *Galaxies* 2022, 10, 63. https://doi.org/10.3390/galaxies10030063

Academic Editor: Maddalena Mantovani

Received: 1 February 2022
Accepted: 29 March 2022
Published: 26 April 2022

Publisher's Note: MDPI stays neutral with regard to jurisdictional claims in published maps and institutional affiliations.

Copyright: © 2022 by the authors. Licensee MDPI, Basel, Switzerland. This article is an open access article distributed under the terms and conditions of the Creative Commons Attribution (CC BY) license (https://creativecommons.org/licenses/by/4.0/).

1. Graduate School of Science, Tokyo Institute of Technology, Meguro-ku, Tokyo 152-8551, Japan
2. Gravitational Wave Science Project, National Astronomical Observatory of Japan (NAOJ), Tokyo 181-8588, Japan
3. Department of Physics, The University of Tokyo, Bunkyo-ku, Tokyo 113-0033, Japan
4. Earthquake Research Institute, The University of Tokyo, Bunkyo-ku, Tokyo 113-0032, Japan
5. Department of Mathematics and Physics, Gravitational Wave Science Project, Hirosaki University, Hirosaki 036-8561, Japan
6. Kamioka Branch, National Astronomical Observatory of Japan (NAOJ), Kamioka-cho, Gifu 506-1205, Japan
7. Korea Institute of Science and Technology Information (KISTI), Yuseong-gu, Daejeon 34141, Korea
8. School of High Energy Accelerator Science, The Graduate University for Advanced Studies (SOKENDAI), Ibaraki, Tsukuba 305-0801, Japan

9. Research Center for the Early Universe (RESCEU), The University of Tokyo, Bunkyo-ku, Tokyo 113-0033, Japan
10. Department of Astronomy, Beijing Normal University, Beijing 100875, China
11. Department of Applied Physics, Fukuoka University, Jonan, Fukuoka 814-0180, Japan
12. Department of Physics, National Tsing Hua University, Hsinchu 30013, Taiwan
13. Laboratoire d'Annecy de Physique des Particules (LAPP), University Grenoble Alpes, Université Savoie Mont Blanc, CNRS/IN2P3, F-74941 Annecy, France
14. Faculty of Engineering, Niigata University, Nishi-ku, Niigata 950-2181, Japan
15. Department of Physics, Graduate School of Science, Osaka City University, Sumiyoshi-ku, Osaka 558-8585, Japan
16. Center for High Energy and High Field Physics, Department of Physics, National Central University, Taoyuan City 32001, Taiwan
17. Institute of Physics, Academia Sinica, Taipei 11529, Taiwan
18. Shanghai Astronomical Observatory, Chinese Academy of Sciences, Shanghai 200030, China
19. College of Industrial Technology, Nihon University, Narashino 275-8575, Japan
20. Institute for Cosmic Ray Research (ICRR), KAGRA Observatory, The University of Tokyo, Kashiwa 277-8582, Japan
21. Institute of Astronomy, National Tsing Hua University, Hsinchu 30013, Taiwan
22. Department of Physics, Tamkang University, New Taipei City 25137, Taiwan
23. State Key Laboratory of Magnetic Resonance and Atomic and Molecular Physics, Innovation Academy for Precision Measurement Science and Technology (APM), Chinese Academy of Sciences, Wuhan 430071, China
24. Department of Astronomy & Space Science, Chungnam National University, Yuseong-gu, Daejeon 34134, Korea
25. Kavli Institute for Astronomy and Astrophysics, Peking University, Haidian District, Beijing 100871, China
26. National Institute for Mathematical Sciences, Yuseong-gu, Daejeon 34047, Korea
27. Department of Physics, Ewha Womans University, Seodaemun-gu, Seoul 03760, Korea
28. Department of Physics, Myongji University, Yongin 17058, Korea
29. Department of Physics, Ulsan National Institute of Science and Technology (UNIST), Ulju-gun, Ulsan 44919, Korea
30. Institute of Particle and Nuclear Studies (IPNS), High Energy Accelerator Research Organization (KEK), Ibaraki, Tsukuba 305-0801, Japan
31. School of Physics and Astronomy, Cardiff University, Cardiff CF24 3AA, UK
32. Instituto de Fisica Teorica, 28049 Madrid, Spain
33. Department of Computer Simulation, Inje University, Gyeongsangnam-do, Gimhae 50834, Korea
34. Department of Physics, National Cheng Kung University, Tainan City 70101, Taiwan
35. School of Physics and Technology, Wuhan University, Wuhan 430072, China
36. National Center for High-Performance Computing, National Applied Research Laboratories, Hsinchu Science Park, Hsinchu 30076, Taiwan
37. Institute for Photon Science and Technology, The University of Tokyo, Bunkyo-ku, Tokyo 113-8656, Japan
38. Faculty of Law, Ryukoku University, Fushimi-ku, Kyoto 612-8577, Japan
39. California Institute of Technology, Pasadena, CA 91125, USA
40. Department of Physics, University of Notre Dame, Notre Dame, IN 46556, USA
41. Department of Physics and Mathematics, Aoyama Gakuin University, Kanagawa, Sagamihara 252-5258, Japan
42. Korea Astronomy and Space Science Institute (KASI), Yuseong-gu, Daejeon 34055, Korea
43. Department of Electronic Control Engineering, National Institute of Technology, Nagaoka College, Niigata 940-8532, Japan
44. Faculty of Science, Toho University, Funabashi 274-8510, Japan
45. Graduate School of Science and Technology, Gunma University, Maebashi 371-8510, Japan
46. Accelerator Laboratory, High Energy Accelerator Research Organization (KEK), Ibaraki, Tsukuba 305-0801, Japan
47. Faculty of Information Science and Technology, Osaka Institute of Technology, Hirakata 573-0196, Japan
48. Department of Space and Astronautical Science, The Graduate University for Advanced Studies (SOKENDAI), Kanagawa, Sagamihara 252-5210, Japan
49. Research Center for Space Science, Advanced Research Laboratories, Tokyo City University, Setagaya, Tokyo 158-0082, Japan
50. Yukawa Institute for Theoretical Physics (YITP), Kyoto University, Sakyou-ku, Kyoto 606-8502, Japan
51. Faculty of Science, Department of Physics, The Chinese University of Hong Kong, Hong Kong 518172, China
52. Department of Communications Engineering, National Defense Academy of Japan, Kanagawa, Yokosuka 239-8686, Japan
53. Department of Physics and Astronomy, Sejong University, Gwangjin-gu, Seoul 143-747, Korea
54. Faculty of Science, University of Toyama, Toyama 930-8555, Japan
55. Department of Physics, Rikkyo University, Toshima-ku, Tokyo 171-8501, Japan

* Correspondence: masayuki@caltech.edu (M.N.); ushiba@icrr.u-tokyo.ac.jp (T.U.); tatsuki.washimi@nao.ac.jp (T.W.)
† These authors contributed equally to this work.

Abstract: KAGRA is a gravitational-wave (GW) detector constructed in Japan with two unique key features: It was constructed underground, and the test-mass mirrors are cooled to cryogenic temperatures. These features are not included in other kilometer-scale detectors but will be adopted in future detectors such as the Einstein Telescope. KAGRA performed its first joint observation run with GEO600 in 2020. In this observation, the sensitivity of KAGRA to GWs was inferior to that of other kilometer-scale detectors such as LIGO and Virgo. However, further upgrades to the detector are ongoing to reach the sensitivity for detecting GWs in the next observation run, which is scheduled for 2022. In this article, the current situation, sensitivity, and future perspectives are reviewed.

Keywords: gravitational wave detector; laser interferometer; cryogenics; underground

1. Introduction

A gravitational wave (GW) is a physical phenomenon predicted by Einstein in his general theory of relativity in 1916. A GW is a wave of spacetime distortion caused by the motion of mass. It travels at the speed of light. The amplitude and waveform of a GW depend on the acceleration and mass of the source. A heavier mass that changes its motion at a faster rate generates stronger GWs. For instance, astronomically massive phenomena, such as a merger of binary neutron stars or black holes, are powerful sources and represent the main targets of GW detectors that are currently in operation. Because GWs have a different emission process than other measures used in astronomy, such as visible light, X-rays, infrared rays, radio waves, cosmic rays, and neutrinos, unique information can be obtained by observing GWs. In addition, because the interaction between GWs and objects is relatively weak, GWs can propagate through space without being scattered or absorbed by objects. Therefore, even GWs generated just after the birth of the universe can reach Earth, and they are therefore expected to act as probes for the history of the universe using future space GW detectors.

GWs distort spacetime and result in a fluctuation of the distance between two points; therefore, the detection of GWs is possible by precisely measuring this distance fluctuation. However, as mentioned above, the amplitude of the distance variation can be as small as 10^{-18} m for current GW detectors, which makes GW detection challenging. Thus far, an optical interferometer is the only instrument that allows for direct GW detection. An interferometer is an L-shaped optical instrument that can convert the arm length fluctuation caused by GWs into a laser intensity fluctuation. A GW interaction can also be described as the tidal force, and the L-shaped interferometer can detect the tidal force efficiently as a differential component of the arm length fluctuation. Because the distance fluctuation is proportional to the distance between two points, a longer-arm interferometer is more sensitive to GW interactions. Thus, GW detectors have continued to increase in size over the last few decades, and current GW detectors have a large kilometer-scale arm. Nevertheless, typical GWs from a target source cause arm-length fluctuations of only 10^{-18} m. Currently, the GW detection network consists of two Advanced LIGOs in the US [1], an Advanced Virgo in Italy [2], and the GEO600 in Germany [3].

The Advanced LIGO and Advanced Virgo detectors are interferometric GW detectors with a kilometer-scale arm length, whereas GEO600 has a 600-m arm length. The Advanced LIGO detector succeeded in the world's first detection of GWs in 2015, opening up a new astronomical field of GW astronomy. The first GW event observed by the two Advanced LIGO detectors, GW150914 [4], was the merger of binary black holes. Since then, the GW observation network with Virgo has observed several dozen GW events [5,6], including GW170817 [7], a GW emitted by the merger of binary neutron stars.

After the development of three kilometer-scale detectors, the construction of a kilometer-scale GW observatory began in Japan. This detector, named KAGRA, has been under construction since 2012, and it achieved its first joint observation run with other observatories in April 2020 [8]. KAGRA is currently being upgraded for further sensitivity improvements. KAGRA is built underground and uses cryogenic mirrors to lower its thermal noise to improve sensitivity. These features differ from those of other GW detectors. While the Advanced LIGO and Virgo are considered second-generation detectors, these features make KAGRA a 2.5 generation detector, that is, the intermediate generation before third-generation detectors, such as the Einstein Telescope (ET) [9] and Cosmic Explorer (CE) [10]. In this article, the design concept of KAGRA, its performance during the first joint observation run, an evaluation of new technologies and the underground environment, and future plans are described.

2. The Design of KAGRA

2.1. Location

The KAGRA experimental site is located under Mount Ikenoyama (elevation of 1369 m), Gifu Prefecture, Japan. Figure 1 presents a schematic of the KAGRA experimental site. It consists of three stations (Corner, X-end, and Y-end), two arm tunnels (X-arm and Y-arm) 3 km in length, and several access tunnels. Under the same mountain, there are many neutrino experiments (Super-Kamiokande [11], KamLAND [12], and CANDLES [13]), dark matter experiments (NEWAGE [14], PICOLON [15], and XMASS (closed) [16]), and other R&D experiments, including those of CLIO [17], which is the prototype of KAGRA.

Japan is famous for its frequent earthquakes, especially on the side facing the Pacific Ocean, where two tectonic plates converge. However, earthquake waves are weakened when they propagate across the Tateyama mountain range, standing northeast of the KAGRA site. This is because the low-density ground (1.4–2.2 g/cm^3; for example, the normal area is 2.6 g/cm^3) is distributed at an altitude of approximately −5 km acts as a cushion [18,19], minimizing the site's propensity for earthquakes.

Figure 1. Location and schematic view of the KAGRA experimental site [20].

2.2. Interferometer Configuration

The simplest configuration of an interferometer is called a Michelson interferometer (MICH, shown in Figure 2a). A Michelson interferometer consists of a laser source, beam splitter (BS) that splits the light into two paths, end mirrors (or end test masses—ETMs) to reflect the split light back to the BS, and photodetector (PD) for measuring the intensity of the recombined light on the BS. The differential component of the variation in the distance from the BS to each ETM (called the arm length) changes the relative phase of the reflected light beams and, consequently, the intensity of the recombined light fluctuates.

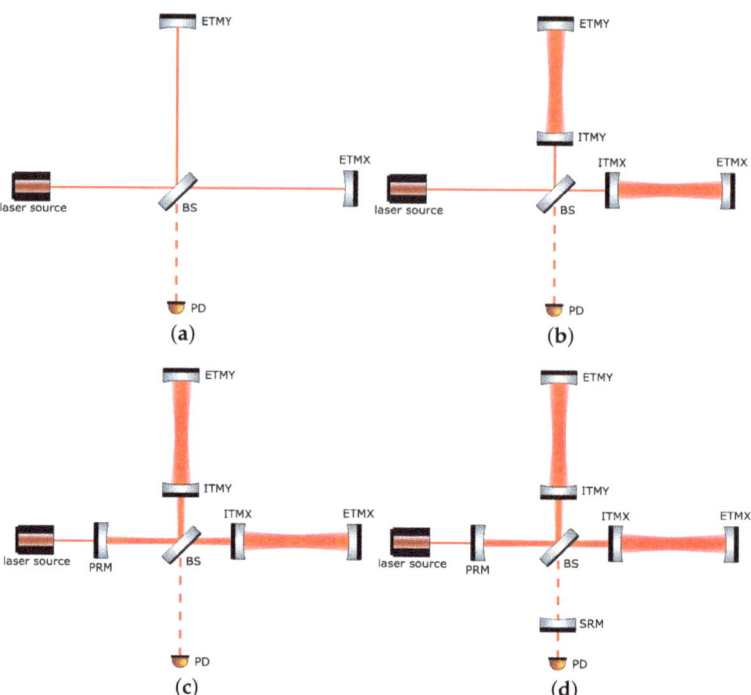

Figure 2. Schematic image of the interferometer configuration. A basic Michelson interferometer (**a**) consists of a laser source, beam splitter (BS), end test masses (ETMX and ETMY), and photodetector (PD). The Fabry–Pérot arm cavities, which are composed of ETMs and input test masses (ITMX and ITMY), extend the effective arm length (**b**). The power-recycling mirror (PRM) and signal-recycling mirror (SRM) improve the sensitivity using the power-recycling technique and resonant sideband extraction technique, respectively (**c,d**). (**a**) Michelson interferometer (MICH). (**b**) Fabry–Pérot Michelson interferometer (FPMI). (**c**) Power-recycling FPMI (PRFPMI). (**d**) Resonant sideband extraction (RSE) interferometer.

Because interferometers with a longer arm are more sensitive to GWs, KAGRA has 3 km-long arms, as in the other GW observatories. However, because a Michelson interferometer with an arm length of the kilometer order is not sufficient to achieve the required sensitivity for detecting a GW, current GW observatories combine multiple optical cavities with a Michelson interferometer to improve sensitivity, as shown in Figure 2.

First, two Fabry–Pérot optical cavities are incorporated into the arms, forming a configuration called the Fabry–Pérot Michelson interferometer (FPMI, shown in Figure 2b). These arm cavities are composed of input mirrors (or input test masses—ITMs) and ETMs, and they extend the effective arm length of the interferometer. In the case of KAGRA, the arm cavities extend the effective arm length by a factor of approximately 1000, resulting in a 1000-fold increase in the GW sensitivity.

Second, another optical cavity, called the power-recycling cavity, is composed of a power-recycling mirror (PRM) and ITMs. In this power-recycling FPMI configuration (PRFPMI, shown in Figure 2c), the PRM reflects the returning laser beam from the FPMI, and the internal power of the interferometer is amplified [21]. Because the signal-to-noise ratio (SNR) of the GW signal to the quantum shot noise is proportional to the inverse of the square root of the laser power circulating in the arm cavities, the power-recycling cavity further improves sensitivity. In the case of KAGRA, the power-recycling cavity amplifies the laser power in the interferometer by a factor of ten [22].

Then, the other optical cavity is added to the signal port, and it configures the resonant sideband extraction (RSE) interferometer [23] (shown in Figure 2d). The additional optical cavity, called a signal-recycling cavity, is composed of the PRFPMI and a signal-recycling mirror (SRM) placed between the BS and PD. The RSE interferometer works to compensate for the signal cancellation at high frequencies, which is a drawback of the PRFPMI, using the resonant sideband extraction technique. For GWs with a frequency higher than the storage time of laser light in the arm cavity, the obtained signal is averaged, resulting in a weak signal and low sensitivity. The signal-recycling cavity in the RSE interferometer allows for the extraction of the signal sideband of the GWs before cancellation. Furthermore, by detuning the length of the signal-recycling cavity microscopically from the resonance point, the signal-recycling cavity can significantly improve the sensitivity in a specific frequency band. This technique is called detuned RSE [24].

For GW detection, all of the optical resonators must be held in resonance. To achieve this, the distance between the mirrors of the interferometer must be precisely controlled with an accuracy of a few hundred picometers. GW detection is possible only when the interferometer is maintained in a resonant state, which is referred to as "the interferometer is locked".

During the last observation run, the interferometer configuration of KAGRA was that of the PRFPMI. For future observations, a signal-recycling cavity will be installed, and KAGRA will be operated as an RSE interferometer. The design sensitivity was also calculated with the RSE interferometer configuration. The successful operation of the RSE interferometer is one of the major milestones for KAGRA.

2.3. Design Sensitivity

GWs are detected as arm length fluctuations; however, their magnitude is very small, that is, the fluctuations are only of the order of 10^{-18} m. Thus, even a tiny noise can mask the GW signal. The process for improving the sensitivity of GW detectors can be summarized as noise reduction. The sensitivity curves of the KAGRA design are shown in Figure 3 [25], which presents the fundamental noises that limit the sensitivity of KAGRA. Noise in GW detectors can be roughly divided into two categories based on its effects on the detectors. One is noise that physically shakes the arm's length, which is indistinguishable from arm length fluctuations due to GWs. As shown in Figure 3, seismic, thermal, and quantum radiation pressure noises are categorized as this type of noise. The others, which are represented by quantum shot noise in the sensitivity curve, are those that do not actually shake the test masses but produce a signal resembling an arm length fluctuation, which again makes it indistinguishable from the actual arm length fluctuation. Because these noises have different frequency characteristics, the design sensitivity is limited by the different noises in each frequency band. Roughly speaking, the former noise limits the sensitivity at lower frequencies, since it needs to shake things up, and it gets smaller at higher frequencies, whereas the latter noise is dominant at higher frequencies. Although fundamental noise appears even in a physically ideal detector, a GW detector's sensitivity can easily be polluted by noise from non-ideal features of the system. This type of noise is called technical noise. The technical noise will eventually be reduced to a point lower than the fundamental noise and will not limit sensitivity.

Seismic noise limits the design sensitivity in the frequency band below 5 Hz. The Earth's surface vibrates by approximately 1 µm even in the absence of an earthquake, and the mirror of an interferometer placed on the ground is not immune. In addition, it is difficult to reduce seismic vibration itself. Therefore, in a GW detector, the mirrors are suspended by a pendulum to reduce the transmission of seismic vibrations to the mirrors because seismic noise is attenuated proportional to f^{-2N} above the resonant frequencies of the pendulum, where N is the number of pendulum stages. In the case of KAGRA, the effect of seismic vibration is also minimized by its underground construction, as explained in the next section. The seismic noise is estimated by considering the seismic vibrations of the ground in the mine, the seismic isolation performance of the pendulums, and the coupling of 1/200 from the vertical seismic vibration, as shown in Figure 3.

Thermal noise, which is caused by the thermal vibration of molecules, is a type of noise that limits the sensitivity at low frequencies below 140 Hz. The thermal vibration of molecules causes the motion of mirrors, their surfaces, and their suspensions, thereby inhibiting GW detection. The thermal noise of a mirror is proportional to the inverse of the square root of the frequencies and limits the sensitivity between 50 and 140 Hz. The thermal noise of a mirror suspension has a noise floor proportional to the inverse of the square of the frequencies and limits the sensitivity below 50 Hz. Several peaks in the thermal noise of the suspension are due to the mechanical resonance of the suspension. The details are summarized in [8]. There are several ways to reduce thermal noise. One is to increase the beam spot size on the mirror to reduce the mirror's thermal noise, which is caused by the vibration of the mirror substrates and coatings, because the correlation of the thermal mirror surfaces between two distant points is small. Another is to use low-mechanical-loss materials for mirrors and their suspensions because thermal noise is proportional to the square root of the mechanical losses of the system [26]. A further method is to reduce the vibration of the molecules by cooling the test-mass mirrors and their suspensions to cryogenic temperatures, as described in the following section. Because this is the first kilometer-scale cryogenic interferometer, the demonstration of cryogenic technology is highly anticipated and is expected to be introduced in future GW detectors.

In the frequency band between 5 and 80 Hz, the sensitivity is limited by quantum radiation pressure noise, which is included as quantum noise in Figure 3. The reflection of light is described in quantum mechanics as the collision of photons on a mirror's surface, which exerts a force called radiation pressure. Because the number of photons in light exhibits quantum fluctuations, the radiation pressure also exhibits inevitable fluctuations, and these fluctuations cause quantum radiation pressure noise.

Quantum shot noise limits the design sensitivity at frequencies above 100 Hz, which is another noise included as quantum noise in Figure 3. A photodetector detects the light intensity by counting the number of photons, which causes its output to fluctuate owing to uncertainty in the number of photons. As described above, an interferometer is an instrument that converts arm-length fluctuations into laser-intensity fluctuations. Therefore, quantum shot noise is inevitable and difficult to reduce in GW detectors.

Both shot and radiation pressure noises are caused by quantum fluctuations of light; however, the relationship between the laser power and SNR is the opposite: the SNR of the radiation pressure noise is proportional to the square root of the power, whereas the SNR of the shot noise is inversely proportional. The frequency response is also different in the two noises: the radiation pressure noise is inversely proportional to the square of the frequency, whereas the shot noise has no frequency dependence, except for its deterioration at high frequencies owing to low-pass filtering for the signal of the optical cavity. Therefore, the optimal laser power is determined by the targeted frequency band. To increase the sensitivity in the high-frequency band, it is necessary to increase the laser power to reduce the shot noise. In the case of the current GW detectors, whose target frequencies are approximately 100 Hz, the intracavity power is designed to be of the order of 1 MW.

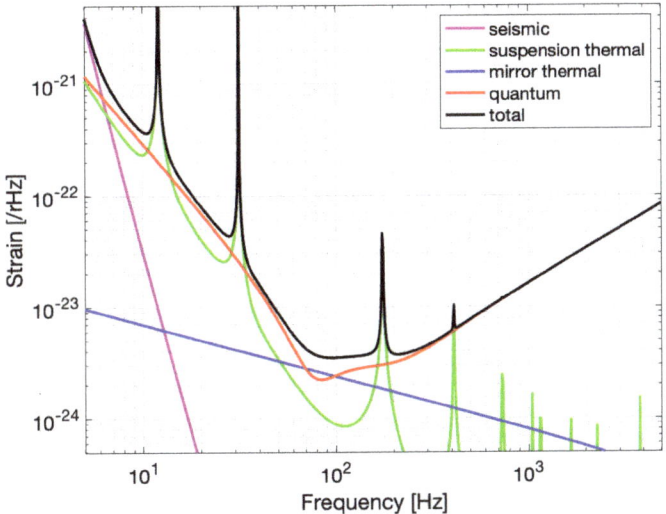

Figure 3. Design sensitivity curve of KAGRA [25]. The horizontal axis shows the frequency, and the vertical axis shows the detectable GW signal amplitude. Several fundamental noises are shown: seismic noise, mirror and suspension thermal noise, and quantum noise. Quantum noise is shown as the sum of the quantum radiation pressure noise and shot noise.

Technical noises are caused by imperfections in the interferometer. For example, in an ideal detector, the wavelength of the laser light is considered to contain no fluctuations, other than quantum fluctuations. However, actual laser light exhibits classical wavelength fluctuations, which cause sensing noise. In many cases, the amplitude of these noises, and sometimes even their presence, is difficult to predict. While the magnitude of the fundamental noise is determined by the interferometer design, the magnitude of technical noise is determined by the performance of the interferometer as a whole system; therefore, the interferometer's performance must be optimized after being operated to improve the sensitivity. This sensitivity improvement process is called noise hunting and is the main task in the sensitivity improvement of GW detectors.

2.4. Key Features of KAGRA

The fundamental noises described above were reduced by designing KAGRA with two key features. One was the utilization of an underground site to reduce seismic noise. The other was the utilization of cryogenic mirrors to reduce thermal noise. The details are summarized in the following subsections.

2.4.1. Underground

Seismic noise is problematic for ground-based GW detectors for two main reasons. The first is sensitivity degradation, as mentioned in the previous section. This can be caused not only by longitudinal motion but also by angular motions of the mirrors through angular-to-longitudinal coupling. The other is the duty-cycle deterioration caused by the angular motions of the mirrors, which disturbs the locking of the interferometer. Owing to the 3 km-long arm, which amplifies the tiny angular motions of the mirrors with respect to the motion of the beam spot, stable operation of the GW detector becomes difficult. There are several technical approaches to reducing these effects, such as utilizing passive vibration isolation with multi-stage suspension and active vibration isolation with inertial sensors; however, further reduction of seismic noise is important for current and future

GW detectors. Because underground sites have low levels of seismic motion with respect to the ground surface, building GW detectors at underground sites is highly beneficial.

The site search for KAGRA was conducted in the late 1990s, and Kamioka in Gifu Prefecture, Japan, was finally selected [27], which is the same location as the two prototype interferometers, a 20 m-scale interferometer, LISM [28], and a 100-m cryogenic interferometer, CLIO [17]. KAGRA was constructed in a horizontal tunnel excavated from a mountain and consists of two 3 km arm tunnels with 1/300 slopes, two end stations, and one corner station. All the stations are located more than 200 m below the surface of the mountain, where the seismic motion is significantly low based on past experience with CLIO [27]. After construction, the seismic motion of the KAGRA site was measured, as shown in Figure 4. Because the seismic motion of the KAGRA site at the observation bands was significantly smaller than that of TAMA300 [29] around the suburbs of Tokyo, the KAGRA location is highly advantageous in terms of seismic noise.

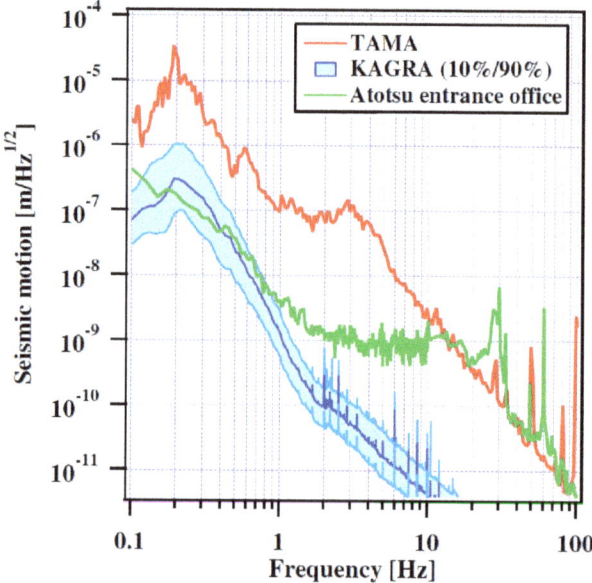

Figure 4. Seismic noise at the TAMA300 site (TAMA), the entrance of the KAGRA tunnel (Atotsu entrance), and the KAGRA site (KAGRA). For the seismic noise of the KAGRA site, the 10th and 90th percentile lines (upper and lower cyan lines, respectively) are shown in the figure. Reprinted with permission from Ref. [8], ©2021 Oxford University Press.

Another important benefit of lower seismic motion is the stability of the interferometer lock, because large mirror motions, especially those below 10 Hz, often cause lock loss in the interferometer. In addition, large motions make it difficult to lock the interferometer. Because seismic motion below 10 Hz at the underground site is smaller than that on the ground surface, the KAGRA site has an advantage in terms of stability and sensitivity. In particular, ground motion of approximately 0.2 Hz, which is called microseismic noise, is problematic; however, microseismic noise at the KAGRA site is approximately ten times smaller than that at the TAMA300 site, even in the 90th percentile, as shown in Figure 4. Therefore, the KAGRA site also has the benefit of seismic motion in microseismic bands between 0.1 and 0.4 Hz.

An additional advantage of underground sites is the ability to construct a huge suspension without tall support structures. Because a longer suspension has a better vibration isolation performance in the observation band, it is beneficial to utilize tall suspensions to reduce seismic noise. To achieve a long suspension on the ground, it is necessary to construct a tall support structure and hang the mirrors from the top, as in the superattenuator in Virgo [30]. In contrast, it is unnecessary to build a tall support in KAGRA because KAGRA involves excavation of a two-story tunnel, and the mirrors can be hung from the second floor. Therefore, although the total height of the test-mass suspension in KAGRA is approximately 13.5 m, the support structure is less than 1 m. Because a shorter support structure is more rigid, using this underground site is advantageous for constructing a tall mirror suspension.

2.4.2. Cryogenics

The thermal noise of mirrors and their suspensions is a fundamental noise source for laser interferometric GW detectors. A promising way to reduce thermal noise is to use cooling mirrors and their suspensions at cryogenic temperatures. Therefore, the mirrors and suspensions of the arm cavities in KAGRA were designed to be cooled to 20 K.

The KAGRA test-mass suspension, which is called a Type-A suspension, consists of nine stages: the upper five stages are at room temperature and the lower four stages are at cryogenic temperatures; they are called the Type-A tower and cryogenic payload, respectively. The cryogenic payload is suspended from the Type-A bottom filter, which is the bottom stage of the Type-A tower, and is stored in a cryostat. Figure 5 shows a schematic of the KAGRA cryogenic system. KAGRA's test masses are located at the bottom of a cryogenic payload in the bottom four stages of the main mirror suspension (the platform (PF), marionette (MN), intermediate mass (IM), and test mass (TM)). The MN, IM, and TM are surrounded by the corresponding recoil masses (marionette recoil mass, intermediate recoil mass, and recoil mass, respectively) to control the position and angle of the mirror. The mirror is made of monocrystalline sapphire, which has an extremely low mechanical loss of 10^{-8} at cryogenic temperatures [31], thereby reducing thermal noise. The sapphire mirror has a cylindrical shape with a diameter of 22 cm and a thickness of 15 cm. It is suspended using four sapphire fibers of 1.6 mm thickness and 350 mm length, which can extract heat from sapphire mirrors effectively owing to their high thermal conductivity at low temperatures [32]. In addition, sapphire mirrors have relatively low absorption at the laser wavelength (1064 nm) [33], resulting in less heat being generated during operation. The cryogenic payload is cooled through 6N (99.9999%) pure aluminum heat links [34], which yield high thermal conductivity while maintaining low stiffness, thus reducing the vibration transfer via heat links. In addition, they are connected to the MN stage to avoid direct coupling of the vibration via heat links to sapphire mirror motions.

The cryogenic payload is stored in two layers of radiation shields to avoid heating by thermal radiation. Sufficient cooling performance is obtained by cooling the inner and outer radiation shields to 8 K and 80 K, respectively. The payload, except for the sapphire parts and the inner side of the radiation shields, is coated with black plating called SOLBLACK and diamond-like carbon, thus effectively utilizing thermal radiation to cool the payload by obtaining a large emissivity. For continuous operation of the cooling system, KAGRA uses four one-watt cryocoolers to cool the cryogenic payload and radiation shields. Furthermore, two cryocoolers are used to cool the payload, and the others are used to cool the radiation shields. However, this generates large vibrations during operation and contaminates the sensitivity of the detector. Therefore, pulse-tube cryocoolers, which have very low vibrations [35], are used, and a heat-link vibration isolation system (HLVIS) is configured to further reduce the vibration transfer to the sapphire mirror via heat links.

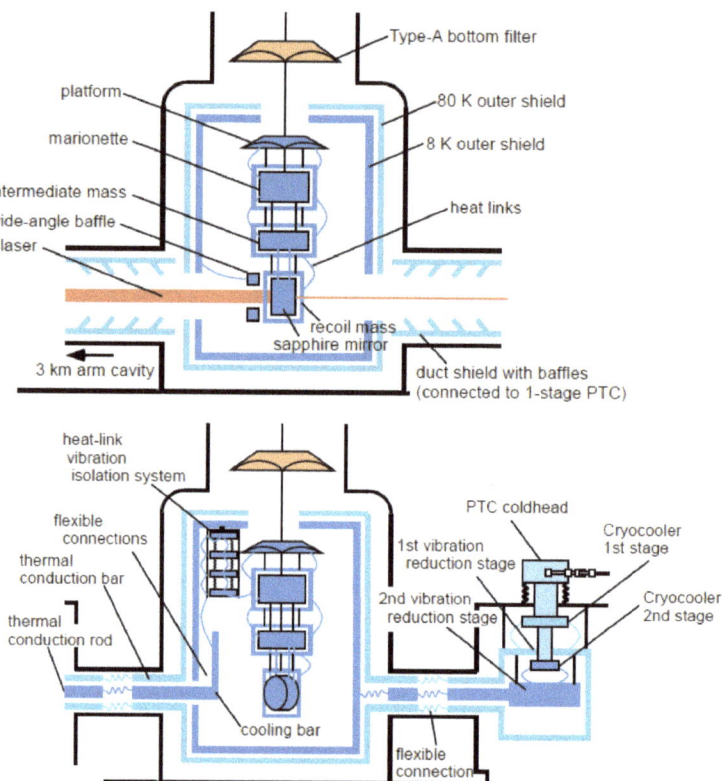

Figure 5. Schematic view of KAGRA's cryogenic system. A side view of the cryostat from the direction orthogonal to the arm (**top**) and another side view at an angle of 45° from the direction indicated in the left panel (**bottom**). Adapted with permission from Ref. [8], ©2021 Oxford University Press.

3. Recent Status
3.1. Detector Performance during the O3GK Observation Run

In April 2019, the Advanced LIGO detectors and the Virgo detector started their observation runs, which are called O3 [36]. In late March 2020, KAGRA was accepted to join O3 as a member of the scientific collaboration with LIGO and Virgo. However, LIGO and Virgo stopped their operations in March 2020 because of the COVID-19 pandemic. In this situation, GEO 600, which is the interferometric GW observatory in Germany with an arm length of 600 m [3], continued the observation, and GEO 600 and KAGRA started a joint observation run called O3GK. This was the first international observation run and a significant milestone for KAGRA.

One of the parameters describing the detector performance is the BNS inspiral range. This is the average distance at which the detector can detect typical binary neutron star mergers. The average BNS inspiral range of KAGRA in the O3GK was 660 kpc [37], although the best value was approximately 1 Mpc, which was recorded during the commissioning period. The interferometer configuration was PRFPMI, and the input power before PRM was 5 W, corresponding to an intracavity power of 50 kW.

The sensitivity with the dominant noise in the O3GK observation run is shown in Figure 6 [37]. As shown in the figure, most of the noise limiting the sensitivity was revealed. The sensitivity at frequencies lower than 100 Hz was limited by the suspension control noise. The details of the suspension control noise are described in Section 3.2.2.

From 100 to 400 Hz, acoustic noise was found to pollute the sensitivity. At the experimental site, many instruments generate sound, and the vibrations of the vacuum chamber caused by these sounds deteriorate the sensitivity. At the frequencies between 400 Hz and 2 kHz, the shot noise limits the sensitivity. Laser frequency noise is another noise that limits the sensitivity at high frequencies above 2 kHz. Although a frequency noise stabilization system was implemented, it was not optimized in the observation run. By optimizing the servo parameter, it will be reduced to lower than the shot noise.

Another important factor in gravitational wave detectors is the duty factor, which is the ratio of the time for which the interferometer is kept locked to the time of the observation period. Because the interferometer can lose its lock owing to external disturbances, such as earthquakes, a high duty factor is one of the major issues in constructing a GW detector. The duty factor of KAGRA during O3GK was 53%, whereas that of GEO 600 was 78% [37].

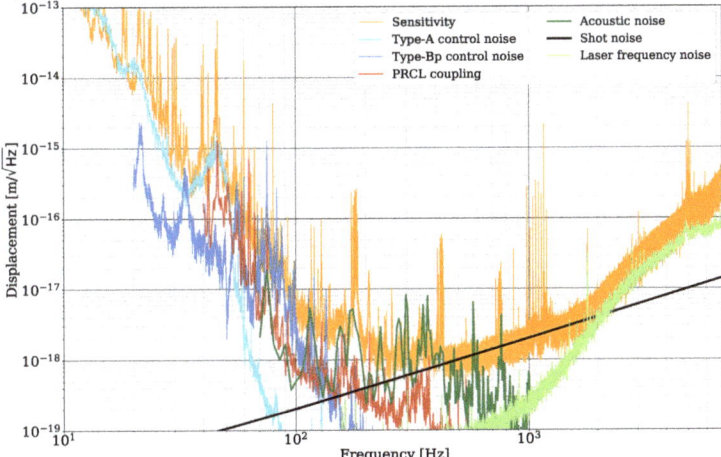

Figure 6. KAGRA's sensitivity with dominant noises. Suspension control noise (<100 Hz), acoustic noise (100 Hz~400 Hz), shot noise (400 Hz~2 kHz), and laser frequency noise (>2 kHz) limit the sensitivity. The average BNS inspiral range was 660 kpc for the O3GK period. Further details are shown in Ref. [37].

3.2. Toward the O4 Observation Run

The interferometer was sometimes difficult to lock during O3GK, especially on days with large microseismic motions (the details are explained in Section 4.1.1). KAGRA plans to upgrade the detector to improve the duty factor. In addition, because the sensitivity of KAGRA during O3GK was limited by two primary noise sources, quantum shot noise at high frequencies and suspension control noise at low frequencies, KAGRA also plans to improve the detector sensitivity for the international joint observation run starting from mid-December 2022 (O4) [38]. Furthermore, some technical difficulties inhibited the cooling of the sapphire mirrors during O3; therefore, several studies for achieving cryogenic operation have been performed for O4. KAGRA will start the O4 observation run with a sensitivity of over 1 Mpc and will work to improve the sensitivity toward the end of O4 by taking an observation break. In the following sections, the KAGRA upgrade plans and recent results on cryogenics are briefly reviewed.

3.2.1. Upgrade for Improving the Duty Factor

Seismic noise at low frequencies, especially microseismic noise, needs to be mitigated to improve the duty factor because it significantly affects the detector's stability. However, passive vibration isolation systems for such low frequencies are challenging; thus, active vibration isolation using inertial sensors, such as a speed meter or accelerometer, is implemented to control the vibration isolation system for sapphire mirrors. Three accelerometers were installed on the main mirror suspensions for inertial control of the suspensions after O3GK. They can detect seismic motion at the level of 10^{-7} m/$\sqrt{\text{Hz}}$ at 0.2 Hz, which is approximately the same as the microseismic motion on a typical day and one order of magnitude smaller than that on a noisy day.

Another measure for improving detector stability is the installation of stronger actuators on the payload of the main mirror suspensions. Cryogenic payloads have coil–magnet actuators consisting of a coil and magnet, which move the suspension through electromagnetic force. However, sometimes the actuator was saturated during lock acquisition and observation, which triggered a lock loss in the interferometer. Therefore, a stronger actuator avoids saturation of the actuators and improves the duty factor. However, the electrical noise of analog circuits and DAC noise are coupled to sensitivity through actuators if the actuator efficiency is too large. Therefore, it is necessary to make the actuator efficiency as large as possible while maintaining a sufficiently low noise coupling in the observation band. Figure 7 shows the actuator efficiencies of the MN and IM stages. The new MN and IM actuators have efficiencies of 1.1 N/A and 55 mN/A, respectively, while the old MN and IM actuators had efficiencies of 0.47 N/A and 18 mN/A, respectively [39]. Based on the measured actuator efficiencies, the noise of analog electronics, and DAC noise, the noise caused by the MN and IM actuators can be estimated as 8.8×10^{-20} m/$\sqrt{\text{Hz}}$ and 1.6×10^{-19} m/$\sqrt{\text{Hz}}$ at 10 Hz, respectively, which are below the target sensitivity of KAGRA.

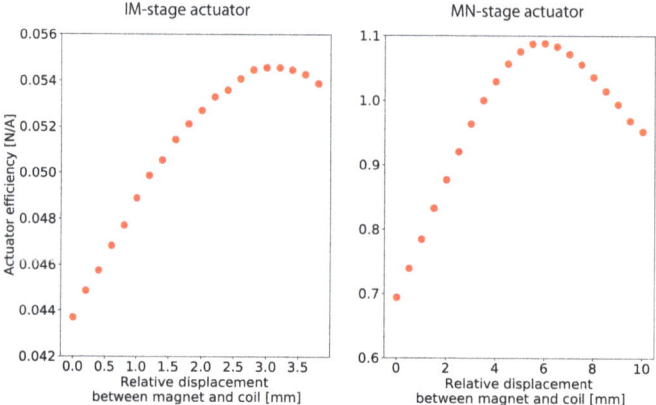

Figure 7. Actuator efficiencies of new coil–magnet actuators of the IM stage (**left**) and MN stage (**right**) as functions of the relative displacement between coils and magnets.

3.2.2. Upgrade for Improving Sensitivity

The sensitivity of KAGRA during O3GK was limited by the quantum shot noise in the high-frequency region. Thus, the replacement of the laser source with one of a higher power is planned for O4. Because quantum shot noise is proportional to $1/\sqrt{P}$, where P is the intracavity power of an arm cavity, increasing the laser power can improve the sensitivity at high frequencies. A new laser source can output 60 W, while the maximum laser power of the current KAGRA laser source is 40 W. The performance of the new laser is currently under evaluation.

The sensitivity in the low-frequency region is limited by the suspension control noise. Especially below 50 Hz, it was contaminated by suspension control noise from the main mirror suspensions. Because the suspension system in a GW detector has a very complex structure, the suspensions have many resonant modes, which disturb the interferometer's operation. Therefore, local controls for damping these suspension resonances are necessary, but can contaminate the sensitivity. Reducing the sensor noise for damping controls is an effective way to mitigate control noise. The payload of a main mirror suspension has reflective photosensors for damping controls [39]; however, it has a large noise above 10 Hz, approximately 6×10^{-9}m/$\sqrt{\text{Hz}}$ for lateral motion and 4×10^{-8}rad/$\sqrt{\text{Hz}}$ for rotation. Therefore, optical levers [40] were installed at the MN and PF stages, which have approximately 2×10^{-9}m/$\sqrt{\text{Hz}}$ for lateral motion and 3×10^{-10}rad/$\sqrt{\text{Hz}}$ for rotation.

3.2.3. Recent Results on Cryogenics

Cooling mirrors for reducing thermal noise are a unique feature of KAGRA, adding certain difficulties related to cryogenics. One of them is molecular adsorption on the cryogenic mirror surface, which causes variations in the reflectivity of the mirrors and laser absorption in the molecular layers [41]. Because molecular layers of a few micrometers cause significant changes in the sensitivity of KAGRA, the mirrors need to be frequently warmed to desorb the molecules from the mirror surface. For this purpose, new heaters for the desorption of molecules were newly installed on the IM stage of the cryogenic payload to mitigate the downtime of observation. Owing to these new heaters, the downtime of the desorption process is expected to reduce from several weeks to a few days.

Four sapphire mirrors were cooled to cryogenic temperatures in 2019. Figure 8 shows an example of the cooling curve of the cryogenic system at the Y-end station from April to May 2019. Because thermal radiation is the dominant cooling path over 100 K, the inner radiation shield, mirror, marionette recoil mass, and HLVIS are cooled simultaneously. On the other hand, because conductive cooling is the dominant path of cooling below 100 K, cooling proceeds from the elements that are closer to the cryocoolers, in the order of HLVIS, marionette recoil mass, and mirror.

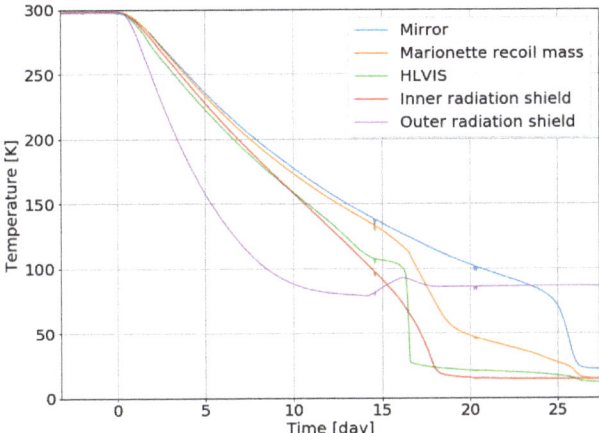

Figure 8. Example of the cooling curves of KAGRA's cryogenic system. The mirror reached 22 K at 27 days after the start of cooling. The cooling speed drastically changed below 100 K because of the increase in the thermal conductivity of the heat links and decrease in the specific heat. Each component is shown in Figure 5.

During cooling in 2019, KAGRA faced a more serious problem. The molecular adsorption during the initial cooling was much greater than expected, and visible frost was formed on the mirror surface. Figure 9 shows photographs of the mirror surface illuminated by a green laser, with and without frost on the mirror. As shown in Figure 9, a very thick frost was formed on the cryogenic mirror surface and caused significant scattering of the green beam. Once the thick frost was formed, the cavity finesse for the 1064 nm laser dropped to several hundred or less, while the finesse at room temperature was approximately 1500.

Therefore, a new cooling scheme to prevent frost formation was considered and tested from November 2020 to February 2021. The scheme involved cooling the mirrors step by step and trapping molecules not on the mirror surface but on the surface of the radiation shields. Owing to this new scheme, the KAGRA mirror was successfully cooled without any thick frost that could be visually inspected.

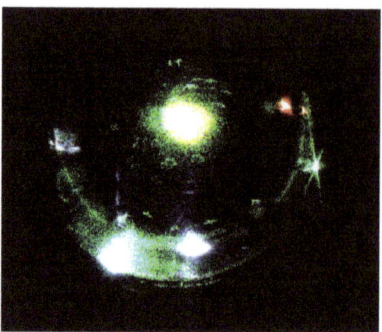 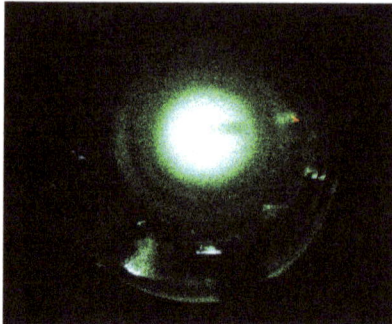

Figure 9. Images of the mirror illuminated with a green laser. (**Left**) Image at room temperature. The mirror surface is clean, and the green beam scattering is smaller than that at cryogenic temperature. (**Right**) Image at cryogenic temperature. The mirror surface is covered with thick frost, and the green beam is scattered on the surface.

4. Evaluations of the Underground Environment

A GW detector is a delicate system that is easily affected by environmental disturbances. The underground environment is expected to be quieter than that of the ground surface, and its actual evaluation is important not only for KAGRA, but also for further GW observatories, such as the ET. In this section, the current results of environmental studies in KAGRA are explained in terms of both their benefits and difficulties. An overview of the physical environmental monitoring system in KAGRA is described in Ref. [42].

4.1. Seismic Motion

4.1.1. Microseismic Motion

As discussed in Section 2.4.1, seismic motion at the frequency of the observational windows at the experimental site is significantly reduced compared with that on the ground surface. However, this reduction is inefficient at lower frequencies. Sometimes, microseismic motions caused by sea waves disrupt the control of suspensions and the interferometer. Japan is surrounded by two seas, the Pacific Ocean and the Sea of Japan, which exhibit different seasonal behaviors. Figure 10 (top) shows the wave height of the Pacific Ocean (Omaesaki in Shizuoka prefecture) and Sea of Japan (Wajima in Ishikawa prefecture) from July 2019 to June 2020 [43]. Figure 10 (bottom) shows the seismic spectrum at the KAGRA site on 12 October 2019 (green), December 2019 (cyan), and March 2020 (red). In the winter season, the waves of the Sea of Japan and the seismic motion at the KAGRA site became relatively larger. In summer and autumn, the level of the sea waves was usually low; however, sometimes it increased owing to a typhoon (for example, on 12 October 2019).

The relationship between the microseismic level and lock state of KAGRA's main interferometer during O3GK was studied [44]. Figure 11 shows the sea waves, seismic level at the KAGRA site, and lock state of the KAGRA interferometer with a focus on the O3GK term. The correlation between the sea waves and seismic level could be observed, and the interferometer could not be locked when the sea was rough (>2 m).

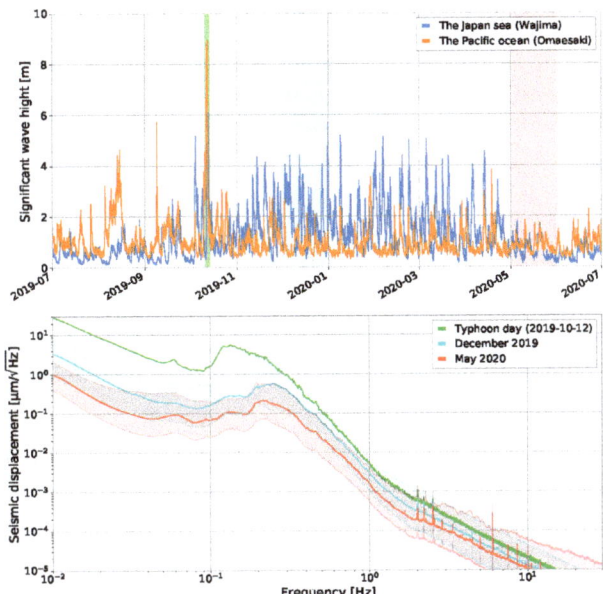

Figure 10. (**Top**): One-year data of the significant wave height in the Sea of Japan (Wajima) and Pacific Ocean (Omaesaki), opened in NOWPHAS [43]. (**Bottom**): Amplitude spectral density of the horizontal seismic displacement measured at the X-end of KAGRA. Each color corresponds to the period shown in the top graph. The solid lines represent the medians and the bands represent the 10th–90th percentiles during the one-month period.

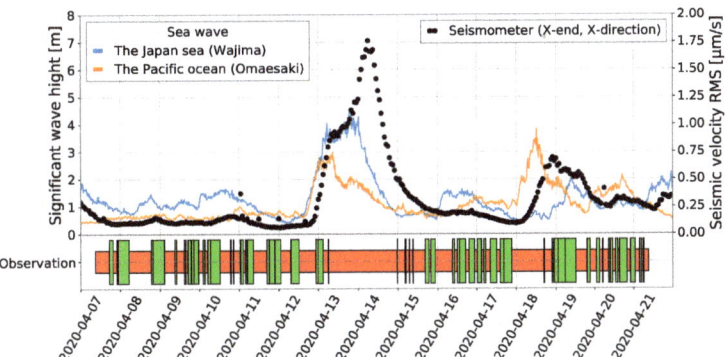

Figure 11. Comparison of the microseisms and the observation state of KAGRA during O3GK [44]. The blue and orange lines show the significant wave height in the Sea of Japan (Wajima) and Pacific Ocean (Omaesaki), respectively, opened in NOWPHAS [43]. The black markers are the RMS values of the seismic velocity in the 0.1–0.3 mHz band for every hour, measured at the X-end of KAGRA. The bottom bar graph shows the observation status of KAGRA during O3GK [37], with the science mode (green) and others (red, mainly the unlocked period).

4.1.2. Seismic Newtonian Noise

The motion of the mass around the experimental site induces a fluctuation in Newton's gravity and shakes the test-mass mirrors. This is called Newtonian noise (NN) [45]. It cannot be shielded against and is counted as fundamental noise.

Seismic motion is known to be the primary source of NN and has been intensively studied in GW detector research. For example, it is known that seismic Rayleigh waves propagating on a surface are reduced in underground facilities. Figure 12 shows the estimation of the NN caused by seismic body waves, seismic Rayleigh waves, and room acoustic waves for KAGRA [46]. All lines are significantly below the design sensitivity of KAGRA.

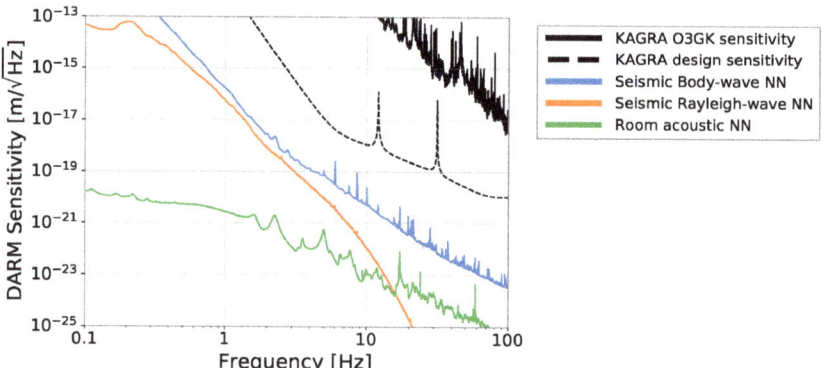

Figure 12. The estimated Newtonian noise from the seismic body waves (blue), seismic Rayleigh waves (orange), and acoustic fields in the experimental site (green) for KAGRA [46] compared with the O3GK sensitivity (black, solid) and design sensitivity (black, dashed) [37] of KAGRA.

4.2. Acoustic Field

The sound at the experimental site is considered environmental noise. Most of the main optics, such as test-mass mirrors or photodetectors for the GW detection port, are suspended in vacuum chambers and isolated from the acoustic field in the experimental room. However, the laser source and other auxiliary optics are not located in vacuum (this is not specified for the underground environment; however, the acoustic response of the KAGRA interferometer was carefully studied for the O3GK configuration [47]). Infrasound, which is a low-frequency sound that the human ear cannot detect, is also of interest because it causes the expansion and contraction of the arm tunnel [42]. The spectrum of the acoustic field in KAGRA's corner station (CS) and X-arm is compared with those of the Virgo central experimental building (CEB, a ground-surface facility) and Matra Gravitational and Geophysical Laboratory (MGGL, an underground facility) in Figure 13 under quiet conditions without human activity. The acoustic levels are similar for both datasets, and the difference between the underground and on-surface environments is not significant. Notably, however, the underground environment is quieter and more stable than the on-surface environment with respect to transient external acoustic disturbances, such as agricultural work or airplanes.

One unique aspect of the acoustic properties of KAGRA is that the reverberation time at the experimental site is much shorter than those of LIGO and Virgo; therefore, a transient sound decays quickly in KAGRA. This is because of the difference in the inner surfaces of the walls rather than the underground location. LIGO and Virgo have painted hard concrete walls, and they reflect the sound efficiently. On the other hand, the walls of KAGRA are coated with bubbling urethane and plastic paint, and they work as acoustic absorbers (Figure 14). A paper on the quantitative evaluation of this topic is in preparation.

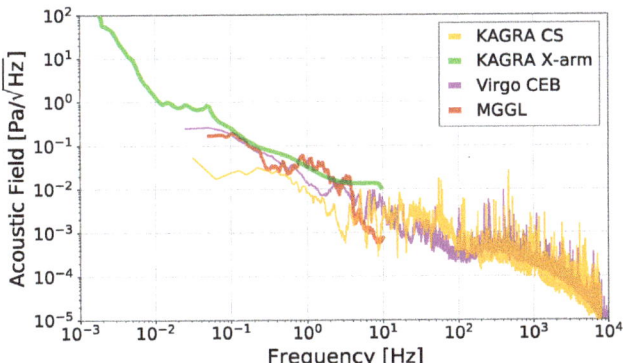

Figure 13. Comparison of the acoustic fields for the gravitational experimental sites: KAGRA CS [48], KAGRA X-arm [42], Virgo CEB [48], and MGGL [49].

Figure 14. Schematic view of the walls in the experimental sites of KAGRA and LIGO/Virgo.

4.3. Magnetic Field

4.3.1. Magnetic Noise Estimation

A magnetic field can cause displacement noise through the force on the mirrors and/or sensing noise through the electronics.

The magnetic field in the cryostat was measured at the X-end. The results are presented in Figure 15 (top, red graph), and the peaks at 1 and 1.7 Hz correspond to the periods of the motors for the cryocoolers (1 and 0.6 s). The coupling functions in case 1 (measured for LIGO) and case 2 (measured for Virgo) were used to estimate the contribution of magnetic noise to the sensitivity of the DARM because it has not yet been measured for KAGRA. The approximated coupling function between the magnetic field and DARM displacement is written as

$$C(f) = \kappa \times \left(\frac{f}{f_0}\right)^{-\beta} \quad [\text{m/T}], \tag{1}$$

where κ, β, and f_0 ($\kappa = 8 \times 10^{-8}$ m/T, $\beta = 2.67$ in LIGO [50], $\kappa = 5.6 \times 10^{-8}$ m/T, $\beta = 3.3$ in Virgo [51], and $f_0 = 10$ Hz for both detectors) are the experimental parameters used to characterize the data. Using these coupling functions, the magnetic noise is projected onto the DARM sensitivity, as shown in Figure 15 (bottom). According to the estimation, magnetic noise will not contaminate the design sensitivity.

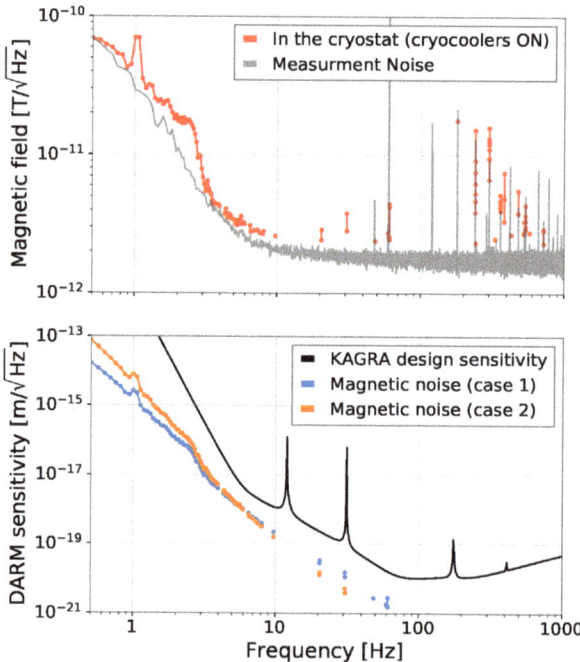

Figure 15. (**Top**) Magnetic field measured in a cryostat for the ETMX with cryocoolers. The gray line shows the measurement limit, including the sensor and ADC noises. (**Bottom**) Expected magnetic noise in the DARM sensitivity of KAGRA, calculated using the magnetic field in the top plot and the coupling functions evaluated for LIGO (blue) and Virgo (orange).

4.3.2. Schumann Resonance

The Schumann resonance is a global electromagnetic resonance with frequencies of 7.8, 14.1, 20.3 Hz, and so on, and an amplitude of approximately 1 pT/$\sqrt{\text{Hz}}$, which is generated and excited by lightning discharges in the cavity formed by the Earth's surface and ionosphere. Its contribution to a single GW detector as noise is expected to be smaller than that of the local magnetic field (for example, coming from power lines or electrical apparatuses); however, it has coherence between far-away points on Earth and is a common noise for the global GW observation network, especially when searching for stochastic background GWs [52,53].

Short-term Schumann resonance measurements were performed at the KAGRA experimental site during the construction phase [54,55]. Figure 16 shows the recent results of the measurements outside the tunnel and inside the KAGRA X-arm tunnel. The amplitude of the Schumann resonance (X-direction) is larger inside the tunnel than outside, a behavior that was also observed in the previous two measurements. More detailed studies, such as remeasurements and simulations, are ongoing to understand this behavior.

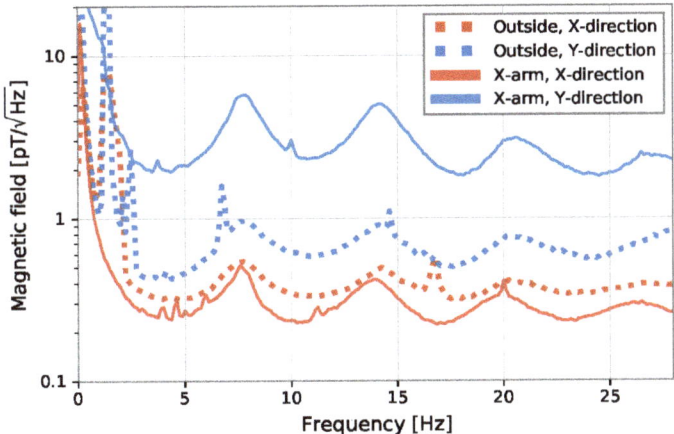

Figure 16. Schumann resonance of magnetic fields measured outside the tunnel (dashed) and inside the X-arm (solid). Red (blue) corresponds to the direction along the X(Y)-arm.

4.3.3. Transient Magnetic Noise from Lightning Strikes

Lightning strikes are well-known high-energy phenomena that emit transient magnetic noise to the atmosphere. When a lightning strike occurs close to KAGRA, a glitch event can be detected by both magnetometers and the GW channel of the main interferometer of KAGRA. Figure 17 shows an example of a lightning event [56]. This is the first evidence that a GW detector constructed in an underground facility is excited by lightning strikes in the atmosphere. This means that lightning is a background event of a burst-GW search, but it can be easily identified using the current system of environmental monitoring.

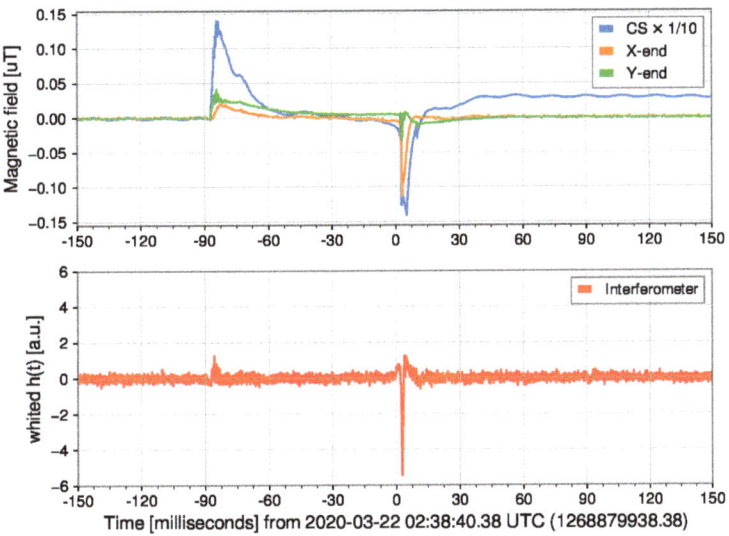

Figure 17. Time–series data of the magnetometers inside the KAGRA site (**top**) and KAGRA's main interferometer (whitened strain signal) (**bottom**) for nearby lightning. The origin of the horizontal axis (22 March 2022, 02:38:40.38) is the time of a lightning strike. For the magnetometers, the DC value of geomagnetism ($\sim$50 μT) is subtracted. Reprinted with permission from Ref. [56], ©2021 IOP Publishing.

4.4. Facility Issues

Although underground facilities provide many benefits, they also present challenges, as explained in this paper. A limitation in space leads to poor extensibility, making it tough (and expensive) to build a filter cavity or long signal-recycling cavity in KAGRA.

In general, the temperature of an underground cave is stable throughout the seasons. However, at the KAGRA experimental site, the room temperature easily changes when the working status of the apparatus changes. The room-temperature change affects the control and alignment of the interferometer. For example, it causes a drift in the geometrical anti-spring filters for vibration isolation in the vertical direction. Typically, room temperature must be maintained within 0.2 °C.

Springwater is another practical issue for underground facilities. Because it can easily pass through the ground and reach the experimental area, it should be removed using pumps and waterways to avoid any accidents. These devices generate additional environmental noise for the GW detector, which must be mitigated. Newtonian noise coming from fluid in a drainage pipe is one possible noise, and its study in simulations is ongoing.

5. Future Plan

GW detection has opened up a new window in astronomy and astrophysics, with further developments expected in the future. Increasing the number of observable events by expanding the observation range and improving the estimation accuracy of source parameters with higher SNR signals are essential. A new detector in the same frequency band with a sensitivity one order of magnitude higher than that of the current GW detectors is under development. ET, which is proposed to be built in Europe, has an arm length of 10 km, mirrors cooled to cryogenic temperatures [9], and underground construction. In addition, the LIGO project proposes the construction of a detector named Cosmic Explorer with an arm length of 40 km, whose sensitivity will be an order of magnitude higher than that of the Advanced LIGO detectors [10]. Another approach to advancing GW astronomy is launching GW observatories into space to observe GWs in lower frequency bands, such as with LISA [57], DECIGO [58], and TianQuin [59].

Although these attempts are being vigorously pursued, construction may take more than a decade. In the meantime, further improvement in the sensitivity of existing detectors is essential for the continuous development of GW astronomy. Advanced LIGO plus (A+) and Advanced Virgo Plus (AdV+) [60], which are upgraded detectors of Advanced LIGO and Advanced Virgo, are planned, and each is expected to improve the sensitivity by a factor of two compared to the current design sensitivity. In addition, in KAGRA, various proposals have been discussed [61]. In this section, some of the proposed plans are introduced.

One of the proposals involves improvement of the sapphire mirror. By making the mirror larger and heavier, domination of the thermal noise of the suspension and the quantum radiation pressure noise over the sensitivity in the low-frequency region will be reduced. Moreover, by increasing the beam size, the coating's thermal noise is expected to be reduced. The currently used sapphire mirror is 22 cm in diameter, 15 cm thick, and weighs 23 kg, which was the largest size that could be made when it was constructed. On the other hand, as a result of research and development, it is expected that a 100 kg sapphire crystal with a diameter of 36 cm and thickness of 25 cm will be created in a few years.

According to the quantum uncertainty principle, the product of the amplitude and phase fluctuations of light has a finite magnitude, and the two fluctuations cannot be simultaneously reduced to zero. A quantum squeezing technique is used to reduce only one of these fluctuations without violating the quantum uncertainty principle by sacrificing the other fluctuation. In Advanced LIGO and Advanced Virgo, reduction of the quantum shot noise, which is caused by quantum phase fluctuations, has been successful [62,63]. However, the intensity fluctuation becomes larger under the squeezed condition in the phase fluctuation, and the radiation pressure noise, which is caused by the quantum amplitude fluctuation, becomes larger. Therefore, a new technique, called frequency-dependent squeezing, is currently under development. This technique uses an optical resonator called a filter cavity to add frequency dependence to the squeezing process. While the quantum phase fluctuation is squeezed in the high-frequency region, where quantum shot noise is dominant, the quantum amplitude fluctuation is squeezed in the low-frequency region, where quantum radiation pressure noise is dominant. Thus, effective quantum noise reduction across the entire bandwidth is achieved. The frequency-dependent squeezing technique was demonstrated by the MIT group in the U.S. [64] and the NAOJ group in Japan [65–67] and will be installed in Advanced LIGO and Advanced Virgo before O4. It is anticipated that this technique will be adopted by KAGRA.

The improved sensitivity obtained by combining these techniques is shown in Figure 18. KAGRA's sensitivity can be improved to the same level as that of A+ and AdV+. Because the mirrors of KAGRA are cooled to cryogenic temperatures, it is difficult to reduce the noise by increasing the laser power, as is planned for A+ and AdV+. Increasing the laser power makes it difficult to cool the mirror to a cryogenic temperature owing to the heat caused by the absorption of the mirror. Because the quantum and thermal noise can be reduced without increasing the laser power, the frequency-dependent squeezing technique and the use of a larger sapphire mirror are the best strategies for improving the sensitivity of KAGRA. This is also the case for the next generation of GW detectors, for some of which cryogenic mirrors are planned, and the improved sensitivity of KAGRA can serve as a case study for them.

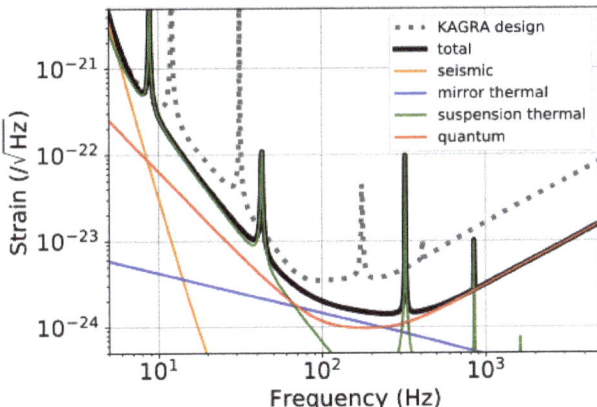

Figure 18. Estimated sensitivity curve after the modifications described in this section. Adapted with permission from Ref. [61], ©2020 American Physical Society.

6. Conclusions

In this article, the current status and future upgrades of KAGRA were reviewed. The first joint observation run in 2020 was a major milestone for KAGRA; however, further upgrades are necessary in order to contribute to gravitational wave astrophysics. KAGRA's key features, the suspensions and cryogenic system, are being upgraded, which is significantly important for the next observation run. Evaluations of the unique underground environment of KAGRA have also progressed, and some topics are progressing ahead of LIGO and Virgo. GW detection with KAGRA is vital for promoting GW astronomy and will also serve as the basis for introducing new technologies in future GW observatories.

Author Contributions: Corresponding authors wrote all the manuscript. M.N. summarized IFO configuration, design sensitivity, and future plans. T.U. described on suspensions, cryogenic systems, and upgrade plans for O4. T.W. wrote on the underground environments. All authors were contributing to KAGRA project in 2020 and agreed to publish the manuscript. All authors have read and agreed to the published version of the manuscript.

Funding: This work was funded by MEXT, JSPS Leading-edge Research Infrastructure Program, JSPS Grant-in-Aid for Specially Promoted Research 26000005, JSPS Grant-in-Aid for Scientific Research on Innovative Areas 2905: JP17H06358, JP17H06361, and JP17H06364, JSPS Core-to-Core Program A. Advanced Research Networks, JSPS Grant-in-Aid for Scientific Research (S) 17H06133 and 20H05639, JSPS Grant-in-Aid for Transformative Research Areas (A) 20A203: JP20H05854, the joint research program of the Institute for Cosmic Ray Research, University of Tokyo, National Research Foundation (NRF), and Computing Infrastructure Project of KISTI-GSDC in Korea, Academia Sinica (AS), AS Grid Center (ASGC), and the Ministry of Science and Technology (MoST) in Taiwan under grants including AS-CDA-105-M06.

Institutional Review Board Statement: Not applicable.

Informed Consent Statement: Not applicable.

Data Availability Statement: Not applicable.

Acknowledgments: M. Nakano, T. Ushiba, and T. Washimi are grateful to Gabriele Vajente for inviting them to write the present manuscript for publication in Galaxies. This work was supported by Advanced Technology Center (ATC) of NAOJ, Mechanical Engineering Center of KEK, the LIGO project, and the Virgo project. Help in the study of the underground environment was provided by the Virgo/ET members, especially F. Paoletti, I. Fiori, J. Harms, and F. Badaracco.

Conflicts of Interest: The authors declare no conflict of interest.

References

1. The LIGO Scientific Collaboration. Advanced LIGO. *Class. Quantum Gravity* **2015**, *32*, 074001. [CrossRef]
2. Acernese, F.; Agathos, M.; Agatsuma, K.; Aisa, D.; Allemandou, N.; Allocca, A.; Amarni, J.; Astone, P.; Balestri, G.; Ballardin, G.; et al. Advanced Virgo: A second-generation interferometric gravitational wave detector. *Class. Quantum Gravity* **2014**, *32*, 024001. [CrossRef]
3. Dooley, K.; Leong, J.; Adams, T.; Affeldt, C.; Bisht, A.; Bogan, C.; Degallaix, J.; Gräf, C.; Hild, S.; Hough, J.; et al. GEO 600 and the GEO-HF upgrade program: Successes and challenges. *Class. Quantum Gravity* **2015**, *33*. [CrossRef]
4. LIGO Scientific Collaboration; Virgo Collaboration. Observation of Gravitational Waves from a Binary Black Hole Merger. *Phys. Rev. Lett.* **2016**, *116*, 061102. [CrossRef] [PubMed]
5. LIGO Scientific Collaboration; Virgo Collaboration. GWTC-1: A Gravitational-Wave Transient Catalog of Compact Binary Mergers Observed by LIGO and Virgo during the First and Second Observing Runs. *Phys. Rev. X* **2019**, *9*, 031040. [CrossRef]
6. LIGO Scientific Collaboration; Virgo Collaboration. GWTC-2: Compact Binary Coalescences Observed by LIGO and Virgo during the First Half of the Third Observing Run. *Phys. Rev. X* **2021**, *11*, 021053. [CrossRef]
7. LIGO Scientific Collaboration; Virgo Collaboration. GW170817: Observation of Gravitational Waves from a Binary Neutron Star Inspiral. *Phys. Rev. Lett.* **2017**, *119*, 161101. [CrossRef]
8. KAGRA Collaboration. Overview of KAGRA: Detector design and construction history. *Prog. Theor. Exp. Phys.* **2020**, *2021*, 05A101. [CrossRef]
9. Maggiore, M.; Broeck, C.V.D.; Bartolo, N.; Belgacem, E.; Bertacca, D.; Bizouard, M.A.; Branchesi, M.; Clesse, S.; Foffa, S.; García-Bellido, J.; et al. Science case for the Einstein telescope. *J. Cosmol. Astropart. Phys.* **2020**, *2020*, 050–050. [CrossRef]
10. Reitze, D.; Adhikari, R.X.; Ballmer, S.; Barish, B.; Barsotti, L.; Billingsley, G.; Brown, D.A.; Chen, Y.; Coyne, D.; Eisenstein, R.; et al. Cosmic Explorer: The U.S. Contribution to Gravitational-Wave Astronomy beyond LIGO. *Bull. AAS* **2019**, *51*, 1–12. Available online: https://baas.aas.org/pub/2020n7i035 (accessed on 17 April 2022).
11. Fukuda, S.; Fukuda, Y.; Hayakawa, T.; Ichihara, E.; Ishitsuka, M.; Itow, Y.; Kajita, T.; Kameda, J.; Kaneyuki, K.; Kasuga, S.; et al. The Super-Kamiokande detector. *Nucl. Instrum. Methods Phys. Res. Sect. A* **2003**, *501*, 418–462. [CrossRef]
12. Suekane, F. The 1000ton liquid scintillation detector project at Kamioka (Kam-LAND). *AIP Conf. Proc.* **1997**, *412*, 969–975. [CrossRef]
13. Umehara, S.; Kishimoto, T.; Nomachi, M.; Ajimura, S.; Iida, T.; Takemoto, Y.; Matsuoka, K.; Trang, V.T.T.; Yoshida, S.; Wang, W.; et al. Search For Neutrino-less Double Beta Decay Of 48Ca- Candles. *Proc. Sci.* **2017**, *281*, 246. [CrossRef]
14. Nakamura, K.; Miuchi, K.; Tanimori, T.; Kubo, H.; Nishimura, H.; Parker, J.D.; Takada, A.; Mizumoto, T.; Sawano, T.; Matsuoka, Y.; et al. NEWAGE—Direction-sensitive Dark Matter Search Experiment. *Phys. Procedia* **2015**, *61*, 737–741. [CrossRef]
15. Fushimi, K.I.; Chernyak, D.; Ejiri, H.; Hata, K.; Hazama, R.; Hirata, S.; Iida, T.; Ikeda, H.; Inoue, K.; Imagawa, K.; et al. PICOLON dark matter search development of highly redio-pure NaI(Tl) scintilltor. *J. Phys. Conf. Ser.* **2020**, *1468*, 012057. [CrossRef]

16. Abe, K.; Hieda, K.; Hiraide, K.; Hirano, S.; Kishimoto, Y.; Kobayashi, K.; Moriyama, S.; Nakagawa, K.; Nakahata, M.; Nishiie, H.; et al. XMASS detector. *Nucl. Instrum. Methods Phys. Res. Sect. A* **2013**, *716*, 78–85. [CrossRef]
17. Uchiyama, T.; Miyoki, S.; Telada, S.; Yamamoto, K.; Ohashi, M.; Agatsuma, K.; Arai, K.; Fujimoto, M.; Haruyama, T.; Kawamura, S.; et al. Reduction of thermal fluctuations in a cryogenic laser interferometric gravitational wave detector. *Phys. Rev. Lett.* **2012**, *108*, 141101. [CrossRef]
18. Katsumata, K. Seismic attenuation and low-velocity anomalies under the Hida mountain range. *Chikyu Mon.* **1996**, *18*, 109–115. (In Japanese)
19. Gennai, N.; Hiramatsu, Y.; Kono, Y. Three-dimensional Distribution of an Extremely Low-Density Body Beneath the Hida Mountains, Central Japan, as Estimated from Gravity Anomalies. *Kazan* **2002**, *47*, 411–418. (In Japanese) [CrossRef]
20. KAGARA Gallery. Available online: https://gwcenter.icrr.u-tokyo.ac.jp/kagra-gallery (accessed on 17 April 2022).
21. Meers, B.J. Recycling in laser-interferometric gravitational-wave detectors. *Phys. Rev. D* **1988**, *38*, 2317–2326. [CrossRef]
22. KAGRA Collaboration. The status of KAGRA underground cryogenic gravitational wave telescope. *J. Phys. Conf. Ser.* **2020**, *1342*, 012014. [CrossRef]
23. Mizuno, J.; Strain, K.; Nelson, P.; Chen, J.; Schilling, R.; Rüdiger, A.; Winkler, W.; Danzmann, K. Resonant sideband extraction: A new configuration for interferometric gravitational wave detectors. *Phys. Lett. A* **1993**, *175*, 273–276. [CrossRef]
24. Kawamura, S.; Nakano, M. Chapter 2: Interferometer configuration and response. In *Advanced Interferometric Gravitational-Wave Detectors*; World Scientific Publishing: Hackensack, NJ, USA, 2019; pp. 33–58. [CrossRef]
25. KAGRA Official Sensitivity Limit. Available online: https://gwcenter.icrr.u-tokyo.ac.jp/en/researcher/parameter (accessed on 17 April 2022).
26. Saulson, P.R. Thermal noise in mechanical experiments. *Phys. Rev. D* **1990**, *42*, 2437–2445. [CrossRef] [PubMed]
27. KAGRA Collaboration. Construction of KAGRA: An underground gravitational-wave observatory. *Prog. Theor. Exp. Phys.* **2018**, *2018*, 013F01. [CrossRef]
28. Sato, S.; Miyoki, S.; Telada, S.; Tatsumi, D.; Araya, A.; Ohashi, M.; Totsuka, Y.; Fukushima, M.; Fujimoto, M. Ultrastable performance of an underground-based laser interferometer observatory for gravitational waves. *Phys. Rev. D* **2004**, *69*, 102005. [CrossRef]
29. Takahashi, R.; The TAMA Collaboration. Status of TAMA300. *Class. Quantum Gravity* **2004**, *21*, S403–S408. [CrossRef]
30. Virgo Collaboration. Virgo: A laser interferometer to detect gravitational waves. *J. Instrum.* **2012**, *7*, P03012. [CrossRef]
31. Uchiyama, T.; Tomaru, T.; Tobar, M.E.; Tatsumi, D.; Miyoki, S.; Ohashi, M.; Kuroda, K.; Suzuki, T.; Sato, N.; Haruyama, T.; et al. Mechanical quality factor of a cryogenic sapphire test mass for gravitational wave detectors. *Phys. Lett. Sect. A* **1999**, *261*, 5–11. [CrossRef]
32. Khalaidovski, A.; Hofmann, G.; Chen, D.; Komma, J.; Schwarz, C.; Tokoku, C.; Kimura, N.; Suzuki, T.; Scheie, A.O.; Majorana, E.; et al. Evaluation of heat extraction through sapphire fibers for the GW observatory KAGRA. *Class. Quantum Gravity* **2014**, *31*, 105004. [CrossRef]
33. Hirose, E.; Billingsley, G.; Zhang, L.; Yamamoto, H.; Pinard, L.; Michel, C.; Forest, D.; Reichman, B.; Gross, M. Characterization of Core Optics in Gravitational-Wave Detectors: Case Study of KAGRA Sapphire Mirrors. *Phys. Rev. Appl.* **2020**, *14*, 014021. [CrossRef]
34. Yamada, T.; Tomaru, T.; Suzuki, T.; Ushiba, T.; Kimura, N.; Takada, S.; Inoue, Y.; Kajita, T. High performance thermal link with small spring constant for cryogenic applications. *Cryogenics* **2021**, *116*, 103280. [CrossRef]
35. Ikushima, Y.; Li, R.; Tomaru, T.; Sato, N.; Suzuki, T.; Haruyama, T.; Shintomi, T.; Yamamoto, A. Ultra-low-vibration pulse-tube cryocooler system-cooling capacity and vibration. *Cryogenics* **2008**, *48*, 406–412. [CrossRef]
36. Georgescu, I. O3 highlights. *Nat. Rev. Phys.* **2020**, *2*, 222–223. [CrossRef] [PubMed]
37. KAGRA Collaboration. Performance of the KAGRA detector during the first joint observation with GEO 600 (O3GK). *arXiv* **2022**, arXiv:2203.07011.
38. LIGO, Virgo and Kagra Observing Run Plans. Available online: https://www.ligo.caltech.edu/news/ligo20211115 (accessed on 17 April 2022).
39. Ushiba, T.; Akutsu, T.; Araki, S.; Bajpai, R.; Chen, D.; Craig, K.; Enomoto, Y.; Hagiwara, A.; Haino, S.; Inoue, Y.; et al. Cryogenic suspension design for a kilometer-scale gravitational-wave detector. *Class. Quantum Gravity* **2021**, *38*, 085013. [CrossRef]
40. Zeidler, S. Length-Sensing OpLevs for KAGRA. Technical Report, JGW-T1605788-v11. Available online: https://gwdoc.icrr.u-tokyo.ac.jp/cgi-bin/DocDB/ShowDocument?docid=5788 (accessed on 17 April 2022).
41. Hasegawa, K.; Akutsu, T.; Kimura, N.; Saito, Y.; Suzuki, T.; Tomaru, T.; Ueda, A.; Miyoki, S. Molecular adsorbed layer formation on cooled mirrors and its impacts on cryogenic gravitational wave telescopes. *Phys. Rev. D* **2019**, *99*, 22003. [CrossRef]
42. KAGRA Collaboration. Overview of KAGRA: Calibration, detector characterization, physical environmental monitors, and the geophysics interferometer. *Prog. Theor. Exp. Phys.* **2021**, *2021*, 05A102. [CrossRef]
43. Ports and Harbours Bureau, Ministry of Land, Infrastructure and Transport, Japan. NOWPHAS: Nationwide Ocean Wave information network for Ports and HArbourS. 2021. Available online: https://www.mlit.go.jp/kowan/nowphas/index_eng.html (accessed on 17 April 2022).
44. Fujikawa, Y. Development of Cause Estimation System for Interferometer Lock Loss in Large-Scale Cryogenic Gravitational Waves Telescope, KAGRA. Master's Thesis, Niigata University, Niigata, Japan, 2020. (In Japanese)
45. Harms, J. Terrestrial gravity fluctuations. *Living Rev. Relativ.* **2019**, *18*, 3. [CrossRef]

46. Badaracco, F.; Harms, J.; Rossi, C.D.; Fiori, I.; Miyo, K.; Tanaka, T.; Yokozawa, T.; Paoletti, F.; Washimi, T. KAGRA underground environment and lessons for the Einstein Telescope. *Phys. Rev. D* **2021**, *104*, 042006. [CrossRef]
47. Washimi, T.; Yokozawa, T.; Tanaka, T.; Itoh, Y.; Kume, J.; Yokoyama, J. Method for environmental noise estimation via injection tests for ground-based gravitational wave detectors. *Class. Quantum Gravity* **2021**, *38*, 125005. [CrossRef]
48. Washimi, T. Status of KAGRA physical environmental monitors toward the O3. In Proceedigs of the 6th KAGRA International Workshop, Wuhan, China, 21 June 2019.
49. Fenyvesi, E.; Molnár, J.; Czellár, S. Investigation of Infrasound Background Noise at Mátra Gravitational and Geophysical Laboratory (MGGL). *Universe* **2020**, *6*, 10. [CrossRef]
50. Thrane, E.; Christensen, N.; Schofield, R.M.S.; Effler, A. Correlated noise in networks of gravitational-wave detectors: Subtraction and mitigation. *Phys. Rev. D* **2014**, *90*, 023013. [CrossRef]
51. Cirone, A.; Fiori, I.; Paoletti, F.; Perez, M.M.; Rodríguez, A.R.; Swinkels, B.L.; Vazquez, A.M.; Gemme, G.; Chincarini, A. Investigation of magnetic noise in advanced Virgo. *Class. Quantum Gravity* **2019**, *36*, 225004. [CrossRef]
52. Himemoto, Y.; Taruya, A. Impact of correlated magnetic noise on the detection of stochastic gravitational waves: Estimation based on a simple analytical model. *Phys. Rev. D* **2017**, *96*, 022004. [CrossRef]
53. Himemoto, Y.; Taruya, A. Correlated magnetic noise from anisotropic lightning sources and the detection of stochastic gravitational waves. *Phys. Rev. D* **2019**, *100*, 082001. [CrossRef]
54. Atsuta, S.; Ogawa, T.; Yamaguchi, S.; Hayama, K.; Araya, A.; Kanda, N.; Miyakawa, O.; Miyoki, S.; Nishizawa, A.; Ono, K.; et al. Measurement of Schumann Resonance at Kamioka. *J. Phys.* **2016**, *716*, 012020. [CrossRef]
55. Coughlin, M.W.; Cirone, A.; Meyers, P.; Atsuta, S.; Bosch, V.; Chincarini, A.; Christensen, N.L.; Rosa, R.D.; Effler, A.; Fiori, I.; et al. Measurement and subtraction of Schumann resonances at gravitational-wave interferometers. *Phys. Rev. D* **2018**, *97*, 102007. [CrossRef]
56. Washimi, T.; Yokozawa, T.; Nakano, M.; Tanaka, T.; Kaihotsu, K.; Mori, Y.; Narita, T. Effects of lightning strokes on underground gravitational waves observatories. *J. Instrum.* **2021**, *16*, P07033. [CrossRef]
57. Babak, S.; Gair, J.; Sesana, A.; Barausse, E.; Sopuerta, C.F.; Berry, C.P.L.; Berti, E.; Amaro-Seoane, P.; Petiteau, A.; Klein, A. Science with the space-based interferometer LISA. V. Extreme mass-ratio inspirals. *Phys. Rev. D* **2017**, *95*, 103012. [CrossRef]
58. Kawamura, S.; Ando, M.; Nakamura, T.; Tsubono, K.; Tanaka, T.; Funaki, I.; Seto, N.; Numata, K.; Sato, S.; Ioka, K.; et al. The Japanese space gravitational wave antenna—DECIGO. *J. Phys.* **2008**, *122*, 012006. [CrossRef]
59. Luo, J.; Chen, L.S.; Duan, H.Z.; Gong, Y.G.; Hu, S.; Ji, J.; Liu, Q.; Mei, J.; Milyukov, V.; Sazhin, M.; et al. TianQin: A space-borne gravitational wave detector. *Class. Quantum Gravity* **2016**, *33*, 035010. [CrossRef]
60. Abbott, B.P.; Abbott, R.; Abbott, T.D.; Abraham, S.; Acernese, F.; Ackley, K.; Adams, C.; Adya, V.B.; Affeldt, C.; Agathos, M.; et al. Prospects for observing and localizing gravitational-wave transients with Advanced LIGO, Advanced Virgo and KAGRA. *Living Rev. Relativ.* **2020**, *23*, 3. [CrossRef] [PubMed]
61. Michimura, Y.; Komori, K.; Enomoto, Y.; Nagano, K.; Nishizawa, A.; Hirose, E.; Leonardi, M.; Capocasa, E.; Aritomi, N.; Zhao, Y.; et al. Prospects for improving the sensitivity of the cryogenic gravitational wave detector KAGRA. *Phys. Rev. D* **2020**, *102*, 022008. [CrossRef]
62. Tse, M.; Yu, H.; Kijbunchoo, N.; Fernandez-Galiana, A.; Dupej, P.; Barsotti, L.; Blair, C.D.; Brown, D.D.; Dwyer, S.E.; Effler, A.; et al. Quantum-Enhanced Advanced LIGO Detectors in the Era of Gravitational-Wave Astronomy. *Phys. Rev. Lett.* **2019**, *123*, 231107. [CrossRef] [PubMed]
63. Virgo Collaboration. Increasing the Astrophysical Reach of the Advanced Virgo Detector via the Application of Squeezed Vacuum States of Light. *Phys. Rev. Lett.* **2019**, *123*, 231108. [CrossRef]
64. McCuller, L.; Whittle, C.; Ganapathy, D.; Komori, K.; Tse, M.; Fernandez-Galiana, A.; Barsotti, L.; Fritschel, P.; MacInnis, M.; Matichard, F.; et al. Frequency-Dependent Squeezing for Advanced LIGO. *Phys. Rev. Lett.* **2020**, *124*, 171102. [CrossRef]
65. Zhao, Y.; Aritomi, N.; Capocasa, E.; Leonardi, M.; Eisenmann, M.; Guo, Y.; Polini, E.; Tomura, A.; Arai, K.; Aso, Y.; et al. Frequency-Dependent Squeezed Vacuum Source for Broadband Quantum Noise Reduction in Advanced Gravitational-Wave Detectors. *Phys. Rev. Lett.* **2020**, *124*, 171101. [CrossRef]
66. Capocasa, E.; Barsuglia, M.; Degallaix, J.; Pinard, L.; Straniero, N.; Schnabel, R.; Somiya, K.; Aso, Y.; Tatsumi, D.; Flaminio, R. Estimation of losses in a 300 m filter cavity and quantum noise reduction in the KAGRA gravitational-wave detector. *Phys. Rev. D* **2016**, *93*, 082004. [CrossRef]
67. Capocasa, E.; Guo, Y.; Eisenmann, M.; Zhao, Y.; Tomura, A.; Arai, K.; Aso, Y.; Marchiò, M.; Pinard, L.; Prat, P.; et al. Measurement of optical losses in a high-finesse 300 m filter cavity for broadband quantum noise reduction in gravitational-wave detectors. *Phys. Rev. D* **2018**, *98*, 022010. [CrossRef]

Review

Review of the Advanced LIGO Gravitational Wave Observatories Leading to Observing Run Four

Craig Cahillane [1,*] and Georgia Mansell [1,2,3]

1 LIGO Hanford Observatory, Richland, WA 99352, USA; georgia.mansell@ligo.org
2 LIGO, Massachusetts Institute of Technology, Cambridge, MA 02139, USA
3 Department of Physics, Syracuse University, Syracuse, NY 13244, USA
* Correspondence: craig.cahillane@ligo.org

Abstract: Gravitational waves from binary black hole and neutron star mergers are being regularly detected. As of 2021, 90 confident gravitational wave detections have been made by the LIGO and Virgo detectors. Work is ongoing to further increase the sensitivity of the detectors for the fourth observing run, including installing some of the A+ upgrades designed to lower the fundamental noise that limits the sensitivity to gravitational waves. In this review, we will provide an overview of the LIGO detectors optical configuration and lock acquisition procedure, discuss the detectors' fundamental and technical noise limits, show the current measured sensitivity, and explore the A+ upgrades currently being installed in the detectors.

Keywords: gravitational wave detectors; optomechanics; low-noise high-power laser interferometry

Citation: Cahillane, C.; Mansell, G. Review of the Advanced LIGO Gravitational Wave Observatories Leading to Observing Run Four. *Galaxies* **2022**, *10*, 36. https://doi.org/10.3390/galaxies10010036

Academic Editor: Gabriele Vajente

Received: 10 January 2022
Accepted: 4 February 2022
Published: 15 February 2022

Publisher's Note: MDPI stays neutral with regard to jurisdictional claims in published maps and institutional affiliations.

Copyright: © 2022 by the authors. Licensee MDPI, Basel, Switzerland. This article is an open access article distributed under the terms and conditions of the Creative Commons Attribution (CC BY) license (https://creativecommons.org/licenses/by/4.0/).

1. Introduction

On 14 September 2015, the Advanced LIGO detectors made the first direct detection of gravitational waves (GWs) from a binary black hole merger [1]. The detectors had just achieved full operation after a five-year hiatus while they were upgraded from initial to Advanced LIGO. The Advanced LIGO detectors featured new technologies and new optical configuration, designed to improve the signal-to-noise ratio of GW signals across the audio frequency spectrum [2–4]. The upgraded detectors drastically improved the sensitivity to intermediate mass black hole merger GW signals, enabling the detection of GW150914 [5].

On 17 August 2017, the Advanced LIGO and Virgo detectors discovered gravitational waves from a binary neutron star merger with a gamma-ray-burst counterpart [6]. This event triggered telescopes to point in the direction of the merger, in order to catch electromagnetic radiation from across the energy spectrum [7].

Today, the detectors have progressed significantly toward the goal of achieving design sensitivity [8]. Through the third observing run (O3), 90 confident gravitational wave detections from astrophysical compact binary mergers have been reported, along with many more low-confidence detections [9].

Now, in the period between observing runs three and four, major infrastructure improvements known as the A+ upgrades are being installed at the LIGO detectors [10,11]. These upgrades are focused on lowering the fundamental noise limit of the Advanced LIGO detectors, making higher levels of sensitivity to gravitational waves possible.

Here we will review the design and performance of the Advanced LIGO detectors leading into to observing run four (O4), scheduled to begin in December 2022. Section 2 will briefly overview the gravitational wave signals we expect. Section 3 will overview the Advanced LIGO optical configuration and lock acquisition process. Section 4 will review the fundamental limits of the Advanced LIGO detectors' sensitivity, as well as the current achieved sensitivity. Section 5 will discuss the current performance of the detectors, introducing the topics of point absorbers on optics and squeezed states of light. Section 6 will overview the upgrades currently being installed in preparation for O4. Section 7 will comment on future avenues for increasing detector sensitivity. Appendices A and B will overview the basics of the Michelson and Fabry–Pérot interferometric configurations, the fundamental building blocks of the full Advanced LIGO interferometer.

2. Gravitational Waves

A gravitational wave can be described as a small perturbation $h_{\mu\nu}$ on a flat spacetime metric $\eta_{\mu\nu}$ [12,13]:

$$g_{\mu\nu} = \eta_{\mu\nu} + h_{\mu\nu}. \tag{1}$$

In the transverse–traceless gauge, a gravitational wave propagating in the z direction can be expressed as

$$h_{\mu\nu}(t,x,y,z) = \begin{pmatrix} 0 & 0 & 0 & 0 \\ 0 & h_+ & h_\times & 0 \\ 0 & h_\times & -h_+ & 0 \\ 0 & 0 & 0 & 0 \end{pmatrix} \cos(\omega t - kz), \tag{2}$$

where h_+ is the plus-polarization gravitational wave strain, $h_\times$ is the cross-polarization strain, and ω and k are the frequency and wavenumber of the GW. In Equation (2), we have defined the usual coordinate system (t,x,y,z) for the Greek indices ranging from 0 to 3. In this gauge choice, the trace of the matrix in Equation (2) is zero, and the spacetime strain is only in the x and y directions, transverse to the z direction of propagation.

Next, we will show that a gravitational wave modulates the spacetime interval ds, and show how this can be interpreted as a change in length ΔL [14,15]. In general, the spacetime interval between any two points is

$$ds^2 = g_{\mu\nu} dx^\mu dx^\nu \tag{3}$$
$$= (\eta_{\mu\nu} + h_{\mu\nu}) dx^\mu dx^\nu \tag{4}$$
$$= -c^2 dt^2 + (1+h_+)dx^2 + (1-h_+)dy^2 + 2h_\times dx\, dy + dz^2, \tag{5}$$

where we have set our coordinate vector $dx^\mu = dx^\nu = (cdt, dx, dy, dz)^T$.

Gravitational wave detectors use laser light to sense spacetime. Light always has a spacetime interval $ds = 0$. If we set up a test particle on the x-axis a length L_x from the origin, and look at the spacetime interval ds for a light wave traveling between the origin and particle when only a h_+ wave is incident, assuming $h_+ \ll 1$, we obtain

$$ds^2 = 0 = -c^2 dt^2 + (1+h_+)dx^2 \tag{6}$$

$$c \int_0^{t_0} dt = \int_0^{L_x} \sqrt{1+h_+} dx \approx \int_0^{L_x} \left(1 + \frac{1}{2} h_+\right) dx \tag{7}$$

$$ct_0 = \left(1 + \frac{1}{2} h_+\right) L_x. \tag{8}$$

Equation (8) emphasizes that, in the chosen gauge and coordinates, the passing gravitational wave h_+ modulates the light travel time t_0 between the two stationary points $(0,0,0)$ and $(L_x,0,0)$. Equivalently, the GW strain can be said to modulate the x length: $\Delta L_x = h_+ L_x/2$. Along the y-axis between the points $(0,0,0)$ and $(0,L_y,0)$, the sign of the h_+ GW modulation is flipped, as seen from Equation (5): $\Delta L_y = -h_+ L_y/2$.

The differential length ΔL in the x- and y-axis, assuming $L_x = L_y = L$, yields

$$\Delta L = \Delta L_x - \Delta L_y = h_+ L \tag{9}$$

$$h_+ = \frac{\Delta L}{L}. \tag{10}$$

Equation (10) is the usual strain-to-length relation used in GW detection based on Michelson interferometers, which feature two orthogonal optical cavities filled with laser light. This motivates the choice for extremely long interferometer arms: generally, the longer the arms, the larger the differential length change ΔL will be. This holds as long as the long-wavelength approximation $\lambda_{GW} \gg L$ is true: if not, Equation (10) breaks down because the GW oscillates spacetime faster than the light can complete a round trip in the optical cavities [16].

3. Advanced LIGO Detectors

Each Advanced LIGO detector is a long-baseline laser interferometer with two 4 km-long orthogonal arms. The interferometer acts as a transducer, transforming the GW signal into observable laser power fluctuations at the antisymmetric port.

The interferometer is supported by several auxiliary subsystems required to detect gravitational waves. Auxiliary subsystems include the core optics length controls [17–23], angular controls [24–31], high-powered stabilized laser [32–34], vacuum system [35–37], optics suspensions [38–40], seismic isolation [41–44], and electronics and data acquisition systems [45–48]. This review will focus on the optical configuration and operation of the interferometers.

The core of the Advanced LIGO detectors are dual-recycled, Fabry–Pérot, Michelson interferometers [2,3], enhanced with an input and an output mode cleaner [49,50], and filled with pre-stabilized laser light [32]. The entire LIGO optomechanical control system is based on the Pound–Drever–Hall frequency stabilization technique [17].

Figure 1 shows a simplified optical configuration planned for O4. The optical configuration is the same as O3, except for the addition of the 300 m filter cavity [51–53].

In this section, we will overview the Advanced LIGO optical configuration and the lock acquisition process. Appendix A overviews the optical components that make up the Advanced LIGO design.

3.1. Main Interferometer

The main interferometer consists of seven core optics, shown in Figure 1: the power-recycling mirror, the signal-recycling mirror, the beamsplitter, and the four arm cavity optics known as input test masses (ITMs) and end test masses (ETMs).

The main interferometer relies on *constructive interference* to build up high levels of laser power inside the 4 km Fabry–Pérot arm cavities (see Appendix B). With more laser power built up in the interferometer, more light is modulated by a passing GW, creating a stronger detected response to GWs at the detection port.

In the Michelson interferometer formed by the two arms and the beamsplitter, *destructive interference* occurs at the antisymmetric (detection) port, where the the beams from the two arms are recombined out of phase, so no light appears. At the input port, constructive interference occurs, so all the light input is reflected back toward the laser in the Michelson interferometer (see Appendix A).

Differential phase changes in the light in each arm, such as those caused by gravitational waves, will cause light to exit out the Michelson detection port. Common phase changes, on the other hand, will have no effect on the light levels at either the input or detection port. Thus, the Michelson detection port is said to have high *common mode rejection*, as both frequency and intensity fluctuations in the input laser light are largely rejected from the detection port.

3.1.1. Basic Signal

The gravitational wave *signal-to-noise ratio* (SNR) at the antisymmetric port is formed by the laser power signal due to GWs P_{as}, as well as the laser power noise $\sqrt{S_P}$, i.e., fluctuations not due to GWs. The gravitational wave SNR for the shot-noise-dominated regime can be approximately written as

$$\text{SNR} \approx \frac{P_{\text{as}}}{\sqrt{S_P}}\sqrt{t_{\text{sig}}} \propto \frac{L\sqrt{P_{\text{arm}}t_{\text{sig}}}}{\lambda}h, \qquad (11)$$

where L is the length of the Fabry–Pérot arm cavities, P_{arms} is the full power buildup in the arms, t_{sig} is the duration of the GW signal in the detector bandwidth, λ is the laser wavelength, and h is the GW strain amplitude. The full detector response is derived in [54,55], and expanded upon in [23,56–58]. A more complete understanding of detector signal and noise processing can be found in [59,60].

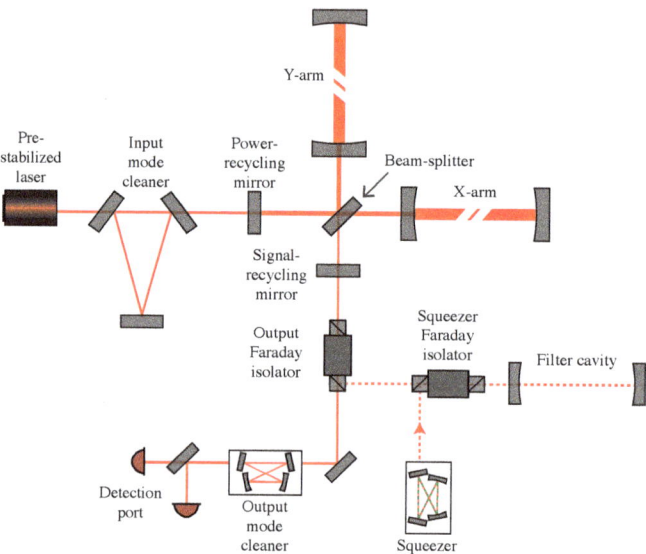

Figure 1. Simplified optical layout of the LIGO detectors for the fourth observing run. The pre-stabilized laser first traverses the input mode cleaner to further stabilize the laser light before entering the main interferometer. The main interferometer consists of the seven core optics in the upper right, including the Fabry–Pérot arm cavities, 50:50 beamsplitter, and recycling mirrors. The GW signal from the main interferometer (solid red) transmits through the signal-recycling mirror, output Faraday isolator, and output mode cleaner to the detection photodetectors at the detection (or antisymmetric) port. The dashed red represents the squeezed light input path from the squeezer cavity, reflected off the filter cavity, and input on the back of the signal-recycling mirror. The filter cavity is discussed in Section 6.3.

Several major considerations in detector design are captured in Equation (11). First, the simplest way to amplify the signal is to extend the arm length L. The main limit on making detectors longer is the cost of the facility, particularly the evacuated beamtube, which currently limits the LIGO detectors to the 4 km scale. Maximizing the arm power P_{arm} increases the detectable laser signal created by GWs, and is limited by input power and losses in the interferometer from absorption and scatter. Reducing the detector wavelength λ would naïvely increase sensitivity to GWs, but would require all major detector infrastructure, such as the source laser, optical coatings, substrates, and photodetectors, to perform at or better than the current noise levels.

3.1.2. Dual-Recycling

Dual-recycling refers to the two recycling cavities formed by the mirrors at the input and output of the main interferometer [61–64]. The mirror at the input is the *power-recycling mirror*, and is used to reflect light back into the main interferometer, enabling greater levels of light circulating inside the interferometer [55,65,66]. The mirror at the output is the *signal-recycling mirror*, and is used to broaden the detector bandwidth [54].

The Advanced LIGO recycling cavities are designed to be geometrically stable to better control spatial mode of the beam entering and exiting the Michelson [67], although point absorbers on the mirrors are suspected of polluting the main spatial mode (see Section 5.3.2). Control schemes for the interferometer degrees of freedom associated with the recycling cavities have been designed and implemented for length [18–21,23] and angular controls [26,29,30,68].

3.1.3. Squeezer

Heisenberg uncertainty in the form of shot noise and radiation pressure noise (Section 4.2) limits the sensitivity of the interferometer [69,70]. The *squeezer* is a squeezed vacuum source, and refers to the optics producing entangled photons for injection into the antisymmetric port of the interferometer [71–74]. The ensemble of entangled photons produce a quantum *squeezed-vacuum* electromagnetic field. By squeezing the quantum vacuum, quantum shot noise can be lowered across the bandwidth of the detector. This is known as *frequency-independent* squeezing.

The filter cavity shown in Figure 1 will enable *frequency-dependent* squeezed light injection. The results of squeezing in O3 are explained in Section 5.4. The filter cavity is explained further in Section 6.3.

3.1.4. Detector Bandwidth and Linewidth

The LIGO *detector bandwidth* refers to the frequency at which the differential arm (DARM) frequency response begins falling off. This value is also known as the *DARM coupled-cavity pole* or simply the *DARM pole*. This frequency is defined primarily by the DARM coupled cavity, which is formed by the arm cavities and the signal-recycling cavity [23]. As mentioned in Section 3.1.2, the signal recycling mirror is locked exactly off-resonance to broaden the detector bandwidth, in a scheme known as *resonant-sideband extraction* [54,56]. During mid-2021 locking, the detector bandwidth at LIGO Hanford was about 450 Hz.

Similarly, the *detector linewidth* refers to the full-width half-maximum of the laser frequency noise when the detector is locked. With a long-baseline, high-finesse interferometer such as Advanced LIGO, this is identical to twice the frequency at which the common arm (CARM) frequency response begins falling off. This is known as the *CARM coupled-cavity pole* or the *CARM pole*. The CARM coupled cavity is formed by the arm cavities and the power-recycling cavity, which in this case is locked on-resonance to enhance the resonating power [23]. This, paired with the 4 km-long baseline, makes the linewidth very small, and the laser ultrastable in the detector bandwidth [75]. The detector linewidth is estimated to be about 1 Hz.

3.1.5. Calibration

Calibration is the process of converting the detector output P_{as} into gravitational wave units of strain h [76–82]. The calibration reference is the *photon calibrator*, which uses an auxiliary laser to apply a known force on the optics via radiation pressure [83,84]. The O3 calibration response upper limit on systematic error and associated uncertainty is ∼11% in magnitude and ∼9° in phase (68% confidence interval) in the sensitive frequency band 20–2000 Hz [78,79]. The systematic error alone is estimated at levels of <2% in magnitude and <4° in phase [79].

Newtonian calibrators, which employ rapidly spinning masses near the optics, are also under development [85–87]. During O3, a Newtonian calibrator with a quadrupole and hexapole was installed at Hanford, and successfully induced motion on the X-end test mass (ETMX) [88]. Due to problems with precision installation and distance uncertainty analysis, the Newtonian calibrator will not be pursued by LIGO as a precision calibration instrument in O4.

3.2. Input Mode Cleaner

The input mode cleaner is a three-mirror, 33 m round trip triangular cavity used to further stabilize the frequency, intensity, and spatial mode content of the input laser before it enters the main interferometer [49]. The RMS laser frequency noise is limited by the linewidth of the interferometer, which is extremely low (1.2 Hz). The laser frequency is locked to the input mode cleaner length, providing high-gain high-bandwidth feedback (∼100 kHz) to massively suppress frequency noise intrinsic to the NPRO laser [20,75,89]. A small sample of the transmission through the input mode cleaner is used to stabilize the intensity of the laser input into the main interferometer.

3.3. Output Mode Cleaner

The output mode cleaner is a four-mirror, 1.1 m round trip bowtie cavity used to transmit only the main interferometer GW signal [50,90–92].

The GW readout scheme is known as *DC readout* [22,93]. A picometer-scale offset in the differential arm length is deliberately introduced and is controlled to let 20 mW of light leak out to the detection port. This light used as a local oscillator, beating against the GW signal light, rendering it detectable on a photodetector.

The radio-frequency sidebands used for controlling interferometer degrees of freedom, and higher-order modes from the main interferometer, are both reflected away from the detection port by the output mode cleaner. Backscatter, i.e. reflection from the output mode cleaner along the main beam path, is rejected by the output Faraday isolator.

3.4. Lock Acquisition

The lock acquisition process is a sequence of steps taken to bring the interferometer from a free-swinging uncontrolled state to an observation-ready state [2,21,94,95]. The optical cavities shown in Figure 1 must be held on resonance (locked) and in the correct alignment. This section will review the lock acquisition process used during O3, which was also described in [8].

Each cavity is locked using the Pound–Drever–Hall (PDH) technique [17]. Four sets of radio-frequency (RF) phase-modulated sidebands are added to the input laser using an electro-optic modulator (9 MHz, 24 MHz, 45 MHz, 118 MHz). The RF sideband frequencies are chosen to be resonant in some cavities and antiresonant in others. The RF beat notes are detected on reflection of the interferometer, at the antisymmetric (detection) port, or through a pick-off on transmission of the power-recycling cavity. RF photodetectors at each port are then used to sense the length and angular degrees of freedom.

The lock acquisition process is coded using the Guardian finite state machine [47]. During O3, the lock acquisition sequence took roughly 25 min, but depends strongly on environmental factors including seismic activity and wind speed [8]. The lock acquisition sequence is always undergoing improvements in speed and versatility.

3.4.1. Prestabilized Laser and Input Optics

The first step of the lock process is to ensure a laser stabilized in frequency, intensity, and spatial mode is entering the main interferometer. Inside a clean room, several important optical components reside on an optical table, making up a full system known as the *pre-stabilized laser*, or PSL [32]. Included in the pre-stabilized laser is a 2-Watt NPRO 1064 nm laser source, a high-powered amplifier to increase the input laser power, a pre-mode cleaner to clean the the laser beam spatial mode, a reference cavity to stabilize the laser frequency, and two photodetectors on a pickoff to stabilize the laser intensity.

Next, the pre-stabilized laser beam is input onto the first in-vacuum, suspended cavity, the input mode cleaner [49]. The beam is further cleaned and stabilized by the input mode cleaner (Section 3.2), and traverses the *input Faraday isolator* which prevents the formation of a parasitic interferometer and provides access to the interferometer reflected beam. Finally, the beam is incident on the first mirror of the main interferometer, the power-recycling mirror.

3.4.2. Arm-Length Stabilization

Next, the arms are brought under control using green light, known as the *arm-length stabilization* system [96–98]. Green light is used so that the arm lengths can be independently controlled while infrared is used to lock the corner. Figure 2 shows the interferometer configuration during arm-length stabilization.

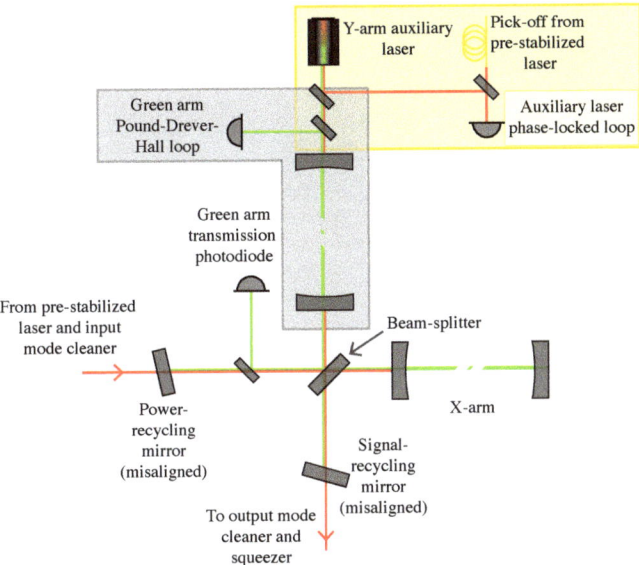

Figure 2. Interferometer layout during the first stage of lock acquisition: arm-length stabilization. The arm-length stabilization uses auxiliary lasers in the end stations (only the Y-arm is shown for simplicity), which emit beams at 1064 nm and 532 nm. The lasers are phase-locked to the pre-stabilized laser which is delivered to the end station by optical fiber (yellow box). The green laser is then locked to the arm cavity through a Pound–Drever–Hall loop on reflection (gray box).

The ALS system consists of two auxiliary green laser sources at each end station. The end station lasers are phase-locked to the main laser, then frequency-doubled to generate 532 nm (green) light which is injected into the arm cavities. Each ALS laser is then locked to their respective arm lengths.

3.4.3. Dual-Recycled Michelson Locking

The next step in the lock acquisition is to lock the dual-recycled Michelson interferometer (DRMI) with infrared light. The dual-recycled Michelson interferometer is formed by the five optics in the corner: the power- and signal-recycling mirror, beamsplitter, and input test masses to the arm cavities. Crucially, the end test masses are *not* included. Figure 3 shows the interferometer configuration during dual-recycled Michelson locking.

During the green locking of the arms, the corner optics are purposely misaligned. Then, the arms are purposely held off-resonance for infrared using the information from the green lock. Finally, the three corner degrees of freedom (the Michelson length, power-recycling length, and signal-recycling length) are brought under control simultaneously using the *3f-PDH locking* technique [96,99]. As the interferometer arms are brought onto resonance for infrared, the usual 1f PDH locking signals flip sign, which would cause the interferometer corner to lose control. The 3f locking signals do not suffer from the sign flip, and are used to maintain control while the arms are brought onto resonance.

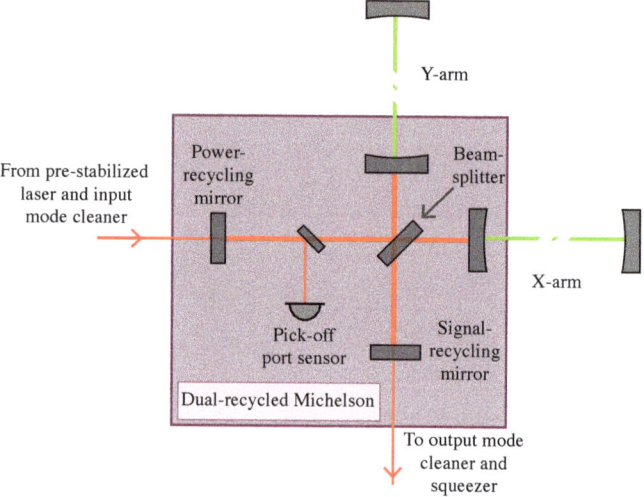

Figure 3. Interferometer layout during the second stage of lock acquisition: dual-recycled Michelson locking. With the arms locked on green, the arms are held off-resonance for infrared so the corner degrees of freedom can be locked independently of the arms. The dual-recycled Michelson is shown in the pink box. DRMI has three length degrees of freedom: the Michelson length (MICH), signal-recycling cavity length (SRCL), and power-recycling cavity length (PRCL). The photodiode at the pick-off port is used to sense all degrees of freedom: each degree of freedom is detected via different phase modulation sideband frequencies which resonate in different cavities [3].

3.4.4. Full Interferometer Locking

Having locked the dual-recycled Michelson with infrared light, the arms are brought onto resonance for infrared light. As the arms move into resonance, $\sim$10 kW of infrared laser power begins resonating in each interferometer arm.

In O3, the noise in the arm length stabilization system is around $\sim$2 Hz [100,101]. However, the linewidth of the interferometer is $\sim$1 Hz. This renders it impossible to directly transition from ALS to full interferometer PDH locking [94,96].

Therefore, the infrared transmission through the arms is used as an error signal to sense the common arm length as it is brought to full power. Once full power is very nearly reached, the common and differential arm length error signal is transitioned to the PDH error signal.

Once the full interferometer is fully locked on infrared, the corner degrees of freedom are switched from 3f to 1f PDH error signals, differential arm control is switched to DC readout [22], and all the angular controls are turned and allowed to converged on the best alignment in preparation for high power.

3.4.5. High-Power, Low-Noise Lock

Until this point, the laser input power is kept at 2 W. Once full lock is achieved, the input power is increased to the highest achievable power.

At this point, the suspension actuators are brought from acquisition mode—with high range and high noise—to low-noise mode, and the control loop bandwidths for the length and angular controls are cut off to achieve the lowest noise state.

Finally, squeezed light is injected to further reduce quantum shot noise; the squeezer subsystem is further discussed in Sections 3.1.3 and 5.4. The interferometer is now ready to observe gravitational waves.

During full lock, the circulating power in the interferometer heats the optics until the heat absorbed and emitted reaches a steady state. This heating process is known as *thermalization*, and takes about 30 minutes after full lock to reach a steady-state. Thermalization affects many aspects of the interferometer, most notably the radius of curvature of the main optics, which affects the scattering of laser light out of the laser's fundamental spatial mode [102]. The optical gain of the interferometer is also affected, although this is tracked via calibration lines [81].

The *thermal compensation system* is a subsystem dedicated to monitoring and controlling negative changes in the interferometer at full power [103]. The thermal compensation system is comprised of ring heater actuators to adjust the test mass optics radii of curvature, spatially tunable CO_2 laser projectors to heat optical surfaces, and Hartmann wavefront sensors to monitor optic surface changes. This system is primarily used to repair spatial distortions in the main beam, enabling higher power buildup inside the interferometer. It is also used to minimize measured noise couplings to the gravitational wave data channel.

4. Detector Sensitivity to Gravitational Waves

Detector sensitivity refers to the gravitational wave *signal-to-noise ratio*. The GW signal is imprinted on the laser light resonating in the detector, and sensed by photodetectors at the detection port.

Noise is any laser power fluctuations sensed at the detection port that are *not* due to gravitational waves. The are two main types of noise: *fundamental* and *technical*.

Fundamental noise is intrinsic to the design of the detector. Fundamental noises include quantum uncertainty, thermal noise in the optics, seismic noise, and Newtonian noise. These often cannot be improved without major upgrades to the detector, such as increasing the arm length or replacing the optical coatings.

Technical noise is not intrinsic to the detector design, but can limit the performance of the detectors. Technical noises are wide in variety, and most detector work is dedicated to eliminating it. Important examples of technical noise include

- Length and angular controls noise;
- Laser frequency and intensity noise;
- Scattered light;
- Residual gas noise;
- Photodetector dark noise;
- Electromagnetic noise.

All of these noise sources and more are considered carefully in [8], but controls noise is the main technical limit to gravitational wave detectors at low frequencies.

A *noise budget* is a way of quantifying the contributions to the measured noise curve [104]. Figure 4 shows a simplified noise budget of the O3 LIGO Hanford interferometer. To produce the measured noise curve in Figure 4, the time series of the detector output is Fourier-transformed to represent the frequency content of the noise as an amplitude spectral density (ASD), then calibrated into units of gravitational wave strain h.

4.1. Design Sensitivity

Design sensitivity is the ultimate sensitivity Advanced LIGO is expected to achieve given the detector configuration and estimated performance. It is formed by the sum of all fundamental noises. Design sensitivity has not yet been achieved by the current detectors, due to technical noises and insufficient power buildup.

Figure 4 shows the Advanced LIGO design sensitivity as the black dashed curve [2,105]. No squeezing is included in the design sensitivity curve. This affects the quantum noise, lowering the design's strain-referenced quantum shot noise but increasing the quantum radiation pressure noise (Section 4.2).

For design sensitivity, 125 W of laser input power is assumed, resulting in 750 kW of circulating power in the arm cavities. The O3 input power was much lower, ∼34 W at Hanford and ∼38 W at Livingston.

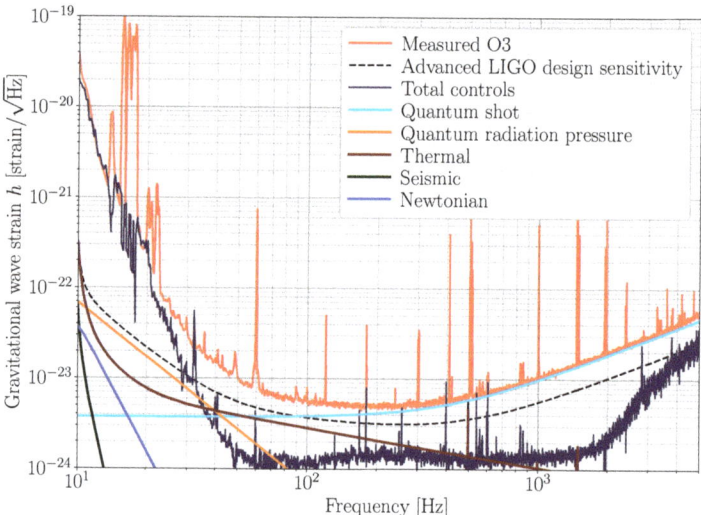

Figure 4. O3 LIGO Hanford gravitational wave noise budget, simplified [8]. The measured curve in red represents the calibrated sensitivity to GWs. The dashed black curve is the Advanced LIGO design sensitivity curve, with 125 W of input power and no squeezing [2,105]. All other curves are measured or estimated contributions to the total measured noise. Here we have only included significant known noise sources for simplicity.

4.2. Quantum Noise

Fluctuations of the vacuum electric field at the interferometer readout port impose the main fundamental limit to the interferometer sensitivity [54,69,70,106]. Quantum noise appears as *shot noise* and *quantum radiation pressure noise*.

4.2.1. Shot Noise

In general, shot noise arises from Poisson fluctuations in the arrival time of discrete objects. In the case of interferometers, the discrete objects are photons at the detection port.

Heisenberg uncertainty in the measured laser amplitude at the detection port cannot be distinguished from actual mirror motion due to GWs. The power detected on the photodetector is made up of a finite number of photons which arrive randomly and independently of one another, leading to a detected white noise amplitude spectral density $\sqrt{S_{\text{shot}}}$ proportional to the total power P_{dc} on the photodetector:

$$\sqrt{S_{\text{shot}}} = \sqrt{2\hbar\omega_0 P_{dc}}. \tag{12}$$

where ω_0 is the fundamental angular frequency of the laser.

Equation (12) is white noise in units of W/$\sqrt{\text{Hz}}$, meaning it has no frequency dependence. However, when this noise is referenced against the GW detector response to yield units strain/$\sqrt{\text{Hz}}$, it begins to rise above the detector bandwidth of around 450 Hz. In Figure 4, the cyan curve shows the estimated GW-referenced quantum shot noise.

4.2.2. Radiation Pressure Noise

Quantum radiation pressure noise (QRPN) is displacement noise arising from amplitude fluctuations of the electric field in the arms. These amplitude fluctuations, again due to Heisenberg uncertainty, mean the arm power is spontaneously increasing and decreasing. This induces forces on the optics via radiation pressure, moving the optics in the arm [69].

For a Michelson interferometer with Fabry–Pérot arms, the displacement amplitude spectral density due to QRPN $\sqrt{S_{\text{QRPN}}}$ can be described as [55]

$$\sqrt{S_{\text{QRPN}}}(f) = \frac{1}{mL(2\pi f)^2} \sqrt{\frac{32 P_{\text{bs}} \hbar \omega_0}{\omega_c^2 + (2\pi f)^2}} \tag{13}$$

where P_{bs} is power on the beamsplitter, m is the mirror mass, L is the arm length, ω_0 is the laser frequency, ω_c is the arm pole describing the number of reflections inside the Fabry–Pérot cavity, and f is the GW signal frequency. Equation (13) is plotted in Figure 4 as the orange curve.

4.3. Thermal Noise

Thermal noise refers to the actual displacement in the mirrors induced by thermal fluctuations in the atoms making up the test mass suspension, substrate, and optical coatings [107–110]. In general, thermal noise increases with mechanical loss in the materials making up the optics, as described by the fluctuation-dissipation theorem [111–113].

For LIGO test masses, the observable fluctuation is the optic displacement due to dissipation from thermal excitations. The dominant source of mechanical loss, and thus thermal noise, is the optical coatings deposited on the optical surface. For a single coating with thickness d, the dissipated power and coating displacement noise $\sqrt{S_x}$ due to thermal fluctuations can be calculated [114,115]:

$$\sqrt{S_x}(f) = \sqrt{\frac{8 k_B T (1+\sigma)(1-2\sigma) d}{\pi w^2 E} \frac{\phi}{2\pi f}} \tag{14}$$

where T is temperature, σ is the coating Poisson ratio, d is the coating thickness, E is the Young's modulus, w is the beam radius, and ϕ is the mechanical loss angle of the coating.

The actual LIGO coatings have more than a single layer, and their thermal noise properties are measured directly in the lab [116,117]. Other thermal noise contributions include thermal noise vibrations in the optic suspensions [113,118]. The total thermal noise estimate, largely from coatings at high frequency and suspensions at low frequency, are plotted as the maroon line in Figure 4.

4.4. Seismic Noise

Seismic noise is optical displacement due to the motion of the Earth physically shaking the mirrors resting on the Earth's surface. Unmitigated, the vibrations of the Earth are much larger than LIGO optics can tolerate. Enormous effort is put into isolating the core optics from the ground vibrations, particularly in the GW-sensitive range. Additionally, earthquakes and windy conditions can make holding the detector lock impossible.

The main LIGO optics are suspended from a quadruple-stage pendulum chain to passively isolate them from ground motion [39]. These pendulums are suspended from active seismic isolation platforms [43] which themselves are supported by hydraulically actuated pre-isolation structures [42].

Ultimately, the linear coupling due to seismic motion is largely suppressed in the GW-detection band, as seen by the green trace in Figure 4. This curve comes from the measured differential displacement of the seismic isolation platforms, multiplied by the isolation of the suspensions which hang from those platforms.

However, at very low frequencies (<1 Hz), below the pendulum resonance frequencies, seismic motion still dominates. Worse, high motion at very low frequencies can couple to higher frequencies via bilinear or nonlinear coupling mechanisms. Work continues to suppress seismic motion further, via monitoring systems and more advanced control schemes [44].

4.5. Newtonian Noise

Newtonian noise, or gravity-gradient noise, is from fluctuations in the ground creating changes in the local gravitational potential around the optics, moving them [119–121]. Newtonian noise is related to seismic noise, but the coupling mechanism is not from ground motion propagating down a pendulum chain, but changes in ground density due to seismic activity. Therefore, Newtonian noise cannot be isolated away with longer pendulums, but can be monitored and actively subtracted [122–124].

Upper limits have been placed on Newtonian noise contributions to LIGO, but have never been directly observed [125]. The blue trace in Figure 4 represents an estimate of Newtonian noise coupling to the GW spectrum given local seismic activity, but is highly uncertain.

4.6. Controls Noise

Controls noise is the noise associated with the sensor and feedback system required to hold the interferometer optics on resonance. This includes both length control loops, which manage the optic's position [18–23,75,93], and angular control loops, which point the optics at each other [24–31,68].

Controls noise is the result of multiple effects. The control loops are required to suppress real motion in the optics, known as *displacement noise*. The controllers must be strong enough to hold the optics in place. To hold the optics in place, electromagnetic coil actuators or electrostatic drives are employed [39,40].

However, the controllers must know where to hold the optics. The Pound–Drever–Hall error signals hold the information about where each optic must be held [2,3,17]. The PDH error signals are detected with radio-frequency photodetectors (RFPDs). These RFPD sensors are limited by sources of *sensor noise*, largely shot noise, but also potentially "dark" noise and analog-to-digital conversion noise. Sensor noise is indistinguishable from actual displacement noise, and dominates most control loop noise floors above $\sim$50 Hz.

4.6.1. Tradeoff

This sets up the fundamental tradeoff involved in LIGO control loop design. Make the controllers too strong, and sensor noise will be reinjected into the controller actuators, creating true, unintended displacement. Make the controllers too weak, and excess displacement noise will pollute the spectrum and make it difficult to hold the interferometer on resonance.

LIGO controllers are designed to be overtly strong during the locking phase, in order to hold the optics on resonance and avoid lock losses. This injects excess sensor noise. Near the end of the locking process, the loop bandwidths are reduced, weakening the hold but avoiding sensor noise injection.

4.6.2. Feedforward

Even with loop bandwidth reduction, optical cross-couplings cause controllers to inject noise into other loops [23]. In fact, sensor noise in the auxiliary length degrees of freedom is injected into the GW spectrum, causing a major limitation.

However, we have information on this sensor noise, since we are constantly measuring it. Therefore, we can *feedforward* the sensor noise, with a negative sign, to the interferometer optics [8]. This creates an optic displacement which counteracts the displacement caused by auxiliary length sensor noise.

4.6.3. Results

Controls noise dominates the GW spectrum at low frequencies, as seen by the purple curve in Figure 4. This curve represents the sum of the noise measured via excess power injection into each length, angular, and laser control loop [8].

The problem is more difficult than summarized above. Optical cross-couplings affect not just the GW spectrum, but all degrees of freedom. Bilinear and nonlinear couplings can be hard to fully quantify, even with excess power injections. Damping loops on suspensions and seismic isolation platforms that reduce large low-frequency seismic motion can leak noise into higher frequencies [15].

Work to lower controls noise further is the highest priority of the commissioning team. A more advanced feedforward scheme is under consideration to reduce angle-to-length coupling. Multiple-input multiple-output controls models are under development. Controls noise for the output mode cleaner are being analyzed. Efforts to better quantify important interferometer parameters, such as optical losses and beam mode matching, are being implemented.

5. Current Performance of the Advanced LIGO Detectors

The performance of the detectors is their overall sensitivity and uptime to astrophysical gravitational wave events. There are currently 90 gravitational wave candidate detections, consisting of binary mergers across the universe from the first three observing runs (O1, O2, and O3) [9]. Figure 5 shows representative GW sensitivity spectra for each observing run.

In this section, we will review the astrophysical range and duty cycle of the detectors, discuss the power budget and major technical limitations involved with high power interferometry, the status of squeezing in LIGO interferometers, and environmental disturbance sources and mitigation efforts.

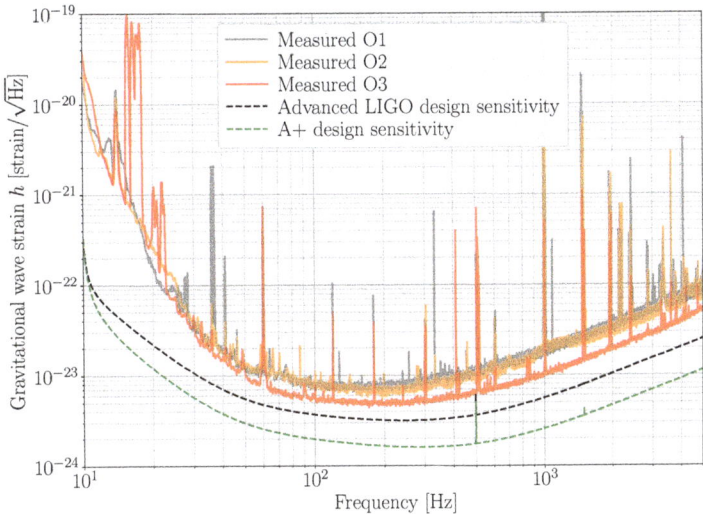

Figure 5. Comparison of LIGO Hanford gravitational wave noise spectra from O1 [4], O2 [126], and O3 [8]. Only the measured O3 spectrum includes squeezed light injection. The Advanced LIGO design sensitivity assumes no squeezing, with 125 W input laser power input yielding 750 kW circulating arm power [2,105]. The A+ design sensitivity includes 12 dB squeezing and a factor of two lower coatings thermal noise [10,11,127].

5.1. Astrophysical Range

A common performance gauge for the LIGO interferometers is the *binary neutron star inspiral range,* or simply the *range* [128–130]. The range refers to the luminosity distance at which the detector is sensitive to a 1.4 $M_\odot$ neutron star merger with an SNR of 8, averaged over sky location and GW polarization.

During O3, the LIGO Livingston Observatory achieved a median binary neutron star range of 134 Mpc, while the LIGO Hanford Observatory achieved a median range of 111 Mpc [8]. The detector sensitivity to heavier binary black holes extends much further than binary neutron stars, since the signals produced by black hole mergers are stronger.

5.2. Duty Cycle

The duty cycle is the uptime of the detectors, in other words, how often the detectors are sensitive to GWs. Also important is coincident observation time, where both the Hanford and Livingston detectors are online at the same time. Coincident observation is critical for extracting maximum information from detections, particularly, verifying the detection is not a false positive and generating sky location data [10].

During O3, both detectors were operational for a greater percentage of the time compared to the previous two observing runs, with Hanford and Livingston achieving observation duty cycles of 74.6% and 77.0%, respectively, with coincident observation 62.2% of the time [8].

5.3. High-Power Interferometry

Gravitational wave observatories are dedicated to pushing the limits on maximum circulating laser power. In Equation (11), we see that as power in the arms P_{arms} increases, so does the detector response to gravitational waves.

The biggest limit on power buildup in the interferometer is imposed by the presence of small, absorbing defects in the test mass optical coatings, known as point absorbers [131]. In this section, we will review how we quantify the power budget in the interferometer, what point absorbers are and how we can mitigate their effect, and other technical problems with high power, including parametric instability and radiation pressure-based optomechanics.

5.3.1. Power Budget

Laser power must be conserved inside the interferometer, i.e. $P_{\text{in}} = P_{\text{out}}$. A *power budget* is a record of where the input power of an interferometer is lost in the interferometer steady-state at full lock. Losses can be from absorption by the optics themselves, or scattered off imperfections in the mirror surfaces into higher-order modes [102,132].

For the carrier laser light, thanks to the common-mode rejection of the Michelson, we can model the interferometer power buildup using a simple plane–wave *coupled cavity*, i.e. three-mirror cavity [65,66]. The three mirrors are the power-recycling mirror, an input test mass, and an end test mass.

The laser resonates inside the coupled cavity, building up power until losses exactly equal the input power. In the coupled-cavity model, there are two main sources of power losses: power-recycling losses $\mathcal{L}_P$ and round-trip arm cavity losses $\mathcal{L}_A$. There is also the promptly reflected power P_{refl} and transmitted power through the arms P_{trans}. The transmission of the power-recycling mirror T_P must be strategically selected to be *impedance-matched* with the overall interferometer losses, or else too much carrier light will be promptly reflected [2,3,61,65,66].

A convenient proxy for power buildup in the interferometer is the *power-recycling gain*, or PRG. The power-recycling gain G_P can be expressed as [131],

$$G_P = \left(\frac{t_p}{1 - r_p \left(1 - \frac{G_A(t_e^2 + \mathcal{L}_A) + \mathcal{L}_P}{2}\right)} \right)^2 \tag{15}$$

where t_p is the power-recycling mirror amplitude transmission, r_p is the power-recycling mirror amplitude reflectivity, t_e is the end test mass amplitude transmission, G_A is the arm power gain ∼265, $\mathcal{L}_A$ is the round-trip arm cavity loss, $\mathcal{L}_P$ is the power-recycling cavity loss. Equation (15) shows how losses in the arms matter more than losses in the power-recycling cavity, because the arm gain G_A scales the arm loss to account for the multiple reflections inside the arm cavity.

For LIGO Hanford in mid-2021, preliminary results suggest that interferometer round-trip losses $\mathcal{L}_A$ may now be lower than assumed for Advanced LIGO design [2,133,134]. There are metrics other than the PRG for measuring the power buildup in the interferometer, including the total interferometer reflection measurement and direct radiation-pressure-based arm power measurement [8,135]. These provide more information on the true power budget, and indicate that the simple plane-wave coupled-cavity model is not sufficient to fully explain power in the interferometer.

5.3.2. Point Absorbers

When the beam circulating in the interferometer encounters the test mass it uniformly heats an area of the test mass across its Gaussian profile. The absorber power in this uniform cross section is determined by the power in the beam and the properties of the fused silica and the optical coating.

Point absorbers are submillimeter points of nonuniform, anomalously high optical absorption found on the test masses. A full discussion of the point absorbers in LIGO can be found in Brooks et. al. [131]. Point absorbers have been identified on multiple test masses in LIGO during the first three observing runs. Their deformation is visible on Hartmann wavefront sensors, an auxiliary sensing system which measures the test mass surface and substrate deformation during power up. Point absorbers have also been imaged on test masses which have been removed from the interferometers, using dark-field microscopy.

The origin of point absorbers is under active investigation. Point absorbers have been observed in the lab on spare test masses which have never been exposed to high optical power. They appear to be embedded in the optical coating and are thought to originate during the coating deposition process. Initial elemental analysis of some point absorbers show high concentrations of aluminum.

The circulating optical power in the interferometer heats up a point absorber, causing light to be scattered out of the arm cavity or into higher-order cavity modes. Depending on the geometry of the cavity, the higher-order modes may be resonantly enhanced, causing additional loss to the fundamental mode and coupling unwanted modes to the GW detection port. As the input power to the interferometer increases, the power scattered into higher-order modes increases, as does the optical loss. Point absorbers on the input test mass affect the arm cavity gain and power-recycling cavity gain, while the end test mass point absorbers only affect the arm cavity. The thermal timescale of losses due to point absorbers are roughly an order or magnitude faster than that of uniform absorption. Point absorbers have been observed to increase coupling of scattered light, laser frequency noise, and laser intensity noise to the gravitational wave readout [8].

To avoid the negative effects of point absorbers, the interferometer alignment can be adjusted such that the beam spot overlap with the point absorbers is minimized. In O3, both Hanford and Livingston operated with the spot position offset from center by ∼10 s of millimeters for certain test masses with known point absorbers [131,136]. However, beam spot position offsets cannot exceed the size of the optic itself (34 cm diameter for test masses), and even small offsets risk scattering excess light out of the fringe of the main Gaussian beam (∼12 cm diameter).

5.3.3. Parametric Instability

Parametric instabilities (PIs) are mechanical modes of the test masses that sap energy from the fundamental mode, putting it into higher-order optical modes of the resonating laser [137,138]. As the mechanical modes begin to oscillate, more laser light is scattered into the higher-order optical mode, further increasing the mechanical oscillations in runaway positive feedback loop.

Mitigation of PIs is essential to avoid runaway mechanical oscillations causing lock-losses. Ring-heaters on the core optics can change the radius of curvature of the optic, which in turn changes the eigenfrequency of the cavity higher-order modes, eliminating the overlap between the optical and mechanical mode frequencies. The electrostatic drive can be used to directly damp parametric instabilities that ring up at high circulating power [139–141].

During O1 and O2, the ring-heaters and electrostatic drive damping were the only ways to combat PI ringups. However, with the higher circulating laser power in O3, dozens to hundreds of potential PIs were expected.

Therefore, acoustic mode dampers (AMDs) were installed on all core test masses [142]. AMDs are mechanical tuned mass dampers glued to the sides of the test mass, with a piezoelectric transducer and shunt resistor designed to dissipate mechanical energy by converting it to electric charge and running it through the resistor. The AMDs passively damp the mechanical oscillations, making it far more difficult for PIs to ring up.

Parametric instabilities have been observed even with the AMDs installed, as expected, but the overall parametric gain of all PIs is drastically reduced. This makes the problem far more tractable to solve with the ring-heaters and electrostatic drive damping. This work enables the higher circulating laser power seen in O3 and beyond (Section 5.3.1).

5.3.4. Radiation Pressure Optomechanics

With the advent of high-power interferometry comes a new era of radiation-pressure-based optomechanics, particularly *optical springs* and *optical torques* for suspended optical cavities. The laser power in the interferometer arm cavities couples the optic suspensions together such that the length and angular degrees of freedom must be considered together. As circulating laser power increases, the dynamics of the optomechanical plants also change, presenting an additional challenge to high-powered interferometry.

Optical springs occur when the radiation pressure in a cavity creates a non-negligible restoring force (or non-restoring force) that affects the usual pendulum response [143–146]. The differential arm degree of freedom at Hanford has exhibited an optical spring effect since O1 [57,77,78,82].

Optical torques refer to radiation pressure causing additional torques on the mirrors that affect the usual pendulum angular response [27]. The *hard modes* refer to the angular modes where the torsional stiffness increases due to the laser power torques. Likewise, the *soft modes* are angular modes where the torsional stiffness decreases due to the laser power torques. One set of these modes must be statically unstable.

The radius of curvature of the test masses plays a strong role in governing the stability of the angular modes. In Advanced LIGO, the soft modes have been chosen to be statically unstable, as they have a lower stiffness parameter and are easier to manage with a feedback control loop. Optical torques have been observed in initial LIGO [28,30], and accounted for in Advanced LIGO design [29].

5.4. Quantum Squeezing

As explained in Section 3.1.3, quantum shot noise limits the sensitivity of interferometers to GWs. A squeezed light source reflected off the output port of the interferometer can decrease quantum shot noise, increasing the detector sensitivity.

Frequency-independent squeezing was injected into both LIGO detectors for the duration of O3, reducing quantum shot noise and increasing the expected gravitational wave detection rate by the cube of the range increase (40% at LIGO Hanford Observatory and 50% at LIGO Livingston Observatory) [71]. Though the squeezer subsystems at both LIGO sites are identical, small differences in the optical loss in their beam paths result in slightly different squeezer performance. During O3, LIGO Hanford Observatory measured 2.0 dB of shot noise improvement from squeezing and LIGO Livingston Observatory measured 2.7 dB in the 1.1–1.4 kHz regime [71]. At LIGO Livingston, additional squeezing injection was possible, but would cause a measurable increase in radiation pressure noise and worsen detector range. In addition to improved range, squeezed state injection facilitated interesting investigations into the quantum nature of the LIGO interferometers [73,74,147].

A filter cavity is being installed at both LIGO sites to improve the quantum noise limit. The filter cavity is discussed in Section 6.3. A full review of the current status of squeezing in LIGO detectors will be published alongside this review [148].

5.5. Environmental Disturbances

Every effort is made to isolate the LIGO optics from environmental noise. Environmental disturbances such as ground motion, acoustic noise, and magnetic noise can couple to the interferometer and cause excess noise in the gravitational wave readout, masking gravitational wave signals and limiting sensitivity. The physical environment monitoring system includes of a variety of sensors and noise injection tools around the main interferometer and is used to monitor environmental noise and characterize coupling to gravitational readout [149]. Sensors include seismometers, accelerometers, thermometers, microphones, magnetometers, electrometers, radio receivers, infrasound microphones, tilt meters, anemometers, voltage monitors, and hygrometers. In this section we discuss some egregious environmental disturbances and their coupling to the interferometer.

5.5.1. Earthquakes

In general, the gravitational wave detector sensitivity is not limited by seismic noise, see Figure 4 and Section 4.4. However, when the seismic waves generated by an earthquake pass through the detector site, the ground motion can become so high that the active seismic control system [42,43] cannot sufficiently suppress the motion.

Earthquakes and large seismic motion accounted for 5% of the unplanned downtime of the LIGO detectors during O1 and O2. For O3, a new seismic controls mode was implemented during earthquakes, aimed at reducing actuator saturation and gain peaking to maintain interferometer lock during earthquakes [150]. When the detector is taken to earthquake mode, two major seismic configuration changes occur: the seismic loops are set to have reduced gain in the 50–60 mHz band, and the common motion measured by seismometers in the corner and end stations is subtracted from the feedback signal. Earthquake mode has allowed the LIGO detectors to remain locked through large earthquakes causing ground velocities up to 3.9 µm/s RMS.

5.5.2. Wind

High-velocity wind can cause the corner and end station buildings to tilt, confusing seismometers and making it difficult (or impossible) to maintain lock. This has been a problem particularly at LIGO Hanford, where gusts over 60 mph have been measured. Between O1 and O2, tilt meters (or ground-rotation sensors) were installed at LIGO Hanford, and used to subtract ground tilt from seismometer signals [151]. More recently, wind fences have been installed at LIGO Hanford, and their effectiveness is under study.

5.5.3. Anthropogenic Noise

Anthropogenic ground motion, caused by human activity near the site, typically occurs in the 1–5 Hz frequency band and is particularly problematic at the LIGO Livingston observatory. At LIGO Livingston, trains passing near the Y-arm, as well as elevated anthropogenic noise during the daytime, which cause scattering noise to be visible in the gravitational wave data in the 10–50 Hz band (see Section 5.5.4).

5.5.4. Scattered Light

The sources of ground motion discussed above can couple to the gravitational wave readout through scattered light. Tiny imperfections in the main and auxiliary optics can cause light to scatter out of the main interferometer beam. This scattered light can then reflect off surfaces in the vacuum system, such as the suspension cages, chamber walls, or viewports. If the light then couples back into the main interferometer beam, it will carry phase modulation from ground motion, and inject noise into the gravitational wave readout. The characteristic morphology of scattering noise in the gravitational wave stain data is arches in the time–frequency domain—see examples in References [149,152]. Low-frequency ground motion caused by earthquakes (0.03–0.1 Hz) or microseism (0.1–0.3 Hz) cause excess noise in the gravitational wave readout in the 10–100 Hz band. In O3, scattered light coupling to the gravitational wave readout was improved compared to previous runs, thanks to a suite of stray light baffles, and improved vibration isolation in the pre-stabilized laser room improved test mass suspension control techniques.

6. Upgrades for Observing Run Four

Observing run three ended in March 2020, and observing run four is scheduled to begin in December 2022. Between these runs, there are several key upgrades being made to the LIGO detectors to improve sensitivity as part of the A+ upgrades [10,11].

6.1. Y-Arm Input Test Mass Replacement at Hanford

During O3, a significant point absorber was identified on the Y-arm input test mass (ITMY) at LIGO Hanford (see Section 5.3.2). In December 2020, during the first part of the break between O3 and O4, the old ITMY was removed and a new test mass installed. Preliminary results from the mid-2021 commissioning period showed no significant absorbers on the new ITMY and improvement in power buildups (see Section 5.3.1).

6.2. End Test Mass Replacements at Livingston

The end test masses at Livingston exhibit strong point absorbers limiting the overall circulating power. In order to achieve the O4 circulating power goal of 400 kW, new end test masses (ETMs) are planned to be installed at LIGO Livingston in 2022.

LIGO Hanford also has exhibited point absorbers on its end test masses, but preliminary results from mid-2021 locking suggest these do not limit power buildup as much as those at Livingston. The possibility for replacing Hanford's ETMs remains open, depending on commissioning results with the higher input powers from the PSL (see Section 6.4).

6.3. Filter Cavity

One side effect of frequency-independent squeezing is that quantum radiation pressure noise increases [54,55,73]. This can be mitigated by reflecting the squeezed light off of a *filter cavity* [51–53,153–155] before injecting it into the interferometer, as shown in Figure 1.

In short, the filter cavity rotates the quadrature of the squeezed light for frequencies below the filter cavity pole frequency, but leaves unrotated the squeezed light quadrature above the filter cavity pole frequency. This is known as *frequency-dependent* squeezing, since the squeezing uncertainty ellipse rotates about the filter cavity pole frequency. This can lower quantum uncertainty across the entire detector bandwidth, not just the shot noise dominated regime.

Currently, the facilities infrastructure for the filter cavity is under construction at both Hanford and Livingston. The filter cavity is expected to be fully built and commissioned in time for O4, starting in December 2022.

6.4. Higher Input Laser Power

While commissioning the LIGO detectors, the input laser power is maximized to reduce shot noise, while maintaining stable operation. During O3, the pre-stabilized laser (PSL) was able to generate $\sim$50 W of optical power at the input mode cleaner, and the detectors operated with 34–38 W input power [8]. Higher power operations were limited by point absorbers.

The goal for O4 is to double the power in the interferometer, from $\sim$200 kW to 400 kW in the arms. Higher input powers are expected to be possible, especially after the test mass replacements. Therefore, the pre-stabilized laser is being upgraded to produce more power.

The new PSL configuration features two NeoLASE NeoVAN-4s-HP solid-state amplifiers in series, amplifying a seed beam from 2 W to 125 W [156]. The seed laser is the same as previous runs: a nonplanar ring oscillator (NPRO) Nd-YAG 1064 nm infrared laser [89].

6.5. Output Path Active Mode Matching

When the squeezed vacuum state encounters any imperfect optical interface, the squeezed state is degraded slightly. Additionally, *mode mismatch* is when the spacial mode of the squeezed state is not exactly matched to the spacial mode of the interferometer. The squeezing improvement to quantum noise is limited by total optical losses from mode mismatch and imperfect optical surfaces.

Of the budgeted sources of loss in O3, mode mismatch was the largest, estimated at 10% loss [71]. Further modeling and analysis of the squeezing over the full detection band has revealed that mode mismatch within the detector itself also induces frequency-dependent loss [74]. For O4, active mode matching elements are being installed between the elements of the squeezer and the interferometer to improve the mode matching.

In the O4 interferometer layout, problematic mode mismatch can occur in several locations. The squeezer mode must match the cavity modes of the output mode cleaner, the filter cavity and the interferometer mode (i.e. the mode circulating in the signal-recycling cavity). While the layout is designed such that these cavity modes are matched, in reality there is some uncertainty in the signal-recycling cavity mode, as well as uncertainty in the placement of optics as they are installed in vacuum. The active mode-matching elements will allow for changes to the spacial modes propagating between these optical cavities.

Two types of active mode-matching element are being installed. A thermally-actuated mirror with large actuation range (200 millidiopters) and slower response time is being installed on the path between the interferometer and the output mode cleaner [157]. Three piezoelectric deformable mirrors, with reduced actuation range (120 millidiopters) but faster response time, are being installed between the squeezer and the filter cavity, and between the filter cavity and the interferometer [158].

7. Conclusions

Powerful black hole and neutron star mergers are now revealed by their imprint on spacetime itself, traveling to the Earth from the distant past, carrying a wealth of information about the events that created them. Advanced LIGO has already revolutionized our understanding of astrophysics and astronomy, with 90 detections of gravitational waves. More detections and higher SNR detections from a more sensitive detector will make new results in astrophysics, general relativity, and cosmology possible.

The Advanced LIGO detectors switch between periods of upgrades and installs, commissioning those upgrades to work as intended, and observation runs. O4 is scheduled to run for one year of coincident observation time between the LIGO detectors, starting in December 2022 with 400 kW circulating power and $\sim$175 Mpc binary neutron star range. O5 is when we plan to achieve the A+ sensitivity shown in Figure 5.

Advanced LIGO's success would not have been possible if not for the lessons learned and support from the first generation of long-baseline interferometers from around the world, including initial LIGO [159–161], Virgo [162,163], GEO600 [164,165], and TAMA [166].

Advanced Virgo [167] currently runs alongside Advanced LIGO, and is the only detector other than LIGO Hanford and LIGO Livingston to have sensed gravitational waves. KAGRA is anticipated to join O4 in observations [168–170]. LIGO India is expected to begin constructing a new observatory soon [171].

More ambitious upgrades to the current facilities are possible for LIGO Voyager, including a new laser wavelength (2 µm) and cryogenically cooled optics [172]. Third-generation detector designs are currently being proposed based on results and designs from Advanced LIGO and A+, including Einstein Telescope [173] in Europe and Cosmic Explorer in the United States [174]. Space-based interferometers with very long baselines are also being designed and constructed. The LISA mission is anticipated to detect much lower frequency GWs than LIGO [175], with the initial LISA Pathfinder results being extremely promising [176].

The technological achievements made with Advanced LIGO will reverberate into the future, just as the knowledge gained by first generation detectors paved the way for Advanced LIGO. Every step toward design sensitivity brings the furthest reaches of the universe closer.

Author Contributions: Both authors have researched and wrote significant portions of this review. All authors have read and agreed to the published version of the manuscript.

Funding: This research was funded by the National Science Foundation grant number PHY-1764464 and PHY-1834382.

Institutional Review Board Statement: Not applicable.

Informed Consent Statement: Not applicable.

Data Availability Statement: Not applicable.

Acknowledgments: The authors acknowledge the vast amount of work that goes into designing, building, operating, and maintaining the LIGO Laboratory and facilities. For locking the interferometer, bringing it to its lowest-noise state, and characterizing the noise sources, we acknowledge the 2021 LIGO Hanford commissioning team, including Sheila Dwyer, Jenne Driggers, Anamaria Effler, Valary Frolov, Keita Kawabe, Jeff Kissel, Robert Schofield, Daniel Sigg, and Varun Srivastava. We acknowledge the calibration working group for producing the infrastructure to calibrate the interferometer data. We acknowledge the LIGO lab operations teams for locking, running, and managing the detector. We acknowledge the LIGO lab detector engineers for fabricating and installing the new Y-arm input test mass that was critical for removing point absorbers from the interferometer core optics. We acknowledge the LIGO facilities crew for building the facility, including the new filter cavity infrastrucuture. This material is based upon work supported by NSF's LIGO Laboratory which is a major facility fully funded by the National Science Foundation.

Conflicts of Interest: The authors declare no conflict of interest.

Abbreviations

The following abbreviations are used in this manuscript:

GW	gravitational waves
LIGO	laser interferometer gravitational wave observatory
O1	observing run one
O2	observing run two
O3	observing run three
O4	observing run four
SNR	signal-to-noise ratio
PDH	Pound–Drever–Hall
RF	radio-frequency
PSL	pre-stabilized laser
ALS	arm-length stabilization
DRMI	dual-recycled Michelson interferometer
DARM	differential arm (length)
ASD	amplitude spectral density
QRPN	quantum radiation pressure noise
MICH	Michelson length
PRCL	power-recycling cavity length
SRCL	signal-recycling cavity length
RFPD	radio-frequency photodetectors
PRG	power-recycling gain
PI	parametric instability
ITMY	input test mass (Y-arm)
ETM	end test mass

Appendix A. Michelson Interferometer

Gravitational waves produce differential motion in orthogonal directions of spacetime (Section 2). Michelson interferometers were originally created to precisely measure differential light velocity in each arm [177]. Today, a Michelson interferometer forms the core of the Advanced LIGO detector, and is used to detect differential motion in the arms [146]. This section will overview how a Michelson is sensitive to differential motion.

First, we will assume the plane-wave approximation is valid, so all electric fields will be simplified into a single complex number $E_0 = |E_0|e^{i\phi}$. Second, we will assume our mirrors are thin mirrors with no losses, so $r^2 + t^2 = R + T = 1$ where r and t are the amplitude reflection and transmission coefficients of the mirrors and R and T are the power reflection and transmission coefficients of the mirrors. Third, we will use the "+/−" mirror reflection convention based on the Fresnel relations, which states that a beam reflected off the back of the mirror suffers a 180° phase flip, but a beam reflected off the front suffers no phase flip.

Appendix A.1. Basics

Figure A1 shows a Michelson interferometer, which consists of an input laser, a 50:50 beamsplitter, and two "arms" of laser light with highly reflective mirrors at the end. The laser input amplitude E_{in} is split into the arms equally by the beamsplitter $r_{bs} = t_{bs} = 1/\sqrt{2}$. The light in each arm E_x, E_y propagates the length of its arm L_x, L_y, is reflected off the end mirrors $r_x = r_y = 1$ accruing different amounts of phase ϕ_x, ϕ_y:

$$E_x = r_x t_{bs} E_{in} e^{i\phi_x}, \qquad E_y = r_y r_{bs} E_{in} e^{i\phi_y} \qquad (A1)$$

$$E_x = \frac{1}{\sqrt{2}} E_{in} e^{i2kL_x}, \qquad E_y = \frac{1}{\sqrt{2}} E_{in} e^{i2kL_y} \qquad (A2)$$

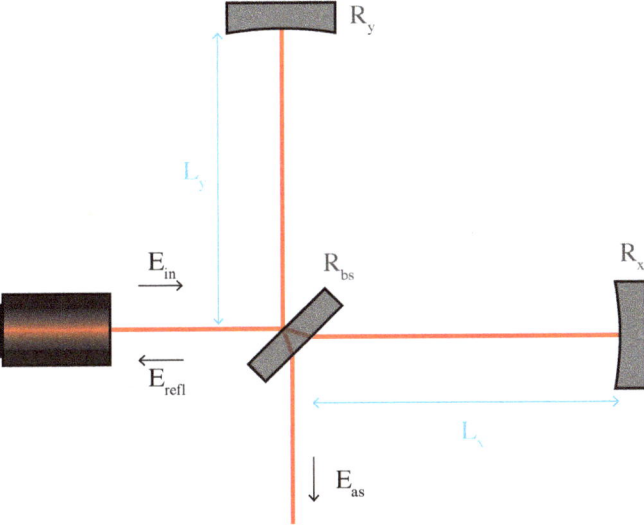

Figure A1. Optical layout of a Michelson interferometer. The input laser electric field is E_{in}, the field reflected from the Michelson is E_{refl}, and the field transmitter through the Michelson antisymmetric port is E_{as}. The 50:50 beamsplitter $R_{bs} = r_{bs}^2 = 1/2$ reflects half the laser power to the Y-arm and transmits half to the X-arm. The highly reflecting end mirrors $R_x \approx R_y \approx 1$ send most of the light directly back to the beamsplitter.

The light from each arm is then recombined at the beamsplitter, producing the reflected beam E_refl and transmitted, or antisymmetric, beam E_as:

$$E_\text{refl} = t_\text{bs} E_x + r_\text{bs} E_y, \qquad E_\text{as} = -r_\text{bs} E_x + t_\text{bs} E_y \qquad \text{(A3)}$$

$$E_\text{refl} = \frac{1}{2} E_\text{in} \left(e^{i2kL_x} + e^{i2kL_y} \right), \qquad E_\text{as} = \frac{1}{2} E_\text{in} \left(-e^{i2kL_x} + e^{i2kL_y} \right) \qquad \text{(A4)}$$

$$E_\text{refl} = E_\text{in} e^{i2kL} \cos(2k\Delta L), \qquad E_\text{as} = -i E_\text{in} e^{i2kL} \sin(2k\Delta L) \qquad \text{(A5)}$$

where between Equations (A4) and (A5) we have defined the common length $L = (L_x + L_y)/2$ and differential length $\Delta L = (L_x - L_y)/2$.

Calculating the power at the reflected and antisymmetric ports $P_\text{refl}, P_\text{as}$:

$$P_\text{refl} = |E_\text{refl}|^2 = P_\text{in} \cos(2k\Delta L)^2 \qquad \text{(A6)}$$

$$P_\text{as} = |E_\text{as}|^2 = P_\text{in} \sin(2k\Delta L)^2 \qquad \text{(A7)}$$

where $P_\text{in} = |E_\text{in}|^2$ is the input power. The power at the antisymmetric port in Equation (A7) depends on the static differential length ΔL.

Appendix A.2. Transfer Function

Suppose we inject a small differential length oscillation $\Delta x \cos(\omega t)$ into the Michelson, such that $\Delta L = \Delta L_0 + \Delta x \cos(\omega t)$. The *transfer function* from the differential length to antisymmetric power at the frequency of injection ω is

$$\frac{P_\text{as}}{\Delta x}(\omega) = k P_\text{in} \sin(4k\Delta L_0). \qquad \text{(A8)}$$

The transfer function Equation (A8) defines the frequency response of antisymmetric power to length motion of the Michelson interferometer. In this case, the transfer function is flat for all ω.

The easiest way to see the effect of the length oscillation Δx on P_as is to think about the derivative of Equation (A7) with respect to ΔL. The small oscillation will vary P_as at the same frequency as $\Delta x \cos(\omega t)$, $\Delta P_\text{as}(\omega)$. The derivative of Equation (A7) is a slight simplification, as it would be missing a factor of two compared to Equation (A8).

The transfer function of a gravitational wave h to power at the antisymmetric port is more complicated, as seen in [14]:

$$\frac{P_\text{as}}{h}(\omega) = k P_\text{in} L \sin(4k\Delta L_0) \operatorname{sinc}\left(\frac{\omega L}{c}\right) e^{-\frac{i\omega L}{c}} \qquad \text{(A9)}$$

Equation (A9) is not flat: when the signal $\omega = 2\pi$ FSR where the *free spectral range* FSR $= c/2L$, the transfer function dips to zero. This is from the laser in the Michelson integrating over one full period of the gravitational wave from Equation (2), yielding zero overall phase change at that frequency. For the full derivation, see either [14,146] or Appendix B of [58].

Appendix B. Fabry–Pérot Interferometer

The Fabry–Pérot interferometer forms a core optomechanical technology in LIGO, with its resonantly enhanced sensitivity to length motion. The beam reflected from the Fabry–Pérot E_refl has a phase strongly dependent on the cavity length L. Combined with a Michelson interferometer, the Fabry–Pérot phase shift can be preferentially "picked-off" and sent out the antisymmetric port, enhancing a normal Michelson's sensitivity to differential motion, and gravitational waves. In the below sections, we will make the same assumptions as Appendix A.

Appendix B.1. Basics

Figure A2 shows a Fabry–Pérot interferometer, which is just a two-mirror aligned optical cavity. The input mirror has reflectivity R_i, and the end mirror has reflectivity R_e.

The input beam E_in is partially reflected into E_refl, and partially transmitted into the cavity E_circ. The circulating beam E_circ makes round trips in the cavity with length L, accruing a phase e^{i2kL} with every round trip, but also partially transmits through the end mirror E_trans and back through the input mirror E_refl.

We can write out the equations for the plane-wave Fabry–Pérot beams as

$$E_\text{circ} = t_i E_\text{in} + r_i r_e e^{i2kL} E_\text{circ} \tag{A10}$$

$$E_\text{refl} = -r_i E_\text{in} + t_i r_e e^{i2kL} E_\text{circ} \tag{A11}$$

$$E_\text{trans} = t_e E_\text{circ} \tag{A12}$$

where t_i, r_i are the amplitude transmission and reflection coefficients of the input mirror, t_e, r_e are the same for the end mirror, and k is the laser wavenumber. In Equation (A11), r_i has a negative sign due to the "+/−" convention, where we have chosen the left side of the input mirror to suffer a phase flip.

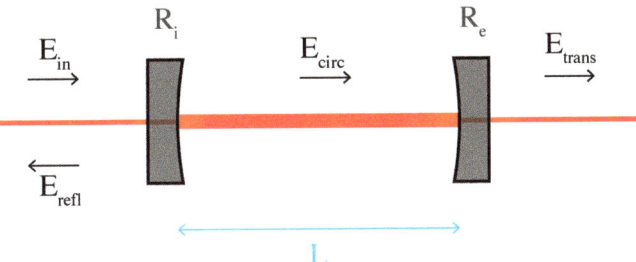

Figure A2. Optical layout of a Fabry–Pérot interferometer.

Using Equation (A10), we can solve for E_circ, and use that result for Equations (A11) and (A12):

$$E_\text{circ} = \frac{t_i}{1 - r_i r_e e^{i2kL}} E_\text{in} \tag{A13}$$

$$E_\text{refl} = \frac{-r_i + (r_i^2 + t_i^2) r_e e^{i2kL}}{1 - r_i r_e e^{i2kL}} E_\text{in} \tag{A14}$$

$$E_\text{trans} = \frac{t_i t_e e^{ikL}}{1 - r_i r_e e^{i2kL}} E_\text{in} \tag{A15}$$

From Equation (A13), we can examine how the resonant buildup works for E_circ. Normally, the product $r_i r_e$ in the denominator is selected to be very close to one. This leaves the phasor e^{i2kL}, which can make the resonant power very large when it equals one. The phasor can equal one when $2kL = n2\pi$, where n is any positive integer. Simplifying yields the *resonance condition* for the cavity length L:

$$L = \frac{\lambda}{2} n \tag{A16}$$

where λ is the laser wavelength.

One important quantity is the *cavity pole* f_p, which can be derived by setting the denominator of Equations (A13)–(A15) to zero:

$$i f_p = -\frac{1}{2\pi} \frac{c}{2L} \log(r_i r_e) \tag{A17}$$

The cavity pole is the frequency at which the Fabry–Pérot frequency response to length motion falls by half, see Equation (A20).

Now we examine Equation (A14), the reflection from the Fabry–Pérot. First, we'll assume $r_i^2 + t_i^2 = 1$, which is true for a lossless mirror. Next, we'll assume that we are near resonance except for a small deviation $\Delta L \ll 1$ such that $L \to L + \Delta L$, then $e^{i2k(L+\Delta L)} \approx 1 + i2k\Delta L$. A first-order series expansion of Equation (A14) about ΔL yields

$$E_{\text{refl}} \approx E_{\text{in}} \left[\frac{-r_i + r_e}{1 - r_i r_e} - ik\Delta L \frac{t_i^2 r_e}{(1 - r_i r_e)^2} \right] \quad (A18)$$

The key of Equation (A18) is the term that depends on ΔL is entirely imaginary and very large. This means that the phase of the reflected light E_{refl} is strongly responding to small changes in length ΔL.

Appendix B.2. Transfer Function

Here, we report the frequency response from end mirror displacement modulation $\Delta x \cos(\omega t)$ to the reflected light E_{refl}. Assuming the cavity is resonant per Equation (A16), we can write the length to reflected field transfer function as

$$\frac{E_{\text{refl}}}{\Delta x}(\omega) = ikE_{\text{in}} \frac{t_i^2 r_e e^{i\omega L/c}}{(1 - r_i r_e)(1 - r_i r_e e^{i2\omega L/c})} \quad (A19)$$

$$\approx ikE_{\text{in}} r_e G_{\text{cav}} \frac{1}{1 + i\frac{\omega}{2\pi f_p}} \quad (A20)$$

where $G_{\text{cav}} = t_i^2/(1 - r_i r_e)^2$ is the ideal cavity power gain, and f_p is the cavity pole from Equation (A17). Between Equations (A19) and (A20) we have assumed the end mirror length modulation Δx is small.

Again, it is easiest to think of the frequency response in Equations (A19) and (A20) as the derivative of Equation (A14) with respect to L. In reality, we must consider the full audio sideband picture to obtain the more accurate Equation (A19). More complete derivations of the Fabry–Pérot frequency response can be found in [57,146,178–180].

References

1. Abbott, B.P.; Abbott, R.; Abbott, T.D.; Abernathy, M.R.; Acernese, F.; Ackley, K.; Adams, C.; Adams, T.; Addesso, P.; Adhikari, R.X.; et al. Observation of Gravitational Waves from a Binary Black Hole Merger. *Phys. Rev. Lett.* **2016**, *116*, 061102. [CrossRef] [PubMed]
2. Aasi, J.; Abbott, B.P.; Abbott, R.; Abbott, T.; Abernathy, M.R.; Ackley, K.; Adams, C.; Adams, T.; Addesso, P.; Adhikari, R.X.; et al. Advanced LIGO. *Class. Quantum Gravity* **2015**, *32*, 074001. [CrossRef]
3. Abbott, R.; Adhikari, R.; Ballmer, S.; Barsotti, L.; Evans, M.; Fritschel, P.; Frolov, V.; Mueller, G.; Slagmolen, B.; Waldman, S. Advanced LIGO Length Sensing and Control Final Design. *Tech. Rep.* **2010**, *1000298*, 2010.
4. Martynov, D.V.; Hall, E.D.; Abbott, B.P.; Abbott, R.; Abbott, T.D.; Adams, C.; Adhikari, R.X.; Anderson, R.A.; Anderson, S.B.; Arai, K.; et al. Sensitivity of the Advanced LIGO detectors at the beginning of gravitational wave astronomy. *Phys. Rev. D* **2016**, *93*, 112004. [CrossRef]
5. Abbott, B.P.; Abbott, R.; Abbott, T.D.; Abernathy, M.R.; Acernese, F.; Ackley, K.; Adams, C.; Adams, T.; Addesso, P.; Adhikari, R.X.; et al. GW150914: The Advanced LIGO Detectors in the Era of First Discoveries. *Phys. Rev. Lett.* **2016**, *116*, 131103. [CrossRef]
6. Abbott, B.P.; Abbott, R.; Abbott, T.D.; Acernese, F.; Ackley, K.; Adams, C.; Adams, T.; Addesso, P.; Adhikari, R.X.; Adya, V.B.; et al. GW170817: Observation of Gravitational Waves from a Binary Neutron Star Inspiral. *Phys. Rev. Lett.* **2017**, *119*, 161101. [CrossRef]
7. Abbott, B.P.; Bloemen, S.; Canizares, P.; Falcke, H.; Fender, R.P.; Ghosh, S.; Groot, P.; Hinderer, T.; Hörandel, J.R.; Jonker, P.G.; et al. Multi-messenger Observations of a Binary Neutron Star Merger. *Astrophys. J. Lett.* **2017**, *848*, L12. [CrossRef]
8. Buikema, A.; Cahillane, C.; Mansell, G.L.; Blair, C.D.; Abbott, R.; Adams, C.; Adhikari, R.X.; Ananyeva, A.; Appert, S.; Arai, K.; et al. Sensitivity and performance of the Advanced LIGO detectors in the third observing run. *Phys. Rev. D* **2020**, *102*, 062003. [CrossRef]

9. Abbott, R.; Abbott, T.D.; Acernese, F.; Ackley, K.; Adams, C.; Adhikari, N.; Adhikari, R.X.; Adya, V.B.; Affeldt, C.; Agarwal, D.; et al. GWTC-3: Compact Binary Coalescences Observed by LIGO and Virgo During the Second Part of the Third Observing Run. *arXiv* **2021**, arXiv:2111.03606.
10. Abbott, B.P.; Abbott, R.; Abbott, T.D.; Abraham, S.; Acernese, F.; Ackley, K.; Adams, C.; Adya, V.B.; Affeldt, C.; Agathos, M.; et al. Prospects for observing and localizing gravitational-wave transients with Advanced LIGO, Advanced Virgo and KAGRA. *Living Rev. Relativ.* **2020**, *23*, 1–69. [CrossRef]
11. Fritschel, P.; Reid, S.; Vajente, G.; Hammond, G.; Miao, H.; Brown, D.; Quetschke, V.; Steinlechner, J. *Instrument Science White Paper 2021*; Technical Report LIGO-T2100298; LIGO Scientific Collaboration: Pasadena, CA, USA, 2021.
12. Misner, C.W.; Thorne, K.S.; Wheeler, J.A. *Gravitation*; Macmillan: Basingstoke, UK, 1973.
13. Sathyaprakash, B.S.; Schutz, B.F. Physics, Astrophysics and Cosmology with Gravitational Waves. *Living Rev. Relativ.* **2009**, *12*, 2. [CrossRef] [PubMed]
14. Saulson, P.R. *Fundamentals of Interferometric Gravitational Wave Detectors*; World Scientific: Singapore, 1994.
15. Adhikari, R.X. Gravitational radiation detection with laser interferometry. *Rev. Mod. Phys.* **2014**, *86*, 121–151. [CrossRef]
16. Rakhmanov, M.; Romano, J.D.; Whelan, J.T. High-frequency corrections to the detector response and their effect on searches for gravitational waves. *Class. Quantum Gravity* **2008**, *25*, 184017. [CrossRef]
17. Drever, R.W.; Hall, J.L.; Kowalski, F.V.; Hough, J.; Ford, G.M.; Munley, A.J.; Ward, H. Laser phase and frequency stabilization using an optical resonator. *Appl. Phys. Photophysics Laser Chem.* **1983**, *31*, 97–105. [CrossRef]
18. Regehr, M.W.; Raab, F.J.; Whitcomb, S.E. Demonstration of a power-recycled Michelson interferometer with Fabry–Perot arms by frontal modulation. *Opt. Lett.* **1995**, *20*, 1507–1509. [CrossRef]
19. Sigg, D.; Mavalvala, N.; Giaime, J.; Fritschel, P.; Shoemaker, D. Signal extraction in a power-recycled Michelson interferometer with Fabry-Perot arm cavities by use of a multiple-carrier frontal modulation scheme. *Appl. Opt.* **1998**, *37*, 5687–5693. [CrossRef]
20. Fritschel, P.; Bork, R.; González, G.; Mavalvala, N.; Ouimette, D.; Rong, H.; Sigg, D.; Zucker, M. Readout and control of a power-recycled interferometric gravitational-wave antenna. *Appl. Opt.* **2001**, *40*, 4988–4998. [CrossRef]
21. Strain, K.A.; Müller, G.; Delker, T.; Reitze, D.H.; Tanner, D.B.; Mason, J.E.; Willems, P.A.; Shaddock, D.A.; Gray, M.B.; Mow-Lowry, C.; et al. Sensing and control in dual-recycling laser interferometer gravitational-wave detectors. *Appl. Opt.* **2003**, *42*, 1244–1256. [CrossRef]
22. Fricke, T.T.; Smith-Lefebvre, N.D.; Abbott, R.; Adhikari, R.; Dooley, K.L.; Evans, M.; Fritschel, P.; Frolov, V.V.; Kawabe, K.; Kissel, J.S.; et al. DC readout experiment in Enhanced LIGO. *Class. Quantum Gravity* **2012**, *29*, 065005. [CrossRef]
23. Izumi, K.; Sigg, D. Advanced LIGO: Length sensing and control in a dual recycled interferometric gravitational wave antenna. *Class. Quantum Gravity* **2017**, *34*, 015001. [CrossRef]
24. Anderson, D.Z. Alignment of resonant optical cavities. *Appl. Opt.* **1984**, *23*, 2944–2949. [CrossRef] [PubMed]
25. Morrison, E.; Meers, B.J.; Robertson, D.I.; Ward, H. Automatic alignment of optical interferometers. *Appl. Opt.* **1994**, *33*, 5041–5049. [CrossRef] [PubMed]
26. Mavalvala, N.; Sigg, D.; Shoemaker, D. Experimental test of an alignment-sensing scheme for a gravitational-wave interferometer. *Appl. Opt.* **1998**, *37*, 7743–7746. [CrossRef] [PubMed]
27. Sidles, J.A.; Sigg, D. Optical torques in suspended Fabry—Perot interferometers. *Phys. Lett. A* **2006**, *354*, 167–172. [CrossRef]
28. Hirose, E.; Kawabe, K.; Sigg, D.; Adhikari, R.; Saulson, P.R. Angular instability due to radiation pressure in the LIGO gravitational-wave detector. *Appl. Opt.* **2010**, *49*, 3474–3484. [CrossRef]
29. Barsotti, L.; Evans, M.; Fritschel, P. Alignment sensing and control in advanced LIGO. *Class. Quantum Gravity* **2010**, *27*, 084026. [CrossRef]
30. Dooley, K.L.; Barsotti, L.; Adhikari, R.X.; Evans, M.; Fricke, T.T.; Fritschel, P.; Frolov, V.; Kawabe, K.; Smith-Lefebvre, N. Angular control of optical cavities in a radiation-pressure-dominated regime: The Enhanced LIGO case. *J. Opt. Soc. Am. A* **2013**, *30*, 2618–2626. [CrossRef]
31. Enomoto, Y.; Nagano, K.; Kawamura, S. Standard quantum limit of angular motion of a suspended mirror and homodyne detection of a ponderomotively squeezed vacuum field. *Phys. Rev. A* **2016**, *94*, 012115. [CrossRef]
32. Kwee, P.; Bogan, C.; Danzmann, K.; Frede, M.; Kim, H.; King, P.; Pöld, J.; Puncken, O.; Savage, R.L.; Seifert, F.; et al. Stabilized high-power laser system for the gravitational wave detector advanced LIGO. *Opt. Express* **2012**, *20*, 10617–10634. [CrossRef]
33. Seifert, F.; Kwee, P.; Heurs, M.; Willke, B.; Danzmann, K. Laser power stabilization for second-generation gravitational wave detectors. *Opt. Lett.* **2006**, *31*, 2000–2002. [CrossRef]
34. Kwee, P.; Willke, B.; Danzmann, K. Shot-noise-limited laser power stabilization with a high-power photodiode array. *Opt. Lett.* **2009**, *34*, 2912–2914. [CrossRef] [PubMed]
35. Zucker, M.E.; Whitcomb, S.E. Measurement of optical path fluctuations due to residual gas in the LIGO 40 meter interferometer. In Proceedings of the Seventh Marcel Grossman Meeting on Recent Developments in Theoretical and Experimental General Relativity, Gravitation, and Relativistic Field Theories, Stanford, CA, USA, 24–30 July 1994; World Scientific: Singapore, 1996; pp. 1434–1436.
36. Dolesi, R.; Hueller, M.; Nicolodi, D.; Tombolato, D.; Vitale, S.; Wass, P.J.; Weber, W.J.; Evans, M.; Fritschel, P.; Weiss, R.; et al. Brownian force noise from molecular collisions and the sensitivity of advanced gravitational wave observatories. *Phys. Rev. D* **2011**, *84*, 063007. [CrossRef]

37. Phelps, M.H.; Gushwa, K.E.; Torrie, C.I. Optical contamination control in the Advanced LIGO ultra-high vacuum system. *Int. Soc. Opt. Photonics* **2013**, *8885*, 314–327. [CrossRef]
38. Robertson, N.A.; Cagnoli, G.; Crooks, D.R.; Elliffe, E.; Faller, J.E.; Fritschel, P.; Goßler, S.; Grant, A.; Heptonstall, A.; Hough, J.; et al. Quadruple suspension design for Advanced LIGO. *Class. Quantum Gravity* **2002**, *19*, 4043. [CrossRef]
39. Aston, S.M.; Barton, M.A.; Bell, A.S.; Beveridge, N.; Bl, B.; Brummitt, A.J.; Cagnoli, G.; Cantley, C.A.; Carbone, L.; Cumming, A.V.; et al. Update on quadruple suspension design for Advanced LIGO. *Class. Quantum Gravity* **2012**, *29*, 235004. [CrossRef]
40. Carbone, L.; Aston, S.M.; Cutler, R.M.; Freise, A.; Greenhalgh, J.; Heefner, J.; Hoyl, D.; Lockerbie, N.A.; Lodhia, D.; Robertson, N.A.; et al. Sensors and actuators for the Advanced LIGO mirror suspensions. *Class. Quantum Gravity* **2012**, *29*, 115005. [CrossRef]
41. Daw, E.J.; Giaime, J.A.; Lormand, D.; Lubinski, M.; Zweizig, J. Long-term study of the seismic environment at LIGO. *Class. Quantum Gravity* **2004**, *21*, 2255–2273. [CrossRef]
42. Wen, S.; Mittleman, R.; Mason, K.; Giaime, J.; Abbott, R.; Kern, J.; O'Reilly, B.; Bork, R.; Hammond, M.; Hardham, C.; et al. Hydraulic external pre-isolator system for LIGO. *Class. Quantum Gravity* **2014**, *31*, 235001. [CrossRef]
43. Matichard, F.; Lantz, B.; Mittleman, R.; Mason, K.; Kissel, J.; Abbott, B.; Biscans, S.; McIver, J.; Abbott, R.; Abbott, S.; et al. Seismic isolation of Advanced LIGO: Review of strategy, instrumentation and performance. *Class. Quantum Gravity* **2015**, *32*, 185003. [CrossRef]
44. Biscans, S.; Warner, J.; Mittleman, R.; Buchanan, C.; Coughlin, M.; Evans, M.; Gabbard, H.; Harms, J.; Lantz, B.; Mukund, N.; et al. Control strategy to limit duty cycle impact of earthquakes on the LIGO gravitational-wave detectors. *Class. Quantum Gravity* **2018**, *35*, 055004. [CrossRef]
45. Bork, R.; Abbott, R.; Barker, D.; Heefner, J. An Overview of the LIGO Control and Data Acquisition System. *arXiv* **2001**, arXiv:0111077.
46. Bartos, I.; Bork, R.; Factourovich, M.; Heefner, J.; Mrka, S.; Mrka, Z.; Raics, Z.; Schwinberg, P.; Sigg, D. The Advanced LIGO timing system. *Class. Quantum Gravity* **2010**, *27*, 084025. [CrossRef]
47. Rollins, J.G. Distributed state machine supervision for long-baseline gravitational-wave detectors. *Rev. Sci. Instrum.* **2016**, *87*, 094502. [CrossRef] [PubMed]
48. Bork, R.; Hanks, J.; Barker, D.; Betzwieser, J.; Rollins, J.; Thorne, K.; von Reis, E. advligorts: The Advanced LIGO real-time digital control and data acquisition system. *SoftwareX* **2021**, *13*, 100619. [CrossRef]
49. Mueller, C.L.; Arain, M.A.; Ciani, G.; Derosa, R.T.; Effler, A.; Feldbaum, D.; Frolov, V.V.; Fulda, P.; Gleason, J.; Heintze, M.; et al. The advanced LIGO input optics. *Rev. Sci. Instrum.* **2016**, *87*, 014502. [CrossRef] [PubMed]
50. Arai, K.; Barnum, S.; Fritschel, P.; Lewis, J.; Waldman, S. *Output Mode Cleaner Design*; Technical Report LIGO-T1000276-v5; LIGO Scientific Collaboration: Pasadena, CA, USA, 2013.
51. Evans, M.; Barsotti, L.; Kwee, P.; Harms, J.; Miao, H. Realistic filter cavities for advanced gravitational wave detectors. *Phys. Rev. D* **2013**, *88*, 022002. [CrossRef]
52. McCuller, L.; Whittle, C.; Ganapathy, D.; Komori, K.; Tse, M.; Fernandez-Galiana, A.; Barsotti, L.; Fritschel, P.; MacInnis, M.; Matichard, F.; et al. Frequency-Dependent Squeezing for Advanced LIGO. *Phys. Rev. Lett.* **2020**, *124*, 171102. [CrossRef]
53. McCuller, L.; Barsotti, L. *Design Requirement Document of the A+ Filter Cavity and Relay Optics for Frequency Dependent Squeezing*; Technical Report T1800447-v7; Massachusetts Institute of Technology: Cambridge, MA, USA, 2020.
54. Buonanno, A.; Chen, Y. Quantum noise in second generation, signal-recycled laser interferometric gravitational-wave detectors. *Phys. Rev. D* **2001**, *64*, 042006. [CrossRef]
55. Kimble, H.J.; Levin, Y.; Matsko, A.B.; Thorne, K.S.; Vyatchanin, S.P. Conversion of conventional gravitational-wave interferometers into quantum nondemolition interferometers by modifying their input and/or output optics. *Phys. Rev. D* **2001**, *65*, 022002. [CrossRef]
56. Ward, R.L. Length Sensing and Control of a Prototype Advanced Interferometric Gravitational Wave Detector. Ph.D. Thesis, California Institute of Technology, Pasadena, CA, USA, 2010. [CrossRef]
57. Hall, E.D. Long-Baseline Laser Interferometry for the Detection of Binary Black-Hole Mergers. Ph.D. Thesis, California Institute of Technology, Pasadena, CA, USA, 2017. [CrossRef]
58. Cahillane, C. Controlling and Calibrating Interferometric Gravitational Wave Detectors. Ph.D. Thesis, California Institute of Technology, Pasadena, CA, USA, 2021. [CrossRef]
59. Abbott, B.P.; Abbott, R.; Abbott, T.D.; Abraham, S.; Acernese, F.; Ackley, K.; Adams, C.; Adya, V.B.; Affeldt, C.; Agathos, M.; et al. A guide to LIGO–Virgo detector noise and extraction of transient gravitational-wave signals. *Class. Quantum Gravity* **2020**, *37*, 055002. [CrossRef]
60. Allen, B.; Anderson, W.G.; Brady, P.R.; Brown, D.A.; Creighton, J.D.E. FINDCHIRP: An algorithm for detection of gravitational waves from inspiraling compact binaries. *Phys. Rev. D* **2012**, *85*, 122006. [CrossRef]
61. Meers, B.J. Recycling in laser-interferometric gravitational-wave detectors. *Phys. Rev. D* **1988**, *38*, 2317. [CrossRef]
62. Strain, K.A.; Meers, B.J. Experimental demonstration of dual recycling for interferometric gravitational-wave detectors. *Phys. Rev. Lett.* **1991**, *66*, 1391. [CrossRef] [PubMed]

63. Heinzel, G.; Strain, K.A.; Mizuno, J.; Skeldon, K.D.; Willke, B.; Winkler, W.; Schilling, R.; Rüdiger, A.; Danzmann, K. Experimental demonstration of a suspended dual recycling interferometer for gravitational wave detection. *Phys. Rev. Lett.* **1998**, *81*, 5493–5496. [CrossRef]
64. Grote, H.; Freise, A.; Malec, M.; Heinzel, G.; Willke, B.; Lück, H.; Strain, K.A.; Hough, J.; Danzmann, K. Dual recycling for GEO 600. *Class. Quantum Gravity* **2004**, *21*, S473. [CrossRef]
65. Fritschel, P.; Shoemaker, D.; Weiss, R. Demonstration of light recycling in a Michelson interferometer with Fabry-Perot cavities. *Appl. Opt.* **1992**, *31*, 1412–1418. [CrossRef] [PubMed]
66. Ando, M. Power Recycling for an Interferometric Gravitational Wave Detector. Ph.D. Thesis, University of Tokyo, Tokyo, Japan, 1998.
67. Arain, M.A.; Mueller, G. Design of the Advanced LIGO Recycling Cavities. *Optics Express* **2008**, *16*, 10018–10032. [CrossRef]
68. Fritschel, P.; Mavalvala, N.; Shoemaker, D.; Sigg, D.; Zucker, M.; González, G. Alignment of an interferometric gravitational wave detector. *Appl. Opt.* **1998**, *37*, 6734–6747. [CrossRef]
69. Caves, C.M. Quantum-Mechanical Radiation-Pressure Fluctuations in an Interferometer. *Phys. Rev. Lett.* **1980**, *45*, 75–79. [CrossRef]
70. Caves, C.M. Quantum-mechanical noise in an interferometer. *Phys. Rev. D* **1981**, *23*, 1693–1708. [CrossRef]
71. Tse, M.; Yu, H.; Kijbunchoo, N.; Fernandez-Galiana, A.; Dupej, P.; Barsotti, L.; Blair, C.; Brown, D.; Dwyer, S.; Effler, A.; et al. Quantum-Enhanced Advanced LIGO Detectors in the Era of Gravitational-Wave Astronomy. *Phys. Rev. Lett.* **2019**, *123*, 231107. [CrossRef]
72. Oelker, E.; Mansell, G.; Tse, M.; Miller, J.; Matichard, F.; Barsotti, L.; Fritschel, P.; McClelland, D.E.; Evans, M.; Mavalvala, N. Ultra-low phase noise squeezed vacuum source for gravitational wave detectors. *Optica* **2016**, *3*, 682–685. [CrossRef]
73. Yu, H.; McCuller, L.; Tse, M.; Kijbunchoo, N.; Barsotti, L.; Mavalvala, N. Quantum correlations between light and the kilogram-mass mirrors of LIGO. *Nature* **2020**, *583*, 43–47. [CrossRef] [PubMed]
74. McCuller, L.; Dwyer, S.E.; Green, A.C.; Yu, H.; Kuns, K.; Barsotti, L.; Blair, C.D.; Brown, D.D.; Effler, A.; Evans, M.; et al. LIGO's quantum response to squeezed states. *Phys. Rev. D* **2021**, *104*, 062006. [CrossRef]
75. Cahillane, C.; Sigg, D.; Mansell, G.L.; Sigg, D. Laser frequency noise in next generation gravitational-wave detectors. *Opt. Express* **2021**, *29*, 42144–42161. [CrossRef]
76. Abbott, B.P.; Abbott, R.; Abbott, T.D.; Abernathy, M.R.; Ackley, K.; Adams, C.; Addesso, P.; Adhikari, R.X.; Adya, V.B.; Affeldt, C.; et al. Calibration of the Advanced LIGO detectors for the discovery of the binary black-hole merger GW150914. *Phys. Rev. D* **2017**, *95*, 062003. [CrossRef]
77. Cahillane, C.; Betzwieser, J.; Brown, D.A.; Goetz, E.; Hall, E.D.; Izumi, K.; Kandhasamy, S.; Karki, S.; Kissel, J.S.; Mendell, G.; et al. Calibration uncertainty for Advanced LIGO's first and second observing runs. *Phys. Rev. D* **2017**, *96*, 102001. [CrossRef]
78. Sun, L.; Goetz, E.; Kissel, J.S.; Betzwieser, J.; Karki, S.; Viets, A.; Wade, M.; Bhattacharjee, D.; Bossilkov, V.; Covas, P.B.; et al. Characterization of systematic error in Advanced LIGO calibration. *Class. Quantum Gravity* **2020**, *37*, 225008. [CrossRef]
79. Sun, L.; Goetz, E.; Kissel, J.S.; Betzwieser, J.; Karki, S.; Bhattacharjee, D.; Covas, P.B.; Datrier, L.E.H.; Kandhasamy, S.; Lecoeuche, Y.K.; et al. Characterization of systematic error in Advanced LIGO calibration in the second half of O3. *arXiv* **2021**, arXiv:2107.00129.
80. Lindblom, L. Optimal calibration accuracy for gravitational-wave detectors. *Phys. Rev. D* **2009**, *80*, 042005. [CrossRef]
81. Tuyenbayev, D.; Karki, S.; Betzwieser, J.; Cahillane, C.; Goetz, E.; Izumi, K.; Kandhasamy, S.; Kissel, J.S.; Mendell, G.; Wade, M.; et al. Improving LIGO calibration accuracy by tracking and compensating for slow temporal variations. *Class. Quantum Gravity* **2017**, *34*, 015002. [CrossRef]
82. Vitale, S.; Haster, C.J.; Sun, L.; Farr, B.; Goetz, E.; Kissel, J.; Cahillane, C. Physical approach to the marginalization of LIGO calibration uncertainties. *Phys. Rev. D* **2021**, *103*, 063016. [CrossRef]
83. Karki, S.; Tuyenbayev, D.; Kandhasamy, S.; Abbott, B.P.; Abbott, T.D.; Anders, E.H.; Berliner, J.; Betzwieser, J.; Cahillane, C.; Canete, L.; et al. The Advanced LIGO photon calibrators. *Rev. Sci. Instrum.* **2016**, *87*, 114503. [CrossRef] [PubMed]
84. Bhattacharjee, D.; Lecoeuche, Y.; Karki, S.; Betzwieser, J.; Bossilkov, V.; Kandhasamy, S.; Payne, E.; Savage, R.L. Fiducial displacements with improved accuracy for the global network of gravitational wave detectors. *Class. Quantum Gravity* **2020**, *38*, 015009. [CrossRef]
85. Estevez, D.; Lieunard, B.; Marion, F.; Mours, B.; Rolland, L.; Verkindt, D. First tests of a Newtonian calibrator on an interferometric gravitational wave detector. *Class. Quantum Gravity* **2018**, *35*, 235009. [CrossRef]
86. Inoue, Y.; Haino, S.; Kanda, N.; Ogawa, Y.; Suzuki, T.; Tomaru, T.; Yamamoto, T.; Yokozawa, T. Improving the absolute accuracy of the gravitational wave detectors by combining the photon pressure and gravity field calibrators. *Phys. Rev. D* **2018**, *98*, 022005. [CrossRef]
87. Estevez, D.; Mours, B.; Pradier, T. Newtonian calibrator tests during the Virgo O3 data taking. *Class. Quantum Gravity* **2021**, *38*, 075012. [CrossRef]
88. Ross, M.P.; Mistry, T.; Datrier, L.; Kissel, J.; Venkateswara, K.; Weller, C.; Kumar, K.; Hagedorn, C.; Adelberger, E.; Lee, J.; et al. Initial Results from the LIGO Newtonian Calibrator. *arXiv* **2021**, arXiv:2107.00141.
89. Kane, T.J.; Byer, R.L. Monolithic, unidirectional single-mode Nd:YAG ring laser. *Opt. Lett.* **1985**, *10*, 65–67. [CrossRef]
90. Korth, Z. Mitigating Noise in Interferometric Gravitational Wave Detectors. Ph.D. Thesis, California Institute of Technology, Pasadena, CA, USA, 2019. [CrossRef]

91. Hoak, D. Gravitational Wave Astrophysics: Instrumentation, Detector Characterization, and a Search for Gravitational Signals from Gamma-ray Bursts. Ph.D. Thesis, University of Massachusetts Amherst, Amherst, MA, USA, 2015. [CrossRef]
92. Venugopalan, G. Prototype Interferometry in the Era of Gravitational Wave Astronomy. Ph.D. Thesis, California Institute of Technology, Pasadena, CA, USA, 2021. [CrossRef]
93. Hild, S.; Grote, H.; Degallaix, J.; Chelkowski, S.; Danzmann, K.; Freise, A.; Hewitson, M.; Hough, J.; Lück, H.; Prijatelj, M.; et al. DC-readout of a signal-recycled gravitational wave detector. *Class. Quantum Gravity* **2009**, *26*, 055012. [CrossRef]
94. Martynov, D.V. Lock Acquisition and Sensitivity Analysis of Advanced LIGO Interferometers. Ph.D Thesis, California Institute of Technology, Pasadena, CA, USA, 2015. [CrossRef]
95. Staley, A.N. Locking the Advanced LIGO Gravitational Wave Detector: With a focus on the Arm Length Stabilization Technique. Ph.D. Thesis, Columbia University, New York, NY, USA, 2015. [CrossRef]
96. Staley, A.; Martynov, D.; Abbott, R.; Adhikari, R.X.; Arai, K.; Ballmer, S.; Barsotti, L.; Brooks, A.F.; Derosa, R.T.; Dwyer, S.; et al. Achieving resonance in the Advanced LIGO gravitational-wave interferometer. *Class. Quantum Gravity* **2014**, *31*, 245010. [CrossRef]
97. Izumi, K.; Arai, K.; Barr, B.; Betzwieser, J.; Brooks, A.; Dahl, K.; Doravari, S.; Driggers, J.C.; Korth, W.Z.; Miao, H.; et al. Multicolor cavity metrology. *J. Opt. Soc. Am. A* **2012**, *29*, 2092–2103. [CrossRef] [PubMed]
98. Mullavey, A.J.; Slagmolen, B.J.J.; Miller, J.; Evans, M.; Fritschel, P.; Sigg, D.; Waldman, S.J.; Shaddock, D.A.; McClelland, D.E. Arm-length stabilisation for interferometric gravitational-wave detectors using frequency-doubled auxiliary lasers. *Opt. Express* **2012**, *20*, 81–89. [CrossRef] [PubMed]
99. Arai, K.; Ando, M.; Moriwaki, S.; Kawabe, K.; Tsubono, K. New signal extraction scheme with harmonic demodulation for power-recycled Fabry-Perot-Michelson interferometers. *Phys. Lett. A* **2000**, *273*, 15–24. [CrossRef]
100. Cahillane, C.; Sigg, D. Out of Loop ALS COMM Frequency Measurement via IR. LHO alog 43119. Available online: https://alog.ligo-wa.caltech.edu/aLOG/index.php?callRep=43119 (accessed on 29 July 2018).
101. Cahillane, C.; Dwyer, S.; Sigg, D. Out of Loop ALS COMM Frequency Measurement—Take Two. LHO alog 43214. Available online: https://alog.ligo-wa.caltech.edu/aLOG/index.php?callRep=43214 (accessed on 2 August 2018).
102. Vajente, G. In situ correction of mirror surface to reduce round-trip losses in Fabry-Perot cavities. *Appl. Opt.* **2014**, *53*, 1459–1465. [CrossRef]
103. Brooks, A.F.; Heptonstall, A.; Lynch, A.; Cole, A.; Abbott, B.; Vorvick, C.; Guido, C.; Ottaway, D.; King, E.; Gustafson, E.; et al. Overview of Advanced LIGO adaptive optics. *Appl. Opt.* **2016**, *55*, 8256–8265. [CrossRef]
104. Weiss, R. *Electronically Coupled Broadband Gravitational Antenna*; Massachusetts Institute of Technology: Cambridge, MA, USA, 1972; p. 54.
105. Barsotti, L.; Fritschel, P.; Evans, M.; Gras, S. *Updated Advanced LIGO Sensitivity Design Curve*; Technical Report LIGO-T1800044; LIGO Scientific Collaboration: Cambridge, MA, USA, 2018.
106. Braginsky, V.B.; Khalili, F.Y.; Thorne, K.S. *Quantum Measurement*; Cambridge University Press: Cambridge, UK, 1992. [CrossRef]
107. Braginsky, V.; Vyatchanin, S. Thermodynamical fluctuations in optical mirror coatings. *Phys. Lett. A* **2003**, *312*, 244–255. [CrossRef]
108. Levin, Y. Internal thermal noise in the LIGO test masses: A direct approach. *Phys. Rev. D* **1998**, *57*, 659–663. [CrossRef]
109. Hong, T.; Yang, H.; Gustafson, E.K.; Adhikari, R.X.; Chen, Y. Brownian thermal noise in multilayer coated mirrors. *Phys. Rev. D* **2013**, *87*, 082001. [CrossRef]
110. Yam, W.; Gras, S.; Evans, M. Multimaterial coatings with reduced thermal noise. *Phys. Rev. D* **2015**, *91*, 042002. [CrossRef]
111. Callen, H.; Greene, R. On a Theorem of Irreversible Thermodynamics. *Phys. Rev.* **1952**, *86*, 702–710. [CrossRef]
112. Kubo, R. The fluctuation-dissipation theorem. *Rep. Prog. Phys.* **1966**, *29*, 255–284. [CrossRef]
113. Saulson, P.R. Thermal noise in mechanical experiments. *Phys. Rev. D* **1990**, *42*, 2437–2445. [CrossRef] [PubMed]
114. Nakagawa, N.; Gretarsson, A.M.; Gustafson, E.K.; Fejer, M.M. Thermal noise in half-infinite mirrors with nonuniform loss: A slab of excess loss in a half-infinite mirror. *Phys. Rev. D* **2002**, *65*, 102001. [CrossRef]
115. Chalermsongsak, T.; Seifert, F.; Hall, E.D.; Arai, K.; Gustafson, E.K.; Adhikari, R.X. Broadband measurement of coating thermal noise in rigid Fabry–Pérot cavities. *Metrologia* **2014**, *52*, 17–30. [CrossRef]
116. Gras, S.; Yu, H.; Yam, W.; Martynov, D.; Evans, M. Audio-band coating thermal noise measurement for Advanced LIGO with a multimode optical resonator. *Phys. Rev. D* **2017**, *95*, 022001. [CrossRef]
117. Gras, S.; Evans, M. Direct measurement of coating thermal noise in optical resonators. *Phys. Rev. D* **2018**, *98*, 122001. [CrossRef]
118. Cagnoli, G.; Hough, J.; DeBra, D.; Fejer, M.M.; Gustafson, E.; Rowan, S.; Mitrofanov, V. Damping dilution factor for a pendulum in an interferometric gravitational waves detector. *Phys. Lett. A* **2000**, *272*, 39–45. [CrossRef]
119. Saulson, P.R. Terrestrial gravitational noise on a gravitational wave antenna. *Phys. Rev. D* **1984**, *30*, 732–736. [CrossRef]
120. Hughes, S.A.; Thorne, K.S. Seismic gravity-gradient noise in interferometric gravitational-wave detectors. *Phys. Rev. D* **1998**, *58*, 122002. [CrossRef]
121. Harms, J. Terrestrial Gravity Fluctuations. *Living Rev. Relativ.* **2015**, *18*, 3. [CrossRef] [PubMed]
122. Driggers, J.C.; Harms, J.; Adhikari, R.X. Subtraction of Newtonian noise using optimized sensor arrays. *Phys. Rev. D* **2012**, *86*, 102001. [CrossRef]
123. Coughlin, M.; Mukund, N.; Harms, J.; Driggers, J.; Adhikari, R.; Mitra, S. Towards a first design of a Newtonian-noise cancellation system for Advanced LIGO. *Class. Quantum Gravity* **2016**, *33*, 244001. [CrossRef]

124. Coughlin, M.W.; Harms, J.; Driggers, J.; McManus, D.J.; Mukund, N.; Ross, M.P.; Slagmolen, B.J.J.; Venkateswara, K. Implications of Dedicated Seismometer Measurements on Newtonian-Noise Cancellation for Advanced LIGO. *Phys. Rev. Lett.* **2018**, *121*, 221104. [CrossRef]
125. Harms, J.; Bonilla, E.L.; Coughlin, M.W.; Driggers, J.; Dwyer, S.E.; McManus, D.J.; Ross, M.P.; Slagmolen, B.J.J.; Venkateswara, K. Observation of a potential future sensitivity limitation from ground motion at LIGO Hanford. *Phys. Rev. D* **2020**, *101*, 102002. [CrossRef]
126. Driggers, J.C.; Vitale, S.; Lundgren, A.P.; Evans, M.; Kawabe, K.; Dwyer, S.E.; Izumi, K.; Schofield, R.M.; Effler, A.; Sigg, D.; et al. Improving astrophysical parameter estimation via offline noise subtraction for Advanced LIGO. *Phys. Rev. D* **2019**, *99*, 042001. [CrossRef]
127. Barsotti, L.; McCuller, L.; Evans, M.; Fritschel, P. *The A+ Design Curve*; Technical Report T1800042-v5; LIGO Scientific Collaboration: Cambridge, MA, USA, 2018.
128. Finn, L.S.; Chernoff, D.F. Observing binary inspiral in gravitational radiation: One interferometer. *Phys. Rev. D* **1993**, *47*, 2198. [CrossRef]
129. Finn, L.S. Binary inspiral, gravitational radiation, and cosmology. *Phys. Rev. D* **1996**, *53*, 2878–2894. [CrossRef]
130. Chen, H.Y.; Holz, D.E.; Miller, J.; Evans, M.; Vitale, S.; Creighton, J. Distance measures in gravitational-wave astrophysics and cosmology. *Class. Quantum Gravity* **2021**, *38*, 055010. [CrossRef]
131. Brooks, A.F.; Vajente, G.; Yamamoto, H.; Abbott, R.; Adams, C.; Adhikari, R.X.; Ananyeva, A.; Appert, S.; Arai, K.; Areeda, J.S.; et al. Point absorbers in Advanced LIGO. *Appl. Opt.* **2021**, *60*, 4047–4063. [CrossRef]
132. Isogai, T.; Miller, J.; Kwee, P.; Barsotti, L.; Evans, M.; Hinkley, N.; Sherman, J.A.; Phillips, N.B.; Schioppo, M.; Lemke, N.D.; et al. Loss in long-storage-time optical cavities. *Opt. Express* **2013**, *21*, 30114–30125. [CrossRef] [PubMed]
133. Cahillane, C. Power Trend of Latest High Power Lock. LHO alog 58772. Available online: https://alog.ligo-wa.caltech.edu/aLOG/index.php?callRep=58772 (accessed on 28 April 2021).
134. Cahillane, C. Power Trends for a Lock Today. LHO alog 58794. Available online: https://alog.ligo-wa.caltech.edu/aLOG/index.php?callRep=58794 (accessed on 29 April 2021).
135. Cahillane, C. Power in the Interferometer—Pre-O4. LHO alog 59142. Available online: https://alog.ligo-wa.caltech.edu/aLOG/index.php?callRep=59142 (accessed on 4 June 2021).
136. Martynov, D. PRG and Optical Gain Increase. LLO alog 43121. Available online: https://alog.ligo-la.caltech.edu/aLOG/index.php?callRep=43121 (accessed on 3 February 2019).
137. Evans, M.; Barsotti, L.; Fritschel, P. A general approach to optomechanical parametric instabilities. *Phys. Lett. A* **2010**, *374*, 665–671. [CrossRef]
138. Green, A.C.; Brown, D.D.; Dovale-Alvarez, M.; Collins, C.; Miao, H.; Mow-Lowry, C.M.; Freise, A. The influence of dual-recycling on parametric instabilities at Advanced LIGO. *Class. Quantum Gravity* **2017**, *34*, 205004. [CrossRef]
139. Miller, J.; Evans, M.; Barsotti, L.; Fritschel, P.; MacInnis, M.; Mittleman, R.; Shapiro, B.; Soto, J.; Torrie, C. Damping parametric instabilities in future gravitational wave detectors by means of electrostatic actuators. *Phys. Lett. A* **2011**, *375*, 788–794. [CrossRef]
140. Blair, C.; Gras, S.; Abbott, R.; Aston, S.; Betzwieser, J.; Blair, D.; Derosa, R.; Evans, M.; Frolov, V.; Fritschel, P.; et al. First Demonstration of Electrostatic Damping of Parametric Instability at Advanced LIGO. *Phys. Rev. Lett.* **2017**, *118*, 151102. [CrossRef] [PubMed]
141. Hardwick, T. High Power and Optomechanics in Advanced LIGO Detectors. Ph.D. Thesis, Louisiana State University, Baton Rouge, LA, USA, 2019.
142. Biscans, S.; Gras, S.; Blair, C.D.; Driggers, J.; Evans, M.; Fritschel, P.; Hardwick, T.; Mansell, G. Suppressing parametric instabilities in LIGO using low-noise acoustic mode dampers. *Phys. Rev. D* **2019**, *100*, 122003. [CrossRef]
143. Buonanno, A.; Chen, Y. Signal recycled laser-interferometer gravitational-wave detectors as optical springs. *Phys. Rev. D* **2002**, *65*, 042001. [CrossRef]
144. Sheard, B.S.; Gray, M.B.; Mow-Lowry, C.M.; McClelland, D.E.; Whitcomb, S.E. Observation and characterization of an optical spring. *Phys. Rev. A* **2004**, *69*, 051801. [CrossRef]
145. Aspelmeyer, M.; Kippenberg, T.J.; Marquardt, F. Cavity optomechanics. *Rev. Mod. Phys.* **2014**, *86*, 1391–1452. [CrossRef]
146. Bond, C.; Brown, D.; Freise, A.; Strain, K.A. Interferometer techniques for gravitational-wave detection. *Living Rev. Relativ.* **2017**, *19*, 1–217. [CrossRef]
147. Whittle, C.; Hall, E.D.; Dwyer, S.; Mavalvala, N.; Sudhir, V.; Abbott, R.; Ananyeva, A.; Austin, C.; Barsotti, L.; Betzwieser, J.; et al. Approaching the motional ground state of a 10-kg object. *Science* **2021**, *372*, 1333–1336. [CrossRef] [PubMed]
148. Dwyer, S.; Mansell, G.; McCuller, L. Squeezing in gravitational wave detectors. *Galaxies* 2022, *under review*.
149. Nguyen, P.; Schofield, R.M.; Effler, A.; Austin, C.; Adya, V.; Ball, M.; Banagiri, S.; Banowetz, K.; Billman, C.; Blair, C.D.; et al. Environmental noise in advanced LIGO detectors. *Class. Quantum Gravity* **2021**, *38*, 14500. [CrossRef]
150. Schwartz, E.; Pele, A.; Warner, J.; Lantz, B.; Betzwieser, J.; Dooley, K.L.; Biscans, S.; Coughlin, M.; Mukund, N.; Abbott, R.; et al. Improving the robustness of the advanced LIGO detectors to earthquakes. *Class. Quantum Gravity* **2020**, *37*, 235007. [CrossRef]
151. Ross, M.P.; Venkateswara, K.; Mow-Lowry, C.; Cooper, S.; Warner, J.; Lantz, B.; Kissel, J.; Radkins, H.; Shaffer, T.; Mittleman, R.; et al. Towards windproofing LIGO: Reducing the effect of wind-driven floor tilt by using rotation sensors in active seismic isolation. *Class. Quantum Gravity* **2020**, *37*, 185018. [CrossRef]

152. Soni, S.; Austin, C.; Effler, A.; Schofield, R.M.S.; González, G.; Frolov, V.V.; Driggers, J.C.; Pele, A.; Urban, A.L.; Valdes, G.; et al. Reducing scattered light in LIGO's third observing run. *Class. Quantum Gravity* **2021**, *38*, 025016. [CrossRef]
153. Kwee, P.; Miller, J.; Isogai, T.; Barsotti, L.; Evans, M. Decoherence and degradation of squeezed states in quantum filter cavities. *Phys. Rev. D* **2014**, *90*, 062006. [CrossRef]
154. Whittle, C.; Komori, K.; Ganapathy, D.; McCuller, L.; Barsotti, L.; Mavalvala, N.; Evans, M. Optimal detuning for quantum filter cavities. *Phys. Rev. D* **2020**, *102*, 102002. [CrossRef]
155. Komori, K.; Ganapathy, D.; Whittle, C.; McCuller, L.; Barsotti, L.; Mavalvala, N.; Evans, M. Demonstration of an amplitude filter cavity at gravitational-wave frequencies. *Phys. Rev. D* **2020**, *102*, 102003. [CrossRef]
156. Bode, N.; Meylahn, F.; Willke, B. Sequential high power laser amplifiers for gravitational wave detection. *Opt. Express* **2020**, *28*, 29469–29478. [CrossRef]
157. Cao, H.T.; Brooks, A.; Ng, S.W.S.; Ottaway, D.; Perreca, A.; Richardson, J.W.; Chaderjian, A.; Veitch, P.J. High dynamic range thermally actuated bimorph mirror for gravitational wave detectors. *Appl. Opt.* **2020**, *59*, 2784–2790. [CrossRef] [PubMed]
158. Srivastava, V.; Mansell, G.; Makarem, C.; Noh, M.; Abbott, R.; Ballmer, S.; Billingsley, G.; Brooks, A.; Cao, H.T.; Fritschel, P.; et al. Piezo-deformable Mirrors for Active Mode Matching in Advanced LIGO. *arXiv* **2021**, arXiv:2110.00674.
159. Sigg, D. Status of the LIGO detectors. *Class. Quantum Gravity* **2008**, *25*, 114041. [CrossRef]
160. Abbott, B.P.; Abbott, R.; Adhikari, R.; Ajith, P.; Allen, B.; Allen, G.; Amin, R.S.; Anderson, S.B.; Anderson, W.G.; Arain, M.A.; et al. LIGO: The Laser Interferometer Gravitational-Wave Observatory. *Rep. Prog. Phys.* **2009**, *72*, 076901. [CrossRef]
161. Aasi, J.; Abadie, J.; Abbott, B.P.; Abbott, R.; Abbott, T.; Abernathy, M.R.; Accadia, T.; Acernese, F.; Adams, C.; Adams, T.; et al. Characterization of the LIGO detectors during their sixth science run. *Class. Quantum Gravity* **2015**, *32*, 115012. [CrossRef]
162. Caron, B.; Dominjon, A.; Drezen, C.; Flaminio, R.; Grave, X.; Marion, F.; Massonnet, L.; Mehmel, C.; Morand, R.; Mours, B.; et al. The VIRGO interferometer for gravitational wave detection. *Nucl. Phys. B Proc. Suppl.* **1997**, *54*, 167–175. [CrossRef]
163. Acernese, F.; Alshourbagy, M.; Amico, P.; Antonucci, F.; Aoudia, S.; Astone, P.; Avino, S.; Baggio, L.; Ballardin, G.; Barone, F.; et al. Status of Virgo. *Class. Quantum Gravity* **2008**, *25*, 114045. [CrossRef]
164. Grote, H.; Allen, B.; Aufmuth, P.; Aulbert, C.; Babak, S.; Balasubramanian, R.; Barr, B.W.; Berukoff, S.; Bunkowski, A.; Cagnoli, G.; et al. The status of GEO 600. *Class. Quantum Gravity* **2005**, *22*, S193–S198. [CrossRef]
165. Grote, H.; LIGO Scientific Collaboration. The GEO 600 status. *Class. Quantum Gravity* **2010**, *27*, 084003. [CrossRef]
166. Ando, M.; Collaboration, t.T. Current status of TAMA. *Class. Quantum Gravity* **2002**, *19*, 1409. [CrossRef]
167. Acernese, F.; Agathos, M.; Agatsuma, K.; Aisa, D.; Allemandou, N.; Allocca, A.; Amarni, J.; Astone, P.; Balestri, G.; Ballardin, G.; et al. Advanced Virgo: A second-generation interferometric gravitational wave detector. *Class. Quantum Gravity* **2015**, *32*, 024001. [CrossRef]
168. Somiya, K. Detector configuration of KAGRA–the Japanese cryogenic gravitational-wave detector. *Class. Quantum Gravity* **2012**, *29*, 124007. [CrossRef]
169. Aso, Y.; Michimura, Y.; Somiya, K.; Ando, M.; Miyakawa, O.; Sekiguchi, T.; Tatsumi, D.; Yamamoto, H. Interferometer design of the KAGRA gravitational wave detector. *Phys. Rev. D* **2013**, *88*, 043007. [CrossRef]
170. Akutsu, T.; Ando, M.; Arai, K.; Arai, Y.; Araki, S.; Araya, A.; Aritomi, N.; Aso, Y.; Bae, S.; Bae, Y.; et al. Overview of KAGRA: Detector design and construction history. *Prog. Theor. Exp. Phys.* **2021**, *2021*, 49. [CrossRef]
171. Padma, T. India's LIGO gravitational-wave observatory gets green light. *Nature*, 22 January 2019. [CrossRef]
172. Adhikari, R.X.; Arai, K.; Brooks, A.F.; Wipf, C.; Aguiar, O.; Altin, P.; Barr, B.; Barsotti, L.; Bassiri, R.; Bell, A.; et al. A cryogenic silicon interferometer for gravitational-wave detection. *Class. Quantum Gravity* **2020**, *37*, 165003. [CrossRef]
173. Hild, S.; Abernathy, M.; Acernese, F.; Amaro-Seoane, P.; Andersson, N.; Arun, K.; Barone, F.; Barr, B.; Barsuglia, M.; Beker, M.; et al. Sensitivity studies for third-generation gravitational wave observatories. *Class. Quantum Gravity* **2011**, *28*, 094013. [CrossRef]
174. Evans, M.; Adhikari, R.X.; Afle, C.; Ballmer, S.W.; Biscoveanu, S.; Borhanian, S.; Brown, D.A.; Chen, Y.; Eisenstein, R.; Gruson, A.; et al. A Horizon Study for Cosmic Explorer: Science, Observatories, and Community. *arXiv* **2021**, arXiv:2109.09882.
175. Baker, J.; Bellovary, J.; Bender, P.L.; Berti, E.; Caldwell, R.; Camp, J.; Conklin, J.W.; Cornish, N.; Cutler, C.; DeRosa, R.; et al. The Laser Interferometer Space Antenna: Unveiling the Millihertz Gravitational Wave Sky. *arXiv* **2019**, arXiv:1907.06482.
176. Sumner, T.J.; Mueller, G.; Conklin, J.W. LISA Pathfinder: First steps to observing gravitational waves from space. *J. Phys. Conf. Ser.* **2017**, *840*, 012001. [CrossRef]
177. Michelson, A.A.; Morley, E.W. On the Relative Motion of the Earth and the Luminiferous Ether. *Am. J. Sci.* **1887**, *34*, 333–345. [CrossRef]
178. Willke, B.; Gustafson, E.K.; Husman, M.E.; Lawrence, M.J.; Byer, R.L. Dynamic response of a Fabry-Perot interferometer. *JOSA B* **1999**, *16*, 523–532. [CrossRef]
179. Rakhmanov, M.; Savage, R.; Reitze, D.; Tanner, D. Dynamic resonance of light in Fabry-Perot cavities. *Phys. Lett. A* **2002**, *305*, 239–244. [CrossRef]
180. Bondu, F.; Debieu, O. Accurate measurement method of Fabry-Perot cavity parameters via optical transfer function. *Appl. Opt.* **2007**, *46*, 2611–2614. [CrossRef]

Review

Detecting Gravitational Waves with Advanced Virgo

Ilaria Nardecchia

INFN, Sezione di Roma Tor Vergata, I-0133 Roma, Italy; ilaria.nardecchia@roma2.infn.it

Abstract: Advanced Virgo is the European gravitational-wave detector that, along with the American ones, is part of the global network of detectors that have been pinpointing gravitational waves since 2015. These kilometer-scale laser interferometers, measuring the distance between quasi-free-falling mirrors, represent the suitable detectors to explore the Universe through gravitational radiation. The initial Virgo experiment completed several runs of scientific data between 2007 and 2011, establishing the upper limits on the gravitational-wave rate expected for several astrophysical sources. The Advanced Virgo project led this instrument to unprecedented sensitivities making gravitational wave detections a routine occurrence. In this review, the basic techniques to build gravitational-waves interferometers and the upgrades needed to boost their sensitivities, even beyond the classical limit, are presented. The particular case of Advanced Virgo will be described hinting at its future developments, as well.

Keywords: gravitational waves; interferometers; ground based gravitational-wave detector; Advanced Virgo

Citation: Nardecchia, I. Detecting Gravitational Waves with Advanced Virgo. *Galaxies* **2022**, *10*, 28. https://doi.org/10.3390/galaxies10010028

Academic Editor: Yi-Zhong Fan

Received: 31 December 2021
Accepted: 28 January 2022
Published: 2 February 2022

Publisher's Note: MDPI stays neutral with regard to jurisdictional claims in published maps and institutional affiliations.

Copyright: © 2022 by the authors. Licensee MDPI, Basel, Switzerland. This article is an open access article distributed under the terms and conditions of the Creative Commons Attribution (CC BY) license (https://creativecommons.org/licenses/by/4.0/).

1. Introduction

Almost one hundred years ago, Albert Einstein predicted the existence of gravitational waves [1], ripples in the fabric of space-time set off by extremely violent, cosmic cataclysms in the early Universe, supernovae explosions, colliding black holes and neutron stars. With the technology available in 1916, Einstein assumed that such ripples would be vanishingly small and nearly impossible to detect. The technological advancements over the past century have changed those prospects and, on 14 September 2015, the LIGO-Virgo Collaboration detected for the first time the ripples in space-time caused by two coalescing black holes (GW150914) [2].

Six years after the first observation, about one hundred detections have followed [3,4]. Among them, the Gravitational Wave (GW) signal detected by two colliding neutron stars in August 2017 (GW170817) [5], marked the first time a cosmic event has been viewed in both gravitational and electromagnetic windows.

These impressive results have been achieved thanks to the global network of second generation of kilometer-scale Michelson laser interferometers Advanced LIGO and Advanced Virgo [6,7].

The purpose of this review is to provide the operating principles of gravitational-wave detectors discussing in details the Advanced Virgo case: Section 2 provides an overview of the main techniques used in GW interferometers, and in Section 3 the main noise sources affecting the performances of the GW detectors are described. In Section 4, the implementation in Advanced Virgo of all the techniques described in the previous sections will be detailed, portraying the interferometer configuration during the latest observing run. Finally, in Section 5 the future instrument upgrades for Advanced Virgo to push the detector sensitivity towards the maximum achievable limit will be described.

2. Gravitational Wave Interferometric Detectors

The effect of a gravitational wave is a change in the local space–time metric, which can be considered equivalent to a change in the distance measured between free-falling test masses.

The GW polarization implies that the distance variation is intrinsically differential: two measurements performed along orthogonal directions provide opposite results.

If the test masses are mirrors, one could reflect laser light off them and observe this GW-induced stretching and compressing of space-time by measuring the light travel time. Interferometric GW detectors are based on this principle.

GW detection is so hard since they are expected to be extremely weak when they finally reach the Earth. The amount by which a distance L would shrink or stretch due to a GW is proportional to the strain amplitude h, that is [8]:

$$\Delta L = \frac{hL}{2}. \quad (1)$$

Since the expected strain amplitudes are of the order of 10^{-22}, we are faced with the prospect of measuring changes in separation of 10^{-19} m even for a 1 km scale interferometer.

In a Michelson interferometer, laser light is incident on a beam splitter that reflects one half of it and transmits the other half. Each light beam travels some distance before being reflected back by a mirror towards the beam splitter where the two beams interfere. The interference provides an output beam, whose power carries information about the difference of the path traveled by the two beams. The GW passage causes one arm of the interferometer to grow longer while the other grows shorter, then vice versa, back and forth as long as the wave is passing.

It can be considered as a transducer which converts a length variation to a variation of the phase of a laser field.

The simple Michelson configuration is not enough to make the detector sensitive to expected GW signals, thus many techniques need to be employed to make possible the GW detection.

The main differences with respect to the simple Michelson scheme are related to the mirrors defining the light paths: they are hang freely on pendula instead of being fixed to a rigid structure and they are several kilometers apart, instead of a few meters.

Despite this improvement, the arms would still be too short to enable the detection of gravitational waves. Thus, an additional mirror is placed into each arm, near the beam splitter, at about a few km from the mirror at the end of that arm forming a Fabry–Perot (FP) optical cavity. As result, the laser into each arm bounces between its two mirrors about 300 times before being merged with the beam from the other arm. These reflections build up the laser power within the interferometer and increase the distance traveled by each laser beam from a few to thousands of km. GW interferometers reach their maximum sensitivity operating at dark fringe so that most of the light is reflected back towards the laser, the so called bright port.

At this point quantum physics enters in the GW detection. First of all, the light's energy can only be absorbed in discrete quanta (photons), resulting in photon-counting noise or shot noise. The GW signal-to-shot-noise ratio can be improved by detecting more photons.

Consequently, GW detectors use high-power laser systems and optical resonators to maximize their shot noise limited sensitivity.

The dark fringe working point allows to increase the laser power circulating into the detector by introducing an additional mirror, called Power Recycling Mirror (PRM). It is located between the laser source and the beam splitter continuously reflecting back into the interferometer the laser light that has traveled through the instrument.

Thanks to this recycling mechanism, the power circulating into the detector can reach values of the order of MW starting from a Nd:YAG laser source delivering only few hundred watts of power. Thus, the power recycling cavity greatly boosts the power of the laser beam inside the FP cavities without the need to generate such a powerful laser beam at the outset.

Moreover, the quantum noise of light disturbs a GW detector. The quantum nature of light produces a fluctuating radiation pressure force on the test-mass mirrors. The mirrors are displaced by the light, an effect that cannot be distinguished from a GW signal. In order to reduce this effect, GW detectors use test masses of up to 40 kg.

With the addition of the power recycling cavity, first generation GW detectors are known as Power Recycled, Fabry–Perot Michelson interferometers.

To date, the basic scheme of a GW interferometer is described, but many other techniques are applied to minimize all the noises affecting its performance.

One of the major obstacles to reach the desired detector sensitivity at frequencies around 10 Hz is the effect of local environmental disturbances causing the motion of the interferometer optics, coupled as noise in the gravitational wave data output.

In the interferometer's most sensitive frequency band (few Hz-300 Hz), the main limitation of the sensitivity is represented by the thermal noise. The mirrors and their suspensions are built from materials having exquisitely high mechanical quality factors. They are made of very pure fused silica glass absorbing only just one in 3-million photons hitting them, making the mirrors not prone to heating. Fused silica exhibits very low thermal noise making it a natural choice to realize the interferometer optics.

The technological enhancement of noise reduction techniques led to the upgrade of the first generation of GW detectors to the second one, the so-called advanced, whose main features are the replacement of steel wires with fused silica fibers to suspend the mirrors, the installation of another partially reflecting mirror, i.e., Signal Recycling Mirror (SRM), placed between the beam splitter and the detector output port to improve the GW signal [9], the injection of squeezed states of light into the dark port of the interferometer to reduce the quantum noise and the implementation of more performing thermal compensation system to cope with the power increase.

Due to the combination of power and signal recycling techniques, the second generation of GW detectors are known as Double Recycled, Fabry–Perot Michelson interferometers (Figure 1).

These so-called advanced detectors replaced the existing interferometers, aiming for a 10 times increased sensitivity.

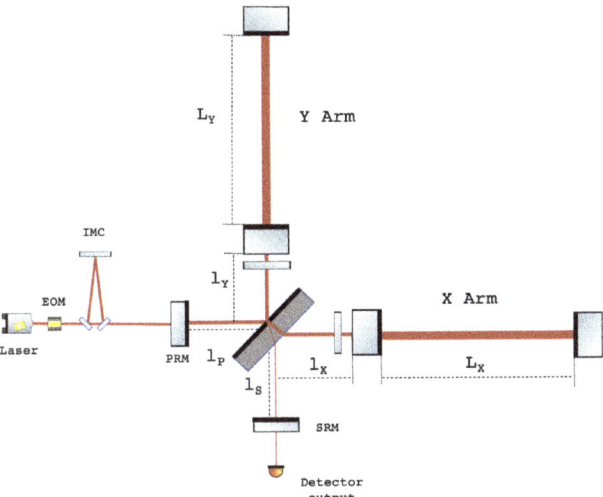

Figure 1. Double Recycled Fabry–Perot Michelson interferometer configuration: PRM indicates the power recycling mirror, SRM the signal recycling mirror and input mirror and end mirror form the Fabry–Perot optical cavities in each arm. The thickness of the red lines indicating the beam path, is proportional to the amount of power circulating into the detector. The image uses the graphic library from [10].

The GW detectors combine a number of advanced technologies to push the limits of precision length measurement even beyond the classic one. The simple Michelson topology integrates additional optical elements, which significantly change the properties of the optical system. In the next paragraphs, an overview of the aforementioned techniques, adopted to make the simple Michelson interferometer a gravitational-wave detector, will be described.

2.1. Free-Falling Mirrors

The optical and mechanical properties of the mirrors play a crucial role to detect GW. Their spherical shape matches the fundamental Gaussian mode of the main laser beam propagating into the detector, their diameter is dimensioned accordingly to the current technology and, finally, their thickness and, consequently their weight, are optimized to cope with the radiation pressure depending on the power circulating into the detector. The mirror aspect ratio is properly chosen to minimize the thermal noise contribution. The advanced GW detector glass mirrors have the same diameter as the first generation ones (around 35 cm) but are twice as thick (20 cm) and, consequently, twice as heavy (around 42 kg).

According to the General Relativity [1], these mirrors are designed to be quasi-free falling in the direction of propagation of the laser beam to respond to the GW, thereby acting as test masses that probe space-time [11]. This is achieved by suspending the mirrors as sophisticated pendula through four tiny fibers of 0.4 mm of diameter. Above the pendulum's resonant frequency, typically around 1 Hz, the suspension system isolates the mirror from vibrations of the ground and the structures on which it is mounted, making it quasi-free. The targeted detection band of earth-based detectors is therefore restricted to the audio band in the range 10 Hz–10 kHz. At lower frequencies, disturbances from the environment are too high, at higher frequencies no strong GW signals are expected [12].

2.2. Michelson Interferometer

In a Michelson interferometer, laser light is incident on a beam splitter that reflects half of it and transmits the other half. Each light beam travels some distance before it is reflected back by a mirror towards the beam splitter where the two beams interfere. The interference provides an output beam, the power of which carries information about the laser path difference. The power measured at the output of the detector, after the recombination of the two beams, is proportional to [8]:

$$P_{out} \propto P_{in} \sin^2\left[k(L_y - L_x)\right] = P_{in} \sin^2 \delta\phi, \qquad (2)$$

where P_{in} is the input power, k is the wavenumber of the laser light defined as $k = 2\pi/\lambda$ with λ the wavelength of the laser and L_x and L_y are the lengths of the two arms. Therefore, any variation in the length of the two arms causes a variation of the phase $\delta\phi$, resulting in a variation of the power measured at the output of the detector.

2.3. Fabry-Perot Optical Cavity

Each arm of gravitational-wave Michelson interferometers hosts a linear two-mirror cavity formed by the input mirror, partially reflective, and the end mirror, almost completely reflective. The behaviour of the cavity is described by its length L, the wavelength of the laser λ and the reflectivity and transmissivity of both mirrors r_1, r_2, t_1 and t_2, respectively. The power circulating inside the cavity is given by:

$$P_{circ} = P_{in} \frac{t_1^2}{(1 - r_1 r_2)^2 + 4 r_1 r_2 \sin^2(kL)} \qquad (3)$$

with $k = 2\pi/\lambda$ and P_{in} the power injected into the cavity.

The maximum power, obtained when the sine function becomes equal to zero, i.e., at $kL = N\lambda$ with N an integer, corresponds to the cavity resonance condition and the power circulating in the cavity is:

$$P_{res} = P_{in} \frac{t_1^2}{(1 - r_1 r_2)^2}. \tag{4}$$

Multiple resonant peaks are present, spaced in length by half wavelength and in frequency by the cavity free spectral range, defined as:

$$\Delta f_{FSR} = \frac{c}{2L}. \tag{5}$$

Another characteristic parameter of a cavity is its linewidth, usually defined as the Full Width at Half Maximum (FWHM) of the resonance peak:

$$FWHM = \frac{2\,\Delta f_{FSR}}{\pi} \arcsin\left(\frac{1 - r_1 r_2}{2\sqrt{r_1 r_2}}\right), \tag{6}$$

that indicates the frequency range resonating inside the cavity. The ratio of the linewidth to the FSR defines the *finesse* (F) of the cavity:

$$F = \frac{\Delta f_{FSR}}{FWHM} = \frac{\pi}{2\,\arcsin\left(\frac{1-r_1 r_2}{2\sqrt{r_1 r_2}}\right)}. \tag{7}$$

In the case of high finesse ($F > 100$), as for GW detectors, i.e., r_1 and r_2 are close to 1, the argument of the arcsin function is small, so:

$$F \approx \frac{\pi \sqrt{r_1 r_2}}{1 - r_1 r_2}. \tag{8}$$

and Equation (3) can be approximated as:

$$P_{res} = P_{in} \frac{t_1^2}{(1 - r_1 r_2)^2} \approx P_{in} \frac{2F}{\pi}. \tag{9}$$

The build-up factor $2F/\pi$ can be interpreted as the number of round-trips inside the cavity. The average time spent by the photons inside the cavity is related to the finesse by the expression:

$$\tau_s = \frac{L}{c} \frac{F}{\pi} \tag{10}$$

and the pole frequency of the cavity is given by:

$$f_p = \frac{1}{4\pi \tau_s}. \tag{11}$$

Thus, in the limit of high finesse, the effective storage time of the light, which in the arm of a Michelson interferometer is $2L/c$, is enhanced by a factor $F/(2\pi)$.

The use of FP cavities not only allows to increase the circulating power in the detector but also provides an important help to improve the sensitivity of gravitational-wave detectors.

The field reflected by the FP cavity is described by:

$$E_{ref} = -\frac{r_1 - r_2(1 - L_1)e^{2ikL}}{1 - r_1 r_2 e^{2ikL}} E_{in} \tag{12}$$

where L_1 are the losses of the input mirror[1]. When the over-coupled cavity condition is satisfied, i.e., $r_1 < r_2$, the phase of the reflected beam rotates by 2π, changing sign between resonance and anti-resonance conditions. It can be demonstrated that, expanding at first order the cavity displacement δL, assuming $L_1 = 0$ and solving for the resonance condition $e^{2ikL} = 1$, Equation (12) can be written in first approximation as [13]:

$$E_{ref}^{res}(\delta L) = \frac{r_2 - r_1}{1 - r_1 r_2}\left(1 + i2k\delta L \frac{r_2(1-r_1)^2}{(1-r_1 r_2)(r_2-r_1)}\right) = E_{ref}^{res} e^{i\phi_{FP}(\delta L)}, \qquad (13)$$

where $E_{ref}^{res} = \frac{r_2 - r_1}{1 - r_1 r_2}$ is the reflected field at resonance and $\phi_{FP}(\delta L)$ is the phase of the field reflected by the Fabry–Perot cavity due to δL. Considering $r_2 \approx 1$, $\phi_{FP}(\delta L)$ can be written as:

$$\phi_{FP}(\delta L) = 2k\frac{2F}{\pi}\delta L, \qquad (14)$$

showing that the phase variation due to a length change is directly proportional to the cavity finesse. Away from the resonances, the phase of the reflected beam is almost flat, so it is insensitive to the changes of the cavity length. The phase of the reflected field changes rapidly when the length is close to resonance. When the reflectivity of the input mirror is close to unit, the sensitivity to a change in the phase term $2kL$ is enhanced by a factor $2F/\pi$ compared to the arm of the simple Michelson interferometer.

Thus, the use of the Fabry–Perot cavities at the resonance condition allows to build up the laser power within the interferometer and amplifies the phase change induced by GW by the same factor $2F/\pi$.

2.4. Interaction of Fabry–Perot Michelson Interferometer with Gravitational Waves

The response of laser interferometers to gravitational waves has been calculated in different ways, particularly in the transverse–traceless (TT) gauge and in the proper detector frame. In the TT gauge, the proper distance between the two test masses changes as a consequence of the GW passage while the coordinate position of the mirrors, initially at rest, does not vary. In the detector frame, the effect of the passage of GW is a displacement of the test masses from their original position and, if the distance between the FP mirrors L is small compared to the GW wavelength, this displacement can be derived using the geodesic deviation equation [8].

In the following, the phase shift induced by GW in the FP cavity will be derived in the proper detector frame.

Consider a FP cavity oriented along the x axis and a GW with only the plus polarization whose amplitude is h_0 and frequency f_{gw}, propagating perpendicularly to the x-y plane of the detector. In the proper detector frame, the distance variation δL_x between the two mirrors induced by the GW derived by the geodesic deviation equation is:

$$\delta L_x = \frac{Lh_0}{2}\cos(2\pi f_{gw} t). \qquad (15)$$

This induces a change $\delta\phi_x$ of the field reflected from the cavity along the X arm equal to:

$$\delta\phi_{FP,x} \approx \frac{4F}{\pi}k\delta L_x. \qquad (16)$$

The phase shift of the FP cavity along the Y direction is obtained by reversing the sign of h_0: $\delta\phi_{FP,y} = -\delta\phi_{FP,x}$. Thus, the total shift in the Michelson FP interferometer is:

$$\delta\phi_{M-FP} = \delta\phi_{FP,x} - \delta\phi_{FP,y} = 2\delta\phi_{FP,x} \approx \frac{8F}{\pi}k\delta L_x. \qquad (17)$$

By replacing Equation (15) into Equation (17), it becomes:

$$\Delta\phi_{M-FP} = \frac{4F}{\pi}kLh_0\cos(2\pi f_{gw} t). \qquad (18)$$

This result is exhaustive only when the period of GW is higher than the cavity storage time τ_s. To evaluate the response of the detector when the period of the incoming GW is comparable to the cavity round-trip time, the TT gauge frame must be considered[2]. In this reference system the phase shift of the Michelson FP interferometer becomes:

$$\delta\phi_{M-FP} = \frac{4F}{\pi} k L h_0 \cos(2\pi f_{gw} t) \frac{1}{\sqrt{1+(f_{gw}/f_p)^2}}. \tag{19}$$

Thus, for $f_{gw} \ll f_p$, the detector response to the GW passage is maximum (Equation (19) reduced to Equation (18) in the proper detector frame), when $f_{gw} = f_p$ the cavity response decreases by factor $\sqrt{2}$ with respect to its maximum and, if $f_{gw} \gg f_p$, the detector response decreases linearly with f_{gw}.

Summarizing, the power stored inside the cavity is amplified with respect to the input power by a factor $G_{FP} = 2F/\pi$. The same amplification applies to the phase response of the reflected beam to GWs, but only for frequencies below the cavity pole:

$$\delta\phi_{FP,x} \approx 2k\delta L_x G_{FP} \frac{1}{\sqrt{1+(f_{gw}/f_p)^2}}. \tag{20}$$

The effect of a GW on the field propagating through the FP cavity can be also described in terms of signal sidebands generated in each arm cavity as a consequence result of the GW passage. Their amplitude is proportional to the power circulating inside the arm, and to a frequency-dependent component related to the FP cavity pole. Since the GW effect is differential, the signal sidebands generated in the two orthogonal arms have opposite sign. Thus, once reached the beam splitter, they interfere in the opposite way with respect to the main laser beam: they are maximized propagating toward the anti-symmetric port, and minimized toward the power recycling mirror.

2.5. Detection at the Dark Fringe

In a Michelson interferometer, any variation in the length of the two arms causes a variation of the phase $\delta\phi$, resulting in a variation of the power measured at the output of the detector. This is described by Equation (2) where $\delta\phi$ can be written as $\delta\phi = \phi_0 + \phi_{gw}$ where ϕ_{gw} contains the GW phase shift contribution and ϕ_0 is the Michelson interferometer working point chosen to maximize the performance of the detector. The choice of tuning the interferometer in dark fringe to detect GW may seem counterintuitive but, is a consequence of use of *real* devices that are, therefore, affected by noise. The presence of the so-called technical noises[3], makes the dark fringe configuration the one with the highest sensitivity [8].

The sinusoidal detector response, shown in Figure 2, indicates the half fringe ($\phi_0 = \pi/4$) as the best working point for the detector since the derivative $\partial P/\partial \phi_0$ is maximum and the sensitivity to a small displacement is the highest. Nevertheless, in this point, any fluctuation in the laser power P_{in} causes a variation of the power measured at the output of the instrument, which can be mistakenly interpreted as the consequence of a GW passage.

Bringing the detector at the dark fringe, it results insensitive to the laser power fluctuations and, in absence of GW, the output power is null. However, it has to be considered that, in this configuration, also the derivative $\partial P/\partial \phi_0$ is zero. Thus, for an incoming GW, the power variation measured at the dark fringe would be of the order of h^2. Such a signal is of course invisible.

To overcome this issue, the laser light is modulated through an Electro Optical Modulator (EOM) before being injected into the interferometer. A variable refractive index crystal placed inside the EOM introduces a phase shift on the beam proportional to the applied voltage, generating some sidebands.

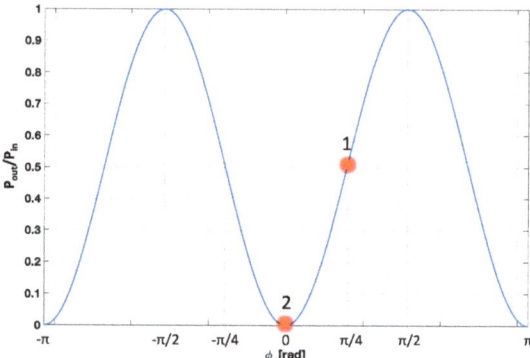

Figure 2. The response of a Michelson interferometer as a function of the fringe level. The half and dark fringe conditions are marked as **1** and **2**, respectively.

The incident electromagnetic field of the laser, passing through the modulator, acquires a time-varying phase and the electromagnetic field becomes:

$$\psi(t) = \psi_0 e^{-i(\omega_0 t + m \sin(\Omega t))}, \qquad (21)$$

where ψ_0 is the amplitude of the input beam, ω_0 is the laser frequency, m is the modulation index and Ω is the modulation frequency.

Equation (21) can be expanded in Fourier modes as:

$$\psi(t) = \psi_0 \sum_{n=-\infty}^{+\infty} J_n(m) e^{-i(\omega_0 + n\Omega)t}, \qquad (22)$$

where $J_n(m)$ are the Bessel functions. For $m \ll 1$, only three terms of the expansion can be considered:

$$\psi(t) \approx \psi_0 \left[J_0(m) e^{-i\omega_0 t} + J_1(m) e^{-i(\omega_0 + \Omega)t} + J_{-1}(m) e^{-i(\omega_0 - \Omega)t} \right], \qquad (23)$$

where the first term represents the *carrier*, and the other two terms correspond to the first upper and lower *sidebands* with frequencies $\omega_\pm = \omega_0 \pm \Omega$. Equation (23) describes the beam impinging on the Fabry–Perot resonant cavity as composed of three independent fields: the carrier and the sideband ones.

If the distance between the beam splitter and the input mirror of the FP cavity along X and Y arms is the same, carrier and sidebands are both on the dark fringe. However, introducing a macroscopic arm length difference of several centimeter equal to an integer number of laser wavelength, called Schnupp asymmetry ($l_X - l_Y$ in Figure 1), the sidebands are no longer on the dark fringe, allowing to be transferred through the interferometer to the output port even if the carrier is at the dark fringe.

When a GW propagates through the interferometer, the term of the electromagnetic field at the dark port containing the contributions of beats of the carrier with the sidebands, encodes the GW signal, which is linear in h and oscillates at frequency Ω [8]. In a second demodulation process the photo-current is then electronically demodulated at Ω in order to finally derive the GW signal stream at f_{gw}.

In conclusion, operating at dark fringe and introducing a small asymmetry in the distance between the beam splitter and the input mirrors of the FP cavities, make the signal insensitive to the laser power fluctuations and allow the extraction of the GW signal from the component demodulated at Ω which is linear (and not quadratic) in h.

This technique, based on the use of the sidebands as optical local oscillator to extract the gravitational wave signal, called heterodyne readout, was commonly used in the first generation of gravitational wave detectors. However, the experience gained running these interferometers indicates several limitations connected to the heterodyne readout, mainly related to the arise of thermal effects in the core optics, due to the high power circulating into the detector, that spoils the quality of the sidebands. Thus, the second generation of gravitational wave detectors uses a detection scheme known as DC readout [14], where a small differential detuning is introduced in the interferometer so that it is no longer locked on a dark fringe. This allows a small amount of carrier light to exit the interferometer to be used as a local oscillator field. A crucial element in the DC readout detection scheme is the Output Mode Cleaner (OMC), which is an optical cavity that transmits only the fundamental Gaussian mode at the carrier frequency. The purpose is to keep only light which leaves the interferometer due to a gravitational wave signal and remove Higher-Order Modes (HOM) caused by interferometer mirror defects and radio-frequency sidebands.

2.6. Power Recycling Cavity

The Power Recycling Cavity (PRC) greatly boosts the power of the laser beam inside the Fabry–Perot cavities without the need to generate such a powerful laser beam at the outset.

It is composed of the power recycling mirror and the compound mirror formed by the Michelson FP interferometer. At resonance, the power circulating into the detector is built up with respect to the input power by the so-called gain that is:

$$G_{PRC} = \frac{1 - r_{PR}^2}{\left[1 - r_{PR}\left(1 - \frac{F}{\pi}L_{RT}\right)\right]^2}, \qquad (24)$$

where r_{PR} is the reflectivity of the power recycling mirror and L_{RT} are the round trip losses obtained by summing those of the mirrors forming the FP cavity.

2.7. Signal Recycling Cavity

For a power recycled high-finesse Fabry–Perot–Michelson interferometer, when $f_{gw} >> f_p$, the measurable phase shift decreases linearly with f_{gw} limiting the detector bandwidth of the detectors (Equation (19)). The installation of another partially reflecting mirror between the beam splitter and the output port to form the Signal Recycling Cavity (SRC) allows to move the pole frequency of the cavity at higher frequency, extending the frequency range where the response of the detector to the passage of the gravitational wave is maximized [13].

The effect induced by GW on the laser beam is to generate differential signal sidebands in the light propagating in the two arms, having the same amplitude but opposite sign. Once constructively recombined at the beam splitter, they are transmitted toward the signal recycling mirror. The differential sidebands see an equivalent input mirror formed by the FP input mirror and the signal recycling one. The reflection and transmission coefficients, r_{SRC} and t_{SRC}, of the equivalent mirror depends on the microscopic tuning of the signal recycling cavity length l_S, that is the distance between the signal recycling mirror and the input mirror. The beam phase propagating through the signal recycling cavity is:

$$\phi_{SRC} = kl_{SRC} = k\left[l_S + \frac{l_X + l_Y}{2}\right], \qquad (25)$$

where l_X and l_Y are the distances of the two input mirrors of the Fabry-Perot cavities from the beam splitter (Figure 1) and the reflection and transmission coefficients can be written as:

$$r_{SRC} = \frac{r_i - r_s e^{2i\phi_{SRC}}}{1 - r_i r_s e^{2i\phi_{SRC}}}, \quad t_{SRC} = \frac{t_i t_s e^{i\phi_{SRC}}}{1 - r_i r_s e^{2i\phi_{SRC}}}, \qquad (26)$$

where r_i, r_s, t_i and t_s are the input mirror and the signal recycling reflectiviy and transmissivity. When $\phi_{SRC} = 0$, the signal recycling cavity is tuned to be resonant for the carrier field. In this configuration the reflectivity of the equivalent input mirror is lower than the FP input mirror decreasing the finesse of the FP cavity seen by the GW sideband signals by the quantity:

$$\frac{F_{\phi_{SRC}=0}}{F_{FP}} = \frac{1 - r_i r_s}{1 + r_s}. \tag{27}$$

Consequently, the pole frequency of the cavity is moved toward high frequency increasing the detector bandwith sensitivity. This signal recycling cavity working point, defined broad-band, is currently implemented in all the advanced GW detectors.

2.8. Laser Source and Injection System

The laser source is an ultra-stable, high-power continuous-wave Nd:YAG laser system. GW detectors set highly demanding requirements in their laser light sources. None of the laser parameters as delivered have adequate stability to allow direct injection of the laser beam into the interferometer [15]. Hence, the beam is injected into the detector after propagating through an extremely complex optical system, installed both in air and in vacuum, to stabilize important laser observables like the power, the frequency, the beam pointing and the spatial filtering. In all GW detectors the high power laser generation and its stabilization are conceptually similar.

The beam is produced by a low power stable laser (master laser), and then a multistage amplification scheme is implemented to deliver hundreds watts of input power. Passive stabilization methods, based on the use of a hierarchical scheme of three optical cavities in cascade composed of the pre-mode cleaner (PMC), the Input Mode Cleaner (IMC) and the Reference Frequency Cavity (RFC), concur to stabilize the laser frequency and power in synergy with nested feedback control acting to minimize the beam jitter and to preserve the beam pointing into the detector. Finally, the laser beam geometrical properties, needed to be matched with the interferometer optical cavities, are defined through the Mode Matching Telescope (MMT).

2.9. Thermal Effects

The FP cavities boost the power circulating by a factor around 300 with respect to simple Michelson configuration. The absorptions of the optical power by the coating of the core optics, albeit of the order of ppm (parts per milion), result in a radial temperature gradient within the mirrors [16] causing thermo-refractive substrate lenses in the recycling cavities (due to the dependence of the refractive index on the temperature) and thermo-elastic surface deformation in the Fabry–Perot mirrors. Both these mechanisms induce wavefront aberrations in the sideband and the carrier fields[4] triggering HOMs that, depending on the stability of the cavity, could be scattered out from the cavity losing circulating power or could become resonant inside it spoiling the control signals.

The optical aberrations are not induced only by thermal effects but also by the cold defects coming from the residual imperfections due to the state of the art of the mirror production procedure.

The Thermal Compensation System (TCS) [17] is conceived to tackle the aberrations coming both from cold defects and thermally driven effects. The thermal compensation strategy is to induce in the optics a complementary distortion with respect to the main laser one restoring the nominal optical configuration of the interferometer. The complex system of thermal actuators and sensors composing the TCS is fundamental to guarantee the operation at high power of the GW detector. Moving from the first generation of gravitational-wave detectors to the second one, new high-performance sensors and actuators have been included in the TCS making it a dynamical adaptive optical system. Wavefront aberrations on each core optics are sensed by the Hartmann Wavefront Sensors (HWSs) [18], probing the optics through an auxiliary beam, usually a SLED (SuperLuminescent Light Emitting Diode), which accumulates wavefront distortions after being transmitted through or reflected from the deformed optics.

The wavefront aberration local sensing provided by HWSs is complementary to the global one measured by the phase camera encoding the amplitude and phase of the main beam circulating into the detector [19]. This sensor scans over a photodiode the beam resulting from the recombination of the pick off of the main laser beam with the one picked up at the strategical ports of the detector. The heterodyne technique is used to independently assess the information in the carrier, upper and lower sidebands at different frequencies.

Two different actuators are designed to cope with thermal effects and cold defects: the CO_2 lasers[5] to correct both cold and thermal lenses and the ring heaters to decrease the radii of curvature of the mirrors. The formers project the suitably shaped heating pattern on an additional transmissive fused silica plate, the so-called Compensation Plate (CP), installed between the beam splitter and the input mirrors.

Ring heaters are thermal actuators conceived to precisely tune the radius of curvature of the highly reflective surface of the mirrors. They are provided by heating elements radiatively coupled to the mirror barrel that induce a thermal gradient in the optics reducing its Radius of Curvature (RoC).

The requested accuracy for the TCS sensors and actuators is strictly dependent from the peculiar design of the interferometer optical cavities.

2.10. Working Point

Length sensing and control is vital to ensure the operation of GW detectors: the carrier must resonate in all the optical cavities and the two beams reflected back by the FP cavities must destructively interfere. The achievement of this configuration, from the uncontrolled mirrors to the final working point, takes place through a complex procedure called lock acquisition. The mirrors are free to swing along the optical axis and to rotate around the horizontal (pitch angle) and vertical (yaw angle) axes in the mirror plane. The former is the longitudinal Degree of Freedom (DoF) which must be controlled within a precision of about $[10^{-12}$–$10^{-10}]$ m to ensure the carrier resonance condition in the optical cavities, the latters define the angulars DoFs to be controlled with nano-radian accuracy.

The working point of a power recycled Fabry–Perot–Michelson interferometer can be described by four longitudinal degrees of freedom[6] (cf. Figure 1):

- the length difference between the two input mirrors of the FP cavities from the beam splitter, MICH: $l_X - l_Y$;
- the differential length of the Fabry–Perot arms, DARM: $(L_X - L_Y)/2$. This is the most important DoF, since it contains the GW signal;
- the average (Common) length of the Fabry–Perot arms, CARM: $(L_X + L_Y)/2$;
- the length of the power recycling cavity, PRCL: $l_P + (l_X + l_Y)/2$, where l_P is the distance between the power recycling mirror and the beam splitter.

The FP and power-recycling cavities (CARM, DARM and PRCL) need to be kept on resonance to maximize the optical path traveled by the light inside the interferometer. In addition, the Michelson interferometer is brought to the dark fringe and the working point is achieved. The longitudinal DoFs are controlled by using the Pound-Drever-Hall (PDH) technique [22,23]: the output of different photodiodes located in strategical part of the detector are used to extract the error signals for each DoF by measuring the beating between the carrier, resonating in all the optical cavities, and the radio-frequency sidebands, anti-resonant in the FP cavities and resonant in the recycling cavities.

Once the longitudinal DoFs controls are engaged, different angular controls act to overlap the input laser beam to the optical cavity axis (the straight line that intersects the centers of curvature of the two spherical mirrors forming the cavity). At the first stage, the angular motions in pitch and yaw of every single mirror are controlled using optical lever signals provided by an auxiliary probe beam reflected by the mirror surface impinging on a positioning sensing device. This type of control is defined *local* since it is independent from the main laser beam pointing and from the mutual position of the optics.

The noise performance of the local controls is not enough to meet the noise and accuracy requirements. Therefore, during the last steps of the lock acquisition sequence, such control is replaced with an angular global control scheme reaching the nano-radian accuracy, based on error signals provided by quadrant photodiodes (QPD) installed in strategical places of the laser beam path, encoding tilt and shift information about the cavity angular DoFs.

Once the dark fringe configuration is achieved, the effects induced by radiation pressure arise in the FP arm cavities inducing an optical spring between the cavity mirrors. Thus, in this condition, a basis of *Common* and *Differential* DoFs, both (+) and (−), are introduced to describe the global misalignment of the optical cavities (Figure 3):

- Common tilt of the arm cavities, COMM(+): the two beams recombine in the same spot on the BS mirror;
- Differential tilt of the arm cavities, DIFF(+): the two beams recombine on the two opposite sides of the BS mirror;
- Common shift of the arm cavities, COMM(−): the effect is two beams recombining in the same spot on the BS mirror;
- Differential shift of the arm cavities, DIFF(−): the effect is two beams recombining on the two opposite sides of the BS mirror.

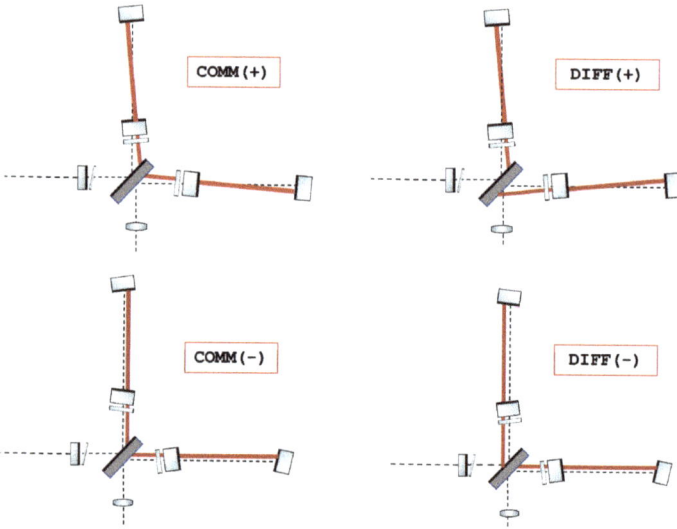

Figure 3. Schematic view of the angular DoFs used to describe the interferometer alignment once reached the dark fringe working point.

The error signals associated with these DoFs satisfy the required accuracy for the control of the orientation of the optics needed to ensure a robust and reliable working point to acquire scientific data.

3. Noises

As described before, GWs are detected by looking at a small transient fluctuation in the amount of power emerging from the output of the detector, but there can be other reasons for the power to fluctuate besides the passage of a gravitational wave through the apparatus. In this section, several of the most important reasons for a false indication of a GW passage, the so-called noises, will be discussed. In a GW interferometer, each noise manifests itself as an apparent or real variation of the position of the mirrors, simulating the effect of the incidence of a GW. In order to distinguish the noise source from the gravitational signal, the amplitude spectral sensitivity $h(f)$ is defined for each noise:

$$h(f) = \frac{\sqrt{\tilde{x}^2(f)}}{L}, \tag{28}$$

where L is the arm length of the interferometer and $\tilde{x}^2(f)$ is the power spectral density of the displacement due to the noise source. The quantity $h(f)$, which has dimension $1/\sqrt{\text{Hz}}$, indicates the amplitude of the gravitational wave signal that would produce the displacement caused by the noise.

The sensitivity of a GW detector is expressed in terms of the strain sensitivity obtained by summing quadratically the amplitude spectral densities of the noises affecting the detector:

$$h(f) = \sqrt{\sum_{i=1}^{n} h_i^2(f)}, \tag{29}$$

where i runs on the total number of the noises.

The sensitivity curve represents the minimum intensity of the gravitational signal detectable by an interferometer.

3.1. Quantum Noise

Quantum noise limits the ability to read out the arm length difference in an interferometer. It comes from the quantum nature of light, which reveals itself through two fundamental mechanisms: photon counting noise (shot noise), arising from statistical fluctuations in the arrival time of photons at the interferometer output; and radiation pressure noise, which is the recoil of the mirrors due to the quantum fluctuations in the photon flux.

The spectral density of the shot noise for a power recycled, Fabry–Perot–Michelson interferometer is given by:

$$h_{shot}(f) = \frac{1}{8FL} \left(\frac{4\pi\hbar\lambda c}{P_{bs}} \right)^{1/2} \sqrt{1 + (f/f_p)^2}, \tag{30}$$

where λ is the wavelength of the main laser and P_{bs} is the power on the beam splitter after the recycling. The radiation pressure noise spectral density is described by:

$$h_{rp}(f) = \frac{16\sqrt{2}F}{ML(2\pi f)^2} \left(\frac{\hbar P_{bs}}{2\pi\lambda c} \right)^{1/2} \frac{1}{\sqrt{1 + (f/f_p)^2}}, \tag{31}$$

where M is the mass of each of the interferometer's four test masses. At low frequencies, the radiation pressure noise term, proportional to $1/f^2$, dominates, while at high frequencies the shot noise is the major contribution. The radiation pressure amplitude spectral density is proportional to the square root of the laser light power while the shot noise amplitude spectral density is inversely proportional to the same quantity. Therefore, while it is possible to improve the strain sensitivity of an interferometer at high frequencies by increasing the circulating light power, inevitably at the same time the sensitivity will worsen at low frequencies, as the radiation pressure increases with the light power.

The so-called optical readout noise is given by the quadrature sum of these two noises:

$$h_{opr} = \sqrt{h_{shot}^2 + h_{rp}^2}. \tag{32}$$

By equalizing the contributions of h_{shot} (Equation (30)) and h_{rp} (Equation (31)), an optimal power, which results in identical magnitude contributions from shot noise and quantum radiation pressure noise for each observation frequency f, can be evaluated:

$$P_{opt} = \frac{\pi^3 c \lambda M f^2}{16 F^2}\left[1 + \left(\frac{f}{f_p}\right)^2\right]. \tag{33}$$

By replacing Equation (33) into Equation (30) (or Equation (31)), the optical read-out noise (Equation (32)) corresponding to the the Standard Quantum Limit (SQL) can be evaluated:

$$h_{SQL} = \frac{1}{2\pi f L}\sqrt{\frac{8\hbar}{M}}. \tag{34}$$

The SQL is defined as the lower bound envelope of the quantum noise spectra for all the optical powers circulating in the interferometer with arm length L and mirror mass M. However, it is possible to beat the SQL by applying quantum techniques [24]. An intuitive understanding of quantum noise can be given through the quadrature pictures in the realm of quantum mechanics, where the uncertainty of the amplitude and phase of the light beam are encoded in the amplitude and phase quadratures, respectively. Both quadratures obey to the Heisenberg Uncertainty principle that imposes a limit on the precision achievable when they are measured simultaneously. The so-called Quantum-Non-Demolition techniques [25,26] allow to redistribute the quadrature uncertainty, reducing the variance in one quadrature at the expense of increased variance in the orthogonal quadrature. A squeezed state can be represented in the quadrature plane as an ellipse, characterized by two frequency-dependent parameters: the squeezing magnitude (the ratio of the ellipse axes with respect to the unsqueezed state) and the squeezing angle (the ellipse orientation).

The first proposal to use the quantum entanglement to improve the measurement precision beyond the limit set by measurement-counting noise, was made by Caves in 1981 [27], when he suggested the use of squeezed states of light as an additional input for laser interferometric GW detectors.

Their sensitivity is limited by the interference caused by the quantum-level creation and annihilation of photons in the vacuum, the so-called vacuum noise that is all-pervasive in space at every frequency.

The vacuum noise introduces noise fluctuations at the output port of the detector imposing the classical-limit of the detector sensitivity. To overcome this limit, a squeezed beam, with the same size, shape and frequency of the main interferometer beam, is injected into the detector and overimposed to the main laser. By replacing the classic vacuum with the squeezed light, the quantum noise contributions can be manipulated. In the GW advanced detectors operating up to date, the radiation pressure did not limit the low frequency range, thus a purely phase-squeezed has been applied to minimize the phase quadrature and therefore the shot noise.

This configuration is defined frequency-independent squeezing. Clearly, the improvement of the current sensitivity at low frequency, could make the radiation pressure noise the dominant contribution. Thus, to simultaneously reduce shot noise and quantum radiation pressure noise in the entire detection frequency range, the squeezed quadrature must be rotated as a function of frequency producing the so-called frequency-dependent squeezing.

The interaction of a frequency-independent squeezed state with an optical Fabry-Perot resonator, referred to as filter cavity, is able to induce such rotation of the squeeze ellipse [28]. The first demonstration of a squeezing source able to reduce quantum noise in the whole spectrum of advanced gravitational-wave detectors is reported in [29].

3.2. Thermal Noise

The thermal excitation of the mechanical degrees of freedom of the test masses, as well as those of their suspension system, results in a spurious contribution to the output of an interferometric detector, setting up a limit to the sensitivity of GW interferometers in a wide frequency band between few Hz and 300 Hz. Thermal noise is intrinsic to all bodies at thermodynamic equilibrium: in a body at steady-state temperature T, the energy equipartition theorem assigns to each degree of freedom a mean energy of $k_B T/2$ where k_B is the Boltzmann constant. Due to the interactions among the microscopic elements, this energy is subject to time fluctuations that generate random oscillations of macroscopic observables mimicking the effect of the GW passage. This phenomenon is described by the Fluctuation–Dissipation Theorem [30], which identifies the link between a generic dissipative mechanism inside a mechanical system and its thermal fluctuations. This theorem asserts that the thermal noise power spectral density is given by:

$$\tilde{x}^2(\omega) = \frac{4 k_B T}{\omega^2} \mathbb{R}\left[\frac{1}{Z(\omega)}\right], \qquad (35)$$

where $Z(\omega)$ is the impedance of the system whose real part represents the dissipative mechanism due to the internal friction in the material quantified by the so called *loss angle parameter* ϕ. In the GW detectors, the thermal noise has two different origins: the first one is due to dissipation in the wires used to suspend the optics and it is dominant up to 30 Hz; the so-called suspension thermal noise. The second one is due to dissipation processes inside the mirrors themselves; the so-called mirror thermal noise.

The suspension thermal noise is given by three contributions, the horizontal and the vertical oscillations due to the pendulum configuration and the violin modes of the fibers suspending the mirrors. The suspension mechanical losses ϕ result from the combination of losses of different nature: the material intrinsic losses, the thermo-elastic ones, deriving from the expansion coefficient of the material, the surfaces losses due to external pollution, and, finally, the losses due to the coupling system between mirror and fibers.

According to the fluctuation–dissipation theorem, thermal noise can be reduced by minimizing the amount of mechanical loss in the suspensions. When a pendulum is displaced in the horizontal direction from its rest position, a restoring force is exerted mainly by the *lossless* gravitational field acting as a constant spring. Therefore, the total losses of the suspension could be lower than the ones of the material of which it is composed, by the ratio of the elastic energy to the gravitational energy, the so-called dilution factor [11]. The mechanism in the vertical direction is different, if the mass is displaced vertically, the restoring elastic force of the fiber acts on the mirror as a simple harmonic oscillator motion with a frequency determined by the elastic spring constant associated with the elongation of the wire. Finally, the suspension wires, subjected to tension, behave like vibrating ropes shaping the violin modes that appear as a nearly harmonic sequence.

The fused silica has a very low loss angle ($\phi \approx 10^{-9}$) making it the natural choice to realize the mirrors. In the first gravitational wave detectors the suspension fibers were of stainless steel, but the high structural losses of steel ($\phi \approx 10^{-4}$) made this solution unsuitable for the second generation detectors. Therefore, fused silica was also employed to produce the suspension fibers forming with the mirror, the so-called *monolithic payload* [31,32]. This upgrade allowed to reduce the suspension thermal noise contribution by factor up to 10 at 30 Hz. Thus, it was used in all the advanced GW detectors to suspend the FP cavity mirrors.

In the frequency band from 30 Hz to 300 Hz, the sensitivity of the detector is limited by the thermal noise of the coating layers deposited on the surfaces of the core optics to make them highly reflective[7]. A HR coating is made of a stack of alternate layers of two materials with high and low refractive index. The reflectivity improves by increasing the refractive index difference between the employed materials and by enhancing the number of layers.

The thermal noise power spectral density of the mirrors coating is proportional to:

$$\tilde{x}^2(\omega) \propto \frac{k_B T}{\omega} \frac{d}{w^2} \phi_{coat}, \tag{36}$$

where w is the radius of the laser beam impinging on the mirror, ϕ_{coat} is the coating loss angle and d is the coating thickness. Thus, besides lowering the temperature of the mirrors, the thermal noise could be minimized by reducing the coating thickness, by identifying new materials with lower losses and by increasing the laser beam size. Various numbers of different dielectric material pairs for reflective coatings have been investigated. It has been found that a coating made by alternating layers of titania doped tantala (TiO_2:Ta_2O_5) and silica (SiO_2) gives the desired reflectivity satisfying the strict limits on the thermal noise and on the optical absorption [33]. The laser beam radius on the mirrors is set around 60 mm according to the technology limitations for the realization of mirrors having a diameter greater than 35 cm.

3.3. Seismic and Newtonian Noise

Another source of displacement noise to deal with is the vibration of the terrestrial environment known as seismic noise. In the region 1–10 Hz, it is mostly due to human activity, natural phenomena in the atmosphere, and many other forms of ground born oscillations. Furthermore, there is a micro-seismic background, which affects a GW interferometer mostly in the form of surface waves that shake the suspension mechanisms and the mirrors. This noise is strongly dependent on the geographical localization of the detector. In general, the amplitude spectral density is of the order of $10^{-11} 1/\sqrt{Hz}$ at 10 Hz, 10 order of magnitudes larger than the expected GW amplitude. Therefore, to build a GW detector it is crucial to implement techniques for the vibration isolation of the test masses able to adequately attenuate this noise.

The vibration isolation system is obtained using a set of pendula in cascade. A single pendulum with resonance frequency f_0 attenuates the vibrations transferred to the mirror by a factor f_0^2/f^2. Thus, a multistage filter made by N pendula provides an attenuation factor $(f_0^2/f^2)^N$.

The Newtonian noise, also known as gravity gradient noise, is due to the time-varying Newtonian gravitational forces acting on the mirrors as a consequence of density fluctuations to density fluctuations caused by seismic activity as well as acoustic and turbulent phenomena in the Earth's atmosphere [34,35]. Given the direct coupling of gravitational fields to the mirrors, they cannot be shielded from this noise. The approach identified to minimize this noise is based on the use of algorithms to process the data acquired by arrays of seismic sensors located near the vacuum chambers hosting the mirrors and, then to subtract its contribution from the ouput data of the interferometer [36]. This noise did not limit the sensitivity of the first generation interferometers, since its magnitude, expected to be $10^{-21} 1/\sqrt{Hz}$ at 10 Hz, was much lower than the radiation pressure one. Its contribution will become non-negligible in the next generations of detectors.

3.4. Technical Noise Sources

Besides these fundamental noises, other disturbances, the so-called technical noises, affect the detector performance requiring advanced technologies to be minimized. The largest contribution to technical noises are the control noises related to the lock and the alignment of the interferometer. Another of the most limiting noise at low-medium frequency range is the scattered light, i.e., diffused light due to the imperfections on the optics surfaces that is scattered out along the main laser beam path introducing additional noise in the detector signals [37]. In order to reduce this spurious light, the optical benches hosting the optical systems devoted to inject the beam into the detector, to monitor its performance and to extract the GW signals, are isolated from the ground replicating the same operating principle of the core optics suspensions. Moreover, the optical benches are studded by light dumpers to suppress spurious beams and some *baffles*, made of absorbing materials, surrounding the core optics [7]. The reduction of the diffused light is also one of the main reason why GW detectors are placed inside the largest vacuum chambers in the world. Indeed, the light propagates through the interferometer into ultra high-vacuum pipes, in order to reduce the refractive index fluctuation caused by the presence of residual air molecules.

4. Advanced Virgo Interferometer

Advanced Virgo is the European gravitational-wave interferometric detector, being part of the global network of interferometers built to detect GW [7]. The Virgo project takes its name from the Virgo cluster, a group of 2000 galaxies 15 Mpc distant from the Earth. Its target sensitivity was $10^{-21} 1/\sqrt{Hz}$ according to the gravitational wave amplitude $h \approx [10^{-21} - 10^{-22}] 1/\sqrt{Hz}$ expected for the coalescence of two neutron stars of masses 1.4 $M_\odot$ at distance of 15 Mpc from the Earth. The history of this experiment begins about 30 years ago, the approval by the scientific community dates back to 1994 and its construction started in 1996, two years later, in Italy, in the countryside around Pisa.

The Virgo experiment acquired scientific data between 2007 and 2011 in four different observing runs. Before the beginning of the third one, the monolithic suspensions have been integrated in the instrument, and Virgo became Virgo plus, an intermediate configuration between the first and second generation of gravitational-wave detectors. Once the last scientific run was over, it was switched off in order to upgrade the experiment to the second generation project, called Advanced Virgo.

This detector joined the second observing run O2 with Advanced LIGO in August 2017, contributing to the first detection of GW emitted by a Binary Neutron Star (BNS) coalescence, GW170817 [5].

After a time break of about two years to upgrade the instruments, Advanced Virgo started the observation period O3 together with Advanced LIGO in April 2019. It should have ended on 30 April 2020 but, due to the COVID-19 pandemic, the conclusion of the observational period was changed to 27 March 2020.

Despite the early closure, the sensitivity of Advanced Virgo and Advanced LIGO in O3 enabled to increase the number of gravitational wave detections more than three-fold over the O2 observing run.

At the end of O3, Advanced Virgo increased its BNS range up to 60 Mpc[8] from the Earth, doubling the best sensitivity achieved during O2.

In Figure 4, the best sensitivity curves during O2 and during O3 are shown compared to the design sensitivity target.

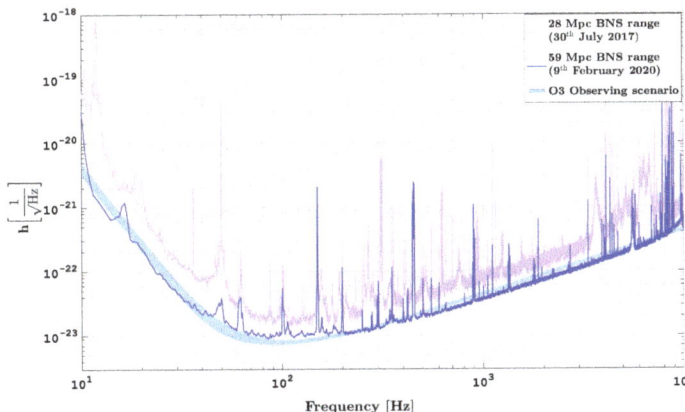

Figure 4. Representative amplitude spectral density of Advanced Virgo during the second half of O3 observational run (blue curve) compared to its design sensitivity target (light blue area). The best sensitivity curve during the second observing run is also depicted (lilac curve) [38,39].

In the following, the instrument configuration during the last part of O3, that made achievable 60 Mpc BNS range, will be described.

4.1. Mirrors and Their Suspensions

The core optics of Advanced Virgo, 20 cm thick, with diameter of 35 cm and weight of 42 kg, are high-purity fused silica cylinders, ultra-fine polished to achieve sub-nanometric roughness, and properly coated to reach the desired reflectivity.

They are suspended by four fused silica fibers to the last stage of the *Superattenuator* (SA) [40], to make them quasi-free and to reduce the seismic noise by ten order of magnitudes above 2 Hz. SA suppresses the seismic horizontal vibrations through a chain of five mechanical filters 8 m-long supported by a three-leg elastic structure (inverted pendulum), connected to ground through flexible joints at the base of each leg. The vertical seismic movements are attenuated by replacing each mass of the multi-stage pendulum by a cylindrical mechanical filter with a set of blade springs with low stiffness. The blades support the next mechanical filter through 1 m-long steel wire, forming a chain of low frequency oscillators. The blades act in parallel to a magnetic anti-spring system, assembled on each filter, to reduce its fundamental vertical frequency from about 1.5 Hz down to below 0.5 Hz [41]. The mirror's suspension wires are anchored to the *marionette*, a rigid plate suspended to the last filter of the SA, through a single steel cable, hosting the magnets faced to the coils attached to the last filter of the SA. This coil–magnet system allows to steer the payload in four degrees of freedom: the translation along the beam and the rotations around the vertical axis and around the horizontal ones, perpendicular and parallel to the beam. Finally, the mirror is enfolded in the *actuator cage* fixed to the last steering filter of the SA, providing the support frame for the baffles, the compensation plate on the input payloads and ring heaters. On the actuator cage, a further set of coils are installed faced on the magnets glued to the anti-reflective surface of the mirror. The SA is the same for both recycling and FP mirrors, while the last stage of suspension is different depending on the mirror and its position in the interferometer.

The lateral surface of each mirror is machined to make flat two small areas to allow the bonding of the *ears*, rectangular silica pieces, hosting the end part of the fibers properly shaped to be anchored. The suspension wires of the recycling cavity mirrors and the beam splitter are made of steel and not of fused silica since they are outside the FP cavities and, therefore, the coupling of the noise to the detector sensitivity is reduced by factor $2F/\pi$ where F is the finesse of the FP cavity. For these mirrors, four triangular silica spacers are glued to the two flat areas allowing the steel fibers to envelop the mirror like a cradle. The same approach has been applied to suspend the beam splitter, the largest optics ever suspended in an interferometric gravitational-wave detector, having a diameter of 550 mm and thickness of 65 mm. The suspension systems of all mirrors are described in details in [42].

4.2. Optical Layout

The two 3 km-long FP cavities are identified as *North* and *West*, following their geographical orientation. The beam transmitted and reflected by the beam splitter propagates through the North and West arms, respectively. In the North arm, Input and End mirrors are called North Input (NI) and North End (NE). Similarly, in the West arm, the two mirrors are identified as West Input (WI) and West End (WE). The FP cavities, have a bi-concave geometry. The nominal mirror's radii of curvature are 1420 m and 1683 m for the input and end mirrors, respectively. With this type of topology, the cavity waist is near the middle of the cavity and the beam radius is about 49 mm on the input test mass and 58 mm on the end one.

The reflectivities of the input and the end mirrors are 98.6 % and 99.9995%. Therefore the finesse is 450 and the pole frequency is at 55 Hz. The FP mirror radii of curvature have been defined in order to maximize the beam size on the FP end mirrors to reduce as much as possible the mirror coating thermal noise. This choice imposed the power recycling mirror radius of curvature of 1430 m for the length of the cavity equal to 11.952 m, pushing the power recycling cavity stability condition very close to the instability limit ($g = 0.9999885$).

The power recycling mirror reflectivity is 95%, thus the finesse of the power recycling cavity is 48.

The distances between the beam splitter and the two input mirrors differ of the Schnupp asymmetry, equal to 0.23 m.

During O3, the signal recycling mirror has been used as a lens, thus Advanced Virgo runned in the power-recycled Michelson configuration.

4.3. High Power Laser and Injection System

During O3, the high power continuous wave laser could deliver about 100 W at the input of the injection system whose role is to further stabilize the laser frequency, to improve the beam shape, to match and to steer the laser beam toward the interferometer core optics.

The laser system was based on a high power oscillator (HPO) configuration: a 500 mW non-planar ring oscillator laser, the master one, is amplified up to 100 W by two medium power solid state amplifiers, the first one called slave laser that amplifies the seeder up to 20 W and the second one, the NeoVan, providing about 100 W at the output.

The optical amplifier is based on four Nd^{3+}:YVO4 crystals, each longitudinally pumped with 50 W at 878.7 nm emitted by Bragg grating diode lasers. The amplified laser beam propagates through a bow-tie pre-mode cleaner cavity 308 mm-long, which cleans the spatial profile and reduce the jitter of the laser beam [43].

Then, the pre-stabilized high power beam propagates through electro-optical modulators providing the radio frequency sidebands used to control the interferometer: the 6,270,777 Hz and 56,433,933 Hz sidebands are anti-resonant in the FP arms and resonant in the power recycling cavity, the 8,361,036 Hz sidebands are anti-resonant in all optical cavities and, finally, the 22.38 MHz sidebands are used to control the input mode cleaner, the in-vacuum 144 m-long triangular cavity with finesse of 1200.

Then, about 30 mW of the laser beam transmitted by the IMC are picked up to feed the monolithic RFC providing the reference to pre-stabilize the master laser frequency. Indeed, the IMC is locked on the reference cavity and the master laser frequency is locked on the IMC length by tuning the temperature and, consequently, the refractive index of its laser crystal. Finally, the PMC is locked on the master laser by tuning the length of the PMC cavity itself. These optical cavities operate in a hierarchical configuration allowing to reduce the frequency noise at the level of $10^{-6} Hz/\sqrt{Hz}$ between 10 Hz and 10 kHz.

Finally, the beam propagates through the Mode Matching Telescopes before being injected into the power recycling cavity. It is used to match the beam onto the detector at the best of 99%. This telescope consists of an afocal off-axis parabolic telescope made of two mirrors that increases the beam size by a factor 8.5 (from 2.6 to 22 mm) [44]. Then, a diverging lens is used in combination with the PR mirror to match the beam to the interferometer.

The power available to be injected inside the detector after the propagation through the injection system was more than 65 W. After some commissioning activities at different power values, the input laser power was set to 19 W during the first part of O3 observing run and increased up to 26 W during the second half.

4.4. Detection System

After the recombination on the beam splitter, the beam propagates through the SR lens and the second MMT, another afocal off-axis parabolic telescope, that reduces the beam size from 49 mm to 1.3 mm to adapt the beam itself to the output mode cleaner cavity. As anticipated in Section 2.5, the goal of the OMC is to clean the dark fringe beam from the spurious light not carrying information on the differential arm displacement. Thus, the OMC filters out the main beam HOMs as well as the 6.27 MHz and 56.44 MHz sidebands transmitted at the dark port.

The OMC is composed of two fused-silica monolithic cavities in series in the bow-tie configuration with finesse 120 [42].

The beam filtered out by OMC encodes only the valuable information about the gravitational wave signal.

4.5. Thermal Compensation System

The marginally stable geometry of the power recycling cavity makes it extremely sensitive to the HOMs occurring in presence of optical aberrations that degrade the quality of the error signals, making the interferometer global working point not reliable. The Advanced Virgo Thermal Compensation System is conceived to tackle the aberrations coming both from cold defects and thermally driven effects (Section 2.9) so that the residual optical path length increase in the recycling cavities is below 2 nm Gaussian weighted RMS, and the RoCs of the FP cavity mirrors are within ± 2 m from their design values [42]. These requirements ensure the quality of the sidebands used to control the detector, the optimization of the circulating power into the FP cavities and the improvement of the destructive interference at the output port of the detector.

TCS features both wavefront sensors and actuators, so that it can be operated as a control loop keeping the detector at the optimal working point.

The CO_2 actuation optical systems are hosted on two optical benches, acoustically isolated from the environment, installed in the two corners between the vacuum chambers of the beam splitter and of each input mirror.

The projectors have been designed to produce two different actuation patterns on the CPs: the Double Axicon System (DAS) and the Central Heating (CH). The first one is obtained by superimposing two annular beams with different sizes and radii in order to shape a *donut*. The name of this actuator derives from axicon, an optic with a conical surface, used to convert the CO_2 Gaussian beam into an annular one. The DAS is used mainly to correct the thermal lensing due to uniform coating absorption in the input mirrors and the cold defects showing a high degree of spherical aberration. The CH actuator, having a Gaussian shape of the same size of the main laser beam, is used to mitigate the thermal transients when the interferometer loses lock.

The laser beam induces a bump on the mirror high-reflectivity surfaces making their profiles non-spherical. To compensate this deformation, a ring heater surrounds each FP mirror. The Advanced Virgo RH consists of two parallel, thin o-rings made of borosilicate-glass (Pyrex), that encircle the mirror. Each ring is powered by Joule heating through a Nickel Crome conductive wire tightly wrapped in helical coils around it, then acting as a radiator. To increase the efficiency of the system, the heat that radiates away is gathered and conveyed toward the mirror barrel by a copper shield enclosing the rings. The same shield provides, in addition, a stable and protective support for holding the rings around the TM. The shield has a c-shaped rectangular cross section and it is internally polished to enhance its reflectivity.

The TCS actuators require error signals for their optimized operation.

In Advanced Virgo six HWSs are used to measure the optical aberrations on the FP mirrors. In particular, two of them measure the thermal lens on the two input mirrors crossed by the laser beam, the so-called HWS in transmission, while four wavefront sensing setups, identified as HWS in reflection, have been designed to measure the thermoelastic deformation on the input and end mirrors. The two HWSs in trasmission and their probe beam SLEDs at 790 nm are hosted on the injection (HWS-INJ) and detection (HWS-DET) areas to sense the thermal lenses on the WI and NI mirrors, respectively. They propagate overimposed to the main laser beam, through the power recycling and signal recycling cavities up to the high reflectivity mirror surfaces of the input mirrors that reflect the beams toward the HWSs allowing for double pass measurement. An afocal telescope with magnification 11 is used to increase the SLED beam size to probe the optics area of around 100 mm-radius and then to reduce it to 9 mm to be matched with the HWS size.

The HWS in reflection are conceptually similar but the probe beam at 880 nm is magnified by a factor of 7 and impinges on the mirror with an angle of 45°, then, it is reflected by the high-reflectivity mirror surface on an auxiliary mirror installed in the same vacuum chamber and it is reflected back towards the wavefront sensor hosted on an in-air optical optical bench installed outside of the mirrors' vacuum chamber.

Two high-performance phase cameras are also installed in the power recycling cavity and on the dark port to sense the real-time status of the phases and amplitudes of the carrier and the sidebands used to control the interferometer. The reference signal is picked up before the IMC and brought to the desired positions through two polarization maintaining fibers. The pickoff beam in the power recycling cavity is extracted by using the Pickoff Plate (POP) placed in front of the PR mirror.

The detailed description of these sensors are addressed in [45,46].

As a reference, a scheme of the TCS sensors and actuators integrated in Advanced Virgo is shown in Figure 5.

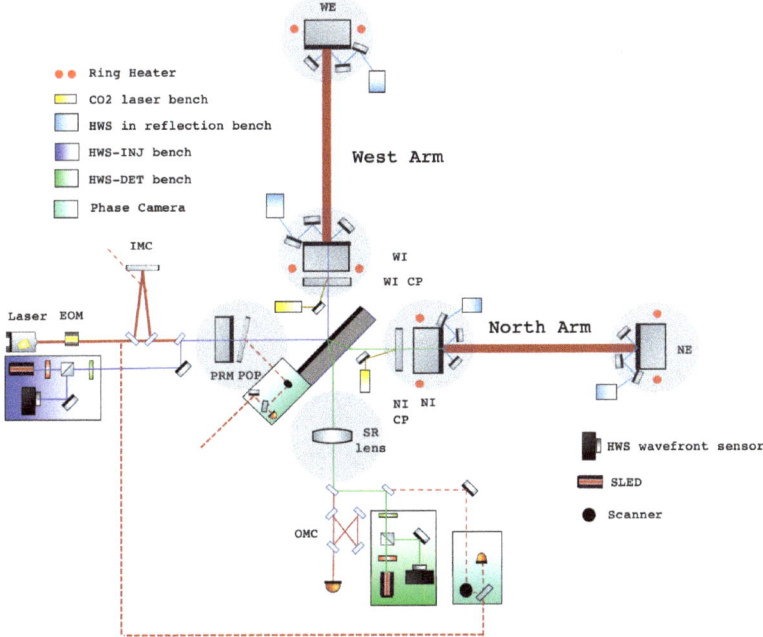

Figure 5. Scheme of the Advanced Virgo TCS superimposed on the optical layout of the detector. Blue and green beams (HWS-INJ and HWS-DET) represent the two HWS probe beams in transmission that allow to measure the thermal lensing in the West Input and on the North Input test masses, respectively. The HWSs devoted to the measurement of the thermo-elastic deformation are shown in light-blue. The phase camera optical layout represented by dashed red line to sense wavefront aberrations in the power recycling cavity and on the dark fringe are also visible. The red circles represent the RH actuators and the yellow rectangles the CO_2 laser benches. The grey circles identifies the vacuum chambers hosting the main optics.

During O3, the DAS shined the CPs to compensate the thermal lensing induced by the main laser beam at 26 W, stabilizing the power recycling cavity and increasing the robustness of the detector. The CH actuator has been switched on during the lock acquisition sequence to avoid thermal transients which slowed down the whole procedure. Finally, the end mirror's RH have been used to tune the RoC in order to maximize the intra-cavity power and minimize the power at the anti-symmetric port. As result, the

FP circulating power increased of about 15% and the power exiting the interferometer decreased by factor 2.

4.6. Interferometer Read-Out

The output of several photodiodes located in strategical parts of the detector are used to extract the gravitational wave strain and the error signals needed to control the interferometer. The read-out scheme of all photodiodes (PDs) installed in Advanced Virgo is shown in Figure 6.

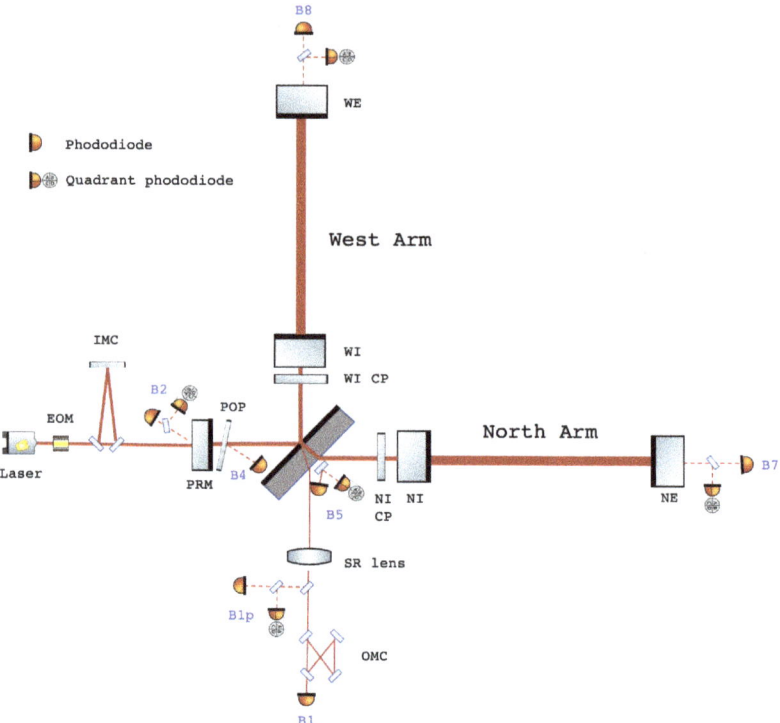

Figure 6. Basic optical layout of Advanced Virgo interferometer and its read-out scheme.

The photodiodes located at the output port of the detector, $B1p$ and $B1$ before and after the output mode cleaner, respectively, carry the information about the DARM DoF and, they are sensitive to the GW passage. At the symmetric port, $B2$ PD senses the beam reflected from the interferometer towards the laser source. The photodiode $B4$ measures the pickoff beam in the PRC reflected by the POP and $B5$ measures the pickoff beam originating from the reflection coming from the North arm on the anti-reflective surface of the beam splitter. Finally, the photodiodes $B7$ and $B8$ measure the powers transmitted by the North and West arm cavities, respectively.

In parallel to aforementioned PDs, quadrant photodiodes are used to provide the error signals needed to control the cavity angular degrees of freedom.

4.7. Interferometer Sensing and Control

The Interferometer Sensing and Control (ISC) allows to achieve and maintain the correct working point of the detector through the lock acquisition procedure (Section 2.10). At the starting point of the lock acquisition, the power recycling mirror is misaligned and FP mirrors are kept in place by optical lever signals. During the first phase of the locking sequence, the two FP cavities are brought to the resonance by using the PDH signals demodulated at 6 MHz provided by B7 and B8 PDs. Then, the MICH DoF is settled at half fringe by using the DC signal measured by B1p normalized by the sum of B4 and B1p DC signals, their ratio is 1 in the bright fringe configuration and 0 in the dark fringe, so when it is equal to 0.5, half of power is reflected toward the symmetric port and the other half toward the antisymmetric port.

During this phase, the dithering control technique [38] is applied in order to overlap the cavity axis to the mirror center minimizing the coupling between longitudinal and angular DoFs: the error signals are provided by mechanically exciting both angular DoFs of each test mass at a specific frequency once the longitudinal DoFs have been fixed. When the beam impinges far from the optics center, the two DoFs are strongly coupled. On the contrary, this coupling is minimized in the mirror center. The mirror angular position which minimize this coupling is chosen. Then, the same strategy is implemented to align the input beam on the cavity axes acting on the PRM and BS. Since the PR rear surface is a strong converging lens (RoC = 3.62 m), its translational DoFs are mechanically exciting at specific frequency to steer the input beam along the North cavity. The error signal, encoding the mutual tilt between the input beam and the cavity axis, is obtained by demodulating the excitation line in the North arm transmitted power. The same purpose is reached for the West Arm by moving the beam splitter in the two angular DoFs. When the powers transmitted by the FP cavities are maximized, the input beam and the cavity axis are overlapped.

During the second phase of the lock acquisition, the power recycling mirror is aligned to achieve the resonance position and MICH is reduced to attain the destructive interference working point [47,48]. During this phase, the power circulating into the detector increases significantly, making very critical the alignment of the power recycling mirror. Thus, during this phase, the PR mirror angular control is performed by using the B2 QPD signal reflected by the power recycling cavity looking at the signal demodulated at 8 MHz.

Once the dark fringe condition is achieved, the error signals associated with the *Common* and *Differential* DoFs (Section 2.10) are used to improve the accuracy of the working point. In particular, the B1p QPD demodulated at 56 MHz provides the errors signals for the most critical DoFs, i.e., COMM(+) and DIFF(+), improving the FP mirror angular DoFs accuracy at the nano-radian level.

The last steps of the lock acquisition are the control of the OMC cavity and the engagement of the DC read-out by adding a DARM offset to have few mW on B1 PD that becomes the final error signal for DARM. Once the procedure is concluded, the squeezing beam is injected and aligned in the interferometer. The duration of the whole looking procedure is about twenty minutes and it is completely automatized on the Metatron environment [49]. The detailed description of the whole acquisition sequence can be found in [38,50].

Thanks to the combined action between ISC and TCS, the longest lock (132 h) has been achieved in the week between 1 and 7 January 2020 [38][9].

4.8. Squeezed Light Injection

The routinely injection of the frequency-independent squeezing in Advanced Virgo to reduce its quantum noise at high frequency was one of the major upgrade implemented before O3. The two optical systems needed to generate squeezed light and to inject it into the dark port of the interferometer are installed in-air, on a single optical bench close to the vacuum chambers hosting the output system. The squeezing light generation is a stand-alone system developed at Albert Einstein Institute (AEI) in Hannover [51] that mainly includes two commercial lasers at 1064 nm. The main one, locked to the Virgo laser frequency, is used to produce the beam at 532 nm (pump beam), that seeds the squeezing generation. The auxiliary laser, locked to the main laser frequency one, shifted by 7 MHz, is used to perform the coherent control needed to produce squeezing at the audio frequencies. The squeezing light at 1064 nm is produced by the green beam pumping the OPA, a linear doubly resonant cavity consisting of a piezo-actuated coupling mirror and a periodically poled potassium titanyl phosphate (PPKTP) nonlinear crystal whose temperature is stabilized to mK to simultaneously ensure phase matching and co-resonance of both wavelengths. The cavity length is controlled via PDH technique using the green beam reflected by the OPA.

A mode matching telescope, made by two spherical mirrors, shapes the squeezing beam size to be equal to the interferometer's one and a pair of piezo-actuated tip-tilt mirrors are used to steer the squeezed beam into the Faraday isolator installed between the detection mode matching telescope and the output mode cleaner where the squeezed and the interferometer beams overlap (Figure 7).

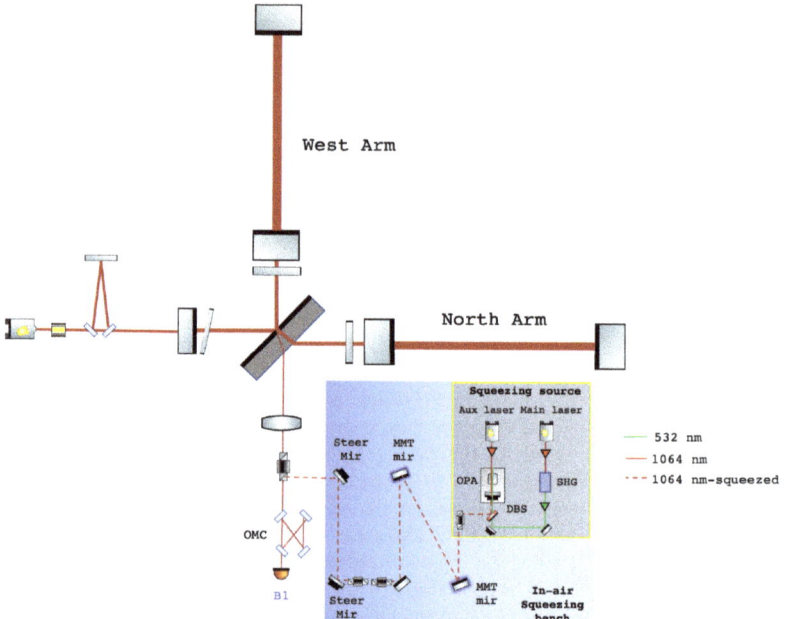

Figure 7. Simplified scheme of the quantum enhanced Advanced Virgo gravitational-wave detector. The squeezed layout optics are hosted on an in-air optical bench (blue box) including the squeezed light source (yellow box), the mode matching telescope, the Faraday isolators, and alignment steering mirrors. Finally, the squeezed beam is injected into the interferometer vacuum system through an antireflective coated viewport.

The squeezing system has its own hierarchical locking scheme, independent of the interferometer one, that takes care of the working point of the squeezed light source and of the injection of the squeezed states into the interferometer.

During O3, the injection of phase-squeezed vacuum states reduced the shot noise level by about 3 dB improving the binary neutron star range by 8% [52].

5. Advanced Virgo + Phase I and II

After the end of O3 run, both Advanced LIGO and Advanced Virgo implemented mid-scale upgrades, designated as A+ and AdV+, aiming to improve their sensitivities by more than two times the current levels [53].

The Advanced Virgo short-term planned upgrades included the installation of the signal recycling mirror, the installation of a more powerful laser and the construction of a filter cavity to provide frequency dependent squeezed light to reduce and reshape the impact of quantum noise. The goal of these upgrades, identified as Phase I, is to detect gravitational waves from the coalescence of binary neutron stars at distances of the order of

100 Mpc. Now the instrument is being prepared for the fourth data taking O4 that should start by the end of 2022. After the end of O4, in view of the fifth observing run O5, a new installation phase, called Phase II, including larger mirrors with lower thermal noise optical coatings, will start. The target will be to detect gravitational waves from the coalescence of binary neutron stars at distances of the order of 200 Mpc.

The detector sensitivities expected for the next observing runs are shown in Figure 8 [54].

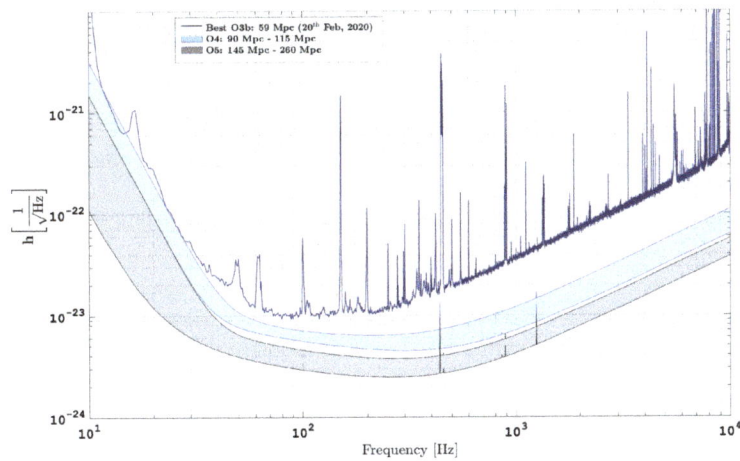

Figure 8. The Advanced Virgo best sensitivity during O3 compared to the expected sensitivity scenarios for the next two observing runs O4 (light blue area) and O5 (grey area).

6. Conclusions

A network of worldwide distributed interferometers operating as a unified detector allowed to detect gravitational waves challenging the most established astrophysical and cosmological scenarios. The Advanced LIGO and Advanced Virgo detectors have actively searched GWs in a highly coordinated campaign during a series of observing runs carried out from 2015.

This overview covers the basic physics behind the gravitational wave interferometers involving the combination of relatively simple optical systems into more and more complex assemblies. The current generation of GW interferometer, such as Advanced Virgo and Advanced LIGO, operates in high-power and quantum regime configuration.

In this paper, the Advanced Virgo experiment is described focusing on the hardware features that allowed to reach a BNS range of 60 Mpc.

Advanced Virgo shut down on 27 March 2020 together with Advanced LIGO, earlier than planned owing to the COVID-19 pandemic, and have been undergoing major upgrades in order to improve the BNS range at distances about 100 Mpc during O4 and as far as more than 200 Mpc during O5.

Funding: This research received no external funding.

Institutional Review Board Statement: Not applicable.

Informed Consent Statement: Not applicable.

Data Availability Statement: The experimental gravitational wave strain data reported in this work is from the Gravitational-wave Open Science Center (GWOSC) [39].

Acknowledgments: The authors gratefully acknowledge the Italian Istituto Nazionale di Fisica Nucleare (INFN), the French Centre National de la Recherche Scientifique (CNRS) and the Netherland Organization for Scientific Research, for the construction and operation of the Virgo detector and the creation and support of the EGO consortium. The authors also gratefully acknowledge research support from these agencies as well as by the Spanish Agencia Estatal de Investigació, the Consellera d'Innovació, Universitats, Ciència i Societat Digital de la Generalitat Valenciana and the CERCA Programme Generalitat de Catalunya, Spain, the National Science Centre of Poland and the Foundation for Polish Science (FNP), the European Commission, the Hungarian Scientific Research Fund (OTKA), the French Lyon Institute of Origins (LIO), the Belgian Fonds de la Recherche Scientifique (FRS-FNRS), Actions de Recherche Concertes (ARC) and Fonds Wetenschappelijk Onderzoek-Vlaanderen (FWO), Belgium. The authors gratefully acknowledge the support of the NSF, STFC, INFN, CNRS and Nikhef for provisional of computational resources.

Conflicts of Interest: The authors declare no conflict of interest.

Notes

1. The minus sign is due to the reflection on the rear face of the input mirror.
2. The detailed discussion about the study of the GW interaction in the different coordinate frames is addressed in [8].
3. The main technical noises contribution will be be discussed in Section 3.4.
4. A wavefront distortion is any transverse or spatial variation with respect to the nominal one accumulated after reflection from or transmission through an optical element.
5. Their wavelength is $\lambda = 10.6$ μm, completely absorbed by the fused silica.
6. The integration of the signal recycling mirror, adds a further longitudinal DoF to be controlled, the length of the signal recycling cavity, defined as $l_S + (l_X + l_Y) = 2$, where l_S is the distance between the signal recycling mirror and the beam splitter. The high number of DoFs to be controlled, prompts the use of two auxiliary green lasers to lock individually the two FP cavities removing two DoFs from the global locking scheme easing the lock acquisition [20,21].
7. The thermal noise of the mirror substrate is negligible with respect to the coating contribution.
8. The so-called BNS range is quoted as the average distance to which a signal generated by a BNS system with 1.4 $M_\odot$–1.4 $M_\odot$ could be detected. It is commonly used in the gravitational wave community to quantify the detector sensitivity.
9. The lock duration is constrained by the time windows for the weekly maintenance and calibration of the detector scheduled once a week.

References

1. Einstein, A. Die Grundlage der allgemeinen Relativitätstheorie. *Ann. Phys.* **1916**, *49*, 769–822. [CrossRef]
2. Abbott, B.P.; Abbott, R.; Abbott, T.D.; Abernathy, M.R.; Acernese, F.; Ackley, K.; Adams, C.; Adams, T.; Addesso, P.; Adhikari, R.X.; et al. (LIGO Collaboration and Virgo Collaboration). Observation of Gravitational Waves from a Binary Black Hole Merger. *Phys. Rev. Lett.* **2016**, *116*, 061102. [CrossRef] [PubMed]
3. Abbott, B.P.; Abbott, R.; Abbott, T.D.; Abraham, S.; Acernese, F.; Ackley, K.; Adams, C.; Adhikari, R.X.; Adya, V.B.; Affeldt, C.; et al. (LIGO Scientific Collaboration and Virgo Collaboration). GWTC-1: A Gravitational-Wave Transient Catalog of Compact Binary Mergers Observed by LIGO and Virgo during the First and Second Observing Runs. *Phys. Rev. X* **2019**, *9*, 031040.
4. Abbott, R.; Abbott, T.D.; Abraham, S.; Acernese, F.; Ackley, K.; Adams, A.; Adams, C.; Adhikari, R.X.; Adya, V.B.; Affeldt, C.; et al. (LIGO Collaboration and Virgo Collaboration). GWTC-2: Compact Binary Coalescences Observed by LIGO and Virgo During the First Half of the Third Observing Run. *Phys. Rev. X* **2020**, *11*, 021053.
5. Abbott, B.P.; Abbott, R.; Abbott, T.D.; Acernese, F.; Ackley, K.; Adams, C.; Adams, T.; Addesso, P.; Adhikari, R.X.; Adya, V.B.; et al. (LIGO Collaboration and Virgo Collaboration). GW170817: Observation of gravitational waves from a binary neutron star inspiral. *Phys. Rev. Lett.* **2017**, *119*, 161101. [CrossRef]
6. Aasi, J.; Abbott, B.P.; Abbott, R.; Abbott, T.; Abernathy, M.R.; Ackley, K.; Adams, C.; Adams, T.; Addesso, P.; Adhikari, R.X.; et al. (LIGO Collaboration). Advanced LIGO. *Class. Quantum Grav.* **2015**, *32*, 074001.
7. Acernese, F.; Agathos, M.; Agatsuma, K.; Aisa, D.; Allemandou, N.; Allocca, A.; Amarni, J.; Astone, P.; Balestri, G.; Ballardin, G.; et al. (Virgo Collaboration). Advanced Virgo: A second-generation interferometric gravitational wave detector. *Class. Quantum Grav.* **2015**, *32*, 024001. [CrossRef]
8. Maggiore, M. *Gravitational Waves*; OXFORD University Press: Oxford, UK, 2007.
9. Meers, B.J. Recycling in laser-interferometric gravitational-wave detectors. *Phys. Rev. D* **1988**, *38*, 2317–2326. [CrossRef]
10. Franzen, A. Component Library (A Vector Graphics Library fot Illustrations of Optics Experiment). 2015. Available online http://www.gwoptics.org/ComponentLibrary/ (accessed on 4 December 2020).
11. Saulson, P.R. *Fundamentals of Interferometric Gravitational Wave Detectors*; World Scientific Publishing Co.: Singapore, 1994.
12. Sathyaprakash, B.S.; Schutz, B.F. Physics, astrophysics and cosmology with gravitational waves. *Living Rev. Relativit.* **2009**, *12*, 2. [CrossRef]
13. Vajente, G. Gravitational Waves Experimental Techniques. In Proceedings of the Tri-Institute Summer School on Elementary Particles, Waterloo, ON, Canada, 9–20 July 2018; Available online: https://www.trisep.ca/2018/program/ (accessed on 21 July 2018).

14. Hild, S.; Grote, H.; Degallaix, J.; Chelkowski, S.; Danzmann, K.; Freise, A.; Hewitson, M.; Hough, J.; Lück, H.; Prijatelj, M.; et al. DC-readout of a signal-recycled gravitational wave detector. *Class. Quant. Grav.* **2009**, *26*, 055012. [CrossRef]
15. Reitze, D.; Saulson, P.R.; Grote, H. *Advanced Interferometric Gravitational-Wave Detectors*; World Scientific Publishing Co.: Singapore, 2019; Volume 2.
16. Hello, P.; Vinet, J.Y. Analytical models of thermal aberrations in massive mirrors heated by high power laser beams. *J. Phys. Paris* **1990**, *51*, 1267–1282. [CrossRef]
17. Lawrence, R.C. Active Wavefront Correction in Laser Interferometric Gravitational Wave Detectors. Ph.D. Thesis, MIT, Cambridge, MA, USA, 2003.
18. Kelly, T.L.; Veitch, P.J.; Brooks, A.F.; Much, J. Accurate and precise optical testing with a differential Hartmann wavefront sensor. *Appl. Opt.* **2007**, *46*, 861–866. [CrossRef] [PubMed]
19. Goda, K.; Ottaway, D.; Connelly, B.; Adhikari, R.; Mavalvala, N.; Gretarsson, A. Frequency-resolving spatiotemporal wave-front sensor. *Opt. Lett.* **2004**, *29*, 1452. [CrossRef] [PubMed]
20. Mullavey, A.J.; Slagmolen, B.J.J.; Miller, J.; Evans, M.; Fritschel, P.; Sigg, D.; Waldman, S.J.; Shaddock, D.A.; McClelland, D.E. Arm-length stabilisation for interferometric gravitational-wave detectors using frequency-doubled auxiliary lasers. *Opt. Express* **2012**, *20*, 81. [CrossRef] [PubMed]
21. Izumi, K.; Arai, K.; Barr, B.; Betzwieser, J.; Brooks, A.; Dahl, K.; Doravari, S.; Driggers, J.C.; Korth, W.Z.; Miao, H.; et al. Multicolor cavity metrology. *J. Opt. Soc. Am. A* **2012**, *29*, 2092. [CrossRef]
22. Drever, R.W.P.; Hall, J.L.; Kowalski, F.V.; Hough, J.; Ford, G.M.; Munley, A.J.;Ward, H. Laser phase and frequency stabilization using an optical resonator. *Appl. Phys. B* **1983**, *31*, 97–105. [CrossRef]
23. Black, E.D. An introduction to Pound-Drever-Hall laser frequency stabilization. *Am. J. Phys.* **2001**, *69*, 79. [CrossRef]
24. Schnabel, R.; Mavalvala, N.; McClelland D.E.; Lam, P.K. Quantum metrology for gravitational wave astronomy. *Nat. Commun.* **2010**, *1*, 121. [CrossRef]
25. Thorne, K.S.; Drever, R.W.P.; Caves, C.M.; Zimmerman, M.; Sandberg, V.D. Quantum nondemolition measurements of harmonic oscillators. *Phys. Rev. Lett.* **1978**, *40*, 667–671. [CrossRef]
26. Braginsky, V.B.; Khalili, F.Y. Quantum nondemolition measurements: The route from toys to tools. *Rev. Mod. Phys.* **1996**, *68*, 1–11. [CrossRef]
27. Caves, C. M. Quantum-mechanical noise in an interferometer. *Phys. Rev. D* **1981**, *23*, 1693–1708. [CrossRef]
28. Kimble, H.J.; Levin, Y.; Matsko, A.B.; Thorne, K.S.; Vyatchanin, S.P. Conversion of conventional gravitational-wave interferometers into quantum nondemolition interferometers by modifying their input and/or output optics. *Phys. Rev. D* **2001**, *65*, 022002. [CrossRef]
29. Zhao, Y.; Aritomi, N.; Capocasa, E.; Leonardi, M.; Eisenmann, M.; Guo, Y.; Polini, E.; Tomura, A.; Arai, K.; Aso, Y.; et al. Frequency-Dependent Squeezed Vacuum Source for Broadband Quantum Noise Reduction in Advanced Gravitational-Wave Detectors. *Phys. Rev. Lett.* **2020**, *124*, 171101. [CrossRef] [PubMed]
30. Callen, H.B.; Welton, T.A. Irreversibility and Generalized Noise. *Phys. Rev.* **1951**, *83*, 34–40. [CrossRef]
31. Lorenzini, M. The monolithic suspension for the Virgo interferometer. *Class. Quant. Grav.* **2010**, *27*, 084021. [CrossRef]
32. Cagnoli. G.; Gammaitoni, L.; Hough, J.; Kovalik, J.; McIntosh, S.; Punturo, M.; Rowan, S. Very High Q Measurements on a Fused Silica Monolithic Pendulum for Use in Enhanced Gravity Wave Detectors. *Phys. Rev. Lett.* **2000**, *85*, 2442–2445. [CrossRef]
33. Pinard, L.; Michel, C.; Sassolas, B.; Balzarini, L.; Degallaix, J.; Dolique, V.; Flaminio, R.; Forest, D.; Granata, M.; Lagrange, B.; et al. Mirrors used in the LIGO interferometers for first detection of gravitational waves. *Appl. Opt.* **2017**, *56*, C11–C15. [CrossRef]
34. Beker, M.G.; van den Brand, J.F.J.; Hennes, E.; Rabeling, D.S. Newtonian noise and ambient ground motion for gravitational wave detectors. *J. Phys. Conf. Ser.* **2012**, *363*, 012004. [CrossRef]
35. Harms, J. Terrestrial Gravity Fluctuations. *Living Rev. Relativ.* **2019**, *22*, 6. [CrossRef]
36. Harms, J.; Venkateswara, K. Newtonian-noise cancellation in large-scale interferometric GW detectors using seismic tiltmeters. *Class. Quant. Grav.* **2016**, *33*, 234001. [CrossRef]
37. Ottaway, D.J.; Fritschel, P.; Waldman S.J. Impact of upconverted scattered light on advanced interferometric gravitational wave detectors. *Opt. Express* **2012**, *20*, 8329–8336. [CrossRef] [PubMed]
38. Allocca, A.; Bersanetti, D.; Casanueva Diaz, J.; De Rossi, C.; Mantovani, M.; Masserot, A.; Rolland, L.; Ruggi, P.; Swinkels, B.; Tapia San Martin, E.T.; et al. Interferometer Sensing and Control for the Advanced Virgo Experiment in the O3 Scientific Run. *Galaxies* **2020**, *33*, 182–189. [CrossRef]
39. Abbott, R.; Abbott, T.D.; Abraham, S.; Acernese, F.; Ackley, K.; Adams, C.; Adhikari, R.X.; Adya, V.B.; Affeldt, C.; Agathos, M.; et al. Open data from the first and second observing runs of Advanced LIGO and Advanced Virgo. *SoftwareX* **2021**, *13*, 100658.
40. Accadia, T.; Acernese, F.; Antonucci, F.; Astone, P.; Ballardin, G.; Barone, F.; Barsuglia, M.; Bauer, T.S.; Beker, M.; Belletoile, A.; et al. the seismic Superattenuators of the Virgo gravitational waves interferometer. *J. Low Freq. Noise Act. Control* **2011**, *30*, 63–79. [CrossRef]
41. Acernese, F.; Antonucci, F.; Aoudia, S.; Arun, K.G.; Astone, P.; Ballardin, G.; Barone, F.; Barsuglia, M.; Bauer, T.S.; Beker, M.; et al. Measurements of Superattenuator seismic isolation by Virgo interferometer. *Astropart. Phys.* **2010**, *33*, 182–189. [CrossRef]
42. Virgo Collaboration. *Virgo-Technical Documentation System*; Virgo Internal Note; VIR-0128A-12; 2012. Available online: https://tds.virgo-gw.eu/ql/?c=8940 (accessed on 13 April 2012).

43. Cleva, F.; Coulon, J. P.; Kéfélian, F. *Characterization, Integration and Operation of a 100-W Solid State Amplifier in the Advanced-VIRGO Pre-Stabilized Laser System*; Conference Paper; CLEO Europe: Munich, Germany, 2019.
44. Buy, C.; Genin, E.; Barsuglia, M.; Gouaty, R.; Tacca, M. Design of a high-magnification and low-aberration compact catadioptric telescope for the Advanced Virgo gravitational-wave interferometric detector. *Class. Quant. Grav.* **2017**, *34*, 095011. [CrossRef]
45. Agatsuma, K.; van der Schaaf, L.; van Beuzekom, M.; Rabeling, D.; van den Brand, J. High-performance phase camera as a frequency selective laser wavefront sensor for gravitational wave detectors. *Opt. Express* **2019**, *27*, 18533–18548. [CrossRef]
46. van der Schaaf, L.; Agatsuma, K.; van Beuzekom, M.; Gebyehu, M.; van den Brand, J. Advanced Virgo phase camera. *J. Phys. Conf. Ser.* **2016**, *718*, 072008. [CrossRef]
47. Acernese, F.; Amico, P.; Al-Shourbagy, M.; Aoudia, S.; Avino, S.; Babusci, D.; Ballardin, G.; Barille', R.; Barone, F.; Barsotti, L.; et al. (Virgo Collaboration). The variable finesse locking technique. *Class. Quantum Grav.* **2006**, *23*, S85–S89. [CrossRef]
48. Bersanetti, D.; Casanueva Diaz, J.; Allocca, A.; Heitmann, H.; Hoak, D.; Mantovani, M.; Ruggi, P.; Swinkels, B. New algorithm for the Guided Lock technique for a high-Finesse optical cavity. *Astropart. Phys.* **2020**, *117*, 102405. [CrossRef]
49. Carbognani, F. *Virgo-Technical Documentation System*; Virgo Internal Note; VIR-0234C-17; 2019. Available online https://tds.virgo-gw.eu/ql/?c=12159 (accessed on 2 November 2019).
50. Acernese, F.; Agathos, M.; Aiello, L.; Allocca, A.; Aloy, M.A.; Amato, A.; Antier, S.; Arene, M.; Arnaud, N.; Ascenzi, S.; et al. The Advanced Virgo longitudinal control system for the O2 observing run. *Astropart. Phys.* **2020**, *116*, 231108. [CrossRef]
51. Mehmet, M.; Vahlbruch, H. The Squeezed Light Source for the Advanced Virgo Detector in the Observation Run O3. *Galaxies* **2020**, *8*, 79. [CrossRef]
52. Acernese, F.; Agathos, M.; Aiello, L.; Allocca, A.; Amato, A.; Ansoldi, S.; Antier, S.; Arène, M.; Arnaud, N.; Ascenzi, S.; et al. Increasing the Astrophysical Reach of the Advanced Virgo Detector via the Application of Squeezed Vacuum States of Light. *Phys. Rev. Lett.* **2019**, *123*, 231108. [CrossRef]
53. Virgo Collaboration. *Virgo-Technical Documentation System*; Virgo Internal Note; VIR-0596A-19; Advanced Virgo Plus Phase I Design Report; 2019. Available online: https://tds.virgo-gw.eu/ql/?c=14430 (accessed on 11 August 2021).
54. LIGO Scientific Collaboration; Virgo Collaboration; KAGRA Collaboration. Prospects for observing and localizing gravitational-wave transients with Advanced LIGO, Advanced Virgo and KAGRA. *Living Rev. Relativ.* **2020**, *23*, 3. [CrossRef] [PubMed]

Article

Research Facilities for Europe's Next Generation Gravitational-Wave Detector Einstein Telescope

Sibilla Di Pace [1,2,†], Valentina Mangano [1,2,†], Lorenzo Pierini [1,2,†], Amirsajjad Rezaei [1,2,†], Jan-Simon Hennig [3,4,‡], Margot Hennig [3,4,‡], Daniela Pascucci [5,‡], Annalisa Allocca [6,7,§], Iara Tosta e Melo [8,§], Vishnu G. Nair [9,10,||], Philippe Orban [11,||], Ameer Sider [9,||], Shahar Shani-Kadmiel [12,||] and Joris van Heijningen [13,*]

1. Dipartimento di Fisica, Università degli Studi di Roma "La Sapienza", I-00185 Roma, Italy
2. Istituto Nazionale di Fisica Nucleare (INFN), Sezione di Roma, I-00185 Roma, Italy
3. Department of Gravitational Waves and Fundamental Physics, Maastricht University, P.O. Box 616, 6200 MD Maastricht, The Netherlands
4. Nikhef, Science Park 105, 1098 XG Amsterdam, The Netherlands
5. Department of Physics and Astronomy, Universiteit Gent, B-9000 Gent, Belgium
6. Dipartimento di Fisica, Università di Napoli Federico II, I-80126 Napoli, Italy
7. Istituto Nazionale di Fisica Nucleare (INFN), Sezione di Napoli, Complesso Universitario di Monte S. Angelo, I-80126 Napoli, Italy
8. Laboratori Nazionali del Sud, Istituto Nazionale di Fisica Nucleare (INFN), I-95123 Catania, Italy
9. Precision Mechatronics Laboratory, Université de Liège, B-4000 Liège, Belgium
10. Manipal Institute of Technology, Manipal Academy of Higher Education, Manipal 576104, India
11. Urban and Environmental Engineering, Faculty of Applied Sciences, Université de Liège, B-4000 Liège, Belgium
12. R&D Department of Seismology and Acoustics, Royal Netherlands Meteorological Institute (KNMI), 3731 GA De Bilt, The Netherlands
13. Centre for Cosmology, Particle Physics and Phenomenology (CP3), Université Catholique de Louvain, B-1348 Louvain-la-Neuve, Belgium
* Correspondence: joris.vanheijningen@uclouvain.be
† On behalf of the Amaldi Research Center Collaboration.
‡ On behalf of the ETpathfinder Collaboration.
§ On behalf of the SarGrav Collaboration.
|| On behalf of the E-TEST Collaboration.

Citation: Di Pace, S.; Mangano, V.; Pierini, L.; Rezaei, A.; Hennig, J.-S.; Hennig, M.; Pascucci, D.; Allocca, A.; Tosta e Melo, I.; Nair, V.G.; et al. Research Facilities for Europe's Next Generation Gravitational-Wave Detector Einstein Telescope. *Galaxies* **2022**, *10*, 65. https://doi.org/10.3390/galaxies10030065

Academic Editor: Gabriele Vajente

Received: 29 January 2022
Accepted: 10 March 2022
Published: 28 April 2022

Publisher's Note: MDPI stays neutral with regard to jurisdictional claims in published maps and institutional affiliations.

Copyright: © 2022 by the authors. Licensee MDPI, Basel, Switzerland. This article is an open access article distributed under the terms and conditions of the Creative Commons Attribution (CC BY) license (https:// creativecommons.org/licenses/by/ 4.0/).

Abstract: The Einstein Telescope is Europe's next generation gravitational-wave detector. To develop all necessary technology, four research facilities have emerged across Europe: The Amaldi Research Center (ARC) in Rome (Italy), ETpathfinder in Maastricht (The Netherlands), SarGrav in the Sos Enattos mines on Sardinia (Italy) and E-TEST in Liége (Belgium) and its surroundings. The ARC pursues the investigation of a large cryostat, equipped with dedicated low-vibration cooling lines, to test full-scale cryogenic payloads. The installation will be gradual and interlaced with the payload development. ETpathfinder aims to provide a low-noise facility that allows the testing of full interferometer configurations and the interplay of their subsystems in an ET-like environment. ETpathfinder will focus amongst others on cryogenic technologies, silicon mirrors, lasers and optics at 1550 and 2090 nm and advanced quantum noise reduction schemes. The SarGrav laboratory has a surface lab and an underground operation. On the surface, the Archimedes experiment investigates the interaction of vacuum fluctuations with gravity and is developing (tilt) sensor technology for the Einstein Telescope. In an underground laboratory, seismic characterisation campaigns are undertaken for the Sardinian site characterisation. Lastly, the Einstein Telecope Euregio meuse-rhine Site & Technology (E-TEST) is a single cryogenic suspension of an ET-sized silicon mirror. Additionally, E-TEST investigates the Belgian–Dutch–German border region that is the other candidate site for Einstein Telescope using boreholes and seismic arrays and hydrogeological characterisation. In this article, we describe the Einstein Telescope, the low-frequency part of its science case and the four research facilities.

Keywords: gravitational waves; einstein telescope; seismic noise; newtonian noise; thermal noise; coating noise; silicon; suspensions; cryogenics; payload; cryostat

1. Introduction

Nearly everything in the universe is almost completely transparent to gravitational waves (GWs), which is both why they were so incredibly difficult to detect but also why, since 2015, they have been helping us see things that no other form of energy does. Over the past 5 years, the current generation of ground-based GW detectors [1–4] have ushered in the detection of the first GW from colliding black holes [5], from colliding neutron stars [6], and with now over 90 other detections [7–9] have solidified a brand new corner of astronomy [10] and cosmology [11].

These monumental achievements would not have been possible without decoupling the instruments from the Earth's ever present motion using complex mirror suspensions [12–14] and sophisticated control systems. This decoupling uncovers a whole slew of other noise sources masking the GW signal, including other seismic effects, thermal noises and quantum noises. Over four decades of development have made the current GW detectors sufficiently sensitive to signals once they move inside the detector bandwidth from about 30 Hz. The current infrastructures of 3- or 4-km long armed interferometers can be made more sensitive with significant effort until infrastructure limits are reached.

The next generation of GW detectors includes the Cosmic Explorer [15] and Einstein Telescope (ET) [16]—the American and European effort, respectively—to be constructed in the 2030s. As shown in Figure 1, the ET design features an equilateral triangular tunnel complex with sides of 10 km. ET uses two interferometer designs: one low-power, low-frequency cryogenic and one high-power, high-frequency room temperature detectors. The low-frequency ET detector, ET-LF, cools its mirrors down to 10–20 K and aims to ensure its seismic wall and thermal noises limitations are moved down to 3 Hz.

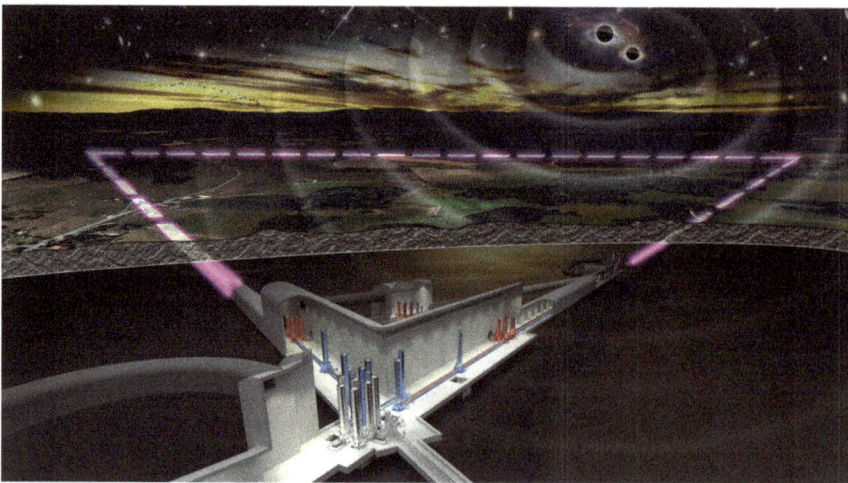

Figure 1. An artist's perspective of the Einstein Telescope. Underground infrastructure near one of the three detector vertices. In halls of different volumes, seismic isolation vacuum towers—blue for the cryogenic ET-LF and red for ET-HF—are housed. The largest hall is the cross-road between the detector arms (in bright dashed magenta), a tunnel for the filter cavity (towards lower right) and an access tunnel (towards lower left). Reproduced from Ref. [16], image courtesy of Marco Kraan, Nikhef.

The high-frequency interferometer, ET-HF operates at room temperature but at 3 MW, which is roughly 20 times the intra-cavity power of the current detectors. Each of the three corner stations houses the laser, input and output optics for one ET-LF and one ET-HF detector. In total, there are six interferometers with 10-kilometer-long Fabry–Perot cavities. To be able to detect GWs < 10 Hz, the detector will be several hundred meters underground, where the seismic noise is lower.

1.1. Science Case for Detector Sensitivity Improvements below 10 Hz

Improving detector sensitivity at low frequencies provides significant benefits to a large spectrum of searches. At present, we have only observed GWs related to the coalescence of compact binaries (CBC). We have gained some understanding on their physics and rates and we are able to make predictions on future observations [10]. The Advanced LIGO/Virgo infrastructures limit us to observe CBC events, such as binary black holes (BBH) or neutron star-black hole (NSBH), with total mass (2–1000) $M_\odot$ within redshift $z \leq 2.0$ [17].

Due to the strong improvements described in the following sections, such signals will be visible by ET up to $z \leq 100$, with detection rates of order 10^5–10^6 coalescences per year [18]. Regarding Binary Neutron Stars (BNS), whose total mass is bounded to 3 $M_\odot$, they would be detected up to $z \leq 3$, while the already observed signals, such as GW170817 [6] are at $z \sim 0.01$, and their expected detection rate is about 7×10^4 coalescences per year [18].

Due to these expected rates and redshifts, we will be able to perform studies on Black Hole (BH) population as function of their masses and distances in order to test BH formation theories. As ET will be able to watch beyond the $z \sim 2$ peak of the star formation, it will be possible to disentangle the contribution of stellar origin BHs from that of possible primordial origin BHs. Observing BBH mergers beyond the reionization epoch, at $z \geq 6$, will enable the determination of the masses of the first metal-poor progenitor stars [19].

Moreover, the frequency at which signals enter the detector sensitivity band will significantly lower: while for Advanced LIGO/Virgo, this frequency is about 20–30 Hz [8,9,20], in ET it will become 2 Hz. This improvement has a strong impact on the observed early inspiral phase of CBC signals: according to [21], they will last in ET sensitivity band for a time longer by a factor $\sim(0.5$–$1.4) \times 10^3$ with respect to current GW detectors.

The increased signal duration, combined with the lowered noise floor, will result in highly enhanced Signal-to-Noise Ratios (SNR) and in extraordinarily precise parameter estimation. We can therefore obtain better understanding of the binaries dynamics, such as their formation mechanisms, the impact of star clusters and galactic nuclei on the production of binary systems.

Tests of General Relativity (GR) will also benefit, with particular attention to post-Newtonian (PN) parameters, which encode GR predictions: through their measure, we see how well experimental results are consistent with GR assumptions. With the present detectors, we were able to measure them with precision of about 10%—the most recent results are shown in [22]. Due to ET, we will be able to determine deviations of PN coefficients from GR predictions with $\leq 10^{-2}$–10^{-3} accuracy.

The observation of CBCs from BNS will permit to determine the nature of matter and interactions in neutron star interior. An event like the first observed BNS coalescence, GW170817, would be seen with a SNR larger by a factor of $\mathcal{O}(50)$ with respect to the actually observed in Advanced LIGO/Virgo. Observing BNS and NSBH coalescences starting from 2 Hz and with high SNRs would allow us to measure magnetic and rotational tidal Love numbers, which parametrize the perturbation on the quadrupole momentum of the system as consequence of the star tidal deformability [23].

In [24,25], it is shown that, with ET, we will be able to infer the Love numbers with an accuracy improved by one order of magnitude: thus, we will obtain stronger constraints on neutron stars Equation of State (EoS), with respect to the ones found in [26,27]. This will provide an unique window onto the behaviour of QCD at energy scales unreachable in Earth-based experiments.

ET will detect, for the first time, gravitational waves from still undetected sources: the instrumental improvements described in this paper will significantly enhance the detection chances of those signals. Regarding the search of Continuous Waves (CWs) emitted by non-axisymmetric neutron stars, opening the observable window to <10 Hz frequencies will permit the search for a huge number of known sources, already observed as pulsars through electromagnetic emission, never searched with current detector sensitivities.

However, since the CW signal amplitude is proportional to the squared rotational frequency of the star, these low-frequency sources will need to have ellipticities ε in the range of 10^{-1}–10^{-5} to be detected [28]. These values are quite high with respect to current upper limits (10^{-5}–10^{-6}) on known sources at >20 Hz [29] but are still possible according to exotic proposed EoSs [30], mostly if we admit that neutron stars can have different internal composition depending on their particular formation history. The search of all sources at higher frequencies will clearly benefit, as their minimum detectable ellipticities will lower by more than one order of magnitude [28].

There are also other proposed CW sources. For instance, a variety of theories beyond standard model physics predict the existence of ultralight dark matter, with masses $m_b \ll 1$ eV. Recently, the proposal that boson clouds could form around spinning black holes through the superradiance mechanism and emit CWs [31] has received growing interest, and searches during the last advanced LIGO/Virgo O3 run have already been performed [32].

Since, at first order, the expected CW should have source-frame frequency proportional to ~ 480 Hz $\cdot m_b / (10^{-12}$ eV$)$ [31], the current detectors sensitivity window allow us to search for boson masses in the range $[5 \times 10^{-14}$–$10^{-11}]$ eV, coupled with solar-mass black holes within few-kpc distances [32].

With the lower noise floor of ET, we will be sensitive to those sources within the whole galaxy and even up to the nearby universe. Moreover, thanks to the frequency cut lowering from 20–30 Hz for current detectors to 3 Hz for ET, we can extend the searched boson mass down to 5×10^{-15} eV, which, in this case, would be associated with intermediate mass black holes of about 1000 $M_\odot$. In this way, we could make a bridge with the masses that could be covered due to future space-based detectors, such as LISA [33].

From what we presented here, a large amount of new science is achievable through the strong noise reduction at low frequencies that will be realized by next generation earth-based detectors, such as ET. On the other hand, further important windows will be opened due to the full band noise reduction up to the kHz regime, the GW produced in the post-merger of BNS, or by the remnant of core-collapse supernovae.

If they result in a neutron star: high frequency normal modes are expected to be excited, related to their interior composition, and produce GWs. Long transient GWs produced by newborn magnetars are also expected, up to a ~ 1 per year rate at distances within 30–40 Mpc: the observation of these signals would give us important information on the initial life of magnetars [6,34]. Last, the observation of quasi-normal modes on post-merger BHs will allow us to test near-horizon effects, such as evidences for exotic compact objects [35] and signals from quantum gravity [36].

1.2. The Challenges for ET at Low-Frequency

The main limitations at frequencies below 10 Hz for ET are the seismic noise, the thermal noises and Newtonian noise, as shown in Figure 2. Newtonian noise arises from the gravitational coupling of the main mirrors of a GW detector with a varying local mass distribution because of passing seismic waves. As with KAGRA, ET will operate underground, which will reduce the ambient seismic and Newtonian noise. Seismic noise will be further reduced by improving vibration isolation technology in combination with underground operation.

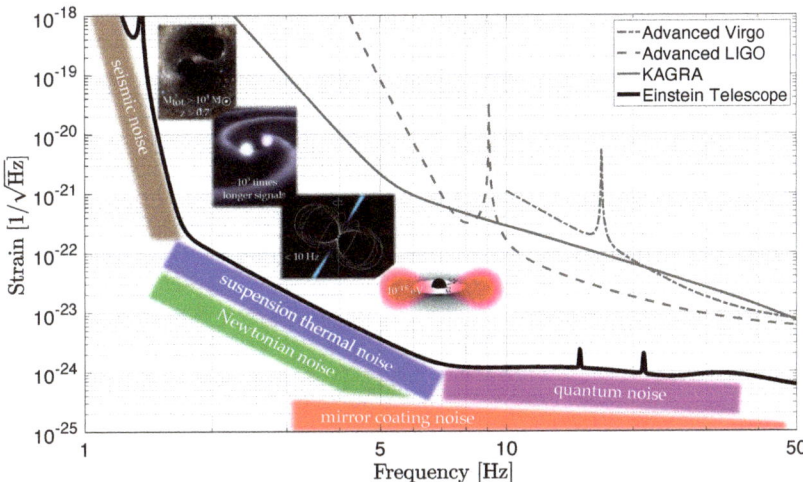

Figure 2. Low-frequency part of the Einstein Telescope strain sensitivity [16] compared to the design sensitivity of second generation GW detectors. Opening up the 2–10 Hz band will allow ET to study BBH systems with $M_{tot} > 10^3$ $M_\odot$ at $z > 0.7$, BNS systems with a 10^3 longer signal length, <10 Hz continuous waves from non-spherical NS and boson clouds. Below the ET curve are the dominant noise sources, which are the regions of research for the four research facilities. More details can be found in the text.

Newtonian noise subtraction by about two orders of magnitude [16] is achieved by vast seismometer arrays. Both suspension and coating thermal noise can be reduced by use of low mechanical loss materials at cryogenic temperatures. Current room temperature detectors use fused silica and the optical technology in combination with a laser wavelength of 1064 nm is now well mastered [37].

However, the mechanical loss of fused silica increases by several orders of magnitude at cryogenic temperatures [38] and therefore many future cryogenic GW detector designs [15,16,39] feature silicon mirrors. ET-LF will feature a 45 cm diameter, 57 cm thick and 211 kg silicon mirror cooled to 10–20 K [16]. The relatively large mirror mass is necessary to ensure the radiation pressure noise caused by the quantum uncertainty on the impinging photon momentum does not endanger the low-frequency goals.

Silicon has excellent mechanical and thermal properties, including the special property that its coefficient of thermal expansion is zero around 18 and 123 K [40]. The contribution of thermo-elastic noise will therefore vanish at these temperatures. Q-factor measurements show that silicon bulk samples can reach a mechanical loss angle as low as 10^{-9} at 10 K [41]. For ET-LF, the mirrors are operated at a cryogenic temperature of 10–20 K to reduce both suspension and coating thermal noise.

The currently used laser wavelength of 1064 nm is absorbed by silicon and longer wavelengths, e.g., 1550 nm or around 2 µm, are therefore required. The requirement for optical absorption in the test masses of ET is <5 ppm/cm [16]. One of the largest challenges for ET is the switch to a new mirror material, new suspensions that cool the mirrors without noise injection from the cryogenic system and with technology at a new laser wavelength.

Although the development of high purity silicon is driven by the semi-conductor industry, procurement of a >100 kg, un-doped, high resistivity, silicon substrate in a precision-cut cylindrical shape is no trivial task. Float-zone (FZ) [42] or magnetic Czochralski (mCz) [43] are the two manufacturing techniques that can provide high quality ingots, in terms of purity and thus low optical absorption, for production of optical substrates for advanced GW detectors.

Currently, the dominant impurities in mCz silicon are sites of interstitial oxygen, which can turn into thermal charge carrier donors during annealing [39]. Unfortunately, the optical absorption of silicon has been found to correlate with an increase in oxygen content and/or a decrease in resistivity [44]. Float Zone silicon produces the purest quality ingots with the lowest levels of oxygen, resulting in optical absorption of <5 ppm/cm. However, this approach does not allow for cylindrical diameters >20 cm. For larger diameters a different approach must be found. Thus, mCz silicon is of interest, as diameters up to 45 cm can currently be produced.

Due to the higher levels of oxygen found in mCz silicon, this increase in diameter comes with higher optical absorption of ∼20 ppm/cm [16]. The requirements for a pre-stabilised laser system (PSL) used in current second generation GW detectors consist of its output power, as well as the frequency, power and pointing noise [45]. For the low-frequency detector of ET, an output power of at least 5 W at 1550 nm or ∼2000 nm in the fundamental TEM_{00} mode with similar and improved requirements for the power, frequency and pointing noise with respect to [45] is needed.

Specifically, the frequency noise should be about $10\,\text{mHz}/\sqrt{\text{Hz}}$, the beam pointing noise (relative lateral and angular beam fluctuations) in the range of $10^{-6}/\sqrt{\text{Hz}}$, and a relative power noise of roughly $3 \times 10^{-10}/\sqrt{\text{Hz}}$ [16]. No such laser system is available at the moment at the proposed wavelengths for ET-LF, and extensive research and development is required.

The coming 10 years will see many ET technology developments taking place at the four research institutes described in detail below. The experience with Advanced Virgo has taught us that it takes more than 10 years from prototype to having a working detector. Even though successful GW detectors have been built, the move towards underground and cryogenic operation at different wavelengths brings many challenges that necessitate these efforts. Table 1 provides a strategic overview of the main research lines towards ET-LF, followed by descriptions of the four research facilities.

Table 1. An overview of the research lines to inform the ET design, including limited details where relevant or fitting. The top block shows the site characterization studies, and the bottom block shows the detector technology developments.

Research Line	ARC	ETpf	SarGrav	E-TEST
Seismic study	-	-	yes	yes
Hydrogeology	-	-	-	yes
Tilt measurement	-	-	yes	-
Magnetic study	-	-	yes	-
290 K suspension	-	double inverted pendulum	-	active/passive combination
Mirror	sapphire/silicon 130 kg	silicon phase 1: 3 kg phase 2: ~100 kg	-	silicon >100 kg
Cryo-suspension	sapphire/silicon	silicon	-	silicon
Temperature	10 K	120 K 15 K	-	20 K
Cooling	low-vibration cold link	120 K radiative 15 K conductive & "jellyfish"	-	suspended cryostat with radiative link
Coating testing	yes	yes	-	yes
Optical technology	-	1550 nm 2090 nm	-	2090 nm
Quantum noise reduction	EPR and ponderomotive	yes	-	-
Photodiodes	-	yes	-	yes
Inertial sensor development	-	-	yes	yes
Superconducting technology	-	-	yes	yes

At Sapienza University of Rome, the ARC was created with the main goal of combining inter-disciplinary research branches focused on experimental GW science. Research activities at ARC include GW physics and data analysis techniques, the improvement of mirror optical coatings, the development of quantum noise reduction strategies (EPR [46,47] and ponderomotive squeezing techniques [48,49]) as well as the development of a facility devoted to test a full-scale cryogenic payload. A dedicated laboratory infrastructure is presently under construction and will host the full-scale cryogenic payload with a large cryostat equipped with low-vibration cooling lines is described in Section 2.

ETpathfinder is an R&D facility located in Maastricht (The Netherlands), which will be used to test new technologies for third generation GW detectors, like ET. Specifically, the main goal is to test new laser wavelengths (1550 and 2090 nm) at low temperatures (15 and 120 K) and a new mirror material (silicon), as well as advanced quantum noise reduction techniques. As described in Section 3, the final configuration will be a full Michelson interferometer with 10 m Fabry–Perot cavities, working at cryogenic temperatures. During a preliminary phase two interferometers—one in each arm—will be working at different temperatures and wavelengths, in order to identify the optimal ones to be used for the second phase.

The SarGrav laboratory is an infrastructure located near the Sos Enattos mine in Lula (Nuoro, Sardinia), which is a potential site for ET. It aims to host underground experiments, such as low seismic noise experiments, cryogenic final stage mirror suspensions and cryogenic low-frequency sensor development. The combination of the Sardinian site characterization and the development of Archimedes, the first experiment in the surface-level laboratory, which will investigate the interaction between quantum vacuum fluctuations and gravity, is described in Section 4.

Lastly, in the heart of the Meuse-Rhine region—the Belgian-Dutch-German border area—E-TEST follows a two-pronged approach towards underground cryogenic detector technology. A prototype cryogenic suspension of a 100 kg silicon mirror will allow to investigate deep-cryogenic radiative cooling, combining active and passive vibration isolation systems and (cryogenic) sensor development. Additionally, E-TEST researchers will perform an underground study to map and model the geology of the Meuse-Rhine region by drilling boreholes, passive and active seismic array campaigns and hydrogeological characterisation. The project will run until the end of 2023 after which the suspension prototype will find a new home at ULiège (Belgium). The full approach is presented in Section 5.

We end with a summary and an overview of author contributions, funding and further acknowledgment.

2. Amaldi Research Center (ARC)

The Amaldi Research Center (ARC) was funded in 2018 by the Italian Ministry of University and Research (MIUR) as an excellence centre at the Department of Physics of Sapienza University of Rome [50]. ARC activities are inter-disciplinary research branches pivoting on the theme of observational GWs science of research, ranging from quantum optics to R&D developments concerning cryogenic payloads for the Einstein Telescope [51]. ARC is partially supported by INFN Roma Sapienza branch. This report touches only the activities conducted towards the realization of cryogenic Laboratory and the foreseen installation of related apparatuses.

In Section 2.1, an overview on the status of current GW detectors payloads is provided, leading to Advanced Virgo+ Phase II Large-Mass payload, and KAGRA cryogenic payloads, which are paving the way towards ET. Section 2.2 at first hints the connection between the existing payload apparatuses in operational GW detection facilities and that envisaged for ET. Then, it covers the essential requirements to be taken into account while designing the payload of interest. ARC plans and objectives are briefly highlighted. The construction of ARC Laboratory infrastructure has already commenced, and the commitment in designing the cryogenic facility to be installed was pursued in parallel. In Section 2.3 the state of the art is illustrated. We started from the cooling line prototype, following the key concept of developing a cryostat suitably designed to hold a full-scale scale basic payload prototype that accounts for all the known and most relevant issues derived from the current experience.

Given the overall commitment of experimental activities at ARC, directly focused on GW, further aspects are also included, including the improvement of the optical coatings of mirrors and development of quantum noise reduction strategies, such as frequency dependent squeezing via quantum entanglement (EPR) [46,47] and ponderomotive techniques [48,49].

2.1. State of the Art: Lessons Learned from Current GW Detectors

The present subsection summarizes the main technologies concerning test mass payload that can be exploited in ET to build up a feasible project for a cryogenic payload.

2.1.1. Advanced Virgo Suspension System

Several aspects and features of Advanced Virgo are relevant to the activities of ARC regarding the design of ET. Among those (see Figure 3), the seismic attenuation system and the mechanical structure of the payload are of great interest. The seismic attenuation system, called Superattenuator (SA) [52–55], is used to isolate the test-mass payload (see Figure 3), it was designed in the nineties and it is very close to what is needed for ET-LF.

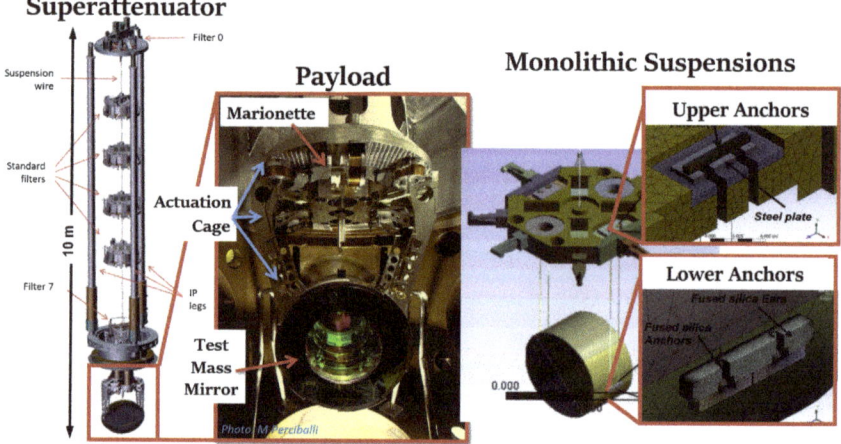

Figure 3. Suspension system of an Advanced Virgo test mass mirror. The Superattenuator (SA, left), a zoom of the payload (centre) and a detail of the monolithic suspension system (right) are shown here. Elaborated from [56].

The mechanical structure of the payload is of importance, being suspended from a single wire. This allows locating the suspension bending points of both steering stages (marionette and mirror) close to their respective center of mass, leading to the optimization of angular modes to the lowest values (∼50 mHz for pitch and roll). Advanced Virgo (AdV) also enables the realization of a composite monolithic suspension, which may be designed in separate components and subsequently assembled. Furthermore, ARC can learn a lot from the challenges of the next upgrade of Virgo (AdV+ Phase II, 2024), as shown in Figure 4, where the mass of end mirrors will be increased from 40 to 105 kg. This is mainly due to the fact that the assembly of a suitable payload with large mass mirrors is not so trivial, in common with ET.

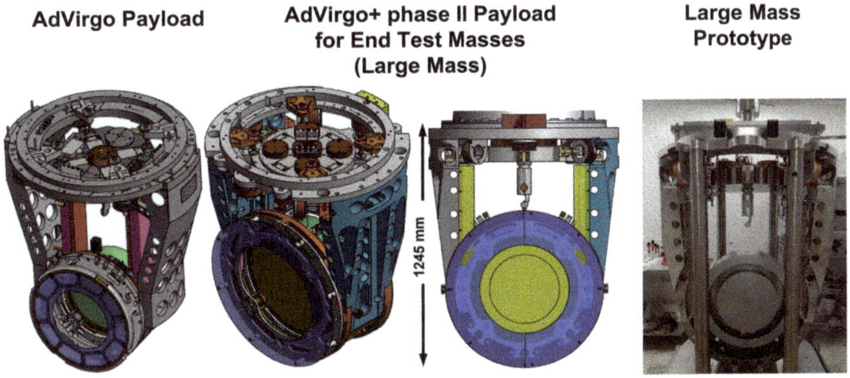

Figure 4. CAD drawings of Advanced Virgo payload (left) and Large Mass (LM) payload design for AdV+ phase II (centre). On the right is a picture of the AdV+ LM prototype. All payloads of AdV+ phase I and Input mirror payloads of AdV+ phase II will still be the same of AdV. The picture shows a circular trench in the (dummy) mirror marking the present diameter (35 cm), to be compared with the diameter of the LM mirror (55 cm). During the assembly, the actuation cage is mounted on four vertical shafts. The overall mass to be integrated in the SA increases from 328 to 500 kg, which requires an upgrade of the SA filters and suspension wires.

2.1.2. KAGRA'S Cryogenic Suspension System

KAGRA, which belongs to the current generation of ground-based GW detectors [3], represents an important step towards ET-LF as it adopts both underground and cryogenics operations [16], and for this reason, it is often referred as a "2.5G" GW detector. Its installation in Japan finished in 2019 and, after one year of commissioning, in February 2020, KAGRA started its first observing run, terminated in April 2020 [3].

Concerning test masses and the whole isolation and suspension system, KAGRA inherited and further developed a configuration that arose through a worldwide collaborative effort. In fact, the passive attenuation system is inspired by Virgo concept, while the digital control hardware (and software) is the same as in LIGO. Interestingly, the payload merges mechanical and electromechanical aspects of both Virgo and LIGO cases.

Some of the important choices already adopted in KAGRA have been regarded as guidelines for the cryogenic project now being developed at ARC, which will be explored in detail in the following subsections. To name a few, conduction is considered as the primary cooling technique (no use of fluids), and cryogenic ducts are regarded as separating the cryocoolers from the cryostat to prevent transmission of vibration. Additionally, the possibility of Hydroxide Catalysis Bonding (HCB), developed in KAGRA to reduce the thermal noise at interfaces of sapphire elements [3,57], for Al2O3 and also for Silicon (possible alternative materials) should be investigated.

Figure 5 shows a schematic diagram of the KAGRA suspension system and cryogenic payload. Structurally, the design appears inspired by the first generation of room temperature Virgo payloads, but with two new features. The marionette is split in two (lumped) parts: DC motorized steering and actively controlled part (IM) for operation set-point lock.

Given the foregoing context, the primary emphasis of ARC's activities are payload concept design and cryogenic testing. On one hand, ARC uses computer simulations to arrive at a desirable mechanical design for ET's payload that exhibits acceptable thermo-mechanical behavior. This is covered in further depth in Section 2.2. Section 2.3, on the other hand, offers some information on ARC's efforts related to the construction of a facility that will allow cryogenic testing on a full-scale prototype of the model after it has been finished.

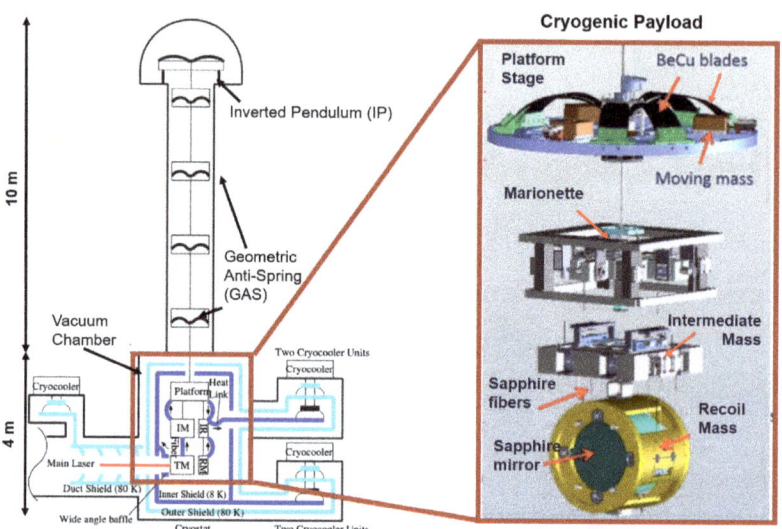

Figure 5. A schematic diagram of KAGRA suspension system is shown on the left, and a detail of the cryogenic payload is on the right. The test mass mirror (TM) is suspended from a seismic attenuation system (SAS) consisting of seven stages of pendulum. The cryogenic payload is composed of a TM, a recoil mass (RM), an intermediate mass (IM), an intermediate recoil mass (IR) and a platform. All these elements are surrounded by an inner and outer radiation shields. The sapphire TM is suspended from the IM by sapphire fibres. The arrows in the scheme show the direction of the heat flow. Heat is extracted from the mirror to the IM through the fibres and transferred to the platform, the IR and the cryocoolers by thin metal wires called heat links. Duct shields are used to reduce thermal radiation [58,59].

2.2. Payload Development at ARC

While providing early payload design for ET, ARC attempts to cherish the valuable experiences gained by the community over the past few decades: Virgo (AdV) experience with low frequency room-temperature payloads, pioneering cryogenic prototype developed in Rome since 2006 (EU-FP6), and later at the EGO site [60], and the major and unique vein developed by the Japanese GW groups expressed by KAGRA [61]. The main components of the envisaged prototype at ARC include the platform (as in KAGRA), reaction actuation cage (a single body), marionette and a hanging dummy mirror. Splitting the marionette in two bodies will also be considered but not at the first stage of development. The purpose of the project is the following:

1. Defining a reasonable size for the inner shield of the cryostat (see Section 2.3), mainly the height while also paying attention to the horizontal section.
2. Designing a feasible configuration for the prototype, accounting realistic prediction of thermal noise and seismic noise through the cooling system [62].

The key features are the following. First, the adoption of long fibres for both marionette and mirror (approximately 100 cm), made of materials with high thermal conductivity and high quality factor, such as sapphire or crystalline silicon. The production of properly sized sapphire fibres is already feasible, though further optimization is expected in the next years [63].

To evaluate the production limits of quality sapphire and silicon fibres in terms of length and purity, collaborations with Institut Lumière Matière of the University of Lyon and Norwegian University of Science and Technology (NTNU) are ongoing. In order to pursue this plan, the issue of anchoring crystalline suspension is of principal relevance and will be the topic of the main R&D, leading to the construction and test of double hooked suspension element. The "quasi-monolithic" solution chosen for KAGRA ensures thermal conductivity, but the monolithic double-head suspension element must still be fully developed in order to achieve the high quality factor demand.

The third crucial element being studied at ARC is the marionette, whose structure, especially in case of sapphire suspension, will adopt high quality factor blades. It is also foreseen to adopt a solution, which permits easy removal of suspension elements (without causing damage) is advantageous due to high manufacturing cost of suspension elements.

The finite element method (FEM) is implemented to analyse and study the corresponding thermo-mechanical response of the early payload design, developed at ARC. This consists of a full-scale prototype with Si_2O_3 or sapphire mirror (diameter of 550 mm and mass of 130 kg), a marionette of same mass, and sapphire wires of 2.2 mm and 5.4 mm for the mirror and marionette, respectively.

All the suspension elements will be tested at low temperature concerning the breaking strength, mechanical quality factor and thermal conductivity through collaboration with Urbino, Perugia, Tor Vergata at EGO (Virgo site), in close collaboration with KAGRA. ARC is not considering small-scale prototyping to be rescaled at later stages; rather, the entire design process is built around the idea of a full-scale prototype since the beginning. Technology should be gradually developed and, eventually, the payload prototype will be assembled with a dummy mirror with the equivalent mechanical dynamics.

The payload structure will embed all the crucial crystalline components involved in the cooling process. The actuation cage, suspended by means of wires, will be inspired by both Virgo and KAGRA experience. The same body can be used to actuate on both marionette and test-mass. Very low stiffness heat links [64] will be certainly needed to connect the actuation cage to thermal radiation shields, but the concept ARC will pursue is the minimization of their presence in the lumped chain marionette-mirror. At the level of the mirror, KAGRA-like ears, attached using hydroxide catalysis bonding, can be adopted [65].

2.3. Cryostat and Cryogenic Cooling System

The laboratory infrastructure at Sapienza University is under construction as shown in Figure 6. Its first purpose is testing a cooling line module (Figure 7), which has been designed and is now under construction, leading to the installation of a full cryogenic facility. The pulse tube cooling station design is the result of local cryogenics experience and collaborative contributions inspired by the pioneering work of KAGRA team [14,58,61,66,67] and CUORE (Cryogenic Underground Observatory for Rare Events) [68].

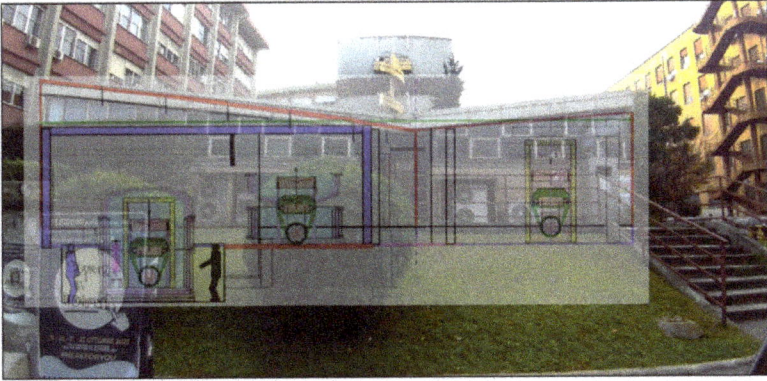

Figure 6. Amaldi Research Center at the University of Rome Sapienza will be dedicated to the development and test of the ET-LF cryogenic payload. The laboratory is under re-construction to allow the assembly of full-scale payload and to insert it into the cryostat, as shown in the pictorial view. For that matter, the floor has been lowered.

Two pulse tubes Cryomech PT400 (1.8 W at 4.2 K) have already been bought by Amaldi Research Center. They are meant to operate in counterphase, and connected to a 5 N pure aluminium (Al5N) thermal duct, mechanically suspended and decoupled from the cryostat. Soft heat links (Al6N) are being designed, following the Japanese experience [58,67], to connect the bar to the cold stages and the cryostat inner shields. Initially, the device will be tested using a service small cryogenic chamber equipped with vibration sensors (on the left in Figure 7).

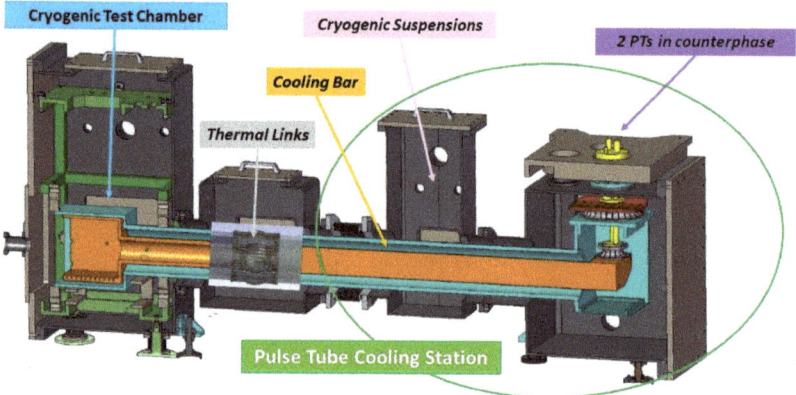

Figure 7. Schematic diagram of the cooling unit that will be hosted in the ARC cryogenic laboratory under construction and that may be implemented in Einstein Telescope as well [69,70].

The application for the large cryostat funding has not been finalized at the moment. We envisage a test cryostat of about 3.5 m in diameter and 3.5 m in height (dimensions limited by the host building). It will be designed to be as close as possible to the ET requirements but focused only on the local test of a full-scale payload. Namely, there will not be any super attenuation system installed above the vacuum chamber, and the access will be implemented through a side flange. We also plan to install a prototype pipe, cooled down by another refrigerator, to test the radiation input impinging on the dummy mirror. In ET, we foresee the use of four cooling units similar to the prototype we are building.

The schedule of the activities is the following:

1. Test of the pulse tube cooling station (equipped with two Cryomech PT400) under construction.
2. Payload design followed by one-by-one tests on crucial parts and then by prototype construction.
3. Cryostat design driven by the overall suspension structure and cooling procedure.
4. Test of the payload prototype in clean room at room temperature and study of the characteristic frequencies with their dissipation at high and low frequency.
5. Cryostat construction followed by cryogenic tests.
6. Payload integration and test of the integrated system.

We plan to have a prototype payload by 2024 and, if suitable funding is granted, to start the commitment for the cryostat construction in 2023. The cryogenic facility will be available for cryogenic tests on different type of full-scale payloads for the Einstein Telescope.

3. Etpathfinder

3.1. Introduction

ETpathfinder [71,72] is currently in its initial construction phase in Maastricht in the Netherlands. This project will develop and integrate suspended silicon mirrors with novel suspension elements in a 10 m prototype facility and aims to verify the technical readiness of subsystems, such as laser systems as well as photo-detectors, that are currently under development at new laser wavelengths applicable to ET (1550 and 2090 nm).

As outlined in the introduction of this article, the requirements on a pre-stabilised laser system (PSL) are quite stringent. While the development for a 1550 nm PSL is on a very promising path [73] (this system will be implemented and tested in ETpathfinder), the availability of a suitable ∼2000 nm laser source and PSL is a large challenge. This statement can also be transferred to suitable photo-detectors.

While the availability for 1550 nm high quantum-efficiency (QE) photo-detectors is promising with state-of-the-art InGaAs photo-diodes, there is currently no suitable solution for ∼2000 nm. ETpathfinder will help and push the development of these subsystems and will be able to test them in a full interferometric setting. To give an example, for a laser system at ∼2000 nm, ETpathifnder will use a laser source at 2090 nm and develop a suitable PSL.

The necessity of moving away from the well-known NPRO laser source at 1064 nm (at which all current GW detectors, including KAGRA, operate [1–4]), stems from the aspiration to operate the interferometer at cryogenic temperatures with silicon optics. The new cryogenic operating temperature requires to abolish the amorphous mirror material fused silica due to high mechanical loss at low temperature and to move to crystalline materials, such as silicon or sapphire. Figure 8 outlines the changes and challenges when moving from the second generation GW detectors to the Einstein Telescope or other third generation GW detectors.

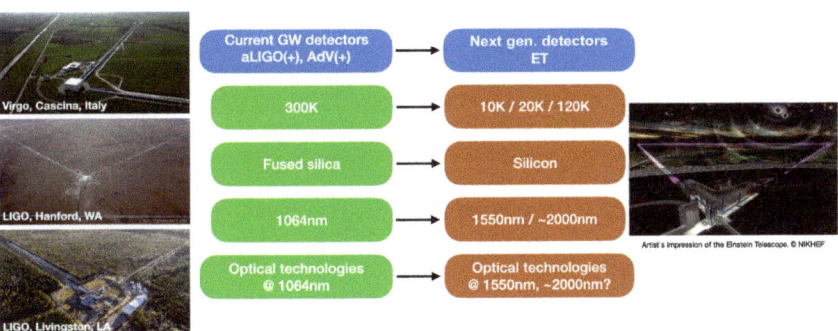

Figure 8. Major changes in detector design towards the next generation GW detectors. Listed are the key parameters of current GW detectors and the counterpart for the next generation detectors.

In the ETpathfinder project, the baseline for Phase 1 is to operate two independent interferometers with 15 cm diameter, 8 cm thick float zone (FZ) silicon mirrors to minimize optical absorption in the input test masses of the Fabry–Perot (FP) arm cavities. A detailed description of the ETpathfinder test masses can be found in Section 3.2.2. ETpathfinders uniqueness stems from the fact that it will operate two interferometers at the same time, while utilizing two new laser wavelength, 1550 and 2090 nm; both potential solutions for ET.

At the same time, it will be able to investigate these two interferometers at two cryogenic temperatures, 15 and 120 K; chosen to be near the zero crossings of the thermal expansion coefficient of silicon. Due to its cryogenic nature, ETpathfinder will also be able to investigate new challenges, such as the growth of ice on its main mirrors that has recently been observed in the KAGRA detector [74].

Based on the findings in ETpathfinder mitigation techniques for this new challenge can be developed and tested in the ETpathfinder prototype interferometer. As a unique full cryogenic Fabry–Perot Michelson interferometer utilizing silicon mirrors and new laser wavelengths, ETpathfinder will address all the challenges outlined in Figure 8. This includes investigations of advanced quantum noise reduction technologies, such as frequency dependent squeezing [75], or a speedmeter topology [76].

These techniques can be investigated in a full interferomteric setting, and ETpathfinder will be able to achieve this while operating with novel technologies. The R&D programme to outline a set of verification experiments is currently under development. For this article, we give examples where applicable, and we focus on highlighting a subset of the design choices for the ETpathfinder project as per design report [71].

3.2. Key Technologies

This section highlights three selected key technologies that make ETpathfinder the unique research facility it aspires to be. Starting with the general mechanical and optical layout, the cryogenic system and the silicon mirror-suspensions of ETpathfinder will be described in more detail. Due to the nature of this article, not all ETpathfinder key technologies can be described here. For an in-depth description of the project and its key technologies, further information can be found in the ETpathfinder design report [71] and the ETpathfinder reference paper [72].

3.2.1. Layout of ETpathfinder

The goal of ETpathfinder in Phase 1 is to verify the technological readiness of the subsystems that are being planned to be implemented in the Einstein Telescope [16]. The parameter matrix that ETpathfinder is going to investigate is of different laser wavelengths (1550 vs. 2090 nm) and different operating temperature (15 vs. 120 K). Despite being hosted in an L-shaped vacuum system, in Phase 1, ETpathfinder will operate with two complete and folded Fabry–Perot Michelson Interferometers (FPMIs); one in each arm. The silicon mirrors used as input end end mirrors of the FPMIs are 15 cm in diameter and with 8 cm thickness. The simplified optical layout for this configuration can be seen in part (a) of Figure 9.

In Phase 2 of the ETpathfinder project, the plan is that the two arms of the L-shaped vacuum system will be equipped with large, ET-like test masses of order 100 kg, with diameter ~45 cm. It is yet to be determined what type of silicon material will be available at that time and what will be used.

The mechanical layout of ETpathfinder can be seen in part b of Figure 9. The vacuum system consists of six towers in an L-shaped arrangement. Two table towers host optical benches that will be populated with the input and output optics, as well as steering optics and the main beam splitter. The four mirror towers are equipped with a sophisticated seismic isolation system in the form of a dual inverted pendulum system with an active platform in between. From this system a four stage pendulum is suspending the mirror to further reduce coupling from seismic motion. The layout of the lowest suspension stage is described in detail in Section 3.2.2.

In order to operate the interferometer at cryogenic temperatures the input and end mirror of the 10 m Fabry–Perot resonators in the interferometer arms are cooled. To reach the cryogenic temperatures via either radiative cooling to 120 K or conductive cooling to 15 K, the mirrors are housed in a suspended cryostat with a multi-layered cryogenic shield around them. The specifics of this system are summarised in Section 3.2.3.

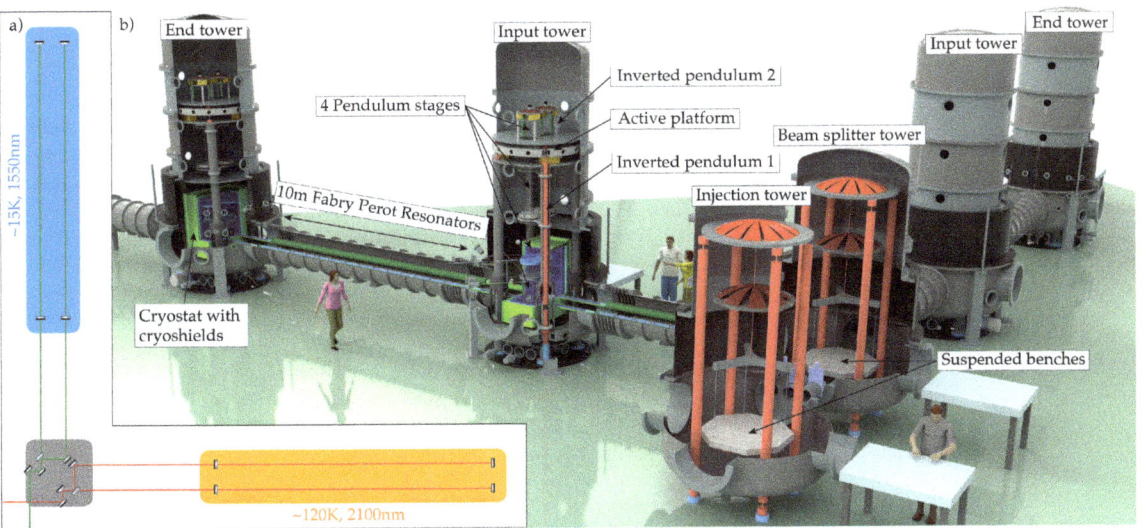

Figure 9. Panel (**a**) shows the simplified optical layout of ETpathfinder Phase 1, in which the two arms of the vacuum system host a full FPMI each, while operating with different parameters. Panel (**b**) shows a rendered model of the ETpathfinder vacuum system with a cross section (image courtesy of Marco Kraan, Nikhef).

3.2.2. Silicon Mirror-Suspensions

As mentioned in the introduction, utilising a new material for the optics and suspension elements in a GW detector will require extensive research and development. Although silicon has ideal thermal conductivity and low mechanical loss at cryogenic temperatures, it is also a crystalline semi-conductor, which can lead to some additional challenges when understanding its optical and mechanical properties. Thus, the entire process of creating a coated silicon optic that is suitable to be used in a next generation GW detector, such as ET is still to be defined.

The silicon test masses of the Einstein Telescope are planned to be 45 cm in diameter and ~200 kg in size [16], with a substrate purity that is high enough to allow a 1550 nm or 2 µm laser beam to pass through it without absorbing more than 5 ppm/cm of the laser power. Thus, the first step of finding a silicon mass for ET is finding a source that can grow a large enough diameter and high resistivity monocrystalline silicon ingot. Then, this ingot must be cut, shaped, polished, and optically coated. All these subsequent steps are not currently defined and require further research and development.

In Phase 1 of the ETpathfinder project, it is planned to operate the two interferometers with 15 cm diameter, 8 cm thick FZ silicon test masses. The FZ silicon ingots that were acquired for ETpathfinder have an average diameter of 155 mm and a resistivity of >10 kΩcm. Within the ETpathfinder project the optical absorption of this material will be measured in a Photothermal Common-Path Interferometer (PCI) [77], to verify its usability. The stringent requirements for polishing the test masses of the ETpathfinder project, follow closely the requirements, such as in advanced LIGO for a fused silica test mass [37] and can be transferred to ET.

Due to its crystalline nature, the polishing of silicon compared to silica is another challenge; however, it should be within the reach of current technologies due to industrial experience regarding *X*-ray mirrors [16]. In the ETpathfinder project, the aim is to find such suitable polishing companies and work closely together with these companies to receive the highest possible quality of surface polish for the silicon mirrors and to verify their quality in an interferometric measurement in the ETpathfiner interferometer.

In Phase 2 of the ETpathfinder project, starting in 2025, it is planned to operate only one FPMI in the facility, utilising larger silicon mirrors of order 100 kg and with a diameter similar to ET, e.g., 45 cm.

The outcomes from Phase 1 will determine what operating temperature and what laser system will be used in Phase 2. In the design for ET, the plan for the cryogenic silicon suspensions is to have silicon optics attached to silicon suspension elements, hanging on small diameter silicon fibres that, together, would form the quasi-monolithic last stage of the suspension.

Here, the silicon suspension elements fulfil a crucial role, both as a cryogenic heat link between the upper suspension stages and the test mass, and as a low thermal noise connection that is strong enough to hold the $\sim$200 kg mass. In practice, creating silicon suspension elements presents a considerable mechanical challenge. This is due in part to the crystalline nature of silicon and its high thermal conductivity. Its crystalline nature means that the silicon needs to be grown as one monocrystalline ingot, instead of simply being heated and pulled into a fibre, as is done for fused silica fibres [78].

Grinding down a larger diameter ingot to a smaller diameter fibre and then further processing it in order to attain a well polished surface pushes the limits of what industry can currently provide. Additionally, silicon's thermal conductivity and tendency to develop high local thermal stress when melted means that connecting the silicon fibres to another suspension element, which is required to connect to the optic, is also challenging. Thus, the CO_2 laser welding used in the fused silica suspensions of AdV and aLIGO is unfeasible in case of silicon.

In the ETpathfinder project, this challenge is increased by the necessity of even thinner silicon suspension fibres that for ET, due to the lighter weight of the mirrors. The development of suspensions and suspension elements for the ETpathfinder project is active research and different methods are under investigation. Currently, mechanically polished suspension rods are being assessed for their quality and usability in the ETpathfinder monolithic suspension. For this, the mechanical loss of these silicon suspension fibres will be measured in a Gentle Nodal Suspension (GeNS) setup [79]. It is further planned to measure the thermal conductivity, and ultimately the breaking strength of these suspension fibres. However, in parallel it will also be investigated if silicon suspension fibres can be grown in a suitable small diameter.

The ETpathfinder project will approach the challenges connected with the use of silicon in different stages. In Phase 1 of the project, state-of-the-art silicon optics will be created, using the highest quality silicon, silicon polish, and optical coatings that are currently available. These optics will first be suspended via metal wires in a newly developed multi-stage cryogenic suspension shown in full in Figure 10a. In Figure 10c, the prototype in its current state can be seen.

In a later stage of Phase 1, the cryogenic suspension will be upgraded with silicon suspension elements and fibres, quasi-monolithicly connecting the silicon optics to the upper mass, as in Figure 10b. As reported above, in Phase 2 ETpathfinder will operate a single interferometer in which large, ET-like test masses will be implemented. This multi-stage approach allows the ETpathfinder collaboration more time to develop methods to create and attach silicon suspension elements, in parallel with developing the process for creating large silicon optics.

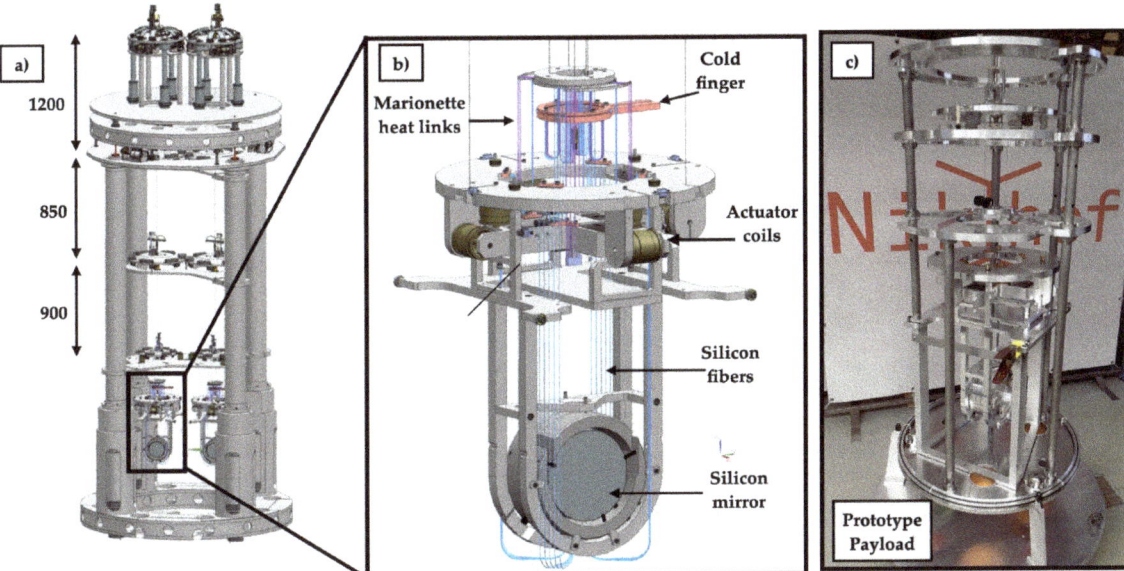

Figure 10. Part (**a**) The full suspension chain as it will be inside the vacuum system. In this picture, also the seismic pre-isolation system can be seen. Part (**b**) The payload [71] of ETpathfinder. Please note the conductive blue heat links that connect to the cold finger. These are thin wires to minimise vibrational coupling from the cryogenic system. Part (**c**) A photograph of the Nikhef payload prototype. In this prototype, the aforementioned coupling strengths are investigated.

3.2.3. Cryogenics

One of the new technologies that ETpathfinder will test is the cryogenic system for the mirrors. The goal is to be able to operate the interferometer at different temperatures: first at room temperature, i.e., 300 K and then at 120 and at 15 K. This means that we need to be able to control the mirror at these temperatures and that the cryogenic system will not limit the sensitivity. We aim to keep the amplitude spectral density of the vibrational motions of the mirrors surfaces below 10^{-18} m/$\sqrt{\text{Hz}}$ at 10 Hz. Part (a) of Figure 11 shows the cross section of the tower of the end mirrors.

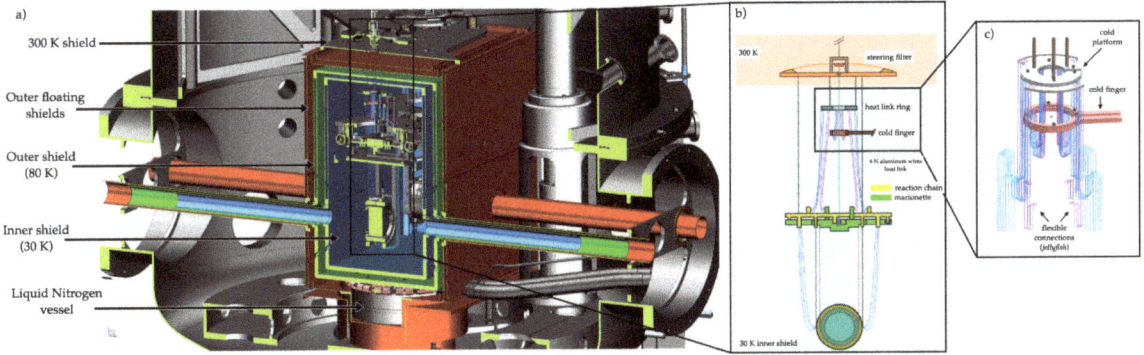

Figure 11. (**a**) Cross section of the tower of the end mirrors. The liquid nitrogen vessel and the thermal shields that enclose the mirrors are shown. (**b**) Jellyfish connections that will be used to cool the suspended test masses. (**c**) Detail of the Jellyfish connections with the cold platform and the cold finger. Adapted from Ref. [71].

The mirrors, marionettes and reaction masses are surrounded by three double-walled thermal radiation shields. The inner one (in blue in the picture) is used to keep a temperature of 30 K. The outer shield (in green) is connected to the vessel at the bottom, that contains 40 L of liquid nitrogen and maintains a temperature of 80 K. The floating outer shield (in red) is used to reduce the radiation load on the first shield. In addition, there will be another shield at 300 K (in grey) used to stabilize the temperature of the filter present on the top.

While 120 K can be reached using radiative cooling without introducing significant vibrational noise, going below 100 K requires conductive cooling. This is done using flexible connections of ultra-pure aluminium wires, called "jellyfish" (see part (b) and (c) of Figure 11).

The cold finger (in pink in the figure), which is connected to the inner shield, is the lowest temperature heat link and it ends into two rings, one for each test mass. The rings are connected to the cold platform through the "jellyfish" construction. The "jellyfish" wires connect the cold platform to the marionette (in purple in the figure) and to the reaction chain (in blue), that is hanging from the geometric anti-spring (GAS) filter present on the top of the thermal shields. The presence of two stages helps to reduce the vibrational noise. The mechanical transfer function of the "jellyfish" is measured at Nikhef beforehand on the payload prototype shown in part c) of Figure 10.

3.3. Status and Future Plans

ETpathfinder is under construction at the University of Maastricht and its timeline is shown in Figure 12. We are currently in Phase 1, at the end of "ETPF infrastructure" phase, with only the vacuum system that still needs to be completed. While the infrastructure works are underway, payload prototypes for preliminary tests are being built.

The prototype of the payload, aka "Proto-0" (shown in part c) of Figure 10), is ready and measurements of the transfer function are in progress. This prototype includes the test mass, the reaction mass and the marionette. Meanwhile "Proto-1", which includes the inverted pendulum, is being built and it will be ready soon. During Phase 1 two temperatures (15 and 120 K) and two wavelengths (1550 and 2090 nm) will be studied, one in each arm of the L-shaped vacuum system.

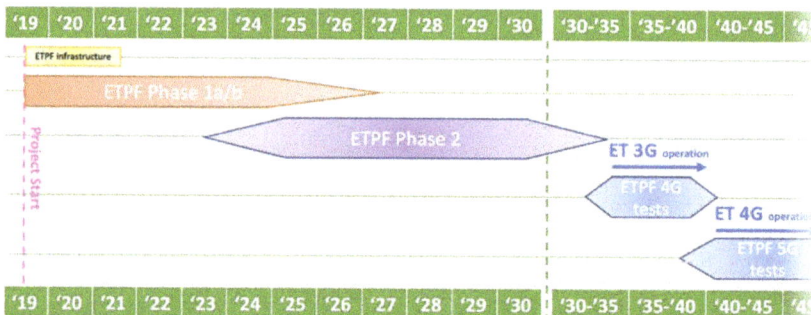

Figure 12. Overview of the timeline of ETpathfinder. The dashed green line shows approximately the start of the ET observation run (not yet defined), after which ETpathfinder will continue to be used as prototype facility for future upgrades [71].

Around 2025, ETpathfinder will enter Phase 2. In this phase, it will work on a single temperature and wavelength, which will be chosen depending on the outcome of Phase 1, and with test masses similar to the ones that will be used for ET. Phase 2 is planned to end around 2030, in order to be able to give useful inputs for the ET final design.

Apart from the already mentioned new technologies, new Quantum Noise reduction techniques are also planned to be tested in ETpathfinder. These techniques could further reduce low-frequency noise in next generation detectors.

The life of ETpathfinder, however, will not end with the birth of ET. ETpathfinder has been designed to be as flexible as possible, in order to be used also as a test facility for future upgrades of any third generation GW detector.

4. Sargrav Laboratory

The surroundings of the Sos Enattos mine in Sardinia are considered as a possible location for ET due to its very low seismic and anthropogenic noise. Such local characteristics allowed the construction of the SarGrav laboratory aiming to host underground experiments, such as low seismic noise experiments, cryogenic payloads, low frequency and cryogenic sensor development. Nonetheless, a fundamental physics experiment, Archimedes, is the first experiment in Sos Enattos' surface area.

4.1. Sos-Enattos Site

The Sos Enattos Mine, located in Sardinia in the territory of Lula, stands on a European tectonic plate far away from any fault lines making its micro-seismic activity among the lowest on Earth, and it has one of the lowest population density in Europe resulting in an area of low anthropogenic disturbances.

Since the site has been nominated to host ET, a strong effort has been conducted to characterise the site in terms of geology, environmental and seismic noise, and a laboratory located at the mine was build, namely SarGrav. Such a laboratory currently hosts sensors and experiments: four broadband triaxial seismometers (one surface vault installation, three underground); three short-period triaxial seismometers; two magnetometers (one buried at the surface and one underground); one tiltmeter (the Archimedes prototype); and one weather station.

Long-term measurements at different depths are ongoing, exploiting the potentialities offered by the Sos Enattos mine. The seismic data from 1 January to 30 April 2020 at two different depths around Sos Enattos were analysed (SOE0 is 400 m above sea level and SOE2 is −110 m with respect to SOE0). In Figure 13 ([80]), the probabilistic power spectra density (PPSD) was obtained using Ref. [81]. A PPSD study implies that transient noise lines (if not stationary disturbances) disappear against the stability of the natural background.

The PSD calculation was done with the obspy tool [82] and a Konno–Omachi smoothing procedure was applied [83]. Between 5×10^{-3} Hz and 2×10^{-1} Hz the PPSD of the underground station SOE2 follows the new low-noise approaches Peterson's New Low Noise Model ([84], NLNM).

The seismic noise between 0.1–1 Hz is dominated by microseismic peaks from sea waves, which are seasonal features. A peak around $f \approx 0.2$ Hz is seen in the Figure and it is caused by secondary microseism. In the frequency interval of 1–10 Hz (Figure 13c,d) the noise of both stations reach their lowest values respectively at 3.5 Hz (≈ -154 dB) and 4.5 Hz (≈ -157 dB) meeting ET's criteria of a noise level of −154 dB at 4 Hz even at surface [80]. The PPSD is affected by the self noise of the digitizer, increasing the noise above 3 Hz. New measurements at Sos Enattos with a reduced input range of the digitizer shows that the seismic noise at Sos Enattos (SOE2) between 3 Hz and 7 Hz crosses the NLNM (Ref. [85], Figure 14).

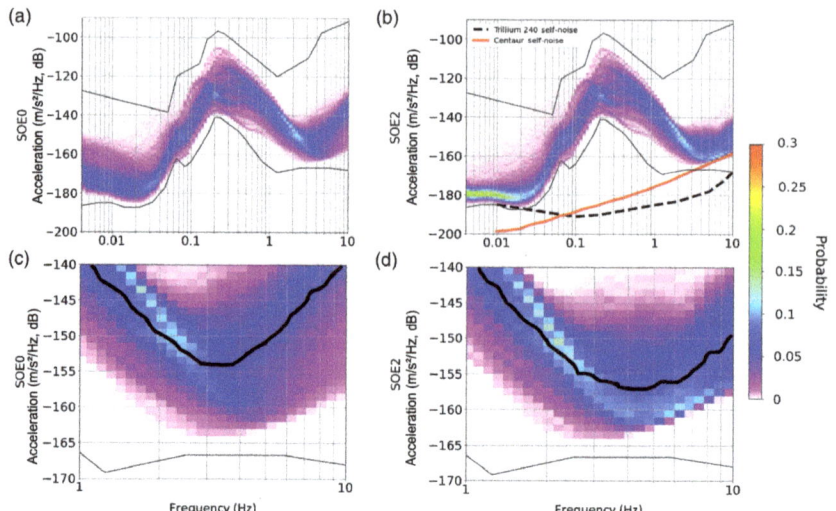

Figure 13. Acceleration power spectral density in Sos Enattos for two sensors: SOE0 (**a**), which is located 400 m above sea and SOE2 (**b**) located at −110 m with respect to SOE0. The data of both sensors were taken in 2020 showing the acceleration spectra versus frequency. Plots (**c**,**d**) are zooms of (**a**,**b**) in the 1 to 10 Hz interval including the median (black line). Reproduced from Ref. [80].

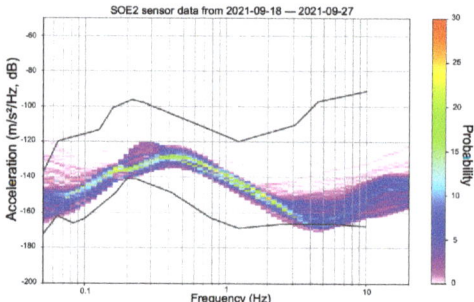

Figure 14. New measurements at Sos Enattos with a reduced input range of the digitizer shows that the seismic noise at Sos Enattos, SOE2 seismometer (−111 m), between 3 Hz and 7 Hz [85]. Acceleration PSD of the horizontal EW channel.

Above 1 Hz, the noise is mainly due to the low population density of the region. Nonetheless, the acoustic noise in the mine has not been affected by any artificial ventilation systems as the mine has a natural airflow (see [86]). Additionally, the main magnetic noise contribution at Sos Enattos is related to the Schumann resonances of the Earth's magnetic field (see [86]).

The correlation between the seismic PSD amplitude with the wave height provided by Copernicus Marine Environment Monitoring Service (CMEMS) in the western Mediterranean sea and the Biscay Bay (Atlantic Ocean) from April to August 2019 at Sos Enattos was also performed [86].

CMEMS provides reference information on the dynamics of the ocean and marine ecosystems for the global ocean and Europeans seas. Such a study showed that the dominant noise contribution comes from the Tyrrhenian Sea, and the best correlation between microseism and sea waves was found for waves with a period of 4.5 s. The maximized ground vibration, due to sea waves at T = 4.5 s, is on the west part of the island with microseismic peaks at $f = 0.22$ Hz [86].

The mine per se has a significant infrastructure, and studies as well as an experiment are in motion to scientifically explore the area proposed for ET.

4.2. Archimedes, the First Experiment in the SarGrav Surface Laboratories

Due to the very low seismic and anthropic noise, SarGrav laboratories are suitable to host experiments requiring a very quiet environment. Archimedes is a fundamental physics experiment currently installed in the SarGrav surface facilities, which aims at measuring the interaction between quantum vacuum fluctuations and gravity. Due to its configuration, Archimedes prototype contributed to the direct ground tilt measurement (which is defined as the absolute angular motion of the ground) at the Sos Enattos site in the frequency region between 2 and 20 Hz, which is a region of interest for ET seismic noise characterization. Hence, it has shown to be a suitable sensor that can contribute to the Newtonian noise cancellation.

4.2.1. Aim of the Experiment

The Archimedes experiment comes within the debate around one of the longstanding problems of fundamental physics: the incompatibility between General Relativity and Quantum Theory [87–89]. To add a contribution to this topic, Archimedes will measure the force exerted by the gravitational field on a Casimir cavity whose vacuum energy is modulated with a superconductive transition.

More precisely, an YBCO (Yttrium Barium Copper Oxide) crystal is exploited as a stack of Casimir cavities. Indeed, when the crystal temperature is lowered below the superconductive transition point, the crystal layers become reflective, and they form a series of Casimir cavities on top of one another. In this condition, only zero-point electromagnetic modes that satisfy the boundary conditions can survive inside each cavity.

On the other hand, when the crystal temperature is increased, it goes back to the normal state and behaves like a dielectric; therefore, no boundary conditions for the EM field must be satisfied and all the zero-point modes can survive inside the YBCO sample. In the hypothesis that vacuum energy interacts with gravity, a force directed upwards should act on the Casimir cavity due to the missing weight of the expelled EM modes. This situation is analogous to the Archimedes buoyancy of fluid, after which the experiment takes its name.

The expected torque generated with this modulation is of the order of 5×10^{-13} N m/$\sqrt{\text{Hz}}$ when integrated over 2 months. The measurement strategy consists of modulating the reflectivity of the Casimir cavity plates by performing a superconducting transition of the two YBCO samples suspended to the balance arms, as shown in Figure 15. In this way, vacuum energy will be periodically expelled from the Casimir cavity, and its weight will be modulated. To measure this effect, a beam-balance will be used as a small force detector.

To allow the superconductive transition, the whole experiment will be cooled in a cryostat, at liquid nitrogen temperature. Moreover, each suspended sample will be surrounded by a shield, which will periodically heat up the sample to bring it from superconductive to normal state. To allow the system thermalization, the modulation will be performed at few tens of mHz. For such a small force to be detected, a very sensitive beam-balance has been suitably designed, and a first prototype has been realized to test its performances.

4.2.2. The Balance Prototype and the Final Setup

A first prototype of the experiment has been built and commissioned in Naples Federico II University laboratories. Few updates have been performed to improve the prototype performances and sensitivity. The main characteristics of the current version are described hereafter.

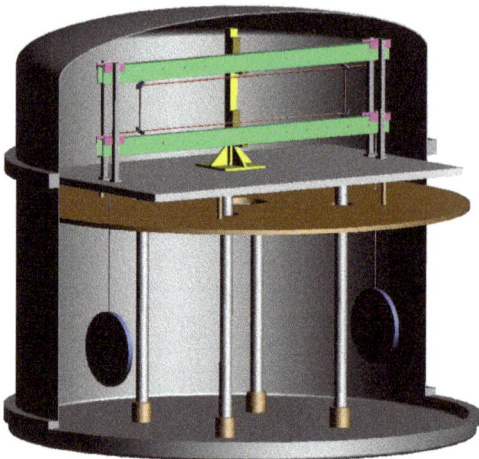

Figure 15. Overview of the Archimedes experiment. The two disks are two YBCO samples, which represent a stack of Casimir cavities. See text for more details.

Mechanics

A schematic of the beam-balance is shown in Figure 16. The balance arm is 50 cm long and is suspended to two solid columns through two thin wire-like suspensions. Since the balance requires a very high torque-to-tilt transfer function, the moment of inertia and the suspension restoring force must be kept as low as possible.

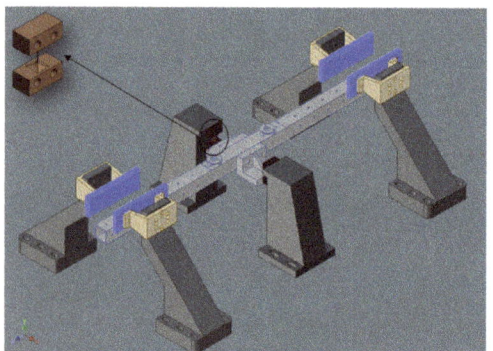 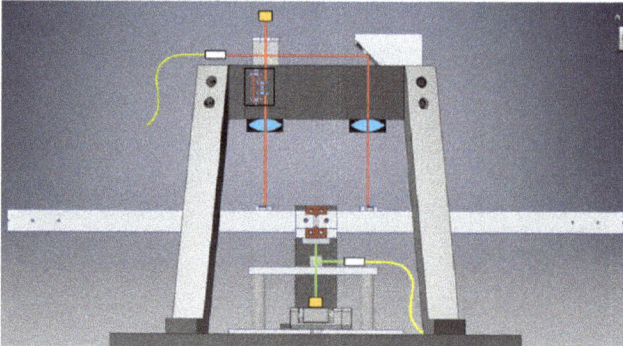

Figure 16. (**Left**): balanced arm (in grey) suspended through two thin Cu-Be joints (highlighted in brown, upper-left corner). The two interferometer mirrors are on the top of the arm and at its end electrostatic actuators are sketched in blue. (**Right**): optical scheme of the Archimedes prototype. The balanced arm shown on the left corresponds to the horizontal bar in this figure. Here, the red trace corresponds to the optical path of the interferometric readout. The optical path length between the two arms is equalized using an optical delay line, which is visible below the beam splitter. The green trace, instead, corresponds to the path of the optical lever beam. Adapted from Ref. [90].

To satisfy the first condition, the arm is hollow and made of aluminium, which keeps its weight low. To accomplish the second requirement, the suspensions section is made as thin as possible, and two flexible joints of Cu-Be 0.5 mm× 0.1 mm are used for this purpose. If the balance centre of mass is kept within 10 μm from the suspension point, its resonance frequency results as around 25 mHz.

Optical Readout

A coarse and a fine optical readout are used to monitor the balance angular position, both anchored to the ground, so that any arm angular motion is referred to it. An optical lever using a SLED (superluminescent diode) is positioned to have the beam impinging perpendicularly on a mirror placed on the lower face of the balance arm (green trace in Figure 16). The beam displacement is sensed by a quadrant photodiode. This optical readout is used as an initial reference position for the arm tilt (coarse positioning).

The finer positioning is provided by a Michelson interferometer, which warrants a high sensitivity. Represented with the red trace in Figure 16, the interferometer beam impinges perpendicularly on the mirrors, to minimize the coupling with undesired degrees of freedom. The interferometer has two unequal arms. However, to avoid common noises coupling in the output channel, an optical delay line located after the beam splitter reflection and made of four right-angle prisms is used to equalize the optical paths. Finally, amplitude noise subtraction is performed by normalizing the output signal by the input power.

Actuation and Control

To keep the prototype arm in its working point (interferometer output on half-fringe), electrostatic actuators are used. Highlighted in blue in Figure 16, they are made of two metallic 2×10 cm plates located along each of the arm ends. A digital filter fed with the interferometer output provides the control, suppressing the low frequency motion and leaving the arm free to oscillate at frequencies higher than the unity gain frequency (0.3 Hz).

The final setup of the Archimedes experiment is currently being installed in the SarGrav surface laboratories, in a dedicated hangar. Unlike the prototype, in the final setup, the measurement arm will be 1.4 m long, and an additional reference arm will be employed for ground tilt cancellation, as shown in Figure 15. The whole setup is installed on a solid support (Figure 17), which will be enclosed in the inner of three vacuum chambers, shown in Figure 17.

Figure 17. (**Left**): Picture of the final setup (still under construction) positioned on a solid table grounded to the cryostat basis. It is positioned inside the Archimedes hangar. (**Right**): Tent structure hosting the cryostat cover.

4.3. Archimedes Prototype as Tiltmeter

Archimedes prototype represents a good inertial reference for ground tilts in the Newtonian Noise frequency region, since the balance arm is free above the control bandwidth, which is above the Unity Gain Frequency ($\approx$300 mHz). When no samples are suspended at the end of its arms, indeed, the beam-balance can be used as a rotational sensor, i.e., a tiltmeter.

First Tilt Measurements at Virgo and Sos-Enattos

Prior to the start of the Virgo observation run O3, the tiltmeter was installed at the Virgo site, and remained there for several months for a joint data taking with the Virgo interferometer. In particular, the tiltmeter was positioned at the North-end building, on the same floor where seismometers and other sensors are located. This period of data taking allowed the ground tilt measurements at the Virgo site, and close attention was paid to the frequency band of 2–20 Hz.

The results are reported in [91]. At a few Hz, a tilt of 8×10^{-11} rad/$\sqrt{Hz}$ was measured. Above 10 Hz, the spectrum presents few resonances, which resulted to be partially coherent with the signals from neighbouring seismometers or interferometer dark fringe signal. Moreover, the tilt noise level detected between 10 and 20 Hz was found to be compatible with the tilt measurements performed at the LIGO sites [92]. Finally, very interesting results where found by comparing the reconstructed tilt signal from seismometer array and the tiltmeter signal [93].

In February 2020, the balance prototype was moved to the SarGrav laboratories in Lula. After few months of updates, devoted to the optical delay line installation and to the amplitude noise subtraction implementation described above, the site tilt was measured in the NN frequency region (2–20 Hz). The results are reported in [90].

In Figure 18, the ground tilt measured at Sos-Enattos site (blue curve) is compared to the ground tilt measured at Virgo (red curve). The level of ground tilt measured at Sos-Enattos is around 10^{-12} rad/$\sqrt{Hz}$, which is two orders of magnitude below the tilt noise level at the Virgo site. To stay conservative, the value of tilt measured at Sos-Enattos is taken as the tiltmeter sensitivity. This means that the instrument can measure the Virgo site tilt with an SNR greater than 100, which is sufficient to be used for the NN reduction in Virgo. On the other hand, this measurement also shows that the tilt level at the Sos-Enattos site is at least two orders of magnitude lower than the Virgo site.

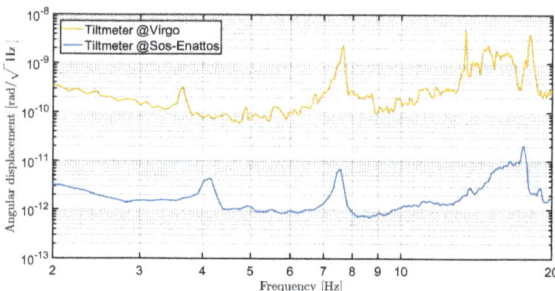

Figure 18. Ground tilt measurement at Virgo and Sos Enattos. Adapted from Ref. [90].

As a plan for the near future, the tiltmeter will be installed at the Virgo site before the start of the next observation run O4 and beyond, to participate to the NN cancellation campaign. At the same time, a similar tiltmeter will still be kept in Sos-Enattos, in order to continue the tilt noise characterization of the site, possibly also underground.

This will surely be helpful for Archimedes ground noise subtraction. At the same time, a further improvement of the sensitivity will allow a more precise measurement of the ground tilt level in Sos-Enattos, which can add important knowledge about the tilt noise level at the Sardinian site, providing a reliable projection of this kind of noise source on the ET sensitivity curve.

5. Einstein Telescope EMR Site and Technology (E-TEST)

The main activities and technologies used in the E-TEST are addressed in this section. It first presents the objectives of the E-TEST and its main tasks. Then, an overview on the cryogenic and suspension design are demonstrated. Lastly, a detailed description of the site characterization is presented. Further details are shown in the following subsections below.

5.1. Introduction and Objectives

Two directions of research relevant to ET are conducted within E-TEST. A prototype mirror suspension system at cryogenic temperature is being developed and the geological characteristics of Euregio Meuse-Rhine (EMR) region are mapped and investigated.

E-TEST results will shape the ET mirror suspension, auxiliary optics and cryogenic design as well as a thorough study of the EMR region. the main tasks of the E-TEST geological research campaign are:

- characterisation of the ambient seismic field in the region to optimally select the location of the corner points and to guide the seismic isolation system design; and
- characterisation of the subsurface geology in terms of material properties to guide the geotechnical engineering efforts of such underground infrastructure.

To build a cryogenic suspension prototype for the silicon mirror suspension, a novel approach is adopted mainly to reduce the overall height and the infrastructure complexity. The currently proposed ET suspension system is a 17-m long Virgo-style superattenuator [54]. The E-TEST approach combines a LIGO-style active tables and a Virgo-style inverted pendulum (IP) stage. This will provide better isolation performance particularly at low frequency since the active control stage provides attenuation below its resonance frequencies. The mirror and the penultimate stage will be in a cryostat at $T \approx 20$ K. The main features of the E-TEST prototype design are the design and the development of:

- ultra-cold vibration control, which includes vacuum and cryogenics, active vibration isolation and the design of a seismic isolation system; and
- optical engineering, which includes silicon mirror manufacture and test, laser and optics at 2 microns wavelength and assembly and validation of the whole setup.

The E-TEST prototype will not provide the desired isolation performance of ET since the overall height of the prototype is limited by the vacuum chamber height (4.2 m). However, it will validate the above strategies that make significant improvements to the current design possible.

5.2. Design of the Cryogenic Suspension Prototype

As part of E-TEST, a novel approach combining an actively controlled inertial platform, such as LIGO suspension system [12] and an IP stage, such as used in Virgo [94] or KAGRA [95] is investigated. The aim is to decrease the overall height and infrastructure complexity of the initially proposed 17-m-long suspension system of ET [16], which was first presented as a fiducial design in the 2011 conceptual design report [28].

Better isolation performance at low frequency is expected since the inertial control approach yields isolation below the system's resonant modes, which is not possible with passive isolation systems [96]. The suspension system will be mounted inside a large vacuum chamber in order to eliminate acoustic noise.

The E-TEST suspension system, shown in Figure 19, consists of one active platform that provides inertial control in the six degrees of freedom. The three legs of the IPs are mounted on the active platform and support the top stage. The IP provides a large amount of isolation in the horizontal direction as the resonance frequency can be tuned to extremely low values (about 70 mHz in KAGRA [96] and 30 mHz in Virgo [94]). Additionally, the IP stage provides means for positioning the parts suspended from the top stage, which can compensate for the tidal drift [28,97]. The top stage houses a large Geometric Anti-Spring (GAS) filter for vertical isolation. From the GAS filter, a marionette is suspended, which is mainly used to position the cryogenic payload.

This cryogenic part contains the cold platform and the test mass, which will be operated at cryogenic temperature (20 K). The cold platform is a cryogenic test-bed for sensors, such as the cryogenic superconducting inertial sensors [98,99] and the test mass is suspended. Additionally, a smaller cryostat has been developed with a cylindrical cold volume—down to 6 K-of 15 cm diameter and 15 cm height to test the performance of the cryogenic sensors and equipment before mounting them inside the E-TEST cryostat to validate their operation.

The radiative cooling is provided by a cryostat of which half is part of the suspended penultimate mass, i.e., attached to the cold platform. GW detector designs that use higher mirror temperatures can employ radiative cooling more easily. This is because the total radiated power P_{rad} of an object with emissivity ϵ is directly proportional to the fourth power of the object temperature T as $P_{rad} = \epsilon \sigma A T^4$, where σ is the Stefan–Boltzmann constant and A the radiating area. Additionally, ϵ typically reduces significantly for even the most emissive materials and coating at $T < 50$ K. The only way to radiatively cool mirrors at ET temperatures, i.e., $T < 20$ K is to increase the radiating area. The E-TEST design achieves this by interlacing a large suspended array of fins with another actively cooled array. The fin structure increases the surface area by more than a factor of 10.

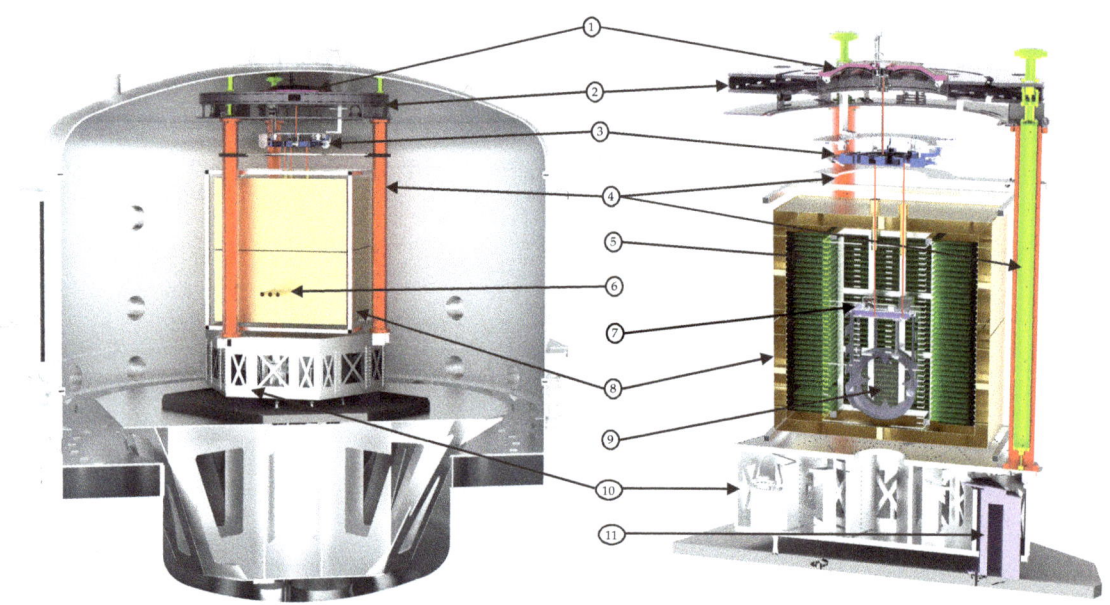

Figure 19. Overview of the E-TEST prototype design. A large vacuum tank (**left**) hosts the cryogenic mirror suspension (**right**). From top to bottom we can see (1) the top GAS filter, (2) the top stage, (3) the marionette and (4) the inverted pendulum legs within pipes that support a reference ring below the top stage. The cryogenic part features (5) the inner cryostat, which has the interlacing fin type heat exchanger. The whole cryostat features (6) three access points for outside experiments to interact with the cryogenic mirror. The inner cryostat is attached to (7) the cold platform. The inner cryostat fins interlace into the fins of the (8) outer cryostat, which provides a cold environment and houses the (9) 100 kg silicon mirror. All of this is supported by (10) an active platform, which provides a stable and quiet environment. In turn, the active platform hangs from three large blades with have a (11) support pillar on the ground.

5.2.1. Optical Engineering

Hanging from the suspensions in a cryogenic environment is the large silicon mirror. The goal is to acquire a >100 kg silicon test mass, with an as large as possible diameter to approach the envisioned 45 cm for ET. As mentioned before, a switch to silicon is necessary for cryogenic GW detectors as fused silica becomes mechanically lossy at low temperature.

An additional switch to a longer wavelength laser, e.g., 1550 nm or around 2 micron, is necessary as silicon is only transmissive there. Using longer wavelengths will decrease the shot noise at the same laser power as the lower energy per photon means the number of photons per second, and thus the quantum statistics improve. The silicon test mass will be polished, coated and characterised by various experiments.

Once the test mass is suspended and in the cryostat, the three tubes visible in Figure 19 provide access to the cold mirror. Outside the vacuum tank, a 5–10 W single mode laser with around 2090 nm wavelength is developed. High quality photodetectors at that wavelength are also developed. Lastly, low-loss optical coatings operating at these wavelengths, and conditions unfamiliar to GW scientists and engineers, are under investigation.

The goals for the laser include single mode beam quality and a high stability in output power and frequency combined with a narrow linewidth. To achieve that, a seed-source and a two-stage amplifier system with additional internal stabilization mechanisms will be developed. This approach follows basic laser design based on a Ho:YAG crystal-based seed source to define the spectral properties as well as holmium-doped fibre amplifiers for the power scaling. The photodiode development is strongly coupled to the laser developments to end up with an optimal wavelength match. The photodetectors are characterised in terms of spectral dependence of quantum efficiency, (dark) noise and overall stability. Additionally, optimization of readout protocols is targeted in terms of signal-to-noise ratio and readout speed.

The E-TEST prototype aspires to acquire a substrate with a mass, purity and dimensions well on track towards the ET mirrors (45 cm diameter, 210 kg). After polishing, characterisation of the substrate will take place using three experiments of which two are shown in Figure 20: a white light interferometer for precise mirror surface quality characterisation, an interferometric measurement scheme using the silicon substrate as a Fabry–Perot etalon to determine its temperature [100] and mechanical loss measurements of internal mechanical modes using a fm/$\sqrt{Hz}$ interferometer [101] excited by a tiny hammer, i.e., a small mass-spring element.

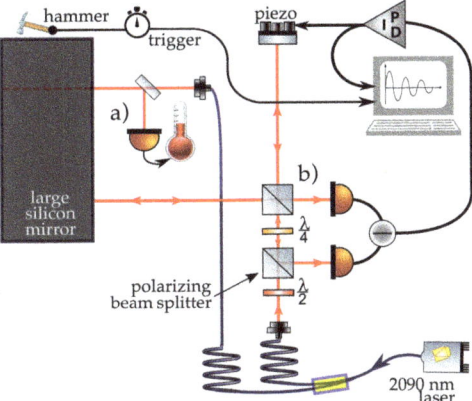

Figure 20. The E-TEST prototype optical experiments: (**a**) the temperature measurement and (**b**) the quality factor measurement. The experiments probe the mirror by having access through the threex tubes into the cryostat visible in Figure 19.

Finally, crystalline coating layers are characterised regarding, e.g., their optical and elastic properties, which are important to estimate the noise behaviour of the ultimate coatings.

5.3. Site Characterization

The ET corner points should be as vibration free as possible. In order to identify candidate sites and optimally select the corner point locations, a series of passive seismic campaigns are planned to capture the ambient seismic field. Two data from two campaigns were previously collected and are openly available online through KNMI/ORFEUS [102]. Figure 21 presents the EMR region and the locations of the concluded seismic campaigns.

Additional campaigns are planned, and the data collected will be added to the 3T network (see Figure 21) data archive. The data collected by these campaigns will be used to model the spatial distribution of the noise in several frequency bands. In addition to the broadband response in the 0.5 to 20 Hz band, we will study the response at narrow-band intervals. Additionally, the data will be used to image the subsurface.

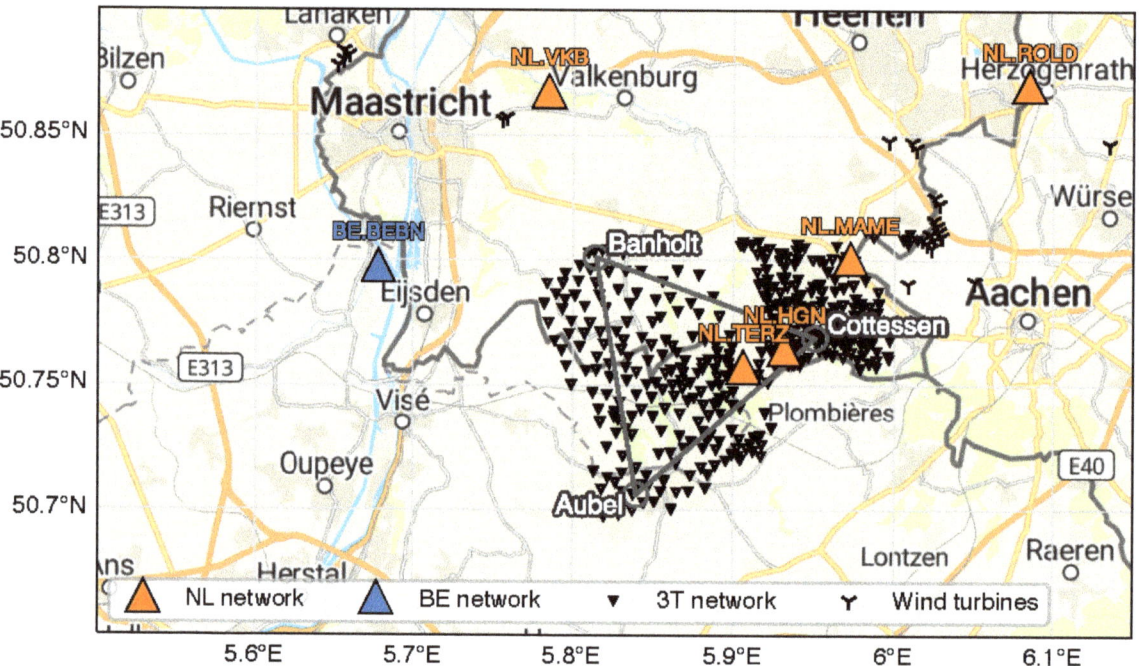

Figure 21. Overview map of the EMR region. The existing permanent seismic stations (triangles) are labelled with the network and stations codes. The 3T seismic campaign stations are indicated by upside-down triangles. The wind turbines in the region are indicated with a "Y" symbol. Note the large cluster of wind turbines North-West of the city of Aachen. The proposed corner point locations are labelled with small black circles.

5.3.1. Noise at the Surface vs. Noise at Depth

The first borehole station in the region is the NL.TERZ in Terziet, as shown in Figure 21. The station hosts a broadband seismometer at the surface and at a depth of 250 m. Seismic noise at the surface is generally attenuated with increasing depth, especially when soft, unconsolidated soil layers at the surface overlay hard rock layers. This attenuation is visible in the power spectral density (PSD) calculated for the surface and borehole seismometers. At frequencies above 1 Hz, noise from anthropogenic activity becomes significant. The noise is attenuated by 10 to 40 dB relative to the surface (see Figure 22). However, several spectral peaks are visible both at the surface and at depth.

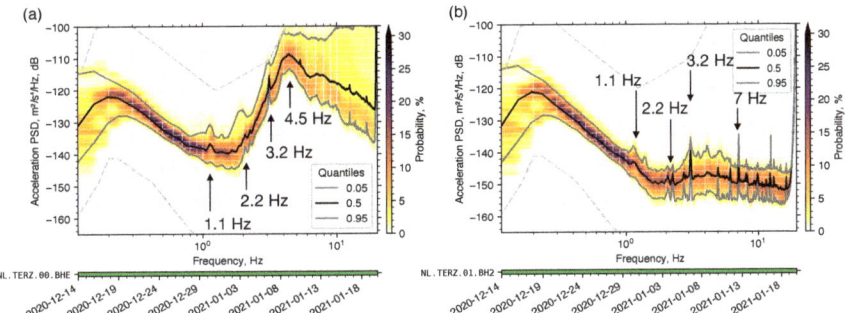

Figure 22. Acceleration PSD at the NL.TERZ (The Netherlands, Terziet) station. (**a**) Surface seismometer, and (**b**), Borehole seismometer at 250 m depth. PSD was calculated using the McNamara and Buland [81] method with half-hour long windows overlapping by 50% between 14 December 2020 and 20 January 2021. No smoothing has been applied to the spectra.

5.3.2. Spectral Peaks Associated with the Wind Turbines

To trace the origin of the spectral peaks identified in Figure 22a, a seismic monitoring campaign was deployed to the west of the Aachen windpark. The sensors were deployed on 14 December 2020 and retrieved on 19 January 2021. This period was chosen to capture the ambient seismic field during the relatively quiet holiday period (Christmas and New Year's) and the typically strong winds in the region.

During this period, there were days with almost no wind, and there were days with more than 25 m/s (90 km/h) wind. During this campaign there was also an active swarm of earthquakes unravelling in the vicinity of Rott, Germany, roughly 20 km south-east to the deployed sensors. These were well recorded by the seismic campaign as-well-as by the NL and BE seismic networks.

Figure 23a presents PSDs from select stations at varying distances from the Aachen wind park. The amplitude at the 1.1, 2.2 and 3.2 Hz spectral peaks, which are observed at all stations in the region, are consistently decreasing as a function of distance from the Aachen wind park. Additionally, the amplitude of the entire spectrum, but specifically of the above spectral peaks, is in correlation with wind speed as presented in Figure 23 for the borehole seismometer at 250 m depth in Terziet. The 7 Hz peak is caused by the fundamental vertical resonance frequency in the steel casing lining the inside of the borehole.

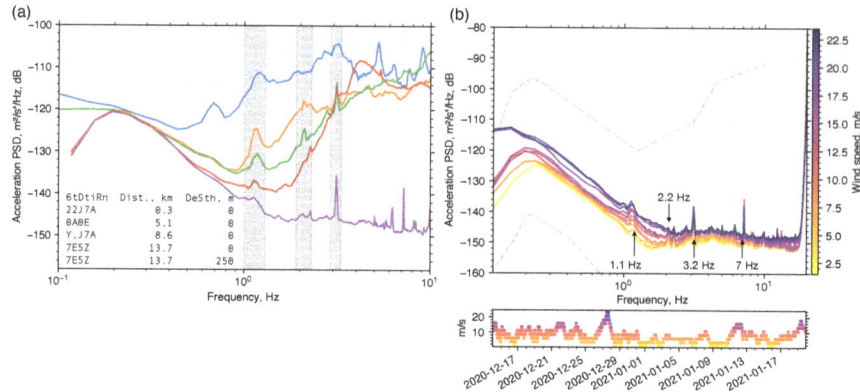

Figure 23. Acceleration PSD (**a**) of select stations at varying distances from the Aachen wind park, and (**b**) as a function of wind speed. The 1.1, 2.2, and 3.2 Hz spectral peaks are associated with the wind turbines north-west of Aachen and the amplitudes at these frequencies decrease as a function of distance from the Aachen wind park and are in correlation with the wind speed measured at the top of the wind turbines.

5.3.3. Geological Characterisation

The site investigated within the E-TEST project is located in the Euregio Meuse-Rhine region between Belgium (including Flanders and Wallonia), The Netherlands and Germany. Within this region, existent sources of noises have been identified and potential locations of the ET infrastructures minimizing the impact of these noises are defined. In this region, Paleozoic rocks of Devonian to Namurian–Wesphalian ages are found. In the North, these rocks are overlain by Cretaceous and Quaternary soft sediments.

These rocks were faulted and folded by different episodes of tectonic activity. A detailed study of the subsurface is required to consider the feasibility of installing an Einstein Telescope infrastructure a few hundreds of meters at depth given the large uncertainty on geological conditions and the lack of data in the underground. In the E-TEST project, deep investigations are therefore deployed to characterise the EMR underground in terms of geological structures, rocks properties and hydraulic properties.

Different geophysical methods, including active seismic (with sledge hammer and vibro-trucks) or passive seismic surveys, classical or deep (up to 300 m) electrical resistivity tomographies (ERT) surveys, are conducted to collect data from various depth ranges and different resolutions in order to image the shallow and deep subsurface. Deep boreholes (up to 300 m) are drilled along the potential axes of the tunnels and corners of the ET infrastructures.

The cores sampled during drillings are used to perform geomechanical tests to determine the mechanical properties of the rocks. Geophysical and hydraulic testing of these boreholes will be performed after their completion. Seismometers will be installed in these boreholes to study the ambient seismic field at the depth of the ET infrastructures.

All the collected data are used to build a 3D geological model of the EMR region and to select the most appropriate area for the ET infrastructures. The specific implementation of ET for this site will be proposed based on the results of the geomechanical tests. A 3D groundwater flow model of the region is also developed to anticipate and organize potentially needed drainage and pumping during the building and operation of the ET infrastructures. The model will also be used to identify the potential impact of the underground infrastructures on its surroundings.

6. Summary

The research described above works towards the low-frequency goals of ET. The current GW detectors do not reach their design sensitivity below 30 Hz. This is largely due to technical noise, such as couplings between different interferometer control degrees of freedom, some of which are not fully understood [1]. While beyond the scope of this article, we can report on an effort towards improved system design with the control systems in mind, something that was largely lacking in the design of current detector systems. This will enable the fruition of the efforts of the four facilities described here to reach the low-frequency fundamental noise projection shown earlier in Figure 2. In the following, we summarize the research efforts of each research facility.

The experience with a large mass payload for Advanced Virgo will be fundamental for designing a prototype payload for ET. Moreover, given the long-term experience of the ARC team on test-mass payload topics and the close collaboration with KAGRA teams, the promised development foreseen in ET context is sustainable. The construction of the building that will host the next generation GW laboratory in Rome has finally started. The facility is designed to allow the development of a full-scale cryogenic payload prototype. Its design started in 2021 in parallel with the construction of a low-vibration cooling line prototype.

ETpathfinder is a state-of-the-art research facility located at the University of Maastricht. This facility will operate two 10-meter-long interferometers operating at cryogenic temperatures, allowing the team to develop and test technologies for next generation GW detectors within a fully integrated system. Key technologies that are in development at ETpathfinder are the following. The fabrication of mirrors and suspension elements from silicon, a material new to our field. These suspended silicon optics will be cooled to different cryogenic temperatures, e.g., 15 and 120 K, using new cryogenic approaches at two different laser wavelengths: 1550 and 2090 nm.

SarGrav facility is a laboratory located in Sardinia, Italy, intended to explore the potential of the region in terms of seismic noise to host ET. The laboratory has several extremely low noise infrastructures, designed to host low-frequency seismic noise experiments and cryogenic payloads. Throughout the old mine ducts and elsewhere, there are several underground stations available for site monitoring. This has a strong synergy with ET candidature activities, namely site monitoring, support in terms of logistics and person power, mechanics and masonry services.

Archimedes was the first fundamental physics experiment installed in SarGrav surface laboratories, aiming at investigating the interaction between quantum vacuum fluctuations and gravity. The Archimedes prototype is currently working as a tiltmeter, and has measured a rotational displacement two orders of magnitude lower than the Virgo site in the Newtonian noise band, showing the suitability of the Sos Enattos site.

The 17-m-tall suspension in the current ET designs are largely regarded as placeholders for solutions that are under development. One such development is the E-TEST suspension prototype, which combines active and passive isolation strategies to suspend a >100 kg silicon mirror as well as a radiatively cooled cryostat. The facility is being built at the Centre Spatial de Liège in Belgium. In parallel, the region in the South of the Netherlands, East of Belgium, and West of Germany is subject to geological and hydrogeological investigations to determine the suitability of the said region to host ET.

The research into developing and testing the key technologies described throughout this article will inform the design of next generation GW detectors, such as ET and its many upgrades to come.

Author Contributions: The authors wish to thank their respective collaborations for being allowed to represent the research facilities on this early career researcher writing team. L.P. presented the low-frequency science case as part of the introduction. The ARC team consists of S.D.P., V.M. and A.R. and the ETpathfinder section was written by M.H., J.-S.H. and D.P. SarGrav was described by A.A. (Archimedes) and I.T.e.M. (site characterisation) and E-TEST by V.G.N. and A.S. (cryo-suspension) and P.O. and S.S.-K. (site characterisation). Finally, J.v.H. conceptualised the structure and focused on general logistics, the abstract, introduction, Section 5.2.1 and closing sections. All authors have read and agreed to the published version of the manuscript.

Funding: Amaldi Research Center is an excellence centre in the Sapienza University (Department of Physics) in Rome and it is funded for five years period (2018–2022) by MIUR with an associated CUP number B81I18001170001. The ETpathfinder project in Maastricht is funded by Interreg Vlaanderen-Nederland, the province of Dutch Limburg, the province of Antwerp, the Flamish Government, the province of North Brabant, the Smart Hub Flemish Brabant, the Dutch Ministry of Economic Affairs, the Dutch Ministry of Education, Culture and Science, and by own funding of the involved partners. The SarGrav laboratory is supported by: INFN with Protocollo di Intesa tra Ministero dell'Universita' e della Ricerca, la Regione Autonoma della Sardegna, l'Istituto Nazionale di Fisica Nucleare e l'Università degli Studi di Sassari; University of Sassari with Accordo di Programma tra la Regione Autonoma della Sardegna, l'Università degli Studi di Sassari, l'Istituto Nazionale di Fisica Nucleare, l'Istituto Nazionale di Geofisica e Vulcanologia, l'Università degli Studi di Cagliari e l'IGEA S.p.a (progetto SAR-GRAV, funds FSC 2014–2020 Patto per lo sviluppo della Regione Sardegna); Università degli Studi di Sassari with "Fondo di Ateneo per la ricerca 2019" ; Istituto Nazionale di Fisica Nucleare and by the Italian Ministero dell' Università e della Ricerca with PRIN 2017 Research Program Framework, n. 2017SYRTCN. L. Loddo and IGEA miners supported the operation in Sos Enattos. Interreg is the European Union's tool to support cross-border projects, which otherwise would not be conducted. The Interreg V-A Euregio Meuse-Rhine (EMR) programme invests almost EUR 100 million in the development of our region until the end of 2020. The E-TEST project is perfored within the framework of the Interreg V-A Euregio Meuse-Rhine Programme, with 50% funding from the European Regional Development Fund (ERDF). By investing EU funds in Interreg projects, the European Union is investing directly in economic development, innovation, territorial development, social inclusion and education in the Euregio Meuse-Rhine. The E-TEST project is co-funded by the Walloon Region, the Flanders Region, the Province of Flemish Brabant, the Province of Belgian Limburg, the Dutch Ministry of Economic Affairs, the Province of Dutch Limburg, the North Rhine-Westphalia, and by own funding of the involved partners.

Institutional Review Board Statement: Not applicable.

Data Availability Statement: All seismic data for the SarGrav site and the Python code used to produce the plots are available at the site repository https://etrepo.df.unipi.it:8000/ (accessed on 12 January 2022). Accounts can be requested by contacting the authors. All seismic data for the EMR site is freely and openly available through https://www.fdsn.org/networks/detail/3T_2020/ (accessed on 8 January 2022) for the 3T network and https://www.fdsn.org/networks/detail/NL/ (accessed on 8 January 2022) for the NL network.

Acknowledgments: For a thorough review, the authors would like to thank Edwige Tournefier and Mario Martinez on behalf of the ET steering committee, and Jeff Kissel on behalf of the LIGO Scientific Collaboration. We additionally express out gratitude for the research performed by all partner institutes. For ARC, these are KAGRA team and CUORE collaboration. For ETpathfinder these are Nikhef, Maastricht University, University of Antwerp, Ghent University, Katholieke Universiteit Leuven, Université catholique de Louvain, Hasselt University, Vrije Universiteit Brussel, Fraunhofer Institute for Laser Technology ILT, RWTH Aachen, University of Twente, Eindhoven University of Technology, Université de Liège, VITO, TNO, LAPP, Albert Einstein Institute, Universitat de Barcelona, Vrije Universiteit Amsterdam and University of Birmingham. For SarGrav these are Regione Sardegna, University of Sassari, INFN, University of Napoli, University of Rome "La Sapienza", University of Sassari, Ego-Virgo, CNR-INO, Université Aix Marseille. And for E-TEST these are ULiège, Fraunhofer Institute for Laser Technology ILT, RWTH Aachen, UHasselt, KULeuven, Nikhef, UBonn, the NMWP, KNMI, UMaastricht and UCLouvain.

Conflicts of Interest: The authors declare no conflict of interest.

References

1. Buikema, A.; Cahillane, C.; Mansell, G.L.; Blair, C.D.; Abbott, R.; Adams, C.; Adhikari, R.X.; Ananyeva, A.; Appert, S.; Arai, K.; et al. Sensitivity and performance of the Advanced LIGO detectors in the third observing run. *Phys. Rev. D* **2020**, *102*, 062003. [CrossRef]
2. Acernese, F. et al. [Virgo Collaboration]. Increasing the Astrophysical Reach of the Advanced Virgo Detector via the Application of Squeezed Vacuum States of Light. *Phys. Rev. Lett.* **2019**, *123*, 231108. [CrossRef] [PubMed]
3. Akutsu, T. et al. [KAGRA Collaboration]. Overview of KAGRA: Detector Design and Construction History. *Prog. Theor. Exp. Phys.* **2020**, *2021*, 05A101. [CrossRef]

4. Lough, J.; Schreiber, E.; Bergamin, F.; Grote, H.; Mehmet, M.; Vahlbruch, H.; Affeldt, C.; Brinkmann, M.; Bisht, A.; Kringel, V.; et al. First Demonstration of 6 dB Quantum Noise Reduction in a Kilometer Scale Gravitational Wave Observatory. *Phys. Rev. Lett.* **2021**, *126*, 041102. [CrossRef]
5. Abbott, B.P. et al. [LIGO Scientific Collaboration and Virgo Collaboration]. Observation of Gravitational Waves from a Binary Black Hole Merger. *Phys. Rev. Lett.* **2016**, *116*, 061102. [CrossRef]
6. Abbott, B.P. et al. [LIGO Scientific Collaboration and Virgo Collaboration]. GW170817: Observation of Gravitational Waves from a Binary Neutron Star Inspiral. *Phys. Rev. Lett.* **2017**, *119*, 161101. [CrossRef]
7. Abbott, B.P. et al. [LIGO Scientific Collaboration and Virgo Collaboration]. GWTC-1: A Gravitational-Wave Transient Catalog of Compact Binary Mergers Observed by LIGO and Virgo during the First and Second Observing Runs. *Phys. Rev. X* **2019**, *9*, 031040. [CrossRef]
8. Abbott, R. et al. [LIGO Scientific Collaboration and Virgo Collaboration]. GWTC-2: Compact Binary Coalescences Observed by LIGO and Virgo during the First Half of the Third Observing Run. *Phys. Rev. X* **2021**, *11*, 021053. [CrossRef]
9. Abbott, R. et al. [LIGO Scientific Collaboration, Virgo Collaboration and KAGRA Collaboration]. GWTC-3: Compact Binary Coalescences Observed by LIGO and Virgo During the Second Part of the Third Observing Run. *arXiv* **2021**, arXiv:2111.03606.
10. Abbott, R. et al. [LIGO Scientific Collaboration, Virgo Collaboration and KAGRA Collaboration]. The population of merging compact binaries inferred using gravitational waves through GWTC-3. *arXiv* **2021**, arXiv:2111.03634.
11. Abbott, R. et al. [LIGO Scientific Collaboration, Virgo Collaboration and KAGRA Collaboration]. Constraints on the cosmic expansion history from GWTC-3. *arXiv* **2021**, arXiv:2111.03604.
12. Matichard, F.; Lantz, B.; Mittleman, R.; Mason, K.; Kissel, J.; Abbott, B.; Biscans, S.; McIver, J.; Abbott, R.; Abbott, S.; et al. Seismic isolation of Advanced LIGO: Review of strategy, instrumentation and performance. *Class. Quantum Gravity* **2015**, *32*, 185003. [CrossRef]
13. Acernese, F.; Antonucci, F.; Aoudia, S.; Arun, K.G.; Astone, P.; Ballardin, G.; Sturani, R. Measurements of Superattenuator seismic isolation by Virgo interferometer. *Astropart. Phys.* **2010**, *33*, 8. [CrossRef]
14. Ushiba, T.; Akutsu, T.; Araki, S.; Bajpai, R.; Chen, D.; Craig, K.; Enomoto, Y.; Hagiwara, A.; Haino, S.; Inoue, Y.; et al. Cryogenic suspension design for a kilometer-scale gravitational-wave detector. *Class. Quantum Gravity* **2021**, *38*, 085013. [CrossRef]
15. Evans, M.; Adhikari, R.X.; Afle, C.; Ballmer, S.W.; Biscoveanu, S.; Borhanian, S.; Weiss, R. A Horizon Study for Cosmic Explorer Science, Observatories, and Community. Tech. Rep. CE DCC Number P2100003. 2021. Available online: https://dcc.cosmicexplorer.org/CE-P2100003 (accessed on 12 November 2021).
16. ET Steering Committee. ET Design Report Update 2020 (Einstein Telescope Collaboration, 2020). 2020. Available online: https://apps.et-gw.eu/tds/ql/?c=15418 (accessed on 6 January 2022).
17. Abbott, B.P.; Abbott, R.; Abbott, T.; Abraham, S.; Acernese, F.; Ackley, K.; Adams, C.; Adya, V.; Affeldt, C.; Agathos, M.; et al. Prospects for observing and localizing gravitational-wave transients with Advanced LIGO, Advanced Virgo and KAGRA. *Living Rev. Relativ.* **2018**, *24*, 1–69. [CrossRef]
18. Maggiore, M.; Broeck, C.V.D.; Bartolo, N.; Belgacem, E.; Bertacca, D.; Bizouard, M.A.; Branchesi, M.; Clesse, S.; Foffa, S.; García-Bellido, J.; et al. Science case for the Einstein telescope. *J. Cosmol. Astropart. Phys.* **2020**, *2020*, 50. [CrossRef]
19. Zaroubi, S. The epoch of reionization. *First Galaxies* **2013**, *396*, 45–101.
20. Abbott, R.; Abbott, T.D.; Acernese, F.; Ackley, K.; Adams, C.; Adhikari, N.; Adhikari, R.X.; Adya, V.B.; Affeldt, C.; Agarwal, D.; et al. All-sky search for short gravitational-wave bursts in the third Advanced LIGO and Advanced Virgo run. *Phys. Rev. D* **2021**, *104*, 122004. [CrossRef]
21. Maggiore, M. *Gravitational Waves: Volume 1: Theory and Experiments*; Oxford University Press: Oxford, UK, 2008; Volume 1.
22. Abbott, R. et al. [The LIGO Scientific Collaboration, the Virgo Collaboration and the KAGRA Collaboration]. Tests of General Relativity with GWTC-3. *arXiv* **2021**, arXiv:gr-qc/2112.06861.
23. Hinderer, T.; Lackey, B.D.; Lang, R.N.; Read, J.S. Tidal deformability of neutron stars with realistic equations of state and their gravitational wave signatures in binary inspiral. *Phys. Rev. D* **2010**, *81*, 123016. [CrossRef]
24. Broeck, C.V.D. Astrophysics, cosmology, and fundamental physics with compact binary coalescence and the Einstein Telescope. *J. Phys. Conf. Ser.* **2014**, *484*, 012008. [CrossRef]
25. Lackey, B.D.; Kyutoku, K.; Shibata, M.; Brady, P.R.; Friedman, J.L. Extracting equation of state parameters from black hole-neutron star mergers: Nonspinning black holes. *Phys. Rev. D* **2012**, *85*, 044061. [CrossRef]
26. Abbott, B.P.; Abbott, R.; Abbott, T.D.; Acernese, F.; Ackley, K.; Adams, C.; Adams, T.; Addesso, P.; Adhikari, R.X.; Adya, V.B.; et al. GW170817: Measurements of Neutron Star Radii and Equation of State. *Phys. Rev. Lett.* **2018**, *121*, 161101. [CrossRef] [PubMed]
27. Abbott, B.P.; Abbott, R.; Abbott, T.D.; Abraham, S.; Acernese, F.; Ackley, K.; Adams, C.; Adhikari, R.X.; Adya, V.B.; Affeldt, C.; et al. GW190425: Observation of a Compact Binary Coalescence with Total Mass∼3.4 M⊙. *Astrophys. J. Lett.* **2020**, *892*, L3. [CrossRef]
28. Abernathy, M.; Acernese, F.; Ajith, P.; Allen, B.; Amaro Seoane, P.; Andersson, N.; Aoudia, S.; Astone, P.; Krishnan, B.; Barack, L.; et al. Einstein Gravitational Wave Telescope Conceptual Design Study. 2011. Available online: https://tds.virgo-gw.eu/?call_file=ET-0106C-10.pdf (accessed on 4 January 2022).
29. Abbott, R. et al. [The LIGO Scientific Collaboration, the Virgo Collaboration and the KAGRA Collaboration]. Searches for Gravitational Waves from Known Pulsars at Two Harmonics in the Second and Third LIGO-Virgo Observing Runs. *arXiv* **2021**, arXiv:astro-ph.HE/2111.13106.

30. Johnson-McDaniel, N.K.; Owen, B.J. Maximum elastic deformations of relativistic stars. *Phys. Rev. D* **2013**, *88*, 044004. [CrossRef]
31. Brito, R.; Ghosh, S.; Barausse, E.; Berti, E.; Cardoso, V.; Dvorkin, I.; Klein, A.; Pani, P. Gravitational wave searches for ultralight bosons with LIGO and LISA. *Phys. Rev. D* **2017**, *96*, 064050. [CrossRef]
32. Abbott, R.; Abe, H.; Acernese, F.; Ackley, K.; Adhikari, N.; Adhikari, R.; Adkins, V.; Adya, V.; Affeldt, C.; Agarwal, D.; et al. All-sky search for gravitational wave emission from scalar boson clouds around spinning black holes in LIGO O3 data. *arXiv* **2021**, arXiv:2111.15507.
33. Brito, R.; Cardoso, V.; Pani, P. *Superradiance: New Frontiers in Black Hole Physics*; Springer: Berlin/Heidelberg, Germany, 2020. [CrossRef]
34. Dall'Osso, S.; Stella, L. Millisecond Magnetars. *arXiv* **2021**, arXiv:astro-ph.HE/2103.10878.
35. Cardoso, V.; Franzin, E.; Maselli, A.; Pani, P.; Raposo, G. Testing strong-field gravity with tidal Love numbers. *Phys. Rev. D* **2017**, *95*, 084014. [CrossRef]
36. Agullo, I.; Cardoso, V.; del Rio, A.; Maggiore, M.; Pullin, J. Potential Gravitational Wave Signatures of Quantum Gravity. *Phys. Rev. Lett.* **2021**, *126*, 041302. [CrossRef] [PubMed]
37. Pinard, L.; Michel, C.; Sassolas, B.; Balzarini, L.; Degallaix, J.; Dolique, V.; Flaminio, R.; Forest, D.; Granata, M.; Lagrange, B.; et al. Mirrors used in the LIGO interferometers for first detection of gravitational waves. *Appl. Opt.* **2017**, *56*, C11–C15. [CrossRef] [PubMed]
38. Schroeter, A.; Nawrodt, R.; Schnabel, R.; Reid, S.; Martin, I.W.; Rowan, S.; Schwarz, C.; Koettig, T.; Neubert, R.; Thurk, M.; et al. On the mechanical quality factors of cryogenic test masses from fused silica and crystalline quartz. *arXiv* **2007**, arXiv:0709.4359.
39. Adhikari, R.X.; Arai, K.; Brooks, A.F.; Wipf, C.; Aguiar, O.; Altin, P.; Barr, B.; Barsotti, L.; Bassiri, R.; Bell, A.; et al. A cryogenic silicon interferometer for gravitational-wave detection. *Class. Quantum Gravity* **2020**, *37*, 165003. [CrossRef]
40. Lyon, K.; Salinger, G.; Swenson, C.; White, G. Linear thermal expansion measurements on silicon from 6 to 340 K. *J. Appl. Phys.* **1977**, *48*, 865–868. [CrossRef]
41. McGuigan, D.; Lam, C.; Gram, R.; Hoffman, A.W.; Douglass, D.H.; Gutche, H.W. Measurements of the mechanical Q of single-crystal silicon at low temperatures. *J. Low Temp. Phys.* **1978**, *30*, 621–629. [CrossRef]
42. Theuerer, H.C. Method of Processing Semiconductive Materials. U.S. Patent 3060123A, 23 October 1962.
43. Lin, W.; Huff, H. *Handbook of Semiconductor Manufacturing Technology*; Doering, R., Nishi, Y., Eds.; CRC Press: Boca Raton, FL, USA, 2008; Chapter 8.
44. Goodman, W.A.; Goorsky, M.S. Reduction of the bulk absorption coefficient in silicon optics for high-energy lasers through defect engineering. *Appl. Opt.* **1995**, *34*, 3367–3373. [CrossRef]
45. Kwee, P.; Bogan, C.; Danzmann, K.; Frede, M.; Kim, H.; King, P.; Pöld, J.; Puncken, O.; Savage, R.L.; Seifert, F.; et al. Stabilized high-power laser system for the gravitational wave detector advanced LIGO. *Opt. Express* **2012**, *20*, 10617–10634. [CrossRef]
46. Valeria, S.; Matteo, B.; Mateusz, B.; Marco, B.; Giacomo, C.; Livia, C.; Beatrice, D.; Martina, D.L.; Sibilla, D.P.; Viviana, F.; et al. EPR experiment for a broadband quantum noise reduction in gravitational wave detectors. In Proceeding of the GRAvitational-Waves Science & technology Symposium (GRASS) 2019, Padova, Italy, 24–25 October 2019. [CrossRef]
47. Sibilla, D.P.; Luca, N.; Ettore, M.; Laura, G.; Paola, P.; Fulvio, R.; Piero, R.; Maurizio, P.; Martina, D.L.; Enrico, C.; et al. Small scale Suspended Interferometer for Ponderomotive Squeezing (SIPS) as test bench of the EPR squeezer for Advanced Virgo. In Proceeding of the GRAvitational-Waves Science & Technology Symposium (GRASS) 2019, Padova, Italy, 24–25 October 2019. [CrossRef]
48. Di Pace, S.; Naticchioni, L.; De Laurentis, M.; Travasso, F. Thermal noise study of a radiation pressure noise limited optical cavity with fused silica mirror suspensions. *Eur. Phys. J. D* **2020**, *74*, 227. [CrossRef]
49. Giacoppo, L.; Majorana, E.; Di Pace, S.; Naticchioni, L.; De Laurentis, M.; Sequino, V.; Basti, A. Towards ponderomotive squeezing with SIPS experiment. *Phys. Scr.* **2021**, *96*, 114007. [CrossRef]
50. Amaldi Research Center Webpage. Available online: https://www.phys.uniroma1.it/fisica/arc_amaldi_research_center (accessed on 6 January 2022).
51. Amaldi Research Center Webpage. Research Activities at ARC. Available online: https://www.phys.uniroma1.it/fisica/arc_research_activities (accessed on 6 January 2022).
52. Acernese, F.A.; Agathos, M.; Agatsuma, K.; Aisa, D.; Allemandou, N.; Allocca, A.; Meidam, J. Advanced Virgo: A second-generation interferometric gravitational wave detector. *Class. Quantum Gravity* **2015**, *32*, 024001. [CrossRef]
53. [The Virgo Collaboration]. Advanced Virgo Technical Design Report Technical Report VIR-0128A-12, Virgo Collaboration, 2012. Available online: https://tds.virgo-gw.eu/ql/?c=8940 (accessed on 6 January 2022).
54. Braccini, S.; Barsotti, L.; Bradaschia, C.; Cella, G.; Di Virgilio, A.; Ferrante, I.; Vinet, J.Y. Measurement of the seismic attenuation performance of the VIRGO Superattenuator. *Astropart. Phys. J.* **2005**, *23*, 557–565. [CrossRef]
55. Naticchioni, L.; on behalf of the Virgo Collaboration. The payloads of Advanced Virgo: Current status and upgrades. *J. Phys. Conf. Ser.* **2018**, *957*, 012002. [CrossRef]
56. [The Virgo Collaboration]. Virgo Suspensions and Payloads. Public Media. Available online: http://public.virgo-gw.eu/index.php?gmedia=zK53B&t=g (accessed on 6 January 2022).
57. Haughian, K.; Chen, D.; Cunningham, L.; Hofmann, G.; Hough, J.; Murray, P.; Nawrodt, R.; Rowan, S.; van Veggel, A.; Yamamoto, K. Mechanical loss of a hydroxide catalysis bond between sapphire substrates and its effect on the sensitivity of future gravitational wave detectors. *Phys. Rev. D* **2016**, *94*, 082003. [CrossRef]

58. Sakakibara, Y. A Study of Cryogenic Techniques for Gravitational Wave Detection. Ph.D. Thesis, University of Tokyo, Tokyo, Japan, 2014.
59. Kumar, R.; Chen, D.; Hagiwara, A.; Kajita, T.; Miyamoto, T.; Suzuki, T.; Sakakibara, Y.; Tanaka, H.; Yamamoto, K.; Tomaru, T. Status of the cryogenic payload system for the KAGRA detector. *J. Phys. Conf. Ser.* **2016**, *716*, 012017. [CrossRef]
60. Basti, F.; Frasconi, F.; Majorana, E.; Naticchioni, L.; Perciballi, M.; Puppo, P.; Rapagnani, P.; Ricci, F. A cryogenic payload for the third generation of gravitational wave interferometers. *Astropart. Phys.* **2011**, *35*, 67–75. [CrossRef]
61. Somiya, K. Detector configuration of KAGRA—The Japanese cryogenic gravitational-wave detector. *Class. Quantum Gravity* **2012**, *29*, 12. [CrossRef]
62. Majorana, E. Outline of Cryogenic Payload Compliance with Einstein Telescope LF. GWADW2021 Gravitational Wave Advanced Detector Workshop, 17–21 May 2021. Available online: https://agenda.infn.it/event/26121/contributions/136321/attachments/81472/106807/GWDAW21_majorana_1.pdf (accessed on 6 January 2022).
63. Bouaita, R.; Alombert-Goget, G.; Ghezal, E.; Nehari, A.; Benamara, O.; Benchiheub, M.; Cagnoli, G.; Yamamoto, K.; Xu, X.; Motto-Ros, V.; et al. Seed orientation and pulling rate effects on bubbles and strain distribution on a sapphire crystal grown by the micro-pulling down method. *CrystEngComm* **2019**, *21*, 4200–4211. [CrossRef]
64. Yamada, T.; Tomaru, T.; Suzuki, T.; Ushiba, T.; Kimura, N.; Takada, S.; Inoue, Y.; Kajita, T. High performance thermal link with small spring constant for cryogenic applications. *Cryogenics* **2021**, *116*, 103280. [CrossRef]
65. Douglas, R.; Van Veggel, A.; Cunningham, L.; Haughian, K.; Hough, J.; Rowan, S. Cryogenic and room temperature strength of sapphire jointed by hydroxide-catalysis bonding. *Class. Quantum Gravity* **2014**, *31*, 045001. [CrossRef]
66. Tokoku, C.; Kimura, N.; Koike, S.; Kume, T.; Sakakibara, Y.; Suzuki, T.; Kuroda, K. Cryogenic System for the Interferometric Cryogenic Gravitational Wave Telescope, KAGRA-Design, Fabrication, and Performance Test. *AIP Conf. Proc.* **2014**, *1573*, 1254–1261. [CrossRef]
67. Yamada, T. Low-Vibration Conductive Cooling of KAGRA Cryogenic Mirror Suspension. Ph.D. thesis, University of Tokyo, Tokyo, Japan, 2020.
68. Arnaboldi, C.; Avignone, F.T., III; Beeman, J.; Barucci, M.; Balata, M.; Brofferio, C.; Vanzini, M. Physics potential and prospects for the CUORICINO and CUORE experiments. *Astropart. Phys.* **2003**, *20*, 91–110. [CrossRef]
69. Rapagnani, P. Cryogenics for the Einstein Telescope. GWADW2019-Gravitational-Wave Advanced Detector Workshop—From Advanced Interferometers to Third Generation Observatories, 19–25 May 2019. Available online: https://agenda.infn.it/event/15928/contributions/89753/ (accessed on 6 January 2022).
70. Rapagnani, P. The Amaldi Research Center ET Cryogenic Lab in Rome. GWADW2021 Gravitational Wave Advanced Detector Workshop, 17–21 May 2021. Available online: https://agenda.infn.it/event/26121/timetable/?view=standard (accessed on 6 January 2022).
71. [The ETpathfinder Collaboration]. ETpathfinder Design Report. ET TDS 2020, ET-0011A-20. Available online: https://apps.et-gw.eu/tds/ql/?c=15645 (accessed on 20 January 2022).
72. Untina, A.; Amato, A.; Arends, J.; Arina, C.; Baars, M.; Baer, P.; Beaumont, W.; Bertolini, A.; Biersteker, S.; Binetti, A.; et al. ETpathfinder: A cryogenic testbed for interferometric gravitational-wave detectors. 2022, *in preparation*.
73. Meylahn, F.; Willke, B. Stabilized laser systems at 1550nm wavelength for future gravitational wave detectors. *arXiv* **2021**, arXiv:physics.optics/2112.03792.
74. Hasegawa, K.; Akutsu, T.; Kimura, N.; Saito, Y.; Suzuki, T.; Ueda, A.; Miyoki, S. Molecular adsorbed layer formation on cooled mirrors and its impacts on cryogenic gravitational wave telescopes. *Phys. Rev. D* **2019**, *99*, 022003. [CrossRef]
75. McCuller, L.; Whittle, C.; Ganapathy, D.; Komori, K.; Tse, M.; Fernandez-Galiana, A.; Barsotti, L.; Fritschel, P.; MacInnis, M.; Matichard, F.; et al. Frequency-Dependent Squeezing for Advanced LIGO. *Phys. Rev. Lett.* **2020**, *124*, 171102. [CrossRef]
76. Danilishin, S.L.; Knyazev, E.; Voronchev, N.V.; Khalili, F.Y.; Gräf, C.; Steinlechner, S.; Hennig, J.S.; Hild, S. A new quantum speed-meter interferometer: Measuring speed to search for intermediate mass black holes. *Light. Sci. Appl.* **2018**, *7*, 11. [CrossRef]
77. Alexandrovski, A.; Fejer, M.; Markosian, A.; Route, R. Photothermal common-path interferometry (PCI): New developments. In *Solid State Lasers XVIII: Technology and Devices*; Clarkson, W.A., Hodgson, N., Shori, R.K., Eds.; International Society for Optics and Photonics: Bellingham, WA, USA, 2009; Volume 7193, pp. 79–91. [CrossRef]
78. Cumming, A.V.; Bell, A.S.; Barsotti, L.; Barton, M.A.; Cagnoli, G.; Cook, D.; Cunningham, L.; Evans, M.; Hammond, G.D.; Harry, G.M.; et al. Design and development of the advanced LIGO monolithic fused silica suspension. *Class. Quantum Gravity* **2012**, *29*, 035003. [CrossRef]
79. Cesarini, E.; Lorenzini, M.; Campagna, E.; Martelli, F.; Piergiovanni, F.; Vetrano, F.; Losurdo, G.; Cagnoli, G. A "gentle" nodal suspension for measurements of the acoustic attenuation in materials. *Rev. Sci. Instrum.* **2009**, *80*, 053904. [CrossRef]
80. Di Giovanni, M.; Giunchi, C.; Saccorotti, G.; Berbellini, A.; Boschi, L.; Olivieri, M.; De Rosa, R.; Naticchioni, L.; Oggiano, G.; Carpinelli, M.; et al. A Seismological Study of the Sos Enattos Area—The Sardinia Candidate Site for the Einstein Telescope. *Seismol. Res. Lett.* **2020**, *92*, 352–364. [CrossRef]
81. McNamara, D.E.; Buland, R.P. Ambient Noise Levels in the Continental United States. *Bull. Seismol. Soc. Am.* **2004**, *94*, 1517–1527. [CrossRef]
82. Obspy: A Python Framework for Processing Seismological Data. Available online: https://docs.obspy.org/ (accessed on 15 December 2021).

83. Konno, K.; Ohmachi, T. Ground-motion characteristics estimated from spectral ratio between horizontal and vertical components of microtremor. *Bull. Seismol. Soc. Am.* **1998**, *88*, 228–241. [CrossRef]
84. Peterson, J. *Observations and Modeling of Seismic Background Noise*; Open-File Report 93-322; U.S. Geological Survey: Denver, CO, USA, 1993. [CrossRef]
85. Naticchioni, L.; Saccorotti, G.; Giunchi, C.; D'Orso, D. *Seismometer Installation in Two Boreholes for the Sardinia Site Characterisation*; Internal Note–Technical Report-ET-0426A-21. Available online: https://apps.et-gw.eu/tds/ql/?c=16147 (accessed on 4 October 2021).
86. Naticchioni, L.; Boschi, V.; Calloni, E.; Capello, M.; Cardini, A.; Carpinelli, M.; Cuccuru, S.; D'Ambrosio, M.; de Rosa, R.; Giovanni, M.D.; et al. Characterization of the Sos Enattos site for the Einstein Telescope. *J. Phys.* **2020**, *1468*, 012242. [CrossRef]
87. Bimonte, G.; Calloni, E.; Esposito, G.; Rosa, L. Energy-momentum tensor for a Casimir apparatus in a weak gravitational field. *Phys. Rev. D* **2006**, *74*, 085011. [CrossRef]
88. Calloni, E.; De Laurentis, M.; De Rosa, R.; Garufi, F.; Rosa, L.; Di Fiore, L.; Esposito, G.; Rovelli, C.; Ruggi, P.; Tafuri, F. Towards weighing the condensation energy to ascertain the Archimedes force of vacuum. *Phys. Rev. D* **2014**, *90*, 022002. [CrossRef]
89. Avino, S.; Calloni, E.; Caprara, S.; De Laurentis, M.; De Rosa, R.; Di Girolamo, T.; Errico, L.; Gagliardi, G.; Grilli, M.; Mangano, V.; et al. Progress in a Vacuum Weight Search Experiment. *Physics* **2020**, *2*, 1–13. [CrossRef]
90. Allocca, A.; Avino, S.; Calloni, E.; Archimedes Collaboration. Picoradiant tiltmeter and direct ground tilt measurements at the Sos Enattos site. *Eur. Phys. J. Plus* **2021**, *136*, 1069. [CrossRef]
91. Enrico, C. Archimedes Collaboration and Virgo Collaboration High-bandwidth beam balance for vacuum-weight experiment and Newtonian noise subtraction. *Eur. Phys. J. Plus* **2021**, *136*, 335. [CrossRef]
92. Coughlin, M.W.; Harms, J.; Driggers, J.; McManus, D.J.; Mukund, N.; Ross, M.P.; Slagmolen, B.J.J.; Venkateswara, K. Implications of Dedicated Seismometer Measurements on Newtonian-Noise Cancellation for Advanced LIGO. *Phys. Rev. Lett.* **2018**, *121*, 221104. [CrossRef]
93. Singha, A.; Hild, S.; Harms, J.; Tringali, M.C.; Fiori, I.; Paoletti, F.; Bulik, T.; Idzkowski, B.; Bertolini, A.; Calloni, E.; et al. Characterization of the seismic field at Virgo and improved estimates of Newtonian-noise suppression by recesses. *Class. Quantum Gravity* **2021**, *38*, 245007. [CrossRef]
94. Accadia, T.; Acernese, F.; Antonucci, F.; Astone, P.; Ballardin, G.; Barone, F.; Barsuglia, M.; Bauer, T.S.; Beker, M.; Belletoile, A.; et al. The seismic Superattenuators of the Virgo gravitational waves interferometer. *J. Low Freq. Noise Vib. Act. Control* **2011**, *30*, 63–79. [CrossRef]
95. Peña Arellano, F.E.; Sekiguchi, T.; Fujii, Y.; Takahashi, R.; Barton, M.; Hirata, N.; Shoda, A.; van Heijningen, J.; Flaminio, R.; DeSalvo, R.; et al. Characterization of the room temperature payload prototype for the cryogenic interferometric gravitational wave detector KAGRA. *Rev. Sci. Instrum.* **2016**, *87*, 034501. [CrossRef] [PubMed]
96. Okutomi, K. Development of 13.5-Meter-Tall Vibration Isolation System for the Main Mirrors in KAGRA. Ph.D. Thesis, University of Tokyo, Tokyo, Japan, 2019.
97. Takamori, A. Low Frequency Seismic Isolation for Gravitational Wave Detectors. Ph.D. Thesis, University of Tokyo, Tokyo, Japan, 2002.
98. van Heijningen, J.V. A fifty-fold improvement of thermal noise limited inertial sensitivity by operating at cryogenic temperatures. *J. Instrum.* **2020**, *15*, P06034. [CrossRef]
99. Ferreira, E.; Bocchese, F.; Badaracco, F.; van Heijningen, J.; Lucas, S.; Perali, A. Superconducting thin film spiral coils as low-noise cryogenic actuators. *J. Phys. Conf. Ser.* **2021**, *2156*, 012080. [CrossRef]
100. Komma, J.; Schwarz, C.; Hofmann, G.; Heinert, D.; Nawrodt, R. hermo-optic coefficient of silicon at 1550 nm and cryogenic temperatures. *Appl. Phys. Lett.* **2012**, *101*, 041905. [CrossRef]
101. Badaracco, F.; van Heijningen, J.V.; Ferreira, E.C.; Perali, A. A cryogenic and superconducting inertial sensor for the Lunar Gravitational–Wave Antenna, the Einstein Telescope and Selene-physics. *arXiv* **2022**, arXiv:2204.04150. Available online: https://arxiv.org/abs/2204.04150 (accessed on 15 October 2021).
102. Shani-Kadmiel, S.; Linde, F.; Evers, L.; Vin, B. Einstein Telescope Seismic Campaigns. [Data Set]. Royal Netherlands Meteorological Institute (KNMI). 2020. Available online: https://www.fdsn.org/networks/detail/3T_2020/ (accessed on 15 October 2021). [CrossRef]

Review

Cosmic Explorer: A Next-Generation Ground-Based Gravitational-Wave Observatory

Evan D. Hall

Department of Physics and LIGO Laboratory, Massachusetts Institute of Technology, Cambridge, MA 02139, USA; evanhall@mit.edu

Abstract: Cosmic Explorer is a concept for a new laser interferometric observatory in the United States to extend ground-based gravitational-wave astrophysics into the coming decades. Aiming to begin operation in the 2030s, Cosmic Explorer will extend current and future detector technologies to a 40 km interferometric baseline—ten times larger than the LIGO observatories. Operating as part of a global gravitational-wave observatory network, Cosmic Explorer will have a cosmological reach, detecting black holes and neutron stars back to the times of earliest star formation. It will observe nearby binary collisions with enough precision to reveal details of the dynamics of the ultradense matter in neutron stars and to test the general-relativistic model of black holes.

Keywords: gravitational waves; laser interferometers; black holes; neutron stars

Citation: Hall, E.D. Cosmic Explorer: A Next-Generation Ground-Based Gravitational-Wave Observatory. *Galaxies* **2022**, *10*, 90. https://doi.org/10.3390/galaxies10040090

Academic Editor: Gabriele Vajente

Received: 15 April 2022
Accepted: 6 July 2022
Published: 18 August 2022

Publisher's Note: MDPI stays neutral with regard to jurisdictional claims in published maps and institutional affiliations.

Copyright: © 2022 by the author. Licensee MDPI, Basel, Switzerland. This article is an open access article distributed under the terms and conditions of the Creative Commons Attribution (CC BY) license (https://creativecommons.org/licenses/by/4.0/).

1. Introduction

By the latter half of the 2030s, the field of gravitational-wave astronomy will be very different from what it is today. Space-based interferometers will collect millihertz signals from merging black holes with thousands to millions of solar masses [1,2]. Pulsar timing arrays will observe a nanohertz background of signals from black hole binaries with billions of solar masses [3]. Polarimetry of the cosmic microwave background may capture the imprint of gravitational waves from the early universe [4]. New experimental efforts will look for mega- and gigahertz gravitational waves arising from physics beyond the Standard Model [5], and for decihertz gravitational waves from astrophysical sources [6–9]. This multibanded array of observations will enhance a catalog of observations in the audio band (roughly ten hertz to several kilohertz) from the global network of ground-based, laser-interferometric gravitational-wave observatories—Advanced LIGO, Advanced Virgo, KAGRA, and GEO600—which should reach full sensitivity in this decade [10–14].

Given this wide spectrum of expected gravitational-wave data, what is the role of continued observation in the audio band? As will be argued in this review, even with a fulsome catalog of data from the current generation of audio-band gravitational-wave detectors, including from the incremental upgrades LIGO A+ and AdVirgo+ [15,16], many questions about stellar-mass binary systems or other phenomena in the gravitational-wave universe will remain unanswered until a network of more sensitive observatories comes online that can collect signals with higher fidelity and from further back in cosmic history. Other than switching to a radically different detection strategy, there are two ways to realize greater sensitivity across the audio band. The first way is to pursue technology improvements to realize a less noisy detector with a similar length as today's detectors, in an existing or potentially new observatory facility. The Voyager concept proposes shifting to a cryogenic test mass material and a longer laser wavelength, among other changes; if installed in the 4 km LIGO facilities, it would give a two- to threefold improvement in amplitude sensitivity over LIGO A+ [17]. This technology can also enable a kilohertz-focused gravitational-wave detector, which leads to the NEMO concept for a 4 km observatory in Australia [18,19]. The second way to realize greater sensitivity is to increase the detector length, since the strength of the gravitational-wave-induced optical signal grows linearly with the detector length, while most noises in the detector grow sublinearly. (This scaling holds so long as the travel time of the laser light down the detector arms is smaller than the period of the gravitational wave).

If technology improvements are coupled with a longer detector arm length, it seems possible to achieve a broadband tenfold improvement in amplitude sensitivity over today's detectors, and to push the lower end of the observation band to well below 10 Hz. In Europe, this idea has developed into the Einstein Telescope project, which aims to construct an underground observatory comprising six interferometers with 10 km arm length [20]. In the United States, the Cosmic Explorer project aims to construct a surface facility hosting a single 40 km interferometer, with current plans additionally calling for a second facility, widely separated from the first, hosting a single 20 km interferometer. The Einstein Telescope and Cosmic Explorer are both referred to as next-generation gravitational-wave observatories, since they represent a significant increase in sensitivity from the current generation of observatories.[1]

Broadly speaking, the ethos of Cosmic Explorer is to "just scale up" a LIGO facility and install a single interferometer with the best technology available. The germ of this idea goes back to at least 2013, when a noise analysis of a 40 km facility with the Advanced LIGO technology set was presented at the Advanced Detector Workshop in Elba [21]. Dwyer et al. [22] elaborated this analysis, demonstrating that such a detector could achieve cosmological reach (redshift $z > 1$) over a wide mass range of binary stellar remnants. An analysis of the noise scalings of such a detector, along with the scalings of a detector using the Voyager technology set, followed thereafter [23]. From 2018 to 2021, the US National Science Foundation funded a horizon study that set out Cosmic Explorer's science case, choice of technology, instrument design, community relationship, project realization, and cost estimate [24]; in parallel, a Cosmic Explorer consortium was established to organize the growing community of interested researchers. Cosmic Explorer intends to come online in the mid-2030s and operate as part of a global next-generation network with Einstein Telescope and potentially other observatories [25,26].

This review will describe the science case for Cosmic Explorer (Section 2) and the observatory concept (Section 3), and give some remarks on the observatory project and its realization (Section 4). We will mostly hew to the vision of Cosmic Explorer as presented in the 2021 horizon study.

2. Science Program

Cosmic Explorer's leap in sensitivity will deliver a catalog of observations that is fundamentally different from the catalog delivered by the current generation of observatories. Whereas today's observatories can detect mergers of binary stellar remnants from redshifts less than 3, Cosmic Explorer will be able to detect them out to cosmological redshifts greater than 10—in other words, from the entire stellar history of the universe (Figures 1 and 2). This also means that the rate of binary merger detections will likely exceed 100,000 per year, enabling detailed inferences about stellar remnant populations. Individual merger signals, especially those in the local universe, will be detected with greatly enhanced signal-to-noise ratio, sometimes exceeding 1000 in amplitude, enabling precision observation of the dynamics at play in these systems.

Cosmic Explorer's broad scientific program has been arranged around four themes. The first is black holes and neutron stars throughout cosmic time (Section 2.1); the second is the dynamics of dense matter (Section 2.2); and the third is extreme gravity and fundamental physics (Section 2.3). A fourth theme, discovery potential (Section 2.4), covers other phenomena and emphasizes the possibility of finding something completely unexpected. Many of these topics overlap with the science case of the Einstein Telescope [27], and the scientific output of both observatories will be enhanced if they operate jointly as part of a worldwide network, particularly due to the improved ability to measure the distance, inclination, and sky location of the systems [28–35].

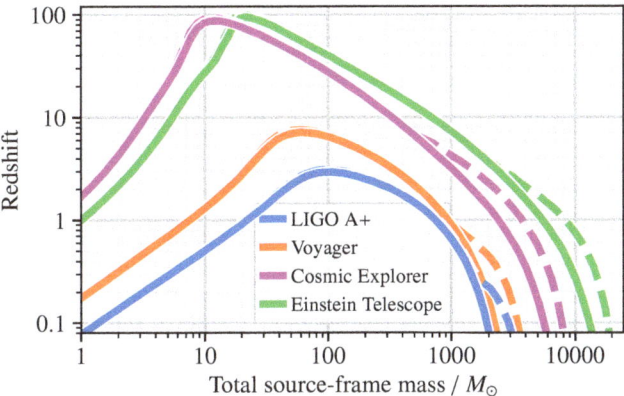

Figure 1. Detection capability of selected current and next-generation gravitational-wave interferometers. Each curve indicates the highest cosmological redshift at which an equal-mass, non-spinning compact binary coalescence could be detected with amplitude signal-to-noise ratio of 8, if the system is optimally oriented on the sky. Solid lines indicate detection using the gravitational radiation from the $(\ell, m) = (2, 2)$ angular mode of the system only; dashed lines show the inclusion of higher-order angular modes using the simulated waveform family IMRPHENOMXHM [36].

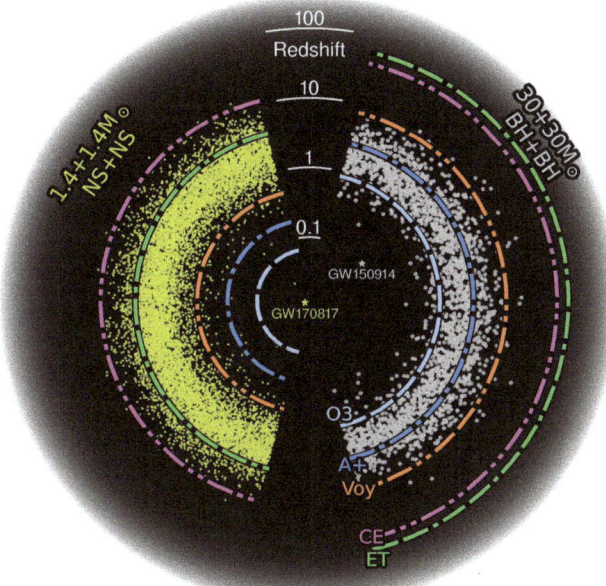

Figure 2. The cosmic history of binary stellar remnant mergers, with $1.4 + 1.4\ M_\odot$ neutron star mergers on the left and $30 + 30\ M_\odot$ black hole mergers on the right; the radial coordinate is cosmological redshift z. The distribution of mergers as a function of redshift assumes the Madau–Dickinson star formation rate and that the typical time from binary formation to merger is 100 million years [37, 38]; under these assumptions, most of these binaries merge at $z \sim 2$. The first gravitational-wave detections of a binary black hole merger (GW150914) and a binary neutron star merger (GW170817) are indicated [39,40]. The colored bands then show the detection capabilities of selected gravitational-wave observatories from Figure 1, as well as the capability of Advanced LIGO during the third LIGO–Virgo observing run.

2.1. Black Holes and Neutron Stars Throughout Cosmic Time

2.1.1. Remnants of the First Stars

The stellar history of the universe extends from the present day back to a redshift higher than 10, beyond which the matter in the universe was predominantly neutral hydrogen. Even the oldest stars that astronomers have observed today, belonging to the so-called Population II, have a metal content that is too high to be explained by direct formation from this neutral hydrogen, leading to a hypothesized cohort of stars (Population III) that would have produced the first phase of stellar nucleosynthesis in the universe [41]. No such Population III star has been observed, but simulations suggest these stars were typically larger than 100 $M_\odot$. If they were sufficiently massive, they would have collapsed into black holes [42,43], implying rich observational prospects for high-redshift gravitational-wave astronomy. Cosmic Explorer will be able to search for the remnant black holes of binary Population III systems at redshift beyond 10 over two decades in mass, about 3–300 $M_\odot$; see Figures 1 and 2).

2.1.2. Seeds of Galaxy Formation

Most galaxies contain at their center a black hole with a mass of millions to billions of solar masses. The formation mechanism of such supermassive black holes has not been conclusively determined, but multiple scenarios rely on seeding from so-called intermediate-mass black holes, with masses ranging from hundreds to hundreds of thousands of solar masses. These intermediate-mass black holes could have formed from accretion onto the black hole remnants of Population III stars, from the collapse of clouds of neutral hydrogen, or from the gravitational collapse of globular clusters [44].

Whatever the mechanism, the formation process must have been underway before $z = 7.5$, given the observation of high-redshift active galactic nuclei likely powered by supermassive black holes (see, for example, Banados et al. [45]). Cosmic Explorer, ideally operating in a network with the Einstein Telescope, will be able to track the growth of high-redshift black holes up to a thousand solar masses, providing key information about the early stages of assembly of intermediate-mass and supermassive black holes [46].

2.1.3. Formation and Evolution of Compact Binaries

The question of how binary systems form, especially with orbits compact enough to coalesce via gravitational-wave emission, is still an open area of research. In regions of high stellar density, such as globular clusters, tightly bound binaries can form from dynamical encounters of stars or stellar remnants; alternatively, an isolated binary can become compact if one star ejects enough gas to form a common envelope around both stars, inducing a drag that tightens the orbit [47]. These formation mechanisms lead to varying predictions about the masses, spins, eccentricities, and other properties of the population of compact binaries, which can be inferred from gravitational-wave observations of the coalescence [48,49].

The existing catalog of gravitational-wave observations already gives hints that multiple formation mechanisms are at work [50]. Next-generation observatories such as Cosmic Explorer will densely sample the compact binary population out to high redshift, and the resulting catalog of observations will be able to not only differentiate between formation channels operating in the present day, but to track the operation of these channels throughout the stellar history of the universe [51].

2.2. Dynamics of Dense Matter

2.2.1. Structure and Composition of Neutron Stars

Neutron stars are known to be cold and ultradense, but the exact behavior of the matter inside them is not known. Particularly in the core, the high pressure and density could cause a phase transition from hadrons to deconfined quarks [52]. This subatomic behavior of the matter determines the equation of state relating pressure, density, and temperature. In neutron stars, the equation of state controls the relation between a star's mass, radius, and deformability in a tidal gravitational field, which are observable in the gravitational waveform of a merging binary neutron star system [53]. Cosmic Explorer will be able to measure hundreds of neutron star radii to within 1% each year, providing a catalog of precise observations of tidal signatures that can be used to distinguish between different models of the neutron star equation of state.

The behavior of cold, dense matter can also be understood through observations of neutron stars in isolation, which could produce gravitational waves through solid body oscillations or through an elliptical mass distribution that rotates with the star [54]. Cosmic Explorer will be able to search for spinning neutron stars with ellipticities on the order of 10^{-9}, testing the initial conclusion from electromagnetic observations that these stars have a minimum ellipticity [55].

2.2.2. New Phases in Quantum Chromodynamics

In the aftermath of a neutron star merger, the cold progenitor stars give way to a hot, dense postmerger remnant, which provides an avenue to probe the behavior of ultradense matter at a finite temperature. Here again the hadronic matter could, given the elevated temperature and density of the postmerger environment, transition to deconfined quarks, and this transition would be imprinted onto the portion of the gravitational waveform resulting from the postmerger oscillations of the remnant [56,57]. Additionally, the postmerger waveform reveals the fate of the remnant: whether it collapses promptly to a black hole, lingers momentarily as a hypermassive neutron star, or survives as a stable neutron star [58,59].

Postmerger oscillations are expected to occur somewhere between 2–4 kHz, which motivates the development of more sensitive gravitational-wave detectors in this frequency range and a careful consideration of their optical configuration [60]. Reliably detecting these postmerger oscillations at least once per year requires a next-generation detector such as the Einstein Telescope or Cosmic Explorer [61], or a dedicated high-frequency detector such as NEMO.

Core-collapse supernovae offer another avenue for witnessing the behavior of matter at extreme temperatures and densities. These supernovae are expected only a few times per century in our galaxy and there is considerable modeling uncertainty in the strength and morphology of their gravitational-wave emission. The detection prospects with the current generation of gravitational-wave observatories is thus uncertain, but a next-generation observatory such as Cosmic Explorer would boost the optimal signal-to-noise ratio by tenfold, vastly increasing the chance of detection [62]. Even so, the rate of detectable core-collapse supernovae is likely to remain low even for the next-generation observatories unless further broadband sensitivity improvements of 100 in amplitude are achieved [63].

2.2.3. Chemical Evolution of the Universe

The observation of a neutron star collision jointly by gravitational-wave and electromagnetic observatories in 2017 (GW170817 [64]) confirmed that these collisions are responsible for the synthesis of many of the heavy elements in the universe [65]. This initial observation anticipates a new set of questions, such as how the properties of the binary affect the rates of nucleosynthesis and the abundances of the products, and whether other systems (especially supernovae and collisions of a neutron star with a black hole) have a significant role in producing these heavy elements. A number of theoretical uncertainties, particularly in the modeling of the optical–infrared afterglow (kilonova), make these questions difficult to answer without a larger sample of joint gravitational-wave and electromagnetic observations of these systems [66]. In concert with next-generation electromagnetic telescopes, Cosmic Explorer will deliver just such a catalog of observations out to $z \sim 1$.

2.2.4. The Engine Powering Short γ-ray Bursts

The observation of a short γ-ray burst nearly simultaneously with GW170817 provided evidence that such bursts originate in neutron star collisions [67], but mysteries linger.

Atypical features in the burst lead to questions about whether it was a canonical burst observed at an unusual angle, or whether some fundamental process differentiates it from the catalog of canonical short γ-ray burst observations [68]. In any case, the central engine driving short γ-ray bursts is still uncertain, and could be accreting black holes or (hyper)massive neutron stars; consequently, these bursts may or may not be observed in the collision of a neutron star with a black hole, in addition to the collision of two neutron stars [68]. Cosmic Explorer will deliver a large catalog of signals from neutron star collisions at a wide variety of observing angles, especially at redshifts $z \lesssim 1$ where systems are accessible with electromagnetic telescopes, enabling an elucidation of the burst mechanism and the engine that drives it [24].

2.3. Extreme Gravity and Fundamental Physics

2.3.1. Testing General Relativity

Gravitational radiation is a powerful tool to test general relativity, particularly in the strong-field regime [69]. Today's gravitational-wave detectors have already begun some of these tests [70,71], and next-generation observatories will continue these tests with greater sensitivity, and enable new kinds of tests not possible today. These observatories will be able to observe mergers with amplitude signal-to-noise ratios in excess of 1000, enabling them to probe theory-agnostic modifications to general relativity with several more orders of magnitude of constraining power than what is possible today [72]. Among the new kinds of tests that will be enabled, Cosmic Explorer and other next-generation detectors will be able to reliably resolve the higher-order multipole moments as a black hole rings down after merger, and they will do so with enough precision to compare the observed signal with the prediction from general relativity that the spectral content is uniquely determined by the mass, spin, and charge of the black hole (the "no hair theorem") [73–75].

2.3.2. Rare and Novel Compact Objects

Cosmic Explorer will detect most of the stellar-mass compact binary coalescences in the low-redshift universe, amounting to hundreds of thousands of events per year. Among these coalescences will be black hole or neutron star systems with rare properties, which could be missed by current observatories. Moreover, Cosmic Explorer may discover that some of the compact objects in its catalog are neither black holes nor neutron stars. A variety of theoretical objects, such as boson stars or gravastars, may superficially mimic the behavior of black holes, but the precise observations enabled by Cosmic Explorer could reveal the absence of a true spacetime horizon; alternatively, observations could reveal new physics associated with black holes [76].

2.3.3. Dark Matter and Dark Energy

The possible gravitational-wave signatures of dark matter are manifold, and essentially every category of astrophysical source targeted by gravitational-wave observatories can be pressed into service to search for dark matter; we will only mention a few here and refer the reader to Bertone et al. [77] for a comprehensive review. By searching for sub-solar-mass binary coalescences, Cosmic Explorer will more tightly constrain the fraction of dark matter that could exist as primordial black holes in the range 10^{-3}–100 $M_\odot$ [78]. Cosmic Explorer can also probe ultralight scalar-field dark matter models in the mass range 0.1–10 peV by searching for a stochastic background of oscillatory gravitational-wave signals from these fields in the vicinity of spinning black holes [79]. Like other interferometers, Cosmic Explorer can be used to directly detect terrestrial dark matter, especially if it couples to Standard Model particles. In particular, it can provide improved constraints on the photon coupling of dark matter for masses below 0.1 peV [80].

Cosmic Explorer will also make contributions to dark energy and cosmology. Joint observation by Cosmic Explorer and the Rubin observatory will yield a sub-percent measurement of the Hubble constant, independent of the traditional cosmic distance ladder.

These observations will additionally yield measurements of the local dark matter density and the local dark energy equation of state to within 20% [81].

2.4. Discovery Potential

Cosmic Explorer's leap in sensitivity may deliver observations not enumerated in the above three science themes. Ultimately, it is impossible to give an exhaustive account of what we might see—perhaps an observational consequence of the unification of quantum mechanics and general relativity, or a new elementary particle, or new physics at work in the early history of the universe. Many potential phenomena in this latter category could appear as a stochastic gravitational-wave background lying beneath the background of merging binary systems; Cosmic Explorer could reveal these phenomena as part of a next-generation network [82–86]. Cosmic Explorer may even reveal phenomena that we cannot yet conceive of: history shows that new, more sensitive astronomical instruments often deliver signals from the Universe that are totally unexpected [87].

3. Observatory

Cosmic Explorer's science goals are premised on achieving a detector with a typical sensitivity of order $10^{-25}/\sqrt{\mathrm{Hz}}$ in the audio band. Achieving such a sensitivity in the 2030s seems possible with further research and development on laser Michelson interferometers, which already can achieve sensitivity better than $10^{-23}/\sqrt{\mathrm{Hz}}$ and with a tenfold increase in the interferometer arm length. Thus, Cosmic Explorer, like the Einstein Telescope, assumes a Michelson interferometer topology, using Fabry–Perot arm cavities along with optical recycling techniques to increase circulating power and achieve broadband operation.

The Cosmic Explorer concept as presented in the 2021 Horizon Study takes as a baseline design the construction of two widely separated facilities on the Earth's surface, one hosting a 40 km detector and the other hosting a 20 km detector, although it considers alternate scenarios in which Cosmic Explorer consists of a single 40 km facility, two 40 km facilities, or two 20 km facilities [24]. In any case, the choice of one detector per facility is different from the Einstein Telescope, which plans for three pairs of interferometric detectors located in a single underground triangular 10 km facility. The trade-off for having only one detector per facility is that each facility then is only sensitive to one gravitational-wave polarization and will not be able to form a null (gravitational-wave-free) diagnostic channel.

There is also the question of what the Cosmic Explorer detector(s) should use as a technology set. Although there is no requirement that the technology set stay fixed over the lifetime of the observatory, the horizon study assumes that Cosmic Explorer will extend the LIGO A+ set, meaning room-temperature fused silica test masses and suspensions, active vibration isolation, and a 1064 nm laser, as well as a new mirror coating technology that is currently still under development and slated for deployment in the next few years. It is also conceivable that a different technology set, such as the cryogenic silicon concept for LIGO Voyager, could be scaled up to Cosmic Explorer, and several previous works have explored that possibility [23,88]. However, the LIGO A+ technology set is more mature, having already been demonstrated on kilometer-scale instruments.

This section presents the expected sensitivity of a 40 km Cosmic Explorer (Section 3.1), and then discusses the detector design (Section 3.2), the vacuum system (Section 3.3), the observatory location (Section 3.4), and the possibility of a 20 km detector (Section 3.5).

3.1. Sensitivity

Figure 3 shows the noise of current and next-generation detectors, including a 40 km Cosmic Explorer, expressed as an equivalent spacetime strain noise. This has by now become the standard way to characterize the sensitivities of gravitational-wave interferometers, and for the current observatories, the construction of these curves is simple: the amplitude spectral density $\sqrt{S_{hh}(\Omega)}$ of the observatory strain noise is found by taking the amplitude spectral density $\sqrt{S_{xx}(\Omega)}$ of the detector's displacement noise and dividing by the arm length L. However, the situation for next-generation observatories is more complicated, firstly because Cosmic Explorer is of comparable size to the wavelengths of kilohertz gravitational waves, and secondly, because the Einstein Telescope comprises multiple interferometers with a 60° opening angle.

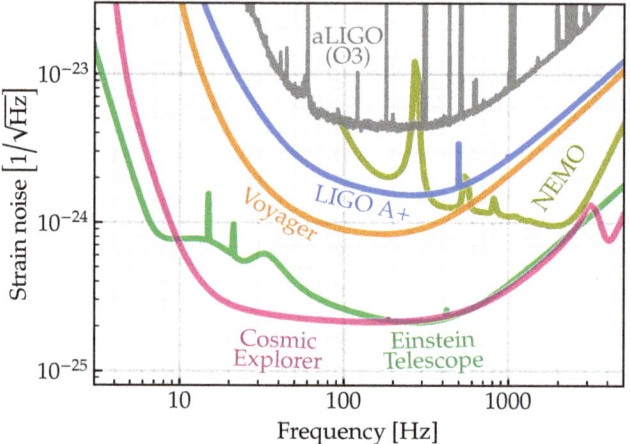

Figure 3. Strain curves for selected current and next-generation detectors, including a 40 km Cosmic Explorer. The curves indicate the sensitivity for an optimally oriented and polarized monochromatic source. Several subtleties of these curves for the next-generation detectors are discussed in Section 3.1.

Each next-generation curve in Figure 3 represents the strain noise of the observatory as a whole corresponding to an optimally oriented and polarized source on the sky at each Fourier frequency. Computing this optimum requires recourse to the antenna response functions $F_+(\theta, \phi, \Omega)$ (for + polarized waves) and $F_\times(\theta, \phi, \Omega)$ (for × polarized waves) of each detector in the observatory, keeping in mind both the source location (θ, ϕ) on the sky and the angular frequency Ω of the arriving waves [89]. In the case of the Einstein Telescope, arriving at the total observatory strain noise requires summing the power collected by each of the three detectors (in other words, treating the Einstein Telescope as a network of three colocated, but rotated, detectors). For Cosmic Explorer, especially, the stipulation of computing the sensitivity separately at each Fourier frequency is important because the optimal sky location and polarization varies significantly with frequency: for a single L-shaped detector such as Cosmic Explorer, the optimum sky location for a zero-frequency source is directly at the detector's zenith or nadir; however, for a source with $\Omega/2\pi = c/2L$ (the free spectral range), the detector is completely insensitive to a source arriving at the zenith or nadir, and the maximum response instead occurs for sources arriving at other angles [90,91]. Figure 4 compares the normalized observatory sensitivities as the gravitational-wave frequency approaches the free spectral range, showing that the antenna pattern of an L-shaped detector is reduced, but not identically zero, at the free spectral range. It also evinces a lack of nulls in the total antenna pattern of the three-detector triangle geometry employed by the Einstein Telescope [20].

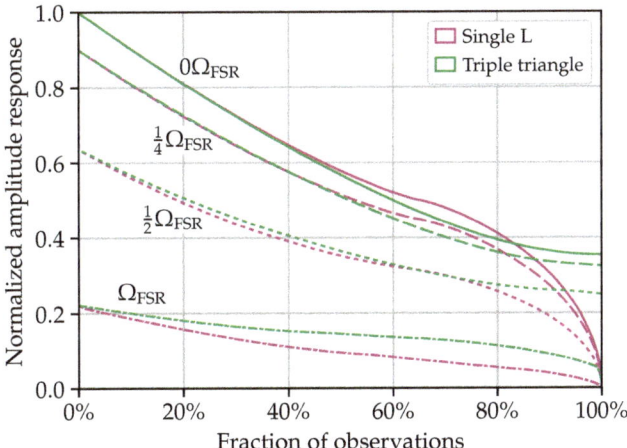

Figure 4. Histogram of normalized, polarization-averaged antenna patterns for a single L-shaped interferometer (such as Cosmic Explorer) and a three-detector triangle (such as the Einstein Telescope), assuming sources distributed isotropically on the sky. Curves are shown for gravitational waves at frequencies 0, $\frac{1}{4}$, $\frac{1}{2}$ and 1 times the detector free spectral range $\Omega_{\text{FSR}}/2\pi = c/2L$. Note that $\Omega_{\text{FSR}}^{(\text{CE})} = \Omega_{\text{FSR}}^{(\text{ET})}/4$.

3.2. Detector

This subsection focuses on the design of a 40 km Cosmic Explorer instrument using an extension of LIGO A+ technology. The fundamental noises in such a detector are shown in Figure 5 (We will return to a 20 km instrument in Section 3.5).

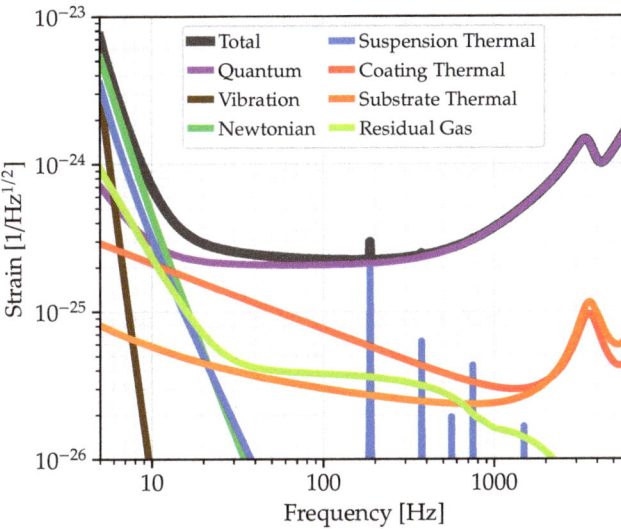

Figure 5. Fundamental noise contributions to the overall strain sensitivity of a 40 km Cosmic Explorer detector, discussed in Section 3.2. The fundamental noises are modeled in `pygwinc` [92], and the noise here is referred to a source arriving from 15° off the detector's zenith.

3.2.1. Optical Configuration

The choice of optical cavity lengths and mirror transmissivities influences many of the noise sources in the detector, particularly the noise arising from quantum mechanical fluctuations of the optical field. In terms of equivalent spacetime strain, most noise sources in the detector decrease with increasing arm length [23,24]; in particular, the amplitude spectral density of quantum shot noise scales as $1/\sqrt{L}$ if the detector bandwidth is held fixed. On the other hand, the free spectral range $c/2L$ limits the maximum bandwidth of the instrument; thus, to achieve the science goals relating to postmerger neutron star physics (Section 2.2.2), the detector cannot be longer than several tens of kilometers. The choice of $L = 40$ km represents a trade-off, yielding a free spectral range of 3.7 kHz while still offering a clear improvement in the shot-noise-limited performance compared to a detector with a shorter baseline. Further consideration of arm length choice is found in Section 3.5.

The optical power circulating in the Cosmic Explorer arm cavities is assumed to be 1.5 MW, which is twice the nominal value for Advanced LIGO; it is not established whether this represents a true upper limit for the detector. Aside from affecting the level of shot noise in the detector, the choice of arm power has several optomechanical implications. First, the quantum backaction (radiation pressure noise) must be counteracted by increasingly heavy test masses; Cosmic Explorer assumes they are each 320 kg, which will already require a scaling up of current fabrication technologies. Second, radiation pressure modifies the angular susceptibility of the suspended masses, and could necessitate feedback control schemes that degrade the sensitivity by injecting servo control noise; however, since Cosmic Explorer plans to use heavier test masses and a near-confocal rather than near-concentric arm cavity resonator geometry, these modifications to the suspension dynamics are weaker than in LIGO A+, even with twice the circulating power [93,94]. Third, high power results in more elastic modes in the test masses being driven into parametric instability by interaction with optical modes [95], although a detailed analysis for Cosmic Explorer is yet to be given. Aside from optomechanical effects, elastic deformation and refractive index changes in the mirrors due to heat absorption in the substrates or coatings can degrade the quantum noise performance of the detector or complicate the feedback control of the mirrors' length or angular degrees of freedom; a quantitative accounting requires fairly detailed models of the detector's optical configuration and sensing and control systems, which have not yet been developed.

The choice of the signal extraction parameters and the transmissivities of the input test mass mirrors depend on the desired quantum-limited bandwidth and peak sensitivity, and on power handling considerations. As in current detectors, the desire to lower the optical power traveling through the beamsplitter and input test mass substrates favors a high arm finesse $\mathcal{F}$. On the other hand, the desire to reduce the effect of noise in the signal extraction cavity favors lower finesse, since losses in this cavity contribute to the quantum noise with a power spectral density $S_{hh}(\Omega) \propto \mathcal{F}\Omega^2$ [96]. Cosmic Explorer assumes the Advanced LIGO finesse of 450. In contrast to the current detectors, Cosmic Explorer's long arm length means that stronger signal extraction is needed to expand the interferometer bandwidth to several hundred hertz; it also means that for any realistic choice of signal extraction cavity length, dispersion in the cavity noticeably alters the level of quantum shot noise. Cosmic Explorer's nominal design assumes a signal extraction cavity length of 20 m, with a 2% transmissive signal extraction mirror, but other length and transmissivity values can be chosen to tune the detector for low-frequency- or high-frequency-focused operation [60]. Cosmic Explorer assumes that the loss in the signal extraction cavity is 500 ppm, including loss due the mismatch of transverse optical modes; this is roughly ten times less than the current value in the LIGO detectors [97].

The quantum noise will be reduced using squeezed vacuum injected into the interferometer's signal port; the goal is 10 dB of quantum noise reduction across the entire sensitive band. Cosmic Explorer proposes to use a 4 km filter cavity with 80 ppm round-trip loss to achieve the simultaneous reduction of radiation pressure and shot noise. Given injection losses of slightly less than 10% and output losses of a few percent, this requires 15–20 dB of squeezed light generation, with the relative path-length fluctuation between the squeezed field and the signal field stabilized to 10 mrad rms.

3.2.2. Test Masses

Cosmic Explorer will need fused silica test masses larger by roughly a factor of two in every linear dimension compared to Advanced LIGO. This is driven first by the need for a large inertia to lessen the effect of radiation pressure fluctuations, to decrease the mechanical susceptibility of the suspension system (Section 3.2.4), and to reduce position fluctuations from gas damping. A mass of 320 kg is enough to keep radiation pressure noise, suspension noise, and gas noise below the geophysical background below 10 Hz. Second, because the radius of the optical mode at each test mass can be no smaller than $\sqrt{\lambda L/\pi}$ due to diffraction [93], the test mass diameter D must be large enough to avoid a significant round-trip power loss due to the finite aperture of the test mass.[2] For Cosmic Explorer's planned operating wavelength of $\lambda = 1$ µm, a test mass diameter of about 70 cm is needed to maintain a sub-part-per-million optical loss while allowing for optical mode sizes slightly larger than the extremal value. If Cosmic Explorer were instead operated with Voyager technology (cryogenic silicon masses and 2 µm laser wavelength), a test mass diameter of more than 80 cm would be needed to maintain similar optical loss, which requires scaling up the current largest monocrystalline silicon ingot size of 45 cm [17].

With larger beam sizes than current detectors, Cosmic Explorer must have test masses that are polished on spatial scales up to tens of centimeters to reduce scattering out of the optical mode of the arm. The most stringent requirements will likely come from the need to control noise arising from scattered light reflecting from a moving surface and then recombining with the optical mode. This is a challenging modeling task, since it requires cataloging and then simulating multiple scattering surfaces in a three-dimensional geometry—notably the baffling in the beam tubes (see Section 3.3).

3.2.3. Mirror Coatings

Cosmic Explorer will use the future state-of-the-art in thin-film mirror coatings, which is likely to be different from the coatings that are used today, which employ fused silica as the low-index material and titania-doped tantala as the high-index material [100]. The Cosmic Explorer model currently adopts the same target as LIGO A+, which is to use a coating whose effective mechanical loss (taking into account coating thickness and elastic parameters) is fourfold less than the LIGO silica–tantala coatings, while still maintaining sub-part-per-million optical absorption and an acceptable level of optical scatter.

Because of the interest from LIGO A+ and AdVirgo+, there is already significant coating development underway. Strategies include retaining fused silica as the low-index material while replacing the high-index material with titania-doped germania, some other metal oxide, or silicon nitride [101,102]. Other strategies include crystalline material pairs such as gallium arsenide and aluminum-doped gallium arsenide [103]. The chief development for Cosmic Explorer will be to scale up the area of the coating to the larger test mass size. The coatings will require low contamination to avoid thermal deformations that degrade the buildup of power in the arm cavities [104,105].

3.2.4. Test Mass Suspensions

Cosmic Explorer will adapt the quadruple pendulum suspension design used for Advanced LIGO [106], giving a $1/\Omega^8$ amplitude suppression of horizontal vibrations for frequencies Ω above the normal modes of the suspension. Cosmic Explorer will retain the monolithic design, in which the test mass, penultimate mass, and the suspension fibers between them are all fabricated from fused silica; the upper components are steel.

The chief adaptations for the Cosmic Explorer suspensions focus on decreasing their mechanical susceptibility (the amount of test mass displacement in response to applied forces) at frequencies within the gravitational-wave band. This serves to increase the amount of vibrational isolation. Consistent with the fluctuation–dissipation theorem, this also reduces the thermodynamic fluctuations perturbing the test masses in this band, since these fluctuations are proportional to the imaginary portion of the susceptibility [107]. The susceptibility should also be engineered so that the frequencies of the normal modes associated with motions of the suspension masses lie below the sensitive band of the interferometer (5 Hz), since this prevents resonant enhancement of seismic or thermal noise within the band and allows for more flexible feedback damping of the modes. The frequencies of these modes can be lowered by increasing the length of the pendulum stages. A total length of 4.0 m is sufficient for the longitudinal modes, although it may not by itself provide sufficient reduction in the mode frequencies of the suspension's vertical motion; due to the Earth's finite radius $R_\oplus$, these modes appear in the gravitational-wave readout with a typical amplitude coupling factor $L/2R_\oplus \simeq 0.003$. These vertical frequencies could be lowered even further by attaching the fibers to compliant silica cantilevers ("blade springs") or by decreasing the cross-sectional area of the fibers. In either case, the main limitation is the strength of the fused silica. It is believed that the current tensile stress of 0.8 GPa in the LIGO fibers can be increased to at least 1.2 GPa in Cosmic Explorer [88,108].

3.2.5. Active Vibration Isolation

The Cosmic Explorer test mass suspensions will be attached to actively controlled platforms that provide improved vibration isolation compared to the analogous system in Advanced LIGO [109]. The improvement will come mainly through the use of inertial sensors that have lower self-noise and can measure in six degrees of freedom [110,111]. Cosmic Explorer aims to achieve a residual platform motion of about $30\,\mathrm{fm}/\sqrt{\mathrm{Hz}}$ at 10 Hz, which is ten times better than the LIGO performance and directly impacts the test mass motion within the sensitive frequency band. Additional inertial sensing improvements at 1 Hz and below, including improved tilt sensing, will enhance the instrument performance by lowering the amount of noise in other feedback control loops [88].

3.2.6. Local Gravity Fluctuations

Local fluctuations of the Earth's gravity present an emerging challenge that will soon limit the low-frequency performance of the current generation of observatories [112,113]. For Cosmic Explorer, which aims to achieve roughly ten times less displacement noise at 10 Hz compared to Advanced LIGO, the challenge will be even more acute and will require a concerted effort to account for fluctuations from both seismic and atmospheric fluctuations. Because Cosmic Explorer will be located on the Earth's surface, it is unlikely that the ambient seismicity will be dramatically lower than that of existing observatories.

To reach the sensitivity shown in Figure 5, it is assumed that the effect of local gravity fluctuations due to the seismic field can be mitigated, either by estimating the fluctuations and subtracting them from the observatory's time series data, or by altering the seismic field in the immediate vicinity of the test masses. Current proposals for subtraction techniques involve an array of seismometers or tiltmeters to measure the ground motion and thereby estimate the fluctuation at each test mass [114]. Altering the seismic field could involve displacing soil underneath the test mass to increase the distance from the mass to the source of the gravitational perturbation, or the installation of metamaterials [115]. Regardless of the method, the level of required mitigation to reach the sensitivity goal is 20 dB for the Rayleigh wave field and 10 dB for the body wave field, given ambient noise levels of $1\,(\mathrm{\mu m/s^2})/\sqrt{\mathrm{Hz}}$ in Rayleigh waves and $0.3\,(\mathrm{\mu m/s^2})/\sqrt{\mathrm{Hz}}$ in body waves.

The gravity fluctuation limit shown in Figure 5 is dominated not by the residual seismic contributions, but rather the infrasonic background from the atmosphere. Other than burying the test masses hundreds of meters underground, mitigation strategies for atmospherically induced gravity fluctuations are uncertain [116] and so no infrasound mitigation has been assumed for Cosmic Explorer. Figure 5 assumes that the typical level of the ambient infrasound is $1\,\mathrm{mPa}/\sqrt{\mathrm{Hz}}$, based on long-term global monitoring [117].

3.2.7. Laser System

Cosmic Explorer will use a 1064 nm laser system. The optical design for the instrument (Section 3.2.1) assumes $P_\mathrm{arm} = 1.5\,\mathrm{MW}$ of power in each arm, along with $\mathcal{L}_\mathrm{arm} = 40\,\mathrm{ppm}$ of loss per round-trip pass in each arm. If the power recycling mirror were critically matched to the arms, this would require an input power of $2P_{\text{arm}}\mathcal{L}_{\text{arm}}$; however, to allow for a slightly overcoupled power recycling cavity, the laser power at the interferometer input is assumed to be 140 W. This requirement is only modestly larger than the requirement for Advanced LIGO. The maximum power produced by the laser system will need to be higher than this value to account for propagation through the input optics system, which will prepare the light in a frequency-, intensity-, and pointing-stabilized Gaussian mode.

For Cosmic Explorer, the frequency stabilization requirements are somewhat more stringent than those of Advanced LIGO. In Advanced LIGO, the apparent displacement noise in the gravitational-wave readout channel due to laser frequency noise is dominated by coupling of higher-order transverse optical modes, with a typical value 1 fm/Hz; if the coupling in Cosmic Explorer is similar, then the requirement on the laser frequency noise at the interferometer input is $0.7\,\mu\text{Hz}/\sqrt{\text{Hz}}$ [118]. In contrast to Advanced LIGO, it is unlikely that the laser can be frequency-locked to the Cosmic Explorer interferometer with sufficient bandwidth due to the low free spectral range of 3.7 kHz. Cahillane et al. [118] propose instead to use two suspended, triangular mode-cleaning cavities, rather than the one cavity of Advanced LIGO.

3.2.8. Calibration

The calibration requirements for the Cosmic Explorer data will need to be drawn from the multiple components of its science program, although some initial bounds can already be given. If Cosmic Explorer (along with electromagnetic observatories) is to deliver Hubble constant measurements to better than 0.2% [81], then the systematic error on the amplitude of the gravitational-wave response must be smaller than this value. For measurements of tidal effects in nearby binary neutron star mergers, which could be observed with total amplitude signal-to-noise ratios in the thousands, calibration errors should be about 1% or better [119]. For signals (such as compact binary mergers) that can be precisely modeled a priori, detector calibration requirements are likely to be informed by the level of improvement that can be achieved in the accuracy of gravitational waveform families [120].

Cosmic Explorer could use several calibration techniques. The main calibration apparatus for today's detectors uses a metrologically traceable photon radiation pressure drive, which in the case of LIGO is currently able to deliver a calibrated test mass displacement with a 0.4% uncertainty [121]; anticipated improvements in optical power metrology may be able deliver an uncertainty better than 0.15% [122]. Separately, spinning source masses in the vicinity of the interferometer test masses can be used to apply a known gravitational force. Prototypes employed in current detectors achieved uncertainty smaller than 1% [123,124], and future apparatus could achieve better than 0.2% uncertainty [125].

3.3. Vacuum System

The vacuum system for Cosmic Explorer, particularly the beam tubes that envelop the 40 km arms, is an active area of research and development. The noise requirements on the vacuum system are not too different from those of LIGO, and the thrust of the research is instead focused on reducing construction cost, developing better diagnostic capabilities, and improving robustness. These activities are crucial so that the observatory is not hamstrung by excessive cost during construction or by infrastructure failures during operation.

Gas-induced optical scattering of the laser light in the arms sets upper limits on the partial pressures of various molecular species in the beam tubes. Two especially important species, hydrogen and water, have partial pressure requirements $p_{H_2} < 40\,\text{nPa} \simeq 0.3\,\text{nTorr}$ and $p_{H_2O} < 4\,\text{nPa} \simeq 0.03\,\text{nTorr}$, which are only slightly more stringent than the goals for the LIGO system. In LIGO, the pressure requirements were met through a series of heat treatments ("baking"), first to deplete hydrogen from the raw 304L stainless steel stock, and then to desorb water from the inner surface of the tubes after installation [126]. Cosmic Explorer may be able to reduce costs by using carbon (mild) steel, which already has a low hydrogen content, by coating the interior of the tubes to reduce water adsorption, or by using novel (e.g., double-walled) tube geometries [126]. Stochastic momentum transfer from residual gas to the test masses additionally sets a requirement on the pressure in the vacuum chambers containing the masses. For meter-scale chambers, the pressure requirement is less stringent than the above requirements for the pressures in the arms [88]; however, they must be able to repeatedly attain this pressure after periodic exposure to atmosphere due to detector maintenance activities.

The diameter of the tube, along with the geometry of the interior baffles, must be chosen to pass the beam through the arm without truncation, especially as such truncation can impress the ground-driven motion of the baffles onto the phase and amplitude of the main optical mode. Although Cosmic Explorer's anticipated beam size (11 cm with 1 µm light) is nearly twice that of Advanced LIGO, it appears that a tube of the same diameter as LIGO (4 ft $\simeq$ 120 cm) with a $\sim$100 cm interior clear aperture (set by the inner radius of the annular baffles) is sufficient to avoid problematic truncation of the beam or baffle-induced noise as the light propagates down the arms [127].[3]

As described in Section 3.2.2, the beam tubes and baffles can also mediate the scattering of stray light back into the main optical mode. In the most common scenario considered, light is scattered out of the main optical mode due to the surface figure error of the test mass and then is reflected from the baffles back toward the same test mass. Bai [128] examined this scenario using a power budgeting calculation, and determined that current polishing techniques, if extended to slightly larger spatial scales, could give acceptable noise performance if the Cosmic Explorer beam tube and baffling system is similar to that of LIGO. However, this power budgeting needs to be confirmed by phase-sensitive calculations (e.g., using Fourier optics [129]) before the polishing requirements of the test masses can be finalized.

3.4. Observatory Location

Aside from the overall shape of the observatory, the main contrast between the Einstein Telescope facility [130] and the Cosmic Explorer facility is that the former is planned to be underground, while the latter is planned to be on the Earth's surface. Cosmic Explorer's choice of surface construction is motivated primarily by the expectation that tunneling would be more expensive than surface construction, especially as tunneling projects are typically more expensive per unit length in the Americas than in Europe [131].

If a 40 km facility is laid out on a perfectly spherical earth (with radius $R_\oplus \simeq 6400$ km), one must deal with the $L^2/8R_\oplus \simeq 30$ m difference in ground height between the center and the ends of the arms. This requires that the soil (or rock) is redistributed along the length of the arm to provide a flat grade on which to build the arms' vacuum pipe; the width of this grade must be at least a few meters to accommodate the infrastructure around the pipe, and the slope on either side of the finished grade cannot be steeper than the soil's angle of repose, typically less than 45°. Additionally, the layout should be chosen so that the deviation of the local gravity from vertical at each test mass is not significantly worse than the deviation expected from a perfectly spherical earth, since this will couple vertical motion of the test mass into the detector degree of freedom that is sensitive to gravitational waves. To redistribute soil in this fashion for two 40 km arms on the spherical Earth, roughly 10^7 m^3 of redistribution is required. Local topography, however, can alter the amount of soil redistribution, and several groups have undertaken algorithmic searches using publicly available topography and land-use data to find locations with a reduced volume of redistributed soil. These searches revealed that sites with favorable topographic profiles, yielding total redistributed volumes of order 10^6 m^3 or better, are not uncommon in the United States and around the world, particularly if the requirements on the detector length and opening angle are allowed to deviate slightly from their nominal values of 40 km and 90°, respectively [132].

Long-term seismic and infrasonic studies will be needed to estimate the impact of ambient geophysical noise on the detector performance, with attention paid to a full characterization of the seismic field (e.g., the types of seismic waves and their isotropy) and of the ground (e.g., its homogeneity and isotropy) to evaluate reduction strategies for local gravity fluctuations. Above a few hertz, where ground acceleration directly impacts the detector sensitivity, the ambient seismic field is generated mostly by nearby anthropogenic sources and different sites can display several orders of magnitude difference in their ground acceleration spectra [88,133,134]. Aside from the ambient noise conditions at the initial site, the facility infrastructure also plays an important role: Nguyen et al. [135] showed that the ground acceleration at the LIGO facilities is largely sourced from local elements such as air handler systems, meaning that Cosmic Explorer can likely make modest improvements to the ground noise spectrum by paying attention to civil engineering and other facility design considerations. Below a few hertz, where ground acceleration affects the controllability of the detector, the ambient seismic field is usually dominated by natural processes [133], such as the secondary microseism at decihertz frequencies sourced by storms in the open ocean [136]. At lower frequencies, ground tilt sourced by local atmospheric pressure fluctuations (e.g., wind) induces significant variability in ground motion and introduces a confusion noise in horizontal seismometer measurements [134,137]. Many of the sources responsible for the ambient seismic background also contribute to the ambient infrasonic background. At frequencies above the microbarom (the atmospheric counterpart of the microseism), wind and eddies are the dominant natural contributors to the infrasonic spectrum [117], with anthropogenic sources including local observatory equipment likely playing an important role as well.

Potential observatory sites will also need to be vetted for suitability in other ways. A geotechnical survey must be carried out to establish a realistic cost estimate for the construction of the facility. Environmental impacts must also be identified, along with strategies for avoiding or remediating these impacts. A plan for the eventual decommissioning of the site must be developed. Separately from topographical and geotechnical considerations, the social implications of the observatory location must also be integrated into the planning. Cosmic Explorer must build a mutually beneficial relationship with the local community. This requires taking community input into account from the beginning of the process and integrating it into the trajectory of the project. This includes engagement with local Indigenous communities, focused on ongoing consent for the project [24,138,139].

3.5. A 20 km Cosmic Explorer?

The 2021 horizon study calls for a 20 km Cosmic Explorer facility in addition to a 40 km facility. While two widely separated facilities will improve the estimation of extrinsic parameters for all types of astrophysical systems, a 20 km facility in particular is motivated by the dense matter portion of Cosmic Explorer's scientific program (Section 2.2). This portion of the program relies heavily on measuring gravitational waves at 2–4 kHz, where the optical response of a 40 km detector is reduced due to the travel time of the light down the arms (Section 3.1). The choice of 20 km for the arm length arose from the desire to choose the length of the detector's arms and signal extraction cavity and the transmissivities of the signal extraction mirror to result in "tuned" operation, where the quantum noise is reduced in the 2–4 kHz band at the expense of higher quantum noise elsewhere.[4]

Importantly, this tuning is limited by optical losses in both the arms and the signal extraction cavity, which noticeably reduces the effectiveness of tuning when realistic loss values (on the order of 0.1 %) are included (Section 3.2.1). Martynov et al. [140] studied how to optimize the parameters of a high-frequency-focused detector, including arm length, to best tune to signals in the 2–4 kHz band. The study found that the optimal detector had an arm length slightly less than 20 km and yielded a 30% improvement in average signal-to-noise ratio in the 2–4 kHz band compared to a 40 km detector. Srivastava et al. [60] examined the performance of a 20 km detector versus a 40 km detector against the whole of the Cosmic Explorer science program, finding that while the 20 km detector offers a modest improvement in the detection of post-merger signals, most science themes are better addressed by a 40 km detector; this is because the 40 km detector has superior noise performance outside the 2–4 kHz frequency range (Figure 6).

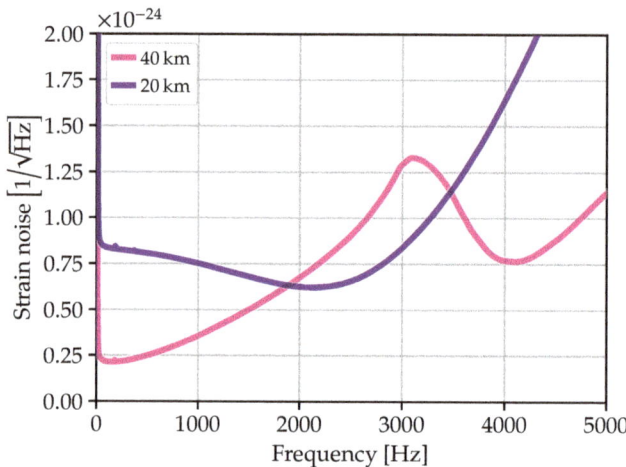

Figure 6. Comparison of a broadband 40 km Cosmic Explorer observatory and a 20 km kilohertz-optimized observatory (Section 3.5).

4. Project and Realization

A key component of the Horizon Study process was the development of an initial cost estimate for Cosmic Explorer. This cost estimate involved extrapolation of detector and facility costs from LIGO, along with the input of civil and vacuum engineers. Based on this process, the cost for the observatory reaches the billion-dollar scale, split in similar proportions between civil engineering, the vacuum system, and the detector, with a smaller portion from management. The anticipated yearly operating cost for two observatories is not significantly larger than LIGO's operating costs [24].

The scale of the Cosmic Explorer effort places it within the category of scientific megaproject. Although the process (and funding source) for realizing Cosmic Explorer is still under discussion, inspiration for the technical aspects of the project trajectory has been taken from the Research Infrastructure Guide from the US National Science Foundation [141]. Under the timeline laid out in the Horizon Study, much of the effort in the 2020s would involve developing a design for the observatory, leading to construction beginning near the end of the decade; installation of the detector would occur in the early 2030s, leading to the first stable operation of the detector (i.e., the first lock) around 2035. The 2020 US Astronomy and Astrophysics Decadal Survey endorsed technology development for Cosmic Explorer as part of the effort in this decade to ensure the advancement of ground-based gravitational-wave astronomy [25,26,142], and Cosmic Explorer is also represented in the 2021 Snowmass Process [9,143–145].

5. Outlook

As part of a global next-generation observatory network, Cosmic Explorer will reach back much further in cosmic time and probe sources with far greater sensitivity than is possible with today's detectors. This promises to revolutionize our understanding of the gravitational-wave universe on multiple fronts: the evolution of black holes and neutron stars throughout cosmic time, the behavior of matter at densities that cannot be probed terrestrially, and the fundamental nature of gravitation and cosmology. This promise can be realized with a research and development program that extends today's gravitational-wave detector technology to a longer baseline, with improvements that include more optical power, larger test masses, and better environmental isolation. To become reality, Cosmic Explorer needs a broad base of support from the gravitational-wave community, the broader astrophysical community, and the local communities where the observatories will be built.

Funding: The author is supported by the MathWorks, Inc. (Apple Hill Drive Natick, MA, USA).

Institutional Review Board Statement: Not applicable.

Informed Consent Statement: Not applicable.

Data Availability Statement: Not applicable.

Acknowledgments: The author thanks Kevin Kuns, Matthew Evans, Joshua Smith, Philippe Landry, B. S. Sathaprakash, Paul Lasky, and David Shoemaker for comments on the manuscript.

Conflicts of Interest: The author declares no conflict of interest.

Notes

1. Elsewhere, Einstein Telescope and Cosmic Explorer are referred to as third-generation observatories, with the current observatories and their incremental upgrades referred to as second generation; the initial detectors in the LIGO and Virgo observatories were first generation.
2. An initial estimate of the round-trip power loss can be found from the clipping loss $2e^{-D^2/2w^2}$ of a Gaussian mode with spot radius w impinging on a test mass with diameter D [22]. However, the Eigenfunction of a finite-aperture cavity is not Gaussian, and accurately computing its round-trip loss requires numerical simulation with Eigenvalue or Fourier-transform methods [93,98,99].
3. For 2 μm light, the transverse motion of the baffles could introduce significant noise due to the larger beam size (16 cm) [127].
4. This tuning of the macroscopic cavity lengths is distinct from "detuned" operation, in which resonant enhancement at kilohertz frequencies is instead achieved by adjusting the *microscopic* length of the signal extraction cavity.

References

1. Amaro-Seoane, P.; Audley, H.; Babak, S.; Baker, J.; Barausse, E.; Bender, P.; Berti, E.; Binetruy, P.; Born, M.; Bortoluzzi, D.; et al. Laser Interferometer Space Antenna. *arXiv* **2017**, arXiv:1702.00786.
2. Mei, J.; Bai, Y.Z.; Bao, J.; Barausse, E.; Cai, L.; Canuto, E.; Cao, B.; Chen, W.M.; Chen, Y.; Ding, Y.W.; et al. The TianQin project: Current progress on science and technology. *Prog. Theor. Exp. Phys.* **2021**, *2021*, 05A107. [CrossRef]
3. Verbiest, J.P.W.; Oslowski, S.; Burke-Spolaor, S. Pulsar Timing Array Experiments. *arXiv* **2021**, arXiv:2101.10081.
4. Kamionkowski, M.; Kovetz, E.D. The Quest for B Modes from Inflationary Gravitational Waves. *Ann. Rev. Astron. Astrophys.* **2016**, *54*, 227–269. [CrossRef]
5. Aggarwal, N.; Aguiar, O.D.; Bauswein, A.; Cella, G.; Clesse, S.; Cruise, A.M.; Domcke, V.; Figueroa, D.G.; Geraci, A.; Goryachev, M.; et al. Challenges and opportunities of gravitational-wave searches at MHz to GHz frequencies. *Living Rev. Rel.* **2021**, *24*, 4. [CrossRef]
6. Kawamura, S.; Ando, M.; Seto, N.; Sato, S.; Musha, M.; Kawano, I.; Yokoyama, J.; Tanaka, T.; Ioka, K.; Akutsu, T.; et al. Current status of space gravitational wave antenna DECIGO and B-DECIGO. *Prog. Theor. Exp. Phys.* **2021**, *2021*, 05A105. [CrossRef]
7. Geiger, R. Future Gravitational Wave Detectors Based on Atom Interferometry; World Scientific: Singapore, 2017; p. 285. [CrossRef]
8. Harms, J.; Ambrosino, F.; Angelini, L.; Braito, V.; Branchesi, M.; Brocato, E.; Cappellaro, E.; Coccia, E.; Coughlin, M.; Della Ceca, R.; et al. Lunar Gravitational-wave Antenna. *Astrophys. J.* **2021**, *910*, 1. [CrossRef]
9. Ballmer, S.W.; Adhikari, R.; Badurina, L.; Brown, D.A.; Chattopadhyay, S.; Evans, M.; Fritschel, P.; Hall, E.; Hogan, J.M.; Jani, K.; et al. Snowmass2021 Cosmic Frontier White Paper: Future Gravitational-Wave Detector Facilities. In Proceedings of the 2022 Snowmass Summer Study, Settle, WA, USA, 17–26 July 2022.
10. Aasi, J.; Abbott, B.; Abbott, R.; Abbott, T.; Abernathy, M.; Ackley, K.; Adams, C.; Adams, T.; Addesso, P.; Adhikari, R.; et al. Advanced LIGO. *Class. Quant. Grav.* **2015**, *32*, 074001. [CrossRef]
11. Acernese, F.; Agathos, M.; Agatsuma, K.; Aisa, D.; Allemandou, N.; Allocca, A.; Amarni, J.; Astone, P.; Balestri, G.; Ballardin, G.; et al. Advanced Virgo: A second-generation interferometric gravitational wave detector. *Class. Quant. Grav.* **2015**, *32*, 024001. [CrossRef]
12. Akutsu, T.; Ando, M.; Arai, K.; Arai, Y.; Araki, S.; Araya, A.; Aritomi, N.; Asada, H.; Aso, Y.; Atsuta, S.; et al. KAGRA: 2.5 Generation Interferometric Gravitational Wave Detector. *Nat. Astron.* **2019**, *3*, 35–40. [CrossRef]
13. Dooley, K.L. Status of GEO 600. *J. Phys. Conf. Ser.* **2015**, *610*, 012015. [CrossRef]
14. Abbott, B.; Abbott, R.; Abbott, T.; Abraham, S.; Acernese, F.; Ackley, K.; Adams, C.; Adya, V.; Affeldt, C.; Agathos, M.; et al. Prospects for observing and localizing gravitational-wave transients with Advanced LIGO, Advanced Virgo and KAGRA. *Living Rev. Rel.* **2018**, *21*, 3. [CrossRef] [PubMed]
15. Barsotti, L.; McCuller, L.; Evans, M.; Fritschel, P. *The A+ Design Curve*; Technical Report T1800042; LIGO. 2018. Available online: https://dcc.ligo.org/public/0149/T1800042/004/T1800042-v4.pdf (accessed on 14 April 2022).
16. Bersanetti, D.; Patricelli, B.; Piccinni, O.J.; Piergiovanni, F.; Salemi, F.; Sequino, V. Advanced Virgo: Status of the Detector, Latest Results and Future Prospects. *Universe* **2021**, *7*, 322. [CrossRef]

17. Adhikari, R.; Arai, K.; Brooks, A.; Wipf, C.; Aguiar, O.; Altin, P.; Barr, B.; Barsotti, L.; Bassiri, R.; Bell, A.; et al. A cryogenic silicon interferometer for gravitational-wave detection. *Class. Quant. Grav.* **2020**, *37*, 165003. [CrossRef]
18. Ackley, K.; Adya, V.; Agrawal, P.; Altin, P.; Ashton, G.; Bailes, M.; Baltinas, E.; Barbuio, A.; Beniwal, D.; Blair, C.; et al. Neutron Star Extreme Matter Observatory: A kilohertz-band gravitational-wave detector in the global network. *Publ. Astron. Soc. Austral.* **2020**, *37*, e047. [CrossRef]
19. Eichholz, J.; Holland, N.A.; Adya, V.B.; van Heijningen, J.V.; Ward, R.L.; Slagmolen, B.J.J.; McClelland, D.E.; Ottaway, D.J. Practical test mass and suspension configuration for a cryogenic kilohertz gravitational wave detector. *Phys. Rev. D* **2020**, *102*, 122003. [CrossRef]
20. Einstein Telescope Steering Committee. *Einstein Telescope: Science Case, Design Study and Feasibility Report*; Technical Report ET–0028A–20; Einstein Telescope. 2020. Available online: http://www.et-gw.eu/index.php/relevant-et-documents (accessed on 14 April 2022).
21. Barsotti, L.; Evans, M.; Mavalvala, N.; Ballmer, S. Long Uncomplicated Next-Generation Gravitational-Wave Observatory. In Proceedings of the Gravitational-Wave Advanced Detector Workshop 2013, Elba, Italy, 19–25 May 2013.
22. Dwyer, S.; Sigg, D.; Ballmer, S.W.; Barsotti, L.; Mavalvala, N.; Evans, M. Gravitational wave detector with cosmological reach. *Phys. Rev. D* **2015**, *91*, 082001. [CrossRef]
23. Abbott, B.P.; Abbott, R.; Abbott, T.D.; Abernathy, M.R.; Ackley, K.; Adams, C.; Addesso, P.; Adhikari, R.X.; Adya, V.B.; Affeldt, C.; et al. Exploring the Sensitivity of Next Generation Gravitational Wave Detectors. *Class. Quant. Grav.* **2017**, *34*, 044001. [CrossRef]
24. Evans, M.; Adhikari, R.X.; Afle, C.; Ballmer, S.W.; Biscoveanu, S.; Borhanian, S.; Brown, D.A.; Chen, Y.; Eisenstein, R.; Gruson, A.; et al. A Horizon Study for Cosmic Explorer: Science, Observatories, and Community. *arXiv* **2021**, arXiv:2109.09882.
25. Reitze, D.; Abbott, B.; Adams, C.; Adhikari, R.; Aggarwal, N.; Anand, S.; Ananyeva, A.; Anderson, S.; Appert, S.; Arai, K.; et al. The US Program in Ground-Based Gravitational Wave Science: Contribution from the LIGO Laboratory. *arXiv* **2019**, arXiv:1903.04615.
26. Reitze, D.; Adhikari, R.X.; Ballmer, S.; Barish, B.; Barsotti, L.; Billingsley, G.; Brown, D.A.; Chen, Y.; Coyne, D.; Eisenstein, R.; et al. Cosmic Explorer: The U.S. Contribution to Gravitational-Wave Astronomy beyond LIGO. *arXiv* **2019**, arXiv:1907.04833.
27. Maggiore, M.; Van Den Broeck, C.; Bartolo, N.; Belgacem, E.; Bertacca, D.; Bizouard, M.A.; Branchesi, M.; Clesse, S.; Foffa, S.; García-Bellido, J.; et al. Science Case for the Einstein Telescope. *JCAP* **2020**, *03*, 050. [CrossRef]
28. Raffai, P.; Gondán, L.; Heng, I.S.; Kelecsényi, N.; Logue, J.; Márka, Z.; Márka, S. Optimal Networks of Future Gravitational-Wave Telescopes. *Class. Quant. Grav.* **2013**, *30*, 155004. [CrossRef]
29. Hu, Y.M.; Raffai, P.; Gondán, L.; Heng, I.S.; Kelecsényi, N.; Hendry, M.; Márka, Z.; Márka, S. Global optimization for future gravitational wave detector sites. *Class. Quant. Grav.* **2015**, *32*, 105010. [CrossRef]
30. Vitale, S.; Evans, M. Parameter estimation for binary black holes with networks of third generation gravitational-wave detectors. *Phys. Rev. D* **2017**, *95*, 064052. [CrossRef]
31. Hall, E.D.; Evans, M. Metrics for next-generation gravitational-wave detectors. *Class. Quant. Grav.* **2019**, *36*, 225002. [CrossRef]
32. Nitz, A.H.; Dal Canton, T. Pre-merger Localization of Compact-binary Mergers with Third-generation Observatories. *Astrophys. J. Lett.* **2021**, *917*, L27. [CrossRef]
33. Li, Y.; Heng, I.S.; Chan, M.L.; Messenger, C.; Fan, X. Exploring the sky localization and early warning capabilities of third generation gravitational wave detectors in three-detector network configurations. *Phys. Rev. D* **2022**, *105*, 043010. [CrossRef]
34. Gossan, S.E.; Hall, E.D.; Nissanke, S.M. Optimizing the Third Generation of Gravitational-wave Observatories for Galactic Astrophysics. *Astrophys. J.* **2022**, *926*, 231. [CrossRef]
35. Borhanian, S.; Sathyaprakash, B.S. Listening to the Universe with Next Generation Ground-Based Gravitational-Wave Detectors. *arXiv* **2022**, arXiv:2202.11048.
36. García-Quirós, C.; Colleoni, M.; Husa, S.; Estellés, H.; Pratten, G.; Ramos-Buades, A.; Mateu-Lucena, M.; Jaume, R. Multimode frequency-domain model for the gravitational wave signal from nonprecessing black-hole binaries. *Phys. Rev. D* **2020**, *102*, 064002. [CrossRef]
37. Madau, P.; Dickinson, M. Cosmic Star Formation History. *Ann. Rev. Astron. Astrophys.* **2014**, *52*, 415–486. [CrossRef]
38. Vitale, S.; Farr, W.M.; Ng, K.; Rodriguez, C.L. Measuring the star formation rate with gravitational waves from binary black holes. *Astrophys. J. Lett.* **2019**, *886*, L1. [CrossRef]
39. Abbott, B.; Abbott, R.; Abbott, T.; Abernathy, M.; Acernese, F.; Ackley, K.; Adams, C.; Adams, T.; Addesso, P.; Adhikari, R.; et al. GW150914: First results from the search for binary black hole coalescence with Advanced LIGO. *Phys. Rev. D* **2016**, *93*, 122003. [CrossRef] [PubMed]
40. Abbott, B.; Abbott, R.; Abbott, T.D.; Acernese, F.; Ackley, K.; Adams, C.; Adams, T.; Addesso, P.; Adhikari, R.X.; Adya, V.B.; et al. GW170817: Observation of Gravitational Waves from a Binary Neutron Star Inspiral. *Phys. Rev. Lett.* **2017**, *119*, 161101. [CrossRef]
41. Salaris, M.; Cassisi, S. *Evolution of Stars and Stellar Populations*; Wiley: Chichester, UK, 2005.
42. Bromm, V.; Larson, R.B. The First stars. *Ann. Rev. Astron. Astrophys.* **2004**, *42*, 79–118. [CrossRef]
43. Madau, P.; Rees, M.J. Massive black holes as Population III remnants. *Astrophys. J. Lett.* **2001**, *551*, L27–L30. [CrossRef]
44. Greene, J.E.; Strader, J.; Ho, L.C. Intermediate-Mass Black Holes. *Ann. Rev. Astron. Astrophys.* **2020**, *58*, 257–312. [CrossRef]
45. Banados, E.; Venemans, B.P.; Mazzucchelli, C.; Farina, E.P.; Walter, F.; Wang, F.; Decarli, R.; Stern, D.; Fan, X.; Davies, F.; et al. An 800-million-solar-mass black hole in a significantly neutral Universe at redshift 7.5. *Nature* **2018**, *553*, 473–476. [CrossRef]

46. Chen, H.Y.; Ricarte, A.; Pacucci, F. Prospects to Explore High-redshift Black Hole Formation with Multi-band Gravitational Waves Observatories. *arXiv* **2022**, arXiv:2202.04764.
47. Mapelli, M. Binary Black Hole Mergers: Formation and Populations. *Front. Astron. Space Sci.* **2020**, *7*, 38. [CrossRef]
48. Rodriguez, C.L.; Amaro-Seoane, P.; Chatterjee, S.; Rasio, F.A. Post-Newtonian Dynamics in Dense Star Clusters: Highly-Eccentric, Highly-Spinning, and Repeated Binary Black Hole Mergers. *Phys. Rev. Lett.* **2018**, *120*, 151101. [CrossRef] [PubMed]
49. Zevin, M.; Romero-Shaw, I.M.; Kremer, K.; Thrane, E.; Lasky, P.D. Implications of Eccentric Observations on Binary Black Hole Formation Channels. *Astrophys. J. Lett.* **2021**, *921*, L43. [CrossRef]
50. Zevin, M.; Bavera, S.S.; Berry, C.P.L.; Kalogera, V.; Fragos, T.; Marchant, P.; Rodriguez, C.L.; Antonini, F.; Holz, D.E.; Pankow, C. One Channel to Rule Them All? Constraining the Origins of Binary Black Holes Using Multiple Formation Pathways. *Astrophys. J.* **2021**, *910*, 152. [CrossRef]
51. Ng, K.K.Y.; Vitale, S.; Farr, W.M.; Rodriguez, C.L. Probing multiple populations of compact binaries with third-generation gravitational-wave detectors. *Astrophys. J. Lett.* **2021**, *913*, L5. [CrossRef]
52. Baym, G.; Hatsuda, T.; Kojo, T.; Powell, P.D.; Song, Y.; Takatsuka, T. From hadrons to quarks in neutron stars: A review. *Rept. Prog. Phys.* **2018**, *81*, 056902. [CrossRef]
53. Chatziioannou, K. Neutron star tidal deformability and equation of state constraints. *Gen. Rel. Grav.* **2020**, *52*, 109. [CrossRef]
54. Haskell, B.; Schwenzer, K. Isolated Neutron Stars. In *Handbook of Gravitational Wave Astronomy*; Springer: Singapore, 2021. [CrossRef]
55. Woan, G.; Pitkin, M.D.; Haskell, B.; Jones, D.I.; Lasky, P.D. Evidence for a Minimum Ellipticity in Millisecond Pulsars. *Astrophys. J. Lett.* **2018**, *863*, L40. [CrossRef]
56. Most, E.R.; Papenfort, L.J.; Dexheimer, V.; Hanauske, M.; Schramm, S.; Stöcker, H.; Rezzolla, L. Signatures of quark-hadron phase transitions in general-relativistic neutron-star mergers. *Phys. Rev. Lett.* **2019**, *122*, 061101. [CrossRef]
57. Prakash, A.; Radice, D.; Logoteta, D.; Perego, A.; Nedora, V.; Bombaci, I.; Kashyap, R.; Bernuzzi, S.; Endrizzi, A. Signatures of deconfined quark phases in binary neutron star mergers. *Phys. Rev. D* **2021**, *104*, 083029. [CrossRef]
58. Sarin, N.; Lasky, P.D. The evolution of binary neutron star post-merger remnants: A review. *Gen. Rel. Grav.* **2021**, *53*, 59. [CrossRef]
59. Kashyap, R.; Das, A.; Radice, D.; Padamata, S.; Prakash, A.; Logoteta, D.; Perego, A.; Godzieba, D.A.; Bernuzzi, S.; Bombaci, I.; et al. Numerical relativity simulations of prompt collapse mergers: Threshold mass and phenomenological constraints on neutron star properties after GW170817. *arXiv* **2021**, arXiv:2111.05183.
60. Srivastava, V.; Davis, D.; Kuns, K.; Landry, P.; Ballmer, S.; Evans, M.; Hall, E.; Read, J.; Sathyaprakash, B.S. Science-Driven Tunable Design of Cosmic Explorer Detectors. *arXiv* **2022**, arXiv:2201.10668.
61. Clark, J.A.; Bauswein, A.; Stergioulas, N.; Shoemaker, D. Observing Gravitational Waves From The Post-Merger Phase Of Binary Neutron Star Coalescence. *Class. Quant. Grav.* **2016**, *33*, 085003. [CrossRef]
62. Abdikamalov, E.; Pagliaroli, G.; Radice, D. Gravitational Waves from Core-Collapse Supernovae. *arXiv* **2020**, arXiv:2010.04356.
63. Srivastava, V.; Ballmer, S.; Brown, D.A.; Afle, C.; Burrows, A.; Radice, D.; Vartanyan, D. Detection Prospects of Core-Collapse Supernovae with Supernova-Optimized Third-Generation Gravitational-wave Detectors. *Phys. Rev. D* **2019**, *100*, 043026. [CrossRef]
64. Abbott, B.; Abbott, R.; Abbott, T.; Acernese, F.; Ackley, K.; Adams, C.; Adams, T.; Addesso, P.; Adhikari, R.; Adya, V.; et al. Multi-messenger Observations of a Binary Neutron Star Merger. *Astrophys. J. Lett.* **2017**, *848*, L12. [CrossRef]
65. Kasen, D.; Metzger, B.; Barnes, J.; Quataert, E.; Ramirez-Ruiz, E. Origin of the heavy elements in binary neutron-star mergers from a gravitational wave event. *Nature* **2017**, *551*, 80. [CrossRef]
66. Barnes, J. The Physics of Kilonovae. *Front. Phys.* **2020**, *8*, 355. [CrossRef]
67. Abbott, B.; Abbott, R.; Abbott, T.; Acernese, F.; Ackley, K.; Adams, C.; Adams, T.; Addesso, P.; Adhikari, R.; Adya, V.; et al. Gravitational Waves and Gamma-rays from a Binary Neutron Star Merger: GW170817 and GRB 170817A. *Astrophys. J. Lett.* **2017**, *848*, L13. [CrossRef]
68. Ciolfi, R. Short gamma-ray burst central engines. *Int. J. Mod. Phys. D* **2018**, *27*, 1842004. [CrossRef]
69. Will, C.M. The Confrontation between General Relativity and Experiment. *Living Rev. Rel.* **2014**, *17*, 4. [CrossRef]
70. Abbott, B.; Abbott, R.; Abbott, T.; Abraham, S.; Acernese, F.; Ackley, K.; Adams, C.; Adhikari, R.; Adya, V.; Affeldt, C.; et al. Tests of General Relativity with the Binary Black Hole Signals from the LIGO-Virgo Catalog GWTC-1. *Phys. Rev. D* **2019**, *100*, 104036. [CrossRef]
71. Abbott, R.; Abbott, T.; Abraham, S.; Acernese, F.; Ackley, K.; Adams, A.; Adams, C.; Adhikari, R.; Adya, V.; Affeldt, C.; et al. Tests of general relativity with binary black holes from the second LIGO-Virgo gravitational-wave transient catalog. *Phys. Rev. D* **2021**, *103*, 122002. [CrossRef]
72. Perkins, S.E.; Yunes, N.; Berti, E. Probing Fundamental Physics with Gravitational Waves: The Next Generation. *Phys. Rev. D* **2021**, *103*, 044024. [CrossRef]
73. Gossan, S.; Veitch, J.; Sathyaprakash, B.S. Bayesian model selection for testing the no-hair theorem with black hole ringdowns. *Phys. Rev. D* **2012**, *85*, 124056. [CrossRef]
74. Meidam, J.; Agathos, M.; Van Den Broeck, C.; Veitch, J.; Sathyaprakash, B.S. Testing the no-hair theorem with black hole ringdowns using TIGER. *Phys. Rev. D* **2014**, *90*, 064009. [CrossRef]

75. Berti, E.; Sesana, A.; Barausse, E.; Cardoso, V.; Belczynski, K. Spectroscopy of Kerr black holes with Earth- and space-based interferometers. *Phys. Rev. Lett.* **2016**, *117*, 101102. [CrossRef]
76. Cardoso, V.; Pani, P. Testing the nature of dark compact objects: A status report. *Living Rev. Rel.* **2019**, *22*, 4. [CrossRef]
77. Bertone, G.; Croon, D.; Amin, M.A.; Boddy, K.K.; Kavanagh, B.J.; Mack, K.J.; Natarajan, P.; Opferkuch, T.; Schutz, K.; Takhistov, V.; et al. Gravitational wave probes of dark matter: Challenges and opportunities. *SciPost Phys. Core* **2020**, *3*, 007. [CrossRef]
78. Chen, Z.C.; Huang, Q.G. Distinguishing Primordial Black Holes from Astrophysical Black Holes by Einstein Telescope and Cosmic Explorer. *JCAP* **2020**, *08*, 039. [CrossRef]
79. Yuan, C.; Brito, R.; Cardoso, V. Probing ultralight dark matter with future ground-based gravitational-wave detectors. *Phys. Rev. D* **2021**, *104*, 044011. [CrossRef]
80. Nagano, K.; Nakatsuka, H.; Morisaki, S.; Fujita, T.; Michimura, Y.; Obata, I. Axion dark matter search using arm cavity transmitted beams of gravitational wave detectors. *Phys. Rev. D* **2021**, *104*, 062008. [CrossRef]
81. Chen, H.Y.; Cowperthwaite, P.S.; Metzger, B.D.; Berger, E. A Program for Multimessenger Standard Siren Cosmology in the Era of LIGO A+, Rubin Observatory, and Beyond. *Astrophys. J. Lett.* **2021**, *908*, L4. [CrossRef]
82. Wu, C.; Mandic, V.; Regimbau, T. Accessibility of the Gravitational-Wave Background due to Binary Coalescences to Second and Third Generation Gravitational-Wave Detectors. *Phys. Rev. D* **2012**, *85*, 104024. [CrossRef]
83. Regimbau, T.; Evans, M.; Christensen, N.; Katsavounidis, E.; Sathyaprakash, B.; Vitale, S. Digging deeper: Observing primordial gravitational waves below the binary black hole produced stochastic background. *Phys. Rev. Lett.* **2017**, *118*, 151105. [CrossRef] [PubMed]
84. Sharma, A.; Harms, J. Searching for cosmological gravitational-wave backgrounds with third-generation detectors in the presence of an astrophysical foreground. *Phys. Rev. D* **2020**, *102*, 063009. [CrossRef]
85. Sachdev, S.; Regimbau, T.; Sathyaprakash, B.S. Subtracting compact binary foreground sources to reveal primordial gravitational-wave backgrounds. *Phys. Rev. D* **2020**, *102*, 024051. [CrossRef]
86. Biscoveanu, S.; Talbot, C.; Thrane, E.; Smith, R. Measuring the primordial gravitational-wave background in the presence of astrophysical foregrounds. *Phys. Rev. Lett.* **2020**, *125*, 241101. [CrossRef]
87. Lang, K.R. Serendipitous Astronomy. *Science* **2010**, *327*, 39–40. [CrossRef]
88. Hall, E.D.; Kuns, K.; Smith, J.R.; Bai, Y.; Wipf, C.; Biscans, S.; Adhikari, R.X.; Arai, K.; Ballmer, S.; Barsotti, L.; et al. Gravitational-wave physics with Cosmic Explorer: Limits to low-frequency sensitivity. *Phys. Rev. D* **2021**, *103*, 122004. [CrossRef]
89. Schutz, B.F. Networks of gravitational wave detectors and three figures of merit. *Class. Quant. Grav.* **2011**, *28*, 125023. [CrossRef]
90. Rakhmanov, M.; Romano, J.D.; Whelan, J.T. High-frequency corrections to the detector response and their effect on searches for gravitational waves. *Class. Quant. Grav.* **2008**, *25*, 184017. [CrossRef]
91. Essick, R.; Vitale, S.; Evans, M. Frequency-dependent responses in third generation gravitational-wave detectors. *Phys. Rev. D* **2017**, *96*, 084004. [CrossRef]
92. Rollins, J.G.; Hall, E.; Wipf, C.; McCuller, L. pygwinc: *Gravitational Wave Interferometer Noise Calculator*; 2020. Available online: https://ascl.net/2007.020 (accessed on 14 April 2022).
93. Kogelnik, H.; Li, T. Laser Beams and Resonators. *Appl. Opt.* **1966**, *5*, 1550–1567. [CrossRef] [PubMed]
94. Sidles, J.A.; Sigg, D. Optical torques in suspended Fabry–Perot interferometers. *Phys. Lett. A* **2006**, *354*, 167–172. [CrossRef]
95. Evans, M.; Gras, S.; Fritschel, P.; Miller, J.; Barsotti, L.; Martynov, D.; Brooks, A.; Coyne, D.; Abbott, R.; Adhikari, R.; et al. Observation of Parametric Instability in Advanced LIGO. *Phys. Rev. Lett.* **2015**, *114*, 161102. [CrossRef]
96. Miao, H.; Smith, N.D.; Evans, M. Quantum limit for laser interferometric gravitational wave detectors from optical dissipation. *Phys. Rev. X* **2019**, *9*, 011053. [CrossRef]
97. McCuller, L.; Dwyer, S.; Green, A.; Yu, H.; Barsotti, L.; Blair, C.; Brown, D.; Effler, A.; Evans, M.; Fernandez-Galiana, A.; et al. LIGO's quantum response to squeezed states. *Phys. Rev. D* **2021**, *104*, 062006. [CrossRef]
98. Siegman, A.E. *Lasers*; University Science Books: Sausalito, CA, USA, 1986.
99. Barriga, P.; Bhawal, B.; Ju, L.; Blair, D.G. Numerical calculations of diffraction losses in advanced interferometric gravitational wave detectors. *J. Opt. Soc. Am. A* **2007**, *24*, 1731–1741. [CrossRef]
100. Granata, M.; Amato, A.; Balzarini, L.; Canepa, M.; Degallaix, J.; Forest, D.; Dolique, V.; Mereni, L.; Michel, C.; Pinard, L.; et al. Amorphous optical coatings of present gravitational-wave interferometers. *Class. Quant. Grav.* **2020**, *37*, 095004. [CrossRef]
101. Vajente, G.; Yang, L.; Davenport, A.; Fazio, M.; Ananyeva, A.; Zhang, L.; Billingsley, G.; Prasai, K.; Markosyan, A.; Bassiri, R.; et al. Low Mechanical Loss TiO2:GeO2 Coatings for Reduced Thermal Noise in Gravitational Wave Interferometers. *Phys. Rev. Lett.* **2021**, *127*, 071101. [CrossRef] [PubMed]
102. Granata, M.; Amato, A.; Cagnoli, G.; Coulon, M.; Degallaix, J.; Forest, D.; Mereni, L.; Michel, C.; Pinard, L.; Sassolas, B.; et al. Progress in the measurement and reduction of thermal noise in optical coatings for gravitational-wave detectors. *Appl. Opt.* **2020**, *59*, A229–A235. [CrossRef] [PubMed]
103. Penn, S.D.; Kinley-Hanlon, M.M.; MacMillan, I.A.O.; Heu, P.; Follman, D.; Deutsch, C.; Cole, G.D.; Harry, G.M. Mechanical Ringdown Studies of Large-Area Substrate-Transferred GaAs/AlGaAs Crystalline Coatings. *J. Opt. Soc. Am. B* **2019**, *36*, C15–C21. [CrossRef]
104. Brooks, A.; Vajente, G.; Yamamoto, H.; Abbott, R.; Adams, C.; Adhikari, R.; Ananyeva, A.; Appert, S.; Arai, K.; Areeda, J.; et al. Point absorbers in Advanced LIGO. *Appl. Opt.* **2021**, *60*, 4047. [CrossRef]

105. Jia, W.; Yamamoto, H.; Kuns, K.; Effler, A.; Evans, M.; Fritschel, P.; Abbott, R.; Adams, C.; Adhikari, R.; Ananyeva, A.; et al. Point Absorber Limits to Future Gravitational-Wave Detectors. *Phys. Rev. Lett.* **2021**, *127*, 241102. [CrossRef]
106. Aston, S.; Barton, M.; Bell, A.; Beveridge, N.; Bland, B.; Brummitt, A.; Cagnoli, G.; Cantley, C.; Carbone, L.; Cumming, A.; et al. Update on quadruple suspension design for Advanced LIGO. *Class. Quant. Grav.* **2012**, *29*, 235004. [CrossRef]
107. Saulson, P.R. Thermal noise in mechanical experiments. *Phys. Rev. D* **1990**, *42*, 2437–2445. [CrossRef]
108. Cumming, A.V.; Jones, R.; Hammond, G.D.; Hough, J.; Martin, I.W.; Rowan, S. Large-scale Monolithic Fused-Silica Mirror Suspension for Third-Generation Gravitational-Wave Detectors. *Phys. Rev. Appl.* **2022**, *17*, 024044. [CrossRef]
109. Matichard, F.; Lantz, B.; Mittleman, R.; Mason, K.; Kissel, J.; Abbott, B.; Biscans, S.; McIver, J.; Abbott, R.; Abbott, S.; et al. Seismic isolation of Advanced LIGO: Review of strategy, instrumentation and performance. *Class. Quant. Grav.* **2015**, *32*, 185003. [CrossRef]
110. Mow-Lowry, C.M.; Martynov, D. A 6D interferometric inertial isolation system. *Class. Quant. Grav.* **2019**, *36*, 245006. [CrossRef]
111. van Heijningen, J.V.; Bertolini, A.; van den Brand, J.F.J. A novel interferometrically read out inertial sensor for future gravitational wave detectors. In Proceedings of the 2018 IEEE Sensors Applications Symposium (SAS), Seoul, Korea, 12–14 March 2018; pp. 1–5. [CrossRef]
112. Harms, J. Terrestrial gravity fluctuations. *Living Rev. Rel.* **2019**, *22*, 6. [CrossRef]
113. Coughlin, M.W.; Harms, J.; Driggers, J.; McManus, D.J.; Mukund, N.; Ross, M.P.; Slagmolen, B.J.J.; Venkateswara, K. Implications of dedicated seismometer measurements on Newtonian-noise cancellation for Advanced LIGO. *Phys. Rev. Lett.* **2018**, *121*, 221104. [CrossRef] [PubMed]
114. Driggers, J.C.; Harms, J.; Adhikari, R.X. Subtraction of Newtonian Noise Using Optimized Sensor Arrays. *Phys. Rev. D* **2012**, *86*, 102001. [CrossRef]
115. Gan, W.S., Seismic Metamaterials. In *New Acoustics Based on Metamaterials*; Springer: Singapore, 2018; pp. 277–288. [CrossRef]
116. Fiorucci, D.; Harms, J.; Barsuglia, M.; Fiori, I.; Paoletti, F. Impact of infrasound atmospheric noise on gravity detectors used for astrophysical and geophysical applications. *Phys. Rev. D* **2018**, *97*, 062003. [CrossRef]
117. Bowman, J.R.; Baker, G.E.; Bahavar, M. Ambient infrasound noise. *Geophys. Res. Lett.* **2005**, *32*, L09803. [CrossRef]
118. Cahillane, C.; Mansell, G.; Sigg, D. Laser Frequency Noise in Next Generation Gravitational-Wave Detectors. *Opt. Express* **2021**, *29*, 42144–42161. [CrossRef]
119. Essick, R. Calibration uncertainty's impact on gravitational-wave observations. *Phys. Rev. D* **2022**, *105*, 082002. [CrossRef]
120. Pürrer, M.; Haster, C.J. Gravitational waveform accuracy requirements for future ground-based detectors. *Phys. Rev. Res.* **2020**, *2*, 023151. [CrossRef]
121. Bhattacharjee, D.; Lecoeuche, Y.; Karki, S.; Betzwieser, J.; Bossilkov, V.; Kandhasamy, S.; Payne, E.; Savage, R.L. Fiducial displacements with improved accuracy for the global network of gravitational wave detectors. *Class. Quant. Grav.* **2021**, *38*, 015009. [CrossRef]
122. Spidell, M.; Lehman, J.; López, M.; Lecher, H.; Kück, S.; Bhattacharjee, D.; Lecoeuche, Y.; Savage, R. A bilateral comparison of NIST and PTB laser power standards for scale realization confidence by gravitational wave observatories. *Metrologia* **2021**, *58*, 055011. [CrossRef]
123. Ross, M.P.; Mistry, T.; Datrier, L.; Kissel, J.; Venkateswara, K.; Weller, C.; Kumar, K.; Hagedorn, C.; Adelberger, E.; Lee, J.; et al. Initial results from the LIGO Newtonian calibrator. *Phys. Rev. D* **2021**, *104*, 082006. [CrossRef]
124. Estevez, D.; Mours, B.; Pradier, T. Newtonian calibrator tests during the Virgo O$_3$ data taking. *Class. Quant. Grav.* **2021**, *38*, 075012. [CrossRef]
125. Inoue, Y.; Haino, S.; Kanda, N.; Ogawa, Y.; Suzuki, T.; Tomaru, T.; Yamanmoto, T.; Yokozawa, T. Improving the absolute accuracy of the gravitational wave detectors by combining the photon pressure and gravity field calibrators. *Phys. Rev. D* **2018**, *98*, 022005. [CrossRef]
126. Dylla, F.; Weiss, R.; Zucker, M.E. (Eds.) In Proceedings of the NSF Workshop on Large Ultrahigh-Vacuum Systems for Frontier Scientific Research, Livingston, LA, USA, 28–31 January 2019. Available online: https://dcc.ligo.org/LIGO-P1900072/public (accessed on 14 April 2022).
127. Vajente, G. *Noise from Clipping on Cosmic Explorer Beam Tube Baffles*; Technical Report CE–T2100011; Cosmic Explorer. 2021. Available online: https://arxiv.org/pdf/2109.09882.pdf (accessed on 14 April 2022).
128. Bai, Y. *Cosmic Explorer: Back-scatter Noise and Design Recommendations*; Technical Report T1900854–v1; LIGO. 2019. Available online: https://dcc.ligo.org/public/ (accessed on 14 April 2022).
129. Day, R. *FFT Simulation Using FOG*; Technical Report G1300532; LIGO. 2013. Available online: https://dcc.ligo.org/LIGO-G1300532/public (accessed on 14 April 2022).
130. Amann, F.; Bonsignorio, F.; Bulik, T.; Bulten, H.J.; Cuccuru, S.; Dassargues, A.; DeSalvo, R.; Fenyvesi, E.; Fidecaro, F.; Fiori, I.; et al. Site-selection criteria for the Einstein Telescope. *Rev. Sci. Instrum.* **2020**, *91*, 9. [CrossRef]
131. Efron, N.; Read, M. *Analysing International Tunnel Costs*; Technical Report; Worcester Polytechnic Institute: Worcester, MA, USA, 2012.
132. Kuns, K. (Massachusetts Institute of Technology, Cambridge, MA, USA); Schiettekatte, F. (University of Montreal, Montréal, QC, Canada); Slagmolen, B.J.J. (Australian National University, Canberra ACT, Australia); Töyra, D. (Australian National University, Canberra ACT, Australia). Personal communication, 2020.

133. Bonnefoy-Claudet, S.; Cotton, F.; Bard, P.Y. The nature of noise wavefield and its applications for site effects studies: A literature review. *Earth-Sci. Rev.* **2006**, *79*, 205–227. [CrossRef]
134. Peterson, J.R. *Observations and Modeling of Seismic Background Noise*; Technical Report; US Geological Survey: Albuquerque, NM, USA, 1993. [CrossRef]
135. Nguyen, P.; Schofield, R.M.; Effler, A.; Austin, C.; Adya, V.; Ball, M.; Banagiri, S.; Banowetz, K.; Billman, C.; Blair, C.D.; et al. Environmental noise in advanced LIGO detectors. *Class. Quant. Grav.* **2021**, *38*, 145001. [CrossRef]
136. Physics of Ambient Noise Generation by Ocean Waves. In *Seismic Ambient Noise*; Cambridge University Press: Cambridge, UK, 2019; pp. 69–108. [CrossRef]
137. De Angelis, S.; Bodin, P. Watching the Wind: Seismic Data Contamination at Long Periods due to Atmospheric Pressure-Field-Induced Tilting. *Bull. Seismol. Soc. Am.* **2012**, *102*, 1255–1265. [CrossRef]
138. Kahanamoku, S.; Alegado, R.A.; Kagawa-Viviani, A.; Kamelamela, K.L.; Kamai, B.; Walkowicz, L.M.; Prescod-Weinstein, C.; de los Reyes, M.A.; Neilson, H. A Native Hawaiian-Led Summary of the Current Impact of Constructing the Thirty Meter Telescope on Maunakea. *arXiv* **2020**, arXiv:2001.00970.
139. Barbu, B. Where science meets the sacred. *Symmetry Magazine*, 2021.
140. Martynov, D.; Miao, H.; Yang, H.; Vivanco, F.H.; Thrane, E.; Smith, R.; Lasky, P.; East, W.E.; Adhikari, R.; Bauswein, A.; et al. Exploring the sensitivity of gravitational wave detectors to neutron star physics. *Phys. Rev. D* **2019**, *99*, 102004. [CrossRef]
141. NSF Large Facilities Office. *Research Infrastructure Guide*; Technical Report NSF 21–107; National Science Foundation: Washington, DC, USA, 2021.
142. Harrison, F.A.; Kennicutt, R.C., Jr. (Eds.) *Pathways to Discovery in Astronomy and Astrophysics for the 2020s*; National Academies of Science, Engineering, and Medicine: Washington, DC, USA, 2021. [CrossRef]
143. Foucart, F.; Laguna, P.; Lovelace, G.; Radice, D.; Witek, H. Snowmass 2021 Cosmic Frontier White Paper: Numerical relativity for next-generation gravitational-wave probes of fundamental physics. *arXiv* **2022**, arXiv:2203.08139.
144. Chakrabarti, S.; Drlica-Wagner, A.; Li, T.S.; Sehgal, N.; Simon, J.D.; Birrer, S.; Brown, D.A.; Bernstein, R.; Bolatto, A.D.; Chang, P.; et al. Snowmass2021 Cosmic Frontier White Paper: Observational Facilities to Study Dark Matter. In Proceedings of the 2022 Snowmass Summer Study, Settle, WA, USA, 17–26 July 2022.
145. Engel, K.; Lewis, T.; Muzio, M.S.; Venters, T.M. Advancing the Landscape of Multimessenger Science in the Next Decade. In Proceedings of the 2022 Snowmass Summer Study, Settle, WA, USA, 17–26 July 2022.

Article

Optimization of Design Parameters for Gravitational Wave Detector DECIGO Including Fundamental Noises

Yuki Kawasaki [1,*], Ryuma Shimizu [1], Tomohiro Ishikawa [1], Koji Nagano [2], Shoki Iwaguchi [1], Izumi Watanabe [1], Bin Wu [1], Shuichiro Yokoyama [3,4] and Seiji Kawamura [1,3]

[1] Department of Physics, Nagoya University, Nagoya 464-8602, Japan; shimizu_r@u.phys.nagoya-u.ac.jp (R.S.); ishikawa_t@u.phys.nagoya-u.ac.jp (T.I.); iwaguchi_s@u.phys.nagoya-u.ac.jp (S.I.); watanabe_i@u.phys.nagoya-u.ac.jp (I.W.); wu_b@u.phys.nagoya-u.ac.jp (B.W.); kawamura@u.phys.nagoya-u.ac.jp (S.K.)
[2] Institute of Space and Astronautical Science, Japan Aerospace Exploration Agency, Sagamihara 252-5210, Japan; knagano@ac.jaxa.jp
[3] The Kobayashi-Masukawa Institute for the Origin of Particles and the Universe, Nagoya University, Nagoya 464-8602, Japan; shu@kmi.nagoya-u.ac.jp
[4] Kavli IPMU (WPI), UTIAS, The University of Tokyo, Kashiwa 277-8583, Japan
* Correspondence: kawasaki_y@u.phys.nagoya-u.ac.jp; Tel.: +81-52-789-6194

Citation: Kawasaki, Y.; Shimizu, R.; Ishikawa, T.; Nagano, K.; Iwaguchi, S.; Watanabe, I.; Wu, B.; Yokoyama, S.; Kawamura, S. Optimization of Design Parameters for Gravitational Wave Detector DECIGO Including Fundamental Noises. *Galaxies* **2022**, *10*, 25. https://doi.org/10.3390/galaxies10010025

Academic Editor: Gabriele Vajente

Received: 25 December 2021
Accepted: 22 January 2022
Published: 1 February 2022

Publisher's Note: MDPI stays neutral with regard to jurisdictional claims in published maps and institutional affiliations.

Copyright: © 2022 by the authors. Licensee MDPI, Basel, Switzerland. This article is an open access article distributed under the terms and conditions of the Creative Commons Attribution (CC BY) license (https://creativecommons.org/licenses/by/4.0/).

Abstract: The DECi-hertz Interferometer Gravitational-Wave Observatory (DECIGO) is a space gravitational wave (GW) detector. DECIGO was originally designed to be sensitive enough to observe primordial GW background (PGW). However, due to the lowered upper limit of the PGW by the Planck observation, further improvement of the target sensitivity of DECIGO is required. In the previous studies, DECIGO's parameters were optimized to maximize the signal-to-noise ratio (SNR) of the PGW to quantum noise including the effect of diffraction loss. To simulate the SNR more realistically, we optimize DECIGO's parameters considering the GWs from double white dwarfs (DWDs) and the thermal noise of test masses. We consider two cases of the cutoff frequency of GWs from DWDs. In addition, we consider two kinds of thermal noise: thermal noise in a residual gas and internal thermal noise. To investigate how the mirror geometry affects the sensitivity, we calculate it by changing the mirror mass, keeping the mirror thickness, and vice versa. As a result, we obtained the optimums for the parameters that maximize the SNR that depends on the mirror radius. This result shows that a thick mirror with a large radius gives a good SNR and enables us to optimize the design of DECIGO based on the feasibility study of the mirror size in the future.

Keywords: gravitational waves; DECIGO; thermal noise; quantum noise; diffraction loss

1. Introduction

The DECi-hertz Interferometer Gravitational-Wave Observatory (DECIGO) is a space gravitational wave (GW) detector [1,2]. One of the most important DECIGO goals is the observation of the primordial GW background (PGW) from the early Universe. It is ideal to observe the PGW in the lowest possible frequency band because the PGW has a larger strain in the lower frequency band. However, in the low-frequency band less than 0.1 Hz, GWs from several astrophysical sources impede the detection of the PGW [3]. Therefore, DECIGO, which has a frequency band between 0.1 Hz and 10 Hz, is optimized for the PGW observation.

Direct detection of PGW could contribute to the determination of inflation models in the early Universe. DECIGO was originally designed to be sensitive enough to observe the PGW, under the assumption that the normalized GW energy density $\Omega_{\rm gw}$ of the PGW is $\Omega_{\rm gw} \approx 2 \times 10^{-15}$ [4]. However, recent observations of CMB by Planck satellite and BICEP/Keck collaboration have lowered the upper limit for the PGW to $\Omega_{\rm gw} \approx 10^{-16}$, and this limit requires improvement of DECIGO's sensitivity [5–7].

In the previous studies, DECIGO's parameters such as mirror reflectivity, arm length, and laser power were optimized for a given mirror radius to maximize signal-to-noise ratio (SNR) of the PGW to quantum noise, including the effect of diffraction loss [8,9]. These parameters affect the magnitude of quantum noise in DECIGO. Specifically, the SNR increased from 6.6 to about 100 by the optimization.

The main noises limiting the detection of PGW are GWs from double white dwarfs (DWDs) and thermal noise. DWDs are fast-rotating binary stars that emit GWs in the form of quadrupole radiation (The frequency of the radiating GW is twice the angular frequency of the binary orbit). GWs from DWDs strongly affect the foreground GWs below around 0.1 Hz [10]. GWs from DWDs that cannot be resolved individually are regarded as noise. It is limiting the detectable frequency band of the PGW. In this paper, we estimate the limitation by GWs from DWDs. In addition, limits to the detector thermal noise cannot be avoided because the mirror and its environment exhibit thermally-driven motion. Thermal noise has larger effects on the SNR in the lower frequency band.

Due to the characteristics of GWs from DWDs and thermal noise, it is important to consider them to calculate the SNR to PGW. Thus, we take GWs from DWDs and thermal noise into consideration. Considering GWs from DWDs and thermal noise, we optimize DECIGO's parameters which are related to the magnitude of the noise and consider the parameters that give a larger SNR.

In this paper, we show the noise by GWs from DWDs in Section 2, the thermal noises in Section 3, the method of optimization in Section 4, the result of optimization in Section 5, and the conclusion in Section 6.

2. GWs from DWDs

GWs from various binaries are believed to affect the foreground GWs significantly in the frequency band between 10^{-5} and 10^{-1} Hz. The contribution of GWs from DWDs is especially relevant in the LISA band [11]. The contribution of galactic DWD is especially relevant in that frequency band. On the other hand, it is considered that the contribution of extragalactic DWD is important in the DECIGO band, which is discussed in e.g., Ref. [10]. There are many DWDs in the Universe [10]. When multiple GW signals from DWDs exist in one frequency bin, which is the frequency resolution of the detector, they cannot be resolved individually and are regarded as noise. A DWD binary system loses a part of energy by emitting GWs. The two stars of a DWD approach each other with increasing rotation frequency. Eventually, they collide at a certain frequency (called a cutoff frequency) which is determined by the mass and size of the binary star components. The DWD does not emit significant GWs after a collision. Therefore, the GWs from DWDs mainly exist in the frequency band below the cutoff frequency.

Due to their typical size and mass, DWDs emit GWs up to around 0.1 Hz. In the previous DECIGO design effort, the lower limit of the calculation range of the SNR was set to be 0.1 Hz to avoid the contamination from the foreground noise from DWDs below 0.1 Hz [8,9]. On the other hand, most of the WDs observed near our galaxy have a mass of 0.8 $M_\odot$ or less. If they form a binary star, they all coalesce at a frequency around 0.07 Hz [3]. Thus, if the observed mass distribution of WDs is extended to the entire Universe, we can consider a model in which the noise from DWDs exists up to 0.07 Hz. Therefore, in this paper, we consider two cases: for a lower limit of calculation of 0.1 Hz and 0.07 Hz. We decided to use these frequencies (0.1 Hz and 0.07 Hz) instead of providing two cases of the corresponding noise spectrums. We call these two cases the standard-DWD-model and the optimistic-DWD-model. In Section 5, we show the result of the calculation and optimized parameters for each model.

3. Thermal Noise

In this section, we estimate the noise caused by the thermal motion of DECIGO's mirrors. We optimize the SNR of DECIGO for the PGW background, considering two sources of thermal noise: thermal noise in a residual gas and internal thermal noise. The former is caused by the collision of residual gas molecules, which thermally move in the satellite, with the mirror. We can calculate this from a simple model (see Section 3.1). The latter comes from the internal dissipation of the mirror itself.

Both power spectrums can be calculated using the Fluctuation-Dissipation Theorem. The theory states that the power spectrum of fluctuating displacement is given as [12]

$$S_x(f) = \frac{k_B T}{\pi^2 f^2} \text{Re}[Y(f)]. \quad (1)$$

The function $Y(f)$, called admittance, is

$$v = Y(f) F_{ext}, \quad (2)$$

where v is the velocity of the mirror. In the following subsections, we use the Fluctuation-Dissipation Theorem to specifically calculate the thermal noise in a residual gas and the internal thermal noise. Table 1 shows the meaning of symbols used in this section.

Table 1. Meaning of each symbol.

Symbol	Meaning
k_B	Boltzmann constant
T (=300 K)	Mirror temperature
m	Mirror mass
R	Mirror radius
S	Mirror cross section
h	Mirror thickness
d	Coating thickness
L	Cavity length
E_0 (=7.4 × 10^{10} N/m^2)	Young's modulus
σ (=0.17)	Poisson's modulus
α	Thermal expansion rate
C	Specific heat per volume
κ	Diffusivity of the mirror
r_0	Beam radius
P	Pressure in the satellite
μ	Mass of a gas molecule in the satellite

3.1. Thermal Noise in a Residual Gas

The dissipation of the system is key in calculations using the Fluctuation Dissipation Theorem. First, we formulate the dissipation of the mirror due to the interaction between the mirror and its surroundings. We model the mirror and its surrounding space [13]. The mirror with mass m and cross-section S floats in the satellite, and residual gas occupies its surroundings.

The pressure of the gas is $P = nk_B T$, where n is the number density of gas molecules. We consider the case where P is low enough so that the mean free path length of molecules is larger than the mirror size. In other words, we do not consider intermolecular collisions.

Then, under this model, we obtain the power spectrum of the thermal noise in a residual gas $S_{x_{gas}}(f)$,

$$S_{x_{gas}}(f) = \frac{k_B T}{\pi^2 f^2} \frac{b}{(2\pi f m)^2 + b^2}, \quad (3)$$

where the factor b is

$$b = 2\pi \left[1.064 \times 10^{13} \left(\frac{1 \times 10^{-8} \text{ Pa}}{P} \right) \left(\frac{400 \text{ cm}^2}{S} \right) \right]^{-1} \text{ [kg/s]}. \quad (4)$$

In Equation (3), b is an important factor that determines the scale of the power spectrum. See Appendix A for how to derive $S_{x_{gas}}(f)$ and b. In the calculation of b, it is assumed that the residual gas in the satellite is nitrogen. If the main gas component is water instead, the coefficient of Equation (4) should be 1.33×10^{13} instead of 1.064×10^{13}. Also, if the main gas component is hydrogen, the coefficient should be 3.98×10^{13}.

Figure 1 shows the amplitude spectral density of the mirror thermal noise in terms of strain $\sqrt{S_h(f)}$, where the cavity length L is 1000 km, the gas pressure is 10^{-8} Pa, and the mirror radius R: 1 m, 0.75 m, and 0.5 m, respectively.

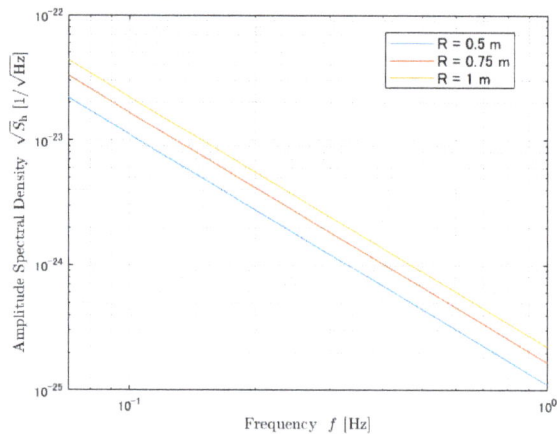

Figure 1. Amplitude spectral density of thermal noise in a residual gas (10^{-8} Pa). The blue line shows the case of $R = 0.5$ m. The red line shows the case of $R = 0.75$ m. The yellow line shows the case of $R = 1.0$ m.

3.2. Internal Thermal Noise

In this subsection, to evaluate the mirror thermal noise, we use Levin's method [14]. At first, it is assumed that the beam radius is much smaller than the mirror radius, and the mirror is regarded as an infinite half-space. According to Levin's method, the power spectrum is given by the following formula [14],

$$S_x(f) = \frac{2k_B T}{\pi^2 f^2} \frac{W_{diss}}{F_0^2}. \tag{5}$$

Here, W_{diss} is the average power that the mirror dissipates, and F_0 is the peak magnitude of the pressure due to the Gaussian laser beam hitting the mirror.

Let's consider the case where the effect of friction appears in the imaginary part of Young's modulus of the mirror. We can calculate W_{diss} using two parameters, ϕ and U_{max}. Here, ϕ is a parameter called the loss angle, and U_{max} is the elastic energy when the expansion and contraction of the mirror are maximized. Consequently, we obtain the power spectrum by assuming an infinite-space mirror [14–16],

$$S_{x_{inf}}(f) = \frac{4k_B T}{2\pi f} \frac{1-\sigma^2}{\sqrt{\pi}E_0 r_0} \phi_{sub}. \tag{6}$$

ϕ_{sub} is the mechanical loss angle of the mirror. We set $\phi_{sub} = 5 \times 10^{-7}$ as being representative of losses seen in fused silica mirrors.

In our simulation, the radius of the beam that hits the mirror is about the same as or larger than the mirror radius except when L is very small. Thus, the assumption of an infinite-space mirror does not hold, and Equation (6) needs to be corrected [17]. Specifically, it is corrected by multiplying Equation (6) by a factor C_{FTM} having the laser radius r_0, the mirror radius R, and the mirror thickness h as parameters. The power spectrum of finite-space mirror is given by,

$$S_{x_{\text{int}}}(f) = C_{\text{FTM}}^2 \times S_{x_{\text{inf}}}(f). \tag{7}$$

See Appendix C for specific C_{FTM} expressions. When the mirror is infinite size, $C_{\text{FTM}} = 1$. In our calculation, we assume that the laser radius r_0 is the distance from the center, where the beam amplitude is $1/e$ of the maximum. For simplicity, we assume $r_0 = R$ at the mirror surface. In calculating h, we assume that the material of the mirror is fused silica, which has a mass density of $\rho = 2.196 \times 10^3$ kg/m^3. We use this corrected $S_{x_{\text{int}}}(f)$ in our simulation.

3.3. Other Sources of Thermal Noise

In the above subsections, we show the power spectrum of the thermal noise in a residual gas (Equation (3)) and the internal thermal noise (Equation (6)). In reality, the mirror has thermal noises other than the above two. Thermoelastic noise and thermal noise of optical coatings are typical examples. Here we demonstrate that they have a negligible effect on the calculation of SNR.

First, assuming that the mirror has infinite size, we obtain the power spectrum of thermoelastic noise of the mirror [18].

$$S_{x_{\text{elas}}}(f) = \frac{16 k_B T^2 (1+\sigma)^2 \alpha^2 \kappa}{\sqrt{\pi} C r_0^3 (2\pi f)^2}. \tag{8}$$

According to the formula of Equation (8), the effect of thermoelastic noise is small. Thermoelastic noise in a finite size mirror is larger than Equation (8), but still not large enough to take into consideration.

Second, when we take the effect of optical coatings into consideration, we must multiply Equation (6) with the factor C_{coat} [19];

$$C_{\text{coat}} \sim \left(1 + \frac{2}{\sqrt{\pi}} \frac{1-2\sigma}{1-\sigma} \frac{\phi_{\text{coat}}}{\phi_{\text{sub}}} \frac{d}{r_0}\right), \tag{9}$$

where ϕ_{coat} is mechanical loss angle of coating. The order of the factor C_{coat} is determined by d/r_0. In this paper, to balance the diffraction loss against the expense and difficulty of large mirrors, we set the beam radius to be comparable to the mirror radius. Since the minimum R is 1 cm in our simulation, the minimum r_0 is also 1 cm. We assume that $d = 4$ µm because the reflectivity of the mirror r is not so high ($r \sim 0.9$). Therefore, $d/r_0 < 10^{-4}$ and $C_{\text{coat}} \sim 1$.

For the above reasons, we treat only thermal noise in a residual gas and internal thermal noise as noise in our simulation.

4. Method of Optimization

DECIGO consists of four clusters that are on the heliocentric orbit of the earth. Two clusters are placed at the same position to detect PGW by combining them. Figure 2 shows the configuration of DECIGO's one cluster. Its features are the following:

- One cluster consists of three interferometers.
- There are differential Fabry-Perot (FP) interferometers with 60° between each arm.
- Each interferometer shares each arm with two other interferometers.

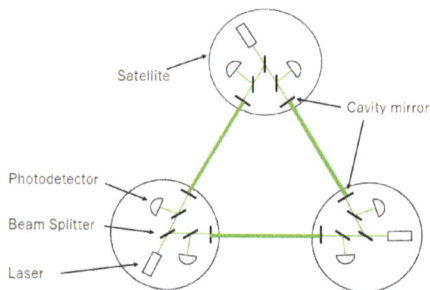

Figure 2. Configuration of one cluster in DECIGO. One cluster has three satellites. Each satellite has two mirrors, and the mirrors compose FP interferometers.

Therefore, the signal and noise obtained from one DECIGO cluster must be properly considered by separating one cluster into two effective interferometers [20]. First, we calculate the sensitivity of one triangular cluster: $S_h^{cluster}$. Then we combine the two clusters at the same position to calculate the SNR. For the detection of PGW, we need two clusters because the PGW is stationary, isotropic, has no polarization, and cannot be detected by one cluster. Then we optimize each of DECIGO's parameters to maximize the SNR for a given mirror radius R. In this paper, we optimize the sensitivity of DECIGO to the PGW ($\Omega_{gw} = 10^{-16}$). The SNR for DECIGO is given by

$$\mathrm{SNR} = \frac{3H_0^2}{10\pi^2}\sqrt{T_{obs}}\left[\int_{f_{min}}^{1}\frac{2\gamma^2(f)\Omega_{gw}^2(f)}{f^6 P_1(f)P_2(f)}df\right]^{\frac{1}{2}}, \qquad (10)$$

where $P_1(f) = P_2(f) = S_h^{cluster}/5$, T_{obs} = 3 years. f_{min} is calculated for the two cases of 0.1 Hz and 0.07 Hz. γ is the normalized overlap reduction function, equivalent to 1 because the two clusters are at the same position.

Considering quantum noises: shot noise $S_{h_{shot}}(f)$ and radiation pressure noise $S_{h_{rad}}(f)$ in addition to thermal noise, $S_h^{cluster}$ is given by [8],

$$S_h^{cluster}(f) = \frac{5\sqrt{2}}{3\sin^2\frac{\pi}{3}}\left[(\sqrt{S_{h_{shot}}(f)})^2 + (\sqrt{S_{h_{rad}}(f)})^2 + (\sqrt{S_{h_{gas}}(f)})^2 + (\sqrt{S_{h_{int}}(f)})^2\right], \qquad (11)$$

where

$$\sqrt{S_{h_{shot}}}(f) = \frac{1}{4\pi L}\frac{(1-r_{eff}^2)^2}{t_{eff}(tD)r_{eff}}\sqrt{\frac{4\pi\hbar c\lambda}{P_0}}\sqrt{1+(\frac{f}{f_p})^2}, \qquad (12)$$

$$\sqrt{S_{h_{rad}}}(f) = \frac{4}{mL(2\pi f)^2}\frac{t_{eff}^2(rD)^2(1+r_{eff}^2)}{(1-r_{eff}^2)^2}\sqrt{\frac{\pi\hbar P_0}{c\lambda}}\sqrt{\frac{1}{1+(\frac{f}{f_p})^2}}, \qquad (13)$$

and $\sqrt{S_{h_{gas,int}}} = \sqrt{S_{x_{gas,int}}}/L$.

In Equation (11), the coefficient $\frac{5\sqrt{2}}{3\sin^2\frac{\pi}{3}}$ represents that one DECIGO cluster consists of three interferometers with $\pi/3$ arm angle.

Table 2 shows the meaning of each symbol in Equations (10)–(13).

Table 2. Meaning of each symbol.

Symbol	Meaning
L	Cavity length
m	Mirror mass
P_0	Laser power entering beam splitter
λ (=515 × 10^{-9} m)	Laser wavelength
r	Mirror reflectivity
t	Mirror transmissivity
D	Effect of diffraction loss
$r_{\text{eff}} \equiv rD^2$	Effective mirror reflectivity
$t_{\text{eff}} \equiv tD^2$	Effective mirror transmissivity
c (=2.9979 × 10^8 m/s)	Light speed
$\hbar$ (=1.0546 × 10^{-34} Js)	Planck constant
H_0 (=70/3.086 × 10^{19} km/s/Mpc)	Hubble constant
$\mathcal{F} \equiv \pi r/(1-r^2)$	Finesse
$f_p \equiv c/4\mathcal{F}_{\text{eff}} L$	Cavity pole frequency
$\mathcal{F}_{\text{eff}} \equiv \pi r_{\text{eff}}/(1-r_{\text{eff}}^2)$	Effective finesse

In the following section, we use the maximized $D = D_{\max}$,

$$D_{\max}^2 = 1 - \exp\left[-\frac{2\pi}{L\lambda}R^2\right]. \tag{14}$$

The cavity setting for the maximizing D is shown in Appendix B. We optimize each of DECIGO's parameter to maximize the SNR for a given mirror radius R.

4.1. Treatment of Each Noise in the Simulation

In this subsection, we show how to treat each noise in our simulation.

For GWs from DWDs, we consider two patterns of the cutoff frequency: 0.07 Hz and 0.1 Hz. Considering the power spectrum of all the noises, we calculate the noise power spectrum of one cluster $S_h^{\text{cluster}}(f)$ by taking the sum of squares with shot noise and radiation pressure noise because all the noises are independent (see Equation (11)).

Note that, $\sqrt{S_{h_{\text{shot}}}}$ and $\sqrt{S_{h_{\text{rad}}}}$ are the strain of quantum noise of one interferometer that has a 90° arm angle. The strain of thermal noise of one mirror is $\sqrt{S_{h_{\text{gas,int}}}}$. Since one arm has two mirrors and their thermal noises are independent of each other, the strain of one arm is $\sqrt{2}$ times larger than that of one mirror. When two arms of one interferometer are correlated, the noise is $\sqrt{2}$ times larger than that of one arm, and the signal is 2 times larger. Therefore, the strain of thermal noise of one interferometer is represented as $\sqrt{S_{h_{\text{gas,int}}}}$.

4.2. Method of Calculation

We calculate the SNR of DECIGO, applying Equation (11) as a function of R, L, r, and P_0.

$$\text{SNR} = \text{SNR}(R, L, r, P_0). \tag{15}$$

Further, we decide the optimized L, r, and P_0 that give the maximum SNR for a given R.

In our simulation, we consider two cases of gas pressure in the satellite: 10^{-8} Pa (high-density-gas case) and 10^{-9} Pa (low-density-gas case). Considering these two cases, we estimate the magnitude of the internal pressure required for the DECIGO's satellites.

In addition, we consider two patterns for the mirror: the constant-mirror-mass model and the constant-mirror-thickness model. In the constant-mirror-mass model, we set the mirror mass to be 100 kg regardless of R. In the constant-mirror-thickness model, we set the mirror mass to be proportional to the square of R.

$$m = \left(\frac{R}{0.5 \text{ m}}\right)^2 \times 100 \text{ kg}. \tag{16}$$

m is decided to be 100 kg at $R = 0.5$ m, which is the default value of DECIGO. In this paper, we consider two mirror models as frameworks with which we can make a further optimization after the limitations of the mirror mass and size are set. We calculate the SNR over the limited range of each parameter shown in Table 3. In addition, we show the results of the optimizations in each case shown in Table 4. That is, we show eight results obtained by combining each model.

Table 3. Limited range of each parameter.

Symbol	Range
R	0 to 1 m
r	0 to 1
P_0	0 to 100 W
L	No limit

Table 4. DECIGO's parameters that have different values depending on the model.

Parameter	Value in Each Model
Cutoff frequency	0.07 Hz/0.1 Hz
Pressure in the satellite	10^{-8} Pa/10^{-9} Pa
Mirror mass	Constant (100 kg)/Proportional to the square of R.

5. Result

5.1. Optimization of SNR and Parameters

In this section, we show the result of the optimization in Figure 3 (optimistic DWD model) and Figure 4 (standard DWD model).

Figures 3 and 4 show the maximized SNR and optimized parameters L, r, and P_0 as a function of R. In Figures 3 and 4a,b show the results of the constant-mirror-thickness model. Figures 3 and 4c,d show the results of the constant-mirror-mass model. Figures 3 and 4a,c show the results of the high-density-gas case. Figures 3 and 4b,d show the results of the low-density-gas case.

First, the figures show very similar characteristics in both DWD models.

In all figures of Figures 3 and 4, the optimized P_0 is 100 W. The maximized SNR and the optimized L increase as the mirror radius R increases. This is because the noise strain is scaled by $1/L$. However, the optimized r has different characteristics in the constant-thickness model and constant-mass model. The optimized r increases as the mirror radius R increases in the constant-thickness model. On the other hand, the optimized r has two characteristics in the constant-mass model. The first one is that it has a dip when R is small due to the extreme cylindrical shape of the mirror, which increases internal thermal noise. The other one is that it decreases with the increase of R because the dominant noise source depends on R.

The features of optimized parameters mentioned in the above paragraph can be explained by the characteristics of shot noise and thermal noises. The large R increases thermal noises and decreases the effect of diffraction loss. At the same R, the large P_0 and the finesse of cavity decreases the shot noise, and the long L decreases the strain of thermal noise (see Equation (11)). When L is extremely long, the effect of diffraction loss is large. If the finesse F (see Table 2) is too high in a situation where the diffraction loss is large, the effect of losing the laser power due to the diffraction loss is greater than the effect of amplifying the laser power in the cavity. Thus, the laser power that can be detected decreases, and the shot noise increases. To reduce the shot noise, it is necessary to lower

r to reduce the finesse to some extent. According to the characteristics of shot noise and thermal noises, when R is small, thermal noises do not matter. Thus, shot noise is dominant when R is small. On the other hand, when R is large, thermal noises are dominant. Since the magnitude of each noise has a continuous dependence on R, the dominant noise is swapped between the shot noise and thermal noises at a specific R. In the range of R, where thermal noises are dominant, the optimized L is long in order constant-mirror-thickness model at the same R. This is because the internal thermal noise due to the distortion of the mirror is significantly larger when R is large.

Let us focus on each gas case. The maximized SNR in the low-density-gas case is about 2 times larger than that in the high-density-gas case. This result indicates that the thermal noise in a residual gas has a significant impact on the total noise spectrum in this model.

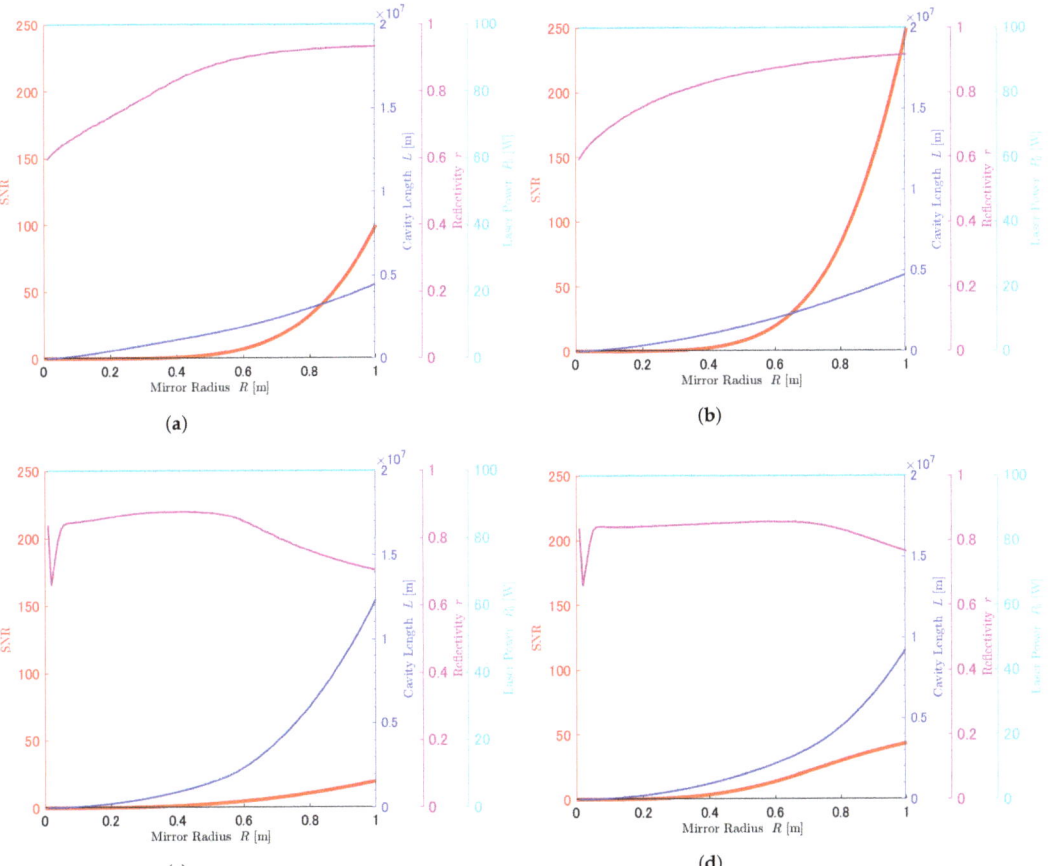

Figure 3. Maximized SNR for R (red line) and optimized L (blue line), r (magenta line), and P_0 (cyan line) in the optimistic DWD model. (**a**,**b**) show the results of the constant-thickness model. (**c**,**d**) show the results of the constant-mass model. (**a**,**c**) show the results of the high-density-gas case. (**b**,**d**) show the results of the low-density-gas case.

It is impossible to reduce all noises at the same time by changing R, L, and r. The SNR is maximized when the dominant noises have approximately the same magnitude in the lower frequency band. Actually, at $R = 1$ m, the shot noise, thermal noise in the high-density-gas case, and internal thermal noise of the constant-mirror-mass model with optimized parameters are about the same around 0.1 Hz (see Figure 5).

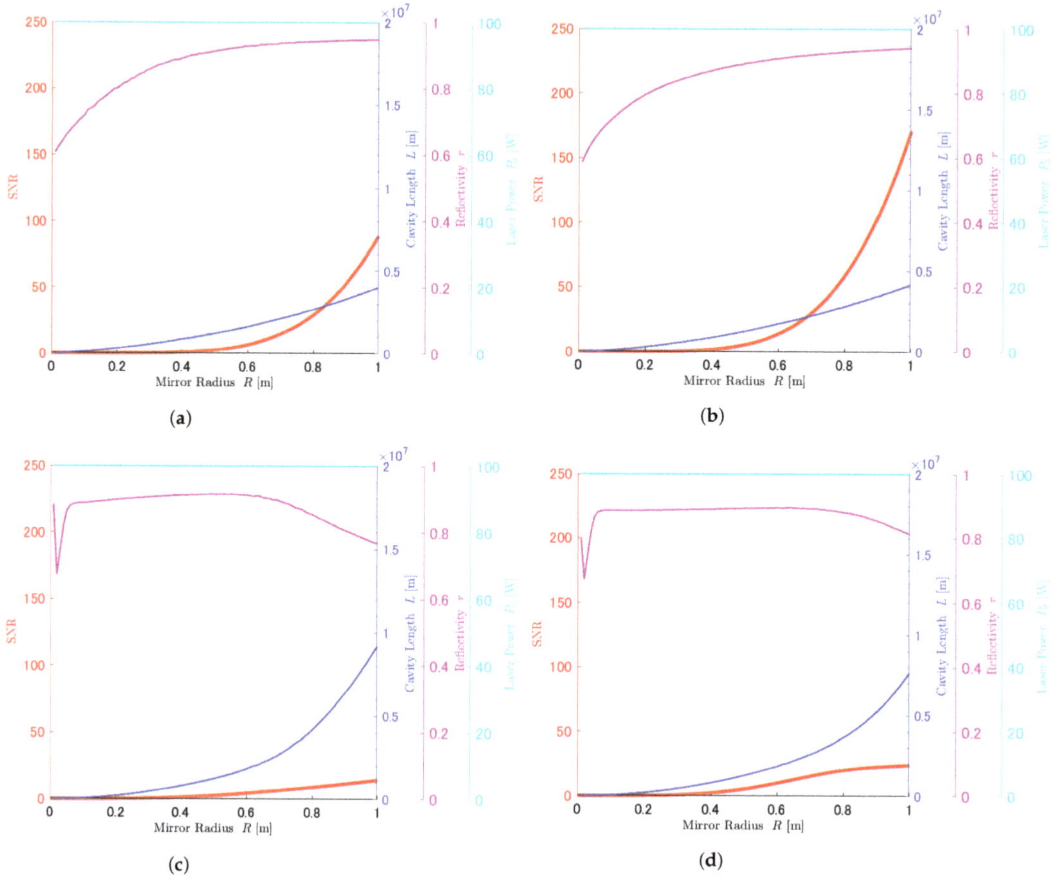

Figure 4. Maximized SNR for R (red line) and optimized L (blue line), r (magenta line), and P_0 (cyan line) in the standard DWD model. (**a**,**b**) show the results of the constant-thickness model. (**c**,**d**) show the results of the constant-mass model. (**a**,**c**) show the results of the high-density-gas case. (**b**,**d**) show the results of the low-density-gas case.

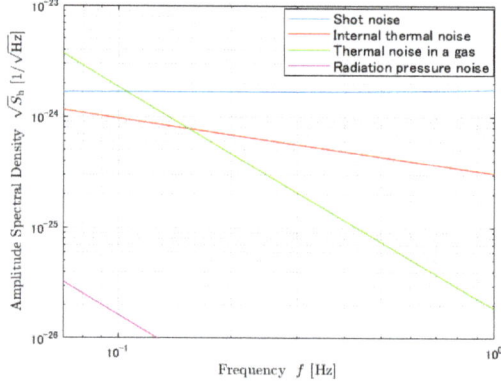

Figure 5. Shot noise (blue line), thermal noise in a residual gas (green line), internal thermal noise (red line), and radiation pressure noise (magenta line) of Figure 3c. All of them are optimized with $L = 1.2 \times 10^7$ m, $r = 0.75$ at $R = 1$ m.

5.2. Comparison of the Estimated Strain Sensitivities, Especially at Large R

The purpose of this paper is to consider the parameters that give a larger SNR; thus, we consider the noise when $R = 1$ m, which has the highest SNR in all cases. In this subsection, we compare the difference in the noise due to the difference in the mirror shape. We note that shot noise does not depend on the mirror thickness and mass. Figure 6 shows the strains of the two thermal noises in the low-density-gas case and radiation pressure noise. In order to show only the effect of mirror models, we set each parameter (excluding mirror thickness) to the optimized value in Figure 3b.

In Figure 6, since the magnitude of the radiation pressure noise is one-third of the thermal noises, we focus on the relationship between the thermal noises and the shape of the mirror. Figure 6 shows that thermal noise due to the gas is 4 times different because the mirror mass and volume are 4 times greater for the constant-mirror-thickness model than for the constant-mirror-mass model. The internal thermal noise has a difference of a magnitude of 10 times between the two mirror models.

The difference in the internal noise between the two mirror models can be explained by the difference in the mirror shape. In the constant-mirror-mass model, which is equal to the constant-mirror-volume model, the mirror thickness h is proportional to R^{-2}. On the other hand, in the constant-mirror-thickness model, h does not depend on R. The dependency of r_0/h differs between the two models by R^2. The factor C_{FTM} for considering the size of the mirror introduced in Section 3.2 is determined by the ratio of the laser radius to the thickness of the mirror r_0/h. When R is large, the increase of r_0/h increases C_{FTM} (see Figure A2). Therefore, the internal thermal noise of the constant-mirror-mass model is larger than that of the constant-mirror-thickness model.

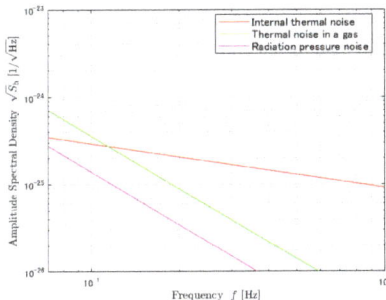
(a) Constant-mirror-thickness model: strain-equivalent noise due to internal thermal noise (red line), thermal noise in a low-density-gas case (green line), and radiation pressure noise (magenta line) of the constant-mirror-thickness model

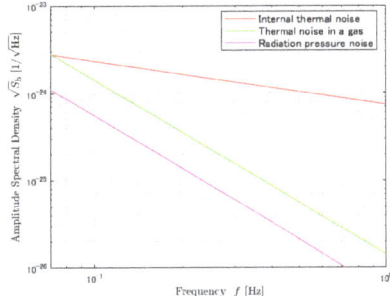
(b) Constant-mirror-mass model: strain-equivalent noise due to internal thermal noise (red line), thermal noise in a low-density-gas case (green line), and radiation pressure noise (magenta line) of the constant-mirror-mass model.

Figure 6. Strain of thermal noises and radiation pressure noise at $R = 1$ m, $L = 5 \times 10^6$ m, $r = 0.9$, and $P_0 = 100$ W. (**a**) shows the optimized noises. (**b**) shows the non-optimized noises.

6. Conclusions

We obtained the optimum parameters that maximize SNR of two correlated DECIGO detector clusters with gravitational waves from double white-dwarf binary systems and detector thermal noises in addition to the quantum noise including the effect of diffraction loss. We have found that we can obtain an extremely good SNR from the most optimistic model among all models we treated in this paper (Figure 3b). In addition, we have also found that the characteristics of the optimized DECIGO's parameters L, r, and P_0 are independent of the DWD's cutoff frequency. Focusing on the DECIGO design, we have found that making the mirror heavier could reduce the total noise. The mirror mass for the best SNR in this paper is four times as large as the default value. For future work, it is necessary to consider the DECIGO's mirror and its surroundings in more detail to improve the accuracy of the simulation. In addition, it is also necessary to investigate the feasibility of large and heavy mirrors to determine the DECIGO parameters for the improvement of the detectability of the PGW. The limitation of mirror mass and size will be determined by the launch capacity of a satellite and the progress in technological development. In the future, we will investigate the limitations of the mirror mass and size to determine the optimum design for DECIGO.

Author Contributions: Conceptualization, Y.K., R.S. and S.K.; Data curation, S.K.; Formal analysis, K.N., S.Y. and S.K.; Investigation, Y.K. and R.S.; Methodology, Y.K, T.I., S.I. and S.K.; Project administration, S.K.; Software, Y.K. and T.I.; Supervision, S.K.; Validation, Y.K., K.N. and S.K.; Visualization, Y.K., R.S. and S.K.; Writing—original draft, Y.K.; Writing—review and editing, Y.K., R.S., T.I., K.N., S.I., I.W., B.W., S.Y. and S.K. All authors have read and agreed to the published version of the manuscript.

Funding: This work was supported by Murata Science Foundation and the Japan Society for the Promotion of Science (JSPS) KAKENHI, grant number JP19H01924.

Institutional Review Board Statement: Not applicable.

Informed Consent Statement: Not applicable.

Data Availability Statement: There is no experimental data for the paper.

Acknowledgments: We would like to thank Kenji Numata and Kentaro Komori for helpful discussion about thermal noises, Tomoya Kinugawa and Gijs Nelemans for helpful advice about gravitational waves from white dwarf binaries, Kazuhiro Nakazawa for helpful advice about the environment in the satellite, and David H. Shoemaker for the editorial comments.

Conflicts of Interest: The authors declare no conflict of interest.

Appendix A. Derivation of Factor b

Here, we derive Equations (3) and (4). Under the model of the mirror and its surroundings in Section 3.1, when the mirror is stationary, gas molecules hit the mirror. On average, the same number of molecules collide on both sides of the mirror. The number of molecules of average velocity $\bar{v}$ coming from one side per unit time is

$$N = \frac{1}{4} n \bar{v} S. \tag{A1}$$

Then, we consider the frictional force F_{fric} that the mirror with velocity v_p receives

$$F_{\text{fric}} = -\frac{1}{4} n S \mu \bar{v} v_p = -b v_p. \tag{A2}$$

The equation of motion of this system is written as

$$F_{\text{ext}} = m\ddot{x} + 2b\dot{x}. \tag{A3}$$

The admittance $Y(f)$ is

$$Y = \frac{1}{i 2\pi f m + b}. \tag{A4}$$

Inserting Equation (A4) into Equation (1), we obtain the power spectrum $S_x(f)$ of Equation (3). In this paper, assuming that the gas is nitrogen, we calculate b of Equation (4).

Appendix B. Effect of Diffraction Loss

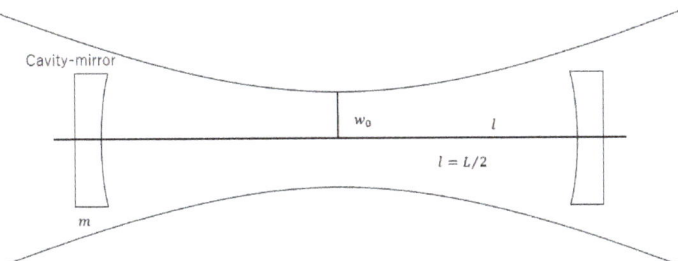

Figure A1. Configuration of a DECIGO's FP cavity. The horizontal line is the line connecting the centers of the mirrors. It coincides with the center of the beam axis when the cavity mirrors are aligned. The curves at the top and bottom of the figure represent the width of the laser beam.

Figure A1 shows the configuration of the DECIGO's FP cavity. The beam waist is located in the middle of each mirror. The beam diameter is greater as the distance from the beam waist increases. At each mirror, a part of the laser light passes outside the mirror. Thus, the power of reflected light is reduced. This is the effect of diffraction loss. We take this effect into consideration using the effective mirror reflectivity $r_{\text{eff}} = rD^2$, where D is the effect of diffraction [9]. In the formula of r_{eff}, the square of D is used because we consider two effects: the leakage loss and the higher-order modes loss. We lose the Gaussian beam of the higher-order mode because the cavity is set to resonate only with the fundamental mode. In this paper, we use the maximized D and it is expressed as follows [8,9]:

$$D_{\max}^2 = 1 - \exp\left[-\frac{2\pi}{L\lambda}R^2\right]. \tag{A5}$$

In order to maximize D, we set the Rayleigh length $Z_R = l = L/2$. Thus, the laser beam radius at the cavity mirrors $r_0 = \sqrt{2}w_0$. We calculate DECIGO's SNR using this $D_{\max}$ as a function of L and R.

Appendix C. Derivation of Factor C_{FTM}

The purpose of this appendix is to derive C_{FTM}^2 of Section 3.2. C_{FTM}^2 is the ratio of the finite-test-mass power spectral density to that for the infinite-test-mass.

In order to calculate the dissipation of test mass, we use the Bessel function of order zero and order one, J_0 and $J_1(x)$. In the following equations, ζ_m is the m'th zero of $J_1(x)$. k_m is related to ζ_m by $k_m = \zeta_m/a$, and p_m is given,

$$p_m = \frac{2}{a^2 J_0^2(\zeta_m)} \int_0^a \frac{e^{-r^2/r_0^2}}{\pi r_0^2} J_0(k_m r) r dr, \tag{A6}$$

where r is the distance of a point on the mirror surface from the beam spot center. a is the test mass radius.

The dissipation of the finite size test mass is obtained

$$W_{\text{diss}} = 2\pi f \phi (U_0 + \Delta U) F_0^2. \tag{A7}$$

Here, U_0 is

$$U_0 = \frac{(1-\sigma^2)\pi a^3}{E_0} \sum_{m=1}^{\infty} U_m \frac{p_m^2 J_0^2(\zeta_m)}{\zeta_m}, \tag{A8}$$

with

$$U_m = \frac{1 - Q_m^2 + 4k_m h Q_m}{(1 - Q_m)^2 - 4k_m^2 h^2 Q_m}, \tag{A9}$$

and
$$Q_m = \exp(-2k_m h). \tag{A10}$$

ΔU is expressed as
$$\Delta U = \frac{a^2}{6\pi h^3 E_0}\left[\pi^2 h^4 p_0^2 + 12\pi H^2 \sigma p_0 s + 72(1-\sigma)s^2\right], \tag{A11}$$

with
$$p_0 = \frac{1}{\pi a^2}, \tag{A12}$$

and
$$s = \pi a^2 \sum_{m=1}^{\infty} \frac{p_m J_0(\zeta_m)}{\zeta_m^2}. \tag{A13}$$

Inserting Equations (A7), (A8) and (A11) into Equation (5), we obtain the noise power spectrum of the finite size test mass,
$$S_{x_{\text{int}}}(f) = \frac{8k_B T}{2\pi f}\phi(U_0 + \Delta U) \tag{A14}$$
$$= C_{\text{FTM}}^2 \times S_{x_{\text{inf}}}(f). \tag{A15}$$

In our calculation, we consider up to $m = 9$ for simplicity because the contribution of large m is small. Figure A2 shows the value of C_{FTM}.

When h/R is not small, the assumption in the calculation of C_{FTM} is incorrect. However, since the effect on the result is small, the correction when R is small (that is, h/R is not small) is not considered.

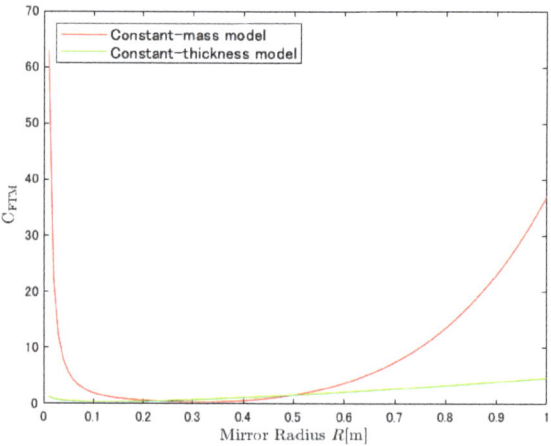

Figure A2. C_{FTM} of constant-mirror-mass model (red line), and constant-mirror-thickness model (green line).

References

1. Seto, N.; Kawamura, S.; Nakamura, T. Possibility of Direct Measurement of the Acceleration of the Universe Using 0.1 Hz Band Laser Interferometer Gravitational Wave Antenna in Space. *Phys. Rev. Lett.* **2001**, *87*, 221103. [CrossRef] [PubMed]
2. Kawamura, S.; Nakamura, T.; Ando, M.; Seto, N.; Akutsu, T.; Funaki, I.; Ioka, K.; Kanda, N.; Kawano, I.; Musha, M.; et al. Space gravitational-wave antennas DECIGO and B-DECIGO. *Int. J. Mod. Phys. D* **2019**, *28*, 1845001. [CrossRef]
3. Kinugawa, T.; Takeda, H.; Yamaguchi, H. Probe for Type Ia supernova progenitor in decihertz gravitational wave astronomy. *arXiv* **2019**, arXiv:1910.01063.
4. Kawamura, S.; Nakamura, T.; Ando, M.; Seto, N.; Tsubono, K.; Numata, K.; Takahashi, R.; Nagano, S.; Ishikawa, T.; Musha, M.; et al. The Japanese space gravitational wave antenna: DECIGO. *Class. Quantum Grav.* **2011**, *28*, 094011. [CrossRef]

5. Planck Collaboration. Planck 2018 results. X. Constraints on inflation. *Astron. Astrophys.* **2020**, *641*, A10. [CrossRef]
6. BICEP/Keck Collaboration. BICEP/Keck XIII. Improved Constraints on Primordial Gravitational Waves using Planck, WMAP, and BICEP/Keck Observations through the 2018 Observing Season. *Phys. Rev. Lett.* **2021**, *127*, 15130.
7. Kuroyanagi, S. Implications of the B-mode Polarization Measurement for Direct Detection of Inflationary Gravitational Waves. *Phys. Rev. D* **2014**, *90*, 063513. [CrossRef]
8. Ishikawa, T.; Iwaguchi, S.; Michimura, Y.; Ando, M.; Yamada, R.; Watanabe, I.; Nagano, K.; Akutsu, T.; Komori, K.; Musha, M.; et al. Improvement of the target sensitivity in DECIGO by optimizing its parameters for quantum noise including the effect of diffraction loss. *Galaxies* **2021**, *9*, 14. [CrossRef]
9. Iwaguchi, S.; Ishikawa, T.; Ando, M.; Michimura, Y.; Komori, K.; Nagano, K.; Akutsu, T.; Musha, M.; Yamada, R.; Watanabe, I.; et al. Quantum Noise in a Fabry-Perot Interferometer Including the Influence of Diffraction Loss of Light. *Galaxies* **2021**, *9*, 9. [CrossRef]
10. Farmer, A.J.; Phinney, E.S. The Gravitational Wave Background from Cosmological Compact Binaries. *Mon. Not. R. Astron. Soc.* **2003**, *346*, 1197–1214. [CrossRef]
11. Boileau, G.; Lamberts, A.; Christensen, N.; Cornish, N.J.; Meyer, R. Spectral separation of the stochastic gravitational-wave background for LISA in the context of a modulated Galactic foreground. *arXiv* **2021**, arXiv:2105.04283.
12. Callen, H.B.; Welton, T.A. Irreversibility and Generalized Noise. *Phys. Rev.* **1951**, *83*, 34. [CrossRef]
13. Saulson, P.R. *Fundamentals of Interferometric Gravitational Wave Detectors*; World Scientific: Singapore, 1994; pp. 107–116.
14. Levin, Y. Internal thermal noise in the LIGO test masses: A Direct approach. *Phys. Rev. D* **1998**, *57*, 659. [CrossRef]
15. Braginsky, V.B.; Gorodetsky, M.L.; Vyatchanin, S.P. Thermodynamical fluctuations and photo-thermal shot noise in gravitational wave antennae. *Phys. Lett. A* **1999**, *264*, 1. [CrossRef]
16. Nakagawa, N.; Gretarsson, A.M.; Gustafson, E.K.; Fejer, M.M. Thermal noise in half-infinite mirrors with nonuniform loss: A slab of excess loss in a half-infinite mirror. *Phys. Rev. D* **2002**, *65*, 102001. [CrossRef]
17. Liu, Y.T.; Thorne, T.S. Thermoelastic noise and homogeneous thermal noise in finite sized gravitational-wave test masses. *Phys. Rev. D* **2000**, *62*, 122002. [CrossRef]
18. Somiya, K.; Yamamoto, K. Coating thermal noise of a finite-size cylindrical mirror. *Phys. Rev. D* **2009**, *79*, 102004. [CrossRef]
19. Numata, K.; Kemery, A.; Jordan, C. Thermal-Noise Limit in the Frequency Stabilization of Lasers with Rigid Cavities. *Phys. Rev. Lett.* **2004**, *93*, 250602. [CrossRef] [PubMed]
20. Prince, T.A.; Tinto, M.; Larson, S.L.; Armstrong, J.W. LISA optimal sensitivity. *Phys. Rev. D* **2002**, *66*, 122002. [CrossRef]

Article

Toward Calibration of the Global Network of Gravitational Wave Detectors with Sub-Percent Absolute and Relative Accuracy

Sudarshan Karki [1,*], Dripta Bhattacharjee [2] and Richard L. Savage [3]

1. Institute for Multi-messenger Astrophysics and Cosmology, Missouri University of Science and Technology, Rolla, MO 65409, USA
2. Department of Physics, Kenyon College, Gambier, OH 43002, USA; bhattacharjee1@kenyon.edu
3. LIGO Hanford Observatory, Richland, WA 99352, USA; rsavage@caltech.edu
* Correspondence: sudarshan.karki@ligo.org

Abstract: The detection of gravitational-wave signals by the LIGO and Virgo observatories during the past few years has ushered us into the era of gravitational-wave astronomy, shifting our focus from detection to source parameter estimation. This has imposed stringent requirements on calibration in order to maximize the astrophysical information extracted from these detected signals. Current detectors rely on photon radiation pressure from auxiliary lasers to achieve required calibration accuracy. These *photon calibrators* have made significant improvements over the last few years, realizing fiducials displacements with sub-percent accuracy. This achieved accuracy is directly dependent on the laser power calibration. For the next observing campaign, scheduled to begin at the end of 2022, a new scheme is being implemented to achieve improved laser power calibration accuracy for all of the GW detectors in the global network. It is expected to significantly improve absolute and relative calibration accuracy for the entire network.

Keywords: calibration; interferometer; gravitational wave; astrophysics; laser metrology

1. Introduction

Recently, gravitational wave (GW) detectors, laser interferometers with kilometer-long arms, have successfully detected gravitational waves. The detectors of the Advanced LIGO and Virgo projects completed their third observing run in 2020. They have detected close to one hundred GW events during the six years since their first detection on 14 September 2015 [1–4]. These signals have been used to test the general theory of relativity in the strong-field regime [5–7], to understand the physics of the evolution of binary star mergers [8–11], to check the validity of the equation of state of neutron stars [12], to estimate the values of cosmological parameters [13], and to measure the speed of gravitational wave propagation [14]. As the sensitivity of the current detectors increases, it is expected that we will soon detect GW signals daily, maybe even several per day [15]. The scientific information that can be extracted from these signals is directly dependent on accurate calibration of the data that are recorded by the detectors. In order to fully exploit the astrophysical content of the GW detections, continuous calibration with accuracy and precision at or beyond the 1% level is required [16]. This requirement includes the amplitude and phase over the entire sensitive frequency band, typically from 10–20 Hz to a few kHz.

Current interferometric GW detectors are variants of Michelson interferometers with optical enhancements that increase their sensitivity to relative arm length variations to the 1×10^{-19} m level [17–19]. The detector arms incorporate optics suspended from multi-stage vibration isolation systems that act as test masses for the passing gravitational waves. A series of optical resonators amplify the phase shift experienced by the circulating laser light. Passing gravitational waves cause differential arm length variations that are encoded in the interferometer output signals that result in laser power fluctuations on the output photodetector of the interferometer. Calibration entails converting these output signals into units of meters of differential arm length variation. These calibrated signals are analyzed to detect gravitational waves and to extract the astrophysical information they carry about the events that generated them. To maintain the optical cavities on resonance, the differential length degree of freedom is controlled using a feedback control servo that suppresses displacements of the test masses via actuators present on parallel cascaded multi-stage pendulums known as reaction chains. Thus, estimating the *external* length variations experienced by the interferometer involves characterization of, and correction for the effect of, the feedback control loop [20]. This is enabled by fiducial periodic displacements of one of the interferometer test masses to measure the response of the interferometer to differential arm length variations. Thus the calibration of the interferometer output signals depends directly on the calibration of these fiducial displacements.

The current generation of GW detectors uses systems referred to as *Photon Calibrators* (Pcals), shown schematically in Figure 1, to generate these calibrated periodic fiducial displacements. These systems employ auxiliary lasers that displace the suspended test masses via laser radiation pressure. The induced displacements are proportional to the amplitude of the modulated laser power and thus the absolute laser power calibration is a crucial aspect of detector calibration. To date, laser power calibration has been achieved using a Pcal laser power transfer standard calibrated by the U. S. National Institute for Standards and Technology (NIST). A series of measurements performed at the LIGO Hanford Observatory (LHO) with this and other transfer standards were used to propagate the NIST calibration to Pcal power sensors operating at the end stations of all interferometers. Using this method, the LIGO Pcal systems achieved 0.41% (1-σ) uncertainty for the fiducial displacements produced during the most recent observing campaign that ended in April 2020 (see Section 3) [21].

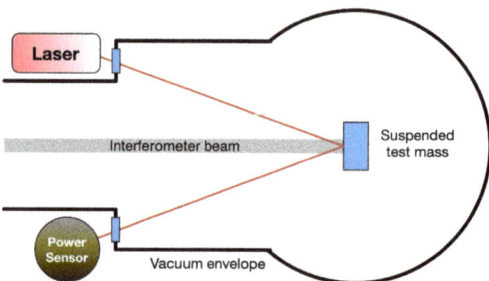

Figure 1. Simplified schematic diagram of a photon calibrator. Variations of this nominal configuration are being employed in all second-generation GW detectors.

The rest of this article provides brief overview of different methods that have been used to generate these fiducial displacements and discusses the working principle of the Pcals as well as their limitations and features. It also elaborates on the method used to achieve fiducial displacements with sub-perecent accuracy using Pcals during the recent LIGO-Virgo observing run. Finally, it discusses the scheme that the network of gravitational-wave detectors plans to employ to achieve sub-percent absolute and relative calibration accuracy for future observing runs using photon calibrators.

2. Evolution of Methods for Generating Calibrated Fiducial Displacements

Over the past two decades, GW interferometers have implemented a variety of techniques to generate calibrated fiducial displacements. During the initial phase of LIGO and even the early period of Advanced Virgo a technique referred to as the *Free-swinging*

Michelson (FSM) method was used to calibrate the detectors [22–25]. This method relies on measurement of Michelson interference fringes and uses the wavelength of the interferometer laser light as a length reference.

Another technique that has been explored in the past is a frequency modulation method [26]. This technique works by modulating the frequency of the laser light to mimic modulation of the test mass position. Modulating the frequency of the laser light creates effective modulation of the arm length given by the dynamic resonance condition for a Fabry-Perot resonator [27]. Another modulation, close in frequency to the laser frequency modulation, is injected using the test mass actuator that is to be calibrated. By comparing the signals from the two modulations detected by the single-arm readout sensor, the test mass actuator strength is calibrated [26].

Recently a technique that uses varying gravitational fields to apply forces directly to a detector's test mass has been explored at various GW interferometers. These systems rely on a combination of rotating masses that produces time-varying forces via periodic changes in the local gravitational field. The force produced by such a system is dependent on the known gravitational constant, the distance between the rotating masses and the detector test mass and the geometrical configuration of the system, shown schematically in Figure 2.

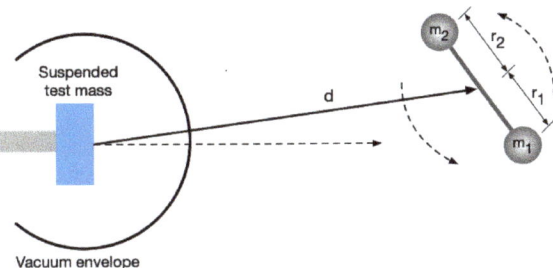

Figure 2. Schematic diagram of a gravity gradient calibrator, commonly referred to as a *Newtonian* or *Gravity* calibrator, located near a suspended test mass.

Such systems have been developed and tested within the Virgo [28,29], KAGRA [30], and LIGO [31] projects during the last few years and have shown promise for providing absolute fiducial displacment with uncertainty better than 1%.

The generation of varying gravitational fields using rotating masses has been used in different experimental settings since the 1960s [32–37]. However, the usefulness of gravity gradient generators for interferometric GW detectors was first proposed by Matone et al. in 2007 [38]. Recently, Inoue et al. proposed a scheme that utilizes these gravity field calibrators, called Gcals, or alternatively Newtonian calibrators (Ncals), in conjunction with a photon calibrator to improve the absolute accuracy of the calibration of the GW detector [30]. However, the first test of a gravity field calibrator in an interferometer setting was carried out at Virgo in 2018 during the second LIGO-Virgo observing run. The Virgo Ncal was an aluminum disk with material removed from two sectors with opening angles of 45 deg. In its first test, the Ncal was spun at 13 Hz and 35 Hz and produced calibrated displacements of the interferometer test mass at twice the rotation frequencies. These calibration lines provided a cross-check of the Free-swinging Michelson method and found agreement within uncertainty limits [28]. Improved, second generation Ncals were tested in Virgo during the third observing run. These Ncals had the ability to inject calibration lines at frequencies up to 110 Hz. Crosschecks with new Pcal systems installed and used during this run indicated a 3% difference between the two methods. However this difference was within their systematic uncertainty estimates [29].

LIGO constructed its own Ncal system made up of an aluminium disk with cylindrical cavities in four-fold and six-fold symmetric patterns. These cavities were alternately filled with tungsten cylinders to form quadrupole and hexapole mass distributions. Thus this system can simultaneously produce time varying forces at twice and three times the Ncal rotation frequency. During the third observing run, using the LIGO Hanford detector, it was demonstrated that a calibrated displacement well above the detector sensitivity could be generated using this system with measurement uncertainty at the 1% level [31].

With further improvements, Ncals have the potential to reach sub-percent absolute accuracy but have a limited frequency range compared with Pcals. Ncals can play an important role in providing a cross-reference for Pcals, but for the foreseeable future the Pcals will remain the primary calibration method for most GW detectors. This is partly due to their ability to provide fiducial displacements for interferometer calibration across the entire detection band, from 10 Hz to a few kHz.

3. Photon Calibrators: Development and the State of the Art

Photon calibrators were first used on the 10-m prototype detector in Glasgow [39], and later at the GEO600 detector in Hannover, Germany [40]. Variations of these instruments have been tested and improved within LIGO over the past 20 years [21,41–44]. During this time, the LIGO Pcals evolved from instruments intended as a sanity check for other calibration methods [23] to the primary absolute calibration tools for the Advanced LIGO interferometers [21,44]. Virgo has developed its own Pcal systems during the last few years and started using them as its primary calibrators during the third observing run [45,46]. KAGRA in Japan has also implemented two Pcal systems similar in design to Advanced LIGO but with lasers 10 times more powerful than LIGO's and the ability to modulate the two Pcal beams independently [47]. The higher laser power provides the ability to make larger calibrated displacements and independent modulations of two beams could be utilized to minimize unintended rotation induced by the Pcal forces.

Photon calibrators work by applying periodic forces to suspended test masses (optics) via photon radiation pressure using auxiliary power-modulated lasers. These forces are given by

$$F_m(\omega) = \frac{2\cos\theta}{c} P_m(\omega), \qquad (1)$$

where θ is the angle of incidence of the laser beams, P_m is the amplitude of the laser power modulated with angular frequency ω and c is the speed of light. At frequencies far above the suspension resonance frequencies, the motion of a suspended test mass is well approximated as a free mass. For Advanced LIGO test masses, with suspension resonance frequencies around 1 Hz, the discrepancy between the actual motion and the free-mass approximation is less than 0.1% above 20 Hz [21]. Thus the periodic longitudinal motion of the test mass is directly proportional to the modulated laser power applied to it, given by [43]

$$x_m(\omega) \approx -\frac{2 P_m(\omega) \cos\theta}{M c \omega^2}, \qquad (2)$$

where M is the mass of the suspended optic and the negative sign indicates that the test mass motion is 180 deg. out of phase with the applied force.

M and $\cos\theta$ are typically determined with accuracies better than 0.1%. The dominant source of uncertainty is the measured laser power.

The forces applied by photon calibrators can also cause unwanted rotation of the suspended test mass if the forces are not centered on the test mass surface or, in the case of multiple beams, if the powers of the beams are not balanced. If the interferometer beam is not centered on the test mass, this rotation will be sensed by the interferometer as a length change. Including rotation-induced length changes, Equation (2) can be rewritten as [43]

$$x_m(\omega) \approx -\frac{2 P_m(\omega) \cos\theta}{M c \omega^2} \left[1 + \frac{M}{I}(\vec{a}\cdot\vec{b})\right], \qquad (3)$$

where I is the moment of inertia of the suspended test mass about the center of its front surface and $\vec{a}$ and $\vec{b}$ are the displacement vectors of the Pcal center of force and the interferometer beam, respectively, from the center of the test mass surface. Ideally, the detectors are designed to operate with the interferometer beam at the center of test masses, but there can be situations where the interferometer beam is offset from the center of the test mass. During the third observing run, LIGO's Hanford detector operated with the interferometer beam displaced from the center of the ETM by as much as a few cm to mitigate the impact of point defects in the mirror coatings [48].

During the first observing run in the advanced LIGO era, cameras were installed as part of the Photon calibrator systems and Pcal beam positions were estimated using the images captured by these cameras. Beam positions were subsequently adjusted using steering mirrors located outside the vacuum envelope [44]. However, these camera systems were removed later, between the first and second observing runs, to mitigate concerns regarding noise introduced by scattered light reflecting from the camera lens and back into the interferometer beam [49]. Currently Pcal beam positions in LIGO are adjusted during vacuum incursions to ensure that the net force acts at the center of the test mass. They are subsequently monitored using the position of the the beams as observed at the entrance of the integrating sphere that receives the light reflected from the test mass [21].

In principle, one could calculate and subtract the contribution from rotation using Equation (3), but because we do not know the magnitude and direction of any unintended displacements of the Pcal beams, maximum estimated displacements are used and the resulting rotation component is treated as an additional source of uncertainty, added in quadrature with other contributions to determine the total uncertainty [43,50].

Earlier LIGO Pcals were designed with a single-beam configuration. In this configuration the force is applied at the center of the optic to minimize unwanted rotation but it elastically deforms the mirror surface at the center of the test mass, the most sensitive region of the interferometer, introducing significant calibration errors if not taken into account. This effect, due to so-called *local elastic deformation*, was first investigated by Hild et al. in 2007 [51]. Goetz et al., in 2009, demonstrated that the errors in calibration due to this effect could be as large as 50% at a few kHz [43] when assuming that the test mass motion is described by free-mass motion. Subsequent LIGO Pcal systems moved to two beam configurations with beams displaced from, and diametrically opposed about, the center of the face of the test mass. This ensured that the local elastic deformations due to the Pcal beams were far away from the region sensed by the interferometer, the center of the test mass [43].

Advanced Virgo Pcals use a single-beam configuration and model their test mass displacement using a combination of free-mass motion and contributions from the excited solid-body modes of the optic, primarily the *drumhead* mode measured at 7813 Hz [45,46]. In this configuration the motion sensed by the interferometer goes to zero at the crossover frequency (~2 kHz) because the free-mass motion is 180 deg. out of phase with, and equal in amplitude to, the elastic deformation as shown in figure 5 in [45]. However, the sensed displacements at frequencies above the crossover are larger than the free-mass motion and they increase dramatically as the excitation frequency approaches that of the drumhead solid-body mode. In principle, if modeled and compensated correctly, this enables probing the interferometer calibration more efficiently at higher frequencies. Advanced LIGO Pcals, designed with two beams that are placed near the nodal circle of the drumhead mode, minimize the contribution from elastic deformation. They thus provide displacement that is closer to the motion of a free mass, but large displacements at high frequencies require significantly more laser power or longer integration times. One can imagine using both configurations in a single Pcal system: using the two beam configuration to calibrate the detector at frequencies where the free-mass motion dominates, then moving both beams to the test mass center to probe the calibration at higher frequencies using the apparent motion due to elastic deformation.

In order to enable calibration of the interferometer with accuracy approaching 1%, the signal-to-noise ratio (SNR) of the Pcal fiducial displacements (calibration lines), some of which are in the interferometer's most sensitive band, must be greater than 100. Because the modulated Pcal forces that generate these lines are applied continuously, directly to the ETM surface, ensuring that displacement noise is not introduced at other frequencies is critical. This could result from either unwanted harmonics of the calibration line modulations or the inherent relative power noise of the laser source. Feedback control systems referred to as *Optical Follower* servos are commonly employed to address both of these potential sources of unwanted displacement noise. LIGO uses analog servos with unity gain frequency near 100 kHz [52]; Virgo uses digital servos. The servos enable deeper power modulation with minimized distortion by compensating for nonlinearities in the acousto-optic modulator drive circuits. This increases the useful range of motion that can be achieved with the available Pcal laser power [44].

4. Laser Power Calibration for Photon Calibrators

Measuring the modulated laser power reflecting from the mirror with the required accuracy is one of the primary challenges for Pcal systems. During the last three observing runs, laser power calibration traceable to SI units has been provided by the US National Institute for Standards and Technology in Boulder, Colorado (NIST) and those calibration were transferred to the Pcal power sensors at the two LIGO observatories as shown schematically in Figure 3.

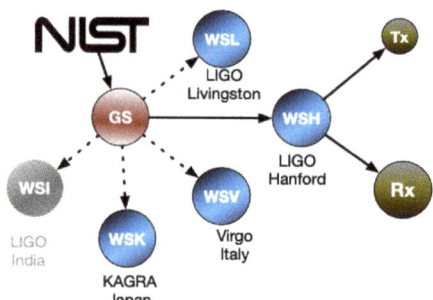

Figure 3. Schematic diagram showing the transfer of laser power calibration from NIST to the Pcal receiver (Rx) and transmitter (Tx) module power sensors (Rx and Tx) at the observatory end stations via a single Gold Standard (GS) and Working Standards (WSi) at each observatory. The Virgo, KAGRA and two LIGO detectors were actively involved in this scheme during the O3 observing run. LIGO India was expected to participate as soon as it became operational. Adapted from [21].

Virgo and KAGRA participated in this scheme during the third observing run that finished in March 2020 and the LIGO India detector was expected to participate once it became operational. In this scheme, the calibration transfer is performed using integrating sphere based power sensors in which a photodetector assembly is mounted on an exit port of the sphere. The inner surface of the integrating sphere is lined with a diffuse scattering material that scatters the light that enters the sphere via multiple reflections, creating a uniform distribution of laser light inside the sphere. One such power sensor, referred to as the Gold Standard, was maintained in one of the optics laboratories at the LIGO Hanford Observatory (LHO). It was calibrated annually at NIST, providing laser power calibration traceable to SI units. During the first and second observing runs the 1-σ uncertainty of the NIST calibrations was 0.44%. The uncertainty of the NIST calibration of the Gold Standard performed at the start of the O3 observing run was 0.32% [53].

The calibration obtained from NIST via the Gold Standard was transferred to similar power sensors called Working Standards. This calibration transfer was realized through a series of responsivity ratio measurements in which two power sensors are placed in a beamsplitter's reflected and transmitted laser beam paths and the time series of the detector outputs are recorded. A second set of time series are recorded with the position of the spheres swapped. The square root of the product of the ratios of these four time series provides the ratio of the responsivities of the two power sensors [44]. The calibration is then transferred to the Pcal power sensors at the interferometer end stations using similar techniques. This process through which the calibration is transferred from a NIST calibrated power sensor to the end station Pcal power sensors, in terms of power reflected from the ETM, has improved significantly within LIGO during the past 15 years and has enabled the calibration of the Pcal power sensors with only a slight increase (less than 0.05%) above the Gold Standard calibration uncertainty [21,44].

Between 2005 and 2007, national metrology institutes (NMIs) from nine countries performed a key comparison for radiant laser power [54]. They measured the responsivity of two thermal laser power sensors at three different laser wavelengths and at three different power levels. Relevant for Pcals are measurements made at 1064 nm, close to the Pcal laser wavelength of 1047 nm, and at power levels of 1 W. Though the comparison results were generally in agreement within the stated uncertainties, in a few cases there were differences between the reported values and and the consensus value that were as large as two percent and exceeded the quoted uncertainties. This triggered some concern regarding the achievable accuracy of laser power calibration within the GW community [55]. This concern and realization of the importance of absolute laser power calibration to the GW community stimulated organization of the *GW Metrology Workshop* that was held at NIST in Boulder, Colorado in the USA in March 2019 [56]. Pursuant to discussions during the workshop, NIST, in collaboration with their German counterpart, the Physiklaisch-Technische Bundesanstalt (PTB) in Braunschweig, Germany, initiated a new bilateral comparison to calibrate an integrating sphere based power sensor of the design currently used by the GW community at 100 mW and 300 mW power levels at the 1047 nm Pcal laser wavelength [57]. The resulting combined degree of equivalence between the NIST and PTB calibration results of -0.15% was well within the 1-σ uncertainties of the Gold Standard calibrations provided by NIST [57]. The report of the comparison concluded that NIST and PTB measurements were sufficiently consistent to support the stated LIGO Pcal displacement uncertainty of 0.41% (1-σ) during the O3 observing run [21,57].

Virgo relied on the Free-swinging Michelson technique to calibrate their detector during the first and second observing runs of the advanced detector era [25], but started using Pcals as their primary calibration tool for the third observing run that began in April 2019. Calibration of Virgo's Pcal systems using a Working Standard (WSV) calibrated at LHO revealed that the Virgo Pcal had a calibration error of 3.92% [46]. The calibration of the Virgo data was corrected to account for this error, thus reducing the relative calibration errors between the LIGO and Virgo detectors. The data from all three detectors were used by the analysis pipelines to detect GW signals and infer source parameters. Virgo was able to propagate the NIST calibration, via the Gold Standard and Virgo Working standard, to their end station Pcal power sensors with overall 1-σ uncertainty of 1.24% [46]. Most of this increase in uncertainty was attributed to uncertainty in the division of optical losses between the test mass incident and reflected paths due to inability to make in-chamber measurements of optical losses. The relative uncertainties in the estimates of the laser power reflecting from the end test masses and in the Pcal-induced displacement fiducials for both LIGO and Virgo during the third observing run, are shown in Table 1.

Table 1. Relative uncertainty estimates (1-σ) for the laser power reflecting from the interferometer test mass, and for the Pcal-induced fiducial displacements, during the third observing run for both the LIGO [21] and the Virgo [46] detectors.

ETM Reflected Power		Fiducial Displacements	
LIGO	Virgo	LIGO	Virgo
0.34%	1.24%	0.41%	1.40%

Similarly, KAGRA's Working Standard (WSK) was calibrated at LHO, using the NIST-calibrated Gold Standard, which was then used to calibrate the KAGRA detector for their first observation run that was held jointly with the GEO600 detector for two weeks in April of 2020 [47].

This process by which Pcals in the network of GW detectors are calibrated using a single NIST-calibrated standard ensures that the relative calibration errors between the detectors are minimized. However, any systematic error in the NIST calibration will manifest as an error in absolute displacement calibration for all observatories and thus in the absolute amplitude of the signals detected. Thus, the accuracy of the NIST calibration directly impacts our ability to determine the amplitude of GW signals.

5. Network Calibration for the O4 Observing Run and Beyond

The scheme described above and used to transfer laser power calibration from NIST to the Pcal power sensors at different observatories relied on a single Gold Standard that was calibrated at NIST and maintained at LHO. This burdened a single observatory with calibration of the working standards for all observatories in the network and necessitated leaving the observatories without calibrated working standards for significant periods while they were in transit and undergoing responsivity ratio measurements at LHO. In consultation with collaborators at NIST and PTB a plan was devised to use two transfer standards to deliver laser power calibration to each observatory in the global network. The observatories then use *local* Gold Standards and Working Standards to propagate the NMI calibrations to the Pcal power sensors at the end stations as shown schematically in Figure 4, using methods that have been developed and improved by LIGO over the past decade (see Section 4).

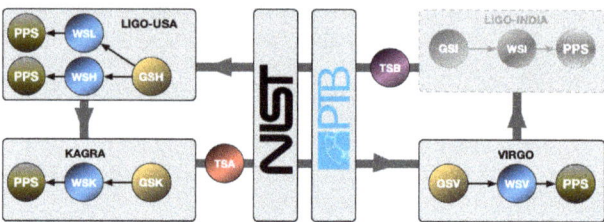

Figure 4. Proposed global network calibration scheme using two transfer standards, TSA and TSB, to deliver laser power calibration from NIST and PTB to each observatory. Local Gold Standards (GSi) and Working Standards (WSi) are then used to transfer the calibrations to Pcal power sensors (PPS) at the end stations. The LIGO, Virgo, and KAGRA detectors are expected to participate in this scheme during the O4 observing run. The LIGO-India detector is expected to participate in subsequent observing runs.

These new transfer standards, labeled TSA and TSB in Figure 4, are updated versions of the previous Gold Standard sensor that incorporate spacers with apertures located between the sphere and the photodetector assembly to minimize temperature dependence of the sensor responsivity [58]. An integrated temperature sensor has also been added for continuous temperature monitoring. The two transfer standards circulate around the loop shown in Figure 4, once per year with a temporal separation of six months. Thus each observatory receives one of the calibrated transfer standard approximately every six months and each transfer standard is calibrated by both NIST and PTB (consecutively) twice per year. Monitoring of the NMI calibrations of the transfer standards together with the derived calibrations of the Gold Standards at each observatory is expected to reveal any changes that may have occurred during shipping. We expect that experience with executing this scheme will reveal potential deficiencies and lead to improvements in the power sensors, the shipping methods, and the loop circulation strategy, if required.

In preparation for implementing this new calibration scheme for the O4 observing run that is scheduled to begin in December 2022, a NIST:PTB bilateral comparison of the transfer standards is planned. The schedule for the comparison is shown in Figure 5.

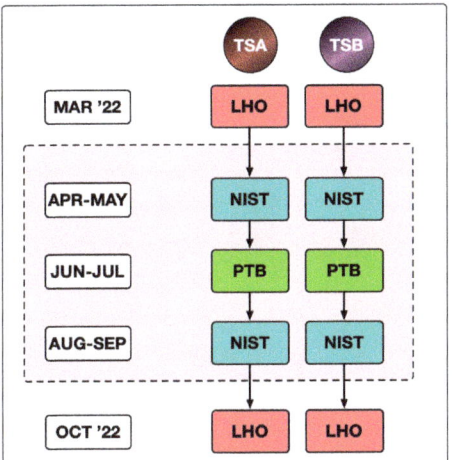

Figure 5. Schedule for the NIST:PTB bilateral comparison to be conducted in coordination with the LIGO Hanford Observatory (LHO) in preparation for the O4 observing run using the upgraded TSA and TSB power sensors.

This comparison will be similar to the recent bilateral comparison reported in [57] except that the updated power sensors will be used and NIST will employ the recently implemented *PARRoT* [59] primary standard. The combined uncertainty in the degree of equivalence for the previous bilateral comparison (see Section 4) was 0.44% (1-σ), dominated by the stated uncertainty in NIST's calibration (0.42%) [57]. The uncertainties in NIST calibrations using the new PARRoT standards are expected to be approximately 0.1%, similar to the uncertainty of the PTB calibrations. This is expected to significantly reduce the uncertainty in the bilateral degree of equivalence for this new comparison and better enable identification of changes in the transfer standards that might occur during shipping. Eventually, this should lead to reductions in the overall uncertainty in the calibration of the Pcal-induced displacements.

When the bilateral comparison is complete, the two calibrated transfer standards will be shipped back to LHO and the modified version of the network calibration scheme shown in Figure 6 will commence.

Figure 6. Simplified version of the scheme shown in Figure 4 to be used at the start of the O4 observing run after the NIST:PTB bilateral comparison outlined in Figure 5 is completed. The KAGRA detector is expected to join this scheme later in the observing run.

The initial scheme involves only the LIGO and Virgo detectors, but we expect that KAGRA will join the calibration scheme during the O4 observing run. Calibrating the KAGRA Working Standard using the LIGO Gold Standard, as carried out during the O3 observing run, will provide calibration traceable to SI units for KAGRA in the meantime. The schedule for the modified calibration scheme is shown in Figure 7. Substantial reductions in the intervals allotted for each measurement may be realized as we gain experience with this plan. In this preliminary scheme, each transfer standard is calibrated by NIST and PTB sequentially, both before and after visiting each observatory. This is intended to rapidly provide data relevant to the stability of the transfer standards, the shipping processes, and the calibration procedures at both the observatories and the NMIs. After gaining experience with this calibration strategy during the first year, we expect to carry out an optimized version of this scheme annually, eventually including the LIGO Aundha Observatory in Maharashtra, India. Based on experience to date propagating the NIST calibrations to the Pcal sensors at the LIGO detector end stations, and assuming that the other observatories will be able to transfer the calibrations with similarly small increases in uncertainty, this scheme should provide relative and absolute calibration of the Pcal-induced displacement fiducials at well below the 1% level for the O4 observing run and beyond.

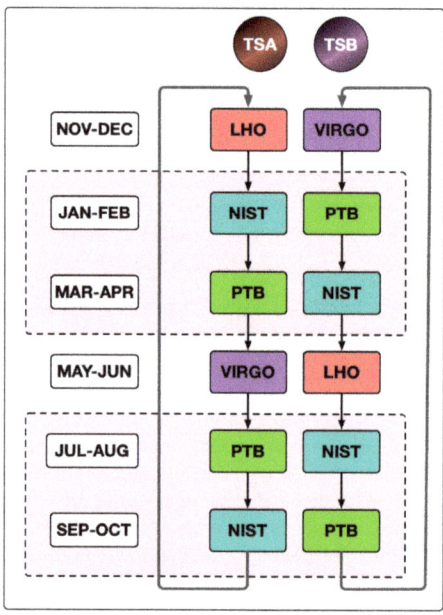

Figure 7. First year schedule during which each transfer standard (TSA and TSB) will be calibrated at NIST and PTB twice per year and arrive at each observatory (Virgo and LHO) once per year.

6. Looking Ahead

Photon calibrators, now the primary calibration tool for all detectors in the global network, have improved significantly over the past fifteen years. These systems provide the calibrated displacement fiducials that determine the overall absolute calibration of the detector output signals. In doing so, they rely on sub-percent accuracy in the calibration of their laser power sensors. Ensuring that the relative calibration errors between all detectors in the network are below the one percent level is enabled by referencing to a common set of measurements or standards, as in the calibration scheme planned for the O4 observing run.

Implementation of Newtonian calibrators is also evolving rapidly, especially at the Virgo observatory. It is possible that they will soon provide continuous, accurate calibration fiducials at the observatories where they are implemented—an important analog to the fiducials generated by the Pcal systems. These Ncal fiducials could obviate the need for in-chamber measurements of the optical efficiencies of the paths between the Pcal transmitter module and the test mass and between the test mass and the receiver module that are required to achieve sub-percent accuracy with the Pcal systems. They could also inform the impact of unintended rotations of the test mass induced by Pcal forces.

Eventually, as the signal-to-noise ratios and frequency of GW detections increase, the GW signals themselves may provide a sufficiently accurate *astrophysical* calibration for comparison with the existing calibration methods. Because waveforms of coalescing compact binary systems are predicted by the Einstein's theory of general relativity, the observed signal amplitudes and phases can be compared with those of the predicted signals to constrain the frequency dependence of the detector responses and the relative calibration between detectors in the network [60,61]. Additionally, if the GW signal has an electromagnetic counterpart, the luminosity distance to the source can be determined using the redshift of the electromagnetic signal, within the limits of the accuracy of the Hubble constant. This estimate of the luminosity distance together with the predicted waveform amplitude provided by general relativity enables absolute amplitude calibration of the detectors via the GW signals detected [60,62]. However, 1% overall amplitude calibration using this method with expected signal SNR levels would require hundreds of GW detections with optical counterparts. Achieving 1% relative calibration accuracy between detectors in the network using GW signals without optical counterparts would require detecting thousands of signals [60]. Another astrophysical calibration method that has the potential to provide percent-level relative calibration of detectors in the network is a *null stream* technique that uses data streams that contain calibration errors as residuals. However this method would still require an independent hardware-based method to determine the absolute scale of the calibration [63].

Calibrating a GW interferometer that operates with numerous resonating optical cavities with suspended mirrors over the entire sensitive frequency band and over year-long periods is a complicated and challenging task. Doing so with sub-percent accuracy has yet to be achieved. But there has been significant progress over the past few years and this goal now seems to be within reach [20,64]. It requires calibrated displacement fiducials with sub-percent accuracy. Experience with the LIGO Pcal systems during the O3 observing run [21], the results of the recent NIST:PTB bilateral comparison using a Pcal power standard [57], and the proposed scheme for absolute and relative calibration of the global network of GW detectors discussed above, indicate that calibration accuracy will not limit the ability of the network to extract astrophysical information from the signals they detect during the upcoming O4 observing run and well into the future.

Author Contributions: Conceptualization, S.K., D.B. and R.L.S.; methodology, S.K., D.B. and R.L.S.; writing—original draft preparation, S.K.; writing—review and editing, S.K., D.B. and R.L.S. All authors have read and agreed to the published version of the manuscript.

Funding: S.K. is supported by NSF awards PHY-1921006 and PHY-2011334 and D.B. is supported by NSF award OAC-2103662. LIGO was constructed by the California Institute of Technology and the Massachusetts Institute of Technology with funding from the National Science Foundation, and operates under cooperative agreement PHY-1764464. Advanced LIGO was built under award PHY-0823459.

Acknowledgments: The authors gratefully acknowledge discussions with J. Lehman, M. Spidell, and M. Stephens at NIST and S. Kück and M. Lopez at PTB regarding bilateral comparisons and the network calibration strategy for the O4 observing run. Fruitful discussions with L. Rolland and colleagues at Virgo, D. Chen and colleagues at KAGRA, and members of the LIGO Calibration Committee are also gratefully acknowledged. The authors thank all of the essential workers who put their health at risk during the COVID-19 pandemic, without whom we would not have been able to complete this work. This paper carries LIGO Document Number LIGO-P2100484.

Conflicts of Interest: The authors declare no conflict of interest.

References

1. Abbott, B.P.; Abbott, R.; Abbott, T.D.; Abernathy, M.R.; Acernese, F.; Ackley, K.; Adams, C.; Adams, T.; Addesso, P.; Adhikari, R.X.; et al. Observation of Gravitational Waves from a Binary Black Hole Merger. *Phys. Rev. Lett.* **2016**, *116*, 061102. [CrossRef] [PubMed]
2. Abbott, B.P.; Abbott, R.; Abbott, T.; Abraham, S.; Acernese, F.; Ackley, K.; Adams, C.; Adhikari, R.X.; Adya, V.B.; Affeldt, C.; et al. GWTC-1: A Gravitational-Wave Transient Catalog of Compact Binary Mergers Observed by LIGO and Virgo during the First and Second Observing Runs. *Phys. Rev. X* **2019**, *9*, 031040. [CrossRef]
3. Abbott, R.; Abbott, T.D.; Abraham, S.; Acernese, F.; Ackley, K.; Adams, A.; Adams, C.; Adhikari, R.X.; Adya, V.B.; Affeldt, C.; et al. GWTC-2: Compact Binary Coalescences Observed by LIGO and Virgo during the First Half of the Third Observing Run. *Phys. Rev. X* **2021**, *11*, 021053. [CrossRef]
4. Abbott, R.; Abbott, T.D.; Acernese, F.; Ackley, K.; Adams, C.; Adhikari, N.; Adhikari, R.X.; Adya, V.B.; Affeldt, C.; Agarwal, D.; et al. GWTC-3: Compact Binary Coalescences Observed by LIGO and Virgo During the Second Part of the Third Observing Run. *arXiv* **2021**, arXiv:gr-qc/2111.03606.
5. Scientific, L.I.; Collaborations, V.; Abbott, B.P.; Abbott, R.; Abbott, T.D.; Abernathy, M.R.; Acernese, F.; Ackley, K.; Adams, C.; Adams, T.; et al. Tests of general relativity with GW150914. *Phys. Rev. Lett.* **2016**, *116*, 221101.
6. Abbott, B.P.; Abbott, R.; Abbott, T.D.; Abraham, S.; Acernese, F.; Ackley, K.; Adams, C.; Adhikari, R.X.; Adya, V.B.; Affeldt, C.; et al. Tests of general relativity with the binary black hole signals from the LIGO-Virgo catalog GWTC-1. *Phys. Rev. D* **2019**, *100*, 104036. [CrossRef]
7. Abbott, R.; Abbott, T.D.; Abraham, S.; Acernese, F.; Ackley, K.; Adams, A.; Adams, C.; Adhikari, R.X.; Adya, V.B.; Affeldt, C.; et al. Tests of general relativity with binary black holes from the second LIGO-Virgo gravitational-wave transient catalog. *Phys. Rev. D* **2021**, *103*. [CrossRef]
8. Abbott, B.P.; Abbott, R.; Abbott, T.D.; Acernese, F.; Ackley, K.; Adams, C.; Adams, T.; Addesso, P.; Adhikari, R.X.; Adya, V.B.; et al. On the Progenitor of Binary Neutron Star Merger GW170817. *Astrophys. J. Lett.* **2017**, *850*, L40. [CrossRef]
9. Abbott, B.P.; Abbott, R.; Abbott, T.D.; Acernese, F.; Ackley, K.; Adams, C.; Adams, T.; Addesso, P.; Adhikari, R.X.; Adya, V.B.; et al. Properties of the binary neutron star merger GW170817. *Phys. Rev. X* **2019**, *9*, 011001. [CrossRef]
10. Abbott, B.P.; Abbott, R.; Abbott, T.D.; Acernese, F.; Ackley, K.; Adams, C.; Adams, T.; Addesso, P.; Adhikari, R.X.; Adya, V.B.; et al. Estimating the Contribution of Dynamical Ejecta in the Kilonova Associated with GW170817. *Astrophys. J. Lett.* **2017**, *850*, L39. [CrossRef]
11. Albert, A.; André, M.; Anghinolfi, M.; Ardid, M.; Aubert, J.J.; Aublin, J.; Avgitas, T.; Baret, B.; Barrios-Martí, J.; Basa, S.; et al. Search for High-energy Neutrinos from Binary Neutron Star Merger GW170817 with ANTARES, IceCube, and the Pierre Auger Observatory. *Astrophys. J. Lett.* **2017**, *850*, L35. [CrossRef]
12. Abbott, B.P.; Abbott, R.; Abbott, T.D.; Acernese, F.; Ackley, K.; Adams, C.; Adams, T.; Addesso, P.; Adhikari, R.X.; Adya, V.B.; et al. GW170817: Measurements of Neutron Star Radii and Equation of State. *Phys. Rev. Lett.* **2018**, *121*, 161101. [CrossRef] [PubMed]
13. Abbott, B.P.; Abbott, R.; Abbott, T.D.; Acernese, F.; Ackley, K.; Adams, C.; Adams, T.; Addesso, P.; Adhikari, R.X.; Adya, V.B.; et al. A gravitational-wave standard siren measurement of the Hubble constant. *Nature* **2017**, *551*, 85–88.
14. Abbott, B.P.; Abbott, R.; Abbott, T.D.; Acernese, F.; Ackley, K.; Adams, C.; Adams, T.; Addesso, P.; Adhikari, R.X.; Adya, V.B.; et al. Gravitational Waves and Gamma-rays from a Binary Neutron Star Merger: GW170817 and GRB 170817A. *Astrophys. J. Lett* **2017**, *848*, L13. [CrossRef]
15. Abbott, B.P.; Abbott, R.; Abbott, T.D.; Abraham, S.; Acernese, F.; Ackley, K.; Adams, C.; Adya, V.B.; Affeldt, C.; Agathos, M.; et al. Prospects for Observing and Localizing Gravitational-Wave Transients with Advanced LIGO, Advanced Virgo and KAGRA. *Living Rev. Relativ* **2020**, *23*, 3. [CrossRef]
16. Lindblom, L. Optimal Calibration Accuracy for Gravitational Wave Detectors. *Phys. Rev.* **2009**, *D80*, 042005. [CrossRef]
17. Aasi, J.; Abbott, B.P.; Abbott, R.; Abbott, T.; Abernathy, M.R.; Ackley, K.; Adams, C.; Adams, T.; Addesso, P.; Adhikari, R.X.; et al. Advanced LIGO. *Class. Quantum Grav.* **2015**, *32*, 074001.
18. Acernese, F.A.; Agathos, M.; Agatsuma, K.; Aisa, D.; Allemandou, N.; Allocca, A.; Amarni, J.; Astone, P.; Balestri, G.; Ballardin, G.; et al. Advanced Virgo: A second-generation interferometric gravitational wave detector. *Class. Quantum Grav.* **2014**, *32*, 024001. [CrossRef]
19. Akutsu, T.; Ando, M.; Arai, K.; Arai, Y.; Araki, S.; Araya, A.; Aritomi, N.; Aso, Y.; Bae, S.; Bae, Y.; et al. Overview of KAGRA: Detector design and construction history. *Prog. Theor. Exp. Phys.* **2021**, *2021*, 05A101. [CrossRef]
20. Sun, L.; Goetz, E.; Kissel, J.S.; Betzwieser, J.; Karki, S.; Viets, A.; Wade, M.; Bhattacharjee, D.; Bossilkov, V.; Covas, P.B.; et al. Characterization of systematic error in Advanced LIGO calibration. *Class. Quantum Grav.* **2020**, *29*, 225008. [CrossRef]
21. Bhattacharjee, D.; Lecoeuche, Y.; Karki, S.; Betzwieser, J.; Bossilkov, V.; Kandhasamy, S.; Payne, E.; Savage, R.L. Fiducial displacements with improved accuracy for the global network of gravitational wave detectors. *Class. Quantum Grav.* **2020**, *38*, 015009. [CrossRef]
22. Adhikari, R.; González, G.; Landry, M.; O'Reilly, B. Calibration of the LIGO detectors for the First LIGO Science Run. *Class. Quantum Grav.* **2003**, *20*, 903–914. [CrossRef]
23. Goetz, E.; Savage, R.L.; Garofoli, J.; Gonzalez, G.; Hirose, E.; Kalmus, P.; Kawabe, K.; Kissel, J.; Landry, M.; O'Reilly, B.; et al. Accurate calibration of test mass displacement in the LIGO interferometers. *Class. Quantum Grav.* **2010**, *27*, 084024. [CrossRef]

24. Accadia, T.; Acernese, F.; Antonucci, F.; Astone, P.; Ballardin, G.; Barone, F.; Barsuglia, M.; Basti, A.; Bauer, T.S.; Beker, M.G.; et al. Calibration and sensitivity of the Virgo detector during its second science run. *Class. Quantum Grav.* **2010**, *28*, 025005. [CrossRef]
25. Accadia, T.; Acernese, F.; Antonucci, F.; Astone, P.; Ballardin, G.; Barone, F.; Barsuglia, M.; Basti, A.; Bauer, T.S.; Beker, M.G.; et al. Calibration of advanced Virgo and reconstruction of the gravitational wave signal h(t) during the observing run O2. *Class. Quantum Grav.* **2018**, *35*, 205004.
26. Goetz, E.; Savage, R.L. Calibration of the LIGO displacement actuators via laser frequency modulation. *Class. Quantum Grav.* **2010**, *27*, 215001. [CrossRef]
27. Rakhmanov, M.; Savage, R.L.; Reitze, D.; Tanner, D.B. Dynamic resonance of light in Fabry-Perot cavities. *Phys. Lett. A* **2002**, *305*, 239–244. [CrossRef]
28. Estevez, D.; Lieunard, B.; Marion, F.; Mours, B.; Roll, L.; Verkindt, D. First Tests of a Newtonian Calibrator on an Interferometric Gravitational Wave Detector. *Class. Quantum Grav.* **2018**, *35*, 235009. [CrossRef]
29. Estevez, D.; Mours, B.; Pradier, T. Newtonian calibrator tests during the Virgo O3 data taking. *Class. Quantum Grav.* **2021**, *38*, 075012. [CrossRef]
30. Inoue, Y.; Haino, S.; Kanda, N.; Ogawa, Y.; Suzuki, T.; Tomaru, T.; Yamanmoto, T.; Yokozawa, T. Improving the absolute accuracy of the gravitational wave detectors by combining the photon pressure and gravity field calibrators. *Phys. Rev.* **2018**, *D98*, 022005. [CrossRef]
31. Ross, M.P.; Mistry, T.; Datrier, L.; Kissel, J.; Venkateswara, K.; Weller, C.; Kumar, K.; Hagedorn, C.; Adelberger, E.; Lee, J.; et al. Initial results from the LIGO Newtonian calibrator. *Phys. Rev. D* **2021**, *104*, 082006. [CrossRef]
32. Forward, R.L.; Miller, L.R. Generation and Detection of Dynamic Gravitational-Gradient Fields. *J. Appl. Phys.* **1967**, *38*, 512–518. [CrossRef]
33. Sinsky, J.; Weber, J. New Source for Dynamical Gravitational Fields. *Phys. Rev. Lett.* **1967**, *18*, 795–797. [CrossRef]
34. Sinsky, J.A. Generation and Detection of Dynamic Newtonian Gravitational Fields at 1660 cps. *Phys. Rev.* **1968**, *167*, 1145–1151. [CrossRef]
35. Hirakawa, H.; Tsubono, K.; Oide, K. Dynamical test of the law of gravitation. *Nature* **2018**, *283*, 184–185. [CrossRef]
36. Suzuki, T.; Tsubono, K.; Kuroda, K.; Hirakawa, H. Calibration of Gravitational Radiation Antenna by Dynamic Newton Field. *Jpn. J. Appl. Phys.* **1981**, *20*, L498–L500. [CrossRef]
37. Ogawa, Y.; Tsubono, K.; Hirakawa, H. Experimental test of the law of gravitation. *Phys. Rev. D* **1982**, *26*, 729–734. [CrossRef]
38. Matone, L.; Raffai, P.; Márka, S.; Grossman, R.; Kalmus, P.; Márka, Z.; Rollins, J.; Sannibale, V. Benefits of artificially generated gravity gradients for interferometric gravitational-wave detectors. *Class. Quantum Grav.* **2007**, *24*, 2217–2229. [CrossRef]
39. Clubley, D.A.; Newton, G.P.; Skeldon, K.D.; Hough, J. Calibration of the Glasgow 10 m prototype laser interferometric gravitational wave detector using photon pressure. *Phys. Lett. A* **2001**, *283*, 85. [CrossRef]
40. Mossavi, K.; Hewitson, M.; Hild, S.; Seifert, F.; Weil, U.; Smith, J.R.; Lück, H.; Grote, H.; Willke, B.; Danzmann, K. A photon pressure calibrator for the GEO600 gravitational wave detector. *Phys. Lett. A* **2006**, *353*, 1. [CrossRef]
41. Bruursema, J. *Calibration of the LIGO Interferometer Using the Recoil of Photons*; T030266; LIGO Document Control Center: Washington, DC, USA, 2003.
42. Sigg, D. *Strain Calibration in LIGO*; T970101; LIGO Document Control Center: Washington, DC, USA, 1997.
43. Goetz, E.; Kalmus, P.; Erickson, S.; Savage, R.L.; Gonzalez, G.; Kawabe, K.; Landry, M.; Marka, S.; O'Reilly, B.; Riles, K.; et al. Precise calibration of LIGO test mass actuators using photon radiation pressure. *Class. Quantum Grav.* **2009**, *26*, 245011. [CrossRef]
44. Karki, S.; Tuyenbayev, D.; Kandhasamy, S.; Abbott, B.P.; Abbott, T.D.; Anders, E.H.; Berliner, J.; Betzwieser, J.; Cahillane, C.; Canete, L.; et al. The Advanced LIGO photon calibrators. *Rev. Sci. Instrum.* **2016**, *87*, 114503. [CrossRef] [PubMed]
45. Accadia, T.; Acernese, F.; Agathos, M.; Allocca, A.; Astone, P.; Ballardin, G.; Barone, F.; Barsuglia, M.; Basti, A.; Bauer, T.S.; et al. Reconstruction of the gravitational wave signal $h(t)$ during the Virgo science runs and independent validation with a photon calibrator. *Class. Quantum Grav.* **2014**, *31*, 165013. [CrossRef]
46. Estevez, D.; Lagabbe, P.; Masserot, A.; Roll, L.; Seglar-Arroyo, M.; Verkindt, D. The Advanced Virgo photon calibrators. *Class. Quantum Grav.* **2021**, *38*, 075007. [CrossRef]
47. Akutsu, T.; Ando, M.; Arai, K.; Arai, Y.; Araki, S.; Araya, A.; Aritomi, N.; Asada, H.; Aso, Y.; Bae, S.; et al. Overview of KAGRA: Calibration, detector characterization, physical environmental monitors, and the geophysics interferometer. *Prog. Theor. Exp. Phys* **2021**, *2021*, 05A102. [CrossRef]
48. Brooks, A.F.; Vajente, G.; Yamamoto, H.; Abbott, R.; Adams, C.; Adhikari, R.X.; Ananyeva, A.; Appert, S.; Arai, K.; Areeda, J.S.; et al. Point absorbers in Advanced LIGO. *Appl. Opt.* **2021**, *60*, 4047–4063. [CrossRef]
49. Schofield, R. *PEM Update*; G1701613; LIGO Document Control Center: Washington, DC, USA, 2007.
50. Goetz, E. Gravitational Wave Studies: Detector Calibration and an All-Sky Search for Spinning Neutron Stars in Binary Systems. Ph.D. Thesis, University of Michigan, Arbor, MI, USA, 2010.
51. Hild, S.; Brinkmann, M.; Danzmann, K.; Grote, H.; Hewitson, M.; Hough, J.; Lück, H.; Martin, I.; Mossavi, K.; Rainer, N.; et al. Photon Pressure Induced Test Mass Deformation in Gravitational-Wave Detectors. *Class. Quantum Grav.* **2007**, *24*, 5681–5688. [CrossRef]
52. Canete, L. *Optical Follower Servo Design for the Calibration of a Gravitational Wave Detector*; T130442; LIGO Document Control Center: Washington, DC, USA, 2013.
53. *Photon Calibrator Gold Standard NIST Calibration*; T1900097; LIGO Document Control Center: Washington, DC, USA, 2018.

54. Kück, S. Final report on EUROMET comparison EUROMET.PR-S2 (Project No. 156): Responsivity of detectors for radiant power of lasers. *Metrologia* **2010**, *47*, 02003. [CrossRef]
55. Tomaru, T. *Private Communication*; National Observatory of Japan: Tokyo, Japan, 2016.
56. Lehman, J. *NIST Workshop 2019 Executive Summary*; LIGO-L1900166; LIGO Document Control Center: Washington, DC, USA, 2019.
57. Spidell, M.; Lehman, J.; López, M.; Lecher, H.; Kück, S.; Bhattacharjee, D.; Lecoeuche, Y.; Savage, R. A bilateral comparison of NIST and PTB laser power standards for scale realization confidence by gravitational wave observatories. *Metrologia* **2021**, *58*, 055011. [CrossRef]
58. Lecoeuche, Y. *Performance Review of Pcal Power Standard Detector Spacers*; T12000714; LIGO Document Control Center: Washington, DC, USA, 2020.
59. Vaskuri, A.K.; Stephens, M.S.; Tomlin, N.A.; Spidell, M.T.; Yung, C.S.; Walowitz, A.J.; Straatsma, C.; Harber, D.; Lehman, J.H. High-accuracy room temperature planar absolute radiometer based on vertically aligned carbon nanotubes. *Opt. Express* **2021**, *29*, 22533–22552. [CrossRef]
60. Essick, R.; Holz, D.E. Calibrating gravitational-wave detectors with GW170817. *Class. Quantum Grav.* **2019**, *36*, 125002. [CrossRef]
61. Mukherjee, S.; Wandelt, B.D.; Nissanke, S.M.; Silvestri, A. Accurate precision cosmology with redshift unknown gravitational wave sources. *Phys. Rev. D* **2021**, *103*, 043520. [CrossRef]
62. Pitkin, M.; Messenger, C.; Wright, L. Astrophysical calibration of gravitational-wave detectors. *Phys. Rev.* **2016**, *D93*, 062002. [CrossRef]
63. Schutz, B.F.; Sathyaprakash, B.S. Self-calibration of Networks of Gravitational Wave Detectors. *arXiv* **2020**, arXiv:2009.10212.
64. Sun, L.; Goetz, E.; Kissel, J.S.; Betzwieser, J.; Karki, S.; Bhattacharjee, D.; Covas, P.B.; Datrier, L.E.; Kandhasamy, S.; Lecoeuche, Y.K.; et al. Characterization of systematic error in Advanced LIGO calibration in the second half of O3. *arXiv* **2021**, arXiv:astro-ph.IM/2107.00129.

Article

Seismic and Newtonian Noise in the GW Detectors

Lucia Trozzo [1,*,†] and Francesca Badaracco [2,*,†]

1. Istituto Nazionale di Fisica Nucleare, Sezione di Napoli, Strada Comunale Cinthia, 80126 Napoli, Italy
2. Centre for Cosmology, Particle Physics and Phenomenology, Université Catholique de Louvain, B-1348 Louvain-La-Neuve, Belgium
* Correspondence: lucia.trozzo@na.infn.it (L.T.); francesca.badaracco@uclouvain.be (F.B.)
† These authors contributed equally to this work.

Abstract: Gravitational wave detectors aim to measure relative length variations of the order of $\Delta L/L \simeq 10^{-21}$, or less. Thus, any mechanism that is able to reproduce such a tiny variation can, in principle, threaten the sensitivity of these instruments, representing a source of noise. There are many examples of such noise, and seismic and Newtonian noise are among these and will be the subject of this review. Seismic noise is generated by the incessant ground vibration that characterizes Earth. Newtonian noise is instead produced by the tiny fluctuations of the Earth's gravitational field. These fluctuations are generated by variations of air and soil density near the detector test masses. Soil density variations are produced by the same seismic waves comprising seismic noise. Thus, it makes sense to address these two sources of noise in the same review. An overview of seismic and Newtonian noise is presented, together with a review of the strategies adopted to mitigate them.

Keywords: seismic noise; Newtonian noise; seismic isolation system; noise subtraction

1. Introduction

Current gravitational wave (GW) detectors are sensitive to signals in a frequency band that ranges between 10 Hz and 10 kHz. Their sensitivity can be affected by several dominant sources of noise, such as ground motion [1], local terrestrial gravity [2], magnetic noise [3], thermal [4] and quantum noise [5].

These noises cause a phase variation of the laser light detected at the interferometer output port in the same way that a passing GW would. If we want to increase the detectors' sensitivity to GWs, it is necessary to reduce these noises as much as possible.

Seismic noise couples with GW detectors via vibrations transmitted through the suspension system and other isolation systems. On the other hand, seismic noise can also directly couple with the detector through what is known in GW physics as Newtonian noise (NN). It is well known from Newtonian physics that a variation in mass density leads to fluctuations in the surrounding gravitational field. Therefore, a passing seismic wave that causes density variations will also produce gravity fluctuations, and thus NN.

In the following sections, we will focus on seismic and Newtonian noise. In Section 2, the origin of seismic noise will be briefly discussed for surface and underground environments. In Section 3, the technologies adopted to mitigate seismic noise will be discussed. In Section 4, a brief introduction of NN will be given, together with a description of atmospheric NN (ANN) and seismic NN (SNN). In Section 5, other sources contributing to NN will be shortly addressed. Finally, the noise subtraction techniques adopted to mitigate NN will be discussed in Section 6.

2. An Introduction to Seismic Noise in GW Detectors

Ground-based GW detector performance is affected by so-called seismic noise. This noise affects detector sensitivity in the range 0.1–10 Hz, also undermining the possibility of operating with a high duty cycle.

What is seismic noise? In geophysics, seismic noise is used to identify the persistent and variable ground vibration that can be detected everywhere on the Earth and that produces a characteristic spectrum.

This kind of vibration is generated by **seismic waves** travelling through the Earth's layers at different speeds and produced by phenomena such as wind, ocean waves, earthquakes, anthropogenic sources, etc. Seismic wave speeds can change depending on the density and the elasticity of the crossed medium, as well as on their depth. Moving from the Earth's crust to the deep mantle, the speed increases from a few m/s up to 13 km/s [6,7].

Seismic waves can be classified as body waves and surface waves.

- **Body waves** include all those waves travelling through the Earth. The density and stiffness of the crossed material depend on temperature, chemical composition, and material phase. For this reason, body waves show different velocities with increasing depth of propagation. They are classified into primary waves (P-waves) and secondary waves (S-waves). P-waves cause a compression/decompression displacement along their propagation direction, whereas S-waves produce a shear displacement perpendicular to their propagation direction. In an earthquake event, S-waves are slower than P-waves (with a typical speed value of about 60% of that of P-waves). S-waves can only travel through solid materials. Indeed, fluids (liquids and gases) do not support shear stresses (see Figure 1). P-waves generate density variations in the medium, so they produce gravity fluctuations. S-waves, being shear waves, can instead produce density variations only in presence of some discontinuity (see Section 4.2).

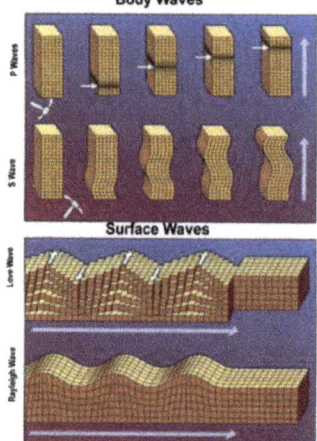

Figure 1. Body and surface waves [8].

- **Surface waves** travel on the Earth's surface and their amplitude decreases exponentially as a function of their depth from the surface. Their speed is slower compared to the speed of body waves (P and S) and their amplitudes can reach several cm in an earthquake event. Mathematically, they arise from the interaction of body waves with a medium discontinuity. They can be distinguished into **Rayleigh waves** (or ground rolls) and **Love waves**. Rayleigh waves produce both longitudinal and transverse motion of surface particles, generating a retrograde vertical ellipse motion in the plane normal to the surface and containing the wave's propagation direction. In a homogeneous and isotropic half-space, Rayleigh waves have a slightly lower velocity than S-waves ($v_R \simeq 0.9\, v_S$) and are non-dispersive (the velocity does not depend on the frequency). Instead, if the half-space is composed of homogeneous and isotropic layers, the waves become dispersive. The dispersion model has an important impact on the gravity fluctuations generated by Rayleigh waves (see Section 4.2).

Love wave polarization is perpendicular to the propagation direction and parallel to the surface. Moreover, these waves have larger amplitudes and speed compared to Rayleigh waves (see Figure 1). Contrary to Rayleigh waves, they cannot propagate in homogeneous and isotropic half-space, but they arise in layered mediums, showing a dispersive model. Being surface shear waves, they do not produce density variations; thus, they are not a source of gravity fluctuations.

2.1. Seismic Noise: NLNM and NHNM Models

Seismic noise is detected and measured with broad-band seismographs everywhere on the Earth. The spectral density associated with this noise is modeled approximately by

$$S(f) \simeq \frac{\alpha}{f^2} \qquad (1)$$

where α depends on the site. For example, the value of α in the Italian site (Cascina, PI) hosting the Virgo detector is about 10^{-7} m $(\text{Hz})^{\frac{3}{2}}$.

With the purpose of monitoring variations in the seismic noise spectral density, in 1993, J. Peterson collected and analysed data from 75 seismic stations around the world. He developed two seismic noise models: the New Low Noise Model (NLNM) and the New High Noise Model (NHNM) [9]. These models, now commonly used as a reference in the scientific community, represent the lowest and the highest seismic background spectra that it is possible to find on the Earth. They were obtained by fitting with straight lines the lower and the upper envelopes of all the spectra measured.

According to Peterson's results (Figure 2), it is possible to split the seismic spectrum into different regions. The region in the 0.05–1 Hz band is dominated by so-called **microseismic noise**, generated every time atmospheric phenomena such as typhoons, storms, and climatic variations occur [10,11]. The most energetic seismic waves that comprise microseisms are Rayleigh waves, but Love and body waves can also contribute.

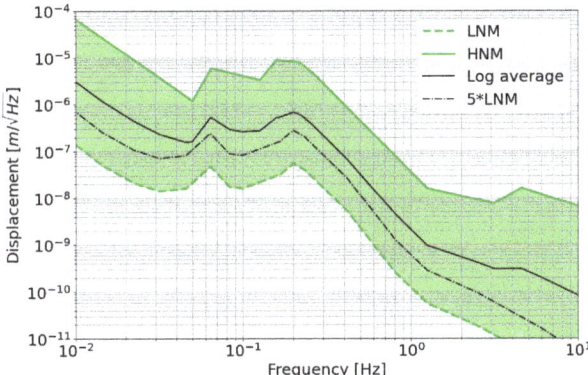

Figure 2. Square root of the power spectral density of the seismic displacement of Peterson's New Low and High Noise Models (NLNM and NHNM), the average of their logarithmic values and 5 times the NLNM.

Microseism signals are non-impulsive, and their amplitudes show strong seasonal modulation, with maxima during winter seasons (when oceans are stormier) and minima during summers. Looking at Figure 2, microseismic noise displays two predominant peaks in the region of 0.05–1 Hz. The weaker peak between 0.05–0.1 Hz is called the "primary peak" and it is explained by the effect of surface gravity waves in shallow waters. It shares the same spectral content as the ocean waves. Its source is associated with the energy transfer of ocean waves breaking on the coast. The stronger peak between 0.1–1 Hz is called the "secondary peak" and it is generated by interactions between waves of the same frequency travelling in opposite directions [12]. It is characterized by twice the frequency of the ocean waves. This peak generally shows a higher amplitude than the primary one.

At frequencies $f < 0.05$ Hz, phenomena such as atmospheric gravity fluctuations and **tidal effects** (generated by the Sun–Moon gravitational attraction), start to manifest themselves in the seismic spectrum, whereas all the vibrations included in the range 1–10 Hz are classified as **anthropogenic noise**, i.e., all the noise produced by human activities such as industrial processes, vehicles, agricultural machinery, wind turbines, etc.

2.2. Seismic Noise in Underground Sites

Seismic classification between low-frequency ($f < 1$ Hz) and high-frequency ($f > 1$ Hz) noise is a way to distinguish natural phenomena from human ones. The heterogeneity of the Earth's crust influences the microseismic spectrum, decreasing or increasing the spectral amplitudes at a specific frequency f. At high frequencies, instead, the amplitude of the seismic spectrum is mainly associated with industrial and transportation activities, but also with drastic weather changes. Seismic noise in underground locations (as well as surface ones) depends on the proximity to the coast, urban areas, and on their geological history.

In underground sites, the atmospheric perturbation influence is minimal. The environmental conditions are more stable; thus, seismic noise is attenuated with respect to the surface. Indeed, the energy content of seismic noise is mainly carried by surface waves, which decay exponentially with increasing depth.

With these considerations in mind, the spectral density of seismic noise in underground locations (depth > 100 m) can be modelled approximately by

$$\frac{10^{-9}}{f^2} \, \text{m} \, \text{Hz}^{\frac{3}{2}} \qquad (2)$$

Comparing Equations (1) and (2), it is evident that seismic noise in underground locations is about 100 times smaller than in surface ones. This can be seen when looking at the spectral noise profiles measured at 1 Hz in some mines: at Kamioka (the experimental site of KAGRA) and Sos-Enattos (Sardinia, Italy) we have $S(f) \simeq \frac{10^{-9} \cdot \text{m}}{\sqrt{\text{Hz}}}$, whereas at Homestake (USA) we have $S(f) \simeq \frac{1.5 \cdot \text{m}}{\sqrt{\text{Hz}}}$. These values are close to the NLNM curve: $S(f) \simeq \frac{10^{-10} \cdot \text{m}}{\sqrt{\text{Hz}}}$ (see Figures 3 and 4).

These values—their geological stability and their distance from industrial activities of underground locations—are the the main reasons why these are considered good candidate sites for the construction of the Einstein Telescope (ET), a third-generation GW detector.

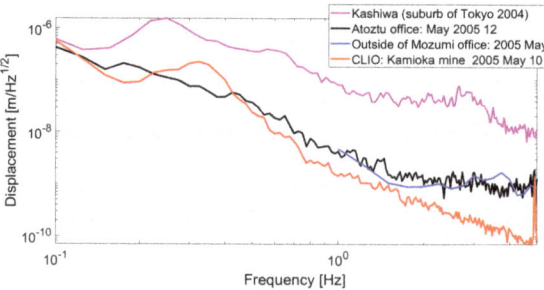

Figure 3. This figure shows the typical spectral density of the seismic noise displacement measured in an underground location at Kamioka (red curve) and compared to those measured at the surface (Tokyo areas). This plot was made using the data shown in Figure 4 in [13].

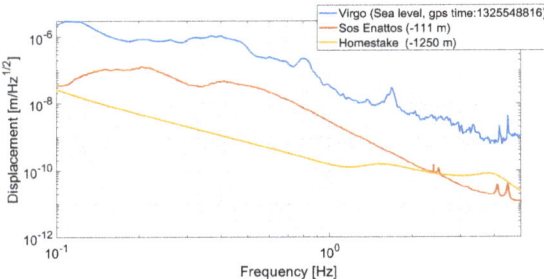

Figure 4. This plot shows the spectral density of the seismic noise displacement measured at the Sos-Enattos mine, compared to those measured near the Central building of Virgo (Pisa, Italy) and at the former mine of Homestake (Lead, SD -USA). The Homestake seismic profile was reconstructed using the data shown in the bottom right of Figure 6.10 in [14].

3. Mechanical Attenuators

Suspending optical components represents a crucial task for the construction of GW interferometers. In fact, the observation of GWs depends on the presence of free-falling (test) masses in the experimental apparatus. For this reason, the test masses must be well isolated (i.e., suspended) from ground vibrations in the frequency band relevant to scientific observations [15].

As discussed in the previous section, seismic noise in the frequency range 0.1–10 Hz represents one of the main limitations to the target sensitivity of GW detectors. Even in underground environments, where the seismic noise is lower than at the surface, ground displacement is eight orders of magnitude larger than that induced by a GW (see Figure 5).

To isolate and suppress the seismic noise transmitted from the ground to the test masses, a GW detector requires complex mechanical suspensions that are essentially low-pass filters and that allow one to consider the test masses as free-falling bodies in the horizontal direction (this is true starting from a few Hz).

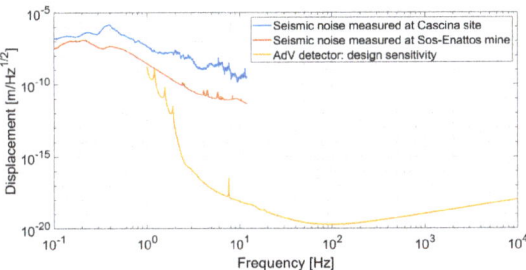

Figure 5. Ground displacement measured at the Cascina site (blue curve) and at the Sos-Enattos mine (red curve) compared to the design sensitivity of the Advanced Virgo detector (AdV). At 10 Hz, the ground displacement is about eight orders of magnitude higher than the sensitivity of the GW detector.

A free-falling mass can be fairly approximated by suspending it through a simple pendulum: this solution allows one to filter out the seismic noise that otherwise would affect the mass.

In order to describe the mechanical response of a simple pendulum to a generic disturbance, it is important to introduce the concept of a mechanical transfer function. In the frequency domain, the transfer function of a system is a linear operator that relates the system's input ($x_i(\omega)$) to its output ($x_o(\omega)$):

$$H(\omega) = \frac{x_o(\omega)}{x_i(\omega)} \qquad (3)$$

The transfer function of a simple pendulum subject to internal friction can be calculated starting from its equation of motion:

$$-M\omega^2 x_o = -k(1 + i\phi)(x_o - x_i) \qquad (4)$$

where x_i and x_o respectively represent the (input) displacement caused by the ground vibrations of the point from which the pendulum is suspended and the (output) displacement of the suspended mass. M is the suspended body mass, k is the oscillator stiffness, and ϕ is the dissipation factor of the system. By taking the ratio between x_o and x_i and using some algebra, it is possible to express the mechanical transfer function magnitude as

$$|H(\omega)| = \frac{\sqrt{1 + \phi^2}}{\sqrt{(1 - \frac{\omega^2}{\omega_0^2})^2 + \phi^2}} \qquad (5)$$

where ω_0 is the resonant mode of the system, defined as $\sqrt{\frac{k}{M}}$. The quality factor Q of such a system is defined as $Q = \frac{1}{\phi}$.

With reference to Figure 6 (blue curve) and considering a harmonic oscillator with resonance mode ω_0 and quality factor Q, we observe that:

- At frequency $\omega \ll \omega_0$, the transfer function is equal to 1 and the force is totally transmitted from the input to the output;
- When $\omega = \omega_0$, the applied force to the input determines a continuous transfer of energy from the input to the output and an amplification of the system motion with a quality factor Q;
- At frequency $\omega \gg \omega_0$, the system behaves as a second-order low-pass mechanical filter.

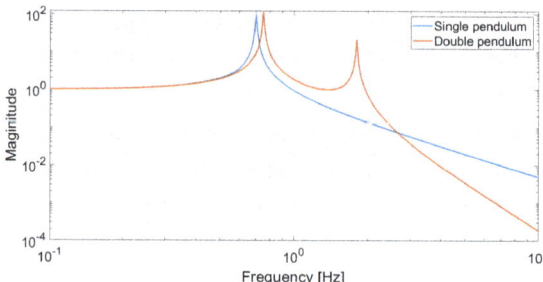

Figure 6. Mechanical transfer functions of a single (blue curve) and a double pendulum (red curve) having the same length.

Increasing the number of stages in a mechanical structure represents a good approach to improving the total attenuation factor of seismic noise at the level of the test masses. In such a way, the magnitude of the transfer function of a cascade of N harmonic oscillators (N stages) can be written as

$$|H(\omega)| = \prod_{i=1}^{N} \frac{\sqrt{1 + \phi_i^2}}{\sqrt{(1 - \frac{\omega^2}{\omega_{0i}^2})^2 + \phi_i^2}} \qquad (6)$$

Above the resonances of the chain, such a system behaves as a low-pass filter of order 2^N that is able to inhibit the transmission of the seismic noise to the suspended body.

3.1. Seismic Isolation Systems

The seismic isolation systems adopted in current GW detectors are based on the idea of suspending a chain of harmonic oscillators in a cascade to filter out the transmitted noise at the test mass level in all its degrees of freedom.

To fulfil the detector requirements, during the last twenty years, a great effort has been made to develop these kind of systems. A few important guidelines were followed: the normal modes of the pendulum mechanical structures must be confined in the low frequency region (below 5 Hz); the pre-isolation stage is used as a mechanical support for the suspension point of the chain, allowing to move it by applying small forces; and finally, the active isolation platform should provide a good level of seismic isolation.

In the following, we will give a brief description of the seismic isolation system used in the LIGO, KAGRA, and Virgo systems.

3.1.1. LIGO Seismic Isolation System

The seismic isolation system adopted by LIGO uses a combination of active and passive stages [16–18]. A conceptual and a CAD model of the **BSC (Basic Symmetric Chamber)**, which houses the test mass and the transfer function of the quadruple pendulum, are shown in Figure 7. The BSC chamber, a 4.5 m tall suspension, consists of three cascade systems. The first system, the active Hydraulic External Pre-Isolator (The HEPI), provides the first isolation stage. The second system, the Internal Seismic Isolation platform (BSC-ISI), provides two stages of isolation. The test mass is suspended by 480 micron-fused silica fibres to a quadruple pendulum. This system shows resonance frequencies ranging from 0.45 to 4 Hz; thus, the isolation from ground vibrations is provided above these frequencies. Finally, vertical attenuation is provided by maraging steel blades installed in the first three stages of the quadruple pendulum.

A remarkable attenuation in the microseismic region is achieved through the use of active controls and noise subtraction techniques [19–22].

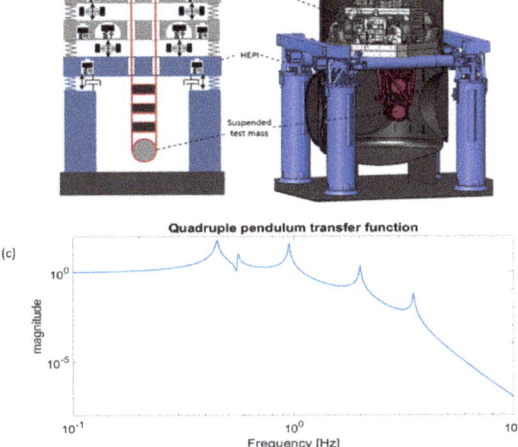

Figure 7. Schematic model (**a**) and technical drawing (**b**) of the BSC chamber supporting the LIGO test masses [17]. For completeness, panel (**c**) shows the quadruple pendulum mechanical transfer function from the ground to the test mass along the longitudinal degree of freedom. This transfer function was reconstructed following Figure 5 in [18].

3.1.2. KAGRA Seismic Isolation System

KAGRA differs from LIGO and Virgo. Indeed, it is the first GW detector built completely underground with cryogenic technologies [23]. Its suspension concept takes inspiration from the Virgo one and it is called the **Type A system**. With reference to Figure 8, it consists of a multi-stage pendulum that is 13.5 m tall. It is based on the second floor of an underground mine, supported by three inverted pendulum legs (1 m). The payload, comprising four stages, is installed inside a cryostat and cooled down to 20 K. The vertical attenuation is provided by triangular maraging blades installed in all the filters present in the chain, which are called Geometrical Anti Spring (GAS) filters.

The attenuation of the suspension is passive but active controls damp the structural modes in the 0.07–3 Hz band.

3.1.3. Virgo Seismic Isolation System

Virgo test masses are suspended using the so-called **Super-Attenuator (SA)**, which is composed of a multi-stage seismic isolation system [24,25]. Referring to Figure 9, it consists of a pre-isolator, which is a soft inverted pendulum (30 mHz), from which is suspended a 9.2 m long multistage chain connected by means of a single wire at the center of mass of each stage. This chain comprises a first filter at the top of the inverted pendulum (filter 0), four standard filters (the pendulums), and a last filter (Filter 7). Below this is the marionette, from which the test mass is suspended by 480 micron-fused silica fibres. To achieve vertical attenuation, the filter chain is equipped with triangular maraging blades and magnetic anti-springs.

The attenuation of the whole suspension from the ground is passive. Active controls are used to damp the structural modes (from 0.03–2 Hz).

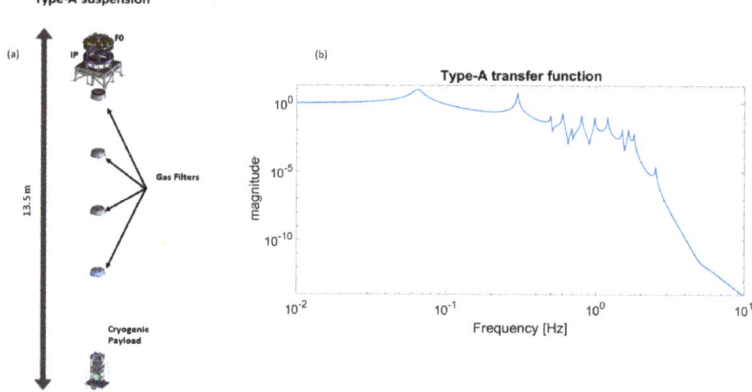

Figure 8. Panel (**a**) shows a technical drawing of a Type A system. From top to bottom, the isolation stages are: the pre-isolator (inverted pendulum and top filter—F0), four GAS filters, and the cryogenic payload (platform, intermediate-mass, marionette, and mirror) [23]. Panel (**b**) shows the Type A mechanical transfer function from the ground to the test mass along the longitudinal degree of freedom.

For completeness, Figure 10 shows the ground displacement, measured at the Cascina site, filtered by means of the SA and compared to AdV sensitivity curve. Looking at this Figure, it is clear that it is thanks to the high-performance suspension system that the current second-generation GW antennas have been able to improve their sensitivity down to 10 Hz. The plan for the future third-generation GW detectors, such as ET [26] and the Cosmic Explorer (CE) [27], is to extend the detection band below 10 Hz. With this intent in mind, an upgrade of the suspension systems is necessary in order to improve seismic attenuation in the low frequency band. Other technological improvements such as cryogenic-payloads and a Newtonian noise subtraction system (see Section 4) will be necessary. Moreover, ET is intended to be sensitive down to 2–3 Hz; for this reason, it will be built underground (see Section 2.2).

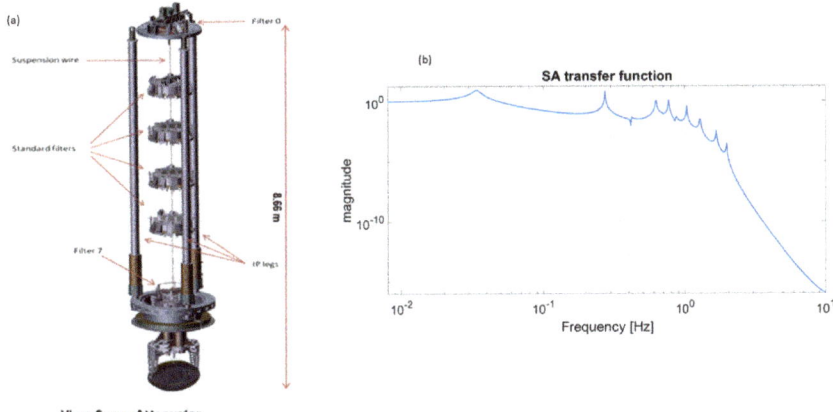

Figure 9. Panel (**a**) shows a technical drawing of the Virgo SA. From top to bottom, the isolation stages are: pre-isolator (inverted pendulum and top filter—F0), five filters and the payload (marionette and mirror). Panel (**b**) shows the SA mechanical transfer function from the ground to the test mass along the longitudinal degree of freedom.

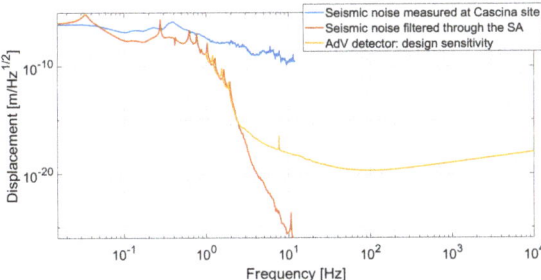

Figure 10. Ground displacement not filtered (blue) and filtered through the SA (red) compared to the design sensitivity of the AdV detector.

4. Newtonian Noise

NN has been foreseen since the beginning of the GW detector era [28], and in 1998, with the contemporaneous works of Beccaria et al. [29] and Hughes and Thorne [30], it was predicted to become the last sensitivity wall in the low frequency band (<30 Hz) of ground-based interferometric detectors. However, it is only with the advent of advanced [31] and third-generation [32] GW detectors that NN will start to threaten their sensitivity and to become the dominant source of noise in the low frequency band. Indeed, in the forthcoming observing runs, quantum and thermal noise will be lowered enough to allow NN to become the dominant noise. For this reason, it will be of utmost importance to reduce NN as much as possible.

Addressing the NN problem will also be a crucial task for 3rd generation gravitational-wave detectors, such as ET and CE.

Due to its gravitational nature, NN cannot be physically shielded or reduced without forcing severe modifications to the already existing infrastructure [30,33]. Therefore, the best approach to suppress it is through active noise cancellation. This aspect will be covered in more detail in Section 6.

The gravity fluctuations induced by a density variations are a simple consequence of the Newtonian law

$$\delta\phi(\vec{r}_0, t) = -G \int dV \frac{\delta\varrho(\vec{r}, t)}{|\vec{r}_0 - \vec{r}|} \quad (7)$$

where $\varrho(\vec{r}, t)$ represents a density variation at a position $\vec{r}$ and at a time t. G is the gravitational constant. Every mechanism that produces a density variation in the media surrounding the test masses represents a source of Newtonian noise. Thus, we can have

$$\delta\varrho_{\text{seis}}(\mathbf{r}, t) = -\nabla \cdot (\rho_{\text{soil}}(\mathbf{r})\boldsymbol{\xi}(\mathbf{r}, t)) \quad (8)$$

$$\delta\varrho_{\text{press}}(\mathbf{r}, t) = \frac{\bar{\rho}_{\text{atm}}}{\gamma \bar{p}_{\text{atm}}} \delta p_{\text{atm}}(\mathbf{r}, t) \quad (9)$$

$$\delta\varrho_{\text{temp}}(\mathbf{r}, t) = -\frac{\bar{\rho}_{\text{atm}}}{\bar{T}_{\text{atm}}} \delta T_{\text{atm}}(\mathbf{r}, t) \quad (10)$$

where $\rho_{\text{soil}}(\mathbf{r}, t)$ is the density of the soil; $\boldsymbol{\xi}(\mathbf{r}, t)$ is the seismic displacement; $p_{\text{atm}}(\mathbf{r}, t)$ and $T_{\text{atm}}(\mathbf{r}, t)$ are the air pressure and temperature; $\gamma \sim 1.4$ is the adiabatic index; and $\bar{\rho}_{\text{atm}}$, $\bar{p}_{\text{atm}}$, and $\bar{T}_{\text{atm}}$ are the average density, pressure, and temperature of the atmosphere, respectively. In the next two Subsections, ANN and SNN will be presented in more detail.

4.1. Atmospheric Newtonian Noise

All the phenomena that can perturb the local gravity field on timescales less than 0.5 s are relevant to present and future ground-based GW detectors. Above this value, their sensitivity is too degraded for NN to be a concern. ANN can be produced by infrasound waves (pressure waves) and temperature fluctuations, as well as shock waves and turbulent phenomena.

Saulson [34] was the first to consider NN produced by atmospheric pressure fluctuations. Creighton [35] analyzed the topic, also discussing the production of NN due to advected temperature fields, high speed objects, and shock waves. Regarding pressure fluctuations generated by turbulent flow, the first model was made in [36] and then resumed in [2], in which a complete review of NN is given.

NN produced by infrasound pressure waves can be divided into two contributions: external and internal. The external contribution is produced by infrasound waves propagating in the atmosphere, which can even be produced by sources far from the detector; indeed, acoustic waves can propagate for long distances with negligible attenuation in the atmosphere [37]. Wind turbines are an example of infrasound and seismic noise sources that should be avoided in the proximity of GW detectors [38,39]. The internal contribution is instead due to the noise generated by the machinery hosted in the buildings (Virgo/LIGO) or caverns (KAGRA/ET). This noise must of course be avoided and mitigated as much as possible. Some studies have been conducted in order to assess its contribution inside underground caverns [40,41].

Concerning the NN generated by the advected temperature field, some more considerations are necessary. Pockets of warm air are mixed with pockets of cool air by convective turbulence, but given the timescales we are interested in, we can consider them as frozen in the atmosphere. However, they can produce gravitational noise when the air flow transports these pockets past the detector. Creighton [35] calculated the NN induced by the density fluctuations caused by the advection of these air pockets. The calculation must involve statistical considerations about the temperature field. Considering a uniform airflow parallel to the ground, we can see that the NN induced by temperature advection strongly depends on wind velocity (see Figure 11). In Figure 11 the ANN produced at the surface is compared with the ET-D sensitivity curve [42]. This shows why building the ET underground is important; reaching the targeted sensitivity would be very challenging in a surface location. Going underground would instead reduce the ANN to a level well below the ET sensitivity curve; indeed, the greater the distance from the source of noise, the lower the induced NN (see Table 1).

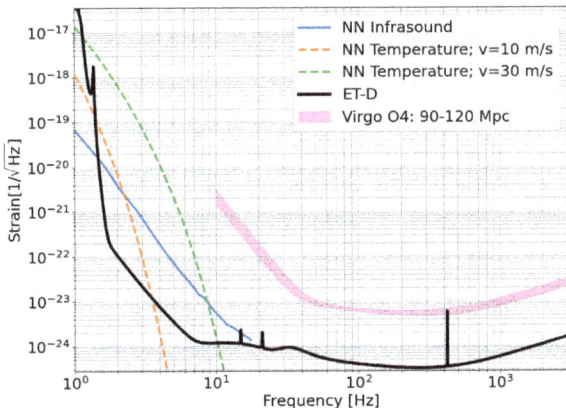

Figure 11. ANN generated by external infrasound and advected temperature fields at the Earth's surface compared with the sensitivity of Virgo foreseen for O4 and with the ET-D sensitivity curve. The ET curve was plotted only to show that building ET on the surface would lead to the requirement of reducing ANN generated by infrasound and advected temperature fields of some orders of magnitude. The ANN produced by infrasound and advected temperature fields were calculated with the models of [35]. The curves for the NN from advected temperature fields were estimated for wind velocities of 10 m/s and 30 m/s. The necessary data to plot the NN produced by infrasound fields were taken from the 75th percentile of Figure 3 in [43].

Table 1. Comparison between the square root of the power spectral densities of the ANN generated by different mechanisms: h is the depth of the underground interferometer, R is the radius of the cavern/room, and d is the shortest distance between the test mass and the moving air flow.

NN Type	Coupling Factor	Condition
External Infrasound	$\propto 1/h^2$	$h \gg \frac{c_s}{4\pi f}$
Internal Infrasound	$\propto R^2$	$R \ll \frac{c_s}{2\pi f}$
Advected Temperature	$\propto e^{-2\pi f d/v}$	$d \gg \frac{v}{2\pi f}$

Table 1 shows how the square root of the power spectral density (PSD) of the strain generated by the different sources of ANN depends on some geometrical parameters such as the distance of the test mass from the atmosphere (external infrasound), the radius of a cavern/room (internal infrasound), and the the minimum distance between the test mass and the air flow (temperature advection). From here, we can easily see that an underground detector would greatly reduce the influence of ANN on the test masses. However, for shallow underground detectors, ANN might still need to be reduced. This can be accomplished by monitoring atmospheric pressure and temperature; however, monitoring the pressure is quite troublesome. Indeed, the infrasound microphones can be affected by nearby turbulent flows (also called wind noise) that can mask the signal in which we are interested [44,45]. This reduces the coherence between two microphones, thus worsening the capabilities of cancelling the NN (see Section 6).

The LIDAR system is a good candidate to measure pressure and temperature fields, but its resolution is not yet sufficient [46] for pressure measurements. Indeed, we are interested in phenomena happening on temporal scales smaller than T = 0.5 s. This means that for pressure waves we need a spatial resolution smaller than $Tc_s/2\pi \sim 27$ m, where c_s is the sound speed in the air ($\simeq$340 m/s).

The possibility of exploiting cosmic rays showers to monitor atmospheric parameters such as the temperature or the pressure has been proposed as well [47]; however, this technique requires a sufficient spatial and temporal resolution (T < 0.5 s) to resolve the fast changes in the density which could give rise to ANN.

4.2. Seismic Newtonian Noise

SNN is produced by seismic waves that are able to locally modify the density of the medium that they are crossing. Rayleigh waves produce density variations through the characteristic elliptical movement that they induce on particles, whereas P-waves occur through the compression and decompression of the soil (see Section 2). Concerning S-waves, we need to be more careful. Shear waves do not produce any density fluctuation (and thus SNN) in a homogeneous volume, but they can if discontinuities (such as a cavern) are present. This is an important point for underground detectors, which are hosted in caverns. The SNN produced by the soil surrounding a cavern of radius a can be written as [2]:

$$\delta \mathbf{a}^{\text{body-waves}}(\mathbf{0}, t) = 4\pi G \rho_0 \left(2\boldsymbol{\xi}^P(\mathbf{0}, t) \frac{j_1(k^P a)}{k^P a} - \boldsymbol{\xi}^S(\mathbf{0}, t) \frac{j_1(k^S a)}{k^S a} \right) \quad (11)$$

where $\delta \mathbf{a}^{\text{body-waves}}(\mathbf{0}, t)$ is the acceleration induced by the SNN at the center of the cavern; G is the gravitational constant; $\boldsymbol{\xi}^P$ and $\boldsymbol{\xi}^S$ are the displacement induced by P- and S-waves, respectively; $j_i(x)$ is the spherical Bessel function of order i; and k^P and k^S are the absolute value of the wave vector of P and S waves, respectively. The equation is obtained by considering a homogeneous and isotropic space with density ρ_0 and the presence of a cavity of radius a. We can note that P-waves contribute to $\delta \mathbf{a}$ with a factor of 2 compared to S-waves. This happens because P-waves contribute to the NN by generating density variations in two ways: through the compression/decompression of the ground and through the displacement of cavity walls. S-waves, instead, enter into play by only generating density variations at the cavity wall discontinuity.

Scattering of seismic waves in the cavern could cause the conversion of P-waves into S-waves and vice versa. However, in [2] it is shown that in the limit of long wavelengths ($k^{P,S} a \to 0$), one can neglect this scattering.

Rayleigh waves dominate the vertical seismic spectrum at the surface and for this reason they are the main source of SNN in detectors such as Virgo and LIGO. These waves are exponentially attenuated underground and contribute less to underground SNN, which instead is dominated by body waves (see Equation (11)). We can model the SNN produced by Rayleigh waves for a surface detector with test masses suspended at h m from the ground as follows [2]:

$$\delta \mathbf{a}^{\text{Rayleigh}}(\mathbf{r}_0, t) = 2\pi G \rho_0 \gamma(\nu) e^{-h k_\rho} \xi_z(\mathbf{0}, 0) e^{i(\mathbf{k}_\rho \cdot \mathbf{r}_0 - \omega t)} \begin{pmatrix} i\cos(\theta) \\ i\sin(\theta) \\ -1 \end{pmatrix} \quad (12)$$

where $\gamma(\nu)$ is a factor determined by the Poisson ratio (i.e. by the elastic properties of the medium) and its value ranges from 0.5 to 1, and θ is the angle that the horizontal wave vector $\mathbf{k}_\rho$ forms with the x-axis. We obtain Equation (12) by calculating the gravity potential induced by a Rayleigh wave, taking its gradient with respect to $\mathbf{r}_0$ and solving for a test mass located above the surface.

However, this model neglects the topology. Indeed, the scattering of seismic waves from an irregular surface topography can vary the composition of the seismic field, leading to complex structures that are not completely characterized by surface displacement [48]. Moreover, for a complete SNN estimation of surface detectors, the underground body wave contribution should also be added to the Rayleigh wave surface contribution.

Rayleigh waves propagating below the surface will generate SNN in an underground test mass through three main mechanisms: surface displacement, rock compression/decompression, and cavern wall displacement. We need to coherently add all these effects to obtain their SNN contribution in the test mass. The PSD of the NN strain induced by Rayleigh waves in an underground detector is given in Equation (2) of [37]. In Figure 12, seismic noise and NN of seismic origin are compared with the ET-D sensitivity curve. The estimate for the NN from Rayleigh waves is calculated using a seismic spectrum lying exactly in the middle between the Peterson NLNM and NHNM (see Figure 2). The estimates for the seismic noise and the SNN from body waves are instead calculated using five times the NLNM. The seismic noise curve was obtained by filtering the ground motion with the transfer function of the 17 m tall suspensions envisaged for ET [42]. The SNN from body waves was calculated based on Equation (11), with a negligible cavity radius compared to the wavelength of the incoming seismic waves and considering an equal energy partition between the two polarizations of S-waves and P-waves. Finally, the SNN produced by Rayleigh waves was estimated using the model of Equation (2) in [37]. However, this estimate must be taken with a grain of salt; indeed, it strongly depends on the velocity dispersion model of Rayleigh waves, as well as on the velocities of P and S-waves.

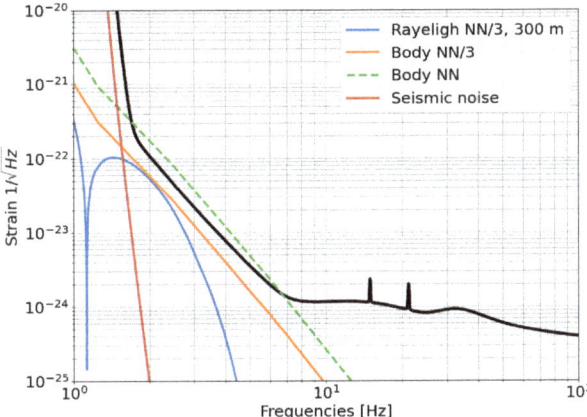

Figure 12. ET-D sensitivity curve compared with the seismic noise and NN of seismic origin. The seismic noise curve was obtained using a seismic spectrum lying exactly at the midpoint between Peterson's NLNM and NHNM (see Figure 2). The same spectrum was used to evaluate the NN generated by Rayleigh waves. For the NN from body waves, we used 5 times the Low Noise Model spectrum, as was done in [37].

5. Other Sources of Newtonian Noise

In principle, NN can be generated by any mass displacement. This means that water flow in underground caverns can also produce such noise. In KAGRA, there can be a large amount of water flowing in the pipes during spring (approximately 1200 tons of water at most per year passes through the drainage pipes near the Y-end station [23]). This could lead to sensitivity limitations of the detector. Indeed, although NN produced by water compression can be considered negligible, the water surface profile can vary during its flow, thus leading to a density variation (the same mechanism by which S-waves can produce NN in presence of a discontinuity). Preliminary models [49] show that NN from turbulent water flow could limit KAGRA's sensitivity.

Another possible source of concern is the NN generated by the vibrations of the cryogenic shielding or by boiling cryogenic liquids. E. Bonilla et al. in [50] studied these effects in relation to the development of LIGO Voyager [51]. They concluded that these sources should not constitute a concern since their NN production will lie below the sensitivity curve of Voyager, as well as that of ET. Structure vibrations will matter only if they have very high Q-factors that can amplify vibrations. Indeed, in [2] (Section 6.5) J. Harms shows that the interaction between an oscillating point mass close to the GW test mass is proportional to the oscillation amplitude, but it is also suppressed by the relative distance between the two objects. This means that, in order to threaten the detector sensitivity, the amplitude should be high and the oscillating objects should be very close to the test mass.

6. Newtonian Noise Cancellation

Given that NN is generated by fluctuations in the gravity field, we cannot easily shield the detector from NN fluctuations. Excavating meter-scale recesses around the test masses would help in reducing nearby density variations and the consequently induced NN by a factor 2–4: this was shown in [33]. A. Singha et al. evaluated, through numerical simulations, the NN originating from an isotropic Rayleigh field in Virgo with and without the recess structure hosting the test masses' clean rooms. They showed that the presence of this empty space leads to a reduction of a factor of two in the estimated NN of Virgo. This result is also supported by the findings of [52], in which seismic data collected in the Virgo West End Building were used to make a first estimate of the SNN affecting the test mass. Concerning ET, cavern dimensions should ideally help in reducing SNN. Plotting the P and S contributions of Equation (11) as a function of $k^P a$ shows that if the cavity radius is 0.4 times the seismic wavelength, then gravity perturbations are reduced by a factor of two. Translated in terms of cavern dimensions, we see that at 30 Hz (the highest interesting frequency for the NN) and considering a conservative P-wave velocity value of 4 km/s, the minimal radius to reduce NN should be of about 50 m [2]. It is clear that such a large radius is unfeasible for underground caverns. In fact, the high rock stress could lead to instabilities that might be fatal [53]. For this reason, it is important to think of other more effective ways to reduce NN both in underground and surface detectors.

Another possible way to reduce both SNN and seismic noise would be the employment of seismic metamaterials, which should provide seismic cloaking that is able to reduce the incoming seismic waves [54,55]. This approach, like the previous one, entails major modifications of the detector infrastructure, so it is not easy to implement in existing GW detectors. Indeed, this would imply building periodic structures around the test masses with dimensions of the order of the seismic waves of interest.

The most immediate way to reduce NN in GW detectors is through active noise cancellation. This method was first suggested by Hughes and Thorne in [30] and then developed by G. Cella in [56]. Active noise cancellation has already been employed in GW interferometers to further suppress noise in the instrument [19–21]. In LIGO, for example, this method is used to actively suppress seismic noise [22].

The basic idea underlying active noise cancellation is to monitor a noise source with some witness sensors and then use these data as an input to a linear filter to reconstruct the noise. In the case of NN, this is possible because the seismic displacement and the induced NN have a linear relationship (see Equations (7) and (8)). The optimal linear filter is calculated to minimize the square error between the estimated signal (the NN) and the real signal and it is known as a Wiener filter (WF) [57].

The main issue in NN cancellation is represented by finding the optimal positions of the N witness sensors in order to maximize the WF capabilities to estimate the SNN. This can be achieved in the frequency domain, but for the final subtraction of NN from GW data, the WF will have to be implemented in the time domain. The distinction between the time-domain WF and the frequency-domain WF lies principally in the fact that in the frequency domain the information regarding the order of the filter disappears. The WF in the frequency domain can be expressed as

$$\hat{X}(\omega) = \mathbf{W}^T(\omega)\mathbf{Y}(\omega) \qquad (13)$$

where both $\mathbf{W}(\omega)$ and $\mathbf{Y}(\omega)$ are N-dimensional vectors containing the Fourier transforms of the WF coefficients and the N witness signals, respectively. The WF is then defined by the coefficients that minimize the ensemble average of the square error function, $E[e^*[\omega]e[\omega]]$, with $e[\omega] = X[\omega] - \hat{X}[\omega]$:

$$\mathbf{W} = (\bar{\mathbf{P}}_{YY})^{-1}\mathbf{P}_{XY} \qquad (14)$$

where $P_{YY_{ij}}(\omega) = E[Y_i^*(\omega)Y_j(\omega)]$ is the element ij of the $N \times N$ matrix of the Cross-PSDs between the ith and j^{th} witness sensors and it is denoted as $\bar{\mathbf{P}}_{YY}$. $P_{XY_i}(\omega) = E[Y_i^*(\omega)X(\omega)]$ is the ith element of the the N-vector of the Cross-PSD between the target signal (the NN in the detector) and the ith witness sensor signal; it is denoted as $\mathbf{P}_{XY}$. With this result we can define the residual as $R = E[e^*e]/P_{XX}$ and obtain

$$R(\omega) = 1 - \frac{\mathbf{P}_{XY}^{\dagger} \tilde{\mathbf{P}}_{YY}^{-1} \mathbf{P}_{XY}}{P_{XX}} \tag{15}$$

where $P_{XX}(\omega) = E[X^*(\omega)X(\omega)]$ is the PSD of the target signal. Note that P_{XX} is a scalar and it is real ($P_{XX} = P_{XX}^*$), whereas $\mathbf{P}_{XY}$ and $\tilde{\mathbf{P}}_{YY}$ are a complex vector and a complex matrix, respectively.

Equation (15) indicates an important point: for effective NN cancellation, correlations between sensors and between them and the test mass are of the utmost importance, but until NN is dominated by other noises (in particular thermal and quantum noises, but also technical noises), evaluating the correlations between the sensors and the test mass strain is hopeless. For this reason, in order to optimize the seismic array positions, we need to rely on coupling models between the seismic displacement and the test mass (see Equation (4) in [52]). The optimal array should be in a configuration that maximizes the correlations between sensors (the elements of $\tilde{\mathbf{P}}_{YY}$). We will come back to this point in the following Subsection, regarding underground NN cancellation.

Ideally, to perform NN cancellation, it would be sufficient to evaluate the WF coefficients of Equation (14). However, this should be done in the time domain, thus implying the inversion of a huge matrix (of the order of NPxNP, since we have to consider also the filter order, P). This could lead to statistical and numerical errors. A way around this would be using a gradient descent algorithm to find the WF coefficients, instead of calculating them through a matrix inversion [58].

In order to perform the cancellation, other sensors rather than seismometers have been proposed. Concerning surface detectors, we know that they are dominated by Rayleigh waves, which can be monitored using an array of vertical seismic sensors. However, a single tiltmeter located under the test mass would be enough to cancel the NN from surface detectors with the only limitation being its own self-noise [59]. The reason that a tiltmeter could perform better is that the vertical displacement under a test mass has zero correlation with the induced NN, whereas the horizontal one correlates in the direction of the test mass displacement. Using seismic sensors to record the horizontal channel would not help, since they are affected by the presence of Love waves, which would spoil the correlations. The tiltmeter, on the other hand, does not have this problem and it could be used for NN cancellation purposes. The possibility of using a tiltmeter is yet to be investigated for the underground case, where instead of Rayleigh waves, there are P and S-waves which mix (see next Subsection).

Another possibility for performing NN cancellation is represented by deep neural networks. Some preliminary works have already been carried out to check how they could perform compared to the WF [60] and to reconstruct the underground seismic field [61].

Newtonian Noise Cancellation in Surface and Underground Detectors

They key to good NN cancellation relies in the search for the optimal array, in order to maximize the WF capabilities to estimate the NN affecting the test mass. Finding such an array means searching for the array configuration that minimizes the residual of Equation (15) for a fixed frequency and number of sensors. If the seismic field is isotropic and homogeneous, this can be accomplished quite easily, especially for surface detectors. In reality, the seismic field, especially at the surface, is never isotropic and/or homogeneous. This leads to the need to use seismic data to reconstruct the surface seismic field by building a surrogate model that will be used to find the optimal array configuration [52]. This has been achieved for Virgo, leading to the array configuration shown in Figure 13 (left).

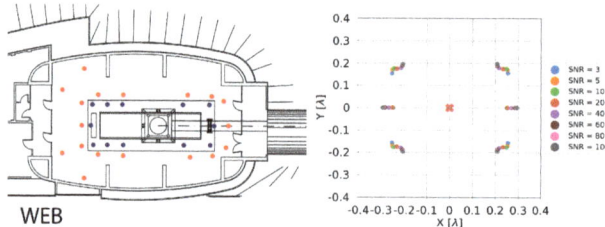

Figure 13. Comparison between the optimal array obtained for the West End Building (WEB) in Virgo (**left**) and the optimal array obtained for an isotropic and homogeneous Rayleigh wave field (**right**). The blue dots in the **left** figure represent sensors placed on the tower platform (which is anchored to the bedrock with pillars), whereas the red dots represent sensors placed on the floor of the building. The optimal array in the **right** figure is represented with different values of SNR. The *right* figure was taken from [62].

In underground detectors, correlations between seismic sensors are greatly spoiled by the mixing of P- and S-waves. Indeed, seismic sensors are only sensitive to the displacement and not to the wave polarization. This means that both P- and S-waves will contribute to the recorded displacement and, since P- and S-waves are uncorrelated, the correlations between the sensors will be degraded. Figure 14 shows a comparison of seismic correlations between the origin and all the other points in the presence of a homogeneous and isotropic seismic field composed only of P-waves in one case (left) and of a mix of P- and S-waves in the other case (right).

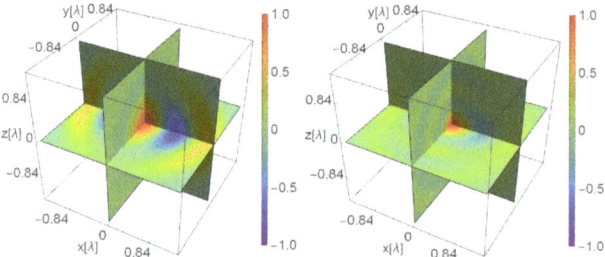

Figure 14. **Left**: seismic correlations between the origin and all the other points in the presence of a homogeneous and isotropic seismic field composed only of P-waves. **Right**: seismic correlations between the origin and all the other points in the presence of a homogeneous and isotropic seismic field composed of 1/3 of P-waves and 2/3 of S-waves (assuming an equal distribution of energy between the three polarizations: one for P-waves and two for S-waves). Figure taken from [62].

For this reason, the WF in the underground environment will never reach the limit imposed by the self noise of the sensors since it is already limited by degraded correlations. This is perhaps the biggest conceptual problem related to NN subtraction in underground detectors because it implies the need for a higher number of sensors to reach a given NN reduction level. Finding a way to disentangle P- and S-components would lead to better performance by the WF (increasing the correlations that could be evaluated separately). Employing tiltmeters, for example, could help in this, but this is something that remains to be investigated.

7. Conclusions

In this paper, two forms of noise present in interferometric GW detectors were reviewed: seismic and Newtonian noise. Newtonian noise has a seismic noise component; it follows then that these two forms of noise are intimately connected and, for this reason, it is natural to address them in the same review.

Seismic noise and its origin are described in detail and an explanation of how this noise can affect GW detection and the techniques employed to reduce its effects in current GW detectors have been provided. Newtonian noise has been described as well: all its contributors (atmospheric, seismic, and some other contributors) were described together, along with the main work carried out in the field.

To conclude, we must point out that third-generation GW detectors require particular care in regard to the design of the suspension system, as well as the design of the Newtonian noise cancellation system. Indeed, seismic and Newtonian noise can become a limiting factor for the detector sensitivity in the low frequency band.

Author Contributions: L.T. and F.B. contributed equally. All authors have read and agreed to the published version of the manuscript.

Funding: This research received no external funding.

Institutional Review Board Statement: Not applicable.

Informed Consent Statement: Not applicable.

Data Availability Statement: Data needed for some figures were taken from Virgo seismic channels, from [43,63] and from ORFEUS, the European Infrastructure for seismic waveform data in EPOS [64].

Acknowledgments: The authors would like to thank Jan Harms, Luciano Di Fiore, and Joris van Heijningen whose insightful comments helped to improve the paper. They would also like to thank Rosario De Rosa, who kindly provided the seismic data of Sos-Enattos site shown in Figures 4 and 5, Kazuhiro Yamamoto, who kindly provided the seismic data to reproduce Figure 3, The Kagra collaboration and Ayaka Shoda who kindly provided the technical drawing of the Type A system, shown in Figure 2 of [23] and the data used in Figure 8.

Conflicts of Interest: The authors declare no conflict of interest.

Abbreviations

The following abbreviations are used in this manuscript:

AdV	Advanced Virgo
ANN	Atmospheric Newtonian Noise
BSC	Basic Symmetric Chamber
CE	Cosmic Explorer
ET	Einstein Telescope
NHNM	New High Noise Model
NLNM	New Low Noise Model
NN	Newtonian Noise
PSD	Power Spectral Density
SA	Super Attenuator
SNN	Seismic Newtonian Noise
WF	Wiener Filter

References

1. Saulson, P.R. *Seismic Noise and Vibration Isolation*; World Scientific: Singapore, 1994; pp. 127–143.
2. Harms, J. Terrestrial gravity fluctuations. *Living Rev. Relativ.* **2019**, *22*, 1–154. [CrossRef]
3. Cirone, A.; Fiori, I.; Paoletti, F.; Perez, M.M.; Rodríguez, A.R.; Swinkels, B.L.; Vazquez, A.M.; Gemme, G.; Chincarini, A. Investigation of magnetic noise in advanced Virgo. *Class. Quantum Gravity* **2019**, *36*, 225004. [CrossRef]
4. Saulson, P.R. Thermal noise in mechanical experiments. *Phys. Rev. D* **1990**, *42*, 2437–2445. [CrossRef] [PubMed]
5. Heurs, M. Gravitational wave detection using laser interferometry beyond the standard quantum limit. *Philos. Trans. R. Soc. Math. Phys. Eng. Sci.* **2018**, *376*, 20170289. [CrossRef] [PubMed]
6. Michael Wysession, S.S. *An Introduction to Seismology, Earthquakes and Earth Structure*; Jon Wiley and Sons: Hoboken, NJ, USA, 2009.
7. Shearer, P.M. *An Introduction to Seismology*; Cambridge University Press: Cambridge, UK, 2012.
8. Seismic Waves. Wikipedia. Available online: https://en.wikipedia.org/wiki/Seismic_wave#/media/File:Pswaves.jpg (accessed on 1 December 2021).

9. Peterson, J.R. *Observations and Modeling of Seismic Background Noise*; USG Report; 1993. Available online: https://pubs.usgs.gov/of/1993/0322/ofr93-322.pdf (accessed on 1 December 2021).
10. Longuet-Higgins, M.S. A theory of the origin of microseisms. *R. Soc.* **1950**, *243*, 1–35.
11. Cessaro, R.K. Sources of primary and secondary microseisms. *Bull. Seismol. Soc. Am.* **1994**, *84*, 142–148. [CrossRef]
12. Nishida, K. Ambient seismic wave field. *Proc. Jpn. Acad. Ser.* **2017**, *93*, 423–448. [CrossRef]
13. Yamamoto, K.; Kamagasako, S.; Uchiyama, T.; Miyoki, S.; Ohashi, M.; Kuroda, K. Measurement of Seismic Motion at Large-Scale Cryogenic Gravitational Wave Telescope Project Site. 2010. Available online: https://gwdoc.icrr.u-tokyo.ac.jp/DocDB/0002/T1000218/001/Kamiokaseis.pdf (accessed on 1 December 2021)
14. Meyers, P. Cross-Correlation Searches for Persistent Gravitational Waves with Advanced LIGO and Noise Studies for Current and Future Ground-Based Gravitational-Wave Detectors. Ph.D. Thesis, University of Minnesota, Minneapolis, MN, USA, 2018.
15. Saulson, P. Vibration isolation for broadband gravitational wave antennas. *Rev. Sci. Instrum* **1984**, *55*, 1315–1320. [CrossRef]
16. Update on Suspension Design for Advanced LIGO. 2012. Available online: https://dcc.ligo.org/public/0001/G0900367/002/G0900367v2.pdf (accessed on 1 December 2021).
17. Matichard, F.; Lantz, B.; Mittleman, R.; Mason, K.; Kissel, J.; Abbott, B.; Biscans, S.; McIver, J.; Abbott, R.; Abbott, S.; et al. Seismic isolation of Advanced LIGO: Review of strategy, instrumentation and performance. *Class. Quantum Gravity* **2015**, *32*, 185003. [CrossRef]
18. Robertson, N.A.; Cagnoli, G.; Crooks, D.R.M.; Elliffe, E.; Faller, J.E.; Fritschel, P.; Goßler, S.; Grant, A.; Heptonstall, A.; Hough, J.; et al. Quadruple suspension design for Advanced LIGO. *Class. Quantum Gravity* **2002**, *19*, 4043. [CrossRef]
19. Driggers, J.C.; Evans, M.; Pepper, K.; Adhikari, R. Active noise cancellation in a suspended interferometer. *Rev. Sci. Instrum.* **2012**, *83*, 024501. [CrossRef] [PubMed]
20. Driggers, J.C.; Vitale, S.; Lundgren, A.P.; Evans, M.; Kawabe, K.; Dwyer, S.E.; Izumi, K.; Schofield, R.M.; Effler, A.; Sigg, D.; et al. Improving astrophysical parameter estimation via offline noise subtraction for Advanced LIGO. *Phys. Rev.* **2019**, *99*, 042001. [CrossRef]
21. DeRosa, R.; Driggers, J.C.; Atkinson, D.; Miao, H.; Frolov, V.; Landry, M.; Giaime, J.A.; Adhikari, R.X. Global feed-forward vibration isolation in a km scale interferometer. *Class. Quantum Gravity* **2012**, *29*, 215008. [CrossRef]
22. Giaime, J.A.; Daw, E.J.; Weitz, M.; Adhikari, R.; Fritschel, P.; Abbott, R.; Bork, R.; Heefner, J. Feedforward reduction of the microseism disturbance in a long-base-line interferometric gravitational-wave detector. *Rev. Sci. Instrum.* **2003**, *74*, 218–224. [CrossRef]
23. Akutsu, T.; M Ando, M.; Arai, K.; Arai, Y.; Araki, S.; Araya, A.; Aritomi, N.; Aso, Y.; Bae, S.; Bae, Y.; et al. Overview of KAGRA: Detector design and construction history. *Prog. Theor. Exp. Phys.* **2021**, *2021*, 05A101. [CrossRef]
24. Braccini, S.; Barsotti, L.; Bradaschia, C.; Cella, G.; Virgilio, A.D.; Ferrante, I.; Fidecaro, F.; Fiori, I.; Frasconi, F.; Gennai, A.; et al. Measurement of the seismic attenuation performance of the virgo superattenuator. *Astropart. Phys.* **2005**, *23*, 557–565. [CrossRef]
25. Trozzo, L. Low Frequency Performance Optimization and Performance of Advanced Virgo Seismic Isolation System. Ph.D. Thesis, Università Degli Studi di Siena, Siena, Italy, 2018.
26. Punturo, M.; Abernathy, M.; Acernese, F.; Allen, B.; Andersson, N.; Arun, K.; Barone, F.; Barr, B.; Barsuglia, M.; Beker, M.; et al. The Einstein Telescope: A third-generation gravitational wave observatory. *Class. Quantum Gravity* **2010**, *27*, 194002. [CrossRef]
27. Evans, M.; Adhikari, R.X.; Afle, C.; Ballmer, S.W.; Biscoveanu, S.; Borhanian, S.; Brown, A.D.; Chen, Y.; Eisenstein, R.; Gruson, A.; et al. A Horizon Study for Cosmic Explorer Science, Observatories, and Community. *arXiv* **2021**, arXiv:2109.09882. Available online: https://arxiv.org/pdf/2109.09882.pdf (accessed on 1 December 2021).
28. Weiss, R.; Muehlner, D. Electromagnetically coupled broadband gravitational antenna. *Final. Q. Rep. Mit Res. Lab. Electron.* **1972**, *105*, 54.
29. Beccaria, M.; Bernardini, M.; Braccini, S.; Bradaschia, C.; Bozzi, A.; Casciano, C.; Cella, G.; Ciampa, A.; Cuoco, E.; Curci, G.; et al. Relevance of Newtonian seismic noise for the VIRGO interferometer sensitivity. *Class. Quantum Gravity* **1998**, *15*, 3339.
30. Hughes, S.A.; Thorne, K.S. Seismic gravity-gradient noise in interferometric gravitational-wave detectors. *Phys. Rev. D* **1998**, *58*. [CrossRef]
31. Acernese, F.; Agathos, M.; Agatsuma, K.; Aisa, D.; Allemandou, N.; Allocca, A.; Amarni, J.; Astone, P.; Balestri, G.; Ballardin, G.; et al. Advanced Virgo: A second-generation interferometric gravitational wave detector. *Class. Quantum Gravity* **2015**, *32*, 024001. [CrossRef]
32. ET Steering Committee Editorial Team. ET Design Report Update 2020. ET-0007A-20. 2020. Available online: https://apps.et-gw.eu/tds/?call_file=ET-0007A-20_ETDesignReportUpdate2020.pdf (accessed on 1 December 2021).
33. Harms, J.; Hild, S. Passive Newtonian noise suppression for gravitational-wave observatories based on shaping of the local topography. *Class. Quantum Gravity* **2014**, *31*, 185011. [CrossRef]
34. Saulson, P.R. Terrestrial gravitational noise on a gravitational wave antenna. *Phys. Rev. D* **1984**, *30*, 732–736. doi: 10.1103/physrevd.30.732. [CrossRef]
35. Creighton, T. Tumbleweeds and Airborne Gravitational Noise Sources for LIGO. *arXiv* **2008**, arXiv:gr-qc/0007050. Available online: https://arxiv.org/pdf/gr-qc/0007050.pdf (accessed on 1 December 2021).
36. Cafaro, C.; Ali, S.A. Analytical Estimate of Atmospheric Newtonian Noise Generated by Acoustic and Turbulent Phenomena in Laser-Interferometric Gravitational Waves Detectors. *arXiv* **2009**, arXiv:0906.4844v2. Available online: https://arxiv.org/pdf/0906.4844.pdf (accessed on 1 December 2021).

37. Amann, F.; Bonsignorio, F.; Bulik, T.; Bulten, H.J.; Cuccuru, S.; Dassargues, A.; DeSalvo, R.; Fenyvesi, E.; Fidecaro, F.; Fiori, I.; et al. Site-Selection Criteria for the Einstein Telescope. *arXiv* **2020**, arXiv:2003.03434. Available online: https://arxiv.org/pdf/2003.03434.pdf (accessed on 1 December 2021).
38. Baumgart, J.; Fritzsche, C.; Marburg, S. Infrasound of a Wind Turbine Reanalyzed as Power Spectrum and Power Spectral Density. *J. Sound Vib.* **2021**, 116310. [CrossRef]
39. Saccorotti, G.; Piccinini, D.; Cauchie, L.; Fiori, I. Seismic Noise by Wind Farms: A Case Study from the Virgo Gravitational Wave Observatory, Italy. *Bull. Seismol. Soc. Am.* **2011**, *101*, 568–578. [CrossRef]
40. Fenyvesi, E.; Molnár, J.; Czellár, S. Investigation of Infrasound Background Noise at Mátra Gravitational and Geophysical Laboratory (MGGL). *Universe* **2020**, *6*, 10. [CrossRef]
41. Badaracco, F.; Harms, J.; Rossi, C.D.; Fiori, I.; Miyo, K.; Tanaka, T.; Yokozawa, T.; Paoletti, F.; Washimi, T. KAGRA underground environment and lessons for the Einstein Telescope. *Phys. Rev. D* **2021**, *104*, 042006. [CrossRef]
42. Einstein Gravitational Wave Telescope Conceptual Design Study—ET-0106C-10. 2011. Available online: http://www.et-gw.eu/ (accessed on 1 December 2021).
43. Posmentier, E.S. 1-to 16-Hz infrasound associated with clear air turbulence predictors. *J. Geophys. Res.* **1974**, *79*, 1755–1760. [CrossRef]
44. Green, D.N. The spatial coherence structure of infrasonic waves: Analysis of data from International Monitoring System arrays. *Geophys. J. Int.* **2015**, *201*, 377–389. [CrossRef]
45. Fiorucci, D.; Harms, J.; Barsuglia, M.; Fiori, I.; Paoletti, F. Impact of infrasound atmospheric noise on gravity detectors used for astrophysical and geophysical applications. *Phys. Rev. D* **2018**, *97*, 062003. [CrossRef]
46. Razenkov, I.I.; Eloranta, E.W. Advances in atmospheric temperature profile measurements using high spectral resolution Lidar. In Proceedings of the 28th International Laser Radar Conference (ILRC 28), Bucharest, Romania, 25–30 June 2018. [CrossRef]
47. Avgitas, T.; Arnaud, N.; Boschi, V.; Fiori, I.; Katsanevas, S.; Marteau, J.; Paoletti, F. Monitoring Newtonian Noise with CREGOVIA. VIR-0125A-20. 2020. Available online: https://tds.virgo-gw.eu/?content=3&r=16753 (accessed on 1 December 2021).
48. Andric, T.; Harms, J. Simulations of Gravitoelastic Correlations for the Sardinian Candidate Site of the Einstein Telescope. *J. Geophys. Res. Solid Earth* **2020**, *125*, e2020JB020401. [CrossRef]
49. Somiya, K. Newtonian Noise from the Underground Water. Available online: http://www-kam2.icrr.u-tokyo.ac.jp/indico/event/3/session/32/contribution/365.pdf (accessed on 1 December 2021).
50. Bonilla, E.; Shapiro, B.; Lantz, B.; Aguiar, O.D.; Constancio, M. Noise requirements of the cryogenic shielding for next generation cryocooled gravitational wave observatories: Newtonian noise. *Phys. Rev. D* **2021**, *104* 122005. [CrossRef]
51. Adhikari, R.X.; Arai1, K.; Brooks, A.F.; Wipf, C.; Aguiar, O.; Altin, P.; Barr, B.; Barsotti, L.; Bassiri, R.; Bell, A.; et al. A cryogenic silicon interferometer for gravitational-wave detection. *Class. Quantum Gravity* **2020**, *37*, 165003. [CrossRef]
52. Badaracco, F.; Harms, J.; Bertolini, A.; Bulik, T.; Fiori, I.; Idzkowski, B.; K Nikliborc, A.K.; Paoletti, F.; Paoli, A.; Rei, L.; et al. Machine learning for gravitational-wave detection: Surrogate Wiener filtering for the prediction and optimized cancellation of Newtonian noise at Virgo. *Class. Quantum Gravity* **2020**, *37*, 195016. [CrossRef]
53. Evert Hoek, Edwin T. Brown, M.A. Empirical strength criterion for rock masses. *J. Geotech. Eng. Div.* **1980**, *106*, 1013–1035. [CrossRef]
54. Seismic Cloaking for LIGO. LIGO-T1800273–v4. 2019. Available online: http://https://dcc.ligo.org/public/0153/T1800273/003/finalReport.pdf (accessed on 1 December 2021).
55. Palermo, A.; Krödel, S.; Marzani, A.; Daraio, C. Engineered metabarrier as shield from seismic surface waves. *Sci. Rep.* **2016**, *6*, 39356. [CrossRef]
56. Cella, G. *Off-Line Subtraction of Seismic Newtonian Noise*; Springer: Milano, Italy, 2000; pp. 495–503. [CrossRef]
57. Vaseghi, S.V. Least Square Errors Filters. In *Advanced Digital Signal Processing and Noise Reduction*; John Wiley & Sons: Hoboken, NJ, USA, 2006; pp. 166–186.
58. Harms, J. Terrestrial Gravity fluctuations as fundamental sensitivity limit of GW detectors. *Living Rev. Relativ.* **2020**, *22*, 6. [CrossRef]
59. Harms, J.; Venkateswara, K. Newtonian-noise cancellation in large-scale interferometric GW detectors using seismic tiltmeters. *Class. Quantum Gravity* **2016**, *33*, 234001. [CrossRef]
60. Cirone, A. Magnetic and Newtonian Noises in Advanced Virgo: Evaluation and Mitigation Strategies. Ph.D. Thesis, Università Degli Studi di Genova, Genova, Italy, 2019.
61. van Beveren, V. Seismonet: A Deep Neural Network for NN Prediction. 2021. Available online: https://agenda.infn.it/event/28070/sessions/20906/#20211110 (accessed on 1 December 2021).
62. Badaracco, F.; Harms, J. Optimization of seismometer arrays for the cancellation of Newtonian noise from seismic body waves. *Class. Quantum Gravity* **2019**, *36*, 145006. [CrossRef]
63. Naticchioni, L.; Perciballi, M.; Ricci, F.; Coccia, E.; Malvezzi, V.; Acernese, F.; Barone, F.; Giordano, G.; Romano, R.; Punturo, M.; et al. Microseismic studies of an underground site for a new interferometric gravitational wave detector. *Class. Quantum Gravity* **2014**, *31*, 105016. [CrossRef]
64. Network IV 1988, Station SENA. 2021. Available online: http://orfeus-eu.org/stationbook/networks/IV/1988/stations/SENA/2019/ (accessed on 1 December 2021).

Review

Squeezing in Gravitational Wave Detectors

Sheila E. Dwyer [1,*,†], Georgia L. Mansell [1,2,3,†] and Lee McCuller [2,4,†]

1. LIGO Hanford Observatory, Richland, WA 99352, USA; gmansell@caltech.edu
2. LIGO, Massachusetts Institute of Technology, Cambridge, MA 02139, USA; mcculler@mit.edu
3. Department of Physics, Syracuse University, Syracuse, NY 13244, USA
4. LIGO, California Institute of Technology, Pasadena, CA 91125, USA
* Correspondence: sheila.dwyer@ligo.org
† These authors contributed equally to this work.

Abstract: Injecting optical squeezed states of light, a technique known as squeezing, is now a tool for gravitational wave detection. Its ability to reduce quantum noise is helping to reveal more gravitational wave transients, expanding the catalog of observations in the last observing run. This review introduces squeezing and its history in the context of gravitational-wave detectors. It overviews the benefits, limitations and methods of incorporating squeezing into advanced interferometers, emphasizing the most relevant details for astrophysics instrumentation.

Keywords: gravitational waves; squeezed states; quantum optics; interferometer; quantum noise

1. Introduction

The study of squeezed states, or squeezing, is a maturing field [1–5], finding applications in experiments limited by the quantum nature of light, including spectroscopy [6], quantum key distribution [7], and imaging [8]. Squeezing has expanded the reach of the LIGO and Virgo gravitational wave detectors in the most recent observing run [9,10] of these second generation detectors. Squeezing has a history in the first generation observatories of the GEO600 and LIGO Hanford detectors as a demonstration of principle [11,12] and reliable, sustained campaign of improving sensitivity of GEO600 through quantum optics [13]. At present, the combination of squeezing and diverse instrumentation improvements [14] has resulted in a nearly ten fold increase in gravitational wave detections in the most recent observing run, with 80 new events [15]. The goal of this review is to provide an overview of how squeezing can improve gravitational wave detectors, in a way that should be accessible to researchers in related fields looking for an introduction. We will introduce key considerations for squeezer performance, emphasizing those that are specific to gravitational wave detectors such as the stringent noise requirements and new techniques such as frequency dependent squeezing.

1.1. Introduction to Quantum Noise in Gravitational Wave Detectors

Gravitational wave detectors are Michelson interferometers that employ optical light to probe the spacetime along their arms. In the interferometer arms, passing gravitational waves shift or modulate the phase of the traversing optical field of carrier light, generating phase modulations at the observation frequency Ω. Wave interference at the Michelson beamsplitter then causes the minuscule phase modulations to be observed as power fluctuations at the interferometer readout. The exquisite sensitivity of the detectors to gravitational waves is ultimately limited by the quantum nature of their probe light in detecting phase modulations.

Experimentally, the quantization of light causes "shot noise" from the independent arrival of photons on the readout detector from the interferometer. The average power on the detector and the observation time gives an expected total number of photons, while measurements of the number have a Poisson distribution. The distribution results in an uncertainty in the interferometer phase measurements, which limits the sensitivity of the current generation of gravitational wave detectors at frequencies above 50 Hz.

Amplitude uncertainty in the interferometer arms causes a fluctuating force on the suspended mirrors from the momentum fluctuations of the optical light. The acceleration from the force causes a displacement of the test mass which adds noise to the phase of the light. Thus, in gravitational wave detectors, quantum amplitude quadrature uncertainty creates phase quadrature uncertainty, with a stronger coupling at lower frequencies. This is quantum radiation pressure noise (QRPN), a manifestation of measurement back action whereby the precise measurements of the test mass positions impart uncertainty into their momentum via Heisenberg uncertainty. The momentum uncertainty causes position uncertainty during continuous observation. This is enforced physically because precise measurements of the test mass position require sufficient optical power that the momentum of the light significantly impacts the momentum of the test mass. This uncertainty results in a mechanical standard quantum limit for measurements of mechanical systems [16]. Increasing the optical power in the interferometer improves the phase sensitivity as well as increases the transfer of optical momentum and its uncertainty. The implication is shown by the dashed curve in Figure 1; as the power is increased the shot noise limited sensitivity improves while the radiation pressure noise increases.

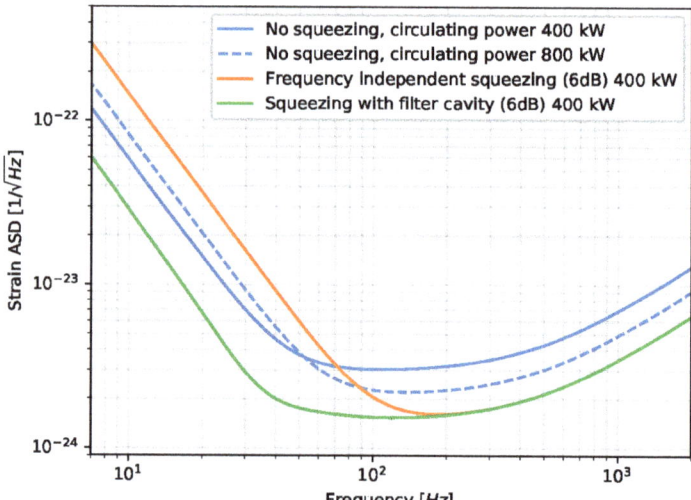

Figure 1. Quantum noise, given in terms of equivalent gravitational-wave detector sensitivity, in the Advanced LIGO design configuration (other noises not shown), calculated using [17]. Gravitational-wave detectors are sensitive to strain, change in arm length over the total arm length. At frequencies above 200 Hz, shot noise is the dominant quantum noise while radiation pressure dominates below 50 Hz. The addition of frequency independent squeezing can reduce one type of quantum noise while increasing the other (see Section 2). Once other noise sources are reduced enough that radiation pressure dominates the low frequency sensitivity of an interferometer, injecting frequency independent squeezing will degrade the sensitivity at some frequencies. Reflecting the squeezed field off of a filter cavity can rotate and filter the squeezing in a frequency dependent way to achieve a broadband sensitivity improvement. The parameters of the injected squeezing, losses, and filter cavity are chosen here so that there is 6 dB of shot noise reduction, and 8 dB of increase in quantum radiation pressure without a filter cavity, and 6 dB improvement in quantum radiation pressure noise with a filter cavity.

1.2. Theoretical Description of Quantum Light, Squeezing

Light can be described by the two quadratures (sine and cosine) of an electric field, both of which have an associated quantum operator, $\hat{X}_1$ and $\hat{X}_2$. Observations of either of these operators have a distribution or uncertainty that is imposed by the quantization of light. Figure 2 shows classic ball and stick style diagrams consisting of a field phasor, representing the quadratures of the classical mean field of the state of the carrier light, with a fuzzy ball showing the magnitude and orientation of the amplitude and phase uncertainties.

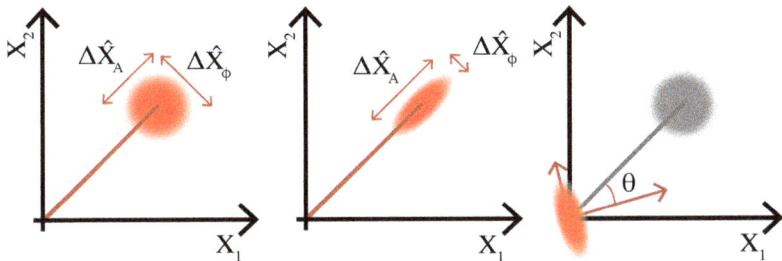

Figure 2. Ball-and-stick diagrams for a coherent state of light (**left**), a squeezed state of light (**center**), and squeezed vacuum (**right**). The red line is a phasor: the amplitude of the state is represented by the length of the line, while the phase is represented by the angle of the line relative to the two quadrature axes—X_1 and X_2. The uncertainty of the state is represented by a fuzzy ball at the end of the stick. The squeezed vacuum field is oriented with angle θ to the quadrature axes.

The first panel of Figure 2 represents a coherent state, the state of ideal laser light. These states have non-zero average field, the carrier amplitude, which provides an orientation of amplitude and phase in the phase space of the quadrature operators. Small modulations of amplitude and phase can be represented as linear combinations of the quadrature operators, $\hat{X}_A$ and $\hat{X}_\phi$.[1]

The uncertainty in the two observable quadratures for vacuum and coherent states are symmetric, and equal, with $\Delta \hat{X}_A^2 = \Delta \hat{X}_\phi^2 = N$. The scale N here represents the standard quantum limit (SQL) for the imprecision of optical measurements [16]. It can be in units of quanta, energy, or spectral density, depending on the experimental context and underlying normalization of the $\hat{X}_A$, $\hat{X}_\phi$ operators. Here, such definitions are omitted, so N represents the scale of the "default" quantum noise from the vacuum state in an optical interferometer.

In the ball-and-stick picture, vacuum states (and squeezed vacuum states) are represented by an uncertainty ball (or ellipse) with no coherent amplitude. Squeezed states have reduced uncertainty in the observations of one quadrature operator compared to a vacuum or coherent state. The quadrature operators do not commute with one another, making them incompatible observables related through the uncertainty relation:

$$\Delta \hat{X}_A \Delta \hat{X}_\phi \geq N. \tag{1}$$

This relation indicates that the quantum phase space of any state has at least the uncertainty area, N, of the vacuum state. The squeezing level, in decibels of phase noise variance reduction with respect to the vacuum state, is given by

$$\mathrm{dB} = -10 \log(\Delta \hat{X}_\phi^2 / N). \tag{2}$$

Due to the uncertainty relation, phase quadrature squeezing causes amplitude quadrature "anti-squeezing", with corresponding increase in its noise variance.

Squeezed states in general are not required to independently affect only $\Delta \hat{X}_A$ or $\Delta \hat{X}_\phi$. One can instead form a squeezed state using operators in a basis rotated by an angle θ with respect to $\hat{X}_A$ and $\hat{X}_\phi$, known as the squeezing angle. More in-depth discussion of quantum optics can be found in [18,19].

To date, this theory describes squeezed states which promise to reduce $\Delta \hat{X}_\phi$ with no apparent limit, arbitrarily improving the sensitivity of interferometers. Realistically, the observed noise reduction of squeezed states is limited through decoherence and degradations of purely-generated squeezed states into impure, mixed states. Those degradations and their implications are detailed in later sections.

1.3. Squeezing in Gravitational Wave Detectors

The "squeezed light upgrade" of gravitational wave detectors surprisingly does not require the main interferometer laser to be modified. Instead, squeezed states are separately produced and injected at the "output" port, see Figure 3. The interferometers are operated with nearly perfect destructive interference, in which case almost all of the input carrier light reflects back towards the laser. Caves realized that the quantum state entering the "output port" *is similarly reflected*, and thus, in conjunction with the input laser power and the mass of the test masses, establishes the quantum state of the light incident on the readout [20]. During its reflection, the state enters, and is modified by, the interferometer.

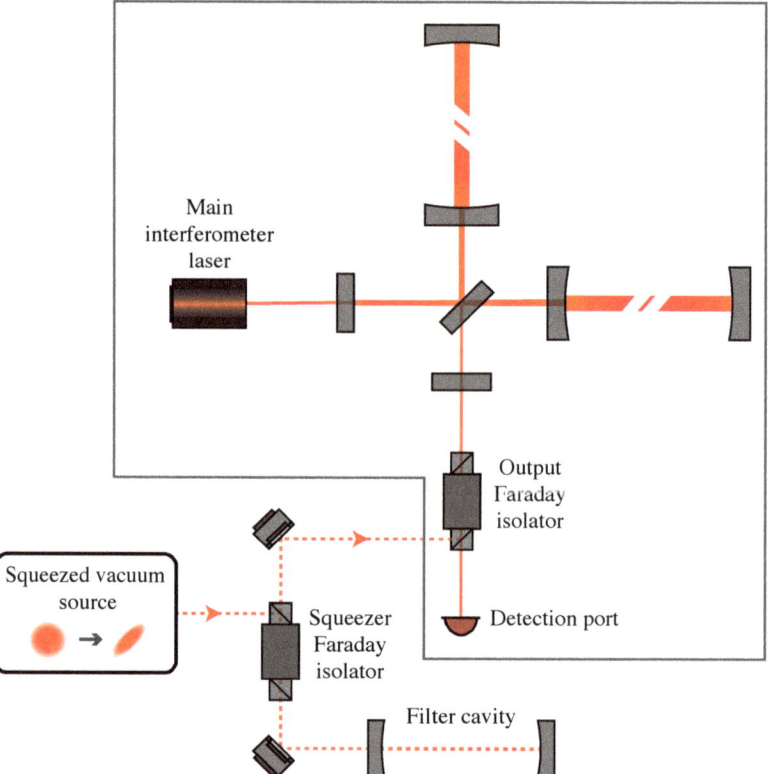

Figure 3. Simplified optical layout of a dual-recycled Fabry–Perot Michelson interferometer (grey box), with frequency-dependent squeezing injected at the output port, as is planned the aLIGO and AdVirgo detectors in Observing Run 4. The squeezed vacuum source generates frequency-independent squeezed light. The squeezed beam (dashed red line) is reflected off the filter cavity, passes back through one or more squeezer Faraday isolators, and is injected into the main interferometer through the output Faraday isolator.

Another example of the phase quadrature displacement is the addition of the fringe light from a static offset in the arm lengths. This displacement adds a large coherent amplitude to the output state without changing the statistics of quadrature observations. By default, vacuum states are perpetually incident on the output port, and the output field consists of the vacuum states mixed with the interferometer field (see Figure 2), causing the readout to have shot noise with Poisson statistics. For squeezing, the vacuum is replaced by squeezed states [20] causing readout noise with sub-Poisson uncertainty for the correct squeezing orientation. This implies—remarkably—that the seemingly passive injection of a field at the output changes the manner by which the classical laser field in the interferometer is emitted and read as photon counts.

Figure 1 shows the impact of both squeezing and carrier power changes on the quantum noise of the Advanced LIGO design. Increasing the optical power in the interferometer improves the phase sensitivity but also directly increases the quantum radiation pressure noise due to backaction, as shown by the dashed curve in Figure 1. Injection of phase squeezing also improves the shot noise limited sensitivity, but increases the radiation pressure noise due to anti-squeezing of the amplitude quadrature.

2. Frequency Dependent Squeezing

The ball-and-stick description of squeezing introduced above shows the squeezing level at a single frequency. The squeezing ellipse can be oriented differently or more or less squeezed at different observation frequencies. Defining the quadrature operators independently for each observation frequency Ω allows the classical description of the frequency response of optical cavities to describe transformations to squeezed states in the frequency domain. The formal description of the relevant frequency domain description of optical states, and its subtleties, is detailed in refs [21,22].

Because of quantum radiation pressure noise, reducing quantum noise throughout the gravitational wave frequency band requires amplitude squeezing at low frequencies and phase squeezing at high frequencies. This can be implemented by continuously rotating the squeezing angle θ as a function of the observation frequency. The appropriate rotation is achieved by reflecting the squeezed beam off of an optical cavity with its resonance detuned (shifted away) from the interferometer's carrier frequency [23–28]. Quantum filter cavities and frequency dependent squeezing are planned to be used in both LIGO and Virgo in the next observing run. Some details of them and their history is included in Section 5.4.

3. Generating Squeezed States of Light

All gravitational-wave detectors currently implementing squeezing use a sub-threshold optical parametric oscillator (OPO), alternately called an optical parametric amplifier, to generate squeezed vacuum [9,10,29]. The squeezer system starts with a laser which is phase locked to have the exact frequency as the main interferometer laser. The squeezer laser pumps a second harmonic generator (SHG) which frequency doubles the 1064 nm light to 532 nm, as shown in Figure 4. The 532 nm light generated by the SHG is then used to pump the optical parametric oscillator.

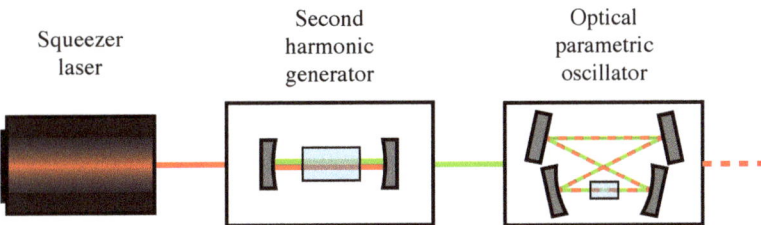

Figure 4. Simplified schematic for squeezed light generation. Red lines indicate 1064 nm beams, green lines are 532 nm, dashed line is squeezed light. The squeezer laser pumps a second harmonic generator which creates the 532 nm light which in turn pumps an optical parametric oscillator.

Since the first experimental realization of squeezing in 1985 [30], several key advances have been made to generate squeezing suitable for use in gravitational wave observatories. The SHG and OPO both use three-wave mixing caused by a second order susceptibility in a crystal, where the induced polarization caused by an applied electric field has a quadratic term allowing exchange of energy between the field at 1064 nm and 532 nm [31]. In the

SHG case, two photons of carrier light convert to frequency-doubled pump light. In OPOs for squeezing, pump photons are down converted into entangled pairs of photons. This process can occur spontaneously or be seeded by an injected field. In either case, the conservation of energy requires that a pump photon at twice the carrier frequency, 2ω, is down converted to a pair of photons at symmetric sideband frequencies $\omega \mp \Omega$, where Ω is the audio band observation frequency. Vacuum fluctuations are incident on the OPO cavity; the correlated pairs of photons generated inside the OPO mean that the field reflected off the cavity can be highly squeezed. More detailed explanations of how an OPO generates squeezing can be found in several references, including [5,19,32,33].

All of the squeezers in use for gravitational wave detectors use a periodically-poled potassium titanyl phosphate (PPKTP) crystal to create their nonlinear interaction, chosen for low loss and high nonlinear coefficient, as discussed in [34]. This crystal is poled for quasi-phase matching [35], which requires that the crystal temperature be controlled to allow for efficient interactions between the two wavelengths. The weak nonlinearity additionally requires high intensity pump light via small beam sizes [36]. The interaction strength is further enhanced using multiple passes in an optical cavity, resonant for the interferometer carrier field. Some OPOs are also doubly resonant, meaning that both the interferometer wavelength and the second-harmonic pump resonate [34]. Doubly resonant cavities require the dispersion between the two wavelengths to be compensated to keep both wavelengths on resonance, while also maintaining the crystal temperature required for phase matching. Several key developments for generating squeezed vacuum states for use in gravitational wave detectors have been made over the last several decades [37,38], as reviewed in [39].

4. Results and History in GEO600, LIGO, Virgo

In the most recent gravitational wave observation run, known as O3, the LIGO, Virgo and GEO600 detectors used squeezing routinely to extend their astrophysical reach [9,10,29]. Figure 5 shows the sensitivity improvements in the LIGO and Virgo detectors, which were the results of decades of research and preparation.

The GEO600 gravitational wave observatory was the first kilometer scale gravitational wave detector to implement squeezing in 2010 [11]. The GEO squeezer uses a linear, hemilithic cavity with a PPKTP crystal resonant for 1064nm and pumped by a single pass 532 nm beam, on an in air optical bench [40]. Efforts at GEO have focused on long term stability [13,41], improvements to the coherent control technique (discussed in Section 5.3) [42], angular controls of squeezing [43], and loss reduction [44]. The GEO detector now routinely runs with 6 dB of shot noise reduction, after several improvements to reduce losses [29].

Virgo implemented squeezing in 2019 with a linear, doubly resonant OPO on an in air opticalTable [45]. The crystal used in this OPO has two regions with separate temperature controllers, most of the crystal is temperature controlled to maintain the phase matching condition, while a small region of the crystal is separately controlled to ensure that both wavelengths are resonant in the cavity. The integration of this squeezed light source with the Virgo controls and automation is described in [46]. The level of squeezing seen in Virgo is limited by optical losses, and shown in Figure 5.

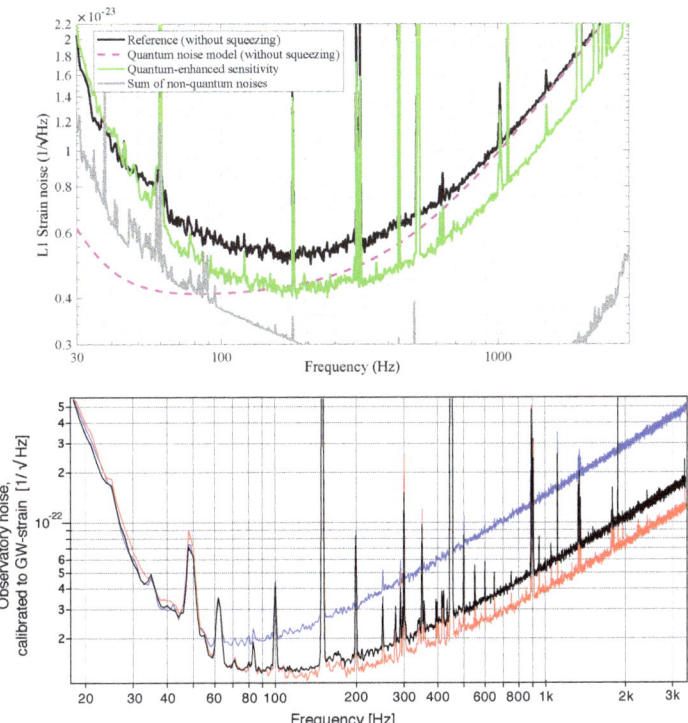

Figure 5. (**Top**) Improved sensitivity of the LIGO Livingston detector in the 3rd observing run, reproduced from [9]. The black trace shows the sensitivity without squeezing injected, while the green trace shows the 2.7 ± 0.1 dB shot noise reduction with squeezing injected. The dashed magenta line shows a model of quantum noise in the detector without squeezing injected, while the gray trace is an estimate of the other noises. (**Bottom**) Improved sensitivity of the Virgo interferometer in the 3rd observing run, reproduced from [10]. The black trace shows the sensitivity without squeezing injected, the red trace shows the 3.2 ± 0.1 dB shot noise reduction with squeezing injected, and blue shows the 8.5 ± 0.1 dB increase in shot noise when the squeezing quadrature is rotated by 90 degrees.

A proof of principle experiment in the LIGO Hanford detector in 2012 demonstrated 2 dB of shot noise reduction [12]. An in air, doubly resonant, traveling wave OPO design with a wedged PPKTP crystal was used to produce squeezing [34]. The crystal temperature is controlled to maintain the phase matching condition in the nonlinear crystal, while a translation stage can adjust the path length in the wedged portion of the crystal to ensure that both wavelengths are resonant in the cavity at the required crystal temperature. This short term squeezing experiment was also used to study the backscatter noise introduced to the detector by squeezing from an in air squeezer [47] and the squeezing angle phase noise [48]. As discussed in Section 5.2, this experiment led LIGO and collaborators at ANU to develop an OPO that could be suspended inside the vacuum system to reduce noise [49–52].

In 2019, LIGO installed in vacuum, doubly resonant bow tie OPOs with wedged PPKTP crystals at both Hanford and Livingston observatories, which resulted in nearly 3 dB of shot noise reduction during the third observation run, as shown in Figure 5 [9]. The quantum radiation pressure noise limited the sensitivity of the Livingston detector, so that the degradation and improvement in quantum radiation pressure noise due to squeezing was observed when squeezing was injected with different squeezing angles [53]. When the maximum level of squeezing available was injected into the interferometer at Livingston, the increased radiation pressure noise degraded the overall sensitivity to astrophysical sources. For this reason the level of squeezing used for routine observations was less than the maximum available [9]. Frequency dependent losses limited the level of squeezing available in both LIGO detectors, as discussed in Section 5.5 and in [54].

5. Integration of Squeezing in Gravitational-Wave Detectors

Gravitational wave detectors are some of the most sensitive meteorology instruments in the world. They impose demanding requirements on optical field stability and physical motion in the audio signal band. High levels of squeezing and frequency dependent squeezing have been developed and demonstrated in lab scale experiments for decades, but require some adaptation to interoperate with gravitational wave interferometers. In this section, we will discuss some of the factors that limit squeezing, ways in which the squeezed light upgrade can add noise to these sensitive instruments, and approaches to improve performance.

5.1. Loss and Phase Noise

The level of squeezing measured in an interferometer or any other squeezing measurement is degraded in three main ways: optical losses, phase noise of the squeezing ellipse [55,56], and coherent light from the interferometer that can be modulated by the squeezer. The first and second degradations are discussed in this section, while the third is discussed in Section 5.2.

The first degradation, optical loss, mixes un-squeezed vacuum states into the squeezed states. This creates mixed states in which the squeezed quadrature is substantially less squeezed, while the anti-squeezed quadrature stays nearly the same. In short, optical losses representing the attenuation of power, Λ, limit the level of observable noise reduction to be $-10\log_{10}(\Lambda)$. Potential sources of losses are intracavity losses in the OPO, characterized by the escape efficiency, losses in relay optics including Faraday isolators [57–59], alignment fluctuations or misalignment of the squeezer beam [52], and mode mismatches between the squeezed beam and mode of the gravitational wave sidebands (or arm cavities) [54].

Fluctuations of the measurement quadrature relative to the squeezed quadrature, called phase noise, mix the increased noise of the anti-squeezed quadrature into the measurement. Phase noise at any frequency limits the useful squeezing level: fluctuations faster than the measurement frequency integrate to limit the measured squeezing while slow fluctuations limit the average interferometer sensitivity to gravitational waves. The phase noise requirements become increasingly stringent at high levels of squeezing [49]. Phase noise is introduced by a variety of mechanisms, including RF sidebands used for interferometer sensing, and sensing errors in the coherent control scheme discussed in Section 5.3. These errors are induced by OPO length noise, temperature fluctuations of the nonlinear crystal, and alignment fluctuations [48].

Levels of loss and phase noise in a squeezing measurement, either in a gravitational wave interferometer or on a balanced homodyne detector, can be characterized by making a series of measurements with different amounts of pump power in the OPO, as shown in Figure 6, and included in [44,48]. As the pump power is increased, the generated states are increasingly squeezed. The loss and phase noise are determined by mapping the dependence between the generated vs. observed noise levels in the squeezing and anti-squeezing quadratures.

Since the maximum level of squeezing is limited by both the losses and phase noise, measurements of the level of noise in the anti-squeezed quadrature are used to distinguish between the two effects. As the pump power and parametric gain increases, the level of anti-squeezing is increased, limited by losses with minimal impact from phase noise. Phase noise causes the squeezing level to decrease at high parametric gains by mixing in the increased noise from the anti-squeezed quadrature, so measurements of the squeezing level at high nonlinear gains provide information about the level of phase noise, as shown by the dashed curves in Figure 6. Because both loss and phase noise can be dependent on the observation frequency in a complex interferometer (see Section 5.5), these measurements may need to be analyzed at multiple frequencies, as in [54].

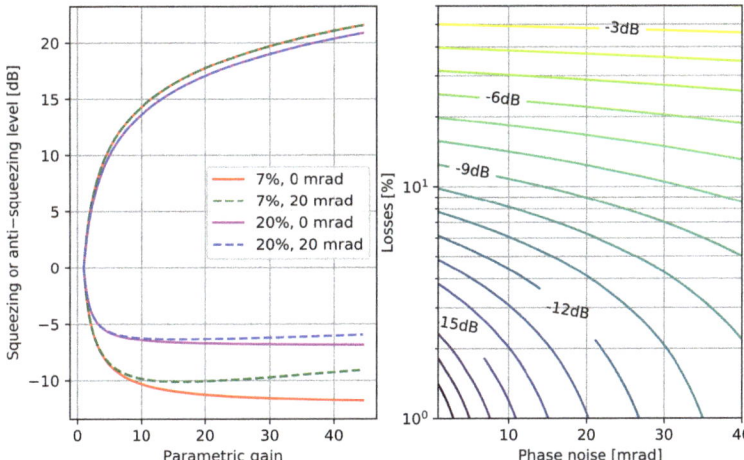

Figure 6. (**Left**) Levels of loss and phase noise in a squeezing measurement can be characterized by measuring the level of squeezing as the parametric gain is varied by changing the OPO pump power. Expressions used to make this plot are explained in [55,56]. The 20% and 7% loss levels are expected requirements for reaching 6 dB and 10 dB of observed squeezing in current and future interferometers. (**Right**) Observable squeezing level with parametric gain optimized for high squeezing [48,52]. This figure shows that to improve from 3 dB to 6 dB of squeezing requires mostly loss reduction, but to reach the 10 dB level of squeezing will also require low phase noise.

For any squeezing measurement there is a nonlinear gain setting that maximizes the level of squeezing given the level of RMS phase noise, and the amount of pump power can be adjusted to adjust the nonlinear gain. This maximum level of measured squeezing is plotted as a function of loss and phase noise in the right panel of Figure 6. While Figure 6 shows the maximum available shot noise reduction, a gravitational wave interferometer which is limited by quantum radiation pressure noise may need to use less than the maximum available to optimize sensitivity, as in [9].

5.2. Backscatter, Technical Noise Introduced by Squeezer

The extreme sensitivity of gravitational wave detectors means that care must be taken to ensure that the squeezer does not introduce noise that will mask gravitational wave signals. Light scattered out of the interferometer towards the squeezer adds coherent light that the squeezer or filter cavity can modulate and then return to the interferometer with the squeezed states, adding a potential noise source via spurious interference paths. This noise can arise both from path length fluctuations which modulate this coherent field in the phase quadrature as well as from noise added to the field within the OPO itself.

A proof of principle squeezing experiment in the LIGO Hanford detector studied noise introduced to the detector by scatter in the phase quadrature, which must be small compared to shot noise [60]. Scatter into the amplitude quadrature also introduces noise by driving differential radiation pressure within the interferometer.

The noise added by these spurious interference paths can be reduced by reducing the motion of the squeezer components and any intermediate path length fluctuations, by moving them into the vacuum system [50,52] and by suspending them [51]. Reducing the amplitude of scattered light can also reduce backscatter noise. Faraday isolators are a key means to reduce the amplitude of backscatter light, but they introduce loss that degrades the squeezing level.

A low loss Faraday isolator is needed to inject squeezing into the interferometer, and typically provides at least 30 dB of isolation between the interferometer and the squeezer components [57–59]. In the third observing run the LIGO, GEO, and Virgo interferometers, respectively, add one, two and three low loss Faraday isolators to further attenuate light reaching the OPO from the interferometer [9,10,29]. Linear OPO cavities reflect all of the scattered light incident on them back towards the interferometer, whereas traveling wave cavities, such as bow-tie cavities, provide nearly 50 dB of backscatter isolation limited by imperfections of the nonlinear crystal and mirrors used [47]. The use of high quality optics in the squeezer can prevent introducing additional sources of scattered light [61]. GEO has reported observing backscatter from the squeezer that is amplified or de-amplified by the nonlinear gain of the OPO [29]. This backscatter noise depends on the nonlinear gain of the OPO, scaling similarly to phase noise and limiting the maximum squeezing level.

5.3. Controls

One of the major challenges for building a squeezer suitable for use in gravitational wave detectors has been the control of the squeezing angle. Introducing a field with a coherent amplitude into the OPO creates several noise couplings that mask any squeezing in the audio frequency band (10 Hz–10 kHz) at which ground based gravitational wave detectors operate [37]. This presents a challenge for control of the squeezer, including the OPO cavity length, filter cavity length, and squeezing angle. To control the OPO cavity length, either a frequency shifted field in the orthogonal polarization [40] or the second harmonic field have been used [34]. In both cases, care has to be taken that the resonance of the field used for sensing is the same as the squeezed field.

Two techniques have been developed to control the squeezing angle without introducing a coherent amplitude at audio frequencies: coherent control [62] and noise locking [63]. The noise lock relies on a dither of the squeezing angle, and demodulation of a measurement of the noise power. This technique ensures that the squeezing angle is locked to a point which minimizes noise in the measurement, however it introduces phase noise which will limit the level of squeezing measured. While the coherent control technique is preferable, the experience at GEO600 has shown that a noise lock in addition to the coherent control can help improve the stability of the squeezing level [13,29].

5.4. Filter Cavity

A filter cavity is required to prepare the correct frequency dependent squeezing if an interferometer's sensitivity is limited by radiation pressure noise, which the LIGO and Virgo detectors currently are [53]. The filter cavity is detuned, meaning that the resonance of the filter cavity is shifted away from the interferometer carrier frequency by a few 10 s of Hz. In reflecting off the detuned filter cavity, upper and lower optical sidebands experience different phase shifts, which rotates the squeezing ellipse [24]. The cavity linewidth must be <100 Hz to rotate the squeezing ellipse at the correct frequency, and can be adjusted for significant changes in interferometer circulating power by changing the filter cavity input coupler [64].

The earliest experiments in frequency dependent squeezing was a proof of the physical effect [25] followed by a demonstration in the audio band [26] using off-carrier control. Frequency dependent squeezing has been observed and characterized recently at the audio frequencies needed for gravitational wave detectors in a 300 m as well as a 16 m linear cavity [27,28]. Work is currently underway to install a 285 m long filter cavity at Virgo [65–67] and a 300 m long filter cavity at both LIGO observatories [68], KAGRA has similar plans for a future upgrade.

Adding a filter cavity to the squeezing path introduces frequency dependent losses from the resonantly-enhanced internal cavity loss and any beam mode mismatch (cf. Section 5.5). The losses reduce the level of squeezing at low frequencies [69]. The loss per length of a filter cavity is the figure to be minimized to preserve low frequency squeezing [70]; longer cavities have been shown to achieve lower loss per unit length [71,72]. Optical losses in the filter cavity not only mix squeezing with the vacuum, they also "dephase" the squeezed state by de-correlating the upper and lower frequency components of the optical quantum state [54]. This creates a noise term that scales with the nonlinear gain.

The filter cavity rotates the squeezing angle only at observation frequencies inside its linewidth, and the rotation angle is determined by the offset ("detuning") between the interferometer carrier frequency and the cavity resonance frequency. Length variations of the filter cavity shift that detuning, creating phase noise that only degrades squeezing in the mid or low frequency audio band [73]. The magnitude of the phase noise depends on the total RMS length noise, establishing requirements on the total environmental noise and the control system to suppress it.

Adding a linear filter cavity also adds an additional backscatter path and can require more Faraday isolators than just the squeezer OPO, especially compared to traveling-wave OPO cavities. Compared to the squeezer, filter cavities have a very high finesse and thus very strict length noise requirements to prevent backscatter noise [68]. The recent laboratory demonstrations of audio-band frequency dependent squeezing [27,28] observe this backscatter noise from the minuscule diffuse scatter from the local oscillator of their balanced homodyne readout. The backscatter power in gravitational-wave interferometers is expected to be substantially higher and drives many integration requirements unique to their implementation into observatories, such as multiple-stage suspensions, active seismic isolation, and new controls techniques [28,74].

5.5. Mode Matching and Frequency Dependence of Interferometer Response

In order to reduce the quantum noise of the interferometer, the transverse spatial field profile ("mode") of the Gaussian beam emitted from the squeezed state source needs to match the optical mode of the interferometer's resonating cavities. When there is a mode mismatch between the spatial profile of the squeezed beam and the interferometer, then the squeezed states do not have a full overlap with the interferometer states. The beam entering the interferometer mode in this case can be decomposed into a mixture of the squeezed field and unsqueezed vacuum in higher order transverse modes.

The mixed states formed from squeezed and vacuum states can behave like an optical loss (degrading squeezing) when observed, but unlike most losses, mode mismatch is a coherent process that depends on how optical cavities and optical telescopes transform the spatial modes. Additionally, optical cavity transmissions and reflections add frequency dependence to these transformations. In total, the optical loss and phase shifts of the squeezing ellipse can pick several frequency dependent changes which are relatively unique to their implementation in advanced gravitational wave interferometers. These effects were first observed, described, and analyzed in both LIGO Hanford and Livingston [54] during observing run three.

There are two key takeaways in the observation of frequency dependent losses. The first is that they indicate that squeezing in interferometers is uniquely more challenging to fully characterize than in broadband laboratory experiments. For interferometers which have both arm and signal extraction cavities, such as LIGO, losses typically increase at higher frequencies where the interferometer spectrum is predominantly quantum noise[2]. The increase in losses can bias estimates of the frequency-independent incoherent losses inferred using only high frequency measurements. More painstaking measurements at lower frequencies, where classical noises must be accounted and removed, are required to characterize the squeezing performance in the audio frequencies of the signal band. The second takeaway is that squeezing losses have a complicated relationship to independent measurements of mode matching between cavities: the impact of mode mismatch on squeezing cannot be simply estimated based on mode matching efficiencies. More fully understanding these relationships will be necessary to produce future specifications of telescope and optical design tolerances and to efficiently commission squeezing systems for interferometers.

Along with mode matching, the optomechanics of radiation pressure also cause frequency dependence in the interferometer response to squeezing. To increase the astrophysical range, this is addressed to first order using the frequency dependent squeezing from a filter cavity, as described above. To fully utilize and optimize filter cavities, we anticipate that yet more complex interactions between the squeezing systems, interferometer cavities, and their optomechanics will be observed. Gravitational wave interferometers are now contributing to squeezing research as well as benefiting from it.

6. Conclusions and Future Plans

6.1. Plans for Upgrading Existing Detectors

In 2023 LIGO, Virgo, and KAGRA plan to start the fourth observing run, with frequency-dependent squeezing implemented at the LIGO and Virgo observatories. The filter cavity is a major squeezer hardware upgrade. With broadband frequency-dependent squeezing, and active wavefront control elements which will reduce loss due to mode mismatch between the cavities of the squeezer and interferometer [75,76], the squeezing improvements to detector sensitivity are expected to be greater than in the third observing run.

Plans beyond the next observing run for the LIGO detectors include the remaining elements of the "A+" upgrade [77]. One of the upgrades for A+ is the detection scheme, which will change from the Michelson fringe to balanced homodyne detection, which will allow the quadrature measured at the detection port to be controlled.

6.2. Plans for Next Generation Detectors

Future ground-based gravitational-wave detectors all include the injection of frequency-dependent squeezed light in their design studies. Cosmic Explorer is a proposed future detector which uses a dual-recycled Fabry–Perot Michelson topology (like LIGO), with proposed arm lengths of 20 and 40 km. The Cosmic Explorer design includes a squeezed light source and 4 km long filter cavity to generate 10 dB of broadband squeezing improvement to the sensitivity [78]. To achieve this level of squeezing improvement, the design targets a total optical loss of $\lesssim 8\%$ and phase noise of $\lesssim 10$ mrad.

The Einstein telescope is another proposed future detector, using a triangular topology and collocated pairs of Michelson interferometers targeting different gravitational-wave frequencies. The Einstein Telescope (ET) also incorporates 10 dB of broadband frequency-dependent squeezing into its design [79]. For the high frequency detector and squeezed light source at 1064 nm and a 300 m filter cavity is proposed. The low frequency detector will operate in a detuned configuration, which means that two filter cavities will be required for frequency dependent squeezing [80] The low frequency ET design also calls for a main laser wavelength of 1550 nm, which means that the squeezed light source will also need to operate at 1550 nm. The ET design is also investigating more elaborate quantum non-demolition schemes to further reduce the quantum noise.

The neutron star extreme matter observatory (NEMO) is another proposed future gravitational-wave detector targeting the high frequency audio band (2–4 kHz) [81]. In this detection band radiation pressure noise no longer limits the detector, and shot noise is the only relevant quantum noise term meaning that NEMO has no need for a filter cavity. The NEMO design thus injects frequency-independent squeezing, with design improvement at 7 dB.

6.3. Summary and Conclusions

Squeezing has become a tool for gravitational wave observatories, with demonstrated reliable performance at LIGO, Virgo and GEO600. The implementation of squeezing at these observatories has been accomplished without introducing noise that limits the sensitivity to gravitational waves, through successful mitigation of scattered light. While these implementations of squeezing have demonstrated improvements to the astrophysical reach of ground based interferometers, realizing the full potential of squeezing for this type of observatory remains a significant challenge.

Both Virgo and LIGO are currently building filter cavities to allow for improvements in quantum noise at frequencies limited by quantum radiation pressure noise as well as shot noise. These cavities need very low losses and creative and precise control schemes to achieve the desired sensitivity for observing runs planned in 2023.

The achievement of 6 dB of squeezing at GEO600 required years of careful effort in loss reduction and controls. LIGO and Virgo are both aiming to increase the level of squeezing in the next observing run. For LIGO, active mode matching will help reach the low levels of effective loss needed to reach 6 dB of squeezing, while challenging, increasing the level of squeezing to 6 dB in combination with filter cavities will provide significant improvements in the rate of gravitational wave observations.

Looking to the future, gravitational-wave observatories will aim to obtain the maximum possible benefit from squeezing, with plans for 10 dB of squeezing. The considerations covered in this review, including control of squeezing and filter cavities, optical losses, phase noise, mode matching and scattered light are going to continue to be crucial in squeezer designs. As ground based gravitational wave astronomy continues to grow as a field, the drive towards better sensitivity will require painstaking attention to each of the factors that can limit squeezing.

Funding: LIGO was constructed by the California Institute of Technology and Massachusetts Institute of Technology with funding from the National Science Foundation, and operates under Cooperative Agreement Grant No. PHY- 1764464. Advanced LIGO was built under Grant No. PHY- 0823459. A+ LIGO is being constructed under Grant PHY-1834382.

Institutional Review Board Statement: Not applicable.

Informed Consent Statement: Not applicable.

Data Availability Statement: Not applicable.

Conflicts of Interest: The authors declare no conflict of interest.

Notes

[1] Note, our definition of phase and amplitude quadrature operators is specifically by choosing a basis of the quadrature operators suitable to describe their respective first-order modulations of a reference classical field. This in contrast to conceptual operators defined to uniquely represent phase and amplitude measurements at all orders (e.g., the Susskind–Glogower or Pegg–Barnett phase operators).

[2] In interferometers with either arm *or* signal extraction cavities, the effect is reversed.

References

1. Stoler, D. Equivalence Classes of Minimum Uncertainty Packets. *Phys. Rev. D* **1970**, *1*, 3217–3219. [CrossRef]
2. Lu, E.Y.C. New Coherent States of the Electromagnetic Field. *Lett. Nuovo C* **1971**, *2*, 1241–1244. [CrossRef]
3. Yuen, H.P. Two-Photon Coherent States of the Radiation Field. *Phys. Rev. A* **1976**, *13*, 2226–2243. [CrossRef]
4. Walls, D.F. Squeezed States of Light. *Nature* **1983**, *306*, 141–146. [CrossRef]
5. Collett, M.J.; Gardiner, C.W. Squeezing of Intracavity and Traveling-Wave Light Fields Produced in Parametric Amplification. *Phys. Rev. A* **1984**, *30*, 1386–1391. [CrossRef]
6. Junker, J.; Wilken, D.; Huntington, E.; Heurs, M. High-precision cavity spectroscopy using high-frequency squeezed light. *Opt. Express* **2021**, *29*, 6053–6068. [CrossRef]
7. Gehring, T.; Haendchen, V.; Duhme, J.; Furrer, F.; Franz, T.; Pacher, C.; Werner, R.F.W.; Schnabel, R. Implementation of continuous-variable quantum key distribution with composable and one-sided-device-independent security against coherent attacks. *Nat. Commun.* **2015**, *6*, 8795. [CrossRef]
8. Lawrie, B.J.; Lett, P.D.; Marino, A.M.; Pooser, R.C. Quantum Sensing with Squeezed Light. *ACS Photonics* **2019**, *6*, 1307–1318. [CrossRef]
9. Tse, M.; Yu, H.; Kijbunchoo, N.; Fernandez-Galiana, A.; Dupej, P.; Barsotti, L.; Blair, C.D.; Brown, D.D.; Dwyer, S.E.; Effler, A.; et al. Quantum-Enhanced Advanced LIGO Detectors in the Era of Gravitational-Wave Astronomy. *Phys. Rev. Lett.* **2019**, *123*, 231107. [CrossRef]

10. Acernese, F.; Agathos, M.; Aiello, L.; Allocca, A.; Amato, A.; Ansoldi, S.; Antier, S.; Arène, M.; Arnaud, N.; Ascenzi, S.; et al. Increasing the Astrophysical Reach of the Advanced Virgo Detector via the Application of Squeezed Vacuum States of Light. *Phys. Rev. Lett.* **2019**, *123*, 231108. [CrossRef]
11. LIGO Scientific Collaboration. A gravitational wave observatory operating beyond the quantum shot-noise limit. *Nat. Phys.* **2011**, *7*, 962–965. [CrossRef]
12. LIGO Scientific Collaboration. Enhanced sensitivity of the LIGO gravitational wave detector by using squeezed states of light. *Nat. Photon* **2013**, *7*, 613–619. [CrossRef]
13. Grote, H.; Danzmann, K.; Dooley, K.L.; Schnabel, R.; Slutsky, J.; Vahlbruch, H. First Long-Term Application of Squeezed States of Light in a Gravitational-Wave Observatory. *Phys. Rev. Lett.* **2013**, *110*, 181101. [CrossRef] [PubMed]
14. Buikema, A.; Cahillane, C.; Mansell, G.L.; Blair, C.D.; Abbott, R.; Adams, C.; Adhikari, R.X.; Ananyeva, A.; Appert, S.; Arai, K.; et al. Sensitivity and Performance of the Advanced LIGO Detectors in the Third Observing Run. *Phys. Rev. D* **2020**, *102*, 062003. [CrossRef]
15. LIGO Scientific Collaboration; Virgo Collaboration; KAGRA Collaboration; Abbott, R.; Abbott, T.D.; Acernese, F.; Ackley, K.; Adams, C.; Adhikari, N.; Adhikari, R.X.; et al. GWTC-3: Compact Binary Coalescences Observed by LIGO and Virgo During the Second Part of the Third Observing Run. *arXiv* **2021**. arXiv:2111.03606.
16. Braginsky, V.B.; Khalili, F.Y. Quantum nondemolition measurements: The route from toys to tools. *Rev. Mod. Phys.* **1996**, *68*, 1–11. [CrossRef]
17. Pygwinc: Python Gravitational Wave Interferometer Noise Calculator. Available online: https://git.ligo.org/gwinc (accessed on 15 September 2021).
18. Walls, D.F.; Milburn, G.J. *Quantum Optics*; Springer: New York, NY, USA, 1995;
19. Gerry, C.; Knight, P. *Introductory Quantum Optics*; Cambridge University Press: Cambridge, UK, 2004. [CrossRef]
20. Caves, C.M. Quantum-mechanical noise in an interferometer. *Phys. Rev. D* **1981**, *23*, 1693–1708. [CrossRef]
21. Caves, C.M.; Schumaker, B.L. New formalism for two-photon quantum optics. I. Quadrature phases and squeezed states. *Phys. Rev. A* **1985**, *31*, 3068–3092. [CrossRef]
22. Schumaker, B.L.; Caves, C.M. New formalism for two-photon quantum optics. II. Mathematical foundation and compact notation. *Phys. Rev. A* **1985**, *31*, 3093–3111. [CrossRef]
23. Unruh, W.G. Quantum Noise in the Interferometer Detector. In *Quantum Optics, Experimental Gravity, and Measurement Theory*; Meystre, P., Scully, M.O., Eds.; NATO Advanced Science Institutes Series; Springer: Boston, MA, USA, 1983; pp. 647–660. [CrossRef]
24. Kimble, H.J.; Levin, Y.; Matsko, A.B.; Thorne, K.S.; Vyatchanin, S.P. Conversion of conventional gravitational-wave interferometers into quantum nondemolition interferometers by modifying their input and/or output optics. *Phys. Rev. D* **2001**, *65*, 022002. [CrossRef]
25. Chelkowski, S.; Vahlbruch, H.; Hage, B.; Franzen, A.; Lastzka, N.; Danzmann, K.; Schnabel, R. Experimental Characterization of Frequency-Dependent Squeezed Light. *Phys. Rev. A* **2005**, *71*, 013806. [CrossRef]
26. Oelker, E.; Isogai, T.; Miller, J.; Tse, M.; Barsotti, L.; Mavalvala, N.; Evans, M. Audio-Band Frequency-Dependent Squeezing for Gravitational-Wave Detectors. *Phys. Rev. Lett.* **2016**, *116*, 041102. [CrossRef]
27. Zhao, Y.; Aritomi, N.; Capocasa, E.; Leonardi, M.; Eisenmann, M.; Guo, Y.; Polini, E.; Tomura, A.; Arai, K.; Aso, Y.; et al. Frequency-Dependent Squeezed Vacuum Source for Broadband Quantum Noise Reduction in Advanced Gravitational-Wave Detectors. *Phys. Rev. Lett.* **2020**, *124*, 171101. [CrossRef] [PubMed]
28. McCuller, L.; Whittle, C.; Ganapathy, D.; Komori, K.; Tse, M.; Fernandez-Galiana, A.; Barsotti, L.; Fritschel, P.; MacInnis, M.; Matichard, F.; et al. Frequency-Dependent Squeezing for Advanced LIGO. *Phys. Rev. Lett.* **2020**, *124*, 171102. [CrossRef] [PubMed]
29. Lough, J.; Schreiber, E.; Bergamin, F.; Grote, H.; Mehmet, M.; Vahlbruch, H.; Affeldt, C.; Brinkmann, M.; Bisht, A.; Kringel, V.; et al. First Demonstration of 6 dB Quantum Noise Reduction in a Kilometer Scale Gravitational Wave Observatory. *Phys. Rev. Lett.* **2021**, *126*, 041102. [CrossRef] [PubMed]
30. Slusher, R.E.; Hollberg, L.W.; Yurke, B.; Mertz, J.C.; Valley, J.F. Observation of Squeezed States Generated by Four-Wave Mixing in an Optical Cavity. *Phys. Rev. Lett.* **1985**, *55*, 2409–2412. [CrossRef]
31. Boyd, R.W. *Nonlinear Optics*; Elsevier: Amsterdam, The Netherlands, 2008.
32. Schnabel, R.; Mavalvala, N.; McClelland, D.E.; Lam, P.K. Quantum Metrology for Gravitational Wave Astronomy. *Nat. Commun.* **2010**, *1*, 121. [CrossRef]
33. Schnabel, R. Squeezed States of Light and Their Applications in Laser Interferometers. *Phys. Rep.* **2017**, *684*, 1–51. [CrossRef]
34. Stefszky, M.; Mow-Lowry, C.M.; McKenzie, K.; Chua, S.; Buchler, B.C.; Symul, T.; McClelland, D.E.; Lam, P.K. An Investigation of Doubly-Resonant Optical Parametric Oscillators and Nonlinear Crystals for Squeezing. *J. Phys. B At. Mol. Opt. Phys.* **2010**, *44*, 015502. [CrossRef]
35. Fejer, M.M.; Magel, G.A.; Jundt, D.H.; Byer, R.L. Quasi-Phase-Matched Second Harmonic Generation: Tuning and Tolerances. *IEEE J. Quantum Electron.* **1992**, *28*, 2631–2654. [CrossRef]
36. Boyd, G.D.; Kleinman, D.A. Parametric Interaction of Focused Gaussian Light Beams. *J. Appl. Phys.* **1968**, *39*, 3597–3639. [CrossRef]

37. McKenzie, K.; Grosse, N.; Bowen, W.P.; Whitcomb, S.E.; Gray, M.B.; McClelland, D.E.; Lam, P.K. Squeezing in the Audio Gravitational-Wave Detection Band. *Phys. Rev. Lett.* **2004**, *93*, 161105. [CrossRef] [PubMed]
38. Vahlbruch, H.; Mehmet, M.; Chelkowski, S.; Hage, B.; Franzen, A.; Lastzka, N.; Goßler, S.; Danzmann, K.; Schnabel, R. Observation of Squeezed Light with 10-dB Quantum-Noise Reduction. *Phys. Rev. Lett.* **2008**, *100*, 033602. [CrossRef]
39. Barsotti, L.; Harms, J.; Schnabel, R. Squeezed vacuum states of light for gravitational wave detectors. *Rep. Prog. Phys.* **2018**, *82*, 016905. [CrossRef]
40. Vahlbruch, H.; Khalaidovski, A.; Lastzka, N.; Gräf, C.; Danzmann, K.; Schnabel, R. The GEO 600 squeezed light source. *Class. Quantum Gravity* **2010**, *27*, 084027. [CrossRef]
41. Khalaidovski, A.; Vahlbruch, H.; Lastzka, N.; Graf, C.; Danzmann, K.; Grote, H.; Schnabel, R. Long-term stable squeezed vacuum state of light for gravitational detectors. *Class. Quantum Gravity* **2012**, *29*, 075001. [CrossRef]
42. Dooley, K.L.; Schreiber, E.; Vahlbruch, H.; Affeldt, C.; Leong, J.R.; Wittel, H.; Grote, H. Phase control of squeezed vacuum states of light in gravitational wave detectors. *Opt. Express* **2015**, *23*, 8235–8245. [CrossRef]
43. Schreiber, E.; Dooley, K.L.; Vahlbruch, H.; Affeldt, C.; Bisht, A.; Leong, J.R.; Lough, J.; Prijatelj, M.; Slutsky, J.; Was, M.; et al. Alignment sensing and control for squeezed vacuum states of light. *Opt. Express* **2016**, *24*, 146–152. [CrossRef]
44. Khalaidovski, A.; Vahlbruch, H.; Lastzka, N.; Gräf, C.; Lück, H.; Danzmann, K.; Grote, H.; Schnabel, R. Status of the GEO 600 squeezed-light laser. *J. Phys. Conf. Ser.* **2012**, *363*, 012013. [CrossRef]
45. Mehmet, M.; Vahlbruch, H. The Squeezed Light Source for the Advanced Virgo Detector in the Observation Run O3. *Galaxies* **2020**, *8*, 79. [CrossRef]
46. Nguyen, C.; Bawaj, M.; Sequino, V.; Barsuglia, M.; Bazzan, M.; Calloni, E.; Ciani, G.; Conti, L.; D'Angelo, B.; De Rosa, R.; et al. Automated source of squeezed vacuum states driven by finite state machine based software. *Rev. Sci. Instrum.* **2021**, *92*, 054504. [CrossRef] [PubMed]
47. Chua, S.; Stefszky, M.; Mow-Lowry, C.; Buchler, B.; Dwyer, S.; Shaddock, D.; Lam, P.K.; McClelland, D. Backscatter tolerant squeezed light source for advanced gravitational-wave detectors. *Opt. Lett.* **2011**, *36*, 4680–4682. [CrossRef] [PubMed]
48. Dwyer, S.; Barsotti, L.; Chua, S.S.Y.; Evans, M.; Factourovich, M.; Gustafson, D.; Isogai, T.; Kawabe, K.; Khalaidovski, A.; Lam, P.K.; et al. Squeezed quadrature fluctuations in a gravitational wave detector using squeezed light. *Opt. Express* **2013**, *21*, 19047–19060. [CrossRef] [PubMed]
49. Oelker, E.; Mansell, G.; Tse, M.; Miller, J.; Matichard, F.; Barsotti, L.; Fritschel, P.; McClelland, D.E.; Evans, M.; Mavalvala, N. Ultra-low phase noise squeezed vacuum source for gravitational wave detectors. *Optica* **2016**, *3*, 682–685. [CrossRef]
50. Wade, A.R.; Mansell, G.L.; Chua, S.S.; Ward, R.L.; Slagmolen, B.J.; Shaddock, D.A.; McClelland, D.E. A squeezed light source operated under high vacuum. *Sci. Rep.* **2015**, *5*, 18052. [CrossRef]
51. Fernández-Galiana, Á.; McCuller, L.; Kissel, J.; Barsotti, L.; Miller, J.; Tse, M.; Evans, M.; Aston, S.M.; Abbott, R.; Shaffer, T.J.; et al. Advanced LIGO squeezer platform for backscattered light and optical loss reduction. *Class. Quantum Gravity* **2020**, *37*, 215015. [CrossRef]
52. Oelker, E.; Barsotti, L.; Dwyer, S.; Sigg, D.; Mavalvala, N. Squeezed light for advanced gravitational wave detectors and beyond. *Opt. Express* **2014**, *22*, 21106–21121. [CrossRef]
53. Yu, H.; McCuller, L.; Tse, M.; Kijbunchoo, N.; Barsotti, L.; Mavalvala, N. Quantum correlations between light and the kilogram-mass mirrors of LIGO. *Nature* **2020**, *583*, 43–47. [CrossRef]
54. McCuller, L.; Dwyer, S.E.; Green, A.C.; Yu, H.; Kuns, K.; Barsotti, L.; Blair, C.D.; Brown, D.D.; Effler, A.; Evans, M.; et al. LIGO's quantum response to squeezed states. *Phys. Rev. D* **2021**, *104*, 062006. [CrossRef]
55. Aoki, T.; Takahashi, G.; Furasawa, A. Squeezing at 946 nm with periodically poled KTiOPO$_4$. *Opt. Express* **2006**, *14*, 6930–6935. [CrossRef]
56. Takeno, Y.; Yukawa, M.; Yonezawa, H.; Furusawa, A. Observation of −9 dB quadrature squeezing with improvement of phasestability in homodyne measurement. *Opt. Express* **2007**, *15*, 4321–4327. [CrossRef] [PubMed]
57. Goetz, R.; Fulda, P.; Martin, R.; Tanner, D. Low Loss Faraday Isolators for Squeezed Vacuum Injection in Advanced LIGO. In *APS April Meeting Abstracts*; APS: College Park, MD, USA, 2016; p. H14.007.
58. Martin, R.; Notte, J.; Reyes, J.; Fulda, P.; Goetz, R.; Tanner, D.B. The A+ Low-Loss Faraday Isolators. LIGO DCC G2101056, LIGO DCC, 2021. Available online: https://dcc.ligo.org/DocDB/0176/G2101056/001/G2101056_APlusLLFI_GWADW2021.pdf.(accessed on 15 December 2021).
59. Genin, E.; Mantovani, M.; Pillant, G.; Rossi, C.D.; Pinard, L.; Michel, C.; Gosselin, M.; Casanueva, J. Vacuum-compatible low-loss Faraday isolator for efficient squeezed-light injection in laser-interferometer-based gravitational-wave detectors. *Appl. Opt.* **2018**, *57*, 9705–9713. [CrossRef] [PubMed]
60. Chua, S.S.Y.; Dwyer, S.; Barsotti, L.; Sigg, D.; Schofield, R.M.S.; Frolov, V.V.; Kawabe, K.; Evans, M.; Meadors, G.D.; Factourovich, M.; et al. Impact of backscattered light in a squeezing-enhanced interferometric gravitational-wave detector. *Class. Quantum Gravity* **2014**, *31*, 035017. [CrossRef]
61. Vahlbruch, H.; Chelkowski, S.; Danzmann, K.; Schnabel, R. Quantum Engineering of Squeezed States for Quantum Communication and Metrology. *New J. Phys.* **2007**, *9*, 371–371. [CrossRef]
62. Chelkowski, S.; Vahlbruch, H.; Danzmann, K.; Schnabel, R. Coherent control of broadband vacuum squeezing. *Phys. Rev. A* **2007**, *75*, 043814. [CrossRef]

63. McKenzie, K.; Mikhailov, E.E.; Goda, K.; Lam, P.K.; Grosse, N.; Gray, M.B.; Mavalvala, N.; McClelland, D.E. Quantum noise locking. *J. Opt. B Quantum Semiclass. Opt.* **2005**, *7*, S421. [CrossRef]
64. Whittle, C.; Komori, K.; Ganapathy, D.; McCuller, L.; Barsotti, L.; Mavalvala, N.; Evans, M. Optimal Detuning for Quantum Filter Cavities. *Phys. Rev. D* **2020**, *102*, 102002. [CrossRef]
65. Abbott, B.P.; Abbott, R.; Abbott, T.D.; Abraham, S.; Acernese, F.; Ackley, K.; Adams, C.; Adya, V.B.; Affeldt, C.; Agathos, M.; et al. Prospects for Observing and Localizing Gravitational-Wave Transients with Advanced LIGO, Advanced Virgo and KAGRA. *Living Rev. Relativ.* **2020**, *23*, 3. [CrossRef]
66. Virgo Collaboration. Advanced Virgo Plus Phase I—Design Report. Technical Report VIR-0596A-19, Virgo TDS. 2019. Available online: https://tds.virgo-gw.eu/?content=3&r=15777. (accessed on 15 December 2021).
67. Sequino, V. Quantum Noise Reduction in Advanced Virgo. *Phys. Scr.* **2021**, *96*, 104014. [CrossRef]
68. McCuller, L.; Barsotti, L. Design Requirements Document of the A+ Filter Cavity and Relay Optics for Squeezing Injection. Technical Report T1800447-v7, LIGO DCC. 2018. Available online: https://dcc.ligo.org/public/0156/T1800447/007/FC_DRD_T1800447-v7.pdf (accessed on 15 November 2021).
69. Corbitt, T.; Mavalvala, N.; Whitcomb, S. Optical cavities as amplitude filters for squeezed fields. *Phys. Rev. D* **2004**, *70*, 022002. [CrossRef]
70. Khalili, F.Y. Optimal configurations of filter cavity in future gravitational-wave detectors. *Phys. Rev. D* **2010**, *81*, 122002. [CrossRef]
71. Evans, M.; Barsotti, L.; Kwee, P.; Harms, J.; Miao, H. Realistic filter cavities for advanced gravitational wave detectors. *Phys. Rev. D* **2013**, *88*, 022002. [CrossRef]
72. Isogai, T.; Miller, J.; Kwee, P.; Barsotti, L.; Evans, M. Loss in long-storage-time optical cavities. *Opt. Express* **2013**, *21*, 30114–30125. [CrossRef] [PubMed]
73. Kwee, P.; Miller, J.; Isogai, T.; Barsotti, L.; Evans, M. Decoherence and degradation of squeezed states in quantum filter cavities. *Phys. Rev. D* **2014**, *90*, 062006. [CrossRef]
74. Aritomi, N.; Leonardi, M.; Capocasa, E.; Zhao, Y.; Flaminio, R. Control of a Filter Cavity with Coherent Control Sidebands. *Phys. Rev. D* **2020**, *102*, 042003. [CrossRef]
75. Srivastava, V.; Mansell, G.; Makarem, C.; Noh, M.; Abbott, R.; Ballmer, S.; Billingsley, G.; Brooks, A.; Cao, H.T.; Fritschel, P.; et al. Piezo-deformable Mirrors for Active Mode Matching in Advanced LIGO. *arXiv* **2021**, arXiv:2110.00674.
76. Cao, H.T.; Brooks, A.; Ng, S.W.S.; Ottaway, D.; Perreca, A.; Richardson, J.W.; Chaderjian, A.; Veitch, P.J. High dynamic range thermally actuated bimorph mirror for gravitational wave detectors. *Appl. Opt.* **2020**, *59*, 2784–2790. [CrossRef]
77. LIGO Scientific Collaboration. Instrument Science White Paper. LIGO-T2000407. Available online: dcc.ligo.org/LIGO-T2000407/public (accessed on 3 November 2021).
78. Evans, M.; Adhikari, R.X.; Afle, C.; Ballmer, S.W.; Biscoveanu, S.; Borhanian, S.; Brown, D.A.; Chen, Y.; Eisenstein, R.; Gruson, A.; et al. A Horizon Study for Cosmic Explorer: Science, Observatories, and Community. *arXiv* **2021**, arXiv:2109.09882.
79. Einstein Telescope Steering Committee Einstein Telescope Design Report Update 2020. Available online: https://gwic.ligo.org/3Gsubcomm/docs/ET-0007B-20_ETDesignReportUpdate2020.pdf (accessed on 15 Novemeber 2021).
80. Jones, P.; Zhang, T.; Miao, H.; Freise, A. Implications of the quantum noise target for the Einstein Telescope infrastructure design. *Phys. Rev. D* **2020**, *101*, 082002. [CrossRef]
81. Ackley, K.; Adya, V.B.; Agrawal, P.; Altin, P.; Ashton, G.; Bailes, M.; Baltinas, E.; Barbuio, A.; Beniwal, D.; Blair, C.; et al. Neutron Star Extreme Matter Observatory: A kilohertz-band gravitational-wave detector in the global network. *Publ. Astron. Soc. Aust.* **2020**, *37*, e047. [CrossRef]

Review

Detector Characterization and Mitigation of Noise in Ground-Based Gravitational-Wave Interferometers

Derek Davis [1,*] and Marissa Walker [2]

1. LIGO, California Institute of Technology, Pasadena, CA 91125, USA
2. Department of Physics, Computer Science, and Engineering, Christopher Newport University, Newport News, VA 23606, USA; marissa.walker@cnu.edu
* Correspondence: dedavis@caltech.edu

Abstract: Since the early stages of operation of ground-based gravitational-wave interferometers, careful monitoring of these detectors has been an important component of their successful operation and observations. Characterization of gravitational-wave detectors blends computational and instrumental methods of investigating the detector performance. These efforts focus both on identifying ways to improve detector sensitivity for future observations and understand the non-idealized features in data that has already been recorded. Alongside a focus on the detectors themselves, detector characterization includes careful studies of how astrophysical analyses are affected by different data quality issues. This article presents an overview of the multifaceted aspects of the characterization of interferometric gravitational-wave detectors, including investigations of instrumental performance, characterization of interferometer data quality, and the identification and mitigation of data quality issues that impact analysis of gravitational-wave events. Looking forward, we discuss efforts to adapt current detector characterization methods to meet the changing needs of gravitational-wave astronomy.

Keywords: LIGO; Virgo; KAGRA; gravitational waves; detector characterization; data quality; noise mitigation

1. Introduction

Within the past decade, advances in the design of gravitational-wave interferometers have allowed the Advanced LIGO and Advanced Virgo detectors to reach the required sensitivity to detect gravitational waves from astrophysical sources [1,2]. These observations [3–7] of the cataclysmic mergers of massive compact objects allowed for the discovery of a new population of black holes [8], insights into the nuclear equation of state [9], precision tests of general relativity [10], and the identification of compact objects that are not predicted to form from stellar evolution [11,12].

These historic discoveries in astrophysics have required measurements of gravitational-wave strains of less than 10^{-21} [3]. To achieve these levels of sensitivity, gravitational-wave detectors rely on a wide array of technologies designed to minimize the sensitivity of the detectors to non-astrophysical sources of noise. However, the complexity of the detectors also provides numerous pathways for introducing instrumental noise into the recorded data. Addressing the presence of noise in the instruments is a crucial aspect of gravitational-wave astrophysics, both for the continual improvement of the detectors themselves and for ensuring appropriate treatment of the noise in the data analyses.

This area of research, focusing on diagnosing and mitigating instrumental problems that impact the quality of recorded gravitational-wave strain data, is known as "detector characterization". Detector characterization was a central element of the initial operation of both first [13–15] and second [16] generation detectors and the first detection of gravitational waves [17]. Figure 1 illustrates the central role of characterizing the detector and its data quality to the flow of LIGO data analysis from the instruments to the final output

of gravitational-wave catalogs. As gravitational-wave astronomy grows, detector characterization and noise mitigation continue to play an important role in the maximization of detector sensitivity and analysis precision [15,18,19].

This article reviews the current state of detector characterization and noise mitigation used in gravitational-wave science. Section 2 focuses on the techniques and approaches to characterizing instrumental performance of gravitational-wave interferometers. Section 3 discusses how problems with the data quality are diagnosed and how this information is propagated to gravitational-wave data analyses. Section 4 focuses on the detector characterization steps taken in response to detected gravitational-wave events. Section 5 then provides an overview of current techniques used to mitigate the impact of instrumental noise in the data. Finally, Section 6 remarks on the current state of the field and potential applicability of these methods to future detectors and analyses.

The focus of this work primarily focuses on techniques used in analyses of data from the LIGO Hanford and LIGO Livingston detectors and analyses completed by the LIGO-Virgo-KAGRA (LVK) collaborations, with examples related to the Virgo detector included when relevant. However, the methods described are broadly applicable to other current and future ground-based interferometric detectors, including GEO600 [20], KAGRA [21], and LIGO India [22] and analyses completed by other groups. All gravitational-wave strain data used for visualizations in this work is from the Gravitational-wave Open Science Center (GWOSC) [23].

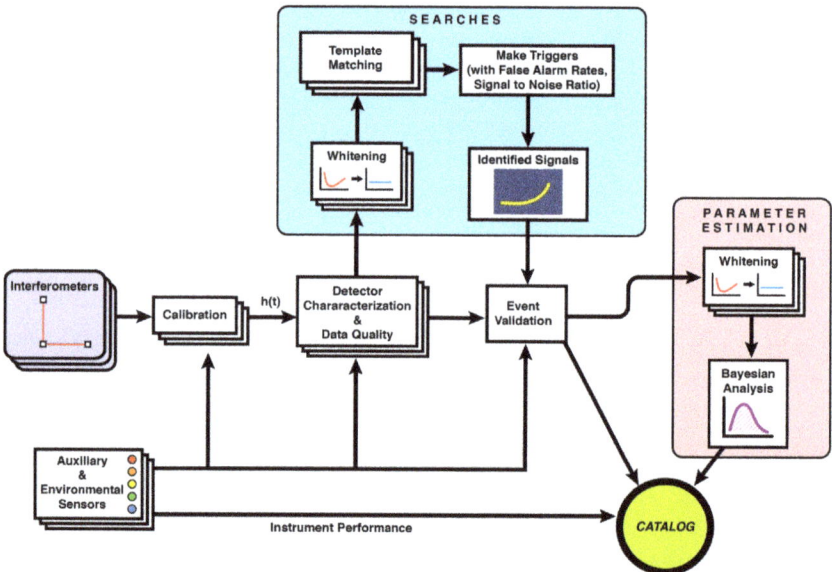

Figure 1. A visualization of the connections between different components of gravitational-wave data analysis. Detector characterization is in the middle, indicating its critical role in gravitational-wave astronomy, as it contributes to many different steps of the process, from improving the detectors to checking candidate gravitational-wave signals for any possible pollution by nose artifacts. Figure reproduced from [24]. © IOP Publishing. Reproduced with permission. All rights reserved.

2. Characterizing Gravitational-Wave Detector Instrumentation

One central goal of detector characterization is finding sources of noise within the instruments and working with on-site staff to mitigate these noise sources to improve the detectors' performance. These investigations may be targeted on improving specific subsystems of the detector or diagnosing particular kinds of noise. This section presents an overview of instrumental investigations for the purposes of making concrete improvements to the detectors, including the detailed analysis of individual detector components and methods for investigating transient and persistent noise in the detectors.

2.1. Subsystem Characterization

Characterization of the instruments for the purpose of improving instrumental performance is carried out at various levels of specificity. To be able to truly characterize the detector as a whole, first individual components have to be well understood, and then the connections between individual subsystems and how they connect to the final output of the detector. Components of each detector are classified into multiple "subsystems" that each focus on a specific element of the overall detector design. The instrumentalists, commissioners, and engineers working on site are faced with the monumental endeavor of finely tuning each subsystem and getting the many different components of the detector to work together in the precise harmony needed to detect gravitational waves. Detector characterization of the individual components of the detector is an integral part of the process, even before the full detector has been installed. Analyzing the data of specific subsystems or combinations of subsystems prior to observing runs is necessary for diagnosing problems and improving the instruments.

For each subsystem, it is important to know its key design features, the important data channels used to monitor its performance, and to develop methods of distinguishing abnormal and nominal behavior. Detailed studies of each subsystem have continued from the earliest engineering runs that were used to characterize the detector and continue to be an important part of the process of identifying issues in the detector during observation runs to detect gravitational waves. This includes having a deep understanding of the physical environment surrounding each instrument [25], the seismic isolation system [26], the suspension systems [27,28], the pre-stabilized laser, individual optical cavities, calibration, thermal compensation system, and the many feedback and control loops required to operate the detectors. At such a detailed level of characterizing the detector, there can be impacts not only on diagnosing specific issues at an early stage of commissioning the detectors, but also on the design of future detectors. For example, the highly sophisticated seismic isolation systems of Advanced LIGO were motivated by an understanding of the significant impact of seismic noise in initial LIGO [29].

2.2. Diagnosing and Mitigating Transient Noise

Characterization of transient noise in the detectors takes into account the overall detector output as well as the behavior of individual subsystems. Several existing papers describe examples of noise investigations in detail [16,18,30–32]. Given the complexity of the detectors and the wide variety of potential noise sources, there is no single way to diagnose all types of instrumental noise. However, these studies tend to follow a similar process, which we describe here. A general overview of this process is shown in Figure 2. These investigations can be focused on tests completed at the detector site or remotely using recorded data and include identification, characterization, and mitigation of instrumental problems. There is generally active collaboration between those at the sites investigating the detectors and those analyzing the detector data, such as diagnostic tests completed by those on site being evaluated by people off-site with additional data analysis tools.

The initial identification of a problem typically begins with analysis of the output of the detector and gathering basic observations about the patterns in the noise, which often gives some initial clues when combined with knowledge of the detector and its environment. This initial analysis is frequently done with the aid of one or more of the many software tools that are run automatically on a daily basis, whose results are displayed on summary web pages internal to LIGO and Virgo and inspected regularly [33,34]. Several of the summary pages show key figures of merit that describe the overall sensitivity and data quality of the strain channel, while numerous additional pages include detailed figures that can be used to trace noise through various subsystems.

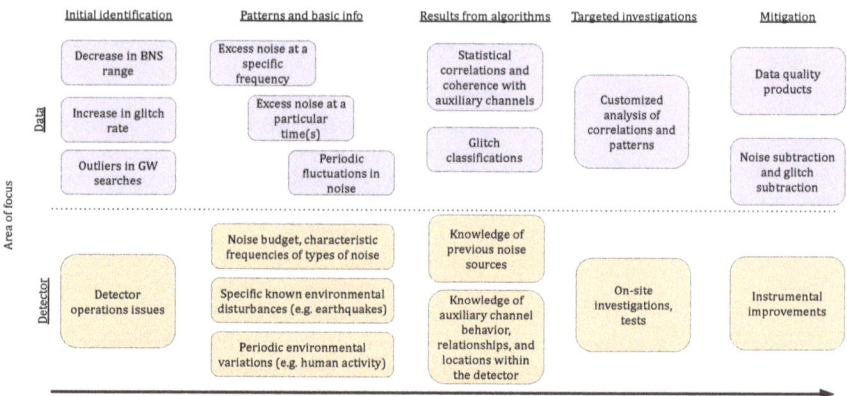

Figure 2. A summary of the general approach to investigating problems from a detector characterization perspective. The two rows show the two main areas of focus in the investigation, either the detector or the data. Rows represent steps in the investigation, while boxes are individual methods. The typical investigation process proceeds from left to right.

One indication of a new problem in the detector is an increase in the rate of "glitches" (short-duration bursts of noise) in the strain data at a particular time or frequency. "Event trigger generators" search for glitches in a time series. One of the most commonly used event trigger generators for detector characterization is Omicron, which is run automatically on a daily basis for the strain channel as well as thousands of auxiliary channels [35,36]. Omicron uses a wavelet basis to transform the time series into a time-frequency representation. Omicron records a variety of metrics for each glitch that it finds, including the peak time, frequency, and signal-to-noise ratio (SNR). Additional event trigger generators are DMT Omega and KleineWelle [37]. Problematic populations of glitches may also be identified by characterizing outliers in the gravitational-wave search backgrounds [17,38] or single-detector GW searches [39,40].

Identified patterns of the noise, such as glitches occurring in a particular frequency range or only during certain times of the day, can already provide useful information about the noise. Combining this knowledge with prior knowledge of the detector based on subsystem characterization or previous instrumental investigations can offer some clues as to the source of the noise. For example, low frequency glitches occurring particularly during the weekdays could relate to elevated seismic noise from human activity.

In addition to the characteristic frequency and SNR of glitches, it is also useful to know the frequency morphology over time. The "Qscan" method [41,42] is based on a similar algorithm to Omicron, and uses overlapping time-frequency tiles of varying widths to create a high resolution spectrogram that shows how the glitch's frequency and amplitude evolve over a short time scale. Based on these images, different classes of glitches have quite distinct shapes, as illustrated in Figure 3.

Since the early science runs of LIGO and Virgo, the detector characterization group began to develop an understanding of particular glitch classes [14,43,44]. Throughout the observing runs, detailed investigations of specific types of glitches (such as "whistle" glitches [16], "blips" [45], and "scattered light glitches" [46]) have continued to be an important facet of detector characterization. These investigations frequently begin with noticing the impact on data quality in the searches, rather than at the specific level of detail of characterizing a particular instrumental monitor. In the noise investigation process, these glitches might be classified visually, but there are now also glitch classification tools that were developed to aid in creating categories of glitches. Gravity Spy [47–49] is a citizen science and machine learning project that offers categorization of glitches based on their appearance in the Qscans. The Gravity Spy glitch collections have been helpful in noise investigations, for example in a study of scattered light glitches that led to improvements in the detector in the third observing run [46].

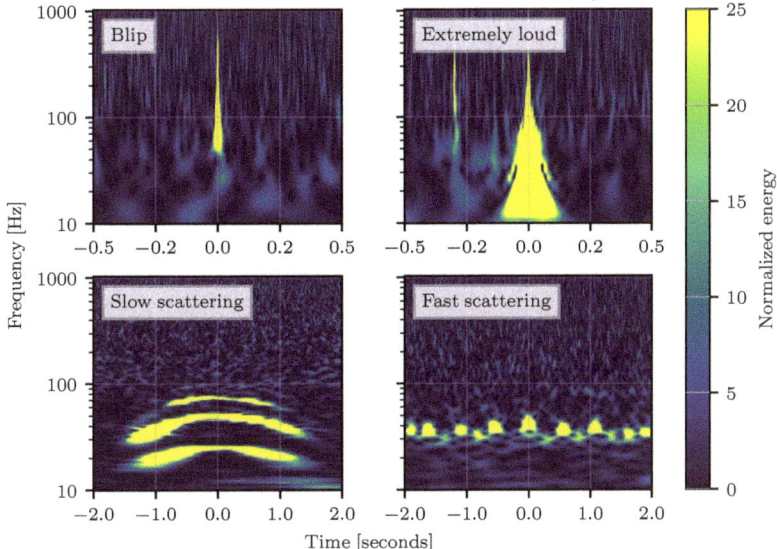

Figure 3. This figure presents Qscans of four common glitch classes present in the LIGO detectors. The glitches' distinct visual appearance in the scans enables them to be categorized visually or through machine learning algorithms. Figure reproduced from [18]. © IOP Publishing. Reproduced with permission. All rights reserved.

To gather more data on the specific parts of the detectors contributing to transient noise, results of automated correlation or classification algorithms can reveal more information, along with knowledge about the detectors to interpret results. Statistical methods are used to compare glitches in the gravitational-wave strain channel with glitches in auxiliary channels [50–53]. There are also methods specifically targeted to identify the source of specific types of noise, such as scattered light [54,55] or lightning [56–59].

Among the algorithms for making statistical comparisons between channels, the Hierarchical Veto (HVeto [25,60–62]) method is especially used for instrumental noise investigations in LIGO. This algorithm begins with the set of all the Omicron triggers in the main gravitational-wave channel and then finds statistically significant time coincidences with glitches in other channels. The hierarchical nature of the method means that it performs multiple rounds of analysis, and after each round it removes the glitches that were found to be correlated with the most significant auxiliary channel. Successive rounds will typically pick up on different types of glitches . The results further include lists of channels that are all related to the most significant channels, and Qscans of the glitches in each round.

Careful studies of the environment around each detector can also further inform the potential sources of transient noise. During each observing run, a series of "injections" that simulate excess environmental noise are regularly performed at each site [25,60–62]. These injections include inducing magnetic noise, loud sounds, and excessive shaking at a level of excitation significantly exceeding the normal environmental level but within the dynamic range of the detector. These injection studies are only completed during time periods when the detector is not actively observing, as they add large amounts of additional noise to the detector data. The coupling between each noise source and the detector can be calculated by measuring the amplitude of the injection using monitors of the physical environment and comparing this to the amount of noise seen in the gravitational-wave strain channel. These measurements allow scientists to know if any sources of noise in the local environment are strong enough to impact the gravitational-wave strain data. If the transfer function between a particular noise source and the detector strain is linear, then the measured coupling is sufficient to estimate the amount of noise each source adds to the detector data. While some noise sources, such as scattered light, do not have a linear coupling, the majority of sources from the local environment are indeed linearly related to the detector strain.

These various methods are used in concert to perform investigations of particular types of glitches, with each method providing particular clues that eventually lead to a deeper understanding of the channels involved in the noise. However, none of the algorithms on their own can provide a solution to the problem without additional knowledge of how the channels are related to the complex inner workings of the detectors, a working knowledge of how noise propagates through the various instrumental systems, and additional targeted analyses of the noise. For example, Figure 4 shows a follow-up study that was done to diagnose a population of glitches in the strain channel that was traced to a compressor switching on and off. This knowledge is built up over time through investigations on the subsystem level, noise injections, and communication with instrumental experts.

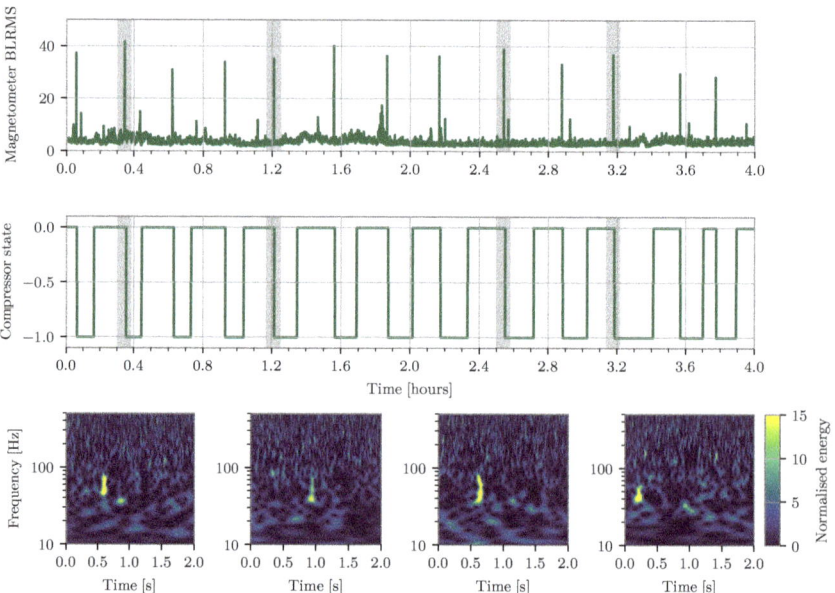

Figure 4. A comparison of time series of a channel showing the band-limited RMS of a magnetometer signal (**top**) and a signal from a compressor (**middle**) over the course of several hours. These channels were found to be significantly correlated with glitches in the strain channel from the HVeto algorithm. For the four peaks in the band-limited RMS time series marked by gray shading, the gravitational-wave strain data are also shown (**bottom**). This analysis provided further evidence that the compressor switching on and off was causing magnetic glitches present in the gravitational-wave strain data. Plotted compressor and magnetometer data are from [30] and strain data are accessed from GWOSC [63].

Finally, targeted investigations on site at the detector are generally applied to further confirm the specific cause of a noise source. These investigations could be types of noise injections to try to simulate the glitch. For example, in the famous thirsty ravens investigations [31], scientists simulated the effects of ravens pecking, and then observed how this introduced similar glitches in the detector.

2.3. Diagnosing and Mitigating Persistent Noise

In addition to investigating glitches in the detector, instrumental investigations also target long-term persistent noise in the detector. Improving the overall sensitivity allows us to see farther into the universe in all types of gravitational wave searches. Lowering the overall noise in the detectors, reducing extra noise at specific frequencies, and keeping the detectors running in a stable state are especially critical for searches for persistent gravitational-wave sources.

Characterization of persistent noise follows a similar process to transient noise investigations, with identification of problematic noise from summary plots of the main output of the detector, gathering information from automated algorithms searching for correlations with auxiliary channels, synthesis of the results from these algorithms with prior knowledge of the detectors, and targeted investigations to continue to build up that knowledge. The types of tools used for these steps of the investigations are different though.

Persistent noise at constant frequencies, or "lines", can be particularly harmful for searches for continuous gravitational waves. Tracking lines in the data and keeping lists of known sources of lines is an important part of the instrumental investigation process [64]. The FScan [65], NoEMi [66], and FineTooth [64] tools are used to track lines in the strain channel and auxiliary channels. FScan produces spectra and spectrograms for each day, and NoEMi tracks lines, follows wandering lines (which change in frequency over time), and indicates coincidences with occurrences in auxiliary channels. Often groups of lines are found to have a constant frequency separation between adjacent lines and are referred to as "combs". FineTooth is a tool for finding and tracking combs of lines in the strain channel as well as magnetometers, which have proven to be useful witnesses of electronics noise that manifests itself in combs. Additionally, noise investigations of lines and combs are frequently aided by analyzing the correlation between the strain channel and auxiliary monitors at specific frequencies, to narrow down the potential sources of noise. In cases when the time in the observing run that the line first appeared can be identified, it is also possible to use the list of instrumental upgrades that occurred near that period to narrow down the search.

Although the long-term performance of the detector is particularly relevant for detecting persistent sources of gravitational waves, numerous metrics were developed to characterize the long-term performance of the ability of each detector to observe transient gravitational-waves. One key figure of merit that describes the overall sensitivity of the detector is the binary neutron star (BNS) "range", a measure of the distance to which the detector could detect a binary neutron star inspiral at an SNR of 8 at any given time, averaged over the entire sky and the different gravitational-wave polarizations. The BNS range fluctuates over time with the noise in the detectors, and significant drops in the BNS range over long periods of time can sometimes be a first clue that something is wrong in the detectors. Detector characterization experts study fluctuations in sensitivity [67] in order to provide clues about what noise sources could be affecting the range of the detector. These investigations are conducted in order to increase the stability of the detectors and maximize their sensitivity, in order to increase the effectiveness of all types of gravitational-wave searches.

The same environmental conditions that lead to changes in the detector range can also lead to a decrease in the amount of time that the detectors are actually in a state that is able to record observational-quality data. Severe environmental disturbances such as nearby earthquakes (or severe earthquakes even far away!) can make the detectors lose the carefully tuned and aligned resonances in the optical cavities required to operate the detector. This loss in observing time affects all astrophysical analyses, so an important aspect of detector characterization is analyzing how the detectors' stability can be increased to be more resilient to such effects. Investigations of the detectors' "duty cycle" are aimed at increasing the amount of time that the detectors are actually operational [68,69]. For example, when an earthquake is known to be coming (based on data from far away seismometers), the detectors can be placed temporarily in an "Earthquake mode", a modified seismic control scheme which allows the detectors to maintain arm cavity resonance during more earthquakes, therefore increasing the amount of usable data [70].

Noise sources that may not be strong enough to be observed in a single detector can still be particularly troublesome if the noise is correlated between detectors. Typically, multiple detectors are used to identify gravitational-wave signals and it is assumed in many analyses that no correlations exist between data from different detectors. Hence, any strongly correlated noise sources that are not accounted for could bias current gravitational-wave analyses. Although multiple potential sources for correlated noise were suggested [17], the only source of noise known to be relevant for ground-based detectors is magnetic noise from "Schumann resonances" [71], fluctuations in the Earth's magnetic field, and strong lighting strikes [72]. The noise contribution from these resonances is currently too low to impact searches for gravitational waves with current detectors, but will become more relevant in the future as detectors increase in sensitivity [73]. Regardless of their expected impact, the noise contributions from correlated magnetic noise is closely monitored using magnetometers and measurements of the coupling between magnetic noise and the strain data at each observatory [18,74].

3. Gravitational-Wave Data Quality

Data quality issues that have not been mitigated in the instrument can be vetoed from the data that is analyzed if these data quality issues can be confidently separated from astrophysical signals. Whether or not data are vetoed depends on several factors, such as the severity of the known problems with the data, the impact of the data quality issues on the astrophysical search backgrounds, and the ability to construct a veto that efficiently removes times of poor data quality without throwing away too much data. This section details how data quality issues are identified and how this information is propagated to gravitational-wave analyses.

3.1. Data Quality Impacts on Searches for Transient Gravitational-Waves

Transient sources of gravitational waves include signals from compact binaries coalescences (CBCs) [3] and other high-energy astrophysical phenomenon, such as supernovae [75]. Searches for these transient gravitational waves must separate bursts of excess power due to gravitational-wave signals from instrumental artifacts. A variety of pipelines were developed that have been used in analyses by both the LVK [76–81] and other groups [82,83]. These searches primarily incorporate information about the data quality using "data quality vetoes", which identify time periods where the data have a high probability of corruption by glitches.

The process of developing data quality vetoes frequently begins much in the same way as general instrumental noise investigations: excess noise is identified through automated pipelines and then traced to try to find correlations with auxiliary monitors. However, in developing data quality vetoes, the primary emphasis is on improving search results rather than improving the detector, so rather than being concerned with any glitches or excess noise, the noise is viewed first from the lens of the search pipelines. For example, if search pipelines show an excessive number of outliers that are due to instrumental artifacts rather than astrophysical signals, there will be more motivation to develop a veto to eliminate the noise. After the initial identification of the problem, similar tools are used to provide a clear picture of when that type of problem occurs, for example using Omicron [35,36] to gather all the glitch times, and Hveto [50,51] or iDQ [53] to find correlations with auxiliary witnesses, often alongside the investigations into the source of different noise source that were discussed in Section 2.

Data quality vetoes are typically applied in separate categories at different points in the search pipeline, and are individualized based on the different types of searches. In recent observing runs, three categories of veto were used, referred to as "category 1", "category 2", and "category 3". In all searches, the first category of veto, category 1, includes data that is deemed to be completely unusable and unreliable, which is eliminated before any of the search pipeline is conducted. Beyond this most severe category of data quality vetoes, other data quality cuts are tuned carefully based on how the noise impacts the different search pipelines. Category 2 vetoes are developed to target small time periods around specific types of glitches, while category 3 vetoes are based on statistical correlations between auxiliary channels and the gravitational-wave strain data. The process for creating data quality vetoes and their impact on the total spacetime volume that searches for compact binary coalescences are sensitive to (referred to as the "sensitivity" of a search) is described in greater detail in [38,84].

Several common strategies exist for creating data quality vetoes. One strategy, which is especially employed in the creation of category 1 vetoes, is to determine segments manually, based on known severe or unusual environmental or instrumental disturbances at a very specific time. The times of these vetoes are frequently taken from the online detector logbook. Examples of this kind of manual determination from O3 are times when forklifts, cranes, or large trucks were operating near the detectors during observing mode [85].

Many types of noise, however, are recurrent and require vetoes to be more finely tuned and programmed in order to select all of the data that needs to be cut. This is how category 2 vetoes are generally developed. Ideally, the noise is traced to a correlated auxiliary witness signal, which can be used to predict any time the noise appears in the strain data. For some types of vetoes, this will involve creating a threshold on an auxiliary witness time series. An example of this type of threshold is shown in Figure 5. For other types of glitches, vetoed times are determined by auxiliary Omicron triggers, usually after a correlation was found by Hveto or a similar algorithm. Whether these vetoes are built using Omicron triggers, an auxiliary channel, or some processing of an auxiliary channel, the exact veto parameters are tuned carefully to maximize the ratio of efficiency (the percent of glitches removed) to deadtime (the percent of total time removed). This ensures that the veto is capturing the most noise while minimizing the risk of removing astrophysical signals.

One important consideration in development of data quality vetoes is to make the primary determination based on auxiliary data and the astrophysical search backgrounds, without using the strain data itself. The exception to this is in cases where there is severely loud noise or noise present in the data which is much louder (e.g., by an order of magnitude) than could be reasonably expected of an astrophysical signal. For the CBC searches, loud glitches are removed from the data before analysis using "gating", described in Section 5.

The channels used to produce vetoes must also be determined to be 'safe' for vetoes, meaning that they are truly witnesses only of auxiliary information, and they will not be influenced by the strain data through control loop feedback. This is important to ensure that the witnesses will only veto noise, not astrophysical signals. The safety of channels is determined by injecting strain noise into the detectors by physically moving the test masses with a known frequency and amplitude [86]. Data from auxiliary channels is then searched for evidence that this injected noise propagated into other channels. If such evidence if found, these channels are not deemed safe.

Different search pipelines make additional data quality cuts or implement additional signal consistency checks or the results of other algorithms, based on the needs determined by reviewing each search's background noise. Searches for generic transient gravitational-wave signals ("bursts") for example, directly use the results of Hveto in their data quality cuts as a category 3 veto.

The amount of time vetoed from the analyses has varied slightly over the different observing runs of Advanced LIGO and different analyses, but typically the total time vetoed is on the order of $\sim 2\%$ or less. In the first observing run, there were several periods of very poor data quality at the Hanford observatory traced to one particular noise source, which ultimately led to vetoing 4.6% of the coincident detector time as a category 1 veto [17]. However, other data quality vetoes and subsequent observing runs have removed less data.

In the second and third observing runs, the vetoes have removed ∼1–2% of the data in total [5,7,18]. Of the confident events identified in the first three observing runs by LVK analyses [4–7], only 2 events have overlapped data quality veto segments. Considering the amount of time removed by these vetoes and the total number of detected events, this number is consistent with the expected rate of chance coincidences. Furthermore, multiple detectors in operation and the diversity of methods that data quality vetoes are used in analyses allowed these events to still be detected despite the overlap with a veto.

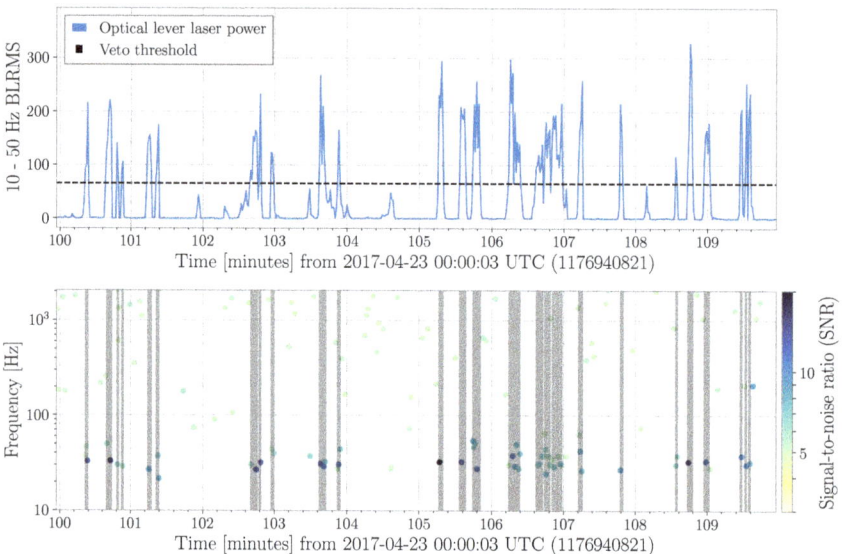

Figure 5. An example of the design and effectiveness of a data quality veto. This data quality veto was designed to remove time periods with glitches from fluctuations in the power of a laser used to control the alignment of a mirror (referred to as an "optical lever"). Top: The root-mean-square of the optical lever laser power after bandpassing between 10 and 50 Hz. The veto threshold is denoted with a black dashed line. Bottom: The time and frequency of glitches in the gravitational-wave strain data as identified by Omicron [35,36]. The color of dots indicates the SNR of the glitch. Time above the veto threshold are shaded in gray. These times represent all of the loud glitches in this time period. Figure reproduced from [18]. © IOP Publishing. Reproduced with permission. All rights reserved.

The benefits of data quality vetoes were reduced in recent observing runs due to improvements in how search pipelines address glitches in the data. In analyses of data from the first observing run, data quality vetoes increased the sensitivity of a search for CBC signals by up to ∼50% [38]. However, the sensitivity of the same search pipeline in the third observing run increased by only ∼5% [18]. As noted in the previous paragraph, the amount of time removed by data quality vetoes changed by only a few percent across these observing runs, suggesting that the difference in sensitivity increase is due to improvements to the search pipeline that were implemented between the two periods considered based on the understanding of detector data from the investigations discussed in this review. One such improvement is accounting for how glitches in the data are similar to only a small portion of the CBC parameter space [87,88]. This change meant that the presence of glitches only reduced the sensitivity of the search in a small portion of the parameter space, which in turn reduced the benefits of mitigating glitches with data quality vetoes. For this reason, it is expected that data quality vetoes will be needed less frequently in future CBC searches. Searches for gravitational-wave bursts have also made improvements that have reduced the benefits of data quality vetoes, but to a lesser extent. Data quality vetoes still significantly improve the sensitivity of burst searches as burst waveforms are more general than CBC waveforms and hence are more likely to be similar to detector artifacts.

In addition to data quality vetoes, another data quality product, the iDQ timeseries, was used in analyses of LIGO data in the third observing run. The iDQ algorithm analyzes the detector state using auxiliary channel information using machine learning techniques to determine the likelihood that there is a glitch present in the strain data. These predictions are made for all times and stored as a time series with a sample rate of 128 Hz. Figure 6 shows an example of the iDQ timeseries near a glitch and near a gravitational-wave signal. At the time of the glitch, the likelihood of a glitch (as predicted by iDQ) is elevated. As expected, no such increase in likelihood is seen at the time of a gravitational-wave signal.

As of the end of the third observing run, only one search algorithm, GstLAL [77], has incorporated this iDQ time series. This CBC search used the value of the iDQ time series to down rank candidates that were predicted to be likely glitches [89]. This method contrasts the approach used with data quality vetoes where times that are likely to contain glitches are removed from the searches completely. This makes it possible to identify loud gravitational-wave candidates that happen to overlap glitches by chance. The use of the iDQ timeseries was found to increase the sensitivity of this CBC search by up to ∼5% [89], comparable with the increase when data quality vetoes were used.

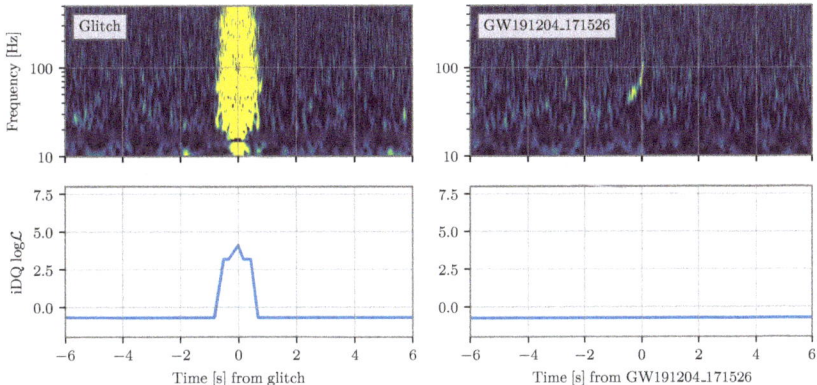

Figure 6. A comparison of the iDQ log-likelihood time series near a glitch and a gravitational-wave signal. Top row: Spectrograms of the LIGO Livingston strain data around a glitch and a gravitational-wave signal (GW191204_171526). Bottom row: iDQ log-likelihood time series for the same two time periods. In the case of the glitch, the iDQ time series is highly elevated at the time of the glitch, while in the case of the gravitational-wave signal no change in the time series is observed. The strain data are from GWOSC [90] while the iDQ data are from [91].

3.2. Data Quality Impacts on Searches for Persistent Gravitational Waves

Persistent gravitational waves include line-like sources of gravitational waves, such as from rotating neutron stars [92], and broadband sources, such as the background signal from weak, unresolved CBC signals [73]. A wide variety of different searches were used to look for persistent gravitational waves, by both the LVK [73,92–94] and other groups [95–97]. As searches for persistent gravitational waves are looking for signals present continuously throughout an observing run, these searches are generally insensitive to short duration bursts of power. For this reason, most of the data quality products used for transient searches are not used by searches for persistent gravitational waves. The only data products that are used by all searches are category 1 vetoes which flag egregious data quality periods. Persistent gravitational-wave searches instead rely on other data quality products and methods that are better suited for their needs.

The data quality product most useful for searches for continuous waves (CW) is lists of known instrumental lines. As mentioned in Section 2.3, lines are particularly harmful for these searches. Each line in the data only impacts a small portion of the frequency parameter space searched by CW searches, so it is not required that these lines be mitigated before searching the data. Instead, any potential candidate that is identified at a frequency of a known instrumental line is not considered astrophysical. This method, however, means that searches for gravitational-waves are not able to detect sources with frequencies very near instrumental lines. These line lists are publicly distributed after the end of each observing run when the bulk data are released [98–100]. Additional details on this process can be found in Section 4.2.

In contrast to CW searches, searches for stochastic gravitational waves look for broadband sources of gravitational waves. These searches can be biased by severe non-stationary data, including particularly loud glitches. For this reason, highly non-stationary data are excluded from the analysis, beyond what is removed by data quality vetoes. Stochastic searches typically remove large amounts of data (sometimes over 20% [73]), balancing the benefits of removing segments with poor data quality against the reduction in sensitivity from a shorter analysis duration. Monitors of the data quality are used throughout the observing run to identify times with poor data quality that could impact stochastic searches.

4. Event Validation

An integral aspect of gravitational wave analysis is investigation of the impact of instrumental artifacts on detected signals. As previously discussed, a large array of sensors is used at each observatory in order to monitor the performance of the detectors and their environment. As instrumental or environmental disturbances could mimic gravitational-wave signals, it is necessary to confirm that no such instrumental artifacts are present to increase confidence in the astrophysical origin of any gravitational-wave detection. Additionally, the presence of noise at the time of a true astrophysical signal could impact the analysis, so it is important to determine whether any additional processing of the data is needed. These investigations are collectively referred to as "event validation".

Event validation is especially important for the first detection of a new type of astrophysical source, particularly if it is known that instrumental artifacts could produce a similar signal to the newly discovered gravitational-wave event. To date, the only confident gravitational-wave detections that have been made are from compact binary coalescences, but even within this class there is a broad range of different timescales that must be considered. These validation procedures were a particularly important component of the first detection of a binary black hole merger (BBH), GW150914 [17], and the first detection of an intermediate mass black hole (IMBH), GW190521 [11]. Event validation will also be an essential element of confirming the observation of gravitational waves from non-CBC sources.

The methods used in event validation procedures rely on many of the same tools previously discussed in Sections 2 and 3. However, rather than analyzing the data or detector status over the entire observation time and all frequencies, event validation procedures focus on a specific part of the parameter space (typically a specific time or frequency). This allows deeper investigation of the state of the detector and data quality than would be typically possible. Furthermore, the properties of the identified gravitational-wave candidate allow additional tests to be used that further constrain how the detector and the data quality could have impacted the caniddate in question.

4.1. Validation of Transient Sources of Gravitational Waves

The validation of transient gravitational-wave events in LVK analyses been previously described in [5,17,18]. In this section, we will highlight the main procedures that were employed.

As transient sources of gravitational waves typically last less than a few minutes, the data surrounding the time of the signal can be more heavily scrutinized than the bulk data. There are three main types of evidence that are investigated as part of transient event validation: evidence of instrumental origin, evidence of transient noise overlapping the signal, and evidence of any detector operating in a non-standard manner at the time of the signal.

First we investigate if there is "evidence that supports an instrumental origin" for the candidate event. Two metrics were used to establish if a candidate has evidence of instrumental origin: (i) evidence that a known class of instrumental artifact is present at the time of the candidate and can cause similar non-astrophysical candidates in a search pipeline (ii) evidence that the observed excess power in at least one detector can be accounted for by instrumental sources. The former metric requires long-term studies of both the detector and the relevant search pipeline, while the latter can be established, in some cases, using only a small amount of data containing the candidate.

The main method of establishing evidence of instrumental origin is with evidence of an auxiliary sensor that can account for the majority of the power observed in the strain data. This is done by examining a wide array of witness sensors to understand if they are correlated with the observed strain power. Multiple methods are used to identify correlations, including manual inspections of visualizations of data [41,42,101–103], machine-learning interpretation of the strain data [47–49], tools that estimate statistical correlations between channels [50,52,53,104,105], and projections of the excess power in the observed strain data based on previous measurements between each auxiliary channel and the strain data [25,60,61].

In addition to testing if the observed power can be accounted for by auxiliary witnesses, the long-term performance of the detectors is investigated to understand if changes to the detector state could create a false candidate. These tests include tests of the stationarity of the data [106,107] and inspection of long-term trends of detector performance [108,109].

Even when there is no evidence of instrumental origin, it is quite common for excess power from instrumental artifacts to be present in the data near an astrophysical signal. This association is coincidental, and was found to occur at a rate expected by chance. Although excess power overlapping a signal is not sufficient cause to doubt the astrophysical origin of a gravitational-wave signal, the excess power should be mitigated before additional analysis of the event is completed. Furthermore, when an event is detected with multiple detectors, it is possible to identify any excess power that is not astrophysical by correlating the multiple data streams. Multiple detectors also allow confirmation that the identified gravitational-wave signal is unrelated to nearby glitches. An example of an event that overlaps excess power from glitches (GW190424_180648) is shown in Figure 7. In this case, two separate types of glitches overlapped the signal. Multiple glitches overlapping a signal is unlikely, but possible, given the recent rate of glitches in gravitational-wave detector data. Mitigation methods used to address these and other similar glitches are discussed in Section 5.

To identify this excess power, methods similar to those used to investigate evidence of instrumental origin are also used. One of the main methods used is visualizations of the data [41,42,101–103]. As an astrophysical signal is coherent between detectors, any incoherent power present in the data must be instrumental in origin. Further simplifying this process is the well-established morphology of astrophysical signals from CBC. There is currently no evidence of measurable deviations from general relativity for these signals [10], meaning that any power not explained by general relativity is also likely to be noise. Hence it is generally much easier to establish evidence of excess power than evidence of instrumental origin. If excess power is identified, other previously mentioned tools are used to potentially identify the cause.

While often considered separately from the event validation procedures, additional, similar, tests of signal morphology and parameters are performed as part of analyses of detected gravitational-wave events. These include tests such as the expected signal in multiple detectors [110] or the generated skymap [111,112]. In the case of events with well-known morphologies, such as CBC signals that follow general relativity, we can use additional signal consistency tests to test the residual power [113]. Correlations between the results of different analyses and specific glitch classes have also been investigated as methods of rejecting non-astrophysical signals [88,114].

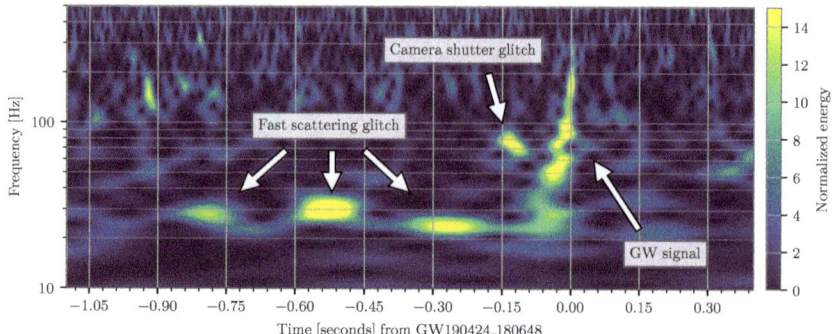

Figure 7. An example of a gravitational-wave signal (GW190424_180648) with two different types of glitches also present nearby in the data. Event validation procedures were able to identify the source of both glitches as well as confirm that there was no evidence the gravitational-wave signal was an instrumental artifact. The source of one of the glitches was vibrations from an automated camera shutter that was inadvertently left running in one of the detector end stations [18] while the source of the second is light scattered off of the main laser beam path that reflects and then interferes with the main beam (referred to as "fast scattering") [46]. This example highlights that it is possible to detect and analyze a gravitational-wave signal despite the presence of nearby glitches. Data plotted is from LIGO Livingston and accessed via GWOSC [90].

The validation process of non-CBC sources of transient gravitational waves, i.e., bursts, is largely similar to that for CBC sources. However, the lack of a known waveform model prevents the use of many of the signal consistency tests available for CBC validation. A similar situation is true for gravitational-wave candidates that are not consistent with general relativity. In the case of a potential burst signal, the most important source of information is the auxiliary channels. Statistical correlations between the strain data and these additional data streams can demonstrate that the observed strain is not astrophysical.

To facilitate rapid follow up of gravitational-wave events by electromagnetic and neutrino observatories, the data from gravitational-wave detectors is continuously analyzed to identify events as quickly as possible. However, these real-time searches are less able to account for the changing state of the detectors and hence are more likely to falsely claim a detection. In recent searches for gravitational waves conducted in real-time, the retraction rate has been high, requiring significant input from event validation investigations. In the third observing run, the retraction rate of candidates released in low latency was 43% [115]. This high retraction rate is expected of low-latency analyses, as quickly changing detector states cannot always be accounted for as part of the analysis. Despite these concerns, low-latency analyses are required for immediate follow up of gravitational-wave signals with other observatories.

For catalogs of gravitational-wave candidates based on post-facto analyses of the data, typically only a small number of candidates are found to have evidence of instrumental origin. For most catalog events, no data quality issues were identified. The main impact of data quality issues is identification of transient noise overlapping the signal, rather than causing the signal. An example of an astrophysical event with transient noise present is shown in Figure 7. Of the 93 unique confident candidates in GWTC-1, -2, -2.1 and -3 [4–7], 18 were found to be coincident with transient noise, while none were found to have instrumental origin.

For low significance catalogs, namely those containing "marginal" triggers, the number of false alarms is much higher. Evidence of instrumental origin was found for 11 out of 25 marginal candidates in GWTC-1 [4], GWTC-3 [7], and the O3 IMBH Search [116]. In much deeper catalogs, such as GWTC-2.1 [6] or 3-OGC [83], many of the candidates likely also have evidence of instrumental origin. However, event validation of these large candidate lists has yet to be attempted.

At present, many of the event validation procedures described in this subsection can only be completed by members of the LIGO, Virgo, and KAGRA collaborations. Many analyses completed as part of event validation almost exclusively rely upon data from auxiliary channels. At the time of writing, these data are not available to those outside of the detector collaborations except for short segments of data [117]. Hence validation completed by other groups [82,83] must only rely upon inspection of the available strain data and publicly available data quality metrics.

4.2. Validation of Persistent Sources of Gravitational Waves

Similar to transient event validation, validation of persistent gravitational-wave candidates relies upon two metrics: investigations of known noise sources and signal-consistency checks. In this subsection, we will briefly outline some of the additional signal consistency checks that are used to vet candidates. No candidate has yet to pass these checks and have high enough significance to be claimed as a detection candidate.

The primary method of validating line-like gravitational-wave candidates is by investigating for evidence of an instrumental line at the same frequency as the signal. Using the line lists discussed in Section 2.3, the list of candidates is filtered. The large number of instrumental lines in the data means that this step vetoes a significant number of candidates. An example of the result of vetoing candidates is shown in Figure 8. All candidates removed due to an association with a known instrumental line are marked with gray circles.

For line-like sources, there is an expected signal morphology and amplitude in each detector that can be used to reject candidates [118–120]. A continuous signal from a gravitational-wave source will be roughly constant in amplitude but will slowly change in frequency due to the Doppler modulation of the Earth's movement around the sun [121]. The rate of the frequency evolution from the Doppler modulation is sky-position dependent, requiring searches for continuous gravitational waves to search each position (or small portions) of the sky separately. While these features complicate the search for these signals, they also can be used to reject instrumental artifacts that do not share these properties. Tests of these properties that have typically been used include: checking that the signal strength is the amplitude expected in each detector; checking that the signal to noise ratio grows in a uniform manner over the course of an observing run; checking that the signal exhibits the expected Doppler modulation of over time is present; and checking that the signal to noise of the candidate drops as the sky localization changes. A candidate that does not behave as expected for an astrophysical signal in all characteristics is likely instrumental in origin. Figure 8 demonstrates how these additional checks can be used to veto many candidates that are not already removed due to their association with known lines. In the displayed example from [118], no candidates remain after applying both the known line and signal consistency tests.

There was also a proposal [122] for signal consistency tests of a potential broadband, stochastic signal candidate. This method relies upon the known frequency-dependent correlation for an astrophysical stochastic background. This correlation is also dependent on the locations and orientations of each gravitational-wave detector in the network, improving the ability of these methods to identify a non-astrophyscial background.

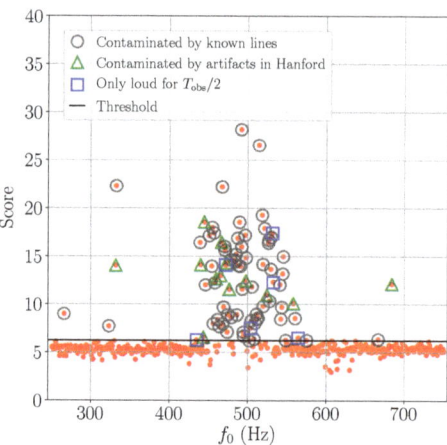

Figure 8. An example of how continuous wave candidates (red dots) are validated based on lists of known lines in the strain data and a variety of signal consistency checks. The threshold for additional followup is shown with a black line. Candidates that are vetoed due to overlapping the known frequency of an instrumental line are marked with gray circles. Candidates that are vetoed because the amplitude of the signal is higher in one detector than expected for an astrophysical signal are marked with green triangles. Candidates that are only significant when considering half of the total analysis time are marked with blue squares. Reprinted figure with permission from [118]; Copyright 2018 by the American Physical Society.

5. Noise Mitigation

In addition to changes to the analysis methods, data quality issues can be mitigated by directly correcting the recorded gravitational-wave strain data. Depending on the frequency resolution, time duration, and the source of the data quality issues, a variety of mitigation methods are used. In the case of long duration noise sources that impact the measured power spectral density of the detector, the noise contributions from sources are modelled and subtracted. This process is typically referred to as "noise subtraction". Modelling and subtraction of short duration transients may use similar methods, but is referred to as "glitch subtraction". Further complicating the picture is the use of alternate glitch mitigation techniques that are agnostic to the glitch time series, and hence require no additional information beyond a time duration and bandwidth. Such techniques include "gating" and "inpainting". Each technique is chosen based on the available time and computational resources in addition to the specific data quality issue in question.

In this section, we outline current methods of noise mitigation that are used to analyze gravitational-wave strain data. Alongside each method, we explain the general uses of the method, and changes that were proposed for future analyses.

5.1. Noise Subtraction

The operational goal of a gravitational-wave interferometer is to have the lowest possible background noise. While numerous advances have recently been able to significantly improve the sensitivity of gravitational-wave interferometers, there remain known sources of noise that contribute to the absolute sensitivity of the interferometer. Some of these known noise sources are theoretically predicted based on the design and location of the interferometer; these are typically referred to as "fundamental" noise sources. Other sources of noise are typically called "technical" noise sources, and stem from a variety of known and unknown sources. For many of these technical noise sources, the time series of the noise contribution and its coupling to the strain channel can be precisely measured, allowing for the possibility of subtracting the relevant noise contributions post-facto. This section explains the techniques used to perform this noise subtraction and the main sources of noise that are targeted.

Multiple proposals for noise subtraction have been explored since the early detector era [123–125], primarily focused on the use of Weiner filtering [126] to calculate the noise contributions from a variety of noise sources. Weiner filtering is particularly useful in cases where a linear coupling exists between the noise source and the gravitational-wave strain data. Additional subtraction procedures based on machine learning [127–129] are also being explored. These new methods have shown promise in subtracting sources of noise that exhibit non-linear couplings to the gravitational-wave strain.

The first extensive use of noise subtracted data occurred in the second observing run of Advanced LIGO. During this observing run, vibrations from turbulent water flow that was used to cool the pre-stabilized laser system introduced significant beam jitter into the interferometer. This jitter added broadband noise from 10 to 2000 Hz at the LIGO Hanford detector. This noise source could not be addressed without an intrusive upgrade to the laser system, meaning that the noise source could not be mitigated until the next observing run.

Two different noise subtraction procedures [130,131] were applied to the O2 dataset. The first [131], based on Weiner filtering, was applied to small segments of data around significant events. The second [130] was based on a similar method of measuring noise contributions [132] and was applied to the entire O2 dataset. In addition to noise from jitter, these noise subtraction procedures removed noise contributions from calibration lines, power line noise, and alignment and length sensing control noise. After applying noise subtraction, the binary neutron star range improved by 25% at LIGO Hanford, which led to a 30% improvement in the overall sensitivity of the gravitational-wave network [130]. Figure 9 shows a comparison of the detector noise curve before and after noise subtraction from a representative time in O2. A broadband decrease in noise can be seen in addition to multiple line features removed.

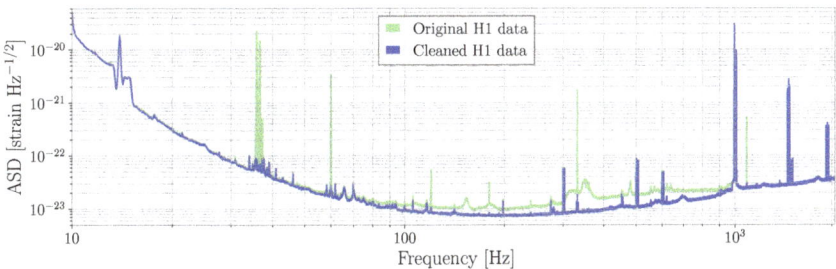

Figure 9. A comparison of the amplitude spectral density (ASD) of the strain data at LIGO Hanford (H1) before (green) and after (blue) subtraction of broadband noise in O2. By using instrumental witnesses to known sources of noise, broadband noise between 80 and 1000 Hz was significantly reduced, as well as elimination of many narrow frequency band spectral artifacts caused by calibration lines and other instrumental factors. Figure is reproduced from [130]. © IOP Publishing. Reproduced with permission. All rights reserved.

In the third observing run, there were no broadband sources of noise that were identified as potential noise subtraction targets at LIGO. For this reason, only noise from line-like sources was subtracted. A new procedure [133] was adopted that was better able to subtract line-like sources. This procedure was applied at the same time as the detector data was calibrated. In addition to this subtraction procedure, LIGO data from the third observing run included subtraction of noise from slow modulations of the 60 Hz power line. These modulations added extra noise as sidebands around the main power line. To subtract this noise, a machine-learning-based method [134] was applied.

Noise subtraction of broadband sources of noise was also used with Virgo data in the third observing run. Noise subtraction with Virgo data used similar procedures to those used with LIGO data [135,136]. The sources of the subtracted noise included laser frequency noise, scattered light noise, and amplitude noise from the laser modulation frequency. This noise subtraction improved the sensitivity by up to 7 Mpc [136].

5.2. Glitch Subtraction

Recent data from ground-based interferometric detectors contains approximately 1 glitch per minute [5,7], which makes it likely that a significant number of gravitational-wave candidates overlap glitches. One of the most prominent examples of such a case is GW170817, when a loud glitch was present within a second of the merger time [9]. In recent catalogs, 20% of candidates overlapped glitches [5]. Signals that are in the sensitive band of the detectors for longer periods, such as binary neutrons, are much more likely to overlap glitches. The Bayesian analyses used to estimate the source properties of gravitational-wave candidates assume that the data are Gaussian and stationary; the presence of glitches severely violates these assumptions and hence may bias the results [137]. It is currently standard procedure to subtract any glitches present in the data with glitch subtraction algorithms prior to performing the final parameter estimation.

The most commonly used algorithm for glitch modelling and subtraction in LVK analyses is BayesWave [138–140]. The BayesWave algorithm is used to measure the power spectral density of data that is used in analyses of gravitational-wave source properties, in addition to modelling non-Gaussian glitches. BayesWave is a Bayesian analysis that uses sine-Gaussian wavelets to model excess power in gravitational-wave data. As more simple models are preferred by the Bayesian analysis, glitch models that use large numbers of wavelets are penalized, reducing the risk of overfitting the model. BayesWave analyses using data from only one detector were used in the second observing run to model glitches, most notably the glitch overlapping GW170817 [138,139]. An example of a case where BayesWave was used in the third observing run is shown in Figure 10. In this case, a blip glitch that overlapped a gravitational-wave signal was modeled and subtracted. This model requires there to be minimal overlap between any glitch and any potential signal.

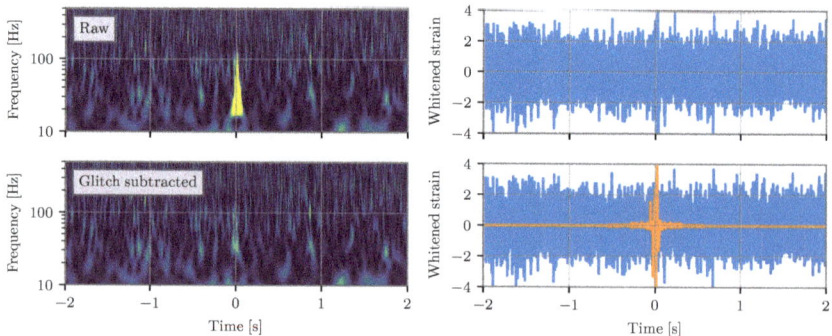

Figure 10. A demonstration of mitigating a glitch by modeling and subtracting the glitch with BayesWave [138–140]. eft column: Spectrograms of whitened strain data from the LIGO Livingston detector before and after subtraction of the glitch. Right column: Time series of the whitened strain before and after subtraction is plotted in blue, while the difference between the data before and after glitch subtraction is plotted in orange. After modeling and subtracting the glitch, the data are consistent with Gaussian noise. Plotted data are from [141].

In addition to modelling excess power in one detector, BayesWave is able to model power coherent between multiple detectors. Recent updates to BayesWave have added support for a "signal plus glitch" configuration that models the coherent signal power at the same time as the incoherent glitch power [140]. This allows the BayesWave model to separate power from a glitch from power that is due to an astrophysical signal. Hence the signal plus glitch configuration is able to model glitches overlapping gravitational-wave signals. Analyses of simulated signals on top of glitches have shown that BayesWave is capable of correctly discriminating between the two sources of excess power [142,143].

Other glitch models [144,145] based on machine learning approaches or class-specific glitch models [146] were also proposed. A subset of these methods have also shown promise in accurate waveform extraction in the presence of non-Gaussian noise.

5.3. Gating and Inpainting

In several use cases, precise glitch modelling is not required to mitigate the impact of glitches on gravitational-wave analyses. Additional methods that are more computationally efficient were developed that remove the data surrounding glitches. While this does lead to some loss of information, the reduced complexity of these techniques allows them to be applied on datasets that contain large numbers of glitches. The two most commonly used techniques to remove segments of data in gravitational-wave analyses are referred to as "gating and "inpainting". Gating can be completed before or after whitening of the data based on the specific analysis technique while inpainting must be done before whitening the data. A comparison of data containing a glitch before and after gating or inpainting is shown in Figure 11.

When gating is completed pre-whitening, the data are typically windowed using an inverted Tukey window [147]. This window zeroes a short segment data containing with a taper at each end. The length of the taper is generally between 0.125 and 0.5 s while the length of the zeroed data can vary based on the duration and strength of the glitch. The use of the taper is to reduce the risk of artifacts introduced during the whitening process, particularly discontinuities that would severely corrupt the data. While the taper does not completely prevent artifacts (typically loud lines in the data "ring" during the gate), these artifacts do not limit the sensitivity of searches for compact binaries that use this gating method for loud glitches. An additional downside of this method is that the length of the taper often is much longer than the duration of the data that is zeroed, increasing the duration of data that is disturbed by this method.

When gating is applied post-whitening, the data are merely zeroed out for the region of interest. This method does not introduce artifacts from the gating method. However, for sufficiently loud glitches, the whitening filter can lead to the data surrounding the glitch to be corrupted. The approximate time segment that is corrupted is given by the the duration of the impulse response of the whitening filter. Hence care must be taken to ensure that the duration of zeroed data is long enough to remove the impact of the whitening filter.

The identification of times to gate is also an important analysis choice. A common choice is to gate a small segment of time around any data points that are above a fixed threshold in the whitened time series. A typical threshold is 25–100 times the amplitude of the standard deviation of the whitened strain data. Around each data point above threshold, a fixed amount of time is added to ensure that the glitch is fully excised. Adaptive methods have also been developed [148], which allow the use of variable gating thresholds and time durations. Additional metrics based on the BLRMS of the strain data [149] or the BNS range [78] have also been used. Gating times have also been chosen based on predictions from auxiliary sensor information, which is able to predict the presence of a loud transient in the gravitational-wave strain data [18].

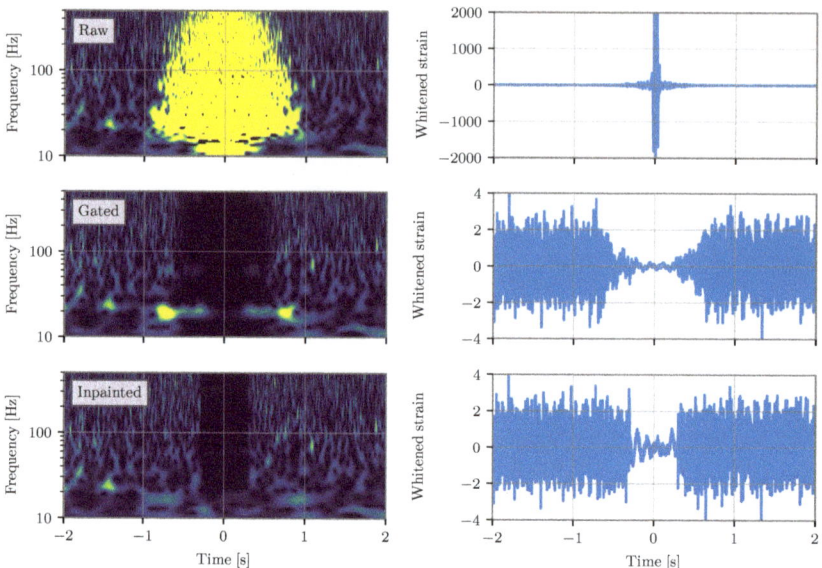

Figure 11. A comparison of the use of gating and inpainting to mitigate a loud noise artifact in the data. Left column: Spectrograms of whitened strain data from the LIGO Livingston detector before mitigation, after mitigation with pre-whitening gating, and after mitigation with inpainting. Right column: Whitened strain time series for the same three cases. Both gating and inpainting methods mitigate the excess power from the instrumental artifact but inpainting introduces fewer artifacts and disturbs less of the time series. This improved mitigation comes at the cost of additional complexity in the method and the requirement that a specific PSD is used to analyze the data after inpainting. Plotted data are accessed from GWOSC [90].

Gating is used extensively in LVK analyses. Pre-whitening gating is currently used by several CBC search algorithms (PyCBC [76], MBTA [78], PyGRB [150]) as well as a search for generic transients (X-pipeline [151]). This method has been used in low latency analyses [152] to manually mitigate loud glitches before localizing the source of gravitational-wave signals. Post-whitening gating is used by two other CBC search algorithms (Gstlal [77] and SPIIR [79]) and a search for generic transient gravitational waves (cWB [80]). In O3, a gated strain dataset was generated for use with searches for persistent gravitational waves [18,149]. Two CBC searches (MBTA and SPIIR) also use pre-whitening gating to remove time periods marked by data quality flags in addition to gating based on a threshold on the whitened strain data.

Inpainting [153] is a similar procedure to gating, but explicitly addresses the impact of whitening on the modified time series. To construct the inpainted time series, the pre-whitened time series is first zeroed over the region of interest. The time series is then whitened and the projection of the zeroed data into the whitened data space is calculated. This calculation is the solution to a Toeplitz system [154], and can be done computationally efficiently. This projection is then subtracted from the original time series so that the whitened time series is approximately zeroed over the region of interest. This method has the advantage of introducing minimal artifacts and removing the need to taper the data. For analyses that use a low rate of gates (less than 1 per few minutes, i.e., typical of LVK analyses) these differences may not have measurable effects. However, the benefits of inpainting allow this method to be applied to the data at a much higher density without corrupting the data stream. This in turn allows for a larger number of non-Gaussian artifacts to be addressed with this method in a single analysis [82].

While glitches are typically addressed by removing data in the time domain, it is possible that only a subset of frequencies are impacted, which can be addressed in the frequency domain. In these cases, the data quality issue can be mitigated by using a reduced frequency bandwidth in the analysis, filtering the data to suppress impacted frequencies, or modifying the PSD used in analyses to suppress impacted frequencies [5].

As these methods remove the excess power from any gravitational-wave signal that is present during the gated or inpainted time, they introduce an bias in the recovered amplitude of any gravitational-wave signal. This bias can be analytically calculated based on the gate configuration [155] or inpainting filter [153] that is used. Additional methods [156] based in machine learning [157] have also been proposed to address this bias.

5.4. Spectral Estimation Methods in the Presence of Non–Gaussian Noise

An essential element of gravitational-wave analyses is the estimate of the power spectral density of the data. Most analyses implicitly or explicitly assume that gravitational-wave data are stationary and Gaussian. This also implies that there is a single true power spectral density that defines the properties of the noise. However, it is well known that this is not the case, although it is still approximately true over short timescales. As gravitational-wave analyses have evolved, the assumptions of stationarity and Gaussianity have begun to be relaxed as new methods were developed to account for the non-ideal nature of the data. This sub-section outlines current techniques to account for variations in the properties of noise over multiple timescales.

Several straightforward techniques were used to calculate the power spectral density of gravitational-wave data. Perhaps the most simple is Welch's method [158], where the noise spectrum is measured over multiple short segments, and each measurement is averaged. If the noise were stationary and Gaussian, this method would be sufficient. However, the averaging employed in this method is easily impacted by the presence of loud glitches. To address this concern, a different method [159], referred to as the "median method", is often used. This method is identical to Welch's method, but uses the median estimate instead of the mean. This method is less susceptible to short, loud transients, but also introduces a known bias into the spectral measurement, even in the idealized case [159]. However, this bias is typically accounted for by normalizing the measured PSD by the expected bias. In cases where the data are not stationary, both methods are unable to account for this variation. Both methods also are known to have biases for spectral measurements of non-stationary, non-Gaussian noise [160,161]. A comparison between the PSD of data containing a glitch estimated using the median method and Welch's method is shown in Figure 12. The PSD estimated using Welch's method shows large deviations from the true PSD due to the presence of the glitch, while the PSD estimating using the median method shows fewer deviations.

To account for these limitations, LVK analyses have typically used the BayesLine algorithm [138,140] for spectral measurements. BayesLine models the noise over fixed timescales as the combination of a stationary and Gaussian noise background with potentially non-Gaussian transients present. The noise curve is fit using a spline and Lorentzians. This model has been shown to model the instantaneous noise of the detectors better than the methods previously described [162]. However, this does not account for potential non-stationarities. For analyses that use a few seconds of data, this is generally not a concern, but may become important as detectors become more sensitive and the duration of astrophysical signals increases. A PSD estimated using BayesLine is also shown in Figure 12. Compared to the other two PSD estimation features, features in the PSD with a small bandwidth are not as well captured by the BayesLine PSD. However, over the small timescales considered in analyses of transient gravitational-wave events, these deviations do not measurable.

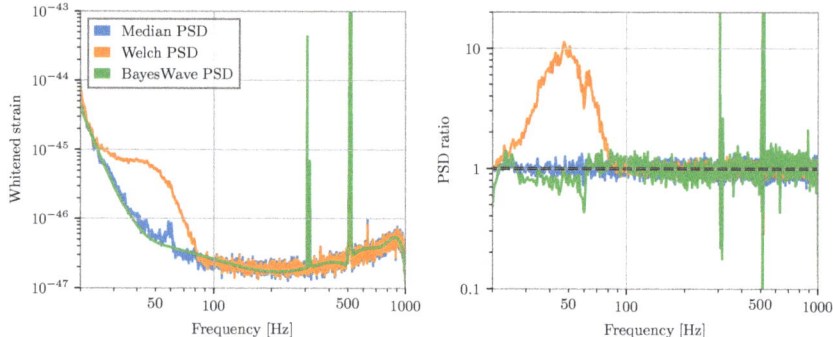

Figure 12. A comparison of different methods to estimate the power spectral density of time domain data that contains a non-Gaussian artifact. Left: The calculated PSD for simulated data using the Median method [159], Welch's method [158], and BayesWave [138,140]. Right: The ratio of the calculated PSD to the known PSD using each method. The PSD calculated with Welch's method is severely biased due to the non-Gaussian artifact in the data. The BayesWave PSD does not capture all of the features in the known PSD due to fitting the PSD with a spline, but has the benefit of using significantly less data than the Median method and hence is less impacted by non-stationary noise. Plotted data are simulated using GWpy [163] and Bilby [164].

Additional Bayesian techniques were proposed, including marginalizing over the power spectral density uncertainty [165] and using different likelihood models that are better suited for non-stationary noise [160,161].

For analyses that use large stretches of data, it is not possible to assume that the noise is stationary over the full timescale considered. Multiple methods are currently used to address this challenge. The simplest solution is to reduce the timescale over which the noise is measured [76]. The measured noise properties can be allowed to change between each segments, and the measured noise spectrum for each segment is only used for analysis of that segment of data. This method is sufficient as long as the timescale over which the PSD is re-measured is shorter than the timescale over which the PSD varies. In practice, it is not possible to measure the PSD over such a short timescale. An alternate method is to allow the measured noise properties to drift with respect to time [166]. The use of a rolling, geometric mean of the noise spectrum can better account for shorter timescale changes than simply analyzing short segments of data.

To account for even shorter fluctuations in the noise properties, it is possible to develop specialized methods that account for the impact of such noise fluctuations on the analysis. In the case of matched filtering, the effect of a mis-measured PSD on the measured variance of the matched filter can be analytically computed [106,153]. This statistic can be measured over short timescales, and the relevant correction can be applied. This method can also be used for the specific PSD used in parameter estimation analyses [167]. While this method does allow for the tracking of short-duration variations in the spectrum, it is not generalizable to all use cases.

6. Ongoing Developments

The characterization of gravitational-wave detectors and mitigation of identified noise artifacts is an essential element of gravitational-wave data analysis. The non-idealized nature of ground-based gravitational-wave detectors ensures that careful studies of these detectors and their data will increase the overall sensitivity of the detector. Even in the best-case scenarios, the high rate of instrumental artifacts in the data means that noise mitigation procedures must be used to confidently detect gravitational waves and make statements about their source properties.

Alongside characterization of currently operating ground-based detectors, research is actively underway to understand how these methods will be a part of observations with next-generation detectors. Metrics that are being used to evaluate potential locations for these instruments include the impact of environmental sources on their overall sensitivity [168–170]. Noise sources that are currently sub-dominant, such as laser frequency noise [171] and correlated magnetic noise [172], are expected to become major limitations for future analyses. The vastly increased sensitivity of these detectors means that common assumptions used in detector characterization analyses, such as the lack of correlated noise between detectors, will no longer be valid. These differences mean that careful monitoring and subtraction of correlated [173] and uncorrelated noise [170,174–176] will play an important role in next-generation analyses.

Detector characterization and noise mitigation efforts are expected to also be a component of analysis of data from space-based detectors. Methods to flag non-stationary noise in LISA [177], separate instrumental artifacts from astrophysical signals [178], and use gap-filling to address missing data [179,180] have already been proposed.

One of the most fundamental changes expected in future detector characterization and noise mitigation developments is an increased reliance on automation and machine learning [18]. The high rate of detection with future detectors will prevent the same level of human involvement in the vast majority of detected gravitational-wave events. Furthermore, the significantly increased size of ground-based detectors will make site-based detector investigations more challenging while space-based investigations may be impossible. However, the methods discussed in this work will lay the groundwork for how detector characterization and noise mitigation will be completed for decades to come.

Author Contributions: Investigation, D.D., M.W.; writing—review and editing, D.D., M.W.; writing—review and editing, D.D., M.W.; visualization, D.D. All authors have read and agreed to the published version of the manuscript.

Funding: DD is supported by the National Science Foundation as part of the LIGO Laboratory, which operates under cooperative agreement PHY-1764464. MW is supported by NSF award PHY-2011975.

Institutional Review Board Statement: Not applicable

Informed Consent Statement: Not applicable

Data Availability Statement: Publicly available datasets were analyzed in this study. All gravitational-wave strain data used for visualizations in this work is from the Gravitational-wave Open Science Center (GWOSC) [23].

Acknowledgments: The authors would like to thanks the other members of the LIGO, Virgo, and KAGRA detector characterization groups who have contributed the wide array of knowledge discussed in this review. We also thank Brennan Hughey for providing numerous helpful comments during the preparation of this article and Laura Nuttall and Ling Sun for providing access to data and figures reproduced in this article. This research has made use of data, software and/or web tools obtained from the Gravitational Wave Open Science Center (https://www.gw-openscience.org/, accessed on 17 December 2021), a service of LIGO Laboratory, the LIGO Scientific Collaboration and the Virgo Collaboration. LIGO Laboratory and Advanced LIGO are funded by the United States National Science Foundation (NSF) as well as the Science and Technology Facilities Council (STFC) of the United Kingdom, the Max–Planck–Society (MPS), and the State of Niedersachsen/Germany for support of the construction of Advanced LIGO and construction and operation of the GEO600 detector. Additional support for Advanced LIGO was provided by the Australian Research Council. Virgo is funded, through the European Gravitational Observatory (EGO), by the French Centre National de Recherche Scientifique (CNRS), the Italian Istituto Nazionale di Fisica Nucleare (INFN) and the Dutch Nikhef, with contributions by institutions from Belgium, Germany, Greece, Hungary, Ireland, Japan, Monaco, Poland, Portugal, Spain.

Conflicts of Interest: The authors declare no conflict of interest.

Abbreviations

The following abbreviations are used in this manuscript:

LIGO	Laser Interferometer Gravitational-wave Observatory
LHO	LIGO Hanford Observatory
LLO	LIGO Livingston Observatory
KAGRA	Kamioka Gravitational Wave Detector
LISA	Laser Interferometer Space Antenna
LVC	LIGO-Virgo Collaboration
GWOSC	Gravitational-Wave Open Science Center
O1	Observing Run 1
O2	Observing Run 2
O3	Observing Run 3
GW	Gravitational Wave
SNR	Signal-to-Noise Ratio
BNS	Binary Neutron Star
CBC	Compact Binary Coalescence
IMBH	Intermediate-Mass Black Hole
GR	General Relativity
ASD	Amplitude Spectral Density
PSD	Power Spectral Density
PEM	Physical Environment Monitoring
DMT	Data Monitoring Tool
UPV	Used Percentage Veto
HVeto	Hierarchical Veto
NoEMi	Noise frequency Event Miner
GstLAL	Gstreamer and the LIGO Algorithm Library search pipeline
MBTA	Multi-Band Template Analysis search pipeline
PyGRB	Python-based Gamma Ray Burst search pipeline
SPIIR	Summed Parallel Infinite Impulse Response search pipeline
cWB	Coherent WaveBurst search pipeline

References

1. Aasi, J.; Abbott, B.P.; Abbott, R.; Abbott, T.; Abernathy, M.R.; Ackley, K.; Adams, C.; Adams, T.; Addesso, P.; Adhikari, R.X.; et al. Advanced LIGO. *Class. Quantum Gravity* **2015**, *32*, 074001, [CrossRef]
2. Acernese, F.; Agathos, M.; Agatsuma, K.; Aisa, D.; Allemandou, N.; Allocca, A.; Amarni, J.; Astone, P.; Balestri, G.; Ballardin, G.; et al. Advanced Virgo: A second-generation interferometric gravitational wave detector. *Class. Quantum Gravity* **2015**, *32*, 024001, [CrossRef]
3. Abbott, B.P.; Abbott, R.; Abbott, T.D.; Abernathy, M.R.; Acernese, F.; Ackley, K.; Adams, C.; Adams, T.; Addesso, P.; Adhikari, R.X.; et al. Observation of Gravitational Waves from a Binary Black Hole Merger. *Phys. Rev. Lett.* **2016**, *116*, 061102, [CrossRef] [PubMed]
4. Abbott, B.P.; Abbott, R.; Abbott, T.D.; Abraham, S.; Acernese, F.; Ackley, K.; Adams, C.; Adhikari, R.X.; Adya, V.B.; Affeldt, C.; et al. GWTC-1: A Gravitational-Wave Transient Catalog of Compact Binary Mergers Observed by LIGO and Virgo during the First and Second Observing Runs. *Phys. Rev. X* **2019**, *9*, 031040, [CrossRef]
5. Abbott, R.; Abbott, T.D.; Abraham, S.; Acernese, F.; Ackley, K.; Adams, A.; Adams, C.; Adhikari, R.X.; Adya, V.B.; Affeldt, C.; et al. GWTC-2: Compact Binary Coalescences Observed by LIGO and Virgo During the First Half of the Third Observing Run. *Phys. Rev. X* **2021**, *11*, 021053, [CrossRef]
6. Abbott, R.; Abbott, T.D.; Acernese, F.; Ackley, K.; Adams, C.; Adhikari, N.; Adhikari, R.X.; Adya, V.B.; Affeldt, C.; Agarwal, D.; et al. GWTC-2.1: Deep Extended Catalog of Compact Binary Coalescences Observed by LIGO and Virgo during the First Half of the Third Observing Run. Available online: https://arxiv.org/abs/2108.01045 (accessed on 17 December 2021).
7. Abbott, R.; Abbott, T.D.; Acernese, F.; Ackley, K.; Adams, C.; Adhikari, N.; Adhikari, R.X.; Adya, V.B.; Affeldt, C.; Agarwal, D.; et al. GWTC-3: Compact Binary Coalescences Observed by LIGO and Virgo During the Second Part of the Third Observing Run. Available online: https://arxiv.org/abs/2111.03606 (accessed on 17 December 2021).
8. Abbott, R.; Abbott, T.D.; Acernese, F.; Ackley, K.; Adams, C.; Adhikari, N.; Adhikari, R.X.; Adya, V.B.; Affeldt, C.; Agarwal, D.; et al. The Population of Merging Compact Binaries Inferred Using Gravitational Waves through GWTC-3. Available online: https://arxiv.org/abs/2111.03634 (accessed on 17 December 2021).
9. Abbott, B.P.; Abbott, R.; Abbott, T.D.; Acernese, F.; Ackley, K.; Adams, C.; Adams, T.; Addesso, P.; Adhikari, R.X.; Adya, V.B.; et al. GW170817: Observation of Gravitational Waves from a Binary Neutron Star Inspiral. *Phys. Rev. Lett.* **2017**, *119*, 161101, [CrossRef]

10. Abbott, R.; Abbott, T.D.; Abraham, S.; Acernese, F.; Ackley, K.; Adams, A.; Adams, C.; Adhikari, R.X.; Adya, V.B.; Affeldt, C.; et al. Tests of general relativity with binary black holes from the second LIGO-Virgo gravitational-wave transient catalog. *Phys. Rev. D* **2021**, *103*, 122002, [CrossRef]
11. Abbott, R.; Abbott, T.D.; Abraham, S.; Acernese, F.; Ackley, K.; Adams, C.; Adhikari, R.X.; Adya, V.B.; Affeldt, C.; Agathos, M.; et al. GW190521: A Binary Black Hole Merger with a Total Mass of 150 $M_\odot$. *Phys. Rev. Lett.* **2020**, *125*, 101102, [CrossRef]
12. Abbott, R.; Abbott, T.D.; Abraham, S.; Acernese, F.; Ackley, K.; Adams, C.; Adhikari, R.X.; Adya, V.B.; Affeldt, C.; Agathos, M.; et al. GW190814: Gravitational Waves from the Coalescence of a 23 Solar Mass Black Hole with a 2.6 Solar Mass Compact Object. *Astrophys. J.* **2020**, *896*, L44, [CrossRef]
13. Kötter, K.; Aulbert, C.; Babak, S.; Balasubramanian, R.; Berukoff, S.; Bose, S.; Churches, D.; Colacino, C.N.; Cutler, C.; Danzmann, K.; et al. Data acquisition and detector characterization of GEO600. *Class. Quantum Gravity* **2002**, *19*, 1399–1407. [CrossRef]
14. Blackburn, L.; Cadonati, L.; Caride, S.; Caudill, S.; Chatterji, S.; Christensen, N.; Dalrymple, J.; Desai, S.; Di Credico, A.; Ely, G.; et al. The LSC Glitch Group: Monitoring Noise Transients during the fifth LIGO Science Run. *Class. Quantum Gravity* **2008**, *25*, 184004, [CrossRef]
15. Aasi, J.; Abadie, J.; Abbott, B.P.; Abbott, R.; Abbott, T.D.; Abernathy, M.; Accadia, T.; Acernese, F.; Adams, C.; Adams, T.; et al. The characterization of Virgo data and its impact on gravitational-wave searches. *Class. Quantum Gravity* **2012**, *29*, 155002, [CrossRef]
16. Nuttall, L.K.; Massinger, T.J.; Areeda, J.; Betzwieser, J.; Dwyer, S.; Effler, A.; Fisher, R.P.; Fritschel, P.; Kissel, J.S.; Lundgren, A.P.; et al. Improving the Data Quality of Advanced LIGO Based on Early Engineering Run Results. *Class. Quantum Gravity* **2015**, *32*, 245005, [CrossRef]
17. Abbott, B.P.; Abbott, R.; Abbott, T.D.; Abernathy, M.R.; Acernese, F.; Ackley, K.; Adamo, M.; Adams, C.; Adams, T.; Addesso, P.; et al. Characterization of transient noise in Advanced LIGO relevant to gravitational wave signal GW150914. *Class. Quantum Gravity* **2016**, *33*, 134001, [CrossRef] [PubMed]
18. Davis, D.; Areeda, J.S.; Berger, B.K.; Bruntz, R.; Effler, A.; Essick, R.C.; Fisher, R.P.; Godwin, P.; Goetz, E.; Helmling-Cornell, A.F.; et al. LIGO detector characterization in the second and third observing runs. *Class. Quantum Gravity* **2021**, *38*, 135014, [CrossRef]
19. Akutsu, T.; Ando, M.; Arai, K.; Arai, Y.; Araki, S.; Araya, A.; Aritomi, N.; Asada, H.; Aso, Y.; Bae, S.; et al. Overview of KAGRA: Calibration, Detector Characterization, Physical Environmental Monitors, and the Geophysics Interferometer. Available online: https://arxiv.org/abs/2009.09305 (accessed on 17 December 2021).
20. Grote, H. The GEO 600 status. *Class. Quantum Gravity* **2010**, *27*, 084003. [CrossRef]
21. Akutsu, T.; Ando, M.; Arai, K.; Arai, Y.; Araki, S.; Araya, A.; Aritomi, N.; Asada, H.; Aso, Y.; Atsuta, S.; et al. KAGRA: 2.5 Generation Interferometric Gravitational Wave Detector. *Nat. Astron.* **2019**, *3*, 35–40. [CrossRef]
22. Iyer, B.; Souradeep, T.; Unnikrishnan, C.S.; Dhurandhar, S.; Raja, S.; Sengupta, A. LIGO-India, Proposal of the Consortium for Indian Initiative in Gravitational-Wave Observations (IndIGO). Available online: https://dcc.ligo.org/LIGO-M1100296/public (accessed on 17 December 2021).
23. Abbott, R.; Abbott, T.D.; Abraham, S.; Acernese, F.; Ackley, K.; Adams, C.; Adhikari, R.X.; Adya, V.B.; Affeldt, C.; Agathos, M.; et al. Open data from the first and second observing runs of Advanced LIGO and Advanced Virgo. *SoftwareX* **2021**, *13*, 100658. [CrossRef]
24. Abbott, B.P.; Abbott, R.; Abbott, T.D.; Abraham, S.; Acernese, F.; Ackley, K.; Adams, C.; Adya, V.B.; Affeldt, C.; Agathos, M.; et al. A guide to LIGO–Virgo detector noise and extraction of transient gravitational-wave signals. *Class. Quantum Gravity* **2020**, *37*, 055002, [CrossRef]
25. Nguyen, P.; Schofield, R.M.S.; Effler, A.; Austin, C.; Adya, V.; Ball, M.; Banagiri, S.; Banowetz, K.; Billman, C.; Blair, C.D.; et al. Environmental noise in advanced LIGO detectors. *Class. Quantum Gravity* **2021**, *38*, 145001, [CrossRef]
26. Matichard, F.; Lantz, B.; Mittleman, R.; Mason, K.; Kissel, J.; Abbott, B.; Biscans, S.; McIver, J.; Abbott, R.; Abbott, S.; et al. Seismic isolation of Advanced LIGO: Review of strategy, instrumentation and performance. *Class. Quantum Gravity* **2015**, *32*, 185003. [CrossRef]
27. Aston, S.M.; Barton, M.A.; Bell, A.S.; Beveridge, N.; Bland, B.; Brummitt, A.J.; Cagnoli, G.; Cantley, C.A.; Carbone, L.; Cumming, A.V.; et al. Update on quadruple suspension design for Advanced LIGO. *Class. Quantum Gravity* **2012**, *29*, 235004. [CrossRef]
28. Walker, M.; Abbott, T.D.; Aston, S.M.; González, G.; Macleod, D.M.; McIver, J.; Abbott, B.P.; Abbott, R.; Adams, C.; Adhikari, R.X.; et al. Effects of transients in LIGO suspensions on searches for gravitational waves. *Rev. Sci. Instrum.* **2017**, *88*, 124501, [CrossRef]
29. MacLeod, D.M.; Fairhurst, S.; Hughey, B.; Lundgren, A.P.; Pekowsky, L.; Rollins, J.; Smith, J.R. Reducing the effect of seismic noise in LIGO searches by targeted veto generation. *Class. Quantum Gravity* **2012**, *29*, 055006, [CrossRef]
30. Nuttall, L.K. Characterizing transient noise in the LIGO detectors. *Philos. Trans. R. Soc. Lond. Math. Phys. Eng. Sci.* **2018**, *376*, 20170286 . [CrossRef] [PubMed]
31. Berger, B.K. Identification and mitigation of Advanced LIGO noise sources. *J. Phys. Conf. Ser.* **2018**, *957*, 012004. [CrossRef]
32. McIver, J.; Massinger, T.J.; Robinet, F.; Smith, J.R.; Walker, M. Diagnostic methods for gravitational-wave detectors. In *ADVANCED INTERFEROMETRIC GRAVITATIONAL-WAVE DETECTORS: Volume I: Essentials of Gravitational-Wave Detectors*; World Scientific: Singapore, 2019; pp. 373–392.
33. Macleod, D.; Urban, A.L.; Isi, M.; Massinger, T.; Paulaltin; Pitkin, M.; Nitz, A. gwpy/gwsumm: 1.0.3. Available online: https://zenodo.org/record/3765457#.Yd9jUS-B1QI (accessed on 17 December 2021).
34. Urban, A.L.; Macleod, D.; Anderson, S.; Baryoga, J. LIGO DetChar Summary Pages. Available online: https://summary.ligo.org (accessed on 17 December 2021).

35. Robinet, F.; Arnaud, N.; Leroy, N.; Lundgren, A.; Macleod, D.; McIver, J. Omicron: A tool to characterize transient noise in gravitational-wave detectors. *SoftwareX* **2020**, *12*, 100620 , [CrossRef]
36. Macleod, D.; Urban, A.L. gwpy/pyomicron: 1.1.0. Available online: https://zenodo.org/record/3973543#.Yd9g0i-B1QI (accessed on 17 December 2021).
37. Blackburn, L. *KleineWelle Technical Document*. Available online: https://dcc.ligo.org/LIGO-T060221/public (accessed on 17 December 2021).
38. Abbott, B.P.; Abbott, R.; Abbott, T.D.; Abernathy, M.R.; Acernese, F.; Ackley, K.; Adams, C.; Adams, T.; Addesso, P.; Adhikari, R.X.; et al. Effects of data quality vetoes on a search for compact binary coalescences in Advanced LIGO's first observing run. *Class. Quantum Gravity* **2018**, *35*, 065010, [CrossRef]
39. Nitz, A.H.; Dal Canton, T.; Davis, D.; Reyes, S. Rapid detection of gravitational waves from compact binary mergers with PyCBC Live. *Phys. Rev. D* **2018**, *98*, 024050, [CrossRef]
40. Gstreamer Plugins for the LSC Algorithm Library. 2016. Available online: https://www.lsc-group.phys.uwm.edu/daswg/projects/gstlal.html (accessed on 17 December 2021).
41. Chatterji, S.; Blackburn, L.; Martin, G.; Katsavounidis, E. Multiresolution techniques for the detection of gravitational-wave bursts. *Class. Quantum Gravity* **2004**, *21*, S1809–S1818, [CrossRef]
42. Chatterji, S. The Search For Gravitational Wave Bursts in Data from the Second LIGO Science Run. Ph.D. Thesis, Massachusetts Institute of Technology, Cambridge, MA, USA, 2005.
43. Christensen, N.; Shawhan, P.; Gonzalez, G. Vetoes for inspiral triggers in LIGO data. *Class. Quantum Gravity* **2004**, *21*, S1747–S1756, [CrossRef]
44. Robinet, F. Data quality in gravitational wave bursts and inspiral searches in the second Virgo Science Run. *Class. Quantum Gravity* **2010**, *27*, 194012. [CrossRef]
45. Cabero, M.; Lundgren, A.; Nitz, A.H.; Dent, T.; Barker, D.; Goetz, E.; Kissel, J.S.; Nuttall, L.K.; Schale, P.; Schofield, R.; et al. Blip glitches in Advanced LIGO data. *Class. Quantum Gravity* **2019**, *36*, 155010, [CrossRef]
46. Soni, S.; Austin, C.; Effler, A.; Schofield, R.M.S.; Gonzalez, G.; Frolov, V.V.; Driggers, J.C.; Pele, A.; Urban, A.L.; Valdes, G.; et al. Reducing scattered light in LIGO's third observing run. *Class. Quantum Gravity* **2020**, *38*, 025016, [CrossRef]
47. Zevin, M.; Coughlin, S.; Bahaadini, S.; Besler, E.; Rohani, N.; Allen, S.; Cabero, M.; Crowston, K.; Katsaggelos, A.K.; Larson, S.L.; et al. Gravity Spy: Integrating Advanced LIGO Detector Characterization, Machine Learning, and Citizen Science. *Class. Quantum Gravity* **2017**, *34*, 064003, [CrossRef] [PubMed]
48. Coughlin, S.; Bahaadini, S.; Rohani, N.; Zevin, M.; Patane, O.; Harandi, M.; Jackson, C.; Noroozi, V.; Allen, S.; Areeda, J.; et al. Classifying the unknown: discovering novel gravitational-wave detector glitches using similarity learning. *Phys. Rev. D* **2019**, *99*, 082002, [CrossRef]
49. Soni, S.; Berry, C.P.L.; Coughlin, S.B.; Harandi, M.; Jackson, C.B.; Crowston, K.; Østerlund, C.; Patane, O.; Katsaggelos, A.K.; Trouille, L.; et al. Discovering features in gravitational-wave data through detector characterization, citizen science and machine learning. newblock *Class. Quantum Gravity* **2021**, *38*, 195016, [CrossRef]
50. Smith, J.R.; Abbott, T.; Hirose, E.; Leroy, N.; Macleod, D.; McIver, J.; Saulson, P.; Shawhan, P. A Hierarchical method for vetoing noise transients in gravitational-wave detectors. *Class. Quantum Gravity* **2011**, *28*, 235005, [CrossRef]
51. Macleod, D.; Urban, A.L.; Smith, J.; Massinger, T. gwdetchar/hveto: 1.0.1. Available online: https://zenodo.org/record/3532131#.Yd9k3i-B1QI (accessed on 17 December 2021).
52. Isogai, T. Used percentage veto for LIGO and virgo binary inspiral searches. *J. Phys. Conf. Ser.* **2010**, *243*, 012005. [CrossRef]
53. Essick, R.; Godwin, P.; Hanna, C.; Blackburn, L.; Katsavounidis, E. iDQ: Statistical inference of non-gaussian noise with auxiliary degrees of freedom in gravitational-wave detectors. *Mach. Learn. Sci. Technol.* **2020**, *2*, 015004. [CrossRef]
54. Valdes, G.; O'Reilly, B.; Diaz, M. A Hilbert–Huang transform method for scattering identification in LIGO. *Class. Quantum Gravity* **2017**, *34*, 235009. [CrossRef]
55. Bianchi, S.; Longo, A.; Valdes, G.; González, G.; Plastino, W. Gwadaptive_Scattering: an Automated Pipeline for Scattered Light Noise Characterization. Available online: https://arxiv.org/abs/2107.07565 (accessed on 17 December 2021).
56. Valdes, G. *Thunderstorms Identification tool in LIGO*. Available online: https://dcc.ligo.org/LIGO-T2000602/public (accessed on 17 December 2021).
57. Valdes, G. Localizing Acoustic Noise Sources Affecting the Sensitivity of LIGO through Multilateration. Available online: https://dcc.ligo.org/LIGO-T2000618/public (accessed on 17 December 2021).
58. Himemoto, Y.; Taruya, A. Correlated magnetic noise from anisotropic lightning sources and the detection of stochastic gravitational waves. *Phys. Rev. D* **2019**, *100*, 082001, [CrossRef]
59. Washimi, T.; Yokozawa, T.; Nakano, M.; Tanaka, T.; Kaihotsu, K.; Mori, Y.; Narita, T. Effects of lightning strokes on underground gravitational waves observatories. *JINST* **2021**, *16*, P07033, [CrossRef]
60. Effler, A.; Schofield, R.M.S.; Frolov, V.V.; Gonzalez, G.; Kawabe, K.; Smith, J.R.; Birch, J.; McCarthy, R. Environmental Influences on the LIGO Gravitational Wave Detectors during the 6th Science Run. *Class. Quantum Gravity* **2015**, *32*, 035017, [CrossRef]
61. Fiori, I.; Paoletti, F.; Tringali, M.C.; Janssens, K.; Karathanasis, C.; Menéndez-Vázquez, A.; Romero-Rodríguez, A.; Sugimoto, R.; Washimi, T.; Boschi, V.; et al. The Hunt for Environmental Noise in Virgo during the Third Observing Run. *Galaxies* **2020**, *8*, 82. [CrossRef]

62. Washimi, T.; Yokozawa, T.; Tanaka, T.; Itoh, Y.; Kume, J.; Yokoyama, J. Method for environmental noise estimation via injection tests for ground-based gravitational wave detectors. *Class. Quantum Gravity* **2021**, *38*, 125005, [CrossRef]
63. LIGO Scientific Collaboration and Virgo Collaboration. *O2 Data Release*. Available online: https://www.gw-openscience.org/O2/ (accessed on 17 December 2021).
64. Covas, P.B.; Effler, A.; Goetz, E.; Meyers, P.M.; Neunzert, A.; Oliver, M.; Pearlstone, B.L.; Roma, V.J.; Schofield, R.M.S.; Adya, V.B.; et al. Identification and mitigation of narrow spectral artifacts that degrade searches for persistent gravitational waves in the first two observing runs of Advanced LIGO. *Phys. Rev. D* **2018**, *97*, 082002, [CrossRef]
65. Coughlin, M. Noise line identification in LIGO S6 and Virgo VSR2. *J. Phys. Conf. Ser.* **2010**, *243*, 012010, [CrossRef]
66. Accadia, T.; Acernese, F.; Agathos, M.; Astone, P.; Ballardin, G.; Barone, F.; Barsuglia, M.; Basti, A.; Bauer, T.S.; Bebronne, M.; et al. The NoEMi (Noise Frequency Event Miner) framework. *J. Phys. Conf. Ser.* **2012**, *363*, 012037. [CrossRef]
67. Walker, M.; Agnew, A.F.; Bidler, J.; Lundgren, A.; Macedo, A.; Macleod, D.; Massinger, T.; Patane, O.; Smith, J.R. Identifying correlations between LIGO's astronomical range and auxiliary sensors using lasso regression. *Class. Quantum Gravity* **2018**, *35*, 225002, [CrossRef]
68. Biscans, S.; Warner, J.; Mittleman, R.; Buchanan, C.; Coughlin, M.; Evans, M.; Gabbard, H.; Harms, J.; Lantz, B.; Mukund, N.; et al. Control strategy to limit duty cycle impact of earthquakes on the LIGO gravitational-wave detectors. *Class. Quantum Gravity* **2018**, *35*, 055004, [CrossRef]
69. Biswas, A.; McIver, J.; Mahabal, A. New methods to assess and improve LIGO detector duty cycle. *Class. Quantum Gravity* **2020**, *37*, 175008, [CrossRef]
70. Schwartz, E.; Pele, A.; Warner, J.; Lantz, B.; Betzwieser, J.; Dooley, K.L.; Biscans, S.; Coughlin, M.; Mukund, N.; Abbott, R.; et al. Improving the robustness of the advanced LIGO detectors to earthquakes. *Class. Quantum Gravity* **2020**, *37*, 235007, [CrossRef]
71. Coughlin, M.W.; Cirone, A.; Meyers, P.; Atsuta, S.; Boschi, V.; Chincarini, A.; Christensen, N.L.; De Rosa, R.; Effler, A.; Fiori, I.; et al. Measurement and subtraction of Schumann resonances at gravitational-wave interferometers. *Phys. Rev. D* **2018**, *97*, 102007. [CrossRef]
72. Ball, M.; Schofield, R.; Frey, R. *Intersite Magnetic Signals from Lightning*. Available online: https://dcc.ligo.org/LIGO-T2000634/public (accessed on 17 December 2021).
73. Abbott, R.; Abbott, T.D.; Abraham, S.; Acernese, F.; Ackley, K.; Adams, A.; Adams, C.; Adhikari, R.X.; Adya, V.B.; Affeldt, C.; et al. Upper Limits on the Isotropic Gravitational-Wave Background from Advanced LIGO and Advanced Virgo's Third Observing Run; Tests of general relativity with binary black holes from the second LIGO-Virgo gravitational-wave transient catalog. *Phys. Rev. D* **2021**, *104*, 022004, [CrossRef]
74. Cirone, A.; Fiori, I.; Paoletti, F.; Perez, M.M.; Rodríguez, A.R.; Swinkels, B.L.; Vazquez, A.M.; Gemme, G.; Chincarini, A. Investigation of magnetic noise in Advanced Virgo. *Class. Quantum Gravity* **2019**, *36*, 225004, [CrossRef]
75. Abbott, B.P.; Abbott, R.; Abbott, T.D.; Abraham, S.; Acernese, F.; Ackley, K.; Adams, C.; Adya, V.B.; Affeldt, C.; Agathos, M.; et al. Optically targeted search for gravitational waves emitted by core-collapse supernovae during the first and second observing runs of advanced LIGO and advanced Virgo. *Phys. Rev. D* **2020**, *101*, 084002, [CrossRef]
76. Usman, S.A.; Nitz, A.H.; Harry, I.W.; Biwer, C.M.; Brown, D.A.; Cabero, M.; Capano, C.D.; Dal Canton, T.; Dent, T.; Fairhurst, S.; et al. The PyCBC search for gravitational waves from compact binary coalescence. *Class. Quantum Gravity* **2016**, *33*, 215004, [CrossRef]
77. Messick, C.; Blackburn, K.; Brady, P.; Brockill, P.; Cannon, K.; Cariou, R.; Caudill, S.; Chamberlin, S.J.; Creighton, J.D.E.; Everett, R.; et al. Analysis Framework for the Prompt Discovery of Compact Binary Mergers in Gravitational-wave Data. *Phys. Rev. D* **2017**, *95*, 042001, [CrossRef]
78. Aubin, F.; Brighenti, F.; Chierici, R.; Estevez, D.; Greco, G.; Guidi, G.M.; Juste, V.; Marion, F.; Mours, B.; Nitoglia, E.; et al. The MBTA Pipeline for Detecting Compact Binary Coalescences in the Third LIGO-Virgo Observing Run. *Class. Quantum Gravity* **2021**, *38*, 095004, [CrossRef]
79. Chu, Q.; Kovalam, M.j; Wen, L.; Slaven-Blair, T.; Bosveld, J.; Chen, Y.; Clearwater, P.; Codoreanu, A.; Du, Z.; Guo, X.; et al. The SPIIR online coherent pipeline to search for gravitational waves from compact binary coalescences. *arXiv* **2020**, arXiv:gr-qc/2011.06787.
80. Klimenko, S.; Yakushin, I.; Mercer, A.; Mitselmakher, G. Coherent method for detection of gravitational wave bursts. *Class. Quantum Gravity* **2008**, *25*, 114029. [CrossRef]
81. Sutton, P.J.; Jones, G.; Chatterji, S.; Kalmus, P.; Leonor, I.; Poprocki, S.; Rollins, J.; Searle, A.; Stein, L.; Tinto, M.; et al. X-Pipeline: An Analysis package for autonomous gravitational-wave burst searches. *New J. Phys.* **2010**, *12*, 053034, [CrossRef]
82. Venumadhav, T.; Zackay, B.; Roulet, J.; Dai, L.; Zaldarriaga, M. New search pipeline for compact binary mergers: Results for binary black holes in the first observing run of Advanced LIGO. *Phys. Rev. D* **2019**, *100*, 023011, [CrossRef]
83. Nitz, A.H.; Capano, C.D.; Kumar, S.; Wang, Y.F.; Kastha, S.; Schäfer, M.; Dhurkunde, R.; Cabero, M. 3-OGC: Catalog of gravitational waves from compact-binary mergers. *Astrophys. J.* **2021**, *922*, 76. [CrossRef]
84. LIGO Scientific Collaboration and Virgo Collaboration. *Data Quality Vetoes Applied to the Analysis of GW150914*. Available online: https://dcc.ligo.org/LIGO-T1600011/public (accessed on 17 December 2021).
85. Davis, D.; Hughey, B.; Massinger, T.; Nuttall, L.; Stuver, A.; Zweizig, J.; Berger, B.; Bruntz, R.; Fisher, R.; Lundgren, A.; et al. LIGO Data Quality Vetoes Applied to the Analysis of O3. Available online: https://dcc.ligo.org/T2100045/public (accessed on 17 December 2021).

86. Biwer, C.; Barker, D.; Batch, J.C.; Betzwieser, J.; Fisher, R.P.; Goetz, E.; Kandhasamy, S.; Karki, S.; Kissel, J.S.; Lundgren, A.P.; et al. Validating gravitational-wave detections: The Advanced LIGO hardware injection system. *Phys. Rev. D* **2017**, *95*, 062002. [CrossRef]
87. Nitz, A.H.; Dent, T.; Dal Canton, T.; Fairhurst, S.; Brown, D.A. Detecting binary compact-object mergers with gravitational waves: Understanding and Improving the sensitivity of the PyCBC search. *Astrophys. J.* **2017**, *849*, 118, [CrossRef]
88. Davis, D.; White, L.V.; Saulson, P.R. Utilizing aLIGO Glitch Classifications to Validate Gravitational-Wave Candidates. *Class. Quantum Gravity* **2020**, *37*, 145001, [CrossRef]
89. Godwin, P.; Essick, R.; Hanna, C.; Cannon, K.; Caudill, S.; Chan, C.; Creighton, J.D.E.; Fong, H.; Katsavounidis, E.; Magee, R.; et al. Incorporation of Statistical Data Quality Information into the GstLAL Search Analysis. Available online: https://arxiv.org/abs/2010.15282 (accessed on 17 December 2021).
90. LIGO Scientific Collaboration and Virgo Collaboration. *O3A Data Release*. Available online: https://www.gw-openscience.org/O3/O3a/ (accessed on 17 December 2021).
91. LIGO Scientific Collaboration, Virgo Collaboration, and KAGRA Collaboration. GWTC-3: Compact Binary Coalescences Observed by LIGO and Virgo During the Second Part of the Third Observing Run—Data Quality Products for GW Searches. Available online: https://zenodo.org/record/5636796#.Yd9rXy-B1QI (accessed on 17 December 2021).
92. Abbott, R.; Abbott, T.D.; Abraham, S.; Acernese, F.; Ackley, K.; Adams, A.; Adams, C.; Adhikari, R.X.; Adya, V.B.; Affeldt, C.; et al. All-sky search for continuous gravitational waves from isolated neutron stars in the early O3 LIGO data. *Phys. Rev. D* **2021**, *104*, 082004, [CrossRef]
93. Abbott, R.; Abbott, T.D.; Abraham, S.; Acernese, F.; Ackley, K.; Adams, A.; Adams, C.; Adhikari, R.X.; Adya, V.B.; Affeldt, C.; et al. All-sky search in early O3 LIGO data for continuous gravitational-wave signals from unknown neutron stars in binary systems. *Phys. Rev. D* **2021**, *103*, 064017, [CrossRef]
94. Abbott, R.; Abbott, T.D.; Acernese, F.; Ackley, K.; Adams, C.; Adhikari, N.; Adhikari, R.X.; Adya, V.B.; Affeldt, C. ; Agarwal, D.; et al. Constraints on Dark Photon Dark Matter Using Data from LIGO's and Virgo's Third Observing Run. Available online: https://arxiv.org/abs/2105.13085 (accessed on 17 December 2021).
95. Steltner, B.; Papa, M.A.; Eggenstein, H.B.; Allen, B.; Dergachev, V.; Prix, R.; Machenschalk, B.; Walsh, S.; Zhu, S.J.; Kwang, S. Einstein@Home All-sky Search for Continuous Gravitational Waves in LIGO O2 Public Data. *Astrophys. J.* **2021**, *909*, 79, [CrossRef]
96. Ashok, A.; Beheshtipour, B.; Papa, M.A.; Freire, P.C.C.; Steltner, B.; Machenschalk, B.; Behnke, O.; Allen, B.; Prix, R. New searches for continuous gravitational waves from seven fast pulsars. *Astrophys. J.* **2021**, *923*, 85. [CrossRef]
97. Renzini, A.; Contaldi, C. Improved limits on a stochastic gravitational-wave background and its anisotropies from Advanced LIGO O1 and O2 runs. *Phys. Rev. D* **2019**, *100*, 063527, [CrossRef]
98. LIGO Scientific Collaboration. O1 Instrumental Lines. Available online: https://www.gw-openscience.org/o1speclines/ (accessed on 17 December 2021).
99. LIGO Scientific and Virgo Collaborations. O2 Instrumental Lines. Available online: https://www.gw-openscience.org/o2speclines/ (accessed on 17 December 2021).
100. LIGO Scientific and Virgo Collaborations. O3 Instrumental Lines. Available online: https://www.gw-openscience.org/O3/o3speclines/ (accessed on 17 December 2021).
101. Areeda, J.S.; Smith, J.R.; Lundgren, A.P.; Maros, E.; Macleod, D.M.; Zweizig, J. LigoDV-web: Providing easy, secure and universal access to a large distributed scientific data store for the LIGO Scientific Collaboration. *Astron. Comput.* **2017**, *18*, 27–34. [CrossRef]
102. Verkindt, D. The Virgo Data Display. Available online: https://tds.virgo-gw.eu/ql/?c=10957 (accessed on 17 December 2021).
103. Verkindt, D. Advanced Virgo: From detector monitoring to gravitational wave alerts. In Proceedings of the 54th Rencontres de Moriond on Gravitation (Moriond Gravitation 2019), La Thuile, Italy, 23–30 March 2019; ARISF: Pars, France, 2019; p. 57.
104. Essick, R.; Mo, G.; Katsavounidis, E. A Coincidence Null Test for Poisson-Distributed Events. *Phys. Rev. D* **2021**, *103*, 042003, [CrossRef]
105. Vajente, G. Analysis of Sensitivity and Noise Sources for the Virgo Gravitational Wave Interferometer. Ph.D. Thesis, Scuola Normale Superiore, Pisa, Italy, 2008.
106. Mozzon, S.; Nuttall, L.K.; Lundgren, A.; Dent, T.; Kumar, S.; Nitz, A.H. Dynamic Normalization for Compact Binary Coalescence Searches in Non-Stationary Noise. *Class. Quantum Gravity* **2020**, *37*, 215014, [CrossRef]
107. Di Renzo, F.; Sorrentino, N. BRISTOL and RAGoUT: Two Tools for Investigating Noise Stationarity and Gaussianity, for Detchar Studies and Data Analysis. Available online: https://tds.virgo-gw.eu/ql/?c=15203 (accessed on 17 December 2021).
108. Macleod, D.; Urban, A.L.; Isi, M.; Paulaltin, T.M.; Pitkin, M.; Nitz, A. gwpy/gwsumm: 1.0.2. Available online: https://zenodo.org/record/3590375#.Yd9lPC-B1QI (accessed on 17 December 2021).
109. Hemming, G.; Verkindt, D. Virgo Interferometer Monitor (VIM) Web User Interface (WUI) User Guide. Available online: https://tds.virgo-gw.eu/ql/?c=11869 (accessed on 17 December 2021).
110. Abbott, B.P.; Abbott, R.; Abbott, T.D.; Acernese, F.; Ackley, K.; Adams, C.; Adams, T.; Addesso, P.; Adhikari, R.X.; Adya, V.B. ; et al. GW170814: A Three-Detector Observation of Gravitational Waves from a Binary Black Hole Coalescence. *Phys. Rev. Lett.* **2017**, *119*, 141101. [CrossRef] [PubMed]
111. Cabero, M.; Mahabal, A.; McIver, J. GWSkyNet: A real-time classifier for public gravitational-wave candidates. *Astrophys. J. Lett.* **2020**, *904*, L9, [CrossRef]

112. Essick, R. *Mutual Information Distance in the "Line-of-Sight" Frame: How to Reject Noise Based on the Basics of Triangulation*. Available online: https://dcc.ligo.org/LIGO-G1602082/public (accessed on 17 December 2021).
113. Abbott, B.P.; Abbott, R.; Abbott, T.D.; Abernathy, M.R.; Acernese, F.; Ackley, K.; Adams, C.; Adams, T.; Addesso, P.; Adhikari, R.X.; et al. Tests of general relativity with GW150914. *Phys. Rev. Lett.* **2016**, *116*, 221101, [CrossRef] [PubMed]
114. Ashton, G.; Thiele, S.; Lecoeuche, Y.; McIver, J.; Nuttall, L.K. Parameterised Population Models of Transient Non-Gaussian Noise in the LIGO Gravitational-Wave Detectors. Available online: https://arxiv.org/abs/2110.02689 (accessed on 17 December 2021).
115. Pace, A.; Prestegard, T.; Moe, B.; Stephens, B. GraCEDb. Available online: https://gracedb.ligo.org (accessed on 17 December 2021).
116. Abbott, R.; Abbott, T.D.; Acernese, F.; Ackley, K.; Adams, C.; Adhikari, N.; Adhikari, R.X.; Adya, V. B.; Affeldt, C.; Agarwal, D.; et al. Search for Intermediate Mass Black Hole Binaries in the Third Observing Run of Advanced LIGO and Advanced Virgo. Available online: https://arxiv.org/abs/2105.15120 (accessed on 17 December 2021).
117. LIGO Scientific Collaboration. *Auxiliary Channel Three Hour Release*. Available online: https://www.gw-openscience.org/auxiliary/GW170814/ (accessed on 17 December 2021).
118. Sun, L.; Brito, R.; Isi, M. Search for ultralight bosons in Cygnus X-1 with Advanced LIGO. *Phys. Rev. D* **2020**, *101*, 063020; Erratum in *Phys. Rev. D* **2020**, *102*, 089902. [CrossRef]
119. Abbott, B.P.; Abbott, R.; Abbott, T.D.; Acernese, F.; Ackley, K.; Adams, C.; Adams, T.; Addesso, P.; Adhikari, R.X.; Adya, V.B.; et al. Search for gravitational waves from Scorpius X-1 in the first Advanced LIGO observing run with a hidden Markov model. *Phys. Rev. D* **2017**, *95*, 122003, [CrossRef]
120. Abbott, B.P.; Abbott, R.; Abbott, T.D.; Abraham, S.; Acernese, F.; Ackley, K.; Adams, C.; Adhikari, R.X.; Adya, V.B.; Affeldt, C.; et al. Search for gravitational waves from Scorpius X-1 in the second Advanced LIGO observing run with an improved hidden Markov model. *Phys. Rev. D* **2019**, *100*, 122002, [CrossRef]
121. Riles, K. Recent searches for continuous gravitational waves. *Phys. Rev. A* **2017**, *32*, 1730035. [CrossRef]
122. Callister, T.; Coughlin, M.W.; Kanner, J.B. Gravitational-wave Geodesy: A New Tool for Validating Detection of the Stochastic Gravitational-wave Background. *Astrophys. J. Lett.* **2018**, *869*, L28, [CrossRef]
123. Driggers, J.C.; Evans, M.; Pepper, K.; Adhikari, R.X. Active noise cancellation in a suspended interferometer. *Rev. Sci. Instrum.* **2012**, *83*, 024501. [CrossRef] [PubMed]
124. Meadors, G.D.; Kawabe, K; Riles, K. Increasing LIGO sensitivity by feedforward subtraction of auxiliary length control noise. *Class. Quantum Gravity* **2014**, *31*, 105014. [CrossRef]
125. Tiwari, V.; Drago, M.; Frolov, V.; Klimenko, S.; Mitselmakher, G.; Necula, V.; Prodi, G.; Re, V.; Salemi, F.; Vedovato, G.; et al. Regression of environmental noise in LIGO data. *Class. Quantum Gravity* **2015**, *32*, 165014. [CrossRef]
126. Wiener, N. *Extrapolation, Interpolation, and Smoothing of Stationary Time Series: With Engineering Applications*; MIT Press: Cambridge, MA, USA, 1964; Volume 8.
127. Ormiston, R.; Nguyen, T.; Coughlin, M.; Adhikari, R.X.; Katsavounidis, E. Noise Reduction in Gravitational-wave Data via Deep Learning. *Phys. Rev. Res.* **2020**, *2*, 033066, [CrossRef]
128. Mukund, N.; Lough, J.; Affeldt, C.; Bergamin, F.; Bisht, A.; Brinkmann, M.; Kringel, V.; Lück, H.; Nadji, S.; Weinert, M.; et al. Bilinear noise subtraction at the GEO 600 observatory. *Phys. Rev. D* **2020**, *101*, 102006, doi:10.1103/PhysRevD.101.102006. [CrossRef]
129. Yu, H.; Adhikari, R.X. Nonlinear Noise Regression in Gravitational-Wave Detectors with Convolutional Neural Networks. Available online: https://arxiv.org/abs/2111.03295 (accessed on 17 December 2021).
130. Davis, D.; Massinger, T.J.; Lundgren, A.P.; Driggers, J.C.; Urban, A.L.; Nuttall, L.K. Improving the Sensitivity of Advanced LIGO Using Noise Subtraction. *Class. Quantum Gravity* **2019**, *36*, 055011, [CrossRef]
131. Drigger, J.C.; Vitale, V.; Lundgren, A.P.; Evans, M.; Kawabe, K.; Dwyer, S.; Izumi, K.; Fritschel, P. Offline Noise Subtraction for Advanced LIGO. Available online: https://dcc.ligo.org/LIGO-P1700260/public (accessed on 17 December 2021).
132. Allen, B.; Hua, W.; Ottewill, A. Automatic Cross-Talk Removal from Multi-Channel Data. Available online: https://arxiv.org/abs/gr-qc/9909083 (accessed on 17 December 2021).
133. Viets, A.; Wade, M. Subtracting Narrow-Band Noise from LIGO Strain Data in the Third Observing Run. Available online: https://dcc.ligo.org/LIGO-T2100058/public (accessed on 17 December 2021).
134. Vajente, G.; Huang, Y.; Isi, M.; Driggers, J.C.; Kissel, J.S.; Szczepańczyk, M.J.; Vitale, S. Machine-learning nonstationary noise out of gravitational-wave detectors. *Phys. Rev. D* **2020**, *101*, 042003. [CrossRef]
135. Estevez, D.; Mours, B.; Rolland, L.; Verkindt, D. *Online h(t) Reconstruction for Virgo O3 Data: Start of O3*; Technical Report VIR-0652B-19. Available online: https://tds.virgo-gw.eu/ql/?c=14486 (accessed on 17 December 2021).
136. Acernese, F.; Agathos, M.; Ain, A.; Albanesi, S.; Allocca, A.; Amato, A.; Andrade, T.; Andres, N.; Andrić, T.; Ansoldi, S.; et al. Calibration of Advanced Virgo and Reconstruction of Detector Strain $h(t)$ during the Observing Run O3. Available online: https://arxiv.org/abs/2107.03294 (accessed on 17 December 2021).
137. Powell, J. Parameter Estimation and Model Selection of Gravitational Wave Signals Contaminated by Transient Detector Noise Glitches. *Class. Quantum Gravity* **2018**, *35*, 155017, [CrossRef]
138. Cornish, N.J.; Littenberg, T.B. BayesWave: Bayesian Inference for Gravitational Wave Bursts and Instrument Glitches. *Class. Quantum Gravity* **2015**, *32*, 135012, [CrossRef]

139. Pankow, C.; Chatziioannou, K.; Chase, E.A.; Littenberg, T.B.; Evans, M.; McIver, J.; Cornish, N.J.; Haster, C.; Kanner, J.; Raymond, V.; et al. Mitigation of the instrumental noise transient in gravitational-wave data surrounding GW170817. *Phys. Rev.* **2018**, *D98*, 084016, [CrossRef]
140. Cornish, N.J.; Littenberg, T.B.; Bécsy, B.; Chatziioannou, K.; Clark, J.A.; Ghonge, S.; Millhouse, M. The BayesWave analysis pipeline in the era of gravitational wave observations. *Phys. Rev. D* **2021**, *103*, 044006. [CrossRef]
141. LIGO Scientific Collaboration and Virgo Collaboration. *Glitch Model for O3a Catalog Events*. Available online: https://dcc.ligo.org/LIGO-T2000470/public (accessed on 17 December 2021).
142. Chatziioannou, K.; Cornish, N.; Wijngaarden, M.; Littenberg, T.B. Modeling compact binary signals and instrumental glitches in gravitational wave data. *Phys. Rev. D* **2021**, *103*, 044013, [CrossRef]
143. Kwok, J.Y.L.; Lo, R.K.L.; Weinstein, A.J.; Li, T.G.F. Investigation on the Effects of Non–Gaussian Noise Transients and Their Mitigations on Gravitational-Wave Tests of General Relativity. Available online: https://arxiv.org/abs/2109.07642 (accessed on 17 December 2021).
144. Torres-Forné, A.; Cuoco, E.; Font, J.A.; Marquina, A. Application of dictionary learning to denoise LIGO's blip noise transients. *Phys. Rev. D* **2020**, *102*, 023011, [CrossRef]
145. Mogushi, K. Reduction of Transient Noise Artifacts in Gravitational-Wave Data Using Deep Learning. Available online: https://arxiv.org/abs/2105.10522 (accessed on 17 December 2021).
146. Merritt, J.; Farr, B.; Hur, R.; Edelman, B.; Doctor, Z. Transient Glitch Mitigation in Advanced LIGO Data with *glitschen*. Available online: https://arxiv.org/abs/2108.12044 (accessed on 17 December 2021).
147. Harris, F. On the use of windows for harmonic analysis with the discrete Fourier transform. *Proc. IEEE* **1978**, *66*, 51–83. [CrossRef]
148. Steltner, B.; Papa, M.A.; Eggenstein, H.B. Identification and Removal of Non-Gaussian Noise Transients for Gravitational Wave Searches. Available online: https://arxiv.org/abs/2105.09933 (accessed on 17 December 2021).
149. Zweizig, J.; Riles, K. Information on Self-Gating of $h(t)$ Used in O3 Continuous-Wave and Stochastic Searches. Available online: https://dcc.ligo.org/LIGO-T2000384/public (accessed on 17 December 2021).
150. Harry, I.W.; Fairhurst, S. A targeted coherent search for gravitational waves from compact binary coalescences. *Phys. Rev.* **2011**, *D83*, 084002, [CrossRef]
151. Abbott, R.; Abbott, T.D.; Acernese, F.; Ackley, K.; Adams, C.; Adhikari, N.; Adhikari, R.X.; Adya, V. B.; Affeldt, C.; Agarwal, D.; et al. Search for Gravitational Waves Associated with Gamma-Ray Bursts Detected by Fermi and Swift during the LIGO-Virgo Run O3b. Available online: https://arxiv.org/abs/2111.03608 (accessed on 17 December 2021).
152. LIGO Scientific Collaboration and Virgo Collaboration. LIGO/Virgo G298048: Further Analysis of a Binary Neutron Star Candidate with Updated Sky Localization. Available online: https://gcn.gsfc.nasa.gov/gcn3/21513.gcn3 (accessed on 17 December 2021).
153. Zackay, B.; Venumadhav, T.; Roulet, J.; Dai, L.; Zaldarriaga, M. Detecting gravitational waves in data with non-stationary and non-Gaussian noise. *Phys. Rev. D* **2021**, *104*, 063034, [CrossRef]
154. Blahut, R.E., Solving Toeplitz Systems. In *Algebraic Methods for Signal Processing and Communications Coding*; Springer: New York, NY, USA, 1992; pp. 89–104. [CrossRef]
155. Talbot, C.; Thrane, E.; Biscoveanu, S.; Smith, R. Inference with finite time series: Observing the gravitational Universe through windows. *Phys. Rev. Res.* **2021**, *3*, 043049, [CrossRef]
156. Mogushi, K.; Quitzow-James, R.; Cavaglià, M.; Kulkarni, S.; Hayes, F. NNETFIX: An artificial neural network-based denoising engine for gravitational-wave signals. *Mach. Learn. Sci. Technol.* **2021**, *2*, 035018, [CrossRef]
157. Cuoco, E.; Powell, J.; Cavaglià, M.; Ackley, K.; Bejger, M.; Chatterjee, C.; Coughlin, M.; Coughlin, S.; Easter, P.; Essick, R.; et al. Enhancing gravitational-wave science with machine learning. *Mach. Learn. Sci. Technol.* **2020**, *2*, 011002. [CrossRef]
158. Welch, P. The use of fast Fourier transform for the estimation of power spectra: A method based on time averaging over short, modified periodograms. *IEEE Trans. Audio Electroacoust.* **1967**, *15*, 70–73. [CrossRef]
159. Allen, B.; Anderson, W.G.; Brady, P.R.; Brown, D.A.; Creighton, J.D.E. FINDCHIRP: An Algorithm for detection of gravitational waves from inspiraling compact binaries. *Phys. Rev. D* **2012**, *85*, 122006, [CrossRef]
160. Talbot, C.; Thrane, E. Gravitational-wave astronomy with an uncertain noise power spectral density. *Phys. Rev. Res.* **2020**, *2*, 043298, [CrossRef]
161. Edy, O.; Lundgren, A.; Nuttall, L.K. Issues of mismodeling gravitational-wave data for parameter estimation. *Phys. Rev. D* **2021**, *103*, 124061, [CrossRef]
162. Chatziioannou, K.; Haster, C.J.; Littenberg, T.B.; Farr, W.M.; Ghonge, S.; Millhouse, M.; Clark, J.A.; Cornish, N. Noise Spectral Estimation Methods and Their Impact on Gravitational Wave Measurement of Compact Binary Mergers. *Phys. Rev. D* **2019**, *100*, 104004, [CrossRef]
163. Macleod, D.; Urban, A.L.; Coughlin, S.; Massinger, T.; Pitkin, M.; Rngeorge ; Paulaltin; Areeda, J.; Singer, L.; Quintero, E.; et al. gwpy/gwpy: 2.0.1. Available online: https://zenodo.org/record/3973364#.Yd9lzS-B1QI (accessed on 17 December 2021).
164. Ashton, G.; Hübner, M.; Lasky, P.D.; Talbot, C.; Ackley, K.; Biscoveanu, S.; Chu, Q.; Divakarla, A.; Easter, P.J.; Goncharov, B.; et al. BILBY: A user-friendly Bayesian inference library for gravitational-wave astronomy. *Astrophys. J. Suppl.* **2019**, *241*, 27, [CrossRef]
165. Biscoveanu, S.; Haster, C.J.; Vitale, S.; Davies, J. Quantifying the Effect of Power Spectral Density Uncertainty on Gravitational-Wave Parameter Estimation for Compact Binary Sources. *Phys. Rev. D* **2020**, *102*, 023008, [CrossRef]

166. Sachdev, S.; Magee, R.; Hanna, C.; Cannon, K.; Singer, L.; SK, J.R.; Mukherjee, D.; Caudill, S.; Chan, C.; Creighton, J.D.E.; et al. An Early-warning System for Electromagnetic Follow-up of Gravitational-wave Events. *Astrophys. J. Lett.* **2020**, *905*, L25, [CrossRef]
167. Zackay, B.; Venumadhav, T.; Dai, L.; Roulet, J.; Zaldarriaga, M. Highly spinning and aligned binary black hole merger in the Advanced LIGO first observing run. *Phys. Rev. D* **2019**, *100*, 023007, [CrossRef]
168. Amann, F.; Bonsignorio, F.; Bulik, T.; Bulten, H.J.; Cuccuru, S.; Dassargues, A.; DeSalvo, R.; Fenyvesi, E.; Fidecaro, F.; Fiori, I.; et al. Site-selection criteria for the Einstein Telescope. *Rev. Sci. Instrum.* **2020**, *91*, 9, [CrossRef]
169. Evans, M.; Adhikari, R.X.; Afle, C.; Ballmer, S.W.; Biscoveanu, S.; Borhanian, S.; Brown, A.; Chen, Y.; Eisenstein, R.; Gruson, A.; et al. A Horizon Study for Cosmic Explorer: Science, Observatories, and Community. Available online: https://arxiv.org/abs/2109.09882 (accessed on 17 December 2021).
170. Badaracco, F.; De Rossi, C.; Fiori, I.; Harms, J.; Miyo, K.; Paoletti, F.; Tanaka, T.; Washimi, T.; Yokozawa, T. The KAGRA underground environment and lessons for the Einstein Telescope. *Phys. Rev. D* **2021**, *104*, 042006, [CrossRef]
171. Cahillane, C.; Mansell, G.; Sigg, D. Laser Frequency Noise in Next Generation Gravitational-Wave Detectors. [CrossRef]
172. Janssens, K.; Martinovic, K.; Christensen, N.; Meyers, P.M.; Sakellariadou, M. Impact of Schumann Resonances on the Einstein Telescope and Projections for the Magnetic Coupling Function. Available online: https://arxiv.org/abs/2110.14730 (accessed on 17 December 2021).
173. Meyers, P.M.; Martinovic, K.; Christensen, N.; Sakellariadou, M. Detecting a stochastic gravitational-wave background in the presence of correlated magnetic noise. *Phys. Rev. D* **2020**, *102*, 102005, [CrossRef]
174. Beker, M.G.; van den Brand, J.F.J.; Hennes, E.; Rabeling, D.S. Newtonian noise and ambient ground motion for gravitational wave detectors. *J. Phys. Conf. Ser.* **2012**, *363*, 012004. [CrossRef]
175. Driggers, J.C.; Harms, J.; Adhikari, R.X. Subtraction of Newtonian noise using optimized sensor arrays. *Phys. Rev. D* **2012**, *86*, 102001. [CrossRef]
176. Coughlin, M.; Mukund, N.; Harms, J.; Driggers, J.; Adhikari, R.; Mitra, S. Towards a first design of a Newtonian-noise cancellation system for Advanced LIGO. *Class. Quantum Gravity* **2016**, *33*, 244001. [CrossRef]
177. Edwards, M.C.; Maturana-Russel, P.; Meyer, R.; Gair, J.; Korsakova, N.; Christensen, N. Identifying and Addressing Nonstationary LISA Noise. *Phys. Rev. D* **2020**, *102*, 084062, [CrossRef]
178. Robson, T.; Cornish, N.J. Detecting Gravitational Wave Bursts with LISA in the presence of Instrumental Glitches. *Phys. Rev. D* **2019**, *99*, 024019, [CrossRef]
179. Baghi, Q.; Thorpe, I.; Slutsky, J.; Baker, J.; Dal Canton, T.; Korsakova, N.; Karnesis, N. Gravitational-wave parameter estimation with gaps in LISA: A Bayesian data augmentation method. *Phys. Rev. D* **2019**, *100*, 022003, [CrossRef]
180. Blelly, A.; Bobin, J.; Moutarde, H. Sparse data inpainting for the recovery of Galactic-binary gravitational wave signals from gapped data. *Mon. Not. R. Astron. Soc.* **2021**, *509*, 5902–5917. [CrossRef]

Article

Gravitational Waves from a Core-Collapse Supernova: Perspectives with Detectors in the Late 2020s and Early 2030s

Marek Szczepańczyk [1,*] and Michele Zanolin [2]

1 Department of Physics, University of Florida, Gainesville, FL 32611, USA
2 Physics and Astronomy Department, Embry-Riddle University, 3700 Willow Creek Road, Prescott, AZ 86301, USA; michele.zanolin@ligo.org
* Correspondence: marek.szczepanczyk@ligo.org

Abstract: We studied the detectability and reconstruction of gravitational waves from core-collapse supernova multidimensional models using simulated data from detectors predicted to operate in the late 2020s and early 2030s. We found that the detection range will improve by a factor of around two with respect to the second-generation gravitational-wave detectors, and the sky localization will significantly improve. We analyzed the reconstruction accuracy for the lower frequency and higher frequency portion of supernova signals with a 250 Hz cutoff. Since the waveform's peak frequencies are usually at high frequencies, the gravitational-wave signals in this frequency band were reconstructed more accurately.

Keywords: gravitational waves; core-collapse supernova; future detectors

1. Introduction

The observation of gravitational waves (GWs) from the binary black hole merger in 2015 [1] marks the beginning of GW astrophysics. In 2017, the binary neutron star was discovered in both GW and electromagnetic spectra [2], while in 2020, the GWs from two neutron star–black hole coalescences were observed [3]. To date, the Advanced LIGO [4] and Advanced Virgo [5] detectors have registered around 90 GW candidates with probability of astrophysical origin greater than 50% [6–8]. The newly born GW astrophysics has already challenged our understanding of the Universe, and we expect this trend will continue. With increased detectors sensitivity, the number of detections is anticipated to grow rapidly. Many GW sources are awaiting discovery, and core-collapse supernovae (CCSNe) are one of them. The next nearby CCSN will be one of the most interesting astronomical events of the century, and GWs will allow us to probe these phenomena's inner engines directly.

The prospects of exploring the Universe with GWs motivate us to improve and expand the current network of gravitational wave detectors. The advanced, second-generation (2G) detectors will reach their designed sensitivities in a few years, and the plans beyond 2G detectors are progressing. Recently the GW network expanded with KAGRA [9]. LIGO detectors could be substantially upgraded to the "LIGO Voyager" [10]. LIGO India [11] is currently under construction, and a neutron star extreme matter observatory (NEMO) detector in Australia is planned [12]. These advances will happen at the end of the 2020s and the beginning of the 2030s [13]. We dub them 2.5G detectors, as they are predicted to operate before the planned third-generation (3G) detectors, such as the Einstein Telescope [14] and Cosmic Explorer [15].

The considerations of exploring the detectability and reconstruction of GWs from CCSN with 2G detectors can be found in [16,17]. This paper focuses on the benefits of an extended 2.5G detectors network. We estimate how well a CCSN source can be localized in the sky.

We quantify how accurately the GW signals, particularly the low- and high-frequency features, can be reconstructed. Section 2 describes the methodology. Our findings are described in Section 3 and the conclusions are presented in Section 4.

2. Methodology

2.1. GW Detectors

The 2.5G network will consist of upgraded existing interferometers and the new detectors are planned for the late 2020s and early 2030s. It is difficult to make accurate predictions in a decade timescale, but we assume six detectors to be operating. Figure 1 shows the detectors' sensitivities considered in this paper. LIGO detectors in Hanford (H) and Livingston (L) will be upgraded to a Voyager sensitivity [10,18]. Virgo (V) will operate at an Advanced Virgo plus [9,19,20] sensitivity, and KA GRA (K) will reach its designed sensitivity [20]. LIGO India (A) is planned to operate at Advanced LIGO plus' sensitivity [20]. While the construction just began in Aundha in India, for simplicity, we assumed the arms to go along geographical directions of longitude and latitude. The NEMO (N) detector is an interferometer primarily targeting the postmerger GW signal from the binary neutron stars. It is optimized to be most sensitive in higher frequencies (around 2 kHz) than the other detectors [12]. This detector has been proposed, and for this study, we assumed its location and arm orientations to be that of AIGO [21]. We note that the location of the NEMO detector could be optimized for maximizing the results but this is beyond the scope of this work.

Given the different sensitivities of each detector, we considered a limited set of network configurations to study. The Voyager detectors are expected to be most sensitive; the networks containing the L and H detectors were considered: LHVKAN, LHVKA, LHVK, LHVK, LHV, LHA, LHK, LHN, LH. We also considered a network that did not contain the Voyager detector, VKA.

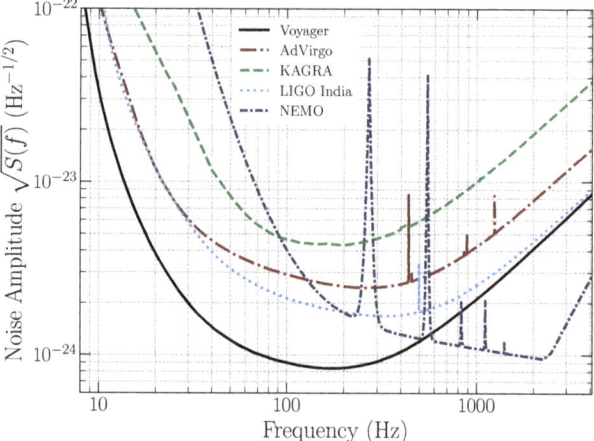

Figure 1. Sensitivities of the detectors projected to operate in the late 2020s and early 2030s. NEMO detector is designed to measure the high-frequency GW signal from binary neutron star postmerger.

2.2. Coherent WaveBurst

Coherent WaveBurst is an excess-power search algorithm for detecting and reconstructing GWs [22]. It does not assume any signal model and uses minimal assumptions on the signal morphologies. The analysis of GW strain data is performed in a wavelet domain [23]. Wavelets with amplitudes above the fluctuations of the detector noise are selected, grouped into clusters, and coherent events are identified. The cWB ranks events with an η_c statistics based on the coherent network energy E_c obtained by cross-correlating detectors data [22]. The η_c is approximately the coherent network signal-to-noise ratio.

While it is not possible to predict a realistic detector noise reliably for the future detectors, we used a Gaussian noise recolored to the detector sensitivities depicted in Figure 1. In our analysis, we accepted events with a signal-to-noise ratio of 12 and those with a correlation coefficient c_c of 0.7 ($c_c \approx 1$ means that an event is coherent across detectors and typically is a GW signal). These thresholds were used in [9]. The LIGO and Virgo detectors network are sensitive to detecting only one GW polarization component. Therefore, in the LIGO/Virgo/KAGRA searches (e.g., [24]) the cWB is typically tuned to reconstruct only one GW polarization component. The second polarization component can also be reconstructed for an extended network of GW detectors. Therefore, we loosened this constraint to allow a fraction of the second GW polarization component to be reconstructed as well.

2.3. CCSNe and GW Signals

CCSN is a violent death of a massive star (above 8 $M_\odot$). During its life, a star burns the fuel by means of nuclear fusion, creating an iron core in the center (see example reviews [25,26]). After exceeding the Chandrasekhar mass (around 1.4 $M_\odot$), the core collapses under the gravitational force forming a hot protoneutron star (PNS). Protons and electrons combine in such a dense environment, creating neutrons and neutrinos. In the so-called *neutrino-driven* mechanism (e.g., [27–32]), 99% of the CCSN energy is released with neutrinos, and they are believed to play a crucial role in the explosion (e.g., [26,33]). Typically, in this scenario, the GW emission comes from the oscillations of the PNS where the restoring force can be gravity, surface, or pressure (g-, f-, p-modes). During the explosion, the shock may also oscillate leading to the standing-accretion shock instability (SASI) [34].

In a case when a progenitor star rotates rapidly, a *magnetorotationally driven* (MHD-driven) mechanism, an explosion might be caused by energetic jets formed by a strong magnetic field (e.g., [35,36]). Alternatively, a failed CCSN may lead to a *black hole formation* (e.g., [37–39]).

The efforts to understand the CCSN engine are more than 50 years old [40]. Still, the explosion mechanism is not yet fully understood (see [25] for a review). Direct observation of GWs from a CCSN event will give us direct insight into the dynamics of this phenomenon. The theoretical and numerical CCSN simulations advanced significantly in recent years, and more accurate GW signal predictions are available. Our analysis used waveforms from multidimensional simulations, five for neutrino-driven explosions, one for MHD-driven explosions, and one for black hole formation.

Andresen et al., 2019 [30] studied the impact of moderate progenitor rotation on the GW signals. GW emission in the pre-explosion phase strongly depended on whether the SASI dominated the postshock flow with neutrino transport and g-mode frequency components in their signals. We used the m15nr model with a strong SASI below 250 Hz.

Kuroda et al., 2016 [41] studied the impact of the equation-of-state (EOS) on the GW signatures using a 15 $M_\odot$ progenitor star. We used the SFHx model with strong SASI at around 100 Hz, and the g-mode had a strong emission around 700 Hz.

Mezzacappa et al., 2020 [27] studied the origins of the GW emission for a 15 $M_\odot$ progenitor star (C15-3D model). The SASI/convection GW emission was present below 200 Hz, while the PNS oscillations occurred primarily above 600 Hz.

O'Connor and Couch, 2018 [31] analyzed the impact of the progenitor asphericities, grid resolution and symmetry, dimensionality, and neutrino physics for a 20 $M_\odot$ progenitor star. We explored the flagship mesa20 model. The resulting GW signals had strong SASI activity, but the g-mode dominated them.

Pan et al., 2020 [39] explored an impact of progenitor star rotation on an explosion and BH formation. We used the SR model for slowly rotating progenitor stars. The star exploded, and the fallback accretion led to a BH formation. The emitted GW energy was large, around $9 \times 10^{-7} M_\odot c^2$.

Radice et al., 2019 [29] studied GW emission depending on the progenitor star mass. The PNS oscillations usually dominated the GW signals. We studied the s13 model, an explosion of a 13 $M_\odot$ progenitor star mass. Besides the PNS oscillations, a strong prompt convection below 100 Hz was present.

Richers et al., 2017 [35] analyzed core-bounce GWs for 18 EOSs from the axisymmetric rapidly rotating stars. We used the A467w0.50_SFHx model. The waveform was around 10 ms long and broadband.

3. Results
3.1. Detection Range

In this analysis, we studied the detectability of GWs as a function of a source distance. We took waveforms from different source angle orientations, rescaled their amplitudes to a given source distance and placed them randomly in the sky. The waveforms were added (injected) to the detector's data stream and reconstructed with cWB. The procedure was repeated for a range of the source distances and allowed us to create a detection efficiency curve as a function of distance. A distance at 50% detection efficiency is referred to as a *detection range*.

The left panel of Figure 2 shows the detection efficiency curves for all considered morphologies and the LHVKA network. The detectability of the most energetic waveforms, SR and A467w0.50_SFHx, exceeds 100 kpc. Less energetic waveforms are detectable at shorter distances. The right panel of Figure 2 considers the s13 model for nine network configurations. Because the noise floor for these two interferometers is the lowest among the 2.5G detectors, the detection distance for the networks with L and H detectors is approximately the same. The least sensitive network is VKA, while the most sensitive is the LHVKA network. The efficiency of the LHVKAN network decreases significantly at low distances, as the N detector is sensitive in a different frequency band than all other detectors. Because the s13 waveform is broadband, the detectors reconstruct different parts of the GW signal. This disbalance can break the coherence and often leads to a rejection of an event by cWB. In such a case, the cWB algorithm needs optimizing, but it is beyond the scope of this paper.

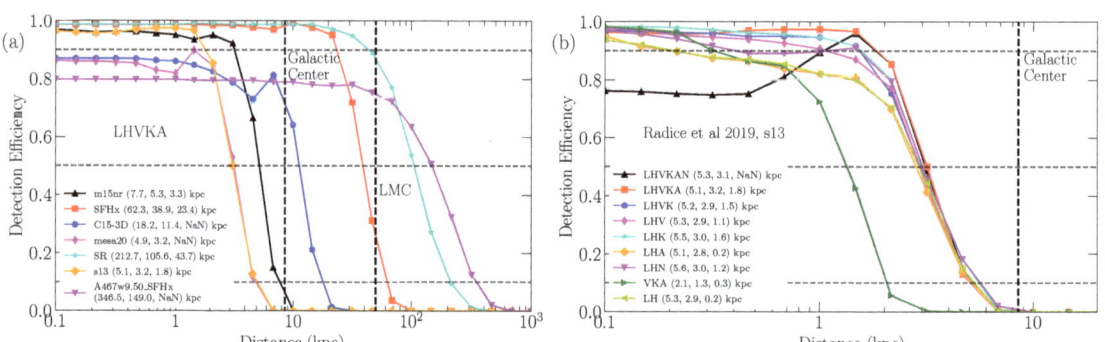

Figure 2. Detection efficiency curves as a function of distance. Numbers in brackets are distances at 10%, 50% and 90% detection efficiency. Plot (**a**) shows how far a CCSN source can be detectable for different models of GW emission [27,29–31,35,39,41] and LHVKA network, and (**b**) different detector networks for the s13 model [29].

Table 1 summarizes the results for all considered waveforms and network configurations. The short A467w0.50_SFHx waveforms are well detectable for all networks containing L and H. Similarly to s13, including NEMO leads to decreased efficiencies at shorter source distances. The least sensitive network is VKA. Compared with [16], the predicted detection ranges for the fifth observing run (O5) for m15nr, SFHx, C15-3D, mesa20, and s13 are 3.3, 21.6, 8.2, 2.0, and 1.8 kpc, respectively. The 2.5G detectors will improve these numbers roughly by a factor of two.

Table 1. Distances at 10%/50%/90% detection efficiency for all considered waveforms and detector networks.

Network	Distance at 10%/50%/90% Efficiency (kpc)						
	m15nr	SFHx	C15-3D	mesa20	SR	s13	A467w0.50_SFHx
LHVKAN	8.6/5.5/-	75.4/45.1/ 4.9	24.1/13.9/-	7.5/0.4/-	165.3/ 50.3/-	5.3/3.1/-	360.9/156.2/-
LHVKA	7.7/5.3/3.3	62.3/38.9/23.4	18.2/11.4/-	4.9/3.2/-	212.7/105.6/43.7	5.1/3.2/1.8	346.5/149.0/-
LHVK	7.8/5.0/2.3	60.2/36.9/19.3	17.6/10.7/1.2	4.6/2.8/1.3	210.6/109.1/32.7	5.2/2.9/1.5	354.2/122.8/-
LHV	8.3/5.1/1.2	60.5/37.0/18.0	18.8/11.2/1.7	4.9/2.9/1.1	215.4/113.4/27.5	5.3/2.9/1.1	366.0/120.0/-
LHA	8.4/5.2/2.4	60.8/37.9/21.1	19.3/11.9/1.8	5.4/3.3/1.5	218.2/110.9/27.8	5.5/3.0/1.6	360.6/130.6/-
LHK	8.0/5.0/0.7	58.8/35.7/11.4	18.2/10.5/0.7	4.5/2.6/0.2	213.4/113.0/14.7	5.1/2.8/0.2	352.5/106.0/-
LHN	9.1/5.7/1.9	70.8/42.6/20.9	26.6/12.9/1.3	8.3/4.8/0.5	183.6/ 48.2/ 8.5	5.6/3.0/1.2	378.3/130.2/-
VKA	3.8/2.2/0.5	25.8/15.9/ 6.4	9.2/ 2.6/0.9	2.9/1.6/0.3	63.5/ 30.5/ 9.5	2.1/1.3/0.3	123.8/ 45.3/-
LH	8.5/5.1/1.0	58.7/34.8/12.1	18.5/10.7/0.7	4.8/2.7/0.5	220.6/112.7/16.7	5.3/2.9/0.2	370.0/104.7/-

3.2. Sky Localization

We studied how well the sky localization will improve with the 2.5G detectors. In this analysis, the waveforms from random source orientations were placed uniformly in volume and then reconstructed. The events were then reconstructed together with the estimated search area. The search area on the sky assigned a probability greater than or equal to the probability assigned to the injected location [42]. Figure 3 shows the search areas for a cumulative number of reconstructed events. The numbers in the brackets are areas at 0.1, 0.5, and 0.9 of the cumulative number of events.

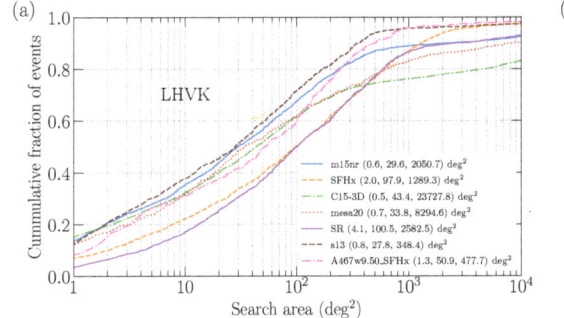
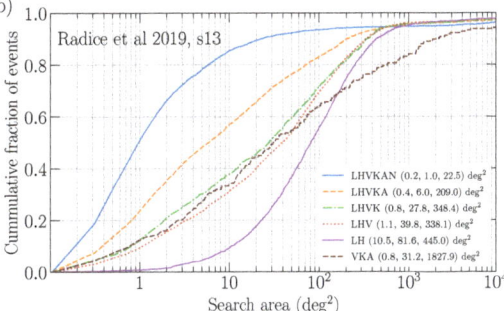

Figure 3. Search areas for (**a**) all GW signals [27,29–31,35,39,41] and (**b**) different detector networks for s13 model [29]. The search area is comparable between GW morphologies. Adding detectors to the network significantly reduces the search area. Numbers in brackets are 0.1, 0.5 and 0.9 of the cumulative number of events.

The left panel of Figure 3 shows the search area curves for all considered waveforms with the LHVK network. The search area curve depends on the waveforms, but it is comparable within the GW morphologies. Some neutrino-driven explosions with broadband GW signals, such as C15-3D, may lead to large search areas. The right panel of Figure 3 compares the search areas for the s13 waveform and different network configurations. The sky location of a GW source is calculated mainly based on the triangulation between the detectors. Clearly, adding more detectors decreases the search area. Comparable performance is seen for the LHV, LHVK, and VKA configurations. Table 2 summarizes the results for all waveforms and networks considered.

Table 2. Search areas for all waveforms and example detector networks.

Waveform	Network	Area at 0.1/0.5/0.9 (deg^2)
m15nr	LHVK	0.6/29.6/2050.7
SFHx	LHVK	2.0/97.9/1289.3
C15-3D	LHVK	0.5/43.4/23727.8
mesa20	LHVK	0.7/33.8/8294.6
SR	LHVK	4.1/100.5/2582.5
s13	LHVKAN	0.2/1.0/22.5
s13	LHVKA	0.4/6.0/209.0
s13	LHVK	0.8/27.8/348.4
s13	LHV	1.1/39.8/338.1
s13	LHV	10.5/81.6/445.0
s13	VKA	0.8/31.2/1827.9
A467w0.50_SFHx	LHVK	1.3/50.9/477.7

3.3. Reconstruction Accuracy

The predicted GW signatures can be divided into low-frequency (LF), such as SASI/convection, and high-frequency (HF) signatures, such as the PNS oscillation. The division can be placed around 250 Hz. We quantified the accuracy of the cWB reconstruction for the full reconstructed waveform, HF, and LF waveform components. We used the waveform overlap, or a match [43] that was defined as a product between a detected $\mathbf{w} = \{w_k(t)\}$ and an injected whitened waveform $\mathbf{h} = \{h_k(t)\}$:

$$O(\mathbf{w}, \mathbf{h}) = \frac{(\mathbf{w}|\mathbf{h})}{\sqrt{(\mathbf{w}|\mathbf{w})}\sqrt{(\mathbf{h}|\mathbf{h})}}, \quad (1)$$

where $(.|.)$ denotes a scalar product in the time domain:

$$(\mathbf{w}|\mathbf{h}) = \sum_k \int_{t_1}^{t_2} w_k(t) h_k(t) dt. \quad (2)$$

The index k is a detector number, and $[t_1, t_2]$ is the time range of the reconstructed event. The waveform overlap ranged from -1 (sign mismatch) to 1 (perfect reconstruction). The HF and LF waveform components were obtained using a high-pass and low-pass Butterworth filter with a 250 Hz cutoff frequency. Similarly to Section 3.2, we used uniform-in-volume injections.

Figure 4 shows a waveform overlap for the m15nr waveform that shows strong SASI and g-mode divided around 250 Hz. The reconstruction accuracy grows with the signal SNR. However, in this example, many waveforms have a poor reconstruction (16% with a waveform overlap below 0.2). The numbers in the brackets show an average waveform overlap at an SNR of 20 and 40, respectively. Only waveforms with a waveform overlap larger than 0.2 are selected. The waveform overlaps for the HF and LF waveform components are typically smaller than those for the full waveform. In this example, the HF component is reconstructed more accurately than the LF part of the signal. Because the waveform peak frequency is around 820 Hz, the HF part of the waveform is reconstructed first. The LF SASI is weaker and relatively long, and the accuracy of its reconstruction is worse.

Table 3 summarizes the results for all considered waveforms and networks. Typically, around 20% of the waveforms are misreconstructed (waveform overlap smaller than 0.2) for the neutrino-driven explosions and LHVK network. In around 56% of the BH formation, the SR waveforms are misreconstructed because the signal is almost 1 s long, and a small portion of the GW signal is reconstructed after the dominant prompt-convection. For the s13 waveform, the least misreconstructions are for the LH and LHV networks, as the cWB is optimized. As in the example of m15nr waveform, typically, the waveform is reconstructed around the peak frequency at low SNR, and reconstruction accuracy in that frequency range is better. Given the peak frequencies of the considered waveforms is above 250 Hz, the waveform overlaps are typically higher in the HF part of the waveform. The LF SASI/convection are weaker parts of the waveforms, resulting in less accurate reconstruction. In the case of the SFHx, the spectrum has distinguished peak frequencies around 100 Hz and 700 Hz, resulting in an accurate reconstruction at low SNR for the HF and LF components. The accuracy decreases with higher SNR values as a more stochastic signal contributes.

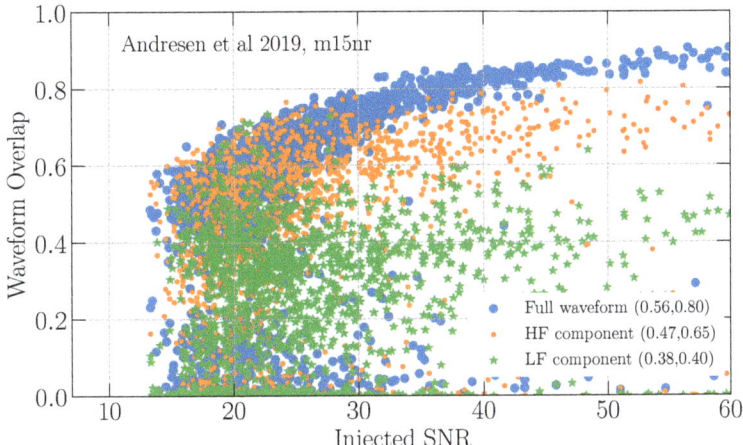

Figure 4. Waveform overlap as a function of injected SNR for m15nr model [30]. The accuracy of the full waveform increases with the SNR. However, in this example, each waveform component is reconstructed less accurately. The numbers in brackets are waveform overlaps at SNR 20 and 40, respectively, (for $O > 0.2$).

Table 3. Waveform overlaps for all waveforms and example detector networks. The reconstruction accuracy depends on the waveforms morphology and typically the waveform component is larger for the part of the signal with the peak frequency.

Waveform	Network	Mis-Recon. $O < 0.2$	O for Full/HF/LF Waveform ($O > 0.2$) SNR = 20	SNR = 40
m15nr	LHVK	16%	0.56/0.47/0.38	0.80/0.65/0.40
SFHx	LHVK	29%	0.61/0.73/0.74	0.87/0.53/0.68
C15-3D	LHVK	18%	0.36/0.40/0.22	0.64/0.57/0.23
mesa20	LHVK	20%	0.43/0.48/0.51	0.62/0.57/0.38
SR	LHVK	56%	0.57/0.27/0.31	0.77/0.45/0.33
s13	LHVKAN	24%	0.60/0.59/0.39	0.73/0.72/0.37
s13	LHVKA	23%	0.66/0.67/0.39	0.81/0.82/0.40
s13	LHVK	23%	0.69/0.69/0.39	0.83/0.76/0.43
s13	LHV	10%	0.70/0.70/0.38	0.82/0.83/0.43
s13	LH	7%	0.73/0.73/0.39	0.86/0.81/0.44
s13	VKA	28%	0.59/0.61/0.34	0.65/0.40/ -
A467w0.50_SFHx	LHVK	16%	0.81/0.61/0.60	0.81/0.72/0.69

4. Conclusions

The era of GW astrophysics has begun, and our understanding of the dynamical Universe is advancing. CCSNe are one of the most interesting cosmic phenomena, and detecting GWs will shed light on understanding the nature of these explosions. The 2.5G detector network will extend around the detection range of around a factor of two, and this improvement will come primarily from the Voyager sensitivity. More detectors in the network will allow significantly improved sky localization of the source than with the 2G detectors. This improvement is important when the galactic dust obscures an optical counterpart of a nearby event. We studied the reconstruction accuracy of the waveforms and their HF and LF components. Typically, the reconstruction was more accurate around the peak frequency of the signal, and the LF waveform component was reconstructed less accurately. The 2.5G detector network will better reconstruct both GW polarization states with respect to the 2G detector network. It will enable a better probing of the supernova's inner engine.

Author Contributions: Conceptualization, M.S.; formal analysis, M.S.; investigation, M.S. and M.Z.; writing—original draft preparation, M.S. and M.Z.; writing—review and editing, M.S. and M.Z. All authors have read and agreed to the published version of the manuscript.

Funding: The work by M.S. was supported by NSF grants no. PHY 1806165 and no. PHY 2110060. M.Z. was supported by NSF grant no. PHY 1806885.

Institutional Review Board Statement: Not applicable.

Informed Consent Statement: Not applicable.

Data Availability Statement: Not applicable.

Acknowledgments: This research has made use of data, software, and/or web tools obtained from the Gravitational Wave Open Science Center, a service of LIGO Laboratory, the LIGO Scientific Collaboration, and the Virgo Collaboration. This material is based upon work supported by NSF's LIGO Laboratory which is a major facility fully funded by the National Science Foundation. We thank David Radice for the insightful comments. This paper has LIGO document number P2200072.

Conflicts of Interest: The authors declare no conflict of interest.

References

1. Abbott, B.; Abbott, R.; Abbott, T.D.; Abernathy, M.R.; Acernese, F.; Ackley, K.; Adams, C.; Adams, T.; Addesso, P.; Adhikari, R.X.; et al. Observation of Gravitational Waves from a Binary Black Hole Merger. *Phys. Rev. Lett.* **2016**, *116*, 61102. [CrossRef] [PubMed]
2. Abbott, B.; Abbott, R.; Abbott, T.D.; Abernathy, M.R.; Acernese, F.; Ackley, K.; Adams, C.; Adams, T.; Addesso, P.; Adhikari, R.X.; et al. GW170817: Observation of Gravitational Waves from a Binary Neutron Star Inspiral. *Phys. Rev. Lett.* **2017**, *119*, 161101. [CrossRef] [PubMed]
3. Abbott, R.; Abbott, T.D.; Abraham, S.; Acernese, F.; Ackley, K.; Adams, A.; Adams, C.; Adhikari, R.X.; Adya, V.B.; Affeldt, C.; et al. Observation of gravitational waves from two neutron star-black hole coalescences. *Astrophys. J. Lett.* **2021**, *915*, L5. [CrossRef]
4. Aasi, J.; Abbott, B.; Abbott, R.; Abbott, T.; Abernathy, M.; Acernese, F.; Ackley, K.; Adams, C.; Adams, T.; Addesso, P.; et al. Advanced LIGO. *Class. Quant. Grav.* **2015**, *32*, 74001. [CrossRef]
5. Acernese, F.; Agathos, M.; Agatsuma, K.; Aisa, D.; Allemandou, N.; Allocca, A.; Amarni, J.; Astone, P.; Balestri, G.; Ballardin, F.; et al. Advanced Virgo: A second-generation interferometric gravitational wave detector. *Class. Quant. Grav.* **2015**, *32*, 24001. [CrossRef]
6. Abbott, R.; Abbott, T.D.; Abraham, S.; Acernese, F.; Ackley, K.; Adams, A.; Adams, C.; Adhikari, R.X.; Adya, V.B.; Affeldt, C.; et al. GWTC-1: A Gravitational-Wave Transient Catalog of Compact Binary Mergers Observed by LIGO and Virgo during the First and Second Observing Runs. *Phys. Rev. X* **2019**, *9*, 31040. [CrossRef]
7. Abbott, R.; Agelova, S.V.; Gier, G.; Hill, P.; Reid, S.; Wallace, G.S. GWTC-2: Compact Binary Coalescences Observed by LIGO and Virgo During the First Half of the Third Observing Run. *arXiv* **2021**, arXiv:2010.14527.
8. Abbott, R.; Abbott, T.D.; Abraham, S.; Acernese, F.; Ackley, K.; Adams, A.; Adams, C.; Adhikari, R.X.; Adya, V.B.; Affeldt, C.; et al. GWTC-3: Compact Binary Coalescences Observed by LIGO and Virgo During the Second Part of the Third Observing Run. *arXiv* **2021**, arXiv:2111.03606.
9. Abbott, R.; Abbott, T.D.; Abraham, S.; Acernese, F.; Ackley, K.; Adams, A.; Adams, C.; Adhikari, R.X.; Adya, V.B.; Affeldt, C.; et al. Prospects for Observing and Localizing Gravitational-Wave Transients with Advanced LIGO, Advanced Virgo and KAGRA. *Living Rev. Rel.* **2018**, *21*, 3. [CrossRef]
10. Adhikari, R.X.; Arai, K.; Brooks, A.F.; Wipf, C.; Aguiar, O.; Altin, P.; Barr, B.; Barsotti, L.; Bassiri, R.; Bell, A. A cryogenic silicon interferometer for gravitational-wave detection. *Class. Quant. Grav.* **2020**, *37*, 165003. [CrossRef]
11. Unnikrishnan, C.S. IndIGO and LIGO-India: Scope and plans for gravitational wave research and precision metrology in India. *Int. J. Mod. Phys. D* **2013**, *22*, 1341010. [CrossRef]
12. Ackley, K.; Adya, V. B.; Agrawal, P.; Altin, P.; Ashton, G.; Bailes, M.; Baltinas, E.; Barbuio, A.; Beniwal, D.; Blair, C.; et al. Neutron Star Extreme Matter Observatory: A kilohertz-band gravitational-wave detector in the global network. *Publ. Astron. Soc. Austral.* **2020**, *37*, e047. [CrossRef]

13. Bailes, M.; Berger, B.K.; Brady, P.R.; Branchesi, M.; Danzmann, K.; Evans, M.; Holley-Bockelmann, K.; Iyer, B.R.; Kajita, T.; Katasanevas, S.; et al. Gravitational-wave physics and astronomy in the 2020s and 2030s. *Nat. Rev. Phys.* **2021**, *3*, 344–366. [CrossRef]
14. Punturo, M.; Abernathy, M.; Acernese, F.; Allen, B.; Andersson, N.; Arun, K.; Barone, F.; Barr, B.; Barsuglia, M.; Beker, M. The Einstein Telescope: A third-generation gravitational wave observatory. *Class. Quantum Gravity* **2010**, *27*, 194002. [CrossRef]
15. Abbott, B.P.; Abbott, R.; Abbott, T.D.; Abernathy, M.R.; Ackley, K.; Adams, C.; Addesso, P.; Adhikari, R.X.; Adya, V.B.; Affeldt, C. Exploring the Sensitivity of Next Generation Gravitational Wave Detectors. *Class. Quant. Grav.* **2017**, *34*, 44001. [CrossRef]
16. Szczepanczyk, M.; Antelis, J.M.; Benjamin, M.; Cavaglia, M.; Gondek-Rosińska, D.; Hansen, T.; Klimenko, S.; Morales, M.D.; Moreno, C.; Mukherjee, S.; et al. Detecting and reconstructing gravitational waves from the next galactic core-collapse supernova in the advanced detector era. *Phys. Rev. D* **2021**, *104*, 102002. [CrossRef]
17. Gossan, S.E.; Sutton, P.; Stuver, A.; Zanolin, M.; Gill, K.; Ott, C.D. Observing Gravitational Waves from Core-Collapse Supernovae in the Advanced Detector Era. *Phys. Rev. D* **2016**, *93*, 42002. [CrossRef]
18. Evans, M.; Sturani, R.; Vitali, S.; Hall, E. *Unofficial Sensitivity Curves (ASD) for aLIGO, Kagra, Virgo, Voyager, Cosmic Explorer, and Einstein Telescope*; Technical Report LIGO-T1500293; LIGO Document Control Center: Washington, DC, USA, 2020.
19. Shoemaker, D. Gravitational wave astronomy with LIGO and similar detectors in the next decade. *arXiv* **2019**, arXiv:1904.03187.
20. Abbott, R. *Noise Curves Used for Simulations in the Update of the Observing Scenarios Paper*; Technical Report LIGO-T2000012; LIGO Document Control Center: Washington, DC, USA, 2020.
21. McClelland, D.E.; Scott, S.M.; Gray, M.B.; Shaddock, D.A.; Slagmolen, B.J.; Searle, A.; Blair, D.G.; Ju, L.; Winterflood, J.; Benabid, F.; et al. Second-generation laser interferometry for gravitational wave detection: ACI GA progress. *Class. Quantum Gravity* **2001**, *18*, 4121–4126. [CrossRef]
22. Klimenko, S.; Vedovato, G.; Drago, M.; Salemi, F.; Tiwari, V.; Prodi, G.A.; Lazzaro, C.; Ackley, K.; Tiwari, S.; Da Silva, C.F.; et al. Method for detection and reconstruction of gravitational wave transients with networks of advanced detectors. *Phys. Rev. D* **2016**, *93*, 1–10. [CrossRef]
23. Necula, V.; Klimenko, S.; Mitselmakher, G. Transient analysis with fast Wilson-Daubechies time-frequency transform. *J. Phys. Conf. Ser.* **2012**, *363*, 1–11. [CrossRef]
24. Abbott, B.P.; Abbott, R.; Abbott, T.D.; Abraham, S.; Acernese, F.; Ackley, K.; Adams, C.; Adhikari, R.X.; Adya,V.B.; Affeldt, C.; et al. All-sky search for short gravitational-wave bursts in the third Advanced LIGO and Advanced Virgo run. *Phys. Rev. D* **2021**, *104*, 122004. [CrossRef]
25. Janka, H.T. Explosion Mechanisms of Core-Collapse Supernovae. *Ann. Rev. Nucl. Part. Sci.* **2012**, *62*, 407–451. [CrossRef]
26. Mezzacappa, A.; Endeve, E.; Messer, O.E.B.; Bruenn, S.W. Physical, numerical, and computational challenges of modeling neutrino transport in core-collapse supernovae. *arXiv* **2020**, arXiv:2010.09013.
27. Mezzacappa, A.; Marronetti, P.; Landfield, R.E.; Lentz, E.J.; Yakunin, K.N.; Bruenn, S.W.; Hix, W.R.; Messer, O.E.B.; Endeve, E.; Blondin, J.M.; et al. Gravitational-wave signal of a core-collapse supernova explosion of a 15 $M_\odot$ star. *Phys. Rev. D* **2020**, *102*, 23027. [CrossRef]
28. Powell, J.; Müller, B. Gravitational Wave Emission from 3D Explosion Models of Core-Collapse Supernovae with Low and Normal Explosion Energies. *Mon. Not. Roy. Astron. Soc.* **2019**, *487*, 1178–1190. [CrossRef]
29. Radice, D.; Morozova, V.; Burrows, A.; Vartanyan, D.; Nagakura, H. Characterizing the Gravitational Wave Signal from Core-collapse Supernovae. *Astrophys. J.* **2019**, *876*, L9. [CrossRef]
30. Andresen, H.; Muller, E.; Janka, H.T.; Summa, A.; Gill, K.; Zanolin, M. Gravitational waves from 3D core-collapse supernova models: The impact of moderate progenitor rotation. *Mon. Not. R. Astron. Soc.* **2019**, *486*, 2238–2253. [CrossRef]
31. O'Connor, E.P.; Couch, S.M. Exploring Fundamentally Three-dimensional Phenomena in High-fidelity Simulations of Core-collapse Supernovae. *Astrophys. J.* **2018**, *865*, 81. [CrossRef]
32. Kuroda, T.; Kotake, K.; Hayama, K.; Takiwaki, T. Correlated Signatures of Gravitational-wave and Neutrino Emission in Three-dimensional General-relativistic Core-collapse Supernova Simulations. *Astrophys. J.* **2017**, *851*, 62. [CrossRef]
33. Janka, H.T. Neutrino-driven Explosions. *arXiv* **2017**, arXiv:1702.08825.
34. Blondin, J.M.; Mezzacappa, A.; DeMarino, C. Stability of Standing Accretion Shocks, with an Eye toward Core-Collapse Supernovae. *Astrophys. J.* **2003**, *584*, 971–980. [CrossRef]
35. Richers, S.; Ott, C.D.; Abdikamalov, E.; O'Connor, E.; Sullivan, C. Equation of state effects on gravitational waves from rotating core collapse. *Phys. Rev. D* **2017**, *95*, 1–29. [CrossRef]
36. Obergaulinger, M.; Aloy, M.A. Magnetorotational core collapse of possible GRB progenitors. III. Three-dimensional models. *arXiv* **2020**, arXiv:2008.07205.
37. Cerdá-Durán, P.; DeBrye, N.; Aloy, M.A.; Font, J.A.; Obergaulinger, M. Gravitational wave signatures in black hole forming core collapse. *Astrophys. J. Lett.* **2013**, *779*, L18. [CrossRef]
38. Kuroda, T.; Kotake, K.; Takiwaki, T.; Thielemann, F.K. A full general relativistic neutrino radiation-hydrodynamics simulation of a collapsing very massive star and the formation of a black hole. *Mon. Not. R. Astron. Soc. Lett.* **2018**, *84*, 80–84. [CrossRef]
39. Pan, K.C.; Liebendorfer, M.; Couch, S.; Thielemann, F.K. Stellar Mass Black Hole Formation and Multi-messenger Signals from Three Dimensional Rotating Core-Collapse Supernova Simulations. *Astrophys. J.* **2020**, *894*, 4.
40. Colgate, S.A.; White, R.H. The Hydrodynamic Behavior of Supernovae Explosions. *Astrophys. J.* **1966**, *143*, 626. [CrossRef]

41. Kuroda, T.; Kotake, K.; Takiwaki, T. A New Gravitational-Wave Signature From Standing Accretion Shock Instability in Supernovae. *Astrophys. J.* **2016**, *829*, L14. [CrossRef]
42. Abadie, J.; Abbott, B.P.; Abbott, R.; Abbott, T.D.; Abernathy, M.; Accadia, T.; Acernese, F.; Adams, C.; Adhikari, R.; Affeldt, C.; et al. First Low-Latency LIGO + Virgo Search for Binary Inspirals and their Electromagnetic Counterparts. *Astron. Astrophys.* **2012**, *541*, A155. [CrossRef]
43. Abbott, R.; Abbott, T.D.; Abraham, S.; Acernese, F.; Ackley, K.; Adams, A.; Adams, C.; Adhikari, R.X.; Adya, V.B.; Affeldt, C.; et al. GW190521: A Binary Black Hole Merger with a Total Mass of 150 $M_\odot$. *Phys. Rev. Lett.* **2020**, *125*, 101102. [CrossRef] [PubMed]

Review

Compact Binary Coalescences: Astrophysical Processes and Lessons Learned

Mario Spera [1,2,3,*], Alessandro Alberto Trani [4,5,6,*] and Mattia Mencagli [1]

1. International School for Advanced Studies—SISSA, Via Bonomea 365, I-34136 Trieste, Italy; mmencagl@sissa.it
2. National Institute for Nuclear Physics—INFN, Sezione di Trieste, I-34127 Trieste, Italy
3. National Institute for Nuclear Physics—INFN, Sezione di Padova, Via Marzolo 8, I-35131 Padova, Italy
4. Research Center for the Early Universe, Graduate School of Science, The University of Tokyo, 7-3-1 Hongo, Bunkyo-ku, Tokyo 113-0033, Japan
5. Department of Earth Science and Astronomy, College of Arts and Sciences, The University of Tokyo, 3-8-1 Komaba, Meguro-ku, Tokyo 153-8902, Japan
6. Okinawa Institute of Science and Technology, 1919-1 Tancha, Onna-son, Okinawa 904-0495, Japan
* Correspondence: mario.spera@sissa.it (M.S.); aatrani@gmail.com (A.A.T.)

Citation: Spera, M.; Trani, A.A.; Mencagli, M. Compact Binary Coalescences: Astrophysical Processes and Lessons Learned. *Galaxies* **2022**, *10*, 76. https://doi.org/10.3390/galaxies10040076

Academic Editor: Gabriele Vajente

Received: 17 March 2022
Accepted: 9 June 2022
Published: 25 June 2022

Publisher's Note: MDPI stays neutral with regard to jurisdictional claims in published maps and institutional affiliations.

Copyright: © 2022 by the authors. Licensee MDPI, Basel, Switzerland. This article is an open access article distributed under the terms and conditions of the Creative Commons Attribution (CC BY) license (https://creativecommons.org/licenses/by/4.0/).

Abstract: On 11 February 2016, the LIGO and Virgo scientific collaborations announced the first direct detection of gravitational waves, a signal caught by the LIGO interferometers on 14 September 2015, and produced by the coalescence of two stellar-mass black holes. The discovery represented the beginning of an entirely new way to investigate the Universe. The latest gravitational-wave catalog by LIGO, Virgo and KAGRA brings the total number of gravitational-wave events to 90, and the count is expected to significantly increase in the next years, when additional ground-based and space-born interferometers will be operational. From the theoretical point of view, we have only fuzzy ideas about where the detected events came from, and the answers to most of the five Ws and How for the astrophysics of compact binary coalescences are still unknown. In this work, we review our current knowledge and uncertainties on the astrophysical processes behind merging compact-object binaries. Furthermore, we discuss the astrophysical lessons learned through the latest gravitational-wave detections, paying specific attention to the theoretical challenges coming from exceptional events (e.g., GW190521 and GW190814).

Keywords: gravitational-wave astrophysics; stars; black holes; stellar evolution; binary stars; stellar dynamics

1. Introduction

Merging compact-object binaries are binary systems composed of two compact objects that are so close to each other to merge via gravitational wave (GW) emission within the age of the Universe. The members of such binaries can be white dwarfs (WDs), neutron stars (NSs), black holes (BHs), and their combinations, e.g., neutron star-black hole binary (NSBH) systems. These systems have been investigated for decades by many authors, who predicted their existence through theoretical studies that go from the formation and evolution of the stellar progenitors to accurate numerical relativity simulations of the final merger phase [1–9].

From the observational point of view, proving the existence of merging compact-object binaries has always been challenging. While such systems are potentially loud GW sources, catching their GW signal is not straightforward. The passage of a GW produces a relative change in the distance between two points which is

$$\frac{\Delta L}{L} \propto \frac{m_1 m_2}{r l_0} \frac{G^2}{c^4}, \qquad (1)$$

where r is the distance from the GW source, l_0 is the orbital separation of the binary, L is the reference distance, m_1 and m_2 are the masses of the GW source, G is the gravitational constant, and c is the speed of light [10]. The factor $G^2 c^{-4}$ is minuscule ($\sim 5 \times 10^{-55}\,\mathrm{m^2\,kg^{-2}}$), thus, when a GW reaches the Earth, it causes an extremely small perturbation, which is very hard to detect.

Even without direct evidences of GWs, the loss of orbital energy of a compact binary via GWs was verified through radio observations of the binary pulsar PSR B1913 + 16 [11]. The observed orbital decay of the **Hulse–Taylor binary** is remarkably consistent with a GW-induced shrinking. This system, which is expected to merge in ~ 300 Myr, provided not only an additional confirmation of the Einstein's theory of general relativity, but it also suggested to us that there might be not just one, but a population of binary neutron stars (BNSs) that can merge in relatively short times via GW emission.

For the first direct evidence of merging compact-object binaries and their GW's fingerprint, we had to wait until 14 September 2015, when the two ground-based interferometers of the Laser Interferometer Gravitational-wave Observatory (LIGO) were able to *measure* the effect of a passing GW. The signal, named **GW150914**, was attributed to the coalescence of two stellar-mass BHs with masses $m_1 = 36^{+5}_{-4}\,\mathrm{M_\odot}$ and $m_2 = 29^{+4}_{-4}\,\mathrm{M_\odot}$ [12,13][1]. The event carried many scientific implications with itself and it laid the foundations of a new way to investigate the Universe by allowing us to access data never collected before.

The initial identification of GW150914 was made through an unmodelled, low-latency search for GW bursts, which is a search procedure that does not assume any particular morphology of the GW signal, i.e., it is agnostic with respect to the source's properties [12,14,15]. Later, the event was recovered also by other matched-filter pipelines [16]. GW150914 established the existence of binary black holes (BBHs) and that stellar-mass BHs can merge in a Hubble time, becoming detectable sources of GWs. However, the biggest surprise came from **the masses of the BHs**: we did not expect to detect stellar BHs with masses $\gtrsim 20\,\mathrm{M_\odot}$.

Prior to GW150914, our knowledge of stellar-mass BHs was limited to electromagnetic observations of Galactic BH X-ray binaries. At the time of GW150914 discovery, there were only a handful of known BHs with confirmed dynamical mass measurements, most of them with mass $\lesssim 15\,\mathrm{M_\odot}$ [17–19]. Theoretical models did not predict the existence of BHs with masses $\gtrsim 20\,\mathrm{M_\odot}$, with a few remarkable exceptions [20–27]; thus, we could have only approximate ideas about where the BHs of GW150914 came from. One of the very few clues we were able to obtain was that the heavy compact objects likely formed in a low-metallicity environment, where stellar winds are quenched and stars can retain enough mass to turn into heavy BHs [13].

The only solid conclusion was that GW150914 marked a new starting point for the astrophysical community. It gave an unprecedented boost to the development of new theoretical models to study the formation and evolution of compact-object binaries and their progenitor stars, with a new goal: providing an astrophysical interpretation to GW sources.

From the theoretical point of view, two main formation channels have been proposed so far for the formation of merging compact objects. In the **isolated binary channel**, two progenitor stars are bound since their formation; they evolve, and then turn into (merging) compact objects at the end of their life, without experiencing any kind of external perturbation [28–44]. This scenario is driven by single and binary stellar evolution processes, and it is sometimes referred to as the "field" scenario, because it assumes that binaries are born in low-density environments, i.e., that they evolve in isolation. In contrast, in the **dynamical channel**, two compact objects get very close to each other after one (or more) gravitational interactions with other stars or compact objects. This evolutionary scenario is quite common in dense stellar environments (e.g., star clusters), and it is driven mainly by stellar dynamics [27,44–61]. In reality, the two formation pathways might have a strong interplay. In star clusters, the orbital parameters of binaries might be perturbed by many passing-by objects. Dynamical interactions might be strong enough to eject the stellar binary from the cluster and to trigger the merger event in the field. Such an apparently isolated merger would not have occurred if the progenitor stars had evolved in isolation.

Such **hybrid scenarios** blur the line between the dynamical and the isolated binary channel, and they have already been investigated by various authors [62–65].

Our theoretical knowledge of the formation scenarios is hampered by the **uncertainties and degeneracies of the astrophysical models**. Single-star evolutionary tracks, the strength of stellar winds (especially for massive stars at low metallicity), core-collapse and pair-instability supernova (PISN), the orbital parameters of binary stars at birth, binary mass transfer, compact-object birth kicks, stellar mergers, tidal interactions, common envelope (CE), and GW recoil, are only part of the uncertain ingredients of the unknown recipe of merging binaries. In contrast, stellar dynamics is simple and elegant, but developing accurate and fast algorithms for the long-term evolution of tight binaries is challenging. Furthermore, studying the evolution of small-scale systems (2 bodies within $\sim 10^{-6}$ pc) in large star clusters ($\gtrsim 10^5$ objects within a few pc) is computationally intensive [66–75].

Therefore, disentangling different shades of flavors by tasting the final result and going back to the responsible ingredients is very challenging. The consequence is that **the GW catalog is growing faster than our theoretical understanding** of merging compact-object binaries. At the time of writing, we have already achieved an historic breakthrough: we have just started talking about a *population* of BHs. Indeed, the latest Gravitational Wave Transient Catalog (GWTC) reports $\sim$90 events[2], mostly BBH mergers, and the count is expected to significantly increase in the next years, at even faster rates than ever because new ground-based interferometers will be operational and the existing ones will increase their sensitivity [79,80].

The catalog already contains many flavors of BBHs that challenge even up-to-date theoretical models. For instance, **GW190814** (see Section 5.1) is an event with very asymmetric masses, a merger that most theoretical models find very difficult to explain [81]. Furthermore, the lightest member is a mystery compact object with an uncertain nature: it can be the heaviest NS or the lightest BH ever observed and its mass falls right into the lower mass gap (see Section 2.7). **GW190521** (see Section 5.2) is the event with the heaviest BHs, with at least one of the two falling in the upper mass gap (see Section 2.9) [82,83]. Its merger product, a BH with mass $148^{+28}_{-16}\,M_\odot$, is the first confirmation of the existence of intermediate-mass BHs. **GW200105_162426** and **GW200115_042309** (see Section 5.4) are the first NSBHs ever observed [84]. **GW170817** is associated with a merger of two NSs and it is the only event observed not only through GWs but also throughout the whole electromagnetic spectrum, a crucial milestone for **multi-messenger astronomy** [85]. There are also 5 events with preference for **negatively aligned spins** with respect to the orbital angular momentum of the binary, including the mentioned GW200115_042309. Spins and their in-plane components might provide important insights on the formation channels (see Section 2.11). The BH mass distribution and the inferred BBH merger rate make the current scenario even more complex. The former seems to have statistically significant **substructures**, that is, it shows up as clumpy, with BHs that tend to accumulate at chirp masses[3] $\mathcal{M} = 8, 14, 27\,M_\odot$, whereas the latter increases with redshift [80,86–88].

Rather than presenting new results, in this work we review our knowledge of the main astrophysical processes that lead to merging compact-object binaries, focusing mainly on BHs. Furthermore, we discuss the clues we can currently collect on the astrophysical origin of some exceptional GW events, and we discuss the main astrophysical lessons learned so far. This is surely a rapidly evolving field (see also the reviews by [89,90]), and most of the topics reported in this work would deserve a review on their own right. Here, we just give an overview of the main aspects that are relevant for the formation of compact objects.

In Section 2 we discuss the evolution of single stars and their relation to compact remnants, Section 3 deals with binary stellar evolution processes, in Section 4 we examine the effects of stellar dynamics, Section 5 presents the astrophysical lessons learned through GW events, and Section 6 contains a summary and a brief outline of future prospects.

2. Single Stars

Throughout this work, we will often refer to **population-synthesis simulations**. To conduct statistical studies on stellar populations and their compact objects, we should follow self-consistently the evolution of any possible type of single and/or binary star from its formation to its death, and possibly beyond. This is prohibitive if we consider that simulating the evolution of just one star from the main sequence until core collapse might take days (if the complex underlying algorithms converge). Thus, for fast population-synthesis studies, the evolution of single stars is approximated through either (i) fitting formulas to detailed stellar evolution calculations (e.g., [35]) or (ii) the interpolation of look-up tables containing pre-evolved stellar evolution tracks for different stars at various metallicity (e.g., [22]). Binary stellar evolution (see Section 3) and other additional processes (e.g., supernova explosions) are generally added through analytical prescriptions on top of the single-star approximations. Fast population-synthesis codes are currently the main resource available to study compact objects from single and binary stars.

2.1. Overview

The life of a star can be thought as a series of gravitational contractions of the whole structure, and expansions under the influence of thermonuclear fusions of increasingly heavy elements in the core, until the formation of the nuclides of the iron group. Each gravitational contraction increases the central temperature until the heaviest element is ignited. After the exhaustion of input elements in the core, the burning process continues in an outer shell while the core contains the heavier products of the previous thermonuclear reactions.

The fusion of elements lighter than iron is an exothermic reaction, which means that it *releases* energy, balancing the thermal energy that stars lose via radiation. However, the average binding energy per nucleon starts to decrease for elements heavier than iron-56, thus forming these elements is an endothermic process, i.e., it *requires* energy. In reality, (i) the chain of nuclear reactions could continue until the formation of nickel-62, which is the nuclide with the highest binding energy per nucleon, but photodisintegration suppresses its formation, and (ii) iron-56 forms as nickel-56 decays ($^{56}_{28}\text{Ni} \rightarrow\, ^{56}_{27}\text{Co} + e^+ + \nu_e + \gamma$ and $^{56}_{27}\text{Co} \rightarrow\, ^{56}_{26}\text{Fe} + e^+ + \nu_e + \gamma$), therefore, **nickel-56** is the heaviest element that stars can produce efficiently through nuclear fusion ($^{52}_{26}\text{Fe} +\, ^{4}_{2}\text{He} \rightarrow\, ^{56}_{28}\text{Ni} + \gamma$).

Stars spend most of their life on the main sequence, that is transforming hydrogen into helium in their innermost regions. The moment when a star ignites hydrogen in its core defines the zero age main sequence (ZAMS). The ZAMS line appears as a quasi-diagonal line in the Hertzsprung-Russell diagram (Figure 1), which is a standard tool for representing the evolutionary stage of stellar populations. While the bulk of the properties of a star is determined only by its mass at the ZAMS (M_{ZAMS}), the mass of the final compact remnant crucially depends also on parameters like the chemical composition and stellar rotation. These parameters control the efficiency of the processes that affect the final mass of the remnant, i.e., they determine how much mass is lost through stellar winds, how much the stellar core can grow, and how much mass is lost in the supernova (SN) explosion.

However, as a first approximation, M_{ZAMS} is indicative of which remnant the star will leave at the end of its life. Very low-mass stars ($M_{\text{ZAMS}} \lesssim 0.26\,M_\odot$) do not reach the threshold temperature for helium ignition, and after their long ($\gtrsim 70$ Gyr) main sequence phase, they become helium WDs (e.g., [91]). Stars with $0.26\,M_\odot \lesssim M_{\text{ZAMS}} \lesssim 8\,M_\odot$ ignite helium and form a carbon-oxygen (CO) core but do not reach temperatures high enough to ignite CO. After the formation of a CO-core, nuclear reactions in the core stop. At this point, the star is supported only by electron degeneracy pressure. At the end of its life, the star will eject most of its outer shells creating a planetary nebula. What is left at the center is a CO WD (e.g., [91]). Stars with ZAMS masses above $\sim 8\,M_\odot$ can reach iron elements, and their life will end with a SN, possibly leaving behind a NS ($8\,M_\odot \lesssim M_{\text{ZAMS}} \lesssim 20\,M_\odot$) or a BH ($M_{\text{ZAMS}} \gtrsim 20\,M_\odot$).

The limits of these mass ranges are quite uncertain. We might say that these limits are the **zero-level uncertainty** to our understanding of the mass spectrum of compact objects.

On the one hand, the uncertainty stems from theoretical modeling of detailed stellar evolution processes, such as convection, dredge up, wind mass loss, and nuclear reaction rates [25,92–96]. On the other hand, the limits also depend on other stellar parameters, such as rotation and chemical composition. These uncertainties affect the masses of stellar cores, which, in turn, have an impact on the nature and abundance of compact remnants that stars may form.

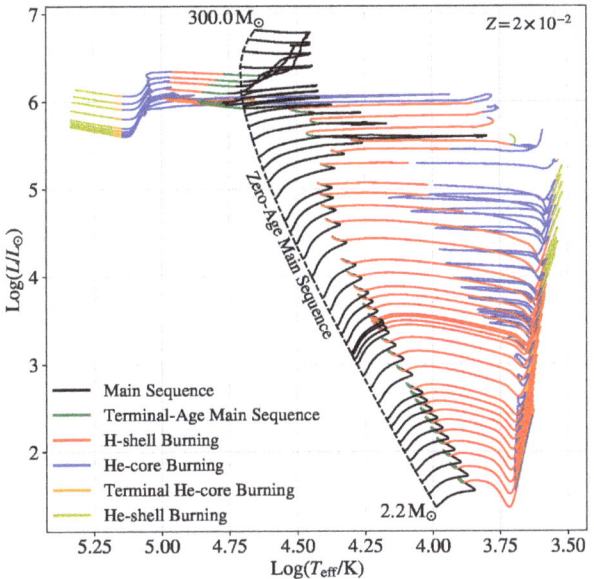

Figure 1. Hertzsprung-Russell diagram (luminosity versus effective temperature) that shows the ZAMS (dashed black line) of stars with masses in the range 2.2 M$_\odot$–300 M$_\odot$, at metallicity $Z = 2 \times 10^{-2}$. The plot also shows the stars' main evolutionary stages (solid lines) until carbon ignition, and it has been obtained through the SEVN population-synthesis code [97] coupled with the look-up tables for single-star evolution from the PARSEC code [98,99].

2.2. The Chandrasekhar Limit

The maximum mass of a WD is well constrained through theoretical arguments, which were firstly outlined by Chandrasekhar [100]. This limit exists because WDs are sustained against gravity by the pressure of electron degeneracy, which can be either non-relativistic or relativistic. Simple stellar polytropic models show that a star supported by a non-relativistic degenerate electron gas has a radius that is inversely proportional to the cube root of its mass, $R \propto M^{-1/3}$ [100]. By looking at the scaling relation, one would expect that the WD radius becomes exceedingly small for exceedingly large masses. However, as the density increases, the electrons become relativistic, and the WD becomes supported by a relativistic degenerate electron gas. In such a state, the corresponding equation of state predicts the existence of a maximum sustainable mass: this is the maximum mass of a WD, also referred to as the **Chandrasekhar mass limit**. Its precise value depends on the average molecular weight per electron, which, in turn, depends on the chemical composition of the WD. For a typical CO or helium WD, the Chandrasekhar limit is $M_c \simeq 1.44\,\mathrm{M}_\odot$.

2.3. The Tolman-Oppenheimer-Volkoff Limit

The maximum mass value for a NS, analogue to the Chandrasekhar limit, is **the Tolman–Oppenheimer–Volkoff (TOV) limit** [101,102]. In this case, support against gravity is provided by the degenerate pressure of a neutron gas. However, unlike in the case of the degenerate electron gas in WDs, neutron-neutron interactions become a crucial (but very uncertain) ingredient to include in the equation of state. Thus, the TOV limit reflects our uncertainties on the NS equation of state. In principle, depending on the adopted equation of state, the TOV limit can be anywhere from $0.5\,M_\odot$ to $3\,M_\odot$ [17,103–114]. The observations of NS masses $\gtrsim 1\,M_\odot$ (e.g., those in binary pulsars, such as PSR B1913 + 16) ruled out the softest equations of state, placing the TOV limit at $M_{\rm TOV} \simeq 1.5$–$3\,M_\odot$. The detection of the GW signal from merging NSs can also be used to constrain the maximum NS mass. In fact, tidal deformations during the last phase of the inspiral affect the properties of the gravitational waveform, which can then be linked to the NS equation of state. The analysis of GW170817 data constrains $M_{\rm TOV} \lesssim 2.3\,M_\odot$ [115,116]. Stellar rotation may also play a role, with rigidly rotating NSs having about 25% larger allowed masses [117–120].

The secondary compact object of GW190814 ($\sim 2.6\,M_\odot$), if a NS, might challenge our understanding of the maximum mass of NSs. Because of the lack of a clear signature of tidal deformations in the GW190814 signal, and the poor constraints on the secondary's spin, no definitive conclusions on the nature of the less massive component of GW190814 exist to date (see also Section 5.1).

2.4. The Role of Stellar Winds

The nature and final mass of a stellar remnant depends crucially on the final properties of the stellar core, which, in turn, depend on the amount of mass a star has lost during its life. Stellar winds have a central role in this picture since they *drive* mass loss over the lifetime of a star. **Stellar winds**, especially for massive stars, are uncertain, and even a factor of 2 uncertainty (typical for state-of-the-art models, e.g., [96]) might have important consequences on the nature and mass spectrum of compact objects.

Wind mass loss originates from the complex **interaction between radiation and matter in stellar atmospheres**. The idea that the outer layers of stars could expand was introduced already at the beginning of the 20th century by Saha [121]. Saha [121] suggested that radiation could be absorbed by matter in the solar atmosphere through an inelastic impact, with a resulting forward velocity of $h\nu/mc$, where h is the Plank length, ν is the frequency of the photon and m the rest mass of matter. We now know that the strongly anisotropic and continuous component of photons from the innermost layers constantly exchanges energy and momentum with free electrons, ions, atoms and dust grains in stellar atmospheres. The momentum equation, considering only a radial direction of the radiation (1D problem), reads

$$v\frac{dv}{dr} = -\frac{GM_*}{r^2} - \frac{1}{\rho}\frac{dp}{dr} + g_{\rm rad} \qquad (2)$$

where M_* is the mass of the star, r is the distance from the center of the star, $v(r)$ is the local wind velocity, $\rho(r)$ is the local density, $p(r)$ is the local pressure of gas, and $g_{\rm rad}$ the radiative acceleration. For the atmospheres of hot massive stars ($T_{\rm eff} \gtrsim 10^4$ K), $g_{\rm rad} = g_{\rm con} + g_{\rm line}$, where $g_{\rm con}$ is the electron scattering acceleration, and $g_{\rm line}$ is the *selective* acceleration caused by spectral line opacity. While $g_{\rm con}$ is quite well established, the challenge is to estimate $g_{\rm line}$[4]. The latter gained increasing importance over the years, especially after the discovery of blue-shifted resonance lines of carbon IV, silicon IV, and nitrogen V, in the OB supergiants δ, ϵ, and ζ Orionis, which suggested expansion velocities $\sim 1400\,\rm km\,s^{-1}$ and mass outflows of $\sim 10^{-6}\,M_\odot\,\rm yr^{-1}$ [122,123].

Castor et al. [124] introduced the idea to express $g_{\rm line}$ through a force multiplier (**CAK theory**), that is

$$v\frac{dv}{dr} = -\frac{GM_*}{r^2} - \frac{1}{\rho}\frac{dp}{dr} + g_{\rm con}[1 + M(\tau)] \qquad (3)$$

where τ is an optical-depth scale for the wind, assumed to depend *only* on the local conditions where the absorption occurs, including the wind velocity gradient [125], and $M(\tau) = k\tau^{-\alpha}$. Castor et al. [124] showed that all spectral lines should be included in the calculation of $M(\tau)$, not only the resonance lines, and that $M(\tau) \gg 1$, that is **stellar winds in hot massive stars are *line driven*.**

More and more spectral lines were included in the CAK theory over the years, and the contribution of **metals**—elements heavier than helium—to stellar winds became increasingly important. Indeed, hydrogen and helium have very few spectral lines in the UV (i.e., the radiation peak frequency of hot massive stars), thus their contribution is expected to be minimal compared to that coming from metals, which have crowded line spectra in the UV band. From CAK theory, it was already clear that **stellar winds are quenched at low metallicity**, that is the mass fraction of metals in a stellar layer. Denoting the mass loss by winds as $\dot{M}_*$ and the metallicity as Z, $\dot{M}_* \propto Z^x$ with x ranging from ∼0.5 [126] to ∼0.9 [127].

It is nowadays understood that the amount and type of metals in the stellar atmosphere affect greatly the mass of the star prior to the SN explosion. Figure 2 shows the typical impact that different values of metallicity have on the final mass of the stars. It is apparent that stars at low Z retain *significantly* more mass than stars at higher Z, thus the former can collapse to significantly heavier BHs.

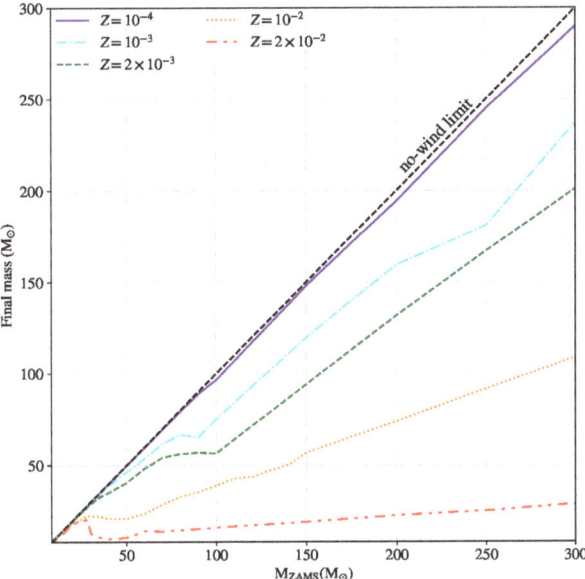

Figure 2. Final mass of the stars as a function of their initial mass, for different values of metallicity. The dashed line at 45 degrees corresponds to the no-wind limit (i.e., final mass = initial mass). Plot obtained with the SEVN population-synthesis code [97] with look-up tables for single-star evolution from the PARSEC code [98].

The precise dependency of winds strength on the amount and kind of metals is still matter of debate. Abbott and Lucy [128] introduced an alternative approach to CAK based on a Monte Carlo method capable of tracking photon paths and includes the possibility of multiple photon scatterings. Vink et al. [129] used this improved approach to re-investigate the $\dot{M}_* - Z$ relation and found $\dot{M}_* \propto Z^{0.69}$ ($\dot{M}_* \propto Z^{0.64}$) for O (B) stars[5]. Vink et al. [129] pointed out that the dominant contribution to the inner (subsonic) stellar wind for O stars at high metallicity ($Z \sim Z_\odot$) comes from the **Fe-group elements**, which are extremely efficient absorbers because their complex atomic structure allows for millions of different lines. At lower metallicity and in the outer (supersonic) wind, the main contribution comes from CNO elements. Furthermore, the recombination of Fe IV to Fe III for T_{eff} going from ∼27,500 K to ∼22,500 K gives a significant boost to mass loss, despite $\dot{M}_* \propto T_{eff}$ in this temperature range (bi-stability jump).

Mass loss is mainly driven by the **Fe-group elements even for Wolf–Rayet (WR) stars**, though the dependence on Z cannot be described as a single power-law. The atmospheres of WR stars are *self-enriched* with metals, (e.g., carbon), so the latter can sustain the mass loss of WR stars for $Z \lesssim 10^{-3} Z_\odot$, where, indeed, $\dot{M}_*$ becomes insensitive to metallicity [130,131]. The mass loss prescriptions developed by Vink et al. [129] and Vink and de Koter [130] are the ones adopted by most state-of-the-art stellar evolution codes. A summary of the prescriptions is given in Section 4 of Vink [96].

Both the CAK theory and the Monte Carlo approach rely on the assumption that a photon with a specific frequency can only be absorbed in an infinitely narrow region of the stellar atmosphere [125]. This approximation breaks down if the wind is not supersonic (e.g., for the inner wind, where $\dot{M}_*$ is set) and for **clumpy winds**. Recent works that do not adopt this assumption predict mass loss rates lower than [129], though the metallicity dependence is remarkably similar (e.g., [132]).

Another important aspect to consider is that the stars that **approach the Eddington limit** during their evolution might experience enhanced mass loss, which may even become insensitive to metallicity and occur in the form of pulsations [99,133–138]. Our knowledge of such continuum-driven winds is hampered by the uncertainties in modeling the interaction between winds and radiation-dominated envelopes.

Another main source of uncertainty is about the **homogeneity** of stellar winds. Several observations seem to suggest that winds are clumpy, though the clumps' formation mechanism and evolution is still under debate [139,140]. The geometry, clumpiness level, and nature of clumps (i.e., optically thin or think) are also uncertain, but they might have a significant impact on stellar winds (e.g., [141]).

Finally, magnetic fields can quench winds and allow the formation of quite massive compact objects even at high metallicities (e.g., [142]), while stellar rotation affects the evolution of stars in many ways, but, overall, it tends to increase mass loss and to allow for the formation of larger stellar cores through enhanced mixing (e.g., [143,144]).

2.5. Core-Collapse Supernovae

As briefly described in Section 2.1, stars with mass $\gtrsim 8 \, M_\odot$ end their life with a SN explosion, ejecting their outer layers in the interstellar medium and leaving a compact remnant behind (either a NS or a BH, depending on the progenitor's mass and structure). The SN process starts with the collapse of the stellar structure, which, after the formation of the Fe-group elements, is not sustained anymore by either the core's nuclear reactions or electron degeneracy pressure. Electron captures on nuclei accelerate core collapse, and when the temperature reaches $\sim 10^{10}$ K the photodisintegration of the Fe-group elements becomes the dominant interaction mechanism ($^{56}\text{Fe} + \gamma \to 13\,^4\text{He} + 4\text{n}$). This process requires very high energies (~ 2 MeV per nucleon), thus the core-collapse accelerates and photons reach enough energies to even photodisintegrate α particles ($^4\text{He} + \gamma \to 2\text{p} + 2\text{n}$). At this stage, electrons have high enough energies ($> m_e c^2$) to collide with protons and forming neutrons and electron neutrinos ($\text{p} + \text{e}^- \to \text{n} + \nu_e$). Thus, it is apparent that there is a significant **enrichment of neutrons**, which eventually form a very compact degenerate structure that can halt the collapse.

The entire collapse process proceeds typically on the dynamical timescale which, for densities $\gtrsim 10^{10}$ g cm^{-3}, might last a few milliseconds. The typical gravitational binding energy of the collapsed core is $\sim 10^{53}$ erg, more than enough to power a typical SN explosion, as long as an effective mechanism that transfers this energy to stellar layers exists.

The mechanism that triggers the actual explosion and, consequently, the link between progenitor stars and their compact remnants, are still matter of debate.

A possible scenario is the **bounce-shock mechanism** (e.g., [145]). During the collapse phase, the core contraction is not self-similar: only the innermost part of the core contracts all together (**homologous core**, ~ 0.5–$1 \, M_\odot$). When the density in the homologous core rises to $\sim 2.7 \times 10^{14}$ g cm^{-3}, the neutron degeneracy pressure would be high enough to sustain the structure against collapse, though the core overshoots its equilibrium state and when $\rho \simeq 5 \times 10^{14}\,\mathrm{g\,cm^{-3}}$ the repulsive nuclear force makes the core bounce back, creating a **shock wave**. The latter might carry enough energy to eject the stellar envelope and power a *prompt explosion*. However, the shock dissipates most of its energy while travelling outwards, through the infalling material, until it stalls at about hundreds of kilometers from the center, well within the Fe core, failing to produce a successful SN.

Neutrinos play a crucial role in reviving the shock through the delayed **neutrino-driven mechanism** (e.g., [146]). At central densities $\sim 5 \times 10^9\,\mathrm{g\,cm^{-3}}$, the mean free path of neutrinos is comparable to the dimension of the homologous core. At higher densities ($\sim 10^{11}\,\mathrm{g\,cm^{-3}}$) neutrinos are basically trapped in the core and they start a congestion that results in the stall of the neutronization process at $\sim 10^{12}\,\mathrm{g\,cm^{-3}}$. The latter completes only seconds after the collapse, when most of the very high-energy neutrinos have had time to escape the core and to deposit part of their energy in the material behind the former shock wave. The rise in pressure in the layer between the proto-NS and the shock wave might revive the latter and power a successful explosion.

One-dimensional simulations of neutrino-driven explosions obtain successful SNe only for low-mass stars with naked O-Ne-Mg cores (ZAMS masses from $\sim 7\,M_\odot$ to $\sim 10\,M_\odot$, electron-capture SNe—see Section 2.6). Two-dimensional simulations revealed that the layer where neutrinos deposit their energy experiences non-radial hydrodynamic instabilities, which (i) generate asymmetric explosions, and (ii) convert thermal energy into kinetic energy, further fueling the explosion (**convection-enhanced neutrino-driven mechanism**, e.g., [147–149]).

State-of-the-art, three-dimensional hydrodynamical simulations of neutrino-driven SNe predict successful explosions for stars up to ~ 25–$30\,M_\odot$. Such sophisticated multi-dimensional simulations are subject to major uncertainties and they are computationally intensive, but most state-of-the-art models seem to agree that blowing up massive stars ($\gtrsim 25\,M_\odot$) is quite challenging (see [150–152] and references therein). For this reason, other explosion mechanisms have been proposed so far (e.g., magnetorotational-driven explosion explosions, [153–161]).

This does not necessarily undermine the foundations of the neutrino-driven mechanism. The detection of heavy stellar-mass BHs through GWs, the lack of observed SNe with massive progenitor stars ($\gtrsim 20\,M_\odot$), and the fact that the observed SN energies are small compared to the energy reservoir of neutrinos ($\lesssim 1\%$), provide clues towards an intrinsically inefficient SN mechanism.

2.6. Electron-Capture SNe

Stars with masses in the range $8\,M_\odot \lesssim M_{ZAMS} \lesssim 10\,M_\odot$ ignite carbon and leave Oxygen-Neon-Magnesium cores. The central temperature and density in the core increase enough to reach electron degeneracy, but never enough to ignite Ne. The increasing electron degeneracy favors electron capture on ^{24}Mg and ^{20}Ne, which lowers pressure support, and initiates the core-collapse phase, which proceeds until the formation of a NS (e.g., [162,163], but see also [164]).

The steep density profile at the edge of O-Ne-Mg cores favors the propagation of the core-bounce shock, preventing its stagnation and the development of significant non-radial hydrodynamical asymmetries in the neutrino-heated layer. This explains why even one-dimensional neutrino-driven simulations produce successful explosions for low-mass progenitors (e.g., [165]). The resulting SN explosion is denoted as an **electron-capture supernova (ECSN)**, and its lack of non-radial asymmetries has implication for the strength of SN kicks (see Section 2.10).

2.7. Compact Remnants and the Lower Mass Gap

The nature and mass of a compact remnant are close relatives of the SN explosion of the progenitor star. Depending on the energy of the explosion, a fraction f_{fb} of the star's material may fall back onto the proto-compact object, which can eventually exceed the TOV limit and transform into a BH. Failed explosions are associated with the collapse of the entire stellar structure and the formation of a massive BH (i.e., $f_{fb} \simeq 1$, **direct collapse**). As such, fallback is a key ingredient to understand the mass spectrum of both NSs and BHs, but constraining it is very challenging.

On the one hand, large grids of self-consistent, multi-dimensional SN explosions are currently not feasible since they are computationally expensive and still require improvements in the implemented physics. On the other hand, one-dimensional simulations predict successful explosions only for low-mass progenitors (no convective engine). For these reasons, grids of SN explosions are generally constructed via one-dimensional models, where the explosion energy is artificially injected either directly into the convective region (**energy-driven models**) or modeled through the expansion of a hard surface placed at a specified mass-cut, generally at the outer border of the iron core (**piston-driven**). In both cases, the convective-enhanced neutrino energy becomes a parameter of the models, and it is generally calibrated using the observed SN luminosities and ^{56}Ni-yields. Following this approach, many authors tried to identify the key parameters of the stellar structure that **drive the explodability of stars** and the amount of fallback.

Fryer et al. [26] studied the outcome of several energy-driven SN explosions and introduced a model where the mass of compact remnants and fallback depend mainly on the final mass of the star and on the mass of the carbon-oxygen core (m_{CO}). Fryer et al. [26] considered two cases: (i) the explosion happens in the first ~250 ms and it is driven mainly by the Rayleigh–Taylor instability (**rapid** model), and (ii) the explosion is delayed (~seconds) and its main engine becomes the standing accretion shock instability (**delayed** model). In both models, fallback has a huge impact on the masses of remnants from stars with $10 M_\odot \lesssim M_{ZAMS} \lesssim 30 M_\odot$. Both models predict direct collapse for $m_{CO} \geq 11 M_\odot$, but the rapid model also for $6 M_\odot \leq m_{CO} \leq 7 M_\odot$, which corresponds to $22 M_\odot \lesssim M_{ZAMS} \lesssim 26 M_\odot$. The latter happens because the rapid mechanism occurs in ~100 ms, i.e., when the infalling ram pressure can be still high enough to prevent a successful explosion. Thus, the rapid approach is more prone to a failed explosion than the delayed model, and it is more sensitive to the compactness of the innermost star's regions. Specifically, in Fryer et al. [26], the stellar models with $22 M_\odot \lesssim M_{ZAMS} \lesssim 26 M_\odot$ develop mixing instabilities and more compact structures during the latest evolutionary stages, causing a failed rapid SN and a **gap** in the remnants mass spectrum between ~$3 M_\odot$ and ~$5 M_\odot$, a dearth which seems in agreement with observations (the **lower mass gap** [17,18,166]). While this argument might suggest a preference for the rapid model, the approach followed by Fryer et al. [26] is simplified and sensitive to the details of the stellar late-stage burning phases. Thus, the existence of the lower mass gap is still matter of debate and there are no conclusive results on the topic.

Figure 3 compares the mass spectrum of compact remnants obtained using the rapid and the delayed SN explosion models applied to the progenitor stars of the SEVN code [97], at $Z = 0.001$ (see also Figure 2 for the progenitors). From Figure 3, it is apparent that the rapid model creates a gap in the BH mass spectrum between ~$2 M_\odot$ and ~$6 M_\odot$ (shaded area), because stars with $23 M_\odot \lesssim M_{ZAMS} \lesssim 26 M_\odot$ evolve through direct collapse, while the delayed model does not.

Ugliano et al. [167] adopted a more sophisticated model than [26], but still 1D, and showed that the **compactness parameter**, $\xi_{2.5}$[6] [168], provides better insights than m_{CO} on the explodability of a star. Ugliano et al. [167] simulations revealed that BHs can form via direct collapse for $M_{ZAMS} \lesssim 20 M_\odot$ and that successful SNe are possible for $20 M_\odot \lesssim M_{ZAMS} \lesssim 40 M_\odot$. This happens because stellar structure does not vary monotonically with M_{ZAMS}, and the SN explosion is sensitive to such variations. Rather than a $\xi_{2.5}$-threshold, it is the **local maxima** in the $\xi_{2.5}$–M_{ZAMS} plane that increase the probability of failed SNe, thus, *islands of explodability* appear for $M_{ZAMS} \lesssim 40 M_\odot$, while direct collapse is dominant for $M_{ZAMS} \gtrsim 40 M_\odot$. Specifically, stars with $22 M_\odot \lesssim M_{ZAMS} \lesssim 26 M_\odot$ tend to have higher $\xi_{2.5}$ than neighboring stars and this creates a dearth of remnants with mass between ~$2 M_\odot$ and $6.5 M_\odot$. While this finding qualitatively agrees with the rapid model of Fryer et al. [26], in Ugliano et al. [167] the gap is naturally produced through a wide range of explosion timescales (from 0.1 s to 1 s) that depend only on the structure of the progenitor at the onset of collapse.

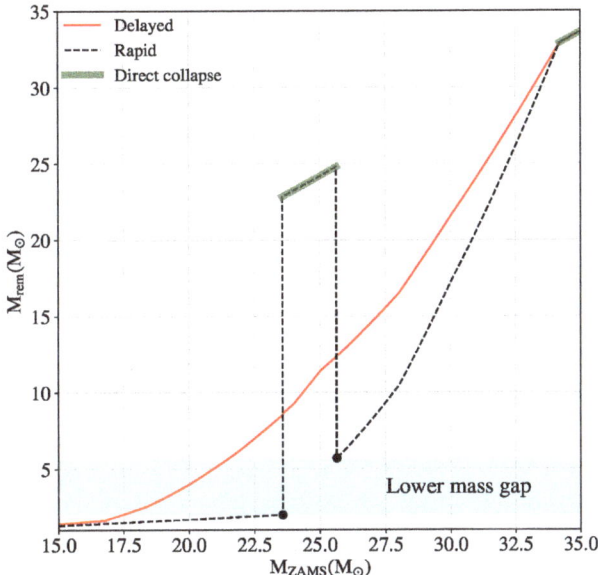

Figure 3. Mass of the compact remnant as a function of the initial mass of its progenitor star obtained with the delayed (solid red line) and the rapid (dashed black line) SN explosion model. The progenitor stars come from the SEVN code [97] with look-up tables from PARSEC [98]. The shaded cyan area shows the location of the lower mass gap, while the semi-transparent green line highlights the region where direct collapse occurs. The two black points define the lower and the upper edge of the mass gap.

Limongi and Chieffi [169] showed that there is a tight monotonic correlation between $\xi_{2.5}$ and m_{CO}, which can be expressed as $\xi_{2.5} = 0.55 - 1.1 m_{CO}^{-1}$, with m_{CO} given in units of $M_\odot$ [170]. This is in qualitative agreement with the simplified approach of Fryer et al. [26], but different assumptions on carbon nuclear reaction rates might significantly affect the correlation (e.g., [171]).

To capture the apparent stochasticity emerging from compactness-based studies, Clausen et al. [172] adopted a probabilistic description to model the NS and BH mass spectrum.

Ertl et al. [173] refined the compactness approach by introducing an even more sophisticated **two-parameter model** to predict the explodability of stars. The first parameter is the normalized enclosed mass for a dimensionless entropy per nucleon of $s = 4$, M_4. This is a good proxy for the proto-NS mass, which corresponds roughly to the iron-core mass at the onset of collapse. The other parameter, μ_4, is the mass derivative at $R(M_4)$. The advantage of the two-parameter model is that the quantities $x \equiv M_4 \mu_4$ and $y \equiv \mu_4$ are strongly connected to the mass accretion rate of the stalling shock and to the neutrino luminosity, respectively, so they are expected to capture the physics of the neutrino-driven explosion better than $\xi_{2.5}$. Ertl et al. [173] predicted successful (failed) SNe for $\mu_4 < y_{sep}(x)$ ($\mu_4 > y_{sep}(x)$), where $y_{sep}(x) = k_1 x + k_2$, and $k_1 \in [0.19; 0.28]$ and $k_2 \in [0.043; 0.058]$, depending on the adopted set of progenitor stars. Ertl et al. [173] (see also [174]) confirmed the presence of islands of explodability, the prevalence of direct collapse for $M_{ZAMS} \gtrsim 30\,M_\odot$, and that fallback SNe are quite rare (i.e., a gap of compact objects with mass between $\sim 2\,M_\odot$ and $5\,M_\odot$).

Recently, Ertl et al. [175] investigated the explodability of a set of evolved naked-helium stars. They confirmed the presence of islands of explodability and the robustness of the two-parameter method to predict progenitors' fate. Furthermore, they showed that the number of fallback SNe that form remnants between $\sim$2 M$_\odot$ and 6 M$_\odot$ is larger than that predicted by Ertl et al. [173] and Sukhbold et al. [174].

It is worth noting that all the features emerging through parametric (1D-based) approaches to the explodability of stars represent only the first step towards an exhaustive scenario for the SN mechanism and the masses of compact remnants. As such, **they should be taken with a grain of salt**, as all the features might be either confirmed or gone by the time we will have a realistic framework for 3D explosion models, which still need improvements and should be considered only as provisional (e.g., [176]).

2.8. Core-Collapse SNe in Population Synthesis Calculations

Performing accurate calculations of the internal structure of stars and sophisticated one-dimensional simulations of the SN mechanism is prohibitive for fast population-synthesis simulations of either single or binary stars.

To calculate the mass of compact remnants, the prescriptions of Fryer et al. [26] are easy to implement and do not require accurate calculations of the internal structure of stars. As such, while very simplified, they are still the most commonly used for fast population-synthesis simulations.

Ertl et al. [175] and Woosley et al. [177] provide tables and fitting formulas to calculate the remnant mass as a function of the initial and pre-SN helium core mass of the star, including also the effect of PISNe and pulsational pair-instability SNe (see Section 2.9). Such relations are expected to capture the physics behind the SN explosion mechanism better than [26].

A similar approach was followed by Patton and Sukhbold [178] who evolved a set of naked carbon-oxygen cores until the onset of collapse and provided values of $\xi_{2.5}$ and M_4 as a function of the initial m_{CO} and carbon abundance X_C. The provided tables can be easily implemented in population-synthesis codes using a compactness- or a two-parameter based method for explodability.

Patton et al. [179] investigated the mass spectrum of NSs and BHs from population-synthesis simulations comparing the different approaches of Fryer et al. [26], Patton and Sukhbold [178], and Woosley et al. [177], for single and binary stars. They found qualitative agreement between the prescriptions of Patton and Sukhbold [178] and Woosley et al. [177], which give results roughly consistent with Ertl et al. [173] and Sukhbold et al. [174]. Significant differences emerge between Patton and Sukhbold [178] and Fryer et al. [26] for the mass distribution of NSs, and for the BH mass spectrum at low masses (10 M$_\odot$–15 M$_\odot$).

2.9. Pair-Instability SNe and the Upper Mass Gap

Theoretical models of single-star evolution predict the existence of another gap in the mass spectrum of compact remnant, which extends from $\sim$60 M$_\odot$ to $\sim$120 M$_\odot$. This is also known as **the upper mass gap**, as opposed to the lower mass gap which corresponds to a dearth of observations of compact objects with mass between $\sim$2.5 M$_\odot$ and $\sim$5 M$_\odot$ [17,18,166] (see also Section 2.7). The pulsational pair-instability supernova (PPISN) [180] and the PISN [181] are the main mechanisms behind the formation of the upper mass gap.

The relation that links the birth mass of a BH (m_{BH}) to M$_{ZAMS}$ is complex because it reflects the uncertainties we have on the evolution of massive stars, on stellar winds, and on the SN explosion mechanism (e.g., [20,26]). Assuming that a progenitor star does not lose mass through stellar winds and that, at the end of its life, the entire stellar structure collapses into a BH without any ejecta, then $m_{BH} \sim$ M$_{ZAMS}$ (e.g., [22] and Figure 2). This is a continuous and monotonically increasing function, thus it predicts no gaps in the BH mass spectrum. Such a simplified relation would work reasonably well for massive stars (M$_{ZAMS} \gtrsim$ 40 M$_\odot$) at low metallicity ($Z \lesssim 10^{-3}$), as long as PPISNe and PISNe are not effective. However, if stars' core temperatures rise above $\sim 7 \times 10^8$ K, photons become energetic enough to **create electron-positron pairs** [180,182–184]. This process converts energy (gamma photons) into rest mass (electrons and positrons), thus it lowers radiation pressure and it triggers stellar collapse. In stars with helium core masses between $\sim 34\,M_\odot$ and $\sim 64\,M_\odot$, the collapse is reversed by oxygen- or silicon- core burning, which shows up as a pulse and makes the core expand and cool. The flash is not energetic enough to disrupt the star and the core begins a series of contractions and expansions (stellar pulsations) that **significantly enhance mass loss**, especially from the outermost stellar layers, and continue until the entropy becomes low enough to avoid the pair instability and stabilize the core until the core-collapse SN explosion. Such pulsational instabilities are referred to as pulsational pair-instability supernova [180,181,185]. In contrast, in stars with helium core masses between $\sim 64\,M_\odot$ and $\sim 130\,M_\odot$, the first pulse is energetic enough to **completely disrupt the entire star** (i.e., PISN [186–188])[7]. Stars with helium cores above $\sim 130\,M_\odot$ experience a rapid pair instability-induced collapse but the energy released by nuclear burning is not enough to reverse the collapse before photodisintegration (endothermic) becomes the dominant photon-interaction mechanism [181]. Thus, the direct collapse to a massive BH (mass $\gtrsim 130\,M_\odot$) becomes unavoidable.

Stars with $Z \gtrsim 5 \times 10^{-3}$ ($Z \gtrsim 2 \times 10^{-2}$) will not evolve through the PISN (PPISN) phase, since their helium core masses cannot grow above $\sim 64\,M_\odot$ ($\sim 34\,M_\odot$) (e.g., [97]), though the metallicity limits are uncertain and depend on the prescriptions adopted to model several processes, including stellar winds, overshooting and stellar rotation.

The main consequence of PPISNe and PISNe is that they create a gap in the BH mass spectrum. At $Z \lesssim 10^{-3}$, the m_{BH} versus M_{ZAMS} relation flattens out for stars with $M_{ZAMS} \gtrsim 60\,M_\odot$ because of the enhanced mass loss caused by PPISNe, which removes all the hydrogen envelopes. Then, the BH mass continues to increase following the growth of the helium core until M_{ZAMS} becomes large enough ($\sim 150\,M_\odot$) to allow for the formation of helium cores $\gtrsim 64\,M_\odot$, when stars evolve through the PISN and $m_{BH} = 0$. This means that the m_{BH} versus M_{ZAMS} relation has a **local maximum** which corresponds to the **lower edge of the upper mass gap** (M_{low}) [63,97,189–193]. Pair creation triggers direct collapse for stars with helium core masses $\gtrsim 130\,M_\odot$ (i.e., $M_{ZAMS} \gtrsim 300\,M_\odot$ for $Z \simeq 10^{-3}$), thus these stars form massive ($\gtrsim 130\,M_\odot$) BHs. This BH mass corresponds to a **local minimum** of the m_{BH}–M_{ZAMS} curve, for $M_{ZAMS} \gtrsim 300\,M_\odot$, and it is referred to as **the upper edge of the upper mass gap** (M_{high}) [97,194–196].

Figure 4 shows a typical example of a BH mass spectrum with the upper mass gap, obtained from a population of single stars, at various metallicities, through the SEVN population-synthesis code [97].

The values of M_{low} and M_{high} are highly uncertain because they strongly depend on metallicity, on the adopted stellar-wind models, on the boundaries of helium core masses for the occurrence of PPISNe and PISNe, on nuclear reaction rates, on stellar rotation, on the treatment of convection, and on the SN explosion mechanism. While most of these processes affect the value of M_{low} and M_{high} by a few percent [170,197–199], the two main sources of uncertainty are our understanding of the failed SN mechanism and of the $^{12}C(\alpha, \gamma)^{16}O$ reaction rate.

As concerns the failed SN mechanism, most theoretical models seem to agree on the occurrence of direct collapse for massive stars but we still do not know if the **hydrogen envelope of the progenitor star** is ejected during the collapse, leaving a remnant with the mass of about the helium core, or if it also contributes to the BH's growth [172,174,200–202]. The collapse of the hydrogen envelope gives an uncertainty on M_{low} of about $20\,M_\odot$ [170].

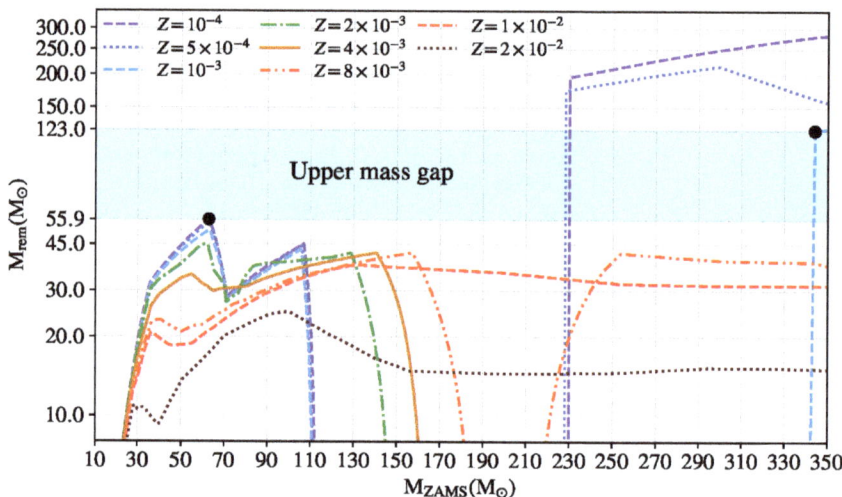

Figure 4. Mass of the BH as a function of the initial mass of its progenitor star, for different values of metallicity $Z \in [10^{-4}; 2 \times 10^{-2}]$. The shaded cyan area shows the location of the upper mass gap. The two black points set the lower edge ($\sim 55.9\,M_\odot$) and the upper edge ($\sim 123\,M_\odot$) of the gap. The plot has been adapted from Spera and Mapelli [97] and it has been obtained through the SEVN code coupled with look-up tables from PARSEC [98] and the delayed SN explosion model [26].

The impact on M_{high} is more difficult to quantify. As example, Spera and Mapelli [97] (see also Figure 4) show that stellar winds of massive stars with $Z \gtrsim 10^{-3}$ are likely strong enough to remove most of the hydrogen envelope during the main sequence phase, preventing the formation of helium cores with mass $\gtrsim 130\,M_\odot$, even for extremely massive stars ($\gtrsim 300\,M_\odot$). Very massive stars ($\gtrsim 350\,M_\odot$) with $Z \simeq 10^{-3}$ might die as Wolf-Rayet stars with mass $\sim 130\,M_\odot$, thus they might be the stars with the smallest M_{ZAMS} to form BHs beyond the gap, setting the value of M_{high} to $\sim 120\,M_\odot$. At $Z \lesssim 10^{-3}$, stars retain a significant fraction of their hydrogen envelope prior to collapse and the stars with the smallest M_{ZAMS} to reach helium core masses above $\sim 130\,M_\odot$ form BHs with masses above the gap. Indeed, at $Z \simeq 10^{-4}$, the stars with the smallest M_{ZAMS} to form BHs beyond the gap have $M_{ZAMS} \simeq 230\,M_\odot$ and $m_{BH} \simeq 210\,M_\odot$ when the hydrogen envelope is accreted by the BH and $m_{BH} \simeq 120\,M_\odot \simeq M_{high}$ when it is not. However, the uncertainties on the evolution of such extremely massive stars are significant and the discussed limits are uncertain. Following these arguments, Woosley [180] pointed out that the upper gap might be seen more as a cut off of BHs with mass $\gtrsim M_{low}$, because BHs with masses $\gtrsim M_{high}$ can form only from the collapse of extremely massive stars, which are supposed to be exceedingly rare and live only for a few Myr (e.g., [203]).

Another significant source of uncertainty is given by our knowledge of **the temperature dependence of the $^{12}C(\alpha, \gamma)^{16}O$ reaction rate** (e.g., [204]). While changing the $^{12}C(\alpha, \gamma)^{16}O$ rate has no significant impact on the stellar structure, it governs the relative amount of oxygen with respect to carbon in the core. Low $^{12}C(\alpha, \gamma)^{16}O$ rates translate into large carbon reservoirs at the end of helium-core burning and into a prolonged carbon-burning phase, which contributes to suppress pair production, stabilize the oxygen core, and delay the latter ignition. In contrast, high $^{12}C(\alpha, \gamma)^{16}O$ rates imply significant carbon depletion in favor of oxygen, which ignites explosively just after the helium burning phase. This has a strong impact on the upper mass gap because low (high) $^{12}C(\alpha, \gamma)^{16}O$ rates push M_{low} and M_{high} towards higher (lower) values [192,193,198,205,206]. Furthermore, massive stars with low $^{12}C(\alpha, \gamma)^{16}O$ rates might experience significant dredge up which tends to stabilize the oxygen core even further. In this scenario, if very low (-3σ) $^{12}C(\alpha, \gamma)^{16}O$ rates are considered together with the collapse of the hydrogen envelope, the upper mass gap might even disappear [206,207]. Conservatively, the impact of $^{12}C(\alpha,\gamma)^{16}O$ rates on both M_{low} and M_{high} is about 15 $M_\odot$.

It is also worth mentioning that the presence of physics beyond the standard model might also significantly affect the edges of the upper mass gap (e.g., [208]).

Overall, considering all the main known uncertainties so far, $M_{low} \in [40\,M_\odot; 75\,M_\odot]$. As for M_{high}, the scenario is more complex. A left endpoint of $\sim 120\,M_\odot$ for the mass interval seems to be a quite robust prediction, while the right endpoint is more uncertain. For instance, considering only stars with $M_{ZAMS} \lesssim 250\,M_\odot$ and the collapse of the entire hydrogen envelope, M_{high} might rise to $\sim 200\,M_\odot$. More conservative limits on M_{ZAMS} (e.g., $M_{ZAMS} \lesssim 150\,M_\odot$) might even cause the mass gap to be seen as a cut off at M_{low}. However, while rare, very massive stars might form from a series of stellar mergers, thus $M_{high} \in [120M_\odot; 200M_\odot]$ might be considered as a reasonable range for M_{high}.

To model the enhanced mass loss predicted by PPISNe, population-synthesis codes generally adopt fitting formulas to detailed stellar evolution calculations (e.g., [97,209]).

2.9.1. Piling-Up BHs

A direct consequence of the enhanced mass loss caused by PPISNe is that most stars with initial mass $60\,M_\odot \lesssim M_{ZAMS} \lesssim 150\,M_\odot$ die as naked helium cores, even at very low metallicity. The final helium cores of these stars have a mass $35\,M_\odot \lesssim m_{HE} \lesssim 65\,M_\odot$, but pair-instability pulses are stronger for heavier cores, thus the helium cores left by PPISNe lie more likely in the range $35\,M_\odot \lesssim m_{HE} \lesssim 45\,M_\odot$. Thus, we might expect **an excess of BHs (pile-up)** with masses in about the same range [97,177,189,210].

Constraining the extent of the BH bump and its mass limits is challenging. From a purely single stellar evolution perspective, the significance of the PPISNe bump depends primarily on the slope of the m_{BH}–M_{ZAMS} theoretical curve for $M_{ZAMS} \lesssim 60\,M_\odot$ (not affected by PPISNe) compared to that for $60\,M_\odot \lesssim M_{ZAMS} \lesssim 150\,M_\odot$ (affected by PPISNe). With a standard initial mass function (e.g., Kroupa [203]), if the m_{BH}–M_{ZAMS} curve at $60\,M_\odot \lesssim M_{ZAMS} \lesssim 150\,M_\odot$ is significantly flatter than the curve at $M_{ZAMS} \lesssim 60\,M_\odot$, then the bump in the BH mass distribution will be more relevant and narrower, especially in correspondence of the kink between the two slopes. However, the relative slopes and the position of the **kink in the m_{BH}–M_{ZAMS} curve are highly uncertain** since they depend on many ingredients including metallicity, stellar winds, the details of the growth of helium cores inside massive stars, nuclear reaction rates (e.g., $^{12}C(\alpha,\gamma)^{16}O$), and the collapse of the hydrogen envelope.

Figure 5 shows the BH mass spectrum (left panel) and the BH mass distribution (right panel) obtained from a population of 10^7 single stars at $Z = 10^{-3}$. The progenitors follow a Kroupa [203] initial mass function with masses in the range $[25; 145]M_\odot$. The black curve does not include the contribution of PPISNe, while the red does. It is apparent that the bumps in the BH mass distribution are close relatives of the kinks of the m_{BH}-M_{ZAMS} curve. The pile-up of BHs through PPISNe happens at about $33\,M_\odot$, around the kinks B and C. However, the **model we adopted** to make Figure 5 has an additional kink in A, which also piles up BHs at $33\,M_\odot$, even without PPISNe. The pile-up at $66.3\,M_\odot$ (kink D) disappears when PPISNe are considered because the latter force $m_{BH} \lesssim 55\,M_\odot$. Therefore, besides depending on metallicity, the existence and position of the kinks A, B, C, and D is *strongly* model-dependent.

A pile-up of compact objects at mass 30–40 $M_\odot$ in GW detections might suggest a PPISNe signature in the BH mass spectrum (e.g., [79,80]). However, the effect of piling up *merging* BHs at specific masses is not only model-dependent (e.g., Figure 5) but it might also have *strong* degeneracies with stellar dynamics and binary stellar evolution processes, thus disentangling the various contributions might be challenging.

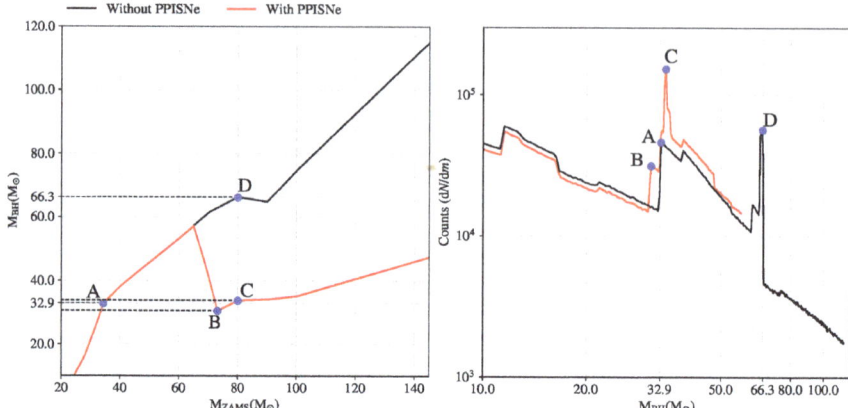

Figure 5. Mass spectrum (m_{BH} vs M_{ZAMS}, left panel) and mass distribution (dN/dm vs m_{BH}, right panel) of BHs obtained evolving a population of 10^7 single stars. The progenitors follow a power-law initial mass function that scales as $dN/dM_{ZAMS} \propto M_{ZAMS}^{-2.3}$ [203] with masses between $25\,M_\odot$ and $145\,M_\odot$. The black (red) curve shows the results without (with) PPISNe. The points A, B, C, and D represent the kinks of the m_{BH}–M_{ZAMS} curve. The plot has been obtained for $Z = 10^{-3}$ through the SEVN population-synthesis code [22] with PPISNe fitting formulas from [97], look-up tables for single stellar evolution from the PARSEC code [98], and the delayed SN explosion mechanism [26].

2.9.2. Populating the Gap

The upper mass gap is a feature in the BH mass spectrum that comes from our theoretical knowledge of *single stellar evolution* processes. However, we know that stars are not born in isolation and, during their life, they may evolve through a series of events that can change their fate in many ways. Specifically, there are various (not exotic) **astrophysical processes that can form BHs in the mass gap**, without contradicting its existence (e.g., [52,56,58,207,211–223]).

For instance, a Nth-generation BH, which is a BH coming from a previous merger of two $(N-1)$th-generation BHs, can easily fall into the upper mass gap. Furthermore, assuming that the hydrogen envelope participates in the BH formation process, stars with an oversized hydrogen envelope (gained through mass accretion from a companion star or even through a merger), but small enough helium cores to avoid the PISN, might form oversized BHs, with masses in the upper mass gap. The latter scenario is quite rare but possible for the isolated binary evolution channel (e.g., [222]).

Nth-generation BHs and oversized BHs coming from binary evolution can be retained, acquire a companion, and merge within a Hubble time in dense stellar environments. Therefore, they can become loud (and detectable) sources of GWs with at least one member in the upper mass gap (e.g., [214,215]).

Testing the presence of the upper mass gap and its underlying stellar astrophysics through GW detections might be challenging. The latest population analysis coming from the GWTC-3 shows a monotonically decreasing BH mass distribution at masses $\gtrsim 50\,M_\odot$ and an inconclusive evidence for the presence of the upper mass gap [80]. On the other hand, observing GW events with members in the upper mass gap might be the distinguishing feature of astrophysical formation channels other than single or isolated binary-star evolution, not necessarily contradicting the existence of the gap itself.

We will explore more scenarios on how to populate the upper mass gap in Section 5.

2.10. SNe Asymmetries and Kicks

Galactic pulsars are observed with **fairly large spatial velocities**, which can be as high as thousands of kilometers per second. Such values are too large to be explained through Blaauw kicks [224] from SN explosions in binary systems. Thus, some, if not all, compact objects should receive quite high **kicks at birth** [225]. Kicks have a huge impact on merging compact objects if they are members of isolated binaries (e.g., change of orbital parameters, unbinding the binary) or if they reside in dense stellar environments (e.g., ejections).

From the observational point of view, Hobbs et al. [226] presented an up-to-date catalogue of Galactic pulsars and showed that the mean three-dimensional velocity of young (age $\lesssim$ 3 Myr) pulsars is $400 \pm 40 \, \mathrm{km \, s^{-1}}$. The three-dimensional speeds are well fit by a Maxwell-Boltzmann distribution with $\sigma_{1D} = 265 \, \mathrm{km \, s^{-1}}$.

A more recent work [227] found that a double-Maxwell-Boltzmann distribution $f(v) = w f_1(v; \sigma_1) + (1-w) f_2(v; \sigma_2)$ with $\sigma_1 \simeq 80 \, \mathrm{km \, s^{-1}}$, $\sigma_2 \simeq 320 \, \mathrm{km \, s^{-1}}$, and $w \simeq 0.4$ significantly improve the theoretical description of the pulsar data.

Analyses of a new dataset of proper motions and parallaxes [228] confirm the bi-modality feature of the velocity distribution with $w = 0.2^{+0.11}_{-0.10}$, $\sigma_1 = 56^{+25}_{-15} \, \mathrm{km \, s^{-1}}$, and $\sigma_2 = 336^{+45}_{-45} \, \mathrm{km \, s^{-1}}$.

From the theoretical point of view, **asymmetries in the SN ejecta** can impart high kicks to newly-born compact objects (e.g., [229]). The kicks can vary from $\sim 10 \, \mathrm{km \, s^{-1}}$ to $\sim 1000 \, \mathrm{km \, s^{-1}}$, depending mainly on the steepness of the density profile at the outer edge of the stellar core (i.e., compactness), and on the stochastic variations of non-radial instabilities associated with the SN engine. Shallow (steeper) density profiles are more (less) prone to SN shock stalling, thus neutrinos will be able to interact with more (less) material and produce more- (less-)asymmetric ejecta (e.g., [230]). As already discussed in Section 2.6, the progenitors of **electron-capture SNe** have very steep density profiles, so the explosion is expected to impart **low kicks** to NSs (tens of $\mathrm{km \, s^{-1}}$, e.g., [231]). Similar results have been obtained for **ultra-stripped stars**, which might form during mass transfer in close binaries [232–234].

Assuming that BHs share the same formation mechanism as NSs and that kicks are driven by the asymmetries in the SN ejecta, BH kicks are expected to be smaller than NSs', with differences coming mainly from the heavier mass of BHs and the smaller amounts of ejecta. This theoretical argument cannot be supported by observations, because BH kicks lack strong observational constraints. Repetto et al. [235] and Repetto and Nelemans [236] showed that the large distances from the Galactic plane of some BH X-ray binaries can only be explained if BHs acquire high kicks at birth (as high as those of NSs), even though they cannot completely rule out smaller BH kicks (see also [237]).

For rapid population-synthesis calculations, most codes assign birth kicks assuming two velocity distributions that distinguish between electron-capture and ultra-stripped SNe from all the other core-collapse SNe. Following [26], compact-object kicks (v_k) are generally assumed to be the same as those coming from observations of pulsars (v_{NS}), but modulated by the fraction of fallback (f_{fb}), so that BHs that form via direct collapse (i.e., no SN ejecta) do not receive kicks:

$$v_k = (1 - f_{fb}) v_{NS} = \frac{m_{ej}}{m_{ej} + m_{rem} - m_{proto}} v_{NS}, \qquad (4)$$

where m_{rem} is the mass of the compact object, m_{proto} is the mass of the proto-compact object, and m_{ej} is the mass of the SN ejecta. A threshold of $m_{rem} = 2\text{–}3 \, M_\odot$ is assumed for distinguishing BHs from NSs.

Adopting small kicks for ECSNe and SNe from ultra-stripped progenitors is crucial to match the rates of merging NSs inferred by the LVK collaboration (e.g., [238,239]), but the simple model by Fryer et al. [26] fails to produce low kicks for compact objects from such channels, because the kick prescription is not very sensitive to m_{ej} (it appears in both the numerator and the denominator of Equation (4)). Here is an instructive example. Case 1: a progenitor star with $m_1 = 10 \, M_\odot$, $m_{He,1} = 6 \, M_\odot$, and $m_{CO,1} = 4 \, M_\odot$. The delayed SN prescription in Fryer et al. [26] predicts $m_{rem,1} \simeq 2.5 \, M_\odot$, $m_{ej,1} \simeq 7.5 \, M_\odot$, and $f_{fb,1} \simeq 0.14$. Case 2: same progenitor that becomes ultra-stripped via binary evolutionary processes. We will have $m_2 \simeq m_{He,2} \simeq m_{CO,2} \simeq 4 \, M_\odot$, and the delayed SN prescription predicts

$m_{\text{rem},2} \simeq 2.1\,\text{M}_\odot$, $m_{\text{ej},2} \simeq 1.9\,\text{M}_\odot$, and $f_{\text{fb},2} \simeq 0.31$. This means that the birth-kick ratio between the two cases would be

$$\frac{v_{\text{k},1}}{v_{\text{k},2}} = \frac{1 - f_{\text{fb},1}}{1 - f_{\text{fb},2}} \simeq 1.2 \tag{5}$$

that is, mostly the same kick for case 1 and case 2, despite the factor of $\simeq 4$ difference in m_{ej}. This is in contrast with both momentum-conserving arguments and with the low kicks obtained through multi-dimensional SN explosions from ultra-stripped progenitors.

Recently, Giacobbo and Mapelli [240] proposed a **unified approach** derived from momentum-conserving arguments, inspired by Bray and Eldridge [239,241]. Independent of the progenitor, the nature of compact remnant, and the SN explosion engine, the birth kick (v_k) is expressed as

$$v_\text{k} = v_{\text{NS}} \frac{m_{\text{ej}}}{m_{\text{rem}}} \frac{\langle m_{\text{NS}} \rangle}{\langle m_{\text{ej}} \rangle} \tag{6}$$

where $\langle m_{\text{NS}} \rangle$ ($\langle m_{\text{ej}} \rangle$) is the average NS (ejecta) mass obtained from a population of isolated stars. This method naturally reproduces the bi-modal kick distribution obtained from observations: it predicts small kicks for compact objects from ECSNe and ultra-stripped progenitors (for which $m_{\text{ej}} \ll \langle m_{\text{ej}} \rangle$), and the normalization $\langle m_{\text{NS}} \rangle / \langle m_{\text{ej}} \rangle$ ensures $v_\text{k} \simeq v_{\text{NS}}$ for isolated progenitors, so that kicks match those observed for Galactic pulsars.

Constraints on the kick magnitudes can be obtained through multi-dimensional simulations of SN explosions, though, as already discussed in Section 2.5, these sophisticated simulations are complex and highly uncertain, thus their results cannot be considered as conclusive.

2.11. Spins

The topic of spins of compact objects would deserve a review in its own right. Here, we discuss the main aspects that are relevant for the current catalog of GW detections, thus we focus mainly on BHs.

The spin rate of compact objects at birth is very uncertain, because it depends on the angular momentum transport mechanisms in the stellar interior, the efficiency of which is still matter of debate. Asteroseismic observations ([242–247]) have shown that the spin rates of red giant cores and WDs are slower than theoretically predicted by nearly all angular momentum transport mechanisms, such as meridional circulation, shear instabilities or propagation of gravity waves [248–258]. The magnetohydrodynamical instability known as the Tayler–Spruit dynamo [259,260] can provide more efficient angular momentum transport than other mechanisms, albeit early works predicted spin rates roughly an order of magnitude too large [252]. The typical BH natal spins predicted by the Tayler-Spruit dynamo are $\chi \sim 0.05$–0.15. Fuller et al. [261] and Fuller and Ma [262] (see also Heger et al. [263]) show that the Tayler–Spruit instability can persist in red giant branch stars despite the existence of strong composition gradients, and they argue that its growth will saturate in a different manner than proposed by Tayler [259] and Spruit [260]. In their formulation, sometimes referred to as the modified Tayler–Spruit dynamo, the instability can grow to larger amplitudes and produce stronger magnetic torques, which lead to an even more efficient angular momentum transport and lower natal spins ($\chi \sim 0.01$). The modified Tayler–Spruit instability proposed by Fuller et al. [261] may correctly explain the angular momentum contained in the core of stars, and hence the spin of the BH that is formed upon the collapse of massive stars. Eggenberger et al. [264] shows that the revised prescription for the transport by the Tayler–Spruit instability does not provide a complete solution to the missing angular-momentum transport revealed by asteroseismology of evolved stars. However, asteroseismic observations and new detailed theoretical models show that the angular momentum transport from the cores to the envelopes of massive stars may be very efficient, thus the first-born BH in a binary may form with low spin (e.g., [261,262,264–266]).

The GW observations of low effective spins in most BBHs also hint at an efficient angular momentum transport in their progenitors [44,80,267,268].

Stars in binaries may spin up via tides, while compact objects in binaries may spin up though accretion. For instance, first-generation, highly spinning BHs can form if their progenitor stars become chemically homogeneous due to tides in close binaries, but BBHs originating from this channel have large and nearly equal masses [39–41]. BHs in X-ray binaries tend to spin faster than BHs observed through GWs, but whether these systems are distinct populations or two sides of the same coin is still matter of debate [19,269]. Spinning up first-born BHs in binaries would require a significant amount of accretion, which is unlikely to occur over the short evolutionary timescale of the massive, non-degenerate companion star or during a common-envelope phase (e.g., [270]). However, Olejak and Belczynski [271] find out that evolutionary sequences that do not involve a CE phase can still lead to an appreciable fraction (∼10%) of systems that are spun up via tides, reaching $\chi \gtrsim 0.4$, considering the classic Tayler-Spruit angular momentum transport. Bavera et al. [272] consider highly efficient angular momentum transport with the modified Tayler-Spruit dynamo, and obtain high spins for the second-born BH at low metallicity due to tidal spin-up. Conversely, they find that at high metallicity the second-born BH has a negligible spin because of wind mass-loss that spins down the progenitor and widens the binaries, weakening tidal interactions.

Finally, the merger remnants of coalescing BBHs will be spinning even if the progenitor BHs were non-spinning. As the two BHs merge, part of the angular momentum of the binary is converted into the spin of the final BH. This has important implications for the signatures of **hierarchical mergers**, wherein GW events are produced by second or higher-generation BHs formed from the coalescence of BBHs, rather than from SN explosions of their progenitor stars. Repeated mergers of BHs can thus produce higher and higher spinning remnants, and naively one might expect to achieve maximally spinning BHs, i.e., BHs with dimensionless spin $\chi \simeq 1$. However, this is not the case, because the spin of the final remnant depends also on the spin of the progenitor BHs and their relative orientation with respect to the binary angular momentum vector. Spins anti-aligned with the binary angular momentum will subtract from the total angular momentum budget of the final BH. Therefore, we expect hierarchical mergers to produce, after several generations of mergers, BHs with an average of $\chi \simeq 0.7$ [190,211,273–277]. The latter is true for nearly-equal mass mergers of higher generation BHs. On the other hand, if many first generation BHs coalesce into a single, massive merger product (as massive BH runaway formation scenarios, e.g., see [278]), the final BH spin will decrease on average. This is because, at next-to-leading order, the decrease in BH spin is proportional to the mass ratio of the binary, and thus on average the spin distribution of merger products will decrease after asymmetric mergers (e.g., [279]). Any hierarchical merger scenario, requires mechanisms to assemble higher-generation BHs into merging binaries, which will be described later in Section 4.

The spins of merging BBHs can be probed via GW observations. GWs carry information about the spin magnitude and orientation of the merging BHs into two phenomenological parameters: the effective inspiral spin parameter χ_{eff} and the effective precession parameter χ_p [280–283]. The effective inspiral spin parameter relates to the component of the BHs' spins aligned to angular momentum of the binary orbit, and can be expressed as:

$$\chi_{\text{eff}} = \frac{m_1 \chi_1 \cos \theta_1 + m_2 \chi_2 \cos \theta_2}{m_1 + m_2} \qquad (7)$$

where m_1 and m_2 are the masses of the two BHs, χ_1 and χ_2 are the two dimensionless spins, and θ_1 and θ_2 are the obliquities, i.e., the angle between the spin direction and the normal to the plane of the binary. The effective spin parameter remains approximatively constant during the inspiral, and it can be used to constrain the individual spins of the BHs. Note that the effective spin parameter is the mass-weighted average of the spin component parallel to the angular momentum vector. Consequently, high-mass-ratio inspirals will mostly carry information about the primary's spin (e.g., GW190412, GW190814, Sections 5.1 and 5.3).

The second phenomenological parameter, χ_p, relates to the orbital precession caused by the in-plane spin component, and is expressed as:

$$\chi_\mathrm{p} = \max\left[\chi_1 \sin\theta_1, \chi_2 \sin\theta_2 \frac{4q+3}{4+3q} q\right] \tag{8}$$

where the indices $_1$ and $_2$ refer to the primary and secondary BHs, so that $m_1 > m_2$, and $q = m_2/m_1 \leq 1$ is the mass ratio.

Correlations between χ_eff and other parameters can be used to disentangle the formation scenarios of GW sources. For example, Zevin and Bavera [284] find that isolated binary evolution cannot produce BBHs with significant mass asymmetry and high spins in the primary BHs, unless either inefficient angular momentum transport or super-Eddington accretion are assumed [272]. The active galactic nuclei (AGN) scenario instead predicts values of χ_eff that are anti-correlated with the mass ratio q, which is roughly consistent with the observed distribution [285,286]. We caution that these studies focus on a small region of the available parameter space of BBH mergers, and more systematic investigations will be required for a better understanding of the correlations between χ_eff and the other observables.

3. Binary Stars

As briefly discussed in Section 1, two main mechanisms to pair compact objects have been proposed. The isolated binary evolution pathway, in which the GW progenitors evolve through various binary evolution processes in isolation, and the dynamical scenario, where the evolution of binaries is mediated by gravitational interactions with other bodies. Here we focus on the isolated binary mechanism, and leave the discussion of the dynamical scenarios for Section 4. We note, however, that some of the formation pathways that have been proposed so far blur the lines between these two categories, requiring elements of both binary stellar evolution and gravitational dynamics.

Many stars, especially the more massive ones, are born in binaries or higher multiple stellar systems. Moe and Di Stefano [287] showed that the multiplicity of stellar systems increases with the stellar mass. This crucial result suggests that **most BH and NS progenitors are not isolated**, but members of binaries, triples, and even quadruple stellar systems. Studying the interactions between close stars is crucial to understand the evolutionary histories of GW mergers.

The timescales of GW coalescence were derived analytically by Peters and Mathews [288], which showed that a circular BBH with masses m_1, m_2 will coalesce in a time t_GW given by:

$$t_\mathrm{GW} = \frac{5}{256} \frac{c^5 a^4}{G^3 m_1 m_2 (m_1 + m_2)} \tag{9}$$

where a is the semimajor axis of the binary. Considering two BHs of $10\,\mathrm{M}_\odot$, it follows that, in order to merge within ~ 13 Gyr, the separation must be smaller than ~ 0.1 au. At solar metallicity, the stellar progenitors of $10\,\mathrm{M}_\odot$ BHs have about $30\,\mathrm{M}_\odot$ ZAMS mass and a radius of $\sim 20\,\mathrm{R}_\odot \simeq 0.18$ au. It is apparent that such a binary could not have been born at a separation of $\lesssim 0.1$ au, because the stars would have collided during the main-sequence phase, even without considering the following giant phase. Therefore, the progenitors of merging BBHs from isolated stellar evolution must have been born at wider separations, and subsequently brought to smaller separations by various mechanisms. Here, we begin by describing the evolutionary processes that can affect binary stars.

3.1. Stellar Tides

When a stellar binary is very tight, **the point mass approximation is not enough** to describe its motion, because finite-size effects (i.e., **tidal forces**) become significant.

An elegant derivation of the equations of motion for a binary affected by tides can be found in [31,289]. The main idea behind these equations is that the star is deformed by its companion, generating a gravitational quadrupole moment. Due to dissipation sources in the stellar interior, the response of the quadrupole moment is not instantaneous with respect to the tidal field. This delay, called time-lag, allows the coupling between the rotational and orbital angular momenta, in addition to the dissipation of orbital energy in the stellar interior.

While the equations of [31] have been used to model a variety of different tidal dissipation mechanisms, the precise source of tidal dissipation depends on the stellar structure [290]. Tidal dissipation in convective layers occurs via the convective motion of large eddies. The convective flows counteracts the tidal flow, which gives rise to dissipation and the lag of the tidal bulges. This kind of tide is referred to as **the equilibrium tide**. For this reason, to quantify the tidal dissipation of evolved stars, we need to characterize the timescale of the convective motion, which is the eddie turnover timescale τ_{conv}. This time scale can be calculated in several ways, either from the bulk properties of the star e.g., [35,291] or from the mixing length parameters adopted in the stellar models [292].

In stars with a radiative envelope, the source of tidal dissipation is the damping of low-frequency gravity waves near the surface of the star [293]. This kind of tide, called **dynamical tide**, is generally modeled following Hut [31], who relies on the ideas of quadrupole deformation and time lag, which are more suitable to describe the equilibrium tide. Nonetheless, just like the equilibrium tide, the tidal dissipation constants of the dynamical tide depend on the details of the stellar structure. The dissipation rate of the dynamical tide scales linearly with a dimensionless tidal torque constant, named E_2, which must be calculated from the stellar density profile e.g., [294,295]. Tabulated values for E_2 were provided by Zahn [293], and were later fitted as a function of stellar mass by Hurley et al. [35], to use in population-synthesis codes. More recent fitting formulae can be found in Qin et al. [265], which, in turn, are based on the ones of Yoon and Cantiello [135]. An alternative formulation for the dynamical tide, which avoids entirely the tidal torque constant E_2, was proposed by Kushnir et al. [296].

Compact stars (WDs, NSs) also experience tides, although their rates of tidal dissipation are poorly constrained [35,297–299].

The main effects of tides are the following. First, they tend to **circularize eccentric binaries**, shrinking their semimajor axis. Second, they tend to **spin-up stars in close binaries**, synchronizing their rotation period to the orbital period, and aligning the spin directions with the angular momentum vector of the binary. Both effects are especially important in the context of GWs. Specifically, tidal spin-up can change both magnitude and orientation of the spins of compact objects with respect to the orbital angular momentum vector, and GW observations may give us insights into these two parameters (see also Section 2.11).

Finally, another crucial consequence of tides is that they can **radically change the structure and evolution of a star**. Tidal spin-up in a close binary introduces rotational mixing of the stellar interior, which tends to flatten its chemical composition gradient. For very close massive binaries, rotational mixing drives large-scale Eddington–Sweet circulations [300,301], so that the entire star is fully mixed. These stars undergo **chemical homogeneous evolution (CHE)**, which has been proposed as a formation pathway for BBHs [36,39–41,302,303]. Chemically-homogeneous stars skip entirely the evolved giant phase because they do not develop a core-envelope boundary. Since such stars remain compact even during the post-MS phases, they can evolve very close to each other without merging via unstable mass transfer (Section 3.2). Therefore, CHE can produce BBHs that merge within the age of the Universe. Because this scenario involves tight binaries with synchronized spins, it predicts BH mergers with large aligned spins. It also favors high BH masses (>20 $M_\odot$) and nearly equal mass ratios ($q \simeq 1$).

3.2. Mass Loss, Mass Transfer and Accretion

As detailed in Section 2.4, stars lose mass through stellar winds. In binaries, such mass loss leads to changes in the orbit of the binary. If the mass loss by winds is isotropic (i.e., no net change in momentum) and adiabatic (slow with respect to the orbital period), the rate of change in orbital semimajor axis a is:

$$\dot{a} = -a\frac{\dot{m}_1 + \dot{m}_2}{m_1 + m_2} \tag{10}$$

where $\dot{m}_1$ and $\dot{m}_2$ are the (negative) mass change rates of the two stars. If the mass loss is slow, the only effect of mass loss is the increase in size of the binary, while its eccentricity remains constant [304,305].

However, the wind lost by one star may be partially accreted by its companion, which introduces a positive rate of mass change. In addition, part of the accreted material may carry linear and angular momentum, further affecting the binary orbit. **The wind accretion rate** can be calculated using the Bondi and Hoyle [306] accretion model. Given a binary with eccentricity e, donor wind speed v_w, and mean orbital velocity $v_{\text{circ}} = \sqrt{G(m_1 + m_2)/a}$, Hurley et al. [35] approximate the mass accretion rate as:

$$\dot{m}_2 = \frac{1}{\sqrt{1-e^2}}\left(\frac{G m_2}{v_w^2}\right)^2 \frac{\alpha_w}{2 a^2}\frac{|\dot{m}_1|}{[1+(v_{\text{circ}}/v_w)^2]^{3/2}} \tag{11}$$

where G is the gravitational constant, $\alpha_w \sim 3/2$ is an efficiency constant, and $\dot{m}_1$ is the donor mass loss rate due to stellar winds. Understanding how the orbit responds to mass transfer is complex, because it depends not only on the amount of mass transferred or lost, but also on the linear and angular momentum that is carried out or accreted. Detailed equations for the orbital response including various mass transfer models were recently developed by Dosopoulou and Kalogera [305,307] and Hamers and Dosopoulou [308].

Another way to transfer mass from a star to its companion is via **Roche lobe overflow**. If the stellar radius is relatively large compared to the size of the binary, the external layers of the star may be stripped out by the gravity of the companion star and the centrifugal force of the binary motion. The region in space where this occurs is approximated by the **Roche lobe**, the equipotential surface shaped like two tear-drops that surround both stars, with the two lobes connected by a saddle point at the center (also known as the first Lagrangian point, L_1) [309–311]. In general, Roche-lobe overflow can be caused by either the primary star entering the giant phase and increasing in radius, or by the shrinking of the binary orbit due to tides.

Commonly, the Roche lobe is approximated as an equal-volume sphere of effective size R_L, the **Roche radius**. A convenient analytic approximation for R_L was given by Eggleton [312]:

$$R_{L,1} = a\frac{0.49\, q^{2/3}}{0.6\, q^{2/3} + \ln(1+q^{1/3})}, \tag{12}$$

where $q = m_1/m_2$ is the mass ratio, and $R_{L,1}$ corresponds to the Roche radius of the star of mass m_1. If the radius of one of the stars exceeds its Roche radius, some material will flow through the saddle point. Part of the material will be accreted by the companion star, while some material will be dispersed in a circumbinary disk. If all the mass lost by one star is accreted by the other and no mass is dispersed, we are in the case of **conservative mass transfer**. The material that is lost during **non-conservative mass transfer** will carry out not only mass but also angular momentum from the binary.

The typical rate at which mass transfer proceeds through L_1 can be estimated, at *order of magnitude*, through Bernoulli's equation, assuming an isentropic, adiabatic, and irrotational fluid, and that the velocity of the flow is parallel to the axis connecting the centers of the two stars. Under these assumptions, the mass transfer rate can be expressed as (e.g., Ge et al. [313])

$$\dot{m}_1 \simeq -\frac{m_1}{P_{\text{orb}}}\left(\frac{\Delta R}{R_{\text{L},1}}\right)^{n+\frac{3}{2}}, \quad (13)$$

where P_{orb} is the binary orbital period, $\Delta R = R_1 - R_{\text{L},1}$ is the Roche-lobe filling factor, and n and R_1 are the envelope's polytropic index and the radius of the donor star, respectively.

Besides changing the binary orbit, mass loss and accretion via Roche lobe overflow will change the structure of both the donor and the accretor. Modeling **the response of the donor star to mass transfer is crucial** to predict the evolution of binary stars but it is also very challenging since it requires an in-depth knowledge of the internal structure of the star and possibly non-equilibrium solutions for it.

To assess the response of the star, we must carefully consider the relevant timescales of stellar evolution. The shortest characteristic time is the dynamical timescale, which is the time on which a star reacts to a perturbation to the hydrostatic equilibrium:

$$t_{\text{dyn}} \simeq \sqrt{\frac{R_1}{g}} \simeq \sqrt{\frac{R_1^3}{Gm_1}}, \quad (14)$$

where $g \approx Gm_1/R_1^2$ is the gravitational acceleration at the stellar surface. The dynamical timescale can be also interpreted as the timescale for the star to collapse (or 'free-fall') if the gas pressure would suddenly disappear. For the Sun, this timescale is about $\tau_{\text{dyn}} \approx 0.5\,\text{h}$, which means that main sequence stars are extremely close to hydrostatic equilibrium.

The thermal timescale, also known as the Kelvin-Helmholtz timescale, describes how fast the changes in the thermal structure of a star can be. A star without a nuclear energy source contracts by radiating away its internal energy content. The Kelvin-Helmholtz timescale is the timescale at which this gravitational contraction occurs:

$$t_{\text{KH}} \simeq \frac{E_{\text{int}}}{L} \simeq \frac{Gm_1^2}{R_1 L}, \quad (15)$$

where $E_{\text{int}} \approx Gm_1^2/R_1$ is the gravitational energy budget of the star, and L is the stellar luminosity. For the Sun, the Kelvin-Helmholtz timescale turns out to be $t_{\text{KH}} \approx 15\,\text{Myr}$.

Finally, the longest stellar timescale is the nuclear timescale, which is the timescale for the nuclear fuel to be exhausted. The energy source of nuclear fusion is the direct conversion of a small fraction ϕ of the rest mass of the reacting nuclei into energy. For hydrogen fusion, $\phi \approx 0.007$, while for helium fusion it is about 10 times smaller. The total nuclear energy supply can be then written as $E_{\text{nuc}} = \phi f_{\text{nuc}} m_1 c^2$, where f_{nuc} is the fraction of stellar mass that can serve as nuclear fuel ($\sim 10\%$). The nuclear timescale can be written as

$$t_{\text{MS}} \simeq \frac{E_{\text{nuc}}}{L} = \phi f_{\text{nuc}} \frac{m_1 c^2}{L}. \quad (16)$$

Using solar values, we obtain $t_{\text{MS}} \approx 10\,\text{Gyr}$, which is consistent with the time the Sun will spend on the main sequence.

During mass transfer, stars continue their evolution in thermal equilibrium if the mass loss rate remains above the **nuclear timescale** but well below the **thermal timescale** for mass transfer, that is

$$t_{\text{MS}} \simeq \frac{\phi X m_{1,c} c^2}{L} < \frac{m_1}{|\dot{m}_1|} < \frac{Gm_1^2}{R_1 L} \simeq t_{\text{KH}}, \quad (17)$$

where X is the initial hydrogen fraction, $m_{1,c}$ the mass of the stellar core, L the luminosity of the star, and c the speed of light. However, if the mass loss timescale becomes comparable or larger than the **thermal timescale**, but remains below the **dynamical timescale**, that is

$$t_{\text{KH}} < \frac{m_1}{|\dot{m}_1|} < \frac{1}{\sqrt{G\rho}} \simeq t_{\text{dyn}}, \tag{18}$$

the star cannot be considered in thermal equilibrium anymore and its response in terms of luminosity and radius variation can be significantly different. In the most extreme cases, mass transfer can reach values as high as the dynamical timescale, crucially altering the response of the donor.

The mass-loss rate depends on the Roche-filling factor (see Equation (13)), which, in turn, depends crucially on how the Roche-lobe radius (Equation (12)) and the donor's radius respond to mass transfer/loss. Generally speaking, if during mass transfer the Roche lobe contracts more than the star does, then the Roche lobe filling factor increases and mass transfer accelerates. Such relative contractions/expansions are evaluated through the ζ **coefficients**:

$$\zeta_* \equiv \frac{\text{d}\log R_1}{\text{d}\log m_1}, \quad \zeta_{\text{L}} \equiv \frac{\text{d}\log R_{\text{L}}}{\text{d}\log m_1} \tag{19}$$

where $\zeta_* = \zeta_{\text{eq}}, \zeta_{\text{th}}, \zeta_{\text{ad}}$, depending on whether the star is in equilibrium, out of thermal equilibrium, or out of both thermal and hydrodynamical equilibrium, respectively.

Approximate Solutions for Population Synthesis Simulations

The ζ_* coefficient is a complex function that depends on many physical stellar parameters, including the star's evolutionary phase. An on-the-fly, self-consistent calculation of such coefficients in population-synthesis simulations is prohibitive, considering also that ζ_{th} and ζ_{ad} refer to non-equilibrium states.

The response of the star in population-synthesis codes is approximated considering the star always in both thermal and hydrodynamical equilibrium, thus the same fitting formulas or look-up tables for single stars apply to stripped/oversized stars in binaries. Furthermore, to predict whether the mass transfer will remain stable (say, at ~ constant ΔR) or not (e.g., runaway Roche-lobe filling), such codes adopt a criterion based on a **critical mass ratio, q_{crit}**. Indeed, if we assume that mass transfer is conservative, i.e., $M = m_1 + m_2 = \text{const.}$, and that the total angular momentum of the binary (J) is conserved as well, then

$$a = \tilde{a}\frac{(1+q)^4}{q^2} \quad \text{and} \quad \zeta_{\text{L}}(q) = (1+q)\frac{\text{d}\log R_{\text{L}}}{\text{d}\log q} \quad \text{with} \quad \tilde{a} = \frac{J^2}{GM^3} \tag{20}$$

and thus, the condition for unstable (hydrodynamical) mass transfer can be thought of as a condition that depends *only* on the mass ratio, that is

$$\zeta_{\text{L}}(q_{\text{crit}}) > \zeta_{\text{ad}}. \tag{21}$$

The ζ_{ad} values are generally approximated with simplified fitting formulas or constant values that depend on the stellar evolution phase, and they are generally calibrated to match the merger rate of compact objects inferred by the LVK and/or on other Galactic observations (e.g., Hurley et al. [35], Leiner and Geller [314], Neijssel et al. [315]).

The values of q_{crit} have a dramatic impact on merging compact-object binaries especially because, if the mass transfer is unstable, the binary orbit shrinks on a dynamical timescale, and the stars are destined to merge. However, if the donor is an evolved star, constituted by a massive core surrounded by a low-density envelope, the binary enters a further phase of binary evolution that has crucial consequences for compact objects: the CE phase.

Figure 6 is a cartoon that shows the normalized Roche-lobe radius ($R_{\text{L}}/\tilde{a}$, see Equation (20)) and the donor's radius response as a function of the mass of the donor star, under the assumptions $J = \text{constant}$ and $m_1 + m_2 = 2 = \text{constant}$, with masses in arbitrary units. In the left panel, a donor with a very steep response to mass stripping ($\zeta_* = 4$) and mass $m_1 \simeq 1.14$ fills its Roche lobe in correspondence to the blue point in the figure. As soon as mass transfer initiates, the star contracts significantly more (black arrow) than R_L does (red arrow), i.e., $\zeta_L < \zeta_*$. Thus, the star remains in thermal equilibrium, and mass transfer stops until nuclear reactions cause a further expansion of the donor. This is a typical case of (nuclear) stable mass transfer. In the right panel, a star with a shallower response ($\zeta_* = 0.5$) and $m_1 \simeq 1.5$ is considered. In this case, R_L shrinks more than R_* (i.e., $\zeta_L > \zeta_*$), therefore increasing the Roche-lobe filling factor and the mass loss rate. This is a typical case of the beginning of a thermally unstable mass transfer, for which $\zeta_* = \zeta_{th}$. By looking at the right panel of Figure 6, this configuration might last until $m_1 \simeq 0.55 \, M_\odot$, though, depending on the R_L-filling factor, mass loss can become fast enough to drive the donor out of dynamical equilibrium, so that $\zeta_* = \zeta_{ad}$. For typical giant stars, mass loss easily evolves towards a very high rate. This happens because $\zeta_{ad} \simeq -0.3$ (e.g., [35]), thus, such donors easily initiate a runaway R_L-filling process that likely leads to CE evolution.

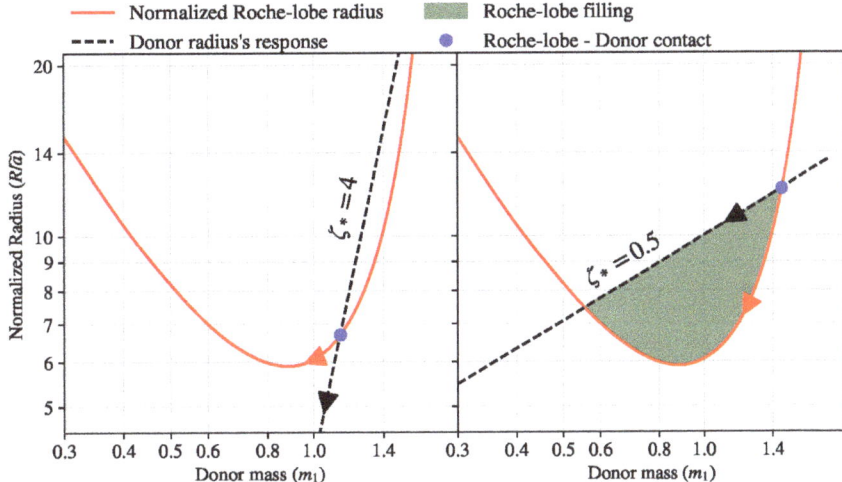

Figure 6. Normalized Roche-lobe radius (solid red line) and donor radius's response (dashed black line) as a function of the donor mass in arbitrary units. Left (right) panel: donor star with steep (shallow) response to mass stripping, $\zeta_* = 4$ ($\zeta_* = 0.5$), and mass $m_1 \simeq 1.14$ ($m_1 \simeq 1.5$). The blue dot is where the donor fills its Roche lobe. The red (black) arrow shows the direction in which the Roche-lobe (donor) radius evolves after mass stripping. The shaded green area represents the amount of Roche-lobe filling. The total angular momentum and the total mass of the system are taken as constants.

3.3. Common Envelope

CE is the process by which one component of a binary gets engulfed in the envelope of its companion [32,37,38,316,317]. The gaseous envelope becomes gravitationally focused and exerts a drag force onto the secondary, which can be considered as a second core within the envelope of the primary. Because of the drag, the two cores begin an inspiral phase, during which orbital energy and angular momentum are transferred to the envelope, which heats up and expands. After the inspiral sets, only two outcomes are possible. If the envelope is too tightly bound, the inspiral continues until the two cores are tidally disrupted and the binary merges into a single star. If, instead, the envelope is ejected, a short-period binary forms.

The CE is a key process in the formation of GW events from isolated binary stars, because it can shrink binary separations by a factor of hundreds, decreasing the coalescence time of compact-object binaries [43,44,266,318–321]. In particular, Dominik et al. [37] found that the coalescence time distribution of post-CE compact object binaries approximately follows a log-uniform distribution, $n(t_{GW}) \propto t_{GW}^{-1}$. The reason for this peculiar scaling comes from Equation (9), which imposes $t_{GW} \propto a^4$. If we assume that the distribution of semimajor axis of post-CE binaries follows a power-law as in

$$\frac{dN}{da} \propto a^{-\gamma}, \tag{22}$$

then, from Equation (9), the distribution of coalescence times can be written as

$$\frac{dN}{dt_{GW}} \propto \frac{dN}{da}\frac{da}{dt_{GW}} \propto t_{GW}^{-(3+\gamma)/4}. \tag{23}$$

Therefore, even a moderately steep ($\gamma \simeq 1$–2) distribution of post-CE semimajor axes will result in a coalescence time distribution very close to a log-uniform distribution.

CE evolution is also important for explaining other astrophysical phenomena related to short period binaries, such as supernovae Ia, X-ray binaries and double neutron stars. In fact, the CE phase was first introduced to explain the existence of short-period dwarf binaries [29].

Due to the complexity of CE evolution, we are still lacking a complete theoretical picture to distinguish between its two possible outcomes—close binary formation or binary merger. Attempts at modeling the CE phase have been mostly limited to two approaches: hydrodynamic simulations [322–330] or analytic prescriptions [29,30,32,331–334]. The latter are particularly convenient because they can be applied to a wide sample of binaries with minimal computing effort.

Hydrodynamic simulations may appear as the best way to model CE evolution, however they come with their limitations. First, hydrodynamic codes can follow only the initial plunge-in stage of CE evolution, which advances on a dynamical timescale. However, the later stages of the CE phase, where the envelope is heated up and expands, proceed on a thermal timescale. In these later stages, the energy deposited by the inspiral is transported to the surface of the star and radiated away. Therefore, modeling this stage requires proper treatment of radiative and convective energy transfer and equation of state for the stellar layers. The pre-CE phase, wherein the binary undergoes unstable mass transfer or other structural instabilities, is also difficult to model with hydrodynamic codes. In fact, many hydrodynamic simulations place the companion stars on a grazing orbit, artificially triggering the plunge-in stage. This approach, however, misses important physics of the early CE stage, such as tidal effects and mass transfer, which can significantly change the stellar structure of the stars prior to the inspiral. Furthermore, hydrodynamic simulations are numerically expensive, which makes them impractical to use for fast population-synthesis calculations.

Analytic models of CE evolution are numerically inexpensive and easy to implement, but they also come with their drawbacks. The most commonly adopted formalism in fast population-synthesis codes is the α–λ **model** [30,32,331], which is based on energy balance considerations. The main idea of this approach is to compare the orbital energy of the binary at the onset of CE with the binding energy of the envelope. By comparing these two energies, it is possible to determine whether or not the binary will survive the CE and to estimate the final size of the binary.

The model depends on two unknown parameters, α and λ, which parametrize the CE efficiency (i.e., how efficienty orbital energy is used to unbind the envelope) and envelope binding energy, respectively. The binding energy of the envelope is parametrized through the λ parameter as [332]

$$E_{bind} = -\frac{Gm_1 m_{1,env}}{\lambda R}, \tag{24}$$

where R is the stellar radius, and $m_{1,env}$ is the mass of the stellar envelope. When both stars are giants at the onset of CE, the binding energy of both envelopes is included in Equation (24). The λ parameter can be estimated from polytropic models or fit to detailed 1D stellar evolution models [35,335–338].

The envelope binding energy is then compared to the difference in orbital energy:

$$\Delta E_{\text{orb}} = -\frac{Gm_{1,c}m_2}{2a_{\text{f}}} + \frac{Gm_1 m_2}{2a_{\text{i}}}, \quad (25)$$

where a_{i} and a_{f} are the pre- and post-CE semimajor axes. α is a dimensionless parameter that measures the efficiency of the CE phase, i.e., how much orbital energy is transferred to the envelope. By equating Equations (24) and (25) we can estimate the size of the final orbit a_{f}:

$$\frac{Gm_1 m_{1,\text{env}}}{R} = \lambda\alpha\left(\frac{Gm_{1,c}m_2}{2a_{\text{f}}} - \frac{Gm_1 m_2}{2a_{\text{i}}}\right). \quad (26)$$

In the above equation, the α parameter appears as a fudge factor that determines how much gravitational binding energy is used up to unbind the binary. For $\alpha = 1$, all the binary orbital energy is used to unbind the envelope, while for $\alpha < 1$ only a fraction of the orbital energy is transferred to the envelope. In other words, the α parameter controls the efficiency of common envelope inspiral.

Because the α and λ parameters appear multiplied together, and are both of order unity, they can be sometime dumped together into a single, unknown parameter. This however neglects differences in envelope binding energies between different stars, which can be instead measured from detailed stellar evolution models [35,335–338]. The α parameter is mostly unconstrained. Some clues on its values can come from observations of post-CE binaries [339–342], and from 3D hydrodynamical simulations of low-mass giant donors (e.g., [343]). However, large values of the α parameter in population-synthesis simulations ($\gtrsim 3$) seem to be necessary to match the merger rate of BNSs inferred by LVK (e.g., [43]). Some recent one-dimensional hydrodynamic simulations also obtain high values for α [344]. Values of α greater than one deserve a particular attention, because according to Equation (26), they imply that more energy than available was used up during the inspiral, or in other words, energy was *generated* during CE phase. One important source of energy is the recombination energy, i.e., energy released during the recombination of the hydrogen plasma into atoms and molecules. Recombination energy has been suggested as a potential driving mechanism for the ejection of the envelope, once it has been expanded by viscous and gravitational drags. Other potential energy sources include nuclear and accretion energies.

The α–λ model is a very simplistic approach, because it hides behind two parameters the complex physics processes that happen during CE evolution. One glaring issue is that it assumes that the entire envelope is ejected, while hydrodynamic simulations have shown that partial envelope ejection is possible. The envelope ejection is also fine-tuned to carry away zero kinetic energy at the infinity, which is not necessarily true. Finally, the α–λ formalism neglects angular momentum transfer, tidal heating, and recombination energy of envelope material [317], all processes that can affect the outcome of CE evolution. Another shortcoming of the α–λ is that it cannot reproduce the eccentricities of observed post-CE binaries, which were shown to deviate from a perfect circular orbit [345–347]. Finally, the α–λ model does not follow the binary inspiral, but prescribes an instantaneous change of the binary orbital parameters. Therefore, it is difficult to incorporate such formalism in numerical models that follow the continuous time-evolution of multiple stellar systems. Recent works have been tackling some of these issues. Progress has been done to include the recombination energy into the λ description e.g., [336–338], and alternative models of CE inspiral that can follow the binary angular momentum are being investigated [348].

3.4. Supernovae: Blaauw and Velocity Kicks

SNe can change the binary orbit because they can impart significant natal kicks to compact objects. The natal kicks are caused by two main physical mechanisms.

The first is the impulsive mass loss caused by the (possible) ejection of mass during the SN explosion. The sudden loss of mass can change the orbit and even unbind the binary, and this process is sometimes referred to as the **Blaauw kick**. This unbinding mechanism was originally proposed to explain runaway O- and B-type stars, because the stars inherit a fraction of the binary orbital velocity following the breakup [224].

Unlike adiabatic mass loss (Section 3.2), the mass ejection during a SN explosion is an impulsive event. Mass loss decreases the gravitational potential, and can therefore even unbind a tight binary without the need of a velocity kick. A circular binary needs to lose half of its total mass during a SN explosion to become unbound, while for an eccentric binary this will depend on the binary phase at the explosion time [349]. If a binary of total mass M and semimajor axis a_0, loses instantaneously a mass Δm, the semimajor axis a_1 after the explosion is:

$$\frac{a_1}{a_0} = \frac{M - \Delta m}{M - 2\Delta m \frac{a_0}{r}}, \qquad (27)$$

where r is the distance between the two bodies at the moment of the explosion ($r \equiv a_0$ for a circular binary).

The second physical mechanism is the velocity kick caused by **the asymmetries in the SN ejecta** (see Section 2.10). The asymmetries can also affect the spin of the newly-born compact remnant [151], by changing its magnitude and orientation.

Unlike the Blaauw kick, the velocity kicks can either tighten or unbind binaries, depending on the relative orientation of the velocity kick with respect to the orbital velocity. Besides changing the orbital energy, velocity kicks also alter the eccentricity of the binary, which can then trigger mass transfer episodes or tides.

Velocity kicks have multiple consequences for the formation of merging compact objects. Besides breaking binaries, they can re-align the binary orbital plane, or misalign it with respect to the stellar spin vectors. However, the velocity magnitude of velocity kicks is poorly constrained, especially those of BHs (see Section 2.10).

Strong velocity kicks are the only mechanism that can form merging BBHs with anti-aligned spins in isolated binary evolution [350–352]. In fact, SN kicks can even flip the orbital plane of the binary, resulting in anti-aligned spin-orbit vectors. On the other hand, extremely strong kicks are required to produce significantly misaligned and anti-aligned spins in isolated binary evolution. The reason is that BBHs that merge within a Hubble time have very short separations ($\ll 0.1$ au) and therefore high orbital velocities ($\gg 400$ km s^{-1}). In order to significantly tilt the binary plane, SN kicks need to be comparable to the orbital velocity, but such extremely high BH natal kicks are in tension with the estimates obtained from the proper motion of X-ray binaries with BH companions [40,235,236] and GW observations (e.g., [353]).

An important consequence of natal kicks is that they can eject compact objects and binaries from their birth star clusters. This prevents them to pair with other compact objects through dynamical interactions, which are described in the next section.

We conclude Section 3 with Figure 7, which shows an example on how binary evolution processes reshape the mass spectrum of compact remnants compared to that obtained for isolated stars. The figure has been obtained by evolving a population of binary stars with the SEVN code, and it has been adapted from Spera et al. [222]. By looking at the left panel of Figure 7, we see that most primaries lose their envelopes through Roche-lobe overflow or CE evolution, thus they form much lighter remnants than those they would have formed as single stars (cfr. curve at $Z = 10^{-4}$ in Figure 4). In contrast, the secondaries can acquire a significant amount of mass from the primary and they can either retain it and form a heavier compact remnant, or lose it through Roche-lobe mass transfer or CE evolution. The lower the metallicity, the larger the deviations from the mass spectrum from single stars: stellar winds are quenched at low Z, thus stars can donate/accrete more mass.

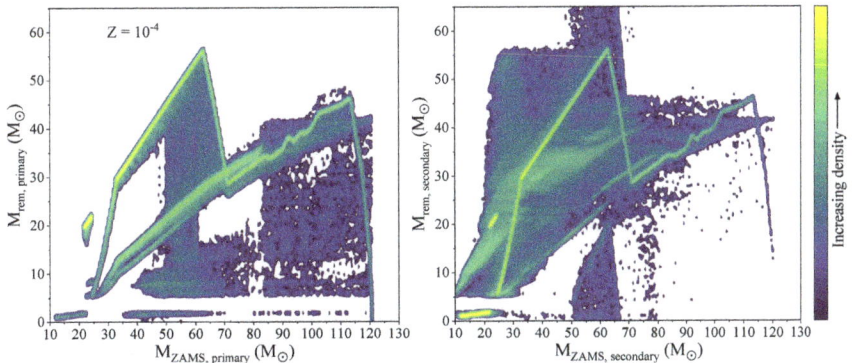

Figure 7. Mass of the compact remnant as a function of the ZAMS mass of its progenitor. The figure has been obtained evolving a population of 10^7 binary stars at $Z = 10^{-4}$ with the SEVN code, as in Spera et al. [222]. The masses of the primary stars are drawn from a Kroupa initial mass function [203] while the secondary masses, initial orbital periods and eccentricities are distributed according to [354]. The left (right) panel refers to primary (secondary) stars, i.e., those that have the largest (smallest) M_{ZAMS} in each binary. The color map represents the number of compact objects at each location of the plot, with counts that increase going from dark to light colors.

4. Stellar Dynamics

Another way to form merging compact-object binaries is through gravitational interactions. Usually, the **dynamical scenario** involves the formation and hardening of binaries through few-body encounters in stellar clusters. However, in recent years, other forms of dynamical scenarios have been proposed, which involve not only massive star clusters but also small multiple systems like triples and quadruples.

4.1. Dense Stellar Environments

Most, if not all, stars are born in stellar clusters: relatively dense ensembles of stars bound together by gravity. The evolution of star clusters is mainly driven by long-range gravitational interactions between individual stars, through a process called **two-body relaxation**. Two-body relaxation leads star clusters to develop a high density core surrounded by a low-density stellar halo. Given their relatively high central density ($\gtrsim 10^3 \, M_\odot \, pc^{-3}$) [355–359], the cores of star clusters are the ideal environments for extreme dynamical interactions between stars and binary stars, including stellar collisions, which are unlikely to occur in the galactic field [57,356].

Star clusters are distinguished according to their age, density and mass. **globular clusters (GCs)** are typically old systems (~Universe's age, ~12 Gyr), very massive ($\geq 10^4 \, M_\odot$) and dense (central density $\rho_c \geq 10^4 \, M_\odot$). They are evolved systems which do not contain gas, dust or young stars. Because of their mass and high central density, many studies for the dynamical formation of compact-object binaries focus on GCs [50,51,54,55,275,319,360–369]. **young dense star clusters (YDSCs)** are relatively young (<100 Myr) systems, thought to be the most common birthplace of massive stars [355,356]. The central density of YDSCs can be as high as that of GCs, although YDSCs have smaller sizes. Some YDSCs can have comparable masses to present-days GCs and, for this reason, they are thought to be close relatives of the ancient progenitors of GCs. However, because of the stellar mass loss during their evolution, YDSCs are not massive enough to evolve into present-day GCs. **open clusters (OCs)** are irregular star clusters composed of 10—a few 10^3 stars. They are generally younger than GCs and they may still contain gas from the molecular cloud from which they formed. Studies of compact binary mergers in young and open clusters include [27,51,57–59,62,63,214,370–374]. Finally, **nuclear star clusters (NSCs)** reside in the nuclei of galaxies. Nuclear star clusters are rather common in galaxies, including our own [375,376]. NSCs are usually more massive and denser than GCs, and may host a super-massive black hole (SMBH) at their center. Regardless of the presence of a NSC, the environment close to SMBHs can also be a site for formation of GW progenitors. Cusps or disks of BHs may form around SMBHs, where they can interact with other compact objects [377–381]. In AGN, BHs can be trapped by the SMBH accretion disk, wherein they can migrate and merge [212,285,380,382–392].

YDSCs and OCs are not long-lived because they inevitably disrupt into the tidal field of their host galaxy as they lose mass during their evolution. Processes that contribute to their disruption include gas expulsion and stellar evaporation. The first may happen during the early life of gas-rich star clusters. Stellar winds and SNe can eject the remaining gas from the cluster, decreasing its gravitational binding and potentially causing its disruption, a process referred to as infant mortality. **Stellar evaporation** is instead the inevitable consequence of two-body relaxation.

4.2. Two-Body Relaxation and the Gravothermal Instability

Two-body relaxation is the consequence of small, but frequent deflections in stellar velocities due to long-range gravitational interactions. Over time, two-body relaxation causes the kinetic energy of stars to be redistributed across the clusters. This process occurs over the timescale [393]:

$$t_{\rm rl} = \frac{\sigma^3}{15.4\, G^2 \langle m \rangle \rho \ln \Lambda}, \tag{28}$$

where σ is the velocity dispersion, G is the gravitational constant, $\langle m \rangle$ the mean stellar mass, ρ the stellar mass density, and $\ln \Lambda$ is the Coulomb logarithm. This last term arises from the uncertain range in impact parameters for the interactions that drive the two-body relaxation, and it is generally assumed to be $\ln \Lambda \sim O(10)$. In simple terms, the two-body relaxation timescale is the time necessary for the system to "forget" its initial conditions through two-body gravitational interactions. The two-body relaxation of star clusters can range from 200 Myr to few Gyr, depending on clusters' size and mass. For reference, the typical timescale for a star to traverse the cluster, called **crossing time**, is:

$$t_{\rm cross} = \frac{R}{\sigma} \simeq \frac{8 \ln N}{N} t_{\rm rl} \tag{29}$$

where R is the cluster size, and N is the number of stars. The crossing time is much shorter than the two-body relaxation timescale. For example, for a cluster of 10^5 stars, the relaxation timescale is about 10^3 times longer than the crossing time.

Two-body relaxation drives a flux of kinetic energy, carried by stars, from the center of the cluster to its outskirts. When stars move from the core of the cluster to the halo, they carry *heat* with them, i.e., kinetic energy. As the core loses energy to support against its gravity, it collapses, thus it increases its velocity dispersion. This causes even more stars to flow into the halo, which expands. As the stellar halo expands, some stars reach high enough velocities to escape the cluster, in a process called **evaporation**. In OCs and YDSCs, the expansion of the cluster accelerates the disruption of the cluster due to the tidal field of the galaxy. This runaway process is called **gravothermal catastrophe**, and in physical terms it is a consequence of the negative heat capacity typical of every self-gravitating system [394]. A system with negative heat capacity loses energy and becomes hotter. To become hotter, a self-gravitating system contracts so that its velocity dispersion (i.e., the average speed of the stars) increases.

In summary, the gravothermal catastrophe is a runaway process that triggers the collapse of the core and the expansion of the halo. This process is accelerated if the stars have a mass spectrum. In fact, massive stars are affected by two more physical processes: **dynamical friction and energy equipartition**.

4.3. Dynamical Friction, Energy Equipartition and Mass Segregation

Dynamical friction is a drag force that acts on massive bodies that travel through a medium of less massive objects. The gravity of the massive body attracts the lighter ones, which form a wake behind it. The overdensity of light bodies tends to decelerate the motion of the massive one via a gravitational drag. The massive body decelerates until it is finally at rest with respect to the lighter bodies. The timescale of dynamical friction for a body of mass M is [395–397]:

$$t_{df} = \frac{3}{4\,(2\,\pi)^{1/2}\,G^2\,\ln\Lambda}\,\frac{\sigma^3}{M\rho} \tag{30}$$

where ρ is the mass density of the lighter bodies. The dynamical friction timescale is much shorter than the two-body relaxation time. In star clusters with a mass spectrum, the core collapse can occur on the dynamical friction timescale, rather than on the two-body relaxation one. The steeper the mass spectrum, the faster the core collapse [398]. The consequence of dynamical friction is that massive stars become slower and sink to the center of the cluster. This phenomenon, called **mass segregation**, is characterized by a varying mass spectrum across the cluster radius, with heavier stars sinking to the cluster's core and the lighter ones crowding the halo. A more dramatic rearrangement of the massive stars in the cluster can be caused by energy equipartition, or rather, the lack of it.

Energy equipartition is the tendency for stars to equalize their average kinetic energy

$$E_k = \frac{1}{2}m\sigma^2 \tag{31}$$

where $\sigma^2 \equiv \langle v^2 \rangle$ is the velocity dispersion of the stars of mass m. Therefore, two populations of masses will have a different velocity dispersion, in order to have the same kinetic energy

$$\frac{1}{2}m_i\sigma_i^2 = \frac{1}{2}m_j\sigma_j^2 \Rightarrow \sigma_i = \sigma_j\sqrt{\frac{m_j}{m_i}}. \tag{32}$$

For $m_i > m_j$, $\sigma_i^2 < \sigma_j^2$, i.e., more massive stars will be on average slower. However, for typical initial mass functions (e.g., $N(m) \propto m^{-2.35}$ [399]), the pathway towards equipartition breaks, and the population of BHs (i.e., the most massive objects one can find in a cluster) decouples from the lightest objects. The BHs interact only among themselves and form an independent sub-cluster, which starts acting as an additional internal energy source for the whole system [362,400–406].

4.4. Halting Core Collapse with Binaries

The core collapse cannot proceed indefinitely. As the density of star increases, so does the chance that stars and binaries have a close gravitational interaction. The rate of encounter between a binary and a single of masses m_{bin} and m is [393]:

$$\Gamma_{1+2\,enc} = 4\sqrt{\pi}n\sigma\,r_{enc}^2\left(1 + \frac{G(m_{bin} + m)}{2r_{enc}\sigma^2}\right) \tag{33}$$

where n is the number density of single stars, m is their average mass, σ the velocity dispersion, and r_{enc} is the maximal closest approach distance. For the encounter to result in energy exchange between the single and the binary, the encounter distance r_{enc} needs to be of the order of the binary semimajor axis, e.g., $r_{enc} \simeq 2a$. If in the core of the cluster there are no binaries, they can be formed via three-body encounters of single stars. These occur on a timescale given by [407]:

$$\Gamma_{1+1+1\,enc} = 126\frac{G^5 m^5 n^3}{\sigma^9} \tag{34}$$

During a three-body encounter between a binary and a single star, a fraction of the internal energy of the binary can be redistributed as translational energy among the interacting bodies. This means that **binaries can considered as a reservoir of kinetic energy**. The kinetic energy released through three-body encounters can be used to *reverse* core collapse.

Statistically, three-body encounters can have different outcomes depending on the kinetic energy of the single,

$$E_k = \frac{1}{2} m_{\text{sin}} v_\infty^2 \tag{35}$$

and the internal energy of the binary

$$E_{\text{bin}} = \frac{G m_1 m_2}{2a} \tag{36}$$

where, m_1 m_2 are the masses of the binary members and a the binary semimajor axis. In the context of stellar clusters, a binary is considered as **hard** if its internal energy E_{bin} is greater than the average kinetic energy E_k of neighboring stars, while it is **soft** in the opposite case. On average, subsequent encounters make hard binaries harder (i.e., their semimajor axis shrinks), while soft binaries tend to become softer (i.e., wider semimajor axis) until they break up [45]. It is worth noting that hardness is a property of the binary relative to its environment. Due to the higher velocity dispersion, the same binary in the core of a cluster might be soft, whereas in the halo it would be hard.

4.5. Forming Merging Compact-Object Binaries

The process of **binary hardening** in stellar clusters is a direct consequence of the core collapse and the gravothermal catastrophe, and it is argued to be one of the most critical processes for the formation of BBHs. Shrinking the semimajor axis of compact object binaries can dramatically shorten the coalescence time of binaries, because the GW coalescence timescale scales as $t_{\text{GW}} \propto a^4$ (Equation (9)). Another important consequence of three-body encounters is that they tend to excite the orbital eccentricity of binaries. In fact, the probability distribution of binary eccentricities after a three-body encounter is close to a thermal distribution ($N(e) \propto e$), and can be even super-thermal in the case of low angular momentum encounters [45,408–413]. The orbital eccentricity has an even greater impact on the GW coalescence timescale, because, for eccentricities close to 1, the coalescence timescale shortens as $t_{\text{GW}} \propto (1 - e^2)^{7/2}$ [414]. An example of the effects of three-body encounters on binary coalescence times is given in Figure 8. In this simulated three-body encounter, a binary and a single meet on a hyperbolic orbit with a small impact parameter and a velocity at infinity of $0.1\,\text{km}\,\text{s}^{-1}$, which is typical of small OCs. The initial binary is not close enough to merge within the age of the Universe. However, the outgoing binary has a shorter separation and a much higher eccentricity, which will cause the binary to coalesce in about 2 Myr after the encounter.

Due to dynamical friction and mass segregation, BHs sink to the core of star clusters [362], where they undergo three-body encounters during the core-collapse phase. A binary will keep undergoing three-body encounters in the core until (i) core collapse is reversed, i.e., the cluster's core "bounces back" and the density in the core decreases, quenching the encounter rate, (ii) the recoil velocity of the binary becomes so high that it is ejected from the core, or (iii) the binary merges due to GW radiation.

The second outcome can happen because when the binary becomes harder, the difference between the initial and final internal binary energies is redistributed as kinetic energy $\Delta E = E_{\text{bin,f}} - E_{\text{bin,i}}$. This kinetic energy is redistributed between the single and the binary following momentum conservation, i.e., a fraction $m_{\text{bin}}/(m_{\text{sin}} + m_{\text{bin}})$ is gained by the single, and a fraction $m_{\text{sin}}/(m_{\text{sin}} + m_{\text{bin}})$ is gained by the binary. In general, the binary recoil velocity is less than the ejection velocity of the single. However, if the injected kinetic energy is sufficiently high, the binary can be ejected from the core and even from the cluster itself. Early studies found that the **dynamical formation of binaries occurs in star clusters**, but most of the merger events happen from binaries that were hardened in the core and then **ejected** [27,51,54,55,369,415].

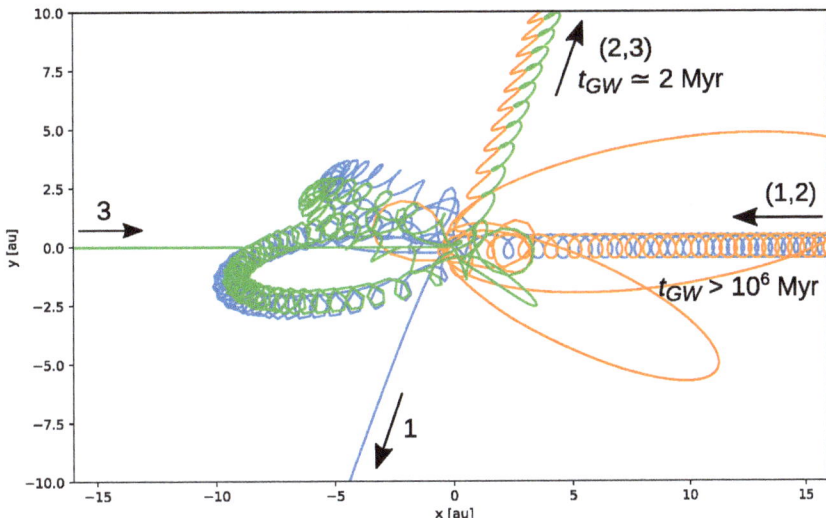

Figure 8. Trajectories during a three-body encounter between a binary (1,2) and a single (3). After a brief chaotic interaction, the binary and the single undergo an exchange. The encounter is concluded by the ejection of the new binary (2,3) and the new single (1). The initial coalescence time of the binary is $t_{GW} > 10^6$ Myr, much greater than a Hubble time. After the interaction, the coalescence time is $t_{GW} \simeq 2$ Myr. The initial approach of the binary-single is hyperbolic, with an impact parameter of $b = 0.6$ au and velocity at infinity of $v_\infty = 0.1$ km/s. All the bodies are 50 $M_\odot$ BHs integrated with TSUNAMI (Trani et al., in prep.), including post-Newtonian corrections of order 1PN, 2PN and 2.5PN to the equations of motion.

Only recently, attention has been brought to **in-cluster mergers that can occur during few-body encounters** in the core (e.g., [211,364,416]). These mergers result from the short pericenter passages that can happen during chaotic three-body encounters, which can trigger rapid gravitational wave coalescence. These kind of mergers can be extremely rapid, due to the initial short separation between the compact objects. For this reason, binaries formed through this scenario can retain detectable eccentricities in the LVK band [417,418]. Another possible scenario for producing eccentric mergers in the LIGO band are GW captures during hyperbolic single-single interactions [379,419,420]. Because the cross section for single-single captures is extremely small compared to binaries, hyperbolic captures are likely to happen only in the most dense environments, like NSCs and GCs.

During three-body encounters, one of the members of the binary might be swapped with the initially single body. Binaries formed through this process are referred to as **exchanged binaries**. Statistically, the lightest body has greater chances to be ejected. For this reason, binaries formed through three-body encounters tend to have higher masses and equal mass ratios. Furthermore, even if binaries formed through dynamical interactions tend to have high eccentricities [45,408], by the time they reach the LVK band, GW emission circularizes them. Therefore, most ejected binaries are not expected to have any residual eccentricity at >10 Hz [13]. Figure 9 illustrates the impact of circularization of GW radiation on merging binaries. In the example, a binary with an initial eccentricity of $e_0 = 0.99$ will be completely circularized by the time it reaches a peak GW frequency of 10 Hz. Only binaries with an extreme eccentricity ($e_0 > 0.999$) can retain some eccentricity at 10 Hz, but their coalescence time will be extremely small ($\sim$days).

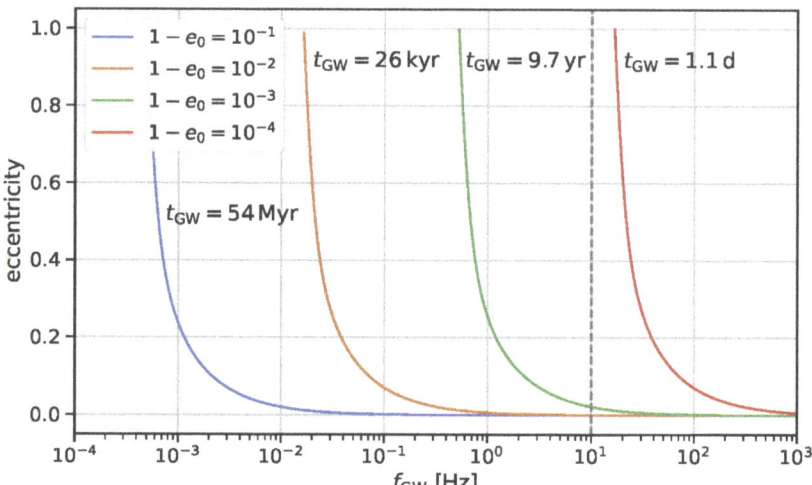

Figure 9. Eccentricity as a function of peak GW frequency for inspiralling binaries. Each curve indicates a binary with the same semimajor axis (1 au), but different initial eccentricity, as indicated in the legend. Coalescence timescales for each initial eccentricity are written next to the respective curves. The curves were calculated using the equations in Peters [414] and the fitting formula for the peak harmonic GW frequency in Hamers [421].

Furthermore, dynamically assembled binaries should not have any correlation between the orientation of BHs spins. Consequently, the predicted $\chi_{\rm eff}$ distribution of dynamically assembled binaries is symmetric and centered around $\chi_{\rm eff} \sim 0$ [211,285,422].

Finally, dense environments have an important consequence for hierarchical mergers, i.e., the GW coalescence of BHs formed from a prior BH coalescence. Asymmetric dissipation of linear momentum during the **GW coalescence imparts a recoil kick** to the final remnant. Depending on the mass ratio and spins of the merging BHs, these GW recoil kicks can be of the order of 100 km s^{-1}, which is much higher then the escape velocity of most clusters [423–428]. Therefore, it is expected that hierarchical mergers only occur in massive stellar environments such as GCs, NSCs, and close to SMBHs [275]. Runaway hierarchical mergers are also a proposed pathway to form intermediate mass BHs from stellar mass BHs [52,276,429–432]).

4.6. Small-N Systems

GW mergers can also be mediated by gravitational interactions in small-N systems, namely **triples, quadruples and higher hierarchical systems**. Hierarchical triple systems are constituted by a binary orbited by an outer object, in a stable configuration. Many stellar triple systems have been observeed so far, and it is reasonable to expect that in many triples the inner binary is composed of compact objects. In fact, massive stars are especially found in triples and higher multiples [433–436]. The fraction of stars found in multiples increases for more massive stars, up to $\sim$50% for B-type stars [287,437–439]. These multiple systems may be formed primordially as a natural outcome of star formation, or may also form dynamically from few-body encounters in stellar clusters.

Gravitational interactions can strongly affect the evolution of triple systems. If the outer object is sufficiently inclined with respect to the inner binary, the latter can exchange angular momentum with the outer orbit on a secular timescale, which is longer than the orbital period of the inner binary. These secular exchanges of angular momentum manifest themselves as the **von Zeipel-Kozai-Lidov (ZKL)** [440–445]. During such oscillations, the eccentricity of the inner binary can reach values very close to 1, inducing very close pericenter passages. If the inner binary is composed of compact objects, GW radiation can be efficiently emitted during these short pericenter passages, leading to the rapid coalescence of the binary. Figure 10 shows the typical evolution of a GW coalescence triggered by ZKL oscillations. There are two main effects of ZKL oscillations. First, they can accelerate the merging of compact object binaries, allowing them to merge within the age of the Universe. Secondly, they excite very high eccentricity in the inner compact binary, which can affect the GW emission waveform, and therefore can be potentially inferred by GW observations at different frequencies [446–448].

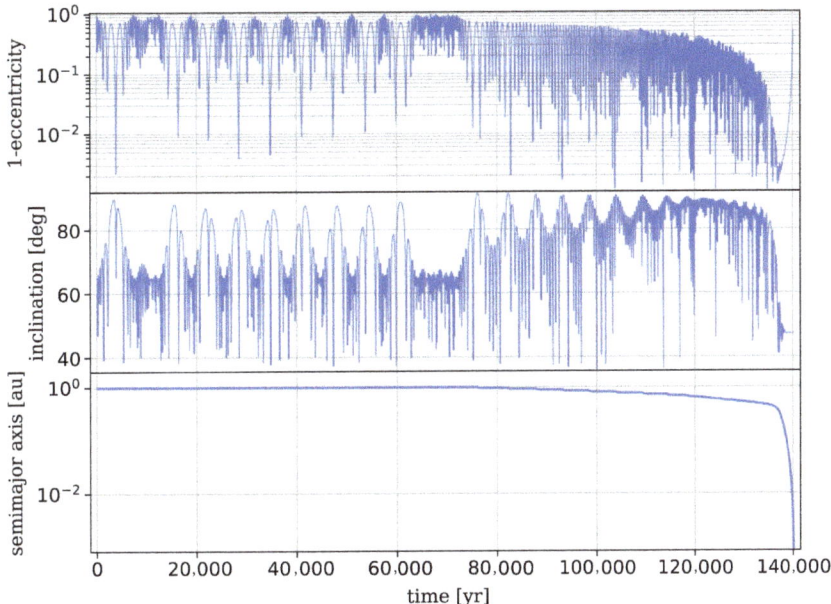

Figure 10. Gravitational-wave merger induced by von Zeipel-Kozai-Lidov evolution in a triple system. Orbital parameters as a function of time for a triple system. Top panel: eccentricity of the inner orbit. Middle panel: inclination of the outer body's orbit with respect to the inner binary. Bottom panel: semimajor axis of the inner binary. The initial orbital parameters of the triples are: mass of the outer body $m_3 = 40\,M_\odot$, mass of the inner bodies $m_1 = 10\,M_\odot$, $m_2 = 20\,M_\odot$, inner semimajor axis $a_1 = 1$ au, outer semimajor axis $a_2 = 16$ au, mutual inclination $i_{mut} = 65°$. Evolved with OKINAMI, which solves the orbit-averaged equations of motion in Delaunay coordinates (Trani et al., in prep.).

The evolution in triple systems can also be affected by all the processes that occur in binary stars, and more. Mass can be lost by the tertiary star and transferred to the inner binary. The outer star could also be affected by tertiary tides [449] or become a giant and undergo a phase of triple CE [450]. In general, modeling the evolution of a triple system is quite complex, because of the strong interplay between dynamics and stellar evolution [451]. Due to the relative lower abundance of triples, the predicted merger rate of BBHs from triples is generally smaller by a factor of ∼100 than that from dynamically assembled binaries [64,211,448,452–460].

The ZKL effect has applications also to triples in which the outer body is a massive BH. This may happen in NSCs hosting a SMBH, which can be orbited by a stellar BBH [461–466]. Just like in the case of a tertiary star, the massive BH can excite the eccentricity of the inner binary, causing the binary to merge.

Other forms of dynamical scenarios include dynamical perturbations of multiple stellar systems in the field [467–469], or interactions of binaries with the tidal fields of star clusters [470].

A few authors have recently started a systematic investigation of the evolution of hierarchical systems with $N > 3$ [471,472]. Specifically, Vynatheya and Hamers [471] investigated compact-object mergers in quadruples, finding that the expected rates for BBHs are of the order of 10 $\text{Gpc}^{-3}\text{yr}^{-1}$ (see also [473]). Other studies on quadruples focused on specific GW events will be discussed in Section 5.

4.7. Hybrid Scenarios

Distinguishing between the isolated binary channel and the dynamical channel might not be straightforward. **Stellar evolution and stellar dynamics are inseparable processes** that are active at the same time. Indeed, besides evolving in complete isolation, stellar binaries can be found in star clusters as well, where they can be affected by close encounters just like compact-object binaries. These stellar binaries can therefore experience processes from both the binary evolution pathway (e.g., mass transfers, CEs) and the dynamical pathway (e.g., exchanges, excitation of eccentricity). For instance, in young star clusters, some BBHs are formed via CE evolution of dynamically-assembled *main sequence* binaries that, at some point of their life, are ejected from the cluster, and merge in the field, appearing as if they had evolved in complete isolation. They can contribute to the merger rate more than dynamically assembled BBHs [62,63,214,474]. These binaries undergo a CE phase, like in the isolated channel, but they also undergo dynamical interactions before and after collapsing to BHs. The CE phase might even be triggered by such dynamical interactions, so that the same binaries would not have merged without the crucial contribution of stellar dynamics. Some specific scenarios require elements from both channels. For example, three-body encounters of tidally spun-up, post-common-envelope binaries have been proposed as a mechanism to produce BBH with misaligned spins [64].

5. Astrophysical Insights from Exceptional Gravitational-Wave Events

In the previous sections, we presented the main astrophysical processes that can drive the formation of merging compact-object binaries. Despite the uncertainties and degeneracies in the astrophysical models, in this section we investigate whether some of the exceptional GW events have distinguishing features that may point us towards a specific formation scenario. An exhaustive analysis of all the exceptional GW events is beyond the scope of this review, which focuses mainly on the astrophysical processes behind merging compact-object binaries. Thus, in this section, we decided to restrict our analysis only to the events containing at least one BH and with physical properties that can be the smoking gun of a specific formation pathway: heavy BHs, as in GW190521, very asymmetric masses, as in GW190814 and GW190412, and mixed components, as in GW200105_162426 and GW200115_042309.

We stress that it is *currently premature to make any kind of conclusive statements*, especially on the origin of *single* GW events, though these exceptional events carry a number of astrophysical traces that are worth exploring here in some detail.

5.1. GW190814

GW190814 is a special LIGO-Virgo Collaboration (LVC) event detected during the first part of the third observing run and presented in Abbott et al. [81]. It is a coalescence with significantly unequal masses (mass ratio $q = 0.112^{+0.008}_{-0.009}$). Furthermore, the secondary component of GW190814 is either the lightest BH or the heaviest NS ever discovered in a compact-object binary system, (secondary mass $m_2 = 2.59^{+0.08}_{-0.09}$). The mass of GW190814's secondary falls into the range of the hypothesized lower mass gap (2.5–5 $\text{M}_\odot$), questioning the existence of this gap. GW190814 is also the GW event with the strongest constraint on the spin precession parameter ($\chi_\text{P} = 0.04^{+0.04}_{-0.03}$) and on the spin of the primary component ($\chi_1 \leq 0.07$), though both of these constraints are consistent with non-spinning components.

The secondary of GW190814 might be either a BH or a NS. The non-detection of any electromagnetic counterparts [475–485], the fact that there were neither clear signatures of tides or spin-induced quadrupole effects in the waveform [486,487], and the uncertainties on both the theoretical estimates of the maximum NS mass and the NS equation of state [488–491], prevent us to determine the nature of the compact object. Post-merger electromagnetic studies suggest that the merger product of GW170817 likely collapsed into a (highly-spinning) BH with a mass comparable to GW190814's secondary ($\sim 2.6 \, M_\odot$) [492]. The latter result has been used by various authors as a starting point to constrain the NS equation of state and the maximum mass of a non-rotating NS, suggesting that the secondary of GW190814 is likely a BH [486,493,494]. However, the hypothesis of a rapidly rotating NS cannot be completely excluded [495–505], even in the context of extended theories of gravity (e.g., Astashenok et al. [506]).

The population analysis of GWTC-3 [80] shows that (i) the secondary of GW190814 is an outlier from the population of NSs of BNS and of the secondaries of NSBH systems detected so far through GWs, and that (ii) GW190814 is an outlier from the population of observed BBHs. These findings support the idea that GW190814 belongs to a distinct population of merging compact-object binaries.

Understanding the formation and evolutionary history of GW190814 is challenging for all current astrophysical models. The challenge is to find a theoretical model that can accommodate, at the same time, the GW190814 mass ratio, masses, and the LVC inferred merger rate. As already discussed in Section 2, most theoretical models do not have predictive power on the nature of compact objects and only a mass-threshold criterion is used to distinguish between NSs and BHs. Thus, depending on the adopted threshold, GW190814-like events might be marked as either NSBH or BBH mergers.

GW190814-like systems are outliers in terms of rates, masses, and mass ratios in most of the distributions of merging NSBH and merging BBH systems predicted by isolated binary evolution models [37,43,218,222,315,318,320,338,507–510]. Zevin et al. [507] identified two possible formation channels for GW190814-like systems, but (i) they form only if the delayed supernova explosion mechanism is adopted (see also Section 2.5), and (ii) their merger rates are at least one order of magnitude below the inferred LVC rates. Furthermore, Zevin et al. [507] showed that the mass of GW190814's secondary is likely its birth mass, therefore GW190814 might give insights on the existence of the lower mass gap and, possibly, on the supernova explosion engine. It is worth mentioning that, in the isolated binary scenario, unlimited super-Eddington accretion onto compact objects might be the key to obtain significantly higher merger rates for GW190814-like systems, within the LVC inferred rate (see e.g., [511,512]).

GW190814 might be a second-generation merger event from a hierarchical triple system [61,439,447,457,513–515]. This is not an exotic formation pathway for GW190814, considering that most massive B-type stars, $\gtrsim 50\%$, are in triples and the percentage tends to increase in low-metallicity environments (see also Section 4.6) [287,437,438,516–521]. Compared to the population of BH mergers from the isolated binary channel, mergers in triples tend to enhance the number of mergers with more unequal masses, resulting in a flatter mass-ratio distribution down to $q \simeq 0.3$ [61,457]. In this context, a possible formation pathway for GW190814 is that the members of the inner binary are two stars that evolve through the CE process and form a tight BNS system. The latter merges within a Hubble time, leaving a low-mass ($\sim 2.6 M_\odot$), highly-spinning BH. The tertiary body is a star that turns into a $\sim 26 M_\odot - $BH at its death. Lu et al. [513] show that there is a non-negligible chance that, at its formation, the low-mass BH is kicked into a low angular momentum orbit so that it can merge with the tertiary compact object within a Hubble time. The merger rate of GW190814-like sources obtained through this channel is consistent with the one inferred in Abbott et al. [81], provided that $\gtrsim 10\%$ of BNS mergers occur in triples and that the tertiary orbital semi-major axis is less than a few au. A high spin of the low-mass BH would be a distinguishing feature of this scenario, but it cannot be corroborated through the analysis of the GW190814 signal because of the uninformative spin posterior of the secondary. Cholis et al. [515] investigated the same formation scenario and obtained similar results as Lu et al. [513], but they considered the possibility that the secondary of GW190814 is a Thorne–Zytkow object, i.e., a metastable object formed from the collision of a NS with a red giant star, possibly turning into a low-mass BH at the end if its life [522]. The local merger rate density from the latter channel can be as high as a few $\text{Gpc}^{-3}\text{yr}^{-1}$, which is within the LVC inferred rate.

Other authors investigated similar dynamical formation pathways for GW190814 involving systems with higher multiplicity, e.g., hierarchical quadruples [523–526], finding similar results.

GW190814-like systems might form in dense stellar environments through binary-single dynamical exchanges. However, the dynamical scenario favors the formation of compact-object binaries with similar masses ($q \gtrsim 0.5$), pairing up the most massive objects (e.g., BHs and their stellar progenitors) in the dense cores of clusters, while low-mass objects (e.g., NSs) are likely ejected from the cluster during close three-body gravitational interactions (see also Section 4) [27,50,51,55,57,275,319,371,527,528]. In contrast, direct GW captures coming from single-single gravitational interactions seem to be exceedingly rare events [419]. Numerical simulations of GCs [529–532] and binary-single scattering experiments in GC-like environments [533–535] show that the local merger-rate density of GW190814-like systems is $\lesssim 0.1\ \text{Gpc}^{-3}\text{yr}^{-1}$, well below the single-event rate inferred by the LVC ($7^{+16}_{-6}\ \text{Gpc}^{-3}\text{yr}^{-1}$). YDSCs might also have an impact in the formation of GW190814-like systems. In contrast to GCs, the dynamical evolution of YDSCs proceeds on much shorter timescales, and they are thought to be the nurseries of massive stars and the building blocks of galaxies. Furthermore, YDSCs form continuously in the Universe, at all redshifts, thus their contribution to the local merger-rate densities of merging compact-object binaries may potentially be higher than that of GCs [27,214,474,535,536]. Specifically, the N-body simulations of YDSCs presented in Rastello et al. [474] support a dynamical formation scenario for GW190814, with an estimated local merger-rate density of GW190814-like systems of $8^{+4}_{-4}\ \text{Gpc}^{-3}\text{yr}^{-1}$. Most of the merging NSBH systems presented in Rastello et al. [474] come from dynamically-perturbed original binaries (i.e., from progenitor stars already bound in the initial conditions, but that would not have formed a merging NSBH if evolved in isolation). Furthermore, all mergers happened in the field because all the progenitor binaries were ejected from the star cluster before the binary members reach coalescence (i.e., hybrid scenario, see Sections 1 and 4.7). In contrast, Fragione and Banerjee [431] performed direct N-body simulations of 65 YDSCs and estimated the local NSBH merger-rate density for these environments to be $\lesssim 3 \times 10^{-2}\ \text{Gpc}^{-3}\text{yr}^{-1}$. However, Fragione and Banerjee [431] and Rastello et al. [474] consider different types of clusters with different initial masses and concentrations, different NS birth kick models, and different fractions of the cosmic star-formation rate that goes into clusters.

GW190814-like systems may also form in AGN. In such crowded environments, the gas-driven formation mechanisms and the hardening process of binaries are effective and gas accretion on compact objects with birth mass $\lesssim 2\,M_\odot$ might be high enough to bring them in (or even beyond) the low-mass gap, before they merge with another compact objects [383,384,537]. Furthermore, the secondary of GW190814 might also be a compact object coming from a previous merger event in an AGN disk. This is not an exotic scenario because merger products are easily retained in AGN thanks to high escape speeds, thus next-generation compact objects can participate in additional mergers [537,538]. Specifically, McKernan et al. [383,384] show that the typical value for the mass ratio of the population of NSBH mergers in AGN disks is $q \simeq 0.1$, with a corresponding local merger rate of about a few $\text{Gpc}^{-3}\text{yr}^{-1}$, both compatible with GW190814.

Bombaci et al. [539] discussed the hypothesis that the secondary of GW190814 is a strange quark star, which is a non-ordinary NS composed of a deconfined mixture of up, down and strange quarks. The authors showed that quark stars can reach masses comparable to the secondary of GW190814 while using physically motivated equations of state for hadrons and quarks, and without assuming an exceedingly large speed of sound.

Various authors investigated the hypothesis of the secondary component of GW190814 being a primordial BH, i.e., a BH formed from density fluctuations in the early Universe, a fraction of second after the big bang [540,541]. Vattis et al. [541] show that the $\sim 2.6\,M_\odot$ member is rather unlikely to be a primordial BH because the typical time needed for a primordial BH to pair and then merge with a $\sim 26\,M_\odot$ stellar-origin BH is very close to (or even larger than) the age of the Universe, contradicting the GW190814 detection (but see also [542,543]).

It is apparent that the parameter space relevant for GW190814-like systems still needs to be fully explored and future GW detections will be crucial to shed light on the nature and formation channels of GW190814-like systems.

5.2. GW190521

GW190521 is currently the GW event with the heaviest BHs in the catalog [80]. The masses of the two BHs are $m_1 = 85^{+21}_{-14}\,M_\odot$ and $m_2 = 66^{+17}_{-18}\,M_\odot$, respectively, and the mass of the merger product is $M = 142^{+28}_{-16}\,M_\odot$ [82,83]. The mass of the primary BH falls confidently into the hypothesized upper mass gap ($\sim 60\,M_\odot$–$120\,M_\odot$) and the merger product is the first strong observational evidence for the existence of intermediate-mass BHs ($\sim 10^2\,M_\odot$–$10^4\,M_\odot$).

Being the shortest-duration signal among the GW detections, GW190521 is a quite difficult event to analyze and measurements of spins and their in-plane components are quite uncertain. The data analysis presented in Abbott et al. [82] supports mild evidences for in-plane spin components with high spin magnitudes for both the BHs, but the values of the BH dimensionless spins remain uninformative at 90% credible intervals (i.e., $\chi_{1,2} \sim$ 0.1–0.9). The hypotheses of a non-precessing signal with orbital eccentricity $e \geq 0.1$ at 10 Hz [544] and of a precessing signal with orbital eccentricity $e \simeq 0.7$ [545] cannot be excluded, even though various authors suggest that GW190521-like binaries likely enter the 10 Hz-band with $e \ll 0.7$ (e.g., [546]). Furthermore, subsequent analysis of the LVC data brought out the intriguing possibility of GW190521 being an intermediate-mass ratio inspiral, with $m_1 = 168^{+15}_{-61}\,M_\odot$ and $m_2 = 66^{+33}_{-3}\,M_\odot$ [195,547].

The formation channel of GW190521 is uncertain. The physical properties of the event seem to favor the dynamical formation pathway, while an explanation through the isolated binary channel is challenging.

Population-synthesis simulations of binary stars show that the most massive BBHs that can form at a given metallicity are unlikely to merge within a Hubble time, making it hard to even explain the formation of systems with lower masses, such as GW170729 [222]. In contrast, Belczynski [350] shows that if heavy ($\gtrsim 180\,M_\odot$) progenitor stars are considered and a very low $^{12}C(\alpha, \gamma)^{16}O$ rate is adopted (-2.5σ with respect to the fiducial value of Farmer et al. [193]), the isolated-binary channel becomes a plausible formation pathway for GW190521. [219] found that GW190521-like systems can be formed from population III (Pop III) binaries, but only for stellar evolution models with a small convective overshooting parameter.

The hypothesis of repeated mergers in dense stellar systems seems to be a promising scenario to explain GW190521 [276,526,548–553].

The escape speed of GCs may be higher than the GW recoil kick imparted to some second-generation BHs, especially if BHs are born with low spins. Thus, second-generation BHs can be retained in GCs and Rodriguez et al. [275] show that the fraction of merging BBHs that have components formed from previous mergers in GCs can be $\gtrsim 10\%$ $\gtrsim 20\%$ for the detectable population. Kimball et al. [553] created a phenomenological population model for merging BBHs derived from [275], and they use that to infer the population properties of BH mergers in the second LVC catalog, finding that the members of GW190521 are likely second-generation (2 g) BHs. Triple systems in GCs may further enhance the retention probability of 2 g BHs, strengthening the Kimball et al. [553] and Rodriguez et al. [275] findings (e.g., [456]). Repeated minor mergers (>2 g) might also have formed the BHs of

GW190521 but only in environments with escape velocities $\gtrsim 200$ km s^{-1}, such as the most massive GCs or nuclear star clusters (e.g., [448,548]).

The escape speed of YDSCs is significantly smaller than globular and nuclear star clusters, thus second-generation BH mergers are expected to be exceedingly rare in such environments [549,554]. However, [63,215,555,556] show that GW190521-like systems can still form in YDSCs via three-body encounters or multiple stellar mergers. In the latter scenario, a heavy BH can originate from the merger of an evolved star with a main-sequence star. If the helium core of the primary star is small enough to avoid PISN and the secondary star is still on the main-sequence, the merger product might be an evolved star with an oversized hydrogen envelope. If a significant fraction of the hydrogen envelope is retained and participate in the final collapse, a BH in the PISN mass gap can form [222]. Such heavy, single BHs can acquire a companion in dense stellar environments and explain the formation of GW190521-like systems. Furthermore, BHs born via this mechanism can preserve most of the spin of the progenitor star, leading to a high-spin BH even if they are 1 g BHs [170], in agreement with the properties of GW190521, even though the efficiency of angular momentum transport inside stars is matter of debate [197]. The same formation pathway has been identified also in GCs [223,557]. It is worth noting that, as in GCs, triple systems in YDSCs may enhance the overall retention probability of 2 g BHs, making the 2 g-channel for GW190521 a viable possibility also for such environments.

Palmese and Conselice [558] investigated the hypothesis that the two BHs of GW190521 were at the centers of two ultra-dwarf galaxies, assuming an extrapolation of the low-end of the central BH-galaxy mass relation (e.g., [559]). This scenario assumes that, after the merger of the two galaxies, the central BHs can merge, and the merger rates for GW190521-like systems from this channel match well those inferred by the LVC.

In AGN, Tagawa et al. [537] show that GW190521-like systems can form either via repeated mergers (>2 g at high metallicity, 2 g at low metallicity), or via mergers of 1g BHs that have grown via super-Eddington accretion. In such gas-rich environments, the interaction between the GW-recoiled merger product and the accretion disk of the active galactic nucleus might generate a delayed (~days after the merger), off-center UV flare, potentially detectable as an electromagnetic transient counterpart of the GW event [560]. About 26 days after the merger of GW190521, the Zwicky transient facility [561] identified a flare from the AGN J124942.3 + 344929, the latter located at the 78% spatial contour and within 1.6σ from the peak marginal luminosity distance of GW190521. Graham et al. [562] identified the flare as a plausible electromagnetic counterpart to the BBH merger GW190521 (ZTF19abanrhr). While the possibility is intriguing and it is a possible distinguishing feature of the AGN formation scenario, the 90% localization area of GW190521 contains thousands of AGN and, currently, it is not possible to establish whether GW190521-ZTF19abanrhr is a real association or a chance coincidence [561,563]. Future high-mass detections and follow-up investigations will be crucial to shed light on this interesting possibility.

Various authors suggest Pop III stars as promising progenitors of the BHs members of GW190521 [207,220,221,321,564]. The key idea is that Pop III stars might retain most of their hydrogen envelope until the end of their life and might form heavy BHs via direct collapse, with masses up to ~ 85 M$_\odot$. Specifically, Liu and Bromm [221] investigated a simplified binary evolution scenario, with an initial binary population taken from N-body simulations of Pop III star clusters [565], and the dynamical hardening process of binaries in high-redshift ($z \simeq 10$) nuclear star clusters. The authors show that both the scenarios can explain the masses and merger rates of GW190521-like systems. In the same context, Safarzadeh and Haiman [218] developed an illustrative toy model showing that the collapse of relatively massive Pop III stars in high-redshift minihalos can form BH seeds that, in $O(10$–$10^2)$ Myr, can double their mass via gas accretion, reach the PISN mass gap, and then merge within a Hubble time, explaining the formation of GW190521. Similar results were obtained by Rice and Zhang [566], who investigated the growth of stellar BH seeds in dense molecular clouds.

De Luca et al. [567] studied the hypothesis of a primordial BH origin for GW190521. Their in-depth analysis shows that the primordial BH scenario is unlikely for GW190521 only if primordial BHs do not accrete mass during their cosmological evolution. In contrast, if accretion is efficient (see also [568]), the scenario can explain the properties of GW190521, including the mild evidence for high BH spins with non-zero in-plane components (see also [569]). A mixed scenario for GW190521-like systems, where primordial BHs coexist, interact and possibly merge with astrophysical (stellar-origin) BHs in dense stellar environments, is also a viable formation scenario [570].

More exotic explanations for the massive BHs of GW190521 are conceivable, and they have been investigated by various authors. They include horizonless vector boson stars, beyond-standard-model physics affecting the edges of the upper mass gap, and dark matter annihilation within stars to avoid PISNe (e.g., [208,571,572]).

5.3. GW190412

At the time of its detection, GW190412 was the first GW event with support for asymmetric masses, and the one with the strongest constraint on the individual spin magnitude of the primary BH [573]. The masses of the BHs are $m_1 = 30.1^{+4.6}_{-5.3}$ M$_\odot$ and $m_2 = 8.3^{+1.6}_{-0.9}$ M$_\odot$, and the mass ratio is $q = 0.28^{+0.12}_{-0.07}$. The signal shows a mild evidence of precession coming from non-zero, in-plane spin components, with $0.15 \leq \chi_p \leq 0.50$ at 90% credibility. The LVC analysis reports a dimensionless spin of the primary BH of $\chi_1 = 0.44^{+0.16}_{-0.22}$, at 90% credibility, obtained using uninformative priors for the spins of both the compact objects ($\chi_{1,2} \in [0, 0.99]$).

In contrast, Mandel and Fragos [574] chose an informative spin prior, assuming that the event formed via the isolated binary channel, and they suggested an alternative interpretation of GW190412 as a merging BBH with a non-spinning primary and a rapidly spinning (tidally spun-up) secondary. Zevin et al. [575] studied the impact of different spin prior assumptions on the analysis of GW190412 and they found that the uninformative prior with both BHs spinning is preferred over other configurations.

Multiple scenarios can explain the formation of GW190412. As already discussed for GW190814, most of the merging BHs that originate from the isolated binary channel have mass ratios $q \gtrsim 0.5$, but the tail of the mass-ratio distributions extends down to $q \sim 0.2$, especially in low-metallicity environments [37,42,43,222,315,338,509]. Furthermore, the assumption of super-Eddington accretion onto compact objects might significantly increase the number of merging systems with $q \lesssim 0.5$ [511,512]. Thus, GW190412 cannot be considered as an outlier for the isolated binary scenario in terms of masses and mass ratio. The moderately high spin of the primary BH may be difficult to reconcile with the isolated channel [218,284], but the uncertainties on the rotation speed and on the dominant mechanisms for angular momentum transport inside massive stars hamper our knowledge of the birth-spin distribution of stellar BHs.

First-generation, highly spinning BHs can form if their progenitor stars undergo CHE, but most of the BHs originating from this channel have large and nearly equal masses, making this scenario unlikely to explain GW190412 [39–41,576].

Repeated mergers of BHs in dense stellar environments might explain the mass ratio and the spin of the primary BH of GW190412. Assuming that BHs have negligible spins at birth, Rodriguez et al. [577] show that GW190412-like systems can form in super star clusters with central escape speeds of, at least, 90 km s^{-1} and that such events are consistent with a first-generation BH of $\sim$10 M$_\odot$ merging with a BH formed from the subsequent merger of three $\sim$10 M$_\odot$ BHs (i.e., a third-generation BH). Gerosa et al. [578] also support the hierarchical merger scenario in dynamical environments with central escape speeds $\gtrsim$150 km s^{-1}, but they discussed the possibility of the primary of GW190412 being a second-generation BH.

The higher central escape speeds of NSCs and AGN can significantly enhance the retention fraction of >1-generation BH mergers, thus naturally producing hierarchical-merger events compatible with GW190412 [56,285,430,579].

On the other hand, Di Carlo et al. [63] and Rastello et al. [474] show that GW190412-like systems can also form in metal-poor YDSCs, but from merging first-generation BHs, because the central escape speed of such clusters is too low to allow for any retention of >1-generation BHs and most binaries are ejected from the cluster before they reach coalescence.

A first-generation origin for GW190412 is also supported by the phenomenological approach to mergers in dense stellar environments presented in Kimball et al. [580] and by von Zeipel-Kozai-Lidov induced mergers in isolated triples [61,457]. The moderately high spin of the primary of GW190412 may be difficult to reconcile with first-generation BHs, even though, as already discussed, the birth spin of BHs is uncertain (see also Section 2.11).

The high spin of the primary BH, the mass ratio, and the masses of GW190412 can also be explained through hierarchical mergers in isolated quadruples [524,581].

5.4. GW200105_162426 and GW200115_042309

GW200105_162426 and GW200115_042309 (hereafter GW200105 and GW200115) are the first two GW events that are consistent with merging NSBH systems. During the first part of the third observing run, GW190426_152155 and GW190814 were also reported as possible merging NSBH candidates. However, the false alarm rate of GW190426_152155 was too high to claim a confirmed detection and the uncertain nature of the secondary compact object prevents us from considering GW190814 as a NSBH merger (see Section 5.1). GW200105 consists of a BH with mass $m_1 = 8.9^{+1.2}_{-1.5}$ $M_\odot$ and a NS of $m_2 = 1.9^{+0.3}_{-0.2}$ $M_\odot$, while GW200115 hosts a BH with mass $m_1 = 5.7^{+1.8}_{-2.1}$ $M_\odot$ and a NS of $m_2 = 1.5^{+0.7}_{-0.3}$ $M_\odot$, using high-spin priors, i.e., $\chi_2 < 0.99$. The effective inspiral spin parameter of GW200105 is peaked at zero ($\chi_{\rm eff} = -0.01^{+0.11}_{-0.15}$) with $\chi_1 = 0.08^{+0.22}_{-0.08}$, while GW200115 has a mild preference for misaligned spins with $\chi_{\rm eff} = -0.19^{+0.23}_{-0.35}$ and $\chi_1 = 0.33^{+0.48}_{-0.29}$, with $\chi_{1,z} = -0.19^{+0.24}_{-0.50}$.

Mandel and Smith [582] reanalyzed the GW200115 signal using astrophysically-motivated spin priors and they obtained better constrains on the masses of the compact objects ($m_1 = 7.0^{+0.4}_{-0.4}$ $M_\odot$, $m_2 = 1.25^{+0.09}_{-0.07}$ $M_\odot$) and a BH spin close to zero ($\chi_{1,z} = 0.00^{+0.04}_{-0.04}$).

The spins of the secondaries are unconstrained and no electromagnetic counterpart has been identified for both the events, in agreement with theoretical expectations for mixed binaries with low-spinning primary BHs (e.g., [583,584], but see [585]).

Taking GW200105 and GW200115 as representative of the whole NSBH population, the inferred merger rate is 45^{+75}_{-33} Gpc^{-3}yr^{-1} [84].

As possible formation channels, very similar considerations as for GW190814 apply here. Indeed, in theoretical models, GW190814 may be identified as either a NSBH or a BBH, depending on the mass threshold adopted to distinguish between BHs and NSs. The main difference with GW190814 is that the masses, mass ratios, and inferred rates of GW200105/GW200115-like events are consistent also with the isolated binary formation channel [34,43,315,318,320,338,507,508,512,586–593].

6. Summary

Merging compact-object binaries, especially BBHs, have been among the main characters of the astrophysical scene over the last ∼5 years. This happened mainly thanks to the discovery of GWs, which gave us access to a new information medium. While the GW catalog continues its inexorable growth, our theoretical knowledge of the formation channels of merging compact objects is still very limited, and most of the parameter space which is relevant for the astrophysical interpretation of GW detections is unexplored.

In this work, we reviewed the main astrophysical processes that may drive the formation of merging compact-object binaries and the lessons learned so far through some exceptional GW events (e.g., GW190814, GW190521). We discussed the degeneracies of the astrophysical models and we showed that some of the uncertainties are large enough to prevent any conclusive statements on merging compact objects.

The main sources of uncertainties come from: (i) our knowledge of the **evolution of massive stars** (e.g., clumpiness and porosity of stellar winds, energy transport in radiation-dominated envelopes, overshooting) – in the next decades, the James Webb Space Telescope and the Extremely Large Telescope will provide crucial insights on the evolution of massive stars, especially those at low metallicity; (ii) the **SN explosion mechanism** (e.g., explodability dependence on progenitor's structure, fallback amount, lower mass gap, pulsational pair-instability SNe, asymmetries in the ejecta) – improvements in self-consistent, 3D simulations will help us to shed light on the SN engine and its byproducts (e.g., compact remnants, yields); (iii) **binary evolution processes** (especially common envelope and the response of donors/accretors to mass transfer) – comparisons with self-consistent, hydrodynamic simulations of binary stars will be crucial to calibrate the main (free) parameters in population-synthesis simulations; (iv) **direct N-body simulations** of star clusters (e.g., they inherit the uncertainties on single and binary stellar evolution processes, and they are computationally challenging) – new software, *natively* developed for state-of-the-art computing accelerators (e.g., Graphics Processing Units), and coupled with up-to-date population-synthesis codes, will give us the opportunity to accurately study merging compact objects in very dense stellar environments, possibly up to the regime of dwarf galaxies.

Meanwhile, detections will not stop, and a stunning collection of GW events will soon be available. The forth observing run (O4) of the LVK collaboration is planned to start later this year (December 2022) [594]. Furthermore, the next years will see the birth of new, next-generation, ground-based and space-born interferometers (e.g., Einsten Telescope, Cosmic Explorer, LISA) that promise to reveal merging compact objects throughout the entire cosmic history and across a much broader frequency range.

Thus, we are heading for exciting times in the field of GWs, with new facilities and detections that will help us to push current astrophysical models beyond the state-of-the-art. In the next decades, such a synergy will be crucial to shed light on the evolutionary histories of merging compact-object binaries across cosmic time.

Author Contributions: Conceptualization: M.S. and A.A.T.; data curation: M.S., A.A.T. and M.M.; writing—original draft preparation: M.S. and A.A.T.; writing—review and editing, M.S., A.A.T. and M.M.; software: M.S. and A.A.T.; supervision: M.S. All authors have read and agreed to the published version of the manuscript.

Funding: A.A.T. received support from JSPS KAKENHI Grant Numbers 17H06360, 19K03907 and 21K13914.

Institutional Review Board Statement: Not applicable.

Informed Consent Statement: Not applicable.

Data Availability Statement: Not applicable.

Acknowledgments: We are indebted to Mike Zevin for his careful reading of the review and for providing comments that helped us to improve the manuscript. We thank the anonymous referees for their careful reading of our manuscript and their insightful comments and suggestions.

Conflicts of Interest: The authors declare no conflict of interest.

Abbreviations

The following abbreviations are used in this manuscript:

AGN	active galactic nuclei
BBH	binary black hole
BH	black hole
BNS	binary neutron star
CO	carbon-oxygen
CE	common envelope
CHE	chemical homogeneous evolution
GC	globular cluster
GW	gravitational wave

GWTC	Gravitational Wave Transient Catalog
ECSN	electron-capture supernova
LIGO	Laser Interferometer Gravitational-wave Observatory
LVC	LIGO-Virgo Collaboration
LVK	LIGO-Virgo-KAGRA
NS	neutron star
NSBH	neutron star-black hole binary
NSC	nuclear star cluster
OC	open cluster
PISN	pair-instability supernova
Pop III	population III
PPISN	pulsational pair-instability supernova
SMBH	super-massive black hole
SN	supernova
TOV	Tolman–Oppenheimer–Volkoff
WD	white dwarf
YDSC	young dense star cluster
ZAMS	zero age main sequence
ZKL	von Zeipel-Kozai-Lidov

Notes

1. Throughout this work, we will use the symbol $M_\odot$ to refer to the Sun's mass.
2. LIGO-Virgo-KAGRA (LVK)-independent analyses have even found a few additional GW candidates (e.g., [76–78]).
3. $\mathcal{M} = \frac{(m_1 m_2)^{3/5}}{(m_1+m_2)^{1/5}}$
4. In cool supergiants ($T_{\text{eff}} < 10^4$ K) the mechanism responsible for winds is the absorption of photons by dust grains, i.e., dust- (or continuum-) driven winds.
5. It is worth noting that wind mass loss does not depend only on metallicity, but also on luminosity, effective temperature, stellar mass, and the velocity of wind at infinity.
6. $\zeta_m = \frac{m}{R(m)}$, where m is a threshold mass in $M_\odot$ and $R(m)$ is the radius enclosing m, in units of 1000 km.
7. It is worth noting that a PISN is driven by a thermonuclear explosion, i.e., very different from neutrino-driven core-collapse SNe.

References

1. Zel'dovich, Y.B.; Podurets, M.A. The Evolution of a System of Gravitationally Interacting Point Masses. *Sov. Astron.* **1966**, *9*, 742.
2. Rees, M.; Ruffini, R.; Wheeler, J.A. *Black Holes, Gravitational Waves, and Cosmology: An Introduction to Current Research*; Gordon and Breach: New York, NY, USA, 1974.
3. Lattimer, J.M.; Schramm, D.N. Black-Hole-Neutron-Star Collisions. *Astrophys. J.* **1974**, *192*, L145. [CrossRef]
4. Clark, J.P.A.; Eardley, D.M. Evolution of close neutron star binaries. *Astrophys. J.* **1977**, *215*, 311–322. [CrossRef]
5. Clark, J.P.A.; van den Heuvel, E.P.J.; Sutantyo, W. Formation of neutron star binaries and their importance for gravitational radiation. *Astron. Astrophys.* **1979**, *72*, 120–128.
6. Hils, D.; Bender, P.L.; Webbink, R.F. Gravitational Radiation from the Galaxy. *Astrophys. J.* **1990**, *360*, 75. [CrossRef]
7. Narayan, R.; Piran, T.; Shemi, A. Neutron Star and Black Hole Binaries in the Galaxy. *Astrophys. J.* **1991**, *379*, L17. [CrossRef]
8. Phinney, E.S. The Rate of Neutron Star Binary Mergers in the Universe: Minimal Predictions for Gravity Wave Detectors. *Astrophys. J.* **1991**, *380*, L17. [CrossRef]
9. Tutukov, A.V.; Yungelson, L.R. The merger rate of neutron star and black hole binaries. *Mon. Not. R. Astron. Soc.* **1993**, *260*, 675–678. [CrossRef]
10. Einstein, A. Über Gravitationswellen. In *Sitzungsberichte der Königlich Preußischen Akademie der Wissenschaften (Berlin)*; Deutsche Akademie der Wissenschaften zu Berlin: Berlin, Germany, 1918; pp. 154–167
11. Hulse, R.A.; Taylor, J.H. Discovery of a pulsar in a binary system. *Astrophys. J.* **1975**, *195*, L51–L53. [CrossRef]
12. Abbott, B.P.; Abbott, R.; Abbott, T.D.; Abernathy, M.R.; Acernese, F.; Ackley, K.; Adams, C.; Adams, T.; Addesso, P.; Adhikari, R.; et al. Observation of Gravitational Waves from a Binary Black Hole Merger. *Phys. Rev. Lett.* **2016**, *116*, 061102. [CrossRef]
13. Abbott, B.P.; Abbott, R.; Abbott, T.D.; Abernathy, M.R.; Acernese, F.; Ackley, K.; Adams, C.; Adams, T.; Addesso, P.; Adhikari, R.X.; et al. Astrophysical implications of the binary black hole merger GW150914. *Astrophys. J.* **2016**, *818*, L22. [CrossRef]
14. Klimenko, S.; Yakushin, I.; Mercer, A.; Mitselmakher, G. A coherent method for detection of gravitational wave bursts. *Class. Quantum Gravity* **2008**, *25*, 114029. [CrossRef]

15. Lynch, R.; Vitale, S.; Essick, R.; Katsavounidis, E.; Robinet, F. An information-theoretic approach to the gravitational-wave burst detection problem. *arXiv* **2015**, arXiv:1511.05955.
16. Abbott, B.P.; Abbott, R.; Abbott, T.D.; Abernathy, M.R.; Acernese, F.; Ackley, K.; Adams, C.; Adams, T.; Addesso, P.; Adhikari, R.; et al. GW150914: First results from the search for binary black hole coalescence with Advanced LIGO. *Phys. Rev. D* **2016**, *93*, 122003. [CrossRef]
17. Özel, F.; Psaltis, D.; Narayan, R.; McClintock, J.E. The Black Hole Mass Distribution in the Galaxy. *Astrophys. J.* **2010**, *725*, 1918–1927. [CrossRef]
18. Farr, W.M.; Sravan, N.; Cantrell, A.; Kreidberg, L.; Bailyn, C.D.; Mandel, I.; Kalogera, V. The Mass Distribution of Stellar-mass Black Holes. *Astrophys. J.* **2011**, *741*, 103. [CrossRef]
19. Fishbach, M.; Kalogera, V. Apples and Oranges: Comparing black holes in X-ray binaries and gravitational-wave sources. *arXiv* **2021**, arXiv:2111.02935.
20. Heger, A.; Fryer, C.L.; Woosley, S.E.; Langer, N.; Hartmann, D.H. How Massive Single Stars End Their Life. *Astrophys. J.* **2003**, *591*, 288–300. [CrossRef]
21. Mapelli, M.; Colpi, M.; Zampieri, L. Low metallicity and ultra-luminous X-ray sources in the Cartwheel galaxy. *Mon. Not. R. Astron. Soc.* **2009**, *395*, L71–L75. [CrossRef]
22. Spera, M.; Mapelli, M.; Bressan, A. The mass spectrum of compact remnants from the PARSEC stellar evolution tracks. *Mon. Not. R. Astron. Soc.* **2015**, *451*, 4086–4103. [CrossRef]
23. Mapelli, M.; Zampieri, L.; Ripamonti, E.; Bressan, A. Dynamics of stellar black holes in young star clusters with different metallicities - I. Implications for X-ray binaries. *Mon. Not. R. Astron. Soc.* **2013**, *429*, 2298–2314. [CrossRef]
24. Belczynski, K.; Bulik, T.; Fryer, C.L.; Ruiter, A.; Valsecchi, F.; Vink, J.S.; Hurley, J.R. On the Maximum Mass of Stellar Black Holes. *Astrophys. J.* **2010**, *714*, 1217–1226. [CrossRef]
25. Woosley, S.E.; Heger, A.; Weaver, T.A. The evolution and explosion of massive stars. *Rev. Mod. Phys.* **2002**, *74*, 1015–1071. [CrossRef]
26. Fryer, C.L.; Belczynski, K.; Wiktorowicz, G.; Dominik, M.; Kalogera, V.; Holz, D.E. Compact Remnant Mass Function: Dependence on the Explosion Mechanism and Metallicity. *Astrophys. J.* **2012**, *749*, 91. [CrossRef]
27. Ziosi, B.M.; Mapelli, M.; Branchesi, M.; Tormen, G. Dynamics of stellar black holes in young star clusters with different metallicities—II. Black hole-black hole binaries. *Mon. Not. R. Astron. Soc.* **2014**, *441*, 3703–3717. [CrossRef]
28. Webbink, R.F. Evolution of Helium White Dwarfs in Close Binaries. *Mon. Not. R. Astron. Soc.* **1975**, *171*, 555–568. [CrossRef]
29. Paczynski, B. Common Envelope Binaries. In *Structure and Evolution of Close Binary Systems*; Eggleton, P., Mitton, S., Whelan, J., Eds.; Springer: Dordrecht, The Netherlands, 1976; Volume 73, p. 75.
30. van den Heuvel, E.P.J. Late Stages of Close Binary Systems. In *Structure and Evolution of Close Binary Systems*; Eggleton, P., Mitton, S., Whelan, J., Eds.; Springer: Dordrecht, The Netherlands, 1976; Volume 73, p. 35.
31. Hut, P. Tidal evolution in close binary systems. *Astron. Astrophys.* **1981**, *99*, 126–140.
32. Webbink, R.F. Double white dwarfs as progenitors of R Coronae Borealis stars and type I supernovae. *Astrophys. J.* **1984**, *277*, 355–360. [CrossRef]
33. Bethe, H.A.; Brown, G.E. Evolution of Binary Compact Objects That Merge. *Astrophys. J.* **1998**, *506*, 780–789. [CrossRef]
34. Belczynski, K.; Kalogera, V.; Bulik, T. A Comprehensive Study of Binary Compact Objects as Gravitational Wave Sources: Evolutionary Channels, Rates, and Physical Properties. *Astrophys. J.* **2002**, *572*, 407–431. [CrossRef]
35. Hurley, J.R.; Tout, C.A.; Pols, O.R. Evolution of binary stars and the effect of tides on binary populations. *Mon. Not. R. Astron. Soc.* **2002**, *329*, 897–928. [CrossRef]
36. de Mink, S.E.; Cantiello, M.; Langer, N.; Yoon, S.C.; Brott, I.; Glebbeek, E.; Verkoulen, M.; Pols, O.R. Rotational mixing in close binaries. In *The Art of Modeling Stars in the 21st Century, Proceedings of the International Astronomical Union (IAU) Symposium, Sanya, China, 6–11 April 2008*; Deng, L., Chan, K.L., Eds.; Cambridge University Press: Cambridge, UK, 2008; Volume 252, pp. 365–370. [CrossRef]
37. Dominik, M.; Belczynski, K.; Fryer, C.; Holz, D.E.; Berti, E.; Bulik, T.; Mandel, I.; O'Shaughnessy, R. Double Compact Objects. I. The Significance of the Common Envelope on Merger Rates. *Astrophys. J.* **2012**, *759*, 52. [CrossRef]
38. Postnov, K.A.; Yungelson, L.R. The Evolution of Compact Binary Star Systems. *Living Rev. Relativ.* **2014**, *17*, 3. [CrossRef] [PubMed]
39. de Mink, S.E.; Mandel, I. The chemically homogeneous evolutionary channel for binary black hole mergers: Rates and properties of gravitational-wave events detectable by advanced LIGO. *Mon. Not. R. Astron. Soc.* **2016**, *460*, 3545–3553. [CrossRef]
40. Mandel, I.; de Mink, S.E. Merging binary black holes formed through chemically homogeneous evolution in short-period stellar binaries. *Mon. Not. R. Astron. Soc.* **2016**, *458*, 2634–2647. [CrossRef]
41. Marchant, P.; Langer, N.; Podsiadlowski, P.; Tauris, T.M.; Moriya, T.J. A new route towards merging massive black holes. *Astron. Astrophys.* **2016**, *588*, A50. [CrossRef]
42. Stevenson, S.; Vigna-Gómez, A.; Mandel, I.; Barrett, J.W.; Neijssel, C.J.; Perkins, D.; de Mink, S.E. Formation of the first three gravitational-wave observations through isolated binary evolution. *Nat. Commun.* **2017**, *8*, 14906. [CrossRef]
43. Giacobbo, N.; Mapelli, M. The progenitors of compact-object binaries: Impact of metallicity, common envelope and natal kicks. *Mon. Not. R. Astron. Soc.* **2018**, *480*, 2011–2030. [CrossRef]

44. Zevin, M.; Bavera, S.S.; Berry, C.P.L.; Kalogera, V.; Fragos, T.; Marchant, P.; Rodriguez, C.L.; Antonini, F.; Holz, D.E.; Pankow, C. One Channel to Rule Them All? Constraining the Origins of Binary Black Holes Using Multiple Formation Pathways. *Astrophys. J.* **2021**, *910*, 152. [CrossRef]
45. Heggie, D.C. Binary Evolution in Stellar Dynamics. *Mon. Not. R. Astron. Soc.* **1975**, *173*, 729–787. [CrossRef]
46. Lightman, A.P.; Shapiro, S.L. The dynamical evolution of globular clusters. *Rev. Mod. Phys.* **1978**, *50*, 437–481. [CrossRef]
47. Hills, J.G.; Fullerton, L.W. Computer simulations of close encounters between single stars and hard binaries. *Astron. J.* **1980**, *85*, 1281–1291. [CrossRef]
48. McMillan, S.; Hut, P.; Makino, J. Star Cluster Evolution with Primordial Binaries. II. Detailed Analysis. *Astrophys. J.* **1991**, *372*, 111. [CrossRef]
49. Hut, P.; McMillan, S.; Goodman, J.; Mateo, M.; Phinney, E.S.; Pryor, C.; Richer, H.B.; Verbunt, F.; Weinberg, M. Binaries in Globular Clusters. *Publ. Astron. Soc. Pac.* **1992**, *104*, 981. [CrossRef]
50. Sigurdsson, S.; Hernquist, L. Primordial black holes in globular clusters. *Nature* **1993**, *364*, 423–425. [CrossRef]
51. Zwart, S.F.P.; McMillan, S.L.W. Black Hole Mergers in the Universe. *Astrophys. J.* **2000**, *528*, L17–L20. [CrossRef]
52. Miller, M.C.; Hamilton, D.P. Four-Body Effects in Globular Cluster Black Hole Coalescence. *Astrophys. J.* **2002**, *576*, 894–898. [CrossRef]
53. O'Leary, R.M.; Rasio, F.A.; Fregeau, J.M.; Ivanova, N.; O'Shaughnessy, R. Binary Mergers and Growth of Black Holes in Dense Star Clusters. *Astrophys. J.* **2006**, *637*, 937–951. [CrossRef]
54. Downing, J.M.B.; Benacquista, M.J.; Giersz, M.; Spurzem, R. Compact binaries in star clusters—I. Black hole binaries inside globular clusters. *Mon. Not. R. Astron. Soc.* **2010**, *407*, 1946–1962. [CrossRef]
55. Rodriguez, C.L.; Morscher, M.; Pattabiraman, B.; Chatterjee, S.; Haster, C.J.; Rasio, F.A. Binary Black Hole Mergers from Globular Clusters: Implications for Advanced LIGO. *Phys. Rev. Lett.* **2015**, *115*, 051101. [CrossRef]
56. Antonini, F.; Rasio, F.A. Merging Black Hole Binaries in Galactic Nuclei: Implications for Advanced-LIGO Detections. *Astrophys. J.* **2016**, *831*, 187. [CrossRef]
57. Mapelli, M. Massive black hole binaries from runaway collisions: The impact of metallicity. *Mon. Not. R. Astron. Soc.* **2016**, *459*, 3432–3446. [CrossRef]
58. Kimpson, T.O.; Spera, M.; Mapelli, M.; Ziosi, B.M. Hierarchical black hole triples in young star clusters: impact of Kozai–Lidov resonance on mergers. *Mon. Not. R. Astron. Soc.* **2016**, *463*, 2443–2452. [CrossRef]
59. Banerjee, S. Stellar-mass black holes in young massive and open stellar clusters and their role in gravitational-wave generation. *Mon. Not. R. Astron. Soc.* **2017**, *467*, 524–539. [CrossRef]
60. Samsing, J.; Ramirez-Ruiz, E. On the Assembly Rate of Highly Eccentric Binary Black Hole Mergers. *Astrophys. J.* **2017**, *840*, L14. [CrossRef]
61. Trani, A.A.; Rastello, S.; Carlo, U.N.D.; Santoliquido, F.; Tanikawa, A.; Mapelli, M. Compact object mergers in hierarchical triples from low-mass young star clusters. *Mon. Not. R. Astron. Soc.* **2022**. [CrossRef]
62. Kumamoto, J.; Fujii, M.S.; Tanikawa, A. Gravitational-wave emission from binary black holes formed in open clusters. *Mon. Not. R. Astron. Soc.* **2019**, *486*, 3942–3950. [CrossRef]
63. Di Carlo, U.N.; Mapelli, M.; Giacobbo, N.; Spera, M.; Bouffanais, Y.; Rastello, S.; Santoliquido, F.; Pasquato, M.; Ballone, A.; Trani, A.A.; et al. Binary black holes in young star clusters: The impact of metallicity. *Mon. Not. R. Astron. Soc.* **2020**, *498*, 495–506. [CrossRef]
64. Trani, A.A.; Tanikawa, A.; Fujii, M.S.; Leigh, N.W.C.; Kumamoto, J. Spin misalignment of black hole binaries from young star clusters: Implications for the origin of gravitational waves events. *Mon. Not. R. Astron. Soc.* **2021**, *504*, 910–919. [CrossRef]
65. Arca Sedda, M.; Mapelli, M.; Benacquista, M.; Spera, M. Population synthesis of black hole mergers with B-POP: The impact of dynamics, natal spins, and intermediate-mass black holes on the population of gravitational wave sources. *arXiv* **2021**, arXiv:2109.12119.
66. Mikkola, S.; Aarseth, S.J. An efficient integration method for binaries in N-body simulations. *New Astron.* **1998**, *3*, 309–320. [CrossRef]
67. Aarseth, S.J. Regularization tools for binary interactions. In *Astrophysical Supercomputing Using Particle Simulations, Proceedings of the IAU Symposium n.208, Tokyo, Japan, 10–13 July 2001*; Makino, J., Hut, P., Eds.; Astronomical Society of the Pacific: San Francisco, CA, USA, 2003; Volume 208, p. 295.
68. Konstantinidis, S.; Kokkotas, K.D. MYRIAD: A new N-body code for simulations of star clusters. *Astron. Astrophys.* **2010**, *522*, A70. [CrossRef]
69. Hypki, A.; Giersz, M. Mocca code for star cluster simulations—I. Blue stragglers, first results. *Mon. Not. R. Astron. Soc.* **2012**, *429*, 1221–1243. [CrossRef]
70. Capuzzo-Dolcetta, R.; Spera, M.; Punzo, D. A fully parallel, high precision, N-body code running on hybrid computing platforms. *J. Comput. Phys.* **2013**, *236*, 580–593. [CrossRef]
71. Capuzzo-Dolcetta, R.; Spera, M. A performance comparison of different graphics processing units running direct N-body simulations. *Comput. Phys. Commun.* **2013**, *184*, 2528–2539. [CrossRef]
72. Rodriguez, C.L.; Morscher, M.; Wang, L.; Chatterjee, S.; Rasio, F.A.; Spurzem, R. Million-body star cluster simulations: comparisons between Monte Carlo and direct N-body. *Mon. Not. R. Astron. Soc.* **2016**, *463*, 2109–2118. [CrossRef]

73. Maureira-Fredes, C.; Amaro-Seoane, P. GraviDy, a GPU modular, parallel direct-summation N-body integrator: Dynamics with softening. *Mon. Not. R. Astron. Soc.* **2017**, *473*, 3113–3127. [CrossRef]
74. Wang, L.; Iwasawa, M.; Nitadori, K.; Makino, J. PETAR: A high-performance N-body code for modelling massive collisional stellar systems. *Mon. Not. R. Astron. Soc.* **2020**, *497*, 536–555. [CrossRef]
75. Mencagli, M.; Nazarova, N.; Spera, M. ISTEDDAS: A new direct N-Body code to study merging compact-object binaries. *J. Phys. Conf. Ser.* **2022**, *2207*, 012051. [CrossRef]
76. Nitz, A.H.; Capano, C.D.; Kumar, S.; Wang, Y.F.; Kastha, S.; Schäfer, M.; Dhurkunde, R.; Cabero, M. 3-OGC: Catalog of Gravitational Waves from Compact-binary Mergers. *Astrophys. J.* **2021**, *922*, 76. [CrossRef]
77. Olsen, S.; Venumadhav, T.; Mushkin, J.; Roulet, J.; Zackay, B.; Zaldarriaga, M. New binary black hole mergers in the LIGO–Virgo O3a data. *arXiv* **2022**, arXiv:2201.02252.
78. Zackay, B.; Venumadhav, T.; Dai, L.; Roulet, J.; Zaldarriaga, M. Highly spinning and aligned binary black hole merger in the Advanced LIGO first observing run. *Phys. Rev. D* **2019**, *100*, 023007. [CrossRef]
79. Abbott, R.; et al. [The LIGO Scientific Collaboration]; [the Virgo Collaboration]; [the KAGRA Collaboration]. GWTC-3: Compact Binary Coalescences Observed by LIGO and Virgo During the Second Part of the Third Observing Run. *arXiv* **2021**, arXiv:2111.03606.
80. Abbott, R.; et al. [The LIGO Scientific Collaboration]; [The Virgo Collaboration]; [The KAGRA Scientific Collaboration]. The population of merging compact binaries inferred using gravitational waves through GWTC-3. *arXiv* **2021**, arXiv:2111.03634.
81. Abbott, R.; Abbott, T.D.; Abraham, S.; Acernese, F.; Ackley, K.; Adams, C.; Adhikari, R.X.; Adya, V.B.; Affeldt, C.; Agathos, M.; et al. GW190814: Gravitational Waves from the Coalescence of a 23 Solar Mass Black Hole with a 2.6 Solar Mass Compact Object. *Astrophys. J.* **2020**, *896*, L44. [CrossRef]
82. Abbott, R.; Abbott, T.D.; Abraham, S.; Acernese, F.; Ackley, K.; Adams, C.; Adhikari, R.X.; Adya, V.B.; Affeldt, C.; Agathos, M.; et al. GW190521: A Binary Black Hole Merger with a Total Mass of 150 $M_\odot$. *Phys. Rev. Lett.* **2020**, *125*, 101102. [CrossRef]
83. Abbott, R.; Abbott, T.D.; Abraham, S.; Acernese, F.; Ackley, K.; Adams, C.; Adhikari, R.X.; Adya, V.B.; Affeldt, C.; Agathos, M.; et al. Properties and Astrophysical Implications of the 150 $M_\odot$ Binary Black Hole Merger GW190521. *Astrophys. J.* **2020**, *900*, L13. [CrossRef]
84. Abbott, R.; Abbott, T.D.; Abraham, S.; Acernese, F.; Ackley, K.; Adams, A.; Adams, C.; Adhikari, R.X.; Adya, V.B.; Affeldt, C.; et al. Observation of Gravitational Waves from Two Neutron Star-Black Hole Coalescences. *Astrophys. J.* **2021**, *915*, L5. [CrossRef]
85. Abbott, B.P.; Abbott, R.; Abbott, T.D.; Acernese, F.; Ackley, K.; Adams, C.; Adams, T.; Addesso, P.; Adhikari, R.X.; Adya, V.; et al. GW170817: Observation of Gravitational Waves from a Binary Neutron Star Inspiral. *Phys. Rev. Lett.* **2017**, *119*, 161101. [CrossRef]
86. Tiwari, V.; Fairhurst, S. The Emergence of Structure in the Binary Black Hole Mass Distribution. *Astrophys. J.* **2021**, *913*, L19. [CrossRef]
87. Karathanasis, C.; Mukherjee, S.; Mastrogiovanni, S. Binary black holes population and cosmology in new lights: Signature of PISN mass and formation channel in GWTC-3. *arXiv* **2022**, arXiv:2204.13495.
88. Mukherjee, S. The redshift dependence of black hole mass distribution: Is it reliable for standard sirens cosmology? *arXiv* **2021**, arXiv:2112.10256.
89. Mapelli, M. Formation Channels of Single and Binary Stellar-Mass Black Holes. In *Handbook of Gravitational Wave Astronomy*; Springer: Singapore, 2021; p. 4. [CrossRef]
90. Mandel, I.; Broekgaarden, F.S. Rates of compact object coalescences. *Living Rev. Rel.* **2022**, *25*, 1. [CrossRef]
91. Eddington, A.S. On the relation between the masses and luminosities of the stars. *Mon. Not. R. Astron. Soc.* **1924**, *84*, 308–332. [CrossRef]
92. Smartt, S.J. Progenitors of Core-Collapse Supernovae. *Annu. Rev. Astron. Astrophys.* **2009**, *47*, 63–106. [CrossRef]
93. Horiuchi, S.; Beacom, J.F.; Kochanek, C.S.; Prieto, J.L.; Stanek, K.Z.; Thompson, T.A. The cosmic core-collapse supernova rate does not match the massive-star formation rate. *Astrophys. J.* **2011**, *738*, 154. [CrossRef]
94. Smartt, S.J. Observational Constraints on the Progenitors of Core-Collapse Supernovae: The Case for Missing High-Mass Stars. *Publ. Astron. Soc. Aust.* **2015**, *32*, e016. [CrossRef]
95. Aguirre, V.S. Stellar Evolution and Modelling Stars. *Asteroseismology and Exoplanets: Listening to the Stars and Searching for New Worlds*; Springer: Berlin/Heidelberg, Germany, 2017; pp. 3–25. [CrossRef]
96. Vink, J.S. Theory and Diagnostics of Hot Star Mass Loss. *arXiv* **2021**, arXiv:2109.08164.
97. Spera, M.; Mapelli, M. Very massive stars, pair-instability supernovae and intermediate-mass black holes with the sevn code. *Mon. Not. R. Astron. Soc.* **2017**, *470*, 4739–4749. [CrossRef]
98. Bressan, A.; Marigo, P.; Girardi, L.; Salasnich, B.; Dal Cero, C.; Rubele, S.; Nanni, A. PARSEC: Stellar tracks and isochrones with the PAdova and TRieste Stellar Evolution Code. *Mon. Not. R. Astron. Soc.* **2012**, *427*, 127–145. [CrossRef]
99. Chen, Y.; Bressan, A.; Girardi, L.; Marigo, P.; Kong, X.; Lanza, A. PARSEC evolutionary tracks of massive stars up to 350 $M_\odot$ at metallicities $0.0001 \leq Z \leq 0.04$. *Mon. Not. R. Astron. Soc.* **2015**, *452*, 1068–1080. [CrossRef]
100. Chandrasekhar, S. The highly collapsed configurations of a stellar mass (Second paper). *Mon. Not. R. Astron. Soc.* **1935**, *95*, 207–225. [CrossRef]
101. Oppenheimer, J.R.; Volkoff, G.M. On Massive Neutron Cores. *Phys. Rev.* **1939**, *55*, 374–381. [CrossRef]
102. Tolman, R.C. Static Solutions of Einstein's Field Equations for Spheres of Fluid. *Phys. Rev.* **1939**, *55*, 364–373. [CrossRef]

103. Rhoades, C.E.; Ruffini, R. Maximum Mass of a Neutron Star. *Phys. Rev. Lett.* **1974**, *32*, 324–327. [CrossRef]
104. Kalogera, V.; Baym, G. The Maximum Mass of a Neutron Star. *Astrophys. J.* **1996**, *470*, L61–L64. [CrossRef]
105. Srinivasan, G. The maximum mass of neutron stars. *Astron. Astrophys. Rev.* **2002**, *11*, 67–96. [CrossRef]
106. Margalit, B.; Metzger, B.D. Constraining the Maximum Mass of Neutron Stars from Multi-messenger Observations of GW170817. *Astrophys. J.* **2017**, *850*, L19. [CrossRef]
107. Shibata, M.; Fujibayashi, S.; Hotokezaka, K.; Kiuchi, K.; Kyutoku, K.; Sekiguchi, Y.; Tanaka, M. Modeling GW170817 based on numerical relativity and its implications. *Phys. Rev. D* **2017**, *96*, 123012. [CrossRef]
108. Linares, M.; Shahbaz, T.; Casares, J. Peering into the Dark Side: Magnesium Lines Establish a Massive Neutron Star in PSR J2215 + 5135. *Astrophys. J.* **2018**, *859*, 54. [CrossRef]
109. Alsing, J.; Silva, H.O.; Berti, E. Evidence for a maximum mass cut-off in the neutron star mass distribution and constraints on the equation of state. *Mon. Not. R. Astron. Soc.* **2018**, *478*, 1377–1391. [CrossRef]
110. Rezzolla, L.; Most, E.R.; Weih, L.R. Using Gravitational-wave Observations and Quasi-universal Relations to Constrain the Maximum Mass of Neutron Stars. *Astrophys. J.* **2018**, *852*, L25. [CrossRef]
111. Ruiz, M.; Shapiro, S.L.; Tsokaros, A. GW170817, general relativistic magnetohydrodynamic simulations, and the neutron star maximum mass. *Phys. Rev. D* **2018**, *97*, 021501. [CrossRef] [PubMed]
112. Cromartie, H.T.; Fonseca, E.; Ransom, S.M.; Demorest, P.B.; Arzoumanian, Z.; Blumer, H.; Brook, P.R.; DeCesar, M.E.; Dolch, T.; Ellis, J.; et al. Relativistic Shapiro delay measurements of an extremely massive millisecond pulsar. *Nat. Astron.* **2020**, *4*, 72–76. [CrossRef]
113. Li, Y.P.; Dempsey, A.M.; Li, S.; Li, H.; Li, J. Orbital Evolution of Binary Black Holes in Active Galactic Nucleus Disks: A Disk Channel for Binary Black Hole Mergers? *Astrophys. J.* **2021**, *911*, 124. [CrossRef]
114. Li, A.; Miao, Z.; Han, S.; Zhang, B. Constraints on the Maximum Mass of Neutron Stars with a Quark Core from GW170817 and NICER PSR J0030 + 0451 Data. *Astrophys. J.* **2021**, *913*, 27. [CrossRef]
115. Shibata, M.; Zhou, E.; Kiuchi, K.; Fujibayashi, S. Constraint on the maximum mass of neutron stars using GW170817 event. *Phys. Rev. D* **2019**, *100*, 023015. [CrossRef]
116. Kashyap, R.; Das, A.; Radice, D.; Padamata, S.; Prakash, A.; Logoteta, D.; Perego, A.; Godzieba, D.A.; Bernuzzi, S.; Bombaci, I.E.A. Numerical relativity simulations of prompt collapse mergers: Threshold mass and phenomenological constraints on neutron star properties after GW170817. *arXiv* **2021**, arXiv:2111.05183.
117. Friedman, J.L.; Ipser, J.R. On the Maximum Mass of a Uniformly Rotating Neutron Star. *Astrophys. J.* **1987**, *314*, 594. [CrossRef]
118. Lasota, J.P.; Haensel, P.; Abramowicz, M.A. Fast Rotation of Neutron Stars. *Astrophys. J.* **1996**, *456*, 300.
119. Lattimer, J.M.; Schutz, B.F. Constraining the Equation of State with Moment of Inertia Measurements. *Astrophys. J.* **2005**, *629*, 979–984. [CrossRef]
120. Breu, C.; Rezzolla, L. Maximum mass, moment of inertia and compactness of relativistic stars. *Mon. Not. R. Astron. Soc.* **2016**, *459*, 646–656. [CrossRef]
121. Saha, M.N. On Radiation-Pressure and the Quantum Theory. *Astrophys. J.* **1919**, *50*, 220. [CrossRef]
122. Morton, D.C. Mass Loss from Three OB Supergiants in Orion. *Astrophys. J.* **1967**, *150*, 535. [CrossRef]
123. Morton, D.C. The Far-Ultraviolet Spectra of Six Stars in Orion. *Astrophys. J.* **1967**, *147*, 1017. [CrossRef]
124. Castor, J.I.; Abbott, D.C.; Klein, R.I. Radiation-driven winds in of stars. *Astrophys. J.* **1975**, *195*, 157–174. [CrossRef]
125. Sobolev, V.V. *Moving Envelopes of Stars*; Harvard University Press: Cambridge, MA, USA,1960.
126. Kudritzki, R.P.; Pauldrach, A.; Puls, J. Radiation driven winds of hot luminous stars. II. Wind models for O-stars in the Magellanic clouds. *Astron. Astrophys.* **1987**, *173*, 293–298.
127. Abbott, D.C. The theory of radiatively driven stellar winds. II. The line acceleration. *Astrophys. J.* **1982**, *259*, 282–301. [CrossRef]
128. Abbott, D.C.; Lucy, L.B. Multiline transfer and the dynamics of stellar winds. *Astrophys. J.* **1985**, *288*, 679–693. [CrossRef]
129. Vink, J.S.; de Koter, A.; Lamers, H.J.G.L.M. Mass-loss predictions for O and B stars as a function of metallicity. *Astron. Astrophys.* **2001**, *369*, 574–588. [CrossRef]
130. Vink, J.S.; de Koter, A. On the metallicity dependence of Wolf-Rayet winds. *Astron. Astrophys.* **2005**, *442*, 587–596. [CrossRef]
131. Sander, A.A.C.; Vink, J.S. On the nature of massive helium star winds and Wolf-Rayet-type mass-loss. *Mon. Not. R. Astron. Soc.* **2020**, *499*, 873–892. [CrossRef]
132. Björklund, R.; Sundqvist, J.O.; Puls, J.; Najarro, F. New predictions for radiation-driven, steady-state mass-loss and wind-momentum from hot, massive stars. II. A grid of O-type stars in the Galaxy and the Magellanic Clouds. *Astron. Astrophys.* **2021**, *648*, A36. [CrossRef]
133. Vink, J.S.; Muijres, L.E.; Anthonisse, B.; de Koter, A.; Gräfener, G.; Langer, N. Wind modelling of very massive stars up to 300 solar masses. *Astron. Astrophys.* **2011**, *531*, A132. [CrossRef]
134. Vink, J.S.; de Koter, A. Predictions of variable mass loss for Luminous Blue Variables. *Astron. Astrophys.* **2002**, *393*, 543–553. [CrossRef]
135. Yoon, S.C.; Cantiello, M. Evolution Of Massive Stars with Pulsation-Driven Superwinds during the Red Supergiant Phase. *Astrophys. J.* **2010**, *717*, L62–L65. [CrossRef]
136. Tang, J.; Bressan, A.; Rosenfield, P.; Slemer, A.; Marigo, P.; Girardi, L.; Bianchi, L. New PARSEC evolutionary tracks of massive stars at low metallicity: Testing canonical stellar evolution in nearby star-forming dwarf galaxies. *Mon. Not. R. Astron. Soc.* **2014**, *445*, 4287–4305. [CrossRef]

137. Gräfener, G.; Vink, J.S.; de Koter, A.; Langer, N. The Eddington factor as the key to understand the winds of the most massive stars. Evidence for a Γ-dependence of Wolf-Rayet type mass loss. *Astron. Astrophys.* **2011**, *535*, A56. [CrossRef]
138. Gräfener, G.; Hamann, W.R. Mass loss from late-type WN stars and its Z-dependence. Very massive stars approaching the Eddington limit. *Astron. Astrophys.* **2008**, *482*, 945–960. [CrossRef]
139. Davies, B.; Oudmaijer, R.D.; Vink, J.S. Asphericity and clumpiness in the winds of Luminous Blue Variables. *Astron. Astrophys.* **2005**, *439*, 1107–1125. [CrossRef]
140. Puls, J.; Markova, N.; Scuderi, S.; Stanghellini, C.; Taranova, O.G.; Burnley, A.W.; Howarth, I.D. Bright OB stars in the Galaxy. III. Constraints on the radial stratification of the clumping factor in hot star winds from a combined H_α, IR and radio analysis. *Astron. Astrophys.* **2006**, *454*, 625–651. [CrossRef]
141. Muijres, L.E.; de Koter, A.; Vink, J.S.; Krtička, J.; Kubát, J.; Langer, N. Predictions of the effect of clumping on the wind properties of O-type stars. *Astron. Astrophys.* **2011**, *526*, A32. [CrossRef]
142. Petit, V.; Keszthelyi, Z.; MacInnis, R.; Cohen, D.H.; Townsend, R.H.D.; Wade, G.A.; Thomas, S.L.; Owocki, S.P.; Puls, J.; ud-Doula, A. Magnetic massive stars as progenitors of 'heavy' stellar-mass black holes. *Mon. Not. R. Astron. Soc.* **2017**, *466*, 1052–1060. [CrossRef]
143. Heger, A.; Langer, N.; Woosley, S.E. Presupernova Evolution of Rotating Massive Stars. I. Numerical Method and Evolution of the Internal Stellar Structure. *Astrophys. J.* **2000**, *528*, 368–396. [CrossRef]
144. Maeder, A.; Meynet, G. Stellar evolution with rotation. VI. The Eddington and Omega -limits, the rotational mass loss for OB and LBV stars. *Astron. Astrophys.* **2000**, *361*, 159–166.
145. Colgate, S.A.; White, R.H. The Hydrodynamic Behavior of Supernovae Explosions. *Astrophys. J.* **1966**, *143*, 626. [CrossRef]
146. Bethe, H.A.; Wilson, J.R. Revival of a stalled supernova shock by neutrino heating. *Astrophys. J.* **1985**, *295*, 14–23. [CrossRef]
147. Janka, H.T.; Mueller, E. The First Second of a Type II Supernova: Convection, Accretion, and Shock Propagation. *Astrophys. J.* **1995**, *448*, L109. [CrossRef]
148. Janka, H.T.; Mueller, E. Neutrino heating, convection, and the mechanism of Type-II supernova explosions. *Astron. Astrophys.* **1996**, *306*, 167.
149. Burrows, A.; Hayes, J.; Fryxell, B.A. On the Nature of Core-Collapse Supernova Explosions. *Astrophys. J.* **1995**, *450*, 830. [CrossRef]
150. Janka, H.T. Neutrino-Driven Explosions. In *Handbook of Supernovae*; Alsabti, A.W., Murdin, P., Eds.; Springer: Cham, Switzerland, 2017; p. 1095. [CrossRef]
151. Janka, H.T. Explosion Mechanisms of Core-Collapse Supernovae. *Annu. Rev. Nucl. Part. Sci.* **2012**, *62*, 407–451. [CrossRef]
152. Mezzacappa, A.; Endeve, E.; Messer, O.E.B.; Bruenn, S.W. Physical, numerical, and computational challenges of modeling neutrino transport in core-collapse supernovae. *Living Rev. Comput. Astrophys.* **2020**, *6*, 4. [CrossRef]
153. LeBlanc, J.M.; Wilson, J.R. A Numerical Example of the Collapse of a Rotating Magnetized Star. *Astrophys. J.* **1970**, *161*, 541. [CrossRef]
154. Bisnovatyi-Kogan, G.S. The Explosion of a Rotating Star As a Supernova Mechanism. *Astron. Zhurnal* **1970**, *47*, 813.
155. Meier, D.L.; Epstein, R.I.; Arnett, W.D.; Schramm, D.N. Magnetohydrodynamic phenomena in collapsing stellar cores. *Astrophys. J.* **1976**, *204*, 869–878. [CrossRef]
156. Mueller, E.; Hillebrandt, W. A magnetohydrodynamical supernova model. *Astron. Astrophys.* **1979**, *80*, 147–154.
157. Fryer, C.L.; Warren, M.S. The Collapse of Rotating Massive Stars in Three Dimensions. *Astrophys. J.* **2004**, *601*, 391–404. [CrossRef]
158. Kotake, K.; Sato, K.; Takahashi, K. Explosion mechanism, neutrino burst and gravitational wave in core-collapse supernovae. *Rep. Prog. Phys.* **2006**, *69*, 971–1143. [CrossRef]
159. Nakamura, K.; Kuroda, T.; Takiwaki, T.; Kotake, K. Impacts of Rotation on Three-dimensional Hydrodynamics of Core-collapse Supernovae. *Astrophys. J.* **2014**, *793*, 45. [CrossRef]
160. Takiwaki, T.; Kotake, K.; Suwa, Y. Three-dimensional simulations of rapidly rotating core-collapse supernovae: Finding a neutrino-powered explosion aided by non-axisymmetric flows. *Mon. Not. R. Astron. Soc.* **2016**, *461*, L112–L116. [CrossRef]
161. Summa, A.; Janka, H.T.; Melson, T.; Marek, A. Rotation-supported Neutrino-driven Supernova Explosions in Three Dimensions and the Critical Luminosity Condition. *Astrophys. J.* **2018**, *852*, 28. [CrossRef]
162. Miyaji, S.; Nomoto, K.; Yokoi, K.; Sugimoto, D. Supernova triggered by electron captures. *Publ. Astron. Soc. Jpn.* **1980**, *32*, 303–329.
163. Nomoto, K.; Sparks, W.; Fesen, R.; Gull, T.R.; Miyaji, S.; Sugimoto, D. The Crab Nebula's progenitor. *Nature* **1982**, *299*, 803–805. [CrossRef]
164. Jones, S.; Röpke, F.K.; Pakmor, R.; Seitenzahl, I.R.; Ohlmann, S.T.; Edelmann, P.V.F. Do electron-capture supernovae make neutron stars?. First multidimensional hydrodynamic simulations of the oxygen deflagration. *Astron. Astrophys.* **2016**, *593*, A72. [CrossRef]
165. Kitaura, F.S.; Janka, H.T.; Hillebrandt, W. Explosions of O-Ne-Mg cores, the Crab supernova, and subluminous type II-P supernovae. *Astron. Astrophys.* **2006**, *450*, 345–350. [CrossRef]
166. Özel, F.; Psaltis, D.; Narayan, R.; Santos Villarreal, A. On the Mass Distribution and Birth Masses of Neutron Stars. *Astrophys. J.* **2012**, *757*, 55. [CrossRef]
167. Ugliano, M.; Janka, H.T.; Marek, A.; Arcones, A. Progenitor-explosion Connection and Remnant Birth Masses for Neutrino-driven Supernovae of Iron-core Progenitors. *Astrophys. J.* **2012**, *757*, 69. [CrossRef]
168. O'Connor, E.; Ott, C.D. Black Hole Formation in Failing Core-Collapse Supernovae. *Astrophys. J.* **2011**, *730*, 70. [CrossRef]

169. Limongi, M.; Chieffi, A. Presupernova Evolution and Explosive Nucleosynthesis of Rotating Massive Stars in the Metallicity Range $-3 \leq$ [Fe/H] ≤ 0. *Astrophys. J.* **2018**, *237*, 13. [CrossRef]
170. Mapelli, M.; Spera, M.; Montanari, E.; Limongi, M.; Chieffi, A.; Giacobbo, N.; Bressan, A.; Bouffanais, Y. Impact of the Rotation and Compactness of Progenitors on the Mass of Black Holes. *Astrophys. J.* **2020**, *888*, 76. [CrossRef]
171. Chieffi, A.; Roberti, L.; Limongi, M.; La Cognata, M.; Lamia, L.; Palmerini, S.; Pizzone, R.G.; Spartà, R.; Tumino, A. Impact of the New Measurement of the ^{12}C + ^{12}C Fusion Cross Section on the Final Compactness of Massive Stars. *Astrophys. J.* **2021**, *916*, 79. [CrossRef]
172. Clausen, D.; Piro, A.L.; Ott, C.D. The Black Hole Formation Probability. *Astrophys. J.* **2015**, *799*, 190. [CrossRef]
173. Ertl, T.; Janka, H.T.; Woosley, S.E.; Sukhbold, T.; Ugliano, M. A Two-parameter Criterion for Classifying the Explodability of Massive Stars by the Neutrino-driven Mechanism. *Astrophys. J.* **2016**, *818*, 124. [CrossRef]
174. Sukhbold, T.; Ertl, T.; Woosley, S.E.; Brown, J.M.; Janka, H.T. Core-Collapse Supernovae from 9 to 120 Solar Masses Based on Neutrino-Powered Explosions. *Astrophys. J.* **2016**, *821*, 38. [CrossRef]
175. Ertl, T.; Woosley, S.E.; Sukhbold, T.; Janka, H.T. The Explosion of Helium Stars Evolved with Mass Loss. *Astrophys. J.* **2020**, *890*, 51. [CrossRef]
176. Burrows, A.; Radice, D.; Vartanyan, D.; Nagakura, H.; Skinner, M.A.; Dolence, J.C. The overarching framework of core-collapse supernova explosions as revealed by 3D FORNAX simulations. *Mon. Not. R. Astron. Soc.* **2020**, *491*, 2715–2735. [CrossRef]
177. Woosley, S.E.; Sukhbold, T.; Janka, H.T. The Birth Function for Black Holes and Neutron Stars in Close Binaries. *Astrophys. J.* **2020**, *896*, 56. [CrossRef]
178. Patton, R.A.; Sukhbold, T. Towards a realistic explosion landscape for binary population synthesis. *Mon. Not. R. Astron. Soc.* **2020**, *499*, 2803–2816. [CrossRef]
179. Patton, R.A.; Sukhbold, T.; Eldridge, J.J. Comparing compact object distributions from mass- and presupernova core structure-based prescriptions. *Mon. Not. R. Astron. Soc.* **2022**, *511*, 903–913. [CrossRef]
180. Woosley, S.E. Pulsational Pair-instability Supernovae. *Astrophys. J.* **2017**, *836*, 244. [CrossRef]
181. Heger, A.; Woosley, S.E. The Nucleosynthetic Signature of Population III. *Astrophys. J.* **2002**, *567*, 532–543. [CrossRef]
182. Fowler, W.A.; Hoyle, F. Neutrino Processes and Pair Formation in Massive Stars and Supernovae. *Astrophys. J. Suppl. Ser.* **1964**, *9*, 201. [CrossRef]
183. Barkat, Z.; Rakavy, G.; Sack, N. Dynamics of Supernova Explosion Resulting from Pair Formation. *Phys. Rev. Lett.* **1967**, *18*, 379–381. [CrossRef]
184. Rakavy, G.; Shaviv, G. Instabilities in Highly Evolved Stellar Models. *Astrophys. J.* **1967**, *148*, 803. [CrossRef]
185. Woosley, S.E.; Blinnikov, S.; Heger, A. Pulsational pair instability as an explanation for the most luminous supernovae. *Nature* **2007**, *450*, 390–392. [CrossRef]
186. Bond, J.R.; Arnett, W.D.; Carr, B.J. The evolution and fate of Very Massive Objects. *Astrophys. J.* **1984**, *280*, 825–847. [CrossRef]
187. Fryer, C.L.; Woosley, S.E.; Heger, A. Pair-Instability Supernovae, Gravity Waves, and Gamma-Ray Transients. *Astrophys. J.* **2001**, *550*, 372–382. [CrossRef]
188. Chatzopoulos, E.; Wheeler, J.C. Effects of Rotation on the Minimum Mass of Primordial Progenitors of Pair-Instability Supernovae. *Astrophys. J.* **2012**, *748*, 42. [CrossRef]
189. Belczynski, K.; Heger, A.; Gladysz, W.; Ruiter, A.J.; Woosley, S.; Wiktorowicz, G.; Chen, H.Y.; Bulik, T.; O'Shaughnessy, R.; Holz, D.E.; et al. The effect of pair-instability mass loss on black-hole mergers. *Astron. Astrophys.* **2016**, *594*, A97. [CrossRef]
190. Fishbach, M.; Holz, D.E. Where Are LIGO's Big Black Holes? *Astrophys. J.* **2017**, *851*, L25. [CrossRef]
191. Stevenson, S.; Sampson, M.; Powell, J.; Vigna-Gómez, A.; Neijssel, C.J.; Szécsi, D.; Mandel, I. The Impact of Pair-instability Mass Loss on the Binary Black Hole Mass Distribution. *Astrophys. J.* **2019**, *882*, 121. [CrossRef]
192. Farmer, R.; Renzo, M.; de Mink, S.E.; Marchant, P.; Justham, S. Mind the Gap: The Location of the Lower Edge of the Pair-instability Supernova Black Hole Mass Gap. *Astrophys. J.* **2019**, *887*, 53. [CrossRef]
193. Farmer, R.; Renzo, M.; de Mink, S.E.; Fishbach, M.; Justham, S. Constraints from Gravitational-wave Detections of Binary Black Hole Mergers on the ^{12}C(α, γ)^{16}O Rate. *Astrophys. J.* **2020**, *902*, L36. [CrossRef]
194. Mangiagli, A.; Bonetti, M.; Sesana, A.; Colpi, M. Merger Rate of Stellar Black Hole Binaries above the Pair-instability Mass Gap. *Astrophys. J.* **2019**, *883*, L27. [CrossRef]
195. Fishbach, M.; Holz, D.E. Minding the Gap: GW190521 as a Straddling Binary. *Astrophys. J.* **2020**, *904*, L26. [CrossRef]
196. Ezquiaga, J.N.; Holz, D.E. Jumping the Gap: Searching for LIGO's Biggest Black Holes. *Astrophys. J. Lett.* **2021**, *909*, L23. [CrossRef]
197. Marchant, P.; Moriya, T.J. The impact of stellar rotation on the black hole mass-gap from pair-instability supernovae. *Astron. Astrophys.* **2020**, *640*, L18. [CrossRef]
198. Woosley, S.E.; Heger, A. The Pair-instability Mass Gap for Black Holes. *Astrophys. J.* **2021**, *912*, L31. [CrossRef]
199. Renzo, M.; Farmer, R.J.; Justham, S.; de Mink, S.E.; Götberg, Y.; Marchant, P. Sensitivity of the lower edge of the pair-instability black hole mass gap to the treatment of time-dependent convection. *Mon. Not. R. Astron. Soc.* **2020**, *493*, 4333–4341. [CrossRef]
200. Nadezhin, D.K. Some Secondary Indications of Gravitational Collapse. *Astrophys. Space Sci.* **1980**, *69*, 115–125. [CrossRef]
201. Lovegrove, E.; Woosley, S.E. Very Low Energy Supernovae from Neutrino Mass Loss. *Astrophys. J.* **2013**, *769*, 109. [CrossRef]
202. Kochanek, C.S. Constraints on core collapse from the black hole mass function. *Mon. Not. R. Astron. Soc.* **2015**, *446*, 1213–1222. [CrossRef]

203. Kroupa, P. On the variation of the initial mass function. *Mon. Not. R. Astron. Soc.* **2001**, *322*, 231–246. [CrossRef]
204. deBoer, R.J.; Görres, J.; Wiescher, M.; Azuma, R.E.; Best, A.; Brune, C.R.; Fields, C.E.; Jones, S.; Pignatari, M.; Sayre, D.; et al. The $^{12}C(\alpha,\gamma)^{16}O$ reaction and its implications for stellar helium burning. *Rev. Mod. Phys.* **2017**, *89*, 035007. [CrossRef]
205. Takahashi, K.; Yoshida, T.; Umeda, H. Stellar Yields of Rotating First Stars. II. Pair-instability Supernovae and Comparison with Observations. *Astrophys. J.* **2018**, *857*, 111. [CrossRef]
206. Costa, G.; Bressan, A.; Mapelli, M.; Marigo, P.; Iorio, G.; Spera, M. Formation of GW190521 from stellar evolution: The impact of the hydrogen-rich envelope, dredge-up, and $^{12}C(\alpha,\gamma)^{16}O$ rate on the pair-instability black hole mass gap. *Mon. Not. R. Astron. Soc.* **2021**, *501*, 4514–4533. [CrossRef]
207. Tanikawa, A.; Yoshida, T.; Kinugawa, T.; Trani, A.A.; Hosokawa, T.; Susa, H.; Omukai, K. Merger Rate Density of Binary Black Holes through Isolated Population I, II, III and Extremely Metal-poor Binary Star Evolution. *Astrophys. J.* **2022**, *926*, 83. [CrossRef]
208. Sakstein, J.; Croon, D.; McDermott, S.D.; Straight, M.C.; Baxter, E.J. Beyond the Standard Model Explanations of GW190521. *Phys. Rev. Lett.* **2020**, *125*, 261105. [CrossRef]
209. Marchant, P.; Renzo, M.; Farmer, R.; Pappas, K.M.W.; Taam, R.E.; de Mink, S.E.; Kalogera, V. Pulsational Pair-instability Supernovae in Very Close Binaries. *Astrophys. J.* **2019**, *882*, 36. [CrossRef]
210. Spera, M.; Giacobbo, N.; Mapelli, M. Shedding light on the black hole mass spectrum. *Mem. Soc. Astron. Ital.* **2016**, *87*, 575.
211. Rodriguez, C.L.; Amaro-Seoane, P.; Chatterjee, S.; Kremer, K.; Rasio, F.A.; Samsing, J.; Ye, C.S.; Zevin, M. Post-Newtonian dynamics in dense star clusters: Formation, masses, and merger rates of highly-eccentric black hole binaries. *Phys. Rev. D* **2018**, *98*, 123005. [CrossRef]
212. Yang, Y.; Bartos, I.; Gayathri, V.; Ford, K.E.S.; Haiman, Z.; Klimenko, S.; Kocsis, B.; Márka, S.; Márka, Z.; McKernan, B.; et al. Hierarchical Black Hole Mergers in Active Galactic Nuclei. *Phys. Rev. Lett.* **2019**, *123*, 181101. [CrossRef] [PubMed]
213. Arca Sedda, M. Birth, Life, and Death of Black Hole Binaries around Supermassive Black Holes: Dynamical Evolution of Gravitational Wave Sources. *Astrophys. J.* **2020**, *891*, 47. [CrossRef]
214. Di Carlo, U.N.; Giacobbo, N.; Mapelli, M.; Pasquato, M.; Spera, M.; Wang, L.; Haardt, F. Merging black holes in young star clusters. *Mon. Not. R. Astron. Soc.* **2019**, *487*, 2947–2960. [CrossRef]
215. Di Carlo, U.N.; Mapelli, M.; Bouffanais, Y.; Giacobbo, N.; Santoliquido, F.; Bressan, A.; Spera, M.; Haardt, F. Binary black holes in the pair instability mass gap. *Mon. Not. R. Astron. Soc.* **2020**, *497*, 1043–1049. [CrossRef]
216. Roupas, Z.; Kazanas, D. Generation of massive stellar black holes by rapid gas accretion in primordial dense clusters. *Astron. Astrophys.* **2019**, *632*, L8. [CrossRef]
217. Natarajan, P. A new channel to form IMBHs throughout cosmic time. *Mon. Not. R. Astron. Soc.* **2020**, *501*, 1413–1425. [CrossRef]
218. Safarzadeh, M.; Haiman, Z. Formation of GW190521 via Gas Accretion onto Population III Stellar Black Hole Remnants Born in High-redshift Minihalos. *Astrophys. J.* **2020**, *903*, L21. [CrossRef]
219. Tanikawa, A.; Susa, H.; Yoshida, T.; Trani, A.A.; Kinugawa, T. Merger Rate Density of Population III Binary Black Holes Below, Above, and in the Pair-instability Mass Gap. *Astrophys. J.* **2021**, *910*, 30. [CrossRef]
220. Farrell, E.; Groh, J.H.; Hirschi, R.; Murphy, L.; Kaiser, E.; Ekström, S.; Georgy, C.; Meynet, G. Is GW190521 the merger of black holes from the first stellar generations? *Mon. Not. R. Astron. Soc.* **2021**, *502*, L40–L44. [CrossRef]
221. Liu, B.; Bromm, V. The Population III Origin of GW190521. *Astrophys. J.* **2020**, *903*, L40. [CrossRef]
222. Spera, M.; Mapelli, M.; Giacobbo, N.; Trani, A.A.; Bressan, A.; Costa, G. Merging black hole binaries with the SEVN code. *Mon. Not. R. Astron. Soc.* **2019**, *485*, 889–907. [CrossRef]
223. Kremer, K.; Spera, M.; Becker, D.; Chatterjee, S.; Di Carlo, U.N.; Fragione, G.; Rodriguez, C.L.; Ye, C.S.; Rasio, F.A. Populating the Upper Black Hole Mass Gap through Stellar Collisions in Young Star Clusters. *Astrophys. J.* **2020**, *903*, 45. [CrossRef]
224. Blaauw, A. On the origin of the O- and B-type stars with high velocities (the "run-away" stars), and some related problems. *Bull. Astron. Inst. Neth.* **1961**, *15*, 265.
225. Gunn, J.E.; Ostriker, J.P. On the Nature of Pulsars. III. Analysis of Observations. *Astrophys. J.* **1970**, *160*, 979. [CrossRef]
226. Hobbs, G.; Lorimer, D.R.; Lyne, A.G.; Kramer, M. A statistical study of 233 pulsar proper motions. *Mon. Not. R. Astron. Soc.* **2005**, *360*, 974–992. [CrossRef]
227. Verbunt, F.; Igoshev, A.; Cator, E. The observed velocity distribution of young pulsars. *Astron. Astrophys.* **2017**, *608*, A57. [CrossRef]
228. Igoshev, A.P. The observed velocity distribution of young pulsars-II. Analysis of complete PSRπ. *Mon. Not. R. Astron. Soc.* **2020**, *494*, 3663–3674. [CrossRef]
229. Wongwathanarat, A.; Janka, H.T.; Müller, E. Three-dimensional neutrino-driven supernovae: Neutron star kicks, spins, and asymmetric ejection of nucleosynthesis products. *Astron. Astrophys.* **2013**, *552*, A126. [CrossRef]
230. Janka, H.T. Neutron Star Kicks by the Gravitational Tug-boat Mechanism in Asymmetric Supernova Explosions: Progenitor and Explosion Dependence. *Astrophys. J.* **2017**, *837*, 84. [CrossRef]
231. Gessner, A.; Janka, H.T. Hydrodynamical Neutron-star Kicks in Electron-capture Supernovae and Implications for the CRAB Supernova. *Astrophys. J.* **2018**, *865*, 61. [CrossRef]
232. Tauris, T.M.; Langer, N.; Podsiadlowski, P. Ultra-stripped supernovae: Progenitors and fate. *Mon. Not. R. Astron. Soc.* **2015**, *451*, 2123–2144. [CrossRef]
233. Müller, B.; Gay, D.W.; Heger, A.; Tauris, T.M.; Sim, S.A. Multidimensional simulations of ultrastripped supernovae to shock breakout. *Mon. Not. R. Astron. Soc.* **2018**, *479*, 3675–3689. [CrossRef]

234. Suwa, Y.; Yoshida, T.; Shibata, M.; Umeda, H.; Takahashi, K. Neutrino-driven explosions of ultra-stripped Type Ic supernovae generating binary neutron stars. *Mon. Not. R. Astron. Soc.* **2015**, *454*, 3073–3081. [CrossRef]
235. Repetto, S.; Davies, M.B.; Sigurdsson, S. Investigating stellar-mass black hole kicks. *Mon. Not. R. Astron. Soc.* **2012**, *425*, 2799–2809. [CrossRef]
236. Repetto, S.; Nelemans, G. Constraining the formation of black holes in short-period black hole low-mass X-ray binaries. *Mon. Not. R. Astron. Soc.* **2015**, *453*, 3341–3355. [CrossRef]
237. Mandel, I. Estimates of black hole natal kick velocities from observations of low-mass X-ray binaries. *Mon. Not. R. Astron. Soc.* **2016**, *456*, 578–581. [CrossRef]
238. Giacobbo, N.; Mapelli, M. The impact of electron-capture supernovae on merging double neutron stars. *Mon. Not. R. Astron. Soc.* **2019**, *482*, 2234–2243. [CrossRef]
239. Bray, J.C.; Eldridge, J.J. Neutron star kicks—II. Revision and further testing of the conservation of momentum 'kick' model. *Mon. Not. R. Astron. Soc.* **2018**, *480*, 5657–5672. [CrossRef]
240. Giacobbo, N.; Mapelli, M. Revising Natal Kick Prescriptions in Population Synthesis Simulations. *Astrophys. J.* **2020**, *891*, 141. [CrossRef]
241. Bray, J.C.; Eldridge, J.J. Neutron star kicks and their relationship to supernovae ejecta mass. *Mon. Not. R. Astron. Soc.* **2016**, *461*, 3747–3759. [CrossRef]
242. Beck, P.G.; Montalban, J.; Kallinger, T.; De Ridder, J.; Aerts, C.; García, R.A.; Hekker, S.; Dupret, M.A.; Mosser, B.; Eggenberger, P.; et al. Fast core rotation in red-giant stars as revealed by gravity-dominated mixed modes. *Nature* **2012**, *481*, 55–57. [CrossRef] [PubMed]
243. Mosser, B.; Goupil, M.J.; Belkacem, K.; Marques, J.P.; Beck, P.G.; Bloemen, S.; De Ridder, J.; Barban, C.; Deheuvels, S.; Elsworth, Y.; et al. Spin down of the core rotation in red giants. *Astron. Astrophys.* **2012**, *548*, A10. [CrossRef]
244. Deheuvels, S.; Doğan, G.; Goupil, M.J.; Appourchaux, T.; Benomar, O.; Bruntt, H.; Campante, T.L.; Casagr, L.; Ceillier, T.; Davies, G.R.; et al. Seismic constraints on the radial dependence of the internal rotation profiles of six Kepler subgiants and young red giants. *Astron. Astrophys.* **2014**, *564*, A27. [CrossRef]
245. Triana, S.A.; Corsaro, E.; De Ridder, J.; Bonanno, A.; Pérez Hernández, F.; García, R.A. Internal rotation of 13 low-mass low-luminosity red giants in the Kepler field. *Astron. Astrophys.* **2017**, *602*, A62. [CrossRef]
246. Hermes, J.J.; Gänsicke, B.T.; Kawaler, S.D.; Greiss, S.; Tremblay, P.E.; Fusillo, N.G.; Raddi, R.; Fanale, S.M.; Bell, K.J.; Dennihy, E.; et al. White Dwarf Rotation as a Function of Mass and a Dichotomy of Mode Line Widths: Kepler Observations of 27 Pulsating DA White Dwarfs through K2 Campaign 8. *Astrophys. J. Suppl. Ser.* **2017**, *232*, 23. [CrossRef]
247. Gehan, C.; Mosser, B.; Michel, E.; Samadi, R.; Kallinger, T. Core rotation braking on the red giant branch for various mass ranges. *Astron. Astrophys.* **2018**, *616*, A24. [CrossRef]
248. Eggenberger, P.; Montalbán, J.; Miglio, A. Angular momentum transport in stellar interiors constrained by rotational splittings of mixed modes in red giants. *Astron. Astrophys.* **2012**, *544*, L4. [CrossRef]
249. Marques, J.P.; Goupil, M.J.; Lebreton, Y.; Talon, S.; Palacios, A.; Belkacem, K.; Ouazzani, R.M.; Mosser, B.; Moya, A.; Morel, P.; et al. Seismic diagnostics for transport of angular momentum in stars. I. Rotational splittings from the pre-main sequence to the red-giant branch. *Astron. Astrophys.* **2013**, *549*, A74. [CrossRef]
250. Ceillier, T.; Eggenberger, P.; García, R.A.; Mathis, S. Understanding angular momentum transport in red giants: The case of KIC 7341231. *Astron. Astrophys.* **2013**, *555*, A54. [CrossRef]
251. Tayar, J.; Pinsonneault, M.H. Implications of Rapid Core Rotation in Red Giants for Internal Angular Momentum Transport in Stars. *Astrophys. J.* **2013**, *775*, L1. [CrossRef]
252. Cantiello, M.; Mankovich, C.; Bildsten, L.; Christensen-Dalsgaard, J.; Paxton, B. Angular Momentum Transport within Evolved Low-Mass Stars. *Astrophys. J.* **2014**, *788*, 93. [CrossRef]
253. Fuller, J.; Lecoanet, D.; Cantiello, M.; Brown, B. Angular Momentum Transport via Internal Gravity Waves in Evolving Stars. *Astrophys. J.* **2014**, *796*, 17. [CrossRef]
254. Belkacem, K.; Marques, J.P.; Goupil, M.J.; Mosser, B.; Sonoi, T.; Ouazzani, R.M.; Dupret, M.A.; Mathis, S.; Grosjean, M. Angular momentum redistribution by mixed modes in evolved low-mass stars. II. Spin-down of the core of red giants induced by mixed modes. *Astron. Astrophys.* **2015**, *579*, A31. [CrossRef]
255. Fuller, J.; Cantiello, M.; Stello, D.; Garcia, R.A.; Bildsten, L. Asteroseismology can reveal strong internal magnetic fields in red giant stars. *Science* **2015**, *350*, 423–426. [CrossRef]
256. Spada, F.; Gellert, M.; Arlt, R.; Deheuvels, S. Angular momentum transport efficiency in post-main sequence low-mass stars. *Astron. Astrophys.* **2016**, *589*, A23. [CrossRef]
257. Eggenberger, P.; Lagarde, N.; Miglio, A.; Montalbán, J.; Ekström, S.; Georgy, C.; Meynet, G.; Salmon, S.; Ceillier, T.; García, R.A.; et al. Constraining the efficiency of angular momentum transport with asteroseismology of red giants: The effect of stellar mass. *Astron. Astrophys.* **2017**, *599*, A18. [CrossRef]
258. Ouazzani, R.M.; Marques, J.P.; Goupil, M.J.; Christophe, S.; Antoci, V.; Salmon, S.J.A.J.; Ballot, J. γ Doradus stars as a test of angular momentum transport models. *Astron. Astrophys.* **2019**, *626*, A121. [CrossRef]
259. Tayler, R.J. The adiabatic stability of stars containing magnetic fields—I. Toroidal fields. *Mon. Not. R. Astron. Soc.* **1973**, *161*, 365. [CrossRef]

260. Spruit, H.C. Dynamo action by differential rotation in a stably stratified stellar interior. *Astron. Astrophys.* **2002**, *381*, 923–932. [CrossRef]
261. Fuller, J.; Piro, A.L.; Jermyn, A.S. Slowing the spins of stellar cores. *Mon. Not. R. Astron. Soc.* **2019**, *485*, 3661–3680. [CrossRef]
262. Fuller, J.; Ma, L. Most Black Holes Are Born Very Slowly Rotating. *Astrophys. J.* **2019**, *881*, L1. [CrossRef]
263. Heger, A.; Woosley, S.E.; Spruit, H.C. Presupernova Evolution of Differentially Rotating Massive Stars Including Magnetic Fields. *Astrophys. J.* **2005**, *626*, 350–363. [CrossRef]
264. Eggenberger, P.; den Hartogh, J.W.; Buldgen, G.; Meynet, G.; Salmon, S.J.A.J.; Deheuvels, S. Asteroseismology of evolved stars to constrain the internal transport of angular momentum. II. Test of a revised prescription for transport by the Tayler instability. *Astron. Astrophys.* **2019**, *631*, L6. [CrossRef]
265. Qin, Y.; Fragos, T.; Meynet, G.; Andrews, J.; Sørensen, M.; Song, H.F. The spin of the second-born black hole in coalescing binary black holes. *Astron. Astrophys.* **2018**, *616*, A28. [CrossRef]
266. Belczynski, K.; Klencki, J.; Fields, C.E.; Olejak, A.; Berti, E.; Meynet, G.; Fryer, C.L.; Holz, D.E.; O'Shaughnessy, R.; Brown, D.A.; et al. Evolutionary roads leading to low effective spins, high black hole masses, and O1/O2 rates for LIGO/Virgo binary black holes. *Astron. Astrophys.* **2020**, *636*, A104. [CrossRef]
267. Miller, S.; Callister, T.A.; Farr, W.M. The Low Effective Spin of Binary Black Holes and Implications for Individual Gravitational-wave Events. *Astrophys. J.* **2020**, *895*, 128. [CrossRef]
268. Abbott, R.; Abbott, T.D.; Abraham, S.; Acernese, F.; Ackley, K.; Adams, A.; Adams, C.; Adhikari, R.X.; Adya, V.B.; Affeldt, C.; et al. Population Properties of Compact Objects from the Second LIGO–Virgo Gravitational-Wave Transient Catalog. *Astrophys. J. Lett.* **2021**, *913*, L7. [CrossRef]
269. Belczynski, K.; Done, C.; Lasota, J.P. All Apples: Comparing black holes in X-ray binaries and gravitational-wave sources. *arXiv* **2021**, arXiv:2111.09401.
270. MacLeod, M.; Ramirez-Ruiz, E. On the Accretion-Fed Growth of Neutron Stars during Common Envelope. *Astrophys. J.* **2014**, *798*, L19. [CrossRef]
271. Olejak, A.; Belczynski, K. The Implications of High Black Hole Spins for the Origin of Binary Black Hole Mergers. *Astrophys. J. Lett.* **2021**, *921*, L2. [CrossRef]
272. Bavera, S.S.; Fragos, T.; Zevin, M.; Berry, C.P.; Marchant, P.; Andrews, J.J.; Coughlin, S.; Dotter, A.; Kovlakas, K.; Misra, D.; et al. The impact of mass-transfer physics on the observable properties of field binary black hole populations. *Astron. Astrophys.* **2021**, *647*, A153. [CrossRef]
273. Berti, E.; Volonteri, M. Cosmological Black Hole Spin Evolution by Mergers and Accretion. *Astrophys. J.* **2008**, *684*, 822–828. [CrossRef]
274. Gerosa, D.; Berti, E. Are merging black holes born from stellar collapse or previous mergers? *Phys. Rev. D* **2017**, *95*, 124046. [CrossRef]
275. Rodriguez, C.L.; Zevin, M.; Amaro-Seoane, P.; Chatterjee, S.; Kremer, K.; Rasio, F.A.; Ye, C.S. Black holes: The next generation—Repeated mergers in dense star clusters and their gravitational-wave properties. *Phys. Rev. D* **2019**, *100*, 043027. [CrossRef]
276. Mapelli, M.; Dall'Amico, M.; Bouffanais, Y.; Giacobbo, N.; Arca Sedda, M.; Artale, M.C.; Ballone, A.; Di Carlo, U.N.; Iorio, G.; Santoliquido, F.; et al. Hierarchical black hole mergers in young, globular and nuclear star clusters: The effect of metallicity, spin and cluster properties. *Mon. Not. R. Astron. Soc.* **2021**, *505*, 339–358. [CrossRef]
277. Tagawa, H.; Haiman, Z.; Bartos, I.; Kocsis, B.; Omukai, K. Signatures of hierarchical mergers in black hole spin and mass distribution. *Mon. Not. R. Astron. Soc.* **2021**, *507*, 3362–3380. [CrossRef]
278. Ebisuzaki, T.; Makino, J.; Tsuru, T.G.; Funato, Y.; Portegies Zwart, S.; Hut, P.; McMillan, S.; Matsushita, S.; Matsumoto, H.; Kawabe, R. Missing Link Found? The "Runaway" Path to Supermassive Black Holes. *Astrophys. J.* **2001**, *562*, L19–L22. [CrossRef]
279. Hughes, S.A.; Blandford, R.D. Black Hole Mass and Spin Coevolution by Mergers. *Astrophys. J.* **2003**, *585*, L101–L104. [CrossRef]
280. Damour, T. Coalescence of two spinning black holes: An effective one-body approach. *Phys. Rev. D* **2001**, *64*, 124013. [CrossRef]
281. Racine, É. Analysis of spin precession in binary black hole systems including quadrupole-monopole interaction. *Phys. Rev. D* **2008**, *78*, 044021. [CrossRef]
282. Schmidt, P.; Hannam, M.; Husa, S. Towards models of gravitational waveforms from generic binaries: A simple approximate mapping between precessing and nonprecessing inspiral signals. *Phys. Rev. D* **2012**, *86*, 104063. [CrossRef]
283. Schmidt, P.; Ohme, F.; Hannam, M. Towards models of gravitational waveforms from generic binaries: II. Modelling precession effects with a single effective precession parameter. *Phys. Rev. D* **2015**, *91*, 024043. [CrossRef]
284. Zevin, M.; Bavera, S.S. Suspicious Siblings: The Distribution of Mass and Spin Across Component Black Holes in Isolated Binary Evolution. *arXiv* **2022**, arXiv:2203.02515.
285. Tagawa, H.; Haiman, Z.; Bartos, I.; Kocsis, B. Spin Evolution of Stellar-mass Black Hole Binaries in Active Galactic Nuclei. *Astrophys. J.* **2020**, *899*, 26. [CrossRef]
286. McKernan, B.; Ford, K.E.S.; Callister, T.; Farr, W.M.; O'Shaughnessy, R.; Smith, R.; Thrane, E.; Vajpeyi, A. LIGO–Virgo correlations between mass ratio and effective inspiral spin: Testing the active galactic nuclei channel. *arXiv* **2021**, arXiv:2107.07551.
287. Moe, M.; Di Stefano, R. Mind Your Ps and Qs: The Interrelation between Period (P) and Mass-ratio (Q) Distributions of Binary Stars. *Astrophys. J. Suppl. Ser.* **2017**, *230*, 15. [CrossRef]
288. Peters, P.C.; Mathews, J. Gravitational Radiation from Point Masses in a Keplerian Orbit. *Phys. Rev.* **1963**, *131*, 435–440. [CrossRef]
289. Eggleton, P.P.; Kiseleva, L.G.; Hut, P. The Equilibrium Tide Model for Tidal Friction. *Astrophys. J.* **1998**, *499*, 853–870. [CrossRef]

290. Zahn, J.P. Reprint of 1977A&A....57..383Z. Tidal friction in close binary stars. *Astron. Astrophys.* **1977**, *500*, 121–132.
291. Rasio, F.A.; Tout, C.A.; Lubow, S.H.; Livio, M. Tidal Decay of Close Planetary Orbits. *Astrophys. J.* **1996**, *470*, 1187. [CrossRef]
292. Brandenburg, A. Stellar Mixing Length Theory with Entropy Rain. *Astrophys. J.* **2017**, *832*, 6. [CrossRef]
293. Zahn, J.P. The dynamical tide in close binaries. *Astron. Astrophys.* **1975**, *41*, 329–344.
294. Claret, A.; Cunha, N.C.S. Circularization and synchronization times in Main-Sequence of detached eclipsing binaries II. Using the formalisms by Zahn. *Astron. Astrophys.* **1997**, *318*, 187–197.
295. Siess, L.; Izzard, R.G.; Davis, P.J.; Deschamps, R. BINSTAR: A new binary stellar evolution code. Tidal interactions. *Astron. Astrophys.* **2013**, *550*, A100. [CrossRef]
296. Kushnir, D.; Zaldarriaga, M.; Kollmeier, J.A.; Waldman, R. Dynamical tides reexpressed. *Mon. Not. R. Astron. Soc.* **2017**, *467*, 2146–2149. [CrossRef]
297. Piran, T. Gamma-ray Bursts and Binary Neutron Star Mergers. In *Compact Stars in Binaries*; van Paradijs, J., van den Heuvel, E.P.J., Kuulkers, E., Eds.; The Astrophysics Spectator: Old Hickory, TN, USA, 1996; Volume 165, p. 489.
298. Thorne, K.S.; Zytkow, A.N. Stars with degenerate neutron cores. I. Structure of equilibrium models. *Astrophys. J.* **1977**, *212*, 832–858. [CrossRef]
299. Fryer, C.L.; Benz, W.; Herant, M. The Dynamics and Outcomes of Rapid Infall onto Neutron Stars. *Astrophys. J.* **1996**, *460*, 801. [CrossRef]
300. Endal, A.S.; Sofia, S. The evolution of rotating stars. II. Calculations with time-dependent redistribution of angular momentum for 7 and 10 M sun stars. *Astrophys. J.* **1978**, *220*, 279–290. [CrossRef]
301. Zahn, J.P. Circulation and turbulence in rotating stars. *Astron. Astrophys.* **1992**, *265*, 115–132.
302. de Mink, S.E.; Cottaar, M.; Pols, O.R. Can Low-Metallicity Binaries Avoid Merging? In *First Stars III*; O'Shea, B.W., Heger, A., Eds.; American Institute of Physics Conference Series; American Institute of Physics: Santa Fe, NM, USA, 2008; Volume 990, pp. 217–219. [CrossRef]
303. de Mink, S.E.; Cantiello, M.; Langer, N.; Pols, O.R.; Brott, I.; Yoon, S.C. Rotational mixing in massive binaries. Detached short-period systems. *Astron. Astrophys.* **2009**, *497*, 243–253. [CrossRef]
304. Hadjidemetriou, J.D. Two-body problem with variable mass: A new approach. *Icarus* **1963**, *2*, 440–451. [CrossRef]
305. Dosopoulou, F.; Kalogera, V. Orbital Evolution of Mass-transferring Eccentric Binary Systems. I. Phase-dependent Evolution. *Astrophys. J.* **2016**, *825*, 70. [CrossRef]
306. Bondi, H.; Hoyle, F. On the mechanism of accretion by stars. *Mon. Not. R. Astron. Soc.* **1944**, *104*, 273. [CrossRef]
307. Dosopoulou, F.; Kalogera, V. Orbital Evolution of Mass-transferring Eccentric Binary Systems. II. Secular Evolution. *Astrophys. J.* **2016**, *825*, 71. [CrossRef]
308. Hamers, A.S.; Dosopoulou, F. An Analytic Model for Mass Transfer in Binaries with Arbitrary Eccentricity, with Applications to Triple-star Systems. *Astrophys. J.* **2019**, *872*, 119. [CrossRef]
309. Sepinsky, J.F.; Willems, B.; Kalogera, V.; Rasio, F.A. Interacting Binaries with Eccentric Orbits: Secular Orbital Evolution Due to Conservative Mass Transfer. *Astrophys. J.* **2007**, *667*, 1170–1184. [CrossRef]
310. Sepinsky, J.F.; Willems, B.; Kalogera, V.; Rasio, F.A. Interacting Binaries with Eccentric Orbits. II. Secular Orbital Evolution due to Non-conservative Mass Transfer. *Astrophys. J.* **2009**, *702*, 1387–1392. [CrossRef]
311. Sepinsky, J.F.; Willems, B.; Kalogera, V.; Rasio, F.A. Interacting Binaries with Eccentric Orbits. III. Orbital Evolution due to Direct Impact and Self-Accretion. *Astrophys. J.* **2010**, *724*, 546–558. [CrossRef]
312. Eggleton, P.P. Aproximations to the radii of Roche lobes. *Astrophys. J.* **1983**, *268*, 368–369. [CrossRef]
313. Ge, H.; Hjellming, M.S.; Webbink, R.F.; Chen, X.; Han, Z. Adiabatic Mass Loss in Binary Stars. I. Computational Method. *Astrophys. J.* **2010**, *717*, 724–738. [CrossRef]
314. Leiner, E.M.; Geller, A. A Census of Blue Stragglers in Gaia DR2 Open Clusters as a Test of Population Synthesis and Mass Transfer Physics. *Astrophys. J.* **2021**, *908*, 229. [CrossRef]
315. Neijssel, C.J.; Vigna-Gómez, A.; Stevenson, S.; Barrett, J.W.; Gaebel, S.M.; Broekgaarden, F.S.; de Mink, S.E.; Szécsi, D.; Vinciguerra, S.; Mandel, I. The effect of the metallicity-specific star formation history on double compact object mergers. *Mon. Not. R. Astron. Soc.* **2019**, *490*, 3740–3759. [CrossRef]
316. Vigna-Gómez, A.; Neijssel, C.J.; Stevenson, S.; Barrett, J.W.; Belczynski, K.; Justham, S.; de Mink, S.E.; Müller, B.; Podsiadlowski, P.; Renzo, M.; et al. On the formation history of Galactic double neutron stars. *Mon. Not. R. Astron. Soc.* **2018**, *481*, 4009–4029. [CrossRef]
317. Ivanova, N.; Justham, S.; Chen, X.; De Marco, O.; Fryer, C.L.; Gaburov, E.; Ge, H.; Glebbeek, E.; Han, Z.; Li, X.D.; et al. Common envelope evolution: Where we stand and how we can move forward. *Astron. Astrophys. Rev.* **2013**, *21*, 59. [CrossRef]
318. Dominik, M.; Berti, E.; O'Shaughnessy, R.; Mandel, I.; Belczynski, K.; Fryer, C.; Holz, D.E.; Bulik, T.; Pannarale, F. Double Compact Objects III: Gravitational-wave Detection Rates. *Astrophys. J.* **2015**, *806*, 263. [CrossRef]
319. Rodriguez, C.L.; Chatterjee, S.; Rasio, F.A. Binary black hole mergers from globular clusters: Masses, merger rates, and the impact of stellar evolution. *Phys. Rev. D* **2016**, *93*, 084029. [CrossRef]
320. Mapelli, M.; Giacobbo, N. The cosmic merger rate of neutron stars and black holes. *Mon. Not. R. Astron. Soc.* **2018**, *479*, 4391–4398. [CrossRef]
321. Tanikawa, A.; Kinugawa, T.; Yoshida, T.; Hijikawa, K.; Umeda, H. Population III binary black holes: Effects of convective overshooting on formation of GW190521. *Mon. Not. R. Astron. Soc.* **2021**, *505*, 2170–2176. [CrossRef]

322. Sandquist, E.L.; Taam, R.E.; Chen, X.; Bodenheimer, P.; Burkert, A. Double Core Evolution. X. Through the Envelope Ejection Phase. *Astrophys. J.* **1998**, *500*, 909–922. [CrossRef]
323. Ricker, P.M.; Taam, R.E. An AMR Study of the Common-envelope Phase of Binary Evolution. *Astrophys. J.* **2012**, *746*, 74. [CrossRef]
324. Passy, J.C.; De Marco, O.; Fryer, C.L.; Herwig, F.; Diehl, S.; Oishi, J.S.; Mac Low, M.M.; Bryan, G.L.; Rockefeller, G. Simulating the Common Envelope Phase of a Red Giant Using Smoothed-particle Hydrodynamics and Uniform-grid Codes. *Astrophys. J.* **2012**, *744*, 52. [CrossRef]
325. Ivanova, N.; Nandez, J.L.A. Common envelope events with low-mass giants: Understanding the transition to the slow spiral-in. *Mon. Not. R. Astron. Soc.* **2016**, *462*, 362–381. [CrossRef]
326. Ohlmann, S.T.; Röpke, F.K.; Pakmor, R.; Springel, V. Constructing stable 3D hydrodynamical models of giant stars. *Astron. Astrophys.* **2017**, *599*, A5. [CrossRef]
327. Iaconi, R.; De Marco, O.; Passy, J.C.; Staff, J. The effect of binding energy and resolution in simulations of the common envelope binary interaction. *Mon. Not. R. Astron. Soc.* **2018**, *477*, 2349–2365. [CrossRef]
328. Reichardt, T.A.; De Marco, O.; Iaconi, R.; Tout, C.A.; Price, D.J. Extending common envelope simulations from Roche lobe overflow to the nebular phase. *Mon. Not. R. Astron. Soc.* **2019**, *484*, 631–647. [CrossRef]
329. Reichardt, T.A.; De Marco, O.; Iaconi, R.; Chamandy, L.; Price, D.J. The impact of recombination energy on simulations of the common-envelope binary interaction. *Mon. Not. R. Astron. Soc.* **2020**, *494*, 5333–5349. [CrossRef]
330. Glanz, H.; Perets, H.B. Common envelope evolution of eccentric binaries. *Mon. Not. R. Astron. Soc.* **2021**, *507*, 2659–2670. [CrossRef]
331. Livio, M.; Soker, N. The Common Envelope Phase in the Evolution of Binary Stars. *Astrophys. J.* **1988**, *329*, 764. [CrossRef]
332. de Kool, M. Common Envelope Evolution and Double Cores of Planetary Nebulae. *Astrophys. J.* **1990**, *358*, 189. [CrossRef]
333. Nelemans, G.; Verbunt, F.; Yungelson, L.R.; Portegies Zwart, S.F. Reconstructing the evolution of double helium white dwarfs: Envelope loss without spiral-in. *Astron. Astrophys.* **2000**, *360*, 1011–1018.
334. Nelemans, G.; Tout, C.A. Reconstructing the evolution of white dwarf binaries: Further evidence for an alternative algorithm for the outcome of the common-envelope phase in close binaries. *Mon. Not. R. Astron. Soc.* **2005**, *356*, 753–764. [CrossRef]
335. Dewi, J.D.M.; Tauris, T.M. On the energy equation and efficiency parameter of the common envelope evolution. *Astron. Astrophys.* **2000**, *360*, 1043–1051.
336. Xu, X.J.; Li, X.D. On the Binding Energy Parameter λ of Common Envelope Evolution. *Astrophys. J.* **2010**, *716*, 114–121. [CrossRef]
337. Claeys, J.S.W.; Pols, O.R.; Izzard, R.G.; Vink, J.; Verbunt, F.W.M. Theoretical uncertainties of the Type Ia supernova rate. *Astron. Astrophys.* **2014**, *563*, A83. [CrossRef]
338. Kruckow, M.U.; Tauris, T.M.; Langer, N.; Kramer, M.; Izzard, R.G. Progenitors of gravitational wave mergers: Binary evolution with the stellar grid-based code COMBINE. *Mon. Not. R. Astron. Soc.* **2018**, *481*, 1908–1949. [CrossRef]
339. Zorotovic, M.; Schreiber, M.R.; Gänsicke, B.T.; Nebot Gómez-Morán, A. Post-common-envelope binaries from SDSS. IX: Constraining the common-envelope efficiency. *Astron. Astrophys.* **2010**, *520*, A86. [CrossRef]
340. Davis, P.J.; Kolb, U.; Willems, B. A comprehensive population synthesis study of post-common envelope binaries. *Mon. Not. R. Astron. Soc.* **2010**, *403*, 179–195. [CrossRef]
341. Davis, P.J.; Kolb, U.; Knigge, C. Is the common envelope ejection efficiency a function of the binary parameters? *Mon. Not. R. Astron. Soc.* **2012**, *419*, 287–303. [CrossRef]
342. De Marco, O.; Passy, J.C.; Moe, M.; Herwig, F.; Mac Low, M.M.; Paxton, B. On the α formalism for the common envelope interaction. *Mon. Not. R. Astron. Soc.* **2011**, *411*, 2277–2292. [CrossRef]
343. Nandez, J.L.A.; Ivanova, N. Common envelope events with low-mass giants: Understanding the energy budget. *Mon. Not. R. Astron. Soc.* **2016**, *460*, 3992–4002. [CrossRef]
344. Fragos, T.; Andrews, J.J.; Ramirez-Ruiz, E.; Meynet, G.; Kalogera, V.; Taam, R.E.; Zezas, A. The Complete Evolution of a Neutron-star Binary through a Common Envelope Phase Using 1D Hydrodynamic Simulations. *Astrophys. J.* **2019**, *883*, L45. [CrossRef]
345. Lynch, R.S.; Freire, P.C.C.; Ransom, S.M.; Jacoby, B.A. The Timing of Nine Globular Cluster Pulsars. *Astrophys. J.* **2012**, *745*, 109. [CrossRef]
346. Kawka, A.; Vennes, S.; O'Toole, S.; Németh, P.; Burton, D.; Kotze, E.; Buckley, D.A.H. New binaries among UV-selected, hot subdwarf stars and population properties. *Mon. Not. R. Astron. Soc.* **2015**, *450*, 3514–3548. [CrossRef]
347. Kruckow, M.U.; Neunteufel, P.G.; Di Stefano, R.; Gao, Y.; Kobayashi, C. A Catalog of Potential Post-Common Envelope Binaries. *Astrophys. J.* **2021**, *920*, 86. [CrossRef]
348. Trani, A.A.; Rieder, S.; Tanikawa, A.; Iorio, G.; Martini, R.; Karelin, G.; Glanz, H.; Portegies Zwart, S. Revisiting Common Envelope Evolution—A New Semi-Analytic Model for N-body and Population Synthesis Codes. *arXiv* **2022**, arXiv:2205.13537.
349. Hills, J.G. The effects of sudden mass loss and a random kick velocity produced in a supernova explosion on the dynamics of a binary star of arbitrary orbital eccentricity. Applications to X-ray binaries and to the binarypulsars. *Astrophys. J.* **1983**, *267*, 322–333. [CrossRef]
350. Belczynski, K. The Most Ordinary Formation of the Most Unusual Double Black Hole Merger. *Astrophys. J.* **2020**, *905*, L15. [CrossRef]

351. Callister, T.A.; Farr, W.M.; Renzo, M. State of the Field: Binary Black Hole Natal Kicks and Prospects for Isolated Field Formation after GWTC-2. *Astrophys. J.* **2021**, *920*, 157. [CrossRef]
352. Steinle, N.; Kesden, M. Pathways for producing binary black holes with large misaligned spins in the isolated formation channel. *Phys. Rev. D* **2021**, *103*, 063032. [CrossRef]
353. Wysocki, D.; Gerosa, D.; O'Shaughnessy, R.; Belczynski, K.; Gladysz, W.; Berti, E.; Kesden, M.; Holz, D.E. Explaining LIGO's observations via isolated binary evolution with natal kicks. *Phys. Rev. D* **2018**, *97*, 043014. [CrossRef]
354. Sana, H.; de Mink, S.E.; de Koter, A.; Langer, N.; Evans, C.J.; Gieles, M.; Gosset, E.; Izzard, R.G.; Le Bouquin, J.B.; Schneider, F.R.N. Binary Interaction Dominates the Evolution of Massive Stars. *Science* **2012**, *337*, 444. [CrossRef] [PubMed]
355. Lada, C.J.; Lada, E.A. Embedded Clusters in Molecular Clouds. *Annu. Rev. Astron. Astrophys.* **2003**, *41*, 57–115. [CrossRef]
356. Portegies Zwart, S.F.; McMillan, S.L.; Gieles, M. Young Massive Star Clusters. *Annu. Rev. Astron. Astrophys.* **2010**, *48*, 431–493. [CrossRef]
357. Ward, J.L.; Kruijssen, J.M.D.; Rix, H.W. Not all stars form in clusters—Gaia-DR2 uncovers the origin of OB associations. *Mon. Not. R. Astron. Soc.* **2020**, *495*, 663–685. [CrossRef]
358. Weidner, C.; Kroupa, P. The maximum stellar mass, star-cluster formation and composite stellar populations. *Mon. Not. R. Astron. Soc.* **2006**, *365*, 1333–1347. [CrossRef]
359. Weidner, C.; Kroupa, P.; Bonnell, I.A.D. The relation between the most-massive star and its parental star cluster mass. *Mon. Not. R. Astron. Soc.* **2009**, *401*, 275–293. [CrossRef]
360. Mapelli, M.; Colpi, M.; Possenti, A.; Sigurdsson, S. The fingerprint of binary intermediate-mass black holes in globular clusters: Suprathermal stars and angular momentum alignment. *Mon. Not. R. Astron. Soc.* **2005**, *364*, 1315–1326. [CrossRef]
361. Tanikawa, A. Dynamical evolution of stellar mass black holes in dense stellar clusters: Estimate for merger rate of binary black holes originating from globular clusters. *Mon. Not. R. Astron. Soc.* **2013**, *435*, 1358–1375. [CrossRef]
362. Breen, P.G.; Heggie, D.C. Dynamical evolution of black hole subsystems in idealized star clusters. *Mon. Not. R. Astron. Soc.* **2013**, *432*, 2779–2797. [CrossRef]
363. Samsing, J.; MacLeod, M.; Ramirez-Ruiz, E. The Formation of Eccentric Compact Binary Inspirals and the Role of Gravitational Wave Emission in Binary-Single Stellar Encounters. *Astrophys. J.* **2014**, *784*, 71. [CrossRef]
364. Samsing, J. Eccentric black hole mergers forming in globular clusters. *Phys. Rev. D* **2018**, *97*, 103014. [CrossRef]
365. Askar, A.; Arca Sedda, M.; Giersz, M. MOCCA-SURVEY Database I: Galactic globular clusters harbouring a black hole subsystem. *Mon. Not. R. Astron. Soc.* **2018**, *478*, 1844–1854. [CrossRef]
366. Arca Sedda, M.; Askar, A.; Giersz, M. MOCCA-Survey Database—I. Unravelling black hole subsystems in globular clusters. *Mon. Not. R. Astron. Soc.* **2018**, *479*, 4652–4664. [CrossRef]
367. Kremer, K.; Rodriguez, C.L.; Amaro-Seoane, P.; Breivik, K.; Chatterjee, S.; Katz, M.L.; Larson, S.L.; Rasio, F.A.; Samsing, J.; Ye, C.S.; et al. Post-Newtonian dynamics in dense star clusters: Binary black holes in the LISA band. *Phys. Rev. D* **2019**, *99*, 063003. [CrossRef]
368. Wang, L.; Fujii, M.S.; Tanikawa, A. Impact of initial mass functions on the dynamical channel of gravitational wave sources. *Mon. Not. R. Astron. Soc.* **2021**, *504*, 5778–5787. [CrossRef]
369. Askar, A.; Szkudlarek, M.; Gondek-Rosińska, D.; Giersz, M.; Bulik, T. MOCCA-SURVEY Database—I. Coalescing binary black holes originating from globular clusters. *Mon. Not. R. Astron. Soc.* **2017**, *464*, L36–L40. [CrossRef]
370. Banerjee, S.; Baumgardt, H.; Kroupa, P. Stellar-mass black holes in star clusters: Implications for gravitational wave radiation. *Mon. Not. R. Astron. Soc.* **2010**, *402*, 371–380. [CrossRef]
371. Banerjee, S. Stellar-mass black holes in young massive and open stellar clusters and their role in gravitational-wave generation—II. *Mon. Not. R. Astron. Soc.* **2018**, *473*, 909–926. [CrossRef]
372. Banerjee, S. Stellar-mass black holes in young massive and open stellar clusters—IV. Updated stellar-evolutionary and black hole spin models and comparisons with the LIGO-Virgo O1/O2 merger-event data. *Mon. Not. R. Astron. Soc.* **2020**, *500*, 3002–3026. [CrossRef]
373. Fujii, M.S.; Tanikawa, A.; Makino, J. The detection rates of merging binary black holes originating from star clusters and their mass function. *Publ. Astron. Soc. Jpn.* **2017**, *69*, 94. [CrossRef]
374. Kumamoto, J.; Fujii, M.S.; Tanikawa, A. Merger rate density of binary black holes formed in open clusters. *Mon. Not. R. Astron. Soc.* **2020**, *495*, 4268–4278. [CrossRef]
375. Böker, T.; Laine, S.; van der Marel, R.P.; Sarzi, M.; Rix, H.W.; Ho, L.C.; Shields, J.C. A *Hubble Space Telescope* Census of Nuclear Star Clusters in Late-Type Spiral Galaxies. I. Observations and Image Analysis. *Astron. J.* **2002**, *123*, 1389–1410. [CrossRef]
376. Graham, A.W.; Spitler, L.R. Quantifying the coexistence of massive black holes and dense nuclear star clusters. *Mon. Not. R. Astron. Soc.* **2009**, *397*, 2148–2162. [CrossRef]
377. Bahcall, J.N.; Wolf, R.A. Star distribution around a massive black hole in a globular cluster. *Astrophys. J.* **1976**, *209*, 214–232. [CrossRef]
378. Szölgyén, Á.; Kocsis, B. Black Hole Disks in Galactic Nuclei. *Phys. Rev. Lett.* **2018**, *121*, 101101. [CrossRef] [PubMed]
379. Gondán, L.; Kocsis, B.; Raffai, P.; Frei, Z. Eccentric Black Hole Gravitational-wave Capture Sources in Galactic Nuclei: Distribution of Binary Parameters. *Astrophys. J.* **2018**, *860*, 5. [CrossRef]

380. Leigh, N.W.C.; Geller, A.M.; McKernan, B.; Ford, K.E.S.; Mac Low, M.M.; Bellovary, J.; Haiman, Z.; Lyra, W.; Samsing, J.; O'Dowd, M.; et al. On the rate of black hole binary mergers in galactic nuclei due to dynamical hardening. *Mon. Not. R. Astron. Soc.* **2018**, *474*, 5672–5683. [CrossRef]
381. Trani, A.A.; Spera, M.; Leigh, N.W.C.; Fujii, M.S. The Keplerian Three-body Encounter. II. Comparisons with Isolated Encounters and Impact on Gravitational Wave Merger Timescales. *Astrophys. J.* **2019**, *885*, 135. [CrossRef]
382. McKernan, B.; Ford, K.E.S.; Bellovary, J.; Leigh, N.W.C.; Haiman, Z.; Kocsis, B.; Lyra, W.; Mac Low, M.M.; Metzger, B.; O'Dowd, M.; et al. Constraining Stellar-mass Black Hole Mergers in AGN Disks Detectable with LIGO. *Astrophys. J.* **2018**, *866*, 66. [CrossRef]
383. McKernan, B.; Ford, K.E.S.; O'Shaugnessy, R.; Wysocki, D. Monte Carlo simulations of black hole mergers in AGN discs: Low χ_{eff} mergers and predictions for LIGO. *Mon. Not. R. Astron. Soc.* **2020**, *494*, 1203–1216. [CrossRef]
384. McKernan, B.; Ford, K.E.S.; O'Shaughnessy, R. Black hole, neutron star, and white dwarf merger rates in AGN discs. *Mon. Not. R. Astron. Soc.* **2020**, *498*, 4088–4094. [CrossRef]
385. Ford, K.E.S.; McKernan, B. Binary Black Hole Merger Rates in AGN Disks versus Nuclear Star Clusters: Loud beats Quiet. *arXiv* **2021**, arXiv:2109.03212.
386. McKernan, B.; Ford, K.E.S.; Lyra, W.; Perets, H.B. Intermediate mass black holes in AGN discs—I. Production and growth. *Mon. Not. R. Astron. Soc.* **2012**, *425*, 460–469. [CrossRef]
387. McKernan, B.; Ford, K.E.S.; Kocsis, B.; Lyra, W.; Winter, L.M. Intermediate-mass black holes in AGN discs—II. Model predictions and observational constraints. *Mon. Not. R. Astron. Soc.* **2014**, *441*, 900–909. [CrossRef]
388. Bellovary, J.M.; Low, M.M.M.; McKernan, B.; Ford, K.E.S. Migration Traps in Disks Around Supermassive Black Holes. *Astrophys. J.* **2016**, *819*, L17. [CrossRef]
389. Bartos, I.; Kocsis, B.; Haiman, Z.; Márka, S. Rapid and Bright Stellar-mass Binary Black Hole Mergers in Active Galactic Nuclei. *Astrophys. J.* **2017**, *835*, 165. [CrossRef]
390. Stone, N.C.; Metzger, B.D.; Haiman, Z. Assisted inspirals of stellar mass black holes embedded in AGN discs: Solving the 'final au problem'. *Mon. Not. R. Astron. Soc.* **2016**, *464*, 946–954. [CrossRef]
391. Secunda, A.; Bellovary, J.; Low, M.M.M.; Ford, K.E.S.; McKernan, B.; Leigh, N.W.C.; Lyra, W.; Sándor, Z. Orbital Migration of Interacting Stellar Mass Black Holes in Disks around Supermassive Black Holes. *Astrophys. J.* **2019**, *878*, 85. [CrossRef]
392. Tagawa, H.; Haiman, Z.; Kocsis, B. Formation and Evolution of Compact-object Binaries in AGN Disks. *Astrophys. J.* **2020**, *898*, 25. [CrossRef]
393. Binney, J.; Tremaine, S. *Galactic Dynamics*, 2nd ed.; Princeton University Press: Princeton, NJ, USA, 2008.
394. Lynden-Bell, D.; Wood, R. The gravo-thermal catastrophe in isothermal spheres and the onset of red-giant structure for stellar systems. *Mon. Not. R. Astron. Soc.* **1968**, *138*, 495. [CrossRef]
395. Chandrasekhar, S. Dynamical Friction. I. General Considerations: The Coefficient of Dynamical Friction. *Astrophys. J.* **1943**, *97*, 255. [CrossRef]
396. Chandrasekhar, S. Dynamical Friction. II. The Rate of Escape of Stars from Clusters and the Evidence for the Operation of Dynamical Friction. *Astrophys. J.* **1943**, *97*, 263. [CrossRef]
397. Chandrasekhar, S. Dynamical Friction. III. A More Exact Theory of the Rate of Escape of Stars from Clusters. *Astrophys. J.* **1943**, *98*, 54. [CrossRef]
398. Fujii, M.S.; Portegies Zwart, S. The moment of core collapse in star clusters with a mass function. *Mon. Not. R. Astron. Soc.* **2014**, *439*, 1003–1014. [CrossRef]
399. Salpeter, E.E. The Luminosity Function and Stellar Evolution. *Astrophys. J.* **1955**, *121*, 161. [CrossRef]
400. Spitzer, L., Jr. Equipartition and the Formation of Compact Nuclei in Spherical Stellar Systems. *Astrophys. J.* **1969**, *158*, L139. [CrossRef]
401. Merritt, D. Two-component stellar systems in thermal and dynamical equilibrium. *Astron. J.* **1981**, *86*, 318–324. [CrossRef]
402. Inagaki, S.; Wiyanto, P. On equipartition of kinetic energies in two-component star clusters. *Publ. Astron. Soc. Jpn.* **1984**, *36*, 391–402.
403. Bianchini, P.; van de Ven, G.; Norris, M.A.; Schinnerer, E.; Varri, A.L. A novel look at energy equipartition in globular clusters. *Mon. Not. R. Astron. Soc.* **2016**, *458*, 3644–3654. [CrossRef]
404. Spera, M.; Mapelli, M.; Jeffries, R.D. Do open star clusters evolve towards energy equipartition? *Mon. Not. R. Astron. Soc.* **2016**, *460*, 317–328. [CrossRef]
405. Webb, J.J.; Vesperini, E. On the link between energy equipartition and radial variation in the stellar mass function of star clusters. *Mon. Not. R. Astron. Soc.* **2017**, *464*, 1977–1983. [CrossRef]
406. Kremer, K.; Ye, C.S.; Chatterjee, S.; Rodriguez, C.L.; Rasio, F.A. How Black Holes Shape Globular Clusters: Modeling NGC 3201. *Astrophys. J.* **2018**, *855*, L15. [CrossRef]
407. Lee, H.M. Evolution of galactic nuclei with 10-$M_\odot$ black holes. *Mon. Not. R. Astron. Soc.* **1995**, *272*, 605–617. [CrossRef]
408. Jeans, J.H. The origin of binary systems. *Mon. Not. R. Astron. Soc.* **1919**, *79*, 408. [CrossRef]
409. Monaghan, J.J. A statistical theory of the disruption of three-body systems—I. Low angular momentum. *Mon. Not. R. Astron. Soc.* **1976**, *176*, 63–72. [CrossRef]
410. Monaghan, J.J. A statistical theory of the disruption of three-body systems—II. High angular momentum. *Mon. Not. R. Astron. Soc.* **1976**, *177*, 583–594. [CrossRef]

411. Valtonen, M.; Karttunen, H. *The Three-Body Problem*; Cambridge University Press: Cambridge, UK, 2005.
412. Stone, N.C.; Leigh, N.W.C. A statistical solution to the chaotic, non-hierarchical three-body problem. *Nature* **2019**, *576*, 406–410. [CrossRef]
413. Kol, B. Flux-based statistical prediction of three-body outcomes. *Celest. Mech. Dyn. Astron.* **2021**, *133*, 17. [CrossRef]
414. Peters, P.C. Gravitational Radiation and the Motion of Two Point Masses. *Phys. Rev.* **1964**, *136*, 1224–1232. [CrossRef]
415. Bae, Y.B.; Kim, C.; Lee, H.M. Compact binaries ejected from globular clusters as gravitational wave sources. *Mon. Not. R. Astron. Soc.* **2014**, *440*, 2714–2725. [CrossRef]
416. Zevin, M.; Samsing, J.; Rodriguez, C.; Haster, C.J.; Ramirez-Ruiz, E. Eccentric Black Hole Mergers in Dense Star Clusters: The Role of Binary-Binary Encounters. *Astrophys. J.* **2019**, *871*, 91. [CrossRef]
417. Lower, M.E.; Thrane, E.; Lasky, P.D.; Smith, R. Measuring eccentricity in binary black hole inspirals with gravitational waves. *Phys. Rev. D* **2018**, *98*, 083028. [CrossRef]
418. Huerta, E.A.; Moore, C.J.; Kumar, P.; George, D.; Chua, A.J.; Haas, R.; Wessel, E.; Johnson, D.; Glennon, D.; Rebei, A.; et al. Eccentric, nonspinning, inspiral, Gaussian-process merger approximant for the detection and characterization of eccentric binary black hole mergers. *Phys. Rev. D* **2018**, *97*, 024031. [CrossRef]
419. Samsing, J.; D'Orazio, D.J.; Kremer, K.; Rodriguez, C.L.; Askar, A. Single-single gravitational-wave captures in globular clusters: Eccentric deci-Hertz sources observable by DECIGO and Tian-Qin. *Phys. Rev. D* **2020**, *101*, 123010. [CrossRef]
420. Hoang, B.M.; Naoz, S.; Kremer, K. Neutron Star-Black Hole Mergers from Gravitational-wave Captures. *Astrophys. J.* **2020**, *903*, 8. [CrossRef]
421. Hamers, A.S. An Improved Numerical Fit to the Peak Harmonic Gravitational Wave Frequency Emitted by an Eccentric Binary. *Res. Notes Am. Astron. Soc.* **2021**, *5*, 275. [CrossRef]
422. Safarzadeh, M.; Farr, W.M.; Ramirez-Ruiz, E. A Trend in the Effective Spin Distribution of LIGO Binary Black Holes with Mass. *Astrophys. J.* **2020**, *894*, 129. [CrossRef]
423. Campanelli, M.; Lousto, C.; Zlochower, Y.; Merritt, D. Large Merger Recoils and Spin Flips from Generic Black Hole Binaries. *Astrophys. J.* **2007**, *659*, L5–L8. [CrossRef]
424. Campanelli, M.; Lousto, C.O.; Zlochower, Y.; Merritt, D. Maximum Gravitational Recoil. *Phys. Rev. Lett.* **2007**, *98*, 231102. [CrossRef]
425. Boyle, L.; Kesden, M.; Nissanke, S. Binary Black-Hole Merger: Symmetry and the Spin Expansion. *Phys. Rev. Lett.* **2008**, *100*, 151101. [CrossRef]
426. Lousto, C.O.; Zlochower, Y. Modeling maximum astrophysical gravitational recoil velocities. *Phys. Rev. D* **2011**, *83*, 024003. [CrossRef]
427. Lousto, C.O.; Zlochower, Y. Nonlinear gravitational recoil from the mergers of precessing black-hole binaries. *Phys. Rev. D* **2013**, *87*, 084027. [CrossRef]
428. Lousto, C.O.; Zlochower, Y. Black hole binary remnant mass and spin: A new phenomenological formula. *Phys. Rev. D* **2014**, *89*, 104052. [CrossRef]
429. Giersz, M.; Leigh, N.; Hypki, A.; Lützgendorf, N.; Askar, A. MOCCA code for star cluster simulations—IV. A new scenario for intermediate mass black hole formation in globular clusters. *Mon. Not. R. Astron. Soc.* **2015**, *454*, 3150–3165. [CrossRef]
430. Antonini, F.; Gieles, M.; Gualandris, A. Black hole growth through hierarchical black hole mergers in dense star clusters: Implications for gravitational wave detections. *Mon. Not. R. Astron. Soc.* **2019**, *486*, 5008–5021. [CrossRef]
431. Fragione, G.; Banerjee, S. Demographics of Neutron Stars in Young Massive and Open Clusters. *Astrophys. J.* **2020**, *901*, L16. [CrossRef]
432. Mapelli, M.; Santoliquido, F.; Bouffanais, Y.; Arca Sedda, M.; Giacobbo, N.; Artale, M.C.; Ballone, A. Mass and rate of hierarchical black hole mergers in young, globular and nuclear star clusters. *arXiv* **2020**, arXiv:2007.15022.
433. Tokovinin, A. Comparative statistics and origin of triple and quadruple stars. *Mon. Not. R. Astron. Soc.* **2008**, *389*, 925–938. [CrossRef]
434. Tokovinin, A. From Binaries to Multiples. I. Data on F and G Dwarfs within 67 pc of the Sun. *Astron. J.* **2014**, *147*, 86. [CrossRef]
435. Tokovinin, A. From Binaries to Multiples. II. Hierarchical Multiplicity of F and G Dwarfs. *Astron. J.* **2014**, *147*, 87. [CrossRef]
436. Tokovinin, A. The Updated Multiple Star Catalog. *Astrophys. J. Suppl. Ser.* **2018**, *235*, 6. [CrossRef]
437. Duchêne, G.; Kraus, A. Stellar Multiplicity. *Annu. Rev. Astron. Astrophys* **2013**, *51*, 269–310. [CrossRef]
438. Sana, H.; Le Bouquin, J.B.; Lacour, S.; Berger, J.P.; Duvert, G.; Gauchet, L.; Norris, B.; Olofsson, J.; Pickel, D.; Zins, G.; et al. Southern Massive Stars at High Angular Resolution: Observational Campaign and Companion Detection. *Astrophys. J. Suppl. Ser.* **2014**, *215*, 15. [CrossRef]
439. Toonen, S.; Hamers, A.; Portegies Zwart, S. The evolution of hierarchical triple star-systems. *Comput. Astrophys. Cosmol.* **2016**, *3*, 6. [CrossRef]
440. Lidov, M. The evolution of orbits of artificial satellites of planets under the action of gravitational perturbations of external bodies. *Planet. Space Sci.* **1962**, *9*, 719–759. [CrossRef]
441. Kozai, Y. Secular perturbations of asteroids with high inclination and eccentricity. *Astron. J.* **1962**, *67*, 591–598. [CrossRef]
442. Zeipel, H.V. Sur l'application des séries de M. Lindstedt à l'étude du mouvement des comètes périodiques. *Astronom. Nachr.* **1909**, *183*, 345–418. [CrossRef]
443. Naoz, S. The Eccentric Kozai-Lidov Effect and Its Applications. *Annu. Rev. Astron. Astrophys.* **2016**, *54*, 441–489. [CrossRef]

444. Shevchenko, I.I. *The Lidov-Kozai Effect—Applications in Exoplanet Research and Dynamical Astronomy*; Springer: Cham, Switzerland, 2017; Volume 441. [CrossRef]
445. Ito, T.; Ohtsuka, K. The Lidov-Kozai Oscillation and Hugo von Zeipel. *Monogr. Environ. Earth Planets* **2019**, *7*, 1–113. [CrossRef]
446. Hoang, B.M.; Naoz, S.; Kocsis, B.; Farr, W.M.; McIver, J. Detecting Supermassive Black Hole-induced Binary Eccentricity Oscillations with LISA. *Astrophys. J.* **2019**, *875*, L31. [CrossRef]
447. Gupta, P.; Suzuki, H.; Okawa, H.; Maeda, K.i. Gravitational waves from hierarchical triple systems with Kozai-Lidov oscillation. *Phys. Rev. D* **2020**, *101*, 104053. [CrossRef]
448. Arca-Sedda, M.; Rizzuto, F.P.; Naab, T.; Ostriker, J.; Giersz, M.; Spurzem, R. Breaching the Limit: Formation of GW190521-like and IMBH Mergers in Young Massive Clusters. *Astrophys. J.* **2021**, *920*, 128. [CrossRef]
449. Gao, Y.; Toonen, S.; Grishin, E.; Comerford, T.; Kruckow, M.U. An empirical fit for viscoelastic simulations of tertiary tides. *Mon. Not. R. Astron. Soc.* **2020**, *491*, 264–271. [CrossRef]
450. Glanz, H.; Perets, H.B. Simulations of common envelope evolution in triple systems: Circumstellar case. *Mon. Not. R. Astron. Soc.* **2021**, *500*, 1921–1932. [CrossRef]
451. Toonen, S.; Portegies Zwart, S.; Hamers, A.S.; Bandopadhyay, D. The evolution of stellar triples. The most common evolutionary pathways. *Astron. Astrophys.* **2020**, *640*, A16. [CrossRef]
452. Thompson, T.A. Accelerating Compact Object Mergers in Triple Systems with the Kozai Resonance: A Mechanism for "Prompt" Type Ia Supernovae, Gamma-Ray Bursts, and Other Exotica. *Astrophys. J.* **2011**, *741*, 82. [CrossRef]
453. Antonini, F.; Toonen, S.; Hamers, A.S. Binary Black Hole Mergers from Field Triples: Properties, Rates, and the Impact of Stellar Evolution. *Astrophys. J.* **2017**, *841*, 77. [CrossRef]
454. Antonini, F.; Chatterjee, S.; Rodriguez, C.L.; Morscher, M.; Pattabiraman, B.; Kalogera, V.; Rasio, F.A. Black Hole Mergers and Blue Stragglers from Hierarchical Triples Formed in Globular Clusters. *Astrophys. J.* **2016**, *816*, 65. [CrossRef]
455. Grishin, E.; Perets, H.B.; Fragione, G. Quasi-secular evolution of mildly hierarchical triple systems: Analytics and applications for GW sources and hot Jupiters. *Mon. Not. R. Astron. Soc.* **2018**, *481*, 4907–4923. [CrossRef]
456. Martinez, M.A.S.; Fragione, G.; Kremer, K.; Chatterjee, S.; Rodriguez, C.L.; Samsing, J.; Ye, C.S.; Weatherford, N.C.; Zevin, M.; Naoz, S.; et al. Black Hole Mergers from Hierarchical Triples in Dense Star Clusters. *Astrophys. J.* **2020**, *903*, 67. [CrossRef]
457. Martinez, M.A.S.; Rodriguez, C.L.; Fragione, G. On the Mass Ratio Distribution of Black Hole Mergers in Triple Systems. *arXiv* **2021**, arXiv:2105.01671.
458. Silsbee, K.; Tremaine, S. Lidov-Kozai Cycles with Gravitational Radiation: Merging Black Holes in Isolated Triple Systems. *Astrophys. J.* **2017**, *836*, 39. [CrossRef]
459. Toonen, S.; Perets, H.B.; Hamers, A.S. Rate of WD-WD head-on collisions in isolated triples is too low to explain standard type Ia supernovae. *Astron. Astrophys.* **2018**, *610*, A22. [CrossRef]
460. Vigna-Gómez, A.; Toonen, S.; Ramirez-Ruiz, E.; Leigh, N.W.C.; Riley, J.; Haster, C.J. Massive Stellar Triples Leading to Sequential Binary Black Hole Mergers in the Field. *Astrophys. J.* **2021**, *907*, L19. [CrossRef]
461. Antonini, F.; Perets, H.B. Secular Evolution of Compact Binaries near Massive Black Holes: Gravitational Wave Sources and Other Exotica. *Astrophys. J.* **2012**, *757*, 27. [CrossRef]
462. VanLandingham, J.H.; Miller, M.C.; Hamilton, D.P.; Richardson, D.C. The Role of the Kozai–Lidov Mechanism in Black Hole Binary Mergers in Galactic Centers. *Astrophys. J.* **2016**, *828*, 77. [CrossRef]
463. Fragione, G.; Grishin, E.; Leigh, N.W.C.; Perets, H.B.; Perna, R. Black hole and neutron star mergers in galactic nuclei. *Mon. Not. R. Astron. Soc.* **2019**, *488*, 47–63. [CrossRef]
464. Hamers, A.S.; Bar-Or, B.; Petrovich, C.; Antonini, F. The Impact of Vector Resonant Relaxation on the Evolution of Binaries near a Massive Black Hole: Implications for Gravitational-wave Sources. *Astrophys. J.* **2018**, *865*, 2. [CrossRef]
465. Hoang, B.M.; Naoz, S.; Kocsis, B.; Rasio, F.A.; Dosopoulou, F. Black Hole Mergers in Galactic Nuclei Induced by the Eccentric Kozai-Lidov Effect. *Astrophys. J.* **2018**, *856*, 140. [CrossRef]
466. Trani, A.A. Do three-body encounters in galactic nuclei affect compact binary merger rates? In *Star Clusters: From the Milky Way to the Early Universe*; Bragaglia, A., Davies, M., Sills, A., Vesperini, E., Eds.; Cambridge University Press: Cambridge, UK, 2020; Volume 351, pp. 174–177. [CrossRef]
467. Michaely, E. From Ultra-wide Binaries to Interacting Binaries in the Field. In Proceedings of the AAS/Division of Dynamical Astronomy Meeting, Boulder, CO, USA, 10–13 June 2019; Volume 51, p. 202.07.
468. Michaely, E.; Perets, H.B. High rate of gravitational waves mergers from flyby perturbations of wide black hole triples in the field. *Mon. Not. R. Astron. Soc.* **2020**, *498*, 4924–4935. [CrossRef]
469. Grishin, E.; Perets, H.B. Chaotic dynamics of wide triples induced by galactic tides: A novel channel for producing compact binaries, mergers, and collisions. *Mon. Not. R. Astron. Soc.* **2022**, *512*, 4993–5009. [CrossRef]
470. Hamilton, C.; Rafikov, R.R. Compact Object Binary Mergers Driven By Cluster Tides: A New Channel for LIGO/Virgo Gravitational-wave Events. *Astrophys. J.* **2019**, *881*, L13. [CrossRef]
471. Vynatheya, P.; Hamers, A.S. How Important Is Secular Evolution for Black Hole and Neutron Star Mergers in 2 + 2 and 3 + 1 Quadruple-star Systems? *Astrophys. J.* **2022**, *926*, 195. [CrossRef]
472. Hamers, A.S.; Fragione, G.; Neunteufel, P.; Kocsis, B. First- and second-generation black hole and neutron star mergers in 2 + 2 quadruples: Population statistics. *Mon. Not. R. Astron. Soc.* **2021**, *506*, 5345–5360. [CrossRef]

473. Liu, B.; Lai, D. Enhanced black hole mergers in binary-binary interactions. *Mon. Not. R. Astron. Soc.* **2019**, *483*, 4060–4069. [CrossRef]
474. Rastello, S.; Mapelli, M.; Di Carlo, U.N.; Giacobbo, N.; Santoliquido, F.; Spera, M.; Ballone, A.; Iorio, G. Dynamics of black hole-neutron star binaries in young star clusters. *Mon. Not. R. Astron. Soc.* **2020**, *497*, 1563–1570. [CrossRef]
475. Dobie, D.; Stewart, A.; Murphy, T.; Lenc, E.; Wang, Z.; Kaplan, D.L.; Andreoni, I.; Banfield, J.; Brown, I.; Corsi, A.; et al. An ASKAP Search for a Radio Counterpart to the First High-significance Neutron Star–Black Hole Merger LIGO/Virgo S190814bv. *Astrophys. J.* **2019**, *887*, L13. [CrossRef]
476. Gomez, S.; Hosseinzadeh, G.; Cowperthwaite, P.S.; Villar, V.A.; Berger, E.; Gardner, T.; Alexander, K.D.; Blanchard, P.K.; Chornock, R.; Drout, M.R.; et al. A Galaxy-targeted Search for the Optical Counterpart of the Candidate NS–BH Merger S190814bv with Magellan. *Astrophys. J.* **2019**, *884*, L55. [CrossRef]
477. Ackley, K.; Amati, L.; Barbieri, C.; Bauer, F.E.; Benetti, S.; Bernardini, M.G.; Bhirombhakdi, K.; Botticella, M.T.; Branchesi, M.; Brocato, E.; et al. Observational constraints on the optical and near-infrared emission from the neutron star-black hole binary merger candidate S190814bv. *Astron. Astrophys.* **2020**, *643*, A113. [CrossRef]
478. Andreoni, I.; Goldstein, D.A.; Kasliwal, M.M.; Nugent, P.E.; Zhou, R.; Newman, J.A.; Bulla, M.; Foucart, F.; Hotokezaka, K.; Nakar, E.; et al. GROWTH on S190814bv: Deep Synoptic Limits on the Optical/Near-infrared Counterpart to a Neutron Star-Black Hole Merger. *Astrophys. J.* **2020**, *890*, 131. [CrossRef]
479. Antier, S.; Agayeva, S.; Aivazyan, V.; Alishov, S.; Arbouch, E.; Baransky, A.; Barynova, K.; Bai, J.M.; Basa, S.; Beradze, S.; et al. The first six months of the Advanced LIGO's and Advanced Virgo's third observing run with GRANDMA. *Mon. Not. R. Astron. Soc.* **2020**, *492*, 3904–3927. [CrossRef]
480. Gompertz, B.P.; Levan, A.J.; Tanvir, N.R. A Search for Neutron Star-Black Hole Binary Mergers in the Short Gamma-Ray Burst Population. *Astrophys. J.* **2020**, *895*, 58. [CrossRef]
481. Morgan, R.; Soares-Santos, M.; Annis, J.; Herner, K.; Garcia, A.; Palmese, A.; Drlica-Wagner, A.; Kessler, R.; García-Bellido, J.; Bachmann, T.; et al. Constraints on the Physical Properties of GW190814 through Simulations Based on DECam Follow-up Observations by the Dark Energy Survey. *Astrophys. J.* **2020**, *901*, 83. [CrossRef]
482. Page, K.L.; Evans, P.A.; Tohuvavohu, A.; Kennea, J.A.; Klingler, N.J.; Cenko, S.B.; Oates, S.R.; Ambrosi, E.; Barthelmy, S.D.; Beardmore, A.; et al. Swift-XRT follow-up of gravitational wave triggers during the third aLIGO/Virgo observing run. *Mon. Not. R. Astron. Soc.* **2020**, *499*, 3459–3480. [CrossRef]
483. Thakur, A.L.; Dichiara, S.; Troja, E.; Chase, E.A.; Sánchez-Ramírez, R.; Piro, L.; Fryer, C.L.; Butler, N.R.; Watson, A.M.; Wollaeger, R.; et al. A search for optical and near-infrared counterparts of the compact binary merger GW190814. *Mon. Not. R. Astron. Soc.* **2020**, *499*, 3868–3883. [CrossRef]
484. Vieira, N.; Ruan, J.J.; Haggard, D.; Drout, M.R.; Nynka, M.C.; Boyce, H.; Spekkens, K.; Safi-Harb, S.; Carlberg, R.G.; Fernández, R.; et al. A Deep CFHT Optical Search for a Counterpart to the Possible Neutron Star–Black Hole Merger GW190814. *Astrophys. J.* **2020**, *895*, 96. [CrossRef]
485. Watson, A.M.; Butler, N.R.; Lee, W.H.; Becerra, R.L.; Pereyra, M.; Angeles, F.; Farah, A.; Figueroa, L.; Gónzalez-Buitrago, D.; Quirós, F.; et al. Limits on the electromagnetic counterpart to S190814bv. *Mon. Not. R. Astron. Soc.* **2020**, *492*, 5916–5921. [CrossRef]
486. Essick, R.; Landry, P. Discriminating between Neutron Stars and Black Holes with Imperfect Knowledge of the Maximum Neutron Star Mass. *Astrophys. J.* **2020**, *904*, 80. [CrossRef]
487. Lackey, B.D.; Wade, L. Reconstructing the neutron-star equation of state with gravitational-wave detectors from a realistic population of inspiralling binary neutron stars. *Phys. Rev. D* **2015**, *91*. [CrossRef]
488. Malik, T.; Ferreira, M.; Agrawal, B.K.; Providência, C. Relativistic description of dense matter equation of state and compatibility with neutron star observables: A Bayesian approach. *arXiv* **2022**, arXiv:2201.12552.
489. Antoniadis, J.; Freire, P.C.; Wex, N.; Tauris, T.M.; Lynch, R.S.; Van Kerkwijk, M.H.; Kramer, M.; Bassa, C.; Dhillon, V.S.; Driebe, T.; et al. A Massive Pulsar in a Compact Relativistic Binary. *Science* **2013**, *340*, 1233232. [CrossRef] [PubMed]
490. Fonseca, E.; Cromartie, H.T.; Pennucci, T.T.; Ray, P.S.; Kirichenko, A.Y.; Ransom, S.M.; Demorest, P.B.; Stairs, I.H.; Arzoumanian, Z.; Guillemot, L.; et al. Refined Mass and Geometric Measurements of the High-mass PSR J0740 + 6620. *Astrophys. J. Lett.* **2021**, *915*, L12. [CrossRef]
491. Romani, R.W.; Kandel, D.; Filippenko, A.V.; Brink, T.G.; Zheng, W. PSR J1810+1744: Companion Darkening and a Precise High Neutron Star Mass. *Astrophys. J. Lett.* **2021**, *908*, L46. [CrossRef]
492. Annala, E.; Gorda, T.; Katerini, E.; Kurkela, A.; Nättilä, J.; Paschalidis, V.; Vuorinen, A. Multimessenger Constraints for Ultra-Dense Matter. *Phys. Rev. X* **2022**, *12*, 011058.
493. Tews, I.; Pang, P.T.H.; Dietrich, T.; Coughlin, M.W.; Antier, S.; Bulla, M.; Heinzel, J.; Issa, L. On the Nature of GW190814 and Its Impact on the Understanding of Supranuclear Matter. *Astrophys. J.* **2021**, *908*, L1. [CrossRef]
494. Fattoyev, F.J.; Horowitz, C.J.; Piekarewicz, J.; Reed, B. GW190814: Impact of a 2.6 solar mass neutron star on the nucleonic equations of state. *Phys. Rev. C* **2020**, *102*, 065805. [CrossRef]
495. Dexheimer, V.; Gomes, R.O.; Klähn, T.; Han, S.; Salinas, M. GW190814 as a massive rapidly rotating neutron star with exotic degrees of freedom. *Phys. Rev. C* **2021**, *103*, 025808. [CrossRef]
496. Tsokaros, A.; Ruiz, M.; Shapiro, S.L. GW190814: Spin and Equation of State of a Neutron Star Companion. *Astrophys. J.* **2020**, *905*, 48. [CrossRef]

497. Nathanail, A.; Most, E.R.; Rezzolla, L. GW170817 and GW190814: Tension on the Maximum Mass. *Astrophys. J.* **2021**, *908*, L28. [CrossRef]
498. Most, E.R.; Papenfort, L.J.; Weih, L.R.; Rezzolla, L. A lower bound on the maximum mass if the secondary in GW190814 was once a rapidly spinning neutron star. *Mon. Not. R. Astron. Soc.* **2020**, *499*, L82–L86. [CrossRef]
499. Biswas, B.; Nandi, R.; Char, P.; Bose, S.; Stergioulas, N. GW190814: On the properties of the secondary component of the binary. *Mon. Not. R. Astron. Soc.* **2021**, *505*, 1600–1606. [CrossRef]
500. Zhang, N.B.; Li, B.A. GW190814's Secondary Component with Mass 2.50–2.67 $M_\odot$ as a Superfast Pulsar. *Astrophys. J.* **2020**, *902*, 38. [CrossRef]
501. Tan, H.; Noronha-Hostler, J.; Yunes, N. Neutron Star Equation of State in Light of GW190814. *Phys. Rev. Lett.* **2020**, *125*, 261104. [CrossRef] [PubMed]
502. Godzieba, D.A.; Radice, D.; Bernuzzi, S. On the Maximum Mass of Neutron Stars and GW190814. *Astrophys. J.* **2021**, *908*, 122. [CrossRef]
503. Wu, X.; Bao, S.; Shen, H.; Xu, R. Effect of the symmetry energy on the secondary component of GW190814 as a neutron star. *Phys. Rev. C* **2021**, *104*, 015802. [CrossRef]
504. Huang, K.; Hu, J.; Zhang, Y.; Shen, H. The Possibility of the Secondary Object in GW190814 as a Neutron Star. *Astrophys. J.* **2020**, *904*, 39. [CrossRef]
505. Kanakis-Pegios, A.; Koliogiannis, P.S.; Moustakidis, C.C. Probing the Nuclear Equation of State from the Existence of a ∼2.6 $M_\odot$ Neutron Star: The GW190814 Puzzle. *Symmetry* **2021**, *13*, 183. [CrossRef]
506. Astashenok, A.V.; Capozziello, S.; Odintsov, S.D.; Oikonomou, V.K. Extended gravity description for the GW190814 supermassive neutron star. *Phys. Lett. B* **2020**, *811*, 135910. [CrossRef]
507. Zevin, M.; Spera, M.; Berry, C.P.L.; Kalogera, V. Exploring the Lower Mass Gap and Unequal Mass Regime in Compact Binary Evolution. *Astrophys. J.* **2020**, *899*, L1. [CrossRef]
508. Broekgaarden, F.S.; Berger, E.; Neijssel, C.J.; Vigna-Gómez, A.; Chattopadhyay, D.; Stevenson, S.; Chruslinska, M.; Justham, S.; de Mink, S.E.; Mandel, I. Impact of Massive Binary Star and Cosmic Evolution on Gravitational Wave Observations I: Black Hole—Neutron Star Mergers. *Mon. Not. R. Astron. Soc.* **2021**. [CrossRef]
509. Olejak, A.; Fishbach, M.; Belczynski, K.; Holz, D.E.; Lasota, J.P.; Miller, M.C.; Bulik, T. The Origin of Inequality: Isolated Formation of a 30+10 $M_\odot$ Binary Black Hole Merger. *Astrophys. J.* **2020**, *901*, L39. [CrossRef]
510. Mandel, I.; Müller, B.; Riley, J.; de Mink, S.E.; Vigna-Gómez, A.; Chattopadhyay, D. Binary population synthesis with probabilistic remnant mass and kick prescriptions. *Mon. Not. R. Astron. Soc.* **2021**, *500*, 1380–1384. [CrossRef]
511. Eldridge, J.J.; Stanway, E.R. BPASS predictions for binary black hole mergers. *Mon. Not. R. Astron. Soc.* **2016**, *462*, 3302–3313. [CrossRef]
512. Eldridge, J.J.; Stanway, E.R.; Xiao, L.; McClelland, L.A.S.; Taylor, G.; Ng, M.; Greis, S.M.L.; Bray, J.C. Binary Population and Spectral Synthesis Version 2.1: Construction, Observational Verification, and New Results. *Publ. Astron. Soc. Aust.* **2017**, *34*, e058. [CrossRef]
513. Lu, W.; Beniamini, P.; Bonnerot, C. On the formation of GW190814. *Mon. Not. R. Astron. Soc.* **2021**, *500*, 1817–1832. [CrossRef]
514. Samsing, J.; Ilan, T. Double gravitational wave mergers. *Mon. Not. R. Astron. Soc.* **2019**, *482*, 30–39. [CrossRef]
515. Cholis, I.; Kritos, K.; Garfinkle, D. Can Thorne-Żytkow Objects source GW190814-type events? *arXiv* **2021**, arXiv:2106.07662.
516. Jiménez-Esteban, F.M.; Solano, E.; Rodrigo, C. A Catalog of Wide Binary and Multiple Systems of Bright Stars from Gaia-DR2 and the Virtual Observatory. *Astron. J.* **2019**, *157*, 78. [CrossRef]
517. Duquennoy, A.; Mayor, M. Multiplicity among solar-type stars in the solar neighbourhood. II—Distribution of the orbital elements in an unbiased sample. *Astron. Astrophys.* **1991**, *500*, 337–376.
518. Sana, H. The multiplicity of massive stars: A 2016 view. In *The Lives and Death-Throes of Massive Stars*; Proceedings of the International Astronomical Union; Eldridge, J.J., Bray, J.C., McClelland, L.A.S., Xiao, L., Eds.; Cambridge University Press: Cambridge, UK, 2017; Volume 329, pp. 110–117. [CrossRef]
519. Gao, S.; Liu, C.; Zhang, X.; Justham, S.; Deng, L.; Yang, M. The Binarity of Milky Way F,G,K Stars as a Function of Effective Temperature And Metallicity. *Astrophys. J.* **2014**, *788*, L37. [CrossRef]
520. Yuan, H.; Liu, X.; Xiang, M.; Huang, Y.; Chen, B.; Wu, Y.; Hou, Y.; Zhang, Y. Stellar Loci II. A Model-Free Estimate of the Binary Fraction for Field FGK Stars. *Astrophys. J.* **2015**, *799*, 135. [CrossRef]
521. Moe, M.; Kratter, K.M.; Badenes, C. The Close Binary Fraction of Solar-type Stars Is Strongly Anticorrelated with Metallicity. *Astrophys. J.* **2019**, *875*, 61. [CrossRef]
522. Thorne, K.S.; Zytkow, A.N. Red giants and supergiants with degenerate neutron cores. *Astrophys. J.* **1975**, *199*, L19–L24. [CrossRef]
523. Safarzadeh, M.; Hamers, A.S.; Loeb, A.; Berger, E. Formation and Merging of Mass Gap Black Holes in Gravitational-wave Merger Events from Wide Hierarchical Quadruple Systems. *Astrophys. J.* **2020**, *888*, L3. [CrossRef]
524. Fragione, G.; Loeb, A.; Rasio, F.A. Merging Black Holes in the Low-mass and High-mass Gaps from 2 + 2 Quadruple Systems. *Astrophys. J.* **2020**, *895*, L15. [CrossRef]
525. Fragione, G.; Kocsis, B. Black hole mergers from quadruples. *Mon. Not. R. Astron. Soc.* **2019**, *486*, 4781–4789. [CrossRef]
526. Liu, B.; Lai, D. Hierarchical black hole mergers in multiple systems: Constrain the formation of GW190412-, GW190814-, and GW190521-like events. *Mon. Not. R. Astron. Soc.* **2021**, *502*, 2049–2064. [CrossRef]

527. Sigurdsson, S.; Phinney, E.S. Dynamics and Interactions of Binaries and Neutron Stars in Globular Clusters. *Astrophys. J. Suppl. Ser.* **1995**, *99*, 609. [CrossRef]
528. Fragione, G.; Kocsis, B. Black Hole Mergers from an Evolving Population of Globular Clusters. *Phys. Rev. Lett.* **2018**, *121*, 161103. [CrossRef]
529. Clausen, D.; Sigurdsson, S.; Chernoff, D.F. Black hole-neutron star mergers in globular clusters. *Mon. Not. R. Astron. Soc.* **2013**, *428*, 3618–3629. [CrossRef]
530. Clausen, D.; Sigurdsson, S.; Chernoff, D.F. Dynamically formed black hole + millisecond pulsar binaries in globular clusters. *Mon. Not. R. Astron. Soc.* **2014**, *442*, 207–219. [CrossRef]
531. Devecchi, B.; Colpi, M.; Mapelli, M.; Possenti, A. Millisecond pulsars around intermediate-mass black holes in globular clusters. *Mon. Not. R. Astron. Soc.* **2007**, *380*, 691–702. [CrossRef]
532. Ye, C.S.; Fong, W.F.; Kremer, K.; Rodriguez, C.L.; Chatterjee, S.; Fragione, G.; Rasio, F.A. On the Rate of Neutron Star Binary Mergers from Globular Clusters. *Astrophys. J.* **2020**, *888*, L10. [CrossRef]
533. Kritos, K.; Cholis, I. Black holes merging with low mass gap objects inside globular clusters. *Phys. Rev. D* **2021**, *104*, 043004. [CrossRef]
534. Arca Sedda, M. Dynamical Formation of the GW190814 Merger. *Astrophys. J.* **2021**, *908*, L38. [CrossRef]
535. Arca Sedda, M. Dissecting the properties of neutron star-black hole mergers originating in dense star clusters. *Commun. Phys.* **2020**, *3*, 43. [CrossRef]
536. Santoliquido, F.; Mapelli, M.; Bouffanais, Y.; Giacobbo, N.; Di Carlo, U.N.; Rastello, S.; Artale, M.C.; Ballone, A. The Cosmic Merger Rate Density Evolution of Compact Binaries Formed in Young Star Clusters and in Isolated Binaries. *Astrophys. J.* **2020**, *898*, 152. [CrossRef]
537. Tagawa, H.; Kocsis, B.; Haiman, Z.; Bartos, I.; Omukai, K.; Samsing, J. Mass-gap Mergers in Active Galactic Nuclei. *Astrophys. J.* **2021**, *908*, 194. [CrossRef]
538. Yang, Y.; Gayathri, V.; Bartos, I.; Haiman, Z.; Safarzadeh, M.; Tagawa, H. Black Hole Formation in the Lower Mass Gap through Mergers and Accretion in AGN Disks. *Astrophys. J.* **2020**, *901*, L34. [CrossRef]
539. Bombaci, I.; Drago, A.; Logoteta, D.; Pagliara, G.; Vidaña, I. Was GW190814 a Black Hole–Strange Quark Star System? *Phys. Rev. Lett.* **2021**, *126*, 162702. [CrossRef] [PubMed]
540. Jedamzik, K. Consistency of Primordial Black Hole Dark Matter with LIGO/Virgo Merger Rates. *Phys. Rev. Lett.* **2021**, *126*, 051302. [CrossRef] [PubMed]
541. Vattis, K.; Goldstein, I.S.; Koushiappas, S.M. Could the 2.6 $M_\odot$ object in GW190814 be a primordial black hole? *Phys. Rev. D* **2020**, *102*, 061301. [CrossRef]
542. Carr, B.; Clesse, S.; García-Bellido, J.; Kühnel, F. Cosmic conundrum explained by thermal history and primordial black holes. *Phys. Dark Universe* **2021**, *31*, 100755. [CrossRef]
543. Clesse, S.; Garcia-Bellido, J. GW190425, GW190521 and GW190814: Three candidate mergers of primordial black holes from the QCD epoch. *arXiv* **2020**, arXiv:2007.06481.
544. Romero-Shaw, I.; Lasky, P.D.; Thrane, E.; Calderón Bustillo, J. GW190521: Orbital Eccentricity and Signatures of Dynamical Formation in a Binary Black Hole Merger Signal. *Astrophys. J.* **2020**, *903*, L5. [CrossRef]
545. Gayathri, V.; Healy, J.; Lange, J.; O'Brien, B.; Szczepanczyk, M.; Bartos, I.; Campanelli, M.; Klimenko, S.; Lousto, C.; O'Shaughnessy, R. GW190521 as a Highly Eccentric Black Hole Merger. *arXiv* **2020**, arXiv:2009.05461.
546. Holgado, A.M.; Ortega, A.; Rodriguez, C.L. Dynamical Formation Scenarios for GW190521 and Prospects for Decihertz Gravitational-wave Astronomy with GW190521-like Binaries. *Astrophys. J.* **2021**, *909*, L24. [CrossRef]
547. Nitz, A.H.; Capano, C.D. GW190521 May Be an Intermediate-mass Ratio Inspiral. *Astrophys. J.* **2021**, *907*, L9. [CrossRef]
548. Fragione, G.; Loeb, A.; Rasio, F.A. On the Origin of GW190521-like Events from Repeated Black Hole Mergers in Star Clusters. *Astrophys. J.* **2020**, *902*, L26. [CrossRef]
549. Fragione, G.; Kocsis, B.; Rasio, F.A.; Silk, J. Repeated mergers, mass-gap black holes, and formation of intermediate-mass black holes in nuclear star clusters. *arXiv* **2021**, arXiv:2107.04639.
550. Mapelli, M.; Santoliquido, F.; Bouffanais, Y.; Arca Sedda, M.A.; Artale, M.C.; Ballone, A. Mass and Rate of Hierarchical Black Hole Mergers in Young, Globular and Nuclear Star Clusters. *Symmetry* **2021**, *13*, 1678. [CrossRef]
551. Baibhav, V.; Berti, E.; Gerosa, D.; Mould, M.; Wong, K.W.K. Looking for the parents of LIGO's black holes. *Phys. Rev. D* **2021**, *104*, 084002. [CrossRef]
552. Anagnostou, O.; Trenti, M.; Melatos, A. Hierarchical Formation Of An Intermediate Mass Black Hole Via Seven Mergers: Implications For GW190521. *arXiv* **2020**, arXiv:2010.06161.
553. Kimball, C.; Talbot, C.; Berry, C.P.L.; Zevin, M.; Thrane, E.; Kalogera, V.; Buscicchio, R.; Carney, M.; Dent, T.; Middleton, H.; et al. Evidence for Hierarchical Black Hole Mergers in the Second LIGO-Virgo Gravitational Wave Catalog. *Astrophys. J.* **2021**, *915*, L35. [CrossRef]
554. Fragione, G.; Banerjee, S. Binary Black Hole Mergers from Young Massive and Open Clusters: Comparison to GWTC-2 Gravitational Wave Data. *Astrophys. J.* **2021**, *913*, L29. [CrossRef]
555. Di Carlo, U.N.; Mapelli, M.; Pasquato, M.; Rastello, S.; Ballone, A.; Dall'Amico, M.; Giacobbo, N.; Iorio, G.; Spera, M.; Torniamenti, S.; et al. Intermediate-mass black holes from stellar mergers in young star clusters. *Mon. Not. R. Astron. Soc.* **2021**, *507*, 5132–5143. [CrossRef]

556. Dall'Amico, M.; Mapelli, M.; Di Carlo, U.N.; Bouffanais, Y.; Rastello, S.; Santoliquido, F.; Ballone, A.; Arca Sedda, M. GW190521 formation via three-body encounters in young massive star clusters. *Mon. Not. R. Astron. Soc.* **2021**, *508*, 3045–3054. [CrossRef]
557. González, E.; Kremer, K.; Chatterjee, S.; Fragione, G.; Rodriguez, C.L.; Weatherford, N.C.; Ye, C.S.; Rasio, F.A. Intermediate-mass Black Holes from High Massive-star Binary Fractions in Young Star Clusters. *Astrophys. J.* **2021**, *908*, L29. [CrossRef]
558. Palmese, A.; Conselice, C.J. GW190521 from the Merger of Ultradwarf Galaxies. *Phys. Rev. Lett.* **2021**, *126*, 181103. [CrossRef]
559. Reines, A.E.; Volonteri, M. Relations between Central Black Hole Mass and Total Galaxy Stellar Mass in the Local Universe. *Astrophys. J.* **2015**, *813*, 82. [CrossRef]
560. McKernan, B.; Ford, K.E.S.; Bartos, I.; Graham, M.J.; Lyra, W.; Marka, S.; Marka, Z.; Ross, N.P.; Stern, D.; Yang, Y. Ram-pressure Stripping of a Kicked Hill Sphere: Prompt Electromagnetic Emission from the Merger of Stellar Mass Black Holes in an AGN Accretion Disk. *Astrophys. J.* **2019**, *884*, L50. [CrossRef]
561. Ashton, G.; Ackley, K.; Hernandez, I.M.; Piotrzkowski, B. Current observations are insufficient to confidently associate the binary black hole merger GW190521 with AGN J124942.3 + 344929. *Class. Quantum Gravity* **2021**, *38*, 235004. [CrossRef]
562. Graham, M.J.; Ford, K.E.S.; McKernan, B.; Ross, N.P.; Stern, D.; Burdge, K.; Coughlin, M.; Djorgovski, S.G.; Drake, A.J.; Duev, D.; et al. Candidate Electromagnetic Counterpart to the Binary Black Hole Merger Gravitational-Wave Event S190521g. *Phys. Rev. Lett.* **2020**, *124*, 251102. [CrossRef] [PubMed]
563. Palmese, A.; Fishbach, M.; Burke, C.J.; Annis, J.; Liu, X. Do LIGO/Virgo Black Hole Mergers Produce AGN Flares? The Case of GW190521 and Prospects for Reaching a Confident Association. *Astrophys. J.* **2021**, *914*, L34. [CrossRef]
564. Kinugawa, T.; Nakamura, T.; Nakano, H. Formation of binary black holes similar to GW190521 with a total mass of ∼150 M$_\odot$ from Population III binary star evolution. *Mon. Not. R. Astron. Soc.* **2021**, *501*, L49–L53. [CrossRef]
565. Liu, B.; Meynet, G.; Bromm, V. Dynamical evolution of population III stellar systems and the resulting binary statistics. *Mon. Not. R. Astron. Soc.* **2021**, *501*, 643–663. [CrossRef]
566. Rice, J.R.; Zhang, B. Growth of Stellar-mass Black Holes in Dense Molecular Clouds and GW190521. *Astrophys. J.* **2021**, *908*, 59. [CrossRef]
567. De Luca, V.; Desjacques, V.; Franciolini, G.; Pani, P.; Riotto, A. GW190521 Mass Gap Event and the Primordial Black Hole Scenario. *Phys. Rev. Lett.* **2021**, *126*, 051101. [CrossRef]
568. Yang, Y. Influences of accreting primordial black holes on the global 21 cm signal in the dark ages. *Mon. Not. R. Astron. Soc.* **2021**, *508*, 5709–5715. [CrossRef]
569. Cruz-Osorio, A.; Lora-Clavijo, F.D.; Herdeiro, C. GW190521 formation scenarios via relativistic accretion. *J. Cosmol. Astropart. Phys.* **2021**, *2021*, 032. [CrossRef]
570. Kritos, K.; De Luca, V.; Franciolini, G.; Kehagias, A.; Riotto, A. The astro-primordial black hole merger rates: A reappraisal. *J. Cosmol. Astropart. Phys.* **2021**, *2021*, 039. [CrossRef]
571. Bustillo, J.C.; Sanchis-Gual, N.; Torres-Forné, A.; Font, J.A.; Vajpeyi, A.; Smith, R.; Herdeiro, C.; Radu, E.; Leong, S.H.W. GW190521 as a Merger of Proca Stars: A Potential New Vector Boson of 8.7×10^{-13} eV. *Phys. Rev. Lett.* **2021**, *126*, 081101. [CrossRef] [PubMed]
572. Ziegler, J.; Freese, K. Filling the black hole mass gap: Avoiding pair instability in massive stars through addition of nonnuclear energy. *Phys. Rev. D* **2021**, *104*, 043015. [CrossRef]
573. Abbott, R.; Abbott, T.D.; Abraham, S.; Acernese, F.; Ackley, K.; Adams, C.; Adhikari, R.X.; Adya, V.B.; Affeldt, C.; Agathos, M.; et al. GW190412: Observation of a binary-black-hole coalescence with asymmetric masses. *Phys. Rev. D* **2020**, *102*, 043015. [CrossRef]
574. Mandel, I.; Fragos, T. An Alternative Interpretation of GW190412 as a Binary Black Hole Merger with a Rapidly Spinning Secondary. *Astrophys. J.* **2020**, *895*, L28. [CrossRef]
575. Zevin, M.; Berry, C.P.L.; Coughlin, S.; Chatziioannou, K.; Vitale, S. You Can't Always Get What You Want: The Impact of Prior Assumptions on Interpreting GW190412. *Astrophys. J.* **2020**, *899*, L17. [CrossRef]
576. Riley, J.; Mandel, I.; Marchant, P.; Butler, E.; Nathaniel, K.; Neijssel, C.; Shortt, S.; Vigna-Gómez, A. Chemically homogeneous evolution: A rapid population synthesis approach. *Mon. Not. R. Astron. Soc.* **2021**, *505*, 663–676. [CrossRef]
577. Rodriguez, C.L.; Kremer, K.; Grudić, M.Y.; Hafen, Z.; Chatterjee, S.; Fragione, G.; Lamberts, A.; Martinez, M.A.S.; Rasio, F.A.; Weatherford, N.; et al. GW190412 as a Third-generation Black Hole Merger from a Super Star Cluster. *Astrophys. J.* **2020**, *896*, L10. [CrossRef]
578. Gerosa, D.; Vitale, S.; Berti, E. Astrophysical Implications of GW190412 as a Remnant of a Previous Black-Hole Merger. *Phys. Rev. Lett.* **2020**, *125*, 101103. [CrossRef]
579. Miller, M.C.; Lauburg, V.M. Mergers of Stellar-Mass Black Holes in Nuclear Star Clusters. *Astrophys. J.* **2009**, *692*, 917–923. [CrossRef]
580. Kimball, C.; Talbot, C.; Berry, C.P.L.; Carney, M.; Zevin, M.; Thrane, E.; Kalogera, V. Black Hole Genealogy: Identifying Hierarchical Mergers with Gravitational Waves. *Astrophys. J.* **2020**, *900*, 177. [CrossRef]
581. Hamers, A.S.; Safarzadeh, M. Was GW190412 Born from a Hierarchical 3 + 1 Quadruple Configuration? *Astrophys. J.* **2020**, *898*, 99. [CrossRef]
582. Mandel, I.; Smith, R.J.E. GW200115: A Nonspinning Black Hole-Neutron Star Merger. *Astrophys. J.* **2021**, *922*, L14. [CrossRef]
583. Fragione, G. Black-hole-Neutron-star Mergers Are Unlikely Multimessenger Sources. *Astrophys. J.* **2021**, *923*, L2. [CrossRef]

584. Hu, R.C.; Zhu, J.P.; Qin, Y.; Zhang, B.; Liang, E.W.; Shao, Y. A Channel to Form Fast-spinning Black Hole–Neutron Star Binary Mergers as Multi-messenger Sources. *arXiv* **2022**, arXiv:2201.09549.
585. D'Orazio, D.J.; Haiman, Z.; Levin, J.; Samsing, J.; Vigna-Gomez, A. Multi-Messenger Constraints on Magnetic Fields in Merging Black Hole-Neutron Star Binaries. *arXiv* **2021**, arXiv:2112.01979.
586. Sipior, M.S.; Sigurdsson, S. Nova Scorpii and Coalescing Low-Mass Black Hole Binaries as LIGO Sources. *Astrophys. J.* **2002**, *572*, 962–970. [CrossRef]
587. Belczynski, K.; Perna, R.; Bulik, T.; Kalogera, V.; Ivanova, N.; Lamb, D.Q. A Study of Compact Object Mergers as Short Gamma-Ray Burst Progenitors. *Astrophys. J.* **2006**, *648*, 1110–1116. [CrossRef]
588. Belczynski, K.; Repetto, S.; Holz, D.E.; O'Shaughnessy, R.; Bulik, T.; Berti, E.; Fryer, C.; Dominik, M. Compact Binary Merger Rates: Comparison with LIGO/Virgo Upper Limits. *Astrophys. J.* **2016**, *819*, 108. [CrossRef]
589. Santoliquido, F.; Mapelli, M.; Giacobbo, N.; Bouffanais, Y.; Artale, M.C. The cosmic merger rate density of compact objects: Impact of star formation, metallicity, initial mass function, and binary evolution. *Mon. Not. R. Astron. Soc.* **2021**, *502*, 4877–4889. [CrossRef]
590. Broekgaarden, F.S.; Berger, E. Formation of the First Two Black Hole-Neutron Star Mergers (GW200115 and GW200105) from Isolated Binary Evolution. *Astrophys. J.* **2021**, *920*, L13. [CrossRef]
591. Kinugawa, T.; Nakamura, T.; Nakano, H. Neutron star black hole binaries in LIGO/Virgo O3b run were formed from Population I/II binaries. *arXiv* **2022**, arXiv:2201.06713.
592. Belczynski, K.; Romagnolo, A.; Olejak, A.; Klencki, J.; Chattopadhyay, D.; Stevenson, S.; Coleman Miller, M.; Lasota, J.P.; Crowther, P.A. The Uncertain Future of Massive Binaries Obscures the Origin of LIGO/Virgo Sources. *Astrophys. J.* **2022**, *925*, 69. [CrossRef]
593. Zhu, J.P.; Wu, S.; Qin, Y.; Zhang, B.; Gao, H.; Cao, Z. Population Properties of Gravitational-Wave Neutron Star–Black Hole Mergers. *arXiv* **2021**, arXiv:2112.02605.
594. Abbott, B.P.; Abbott, R.; Abbott, T.D.; Abernathy, M.R.; Acernese, F.; Ackley, K.; Adams, C.; Adams, T.; Addesso, P.; Adhikari, R.X.; et al. Prospects for observing and localizing gravitational-wave transients with Advanced LIGO, Advanced Virgo and KAGRA. *Living Rev. Relativ.* **2018**, *21*, 3. [CrossRef]

Review

Status and Perspectives of Continuous Gravitational Wave Searches

Ornella Juliana Piccinni [1,2]

1 INFN, Sezione di Roma, I-00185 Roma, Italy; ornella.juliana.piccinni@roma1.infn.it or opiccinni@ifae.es
2 Institut de Física d'Altes Energies (IFAE), Barcelona Institute of Science and Technology, and ICREA, E-08193 Barcelona, Spain

Abstract: The birth of gravitational wave astronomy was triggered by the first detection of a signal produced by the merger of two compact objects (also known as a compact binary coalescence event). The following detections made by the Earth-based network of advanced interferometers had a significant impact in many fields of science: astrophysics, cosmology, nuclear physics and fundamental physics. However, compact binary coalescence signals are not the only type of gravitational waves potentially detectable by LIGO, Virgo, and KAGRA. An interesting family of still undetected signals, and the ones that are considered in this review, are the so-called continuous waves, paradigmatically exemplified by the gravitational radiation emitted by galactic, fast-spinning isolated neutron stars with a certain degree of asymmetry in their mass distribution. In this work, I will review the status and the latest results from the analyses of advanced detector data.

Keywords: continuous gravitational waves; neutron stars; dark matter; LIGO; Virgo; KAGRA

1. Introduction

To date, the LIGO and Virgo interferometric detectors [1–3] have registered 90 gravitational wave (GW) events from the coalescence and merger of two compact bodies, either a pair of black holes (BHs) or neutron stars (NSs) or a mixed NS–BH system [4–7]. Each confirmed detection, starting from the first event in September 2015, has added a big piece of information about our comprehension of nature. However, there is still a huge pile of missing pieces to be added to the puzzle before having a complete picture of the GW sky. Indeed, the GW community is only at the beginning of the newborn GW astronomy. Gathering all the information collected so far, GW scientists have been able to prove, among other things, the existence of GWs, the possibility of having BHs in binaries, and the formation of heavy elements in NSs mergers, etc., just by considering the class of transient GW events. In principle, the number of potentially emitting sources is really large, since any system is able to generate GWs whenever there is a non-vanishing mass quadrupole moment. In particular, other astrophysical systems are able to emit GWs potentially detectable by Earth-based interferometers such as LIGO, Virgo and KAGRA [1,2,8]. In this review, I will focus on the discussion of the prospects of detection for a particular subset of GW signals called continuous waves (CWs). Although the emitted signal in this case might be difficult to catch in the data, a detection would certainly be of wide interest to the full scientific community. In Section 2, I will provide some information about the physical systems that can emit CWs signals. In Section 3, I will provide an up-to-date discussion of the data analysis techniques used for this type of problem. Finally, in Section 4, I will report the latest observational results, while conclusions are given in Section 5.

2. Sources of Continuous GWs

The detection of continuous GW signals represents one of the next milestones to reach in gravitational-wave astronomy. Long-lasting signals, persistent over the full observing run (i.e., the data taking period), or in its shorter duration version, the so-called long CW transients, are typically emitted by fast spinning asymmetric NSs, both in accreting systems or as isolated sources. To this canonical set of sources, recent studies have reported the possibility of also observing the continuous gravitational emission by potential dark matter (DM) candidates. Other potential sources of CWs are boson stars [9,10] and Thorne-Żytkow Objects [11], although no associated search in advanced detector data has been carried out yet.

In this section, I will review the main emission models proposed in the literature. Previous reviews about CW signals and searches can be found in [12–17] or in the more general GW reviews [18,19].

2.1. Neutron Stars

The physical condition of NS matter is unique, making these fascinating compact objects precious laboratories for subatomic and fundamental physics [20,21]. High density and pressure are reached as the inner core is approached, with an average density comparable with terrestrial atomic nuclei ($\rho_0 \sim 2.5 \times 10^{14}$ g/cm^3), up to values one order of magnitude bigger in the inner core. Surface magnetic fields can reach values up to 10^{12} Gauss or 10^{15} Gauss for strongly magnetized NSs, also known as magnetars [22,23]. Given the extreme condition of NS matter, the equation of state (EOS) is not completely known since superfluidity, superconductivity [24,25], exotic states or quantum effects might be present [26–29]. The actual NS composition is still unknown. In particular, when higher densities are reached, the hadronic nuclear matter undergoes a de-confinement transition to a new phase of quarks and gluons [30], although how this phase transition occurs is still unclear. In a different scenario, the NS inner core can be composed of hyperons [31], Bose–Einstein, pion or kaon condensates [32–34] and more. Furthermore, some of the above-mentioned states of matter can be simultaneously present inside the compact object. The NS matter EOS directly reflects on the star's observable global parameters such as the mass and the radius. Theoretical and observational efforts, including those related to GWs, to measure the NS masses and radii are ongoing [35–39]. To set constraints on the EOS of isolated NSs, both mass and radius should be measured, and some assumptions on the pulse profiles should be made (see, e.g., [40]). NS masses are typically measured from pulsar observations, while radius measurements are more challenging and strongly depend on the X-ray emission model assumed. To date, the NS measured masses lie in the range $[1.1; 2.2]$ $M_\odot$, with the most massive source being the millisecond pulsar J0740+6620 with a mass of 2.14 $M_\odot$ [41]. Direct measurements of radii do not exist; however, estimates can be made, for instance, by combining the measured flux and temperature with the source distance. Current estimates report NS radii in the range $[9; 13]$ km [42–44]. Further improvements on the NS radius and mass estimates are provided by the NICER mission [45,46]. The detection of the first NS merger event GW170817 by LIGO and Virgo [47], followed by the electromagnetic (EM) gamma-ray burst GRB170817 [48], and the optical transient signal of a kilonova (AT 2017gfo) [49], provided a new tool for NS mass and radius estimates [50], extending the possible NS mass range. Other GW events involving potential NS have been reported to date: GW190425 [51] with a progenitor mass of $[1.12; 2.52]$ $M_\odot$ and GW190814 [52] involving a compact object with a mass of $2.50 - 2.67$ $M_\odot$. No EM counterpart has been observed from the two events, suggesting that these are the smallest BHs to date, although the possibility of being the most massive NSs measured so far cannot be completely excluded. To this list of GW signals involving at least a (potential) NS, there are the events: GW190917_114630 [6], GW191219_163120 [7], GW200210_092254 [7] and the two GW200105_162426 and GW200115_042309 discussed in [7,53].

The formation of an NS could happen through two main channels: (i) core-collapse supernova explosions (CCSN), forming a very hot proto-neutron star, followed by a cooler stable NS [54], (ii) after a binary NS merger [55]. In these two scenarios, fast-rotating and highly magnetized young NS (in particular magnetars) could be formed.

Spinning NSs are expected to emit GWs continuously if they are asymmetric with respect to their rotation axis [56,57]. Potential targets for Earth-based detectors are galactic sources. The signal produced as the star spins is almost monochromatic and with a frequency proportional to the star's spin frequency. Four different scenarios are considered possible for the observation of CWs, namely (i) very hot newborn NSs, right after the formation, i.e., after merger and core-collapse supernova, reaching rotating frequencies close to their Keplerian limit; (ii) young NSs such as stable supernova remnants during the initial spin-down phase; (iii) accreting low mass X-ray binaries (LMXBs) emitting thermal X-ray radiation and characterized by a small spin-up; (iv) fast-spinning pulsars, i.e., old millisecond pulsars with small spin-down. Different CW emission models are considered (see [56]), and these include the emission due to the presence of non-axisymetries in rigid rotating triaxial bodies, rotating about one of its principal axes (equivalent to a biaxial rotor not spinning about one of the principal axes); oscillation of the star; or more complicated scenarios such as free precessing systems or heterogeneous stars (when multiple phases of component matter are simultaneously present, including superfluidity).

If from one side, some of the GW emission mechanisms are well understood, the actual factors that cause the asymmetry in the star are still under debate. Indeed, the asymmetry could be triggered by the presence of residual crustal deformations (e.g., after a fast cooling of the NS crust), the presence of a strong inner magnetic field not aligned with the star's rotation axis, or the presence of magnetic or thermal "mountains" (see [17] for a review). The maximum ellipticity (i.e., deformability) the star can sustain depends on both the NS EOS and the breaking strain of the crust [15]. I briefly review the two main CW emission mechanisms happening in NSs and how these reflect on the expected signal amplitude.

Ellipticity driven emission: the GW amplitude for an NS with asymmetries can be expressed in terms of the product between the moment of inertia I_3 along the spin axis and the star's degree of asymmetry, also known as ellipticity ε:

$$h_0 = \frac{16\pi^2 G}{c^4} \frac{I_3 \varepsilon f_{\text{spin}}^2}{r} \quad (1)$$

where f_{spin} is the star spin frequency of a source at a distance r. Most of the observed NSs have rotation frequencies below 1 kHz, i.e., in the sensitivity range of ground-based interferometers such as advanced LIGO/Virgo. The ellipticity is given by $\varepsilon = \frac{I_2 - I_1}{I_3}$, assuming $I_1 \neq I_2$. Most of the parameters entering in Equation (1) can be somehow constrained by astronomical observations, except for the ellipticity ε for which only theoretical maxima estimates exist [58–63]. Current estimates only report upper limits in the 10^{-7}–10^{-5} range, while an actual estimate of a fiducial ellipticity of $\sim 10^{-9}$, possibly sustained by millisecond pulsars, is given in [61].

For the case of elastic stresses, the maximum sustainable ellipticity is related to the crustal breaking strain u_{break} as [64]

$$\varepsilon < 2 \times 10^{-5} \left(\frac{u_{\text{break}}}{0.1} \right) \quad (2)$$

with estimated values of $u_{\text{break}} = 0.1$, much larger than standard terrestrial materials [65]. However, these constraints strongly depend on the actual EOS (see, e.g., [15]).

For quadrupolar deformations on spherically symmetric stars due to magnetic fields [66–68], the ellipticity is given by the ratio of the magnetic energy and the GW energy. The actual deformation strongly depends on the magnetic field morphology. Indeed, poloidal fields will oblate the star, while toroidal fields tend to prolate the star. When the magnetic field is purely poloidal, the ellipticity will depend on the average $\bar{B}$ field as

$$\varepsilon \approx 10^{-12} \left(\frac{\bar{B}}{10^{12} \text{G}} \right)^2. \quad (3)$$

In the case of a fully toroidal magnetic field, the star's ellipticity is given by

$$\varepsilon \approx 10^{-11} \left(\frac{\bar{B}}{10^{12} \text{G}} \right)^2. \tag{4}$$

In a realistic scenario, also known as "twisted-torus" configuration, both the poloidal and toroidal components will contribute to the B field (for a detailed discussion, see [15,17,56]). Given the uncertainty connected to the estimation of ε and the moment of inertia I, typically the deviation from axisymmetry is constrained in terms of the quadrupole Q_{22} (assuming that the $l = m = 2$ mode dominates) [59]

$$Q_{22} = \sqrt{\frac{8\pi}{15}} \varepsilon I. \tag{5}$$

R-mode emission: a different emission channel for CW radiation is given by the Rossby (r-)modes oscillations in rotating stars. R-mode emission is provided by the Chandrasekhar–Friedman–Schutz instability, leading to the rapid growth of the r-mode amplitude until a saturation amplitude is reached and the growth of the mode stops [69]. These amplitudes are damped by the viscosity of the star. Given these two opposite effects, where the amplitude increases with the spin of the star and is suppressed by the viscosity, dependent on the temperature, an instability window is defined in the angular velocity-temperature plane [70]. Typically, NSs are unstable to r-modes except at extreme temperatures. At very low temperatures, the shear viscosity dominates the damping, while at very high temperatures, the bulk viscosity takes the lead in the r-mode suppression. Given this strict relation with the inner physics of the NS during the r-mode emission, constraints on the GW observable properties are interesting tools for the study of the EOS [56,71]. A typical parameter constrained in CW searches for r-modes is the r-mode amplitude α. Considering a source at a distance r the GW strain h_0 is given by [72]:

$$h_0 = \sqrt{\frac{2^9 \pi^7}{5}} \frac{G}{c^5} \tilde{J} M R^3 \frac{f_{\text{gw}}^3 \alpha}{r} \tag{6}$$

where the dimensionless constant $\tilde{J}$ is connected to the source density and EOS [69,72]. M and R are the NS mass and radius. The GW frequency f_{gw} is proportional to the oscillation angular frequency $\omega = 2\pi f_{\text{gw}}$, which is related to the rotation angular velocity as $\omega \sim -4\Omega/3$. If relativistic corrections and other effects due to the rotation are considered [73,74], e.g., those related to the EOS, the relation between the GW frequency and the star spin frequency can be parametrized as [74,75]:

$$f_{\text{gw}} = A f_{\text{spin}} + B \left(\frac{f_{\text{spin}}}{f_{\text{Kepler}}} \right)^2 f_{\text{spin}} \tag{7}$$

where f_{Kepler} is the Kepler frequency of the star, i.e., its maximum sustainable spin frequency. The values for A and B lie in a range $1.39 < A < 1.57$ and $0 < B < 0.195$.

Ellipticities are also expected to be present in LMXBs, due to an asymmetric accretion process, producing, for instance, thermal gradients in the crust [58]. In these systems, a spinning NS is accreting matter from a companion, forming a circumstellar accretion disk around it and emitting strong X-ray radiation. These systems represent interesting targets for CW searches [76] given that when the accretion torque balances the GW torque, LMXBs become very stable GW emitters. In particular, the GW amplitude of an LMXBs is proportional to the square root of the X-ray flux. For this reason, very bright sources such as Scorpius X-1 (Sco X-1) or XTE J1751-305 represent ideal targets. It has been observed that all the NSs in LMXB systems have maximum spinning frequencies below their Keplerian breakup limit. Indeed, the fastest LMXB observed has a spin frequency of $\sim$700 Hz, while according to [77], the lowest breakup frequency allowed is $\sim$1200 Hz, although this limit strongly depends on the assumptions made for the EOS of the star. This suggests that this limit is strongly related to the GW torques [77,78] due to oscillations or asymmetries, although it could be due to the interaction of the accreting disk with the NS magnetic field [79]. The search for CWs from accreting sources is complicated mainly by two factors [76]: (i) the source is spun up by the companion during the accretion, and a spin-wandering effect [80] could be present; (ii) an additional Doppler effect by the binary orbital motion is present [81]. Eventually, variations in the matter accretion rate directly reflect into irregular spinning frequency. To make these searches even more complicated, often the spin frequency is not known, as in the case of Sco X-1.

Different approaches are used, tailored to the emission model considered for the search. For instance, some methods are adapted and/or new algorithms have been developed for the case of a long duration transient emitted by postmerger remnants, or for the case of CWs from glitching pulsars. In the postmerger remnant case, the source is expected to have a high spin-down rate; hence, the frequency will strongly vary with time. In the glitching pulsar case, the frequency suddenly changes, a sudden spin-up occurs, which may enhance the GW emission for a short time [82], and then the star relaxes back to the standard spin-down scenario.

In thee case of detection, it is possible to extract some information about the main CW emission mechanism happening in an NS, by looking at the GW frequency measured (see [13]). In particular, it is known that the GW frequency is related to the star spin frequency according to $f_{\rm gw} = k(f_{\rm spin} + f_{\rm prec})$. Here, k is a proportionality factor dependent on the model considered. In the simplest case of no precessing ($f_{\rm prec} = 0$) rigid rotating bodies, with asymmetries supported by elastic and/or magnetic stresses, $k = 2$, and hence, $f_{\rm gw} = 2f_{\rm spin}$. In r-mode oscillations scenarios, the estimated emitted frequency is $f_{\rm gw} \sim \frac{4}{3}f_{\rm spin}$, although deviations from this number are expected when relativistic corrections are included and/or different EOS are considered. In this case, the GW amplitude of the r-mode signal is parametrized in terms of the r-mode amplitude α, and it explicitly depends on the mass and radius of the NS and on the star EOS. For the case of CWs emitted by LMXB systems, accreting matter from a companion star, the relation between the spin frequency and the GW frequency is expected to be $f_{\rm gw} = 2f_{\rm spin}$.

As the star spins, its angular momentum will be radiated away, e.g., via GW emission, decreasing its frequency as [1]

$$\dot{f} = Kf^n \qquad (8)$$

where the negative constant K and the braking index n depend on the energy loss mechanism as $n = f\ddot{f}/\dot{f}^2$. The spin-down process may be more complicated than the simple power law in Equation (8), and in general, it is possible that the energy loss is due to a simultaneous contribution from both the gravitational and magnetic dipole emission. For a spin-down fully dominated by a gravitational emission [83], i.e., a gravitar, $n = 5$ (or $n = 7$ if the GW emission happens via r-mode), while $n = 3$ for magnetic dipole emission. An estimate of the age of the source can be expressed as

$$\tau = -\left[\frac{f}{(n-1)\dot{f}}\right]\left[1 - \left(\frac{f}{f_0}\right)^{(n-1)}\right] \qquad (9)$$

here, f_0 is the star birth rotation frequency. For old sources (with $f \ll f_0$), the age is simplified as

$$\tau \approx -\left[\frac{f}{(n-1)\dot{f}}\right] \qquad (10)$$

More complicated emission scenarios are described in the literature. For instance, when the star is in free precession, dual harmonic emissions can be present at once and twice the star's spinning frequency. A particular case of dual harmonic emission is encountered when the star has a superfluid core pinned to the crust and not aligned with the principal axes of the moment of inertia [84]. More complex emission models exist, e.g., when the configuration is that of a triaxial freely precessing body or for the case of a deferentially rotating two-component star. In this case, the emission may happen on more than two harmonics, complicating the signal waveform to be searched for. Typically these models are not considered in real searches.

The class of CWs signals is then a good benchmark to study the state of matter at higher densities. In addition to this aspect, CW detections can be used to test general relativity (GR). According to GR, only two tensor polarization states exist for GWs. When more generic metric theories of gravity are assumed, the number of polarizations increases up to six, allowing for two scalar and two additional vector modes. In particular, for the Brans–Dicke theory of gravity [85], only one additional scalar polarization state is predicted to be present along with the two tensor polarizations predicted by GR. As discussed in [86–88], it is possible to put constraints on these extra polarizations using CWs detections from known pulsars. Indeed, the detector response function to a given polarization depends on the direction of propagation of the GW along the two detector arms (see, e.g., [89]). Given the long duration nature of CWs, different antenna patterns will produce a different sidereal amplitude modulation. This means that all the relevant information to distinguish between the polarizations is encoded in the sidereal-day-period amplitude modulation of the signal. This is true only if the signal phase evolution for non-GR polarizations is equal to that assumed for GR.

Strain Amplitude Limits

It is possible to identify promising targets for CWs by computing some limits based on the information about the source. These quantities constraint the maximum GW emission of a given source. Three main limits are used in CW searches: the spin-down limit, the age-based limit and the torque balance limit.

Spin-down limit: generally, for known pulsars with precisely measured $f_{\rm spin}$ and $\dot{f}_{\rm spin}$, it is possible to define the so-called spin-down limit on the maximum detectable strain [57]. If all the energy loss during the spin-down is released in the form of GWs, by equating the GW power emission to the time derivative of the rotational kinetic energy, one obtains a source at a distance r:

$$h_0^{\rm sd} = \frac{1}{r}\sqrt{\frac{5}{2}\frac{G}{c^3}I_3\frac{|\dot{f}_{\rm gw}|}{f_{\rm gw}}} = 2.5 \times 10^{-25}\left(\frac{1\,\rm kpc}{r}\right)\sqrt{\left(\frac{1\,\rm kHz}{f_{\rm gw}}\right)\left(\frac{|\dot{f}_{\rm gw}|}{10^{-10}\,\rm Hz/s}\right)\left(\frac{I_3}{I_0}\right)}. \tag{11}$$

where $I_0 = 10^{38}$ kg m^2. This gives an absolute upper limit to the amplitude of the CW signal emitted by a pulsar.

Age-based limit: an alternative way to check the goodness of a potential CW target, when the rotational parameters are unknown, is to look at the so-called indirect age-based limit. Similar to the spin-down limit, assuming that all the energy lost is radiated away with GWs, it is possible to express the spin-down limits in terms of the age of the star τ using Equation (9) and a braking index $n = 5$ [90]

$$h_0^{\rm age} = 2.27 \times 10^{-24}\left(\frac{1\,\rm kpc}{r}\right)\left(\frac{1\,\rm kyr}{\tau}\right)^{1/2}\left(\frac{I_3}{I_0}\right)^{1/2}. \tag{12}$$

Torque balance limit: empirical upper limits can also be defined for accreting binaries. Assuming that the GW emission is completely balanced by the angular momentum added via accretion, the so-called torque-balance limit can be derived [91]. Assuming that the accretion luminosity is fully radiated as X-rays, this provides an estimate on the mass accumulation rate; hence, the limit can be written in terms of the observable X-ray flux F_X and the star spin frequency (GW frequency):

$$h_0^{\text{tb}} = 5 \times 10^{-27} \left(\frac{F_X}{F_\star}\right)^{1/2} \left(\frac{R}{10 \text{ km}}\right)^{1/2} \left(\frac{r_m}{10 \text{ km}}\right)^{1/4} \left(\frac{1.4 M_\odot}{M}\right)^{1/4} \left(\frac{700 \text{ Hz}}{f_{\text{gw}}}\right)^{1/2} \qquad (13)$$

with $F_\star = 10^{-8} \text{ erg cm}^{-2} \text{ s}^{-1}$. M and R are the NS mass and radius and r_m is the lever arm, usually equal to R or to the Alfven radius, i.e., the radius corresponding to the inner edge of the accretion disk.

2.2. Dark Matter Candidates

A CW-like signature is expected to be produced in the data also by several potential DM candidates [92]. For a few years, interferometric detector data have been used to look for evidence of DM, both in terms of GW, emitted by systems made up of particles from the dark sector, and as direct DM detectors, assuming a DM coupling to the detector components. For a review of all the DM candidates that can be investigated using GWs detectors, see [93]. Potential DM candidates may be ultra-light bosons, including dark photons or quantum-chromo-dynamic axions [94–97]. In this section, I review three main scenarios involving DM candidates, where a persistent CW-like signal is expected to be produced and actively searched by the CW community: boson clouds around spinning BHs, vector bosons in form of dark photons, compact dark objects or primordial black holes. The latest observational results will be discussed in Section 4.2.

2.2.1. Boson Clouds

Ultralight bosons condensates can clump around spinning BHs through superradiance [95,96,98]. The BH-boson cloud system can be described using an analogy with the hydrogen atom model when the axion's Compton wavelength is comparable to the size of a BH, turning this system into a "gravitational atom". When boson fields are present nearby a spinning BH, these can interact with the BH and condensate around it, all occupying the same (quantum) state and reaching huge occupation numbers after exponential growth. This process takes place at the expense of the BH angular momentum, and indeed, the axion or axion-like particles scatter on the BH decreasing its spin. When the BH spin is low enough, the superradiance process stops, and the cloud dissipates via axion annihilation into gravitons. During this depletion phase or when transitioning between levels of the gravitational atom, the system generates a quasi-monochromatic and long-duration signal that can be searched with CW methods. It should be noted, however, that the GW contribution from transition levels is sub-dominant. The most interesting scenario for Earth-based detectors such as LIGO, Virgo and KAGRA is the annihilation process. Indeed, the signal produced in this case is in the detector sensitivity band for boson masses in the $10^{-13} - \times 10^{-12}$ eV range. If the boson self-interaction is negligible, the gravitational-wave signal frequency depends mainly on the mass of the boson and weakly on the mass and spin of the BH. When self-interaction is considered, the approximation of the signal with a CW-like shape is no longer valid since the signal is strongly suppressed [99]. In particular, if the self-interaction is stronger than the gravitational binding energy, the cloud becomes unstable, and it collapses in a process known as "bosenova". During this process, the system may produce a burst of GWs [95]. In general, the annihilation signal cannot be fully characterized unless some assumptions on the BH are made. Indeed, the emitted signal depends on the mass, spin, distance, and age of the BH.

Let us briefly review the main characteristic of the signal emitted by BH-boson clouds as in [94,95,98,100,101]. When the superradiant condition is satisfied, i.e., when the boson angular frequency is less than the BH's outer horizon angular frequency, the scalar field starts to clump around the BH. This effect is maximized when the particle's reduced Compton wavelength $\lambda_b = \frac{\hbar c}{m_b}$, which depends on the boson mass m_b, is comparable to the BH Schwarzschild radius $R = \frac{2GM_{\text{BH}}}{c^2}$. This superradiant instability phase has a typical duration of

$$\tau_{\text{inst}} \approx 20 \left(\frac{M_{\text{BH}}}{10 \, M_\odot}\right) \left(\frac{\alpha}{0.1}\right)^{-9} \left(\frac{1}{\chi_i}\right) \text{ days}, \qquad (14)$$

dependent on the BH mass $M_{\rm BH}$ and dimensionless spin χ_i. Returning to the analogy with the hydrogen atom, α is the fine-structure constant in the gravitational atom

$$\alpha = \frac{GM_{\rm BH}}{c^3}\frac{m_b}{\hbar}. \tag{15}$$

As long as the BH spin is above the critical spin $\chi_c \approx \frac{4\alpha}{1+4\alpha^2}$, the cloud will continue to grow and the BH will decrease its spin. Once equilibrium has been reached, the boson cloud mass is dissipated on a timescale[2]

$$\tau_{\rm gw} \approx 6.5 \times 10^4 \left(\frac{M_{\rm BH}}{10\,M_\odot}\right)\left(\frac{\alpha}{0.1}\right)^{-15}\left(\frac{1}{\chi_i}\right) \text{ years.} \tag{16}$$

The GW amplitude decays in time as $(1+t/\tau_{\rm gw})^{-1}$ from a starting strain amplitude determined mainly by the BH and boson masses (entering in the definition of α) and the BH initial spin

$$h_0 \approx 3 \times 10^{-24} \left(\frac{\alpha}{0.1}\right)^7 \left(\frac{\chi_i - \chi_c}{0.5}\right)\left(\frac{M_{\rm BH}}{10\,M_\odot}\right)\left(\frac{1\,\text{kpc}}{r}\right). \tag{17}$$

During this emission phase, the GW emitted frequency, which is twice the frequency of the field, is also dependent on the two-component masses as

$$f_{\rm gw} \simeq 483\,\text{Hz}\left(\frac{m_b}{10^{-12}\,\text{eV}}\right)\left[1 - 7 \times 10^{-4}\left(\frac{M_{\rm BH}}{10\,M_\odot}\frac{m_b}{10^{-12}\,\text{eV}}\right)^2\right] \tag{18}$$

During the depletion phase, a small spin-up is present due to the loss of mass. Indeed, during the cloud formation phase, a large spin-down rate is present, although the expected signal strain is still too low to be detected. This drift changes when the cloud starts to evaporate. The actual spin-up rate during the depletion phase is strongly dependent on the boson self-interaction constant. For simplicity, we consider the case of a negligible self-interaction when the spin-up due to annihilation is the dominant drift:

$$\dot{f}_{\rm gw} \approx 7 \times 10^{-15}\left(\frac{m_b}{10^{-12}\,\text{eV}}\right)^2\left(\frac{\alpha}{0.1}\right)^{17}\,\text{Hz/s.} \tag{19}$$

When the self-interaction starts to be non-negligible, the spin-up rate is enhanced by two contributions, one from the bosons energy level transition and a second from the change in the self-interaction energy as the cloud depletes. At this point, the signal is expected to be shorter or with a smaller amplitude. For a more general discussion on the role of the boson self-interaction parameter, see [99]. In current CW searches, the main contribution to the GW emission considered for these models are those from the main growing state since the second fastest growing state emission is weaker than the first level one and is not fully quadrupolar.

Analogous to the standard CW case for NSs, Doppler modulations should be considered when looking for the signal in the detector data (see Section 4.2 for the latest observing results from this field). Finally, we notice that the same superradiance effect described above is somehow expected also for rotating NS [102,103], although it is not clear if the GW emission is loud enough to be detected by currently operating detectors.

2.2.2. Ultralight Vector Bosons: Dark Photons

DM particles are expected to interact with other DM particles in the same way as standard matter interacts with the EM force mediated by the photon. The equivalent force mediator for the dark sector is the dark photon. According to current theories, the dark photon is not expected to couple directly to standard model particles, although a small mixing-induced coupling to EM currents can be present [104,105]. Here, we focus on an ultralight DM candidate, which behaves as a classical field interacting coherently with the atoms of the test masses. In particular, we assume that the dark photon is a vector boson coupled to the baryon or baryons minus leptons number $U(1)_B/U(1)_{B-L}$. In practice, if sufficiently light, the dark photon has a high phase-space density; hence, it behaves as a coherently oscillating classic field producing an oscillating force on dark charged objects [106–108]. The same type of oscillation is expected for the tensor boson case [109]. The mass of the dark photon could be provided either by a dark Higgs boson or via the Stuckelberg mechanism [104,105,110]. Different production mechanisms have been proposed for the dark photon, such as the misalignment mechanism associated with the inflationary epoch, light scalar decay or cosmic strings [111,112]. Several attempts to set constraints on this type of DM are present in the literature [107,113,114]. The dark photon DM field oscillations act as a time-dependent equivalence principle-violating force acting on the test masses and producing a change in the relative length of the detector's arms. There exist two main signatures when test bodies interact with the dark photon fields: a spatial gradient is present, producing a relative acceleration between the objects due to the different field amplitude; given the equivalence principle-violation of this force, test masses of different materials will experience different accelerations. For all Earth-based detectors, an additional effect due to the finite light travel time should be considered [115,116].

I briefly review the main characteristics of the expected signal from dark photons while search results are discussed in Section 4.2. The Lagrangian of the massive vector field A^μ, which couples to B or $B-L$ current J_D^μ ($D = B$ or $B-L$) as DM is given (in natural units) by

$$\mathcal{L} = -\frac{1}{4}F^{\mu\nu}F_{\mu\nu} + \frac{1}{2}m_A^2 A^\mu A_\mu - \epsilon_D e J_D^\mu A_\mu, \qquad (20)$$

where $F_{\mu\nu} = \partial_\mu A_\nu - \partial_\nu A_\mu$, m_A is the mass of the vector field, and ϵ_D is the coupling constant normalized to the EM one. The dark photon field A_μ can be approximated as a plane wave with a characteristic momentum $\vec{k} \simeq m_A \vec{v}_0/\hbar$, within a coherence time $T_{\text{coh}} \simeq 2\pi\hbar(m_A v_0^2)^{-1}$. The local amplitude $A_{\mu,0}$ of the dark electric gauge field is obtained assuming an energy density, $\frac{1}{2}m_A^2 A_{\mu,0} A_0^\mu$, equal to that of the local DM $\rho_{\text{DM}} = 0.4\,\text{GeV}/\text{cm}^3$. The time-dependent force acting on the test masses produces a strain oscillating at the same frequency and phase as the DM field [106,116–118]. It should be noted that a similar signal may be produced in the case of scalar dark matter particles directly interacting with the mirrors. In particular, as described by [119], the interaction of the scalar bosons with the beam-splitter will induce oscillations in the thickness of the mirror due to the oscillations of the fundamental constants [120–122]. Considering only vector bosons in a non relativistic scenario, the contribution from the magnetic dark field is negligible if compared to the electric dark field[3]. The dark photon DM background field will generate an acceleration on each i-th test mass as:

$$\vec{a}_i(t, \vec{x}_i) = \frac{\vec{F}_i(t, \vec{x}_i)}{M_i} \simeq \epsilon_D e \frac{q_{D,i}}{M_i} \partial_t \vec{A}(t, \vec{x}_i) \qquad (21)$$

M_i and $q_{D,i}$ are the total mass and dark charge of the test mass located at x_i.

This acceleration will cause a tiny differential relative displacement between pairs of test masses that can be converted into a strain by integrating Equation (21) twice over time. Following [116,123], the GW strain will have two contributes, one due to the relative variation of the arm length due to the dark force acting on the mirrors $h_D(t)$, and a second one due to the finite light-traveling time in the arm $h_C(t)$. These two contributions can be averaged over random polarization and propagation directions, and the resulting strain in SI units can be written as:

$$\sqrt{\langle h_D^2\rangle} = C\frac{q}{M}\frac{e\epsilon_D}{2\pi c^2}\sqrt{\frac{2\rho_{\text{DM}}}{\epsilon_0}}\frac{v_0}{f_0} = 6.28\times 10^{-27}\left(\frac{\epsilon_D}{10^{-23}}\right)\left(\frac{100\,\text{Hz}}{f_0}\right) \qquad (22)$$

$$\sqrt{\langle h_C^2\rangle} = \frac{\sqrt{3}}{2}\sqrt{\langle h_D^2\rangle}\left(\frac{2\pi f_0 L}{v_0}\right) \simeq 6.21 \times 10^{-26}\left(\frac{\epsilon_D}{10^{-23}}\right). \qquad (23)$$

The total strain will be the root sum of the squares of the two contributions. The quantity C is a geometric factor dependent on the position and orientation of the interferometer with respect to the DM wind. The signal frequency is then determined by the dark photon mass $f_0 = m_A c^2/(2\pi\hbar)$, corresponding for Earth-based detectors to dark photon masses in the range 10^{-14}–10^{-11} eV/c^2. Given that the velocity of dark photon particles follows a Maxwell–Boltzmann distribution, and assuming a virial velocity of $v_0 = 220$ km/s, the signal frequency will lie in the $(f_0, f_0 + \Delta f)$ range, where:

$$\frac{\Delta f}{f_0} = \frac{1}{2}\frac{v_0^2}{c^2} \approx 2.94 \times 10^{-7}. \qquad (24)$$

Furthermore, for the dark photon DM case, the Doppler shift due to Earth's rotation is present, although the frequency shift due to this effect is an order of magnitude smaller than the one from the Maxwell–Boltzmann spreading.

2.2.3. Compact Dark Objects and Primordial Black Holes

Dark matter can be present in our Universe in the form of macroscopic objects, which we generically refer to as compact dark objects (CDOs). The actual formation channel and the origin of CDOs are still widely debated. According to some hypotheses, CDOs can be also PBHs. CDOs can form pairs and emit an almost monochromatic signal while being far from the coalescence phase. One option for the formation of the pair, proposed in [124], is to assume that these objects can be trapped inside normal matter via non-gravitational interactions, for instance, the Sun or even the Earth [125]. If a second CDO is also trapped inside the same object, these can form a binary CDO emitting GWs with a long lifetime for low mass objects. According to [124], the probability of collisions between CDOs and the Sun is not negligible for CDOs masses $\sim 10^{-10} M_\odot$; hence, there is a non-negligible possibility of having these pairs of CDOs formed in our solar system. Furthermore, PBHs can be constituents of a fraction of the DM in the Universe depending on their formation channels (see [126–129] for the latest reviews about PBHs as DM candidates). In particular, the origin of most of the sub-solar and planetary mass BHs is likely primordial, although speculations on alternative formation channels exist, e.g., created from NSs by the accumulation of DM and subsequent collapse into a BH [130]. For the context of CW signals, PBHs, as well as more generic CDOs, represent potential targets. Indeed, the GW signals emitted by these systems, when the two compact objects are far away from the coalescence and/or their masses are small enough, are modeled as quasi-monochromatic. This approximation is valid until the inspiral orbit does not reach the inner-most stable orbit. When the low-mass/far-from-coalescence conditions are dropped, the frequency evolution of these systems is better represented by a power law with a spin-up.

For the masses considered ($\leq 10^{-5} M_\odot$) in searches for CW signals from a pair of compact objects, the linear approximation is always valid considering the frequencies of the detector sensitivity band. In addition, if the chirp mass is small enough, the frequency can be modeled exactly as the linear frequency Taylor expansion used for standard CW searches. This means that, for instance, a pair of inspiralling PBHs with chirp masses below $10^{-5} M_\odot$ would emit a GW signal indistinguishable from those arising from non-axisymmetric rotating NSs spinning up.

Let us now consider the type of emission that could be released by these systems. The two systems of the two orbiting PBHs/CDOs can be approximated as a two-body problem of point mass objects in a circular orbit. The system loses energy as the inspiralling continues and the two masses approach each other. The signal model discussed in this section is widely described in the classical handbook of GW science [131–133] as well as in [124,134–136]. The expected signal strain amplitude is that of a circular BH binary inspiral at a distance r identified by a chirp mass $\mathcal{M}$ with a time to the coalescence $\tau = t_c - t$:

$$h_0(t) = \frac{4c}{r}\left(\frac{G\mathcal{M}}{c^3}\right)^{5/3}(\pi f_{gw}(t))^{2/3}. \tag{25}$$

The amplitude is time-dependent and scales with the GW frequency, equal to twice the system orbital frequency. The GW frequency emitted is dependent on the system chirp mass $\mathcal{M}$ as

$$f_{gw}(\tau) = \frac{(5/\tau)^{\frac{3}{8}}}{8\pi}\left(\frac{G\mathcal{M}}{c^3}\right)^{-5/8}. \tag{26}$$

In this case, the expected signal frequency variation (the spin-up) due to the change in distance of the inspiralling system is given by:

$$\dot{f}_{gw} = \frac{96}{5}\pi^{8/3}\left(\frac{G\mathcal{M}}{c^3}\right)^{5/3}f_{gw}^{11/3}. \tag{27}$$

Equation (26) is derived by integrating the expression for the spin-up. For low masses, the frequency evolution can be simplified, assuming that the observing time T_{obs} is bigger than τ and assuming a small chirp mass. This means that the PBH/CDO spin-up rate $\dot{f}_{gw}$ can be treated as a constant. In this case, the expected signal can be linearized as $f_{gw}(t) \sim f_0 + (t-t_0)\dot{f}_{gw}$, which coincides with the standard NS case (see Equation (29)). On the other hand, if the spin-up is too high, this approximation is no longer valid, and the frequency evolution should be modeled as a power-law, as discussed in [136]. Furthermore, for this system, the signal undergoes a daily modulation at the detector, which should be considered in the analyses.

3. Searches for CWs Signals with Earth-Based Detectors

Different methods for the search for CW signals have been developed. The variety of methods reflects the different ways it is possible to look for these long-lasting signals, giving priority to the sensitivity of the pipeline (i.e., the search algorithm) or its robustness with respect to deviations of the signal from the assumed model.

3.1. The Signal at the Detector

CWs are by definition all those quasi-monochromatic GW signals characterized by a long duration, ranging from hours to years, and deeply buried in detector noise. When the CW signal reaches the detector, several modulation effects occur. The strain measured at the detector for a triaxial rotor is given by

$$h(t) = h_0\left[F_+(t,\alpha,\delta,\psi)\frac{(1+\cos^2\iota)}{2}\cos\Phi(t) + F_\times(t,\alpha,\delta,\psi)\cos\iota\sin\Phi(t)\right] \tag{28}$$

here, (α,δ) are the right ascension and declination of the source in the sky, ψ is the polarization angle, $F_{+/\times}$ are the detector response to the two $h_{+/\times}$ polarizations of the GW. The signal strain also depends on the inclination of the rotation axis to the line of sight ι and the GW phase $\Phi(t)$ (see, e.g., [132]). The phase of the GW signal is related to the frequency components $(f,\dot{f},\ddot{f},\ldots)$ at a given reference time t_0 as

$$\Phi(t) = \phi_o + 2\pi\left[f(t-t_0) + \frac{\dot{f}}{2!}(t-t_0)^2 + \ldots\right] \tag{29}$$

where ϕ_0 is an initial phase. The signal phase is modulated mainly by the Doppler due to relative motion between the detectors and the source and other relativistic effects, namely the Einstein and Shapiro delays. The frequency at the detector will be spread with respect to the emitted frequency as:

$$f_{\text{gw}}(t) = \frac{1}{2\pi}\frac{d\Phi(t)}{dt} = f_0(t)\left(1 + \frac{\vec{v}(t)\cdot\hat{n}}{c}\right) \qquad (30)$$

where $\vec{v}$ is the velocity vector of the detector, while $\hat{n}$ is the unit vector pointing to the source direction, both expressed in the Solar System Barycenter reference frame. Here, $f_0(t)$ is the GW frequency arriving at the detector at the time t and emitted by the star at the reference time t_0. As mentioned in the previous sections, $f_0(t)$ can be described by a Taylor expansion such as $f_0(t) \simeq f_0 + \dot{f}(t-t_0) + \ldots$, where $\dot{f}$ is the first order spin-down parameter.

The phase modulation due to the Doppler Effect, apart from an irrelevant constant, can be obtained by integrating Equation (30) as:

$$\phi_d(t) = 2\pi \int_{t_0}^{t} f_0(t')\frac{\vec{v}\cdot\hat{n}}{c}dt' \approx \frac{2\pi}{c}p_{\hat{n}}(t)f_0(t) \qquad (31)$$

where $p_{\hat{n}}(t)$ is the position of the detector projected along $\hat{n}$.

The pure signal strain at the detector, assuming the ideal situation where no noise is present, is depicted in Figure 1.

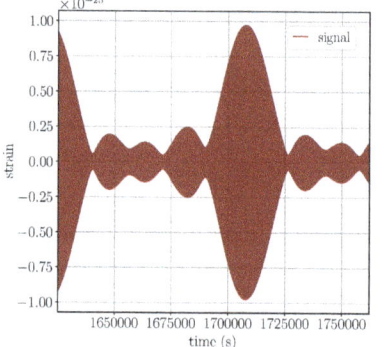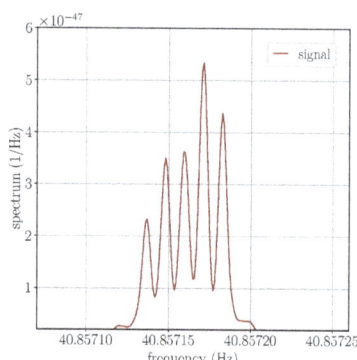

Figure 1. Features of a CW signal without noise. (**Left**): time series of the signal before removing any modulation, the signal is modulated in amplitude and frequency. (**Right**): power spectrum after removing the frequency modulations, the five peaks due to the sidereal modulation are clearly visible.

The figure on the left reproduces a signal as it is received at the detector, and it is visibly modulated both in frequency and in amplitude. Even after the removal of the main modulation effects, namely the Doppler and the spin-down of the source, the power spectrum reported on the right side is very different from the one produced by a purely sinusoidal signal. This amplitude modulation is produced by the antenna sidereal response; hence, by the time dependence of $F_{+/\times}$. In the right plot, five peaks are visible, and those are due to the Earth's sidereal modulation. This last effect produces a splitting of the signal power among five frequencies f_0, $f_0 \pm f_\oplus$ and $f_0 \pm 2f_\oplus$, where $f_\oplus$ is the Earth's sidereal frequency. In a more general formalism where a dual-harmonic emission is assumed, the strain at the detector has two components h_{21} and h_{22}, representing the emission at f_{spin} and $2f_{\text{spin}}$, respectively (see, e.g., Equations (1) and (2) in [137]). The two harmonics are typically represented by the two amplitudes C_{21} and C_{22}. Equation (28) is equivalent to the h_{22} component only, i.e., which corresponds to the case of $C_{21} = 0$ and $C_{22} = h_0/2$.

When the signal is buried in the detector data, it is not possible to appreciate the signal morphology by eye since it is several orders of magnitude lower than the typical data strain amplitude. For this reason, effective data analysis methods are needed to extract the signal from the noise. Some of these methods are reported in the following section, while the results will be discussed in Section 4.

3.2. Search Methods

Given the long-lived and weak nature of CW signals, it is intuitive to think that the more data that are used in the analysis, the more signal power is accumulated, thus increasing the signal-to-noise ratio. The optimal search method to look for these signals, provided that the waveform is completely known and under the assumption of gaussian noise, is the matched filtering. Several methods have been developed to look for sources such as know pulsars, where all the parameters of the source are known. Source parameters may be available from EM observations, i.e., the source sky position and its rotational parameters are known. In this case, the so-called "targeted" searches are performed using matched filtering. Several implementations of the matched filtering techniques, also known as coherent searches, exist based on different detection statistics or algorithms: the 5-vector [138,139] method, the F/B/G statistic [140–144] and the time-domain heterodyne-based pipelines (Bayesian and Band-Sampled-Data) [145–147].

In targeted searches, the phase of the CWs is assumed to be locked to the rotational phase of the crust of the star, which is completely defined by its EM observation. When this assumption is relaxed, "narrow-band" searches are performed. This would allow taking into account, e.g., a differential rotation between the rigid crust and superfluid parts of the star. In these searches, a small region around the EM-inferred signal parameters is investigated. In general, a narrow-band search for a given target is less sensitive than its respective targeted case due to the increased trial factor.

As the knowledge about the source parameters decreases, the parameter space to investigate explodes, making the use of fully coherent searches impractical [148]. For this reason, many semi-coherent techniques have been developed [149,150]. In a typical semi-coherent search, chunks of data may be first analyzed coherently (e.g., using a matched-filter) and then combined incoherently (i.e., not considering the phase information). This incoherent combination can be achieved in many different ways, for instance, by summing the detection statistics in each chunk of data analyzed and computing a single final detection statistic (see [12] for a detailed review of wide parameter space searches for CWs). These searches are suitable in the case when no EM counterpart is present, such as all-sky search surveys for NS or DM candidates, or when the true nature of the source is not completely known, for instance, directed searches pointing to interesting sky regions or supernova remnants hosting potential young NS. Semi-coherent methods include the FrequencyHough [151–153], the SkyHough [154–156], the Time-Domain $\mathcal{F}$-statistic [140,157,158], Weave [159], PowerFlux [160,161], and Einstein@Home, based on the global correlation transform method [162–164]. A comparison of methods for the detection of GWs from unknown NSs is given in [165].

Loosely coherent methods, such as the Falcon pipeline [166–168], have been developed to manage the huge computing cost of all-sky searches while keeping the robustness to a wide family of signals, allowing for a loose phase track in the evolution of the signal frequency. A different approach can be used if one wants to go deep with the sensitivity in an all-sky search but keep the focus on a specific narrow frequency band, as described in [169].

Semi-coherent or incoherent methods can be used when no assumption on the source frequency evolution is made or if it is different from the standard Taylor expansion in time such as in Equation (29). These include the hidden Markov model Viterbi tracker [170–172], the Sidereal Filter [173] and cross-correlation based methods such as CrossCorr [174] STAMP [175], SOAP [176] or Radiometer [177]. Some of these methods—CrossCorr method [178], Viterbi/J-statistic method [179], the 5-vector binary method [180] and the method in [81]—have been adapted for the LMXB searches such as Sco-X1, where also the orbital modulation needs to be considered and a stochastic spin wandering, including spin-up, is sometimes taken into account. Methods specifically tailored for all-sky searches for unknown binaries are the BinarySkyHough [181] and TwoSpect [182].

Different flavors of the above-mentioned techniques have been adapted for the case of long-transient CW signals [183–189] and glitching pulsars [190,191], ensemble of pulsars [144,192,193] or DM candidates [194–196]. Furthermore, several methods have been developed for the search of CW signals using machine learning [197–203]. For the latest review on CW methods and searches, see [12,14,16].

In general, all these pipelines produce the so-called search candidates, i.e., potential astrophysical signals that need to be investigated in detail. These candidates undergo a series of post-processing veto steps, and then, the most interesting ones are followed up with different techniques in order to clearly establish their significance, e.g., [203–214]. A fraction of these candidates is vetoed if found near known instrumental artifacts, also known as spectral lines, typically present in the detectors [215]. Multiple approaches exist for this part of the analysis to discard or pass the outliers to the follow-up stage, as described in [12]. Sometimes the assessment of the real origin of an outlier is the most difficult and less automated part of the analysis, but in general, for most of the follow-up techniques, the final goal is to check if the outlier significance follows an expected theoretical trend. This is achieved, for instance, by checking if the outlier signal-to-noise ratio grows as more data are used to analyze that candidate or by increasing the coherence time. Alternative follow-up methods are based on machine learning techniques (see Section 4 in [12]).

If all the outliers are discarded from being real astrophysical signals during the follow-up stage, no CW signal detection can be claimed. In this case, typically upper limits on the signal strain are provided. These values usually span the full frequency range investigated in the search for the case of wide parameter space searches. For a given confidence level, the upper limit curve determines a watershed on the signal amplitude h_0 above which it is possible to exclude the existence of CW signals. These curves are estimated using a tremendous number of simulated signals added to the data or via less computationally expensive methods based on analytically derived or scaling formulas (the most famous being the "sensitivity depth" [212,216], see also [217,218]). In addition to giving an estimate of how deep a given search can look for a CW signal, upper limits are often used to set astrophysical constraints on some related quantities according to the type of search performed. Typical constraints derived from upper limit curves are those on the ellipticity of the spinning NS (or the quadrupole Q_{22}) or the r-mode amplitude α. In searches looking for DM candidates, these limits can be converted to, e.g., a coupling constant, mass exclusion regions, merging rates and abundances.

According to population studies, an order of 10^8–10^9 NSs is expected to exist in our Galaxy [219]. Only a small fraction of the expected population has been detected electromagnetically or has an associated EM counterpart [220]. Among all the ∼3000 sources reported in the Australian Telescope National Facility (ATNF) catalog [221], about 10% are in a binary system. If sources spinning at frequencies above 10 Hz are considered, this fraction increases to ∼50%. Information provided by astronomers is used to constrain the investigated parameter space. In this sense, CW searches have a strong multi-messenger approach. EM information is fundamental for the search of known pulsars, but it provides interesting inputs for the search of new sources, such as supernova remnants potentially hosting an NS, as well as updated information about these sources. In particular, the detection of CWs from a particularly interesting source or sky region (galactic center, globular clusters, etc…) represents a real discovery; given the long-lasting nature of the signal, EM observations following the detection could be carried out for a long time, opening the possibility to, e.g., perform tests of GR and/or to set interesting constraints on the inner composition of the emitting body and on its EOS. On the other hand, the discovery of EM dark sources, including DM candidates, will provide a new tool for the study of a new population of astrophysical sources, as well as contribute to solving many of the open questions about our Universe.

4. Recent Results

Since the beginning of the advanced detector era, the interest with respect to CW sources has increased, as probed by the increasing number of publications on this topic over the years. Boosted by the enhancement of the sensitivity of the detectors as well as the development of data analysis techniques, different and new searches have taken place. I briefly review the most recent search results for CW signatures in advanced detector data from the latest three observing runs [4,5,7]. The first observing run (O1) started on 11 September 2015 and finished on 19 January 2016. The second observing run (O2) lasted from 30 November 2016 to 25 August 2017. During O1, only the two LIGO interferometers were recording data, while during O2, the Advanced Virgo joined the run at the beginning of August 2017. The O3 run started on 1 April 2019, 15:00 UTC and finished on 27 March 2020, 17:00 UTC. In the following, we refer to the period 1 April 2019–1 October 2019 as O3a, while the second part of O3, O3b, starts on 1 November 2019 after a month-long commissioning break. Wherever possible, the latest and most stringent results will be presented at the beginning of each section, while older results will follow.

4.1. Results from Known Sources (Pulsars, LMXBs, Supernova Remnants)

In this section, I review the latest results for searches of CW from known sources or sources with an EM counterpart, such as the central compact objects in supernova remnants.

4.1.1. Known Pulsars

A targeted search is the most sensitive way to look for persistent signals from known pulsars. These searches strongly rely on the EM information available about the source. Indeed, in these searches, the GW phase evolution is completely determined by the EM observations of the rotational parameters of the star. This in principle gives a full picture of the GW emission from the star. A slightly different type of search, known as narrow-band, is sometimes applied if the coupling model between the GW and EM signal phase evolution is relaxed. This allows to assume a more generic scenario, and typically, a small region around the expected GW frequency and spin-down is investigated.

The latest extensive search for CW from known pulsars is reported in [222]. In this work, 236 pulsars have been analyzed, among which the Crab and the Vela pulsars, using LIGO and Virgo O3 data combined with O2 data. Several pulsars glitched during the considered runs and some have sufficient information from EM observations on their orientation to restrict their priors on the ι and ψ parameters. The ephemerides come from the observations from the CHIME, Hobart, Jodrell Bank, MeerKAT, Nancay, NICER and UTMOST observatories. The search was run using three independent pipelines: the time-domain Bayesian method [145,146], the F/G/D-statistic method [88,140,143] and the 5-vector method [138,139]. All the pipelines searched for the standard single harmonic GW emission from the $l = m = 2$ mass quadrupole mode with a frequency at twice the pulsar rotation frequency. In addition, the Bayesian and the F/G/D-statistic pipelines assumed a dual harmonic emission scenario, i.e., the $l = 2; m = 1, 2$ modes with a GW frequency at once and twice the rotation frequency [84,223]. To complete the search, the 5-vector method limited the search to the single harmonic scenario but at the $l = 2; m = 1$ mode only, hence assuming a GW frequency at the star rotation frequency. Furthermore, the D-statistic has been used to test the dipole radiation as predicted by the Brans–Dicke theory [85,88]. No GW detection has been reported, and upper limits on the strain are given in Figure 2. Blue stars indicate the upper limit of a given pulsar, and those with upper limits below the spin-down limit (see Equation (11)) are marked with yellow circles. Grey triangles mark the spin-down limit of each pulsar. The pink curve is a sensitivity estimate for a generic targeted search, and it is given by $\sim 10\sqrt{S_n(f)/T_{\mathrm{obs}}}$, where $S_n(f)$ is the power spectral density.

From Figure 2, it can be seen that 23 out of the 236 pulsars have strain amplitudes lower than the limits calculated from their electromagnetically measured spin-down rates. Among these, 90 millisecond pulsars have a spin-down ratio, i.e., the ratio between the upper limit and the spin-down limit, less than 10. For instance, J0437-4715 and J0711-6830 have spin-down ratios of 0.87 and 0.57, respectively. For the Crab and Vela pulsars, these limits are factors of $\sim$100 and $\sim$20 lower than their spin-down limits, respectively. Nine of these twenty-three pulsars beat their spin-down limits for the first time. The pulsar with the smallest upper limit on h_0 was J1745-0952 with 4.72×10^{-27}. The best Q_{22} upper limit was achieved by J0711-6830 with 4.07×10^{29} kg m^2, equivalent to a limit on the ellipticity of 5.26×10^{-9}. This result is lower than the maximum values predicted for a variety of NS equations of state [63]. Concerning the dual harmonic search, the most constraining upper limit for C_{21} was 7.05×10^{-27} for J2302+4442. The stringent C_{22} upper limit was 2.05×10^{-27} for J1537-5312.

A previous search using O1 plus O2 data on 222 pulsars is given in [224]. In that search, the percentage of GW emission contributing to the spin-down luminosity for Crab and Vela pulsars was less than 0.017% and 0.18%, respectively. Compared to the O2+O3 search [222] described above, these numbers decrease as expected to 0.009% for Crab but increased for Vela up to a maximum of 0.27%. This unexpected result is due to the presence of a significant noise line in the LIGO Hanford detector at twice Vela's rotational frequency during O3. The O1+O2 search in [224] and the O2+O3 search in [222] certainly improve the results of the previous "CW pulsar catalog" for 200 pulsars in O1 data [225].

Tests for non-GR polarizations are also provided for the 23 pulsars beating the spin-down limit in [222], checking for the additional non-negligible scalar radiation originated from the time-dependent dipole moment [88]. No deviation from GR has been reported, and the stringent upper limit for dipole radiation is obtained for the millisecond pulsar J0437-4715. A previous test on GR from known pulsar searches, not assuming any particular alternative theory of gravity, is given in [226] using O1 data.

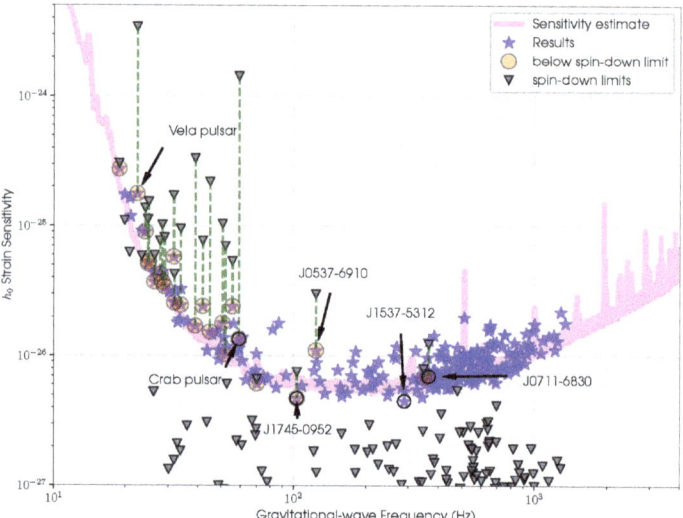

Figure 2. Upper limits on h_0 for the 236 pulsars in the targeted search in [222] are relative to the time-domain Bayesian method. The stars show 95% credible upper limits on the amplitudes of h_0. Grey triangles represent the spin-down limits for each pulsar computed as in Equation (11). Pulsars with upper limits surpassing their spin-down limits are marked with yellow circles. The pink curve gives an estimate of the expected strain sensitivity of all three detectors combined during the course of O3. Figure taken from [222].

A separate dual harmonic search has been performed on the same dataset (O2+O3) for the energetic young pulsar and frequent glitcher PSRJ0537-6910 in [227]. No CW signal has been detected in this search but, for the first time, the spin-down limit for this type of GW emission on this source has been surpassed. Results show that GWs from the $l = m = 2$ mode contribute to less than 14% of the spin-down energy budget. The same target has been investigated by two other searches, tuned for r-modes oscillations, using ephemerides from

NICER [228] in O3 [229] and O1+O2 [230] data. As discussed in Section 2.1, the relation between the gravitational-wave frequency and the star spin frequency in r-mode emission scenarios strongly depends on the NS structure. For this reason, both searches assumed the frequency evolution model proposed in [75]. Searches for the r-mode emission from PSR J0537-6910 are motivated by the fact that this pulsar shows a trend in the inter-glitch behavior that suggests an effective braking index close to $n = 7$ at long times after the glitch [231,232]. A braking index of seven is expected for a spin-down dominated by the r-mode emission. The amplitude's upper limits in the O3 search [229] improve the existing results by a factor of up to three, placing stringent constraints on theoretical models for r-mode-driven spin-down in PSR J0537-6910. Another search for r-mode emissions for the Crab pulsar is reported in [233], providing for the first time upper limits beating the spin-down limit for this source/type of emission in O1 plus O2 data.

Five sources have been the target of a previous single and dual harmonic search for known pulsars [137]. These pulsars have been analyzed in the data from the first two and the first half of the third observing run of advanced detectors (O1+O2+O3a). The targets included three recycled pulsars[4] (J0437-715, J0711-6830, and J0737-3039A) and the two young pulsars Crab and Vela. For Crab, Vela and J0711-6830, a narrow-band search has also been performed using the 5-vector narrow-band method [234,235]. Results from this work constrain the equatorial ellipticities of some of the targets to be less than 10^{-8}, and for the first time, an upper limit below the spin-down limit for a recycled pulsar is reported. This latter aspect is interesting since the evolutionary history of a recycled pulsar is connected to an early accretion phase from a binary companion, very different from the case of young and more slowly spinning pulsars. Another set of seven recycled pulsars is investigated in [236]. The timing information is provided by the Arecibo 327 MHz Drift-Scan Pulsar Survey, and the search is performed on O1+O2+O3a data. All the targets, except for the millisecond pulsar J0154+1833, are in binary systems. The stringent constraint on the ellipticity is 1.5×10^{-8} for PSR J0154+1833.

Data from Fermi-LAT observations have been used in the search for CW from single harmonic emission from PSR J0952-0607 [237] and dual-harmonic emission from PSR J1653-0158 [238], using data from O1 and O2. The results of the search for CW signals from ten sources associated with TeV sources observed by the High Energy Stereoscopic System (H.E.S.S.) are reported in [239]. All the sources are associated with isolated NSs and with estimated distances up to 7 kpc. In particular, two targets are γ-ray pulsars, while eight H.E.S.S. sources are pulsar wind nebulae powered by known pulsars. The ephemerids for each pulsar are provided by the ATNF pulsar catalog. The search is performed using O2 data and tracks, with a hidden Markov model, the three GW frequencies expected to be at 1x, 2x and 4/3x the source spin frequency in a narrow band of 1 Hz around each multiple.

The latest results from the O3 fully coherent narrow-band search can be found in [240]. The search looks for CW from 18 pulsars using the five-vector and F-statistic narrow-band pipelines. For seven of these pulsars, the upper limits are lower than their spin-down limit. These results overcome the corresponding ones from the narrow-band search in O3a [137], improving the upper limits by a factor ~35% for the Crab pulsar, and ~10% for Vela and J0711-6830 pulsars even if the parameter space investigated in this search is 6.5, 1.2 and 7.1 times larger. Results from an additional search for long-duration transient GWs after pulsar glitches are also reported in [240]. Six targets have been investigated by the long-transient search, performed using the transient F-statistic method [185,241]. For these six sources, showing a total of nine glitches, an independent long-transient search is performed after each glitch. None of these targets, neither from the narrow-band or long-transient search, produced an outlier significant enough to be considered as a signal, although two marginal outliers are reported for the last glitch of J0537-6910. The transient F-statistic method has been applied for the search of long-duration transients after glitches in the Vela and Crab pulsars in O2 data [242]. Previous narrow-band searches using O2 and O1 data are given in [243,244].

4.1.2. Supernova Remnants

Another family of interesting targets with EM counterparts, but without precise timing of the rotational parameters, is the supernova remnants. Supernova remnants may host young NSs, which are excellent targets for the search for CWs. Given the lack of information on the spin frequency of the central compact object inside the nebula, directed searches are performed. In these searches, the only information assumed as known is the source sky position, while the remaining parameters $(f, \dot{f}, \ldots)$ are investigated in a wide range. The choice of the parameter space to investigate is only limited by the computing cost of the search, and this may change according to the different algorithms used and to the specific setup chosen. Given an amount of computing power, some regions may have a higher priority over the full GW sensitivity band [245,246]. No CW detection is reported from these sources. In the following, I report the latest search results from these targets.

Searches for supernova remnants in LIGO-Virgo O3a data are reported in [247,248]. To date, the results in [247] are the most stringent for the source targeted: Cassiopeia A (Cas A, G111.7-2.1) and Vela Jr. (G266.2-1.2) supernova remnants. Both sources are extremely young, with inferred lower estimate ages of ∼300 years for Cas A, and ∼700 years for Vela Jr. With these assumptions, these targets have a corresponding indirect age-based limit (see Equation (12)) of ∼1.2×10^{-24} for the central compact object in Cas A, assuming a distance of 3.3 kpc, and 1.4×10^{-23} for Vela Jr. if located at 0.2 kpc. The search is based on the semi-coherent Weave method [159]. No GW signal is detected in the analyzed band, and the best sensitivity to the signal strain amplitude reached in this search is ∼6.3×10^{-26} for Cas A and ∼5.6×10^{-26} for Vela Jr., well below their age-based upper limit. A comparative plot is shown in Figure 3, showing the upper limits provided by the searches in [247–249]. In the search reported in [248], three complementary pipelines have been used: the Band-Sampled-Data directed pipeline, the single harmonic Viterbi and the dual harmonic Viterbi pipelines. Each pipeline used different signal models and methods for the identification of noise artifacts. In particular, the two Viterbi pipelines are robust to sources with spin wandering. This search targets a total of 15 supernova remnants, including Cas A, Vela Jr. and G347.3-0.5. These three targets have also been analyzed in a previous Einstein@Home search [250] using O1 data. The most interesting candidates of this search have been followed up in O2 data, along with new sub-threshold candidates of the same O1 search as reported in [249]. A full deep search for CWs from G347.3-0.5 in the frequency band below 400 Hz in O2 LIGO data is described in [251]. This choice is justified by the existence of a sub-threshold candidate at around 369 Hz that survived the search in [249]. The same candidate has been further investigated with an MCMC method in O2 data [205]. Any significant result has been reported from this search in O2 data, and hence, upper limits are provided, improving those from the same search in O1 data and those from the more robust single harmonic Viterbi tracker in O3a [248].

For the closest target Vela Jr., the best upper limit in [248] is 8.2×10^{-26} for the band-sampled-data pipeline. This result is more constraining than those set by [249,250]; however, it is less stringent than the results in [247] by a factor of 30% (see Figure 3). It should be noted that the searches in [249,250] used O1 and O2 data, while the searches in [247,248] used data from detectors with improved sensitivity (O3a). However, the Einstein@Home O1 searches [249,250] used a coherent integration duration ∼20–150 times longer than the one in the band-sampled-data search in [248], while the Weave search in [247] used a coherence length 10–70 times longer. This guarantees a starting theoretical sensitivity gain of a factor of 2.1–3.5 and 1.7–2.9 for [249,250] and [247], respectively[5]. On the other hand, the use of longer coherence times corresponds to an increase in the computing power needed for the search, as it scales at least as the fourth power of the coherence time. Furthermore, the use of a longer coherence time may negatively impact the robustness of the search. This makes it clear that different approaches are needed when wide parameter space searches are performed, choosing the right balance between computing cost, robustness and sensitivity.

Previous searches for CW from some of the 15 targets investigated in [248] are presented in [252,253] using LIGO O2 data, although using, respectively, a fully coherent method and a less sensitive but model robust Viterbi tracker. A previous fully coherent O1 search is given in [254], also listing among the targets the extrasolar planet candidate Fomalhaut b suggested to be a nearby old NS. The latter is also investigated in [255] using a hidden Markov model Viterbi tracker.

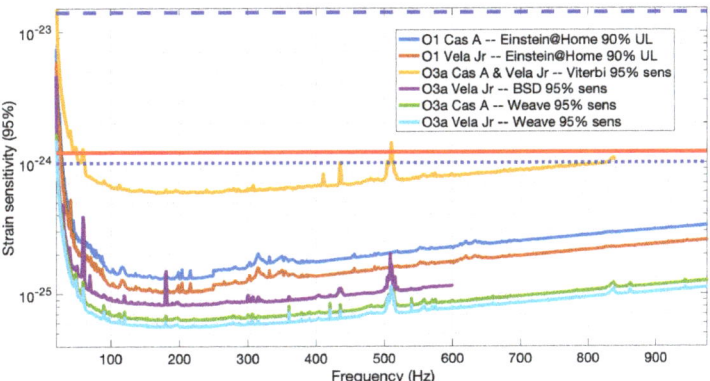

Figure 3. Results taken from the supernova remnant search in LIGO O3a data for Cas A and Vela Jr using Weave [247]. Estimated GW strain amplitude sensitivities are given at the 95% confidence level. Additional results from prior searches for Cas A and Vela Jr. in O1 Einstein@Home 90% C.L. [250] and the O3a model-robust Viterbi method (yellow) and band-sampled-data method (purple) [248]. The solid red horizontal line indicates the age-based upper limit on the Cas A strain amplitude. The dashed (dotted) horizontal blue lines indicate the optimistic (pessimistic) age-based upper limit on Vela Jr. strain amplitude, assuming an age and distance of 700 yr and 0.2 kpc (5100 yr and 1.0 kpc). Figure adapted from [247].

4.1.3. Low-Mass X-ray Binaries and Sco-X1

A significant fraction of observed known NS is in a binary system. Among these, LMXBs are of particular interest for CW searches. Indeed, the presence of a GW torque could explain why the maximum observed spinning frequency 716 Hz for PSR J1748-2446ad is well below the centrifugal breakup frequency, estimated at ∼1400 Hz. These systems are typically formed by an NS (or stellar-mass BH) and a low mass ($\leq 1 M_\odot$) stellar companion. A recent search for CWs from 20 accreting millisecond X-ray pulsars in O3 data is given in [256]. Five of these twenty accreting pulsars have already been analyzed with the same method in O2 data [257]. The search relies on the EM observation of the spin frequencies and orbital parameters of the system, happening during the active outburst phase. The algorithm uses a hidden Markov model (implemented via Viterbi) to track spin wandering [170] and combines its results with the J-statistic to account for the orbital phase modulation [179]. For each target, the search looks for CW signals in sub-bands around $\{1, 4/3, 2\} f_{\rm spin}$. One of the targets, SAX J1808.4-3658, went into outburst during O3a. Given that, according to some models, CWs are only emitted during this outburst phase [258], an opportunistic search for SAX J1808.4-3658 is also provided in [256]. No significant candidates are reported from this search. However, upper limits have been placed on the GW strain amplitude with 95% confidence level. The strictest constraint is 4.7×10^{-26} from IGR J17062-6143. The stringent constraints on the ellipticity for the $f_{\rm gw} = 2 f_{\rm spin}$ case is $\varepsilon^{95\%} = 3.1 \times 10^{-7}$ for the IGR J00291+5934 source. The corresponding upper limit on the r-mode amplitude ($f_{\rm gw} = \frac{4}{3} f_{\rm spin}$) is $\alpha^{95\%} = 1.8 \times 10^{-5}$ for the same source.

To date, several searches have targeted Sco X-1 [259–262] in advanced detector data. The latest results using O3 data are reported in [263]. Sco-X1 is a very interesting candidate for CW searches since it is the brightest extrasolar X-ray source in the sky, which means that it is potentially an optimal source of GWs [264,265]. The system is composed of a 1.4 $M_\odot$ NS and a 0.7 $M_\odot$ companion star [266]. Although being a known source, no EM measurement of the rotation frequency and frequency derivative exists for Sco-X1. In addition to these uncertainties, some of the binary parameters are barely known, making the search for this source very computationally challenging. To date, no CW is reported for this source, while the torque-balance limit (see Equation (13)) has been beaten for the first time in [259], using CrossCorr method [178,267] in O2 data. The best constraints are as low as 7.06×10^{-26}, assuming an NS spin inclination $\iota = 44° \pm 6°$ [266,268]. To date, none of the searches beats the limit if an isotropic prior on ι is made, as reported in Figure 4. A different method has been used in the latest search for Sco-X1 in O3 [263], using a hidden Markov model pipeline implemented with the Viterbi algorithm [179]. This method, although being less sensitive than the cross-correlation search, provides a complementary tool to CrossCorr results. The upper limits from the O3 search are on average $\sim$3 times lower than those from the O2 hidden Markov model search [261] and 13 lower than the same search in O1 data [260]. Previous searches using O1 data and the hidden Markov model and CrossCorr methods are reported in [260,262]. In O3, the lowest $h_0^{95\%}$ for a hidden Markov model tracked signal are $4.56 \times 10^{-26}, 6.16 \times 10^{-26}$, and 9.41×10^{-26} for circular ($\iota = 0°$), electromagnetically restricted ($\iota = 44°$) and unknown polarizations, respectively. Furthermore, for the hidden Markov model search, the torque balance limit is beaten for a fixed ι below 200 Hz and for r_m equal to the NS radius or the Alfven radius [260]. By beating the torque balance limit for r_m at the Alfven radius, it is possible to identify some exclusion region over the mass-radius-magnetic field combination for some equation-of-state models (see [259] for a discussion). Constraints in the mass–radius plane are also possible when r_m equals the NS radius.

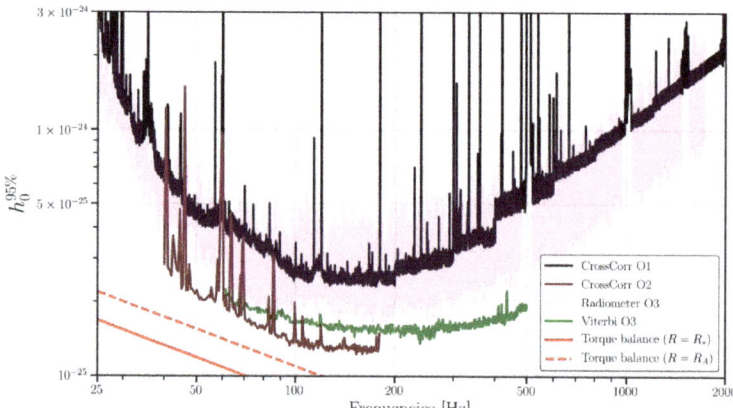

Figure 4. GW strain upper limits at 95% confidence as a function of frequency. No assumption on the ι angle is made for the curves in the figure. The curves are for the CrossCorr O1 search [262] (black line), the CrossCorr O2 search [259] (brown line), the Radiometer O3 search [269] (light pink line), and the O3 hidden Markov model search [263] (green line). The indirect torque-balance upper limits (see Equation (13)), for the $r_m = R$ case (red solid line) and for r_m equal to the Alfven radius (dashed red line), are also plotted. Figure taken from [263].

4.2. Results from Unknown Sources (All-Sky, Spotlight Surveys, Dark Matter Candidates)

In the absence of EM-driven information, wide parameter space searches for unknown sources allow scouring the whole sky in search for EM silent sources. These searches include all-sky surveys for isolated NS and NS in binary systems. It is also usual to look for CWs from a specific and over-populated region in the sky, such as the Galactic Center or some globular clusters. In these cases, sometimes the information provided by EM observations is not enough to shed light on the exact population of the analyzed region, and GWs could help in this direction. Finally, through GWs, we could also look for DM candidates.

4.2.1. All-Sky Surveys

The latest results for all-sky surveys using LIGO-Virgo O3 data are reported in [270] and a summary of the results can be found in Figure 5. Four different analysis methods are used to look for signals from isolated non-axisymmetric NSs: the FrequencyHough [151], Sky-Hough [154], Time-Domain F-statistic [140,157], and SOAP [176], and for the first time, applied in an all-sky CW search. The frequency investigated ranges from 10 to 2048 Hz and from -10^{-8} to 10^{-9} Hz/s for the first frequency derivative[6], each pipeline covers a subset of this parameter space except for the FrequencyHough. The frequency range is wide enough to cover most of the expected sources: young and energetic NS, millisecond pulsars and signals from r-mode oscillations. The search results are generic and are valid for any quasi-monochromatic, persistent signal characterized by the parameters investigated in this search following the linear phase evolution in Equation (29). Constraints on the rate and abundance of inspiraling planetary-mass and asteroid-mass PBHs are also discussed in this search. No GW observation has been reported, and the best constraint on the strain amplitude at the 95% confidence level is $\sim 1.1 \times 10^{-25}$ in the 100–200 Hz frequency range. This is the first all-sky search using Advanced Virgo data.

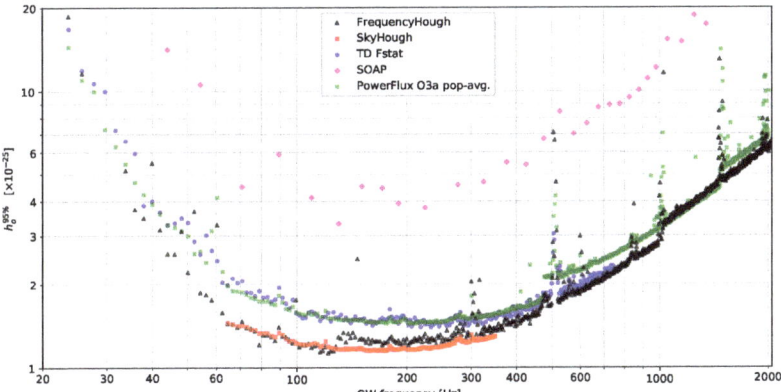

Figure 5. Comparison of 95% confidence upper limits on GW amplitude obtained in the O3 all-sky search by the FrequencyHough pipeline (black triangles), the SkyHough pipeline (red squares), the Time-Domain F-statistic pipeline (blue circles), and the SOAP pipeline (magenta diamonds). Population-averaged upper limits obtained in the Powerflux O3a search are marked with dark-green crosses. Figure taken from [161].

A previous search using the PowerFlux pipeline on O3a data [161] provided an upper limit on the strain, for the most favorable orientation, of 6.3×10^{-26}, improving previous results from O2 data. If compared with the population-averaged upper limit, the lowest 95% C.L. in O3a is 1.4×10^{-25}, less constraining than the full O3 search in [270] (see Figure 5). Results from this search have been used to constrain the rate and abundance of inspiraling PBHs in [271]. To date, only the O2 Falcon search beats the upper limits in [270], although the frequency derivative range is at least 10^3 smaller, making the results in [270], de facto, the most stringent limits for sources with spin-down as low as -1×10^{-8} Hz/s in the 20–2000 Hz frequency range.

Upper limits on the ellipticity are also derived in [270]. The search is able to detect nearby sources, within 100 pc, with ellipticities above 3×10^{-7} emitting at 200 Hz, or even ellipticities as low as $\sim 2 \times 10^{-9}$ for sources spinning at the highest frequencies. For sources located as far as the Galactic Center region (8–10 kpc), the search is able to detect signals with ellipticities bigger than $\sim 3 \times 10^{-6}$ for frequencies above 1500 Hz. Probing very small ellipticities with such a wide parameter space search certainly goes in the right direction for a detection. Indeed, ellipticities below 10^{-7} are in the expected range of sustainable strains in NS crusts [58,60,62–64]. Previous searches performed using O2 data are given in [272–276], and O1 searches can be found in [277–279].

No CW detection is reported from all-sky searches for unknown NSs in binary systems. The latest search, carried out on O3a data [280,281], placed upper limits on the strain at 2.4×10^{-25} for NSs in binary systems spanning orbital periods of 3–45 days. The search, carried out using the BinarySkyHough pipeline in O3a, is the update of the O2 all-sky binary survey presented in [282], reporting an improved result by a factor of 1.6. A good fraction of known NS is in a binary system. Despite this, no other all-sky search, specifically tailored for unknown binaries, has been carried out in advanced detector data. The main reason for this lack is due to the huge computing cost associated with these searches, significantly overcoming the already computationally demanding all-sky searches for isolated NS. However, according to [283], for some combinations of the binary period and semi-major axis parameters, results from wide parameter space searches for unknown isolated sources are also valid for the binary case.

4.2.2. Spotlight Surveys: The Galactic Center and Terzan 5

Directed searches targeting interesting sky regions such as the Galactic Center and the globular cluster Terzan 5 have been carried out in advanced detector data. Indeed, concerning the Galactic Center, a significant population of up to hundreds or even thousands of NSs is expected to exist [284,285]. Moreover, the true composition of this region, showing an extended gamma-ray emission from its center [286–288], is still under debate and could be explained, for instance, by the presence of an unresolved population of millisecond pulsars [289–293]. A recent search for the CW emission from the Galactic center region has been carried out in O3 LIGO and Virgo data [294]. The search uses a semi-coherent method developed in the band-sampled data framework and span a wider parameter space compared to the previous O2 search in [295]. The frequency investigated ranges from 10 Hz to 2000 Hz, while the spin-down/up lies between $[-1.8 \times 10^{-8}; 10^{-10}]$ Hz/s. No CW signal has been detected, and upper limits on the GW amplitude are presented. To date, this search reports the most stringent upper limit for targets located within 30–300 parsecs from the Galactic Center, with a minimum strain of $\sim 7.6 \times 10^{-26}$ at 142 Hz at a 95% confidence level. The same search reports upper limits on the ellipticity and the r-mode amplitude. The same search has been used to identify exclusion regions in the BH/boson cloud mass plane for sources located in the Galactic Center.

A previous search for CW from the Galactic Center and Terzan 5 is reported in [296] using O1 data. The search, based on a loosely coherent method, looks for signals emitting at frequencies in the range [475; 1500] Hz and with frequency time derivatives in the range $[-3.0; 0.1] \times 10^{-8}$ Hz/s. O3 data have already been used to make a lower sensitivity search for an unresolved GW emission from the Galactic Center region using stochastic GW search methods [269].

4.2.3. Dark Matter Candidates—Ultralight Bosons and CDOs

Methods for the search of CW from NSs can be easily adapted to any kind of GW signal with features similar to the standard NS case. An emerging family of searches is the one for DM candidates. This branch of investigations through CW tools is very immature when compared, e.g., with known pulsars searches. Nevertheless, some searches have been carried out in advanced detector data. In Section 2.2, the major DM systems investigated in CW searches have been described: boson clouds around spinning BHs, ultralight vector bosons and CDOs.

The first all-sky survey for persistent, quasi-monochromatic GW signals emitted by ultralight scalar boson clouds around spinning BHs is reported in [297]. The search analyzed the frequency range [20; 610] Hz of the O3 observing run of Advanced LIGO. According to the expected spin wandering signal model from boson clouds, a small range around the $f_{\rm gw}$ parameter has been considered. The main search has been carried out using the method in [194], and the most interesting candidates have been followed up with a FrequencyHough-based method and the Viterbi method. No potential CW candidate remains after the follow-up, and upper limits on the signal strain are provided at the 95% confidence level. The minimum value is 1.04×10^{-25} in the most sensitive frequency region of the detectors ∼130 Hz. These upper limits on the strain can be translated into exclusion regions in the BH-boson cloud mass plane after assuming some parameters of the BH population: the age of the source, its distance and its spin. Along with these exclusion regions, it is possible to derive the maximum distance at which a given BH-boson cloud system, with a certain age, is not emitting CWs, as a function of the boson mass (see Figure 6). In other words, these maximum distances tell us how far we can exclude the presence of an emitting system according to the null detection results obtained by the search. These constraints have been computed by simulating a BH population with masses in the range $[5; 100]$ $M_\odot$ and a uniform spin distribution in the range $[0.2; 0.9]$. The maximum distance corresponds to the distance at which at least 5% of the simulated signal produces a strain amplitude higher than the upper limits of the search, meaning that it would have been detected. The paper in [297] also reports the same figure but for a BH population with maximum masses of 50 $M_\odot$. These constraints strongly depend on the ensemble properties of the simulated BH population. The plot in Figure 6 shows that the presence of systems younger than 10^3 yrs is disfavored within the Galaxy, if formed by bosons with masses above 1.2×10^{-13} eV, for the considered BH mass distribution. Older systems, which produce a smaller strain amplitude, are more difficult to constrain.

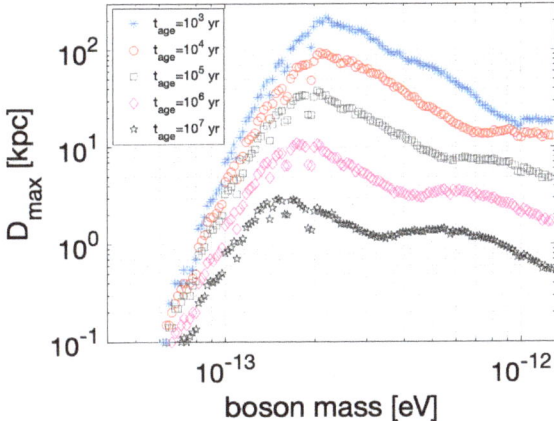

Figure 6. Maximum distance at which at least 5% of a simulated population of BHs-boson cloud would produce a detectable GW signal in the search described in [297]. The simulated population has a maximum BH mass of $100 M_\odot$. The curve is produced for different markers for systems with ages between 10^3 yrs and 10^7 yrs, as indicated in the legend. Figure taken from [297].

The search in [297] is the first of this type, all-sky type and optimized for frequency wandering signals, although it is possible to compute the same exclusion regions of the BH/scalar boson mass parameter space also using upper limits from all-sky searches for spinning NSs as in [100]. A previous directed search for boson clouds from Cygnus X-1 was performed in O2 data in [298] using the same Markov model Viterbi method applied for the follow-up of the all-sky boson cloud O3 search [297].

Another potential candidate for CW signals, in the subset of the ultralight DM particles with masses 10^{-14}–10^{-11} eV/c^2 is a vector boson, the dark photon, which directly couples to GW interferometers (see Section 2.2). The latest O3 LIGO-Virgo data all-sky search for the CW signature from this type of system provided in [123]. The boson mass range probed by this search is $(2-4) \times 10^{-13}$ eV/c^2, corresponding to the detectors frequencies $[10; 2000]$ Hz. The search applies two complementary methods. One pipeline is based on a cross-correlation method [106] and already used in a previous dark photon DM O1 search [117]. The second is a semi-coherent method [196] based on the band-sampled-data framework [147] and adapted from the one used in the latest O3 BH-boson cloud search [194,297]. No evidence of DM signatures has been found, and upper limits on the signal strain are derived. These limits can be converted into upper limits on the coupling factor of the interaction between the dark photon and the baryons in the detector. These constraints surpass the ones provided by existing DM experiments, such as the Eöt–Wash torsion balance [299] and MICROSCOPE [300], and improve previous O1 results by a factor ∼100.

Searches for CW signatures from a pair of CDOs or PBHs far from the coalescence are also possible. The only actual search for systems with a frequency and amplitude evolution described by Equations (25) and (26) has been performed in O1 data [124]. How these CDOs can be formed is still under debate. One option is to assume that these objects can be trapped by normal matter, for instance a planet or even the Sun. Once these objects are formed, binaries can form if orbiting close enough to each other. CDOs emitting GWs from the inspiral phase inside a solar system object should be very dense and in a very close binary orbit. The search in [124] searches for CW signals from CDOs orbiting near the center of the Sun in the GW frequency range 50–550 Hz. No signal is claimed, and upper limits are provided. These limits are converted into upper limits on the mass of CDOs. For almost the full frequency range investigated, these limits are below 10^{-9} $M_\odot$ with a minimum value of 5.8×10^{-10} $M_\odot$ at 525.5 Hz.

Constraints on the rates and abundances of nearby planetary- and asteroid-mass primordial BHs are provided in [270,271]. These constraints are mapped from the upper limits strain results of the O3a Powerflux search and the O3 FrequencyHough search with minimal modeling assumptions on the PBH population. As anticipated in the previous paragraph, the search in [270] targets CW from unknown NS, but the results can be generalized for the case of CDOs or PBHs far from the coalescence as far as they follow a linear frequency evolution. In principle, this search is able to probe GW signals below 250 Hz from inspiralling PBHs binaries with chirp masses smaller than $O(10^{-5})M_\odot$. The constraints obtained from the latest full O3 search in [270] are more stringent than those presented in [271] from the O3a search thanks to the use of a longer observing time. Unfortunately, none of these results are stringent enough to be able to constrain the merging rate of PBHs but will certainly be interesting for future third-generation of detectors [301,302].

5. Conclusions

In recent years, we have witnessed the huge impact that GW science had on our understanding of the Universe. Each detection has provided an interesting tool to test what already is known, but mostly the unknown, about these fascinating compact objects able to emit GWs. The main actors in these scenes have been the well-known merger events, either as a pair of BHs or a system involving at least one NS. We have witnessed the birth of the so-called multi-messenger astronomy, an incredibly powerful way to depict the details of a binary NS merger through EM, neutrino and particle astronomy. However, this is just the beginning, and indeed, the increase in the detectors' sensitivity, expected for the upcoming fourth observing run, along with the improvement of existing pipelines, will certainly bring about the discovery of even more fascinating and unexpected phenomena. In this scenario, CW signals can be the next surprise in GW astronomy. A CW detection from NS could provide evidence for star deformations and shed light on the NS structure and their thermal, spin, and magnetic field evolution. On the other hand, if the CW detection happens to be in the case of a DM candidate such as from a boson cloud around spinning BH, this will lead to the first direct evidence of the existence of DM, solving one of the most intriguing open problems of astrophysics.

Unfortunately, to date, any search has been able to find strong evidence of GW emission from CW sources. However, an increasing number of known pulsars is surpassing their spin-down limit. The lowest constraints on the equatorial ellipticities are very close to realistic expectations for normal EOS. A comment is probably necessary to explain why, even using the most sensitive pipelines for CW searches, any GW has been observed from these sources. It is not unlikely that the assumed models are not well representative of the realistic emission scenario happening for CW, in particular for NS. This is the main reason why, along with improvements in the pipeline's sensitivity, many approaches tend to improve the pipeline's robustness with respect to the model. The final answer to this long-debated issue of the existence (or not) of CW signals is probably just around the corner, and the upcoming O4 run is expected from a wide community of scientists to finally solve this unanswered question. Even if no detection happens during O4, a new generation of detectors—Einstein Telescope, Cosmic Explorer, LISA and more [301–306]—will start their observation in the future, providing even more interesting detection scenarios.

Funding: This work was supported by the L'Oréal-UNESCO fellowship for Women in Science.

Acknowledgments: I thank Cristiano Palomba for the useful suggestion and discussion, improving the first version of this review. I also thank the Continuous Wave working group and the LIGO-Virgo-KAGRA Collaboration for the material used in this review.

Conflicts of Interest: The author declares no conflict of interest.

Notes

1. Given the proportionality between f_{gw} and f_{spin}, here f can indicate any of the two frequencies.
2. for $m = 1$ and for $\alpha \ll 0.1$.
3. Hence, the time derivative of the time component of A_μ is negligible relative to $\vec{A}$.
4. Recycled pulsars are ordinary pulsars that have been spun up by accretion from a companion star in a binary system.
5. The ranges are due to fact that the coherence time used in [248] changes in each 10Hz frequency band.
6. except for the SOAP pipeline that covers the additional small region $[1000; 2048]$ Hz in frequency and $[10^{-9}; 10^{-8}]$ Hz/s in spin-up.

References

1. Aasi, J.; Abbott, B.P.; Abbott, R.; Abbott, T.; Abernathy, M.R.; Ackley, K.; Adams, C.; Adams, T.; Addesso, P.; Adhikari, R.X.; et al. Advanced LIGO. *Class. Quantum Gravity* **2015**, *32*, 074001. [CrossRef]
2. Acernese, F.; Agathos, M.; Agatsuma, K.; Aisa, D.; Allemandou, N.; Allocca, A.; Amarni, J.; Astone, P.; Balestri, G.; Ballardin, G.; et al. Advanced Virgo: A second-generation interferometric gravitational wave detector. *Class. Quantum Gravity* **2014**, *32*, 024001. [CrossRef]
3. Nardecchia, I. Detecting Gravitational Waves with Advanced Virgo. *Galaxies* **2022**, *10*, 28. [CrossRef]
4. Abbott, B.P.; Abbott, R.; Abbott, T.; Abraham, S.; Acernese, F.; Ackley, K.; Adams, C.; Adhikari, R.X.; Adya, V.B.; Affeldt, C.; et al. GWTC-1: A Gravitational-Wave Transient Catalog of Compact Binary Mergers Observed by LIGO and Virgo during the First and Second Observing Runs. *Phys. Rev. X* **2019**, *9*, 031040. [CrossRef]
5. Abbott, R.; Abbott, T.D.; Abraham, S.; Acernese, F.; Ackley, K.; Adams, A.; Adams, C.; Adhikari, R.X.; Adya, V.B.; Affeldt, C.; et al. GWTC-2: Compact Binary Coalescences Observed by LIGO and Virgo during the First Half of the Third Observing Run. *Phys. Rev. X* **2021**, *11*, 021053. [CrossRef]
6. The LIGO Scientific Collaboration; Abbott, R.; Abbott, T.D.; Acernese, F.; Ackley, K.; Adams, C.; Adhikari, N.; Adhikari, R.X.; Adya, V.B.; Affeldt, C.; et al. GWTC-2.1: Deep Extended Catalog of Compact Binary Coalescences Observed by LIGO and Virgo During the First Half of the Third Observing Run. *arXiv* **2021**, arXiv:2108.01045.
7. Abbott, R.; Abbott, T.D.; Acernese, F.; Ackley, K.; Adams, C.; Adhikari, N.; Adhikari, R.X.; Adya, V.B.; Affeldt, C.; Agarwal, D.; et al. GWTC-3: Compact Binary Coalescences Observed by LIGO and Virgo during the Second Part of the Third Observing Run. *arXiv* **2021**, arXiv:2111.03606.
8. Akutsu, T.; Ando, M.; Arai, K.; Arai, Y.; Araki, S.; Araya, A.; Aritomi, N.; Asada, H.; Aso, Y.; Atsuta, S.; et al. KAGRA: 2.5 generation interferometric gravitational wave detector. *Nat. Astron.* **2019**, *3*, 35–40. [CrossRef]
9. Di Giovanni, F.; Sanchis-Gual, N.; Cerdá-Durán, P.; Zilhão, M.; Herdeiro, C.; Font, J.A.; Radu, E. Dynamical bar-mode instability in spinning bosonic stars. *Phys. Rev. D* **2020**, *102*, 124009. [CrossRef]
10. Sanchis-Gual, N.; Di Giovanni, F.; Zilhão, M.; Herdeiro, C.; Cerdá-Durán, P.; Font, J.A.; Radu, E. Nonlinear Dynamics of Spinning Bosonic Stars: Formation and Stability. *Phys. Rev. Lett.* **2019**, *123*, 221101. [CrossRef]
11. DeMarchi, L.; Sanders, J.R.; Levesque, E.M. Prospects for Multimessenger Observations of Thorne-Zytkow Objects. *Astrophys. J.* **2021**, *911*, 101. [CrossRef]
12. Tenorio, R.; Keitel, D.; Sintes, A.M. Search Methods for Continuous Gravitational-Wave Signals from Unknown Sources in the Advanced-Detector Era. *Universe* **2021**, *7*, 474. [CrossRef]

13. Jones, D.I. Learning from the Frequency Content of Continuous Gravitational Wave Signals. *arXiv* **2021**, arXiv:2111.08561.
14. Sieniawska, M.; Bejger, M. Continuous Gravitational Waves from Neutron Stars: Current Status and Prospects. *Universe* **2019**, *5*, 217. [CrossRef]
15. Glampedakis, K.; Gualtieri, L. *Gravitational Waves from Single Neutron Stars: An Advanced Detector Era Survey*; Astrophysics and Space Science Library; Springer: Berlin/Heidelberg, Germany, 2018; pp. 673–736. [CrossRef]
16. Riles, K. Recent searches for continuous gravitational waves. *Mod. Phys. Lett. A* **2017**, *32*, 1730035. [CrossRef]
17. Lasky, P.D. Gravitational Waves from Neutron Stars: A Review. *Publ. Astron. Soc. Aust.* **2015**, *32*, e034. [CrossRef]
18. Bersanetti, D.; Patricelli, B.; Piccinni, O.J.; Piergiovanni, F.; Salemi, F.; Sequino, V. Advanced Virgo: Status of the Detector, Latest Results and Future Prospects. *Universe* **2021**, *7*, 322. [CrossRef]
19. Caudill, S.; Kandhasamy, S.; Lazzaro, C.; Matas, A.; Sieniawska, M.; Stuver, A.L. Gravitational-wave searches in the era of Advanced LIGO and Virgo. *Mod. Phys. Lett. A* **2021**, *36*, 2130022. [CrossRef]
20. Lattimer, J.M.; Prakash, M. The Physics of Neutron Stars. *Science* **2004**, *304*, 536–542. [CrossRef]
21. Haensel, P.; Potekhin, A.Y.; Yakovlev, D.G. *Neutron Stars 1: Equation of State and Structure*; Springer: New York, NY, USA, 2007; Volume 326. [CrossRef]
22. Duncan, R.C.; Thompson, C. Formation of Very Strongly Magnetized Neutron Stars: Implications for Gamma-Ray Bursts. *Astrophys. J. Lett.* **1992**, *392*, L9. [CrossRef]
23. Esposito, P.; Rea, N.; Israel, G.L. Magnetars: A Short Review and Some Sparse Considerations. In *Timing Neutron Stars: Pulsations, Oscillations and Explosions*; Astrophysics and Space Science Library; Springer: Berlin/Heidelberg, Germany, 2020; pp. 97–142. [CrossRef]
24. Haskell, B.; Sedrakian, A. Superfluidity and Superconductivity in Neutron Stars. In *The Physics and Astrophysics of Neutron Stars*; Astrophysics and Space Science Library; Springer: Berlin/Heidelberg, Germany, 2018; pp. 401–454. [CrossRef]
25. Chamel, N. Superfluidity and Superconductivity in Neutron Stars. *J. Astrophys. Astron.* **2017**, *38*, 43. s12036-017-9470-9. [CrossRef]
26. Baym, G.; Hatsuda, T.; Kojo, T.; Powell, P.D.; Song, Y.; Takatsuka, T. From hadrons to quarks in neutron stars: A review. *Rep. Prog. Phys.* **2018**, *81*, 056902. [CrossRef] [PubMed]
27. Oertel, M.; Hempel, M.; Klähn, T.; Typel, S. Equations of state for supernovae and compact stars. *Rev. Mod. Phys.* **2017**, *89*, 015007. [CrossRef]
28. Stone, J.R. Nuclear Physics and Astrophysics Constraints on the High Density Matter Equation of State. *Universe* **2021**, *7*, 257. [CrossRef]
29. Burgio, G.; Schulze, H.J.; Vidaña, I.; Wei, J.B. Neutron stars and the nuclear equation of state. *Prog. Part. Nucl. Phys.* **2021**, *120*, 103879. [CrossRef]
30. Annala, E.; Gorda, T.; Kurkela, A.; Nättilä, J.; Vuorinen, A. Evidence for quark-matter cores in massive neutron stars. *Nat. Phys.* **2020**, *16*, 907–910. [CrossRef]
31. Vidaña, I. Hyperons: The strange ingredients of the nuclear equation of state. *Proc. R. Soc. A Math. Phys. Eng. Sci.* **2018**, *474*, 20180145. [CrossRef]
32. Pethick, C.J.; Schaefer, T.; Schwenk, A. Bose-Einstein condensates in neutron stars. *arXiv* **2015**, arXiv:1507.05839.
33. Baym, G.; Flowers, E. Pion condensation in neutron star matter: Equilibrium conditions and model calculations. *Nucl. Phys. A* **1974**, *222*, 29–64. [CrossRef]
34. Ramos, A.; Schaffner-Bielich, J.; Wambach, J. Kaon Condensation in Neutron Stars. In *Physics of Neutron Star Interiors*; Lecture Notes in Physics; Blaschke, D., Sedrakian, A., Glendenning, N.K., Eds.; Springer: Berlin/Heidelberg, Germany, 2001; Volume 578. [CrossRef]
35. Özel, F.; Freire, P. Masses, Radii, and the Equation of State of Neutron Stars. *Annu. Rev. Astron. Astrophys.* **2016**, *54*, 401–440. [CrossRef]
36. Watts, A.L.; Andersson, N.; Chakrabarty, D.; Feroci, M.; Hebeler, K.; Israel, G.; Lamb, F.K.; Miller, M.C.; Morsink, S.; Özel, F.; et al. Colloquium: Measuring the neutron star equation of state using x-ray timing. *Rev. Mod. Phys.* **2016**, *88*, 021001. [CrossRef]
37. Steiner, A.W.; Lattimer, J.M.; Brown, E.F. The neutron star mass-radius relation and the equation of state of dense matter. *Astrophys. J.* **2013**, *765*, L5. [CrossRef]
38. Lattimer, J.M. Neutron star masses and radii. *AIP Conf. Proc.* **2019**, *2127*, 020001. [CrossRef]
39. Llanes-Estrada, F.J.; Lope-Oter, E. Hadron matter in neutron stars in view of gravitational wave observations. *Prog. Part. Nucl. Phys.* **2019**, *109*, 103715. [CrossRef]
40. Bogdanov, S.; Lamb, F.K.; Mahmoodifar, S.; Miller, M.C.; Morsink, S.M.; Riley, T.E.; Strohmayer, T.E.; Tung, A.K.; Watts, A.L.; Dittmann, A.J.; et al. Constraining the Neutron Star Mass–Radius Relation and Dense Matter Equation of State with NICER. II. Emission from Hot Spots on a Rapidly Rotating Neutron Star. *Astrophys. J.* **2019**, *887*, L26. [CrossRef]
41. Cromartie, H.T.; Fonseca, E.; Ransom, S.M.; Demorest, P.B.; Arzoumanian, Z.; Blumer, H.; Brook, P.R.; DeCesar, M.E.; Dolch, T.; Ellis, J.A.; et al. Relativistic Shapiro delay measurements of an extremely massive millisecond pulsar. *Nat. Astron.* **2019**, *4*, 72–76. [CrossRef]
42. Guillot, S.; Rutledge, R.E. Rejecting proposed dense matter equations of state with Quiescent low-mass X-ray binaries. *Astrophys. J.* **2014**, *796*, L3. [CrossRef]
43. Nattila, J.; Miller, M.C.; Steiner, A.W.; Kajava, J.J.E.; Suleimanov, V.F.; Poutanen, J. Neutron star mass and radius measurements from atmospheric model fits to X-ray burst cooling tail spectra. *Astron. Astrophys.* **2017**, *608*, A31. [CrossRef]

44. Wei, J.B.; Figura, A.; Burgio, G.F.; Chen, H.; Schulze, H.J. Neutron star universal relations with microscopic equations of state. *J. Phys. G Nucl. Part. Phys.* **2019**, *46*, 034001. [CrossRef]
45. Gendreau, K.; Arzoumanian, Z. Searching for a pulse. *Nat. Astron.* **2017**, *1*, 895–895. [CrossRef]
46. Miller, M.C.; Lamb, F.K.; Dittmann, A.J.; Bogdanov, S.; Arzoumanian, Z.; Gendreau, K.C.; Guillot, S.; Harding, A.K.; Ho, W.C.G.; Lattimer, J.M.; et al. PSR J0030+0451 Mass and Radius from NICER Data and Implications for the Properties of Neutron Star Matter. *Astrophys. J.* **2019**, *887*, L24. [CrossRef]
47. Abbott, B.; Abbott, R.; Abbott, T.; Acernese, F.; Ackley, K.; Adams, C.; Adams, T.; Addesso, P.; Adhikari, R.; Adya, V.; et al. GW170817: Observation of Gravitational Waves from a Binary Neutron Star Inspiral. *Phys. Rev. Lett.* **2017**, *119*, 161101. [CrossRef] [PubMed]
48. Abbott, B.P.; Abbott, R.; Abbott, T.D.; Acernese, F.; Ackley, K.; Adams, C.; Adams, T.; Addesso, P.; Adhikari, R.X.; Adya, V.B.; et al. Gravitational Waves and Gamma-Rays from a Binary Neutron Star Merger: GW170817 and GRB 170817A. *Astrophys. J.* **2017**, *848*, L13. [CrossRef]
49. Abbott, B.P.; Abbott, R.; Abbott, T.D.; Acernese, F.; Ackley, K.; Adams, C.; Adams, T.; Addesso, P.; Adhikari, R.X.; Adya, V.B.; et al. Multi-messenger Observations of a Binary Neutron Star Merger. *Astrophys. J.* **2017**, *848*, L12. [CrossRef]
50. Abbott, B.; Abbott, R.; Abbott, T.; Acernese, F.; Ackley, K.; Adams, C.; Adams, T.; Addesso, P.; Adhikari, R.; Adya, V.; et al. GW170817: Measurements of Neutron Star Radii and Equation of State. *Phys. Rev. Lett.* **2018**, *121*, 161101. [CrossRef]
51. Abbott, B.P.; Abbott, R.; Abbott, T.D.; Abraham, S.; Acernese, F.; Ackley, K.; Adams, C.; Adhikari, R.X.; Adya, V.B.; Affeldt, C.; et al. GW190425: Observation of a Compact Binary Coalescence with Total Mass 3.4 $M_\odot$. *Astrophys. J. Lett.* **2020**, *892*, L3. [CrossRef]
52. Abbott, R.; Abbott, T.D.; Abraham, S.; Acernese, F.; Ackley, K.; Adams, C.; Adhikari, R.X.; Adya, V.B.; Affeldt, C.; Agathos, M.; et al. GW190814: Gravitational Waves from the Coalescence of a 23 Solar Mass Black Hole with a 2.6 Solar Mass Compact Object. *Astrophys. J. Lett.* **2020**, *896*, L44. [CrossRef]
53. Abbott, R.; Abbott, T.D.; Abraham, S.; Acernese, F.; Ackley, K.; Adams, A.; Adams, C.; Adhikari, R.X.; Adya, V.B.; Affeldt, C.; et al. Observation of Gravitational Waves from Two Neutron Star–Black Hole Coalescences. *Astrophys. J. Lett.* **2021**, *915*, L5. [CrossRef]
54. Cerda-Duran, P.; Elias-Rosa, N. Neutron Stars Formation and Core Collapse Supernovae. In *The Physics and Astrophysics of Neutron Stars*; Astrophysics and Space Science Library; Springer: Berlin/Heidelberg, Germany, 2018; pp. 1–56. [CrossRef]
55. Baiotti, L.; Rezzolla, L. Binary neutron star mergers: A review of Einstein's richest laboratory. *Rep. Prog. Phys.* **2017**, *80*, 096901. [CrossRef]
56. Haskell, B.; Schwenzer, K. Isolated Neutron Stars. In *Handbook of Gravitational Wave Astronomy*; Bambi, C., Katsanevas, S., Kokkotas, K.D., Eds.; Springer: Singapore, 2021. [CrossRef]
57. Shapiro, S.L.; Teukolsky, S.A. *Black Holes, White Dwarfs, and Neutron Stars: The Physics of Compact Objects*; Wiley: Weinheim, Germany, 1983.
58. Ushomirsky, G.; Cutler, C.; Bildsten, L. Deformations of accreting neutron star crusts and gravitational wave emission. *Mon. Not. R. Astron. Soc.* **2002**, *319*, 902–932. [CrossRef]
59. Owen, B.J. Maximum Elastic Deformations of Compact Stars with Exotic Equations of State. *Phys. Rev. Lett.* **2005**, *95*, 211101. [CrossRef] [PubMed]
60. Johnson-McDaniel, N.K.; Owen, B.J. Maximum elastic deformations of relativistic stars. *Phys. Rev. D* **2013**, *88*, 044004. [CrossRef]
61. Woan, G.; Pitkin, M.D.; Haskell, B.; Jones, D.I.; Lasky, P.D. Evidence for a Minimum Ellipticity in Millisecond Pulsars. *Astrophys. J.* **2018**, *863*, L40. [CrossRef]
62. Gittins, F.; Andersson, N.; Jones, D.I. Modelling neutron star mountains. *Mon. Not. R. Astron. Soc.* **2020**, *500*, 5570–5582. [CrossRef]
63. Gittins, F.; Andersson, N. Modelling neutron star mountains in relativity. *Mon. Not. R. Astron. Soc.* **2021**, *507*, 116–128. [CrossRef]
64. Haskell, B.; Jones, D.I.; Andersson, N. Mountains on Neutron Stars: Accreted versus Non-Accreted Crusts. *Mon. Not. R. Astron. Soc.* **2006**, *373*, 1423–1439. Available online: https://academic.oup.com/mnras/article-pdf/373/4/1423/11177018/mnras0373-1423.pdf (accessed on 2 May 2022). [CrossRef]
65. Horowitz, C.J.; Kadau, K. Breaking Strain of Neutron Star Crust and Gravitational Waves. *Phys. Rev. Lett.* **2009**, *102*, 191102. [CrossRef]
66. Mastrano, A.; Melatos, A.; Reisenegger, A.; Akgün, T. Gravitational Wave Emission from a Magnetically Deformed Non-Barotropic Neutron Star. *Mon. Not. R. Astron. Soc.* **2011**, *417*, 2288–2299. Available online: https://academic.oup.com/mnras/article-pdf/417/3/2288/3826519/mnras0417-2288.pdf (accessed on 2 May 2022). [CrossRef]
67. Suvorov, A.G.; Mastrano, A.; Geppert, U. Gravitational Radiation from Neutron Stars Deformed by Crustal Hall Drift. *Mon. Not. R. Astron. Soc.* **2016**, *459*, 3407–3418. Available online: https://academic.oup.com/mnras/article-pdf/459/3/3407/8110424/stw909.pdf (accessed on 2 May 2022). [CrossRef]
68. Haskell, B.; Samuelsson, L.; Glampedakis, K.; Andersson, N. Modelling Magnetically Deformed Neutron Stars. *Mon. Not. R. Astron. Soc.* **2008**, *385*, 531–542. Available online: https://academic.oup.com/mnras/article-pdf/385/1/531/3465601/mnras0385-0531.pdf (accessed on 2 May 2022). [CrossRef]
69. Owen, B.J.; Lindblom, L.; Cutler, C.; Schutz, B.F.; Vecchio, A.; Andersson, N. Gravitational waves from hot young rapidly rotating neutron stars. *Phys. Rev. D* **1998**, *58*, 084020. [CrossRef]
70. Lindblom, L.; Owen, B.J.; Morsink, S.M. Gravitational Radiation Instability in Hot Young Neutron Stars. *Phys. Rev. Lett.* **1998**, *80*, 4843–4846. [CrossRef]

71. Kokkotas, K.D.; Schwenzer, K. r-mode astronomy. *Eur. Phys. J. A* **2016**, *52*, 38. [CrossRef]
72. Owen, B.J. How to adapt broad-band gravitational-wave searches for r-modes. *Phys. Rev. D* **2010**, *82*, 104002. [CrossRef]
73. Lockitch, K.H.; Friedman, J.L.; Andersson, N. Rotational modes of relativistic stars: Numerical results. *Phys. Rev. D* **2003**, *68*, 124010. [CrossRef]
74. Idrisy, A.; Owen, B.J.; Jones, D.I. R-mode frequencies of slowly rotating relativistic neutron stars with realistic equations of state. *Phys. Rev. D* **2015**, *91*, 024001. [CrossRef]
75. Caride, S.; Inta, R.; Owen, B.J.; Rajbhandari, B. How to search for gravitational waves from r-modes of known pulsars. *Phys. Rev. D* **2019**, *100*, 064013. [CrossRef]
76. Watts, A.L.; Krishnan, B.; Bildsten, L.; Schutz, B.F. Detecting gravitational wave emission from the known accreting neutron stars. *Mon. Not. R. Astron. Soc.* **2008**, *389*, 839–868. [CrossRef]
77. Haskell, B.; Zdunik, J.L.; Fortin, M.; Bejger, M.; Wijnands, R.; Patruno, A. Fundamental physics and the absence of sub-millisecond pulsars. *Astron. Astrophys.* **2018**, *620*, A69. [CrossRef]
78. Gittins, F.; Andersson, N. Population synthesis of accreting neutron stars emitting gravitational waves. *Mon. Not. R. Astron. Soc.* **2019**, *488*, 99–110. [CrossRef]
79. Andersson, N.; Glampedakis, K.; Haskell, B.; Watts, A.L. Modelling the Spin Equilibrium of Neutron Stars in Low-Mass X-ray Binaries without Gravitational Radiation. *Mon. Not. R. Astron. Soc.* **2005**, *361*, 1153–1164. Available online: https://academic.oup.com/mnras/article-pdf/361/4/1153/3885817/361-4-1153.pdf (accessed on 2 May 2022). [CrossRef]
80. Mukherjee, A.; Messenger, C.; Riles, K. Accretion-induced spin-wandering effects on the neutron star in Scorpius X-1: Implications for continuous gravitational wave searches. *Phys. Rev. D* **2018**, *97*, 043016. [CrossRef]
81. Leaci, P.; Astone, P.; D'Antonio, S.; Frasca, S.; Palomba, C.; Piccinni, O.; Mastrogiovanni, S. Novel directed search strategy to detect continuous gravitational waves from neutron stars in low- and high-eccentricity binary systems. *Phys. Rev. D* **2017**, *95*, 122001. [CrossRef]
82. Yim, G.; Jones, D.I. Transient Gravitational Waves from Pulsar Post-Glitch Recoveries. *Mon. Not. R. Astron. Soc.* **2020**, *498*, 3138–3152. Available online: https://academic.oup.com/mnras/article-pdf/498/3/3138/33780576/staa2534.pdf (accessed on 2 May 2022). [CrossRef]
83. Palomba, C. Simulation of a population of isolated neutron stars evolving through the emission of gravitational waves. *Mon. Not. R. Astron. Soc.* **2005**, *359*, 1150–1164. [CrossRef]
84. Jones, D.I. Gravitational wave emission from rotating superfluid neutron stars. *Mon. Not. R. Astron. Soc.* **2010**, *402*, 2503–2519. [CrossRef]
85. Brans, C.; Dicke, R.H. Mach's Principle and a Relativistic Theory of Gravitation. *Phys. Rev.* **1961**, *124*, 925–935. [CrossRef]
86. Isi, M.; Weinstein, A.J.; Mead, C.; Pitkin, M. Detecting beyond-Einstein polarizations of continuous gravitational waves. *Phys. Rev. D* **2015**, *91*, 082002. [CrossRef]
87. Isi, M.; Pitkin, M.; Weinstein, A.J. Probing dynamical gravity with the polarization of continuous gravitational waves. *Phys. Rev. D* **2017**, *96*, 042001. [CrossRef]
88. Verma, P. Probing Gravitational Waves from Pulsars in Brans–Dicke Theory. *Universe* **2021**, *7*, 235. [CrossRef]
89. Schutz, B.F. Networks of gravitational wave detectors and three figures of merit. *Class. Quantum Gravity* **2011**, *28*, 125023. [CrossRef]
90. Wette, K.; Owen, B.J.; Allen, B.; Ashley, M.; Betzwieser, J.; Christensen, N.; Creighton, T.D.; Dergachev, V.; Gholami, I.; Goetz, E.; et al. Searching for gravitational waves from Cassiopeia A with LIGO. *Class. Quantum Gravity* **2008**, *25*, 235011. [CrossRef]
91. Bildsten, L.; Chakrabarty, D.; Chiu, J.; Finger, M.H.; Koh, D.T.; Nelson, R.W.; Prince, T.A.; Rubin, B.C.; Scott, D.M.; Stollberg, M.; et al. Observations of Accreting Pulsars. *Astrophys. J. Suppl. Ser.* **1997**, *113*, 367–408. [CrossRef]
92. Bertone, G.; Hooper, D. History of dark matter. *Rev. Mod. Phys.* **2018**, *90*, 045002. [CrossRef]
93. Bertone, G.; Croon, D.; Amin, M.; Boddy, K.K.; Kavanagh, B.; Mack, K.J.; Natarajan, P.; Opferkuch, T.; Schutz, K.; Takhistov, V.; et al. Gravitational wave probes of dark matter: Challenges and opportunities. *SciPost Phys. Core* **2020**, *3*, 7. [CrossRef]
94. Arvanitaki, A.; Dimopoulos, S.; Dubovsky, S.; Kaloper, N.; March-Russell, J. String axiverse. *Phys. Rev. D* **2010**, *81*, 123530. [CrossRef]
95. Arvanitaki, A.; Dubovsky, S. Exploring the string axiverse with precision black hole physics. *Phys. Rev. D* **2011**, *83*, 044026. [CrossRef]
96. Brito, R.; Cardoso, V.; Pani, P. *Superradiance*; Lecture Notes in Physics; Springer: Berlin/Heidelberg, Germany, 2020. [CrossRef]
97. Peccei, R.D.; Quinn, H.R. CP Conservation in the Presence of Instantons. *Phys. Rev. Lett.* **1977**, *38*, 1440–1443. [CrossRef]
98. Arvanitaki, A.; Baryakhtar, M.; Huang, X. Discovering the QCD axion with black holes and gravitational waves. *Phys. Rev. D* **2015**, *91*, 084011. [CrossRef]
99. Baryakhtar, M.; Galanis, M.; Lasenby, R.; Simon, O. Black hole superradiance of self-interacting scalar fields. *Phys. Rev. D* **2021**, *103*, 095019. [CrossRef]
100. Palomba, C.; D'Antonio, S.; Astone, P.; Frasca, S.; Intini, G.; La Rosa, I.; Leaci, P.; Mastrogiovanni, S.; Miller, A.; Muciaccia, F.; et al. Direct Constraints on the Ultralight Boson Mass from Searches of Continuous Gravitational Waves. *Phys. Rev. Lett.* **2019**, *123*, 171101. [CrossRef] [PubMed]
101. Zhu, S.J.; Baryakhtar, M.; Papa, M.A.; Tsuna, D.; Kawanaka, N.; Eggenstein, H.B. Characterizing the continuous gravitational-wave signal from boson clouds around Galactic isolated black holes. *Phys. Rev. D* **2020**, *102*, 063020. [CrossRef]

102. Cardoso, V.; Pani, P.; Yu, T.T. Superradiance in rotating stars and pulsar-timing constraints on dark photons. *Phys. Rev. D* **2017**, *95*, 124056. [CrossRef]
103. Day, F.V.; McDonald, J.I. Axion superradiance in rotating neutron stars. *J. Cosmol. Astropart. Phys.* **2019**, *2019*, 051. [CrossRef]
104. Graham, M.; Hearty, C.; Williams, M. Searches for dark photons at accelerators. *arXiv* **2021**, arXiv:2104.10280.
105. Fabbrichesi, M.; Gabrielli, E.; Lanfranchi, G. *The Physics of the Dark Photon*; SpringerBriefs in Physics; Springer: Berlin/Heidelberg, Germany, 2021. [CrossRef]
106. Pierce, A.; Riles, K.; Zhao, Y. Searching for Dark Photon Dark Matter with Gravitational-Wave Detectors. *Phys. Rev. Lett.* **2018**, *121*, 061102. [CrossRef]
107. Graham, P.W.; Kaplan, D.E.; Mardon, J.; Rajendran, S.; Terrano, W.A. Dark matter direct detection with accelerometers. *Phys. Rev. D* **2016**, *93*, 075029. [CrossRef]
108. Carney, D.; Hook, A.; Liu, Z.; Taylor, J.M.; Zhao, Y. Ultralight dark matter detection with mechanical quantum sensors. *New J. Phys.* **2021**, *23*, 023041. [CrossRef]
109. Armaleo, J.M.; López Nacir, D.; Urban, F.R. Searching for spin-2 ULDM with gravitational waves interferometers. *J. Cosmol. Astropart. Phys.* **2021**, *2021*, 053. [CrossRef]
110. Raggi, M.; Kozhuharov, V. Results and perspectives in dark photon physics. *Riv. Nuovo Cim.* **2015**, *38*, 449–505. [CrossRef]
111. Co, R.T.; Hall, L.J.; Harigaya, K. QCD Axion Dark Matter with a Small Decay Constant. *Phys. Rev. Lett.* **2018**, *120*, 211602. [CrossRef] [PubMed]
112. Co, R.T.; Pierce, A.; Zhang, Z.; Zhao, Y. Dark photon dark matter produced by axion oscillations. *Phys. Rev. D* **2019**, *99*, 075002. [CrossRef]
113. Guo, H.K.; Ma, Y.; Shu, J.; Xue, X.; Yuan, Q.; Zhao, Y. Detecting dark photon dark matter with Gaia-like astrometry observations. *J. Cosmol. Astropart. Phys.* **2019**, *2019*, 015. [CrossRef]
114. Xue, X.; Xia, Z.Q.; Zhu, X.; Zhao, Y.; Shu, J.; Yuan, Q.; Bhat, N.D.R.; Cameron, A.D.; Dai, S.; Feng, Y.; et al. High-precision search for dark photon dark matter with the Parkes Pulsar Timing Array. *arXiv* **2021**, arXiv:2112.07687.
115. Arvanitaki, A.; Huang, J.; Van Tilburg, K. Searching for dilaton dark matter with atomic clocks. *Phys. Rev. D* **2015**, *91*, 015015. [CrossRef]
116. Morisaki, S.; Fujita, T.; Michimura, Y.; Nakatsuka, H.; Obata, I. Improved sensitivity of interferometric gravitational-wave detectors to ultralight vector dark matter from the finite light-traveling time. *Phys. Rev. D* **2021**, *103*, L051702. [CrossRef]
117. Guo, H.K.; Riles, K.; Yang, F.W.; Zhao, Y. Searching for dark photon dark matter in LIGO O1 data. *Commun. Phys.* **2019**, *2*, 155. [CrossRef]
118. Michimura, Y.; Fujita, T.; Morisaki, S.; Nakatsuka, H.; Obata, I. Ultralight vector dark matter search with auxiliary length channels of gravitational wave detectors. *Phys. Rev. D* **2020**, *102*, 102001. [CrossRef]
119. Vermeulen, S.M.; Relton, P.; Grote, H.; Raymond, V.; Affeldt, C.; Bergamin, F.; Bisht, A.; Brinkmann, M.; Danzmann, K.; Doravari, S.; et al. Direct limits for scalar field dark matter from a gravitational-wave detector. *Nature* **2021**, *600*, 424–428. [CrossRef]
120. Stadnik, Y.V.; Flambaum, V.V. Enhanced effects of variation of the fundamental constants in laser interferometers and application to dark-matter detection. *Phys. Rev. A* **2016**, *93*, 063630. [CrossRef]
121. Stadnik, Y.V.; Flambaum, V.V. Searching for Dark Matter and Variation of Fundamental Constants with Laser and Maser Interferometry. *Phys. Rev. Lett.* **2015**, *114*, 161301. [CrossRef] [PubMed]
122. Grote, H.; Stadnik, Y.V. Novel signatures of dark matter in laser-interferometric gravitational-wave detectors. *Phys. Rev. Res.* **2019**, *1*, 033187. [CrossRef]
123. Abbott, R.; Abbott, T.D.; Acernese, F.; Ackley, K.; Adams, C.; Adhikari, N.; Adhikari, R.X.; Adya, V.B.; Affeldt, C.; Agarwal, D.; et al. Constraints on dark photon dark matter using data from LIGO's and Virgo's third observing run. *arXiv* **2021**, arXiv:2105.13085.
124. Horowitz, C.; Papa, M.; Reddy, S. Search for compact dark matter objects in the solar system with LIGO data. *Phys. Lett. B* **2020**, *800*, 135072. [CrossRef]
125. Horowitz, C.J.; Widmer-Schnidrig, R. Gravimeter Search for Compact Dark Matter Objects Moving in the Earth. *Phys. Rev. Lett.* **2020**, *124*, 051102. [CrossRef]
126. Carr, B.; Kuhnel, F. Primordial Black Holes as Dark Matter Candidates. *arXiv* **2021**, arXiv:2110.02821.
127. Carr, B.; Kohri, K.; Sendouda, Y.; Yokoyama, J. Constraints on primordial black holes. *Rep. Prog. Phys.* **2021**, *84*, 116902. [CrossRef]
128. Green, A.M.; Kavanagh, B.J. Primordial black holes as a dark matter candidate. *J. Phys. G Nucl. Part. Phys.* **2021**, *48*, 043001. [CrossRef]
129. Carr, B.; Kühnel, F. Primordial Black Holes as Dark Matter: Recent Developments. *Annu. Rev. Nucl. Part. Sci.* **2020**, *70*, 355–394. [CrossRef]
130. Kouvaris, C.; Tinyakov, P.; Tytgat, M.H.G. NonPrimordial Solar Mass Black Holes. *Phys. Rev. Lett.* **2018**, *121*, 221102. [CrossRef]
131. Misner, C.W.; Thorne, K.S.; Wheeler, J.A. *Gravitation*; W. H. Freeman: San Francisco, CA, USA, 1973.
132. Maggiore, M. *Gravitational Waves: Volume 1: Theory and Experiments*; Gravitational Waves; OUP Oxford: Oxford, UK, 2008.
133. Creighton, J.; Anderson, W. Gravitational-Wave Physics and Astronomy: An Introduction to Theory, Experiment and Data Analysis. In *Gravitational-Wave Physics and Astronomy: An Introduction to Theory, Experiment and Data Analysis*; Wiley: Hoboken, NJ, USA, 2011. [CrossRef]
134. Peters, P.C. Gravitational Radiation and the Motion of Two Point Masses. *Phys. Rev.* **1964**, *136*, B1224–B1232. [CrossRef]

135. Tiwari, V.; Klimenko, S.; Necula, V.; Mitselmakher, G. Reconstruction of chirp mass in searches for gravitational wave transients. *Class. Quantum Gravity* **2015**, *33*, 01LT01. [CrossRef]
136. Miller, A.L.; Clesse, S.; De Lillo, F.; Bruno, G.; Depasse, A.; Tanasijczuk, A. Probing planetary-mass primordial black holes with continuous gravitational waves. *Phys. Dark Universe* **2021**, *32*, 100836. [CrossRef]
137. Abbott, R.; Abbott, T.D.; Abraham, S.; Acernese, F.; Ackley, K.; Adams, A.; Adams, C.; Adhikari, R.X.; Adya, V.B.; Affeldt, C.; et al. Gravitational-wave Constraints on the Equatorial Ellipticity of Millisecond Pulsars. *Astrophys. J. Lett.* **2020**, *902*, L21. [CrossRef]
138. Astone, P.; D'Antonio, S.; Frasca, S.; Palomba, C. A method for detection of known sources of continuous gravitational wave signals in non-stationary data. *Class. Quantum Gravity* **2010**, *27*, 194016. [CrossRef]
139. Astone, P.; Colla, A.; D'Antonio, S.; Frasca, S.; Palomba, C. Coherent search of continuous gravitational wave signals: Extension of the 5-vectors method to a network of detectors. *J. Phys. Conf. Ser.* **2012**, *363*, 012038. [CrossRef]
140. Jaranowski, P.; Królak, A.; Schutz, B.F. Data analysis of gravitational-wave signals from spinning neutron stars: The signal and its detection. *Phys. Rev. D* **1998**, *58*, 063001. [CrossRef]
141. Prix, R.; Krishnan, B. Targeted search for continuous gravitational waves: Bayesian versus maximum-likelihood statistics. *Class. Quantum Gravity* **2009**, *26*, 204013. [CrossRef]
142. Prix, R. Search for continuous gravitational waves: Metric of the multidetector $\mathcal{F}$-statistic. *Phys. Rev. D* **2007**, *75*, 023004. [CrossRef]
143. Jaranowski, P.; Królak, A. Searching for gravitational waves from known pulsars using the $\mathcal{F}$ and $\mathcal{G}$ statistics. *Class. Quantum Gravity* **2010**, *27*, 194015. [CrossRef]
144. Cutler, C.; Schutz, B.F. Generalized $\mathcal{F}$-statistic: Multiple detectors and multiple gravitational wave pulsars. *Phys. Rev. D* **2005**, *72*, 063006. [CrossRef]
145. Dupuis, R.J.; Woan, G. Bayesian estimation of pulsar parameters from gravitational wave data. *Phys. Rev. D* **2005**, *72*, 102002. [CrossRef]
146. Pitkin, M.; Isi, M.; Veitch, J.; Woan, G. A nested sampling code for targeted searches for continuous gravitational waves from pulsars. *arXiv* **2017**, arXiv:1705.08978.
147. Piccinni, O.J.; Astone, P.; D'Antonio, S.; Frasca, S.; Intini, G.; Leaci, P.; Mastrogiovanni, S.; Miller, A.; Palomba, C.; Singhal, A. A new data analysis framework for the search of continuous gravitational wave signals. *Class. Quantum Gravity* **2018**, *36*, 015008. [CrossRef]
148. Brady, P.R.; Creighton, T.; Cutler, C.; Schutz, B.F. Searching for periodic sources with LIGO. *Phys. Rev. D* **1998**, *57*, 2101–2116. [CrossRef]
149. Brady, P.R.; Creighton, T. Searching for periodic sources with LIGO. II. Hierarchical searches. *Phys. Rev. D* **2000**, *61*, 082001. [CrossRef]
150. Cutler, C.; Gholami, I.; Krishnan, B. Improved stack-slide searches for gravitational-wave pulsars. *Phys. Rev. D* **2005**, *72*, 042004. [CrossRef]
151. Astone, P.; Colla, A.; D'Antonio, S.; Frasca, S.; Palomba, C. Method for all-sky searches of continuous gravitational wave signals using the frequency-Hough transform. *Phys. Rev. D* **2014**, *90*, 042002. [CrossRef]
152. Palomba, C.; Astone, P.; Frasca, S. Adaptive Hough transform for the search of periodic sources. *Class. Quant. Grav.* **2005**, *22*, S1255–S1264. [CrossRef]
153. Antonucci, F.; Astone, P.; D'Antonio, S.; Frasca, S.; Palomba, C. Detection of periodic gravitational wave sources by Hough transform in the f versus $\dot{f}$ plane. *Class. Quantum Gravity* **2008**, *25*, 184015. [CrossRef]
154. Krishnan, B.; Sintes, A.M.; Papa, M.A.; Schutz, B.F.; Frasca, S.; Palomba, C. Hough transform search for continuous gravitational waves. *Phys. Rev. D* **2004**, *70*, 082001. [CrossRef]
155. Sintes, A.M.; Krishnan, B. Improved Hough search for gravitational wave pulsars. *J. Phys. Conf. Ser.* **2006**, *32*, 206–211. [CrossRef]
156. Jordana, L.S.d.l.; Collaboration, t.L.S.C.a. Hierarchical Hough all-sky search for periodic gravitational waves in LIGO S5 data. *J. Phys. Conf. Ser.* **2010**, *228*, 012004. [CrossRef]
157. Aasi, J.; Abbott, B.P.; Abbott, R.; Abbott, T.; Abernathy, M.R.; Accadia, T.; Acernese, F.; Ackley, K.; Adams, C.; Adams, T.; et al. Implementation of an $\mathcal{F}$-statistic all-sky search for continuous gravitational waves in Virgo VSR1 data. *Class. Quantum Gravity* **2014**, *31*, 165014. [CrossRef]
158. Pisarski, A.; Jaranowski, P. Banks of templates for all-sky narrow-band searches of gravitational waves from spinning neutron stars. *Class. Quantum Gravity* **2015**, *32*, 145014. [CrossRef]
159. Wette, K.; Walsh, S.; Prix, R.; Papa, M. Implementing a semicoherent search for continuous gravitational waves using optimally constructed template banks. *Phys. Rev. D* **2018**, *97*, 123016. [CrossRef]
160. Dergachev, V. Description of PowerFlux Algorithms and Implementation. In *LIGO Document T050186*; 2005. Available online: https://dcc.ligo.org/LIGO-T050186/public (accessed on 2 May 2022).
161. Abbott, R.; Abbott, T.; Abraham, S.; Acernese, F.; Ackley, K.; Adams, A.; Adams, C.; Adhikari, R.; Adya, V.; Affeldt, C.; et al. All-sky search for continuous gravitational waves from isolated neutron stars in the early O3 LIGO data. *Phys. Rev. D* **2021**, *104*, 082004. [CrossRef]
162. Pletsch, H.J. Parameter-space correlations of the optimal statistic for continuous gravitational-wave detection. *Phys. Rev. D* **2008**, *78*, 102005. [CrossRef]

163. Pletsch, H.J.; Allen, B. Exploiting Large-Scale Correlations to Detect Continuous Gravitational Waves. *Phys. Rev. Lett.* **2009**, *103*, 181102. [CrossRef]
164. Pletsch, H.J. Parameter-space metric of semicoherent searches for continuous gravitational waves. *Phys. Rev. D* **2010**, *82*, 042002. [CrossRef]
165. Walsh, S.; Pitkin, M.; Oliver, M.; D'Antonio, S.; Dergachev, V.; Krolak, A.; Astone, P.; Bejger, M.; Di Giovanni, M.; Dorosh, O.; et al. Comparison of methods for the detection of gravitational waves from unknown neutron stars. *Phys. Rev. D* **2016**, *94*, 124010,
166. Dergachev, V. On blind searches for noise dominated signals: A loosely coherent approach. *Class. Quantum Gravity* **2010**, *27*, 205017. [CrossRef]
167. Dergachev, V. Loosely coherent searches for sets of well-modeled signals. *Phys. Rev. D* **2012**, *85*, 062003. [CrossRef]
168. Dergachev, V. Loosely coherent searches for medium scale coherence lengths. *arXiv* **2019**, arXiv:1807.02351.
169. Wette, K.; Dunn, L.; Clearwater, P.; Melatos, A. Deep exploration for continuous gravitational waves at 171–172 Hz in LIGO second observing run data. *Phys. Rev. D* **2021**, *103*, 083020. [CrossRef]
170. Suvorova, S.; Sun, L.; Melatos, A.; Moran, W.; Evans, R. Hidden Markov model tracking of continuous gravitational waves from a neutron star with wandering spin. *Phys. Rev. D* **2016**, *93*, 123009. [CrossRef]
171. Sun, L.; Melatos, A.; Lasky, P.D. Tracking continuous gravitational waves from a neutron star at once and twice the spin frequency with a hidden Markov model. *Phys. Rev. D* **2019**, *99*, 123010. [CrossRef]
172. Sun, L.; Melatos, A.; Suvorova, S.; Moran, W.; Evans, R.J. Hidden Markov model tracking of continuous gravitational waves from young supernova remnants. *Phys. Rev. D* **2018**, *97*, 043013. [CrossRef]
173. D'Antonio, S.; Palomba, C.; Frasca, S.; Astone, P.; La Rosa, I.; Leaci, P.; Mastrogiovanni, S.; Piccinni, O.J.; Pierini, L.; Rei, L. Sidereal filtering: A novel robust method to search for continuous gravitational waves. *Phys. Rev. D* **2021**, *103*, 063030. [CrossRef]
174. Romano, J.D.; Cornish, N.J. Detection methods for stochastic gravitational-wave backgrounds: A unified treatment. *Living Rev. Relativ.* **2017**, *20*, 2. [CrossRef]
175. Thrane, E.; Kandhasamy, S.; Ott, C.D.; Anderson, W.G.; Christensen, N.L.; Coughlin, M.W.; Dorsher, S.; Giampanis, S.; Mandic, V.; Mytidis, A.; et al. Long gravitational-wave transients and associated detection strategies for a network of terrestrial interferometers. *Phys. Rev. D* **2011**, *83*, 083004. [CrossRef]
176. Bayley, J.; Messenger, C.; Woan, G. Generalized application of the Viterbi algorithm to searches for continuous gravitational-wave signals. *Phys. Rev. D* **2019**, *100*, 023006. [CrossRef]
177. Mitra, S.; Dhurandhar, S.; Souradeep, T.; Lazzarini, A.; Mandic, V.; Bose, S.; Ballmer, S. Gravitational wave radiometry: Mapping a stochastic gravitational wave background. *Phys. Rev. D* **2008**, *77*, 042002. [CrossRef]
178. Whelan, J.T.; Sundaresan, S.; Zhang, Y.; Peiris, P. Model-based cross-correlation search for gravitational waves from Scorpius X-1. *Phys. Rev. D* **2015**, *91*, 102005. [CrossRef]
179. Suvorova, S.; Clearwater, P.; Melatos, A.; Sun, L.; Moran, W.; Evans, R. Hidden Markov model tracking of continuous gravitational waves from a binary neutron star with wandering spin. II. Binary orbital phase tracking. *Phys. Rev. D* **2017**, *96*, 102006. [CrossRef]
180. Singhal, A.; Leaci, P.; Astone, P.; D'Antonio, S.; Frasca, S.; Intini, G.; Rosa, I.L.; Mastrogiovanni, S.; Miller, A.; Muciaccia, F.; et al. A resampling algorithm to detect continuous gravitational-wave signals from neutron stars in binary systems. *Class. Quantum Gravity* **2019**, *36*, 205015. [CrossRef]
181. Covas, P.; Sintes, A.M. New method to search for continuous gravitational waves from unknown neutron stars in binary systems. *Phys. Rev. D* **2019**, *99*, 124019. [CrossRef]
182. Goetz, E.; Riles, K. An all-sky search algorithm for continuous gravitational waves from spinning neutron stars in binary systems. *Class. Quantum Gravity* **2011**, *28*, 215006. [CrossRef]
183. Oliver, M.; Keitel, D.; Sintes, A.M. Adaptive transient Hough method for long-duration gravitational wave transients. *Phys. Rev. D* **2019**, *99*, 104067. [CrossRef]
184. Miller, A.; Astone, P.; D'Antonio, S.; Frasca, S.; Intini, G.; La Rosa, I.; Leaci, P.; Mastrogiovanni, S.; Muciaccia, F.; Palomba, C.; et al. Method to search for long duration gravitational wave transients from isolated neutron stars using the generalized frequency-Hough transform. *Phys. Rev. D* **2018**, *98*, 102004. [CrossRef]
185. Prix, R.; Giampanis, S.; Messenger, C. Search method for long-duration gravitational-wave transients from neutron stars. *Phys. Rev. D* **2011**, *84*, 023007. [CrossRef]
186. Sun, L.; Melatos, A. Application of hidden Markov model tracking to the search for long-duration transient gravitational waves from the remnant of the binary neutron star merger GW170817. *Phys. Rev. D* **2019**, *99*, 123003. [CrossRef]
187. Banagiri, S.; Sun, L.; Coughlin, M.W.; Melatos, A. Search strategies for long gravitational-wave transients: Hidden Markov model tracking and seedless clustering. *Phys. Rev. D* **2019**, *100*, 024034. [CrossRef]
188. Keitel, D. Robust semicoherent searches for continuous gravitational waves with noise and signal models including hours to days long transients. *Phys. Rev. D* **2016**, *93*, 084024. [CrossRef]
189. Keitel, D.; Ashton, G. Faster search for long gravitational-wave transients: GPU implementation of the transient $\mathcal{F}$-statistic. *Class. Quantum Gravity* **2018**, *35*, 205003. [CrossRef]
190. Ashton, G.; Prix, R.; Jones, D. A semicoherent glitch-robust continuous-gravitational-wave search method. *Phys. Rev. D* **2018**, *98*, 063011. [CrossRef]
191. Ashton, G.; Prix, R.; Jones, D. Statistical characterization of pulsar glitches and their potential impact on searches for continuous gravitational waves. *Phys. Rev. D* **2017**, *96*, 063004. [CrossRef]

192. Pitkin, M.; Messenger, C.; Fan, X. Hierarchical Bayesian method for detecting continuous gravitational waves from an ensemble of pulsars. *Phys. Rev. D* **2018**, *98*, 063001. [CrossRef]
193. Buono, M.; De Rosa, R.; D'Onofrio, L.; Errico, L.; Palomba, C.; Piccinni, O.J.; Sequino, V. A method for detecting continuous gravitational wave signals from an ensemble of known pulsars. *Class. Quantum Gravity* **2021**, *38*, 135021. [CrossRef]
194. D'Antonio, S.; Palomba, C.; Astone, P.; Frasca, S.; Intini, G.; La Rosa, I.; Leaci, P.; Mastrogiovanni, S.; Miller, A.; Muciaccia, F.; et al. Semicoherent analysis method to search for continuous gravitational waves emitted by ultralight boson clouds around spinning black holes. *Phys. Rev. D* **2018**, *98*, 103017. [CrossRef]
195. Isi, M.; Sun, L.; Brito, R.; Melatos, A. Directed searches for gravitational waves from ultralight bosons. *Phys. Rev. D* **2019**, *99*, 084042. [CrossRef]
196. Miller, A.L.; Astone, P.; Bruno, G.; Clesse, S.; D'Antonio, S.; Depasse, A.; De Lillo, F.; Frasca, S.; La Rosa, I.; Leaci, P.; et al. Probing new light gauge bosons with gravitational-wave interferometers using an adapted semicoherent method. *Phys. Rev. D* **2021**, *103*, 103002. [CrossRef]
197. Morawski, F.; Bejger, M.; Ciecielag, P. Convolutional neural network classifier for the output of the time-domain $\mathcal{F}$-statistic all-sky search for continuous gravitational waves. *Mach. Learn. Sci. Technol.* **2020**, *1*, 025016. [CrossRef]
198. Yamamoto, T.S.; Tanaka, T. Use of an excess power method and a convolutional neural network in an all-sky search for continuous gravitational waves. *Phys. Rev. D* **2021**, *103*, 084049. [CrossRef]
199. Miller, A.L.; Astone, P.; D'Antonio, S.; Frasca, S.; Intini, G.; La Rosa, I.; Leaci, P.; Mastrogiovanni, S.; Muciaccia, F.; Mitidis, A.; et al. How effective is machine learning to detect long transient gravitational waves from neutron stars in a real search? *Phys. Rev. D* **2019**, *100*, 062005. [CrossRef]
200. Beheshtipour, B.; Papa, M.A. Deep learning for clustering of continuous gravitational wave candidates. *Phys. Rev. D* **2020**, *101*, 064009. [CrossRef]
201. Dreissigacker, C.; Sharma, R.; Messenger, C.; Zhao, R.; Prix, R. Deep-Learning Continuous Gravitational Waves. *Phys. Rev. D* **2019**, *100*, 044009. [CrossRef]
202. Dreissigacker, C.; Prix, R. Deep-Learning Continuous Gravitational Waves: Multiple detectors and realistic noise. *Phys. Rev. D* **2020**, *102*, 022005. [CrossRef]
203. Bayley, J.; Messenger, C.; Woan, G. Robust machine learning algorithm to search for continuous gravitational waves. *Phys. Rev. D* **2020**, *102*, 083024. [CrossRef]
204. Leaci, P. Methods to filter out spurious disturbances in continuous-wave searches from gravitational-wave detectors. *Phys. Scr.* **2015**, *90*, 125001. [CrossRef]
205. Tenorio, R.; Keitel, D.; Sintes, A.M. Application of a hierarchical MCMC follow-up to Advanced LIGO continuous gravitational-wave candidates. *Phys. Rev. D* **2021**, *104*, 084012. [CrossRef]
206. Tenorio, R.; Keitel, D.; Sintes, A.M. Time-frequency track distance for comparing continuous gravitational wave signals. *Phys. Rev. D* **2021**, *103*, 064053. [CrossRef]
207. Intini, G.; Leaci, P.; Astone, P.; Antonio, S.D.; Frasca, S.; Rosa, I.L.; Miller, A.; Palomba, C.; Piccinni, O. A Doppler-modulation based veto to discard false continuous gravitational-wave candidates. *Class. Quantum Gravity* **2020**, *37*, 225007. [CrossRef]
208. Zhu, S.J.; Papa, M.A.; Walsh, S. New veto for continuous gravitational wave searches. *Phys. Rev. D* **2017**, *96*, 124007. [CrossRef]
209. Keitel, D. Distinguishing transient signals and instrumental disturbances in semi-coherent searches for continuous gravitational waves with line-robust statistics. *J. Phys. Conf. Ser.* **2016**, *716*, 012003. [CrossRef]
210. Ashton, G.; Prix, R. Hierarchical multistage MCMC follow-up of continuous gravitational wave candidates. *Phys. Rev. D* **2018**, *97*, 103020. [CrossRef]
211. Isi, M.; Mastrogiovanni, S.; Pitkin, M.; Piccinni, O.J. Establishing the significance of continuous gravitational-wave detections from known pulsars. *Phys. Rev. D* **2020**, *102*, 123027. [CrossRef]
212. Behnke, B.; Papa, M.A.; Prix, R. Postprocessing methods used in the search for continuous gravitational-wave signals from the Galactic Center. *Phys. Rev. D* **2015**, *91*, 064007. [CrossRef]
213. Keitel, D.; Prix, R.; Papa, M.A.; Leaci, P.; Siddiqi, M. Search for continuous gravitational waves: Improving robustness versus instrumental artifacts. *Phys. Rev. D* **2014**, *89*, 064023. [CrossRef]
214. Tenorio, R.; Modafferi, L.M.; Keitel, D.; Sintes, A.M. Empirically estimating the distribution of the loudest candidate from a gravitational-wave search. *arXiv* **2021**, arXiv:2111.12032.
215. Covas, P.; Effler, A.; Goetz, E.; Meyers, P.; Neunzert, A.; Oliver, M.; Pearlstone, B.; Roma, V.; Schofield, R.; Adya, V.; et al. Identification and mitigation of narrow spectral artifacts that degrade searches for persistent gravitational waves in the first two observing runs of Advanced LIGO. *Phys. Rev. D* **2018**, *97*, 082002. [CrossRef]
216. Dreissigacker, C.; Prix, R.; Wette, K. Fast and accurate sensitivity estimation for continuous-gravitational-wave searches. *Phys. Rev. D* **2018**, *98*, 084058. [CrossRef]
217. Dergachev, V. Novel universal statistic for computing upper limits in an ill-behaved background. *Phys. Rev. D* **2013**, *87*, 062001. [CrossRef]
218. Feldman, G.J.; Cousins, R.D. Unified approach to the classical statistical analysis of small signals. *Phys. Rev. D* **1998**, *57*, 3873–3889. [CrossRef]
219. Treves, A.; Turolla, R.; Zane, S.; Colpi, M. Isolated Neutron Stars: Accretors and Coolers. *Publ. Astron. Soc. Pac.* **2000**, *112*, 297–314. [CrossRef]

220. Rajwade, K.; Chennamangalam, J.; Lorimer, D.; Karastergiou, A. The Galactic halo pulsar population. *Mon. Not. R. Astron. Soc.* **2018**, *479*, 3094–3100. [CrossRef]
221. Manchester, R.N.; Hobbs, G.B.; Teoh, A.; Hobbs, M. The Australia Telescope National Facility Pulsar Catalogue. *Astron. J.* **2005**, *129*, 1993–2006. [CrossRef]
222. Abbott, R.; Abe, H.; Acernese, F.; Ackley, K.; Adhikari, N.; Adhikari, R.X.; Adkins, V.K.; Adya, V.B.; Affeldt, C.; Agarwal, D.; et al. Searches for Gravitational Waves from Known Pulsars at Two Harmonics in the Second and Third LIGO-Virgo Observing Runs. *arXiv* **2021**, arXiv:2111.13106.
223. Pitkin, M.; Gill, C.; Jones, D.I.; Woan, G.; Davies, G.S. First results and future prospects for dual-harmonic searches for gravitational waves from spinning neutron stars. *Mon. Not. R. Astron. Soc.* **2015**, *453*, 4399–4420. [CrossRef]
224. Abbott, B.P.; Abbott, R.; Abbott, T.D.; Abraham, S.; Acernese, F.; Ackley, K.; Adams, C.; Adhikari, R.X.; Adya, V.B.; Affeldt, C.; et al. Searches for Gravitational Waves from Known Pulsars at Two Harmonics in 2015–2017 LIGO Data. *Astrophys. J.* **2019**, *879*, 10. [CrossRef]
225. Abbott, B.P.; Abbott, R.; Abbott, T.D.; Abernathy, M.R.; Acernese, F.; Ackley, K.; Adams, C.; Adams, T.; Addesso, P.; Adhikari, R.X.; et al. First Search for Gravitational Waves from Known Pulsars with Advanced LIGO. *Astrophys. J.* **2017**, *839*, 12. [CrossRef]
226. Abbott, B.P.; et al. First Search for Nontensorial Gravitational Waves from Known Pulsars. *Phys. Rev. Lett.* **2018**, *120*, 031104. [CrossRef] [PubMed]
227. Abbott, R.; Abbott, T.D.; Abraham, S.; Acernese, F.; Ackley, K.; Adams, A.; Adams, C.; Adhikari, R.X.; Adya, V.B.; Affeldt, C.; et al. Diving below the Spin-down Limit: Constraints on Gravitational Waves from the Energetic Young Pulsar PSR J0537-6910. *Astrophys. J. Lett.* **2021**, *913*, L27. [CrossRef]
228. Ho, W.C.G.; Espinoza, C.M.; Arzoumanian, Z.; Enoto, T.; Tamba, T.; Antonopoulou, D.; Bejger, M.; Guillot, S.; Haskell, B.; Ray, P.S. Return of the Big Glitcher: NICER timing and glitches of PSR J0537-6910. *Mon. Not. R. Astron. Soc.* **2020**, *498*, 4605–4614. [CrossRef] [PubMed]
229. Abbott, R.; Abbott, T.D.; Abraham, S.; Acernese, F.; Ackley, K.; Adams, A.; Adams, C.; Adhikari, R.X.; Adya, V.B.; Affeldt, C.; et al. Constraints from LIGO O3 Data on Gravitational-wave Emission Due to R-modes in the Glitching Pulsar PSR J0537–6910. *Astrophys. J.* **2021**, *922*, 71. [CrossRef]
230. Fesik, L.; Papa, M.A. First Search for r-mode Gravitational Waves from PSR J0537-6910. *Astrophys. J.* **2020**, *895*, 11. [CrossRef]
231. Andersson, N.; Antonopoulou, D.; Espinoza, C.M.; Haskell, B.; Ho, W.C.G. The Enigmatic Spin Evolution of PSR J0537–6910: R-modes, Gravitational Waves, and the Case for Continued Timing. *Astrophys. J.* **2018**, *864*, 137. [CrossRef]
232. Antonopoulou, D.; Espinoza, C.M.; Kuiper, L.; Andersson, N. Pulsar spin-down: The glitch-dominated rotation of PSR J0537-6910. *Mon. Not. R. Astron. Soc.* **2017**, *473*, 1644–1655. [CrossRef]
233. Rajbhandari, B.; Owen, B.J.; Caride, S.; Inta, R. First searches for gravitational waves from r-modes of the Crab pulsar. *Phys. Rev. D* **2021**, *104*, 122008. [CrossRef]
234. Mastrogiovanni, S.; Astone, P.; D'Antonio, S.; Frasca, S.; Intini, G.; Leaci, P.; Miller, A.; Palomba, C.; Piccinni, O.J.; Singhal, A. An improved algorithm for narrow-band searches of continuous gravitational waves. *Class. Quantum Gravity* **2017**, *34*, 135007. [CrossRef]
235. Astone, P.; Colla, A.; D'Antonio, S.; Frasca, S.; Palomba, C.; Serafinelli, R. Method for narrow-band search of continuous gravitational wave signals. *Phys. Rev. D* **2014**, *89*, 062008. [CrossRef]
236. Ashok, A.; Beheshtipour, B.; Papa, M.A.; Freire, P.C.C.; Steltner, B.; Machenschalk, B.; Behnke, O.; Allen, B.; Prix, R. New Searches for Continuous Gravitational Waves from Seven Fast Pulsars. *Astrophys. J.* **2021**, *923*, 85. [CrossRef]
237. Nieder, L.; Clark, C.J.; Bassa, C.G.; Wu, J.; Singh, A.; Donner, J.Y.; Allen, B.; Breton, R.P.; Dhillon, V.S.; Eggenstein, H.B.; et al. Detection and Timing of Gamma-Ray Pulsations from the 707 Hz Pulsar J0952-0607. *Astrophys. J.* **2019**, *883*, 42. [CrossRef]
238. Nieder, L.; Clark, C.J.; Kandel, D.; Romani, R.W.; Bassa, C.G.; Allen, B.; Ashok, A.; Cognard, I.; Fehrmann, H.; Freire, P.; et al. Discovery of a Gamma-Ray Black Widow Pulsar by GPU-accelerated Einstein@Home. *Astrophys. J. Lett.* **2020**, *902*, L46. [CrossRef]
239. Beniwal, D.; Clearwater, P.; Dunn, L.; Melatos, A.; Ottaway, D. Search for continuous gravitational waves from ten H.E.S.S. sources using a hidden Markov model. *Phys. Rev. D* **2021**, *103*, 083009. [CrossRef]
240. Abbott, R.; Abbott, T.D.; Acernese, F.; Ackley, K.; Adams, C.; Adhikari, N.; Adhikari, R.X.; Adya, V.B.; Affeldt, C.; Agarwal, D.; et al. Narrowband searches for continuous and long-duration transient gravitational waves from known pulsars in the LIGO-Virgo third observing run. *arXiv* **2021**, arXiv:2112.10990.
241. Modafferi, L.M.; Moragues, J.; Keitel, D.; Collaboration, L.S.; Collaboration, V.; Collaboration, K. Search setup for long-duration transient gravitational waves from glitching pulsars during LIGO-Virgo third observing run. *arXiv* **2022**, arXiv:2201.08785.
242. Keitel, D.; Woan, G.; Pitkin, M.; Schumacher, C.; Pearlstone, B.; Riles, K.; Lyne, A.G.; Palfreyman, J.; Stappers, B.; Weltevrede, P. First search for long-duration transient gravitational waves after glitches in the Vela and Crab pulsars. *Phys. Rev. D* **2019**, *100*, 064058. [CrossRef]
243. Abbott, B.; Abbott, R.; Abbott, T.; Abraham, S.; Acernese, F.; Ackley, K.; Adams, C.; Adhikari, R.; Adya, V.; Affeldt, C.; et al. Narrow-band search for gravitational waves from known pulsars using the second LIGO observing run. *Phys. Rev. D* **2019**, *99*, 122002. [CrossRef]
244. Abbott, B.; Abbott, R.; Abbott, T.; Acernese, F.; Ackley, K.; Adams, C.; Adams, T.; Addesso, P.; Adhikari, R.; Adya, V.; et al. First narrow-band search for continuous gravitational waves from known pulsars in advanced detector data. *Phys. Rev. D* **2017**, *96*, 122006. [CrossRef]

245. Ming, J.; Krishnan, B.; Papa, M.A.; Aulbert, C.; Fehrmann, H. Optimal directed searches for continuous gravitational waves. *Phys. Rev. D* **2016**, *93*, 064011. [CrossRef]
246. Ming, J.; Papa, M.A.; Krishnan, B.; Prix, R.; Beer, C.; Zhu, S.J.; Eggenstein, H.B.; Bock, O.; Machenschalk, B. Optimally setting up directed searches for continuous gravitational waves in Advanced LIGO O1 data. *Phys. Rev. D* **2018**, *97*, 024051. [CrossRef]
247. Abbott, R.; Abbott, T.D.; Acernese, F.; Ackley, K.; Adams, C.; Adhikari, N.; Adhikari, R.X.; Adya, V.B.; Affeldt, C.; Agarwal, D.; et al. Search of the Early O3 LIGO Data for Continuous Gravitational Waves from the Cassiopeia A and Vela Jr. Supernova Remnants. *arXiv* **2021**, arXiv:2111.15116.
248. Abbott, R.; Abbott, T.D.; Abraham, S.; Acernese, F.; Ackley, K.; Adams, A.; Adams, C.; Adhikari, R.X.; Adya, V.B.; Affeldt, C.; et al. Searches for Continuous Gravitational Waves from Young Supernova Remnants in the Early Third Observing Run of Advanced LIGO and Virgo. *Astrophys. J.* **2021**, *921*, 80. [CrossRef]
249. Papa, M.A.; Ming, J.; Gotthelf, E.V.; Allen, B.; Prix, R.; Dergachev, V.; Eggenstein, H.B.; Singh, A.; Zhu, S.J. Search for Continuous Gravitational Waves from the Central Compact Objects in Supernova Remnants Cassiopeia A, Vela Jr., and G347.3–0.5. *Astrophys. J.* **2020**, *897*, 22. [CrossRef]
250. Ming, J.; Papa, M.A.; Singh, A.; Eggenstein, H.B.; Zhu, S.J.; Dergachev, V.; Hu, Y.; Prix, R.; Machenschalk, B.; Beer, C.; et al. Results from an Einstein@Home search for continuous gravitational waves from Cassiopeia A, Vela Jr., and G347.3. *Phys. Rev. D* **2019**, *100*, 024063. [CrossRef]
251. Ming, J.; Papa, M.A.; Eggenstein, H.B.; Machenschalk, B.; Steltner, B.; Prix, R.; Allen, B.; Behnke, O. Results From an Einstein@Home Search for Continuous Gravitational Waves From G347.3 at Low Frequencies in LIGO O2 Data. *Astrophys. J.* **2022**, *925*, 8. [CrossRef]
252. Lindblom, L.; Owen, B.J. Directed searches for continuous gravitational waves from twelve supernova remnants in data from Advanced LIGO's second observing run. *Phys. Rev. D* **2020**, *101*, 083023. [CrossRef]
253. Millhouse, M.; Strang, L.; Melatos, A. Search for gravitational waves from 12 young supernova remnants with a hidden Markov model in Advanced LIGO's second observing run. *Phys. Rev. D* **2020**, *102*, 083025. [CrossRef]
254. Abbott, B.P.; Abbott, R.; Abbott, T.D.; Abraham, S.; Acernese, F.; Ackley, K.; Adams, C.; Adhikari, R.X.; Adya, V.B.; Affeldt, C.; et al. Searches for Continuous Gravitational Waves from 15 Supernova Remnants and Fomalhaut b with Advanced LIGO. *Astrophys. J.* **2019**, *875*, 122. [CrossRef]
255. Jones, D.; Sun, L. Search for continuous gravitational waves from Fomalhaut b in the second Advanced LIGO observing run with a hidden Markov model. *Phys. Rev. D* **2021**, *103*, 023020. [CrossRef]
256. Abbott, R.; Abbott, T.; Acernese, F.; Ackley, K.; Adams, C.; Adhikari, N.; Adhikari, R.; Adya, V.; Affeldt, C.; Agarwal, D.; et al. Search for continuous gravitational waves from 20 accreting millisecond x-ray pulsars in O3 LIGO data. *Phys. Rev. D* **2022**, *105*, 022002. [CrossRef]
257. Middleton, H.; Clearwater, P.; Melatos, A.; Dunn, L. Search for gravitational waves from five low mass x-ray binaries in the second Advanced LIGO observing run with an improved hidden Markov model. *Phys. Rev. D* **2020**, *102*, 023006. [CrossRef]
258. Haskell, B.; Patruno, A. Are Gravitational Waves Spinning Down PSR J1023 + 0038? *Phys. Rev. Lett.* **2017**, *119*, 161103. [CrossRef]
259. Zhang, Y.; Papa, M.A.; Krishnan, B.; Watts, A.L. Search for Continuous Gravitational Waves from Scorpius X-1 in LIGO O2 Data. *Astrophys. J. Lett.* **2021**, *906*, L14. [CrossRef]
260. Abbott, B.; Abbott, R.; Abbott, T.; Acernese, F.; Ackley, K.; Adams, C.; Adams, T.; Addesso, P.; Adhikari, R.; Adya, V.; et al. Search for gravitational waves from Scorpius X-1 in the first Advanced LIGO observing run with a hidden Markov model. *Phys. Rev. D* **2017**, *95*, 122003. [CrossRef]
261. Abbott, B.; Abbott, R.; Abbott, T.; Abraham, S.; Acernese, F.; Ackley, K.; Adams, C.; Adhikari, R.; Adya, V.; Affeldt, C.; et al. Search for gravitational waves from Scorpius X-1 in the second Advanced LIGO observing run with an improved hidden Markov model. *Phys. Rev. D* **2019**, *100*, 122002. [CrossRef]
262. Abbott, B.P.; Abbott, R.; Abbott, T.D.; Acernese, F.; Ackley, K.; Adams, C.; Adams, T.; Addesso, P.; Adhikari, R.X.; Adya, V.B.; et al. Upper Limits on Gravitational Waves from Scorpius X-1 from a Model-based Cross-correlation Search in Advanced LIGO Data. *Astrophys. J.* **2017**, *847*, 47. [CrossRef]
263. Abbott, R.; Abbott, T.D.; Acernese, F.; Ackley, K.; Adams, C.; Adhikari, N.; Adhikari, R.X.; Adya, V.B.; Affeldt, C.; Agarwal, D.; et al. Search for gravitational waves from Scorpius X-1 with a hidden Markov model in O3 LIGO data. *arXiv* **2022**, arXiv:2201.10104.
264. Bildsten, L. Gravitational Radiation and Rotation of Accreting Neutron Stars. *Astrophys. J.* **1998**, *501*, L89–L93. [CrossRef]
265. Wagoner, R.V. Gravitational radiation from accreting neutron stars. *Astrophys. J.* **1984**, *278*, 345–348. [CrossRef]
266. Wang, L.; Steeghs, D.; Galloway, D.K.; Marsh, T.; Casares, J. Precision Ephemerides for Gravitational-wave Searches—III. Revised system parameters for Sco X-1. *Mon. Not. R. Astron. Soc.* **2018**, *478*, 5174–5183. [CrossRef]
267. Meadors, G.D.; Krishnan, B.; Papa, M.A.; Whelan, J.T.; Zhang, Y. Resampling to accelerate cross-correlation searches for continuous gravitational waves from binary systems. *Phys. Rev. D* **2018**, *97*, 044017. [CrossRef]
268. Fomalont, E.B.; Geldzahler, B.J.; Bradshaw, C.F. Scorpius X-1: The Evolution and Nature of the Twin Compact Radio Lobes. *Astrophys. J.* **2001**, *558*, 283–301. [CrossRef]
269. Abbott, R.; Abbott, T.; Abraham, S.; Acernese, F.; Ackley, K.; Adams, A.; Adams, C.; Adhikari, R.; Adya, V.; Affeldt, C.; et al. Search for anisotropic gravitational-wave backgrounds using data from Advanced LIGO and Advanced Virgo's first three observing runs. *Phys. Rev. D* **2021**, *104*, 022005. [CrossRef]

270. Abbott, R.; Abbott, T.D.; Acernese, F.; Ackley, K.; Adams, C.; Adhikari, N.; Adhikari, R.X.; Adya, V.B.; Affeldt, C.; Agarwal, D.; et al. All-sky search for continuous gravitational waves from isolated neutron stars using Advanced LIGO and Advanced Virgo O3 data. *arXiv* **2022**, arXiv:2201.00697.
271. Miller, A.L.; Aggarwal, N.; Clesse, S.; Lillo, F.D. Constraints on planetary and asteroid-mass primordial black holes from continuous gravitational-wave searches. *arXiv* **2021**, arXiv:2110.06188.
272. Dergachev, V.; Papa, M.A. Results from the First All-Sky Search for Continuous Gravitational Waves from Small-Ellipticity Sources. *Phys. Rev. Lett.* **2020**, *125*, 171101. [CrossRef]
273. Dergachev, V.; Papa, M.A. Results from high-frequency all-sky search for continuous gravitational waves from small-ellipticity sources. *Phys. Rev. D* **2021**, *103*, 063019. [CrossRef]
274. Dergachev, V.; Papa, M.A. Search for continuous gravitational waves from small-ellipticity sources at low frequencies. *Phys. Rev. D* **2021**, *104*, 043003. [CrossRef]
275. Steltner, B.; Papa, M.A.; Eggenstein, H.B.; Allen, B.; Dergachev, V.; Prix, R.; Machenschalk, B.; Walsh, S.; Zhu, S.J.; Behnke, O.; et al. Einstein@Home All-sky Search for Continuous Gravitational Waves in LIGO O2 Public Data. *Astrophys. J.* **2021**, *909*, 79. [CrossRef]
276. Abbott, B.; Abbott, R.; Abbott, T.; Abraham, S.; Acernese, F.; Ackley, K.; Adams, C.; Adhikari, R.; Adya, V.; Affeldt, C.; et al. All-sky search for continuous gravitational waves from isolated neutron stars using Advanced LIGO O2 data. *Phys. Rev. D* **2019**, *100*, 024004. [CrossRef]
277. Dergachev, V.; Papa, M.A. Results from an extended Falcon all-sky survey for continuous gravitational waves. *Phys. Rev. D* **2020**, *101*, 022001. [CrossRef]
278. Dergachev, V.; Papa, M.A. Sensitivity Improvements in the Search for Periodic Gravitational Waves Using O1 LIGO Data. *Phys. Rev. Lett.* **2019**, *123*, 101101. [CrossRef]
279. Abbott, B.; Abbott, R.; Abbott, T.; Acernese, F.; Ackley, K.; Adams, C.; Adams, T.; Addesso, P.; Adhikari, R.; Adya, V.; et al. First low-frequency Einstein@Home all-sky search for continuous gravitational waves in Advanced LIGO data. *Phys. Rev. D* **2017**, *96*, 122004. [CrossRef]
280. Abbott, R.; Abbott, T.E.A. All-sky search in early O3 LIGO data for continuous gravitational-wave signals from unknown neutron stars in binary systems. *Phys. Rev. D* **2021**, *103*, 064017. [CrossRef]
281. Tenorio, R.; The LIGO Scientific Collaboration; Virgo Collaboration. An all-sky search in early O3 LIGO data for continuous gravitational-wave signals from unknown neutron stars in binary systems. *arXiv* **2021**, arXiv:2105.07455.
282. Covas, P.; Sintes, A.M. First All-Sky Search for Continuous Gravitational-Wave Signals from Unknown Neutron Stars in Binary Systems Using Advanced LIGO Data. *Phys. Rev. Lett.* **2020**, *124*, 191102. [CrossRef]
283. Singh, A.; Papa, M.A.; Dergachev, V. Characterizing the sensitivity of isolated continuous gravitational wave searches to binary orbits. *Phys. Rev. D* **2019**, *100*, 024058. [CrossRef]
284. Rajwade, K.M.; Lorimer, D.R.; Anderson, L.D. Detecting Pulsars in the Galactic Centre. *Mon. Not. R. Astron. Soc.* **2017**, *471*, 730–739. Available online: https://academic.oup.com/mnras/article-pdf/471/1/730/19376227/stx1661.pdf (accessed on 2 May 2022). [CrossRef]
285. Kim, C.; Davies, M.B. Neutron Stars in the Galactic Center. *J. Korean Astron. Soc.* **2018**, *51*, 165–170. [CrossRef]
286. Ajello, M.; Albert, A.; Atwood, W.B.; Barbiellini, G.; Bastieri, D.; Bechtol, K.; Bellazzini, R.; Bissaldi, E.; Blandford, R.D.; Bloom, E.D.; et al. Fermi-lat observations of high-energy γ-ray emission toward the galactic center. *Astrophys. J.* **2016**, *819*, 44. [CrossRef]
287. Di Mauro, M. Characteristics of the Galactic Center excess measured with 11 years of Fermi -LAT data. *Phys. Rev. D* **2021**, *103*, 063029. [CrossRef]
288. collaboration, H. Acceleration of petaelectronvolt protons in the Galactic Centre. *Nature* **2016**, *531*, 476–479. [CrossRef]
289. Bartels, R.; Krishnamurthy, S.; Weniger, C. Strong Support for the Millisecond Pulsar Origin of the Galactic Center GeV Excess. *Phys. Rev. Lett.* **2016**, *116*, 051102. [CrossRef]
290. Calore, F.; Mauro, M.D.; Donato, F.; Hessels, J.W.T.; Weniger, C. Radio detection prospects for a bulge population of millisecond pulsars as suggested by fermi-lat observations of the inner galaxy. *Astrophys. J.* **2016**, *827*, 143. [CrossRef]
291. Grégoire, T..; Knödlseder, J. Constraining the Galactic millisecond pulsar population using Fermi Large Area Telescope. *Astron. Astrophys.* **2013**, *554*, A62. [CrossRef]
292. Hooper, D.; Linden, T. Millisecond pulsars, TeV halos, and implications for the Galactic Center gamma-ray excess. *Phys. Rev. D* **2018**, *98*, 043005. [CrossRef]
293. Buschmann, M.; Rodd, N.L.; Safdi, B.R.; Chang, L.J.; Mishra-Sharma, S.; Lisanti, M.; Macias, O. Foreground mismodeling and the point source explanation of the Fermi Galactic Center excess. *Phys. Rev. D* **2020**, *102*, 023023. [CrossRef]
294. Abbott, R.; Abbott, T.D.; Acernese, F.; Ackley, K.; Adams, C.; Adhikari, N.; Adhikari, R.X.; Adya, V.B.; Affeldt, C.; Agarwal, D.; et al. Search for continuous gravitational wave emission from the Milky Way center in O3 LIGO–Virgo data. *arXiv* **2022**, arXiv:2204.04523.
295. Piccinni, O.J.; Astone, P.; D'Antonio, S.; Frasca, S.; Intini, G.; La Rosa, I.; Leaci, P.; Mastrogiovanni, S.; Miller, A.; Palomba, C. Directed search for continuous gravitational-wave signals from the Galactic Center in the Advanced LIGO second observing run. *Phys. Rev. D* **2020**, *101*, 082004. [CrossRef]
296. Dergachev, V.; Papa, M.A.; Steltner, B.; Eggenstein, H.B. Loosely coherent search in LIGO O1 data for continuous gravitational waves from Terzan 5 and the Galactic Center. *Phys. Rev. D* **2019**, *99*, 084048. [CrossRef]

297. Abbott, R.; Abbott, T.D.; Acernese, F.; Ackley, K.; Adams, C.; Adhikari, N.; Adhikari, R.X.; Adya, V.B.; Affeldt, C.; Agarwal, D.; et al. All-sky search for gravitational wave emission from scalar boson clouds around spinning black holes in LIGO O3 data. *arXiv* **2021**, arXiv:2111.15507.
298. Sun, L.; Brito, R.; Isi, M. Search for ultralight bosons in Cygnus X-1 with Advanced LIGO. *Phys. Rev. D* **2020**, *101*, 063020. [CrossRef]
299. Schlamminger, S.; Choi, K.Y.; Wagner, T.A.; Gundlach, J.H.; Adelberger, E.G. Test of the Equivalence Principle Using a Rotating Torsion Balance. *Phys. Rev. Lett.* **2008**, *100*, 041101. [CrossRef]
300. Bergé, J.; Brax, P.; Métris, G.; Pernot-Borràs, M.; Touboul, P.; Uzan, J.P. MICROSCOPE Mission: First Constraints on the Violation of the Weak Equivalence Principle by a Light Scalar Dilaton. *Phys. Rev. Lett.* **2018**, *120*, 141101. [CrossRef]
301. Punturo, M.; Abernathy, M.; Acernese, F.; Allen, B.; Andersson, N.; Arun, K.; Barone, F.; Barr, B.; Barsuglia, M.; Beker, M.; et al. The Einstein Telescope: A third-generation gravitational wave observatory. *Class. Quantum Gravity* **2010**, *27*, 194002. [CrossRef]
302. Reitze, D.; Adhikari, R.X.; Ballmer, S.; Barish, B.; Barsotti, L.; Billingsley, G.; Brown, D.A.; Chen, Y.; Coyne, D.; Eisenstein, R.; et al. Cosmic Explorer: The U.S. Contribution to Gravitational-Wave Astronomy beyond LIGO. *arXiv* **2019**, arXiv:1907.04833.
303. Danzmann, K.; The LISA Pathfinder Team.; The eLISA Consortium. LISA and its pathfinder. *Nat. Phys.* **2015**, *11*, 613–615. [CrossRef]
304. Kalogera, V.; Sathyaprakash, B.S.; Bailes, M.; Bizouard, M.A.; Buonanno, A.; Burrows, A.; Colpi, M.; Evans, M.; Fairhurst, S.; Hild, S.; Kasliwal, M.M.; et al. The Next Generation Global Gravitational Wave Observatory: The Science Book. *arXiv* **2021**, arXiv:2111.06990.
305. Kawamura, S.; Ando, M.; Seto, N.; Sato, S.; Musha, M.; Kawano, I.; Yokoyama, J.I.; Tanaka, T.; Ioka, K.; Akutsu, T.; Takashima, T.; et al. Current status of space gravitational wave antenna DECIGO and B-DECIGO. *arXiv* **2020**, arXiv:2006.13545.
306. Luo, J.; Chen, L.S.; Duan, H.Z.; Gong, Y.G.; Hu, S.; Ji, J.; Liu, Q.; Mei, J.; Milyukov, V.; Sazhin, M.; et al. TianQin: A space-borne gravitational wave detector. *Class. Quantum Gravity* **2016**, *33*, 035010. [CrossRef]

Review

Stochastic Gravitational-Wave Backgrounds: Current Detection Efforts and Future Prospects

Arianna I. Renzini [1,2,*], Boris Goncharov [3,4], Alexander C. Jenkins [5,6] and Patrick M. Meyers [7,8,9]

1. LIGO Laboratory, California Institute of Technology, Pasadena, CA 91125, USA
2. Department of Physics, California Institute of Technology, Pasadena, CA 91125, USA
3. Gran Sasso Science Institute (GSSI), I-67100 L'Aquila, Italy; boris.goncharov@gssi.it
4. INFN, Laboratori Nazionali del Gran Sasso, I-67100 Assergi, Italy
5. Department of Physics and Astronomy, University College London, Gower Street, London WC1E 6BT, UK; alex.jenkins@ucl.ac.uk
6. Theoretical Particle Physics and Cosmology Group, Physics Department, King's College London, Strand, London WC2R 2LS, UK
7. Theoretical Astrophysics Group, California Institute of Technology, Pasadena, CA 91125, USA; pmeyers@caltech.edu
8. OzGrav, University of Melbourne, Parkville, VIC 3010, Australia
9. School of Physics, University of Melbourne, Parkville, VIC 3010, Australia
* Correspondence: arenzini@caltech.edu

Citation: Renzini, A.I.; Goncharov, B.; Jenkins, A.C.; Meyers, P.M. Stochastic Gravitational-Wave Backgrounds: Current Detection Efforts and Future Prospects. *Galaxies* **2022**, *10*, 34. https://doi.org/10.3390/galaxies10010034

Academic Editors: Gabriele Vajente, Annalisa Allocca and Yi-Zhong Fan

Received: 16 December 2021
Accepted: 5 February 2022
Published: 14 February 2022

Publisher's Note: MDPI stays neutral with regard to jurisdictional claims in published maps and institutional affiliations.

Copyright: © 2022 by the authors. Licensee MDPI, Basel, Switzerland. This article is an open access article distributed under the terms and conditions of the Creative Commons Attribution (CC BY) license (https://creativecommons.org/licenses/by/4.0/).

Abstract: The collection of individually resolvable gravitational wave (GW) events makes up a tiny fraction of all GW signals that reach our detectors, while most lie below the confusion limit and are undetected. Similarly to voices in a crowded room, the collection of unresolved signals gives rise to a background that is well-described via stochastic variables and, hence, referred to as the stochastic GW background (SGWB). In this review, we provide an overview of stochastic GW signals and characterise them based on features of interest such as generation processes and observational properties. We then review the current detection strategies for stochastic backgrounds, offering a ready-to-use manual for stochastic GW searches in real data. In the process, we distinguish between interferometric measurements of GWs, either by ground-based or space-based laser interferometers, and timing-residuals analyses with pulsar timing arrays (PTAs). These detection methods have been applied to real data both by large GW collaborations and smaller research groups, and the most recent and instructive results are reported here. We close this review with an outlook on future observations with third generation detectors, space-based interferometers, and potential noninterferometric detection methods proposed in the literature.

Keywords: gravitational waves; gravitational-wave backgrounds; stochastic gravitational-wave backgrounds; stochastic searches of gravitational waves; gravitational-wave laser interferometers; pulsar timing arrays

1. Introduction

Gravitational waves (GWs) are perturbations of the spacetime metric caused by extremely energetic events throughout the Universe. Up until now, direct detections of GWs have been coherent measurements of resolved waveforms in detector datastreams which may be traced back to single, point-like sources. These make up a tiny fraction of the gravitational-wave sky: The vast collection of unresolved signals corresponding to multiple point sources or extended sources adds up incoherently, giving rise to gravitational-wave backgrounds (GWBs). A variety of different backgrounds is expected given the range of GW sources in the Universe; however, regardless of their origin, most of these are treated as *stochastic*, as they may be described by a non-deterministic strain signal and are, hence, referred to as stochastic gravitational-wave backgrounds (SGWBs).

Some backgrounds are stochastic by generation processes (e.g., inflationary tensor modes), whereas others are stochastic due to the characteristics or limitations of the specific detector used to observe them (e.g., the cumulative signal from many binary black hole coalescences). An SGWB of this latter nature is by definition at the threshold of detection, making it effectively a detector-dependent observable. Determining whether a signal is a background and also whether it inherently behaves as a stochastic field is then an iterative process, where first all signals present in the detector timestream undergo signal-to-noise ratio (SNR) estimation, which determines their resolvability, and then the background is estimated as the cumulative sum of only the unresolved and/or sub-threshold signals. In practice, each GW detector will be able to access qualitatively different backgrounds, depending on the noise levels and frequency ranges probed.

With this review, we intend to provide a clear and complete yet concise reference for the broader community interested in stochastic search efforts while surveying our field of research. In laying out stochastic background detection techniques, we focus on three categories of detectors: ground-based detector networks, pulsar timing arrays (PTAs) monitored by radio telescopes, and spaceborne detectors comprised of sets of satellites. We do not discuss in detail the impressive work on data acquisition and processing necessary to put the data in the form required for the implementation of the searches we report (see Sections 4 and 5); we refer the reader to several other papers that delineate these efforts (see, e.g., [1–5] for recent discussions of ground-based laser interferometer detector characterization and calibration and [6–8] for reviews of PTA experiments).

We consider the present *second generation* (2G) ground-based detector network to be made up of three detectors that are fully operational: the NSF-funded Laser Interferometer Gravitational-wave Observatory (LIGO) pair of detectors in the United States [9] and the Virgo detector in Italy [10]. To these, we can add the GEO600 [11] detector in Germany, which, however, does not have comparable sensitivity to the others given its smaller size, and the Kamioka Gravitational-wave Detector (KAGRA) in Japan [12], which has not reached initial design sensitivity yet. Future detectors will include the Indian Initiative in Gravitational-wave Observations [13]. Beyond these, we discuss the potential of the upcoming *third generation* (3G) detector network, which will include the Einstein Telescope (ET) [14,15] and Cosmic Explorer (CE) [16–18]. All these monitor frequencies around 10^2 Hz, spanning roughly two orders of magnitude in total, ~ 10–10^3 Hz, depending on specific characteristics.

Regarding nanohertz-frequency stochastic backgrounds, $f \sim 10^{-9}$ Hz, we outline the methodology of pulsar timing array (PTA) experiments and present results from the North American Nanohertz Observatory for Gravitational Waves (NANOGrav [19]), the Parkes Pulsar Timing Array (PPTA [20]), the European Pulsar Timing Array ([EPTA [21,22]), and the consortium of these collaborations known as the International Pulsar Timing Array (IPTA [23,24]), of which the Indian PTA (InPTA [25]) is also now a member. We comment on the common-spectrum noise process reported by the above collaborations that may be related to stochastic GWs or similar noise spectra in timing array pulsars [26]. We describe standard search methods for an isotropic GWB, and we also briefly discuss methods for resolving anisotropies in the GWB. We further comment on the role of future observation efforts such as the Square Kilometer Array (SKA [27]) and the five-hundred-meter aperture spherical radio telescope (FAST [28]).

As for spaceborne interferometers, we primarily discuss the potential detection capabilities of the Laser Interferometer Space Antenna (LISA), which is an ESA-led mission in collaboration with NASA planned to launch in the mid 2030s. LISA will scan a broad range of frequencies, $f \sim 10^{-5}$–10^{-1} Hz, with a maximum sensitivity around a millihertz, allowing us to tune into a new, vast range of the GW sky at unprecedented depth and volume [29].

We will start by introducing the theoretical underpinnings of GWB science in Section 2. In Section 3, we review expected sources of GWBs typically considered in the literature. We outline the different properties of the backgrounds in relation to the detectors that measure

GWs today and those that will probe them in the foreseeable future. We offer a detailed explanation of stochastic search methods in Section 4, differentiating between different observing strategies and detection regimes. In Section 5, we summarise current detection results, reporting the most stringent upper limits yet on SGWBs while highlighting how close we are to detection. Finally, we close this review in Section 6 with an overview of future prospects with the upcoming GW detectors.

2. Theory of Stochastic Backgrounds

In this section, we provide the theoretical foundations of GW science essential to the description of generation and propagation of GWs in the Universe. First, we review the mathematical description of stochastic backgrounds in a common framework, regardless of their astrophysical or cosmological origin, which lies at the basis of (almost) all stochastic search methods reviewed in Section 4. Then, we introduce the fractional energy density of GWs, which is the main observable targeted by stochastic searches.

2.1. Gravitational-Wave Strain and Stokes Parameters

We work in the linearised regime of general relativity, such that the spacetime metric is close to that of flat Minkowski space, with small perturbations that encode GWs, $g_{\mu\nu} = \eta_{\mu\nu} + h_{\mu\nu}$. Neglecting terms of order h^2, the vacuum Einstein field equation can then be written as a wave equation in the De Donder gauge [30],

$$\Box \left(h_{\mu\nu} - \frac{1}{2}\eta_{\mu\nu} h^{\alpha}{}_{\alpha} \right) = 0, \qquad (1)$$

where the box operator is the D'Alembert operator, defined as $\Box = \partial_\mu \partial^\mu$. Solutions to this equation may be constructed as linear superpositions of plane waves,

$$h_{\mu\nu} = A e_{\mu\nu} e^{i(k_\alpha x^\alpha)}, \qquad (2)$$

where $e_{\mu\nu}$ is the normalised polarisation tensor, and k^α is the wave four-vector. By inserting this solution in the equation above, one recovers the dispersion relation $k_\alpha k^\alpha = 0$. This implies that the waves travel at the speed of light in the linearised regime. We may then pick the transverse-traceless (TT) gauge and reduce $h_{\mu\nu}$ to a purely spatial perturbation, h_{ij}, which carries two degrees of freedom or equivalently two independent, spin-2, polarisation states.

Generalising Equation (2) as in [31], for example, the GW strain at time t and position vector x given by an *infinite superposition* of plane waves incoming from all directions on the sky $\hat{n}$,

$$\hat{n} = (\sin\theta\cos\phi, \sin\theta\sin\phi, \cos\theta), \qquad (3)$$

in standard angular coordinates (θ, ϕ) on the 2-sphere may be written as

$$h_{ij}(t, x) = \int_{-\infty}^{+\infty} df \int_{S^2} d\hat{n} \sum_{P=+,\times} h_P(f, \hat{n}) \, \epsilon_{ij}^P(\hat{n}) \, e^{i2\pi f(\hat{n}\cdot x - t)}. \qquad (4)$$

The spatial wave vector is written explicitly as $k = 2\pi f \hat{n}$ (we will use $c = 1$ throughout unless otherwise noted), P labels the polarisation states, and h_P are the respective amplitudes assigned to each state. Choosing the linear polarisation basis $\{+, \times\}$, the orthogonal polarisation base tensors ϵ^P may be written as

$$\epsilon^+ = e_\theta \otimes e_\theta - e_\phi \otimes e_\phi, \qquad (5)$$

$$\epsilon^\times = e_\theta \otimes e_\phi + e_\phi \otimes e_\theta, \qquad (6)$$

with

$$e_\theta = (\cos\theta\cos\phi, \cos\theta\sin\phi, -\sin\theta), \qquad (7)$$
$$e_\phi = (-\sin\phi, \cos\phi, 0), \qquad (8)$$

as defined in [32]. For a stochastic signal, h_P represents a random complex number. Most often, these are assumed to be drawn from a Gaussian probability distribution. This is likely a good approximation for a cosmological GWB, as we will see in Section 3. For a stochastic GWB of astrophysical sources, this assumption may break down but the central limit theorem will guarantee that the statistics approach with respect to a Gaussian random field if the signal is sourced by a sufficiently large number of independent events and that any high signal-to-noise outliers have been subtracted from the detector's timestreams. Under the Gaussian assumption, the statistical properties of the amplitudes are then characterised solely by the second moments of the distribution $\langle h_P(f, \hat{n}) h^\star_{P'}(f', \hat{n}') \rangle$, which, assuming statistical homogeneity, correspond to ensemble averages as [33]

$$\begin{pmatrix} \langle h_+(f,\hat{n}) h^\star_+(f',\hat{n}') \rangle & \langle h_+(f,\hat{n}) h^\star_\times(f',\hat{n}') \rangle \\ \langle h_\times(f,\hat{n}) h^\star_+(f',\hat{n}') \rangle & \langle h_\times(f,\hat{n}) h^\star_\times(f',\hat{n}') \rangle \end{pmatrix} = \delta^{(2)}(n,n')\,\delta(f-f') \times \begin{pmatrix} I(f,\hat{n}) + Q(f,\hat{n}) & U(f,\hat{n}) - iV(f,\hat{n}) \\ U(f,\hat{n}) + iV(f,\hat{n}) & I(f,\hat{n}) - Q(f,\hat{n}) \end{pmatrix}, \qquad (9)$$

where the Stokes parameters I, the intensity, Q and U, giving the linear polarisation, and V, the circular polarisation, have been introduced. The four Stokes parameters completely describe the polarisation of the observed signal in analogy with electromagnetic Stokes parameters for the photon [34]. The difference here is that whilst the electromagnetic Q and U Stokes parameters transform as spin-2 quantities with respect to rotations, their GW strain counterparts transform as spin-4. In both cases, intensity I behaves as a scalar under rotations, while V transforms as a pseudo-scalar. More details on these and their spin-weighted behaviour may be found in [35].

2.2. The Energy Density of Gravitational Waves

The evolution of our Universe is described in terms of its expansion rate, also referred to as the Hubble rate,

$$H(t) \equiv \frac{d}{dt} \ln a, \qquad (10)$$

where $a(t)$ is the cosmological scale factor. Using general relativity, we can write this rate in terms of the different forms of energy density present in the Universe (this is most conveniently performed as a function of redshift z),

$$H(z) = H_0 \left(\Omega_R (1+z)^4 + \Omega_M (1+z)^3 + \Omega_k (1+z)^2 + \Omega_\Lambda \right)^{1/2}, \qquad (11)$$

where $H_0 \approx 70$ km s^{-1} Mpc^{-1} is the Hubble rate today. In Equation (11), $\Omega_i = \rho_i/\rho_c$ are the density parameters of each energy component of the Universe: radiation R, which includes photons and relativistic neutrinos; matter M, which includes baryons and cold dark matter; curvature k; and the cosmological constant Λ. The critical energy density ρ_c is a normalisation that can be interpreted as the energy density required to close our (flat) Universe today, which is explicitly

$$\rho_c = \frac{3H_0^2}{8\pi G}, \qquad (12)$$

where $G = 6.67 \times 10^{-11}$ m^3 kg^{-1} s^{-1} is the universal gravitational constant.

At this stage, one may ask the following: where do GWs fit in? In fact, GWs feature in Equation (11), as a part of the radiation energy density, as they are considered to be carried by massless particles propagating at the speed of light.[1] This allows us to write

$$\Omega_R = \Omega_\gamma + \Omega_\nu + \Omega_{GW} + \cdots, \tag{13}$$

with the terms in the sum representing the energy density in photons, neutrinos, and GWs, respectively. While the present day value of the radiation density is very small ($\Omega_R \sim 10^{-4}$), we see from Equation (11) that at very high redshift, $z \gtrsim \mathcal{O}(10^3)$, it dominated the Universe's expansion. As a result, any additional contributions to the radiation density, including those from primordial GWs, will leave an imprint on cosmological observables generated at these early epochs: principally, the cosmic microwave background (CMB) and the light element abundances predicted by Big Bang nucleosynthesis (BBN) [37]. These imprints are identical for all forms of additional radiation density; thus, by convention they are parameterised in terms of the effective number of neutrino species, N_{eff}. Constraints on N_{eff} can straightforwardly be converted into constraints on GWB energy density. The most up-to-date analysis combines CMB and BBN data with external datasets such as measurements of the baryon acoustic oscillation scale, producing [38]

$$\Omega_{GW} < 1.2 \times 10^{-6} \left(\frac{H_0}{100 \, \text{km} \, \text{s}^{-1} \, \text{Mpc}^{-1}} \right)^{-2}. \tag{14}$$

Given these strong constraints on Ω_{GW}, it is reasonable to consider GWs as perturbations in the Universe, which do not influence the bigger picture but obey the propagation rules, the structure, and the energy content of the Universe that have been set out.

The density parameter appearing in Equation (14) encapsulates the *total* energy density of GWs at all frequencies,[2] as this is what determines the Hubble expansion rate. However, all other searches for gravitational waves focus on particular frequency bands; thus, it is convenient to define the GW energy density frequency spectrum [39],

$$\Omega_{GW}(f) = \frac{1}{\rho_c} \frac{d\rho_{GW}(f)}{d \ln f}; \tag{15}$$

note that the frequency f here is the *measured* frequency, assuming an observer and the intervention of an instrument which mediates the true signal and the measurement. Furthermore, beyond the isotropic value of GWB over the entire sky it is possible to include any anisotropy by adding a directional dependence $\Omega_{GW}(f) \to \Omega_{GW}(f, \hat{n})$ where $\hat{n}$ is the unit vector of a line of sight.

It is now possible to recover the cosmological information contained in the Ω_{GW} parameter, which is effectively the cumulative GW energy history weighted per redshifted frequency bin, as presented in [40]. This may be observed by noting that homogeneity and isotropy throughout the universe imply

$$\rho_{GW} = \int_0^\infty \frac{df}{f} \int_0^\infty dz \frac{N(z)}{1+z} f_r \frac{dE_{GW}}{df_r}, \tag{16}$$

where z is redshift, $N(z)$ is the number of GW emitters as a function of redshift, and f_r is the emission frequency of GWs in the rest frame of the emitter, $f_r = f(1+z)$. dE_{GW}/df_r is then the spectral energy density of the source population. Equation (15) may be rewritten as

$$\rho_{GW} = \int_0^\infty \frac{df}{f} \rho_c \, \Omega_{GW}(f), \tag{17}$$

hence, equating Equations (15) and (16) frequency by frequency yields

$$\Omega_{\rm GW}(f) = \frac{1}{\rho_c} \int_0^\infty dz \, \frac{N(z)}{1+z} \left[f_{\rm r} \frac{dE_{\rm GW}}{df_{\rm r}} \right]_{f_{\rm r}=f(1+z)}. \qquad (18)$$

Equation (18) implies that the fractional energy density of GWs per measured logarithmic frequency intervals at redshift zero, $\Omega_{\rm GW}$, is proportional to the integral over the cosmic history of the comoving number density of the sources multiplied by the emitted energy fraction of each source, in the appropriately redshifted frequency bin. This directly relates $\Omega_{\rm GW}$ to the source event rate as a function of redshift, $N(z)$. In the case of different types of sources, this may be extended to a sum over all contributors,

$$N(z) \left[f_{\rm r} \frac{dE_{\rm GW}}{df_{\rm r}} \right]_{f_{\rm r}=f(1+z)} \longrightarrow \sum_i N_i(z) \left[f_{\rm r} \frac{dE_{\rm GW,i}}{df_{\rm r}} \right]_{f_{\rm r}=f(1+z)}. \qquad (19)$$

$\Omega_{\rm GW}(f)$ may also be re-written in terms of the intensity parameter I defined in Equation (9) [32].

$$\Omega_{\rm GW}(f) = \frac{4\pi^2 f^3}{\rho_c G} I(f). \qquad (20)$$

We can derive this relationship using the Isaacson formula for the energy density of the GWB [41,42],

$$\rho_{\rm GW} = \frac{1}{32\pi G} \langle \dot{h}_{ij} \dot{h}_{ij} \rangle, \qquad (21)$$

where the angle brackets indicate an average over many wavelengths. Inserting the plane-wave decomposition in Equation (4) and rewriting the two-point statistics of each plane wave in terms of the Stokes parameters in Equation (9), we obtain

$$\rho_{\rm GW} = \frac{\pi}{2G} \int_0^\infty df \int_{S^2} d\hat{n} \, f^2 I(f, \hat{n}). \qquad (22)$$

Note that we have assumed ergodicity here such that the spatial average in Equation (21) is equivalent to the ensemble average in Equation (9). If we treat intensity as isotropic, $I(f, \hat{n}) \to I(f)$, then we immediately recover Equation (20). This fundamental relation allows us to connect GWB observations to cosmological implications of the background and may easily be extended to a directional statement as

$$\Omega_{\rm GW}(f, \hat{n}) = \frac{4\pi^2 f^3}{\rho_c G} I(f, \hat{n}). \qquad (23)$$

Note that this implies

$$\Omega_{\rm GW}(f) = \frac{1}{4\pi} \int_{S^2} d\hat{n} \, \Omega_{\rm GW}(f, \hat{n}), \qquad (24)$$

however, one must take care of factors of 4π as other conventions are sometimes used. Note that we are using the conventions as in [32], where all power spectra are one-sided.

As for the other Stokes' parameters, these do not contribute to $\Omega_{\rm GW}$ and are equal to zero in the case of an unpolarised background. This may be easily gleaned by their definitions, in Equation (9), as the second moments of the h_+ and $h_\times$ fields should be equal and the expectation value of any cross correlations between the two should vanish. $\Omega_{\rm GW}$, thus, inherits the spectral properties from the GWB intensity as per Equation (20). As will emerge in the following sections, the spectral dependence is often reduced to a power law, in which case it is common practice to write[3]

$$\Omega_{\rm GW}(f) = \Omega_{\rm GW}(f_{\rm ref}) \left(\frac{f}{f_{\rm ref}} \right)^\alpha, \qquad (25)$$

where α is the spectral index of the signal, and f_{ref} is a reference frequency. This assumption is often extended to be valid in each direction independently, such that the spectral and directional dependence of the GW signal factor out as

$$I(f, \hat{n}) = I(f_{\text{ref}}, \hat{n}) \left(\frac{f}{f_{\text{ref}}} \right)^{\alpha - 3}. \qquad (26)$$

This is particularly useful when performing multiparameter estimations such as mapmaking as it allows one to integrate out the spectral dependence of the reconstructed signal and solve for an intensity sky map. Note that in the ensemble, averaging is required to recover the Stokes' parameters, and all temporal phase information in the GWs is discarded; as argued in [43], no physical information may be recovered from the coherent phase component.

3. Sources of Stochastic Backgrounds

GWBs fall broadly into two distinct categories based on the underlying generation mechanism. The first is a superposition of signals of astrophysical origin, galactic and/or extra-galactic, that are not individually detected or resolved. This type of background will, thus, be unresolved and incoherent in that the temporal phase of the signal is expected to be random and is expected to be stochastic in the limit where the number of sources is very large. The second category is cosmological or primordial backgrounds. These include GWBs generated by the evolution of vacuum fluctuations during an inflationary epoch that end up as superhorizon tensor modes at the end of inflation [44,45]. It also includes GWBs generated by nonlinear phenomena at early times such as phase transitions or via emission by topological defects [46–48]. For the most part, primordial backgrounds are formed via stochastic processes, resulting in stochastic signals; on top of this, propagation effects contribute to isotropising a primordial signal, in most cases erasing any initial anisotropies [49,50]. In particular, stochasticity here implies no initial information is retained by the temporal phase of the background [51]. Cosmological GWBs can also be stochastic due to many overlapping signals, for example, in the case of cosmic strings. Assuming that the orientation of individual astrophysical sources is random on the sky, these are in general expected to be unpolarised, as an equal distribution in the polarisation modes will cancel out any local asymmetry. Primordial signals are also mostly assumed to be unpolarised, as the underlying stochastic process is not expected to select a preferential frame, with some exceptions as we explain below. What then characterises backgrounds of different origin is the spectral dependence of the source energy density in Equation (18): the power spectrum of the signal depends on the specific GW emission mechanism, which is imprinted in the measured strain. Note that this measurement includes non-negligible selection effects, as *qualitatively* different backgrounds contribute from different redshift shells and from different directions.

In this section, we review both astrophysical and cosmological GWBs, providing the necessary background for the targeted searches discussed in Section 5. We also comment on the *observational properties* of the signal which are essential to understand when building an optimal search method. The various sources are also summarised in Figure 1, which includes the sensitivity of several GW detection efforts for reference.

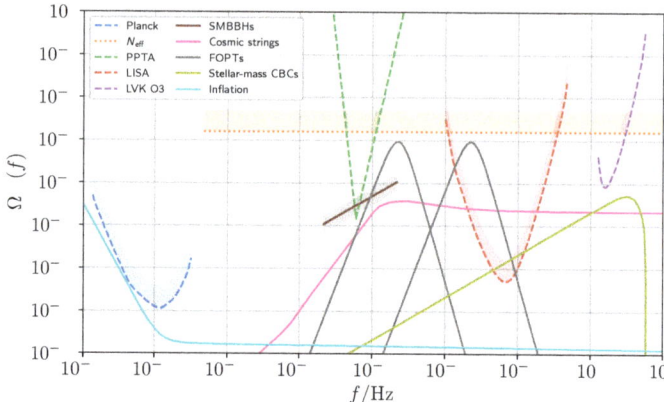

Figure 1. An overview of potential GWB signals across the frequency spectrum. The light blue curve shows the prediction for single-field slow-roll inflation with a canonical kinetic term, with tensor-to-scalar ratio $r_{0.002} = 0.1$ [52]. The pink curve shows a GWB from Nambu–Goto cosmic strings, using "model 2" of the loop network, with a dimensionless string tension of $G\mu = 10^{-11}$ [53]. The brown curve shows a GWB from inspiralling supermassive BBHs, with the amplitude and shaded region shown here corresponding to the common noise process in the NANOGrav 12.5-year data set [54]. The two grey curves show GWBs generated by first-order phase transitions at the electroweak scale (∼200 GeV) and the QCD scale (∼200 MeV), respectively [55]. The yellow curve shows a GWB generated by stellar-mass compact binaries, based on the mass distributions and local merger rates inferred by LVK detections [56]. The dashed curves show various observational constraints, as described further in Section 5 (this includes the PPTA constraint, which intersects the possible NANOGrav SMBBH signal); the dotted curve shows the integrated constraint from measurements of N_{eff}, which cannot be directly compared with the frequency-dependent constraint curves but is shown here for indicative purposes.

3.1. Astrophysical Backgrounds

Astrophysical GWBs are the collection of all GWs generated by astrophysical processes which are individually unresolved by your GW detector. These can be either individual subthreshold signals, or they can be so numerous that they add up incoherently and form a continuous signal in the timestream.

Perhaps the most studied signal in the literature is a background sourced by a collection of inspiralling and merging compact binary systems. These include black hole binaries, neutron star binaries, white dwarf binaries, and systems counting a mixed pair of these objects. Black hole binaries in particular are a vast category of sources, as the mass of each black hole in the binary ranges between 5 and $10^{10} M_\odot$. The lower mass of $5 M_\odot$ here refers to the lack of black holes between the Tolman–Oppenheimer–Volkoff limit (which sets the maximum mass of a neutron star to $2.9 M_\odot$ [57]) and $5 M_\odot$, as seen in low-mass X-ray binary observations [58,59][4]. Specifically, a BH is considered *massive* ($M_{\text{BH}} \sim 10^5\text{--}10^{10} M_\odot$), *intermediate* ($M_{\text{BH}} \sim 10^2\text{--}10^5 M_\odot$), and *stellar mass* ($M_{\text{BH}} \sim 5\text{--}10^2 M_\odot$) [61]. There are binaries that have a mass ratio close to one, where the two black holes in the binary fall within the same mass category, and there are also so-called extreme mass ratio (EMR) binaries where the two objects belong to different families, including extreme mixed binaries such as massive black hole–neutron star pairs. There is a direct relation between binary masses and GW emission frequencies; however, overall, the GW power spectra have a similar shape. In particular, in the early emission stage of the binary, i.e., the *inspiral* phase when the energy emission increases adiabatically as the binary's orbit shrinks very gradually, energy emission can be described by very few parameters and is well-approximated by a power law as explained below. The masses also impact the characteristic amplitude of a

GW signal, which in turn may be linked to the detection threshold via the signal-to-noise ratio (SNR) of each signal. The latter sets the maximum expected redshift depth at which each type of signal may be observed by the detectors probing that frequency range. A good example of this is the background generated by double white dwarfs, which is expected to be observable by the LISA detector only at very low redshift [62] such that LISA will only be sensitive to white dwarfs from the Milky Way and, perhaps, to those in the local group [63].

Other astrophysical sources of GWs include asymmetric supernovae explosions and rotating neutron stars which are not spherically symmetric and may produce triaxial emission [64]. These are considered minor sources of GWs compared to compact binaries as their characteristic signal is weaker. Furthermore, they are also considerably harder to model; hence, the discussion that follows is mainly focused on the former; nevertheless, many equations presented are general and may be applied to these secondary sources as well. In principle, the fact that these are harder to model also implies that they will necessarily be targets of stochastic searches, as the latter may be considered as generic, "un-modelled" searches of GW power.

It may seem odd to use the fractional parameter Ω_{GW} to describe GW energy from astrophysical events, as historically this is considered a cosmological quantity; however, several authors and collaborations have deemed it a useful convention allowing scientists from different fields to easily compare results. With this in mind, it may be considered as a compact measure of the GW history of the low-redshift Universe, after galaxy and star formation have taken place. To see this in more detail, following [40], let N be the number of events of a particular signal type in a comoving volume. This may be decomposed in event rate $\dot{N}$ multiplied by cosmic time slice dt_r/dz,

$$N(z) = \dot{N}\frac{dt_r}{dz} \equiv \frac{\dot{N}}{(1+z)H(z)}. \quad (27)$$

Then, as in [65], the fractional energy density may be rewritten as

$$\Omega_{GW} = \frac{f}{\rho_c} \int_0^{z_{max}} dz \frac{\dot{N}(z)}{(1+z)H(z)} \left\langle \frac{dE_{GW}}{df_r}\bigg|_{f_r=f(1+z)} \right\rangle, \quad (28)$$

where the angle brackets indicate an averaging over particular source population parameters θ, such that

$$\left\langle \frac{dE_{GW}}{df_r} \right\rangle = \int d\theta\, p(\theta) \frac{dE_{GW}(\theta; f_r)}{df_r}, \quad (29)$$

and $p(\theta)$ is the probability distribution of source parameters. In the case of a stochastic background, one would expect the parameter space to be fully sampled by the population; however, note that selection effects imposed by the detector may break this limit. One would expect the event rate $\dot{N}$ to locally increase with redshift, as the volume of each redshift shell increases. In fact, the event rate for stellar mass compact binary coalescences has been found to increase with redshift when analysing the direct detections reported by LIGO [66]. However, this rate cannot increase monotonically out to infinity and must have a turnaround point at some peak redshift $\hat{z}$ and then decay to zero as star formation ceases in the early Universe. In general, this may be modelled phenomenologically with [67]

$$\dot{N}(z) = \mathcal{C}(\alpha_r, \beta_r, \hat{z}) \frac{\dot{N}_0(1+z)^{\alpha_r}}{1 + \left(\frac{1+z}{1+\hat{z}}\right)^{\alpha_r+\beta_r}}, \quad (30)$$

such that at low redshift, the rate increases as $\dot{N} \propto (1+z)^{\alpha_r}$, then reaches a maximum at $z \sim \hat{z}$, and finally decreases at high redshift as $\dot{N} \propto (1+z)^{-\beta_r}$. $\mathcal{C}$ is the normalisation constant

$$\mathcal{C}(\alpha_r, \beta_r, \hat{z}) = 1 + (1+\hat{z})^{-(\alpha_r+\beta_r)} \quad (31)$$

which ensures $\dot{N}(z=0) = \dot{N}_0$. Constraining $\hat{z}$, α_r and β_r provides insight on binary formation history and, consequently, star formation history as well. In practice, however, stochastic searches probe the redshift-integrated observable $\Omega_{GW}(f)$ only. The redshift history may be reconstructed with careful modelling and cross-correlation with direct measurements of individual events for which redshift is estimated; see the approach presented in [65]. Note that selection effects due to the mass distribution of sources need to be taken into account in this sort of analysis. Alternatively to this phenomenological approach, the redshift-dependent event rate may also be probed by conducting a careful study of the specific astrophysical conditions which favour compact binary inspirals and mergers; for example, the evolution of galaxy star formation and chemical enrichment can be combined with prescriptions for merging of compact binaries obtained via stellar evolution simulations [68,69].

To study the spectral dependence of different backgrounds, we can plug in different source models in Equation (18) and calculate the spectral shape of Ω_{GW}. This is particularly useful in the case of an astrophysical background as N and E_{GW} are directly related to the star formation history of the Universe, and astrophysical GWs from different source populations will contribute to Ω_{GW} in different amounts at different times. This may result in a method that differentiates between astrophysical backgrounds and also test different stellar and galaxy evolution models [70].

An example of astrophysical background with a simple expected spectral dependence is that of compact binaries in the adiabatic inspiral phase [71]. In this case, it is sufficient to model GW radiation at leading quadrupole order [72],

$$\frac{dE_{GW}}{d\ln f_r} = \frac{\pi^{2/3}}{3} G^{2/3} \mathcal{M}^{5/3} f_r^{2/3}, \tag{32}$$

where $\mathcal{M}$ is the *chirp mass*, given by

$$\mathcal{M} = \frac{(m_1 m_2)^{3/5}}{(m_1 + m_2)^{1/5}}, \tag{33}$$

where m_1 and m_2 are the masses of the two compact objects in the binary. The co-moving number density will depend on chirp masses in the binary distribution and may be rewritten as an integral over $\mathcal{M}$,

$$N = \int_{\mathcal{M}_{min}}^{\mathcal{M}_{max}} \frac{dN}{d\mathcal{M}} d\mathcal{M}, \tag{34}$$

where the integration extremes will depend on source population characteristics. Rearranging the terms in Equation (28), one obtains

$$\Omega_{GW}^{CB} \propto f^{2/3} \int_0^{z_{max}} dz \frac{1}{(1+z)^{1/3}} \int_{\mathcal{M}_{min}}^{\mathcal{M}_{max}} d\mathcal{M} \frac{dN}{d\mathcal{M}} \mathcal{M}^{5/3}, \tag{35}$$

where the average over the population parameters is simply reduced to the integral over all possible chirp masses. Here, the superscript CB labels compact binaries generically. This provides a simple spectral dependence for Ω_{GW}^{CB}, which may be condensed as[5]

$$\Omega_{GW}^{CB} = \Omega_{GW}^{CB}(f_{ref}) \left(\frac{f}{f_{ref}}\right)^{2/3}, \tag{36}$$

where $\Omega_{GW}^{CB}(f_{ref})$ is the appropriately normalised energy density calculated at a reference frequency f_{ref}.

This simple model may be extended to all general inspiral-dominated GWBs as the same principles apply and has been reprised all over the literature and used in almost every GWB search with data available. The same principle, for example, has been used in the estimation of the expected background from stellar mass black hole and neutron star binaries in the LIGO detector frequency band [73], with some tweaks to account for the chirp signal from merging black holes which has a substantially different energy output per frequency. This result is shown in Figure 2.

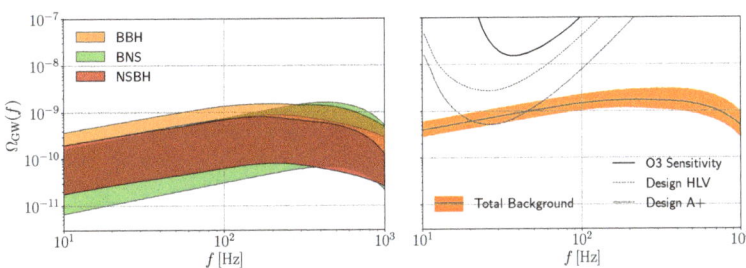

Figure 2. Projections for the CBC stochastic background using the third GW transient catalogue (GWTC-3), first presented in [74]. On the right, the total expected background is compared to the integrated sensitivity of current and future configurations of the 2G detector network. This plot was obtained using open data published in [75].

3.2. Primordial Backgrounds

There are a range of potential physical processes occurring in the primordial Universe which would result in a rich variety of GW signals. We report the most noteworthy here; however, this is a nonexhaustive list of all sources which have been studied in the literature. We focus especially on sources which have corresponding search pipelines and for which constraints have been derived with existing GW data. For a more in-depth review of the subject, see [76].

First and foremost, all inflationary models include an irreducible GWB as a byproduct of inflation [76,77]. Any inflationary process results in the stretching of quantum fluctuations which are parametrically amplified into classical density perturbations, producing particularly tensor perturbations which we identify as GWs. The amplification process causes perturbation wavelengths to expand until they reach the size of the horizon, when they exit causal contact and their evolution remains frozen until the Universe's horizon returns to their scale in the post-inflationary era and they may re-enter. At time of re-entry, the GWB is formed by standing waves, and their phases are correlated between modes with opposite momenta [78]. In most models, the perturbations are adiabatic, Gaussian, and approximately scale-invariant, resulting in a similarly defined GWB. In this case, the fractional energy density will be approximately frequency independent at frequencies $f \gg H_0 \sim 10^{-18}$ Hz,

$$\Omega_{\text{GW}}^{\text{Infl.}}(f) \approx \text{const.},\tag{37}$$

and will be primarily characterised by its amplitude. The perturbations are also expected to imprint a pattern of B-modes in the polarization of the CMB [79], which has not been detected yet and is the aim of numerous CMB experiments [80–83]. This nondetection imposes an upper bound on the inflationary GWB amplitude, setting it well below the reach of present or planned GW detectors. The prevalent opinion in the community is that precision measurements of the CMB are still the best chance to garner decisive evidence of inflation and discriminate between models.

Beyond the irreducible background, however, the inflationary era may also source a second GWB which in certain cases dominates over the irreducible component, often presenting strongly scale-dependent features or characteristic peaks in the power spectrum [76]. For example, the presence of additional fields during the inflationary epoch other than the inflaton could have an effect on GW emission, as these may have interactions resulting in strong particle production or may act as spectator fields and exhibit a sub-luminal propagation speed [84,85]. The presence of additional symmetries in the inflationary sector would also have an impact, as these would result in breaking of space reparametrizations, allowing the graviton to acquire a mass. Alternative theories of gravity (other than general relativity) governing the inflationary era would have an impact on all aspects of primordial GWs. The scalar density perturbations generated during inflation may also source GWs; this may occur either at second order in perturbation theory [86] or by acting as seeds for primordial black holes [87,88]. Finally, GWs can also be produced during preheating [89–92] due to the violent transfer of energy from the inflationary sector to Standard Model plasma. All these possible inflationary scenarios are effectively extremely hard to probe with electromagnetic observations; hence, GWs present a unique window into this epoch. See for example [93] for a discussion of inflationary backgrounds in the LISA band and how a positive detection would revolutionise the current science of inflation. For more details and references to the specific models that may give rise to the effects discussed above, refer to the review [76].

After inflation, primordial GWs may have been generated as a consequence of phase transitions which may have occurred as the primordial Universe cooled down in its post-inflationary adiabatic expansion. First-order phase transitions in particular would proceed via the nucleation of true-vacuum bubbles, sourcing GWs through the collision of these bubbles [44,46], as well as through the resulting acoustic and/or turbulent motion of the primordial plasma [55]. The characteristic power spectrum of a background formed by bubble collisions presents a sharp peak at the frequency related to the energy scale at which the transition occurred, T_*,

$$f_{\text{peak}} \sim 10^{-6} \, \text{Hz} \times \frac{\beta}{H_*} \times \frac{T_*}{200 \, \text{GeV}}, \tag{38}$$

where β/H_* is the rate of the transition in units of the Hubble rate at the transition epoch. For typical values $\beta/H_* \sim 10^3$, we see that this peak lies in the megahertz (mHz) band probed by LISA for transitions at the electroweak scale $T_* \sim 200 \, \text{GeV}$, allowing us to test a myriad of particle physics models which predict such signals.

Phase transitions may also give rise to stable topological defects, the most prominent example of which are *cosmic strings*. These line-like topological defects are generated through spontaneous symmetry breaking in the early Universe [47,48] and are a generic prediction of many theories beyond the Standard Model of particle physics [94]. On macroscopic scales, cosmic strings are effectively described by a single parameter, the dimensionless string tension $G\mu$, which is determined by the energy scale at which they were formed. Once formed, dynamical evolution results in a dense network of cosmic string loops which oscillate at relativistic speeds, producing copious GWs which combine to produce a strong SGWB signal for which its amplitude and spectral shape are set by $G\mu$.

As mentioned above, a potential GW signal of cosmological origin is the SGWB from *primordial black holes* (PBHs); i.e., black holes formed in the early Universe rather than through stellar evolution. Since black holes are massive and non-baryonic and interact only through gravity, PBHs are very natural and well-motivated cold dark matter (CDM) candidates. The cosmic mass density of PBHs is, therefore, usually expressed as a fraction of the total CDM mass density, $f_{\text{PBH}} \equiv \rho_{\text{PBH}}/\rho_{\text{CDM}}$. Similarly to stellar-origin black holes, PBHs can form binaries (either by forming in close proximity to each other or through dynamical encounters) which then inspiral and emit GWs or they can emit GWs through close hyperbolic encounters [95]. The cumulative signal from many such binaries produces a SGWB spectrum which is determined by the PBH mass spectrum and DM mass fraction f_{PBH}.

In general, GWs emitted in the primordial Universe are considered stochastic under the *ergodic* assumption, which equates the ensemble average of an observable with its time and/or spatial average. Essentially, we assume that by observing large enough regions of the Universe today, or a given region for long enough time, we have access to many independent realisations of the system. This is realistic given two fundamental premises of cosmology, namely that the Universe is statistically homogeneous and isotropic, such that the initial conditions of the GW-generating process may be considered the same at every point in space and that the GW source fulfills causality, operating at a time when the typical size of a region of causal contact in the Universe was smaller than today. It can be shown [76] that the correlation scale today of a GW signal from the early Universe is tiny comparable to the present Hubble scale, verifying this requirement.

Stochasticity would also imply the lack of a preferred polarisation mode in the signal, as all mode configurations should be fully sampled in the observation set. While this is intuitively true for astrophysical backgrounds, the argument for primordial GWs is more delicate, and while a background may be stochastic for the reasons described above, there may be specific formation channels which will violate parity and induce an asymmetry in the polarisation modes, effectively generating circularly polarised waves. This effect may be found in alternative theories of gravity, such as Chern–Simons gravity [96] or certain quantum gravity models [97]. The study of parity-violating theories of gravity is inspired by grand unification, as the electro-weak sector of the standard model is chiral and, thus, maximally violates parity [98,99].

3.3. Anisotropies in Stochastic Backgrounds

We can distinguish two root causes of anisotropy in stochastic signals. Firstly, there may be inhomogeneities in the GW source mechanisms, such as a particular distribution of the sources on the sky, which necessarily produces an anisotropic signal. Secondly, as GWs propagate, they accumulate line-of-sight effects [100], crossing different matter density fields which are (if mildly) inhoheneously distributed in our Universe. For astrophysical backgrounds, the spatial distribution of GW events is a biased tracer of the underlying light matter distribution, while primordial backgrounds will present anisotropies linked to the particular physical processes that occurred in the early Universe. In order to investigate these effects, it is useful to define the fractional GW energy density per solid angle $d\hat{n}$,

$$\Omega_{\text{GW}}(f, \hat{n}) = \frac{1}{\rho_c} \frac{d\rho_{\text{GW}}}{d\ln f \, d\hat{n}}, \tag{39}$$

such that

$$\overline{\Omega}_{\text{GW}}(f) = \frac{1}{4\pi} \int_{S^2} d\hat{n} \, \Omega_{\text{GW}}(f, \hat{n}), \tag{40}$$

as in [101,102]. $\overline{\Omega}_{\text{GW}}(f)$ is the GWB monopole, where the bar is introduced to highlight the fact that it is an isotropic all-sky average over the directional fluctuations. The latter may be described by the GW density contrast,

$$\delta_{\text{GW}}(f, \hat{n}) = \frac{\Omega_{\text{GW}}(f, \hat{n}) - \overline{\Omega}_{\text{GW}}(f)}{\overline{\Omega}_{\text{GW}}(f)}, \tag{41}$$

in analogy with the formalism used to quantify the level of anisotropy in CMB temperature [103] and in galaxy clustering [104]. This dimensionless parameter provides an unambiguous metric to compare different results.

At first order in the perturbations, the density contrast may be decomposed into three distinct contributions related to the origin of the anisotropies,

$$\delta_{\text{GW}} \simeq \delta_{\text{GW}}^{\text{s}} + \delta_{\text{GW}}^{\text{los}} + \mathcal{D}\hat{n} \cdot \hat{v}_{\text{obs}}. \tag{42}$$

Here, $\delta_{\text{GW}}^{\text{s}}$ is the *source* term resulting from anisotropies at the GW source, for example, due to the specific distribution of events for astrophysical backgrounds, while $\delta_{\text{GW}}^{\text{los}}$ is the *propagation* term [100], which encapsulates accumulated line-of-sight effects. The final term is the dipole of magnitude $\mathcal{D}$ induced by the observer's peculiar velocity v_{obs}. Note that the propagation term includes contributions similar to those encountered in CMB anisotropy calculations: the Sachs–Wolfe effect, due to the local curvature at emission, and the integrated Sachs–Wolfe effect, due to the curvature perturbations encountered along the line-of-sight [105]; a Doppler term due to the source's peculiar velocity; and higher order effects such as gravitational lensing and redshift-space distortions [106]. All these terms have been the subject of intense study in recent years and both astrophysical and primordial contributions have been modelled extensively (see for example [107–109] for independent calculations of astrophysical background anisotropies and [50,102,110] for examples of primordial ones). The propagation term is often assumed to be negligible in the case of astrophysical backgrounds or it is directly included as part of the source term; in [111,112], it is expressly estimated and shown to account for at most ∼10% of the total anisotropy. In the case of a truly primordial background dating back as far as or before the CMB, however, this term will be considerably larger and will be comparable to the intrinsic anisotropies at large scales as shown in [100].

We analyse here the general scenario where the density contrast at the source behaves as a Gaussian random field, as this is mostly assumed in the literature as well. In this case, δ^s_{GW} is characterised by its two-point correlation function,

$$C_{GW}(f, \cos\theta) = \langle \delta^s_{GW}(f, \hat{n})\, \delta^s_{GW}(f, \hat{n}')\rangle, \tag{43}$$

in analogy with CMB anisotropies, as the first moment $\langle \delta^s_{GW}\rangle$ is zero by definition, and all higher order moments will either vanish or may be expressed in terms of C_{GW} [102]. Here, $\cos\theta = \hat{n}\cdot\hat{n}'$ and the angular brackets represent an averaging over all $\hat{n}$, $\hat{n}'$ direction pairs of aperture θ. $C_{GW}(f,\cos\theta)$ will then be different from zero where there are consistent spatial correlations on the sky associated to θ, at frequency f. To observe this formally, we expand the two-point function in spherical harmonic space as

$$C_{GW}(f, \cos\theta) = \sum_{\ell=0}^{\infty} \frac{2\ell+1}{4\pi} C_\ell^\delta(f) P_\ell(\cos\theta), \tag{44}$$

where P_ℓ is the ℓth Legendre polynomial. By inverting this equation, we obtain the angular power spectrum $C_\ell^\delta(f)$ for the GW energy density contrast,

$$C_\ell^\delta(f) = 2\pi \int_{-1}^{+1} d\cos\theta\, C_{GW}(f, \cos\theta)\, P_\ell(\cos\theta), \tag{45}$$

which may be estimated from observations. Note that quantity $\ell(\ell+1)C_\ell/2\pi$ is roughly the contribution per logarithmic ℓ bin to the variance of δ^s; hence, this will often be the quantity shown in plots quantifying the C_ℓ^δ power spectrum from different signal models and in GW data sets.

Alternatively, we can also calculate the angular power spectrum of the Ω_{GW} parameter itself, first by decomposing it into spherical harmonic components,

$$\Omega_{GW}(f, \hat{n}) = \sum_{\ell=0}^{\infty} \sum_{m=-\ell}^{+\ell} \Omega^{GW}_{\ell m}(f)\, Y_{\ell m}(\hat{n}), \tag{46}$$

and then by defining

$$C_\ell^\Omega = \frac{1}{2\ell+1} \sum_{m=-\ell}^{+\ell} \left\langle \Omega^{GW}_{\ell m}(f)\, \Omega^{GW}_{\ell m}(f) \right\rangle, \tag{47}$$

where angle brackets indicate an ensemble average over random realizations of Ω_{GW}. The information encapsulated in C_ℓ^Ω and C_ℓ^δ is the same, and they are both dimensionless quantities; however, note that the numerical scale of C_ℓ^Ω is roughly that of Ω_{GW}^2, whereas C_ℓ^δ shows the fractional contribution of each mode to the power spectrum with respect to the monopole $\bar{\Omega}_{GW}$.

To quote the expected levels of anisotropy for astrophysical backgrounds from calculations in the references mentioned above, one may compare Figure 2 in [107] and Figure 4 in [108]. It has been pointed out in the literature [102,113–115] that there is a tension between these two predictions; the difference in the estimates highlighted here stems probably from different treatments of the source effects at very low redshift, where the clustering at small scales induces non-linear effects in the field which the overall anisotropy level is very sensitive to. Cosmological backgrounds are expected to present CMB-like anisotropies of $\delta_{GW}^s \sim 10^{-5}$ [100]. A comparison between these estimates and the expected sensitivity-per-multipole of various GW detectors may be found in [116].

Finally, note that to properly assess the sourced GW anisotropies from direct measurements, it is necessary to subtract out the kinematic dipole term induced by the observer's peculiar velocity as seen in Equation (42). This may be performed similarly to CMB analysis, potentially using the independent estimate of v_{obs} from CMB data themselves.

3.4. Observational Properties of Stochastic Backgrounds

The observational properties of the SGWB such as time-domain characteristics and selection effects imposed by the observation method merit special attention as these are crucial for developing effective search methods. For the sake of simplicity, this discussion is focused on astrophysical backgrounds where individual events are clearly defined and are not extremely model dependent. However, most of the following considerations generally apply to primordial backgrounds as well and have intuitive extension to backgrounds from topological defects and primordial black holes for example.

Three main regimes are identified in the literature based on the frequency of occurrence of the events in time. These are referred to as *Poisson noise* regime, where GWs appear as isolated bursts in the timestream, *Gaussian* regime, where the timestream is packed with numerous overlapping signals and the central limit theorem applies, and *popcorn* or *intermittent* regime, which lies somewhere in between. A visualisation of these is provided in Figure 3, generated using mock-data generation open source package presented in [117,118]. The discriminating factor between regimes is encapsulated in the *duty cycle*, which is the mean ratio between event duration and the time interval between consecutive events. This will also be equal to the average number of events present at the detector at a given observation time. While it is intuitively clear that the Gaussian background in Figure 3 is stochastic, this is not obvious of the other regimes. Operationally, a signal may be considered stochastic if it is more effective, in the Bayesian sense of the word, to search for it in the data using a stochastic model for the waveform as opposed to a deterministic one [119]. Furthermore, a signal is defined as *resolvable* if it can be decomposed into non-overlapping and individually detectable signals, in either the time or frequency domain. With this in mind, the only way to know whether a signal is stochastic, is to search for it and see what method yields the best result or more stringent upper limit. In the case of astrophysical GW signals, there is a continuous distribution of events where the highest SNRs are expected to be resolved, and beneath a certain detector-imposed cutoff, the events accumulate to form the background signal. The boundary between the resolved and unresolved population is not obvious, and a few bright signals stand out above the confusion background. When these are resolvable, deterministic signals, they should be subtracted from data, leaving a residual background that may be analysed with stochastic tools. In [119], the authors present simulations designed to establish whether certain signals are best searched for with stochastic or deterministic methods. They find, similarly to [120] and somewhat unsurprisingly, that deterministic signal models are favoured whenever the background is made up of a small number of sources, and stochastic models are preferred for larger source numbers. The boundary between regimes however is not well defined, and hybrid models comprised of a deterministic signal model for individual bright sources and a Gaussian–stochastic signal model for the confusion background are generally most effective to extract the population parameters.

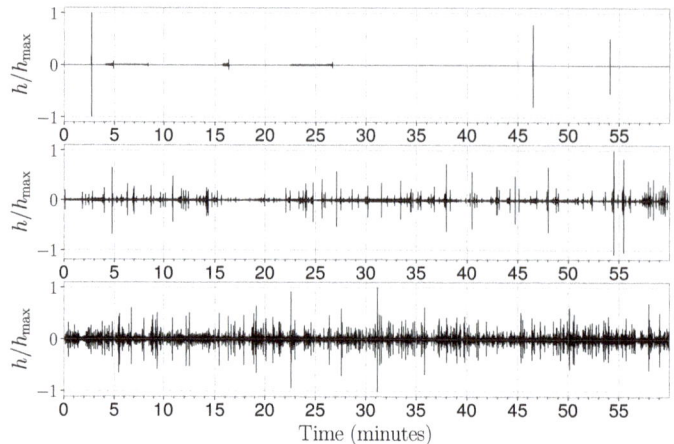

Figure 3. Examples of interferometer timestreams populated by GWBs with different time-domain properties, inspired by [64]: Poisson noise (top panel), popcorn (middle panel), and Gaussian (bottom panel). The strain on the y-axis is normalised to show the fractional contribution of each burst/wavelet to the signal, while the Δ parameter is the *duty cycle*, i.e., the mean ratio between event duration and the time interval between consecutive events.

These analyses highlight the distinction between *event rate* and *detection rate*. The event rate is the actual rate at which binaries are merging in the visible Universe, while the detection rate is the rate with which we can detect them, which is plagued by selection effects depending on both the binary's intrinsic and extrinsic parameters and the detector's characteristics.

There is a further degree of complication caused by these unresolved, bright signals in the timestream which behave as *shot noise* and may hinder the correct interpretation of a detection. These signals represent random, Poissonian fluctuations in the finite population of sources and will induce a white noise component in the angular power spectrum. The observational effect that arises is induced by the fact that nearby, bright sources approximately randomly distributed around the observer will mask the underlying structure of the Universe. This is analysed and quantified in [121–123] for the monopole and anisotropies of an astrophysical background, respectively. Here, Poisson white noise is modelled with a free parameter representing the cutoff distance from Earth beyond which the GW signal may be considered a stochastic background by the definition given above. The cutoff naturally depends on the sensitivity of the detector array under consideration. This is analysed in [122,123] for the anisotropic background, and it is found that the white noise component dominates current LIGO and Virgo detectors; however, the planned upgrades of these detectors and the future 3G detectors may be sufficient to curb this effect. As discussed in [124,125], another strategy to mitigate the shot noise is to cross-correlate the GW signal with a galaxy catalogue, as this cross-correlation spectrum has a much lower level of shot noise. Furthermore, as GW sources are finite in time, then Poisson statistics dictate that this noise decays as the inverse of the observation time; hence, long observing runs will progressively mitigate this effect. Quantifying this distinction is an evergrowing effort. The current event rate estimates based on astrophysical models informed by the LIGO detections show that there is approximately one binary neutron star merger every 13 s and one binary black hole merger every 223 s [73]. Clearly, the vast majority of these lie well beneath the threshold for detection. This is quantified for example in [126] where the detection rate per year is encoded as a function of the merging binary masses. It is shown that there are several astrophysical models for compact binaries which fit the detection rate of ~10 events per year from the aLIGO O1 and O2 data runs. It is clear that the rate of "intermediate" subthreshold events from an astrophysical population following these models is low and remains far from the stochastic limit as defined above.

It is worth pointing out that these observational features of astrophysical backgrounds discussed here may themselves provide insight in compact binary population parameters such as binary coalescence rates for different binary species, as detailed in [127]. Furthermore, the time dependence of astrophysical backgrounds in general may be a powerful discriminating factor between these and backgrounds of primordial origin.

4. Detection Approaches and Methodologies

Given its stochastic nature, the main challenge in measuring an SGWB is confidently distinguishing signal from the (stochastic) noise in GW detectors. The interplay between signal and noise bears a central role in stochastic search methods, and in particular the validity of a given method may depend on the expected *signal-to-noise regime* or *ratio* (SNR): whether the noise dominates the measurement, i.e., the detector operates in the *low signal regime*, or whether the signal is comparable to or stronger than the detector noise, i.e., *high signal regime*. Here, we classify search methods based on assumptions made primarily on the signal, such as Gaussianity and isotropy, starting from minimal assumptions on SNR, and we highlight how the latter then impacts the formulation of the optimal estimators.

Cross-correlation searches have cast a wide net, targeting a variety of stochastic backgrounds within the same style of search and also refining methods to extract specific signals from the data—see, e.g., the dark photon search (e.g., [128]) or the cosmic string search (e.g., [129]). We divide searches into three broad categories. We present the methodology to search for an isotropic stochastic background, which relies on the isotropic assumption to simplify the estimator considerably. Then, we show what happens when this assumption is relaxed in searches for anisotropic backgrounds. Finally, we review special searches which target elusive signatures which may imply deviation from general relativity and/or the standard model. However, first, let us review the common denominators in stochastic searches, namely the *cross-correlation* statistic and the correlated detector response.

4.1. Interdetector and Spatial Correlations

The first step in most stochastic searches is to consider the auto- and cross-correlation of datastreams from one or more detectors, as this operation discards all phase information and targets the signal power directly. To then deconvolve the response of the detectors to the signal, many searches rely on an *overlap function*, which determines the cross-power response of a pair of detectors to a stochastic background. The most common approach is to estimate the significance of excess correlated power in multiple detectors, integrated over all available observing time, often assuming noise in different detectors not to be correlated[6]. Throughout this section, these methodologies will be reviewed in detail; first, however, let us formally introduce the cross-correlation statistic and derive the overlap functions for different detector setups as these will be the building blocks for the rest of this review.

To start, consider a Gaussian, stationary GWB observed through two distinct detectors, 1 and 2. Each detector timestream may be decomposed into signal and noise components as

$$d_1(t) = R_1(t) * h(t) + n_1(t), \qquad d_2(t) = R_2(t) * h(t) + n_2(t), \qquad (48)$$

where R_1 and R_2 represent the individual detector response functions to GW signals, and "$*$" represents a convolution. These are characterised by functional dependencies on intrinsic and extrinsic parameters of the GWs such as polarisation and incoming direction; however, we omit these now as they may be easily included at a later stage.

We consider both h and n fields in Equation (48) as mean zero Gaussian variates; hence, these are fully described by their second-order moments. Let us work in the Fourier domain, where the assumption of stationarity implies that the noise covariance is diagonal, i.e., the noise in each frequency bin is uncorrelated[7],

$$\langle n_i(f) n_i(f') \rangle = \delta_{ff'} P_{f,i}, \tag{49}$$

with P_i as the noise power spectrum in detector i. We define the discrete Fourier transforms of the data streams starting at timestamp τ as $\tilde{d}_1^\tau, \tilde{d}_2^\tau$, and drop the time label immediately for the sake of conciseness. We then take the cross-correlation of these quantities as

$$C_{12}(f) = \tilde{d}_1(f) \tilde{d}_2^\star(f), \tag{50}$$

which, assuming uncorrelated noise between detectors, has expectation value of

$$\langle C_{12}(f) \rangle = R_1(f) R_2^\star(f) \langle \tilde{h}_1(f) \tilde{h}_2^\star(f) \rangle = T_{\text{obs}} \Gamma_{12}(f) I_{\text{GW}}(f). \tag{51}$$

Γ_{12} is the *overlap reduction function*, where the *reduction* comes from the fact that it is a sky-integrated quantity (more details to follow), and $I_{\text{GW}}(f)$ is the sky-integrated power spectrum of the background. Note the normalisation T_{obs} as we assume the observation lasts a finite amount of time. The covariance of the correlated measurement is as

$$\text{Cov}[C_{12\,f,f'}] = \langle C_{12}(f) C_{12}^\star(f') \rangle - \langle C_{12}(f) \rangle \langle C_{12}^\star(f') \rangle \approx T_{\text{obs}} \delta_{ff'} P_{1,f} P_{2,f}, \tag{52}$$

taking the weak signal limit in the final equality. In this case, the cross-correlation statistic has been shown to be a *sufficient statistic* [131], making it a good choice for stochastic searches. This is because there is little information to be drawn out from the auto-correlated measurements, as these are effectively measurements of the detector noise power; conversely, to use auto-correlations to estimate the signal, one would need an independent and accurate measurement of the noise power to model and subtract out the noise. This approach would require an iterative estimator where both signal and noise are included in the fit [132]. Note that using the cross-correlation component only of the data and, thus, ignoring the auto-correlations allows for considerable simplification of the optimal estimators and computations necessary in data analysis.

The functional form of the overlap function of a detector network can be derived from Equation (51) by appropriately combining the individual response functions of each detector. In the case of laser interferometers, the basic response function is the *arm response function*, and arms are then combined to form the detector. This may be performed physically, by using laser interferometry as is performed in LIGO/Virgo [133], or in post-processing, with *time-delayed interferometry* (TDI) as in the case of LISA [134,135]. Considering arm u_{PS} spanning from point P to point S, the one-way arm response $\vec{u} : P \to S$ in the frequency domain is described as [33]

$$R^A_{\vec{u}}(f, \hat{n}) = \frac{1}{2} u \otimes u : \epsilon^A \mathcal{T}_{\vec{u}}(f, \hat{n} \cdot u) e^{i \frac{2\pi f}{c} \hat{n} \cdot x_S}, \tag{53}$$

with the one-way *timing transfer function* relative to a photon travelling along u_{PS}, $\mathcal{T}_u$, as

$$\mathcal{T}_{\vec{u}}(f, \hat{n} \cdot u) = \frac{L}{c} e^{-\frac{\pi f L}{c}(1 + \hat{n} \cdot \hat{u})} \text{sinc}\left(\frac{\pi f L}{c}(1 + \hat{n} \cdot \hat{u})\right). \tag{54}$$

In the case of LIGO-like detectors, which are 90°-arm, Michelson–Morley style interferometers, a laser photon performs a round trip along one arm before interfering with the beam in the other arm; hence, the relevant response function is the *two-way* arm response function along $\overleftrightarrow{u} : P \leftrightarrow S$, which we can write in terms of the one-way timing transfer function as

$$R^A_{\overleftrightarrow{u}}(f, \hat{n}) = \frac{1}{2} u \otimes u : \epsilon^A \left(\mathcal{T}_{\vec{u}}(f, \hat{n} \cdot u) e^{i \frac{2\pi f}{c}(\hat{n} \cdot x_S - L)} + \mathcal{T}_{\overleftarrow{u}}(f, \hat{n} \cdot u) e^{i \frac{2\pi f}{c} \hat{n} \cdot x_P} \right); \tag{55}$$

note the extra $-L$ term which accounts for the extra phaseshift incurred when travelling over the same distance twice. Then, assuming that the detector is not moving during the measurement, we can substitute in $x_S = x_P + u$, and rewrite the above as

$$R^A_{\overleftrightarrow{u}}(f, \hat{n}) = \frac{1}{2} u \otimes u : \epsilon^A \mathcal{T}_{\overleftrightarrow{u}}(f, \hat{n} \cdot u) e^{i \frac{2\pi f}{c} \hat{n} \cdot x_P}, \tag{56}$$

where the two-way timing transfer function along the same arm is derived as

$$\mathcal{T}_{\overleftrightarrow{u}}(f, \hat{n} \cdot u) = \frac{L}{c} e^{-i\frac{2\pi fL}{c}} \left[e^{-i\frac{\pi fL}{c}(1-\hat{n}\cdot\hat{u})} \operatorname{sinc}\left(\frac{\pi fL}{c}(1 + \hat{n} \cdot \hat{u}) \right) \right.$$
$$\left. + e^{i\frac{2\pi fL}{c}(1+\hat{n}\cdot\hat{u})} \operatorname{sinc}\left(\frac{\pi fL}{c}(1 - \hat{n} \cdot \hat{u}) \right) \right]. \tag{57}$$

Note that in the *small antenna limit*, i.e., when the scale of the detector is much smaller than the wavelength probed, $L \ll c/f_{\rm GW}$, we have that $|\mathcal{T}_{\overleftrightarrow{u}}| \longrightarrow 1$, implying that all the frequency dependence of the detector response is encoded in the phase term of Equation (56). Consider now detector 1 which is made up of arms u and v, joined at point P; its polarisation response in frequency space, in the small antenna limit, will simply be

$$F^A_1(f, \hat{n}) = R^A_{\overleftrightarrow{u}}(f, \hat{n}) - R^A_{\overleftrightarrow{v}}(f, \hat{n}) = \frac{1}{2}(u_1 \otimes u_1 - v_1 \otimes v_1) : \epsilon^A e^{i\frac{2\pi f}{c}\hat{n}\cdot x_1}, \tag{58}$$

where we have substituted in x_1 for x_P as we consider it to be the location of the detector itself. Finally, the unpolarised overlap function[8] of a detector pair is given by combining the response functions of the two detectors [33],

$$\gamma_{12}(f, \hat{n}) = F^+_1(f, \hat{n}) F^+_2(f, \hat{n}) + F^\times_1(f, \hat{n}) F^\times_2(f, \hat{n}), \tag{59}$$

while the overlap reduction function Γ is obtained by sky-integrating the above,

$$\Gamma_{12}(f) = \int_{S^2} d\hat{n}\, \gamma_{12}(f, \hat{n}). \tag{60}$$

Note that polarisation F functions here defined specifically for ground-based interferometers correspond to the individual detector response functions seen in Equation (51). We have chosen to incorporate the frequency-dependent phase terms into the response functions directly; however, in the literature, these are sometimes left out of F functions to underline the fact that, in the small antenna limit, there is no interaction between GW frequency and detector geometry [33]. In the overlap function, the phase terms add, giving rise to a time delay term representing the frequency-dependent phase shift between the two detectors; explicitly,

$$\gamma_{12}(f, \hat{n}) = \tilde{\gamma}_{12}(\hat{n}) e^{i\frac{2\pi f}{c}\hat{n}\cdot b}, \tag{61}$$

where $\tilde{\gamma}$ is the geometric component of the overlap function, and b is the *baseline vector* that points from detector 1 to detector 2. The numerical values of $\tilde{\gamma}$ as a function of direction then depend specifically on the coordinate basis chosen to represent the function; often, the choice is to represent it in an Earth-centered celestial frame, where the function will be time-dependent, as the arms sweep round and round on the sky following the Earth's rotation on its axis. This behaviour gives rise to the specific *scan strategy* of the detector array, which is essential for directional stochastic searches. On the other hand, the frequency-dependent phase term highlights the role of the baseline length in a stochastic search: the ratio between $|b|$ and GW wavelength will determine what frequencies will be suppressed in the search; the longer the baseline, the higher the frequencies accessible will be. The overlap reduction functions for the LIGO Hanford and Livingston detector pair (L–H), LIGO Hanford and Virgo (H–V), and LIGO Hanford and Kagra (L–K) are shown in

Figure 4a, while the respective (instantaneous) overlap functions are plotted on the sky in Figure 5 at a particular common time.

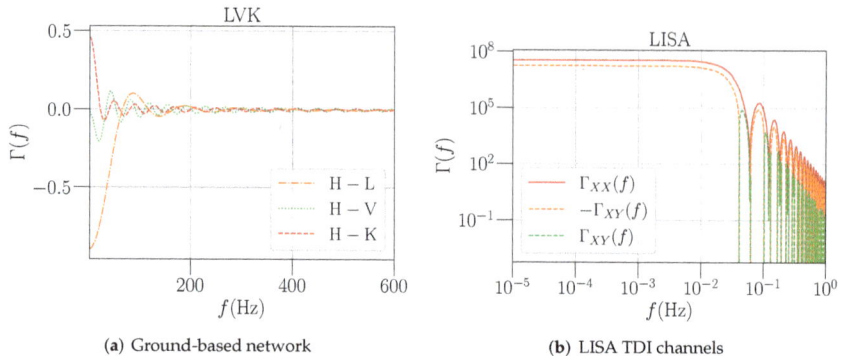

Figure 4. Overlap reduction functions for different GW interferometer detectors: ground-based (**left**) and space-based (**right**). Note that, in panel (**b**), the positive and negative parts of the LISA TDI overlap function Γ_{XY} are plotted separately, as the y-axis is log-scaled.

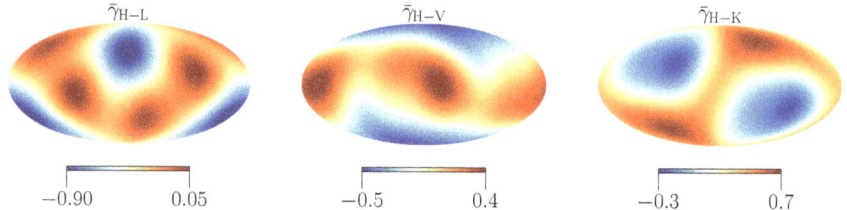

Figure 5. Geometric components of the overlap functions for different ground-based detector combinations mapped on the sky in geocentric celestial coordinates at a common time.

As mentioned above, long arm length, spaceborne detectors such as the future LISA three-satellite constellation, oriented in roughly an equilateral triangle, will measure GWs by combining the one-way arm responses (53) of several arms at different times composing TDI configurations or *channels*[9]. The most basic configuration can be thought of as a TDI–Michelson–Morley interferometer, where one constructs a response such as that in Equation (58). However, the great advantage of TDI is that it is possible to construct channels that suppress detector noise and enhance the signal [138]; this is a very active area of study [139–144]. For the purposes of this review, let us cite the TDI $\{X, Y, Z\}$ set of channels, which are based on the Michelson–Morley style measurement in Equation (58), where nominally X is centered around spacecraft 1, referred to hereafter as S_1; Y around spacecraft 2, S_2; and Z around spacecraft 3, S_3. However, to minimise noise, each light path is "reflected" back and forth between spacecrafts multiple times such that the noise interferes destructively. The total number of reflections is then linked to a version number for the TDI channel; e.g., "TDI 1 X" refers to a channel constructed by "interfering" the following light paths:

$$(S_1 \to S_2 \to S_1 \to S_3 \to S_1) - (S_1 \to S_3 \to S_1 \to S_2 \to S_1). \tag{62}$$

For more details on this calculation, see also official LISA documentation [145]. Another useful set of channels is the orthonormal set which approximately diagonalise the X, Y, Z noise-correlation matrix, A, E, T [146]. This set is often used for simplicity as one may consider the auto-correlations of A and E only, treating them as separate measurements, and use T as a *Sagnac* channel which is mostly sensitive to detector noise and blind to the signal [147,148]. However, in practice diagonalizing X, Y, Z is not a simple task as the detectors continuously move with respect to the measurement. The auto- and cross-correlated overlap functions for LISA are constructed as in Equation (59), where now the polarisation responses are referred to TDI channels. Note that LISA does not operate in the small antenna limit, hence the timing transfer function remains frequency dependent, inducing oscillations in TDI responses at high frequency, as observed in Figure 4b.

In the case of pulsar timing arrays, we can use the one-way transfer function defined in Equation (54), as in this case the arm vector $\hat{u}$, points from the solar system barycenter to the pulsar, and the arm length L is the distance from the solar system barycenter to the pulsar. One can expand the sinc function using Euler's identity and isolate the exponentials with arguments that depend on fL/c. Those exponential terms vary rapidly with sky direction for $fL/c \gg 1$ averaging down to zero in Equation (60) for Earth–pulsar baselines greater than 100 parsec in the nanohertz band (e.g., Figure 1 in [149]). From here, it is straightforward to calculate the (now frequency-independent) overlap reduction function by considering the cross-correlation of data from two pulsars, which serve as one-way timing beams (see, e.g., [33,149,150] for a more complete discussion). The overlap reduction function for a pair of pulsars a and b now depends on the angle between Earth–pulsar baselines, ζ_{ab} [150]:

$$\Gamma_{\text{PTA}}(\zeta_{ab}) = \frac{1}{2} - \frac{1}{4}\left(\frac{1-\cos\zeta_{ab}}{2}\right) + \frac{3}{2}\left(\frac{1-\cos\zeta_{ab}}{2}\right)\ln\left(\frac{1-\cos\zeta_{ab}}{2}\right). \tag{63}$$

where Γ_{PTA} is commonly referred to as the *Hellings–Downs* curve and may be observed in Figure 6.

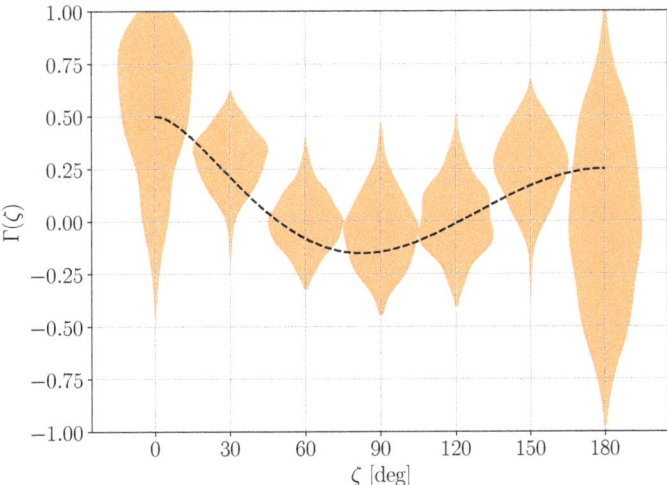

Figure 6. The dashed line is the Hellings–Downs curve described by Equation (63). ζ is the angle between Earth–pulsars baselines, and Γ measures the spatial correlation. At $\zeta = 0$, the function assumes the pulsars located at different distances. When distances are the same, $\Gamma(0) = 1$. Shaded regions correspond to constraints on spatial correlations obtained with the second data release of the Parkes Pulsar Timing Array except PSR J0437−4715 [26].

4.2. Isotropic Background Search Methods

In this section, we review the case of isotropic backgrounds searches. We start by presenting the approach for ground-based interferometers, which may be considered the simplest case as these operate in the low-signal regime. We then lay out the detection strategy of PTAs. The application of these methods on real data and corresponding search results are reviewed in Section 5.

4.2.1. Ground-Based Detectors

The flagship LVK stochastic search targets a Gaussian, isotropic, stationary, and unpolarised background [56]. This set of assumptions results in a simple, ready-to-use estimator which results in a relatively rapid analysis of LIGO-Virgo data. All other collaboration searches use, as a starting point, the breakdown of one of these assumptions, and most extend the estimator to a particular case.

As detailed in Section 3, a stochastic signal which satisfies all assumptions listed above is fully described by its spectral energy density, which may be expressed in terms of the fractional energy density $\Omega_{\rm GW}(f)$. Under the assumption the latter presents a power-law spectrum as in Equation (25), we can use the cross-correlation statistic presented in Equations (51) and (52) to write down an *optimal filter* to apply to the data and draw out an estimate for the amplitude $\Omega_{\rm GW}(f_{\rm ref})$ at reference frequency $f_{\rm ref}$. To start, we remind the reader of Equation (20) relating the measured GWB intensity to the energy density, which we may rewritten as

$$\Omega_{\rm GW}(f_{\rm ref}) = \mathcal{H}(f, f_{\rm ref}) I(f), \qquad (64)$$

with

$$\mathcal{H}(f, f_{\rm ref}) = \frac{4\pi^2}{\rho_c G} f_{\rm ref}^3 \left(\frac{f}{f_{\rm ref}}\right)^{3-\alpha}. \qquad (65)$$

By inspection, we already oberve that $\mathcal{H}(f, f_{\rm ref})$ is an unbiased filter to use on the data to derive an estimate of the background, in the case where the GWB obeys Equations (20) and (51). In general, there are several methods to show that this filter is optimal and write an estimator for $\Omega_{\rm GW}$, and different assumptions on the signal and noise components result in distinct solutions. We report the derivation shown in [151]. The approach here is to find the function which maximises the SNR of the *estimated* GWB signal, defined as

$$\text{SNR} = \frac{\hat{\Omega}_{\rm GW}|_{f_{\rm ref}}}{\sigma_\Omega^2}, \qquad (66)$$

where

$$\sigma_\Omega^2 = \text{Cov}[\hat{\Omega}_{\rm GW}|_{f_{\rm ref}}]. \qquad (67)$$

Re-writing the expectation value for the data correlation $C(f)$ in terms of $\Omega_{\rm GW}(f_{\rm ref})$ using Equations (20) and (51),

$$\langle C(f)\rangle = T_{\rm obs}\Gamma_{12}(f)\mathcal{H}^{-1}(f, f_{\rm ref})\Omega_{\rm GW}(f_{\rm ref}), \qquad (68)$$

and assuming the low-signal limit following Allen and Romano [151], one obtains

$$\hat{\Omega}_{\rm GW}|_{f_{\rm ref}} = F_{f_{\rm ref}}^{-1} \int_0^\infty df \frac{\Gamma_{12}(f)\mathcal{H}(f, f_{\rm ref})}{P_1(f)P_2(f)} C(f), \qquad (69)$$

where $F_{f_{\rm ref}}$ may be thought of as a normalisation which depends on the chosen reference frequency,

$$F_{f_{\rm ref}} = T_{\rm obs} \int_0^\infty df \frac{\Gamma_{12}^2(f)\mathcal{H}^2(f, f_{\rm ref})}{P_1(f)P_2(f)}. \qquad (70)$$

In fact, in deriving the variance σ_Ω^2 as formulated in Equation (67), it turns out that $F_{f_{\rm ref}}$ is equal to the inverse variance of the estimator, up to a factor of 2,

$$\sigma_\Omega^2 = \frac{1}{2}\left[\int_0^\infty df \frac{\Gamma_{12}^2(f)\mathcal{H}^2(f, f_{\rm ref})}{P_1(f)P_2(f)}\right]^{-1} \equiv \frac{F_{f_{\rm ref}}}{2}. \qquad (71)$$

where P_1 and P_2 are the noise power spectra in detectors 1 and 2, respectively, as defined in Equation (49). In principle, these are not known and need to be estimated carefully so as not to bias the search. When operating in the weak signal, it is reasonable to calculate the noise power spectra from the data directly; however, one should be cautious not to use these estimates on *the very same* data stretch they have been estimated from. In practice, for stochastic searches using ground-based interferometers, the data are segmented into short time segments and the full estimator takes the average of Ω_{GW} over the entire dataset. To estimate Ω_{GW} in a single data segment τ, one may use noise power spectra estimated from *other* segments within a time window over which detector noise is stationary; for example, in the LVK stochastic searches, the average of P_i in the adjacent segments is taken. Otherwise, it is also possible to estimate the noise power spectrum using a parametric fit, as in [152–154], or by using a wavelet expansion using methods as shown for example in [155].

Another approach to construct an estimator for the SGWB is to construct a likelihood function for the signal given the data, and maximise it to obtain a maximum likelihood detection statistic. Let us switch to a compact vector notation, where the data vector $\boldsymbol{d} = (d_1, d_2, ..., d_N)$ spans the detector space comprising N detectors, and data covariance is the generalised $N \times N$ correlation matrix $\boldsymbol{C}$, where each entry is $C_{ij} = d_i d_j$. Starting with a zero-mean Gaussian assumption for both the signal h and noise n terms in the data, we can write

$$\mathcal{L}(\boldsymbol{d}) \propto \prod_{f,\tau} \frac{1}{|C|^{1/2}} e^{\frac{1}{2} \boldsymbol{d}^\dagger C^{-1} \boldsymbol{d}}, \tag{72}$$

where all observed time segments τ and frequency modes f are considered independent. A method based on this likelihood employs both auto-correlations and cross-correlations of the datastreams to reconstruct SGWB and is discussed in the context of ground-based detectors in [156]. Using auto-correlations is not recommended in scenarios where the detector noise terms are not independently measured, as these will be inextricable from the auto-power spectra. This likelihood is in fact proposed for future LISA data analysis in [147,148], making full use of the independent estimate of the noise from GW-insensitive channels (see details on Sagnac channels here [157]). A more simple, alternative route can be taken by noting that, in the low-signal approximation, the Gaussian assumption can actually be applied to the average of the two-detector residual $C_{ij} - \langle C_{ij} \rangle$, leading to a different formulation,

$$\mathcal{L}(C_{ij}) \propto \prod_{f,\tau} \frac{1}{\sigma^2} e^{\frac{1}{2}(C_{ij} - \langle C_{ij} \rangle) \sigma^{-2} (C_{ij} - \langle C_{ij} \rangle)^\star}. \tag{73}$$

This holds in the limit where data are averaged over many segments such that the distribution of the residuals approximates a Gaussian; otherwise, a single residual will not follow this distribution [158]. In [131], Matas and Romano show that likelihood (72) is well approximated by (73) in the low-signal limit. In this case, maximising either likelihood with respect to $\Omega_{GW}(f_{\rm ref})$ yields the same solution as above. The extension to include multiple baselines is straightforward, assuming each C_{ij} may be considered as an independent measurement. The full likelihood $\mathcal{L}(C)$ becomes the product over the individual baseline likelihoods as

$$\mathcal{L}(C) \propto \prod_b \mathcal{L}(C_b), \tag{74}$$

where the baseline index b cycles over the detector pairs ij in the set, without double counting baselines.

The approach can be taken one step further to formulate a hybrid frequentist–Bayesian analysis as proposed in [159] by re-expressing the likelihood in terms of Ω and the model parameters we would like to constrain,

$$\mathcal{L}(\hat{\Omega}_{\mathrm{GW}}(f)|\Theta) \propto \exp\left[-\frac{1}{2}\sum_{b,f}\left(\frac{\hat{\Omega}_{\mathrm{GW}}^{b}(f) - \Omega_{\mathrm{M}}(f|\Theta)}{\sigma_{\Omega,b}^{2}(f)}\right)^{2}\right], \tag{75}$$

where Ω_M is the fractional energy density of the *model M* which is being tested, Θ are the parameters on which the model depends, and $\hat{\Omega}_{\mathrm{GW}}^{b}(f)$ is an estimator for the strength of the SGWB in a single frequency bin (see, e.g., [160]).

Equation (75) is used as the basis for parameter estimation of models for the GWB, and Bayesian model selection [159]. In the case of parameter estimation, one estimates the posterior distribution of the parameters of the model, Θ,

$$p(\Theta|\hat{\Omega}_{\mathrm{GW}}(f), M) = \frac{\mathcal{L}(\hat{\Omega}_{\mathrm{GW}}(f)|\Theta) p(\Theta)}{p[\hat{\Omega}_{\mathrm{GW}}(f)|M]}, \tag{76}$$

where now we have specified model M explicitly, $p(\Theta)$ is the prior on the model parameters, and

$$p(\hat{\Omega}_{\mathrm{GW}}(f)) = \int \mathcal{L}(\hat{\Omega}_{\mathrm{GW}}(f)|\Theta) p(\Theta)\, d\Theta \tag{77}$$

is the model evidence or "marginal likelihood". The posterior is typically estimated either by brute force estimation or, in high dimensional cases, by MCMC methods.

In addition to estimating the posterior in Equation (76), one can perform Bayesian model selection by comparing the marginal likelihood for two separate models. This is used to construct an odds ratio between two models $\mathcal{A}$ and $\mathcal{B}$,

$$\mathcal{O}_{\mathcal{B}}^{\mathcal{A}} = \frac{\pi(\mathcal{A})}{\pi(\mathcal{B})} \frac{p[\hat{\Omega}_{\mathrm{GW}}(f)|\mathcal{A}]}{p[\hat{\Omega}_{\mathrm{GW}}(f)|\mathcal{B}]}. \tag{78}$$

The first term on the right-hand side is the *prior odds*, where one specifies any prior information about the preference for one model over the other. The second term is simply the ratio of evidences. Odds ratios, or Bayes factors (simply the second term on the right-hand side, i.e., equal prior odds), can be used to distinguish between models for the GWB. A general heuristic guide for their use is discussed in Chapter 3 of [33]. Bayes factors have been used recently as the detection statistic in searches that seek to measure alternative polarizations of GWs [56,160,161], in searching for a background from superradiant instabilities around black holes [162,163], as well as searching for models of cosmological backgrounds [164–166]. This hybrid-Bayesian methodology has also been proposed in attempting to distinguish between a GWB and globally correlated magnetic noise [167], and simultaneously search for multiple GWB models contributing at once [168]. We discuss the problem of globally correlated magnetic noise for current and future detectors in more detail in Section 5. In addition, a Fisher matrix formalism has also been proposed to simultaneously search for multiple GWB contributions [169].

The detection approaches outlined above have been validated both through mock data challenges [170] and hardware injection campaigns [171]. The latter consisted in generating an isotropic Gaussian stochastic signal by manipulating the test masses at both LIGO sites and successfully recovering the injection via a cross-correlation stochastic search. However, the mock data challenge in [170] considers the case of a semirealistic astrophysical background of binary black holes and neutron stars. Here, the authors prove that the cross-correlation statistical approach assuming a Gaussian background remains valid even in the case of an intermittent astrophysical signal, although it is suboptimal. The fully optimal search methods for this sort of signal are described in Section 4.4.

4.2.2. Pulsar Timing Arrays

In describing the typical Bayesian analysis that is currently performed by most PTAs to search for an isotropic GWB, we follow the methods laid out in, e.g., [172–176], and refer to more specific studies throughout our discussion. Unlike for ground-based interferometers where the detector strain time series is uniformly sampled with equivalent time stamps at each detector, the data collected by PTAs are the arrival times of pulses from an ensemble of pulsars on the sky. Hence, it is preferable to work in the time domain directly, and the typical starting point is the *timing residuals* of all pulsars, δt, which are left over after subtracting off the best-fit timing model constructed using deterministic parameters of the pulsars (e.g., rotation frequency, spin-down, binary parameters, sky position, etc.). The likelihood of obtaining n timing residuals given model parameters θ for a given pulsar is a multivariate Gaussian as

$$\mathcal{L}(\delta t|\theta) \propto \frac{1}{|C|^{1/2}} e^{-\frac{1}{2}(\delta t-s)^T C^{-1}(\delta t-s)}, \tag{79}$$

where s includes contributions from *deterministic* signals with explicitly modelled time dependence, including the evolution of arrival times as described by the timing model. The covariance matrix C represents contributions from *stochastic* processes. Note that while we have used "$\propto$", the specific normalization does matter in this analysis in general, as the spectra of some of the stochastic processes that contribute to C are themselves described by a set of free parameters.

The diagonal elements of C yield "white" noise that is uncorrelated in time whereas off-diagonal elements of C manifest as time-correlated "red" processes, including the GWB. Red processes are modeled in the frequency domain with a power-law for the power spectral density of timing residuals

$$P(f|A,\gamma) = \frac{A^2}{12\pi^2} \text{yr}^3 (f\,\text{yr})^{-\gamma}, \tag{80}$$

where f is the GW or noise frequency, and A and $-\gamma$ are the power-law amplitude and spectral index, respectively. We discuss sources of red noise that affect pulsars individually in more detail in Section 5.2.2. For the GW case, amplitude A corresponds to the GW strain amplitude at the reference frequency $f_{\text{ref}} = \text{yr}^{-1}$ and γ corresponds to α in Equation (25) and α' explained in footnote 3: $\gamma = 3 - 2\alpha' = 5 - \alpha = 13/3$. The lowest frequency and the size of the frequency bin Δf are usually selected to be equal to the inverse of the total observation time T_{obs}, which is typically more than a decade. The data are collected every few weeks. The observed power spectral density of timing residuals $P(f)$ [s^3] is derived from the GW strain power spectral density $S(f)$ (s) in Section A4 in [177]. Neglecting frequencies f other than multiples of T_{obs}^{-1}, the densities and strain are related as

$$P(f) = \frac{S(f)}{12\pi^2 f^2} = \frac{h(f)^2}{12\pi^2 f^3}. \tag{81}$$

With each pulsar modelled by tens of timing model parameters and the necessity to invert the covariance matrix that models both temporal and spatial correlations for every likelihood evaluation, in practice it is necessary to marginalise the likelihood over nuisance parameters, which include timing model parameters and Gaussian coefficients that yield a specific realization of red noise. Below, we describe the marginalization procedure [178,179] that is employed by recent searches (e.g., [26,54,180]). First, the likelihood is rewritten as

$$\mathcal{L}(\delta t|\epsilon, a, \eta) \propto \frac{1}{|N|^{1/2}} e^{-\frac{1}{2}(\delta t-s)^T N^{-1}(\delta t-s)}, \tag{82}$$

$$\text{where } s = M\epsilon + Fa + s'. \tag{83}$$

The covariance matrix N is now diagonal and, thus, represents the white noise associated with each observation; ϵ represents deterministic timing model parameters and the "design matrix" M maps them to the timing residuals; Fa represents low frequency "red" noise. The latter is modelled by a Fourier series with a Fourier amplitudes vector a and a matrix F of unit-norm frequency Fourier modes. Typically, the frequencies of the Fourier series are multiples of $1/T_{\text{obs}}$ [174]. η represents *hyperparameters* that govern the shape of the red noise spectrum defined by F and a, and s' denotes deterministic terms that are not marginalised over. To be precise, the matrix N is block-diagonal, consisting of the nominal error in pulse arrival time, but parameterised by "EFAC," which multiplies arrival time errors; "EQUAD", which is added to the arrival time errors in quadrature; and "ECORR", which accounts for correlated measurement uncertainties in contemporaneous, multi-band observations and contributions to the off-diagonal terms [54,179,180].

Further compactifying the equations, we express

$$T = (M \quad F), \tag{84}$$

$$b = \begin{pmatrix} \epsilon \\ a \end{pmatrix}. \tag{85}$$

Gaussian priors are then placed on b,

$$\pi(b|\eta) = \frac{\exp\left(-\tfrac{1}{2} b^T B^{-1} b\right)}{\sqrt{2\pi \det\{B\}}}, \tag{86}$$

with covariance B, for which its parameters have previously been referred to as η,

$$B = \begin{pmatrix} \infty & 0 \\ 0 & \varphi \end{pmatrix}, \tag{87}$$

where we have left the prior on the timing model parameters unconstrained (the upper left corner indicates a block with diagonal entries of infinity). The posterior is then proportional to the original multivariate likelihood described by Equation (79) times the prior described by Equation (86),

$$\mathcal{P}(b, \eta | \delta t) \propto \mathcal{L}(\delta t | b) \times \pi(b|\eta) \times \pi(\eta). \tag{88}$$

The initial timing model parameters and the design matrix are obtained with least-squares fitting. The matrix φ contains information about the spectrum of low frequency noise, including intrinsic red noise for each pulsar and the GWB. If we label pulsars as a and b and frequency bins (multiples of $1/T_{\text{obs}}$) as i and j, then the elements of this matrix are

$$[\varphi]_{(ai),(bj)} = \Gamma_{ab} \rho_i \delta_{ij} + \eta_{ai} \delta_{ab} \delta_{ij}, \tag{89}$$

where ρ_i is the spectrum of the GWB (and is, therefore, present in all cross-correlations and auto-correlations), and η_{ai} is the spectrum of intrinsic red noise of pulsar a in frequency bin i (and is, therefore, only present on the diagonals). The vectors of maximum-likelihood values of b, $\hat{b}$, are obtained by solving

$$\hat{b} = \Sigma^{-1} d, \tag{90}$$

$$\Sigma = T^T N^{-1} T + \varphi^{-1}, \tag{91}$$

$$d = T^T N^{-1} \delta t. \tag{92}$$

Alternatively, one can explicitly marginalise over b as

$$\mathcal{P}(\eta|\delta t) = \int db\, \mathcal{P}(b, \eta|\delta t)$$
$$= \frac{\exp\left(-\frac{1}{2}\delta t^T C^{-1} \delta t\right)}{\sqrt{2\pi \det C}}, \tag{93}$$

where $C = N + TBT^T$. C can be efficiently inverted using the Woodbury formula to increase computational efficiency.

In principle, φ is block diagonal with independent frequency bins but correlated noise between pulsars when a GWB is present. However, a GWB signal is expected to reveal itself as a strong common red noise process before cross-correlations are evident. Recent analyses have, therefore, first evaluated the term in Equation (89) with $\Gamma_{ab} = \delta_{ab}$ [178] as the null hypothesis and Γ_{ab} given by Equation (63) as the signal hypothesis. As we discuss in Section 5.2, there is strong evidence for a common spectrum process ($\Gamma_{ab} = \delta_{ab}$) compared to the intrinsic red-noise only hypothesis ($\Gamma_{ab} = 0$), but little compelling evidence for cross-correlations compared to a common spectrum process.

The η_{ai} and ρ_i spectra are modeled as a power law,

$$\eta_{a,i} = P_{\text{red}}(f_i | A_{a,\text{red}}, \gamma_{a,\text{red}}) \Delta f, \tag{94}$$
$$\rho_i = P_{\text{GW}}(f_i | A_{\text{GW}}, \gamma_{\text{GW}}) \Delta f, \tag{95}$$

and so instead of having N_{freq} parameters per pulsar (plus N_{freq} more parameters for the GWB), one has $2(N_{\text{pulsar}} + 1)$ free hyper-parameters that specify the shape of noise processes. White noise parameters, such as the typical EFAC, EQUAD, and ECORR parameters are measured on a per-pulsar (and per-observatory or per-observing back-end) basis. Typical pulsar datasets are modelled by tens of such parameters; thus, white noise parameters are often fixed to their maximum likelihood values that were calculated by analyzing pulsars individually.

Bayesian inference with the marginalised likelihood typically yields posterior samples for the $2(N_{\text{pulsar}} + 1)$ hyperparameters, and the Bayesian evidence, which is the integral of the likelihood over the prior. The evidence is used to select a model that best describes the data. In some recent analyses, explicit Bayes factors (the ratio of evidences between models) are calculated using a "product-space" approach that foregoes individual evidence calculations in favor of sampling from multiple models simultaneously [54,180].

It is also common to consider an optimal statistic which is built similar to the one presented for LVK searches [149,181,182]. We follow the conventions and methods in [182], which were implemented in [54]. We start from the auto-covariance and cross-covariance matrices calculated from the timing residuals,

$$C_a = \langle \delta t_a \otimes \delta t_a \rangle, \tag{96}$$
$$S_{ab} = \langle \delta t_a \otimes \delta t_b \rangle|_{a \neq b}. \tag{97}$$

For a GWB with PSD given by $P_{\text{GW}}(f)$, the cross-covariance matrix is given by

$$S_{ab} = P_{\text{GW}}(f)\left(F_a \Gamma_{ab} F_b^T\right). \tag{98}$$

Specifically, for a background dominated by supermassive black hole binaries that evolve solely due to GW emission, $\gamma = 13/3$. The optimal statistic, $\hat{A}^2$, is then given by [149,181,182]

$$\hat{A}^2 = \frac{\sum_{ab} \delta t_a^T C_a^{-1} \tilde{S}_{ab} C_b^{-1} \delta t_b}{\sum_{ab} C_a^{-1} \tilde{S}_{ab} C_b^{-1} \tilde{S}_{ba}}, \tag{99}$$

with
$$A_{\text{GW}}^2 \tilde{S}_{ab} = S_{ab}. \tag{100}$$

In the second line, we define the amplitude-independent cross-correlation matrix, which makes $\langle \hat{A}^2 \rangle = A_{\text{GW}}^2$. If $A_{\text{GW}} = 0$, then the variance of the optimal statistic is given by

$$\sigma_0 = \left[\sum_{ab} C_a^{-1} \tilde{S}_{ab} C_b^{-1} \tilde{S}_{ba} \right]^{-1/2}, \tag{101}$$

which allows us to construct an SNR $\rho = \hat{A}^2/\sigma_0$. The SNR significance can be found by estimating its noise-only distribution using simulations of the data with pulsar sky positions randomly assigned or random phase shifts applied to the data to remove a signal [179,183].

The implementation of the optimal statistic requires evaluating C_a and S_{ab} for a given choice of hyperparameters that define a, which are amplitudes of sinusoids on which the red noise is decomposed. One typically uses hyperparameters that correspond to $\hat{b}$ in Equation (92). One can also use the maximum *a posteriori* estimates of the red noise parameters from the Bayesian analysis, $A_{\text{red},a}^{\max}$, $\gamma_{\text{red},a}^{\max}$, $A_{\text{GW}}^{\max}$, and $\gamma_{\text{GW}}^{\max}$, but this can result in a large bias in the estimate of $\hat{A}^2$ because the individual red noise parameters and the common red noise parameters are highly correlated. In practice, the red noise parameters are drawn from the posterior samples from the Bayesian analysis and for each draw the optimal statistic and its SNR are calculated. One can estimate a value of $\hat{A}^2$ from this distribution, which is significantly less biased than if one calculates the optimal statistic once from the maximum *a posteriori* estimates of the noise parameters [182].

While our focus in this section has been on methods for detecting an isotropic GWB with PTAs, note that there is also a recent paper that aims to measure both continuous sources from individual supermassive black hole binaries as well as an isotropic confusion background [184].

4.3. Anisotropic Background Detection Methods

Mapping an SGWB is a distinct problem from that of tracing back an individual source position. Individual source mapping leverages the coherence of radiation arriving from the source, using the phase information of the signal to estimate both angular and frequency-dependent phase along with other intrinsic and extrinsic source parameters. In either case, however, a basic requirement for directional analyses is multiple observations of the same signal. These multiple observations can be made in different ways. Multiple detectors at different locations will impose a known phase shift on a coherent signal, which can be used to constrain the position on the sky. In the case of a persistent, coherent source, unequal-time auto-correlation of a single detector signal can yield angular phase information, and in the case of some sources of GWs, matched filtering can be used to pinpoint the location on the sky with a significantly larger effective baseline [185]. For the case of a persistent and incoherent source, such as an SGWB, one may use equal-time correlations of data from different detectors and the motion of individual detectors with respect to the frame in which the signal is stationary to reconstruct angular information. We focus on this approach here.

Let us start by discussing the weak signal limit, which applies to the 2G ground-based detector network (e.g., LIGO and Virgo). As we did for the isotropic case, we can assume that the residuals for the data cross-correlation spectra and our model are Gaussian, similarly to Equation (73). The log-likelihood may be written as a function of an anisotropic signal I explicitly as

$$\ln \mathcal{L}(C^\tau(f)|I(f,\hat{n})) \propto \frac{1}{2} \Big[(C^\tau(f) - \langle C^\tau(f) \rangle) \sigma^{-2} (C^\tau(f) - \langle C^\tau(f) \rangle)^\star + \text{Tr} \ln \sigma^2 \Big], \tag{102}$$

where we generically model the correlated data as

$$\langle C^{\tau}(f) \rangle = \int_{S^2} d\hat{n}\, A^{\tau}(f, \hat{n}) I(f, \hat{n}). \qquad (103)$$

The operator *A projects* the sky signal I into the datastream, and contains all the necessary correlated response information of the detectors. For ground- and space-based detectors, A is given by Equation (59) up to appropriate normalisation factors. We have reintroduced the timestamp label τ here as it serves an important purpose: tracking the time-dependence of the detector response on the sky; the sky signal I is considered absolutely stationary[10] and, thus, τ-independent. For ground-based interferometric detectors, operator A depends only upon the sidereal time, which means the data stream can be folded on the sidereal day before we invert Equation (103) to solve for I [186–188]. To probe the effects of the projection operator A on the GW observations, it is useful to simulate a signal as a single point source on the sky and "project" it analytically (or numerically) into cross-correlated mock data, which produces the *point-spread function* of the detector pair. This has often been studied to glean the effective angular resolution of the detectors to a stochastic source—we refer the reader to [189] for a complete presentation of the subject.

We can now derive a *maximum-likelihood mapping* solution by maximising the likelihood with respect to the sky map. To best illustrate the structure of the solution, let us use a compact matrix notation where operators in bold generally span multiple dimensions, i.e., time, frequency, direction, and baseline, such as $A_b^{\tau}(f, \hat{n}) \to \mathbf{A}$. These are contracted appropriately to achieve the desired result,

$$\tilde{\mathbf{I}} = \left(\mathbf{A}^{\dagger} \mathbf{\Sigma}^{-1} \mathbf{A}\right)^{-1} \mathbf{A}^{\dagger} \mathbf{\Sigma}^{-1} \mathbf{C}. \qquad (104)$$

In the simple case of a single frequency and single time segment of data, we can think of $\mathbf{C}$ as a vector containing cross-correlations between different baselines, $\mathbf{\Sigma}$ is the noise covariance of the cross-correlation of the detector pairs, and $\mathbf{A}$ is now a matrix that contains geometric factors that project different sky directions onto correlations between different detectors. Explicitly, $\mathbf{\Sigma}$ entries are of the form

$$\Sigma_b^{\tau}(f, f') = \mathrm{Cov}[P_i^{f} P_j^{f'}]_{\tau}, \qquad (105)$$

where i, j label the two detectors in the baseline b. More details on the calculation may be found in [35,189,190].

In practice, this solution may need to be implemented iteratively as the noise covariance $\mathbf{\Sigma}$ may not be known *a priori* and, hence, may need to be estimated from the data themselves. In the low signal limit however, as is the case with current ground-based networks, the noise covariance is estimated independently of the signal and Equation (104) is, thus, a closed-form mapping solution. The first term on the right-hand side is the *Fisher information matrix*,

$$\mathbf{F} = \mathbf{A}^{\dagger} \mathbf{\Sigma}^{-1} \mathbf{A}, \qquad (106)$$

which is inverted and applied to the *projection map*,

$$\mathbf{z} = \mathbf{A}^{\dagger} \mathbf{\Sigma}^{-1} \mathbf{C}, \qquad (107)$$

to extract the maximum-likelihood solution $\tilde{\mathbf{I}}$. $\mathbf{z}$ is often referred to as the *dirty map* in the literature, as it effectively represents a first, naïve representation of the cross-spectral density on the sky, while $\tilde{\mathbf{I}}$ is considered the *clean map* as it is the result of a deconvolution. The Fisher matrix contains the pixel–pixel covariance information necessary to deconvolve the detector response from the dirty map. In principle, this method can also be employed for anisotropic searches in a strong signal regime; in this case, if the signal is Gaussian, the map point-estimate remains accurate; however, covariance $\mathbf{\Sigma}$ requires extra terms as the signal contribution may not be ignored.

However, in the presence of a strong signal term, it is preferable to include auto-correlation terms in the likelihood, as these contain precious information. This is the case for, e.g., LISA and PTAs. Hence, we consider again the Gaussian likelihood (72), and as in [191–194], we extend it to include directional information,

$$\ln \mathcal{L}(\boldsymbol{d}^\tau(f) | I(f, \hat{\boldsymbol{n}})) \propto \frac{1}{2}\left[\boldsymbol{d}^\tau(f) \boldsymbol{C}^{-1} \boldsymbol{d}^{\tau\star}(f) + \operatorname{Tr} \ln \boldsymbol{C}\right], \quad (108)$$

where the correlation matrix $\boldsymbol{C}^\tau(f)$ (re-introducing the time and frequency dependence explicitly here for clarity) may be estimated as

$$\boldsymbol{C}(f) = \int_{S^2} d\hat{\boldsymbol{n}} A(f, \hat{\boldsymbol{n}}) I(f, \hat{\boldsymbol{n}}) + \boldsymbol{N}, \quad (109)$$

with $\boldsymbol{N}$ as the noise covariance. Note that A is an $N \times N$ matrix representing the correlated response of the full network.

The above notation implies that we are discussing LISA because we have specified the frequency domain and that A depends on τ. In principle, PTA analysis works analogously—note the similarity of Equation (109) to Equation (89), with the added complication of a dependence on direction. However, it is worth briefly reiterating specific differences. First, the "detector response" is time-independent for PTAs, and in general we assume it is frequency independent. In addition, PTAs leave data in the time domain but expand the GW signal and intrinsic red noise in the frequency domain using a set of Fourier basis functions with an appropriate prior to impose a power-law spectrum and correlations between pulsars (see Equations (87)–(92)). It is the correlations between pulsars that are directly affected, with the anisotropy of the background causing a deviation from the Hellings–Downs curve that depends upon the specific realization of the background. This means that Equation (89) changes:

$$\Gamma_{ab}\rho_i \rightarrow \int_{S^2} d\hat{\boldsymbol{n}}\, \Gamma_{ab}(\hat{\boldsymbol{n}})\rho_i(\hat{\boldsymbol{n}}), \quad (110)$$

with i once again specifying the frequency index, a and b specifying pulsars we are correlating, and $\rho_i(\hat{\boldsymbol{n}})$ specifying the GWB amplitude at frequency index i in direction $\hat{\boldsymbol{n}}$. In this case, $\Gamma_{ab}(\hat{\boldsymbol{n}})$ can be considered a direct analogue to $A(f, \hat{\boldsymbol{n}})$.

In [193], the authors show that extracting the maximum-likelihood map solution from Equation (108) yields

$$\tilde{I} = F^{-1} \cdot \frac{1}{2}\operatorname{Tr}\left[C^{-1}\frac{\partial C}{\partial \tilde{I}} C^{-1}\left(\boldsymbol{d} \otimes \boldsymbol{d}^\star - \boldsymbol{N}\right)\right], \quad (111)$$

$$F = \frac{1}{2}\operatorname{Tr}\left[C^{-1}\frac{\partial C}{\partial \tilde{I}} C^{-1}\frac{\partial C}{\partial \tilde{I}}\right], \quad (112)$$

where F is the Fisher information matrix. This solution is in fact structurally identical to the Bond–Jaffe–Knox mapping procedure in CMB [195,196] and requires an iterative implementation: first, a "guess" map is injected in C (Equation (109)), then a first solution $\tilde{I}$ is calculated using Equation (111), which updates the estimate of C and so on until convergence. Beyond SNR considerations, this iterative method is also useful in the case of correlated noise terms as these may be included in the noise model $\boldsymbol{N}$, whereas solution (104) rests upon the assumption that the noise is completely uncorrelated between different detectors/measurements.

Alternatively, in the strong or intermediate signal regime one can employ a fully Bayesian approach to the problem as presented in, e.g., [192,194,197]. In [192], the authors develop a fully Bayesian search pipeline to use PTAs to map the GW sky using the formalism detailed in [191]. In [194], the authors present a Bayesian search for anisotropies in the GWB using LISA, where they decompose the sky onto the first three spherical harmonics, parameterize the noise covariance curve, and use MCMC sampling to map the diffuse sky and estimate the noise properties of the detector simultaneously.

Several different approaches can be taken when applying these map-making methods to real data [157,186,189–192,197–204] based on specific necessities. The spectral dependence of the map is often factored out (although not always, see, e.g., [154,169,202,205]), under the assumption in Equation (26) and integrated over to obtain *broadband* maps of the GW sky. Then, the direction-dependent component of the signal may be expanded and mapped in spherical harmonics,

$$I(\hat{n}) = \sum_{\ell=0}^{\infty} \sum_{m=-\ell}^{\ell} I_{\ell m} Y_{\ell m}(\hat{n}), \tag{113}$$

or discretized directly on the sky in pixel space,

$$I(\hat{n}) = \sum_{p'=1}^{N_{\text{pix}}} I_{p'} \delta_{pp'}, \tag{114}$$

where $Y_{\ell m}$ are the standard spherical harmonics, and we have used p and p' to enumerate pixels on the sky that are specified using some choice of pixelization (e.g., HealPix [206])[11]. Other works have argued for the use of curl and gradient spherical harmonics, as in CMB analyses [199–201], or bipolar spherical harmonics [207], although to our knowledge these have not yet been employed on real data.

In both the pixel and spherical harmonic bases, the Fisher matrix F is usually very poorly conditioned for a single baseline, as the sky coverage is incomplete; this is the case even after time-integration, which takes into account the sky-scanning strategy of the baseline. Regularisation techniques are, therefore, needed to estimate maximum likelihood solutions such as those presented in Equations (112) and (106). Examples of regularization techniques include cutting off the sum in (113) a priori at some maximum ℓ [190], singular value decomposition (SVD) (see, e.g., [208]), and the drastic approach of limiting the calculation to the diagonal of F, ignoring all off-diagonal correlations [198]. In some cases, combinations of these approaches are used.

The spherical harmonic basis has mostly been employed when searching for a diffuse background, which dominates the low-ℓ modes, while pixel space has been employed when searching for point-like stochastic sources, although it has been shown that there is a one-to-one mapping between the two [209] (see, e.g., Figures 1 and 2 of [192] for an illustrative example of how specific anisotropic maps correspond to different spherical harmonic decompositions). There may however be subtle differences between the conditioning in spherical harmonic and pixel space; in interferometry in general, the choice has often been to obtain a spherical harmonic domain solution since the measurements directly constrain this domain (see e.g., [210] for an application to CMB interferometry). The reconstruction of the actual "image" is then left as a separate and straightforward conversion problem.

However, as discussed in [152], in the case of GW detectors, there is a non-trivial coupling of spherical modes in the sky response due to the non-compactness of the beam, indicating that adopting this approach may have significant drawbacks. In particular, there is no isotropic kernel for a primary beam describing the coupling of individual pairs of directions, hence limiting the number of spherical modes in the solution in a piece-wise fashion could make the problem more ill-conditioned than it actually is. Finally, in the case of PTAs it has been shown that, when working in the spherical harmonics basis, the non-uniformity of pulsars on the sky makes it impossible to decouple the monopole from other multipole moments, making the search less sensitive to isotropic backgrounds [203,204]. In those studies, the authors propose using a basis formed with principal component analysis of the direction-dependent sensitivity of the specific PTA.

In fully Bayesian examples, using too many spherical harmonics terms or pixels on the sky can make the problem intractable or, in a detection case, could widen the parameter space beyond what is possible to resolve. Techniques that can be used to make the full Bayesian problem more tractable might be to only search over the first few spherical harmonics, as in, e.g., [192,194]. Other techniques have also been proposed, one of which constructs a set of basis "sky vectors" from only the columns of the SVD matrices that are associated with non-zero singular values of the Fisher matrix. One then samples over their coefficients to reconstruct the map using a lower-dimensional representation of the sky [197,201].

Although notably more challenging when attempting map-making with a singular F, the spectral dependence may be solved for as well, resulting in *narrowband* directional searches. These have been carried out by the LVK collaboration targeting point-like sources which may have an interesting spectral emission (e.g., asymmetric neutron stars, supernova remnants, the galactic bulge) and have been performed in pixel space [187,188,211]. As point sources are not correlated with other points on the sky, this type of search ignores the off-diagonal correlations in the Fisher matrix to avoid the inversion problem. Another approach employed on LIGO data in [154] is that of frequency-banding, where one solves for maps in separate frequency bands spanning several Hz, making minimal assumptions about the spectrum of the signal in each band. This allows both inverting the full Fisher matrix and obtaining full sky maps in each band and attempt a model-free reconstruction of the frequency spectrum. In the case of pulsar timing arrays, the signal is dominated by a small ($\lesssim$10) number of frequencies, and so in the fully Bayesian analysis in [202], they estimate different spherical harmonic coefficients at different frequencies to allow for maps that are dominated by point sources in different directions at different frequencies.

4.4. The Approach towards Non-Gaussian Backgrounds

The cross-correlation searches reviewed above have been shown to be *optimal* in the case of a continuous background, which, for example, presents a timestream as in the third row of Figure 3; however, these will be suboptimal in the case of a background which is intermittent, such as the first row of Figure 3. As argued in [212], an intermittent background will not satisfy the central limit theorem; thus, searching for such a signal under the Gaussian assumption will reduce the sensitivity of the search, resulting in delays until detection (although it will not bias the point estimate). Given the observations of GWs accumulated up until now [213] and the lack of a detection of a Gaussian stochastic background, it is clear that a signal of sub-threshold GW bursts from compact binary coalescences is present in LIGO and Virgo data and may be the first stochastic signal that can be detected with ground-based detectors.

A few optimised search methods for non-Gaussian backgrounds have been proposed: a maximum likelihood approach [212] where each isolated GW making up the background is modelled as a "stochastic burst" of GW strain, correlated between detectors; a Bayesian search method which leverages deterministic parameter estimation [214,215], fitting each burst with a compact binary waveform; and, soon, a fully Bayesian stochastic search [216] which extends the formalism of [212]. This method has also been extended to estimate the anisotropic properties of the subthreshold CBC population [217].

While substantially different in formulation and implementation, these approaches share the premise of re-parametrisation of the background signal based on a *Gaussianity parameter*, ξ, which quantifies the degree of non-Gaussianity. Effectively, this is the same as the duty cycle introduced in Section 3.4 and is linked to the duration of each individual GW burst and the frequency with which they appear in the detector. If normalised, $0 \leq \xi \leq 1$ is the probability that a burst is present in the detector at any given time, and if $\xi = 1$, the background is Gaussian. The detector noise, on the other hand, is usually still assumed to be Gaussian[12]. Then, that assuming we segment data into short segments labelled by i, the likelihood function for the data vector d_i (for a set of detectors) given the data covariance C and signal model h is

$$\mathcal{L}(d_i) \propto \prod_{f,\tau} \frac{1}{|C|^{1/2}} e^{\frac{1}{2}(d_i - h_i) C^{-1} (d_i - h_i)^*} . \tag{115}$$

For an intermittent background, model h_i in the likelihood will be either a GW burst or a CBC waveform, if the data segment d_i has a signal, or simply equal to zero if it does not [215]. The full likelihood $\mathcal{L}_{\text{full}}$ of the data with an intermittent signal may then be written as the mixture of a signal-and-noise likelihood $\mathcal{L}_s$ and a noise-only likelihood $\mathcal{L}_n$ as

$$\mathcal{L}_{\text{full}}(d_i) = \xi \mathcal{L}_s(d_i | h_i) + (1 - \xi) \mathcal{L}_n(d_i | 0) , \tag{116}$$

featuring the duty cycle ξ as a parameter. Maximising this likelihood (with any of these approaches) results in posterior distributions for both the signal parameters that construct h_i, and ξ; furthermore, it is also possible to include noise parameters here such that these also are estimated.

5. Current Detection Efforts of SGWBs

A variety of searches based on the methods described in Section 4 have been implemented in interferometric and timing data, in the case of ground-based detectors and pulsar timing arrays (PTA), respectively, to either detect or constrain a wide range of stochastic backgrounds. Beyond these, many investigations have been carried out to assess the detection potential of future detectors on the ground and in space and their ability to distinguish different background sources.

In this Section, we start by discussing the most recent analysis results from the ground-based detector LIGO–Virgo–KAGRA (LVK) collaboration, obtained with the third observing run (O3) of the 2G detectors: the *Advanced* LIGO and the *Advanced* Virgo. These results build on the previous data runs O1 and O2 of the 2G detectors. The overall sensitivity of the 2G detector network may be observed in Figure 7. We then discuss future detection prospects for the 2G network, which should reach *design* sensitivity with the next few upgrades of the instruments [218]. When representing the sensitivity to a GWB, we use "power-law integrated" sensitivity curves, which show the sensitivity to a GWB at each frequency (at a chosen SNR level) with a power law spectral shape that is tangent to the curve at that frequency [219].

For PTAs, we provide details about existing and proposed collaborations across the world and report on their searches for nanohertz GWBs. We review the upper limits on the amplitude of the isotropic GWB from circular supermassive black hole binaries. Next, we briefly outline main sources of noise that limit the searches and discuss the future of timing array experiments. We close by briefly discussing other interesting GW searches, such as resonant bar experiments and the Moon-based proposals, and highlight their bearing on stochastic searches.

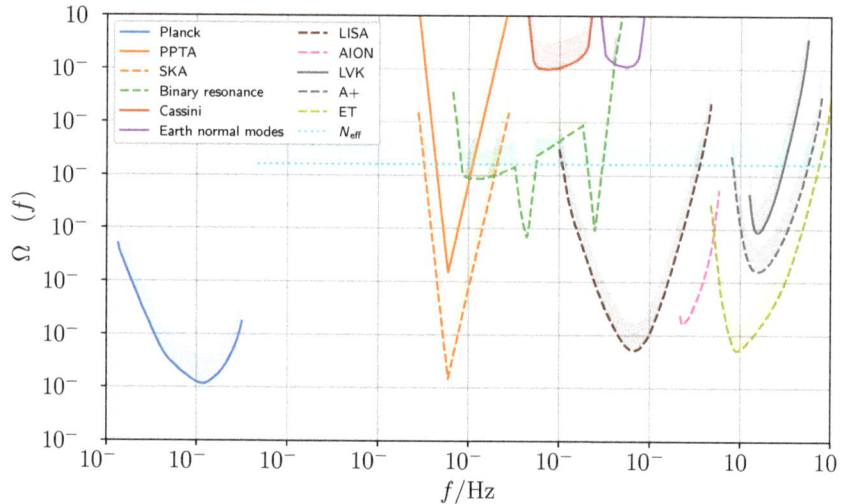

Figure 7. A survey of constraints (all at 95% confidence) on the GWB across the frequency spectrum. Solid curves indicate existing results from LIGO/Virgo's first three observing runs [56], monitoring of the Earth's normal modes [220], Doppler tracking of the Cassini satellite [221], pulsar timing observations by the PPTA [222], and CMB temperature and polarisation spectra measured by Planck [222,223]. Dashed curves are forecast constraints for LIGO at A+ sensitivity, Einstein Telescope [14], AION-km [224], LISA [29], binary resonance searches [225,226], and pulsar timing with the Square Kilometre Array [227]. The dotted curve indicates the level of the integrated constraint from measurements of N_{eff} [38]; note that this is a constraint on the total GW energy density over a broad frequency range and *cannot* be directly compared to the other constraints. Note also that both the Planck and N_{eff} constraints apply only to primordial GWs emitted before the epoch of BBN. See Figure 1 for various GWB signal predictions in relation to these constraints.

5.1. Searches with Ground-Based Laser Interferometers

The ground-based detector communities have put in a continued, concerted effort towards detecting a stochastic GW background between $\sim$10–10^3 Hz. The principal candidate for a stochastic background in the ground-based detector band is one given by inspiralling and merging binary black holes and neutron stars. This is clear given the sensitivity of the LIGO-Virgo network, as shown for example in Figure 7, and the fact that these detectors have *already detected* a large set of CBCs [74]. This background has been exclusively searched for via a cross-correlation search, tailored to the astrophysical background in particular by reweighting the data in frequency according to the expected power-law spectral dependence as derived in Equation (36). First efforts of isotropic stochastic searches date back to 2003 and the first science run [228], followed by several other science runs of the LIGO detectors [16,229–231], and the Advanced detector era since 2016 [161,232], and, finally, the inclusion of Virgo [56]. Beyond these, several other searches have been carried out by targeting specific GWBs; notably, searches which allow for anisotropy in the signal have regularly been carried out [211,233–236], as well as searches for cosmic string networks [129,237,238]. Other targeted searches include searches for non-GR polarisation modes [56,161,239]. Furthermore, several stochastic search efforts have been carried out by small teams outside the LVK collaboration; let us cite here a set of directional searches complementary to the LVK ones [153,154,240], a search for correlations between the anisotropic GWB and galaxy catalogues [241], searches for ultralight vector bosons [162,163], a search for a primordial inflationary background [242], and a search for parity-violating stochastic signals [166].

We focus on current search results in this section, detailing the detector characterisation issues that the Advanced detectors have faced up to now. We discuss future challenges for ground-based detectors in Section 6.1, where we explore SGWB detection strategies with third generation interferometers.

5.1.1. Search Results for an Isotropic Background by LVK

Applying the cross-correlation recipe described in Section 4 to the real LIGO-Virgo datasets requires firstly identifying the valid cross-correlation times at which different detectors are simultaneously online and fully operational and, subsequently, Fourier transforming the measured timestreams to the frequency domain. In practice, it is convenient to divide these into smaller time segments and fast-Fourier transform (FFT) each segment, which is treated as an independent measurement. This reduces the cost of Fourier transforming, excludes frequencies that are far into the $1/f$ tail, and ensures that noise properties are stationary within each segment.

In the most recent isotropic stochastic analysis [56], raw data are segmented into 192 s segments which are then Hann-windowed and FFTed. The data are downsampled from the native sampling rate of 16 kHz to 4096 Hz, and the full frequency band included in the analyses spans 20–1726 Hz; this choice is made so as to exclude the highest and lowest frequencies available where noise becomes prohibitively large. Data quality cuts are applied based on a measure of noise stationarity between segments or when there are known detector artifacts in the data, and these cuts reduce viable data by ∼20% in O3. In addition, frequencies where narrow spectral artifacts ("lines") occur and are caused by known instrumental disturbances or show coherence between detectors are removed [243] and typically cut ∼15–20% of the frequency band. More details on the methodology, exact values of data excised for each baseline in O3, and implementation of the quality checks can be found in [56,243]. Note that this is the first advanced-detector era stochastic analysis to include multiple baselines[13]; we highlight in this section the important implications of adding two long baselines to the network. Specifically, O3 analysis spans Hanford–Livingston (H–L), Hanford–Virgo (H–V), and Livingston–Virgo (L–V).

Several new analysis features were implemented in [56], as the LVK collaboration gears up for a possible SGWB detection. The results are presented by using a log-uniform prior, assigning equal weight to each order of magnitude in Ω_{GW}, in line with our current state of knowledge. Furthermore, a correlated noise analysis targeting magnetic noise resonances was carried out, using the framework set up by the likelihood (75). The analysis confirmed the lack of correlated magnetic noise across the interferometer network and laid out a clear methodology, which will prove essential for similar analyses with future, more sensitive detectors (e.g., 3G). For the first time, short *gates* (∼1 s) were employed to remove frequent, loud glitches which populated the LIGO detector O3 data [244,245]. These were not as frequent nor problematic in previous data runs, and investigations are still under way to determine the sources of these noise artifacts. Without their removal, loud glitches would bias the PSD of a 192-second segment, which would then not pass the stationarity cut, reducing the effective live time of the LIGO detectors to less than 50%, whereas gated datasets are reduced by about 1% of the original total length.

The H–L baseline contributes the most to overall network sensitivity, while Virgo baselines remain important for higher frequencies and, hence, especially for searches employing higher values of the spectral index α. The combined H–L–V spectrum for all three data runs shown in Figure 8 is consistent with Gaussian noise, with symmetric fluctuations around zero. Note that the Virgo baselines contribute information around 64 Hz, where the overlap reduction function of H–L is null. In general, the three baseline combinations are more sensitive given that each detector has different consistent monochromatic noise lines (e.g., the harmonics of the suspension mechanism) which are excluded from analyses, inducing gaps in the frequency spectra.

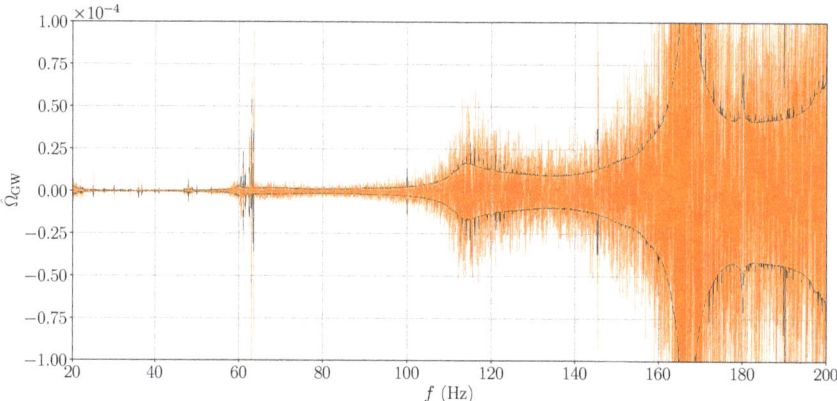

Figure 8. Combined cross-correlation spectra for the three O3 baselines. The grey lines here mark 1σ contours. The data, by eye, appears to follow the Gaussian distribution. Note that adding the Virgo baselines has filled in the gap in the H–L data present around the 60 Hz power line (this broad line is present in both USA-based detectors, but not in Italy). The original version of this plot is presented in [56]; the one shown here was obtained using open data published in [246].

As there is no clear evidence of a GWB, as LVK places upper limits on the three fixed power law models: $\alpha = 0$, typically associated with a scale-invariant, cosmological model [76]; $\alpha = 2/3$, which describes a population of inspiralling compact binaries [64]; and $\alpha = 3$, which corresponds to a flat strain power [151]. These are astrophysically motivated further in Section 3. With 95% confidence, it was found that $\Omega_{GW}|_{25Hz} < 0.6 \pm 1.7 \times 10^{-8}$ ($\alpha = 0$), $0.3 \pm 1.2 \times 10^{-8}$ ($\alpha = 2/3$), and $0.4 \pm 1.3 \times 10^{-9}$ ($\alpha = 3$). In recent analyses, α is also allowed to vary as a parameter of the GWB model in likelihood [75]. In this case, a mean-zero Gaussian prior is assumed, with standard deviation 3.5. Marginalising over α with this method yields a 95% confidence upper limit of $\Omega_{GW}|_{25Hz} < 0.7 \pm 2.7 \times 10^{-8}$. When comparing the hypotheses of signal and noise to noise-only, the $\log_{10}$ Bayes Factor is found to be -0.3. The posteriors for the joint fit of α and $\Omega_{GW}|_{25Hz}$ are shown here in Figure 9.

The results discussed so far assume that the stochastic GW signal is entirely composed of the two transverse-traceless (TT) polarisation modes predicted by GR. However, modified gravity theories generally contain additional polarisations, up to a maximum of six: the two TT modes of GR, one scalar "breathing" mode, and three longitudinal modes—one scalar and two vector [247]. A detection of non-TT polarisation content would provide compelling evidence for the breakdown of GR. Using the method first developed in Ref. [160], LVKs have conducted searches for non-GR polarisations in GWB, using the distinct overlap reduction functions associated with each different set of modes (scalar, vector, and tensor) and marginalising over the power-law slope α as described above [56,239]. The resulting upper limits on the GWB intensity are broadly similar in each case, giving $\Omega_T < 6.4 \times 10^{-9}$ for tensors, $\Omega_V < 7.9 \times 10^{-9}$ for vectors, and $\Omega_S < 2.1 \times 10^{-8}$ for scalars with the O3 dataset [56].

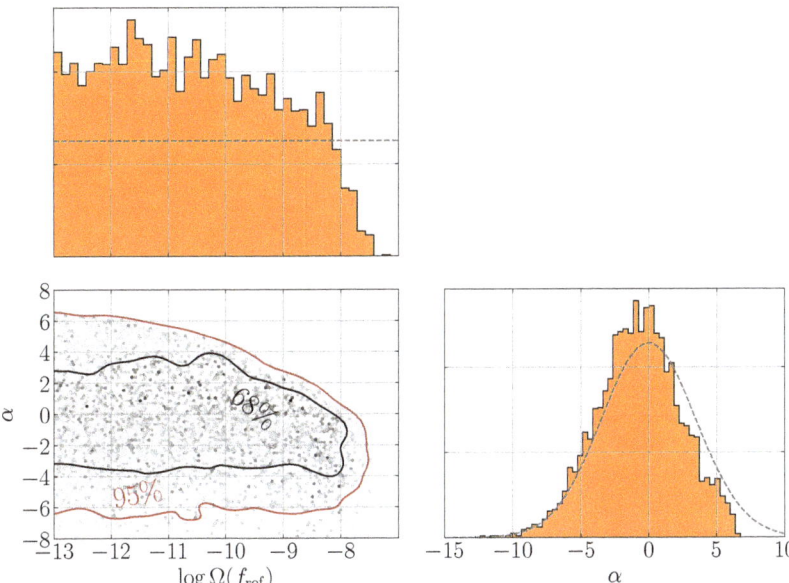

Figure 9. Posterior distributions for the GWB energy density Ω_{GW} at reference frequency $f = 25$ Hz and spectral index α. The dashed grey lines show the priors used in parameter estimation. Note that a log-uniform prior was chosen here on Ω_{GW}, and a mean–zero Gaussian was chosen for α as the detector noise PSD is approximately flat. The original version of this plot is presented in [56]; the one shown here was obtained using the open data published in [246].

LVK assessed future detection prospects by projecting the expected astrophysical background signal, given the current GW detections, onto the expected sensitivities of upcoming detector networks. This comparison is present in Figure 2 in Section 3.1, where we discuss the different contributions to the stochastic background. The expected signal includes contributions from BBHs, BNSs, and BHNSs, all of which have representative direct detections in the advanced LIGO-Virgo runs. We discuss details of the astrophysical background model in Section 3.1; in essence, the total GWB at the selected reference frequency is expected to be $\Omega_{GW}^{CBC}|_{25Hz} < 1.9 \times 10^{-9}$, which is about an order of magnitude away from the upper limit set with $\alpha = 2/3$. Taking Ω_{GW}^{CBC} as an upper limit, it is compared with the 2σ integrated sensitivity curve for O3,2-year projections for the Advanced LIGO-Virgo network operating at design sensitivity [218], and a 2-year, 50% duty cycle A+ network at design sensitivity [248]. Figure 2 shown in Section 3 suggests that by the time design sensitivity is reached for Advanced LIGO-Virgo detectors, these will be marginally sensitive to the background. By the A+ phase, the vast majority of the background signal should be within reach of detection.

Both the astrophysical GWB spectrum and the set of individual BBH signals resolved by LIGO/Virgo are determined by the cosmic BBH merger rate history $\dot{N}(z)$. The non-observation of the GWB from this category of sources sets an upper bound on this function, while the set of resolved signals provides a lower bound at low redshift. By combining both pieces of information, we can, therefore, infer something about this merger history [56,65], potentially revealing interesting astrophysical information about BBH abundances and formation channels, such as whether BBHs are predominantly formed through isolated binary evolution or through dynamical assembly in dense stellar environments. As was recently pointed out in Refs. [249–251], these inferences about the BBH merger rate at high redshift can also be used to set an upper bound on the fraction of individual detections that are expected to undergo strong gravitational lensing. At present (i.e., post-O3), the uncertainty on $\dot{N}(z)$ is still large, spanning several orders of magnitude at redshifts $z \gtrsim 1$ [56], but we can look forward to significant improvements with future LVK observing runs. The inferred redshift shape of $\dot{N}(z)$ is currently consistent with the BBH merger rate directly tracking the cosmic star formation rate (see Figure 10), but there are some tentative hints of a shallower growth at low redshift, as one would expect if there is a non-zero delay time between star formation and the eventual merger event. Note that the star formation rate reported here is arbitrarily normalised.

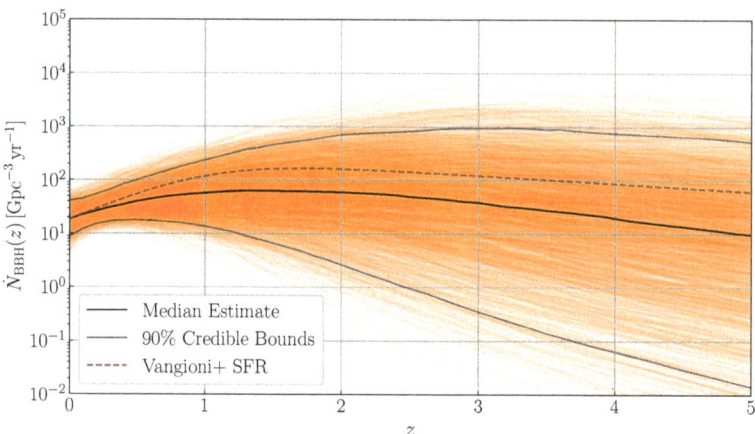

Figure 10. Collection of all posterior draws for the merger rate as a function of redshift $\dot{N}_{\text{BBH}}(z)$ inferred from the combination of the resolved BBH detections in the GWTC-2 catalog [252] and the upper limits on the stochastic background obtained with LIGO/Virgo O3 data. The original version of this plot is presented in [56]; the one shown here was obtained using open data published in [246].

LVK stochastic searches have also been used to search for various cosmological sources of GWs that have been proposed in the literature, which we reviewed in Section 3. Among the most promising of these sources are cosmic strings, and LVK stochastic searches can be used in particular to place upper limits on the cosmic string tension $G\mu$. The precise constraint depends on the model adopted for the string loop network, but the strongest constraint from the first three observing runs is $G\mu < 4 \times 10^{-15}$ [129]. This is the strongest existing constraint on a cosmic string model from any experiment; for comparison, CMB constraints are typically at the level of $G\mu \lesssim 10^{-7}$ [253]. Another potential signal of cosmological origin is SGWB from PBHs. The non-observation of this signal by LIGO/Virgo implies that PBHs in the mass range $2\,M_\odot$–$200\,M_\odot$ cannot make up the entirety of the cosmic CDM budget [254,255], $f_{\text{PBH}} \lesssim 1$; by the time LIGO/Virgo reach design sensitivity, this constraint is expected to improve to $f_{\text{PBH}} \lesssim 10^{-3}$. Searches have also been conducted for the "scalar-induced" SGWB generated by the collapsing overdensities during the process of PBH formation [165]. For GWs in the LVK frequency band, this corresponds to the formation of very light PBHs, with masses $\lesssim 10^{13}$ kg. With future *third-generation* interferometers, these searches are expected to dominate over existing constraints coming from electromagnetic signatures of PBH evaporation.

We have aimed here to provide only a taster of some of the numerous cosmological GW sources that have been probed with LVK stochastic searches. Many other examples exist, including first-order phase transitions [164], superradiant bosonic condensates around black holes [162,163], and even sources which are not associated with GWs, but which couple directly to the LIGO/Virgo test masses to mimic a SGWB signal, such as dark photons [128].

5.1.2. Search Results for an Anisotropic Background by LVK

The anisotropic search methods outlined in Section 4.3 were most recently applied to LIGO and Virgo detector data in [211]. For the first time, data from Virgo was included in the search, leading to a three-baseline network, similarly to the isotropic search presented in Section 4.2.1. The data were pre-processed as in the latter, starting from the *gated* LIGO data-sets. To increase the efficiency of the search, the data were *folded* to one sidereal day before analysis [186]; this effectively reduces the cost of the search by a factor equal to the number of days in the dataset, with extremely little loss of information.

Three different, complementary approaches were employed in the search: a broadband, pixel-based analysis targeting point sources, referenced as the broad-band radiometer (BBR) analysis; a broadband, spherical harmonic decomposition (SHD) analysis, sensitive to extended stochastic sources [190]; and, finally, a narrowband analysis targeting three specific sky locations where a GWB signal may be expected, dubbed the narrowband radiometer (NBR) search. Notably, the so-called "radiometer" searches are both carried out in pixel space and ignore off-diagonal correlations present in the Fisher information matrix (Equation (106)) under the assumption that each direction is fully uncorrelated. The SHD search on the other hand is aimed at diffuse sources which span multiple directions and, thus, requires tackling the Fisher matrix inversion problem. The spherical harmonic domain is chosen here to reduce the effective number of degrees of freedom to a small number of modes on the sky, assuming the measurement is *diffraction-limited*, i.e., the maximum resolvable scale on the sky is directly related to frequency f and aperture D of an interferometric measurement by the following (see, e.g., [235] for a more detailed discussion),

$$\ell_{\max} \sim \frac{2\pi D f}{c}. \tag{117}$$

In a cross-correlation GW analysis with pairs of detectors, D is the length of the baseline for each detector pair. To obtain an estimate for a sensible $\ell_{\max}$ to use in the search, frequency f is assumed to be the frequency at which the detectors are most sensitive to the stochastic signal; in practice, three different spectral indices were employed in the SHD search in [211], which approach LIGO/Virgo sensitivity curves at different "peak" frequencies. These suggest a band-limiting of $\ell_{\max} = 3$, 4, and 16 for $\alpha = 0, 2/3$, and 3, respectively.

The BBR analysis yields sky maps consistent with mean zero Gaussian noise and, thus, provides directional upper limits, as seen in the signal-to-noise ratio (SNR) maps presented in Figure 11. Note that these are obtained by assuming each direction is fully independent and, thus, should not be read as maps at all, but rather each pixel value should be interpreted as the upper limit on stochastic GWs in that particular direction in the case where that direction is the only one contributing to a stochastic signal. Similarly, SHD analysis produces spherical harmonic coefficients for GWB, band-limited according to the prescription above, which are then converted to the pixel domain yielding maps consistent with noise. The angular power spectrum C_ℓ^{GWB} as defined by Equation (47) can be directly estimated from the coefficients; however, as the measurement is noise-dominated, the unbiased estimator is [154,190]

$$\hat{C}'^{\mathrm{GWB}}_\ell = \hat{C}^{\mathrm{GWB}}_\ell - \mathcal{N}_\ell, \qquad \mathcal{N}_\ell = \frac{1}{2\ell+1}\sum_m F^{-1}_{\ell m, \ell m}. \tag{118}$$

Here, $\hat{C}^{\mathrm{GWB}}_\ell$ is the naive angular power spectrum estimator calculated as in Equation (47) using the spherical harmonic coefficients obtained from the data. $\mathcal{N}_\ell$ is an estimate of the noise covariance of the GW measurement, containing the appropriately normalised inverse Fisher matrix F calculated in spherical harmonic coordinates and is taken to be a measure of the uncertainty. Employing the unbiased estimator results in an angular power spectrum estimate fully consistent with zero; thus 95%, upper limits are placed on the spectrum as shown in Figure 12.

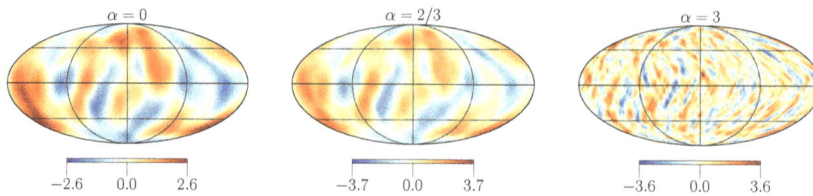

Figure 11. SNR maps obtained with the "broad–band radiometer" search method applied to O1, O2, and O3 data, for different fixed values of the spectral index α, as explained in the text. It is clear there is no significant high SNR signal in the maps. The original version of this plot is presented in [211]; the one shown here was obtained using open data published in [256].

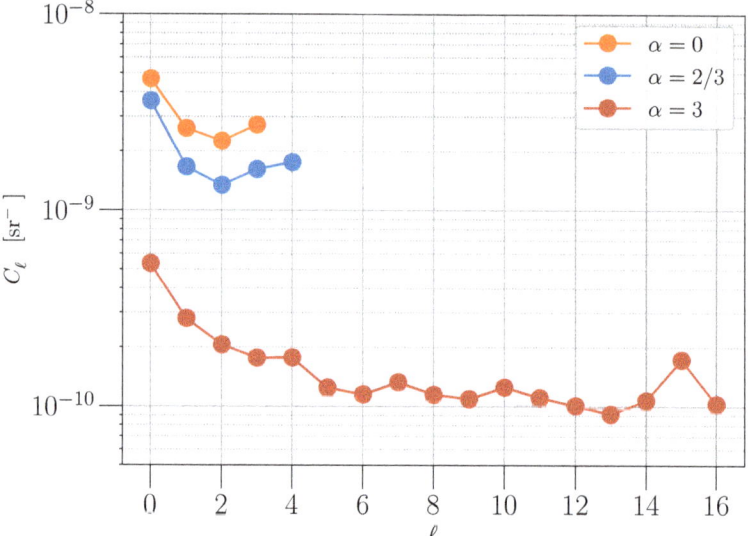

Figure 12. Angular power spectrum upper limits obtained with the "spherical harmonic decomposition" search method applied to O1, O2, and O3 data, for different fixed values of the spectral index α, as explained in the text. The original version of this plot is presented in [211]; the one shown here was obtained by using open data published in [256].

The NBR analysis described in [211] sets upper limits on frequency spectra from three astrophysically relevant sky locations: the direction of the X-ray emitting binary system *Scorpius X-1* [257]; the direction of the remnant of Supernova 1987A [258]; and the center of our Galaxy, which may contain relevant GW sources [259]. No overdensity of GWs is found in any of these directions; hence, narrowband upper limits are placed in each frequency bin. Recently, LVK extended this type of search to an "All–Sky, All–Frequency" (ASAF) search [260], which produces sky maps for each frequency bin, in the pixel domain and at high pixelisation, assuming each pixel is uncorrelated. This type of search is best suited to quickly identify candidates for continuous, quasi-monochromatic GW wave sources coming from point sources on the sky, e.g., rotating neutron stars. The results of this search found a small set of outliers which may be investigated with continuous waves searches, for example, with methods proposed in [261].

5.2. Stochastic Searches with Pulsar Timing Arrays

Unlike ground-based interferometers, the first astrophysical signal observed with PTAs is expected to be a stochastic signal [120] from supermassive black hole binaries. For an insightful review of the astrophysics that can be performed with PTAs, see [262], and for a broader overview of the field, see [263]. The concept of such experiments was proposed by Sazhin [264] and further discussed by Detweiler [265]. To reach nanohertz frequencies, PTAs perform arrival time measurements from an ensemble of millisecond pulsars for a minimum of several years. The first three PTAs are the EPTA [21], NANOGrav [19], and PPTA [20]. The dependence of the Hellings–Downs curve in Equation (63) on the angular coordinates of pulsars implies that timing arrays benefit from observing pulsar pairs across the entire sky. Specifically, it was shown by Siemens et al. [266] that it is important to increase the number of observed pulsar pairs to resolve Earth-term spatial correlations of the background from the spatially uncorrelated pulsar-term component of the background, which manifests as time-correlated noise.

While EPTA and NANOGrav mostly observe pulsars from the northern hemisphere, PPTA has access to pulsars from the southern hemisphere. Recently, two more efforts have emerged: the Indian Pulsar Timing Array (InPTA [25], which is the newest member of IPTA); and the MeerTime project [267], which is based on the MeerKAT [268] facility in South Africa, a precursor of SKA [27]. A recent proposal sees the new telescope FAST [28], the largest "dish" radio telescope in the world, laying the foundations for a PTA collaboration in China. The IPTA [23] is the global effort to accelerate the detection of the nanohertz GWB by combining data sets across the previously mentioned member collaborations.

5.2.1. Search Results for an Isotropic Nanohertz Background

Searches for isotropic GWB constrain the power-law strain amplitude A of the background at the GW frequency $f = 1\,\text{yr}^{-1}$. Following Equation (36) and the relation between spectral indices explained in footnote 3, the strain spectrum of the background has the form $h(f) = A(f/1\,\text{yr}^{-1})^{-2/3}$. The limits on A, denoting either confidence or credibility, are reportedly between 1.1×10^{-14} and 1.0×10^{-15} at 95% [173,180,269–274].

As discussed in Section 4.2.2, it is expected that, prior to the detection of Hellings–Downs spatial correlations, temporal correlations with the same spectra will be observed in pulsar data sets. This phenomenon is now known as the "common-spectrum process", and it was first reported in the search for the background with the NANOGrav 12.5-year data set [54], where the authors for the first time did not place limits on the background amplitude but instead provided the measurement of the amplitude of the common-spectrum process.

After that, the PPTA collaboration reported [26] statistical evidence for the common-spectrum process in a similar fashion, while also suggesting that current analyses do not consider a model where spectra are similar but not common. Furthermore, the authors simulated data set showed evidence for the common-spectrum process, whereas amplitudes of the injected noise power spectra were different by several orders of magnitude. Thus, it was shown that the evidence for the common-spectrum process might arise from pulsar noise described by parameters in a similar range or by model mis-specification.

On the other hand, compared with NANOGrav results [54], PPTA [26] measured the spectral slope $-\gamma$ of the common-spectrum process to be even more consistent with the theoretical prediction for the GWB from supermassive black hole binaries, $\gamma = 13/3$. The relation between this value and the strain spectral index $\alpha' = -2/3$ is explained in Section 4.2.2. Furthermore, under certain analysis conditions, constraints on spatial correlations as a function of pulsar-Earth baselines obtained by the PPTA seem to be even in a better agreement with the Hellings–Down curve. The PPTA measurement is presented here in Figure 6 and the NANOGrav measurement may be seen in Figure 7 of [54]. The PPTA measurement is affected by the pulsar with strong unmodelled excess noise [26]. The EPTA collaboration has also reported evidence for the common-spectrum process with a 24-year-long data set from an observation of six pulsars [275]. Measurements of power-law parameters of the common-spectrum process by NANOGrav, PPTA, and EPTA are presented in Figure 13.

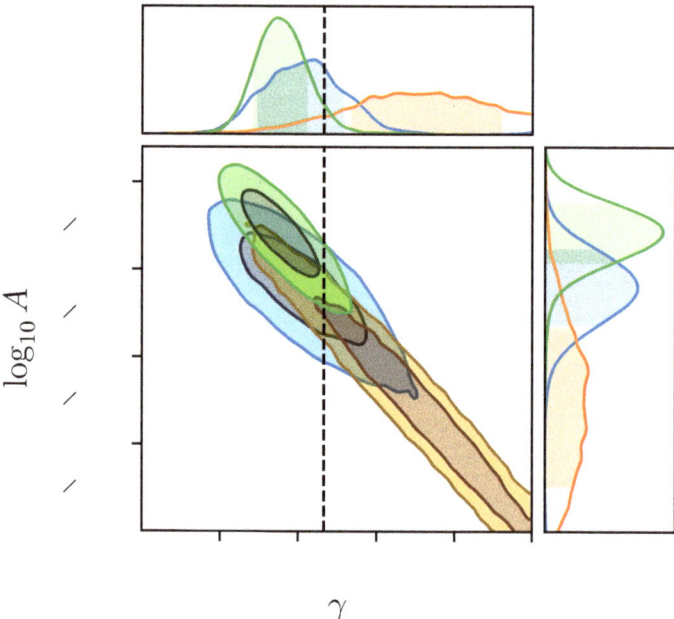

Figure 13. Power-law amplitude A and the negative of the spectral index, γ (see Equation (80)), of the common component of power spectral density of timing residuals δt as reported NANOGrav (orange [54]), PPTA (blue [26]), and EPTA (green [275]).

The results of searches for the isotropic background are summarised in Table 1. The observation time span T_{obs} does not directly increase with publication year due to the inclusion or noninclusion of older data where the limited radio frequency band is not sufficient to model "chromatic" red noise arising from pulse propagation effects in the interstellar medium. One also might notice that a few upper limits on the GW strain amplitude are below the amplitude of the common-spectrum process. This is partly caused by the adoption of the older Solar System ephemerides in earlier publications, which were known to contain systematic errors. The origin of the common-spectrum process is to be clarified in future work through better constraints on spatial and temporal correlations. For a more thorough discussion about the noise with references please refer to the following subsections.

Table 1. Results of searches for the nanohertz-frequency isotropic GWB with the amplitude A and the energy-density spectral index $\alpha = 2/3$ in chronological order. The first three columns list details of corresponding publications. Publications that adopted alphabetical author list are denoted by asterisks. The fourth column contains 95% upper limits on A for the GWB and measurements of A of the common-spectrum process (CP) with credible levels of 1σ in [26] and 5–95% in [54,275,276]. The values in the last two columns are the characteristics of the data set: the total observation time $T_{\rm obs}$ and the number of pulsars in the array $N_{\rm psr}$.

Publication	Collaboration	Year	A ($\times 10^{-15}$)	$T_{\rm obs}$ (yr)	$N_{\rm psr}$
Jenet et al. [269]	PPTA	2006	<11	20	7
van Haasteren et al. [173]	EPTA	2011	<6	11	5
Demorest et al. [270]	NANOGrav	2013	<7	5	17
Shannon et al. [271]	PPTA	2013	<2.4	25	6
Lentati et al. [272]	EPTA	2015	<3.0	18	6
* Arzoumanian et al. [178]	NANOGrav	2015	<1.5	9	37
Shannon et al. [274]	PPTA	2015	<1.0	11	4
Verbiest et al. [24]	IPTA	2016	<1.7	21	4
* Arzoumanian et al. [180]	NANOGrav	2018	<1.45	11.4	45
* Arzoumanian et al. [54]	NANOGrav	2020	CP: $1.9^{+0.8}_{-0.6}$	12.5	45
Goncharov et al. [26]	PPTA	2021	CP: $2.2^{+0.4}_{-0.3}$	15.0	26
Chen et al. [275]	EPTA	2021	CP: $3.0^{+0.9}_{-0.7}$	24.0	6
* Antoniadis et al. [276]	IPTA	2022	CP: $2.8^{+1.2}_{-0.8}$	30.2	53

5.2.2. Challenges in GWB Searches with PTAs

PTAs, as galactic-scale gravitational wave detectors, are affected by a wide variety of noise sources. These include instrumental noise artifacts from the instruments and the hardware that processes raw telescope data; effects induced by the Solar System planets and/or the interstellar medium; and jittering of the neutron stars themselves—sources of radio waves—and their gravitationally bound companions such as other neutron stars, white dwarfs, or black holes. Both instrumental and environmental noise sources play an important role. As discussed in Section 4.2.2, stochastic processes in PTAs can be uncorrelated in time, i.e., white, and time-correlated, i.e., red. Some noise processes introduce spatial correlations between pulse arrival times in pulsars across the sky. Below we briefly discuss prospects for future PTAs given the current knowledge of the noise.

Environmental white noise associated with pulse shape changes is referred to as *jitter* (e.g., [277,278]). Without jitter noise, measurement errors are limited by the radio pulse signal-to-noise ratio. New scientific instruments such as FAST and SKA will significantly improve upon previous radiometer (white instrumental) noise levels, thus expanding the number of pulsars in the array and improving noise power spectra of the observed pulsars. Therefore, the timing precision of the brightest pulsars will be limited by environmental properties. In particular, MPTA reported [267] an extraordinary timing precision for some of the millisecond pulsars previously observed by the PPTA. PSR J1909−3744 showed the root-mean-square of timing residuals (rms[14]) of 66 ns with 11 months of observations, whereas in the second data release of PPTA [279], this pulsar showed rms residuals of 240 ns. Pulse integration times may be increased in the future to further lower white noise levels. Following Equation (81), a pulsar with an achievable timing precision of 10 ns observed biweekly, in 10 years, would be able to probe a GW strain of 5×10^{-17} at 3 nHz. In reality, however, the detection of a nanohertz stochastic background requires timing an ensemble of pulsars, and there are sources of red noise that limit timing arrays at low frequencies.

Red noise is resolved in most pulsars after they are observed for a couple of years. A comprehensive study of this topic for the first data release of the IPTA can be found in [280]. Normally, the strongest red noise in recycled pulsars appears at low radio frequencies ν from variations in the dispersion measure, electron column density towards the line of sight. Due to dependence $P(f) \propto \nu^{-2}$, this noise is easy to model and it is straightforward to separate its contribution from the one of the GWB. Some red noise was found to be affecting only certain radio frequency bands or back-end observing systems. Independent of ν, "achromatic" red noise is also referred to as spin noise as it is associated with pulsar rotational irregularities. Spin noise with a power spectral density which continuously increases towards low frequencies with a power-law might eventually turn over, but no such spectra were found in millisecond pulsars [281,282]. One may find the term "timing noise" in the literature, which is used to denote spin noise and glitches, i.e., sudden changes in pulsar spin periods followed by an exponential relaxation (e.g., [283]). GWBs are separated from spin noise through spatial correlations, although incorrect red noise models may result in incorrect inferences of the GWB [284]. For the EPTA second data release, it was shown [282] that tailored pulsar red noise models with band- and system-related noise marginally increase evidence for Hellings–Downs correlations, whereas PPTA showed that the inclusion of the brightest PSR J0437–4715 (which shows significant red noise and residual excess noise [285]) results in an increase in the inferred correlation coefficients $\Gamma(\zeta_{ab})$ [26]. Before spatial correlations are resolved, both the GWB and spin noise can yield evidence for the common-spectrum process [26]. Inferences of the GWB based on the common-spectrum process at this point in time may be treated as speculative, especially given that spin noise in pulsars may yield a power-law $P(f)$ with $\gamma = 4$ [286], which is close to $\gamma = 13/3 = 4.3(3)$ for the GWB. Some low-frequency noise can also introduce spatial correlations which can still be distinguished from the Hellings–Downs prediction [287]. Time-correlated errors in terrestrial time standards, also known as clock errors, can yield monopolar spatial correlations between pulsars a and b, $\Gamma(\zeta_{ab}) = 1$. Pulse arrival times are referenced to the position of the Solar System barycenter; thus, systematic errors in the barycenter position can yield red noise with dipolar spatial correlations $\Gamma(\zeta_{ab}) = \cos(\zeta_{ab})$. This noise can be mitigated byt improving Solar System ephemerides, and when improvements are not available, it can be modelled as a purely deterministic process [288,289]. In an analysis with the NANOGrav 11 year data set [180], it was demonstrated that the results are affected by the choice of Solar System ephemeris, whereas deterministic modeling of systematic errors in ephemerides renders consistent results. The good news is that the contributions of ephemeris noise are found to be rather weak for current data sets and ephemerides. In particular, in the search for a stochastic background in the second data release of the PPTA [26], the authors computed Bayesian evidence for errors in every parameter of the deterministic ephemeris model: masses and orbital Keplerian parameters of planets from Mars to Saturn, with orbital frequencies in the PTA band. They found marginal evidence for systematic errors in older ephemerides and no evidence for errors in present-day ephemerides used for GW analyses between 2020 and 2021. Red noise is mostly environmental; thus, it might be worth allocating more time to fainter pulsars that do not show evidence of such noise.

With the above in mind, we provide sensitivity projections for a few scenarios of future PTAs in Figure 14. When evaluating the performance of future PTAs, several simplifications are usually made. For example, often, red noise and effects of fitting for the timing model are neglected, as in Figures 1 and 7. We addressed these points in Figure 14 by adopting the formalism from [290] and the relevant code [291]. The sensitivity estimates can be further refined based on more realistic noise properties and observing scenarios—a subject of future work. For a more detailed review of measurement errors in pulsar timing arrays please refer to [292]. Challenges for GW detection with pulsar timing arrays are also discussed in [293].

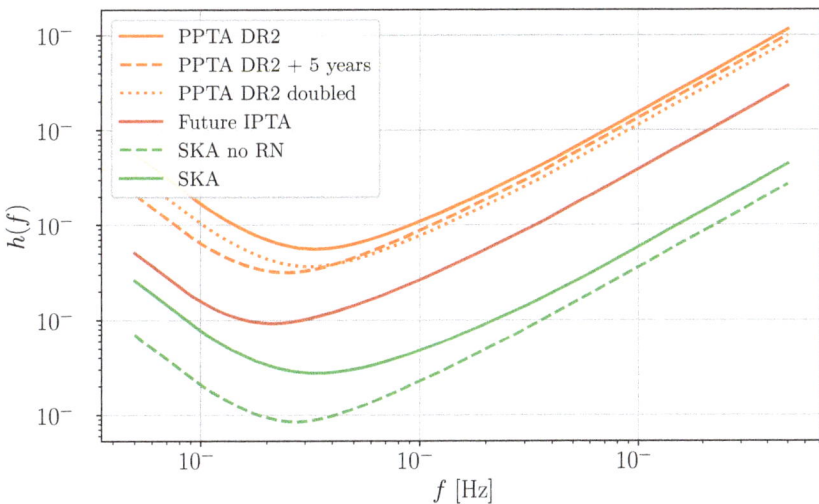

Figure 14. Power-law-integrated sensitivity [290,291] at the level of SNR = 3 of simulated PTAs to the SGWB strain $h(t)$. We demonstrate the effects of timing precision, red noise, and a number of array pulsars. Pulsars are distributed isotropically across the sky and observed biweekly. Orange lines represent variations of the 15-year-long PPTA DR2, with real pulsar T_{obs}, white noise levels based on the rms residuals ranging from 240 ns to 24,050 ns [279] and best-fit red noise parameters from [285]. The dashed line represents PPTA DR2 extended by 5 more years of observation, whereas the dotted line represents PPTA DR2 with a doubled number of pulsars with the same noise properties. Red line is an example of the future IPTA with 20 years of observations of 100 pulsars with white noise rms drawn uniformly between 20 and 500 ns. Red noise $\log_{10} A$ is drawn uniformly from $[-14, -20]$ and γ drawn uniformly from $[1, 7]$, a fiducial choice based on [285]. Green lines represent SKA observing 50 pulsars with white noise rms of 30 ns for 15 years, with (solid line) and without (dashed line) red noise assumed for the IPTA.

5.2.3. Search Results for an Anisotropic Nanohertz Background

To date, one search for an anisotropic GWB with PTAs has been performed [202]. In the latter, the authors use six pulsars from the EPTA with a timing baseline of $T_{obs} = 17.7$ years. While the results indicate that the data are unable to improve upon a physically motivated prior, the search setup, motivation, and results are useful to review.

The authors use a spherical harmonic decomposition with $\ell_{max} = 4$ based on analytical arguments of the PTA resolution established in [294]. They perform three parameterizations and one independent analysis. First, they use a single set of anisotropy coefficients across the entire frequency band (lowest five harmonics of $1/T_{obs}$) and chose a fixed spectral index consistent with a population of supermassive black hole binaries. Second, they allow different anisotropy coefficients at each of the lowest five harmonics of $1/T_{obs}$. Third, they allow different spherical harmonic coefficients for each of the lowest four harmonics of $1/T_{obs}$ and use a single set of spherical harmonics coefficients to describe up to the fiftieth harmonic. In all cases, they impose that the power on the sky in each pixel is positive, as negative power would be unphysical. Fourth, they independently estimate the cross-correlations between individual pulsars and then map these onto a chosen basis.

The results yielded no detection of a GWB, and limits were set on the angular power spectrum C_ℓ for each of the individual parameterizations (and for each individual frequency, where appropriate). The limits on strain amplitude in multipoles with $\ell > 0$ are $\lesssim 40\%$ of the monopole. However, these limits do not improve upon the physically motivated prior. Current astrophysical estimates suggest that the strain amplitude in multipoles with $\ell > 0$ is around 20% of the monopole [295]. In the case of the fourth analysis, the physical prior is not applied, and the authors observed that sensitivity to the dipole is reduced due to the distribution of the six pulsars on the sky, highlighting the desire for using a large number of pulsars that are uniformly distributed on the sky.

5.2.4. Search Results for a Nanohertz Background Not Related to Supermassive Black Hole Binaries

While quite a few sources of a GWB that can be measured by PTAs have been proposed, outside of the generic isotropic background, which is generally assumed to be dominated by unresolved supermassive blackhole binaries, only a few explicit searches have been carried out.

Recently, both the PPTA and NANOGrav have placed constraints on first-order phase transitions in the early Universe [296,297]. In [296], the authors use 45 pulsars to search for a signal from first-order phase transitions using three different models. The common spectrum process first reported in NANOGrav data in [54] is also consistent with a first-order phase transition at temperatures below the electroweak scale, with $T^\star \lesssim 10\,\text{MeV}$ at the 1σ. They calculate posterior distributions on the temperature and bubble nucleation rate when phase transition occurs, as well as the strength of the phase transition and the friction between bubble walls and the plasma. However, it is important to note that these posteriors assume only a GWB from phase transitions is present, while the data cannot distinguish between this model and one described by a GWB from supermassive binary black holes. In addition, no spatial correlations between pulsars are found; hence, no detection of a GWB is claimed. The results of [297] are similar—no evidence of spatial correlations between pulsars is reported, and constraints on the temperature of a potential phase transition are found to be $1\,\text{MeV} \lesssim T^\star \lesssim 100\,\text{MeV}$. For a recent discussion on separating a background from supermassive black hole binaries and first order phase transitions (or other potential sources of a nHz GWB) using a multi-messenger approach, see [298].

Several groups have recently searched NANOGrav, PPTA, and IPTA data sets for evidence of alternative polarizations of GWs. In [299,300], the authors claim a Bayes factor of $\sim$100 in preference of background from spatially correlated scalar-transverse gravitational waves compared to a simple common spectrum red noise process using both NANOGrav and IPTA data. They claim similar significance when comparing a scalar transverse background to a background from tensor transverse gravitational waves. However, they found no such significant evidence when searching PPTA data [301]. In [302], the authors find a preference for a scalar transverse background, but with less significant evidence. However, this significance goes away when the authors account for uncertainties in the solar system ephemeris using [289] or when removing one pulsar, PSR J0030+0451.

5.3. Other Stochastic Background Searches

There are many GW experiments that we have omitted from the discussion above. In this section, we very briefly highlight a few that are of particular interest, some of which are shown in Figure 7. Our focus here is on the nanohertz–kilohertz frequency band; however, see the review article [303] and references therein for a summary of detection methods at MHz frequencies and above.

The oldest method of GW detection, pioneered by Weber [304,305] in the 1960s with his "resonant bar" experiments, is to monitor the resonant frequencies of some macroscopic test object. When acted upon by a GW with a frequency matching one of the object's normal modes, the stretching and squeezing action they induce excites vibrations in these modes which can be amplified and detected. Numerous such resonant-mass experiments have been operated since the 1960s [306], but none has had sufficient sensitivity to place meaningful bounds on the GWB below the $\Omega(f) < 1$ level required to prevent GWs from over-closing the Universe. However, the same idea has been applied with success on a much larger scale, using the Earth itself as a resonant mass. By monitoring the Earth's normal mode frequencies using gravimeter data, Coughlin and Harms [220] placed an upper limit on the GWB in the megahertz frequency band. The corresponding PI curve has a minimum of $\Omega(f) \approx 1.3 \times 10^{-2}$ at $f \approx 1.6\,\text{mHz}$. Recently, a trio of similar experiments have been proposed in which gravimeters installed on the Lunar surface could be used to monitor the Moon's normal modes, providing a cleaner probe of GWs in the megahertz frequency band [307,308].

Another GW experiment which has successfully constrained the GWB below the $\Omega(f) < 1$ level is the work of Armstrong et al. [221], who carried out Doppler-tracking observations of the Cassini spacecraft. The principle here is very similar to IFOs and PTAs in that it tracks the trajectories of photons in the presence of GWs; however, rather than measuring changes in the light-travel time, one attempts to measure changes in the photon frequency due to GW-induced Doppler shifts between the two test masses (this is essentially the time derivative of the perturbation to the light-travel time). This analysis probed GWs in the 1–100 µHz band, with the corresponding PI curve reaching a minimum of $\Omega(f) \approx 9.9 \times 10^{-3}$ at $f \approx 3.9\,\text{µHz}$. This is a particularly interesting frequency range, as it straddles a significant gap between PTA constraints at nanohertz frequencies and future constraints from LISA and other space-based interferometers in the megahertz band; however, the Cassini constraint in this "µHz gap" is not strong enough to be of astrophysical or cosmological interest. Recently, it has been pointed out that much more competitive GWB constraints could be obtained in this frequency band using high-precision observations of binary systems (in particular, binary pulsars and the Earth–Moon system), by searching for the imprints of stochastic GWs on their orbits [225,226]. Other proposals for accessing these frequencies include an extremely long-baseline space-based interferometer such as the µAres concept [309].

In addition to changing the frequency and/or time-of-arrival of photons, GWs can also cause *angular deflections* in photon trajectories, such that distant astronomical objects appear displaced from their true positions on the sky. These GW-induced deflections have a distinctive geometric pattern across the sky, allowing one to search for a GWB signal with high-precision astrometry from observatories such as GAIA and THEIA [310–312]. The resulting PI curve lies in roughly in the same nanohertz frequency band probed by PTAs, albeit with improved high-frequency sensitivity. Forecasts in Ref. [312] indicate that next-generation astrometry with an observatory such as THEIA may be sensitive to $\Omega(f) \sim 10^{-16}$ at nanohertz frequencies, surpassing even the reach of pulsar-timing observations with SKA.

Finally, a GW detection technique which is subject to growing interest in the community is *atom interferometry*, in which, rather than using interference between photons to measure the phase difference between two spatial paths, one exploits the wave-like behaviour of matter on the quantum scale to measure interference between atoms. While first-generation atom interferometry experiments such as AION [224] and MAGIS [313,314] are in their early stages and are not expected to have significant sensitivity to GWs, proposals for future kilometer-scale experiments are forecast to provide extremely useful GWB constraints in the 0.1–1 Hz band. In particular, the AION-km proposal has a forecast sensitivity of $\Omega(f) \approx 2.7 \times 10^{-12}$ at $f \approx 0.12\,\text{Hz}$.

6. Stochastic Background Detection Prospects with Future Gravitational-Wave Detectors

We close this review with an outlook on the detection capabilities of upcoming GW detectors. We first discuss the potential of 3G detectors, which will be considerably more sensitive to GWs in the same frequency bands as LVK instruments, as may be observed in Figure 7, and specifically prospects of performing component separation with ET and CE. We then review the upcoming LISA mission and lay out different stochastic search methods which may be employed with such a detector.

6.1. Stochastic Searches with Third Generation Interferometers

By the mid-late 2030s, it is expected that ground-based gravitational wave detectors will evolve to the third generation of laser interferometers comprising ET and CE. These observatories are expected to outperform current 2G network sensitivity by several orders of magnitude in strain, extending the BBH detection horizon out to the earliest epochs of star formation at $z \approx 20$ and beyond [52,315]. This would allow 3G detectors to individually resolve more than 99.9% of all stellar origin BBH signals in the Universe [316]. This eliminates the motivation to search for the background of stellar origin BBHs with standard cross-correlation methods described in Section 4 because only very few of such signals will remain unresolved, whereas searches for the non-Gaussian background outlined in Section 4.4 might be more appropriate. In between 2G and 3G detectors, there is also the proposed "2.5G" Australian detector NEMO [317], which will use very high laser power to target high frequency signals from tidal effects in the late stages of binary neutron star inspirals.

However, cross-correlation based searches might still be relevant for BNS and BHNS backgrounds because individual events will only be resolved up to redshifts $\gtrsim 1$ [318]. The approach will be then to subtract out all the resolved sources from the timestream and run a stochastic search on the remaining data. This may be performed iteratively and/or assuming different contributions relative to the signal to perform component separation [319].

Furthermore, cross-correlation based stochastic searches are suitable for searches for cosmological gravitational wave backgrounds, following a subtraction of individual compact binary coalescence signals [316,320]. The noise formed by residuals from the subtraction of best-fit compact binary coalescence waveforms can be reduced to negligible levels following the demonstration by [321].

Third-generation detectors also present a unique detection opportunity for primordial black holes. The merger rate of primordial black hole binaries per unit volume is predicted to grow continuously towards redshifts of 50 and beyond [322], producing a high redshift source of stochastic GWs which could be probed with 3G cross-correlation searches. Note that this remains subject to the theoretically uncertain rate of such events that the nature provided us with; let us cite several investigations on the matter [254,323–325]. Attribution of a merged black hole binary to primordial and not stellar origin based on redshift alone will not be statistically strong even with 40-kilometer Cosmic Explorer, 20-kilometer Cosmic Explorer South, and Einstein Telescope [326]. This means that even in the scenario where primordial black holes are abundant, studies of these events will require a combination of fitting for their ensemble properties as well as cross-correlation-based searches for the stochastic background that are sensitive to subthreshold signals. In the case of competing stochastic backgrounds, studies have been performed to carry out simultaneous Bayesian fitting of both astrophysical and primordial components [168,327], and methods have been proposed to distinguish primordial black holes from astrophysical ones [328,329].

Correlating anisotropies in the GWB which electromagnetic observations has also been proposed as a target for future detectors. In some cases, this means using galaxy catalogues to guide the model used for anisotropic GWB searches [241], while in other cases, the proposal is to correlate sub-threshold GW signals with EM transients to probe fundamental physics [127,330].

There are quite a few technological challenges in the development of 3G detectors that are directly relevant for GWB searches, for which its sensitivity to $\Omega_{\rm gw}$ scales with f^{-3} and, therefore, benefit from improved low frequency sensitivity. Below, we discuss two important and probable sources of low frequency noise that are important for GWB searches.

First, globally correlated magnetic noise from, e.g., Schumann resonances [331,332] will, if not subtracted or dealt with in some manner, provide a lower limit on our ability to measure a GWB in the frequency band from $\sim$8–40 Hz [167,333–341], and could even be an issue at higher frequencies [341]. The assumption that a GWB will look like correlated noise between multiple detectors means that correlated magnetic noise could masquerade as a GWB if we are not careful. There are several avenues we can take to avoid this issue. One of the most promising is Wiener filtering using low noise magnetometers near the detectors [334–336,338]. Another option is spectral separation using the hybrid-Bayesian method discussed at the end of Section 4.2, where one models the contribution of the correlated magnetic noise to the cross-correlation statistic and includes it with a model for the GWB [167]. Finally, reducing the coupling of magnetic fields into the strain channel of the detectors will also be vital [341]. In the end, some combination of all three of these ideas will likely be needed.

Second, low frequency noise due to gravity gradients caused by temperature fluctuations in the atmosphere (infrasound) or seismic waves, known as "Newtonian noise," is likely a limiting noise source at frequencies up to $\sim$30 Hz [14,18,342–345]. For a complete review, see [344]. One cannot shield against Newtonian noise and, therefore, need to either subtract [346–350] it or cleverly design the local environment of the detectors to reduce surface seismic waves and atmospheric perturbations [351]. Estimating the specific contribution of Newtonian noise to the detectors from, e.g., seismic waves, is calculable based on a realisation of the seismic wavefield [344], but is very difficult to achieve in practice. Proof of principle tests of using an array of seismometers or geophones to create Wiener filters or use machine learning to clean a "target" seismometer channel are promising, and work on optimal design of local sensor arrays is mature [346–350,352]. However, cleaning a seismometer is quite different from cleaning Newtonian noise from a gravitational wave detector. In the end, it is likely that for 3G detectors, an array of geophones, broadband seismometers, and tiltmeters (which can be used to separate seismic tilt from seismic waves) will be needed to subtract Newtonian noise due to seismic waves [344,353]. Meanwhile, an array of infrasound microphones or LIDAR detectors, along with potentially using wind fences around facilities, will be needed to reduce and cancel Newtonian noise due to atmospheric fluctuations [354,355].

6.2. Stochastic Searches with the Laser Interferometer Space Antenna

Stochastic searches with LISA present distinct challenges from those discussed for PTAs and ground-based interferometer networks, primarily due to the fact that LISA is considered to be a *single* detector; hence, it is not possible to use a cross-correlation search with a second detector which is not co-located with LISA. It is, however, possible to auto- and cross-correlate TDI channels, as we explain here.

The antenna itself will be comprises three spacecrafts which will be positioned on three heliocentric orbits and will specify a plane at a 60° angle with the ecliptic, in an equilateral triangle configuration which will be maintained throughout the entire duration of the mission (4+ years) [29]. Each spacecraft will send a laser beam to each other spacecraft such that, in total, six laser measurements will be made, comprising the *links* of the detector. The links are then combined to form TDI channels, as detailed in Section 4.1. Basic LISA studies start from considering sets of three channels, where each channel is centered around one spacecraft; however, more sophisticated studies are already under way [138,140,356]. These channels produce a set of observations, which we can treat as timestreams for the purposes of this discussion (although these are effectively combined in post-processing and are not the read-out of the detector), $X(t), Y(t), Z(t)$, as introduced in Section 4.1. Taking the same approach as for real interferometer timestreams, we can decompose each of these in their signal and noise components,

$$X(t) = R_X(t) * h(t) + n_X(t), \qquad (119)$$

where R_X is the specific response of the X channel, and n_X is its noise term. The noise terms for the three channels are not independent, as each shares (possibly multiple) links; hence, a residuals analysis such as that based on Likelihood (73) is out of the question. Hence, LISA stochastic analyses are based on Gaussian likelihoods for the data as Likelihood (72), where the data are now a set of TDI channels,

$$\mathcal{L}(d) \propto \prod_{f,\tau} \frac{1}{|C|^{1/2}} e^{\frac{1}{2} T C^{-1} T^*}, \qquad (120)$$

with $\boldsymbol{T} = (X, Y, Z)^T$, and $\boldsymbol{C}$ is the full covariance matrix of the data, $\boldsymbol{C} = \langle \boldsymbol{T} \otimes \boldsymbol{T}^\star \rangle$. The key to detecting a stochastic background with LISA is then understanding how instrument noise and GW signals manifest in different TDI channels and finding an accurate modelling approach to plug into Likelihood (120). The first step consists in picking the specific TDI channels and assumptions to work in—there are several options provided in the literature [134,135,146,357–359].

Both maximum-likelihood methods and Bayesian approaches which compute the full posteriors have been proposed to extract and characterise an SGWB from LISA data. In the first case, it is possible to produce a maximum-likelihood solution by fixing a noise model and iterating over the data until the signal converges to the maximum-likelihood estimate; this is essentially the same approach as that laid out in Section 4.3 for anisotropic searches, based on [193]. Otherwise, one may take a full Bayesian approach, parametrizing signal and noise components in the data and assuming appropriate priors for the two sets of parameters, then sampling the Likelihood to obtain informative posteriors. This is performed for example in [147] for an isotropic stochastic background, where the data were given by the LISA Data Challenge (LDC). Here, the authors show that, using the noise orthogonal A, E, T set of TDI channels, they are able to recover the stochastic signal and independently measure the relevant LISA noise parameters for each arm of the interferometer. Note, however, that this is performed in the absence of competing signals.

In fact, component separation will be a major challenge for LISA data analysis, as a variety of signals will contribute to the same frequency band and overlap in time [360]. In the case of stochastic backgrounds, as detailed in Section 3, LISA will be sensitive to an anisotropic galactic white dwarf binary background which traces the shape of the Milky Way, a mostly isotropic background of either primordial or stellar-origin black hole and neutron star binaries [361], and also potentially other primordial backgrounds, such as those arising from inflation [93], first-order phase transitions [55,362], and cosmic strings [53,363], all of which may be either isotropic or anisotropic. Galactic binaries will by far dominate the measurement, and in fact several approaches have been proposed towards component separation, relying on characteristic, observable differences of each component such as their spectral shape [148,364], or their distribution on the sky, as seen in [193,194]. In any case, it will first be necessary to disentangle the resolvable white dwarf binaries from the unresolvable white dwarf binary background in the data streams, as detailed in [132].

Anisotropic stochastic searches with LISA leverage the motion of the LISA constellation around the sun to map the signal in the solar system barycenter frame. The method proposed in [193] fixes the noise model, simulates mock data assuming the LISA response functions in [365] and uses the Bond–Jaffe–Knox maximum-likelihood solution in Equation (111) to test the mapping capabilities of the detector. It was found that the angular resolution of LISA for stochastic signals highly depends on their SNR as a function of frequency, as the detector response varies greatly as a function of the latter. The stochastic signals compete with the detector noise, which at low SNR dominates the modes of the Fisher information matrix (112). Beyond this, the angular resolution at which LISA "sees" the signal is diffraction-limited; hence, the higher the frequency, the better the angular resolution will be. In the best-case scenario of a high SNR signal dominating at frequencies ~ 0.1 Hz, the angular resolution will be of the order $\ell_{\max} \sim 16$—see Figure 6 of [193]. Another approach proposed in [194] tackles the mapping problem by setting priors on the spherical harmonic modes of the signal and solving for their amplitudes in a Bayesian framework, using a single TDI channel. This is especially useful when the sky distribution of the signal is well known, as is the case for the galactic white dwarf binary background. The technique proposed here is based on the Clebsch–Gordan expansion, which allows one to constrain the spherical harmonics with a non-negative distribution. This method has proven to be effective for the recovery of a mock galactic background and yields an informative set of posteriors on the coefficients of the signal—see Figure 3 of [194]. However, it has only been tested at the low resolution of $\ell_{\max} = 4$ as the solver scales significantly in computational cost with the number of modes one tries to recover.

Author Contributions: Conceptualization: A.I.R., B.G., A.C.J. and P.M.M. Data curation: A.I.R., B.G., A.C.J. and P.M.M. Software: A.I.R., B.G., A.C.J. and P.M.M. Making of figures and tables: A.I.R., B.G. and A.C.J. Writing—original draft: A.I.R., B.G., A.C.J. and P.M.M. Writing—review & editing: A.I.R., B.G., A.C.J. and P.M.M. All authors have read and agreed to the published version of the manuscript.

Funding: AIR acknowledges the support of the National Science Foundation and the LIGO Laboratory. BG is supported by the Italian Ministry of Education, University and Research within the PRIN 2017 Research Program Framework, n. 2017SYRTCN. PMM was supported by the NANOGrav Physics Frontiers Center, National Science Foundation (NSF), award number 2020265. Parts of this research were conducted by the Australian Research Council Centre of Excellence for Gravitational Wave Discovery (OzGrav), through project number CE170100004.

Data Availability Statement: This manuscript shows figures created using the LVK open data [246,256], and publicly available PTA results presented in [26,54,275,285].

Acknowledgments: The authors thank Katerina Chatziioannou and Joseph Romano for precious comments on our original draft.

Conflicts of Interest: The authors declare no conflict of interest.

Notes

1. There are several theories that postulate modifications to this statement, but these modifications are strongly constrained by multimessenger observations of the binary neutron star merger GW170817 [36].
2. Strictly speaking, GWs with wavelengths larger than the size of the cosmological horizon are frozen out by Hubble friction and, thus, do not contribute to the effective energy density. As a result, the density parameter appearing on the left-hand side of Equation (14) should be interpreted as an integral over $\Omega_{\rm GW}(f)$ from a minimum frequency of $f \sim 10^{-15}$ Hz, which corresponds to the size of the horizon at the epoch when the CMB photons were emitted.
3. Often in the literature, the letter α is used to denote a different spectral index, hereby denoted α', of the characteristic strain spectrum of the stochastic gravitational wave background $h(f) \equiv \sqrt{fS(f)} \propto f^{\alpha'}$, where $S(f)$ is the power spectral density of the background. This leads to the power-law index of $2\alpha' + 2$ for $\Omega_{\rm GW}$ in Equation (25) instead of α.
4. There is still much uncertainty around this black hole "lower mass gap" and it remains a main focus of research in the field; see, e.g., the discussions in [58–60].
5. As mentioned in the footnote 3, the energy density spectral index $\alpha = 2/3$ is related to the strain amplitude spectral index α' such that $\alpha = 2\alpha' + 2$. Therefore $\alpha' = -2/3$, which is the quantity often referred to as α in publications. Due to the parametric choices made in the different search pipelines, α is most frequently used in LVK literature, while α' is most frequently used in the PTA literature.
6. There are, in fact, sources of spatially correlated noise. They can be distinguished from SGWBs by either a deterministic component or by an overlap reduction function different to those of SGWBs. We provide more details in Section 5.
7. Time segments with non-stationary noise are removed from analyses of real data [56], the stationarity is usually determined empirically. Note that when applying a non-trivial windowing function to time-domain data, e.g., for computing a discrete Fourier transform, we introduce correlations between frequency bins. This effect and the methods to mitigate it are described in [130].
8. Note that this is result is derived from the detector response to a fully unpolarised stochastic background; in the case of a polarised signal, extra terms need to be considered. More details on this can be found, e.g., in [136,137].
9. Note that directly interfering laser beams in the case of LISA is impossible due to energy dispersion along the arm [29].
10. Note that this is no longer the case in the presence of temporal shot noise, e.g., for the astrophysical GWB from compact binary coalescences [122]. In this case, each time segment will have random GWB intensity fluctuations due to the finite number of sources. The statistical independence of these fluctuations at different times can be leveraged to mitigate the impact of shot noise on measurements of the angular power spectrum [123].
11. Note that in these two cases I_p and $I_{\ell m}$ have different units because in (114) the basis function carry units sr^{-1}.
12. In fact, in [215] the authors discuss the extension of their optimal search method in the presence of non-Gaussian noise as well. The implementation of the method becomes substantially more involved, however practical considerations about the nature and behaviour of the non-Gaussian noise can simplify it considerably.
13. Initial-detector era searches on LIGO Science Run 5 (S5)/Virgo Science Run 1 (VSR1) [16] and LIGO Science Run 6, Virgo Science Runs 2 and 3 (VSR23) [231] used the full Hanford, Livingston, Virgo detector network.

[14] Often used in the literature to quantify noise in a given pulsar. For rms σ^2 of Gaussian white noise, the power spectral density of residuals $P = 2\pi\sigma^2\Delta t$, where Δt is the time between observations, which is typically a couple of weeks. Note, rms residuals may increase with longer data spans due to more sources of noise becoming prominent at longer time scales. Sometimes rms residuals are provided for a particular source of noise.

References

1. Davis, D.; Walker, M. Detector Characterization and Mitigation of Noise in Ground-Based Gravitational-Wave Interferometers. *Galaxies* **2022**, *10*, 12. [CrossRef]
2. Sun, L.; Goetz, E.; Kissel, J.S.; Betzwieser, J.; Karki, S.; Viets, A.; Wade, M.; Bhattacharjee, D.; Bossilkov, V.; Covas, P.B.; et al. Characterization of systematic error in Advanced LIGO calibration. *Class. Quant. Grav.* **2020**, *37*, 225008. [CrossRef]
3. Sun, L.; Goetz, E.; Kissel, J.S.; Betzwieser, J.; Karki, S.; Bhattacharjee, D.; Covas, P.B.; Datrier, L.E.; Kandhasamy, S.; Lecoeuche, Y.K.; et al. Characterization of systematic error in Advanced LIGO calibration in the second half of O3. *arXiv* **2021**, arXiv:2107.00129.
4. Acernese, F.; Agathos, M.; Ain, A.; Albanesi, S.; Allocca, A.; Amato, A.; Andrade, T.; Andres, N.; Andrić, T.; Ansoldi, S.; et al. Calibration of Advanced Virgo and reconstruction of detector strain $h(t)$ during the Observing Run O3. *Class. Quant. Grav.* **2022**, *39*, 045006. [CrossRef]
5. Akutsu, T.; Ando, M.; Arai, K.; Arai, Y.; Araki, S.; Araya, A.; Aritomi, N.; Asada, H.; Aso, Y.; Bae, S.; et al. Overview of KAGRA: Calibration, detector characterization, physical environmental monitors, and the geophysics interferometer. *PTEP* **2021**, *2021*, 05A102. [CrossRef]
6. Verbiest, J.P.W.; Osłowski, S.; Burke-Spolaor, S. Pulsar Timing Array Experiments. In *Handbook of Gravitational Wave Astronomy*; Bambi, C., Katsanevas, S., Kokkotas, K.D., Eds.; Springer: Singapore, 2020; pp. 1–42. [CrossRef]
7. Tiburzi, C. Pulsars Probe the Low-Frequency Gravitational Sky: Pulsar Timing Arrays Basics and Recent Results. *PASA* **2018**, *35*, e013. [CrossRef]
8. Hobbs, G.; Dai, S. Gravitational wave research using pulsar timing arrays. *Natl. Sci. Rev.* **2017**, *4*, 707–717. [CrossRef]
9. Abbott, B.P.; Abbott, R.; Abbott, T.D.; Abernathy, M.R.; Acernese, F.; Ackley, K.; Adams, C.; Adams, T.; Addesso, P.; Adhikari, R.X.; et al. GW150914: The Advanced LIGO Detectors in the Era of First Discoveries. *Phys. Rev. Lett.* **2016**, *116*, 131103. [CrossRef]
10. Accadia, T.; Acernese, F.; Antonucci, F.; Astone, P.; Ballardin, G.; Barone, F.; Barsuglia, M.; Basti, A.; Bauer, T.S.; Bebronne, M.; et al. Status of the Virgo project. *Class. Quantum Gravity* **2011**, *28*, 114002. [CrossRef]
11. Affeldt, C.; Danzmann, K.; Dooley, K.L.; Grote, H.; Hewitson, M.; Hild, S.; Hough, J.; Leong, J.; Lück, H.; Prijatelj, M.; et al. Advanced techniques in GEO 600. *Class. Quantum Gravity* **2014**, *31*, 224002. [CrossRef]
12. Castelvecchi, D. Japan's pioneering detector set to join hunt for gravitational waves. *Nature* **2019**, *562*, 9–10. [CrossRef] [PubMed]
13. LIGO-India, Proposal of the Consortium for Indian Initiative in Gravitational-Wave Observations (IndIGO). Available online: https://dcc.ligo.org/LIGO-M1100296/public (accessed on 1 November 2021).
14. Punturo, M.; Abernathy, M.; Acernese, F.; Allen, B.; Andersson, N.; Arun, K.; Barone, F.; Barr, B.; Barsuglia, M.; Beker, M.; et al. The Einstein Telescope: A third-generation gravitational wave observatory. *Class. Quant. Grav.* **2010**, *27*, 194002. [CrossRef]
15. Sathyaprakash, B.; Abernathy, M.; Acernese, F.; Amaro-Seoane, P.; Andersson, N.; Arun, K.; Barone, F.; Barr, B.; Barsuglia, M.; Beker, M.; et al. Scientific Potential of Einstein Telescope. In Proceedings of the 46th Rencontres de Moriond on Gravitational Waves and Experimental Gravity, La Thuile, Italy, 20–27 March 2011; pp. 127–136.
16. Abadie, J.; Abbott, B.P.; Abbott, R.; Abbott, T.D.; Abernathy, M.; Accadia, T.; Acernese, F.; Adams, C.; Adhikari, R.; Affeldt, C.; et al. Upper limits on a stochastic gravitational-wave background using LIGO and Virgo interferometers at 600–1000 Hz. *Phys. Rev. D* **2012**, *85*, 122001. [CrossRef]
17. Reitze, D.; Adhikari, R.X.; Ballmer, S.; Barish, B.; Barsotti, L.; Billingsley, G.; Brown, D.A.; Chen, Y.; Coyne, D.; Eisenstein, R.; et al. Cosmic Explorer: The U.S. Contribution to Gravitational-Wave Astronomy beyond LIGO. *Bull. Am. Astron. Soc.* **2019**, *51*, 035.
18. Hall, E.D.; Kuns, K.; Smith, J.R.; Bai, Y.; Wipf, C.; Biscans, S.; Adhikari, R.X.; Arai, K.; Ballmer, S.; Barsotti, L.; et al. Gravitational-wave physics with Cosmic Explorer: Limits to low-frequency sensitivity. *Phys. Rev. D* **2021**, *103*, 122004. [CrossRef]
19. McLaughlin, M.A. The North American Nanohertz Observatory for Gravitational Waves. *Class. Quantum Gravity* **2013**, *30*, 224008. [CrossRef]
20. Manchester, R.N.; Hobbs, G.; Bailes, M.; Coles, W.A.; van Straten, W.; Keith, M.J.; Shannon, R.M.; Bhat, N.D.R.; Brown, A.; Burke-Spolaor, S.G.; et al. The Parkes Pulsar Timing Array Project. *PASA* **2013**, *30*, e017. [CrossRef]
21. Kramer, M.; Champion, D.J. The European Pulsar Timing Array and the Large European Array for Pulsars. *Class. Quantum Gravity* **2013**, *30*, 224009. [CrossRef]
22. Desvignes, G.; Caballero, R.N.; Lentati, L.; Verbiest, J.P.W.; Champion, D.J.; Stappers, B.W.; Janssen, G.H.; Lazarus, P.; Osłowski, S.; Babak, S.; et al. High-precision timing of 42 millisecond pulsars with the European Pulsar Timing Array. *Mon. Not. R. Astron. Soc.* **2016**, *458*, 3341–3380. [CrossRef]
23. Hobbs, G.; Archibald, A.; Arzoumanian, Z.; Backer, D.; Bailes, M.; Bhat, N.D.R.; Burgay, M.; Burke-Spolaor, S.; Champion, D.; Cognard, I.; et al. The International Pulsar Timing Array project: Using pulsars as a gravitational wave detector. *Class. Quantum Gravity* **2010**, *27*, 084013. [CrossRef]
24. Verbiest, J.P.W.; Lentati, L.; Hobbs, G.; van Haasteren, R.; Demorest, P.B.; Janssen, G.H.; Wang, J.B.; Desvignes, G.; Caballero, R.N.; Keith, M.J.; et al. The International Pulsar Timing Array: First data release. *MNRAS* **2016**, *458*, 1267–1288. [CrossRef]

25. Joshi, B.C.; Arumugasamy, P.; Bagchi, M.; Bandyopadhyay, D.; Basu, A.; Dhanda Batra, N.; Bethapudi, S.; Choudhary, A.; De, K.; Dey, L.; et al. Precision pulsar timing with the ORT and the GMRT and its applications in pulsar astrophysics. *J. Astrophys. Astron.* **2018**, *39*, 51. [CrossRef]
26. Goncharov, B.; Shannon, R.M.; Reardon, D.J.; Hobbs, G.; Zic, A.; Bailes, M.; Curyło, M.; Dai, S.; Kerr, M.; Lower, M.E.; et al. On the Evidence for a Common-spectrum Process in the Search for the Nanohertz Gravitational-wave Background with the Parkes Pulsar Timing Array. *ApJ* **2021**, *917*, L19. [CrossRef]
27. Dewdney, P.E.; Hall, P.J.; Schilizzi, R.T.; Lazio, T.J.L.W. The Square Kilometre Array. *IEEE Proc.* **2009**, *97*, 1482–1496. [CrossRef]
28. Nan, R.; Li, D.; Jin, C.; Wang, Q.; Zhu, L.; Zhu, W.; Zhang, H.; Yue, Y.; Qian, L. The Five-Hundred Aperture Spherical Radio Telescope (fast) Project. *Int. J. Mod. Phys. D* **2011**, *20*, 989–1024. [CrossRef]
29. Amaro-Seoane, P.; Audley, H.; Babak, S.; Baker, J.; Barausse, E.; Bender, P.; Berti, E.; Binetruy, P.; Born, M.; Bortoluzzi, D.; et al. Laser Interferometer Space Antenna. *arXiv* **2017**, arXiv:1702.00786.
30. Wald, R.M. *General Relativity*; University of Chicago Press: Chicago, IL, USA, 1984.
31. Cornish, N.J. Mapping the gravitational-wave background. *Class. Quantum Gravity* **2001**, *18*, 4277–4291. [CrossRef]
32. Allen, B.; Ottewill, A.C. Detection of Anisotropies in the Gravitational-Wave Stochastic Background. *Phys. Rev. D* **1996**, *56*, 545–563. [CrossRef]
33. Romano, J.D.; Cornish, N.J. Detection methods for stochastic gravitational-wave backgrounds: A unified treatment. *Living Rev. Relativ.* **2017**, *20*, 1–223. [CrossRef]
34. Jackson, J.D. *Classical Electrodynamics*, 3rd ed.; Wiley: New York, NY, USA, 1999.
35. Renzini, A.I. Mapping the Gravitational-Wave Background. Ph.D. Thesis, Imperial College London, London, UK, 2020. [CrossRef]
36. Abbott, B.P.; Abbott, R.; Abbott, T.D.; Acernese, F.; Ackley, K.; Adams, C.; Adams, T.; Addesso, P.; Adhikari, R.X.; Adya, V.B.; et al. Gravitational Waves and Gamma-rays from a Binary Neutron Star Merger: GW170817 and GRB 170817A. *Astrophys. J. Lett.* **2017**, *848*, L13. [CrossRef]
37. Kolb, E.W.; Turner, M.S. *The Early Universe*; Addison-Wesley: Boston, MA, USA, 1990; Volume 69.
38. Pagano, L.; Salvati, L.; Melchiorri, A. New constraints on primordial gravitational waves from Planck 2015. *Phys. Lett. B* **2016**, *760*, 823–825. [CrossRef]
39. Christensen, N. Stochastic Gravitational Wave Backgrounds. *Rep. Prog. Phys.* **2019**, *82*, 016903. [CrossRef] [PubMed]
40. Phinney, E.S. A Practical Theorem on Gravitational Wave Backgrounds. *arXiv* **2001**, arXiv:0108028.
41. Isaacson, R.A. Gravitational Radiation in the Limit of High Frequency. I. The Linear Approximation and Geometrical Optics. *Phys. Rev.* **1968**, *166*, 1263–1271. [CrossRef]
42. Isaacson, R.A. Gravitational Radiation in the Limit of High Frequency. II. Nonlinear Terms and the Effective Stress Tensor. *Phys. Rev.* **1968**, *166*, 1272–1279. [CrossRef]
43. Renzini, A.I.; Romano, J.D.; Contaldi, C.R.; Cornish, N.J. A comparison of maximum likelihood mapping methods for gravitational-wave backgrounds. *Phys. Rev. D* **2022**, *105*, 023519. [CrossRef]
44. Grishchuk, L. Amplification of gravitational waves in an isotropic universe. *Sov. J. Exp. Theor. Phys.* **1975**, *40*, 409.
45. Maggiore, M. Gravitational wave experiments and early universe cosmology. *Phys. Rep.* **2000**, *331*, 283–367. [CrossRef]
46. Hogan, C.J. Gravitational radiation from cosmological phase transitions. *Mon. Not. R. Astron. Soc.* **1986**, *218*, 629–636. [CrossRef]
47. Battye, R.A.; Caldwell, R.R.; Shellard, E.P.S. Gravitational waves from cosmic strings. In *Topological Defects in Cosmology*; World Scientific Pub. Co. Inc.: Singapore, 1997; pp. 11–31.
48. Vilenkin, A.; Shellard, E.S. *Cosmic Strings and Other Topological Defects*; Cambridge University Press: Cambridge, UK, 2000.
49. Bartolo, N.; De Luca, V.; Franciolini, G.; Lewis, A.; Peloso, M.; Riotto, A. Primordial Black Hole Dark Matter: LISA Serendipity. *Phys. Rev. Lett.* **2019**, *122*, 211301. [CrossRef]
50. Bartolo, N.; Bertacca, D.; De Luca, V.; Franciolini, G.; Matarrese, S.; Peloso, M.; Ricciardone, A.; Riotto, A.; Tasinato, G. Gravitational wave anisotropies from primordial black holes. *J. Cosmol. Astropart. Phys.* **2020**, *02*, 028. [CrossRef]
51. Margalit, A.; Contaldi, C.R.; Pieroni, M. Phase Decoherence of Gravitational Wave Backgrounds. *Phys. Rev. D* **2020**, *102*, 083506. [CrossRef]
52. Maggiore, M. *Gravitational Waves. Vol. 2: Astrophysics and Cosmology*; Oxford University Press: Oxford, UK, 2018.
53. Auclair, P.; Blanco-Pillado, J.J.; Figueroa, D.G.; Jenkins, A.C.; Lewicki, M.; Sakellariadou, M.; Sanidas, S.; Sousa, L.; Steer, D.A.; Wachter, J.M.; et al. Probing the gravitational wave background from cosmic strings with LISA. *J. Cosmol. Astropart. Phys.* **2020**, *04*, 034. [CrossRef]
54. Arzoumanian, Z.; Baker, P.T.; Blumer, H.; Bécsy, B.; Brazier, A.; Brook, P.R.; Burke-Spolaor, S.; Chatterjee, S.; Chen, S.; Cordes, J.M.; et al. The NANOGrav 12.5 yr Data Set: Search for an Isotropic Stochastic Gravitational-wave Background. *ApJ* **2020**, *905*, L34. [CrossRef]
55. Caprini, C.; Hindmarsh, M.; Huber, S.; Konstandin, T.; Kozaczuk, J.; Nardini, G.; No, J.M.; Petiteau, A.; Schwaller, P.; Servant, G.; et al. Science with the space-based interferometer eLISA. II: Gravitational waves from cosmological phase transitions. *JCAP* **2016**, *04*, 001. [CrossRef]
56. Abbott, R.; Abbott, T.D.; Abraham, S.; Acernese, F.; Ackley, K.; Adams, A.; Adams, C.; Adhikari, R.X.; Adya, V.B.; Affeldt, C.; et al. Upper limits on the isotropic gravitational-wave background from Advanced LIGO and Advanced Virgo's third observing run. *Phys. Rev. D* **2021**, *104*, 022004. [CrossRef]
57. Kalogera, V.; Baym, G. The maximum mass of a neutron star. *Astrophys. J. Lett.* **1996**, *470*, L61–L64. [CrossRef]

58. Bailyn, C.D.; Jain, R.K.; Coppi, P.; Orosz, J.A. The Mass Distribution of Stellar Black Holes. *ApJ* **1998**, *499*, 367–374. [CrossRef]
59. Özel, F.; Psaltis, D.; Narayan, R.; McClintock, J.E. The Black Hole Mass Distribution in the Galaxy. *ApJ* **2010**, *725*, 1918–1927. [CrossRef]
60. Gupta, A.; Gerosa, D.; Arun, K.G.; Berti, E.; Farr, W.M.; Sathyaprakash, B.S. Black holes in the low mass gap: Implications for gravitational wave observations. *Phys. Rev. D* **2020**, *101*, 103036. [CrossRef]
61. Celotti, A.; Miller, J.C.; Sciama, D.W. Astrophysical evidence for the existence of black holes. *Class. Quantum Gravity* **2000**, *16*, A3. [CrossRef]
62. Cooray, A.R. Gravitational wave background of neutron star-white dwarf binaries. *Mon. Not. R. Astron. Soc.* **2004**, *354*, 25–30. [CrossRef]
63. Korol, V.; Belokurov, V.; Moore, C.J.; Toonen, S. Weighing Milky Way Satellites with LISA. *Mon. Not. R. Astron. Soc.* **2021**, *502*, L55–L60. [CrossRef]
64. Regimbau, T. The astrophysical gravitational wave stochastic background. *Res. Astron. Astrophys.* **2011**, *11*, 369. [CrossRef]
65. Callister, T.; Fishbach, M.; Holz, D.; Farr, W. Shouts and Murmurs: Combining Individual Gravitational-Wave Sources with the Stochastic Background to Measure the History of Binary Black Hole Mergers. *Astrophys. J. Lett.* **2020**, *896*, L32. [CrossRef]
66. Fishbach, M.; Holz, D.E.; Farr, W.M. Does the Black Hole Merger Rate Evolve with Redshift? *Astrophys. J. Lett.* **2018**, *863*, L41. [CrossRef]
67. Madau, P.; Dickinson, M. Cosmic Star Formation History. *Annu. Rev. Astron. Astrophys.* **2014**, *52*, 415–486. [CrossRef]
68. Boco, L.; Lapi, A.; Goswami, S.; Perrotta, F.; Baccigalupi, C.; Danese, L. Merging Rates of Compact Binaries in Galaxies: Perspectives for Gravitational Wave Detections. *Astrophys. J.* **2019**, *881*, 157. [CrossRef]
69. Boco, L.; Lapi, A.; Chruslinska, M.; Donevski, D.; Sicilia, A.; Danese, L. Evolution of Galaxy Star Formation and Metallicity: Impact on Double Compact Objects Mergers. *Astrophys. J.* **2021**, *907*, 110. [CrossRef]
70. Callister, T.; Sammut, L.; Qiu, S.; Mandel, I.; Thrane, E. The limits of astrophysics with gravitational-wave backgrounds. *Phys. Rev. X* **2016**, *6*, 031018. [CrossRef]
71. Sesana, A.; Vecchio, A.; Colacino, C.N. The stochastic gravitational-wave background from massive black hole binary systems: Implications for observations with Pulsar Timing Arrays. *Mon. Not. R. Astron. Soc.* **2008**, *390*, 192–209. [CrossRef]
72. Thorne, K.; Hawking, S.; Israel, W. *Three Hundred Years of Gravitation*; Cambridge University Press: Cambridge, UK, 1987; p. 330.
73. Abbott, B.P.; Abbott, R.; Abbott, T.D.; Acernese, F.; Ackley, K.; Adams, C.; Adams, T.; Addesso, P.; Adhikari, R.X.; Adya, V.B.; et al. GW170817: Implications for the Stochastic Gravitational-Wave Background from Compact Binary Coalescences. *Phys. Rev. Lett.* **2018**, *120*, 091101. [CrossRef] [PubMed]
74. LIGO Scientific Collaboration; Virgo Collaboration; KAGRA Scientific Collaboration. The population of merging compact binaries inferred using gravitational waves through GWTC-3. *arXiv* **2021**, arXiv:2111.03634.
75. LIGO Scientific Collaboration; Virgo Collaboration; KAGRA Collaboration. The Population of Merging Compact Binaries Inferred Using Gravitational Waves through GWTC-3—Data Release. 2021. Available online: https://zenodo.org/record/5655785 (accessed on 1 November 2021).
76. Caprini, C.; Figueroa, D.G. Cosmological backgrounds of gravitational waves. *Class. Quantum Gravity* **2018**, *35*, 163001. [CrossRef]
77. Guzzetti, M.C.; Bartolo, N.; Liguori, M.; Matarrese, S. Gravitational waves from inflation. *Riv. Nuovo Cim.* **2016**, *39*, 399–495. [CrossRef]
78. Contaldi, C.R.; Magueijo, J. Unsqueezing of standing waves due to inflationary domain structure. *Phys. Rev. D* **2018**, *98*, 043523. [CrossRef]
79. Kamionkowski, M.; Kosowsky, A.; Stebbins, A. A Probe of primordial gravity waves and vorticity. *Phys. Rev. Lett.* **1997**, *78*, 2058–2061. [CrossRef]
80. COrE Collaboration; Bouchet, F.R. COrE (Cosmic Origins Explorer) A White Paper. *arXiv* **2011**, arXiv:1102.2181.
81. Matsumura, T.; Akiba, Y.; Borrill, J.; Chinone, Y.; Dobbs, M.; Fuke, H.; Ghribi, A.; Hasegawa, M.; Hattori, K.; Hattori, M.; et al. Mission design of LiteBIRD. *J. Low Temp. Phys.* **2014**, *176*, 733. [CrossRef]
82. Abazajian, K.N.; Adshead, P.; Ahmed, Z.; Allen, S.W.; Alonso, D.; Arnold, K.S.; Baccigalupi, C.; Bartlett, J.G.; Battaglia, N.; Benson, B.A.; et al. CMB-S4 Science Book, First Edition. *arXiv* **2016**, arXiv:1610.02743.
83. Ade, P.; Aguirre, J.; Ahmed, Z.; Aiola, S.; Ali, A.; Alonso, D.; Alvarez, M.A.; Arnold, K.; Ashton, P.; Austermann, J.; et al. The Simons Observatory: Science goals and forecasts. *JCAP* **2019**, *02*, 056. [CrossRef]
84. Kuroyanagi, S.; Chiba, T.; Sugiyama, N. Precision calculations of the gravitational wave background spectrum from inflation. *Phys. Rev. D* **2009**, *79*, 103501. [CrossRef]
85. Chung, D.J.H.; Kolb, E.W.; Riotto, A.; Tkachev, I.I. Probing Planckian physics: Resonant production of particles during inflation and features in the primordial power spectrum. *Phys. Rev. D* **2000**, *62*, 043508. [CrossRef]
86. Ananda, K.N.; Clarkson, C.; Wands, D. The Cosmological gravitational wave background from primordial density perturbations. *Phys. Rev. D* **2007**, *75*, 123518. [CrossRef]
87. Clesse, S.; García-Bellido, J.; Orani, S. Detecting the Stochastic Gravitational Wave Background from Primordial Black Hole Formation. *arXiv* **2018**, arXiv:1812.11011.
88. Garcia-Bellido, J.; Peloso, M.; Unal, C. Gravitational Wave signatures of inflationary models from Primordial Black Hole Dark Matter. *JCAP* **2017**, *09*, 013. [CrossRef]
89. Khlebnikov, S.Y.; Tkachev, I.I. Relic gravitational waves produced after preheating. *Phys. Rev. D* **1997**, *56*, 653–660. [CrossRef]

90. Easther, R.; Lim, E.A. Stochastic gravitational wave production after inflation. *JCAP* **2006**, *04*, 010. [CrossRef]
91. Garcia-Bellido, J.; Figueroa, D.G. A stochastic background of gravitational waves from hybrid preheating. *Phys. Rev. Lett.* **2007**, *98*, 061302. [CrossRef]
92. Easther, R.; Giblin, J.T.; Lim, E.A. Gravitational Wave Production at the End of Inflation. *Phys. Rev. Lett.* **2007**, *99*, 221301. [CrossRef]
93. Bartolo, N.; Caprini, C.; Domcke, V.; Figueroa, D.G.; Garcia-Bellido, J.; Guzzetti, M.C.; Liguori, M.; Matarrese, S.; Peloso, M.; Petiteau, A.; et al. Science with the space-based interferometer LISA. IV: Probing inflation with gravitational waves. *J. Cosmol. Astropart. Phys.* **2016**, *12*, 026. [CrossRef]
94. Jeannerot, R.; Rocher, J.; Sakellariadou, M. How generic is cosmic string formation in SUSY GUTs. *Phys. Rev. D* **2003**, *68*, 103514. [CrossRef]
95. García-Bellido, J.; Jaraba, S.; Kuroyanagi, S. The stochastic gravitational wave background from close hyperbolic encounters of primordial black holes in dense clusters. *arXiv* **2021**, arXiv:2109.11376.
96. Alexander, S.; Marciano, A.; Smolin, L. Gravitational origin of the weak interaction's chirality. *Phys. Rev. D* **2014**, *89*, 065017. [CrossRef]
97. Freidel, L.; Minic, D.; Takeuchi, T. Quantum gravity, torsion, parity violation and all that. *Phys. Rev. D* **2005**, *72*, 104002. [CrossRef]
98. Alexander, S.H. Isogravity: Toward an Electroweak and Gravitational Unification. *arXiv* **2007**, arXiv:0706.4481.
99. Smolin, L. The Plebanski action extended to a unification of gravity and Yang-Mills theory. *Phys. Rev. D* **2009**, *80*, 124017. [CrossRef]
100. Contaldi, C.R. Anisotropies of Gravitational Wave Backgrounds: A Line Of Sight Approach. *Phys. Rev. Lett.* **2017**, *B771*, 9–12. [CrossRef]
101. Jenkins, A.C.; Sakellariadou, M. Anisotropies in the stochastic gravitational-wave background: Formalism and the cosmic string case. *Phys. Rev. D* **2018**, *98*, 063509. [CrossRef]
102. Jenkins, A.C.; O'Shaughnessy, R.; Sakellariadou, M.; Wysocki, D. Anisotropies in the astrophysical gravitational-wave background: The impact of black hole distributions. *Phys. Rev. Lett.* **2019**, *122*, 111101. [CrossRef]
103. Durrer, R. *The Cosmic Microwave Background*; Cambridge University Press: Cambridge, UK, 2008. [CrossRef]
104. Peebles, P.J.E. *The Large-Scale Structure of the Universe*; Princeton University Press: Princeton, NJ, USA, 2020.
105. Sachs, R.; Wolfe, A. Perturbations of a cosmological model and angular variations of the microwave background. *Astrophys. J.* **1967**, *147*, 73–90. [CrossRef]
106. Bartolo, N.; Bertacca, D.; Matarrese, S.; Peloso, M.; Ricciardone, A.; Riotto, A.; Tasinato, G. Anisotropies and non-Gaussianity of the Cosmological Gravitational Wave Background. *Phys. Rev. D* **2019**, *100*, 121501. [CrossRef]
107. Cusin, G.; Dvorkin, I.; Pitrou, C.; Uzan, J.P. First predictions of the angular power spectrum of the astrophysical gravitational wave background. *Phys. Rev. Lett.* **2018**, *120*, 231101. [CrossRef] [PubMed]
108. Jenkins, A.C.; Sakellariadou, M.; Regimbau, T.; Slezak, E. Anisotropies in the astrophysical gravitational-wave background: Predictions for the detection of compact binaries by LIGO and Virgo. *Phys. Rev. D* **2018**, *98*, 063501. [CrossRef]
109. Capurri, G.; Lapi, A.; Baccigalupi, C.; Boco, L.; Scelfo, G.; Ronconi, T. Intensity and anisotropies of the stochastic gravitational wave background from merging compact binaries in galaxies. *JCAP* **2021**, *11*, 032. [CrossRef]
110. Geller, M.; Hook, A.; Sundrum, R.; Tsai, Y. Primordial Anisotropies in the Gravitational Wave Background from Cosmological Phase Transitions. *Phys. Rev. Lett.* **2018**, *121*, 201303. [CrossRef]
111. Bertacca, D.; Ricciardone, A.; Bellomo, N.; Jenkins, A.C.; Matarrese, S.; Raccanelli, A.; Regimbau, T.; Sakellariadou, M. Projection effects on the observed angular spectrum of the astrophysical stochastic gravitational wave background. *Phys. Rev. D* **2020**, *101*, 103513. [CrossRef]
112. Bellomo, N.; Bertacca, D.; Jenkins, A.C.; Matarrese, S.; Raccanelli, A.; Regimbau, T.; Ricciardone, A.; Sakellariadou, M. CLASS_GWB: Robust modeling of the astrophysical gravitational wave background anisotropies. *arXiv* **2021**, arXiv:2110.15059.
113. Cusin, G.; Dvorkin, I.; Pitrou, C.; Uzan, J.P. Comment on the article "Anisotropies in the astrophysical gravitational-wave background: The impact of black hole distributions" by A.C. Jenkins et al. [arXiv:1810.13435]. *arXiv* **2018**, arXiv:1811.03582.
114. Jenkins, A.C.; Sakellariadou, M.; Regimbau, T.; Slezak, E.; O'Shaughnessy, R.; Wysocki, D. Response to Cusin et al's comment on arXiv:1810.13435. *arXiv* **2019**, arXiv:1901.01078.
115. Pitrou, C.; Cusin, G.; Uzan, J.P. Unified view of anisotropies in the astrophysical gravitational-wave background. *Phys. Rev. D* **2020**, *101*, 081301. [CrossRef]
116. Alonso, D.; Contaldi, C.R.; Cusin, G.; Ferreira, P.G.; Renzini, A.I. The N_ℓ of gravitational wave background experiments. *arXiv* **2020**, arXiv:2005.03001.
117. Regimbau, T.; Dent, T.; Del Pozzo, W.; Giampanis, S.; Li, T.G.F.; Robinson, C.; Van Den Broeck, C.; Meacher, D.; Rodriguez, C.; Sathyaprakash, B.S.; et al. Mock data challenge for the Einstein Gravitational-Wave Telescope. *Phys. Rev. D* **2012**, *86*, 122001. [CrossRef]
118. Regimbau, T.; Meacher, D.; Coughlin, M. Second Einstein Telescope mock science challenge: Detection of the gravitational-wave stochastic background from compact binary coalescences. *Phys. Rev. D* **2014**, *89*, 084046. [CrossRef]
119. Cornish, N.J.; Romano, J.D. When is a gravitational-wave signal stochastic? *Phys. Rev. D* **2015**, *92*, 042001. [CrossRef]
120. Rosado, P.A.; Sesana, A.; Gair, J. Expected properties of the first gravitational wave signal detected with pulsar timing arrays. *Mon. Not. R. Astron. Soc.* **2015**, *451*, 2417–2433. [CrossRef]

121. Meacher, D.; Thrane, E.; Regimbau, T. Statistical properties of astrophysical gravitational-wave backgrounds. *Phys. Rev. D* **2014**, *89*, 084063. [CrossRef]
122. Jenkins, A.C.; Sakellariadou, M. Shot noise in the astrophysical gravitational-wave background. *Phys. Rev. D* **2019**, *100*, 063508. [CrossRef]
123. Jenkins, A.C.; Romano, J.D.; Sakellariadou, M. Estimating the angular power spectrum of the gravitational-wave background in the presence of shot noise. *Phys. Rev. D* **2019**, *100*, 083501. [CrossRef]
124. Alonso, D.; Cusin, G.; Ferreira, P.G.; Pitrou, C. Detecting the anisotropic astrophysical gravitational wave background in the presence of shot noise through cross-correlations. *Phys. Rev. D* **2020**, *102*, 023002. [CrossRef]
125. Canas-Herrera, G.; Contigiani, O.; Vardanyan, V. Cross-correlation of the astrophysical gravitational-wave background with galaxy clustering. *Phys. Rev. D* **2020**, *102*, 043513. [CrossRef]
126. Dvorkin, I.; Uzan, J.P.; Vangioni, E.; Silk, J. Exploring stellar evolution with gravitational-wave observations. *Mon. Not. R. Astron. Soc.* **2018**, *479*, 121–129. [CrossRef]
127. Mukherjee, S.; Silk, J. Time-dependence of the astrophysical stochastic gravitational wave background. *Mon. Not. R. Astron. Soc.* **2020**, *491*, 4690–4701. [CrossRef]
128. Abbott, R.; Abbott, T.D.; Acernese, F.; Ackley, K.; Adams, C.; Adhikari, N.; Adhikari, R.X.; Adya, V.B.; Affeldt, C.; Agarwal, D.; et al. Constraints on dark photon dark matter using data from LIGO's and Virgo's third observing run. *arXiv* **2021**, arXiv:2105.13085.
129. Abbott, R.; Abbott, T.D.; Abraham, S.; Acernese, F.; Ackley, K.; Adams, A.; Adams, C.; Adhikari, R.X.; Adya, V.B.; Affeldt, C.; et al. Constraints on Cosmic Strings Using Data from the Third Advanced LIGO–Virgo Observing Run. *Phys. Rev. Lett.* **2021**, *126*, 241102. [CrossRef] [PubMed]
130. Talbot, C.; Thrane, E.; Biscoveanu, S.; Smith, R. Inference with finite time series: Observing the gravitational Universe through windows. *Phys. Rev. Res.* **2021**, *3*, 043049. [CrossRef]
131. Matas, A.; Romano, J.D. Frequentist versus Bayesian analyses: Cross-correlation as an approximate sufficient statistic for LIGO-Virgo stochastic background searches. *Phys. Rev. D* **2021**, *103*, 062003. [CrossRef]
132. Littenberg, T.; Cornish, N.; Lackeos, K.; Robson, T. Global Analysis of the Gravitational Wave Signal from Galactic Binaries. *Phys. Rev. D* **2020**, *101*, 123021. [CrossRef]
133. Aasi, J.; Abbott, B.P.; Abbott, R.; Abbott, T.; Abernathy, M.R.; Ackley, K.; Adams, C.; Adams, T.; Addesso, P.; Adhikari, R.X.; et al. Advanced LIGO. *Class. Quantum Gravity* **2015**, *32*, 074001. [CrossRef]
134. Armstrong, J.W.; Estabrook, F.B.; Tinto, M. Time-Delay Interferometry for Space-based Gravitational Wave Searches. *Astrophys. J.* **1999**, *527*, 814–826. [CrossRef]
135. Tinto, M.; Armstrong, J.W. Cancellation of laser noise in an unequal-arm interferometer detector of gravitational radiation. *Phys. Rev. D* **1999**, *59*, 102003. [CrossRef]
136. Seto, N.; Taruya, A. Measuring a parity-violation signature in the early universe via ground-based laser interferometers. *Phys. Rev. Lett.* **2007**, *99*, 121101. [CrossRef] [PubMed]
137. Seto, N.; Taruya, A. Polarization analysis of gravitational-wave backgrounds from the correlation signals of ground-based interferometers: Measuring a circular-polarization mode. *Phys. Rev. D Part. Fields, Gravit. Cosmol.* **2008**, *77*, 1–27. [CrossRef]
138. Bayle, J.B.; Hartwig, O.; Staab, M. Adapting time-delay interferometry for LISA data in frequency. *Phys. Rev. D* **2021**, *104*, 023006. [CrossRef]
139. Bayle, J.B.; Lilley, M.; Petiteau, A.; Halloin, H. Effect of filters on the time-delay interferometry residual laser noise for LISA. *PRD* **2019**, *99*, 084023. [CrossRef]
140. Vallisneri, M.; Bayle, J.B.; Babak, S.; Petiteau, A. Time-delay interferometry without delays. *Phys. Rev. D* **2021**, *103*, 082001. [CrossRef]
141. Bayle, J.B.; Vallisneri, M.; Babak, S.; Petiteau, A. On the matrix formulation of time-delay interferometry. *arXiv* **2021**, arXiv:2106.03976.
142. Tinto, M.; Dhurandhar, S.; Joshi, P. Matrix representation of time-delay interferometry. *PRD* **2021**, *104*, 044033. [CrossRef]
143. Page, J.; Littenberg, T.B. Bayesian time delay interferometry. *PRD* **2021**, *104*, 084037. [CrossRef]
144. Baghi, Q.; Thorpe, J.I.; Slutsky, J.; Baker, J. Statistical inference approach to time-delay interferometry for gravitational-wave detection. *PRD* **2021**, *103*, 042006. [CrossRef]
145. LISA Data Challenge Manual. 2018. Available online: https://lisa-ldc.lal.in2p3.fr/static/data/pdf/LDC-manual-001.pdf (accessed on 1 November 2021).
146. Tinto, M.; Dhurandhar, S.V. TIME DELAY. *Living Rev. Relativ.* **2005**, *8*, 4. [CrossRef] [PubMed]
147. Adams, M.R.; Cornish, N.J. Discriminating between a stochastic gravitational wave background and instrument noise. *Phys. Rev. D* **2010**, *82*, 022002. [CrossRef]
148. Adams, M.R.; Cornish, N.J. Detecting a stochastic gravitational wave background in the presence of a galactic foreground and instrument noise. *Phys. Rev. D* **2014**, *89*, 022001. [CrossRef]
149. Anholm, M.; Ballmer, S.; Creighton, J.D.E.; Price, L.R.; Siemens, X. Optimal strategies for gravitational wave stochastic background searches in pulsar timing data. *PRD* **2009**, *79*, 084030. [CrossRef]
150. Hellings, R.W.; Downs, G.S. Upper limits on the isotropic gravitational radiation background from pulsar timing analysis. *ApJ* **1983**, *265*, L39–L42. [CrossRef]

151. Allen, B.; Romano, J.D. Detecting a stochastic background of gravitational radiation: Signal processing strategies and sensitivities. *Phys. Rev. D* **1999**, *59*, 102001. [CrossRef]
152. Renzini, A.I.; Contaldi, C.R. Mapping Incoherent Gravitational Wave Backgrounds. *Mon. Not. R. Astron. Soc.* **2018**, *481*, 4650–4661. [CrossRef]
153. Renzini, A.I.; Contaldi, C.R. Gravitational Wave Background Sky Maps from Advanced LIGO O1 Data. *Phys. Rev. Lett.* **2019**, *122*, 081102. [CrossRef]
154. Renzini, A.; Contaldi, C. Improved limits on a stochastic gravitational-wave background and its anisotropies from Advanced LIGO O1 and O2 runs. *Phys. Rev.* **2019**, *D100*, 063527. [CrossRef]
155. Chatziioannou, K.; Haster, C.J.; Littenberg, T.B.; Farr, W.M.; Ghonge, S.; Millhouse, M.; Clark, J.A.; Cornish, N. Noise spectral estimation methods and their impact on gravitational wave measurement of compact binary mergers. *Phys. Rev. D* **2019**, *100*, 104004. [CrossRef]
156. Cornish, N.J.; Romano, J.D. Towards a unified treatment of gravitational-wave data analysis. *Phys. Rev. D* **2013**, *87*, 122003. [CrossRef]
157. Cornish, N.J. Detecting a stochastic gravitational wave background with the Laser Interferometer Space Antenna. *Phys. Rev. D* **2002**, *65*, 022004. [CrossRef]
158. Coughlin, M.; Christensen, N.; Gair, J.; Kandhasamy, S.; Thrane, E. Method for estimation of gravitational-wave transient model parameters in frequency–time maps. *Class. Quantum Gravity* **2014**, *31*, 165012. [CrossRef]
159. Mandic, V.; Thrane, E.; Giampanis, S.; Regimbau, T. Parameter Estimation in Searches for the Stochastic Gravitational-Wave Background. *Phys. Rev. Lett.* **2012**, *109*, 171102. [CrossRef]
160. Callister, T.; Biscoveanu, A.S.; Christensen, N.; Isi, M.; Matas, A.; Minazzoli, O.; Regimbau, T.; Sakellariadou, M.; Tasson, J.; Thrane, E. Polarization-based Tests of Gravity with the Stochastic Gravitational-Wave Background. *Phys. Rev. X* **2017**, *7*, 041058. [CrossRef]
161. Abbott, B.P.; Abbott, R.; Abbott, T.D.; Abraham, S.; Acernese, F.; Ackley, K.; Adams, C.; Adya, V.B.; Affeldt, C.; Agathos, M.; et al. Search for the isotropic stochastic background using data from Advanced LIGO's second observing run. *Phys. Rev. D* **2019**, *100*, 061101. [CrossRef]
162. Tsukada, L.; Callister, T.; Matas, A.; Meyers, P. First search for a stochastic gravitational-wave background from ultralight bosons. *Phys. Rev. D* **2019**, *99*, 103015. [CrossRef]
163. Tsukada, L.; Brito, R.; East, W.E.; Siemonsen, N. Modeling and searching for a stochastic gravitational-wave background from ultralight vector bosons. *Phys. Rev. D* **2021**, *103*, 083005. [CrossRef]
164. Romero, A.; Martinovic, K.; Callister, T.A.; Guo, H.K.; Martínez, M.; Sakellariadou, M.; Yang, F.W.; Zhao, Y. Implications for First-Order Cosmological Phase Transitions from the Third LIGO-Virgo Observing Run. *Phys. Rev. Lett.* **2021**, *126*, 151301. [CrossRef]
165. Romero-Rodriguez, A.; Martinez, M.; Pujolàs, O.; Sakellariadou, M.; Vaskonen, V. Search for a scalar induced stochastic gravitational wave background in the third LIGO-Virgo observing run. *Phys. Rev. Lett.* **2022**, *128*, 051301. [CrossRef]
166. Martinovic, K.; Badger, C.; Sakellariadou, M.; Mandic, V. Searching for parity violation with the LIGO-Virgo-KAGRA network. *Phys. Rev. D* **2021**, *104*, L081101. [CrossRef]
167. Meyers, P.M.; Martinovic, K.; Christensen, N.; Sakellariadou, M. Detecting a stochastic gravitational-wave background in the presence of correlated magnetic noise. *PRD* **2020**, *102*, 102005. [CrossRef]
168. Martinovic, K.; Meyers, P.M.; Sakellariadou, M.; Christensen, N. Simultaneous estimation of astrophysical and cosmological stochastic gravitational-wave backgrounds with terrestrial detectors. *Phys. Rev. D* **2021**, *103*, 043023. [CrossRef]
169. Parida, A.; Suresh, J.; Mitra, S.; Jhingan, S. Component separation map-making for stochastic gravitational wave background. *arXiv* **2019**, arXiv:1904.05056.
170. Meacher, D.; Coughlin, M.; Morris, S.; Regimbau, T.; Christensen, N.; Kandhasamy, S.; Mandic, V.; Romano, J.D.; Thrane, E. Mock data and science challenge for detecting an astrophysical stochastic gravitational-wave background with Advanced LIGO and Advanced Virgo. *Phys. Rev. D* **2015**, *92*, 063002. [CrossRef]
171. Biwer, C.; Barker, D.; Batch, J.C.; Betzwieser, J.; Fisher, R.P.; Goetz, E.; Kandhasamy, S.; Karki, S.; Kissel, J.S.; Lundgren, A.P.; et al. Validating gravitational-wave detections: The Advanced LIGO hardware injection system. *Phys. Rev. D* **2017**, *95*, 062002. [CrossRef]
172. van Haasteren, R.; Levin, Y.; McDonald, P.; Lu, T. On measuring the gravitational-wave background using Pulsar Timing Arrays. *MNRAS* **2009**, *395*, 1005–1014. [CrossRef]
173. van Haasteren, R.; Levin, Y.; Janssen, G.H.; Lazaridis, K.; Kramer, M.; Stappers, B.W.; Desvignes, G.; Purver, M.B.; Lyne, A.G.; Ferdman, R.D.; et al. Placing limits on the stochastic gravitational-wave background using European Pulsar Timing Array data. *MNRAS* **2011**, *414*, 3117–3128. [CrossRef]
174. Lentati, L.; Alexander, P.; Hobson, M.P.; Taylor, S.; Gair, J.; Balan, S.T.; van Haasteren, R. Hyper-efficient model-independent Bayesian method for the analysis of pulsar timing data. *PRD* **2013**, *87*, 104021. [CrossRef]
175. van Haasteren, R.; Vallisneri, M. New advances in the Gaussian-process approach to pulsar-timing data analysis. *PRD* **2014**, *90*, 104012. [CrossRef]
176. Lentati, L.; Alexander, P.; Hobson, M.P.; Feroz, F.; van Haasteren, R.; Lee, K.J.; Shannon, R.M. TEMPONEST: A Bayesian approach to pulsar timing analysis. *MNRAS* **2014**, *437*, 3004–3023. [CrossRef]

177. Hobbs, G.; Jenet, F.; Lee, K.J.; Verbiest, J.P.W.; Yardley, D.; Manchester, R.; Lommen, A.; Coles, W.; Edwards, R.; Shettigara, C. TEMPO2: A new pulsar timing package—III. Gravitational wave simulation. *MNRAS* **2009**, *394*, 1945–1955. [CrossRef]
178. Arzoumanian, Z.; Brazier, A.; Burke-Spolaor, S.; Chamberlin, S.J.; Chatterjee, S.; Christy, B.; Cordes, J.M.; Cornish, N.J.; Crowter, K.; Demorest, P.B.; et al. The NANOGrav Nine-year Data Set: Limits on the Isotropic Stochastic Gravitational Wave Background. *ApJ* **2016**, *821*, 13. [CrossRef]
179. Taylor, S.R.; Lentati, L.; Babak, S.; Brem, P.; Gair, J.R.; Sesana, A.; Vecchio, A. All correlations must die: Assessing the significance of a stochastic gravitational-wave background in pulsar timing arrays. *PRD* **2017**, *95*, 042002. [CrossRef]
180. Arzoumanian, Z.; Baker, P.T.; Brazier, A.; Burke-Spolaor, S.; Chamberlin, S.J.; Chatterjee, S.; Christy, B.; Cordes, J.M.; Cornish, N.J.; Crawford, F.; et al. The NANOGrav 11 Year Data Set: Pulsar-timing Constraints on the Stochastic Gravitational-wave Background. *ApJ* **2018**, *859*, 47. [CrossRef]
181. Chamberlin, S.J.; Creighton, J.D.E.; Siemens, X.; Demorest, P.; Ellis, J.; Price, L.R.; Romano, J.D. Time-domain implementation of the optimal cross-correlation statistic for stochastic gravitational-wave background searches in pulsar timing data. *PRD* **2015**, *91*, 044048. [CrossRef]
182. Vigeland, S.J.; Islo, K.; Taylor, S.R.; Ellis, J.A. Noise-marginalise optimal statistic: A robust hybrid frequentist-Bayesian statistic for the stochastic gravitational-wave background in pulsar timing arrays. *PRD* **2018**, *98*, 044003. [CrossRef]
183. Cornish, N.J.; Sampson, L. Towards robust gravitational wave detection with pulsar timing arrays. *PRD* **2016**, *93*, 104047. [CrossRef]
184. Bécsy, B.; Cornish, N.J. Joint search for isolated sources and an unresolved confusion background in pulsar timing array data. *Class. Quantum Gravity* **2020**, *37*, 135011. [CrossRef]
185. Prix, R.; Itoh, Y. Global parameter-space correlations of coherent searches for continuous gravitational waves. *Class. Quantum Gravity* **2005**, *22*, S1003–S1012. [CrossRef]
186. Ain, A.; Dalvi, P.; Mitra, S. Fast gravitational wave radiometry using data folding. *Phys. Rev. D Part. Fields, Gravit. Cosmol.* **2015**, *92*, 022003. [CrossRef]
187. Ain, A.; Suresh, J.; Mitra, S. Very fast stochastic gravitational wave background map making using folded data. *PRD* **2018**, *98*, 024001. [CrossRef]
188. Goncharov, B.; Thrane, E. All-sky radiometer for narrowband gravitational waves using folded data. *PRD* **2018**, *98*, 064018. [CrossRef]
189. Mitra, S.; Dhurandhar, S.; Souradeep, T.; Lazzarini, A.; Mandic, V.; Bose, S.; Ballmer, S. Gravitational wave radiometry: Mapping a stochastic gravitational wave background. *Phys. Rev. D* **2008**, *77*, 042002. [CrossRef]
190. Thrane, E.; Ballmer, S.; Romano, J.D.; Mitra, S.; Talukder, D.; Bose, S.; Mandic, V. Probing the anisotropies of a stochastic gravitational-wave background using a network of ground-based laser interferometers. *Phys. Rev. D Part. Fields, Gravit. Cosmol.* **2009**, *80*, 122002. [CrossRef]
191. Mingarelli, C.M.F.; Sidery, T.; Mandel, I.; Vecchio, A. Characterizing gravitational wave stochastic background anisotropy with pulsar timing arrays. *PRD* **2013**, *88*, 062005. [CrossRef]
192. Taylor, S.R.; Gair, J.R. Searching for anisotropic gravitational-wave backgrounds using pulsar timing arrays. *PRD* **2013**, *88*, 084001. [CrossRef]
193. Contaldi, C.R.; Pieroni, M.; Renzini, A.I.; Cusin, G.; Karnesis, N.; Peloso, M.; Ricciardone, A.; Tasinato, G. Maximum likelihood map-making with the Laser Interferometer Space Antenna. *Phys. Rev. D* **2020**, *102*, 043502. [CrossRef]
194. Banagiri, S.; Criswell, A.; Kuan, T.; Mandic, V.; Romano, J.D.; Taylor, S.R. Mapping the gravitational-wave sky with LISA: A Bayesian spherical harmonic approach. *MNRAS* **2021**, *507*, 5451–5462. [CrossRef]
195. Bond, J.R.; Jaffe, A.H.; Knox, L. Estimating the power spectrum of the cosmic microwave background. *Phys. Rev.* **1998**, *D57*, 2117–2137. [CrossRef]
196. Rocha, G.; Contaldi, C.; Bond, J.; Gorski, K. Application of XFaster power spectrum and likelihood estimator to Planck. *Mon. Not. R. Astron. Soc.* **2011**, *414*, 823–846. [CrossRef]
197. Cornish, N.J.; van Haasteren, R. Mapping the nano-Hertz gravitational wave sky. *arXiv* **2014**, arXiv:1406.4511.
198. Ballmer, S.W. A radiometer for stochastic gravitational waves. *Class. Quantum Gravity* **2006**, *23*, S179–S185. [CrossRef]
199. Gair, J.; Romano, J.D.; Taylor, S.; Mingarelli, C.M.F. Mapping gravitational-wave backgrounds using methods from CMB analysis: Application to pulsar timing arrays. *PRD* **2014**, *90*, 082001. [CrossRef]
200. Gair, J.R.; Romano, J.D.; Taylor, S.R. Mapping gravitational-wave backgrounds of arbitrary polarisation using pulsar timing arrays. *PRD* **2015**, *92*, 102003. [CrossRef]
201. Romano, J.D.; Taylor, S.R.; Cornish, N.J.; Gair, J.; Mingarelli, C.M.F.; van Haasteren, R. Phase-coherent mapping of gravitational-wave backgrounds using ground-based laser interferometers. *PRD* **2015**, *92*, 042003. [CrossRef]
202. Taylor, S.R.; Mingarelli, C.M.F.; Gair, J.R.; Sesana, A.; Theureau, G.; Babak, S.; Bassa, C.G.; Brem, P.; Burgay, M.; Caballero, R.N.; et al. Limits on Anisotropy in the Nanohertz Stochastic Gravitational Wave Background. *PRL* **2015**, *115*, 041101. [CrossRef]
203. Ali-Haïmoud, Y.; Smith, T.L.; Mingarelli, C.M.F. Fisher formalism for anisotropic gravitational-wave background searches with pulsar timing arrays. *PRD* **2020**, *102*, 122005. [CrossRef]
204. Ali-Haïmoud, Y.; Smith, T.L.; Mingarelli, C.M.F. Insights into searches for anisotropies in the nanohertz gravitational-wave background. *PRD* **2021**, *103*, 042009. [CrossRef]

205. Suresh, J.; Agarwal, D.; Mitra, S. Jointly setting upper limits on multiple components of an anisotropic stochastic gravitational-wave background. *PRD* **2021**, *104*, 102003. [CrossRef]
206. Gorski, K.M.; Hivon, E.; Banday, A.J.; Wandelt, B.D.; Hansen, F.K.; Reinecke, M.; Bartelman, M. HEALPix—A Framework for high resolution discretization, and fast analysis of data distributed on the sphere. *Astrophys. J.* **2005**, *622*, 759–771. [CrossRef]
207. Hotinli, S.C.; Kamionkowski, M.; Jaffe, A.H. The search for statistical anisotropy in the gravitational-wave background with pulsar timing arrays. *Open J. Astrophys.* **2019**, *2*, 8. [CrossRef]
208. Ivezić, Ž.; Connolly, A.; VanderPlas, J.; Gray, A. *Statistics, Data Mining, and Machine Learning in Astronomy: A Practical Python Guide for the Analysis of Survey Data*; Princeton Series in Modern Observational Astronomy; Princeton University Press: Princeton, NJ, USA, 2014.
209. Suresh, J.; Ain, A.; Mitra, S. Unified mapmaking for an anisotropic stochastic gravitational wave background. *PRD* **2021**, *103*, 083024. [CrossRef]
210. Myers, S.T.; Contaldi, C.R.; Bond, J.R.; Pen, U.L.; Pogosyan, D.; Prunet, S.; Sievers, J.L.; Mason, B.S.; Pearson, T.J.; Readhead, A.C.S.; et al. A fast gridded method for the estimation of the power spectrum of the CMB from interferometer data with application to the cosmic background imager. *Astrophys. J.* **2003**, *591*, 575–598. [CrossRef]
211. Abbott, R.; Abbott, T.D.; Abraham, S.; Acernese, F.; Ackley, K.; Adams, A.; Adams, C.; Adhikari, R.X.; Adya, V.B.; Affeldt, C.; et al. Search for anisotropic gravitational-wave backgrounds using data from Advanced LIGO and Advanced Virgo's first three observing runs. *Phys. Rev. D* **2021**, *104*, 022005. [CrossRef]
212. Drasco, S.; Flanagan, E.E. Detection methods for non-Gaussian gravitational wave stochastic backgrounds. *Phys. Rev.* **2003**, *D67*, 082003. [CrossRef]
213. Abbott, R.; Abbott, T.D.; Acernese, F.; Ackley, K.; Adams, C.; Adhikari, N.; Adhikari, R.X.; Adya, V.B.; Affeldt, C.; Agarwal, D.; et al. GWTC-3: Compact Binary Coalescences Observed by LIGO and Virgo During the Second Part of the Third Observing Run. *arXiv* **2021**, arXiv:2111.03606.
214. Thrane, E. Measuring the non-Gaussian stochastic gravitational-wave background: A method for realistic interferometer data. *Phys. Rev. D* **2013**, *87*, 043009. [CrossRef]
215. Smith, R.; Thrane, E. Optimal Search for an Astrophysical Gravitational-Wave Background. *Phys. Rev. X* **2018**, *8*, 021019. [CrossRef]
216. Lawrence, J.; Turbang, K.; Matas, A.; Renzini, A.; Van Remortel, N.; Romano, J. A stochastic-signal-based search for intermittent gravitational-wave backgrounds. 2022, *in preparation*.
217. Banagiri, S.; Mandic, V.; Scarlata, C.; Yang, K.Z. Measuring angular N-point correlations of binary black hole merger gravitational-wave events with hierarchical Bayesian inference. *Phys. Rev. D* **2020**, *102*, 063007. [CrossRef]
218. Barsotti, L.; Fritschel, P.; Evans, M.; Gras, S. Advanced LIGO *Design* Sensitivity Curve. 2018. Available online: https://dcc.ligo.org/LIGO-T1800044/public (accessed on 1 November 2021).
219. Thrane, E.; Romano, J.D. Sensitivity curves for searches for gravitational-wave backgrounds. *Phys. Rev.* **2013**, *D88*, 124032. [CrossRef]
220. Coughlin, M.; Harms, J. Constraining the gravitational wave energy density of the Universe using Earth's ring. *Phys. Rev. D* **2014**, *90*, 042005. [CrossRef]
221. Armstrong, J.W.; Iess, L.; Tortora, P.; Bertotti, B. Stochastic gravitational wave background: Upper limits in the 10**-6-Hz 10**-3-Hz band. *Astrophys. J.* **2003**, *599*, 806–813. [CrossRef]
222. Lasky, P.D.; Mingarelli, C.M.; Smith, T.L.; Giblin, J.T., Jr.; Thrane, E.; Reardon, D.J.; Caldwell, R.; Bailes, M.; Bhat, N.R.; Burke-Spolaor, S.; et al. Gravitational-wave cosmology across 29 decades in frequency. *Phys. Rev. X* **2016**, *6*, 011035. [CrossRef]
223. Akrami, Y.; Arroja, F.; Ashdown, M.; Aumont, J.; Baccigalupi, C.; Ballardini, M.; Banday, A.J.; Barreiro, R.B.; Bartolo, N.; Basak, S.; et al. Planck 2018 results. X. Constraints on inflation. *Astron. Astrophys.* **2020**, *641*, A10. [CrossRef]
224. Badurina, L.; Bentine, E.; Blas, D.; Bongs, K.; Bortoletto, D.; Bowcock, T.; Bridges, K.; Bowden, W.; Buchmueller, O.; Burrage, C.; et al. AION: An Atom Interferometer Observatory and Network. *JCAP* **2020**, *05*, 011. [CrossRef]
225. Blas, D.; Jenkins, A.C. Detecting stochastic gravitational waves with binary resonance. *arXiv* **2021**, arXiv:2107.04063.
226. Blas, D.; Jenkins, A.C. Bridging the μHz gap in the gravitational-wave landscape with binary resonance. *arXiv* **2021**, arXiv:2107.04601.
227. Janssen, G.H.; Hobbs, G.; McLaughlin, M.; Bassa, C.G.; Deller, A.T.; Kramer, M.; Lee, K.J.; Mingarelli, C.M.F.; Rosado, P.A.; Sanidas, S.; et al. Gravitational wave astronomy with the SKA. *PoS* **2015**, *AASKA14*, 037. [CrossRef]
228. Abbott, B.; Abbott, R.; Adhikari, R.; Ageev, A.; Allen, B.; Amin, R.; Anderson, S.B.; Anderson, W.G.; Araya, M.; Armandula, H.; et al. Analysis of first LIGO science data for stochastic gravitational waves. *Phys. Rev. D* **2004**, *69*, 122004. [CrossRef]
229. Abbott, B.; Abbott, R.; Adhikari, R.; Agresti, J.; Ajith, P.; Allen, B.; Allen, R.; Amin, R.; Anderson, S.B.; Anderson, W.G.; et al. Upper limits on a stochastic background of gravitational waves. *Phys. Rev. Lett.* **2005**, *95*, 221101. [CrossRef] [PubMed]
230. Abbott, B.; Abbott, R.; Adhikari, R.; Agresti, J.; Ajith, P.; Allen, B.; Amin, R.; Anderson, S.B.; Anderson, W.G.; Araya, M.; et al. Searching for a Stochastic Background of Gravitational Waves with LIGO. *Astrophys. J.* **2007**, *659*, 918–930. [CrossRef]
231. Aasi, J.; Abbott, B.P.; Abbott, R.; Abbott, T.; Abernathy, M.R.; Accadia, T.; Acernese, F.; Ackley, K.; Adams, C.; Adams, T.; et al. Improved Upper Limits on the Stochastic Gravitational-Wave Background from 2009–2010 LIGO and Virgo Data. *Phys. Rev. Lett.* **2014**, *113*, 231101. [CrossRef]

232. Abbott, B.P.; Abbott, R.; Abbott, T.D.; Abernathy, M.R.; Acernese, F.; Ackley, K.; Adams, C.; Adams, T.; Addesso, P.; Adhikari, R.X.; et al. Upper Limits on the Stochastic Gravitational-Wave Background from Advanced LIGO's First Observing Run. *Phys. Rev. Lett.* **2017**, *118*, 121101; Erratum on **2017**, *119*, 029901. [CrossRef]
233. Abbott, B.; Abbott, R.; Adhikari, R.; Agresti, J.; Ajith, P.; Allen, B.; Amin, R.; Anderson, S.B.; Anderson, W.G.; Arain, M.; et al. Upper limit map of a background of gravitational waves. *Phys. Rev. D* **2007**, *76*, 082003. [CrossRef]
234. Abadie, J.; Abbott, B.P.; Abbott, R.; Abernathy, M.; Accadia, T.; Acernese, F.; Adams, C.; Adhikari, R.; Ajith, P.; Allen, B.; et al. Directional Limits on Persistent Gravitational Waves Using LIGO S5 Science Data. *Phys. Rev. Lett.* **2011**, *107*, 271102. [CrossRef]
235. Abbott, B.P.; Abbott, R.; Abbott, T.D.; Abernathy, M.R.; Acernese, F.; Ackley, K.; Adams, C.; Adams, T.; Addesso, P.; Adhikari, R.X.; et al. Directional Limits on Persistent Gravitational Waves from Advanced LIGO's First Observing Run. *Phys. Rev. Lett.* **2017**, *118*, 121102. [CrossRef]
236. Abbott, B.P.; Abbott, R.; Abbott, T.D.; Abraham, S.; Acernese, F.; Ackley, K.; Adams, C.; Adhikari, R.X.; Adya, V.B.; Affeldt, C.; et al. Directional limits on persistent gravitational waves using data from Advanced LIGO's first two observing runs. *Phys. Rev. D* **2019**, *100*, 062001. [CrossRef]
237. Aasi, J.; Abadie, J.; Abbott, B.P.; Abbott, R.; Abbott, T.; Abernathy, M.R.; Accadia, T.; Acernese, F.; Adams, C.; Adams, T.; et al. Constraints on Cosmic Strings from the LIGO-Virgo Gravitational-Wave Detectors. *Phys. Rev. Lett.* **2014**, *112*, 131101. [CrossRef]
238. Abbott, B.P.; Abbott, R.; Abbott, T.D.; Acernese, F.; Ackley, K.; Adams, C.; Adams, T.; Addesso, P.; Adhikari, R.X.; Adya, V.B.; et al. Constraints on cosmic strings using data from the first Advanced LIGO observing run. *Phys. Rev. D* **2018**, *97*, 102002. [CrossRef]
239. Abbott, B.P.; Abbott, R.; Abbott, T.D.; Acernese, F.; Ackley, K.; Adams, C.; Adams, T.; Addesso, P.; Adhikari, R.X.; Adya, V.B.; et al. Search for Tensor, Vector, and Scalar Polarizations in the Stochastic Gravitational-Wave Background. *Phys. Rev. Lett.* **2018**, *120*, 201102. [CrossRef]
240. Agarwal, D.; Suresh, J.; Mitra, S.; Ain, A. Upper limits on persistent gravitational waves using folded data and the full covariance matrix from Advanced LIGO's first two observing runs. *PRD* **2021**, *104*, 123018. [CrossRef]
241. Yang, K.Z.; Mandic, V.; Scarlata, C.; Banagiri, S. Searching for Cross-Correlation Between Stochastic Gravitational Wave Background and Galaxy Number Counts. *Mon. Not. R. Astron. Soc.* **2020**, *500*, 1666–1672. [CrossRef]
242. Kapadia, S.J.; Lal Pandey, K.; Suyama, T.; Kandhasamy, S.; Ajith, P. Search for the Stochastic Gravitational-wave Background Induced by Primordial Curvature Perturbations in LIGO's Second Observing Run. *Astrophys. J. Lett.* **2021**, *910*, L4. [CrossRef]
243. Covas, P.B.; Effler, A.; Goetz, E.; Meyers, P.M.; Neunzert, A.; Oliver, M.; Pearlstone, B.L.; Roma, V.J.; Schofield, R.M.; Adya, V.B.; et al. Identification and mitigation of narrow spectral artifacts that degrade searches for persistent gravitational waves in the first two observing runs of Advanced LIGO. *Phys. Rev. D* **2018**, *97*. [CrossRef]
244. Available online: https://dcc.ligo.org/T2000384/public (accessed on 1 November 2021).
245. Matas, A.; Dvorkin, I.; Regimbau, T.; Romero, A. Applying Gating to Stochastic Searches in O3. 2021. Available online: https://dcc.ligo.org/P2000546/public (accessed on 1 November 2021).
246. LIGO Scientific Collaboration; Virgo Collaboration; KAGRA Collaboration. Data for Upper Limits on the Isotropic Gravitational-Wave Background from Advanced LIGO's and Advanced Virgo's Third Observing Run. 2021. Available online: https://dcc.ligo.org/LIGO-G2001287 (accessed on 1 November 2021).
247. Will, C.M. The Confrontation between General Relativity and Experiment. *Living Rev. Relativ.* **2014**, *17*, 4. [CrossRef]
248. Abbott, B.P.; Abbott, R.; Abbott, T.D.; Abraham, S.; Acernese, F.; Ackley, K.; Adams, C.; Adya, V.B.; Affeldt, C.; Agathos, M.; et al. Prospects for observing and localizing gravitational-wave transients with Advanced LIGO, Advanced Virgo and KAGRA. *Living Rev. Relativ.* **2020**, *23*, 3. [CrossRef]
249. Mukherjee, S.; Broadhurst, T.; Diego, J.M.; Silk, J.; Smoot, G.F. Inferring the lensing rate of LIGO-Virgo sources from the stochastic gravitational wave background. *Mon. Not. R. Astron. Soc.* **2021**, *501*, 2451–2466. [CrossRef]
250. Buscicchio, R.; Moore, C.J.; Pratten, G.; Schmidt, P.; Bianconi, M.; Vecchio, A. Constraining the lensing of binary black holes from their stochastic background. *Phys. Rev. Lett.* **2020**, *125*, 141102. [CrossRef]
251. Buscicchio, R.; Moore, C.J.; Pratten, G.; Schmidt, P.; Vecchio, A. Constraining the lensing of binary neutron stars from their stochastic background. *Phys. Rev. D* **2020**, *102*, 081501. [CrossRef]
252. Abbott, R.; Abbott, T.D.; Abraham, S.; Acernese, F.; Ackley, K.; Adams, A.; Adams, C.; Adhikari, R.X.; Adya, V.B.; Affeldt, C.; et al. GWTC-2: Compact Binary Coalescences Observed by LIGO and Virgo During the First Half of the Third Observing Run. *Phys. Rev. X* **2021**, *11*, 021053. [CrossRef]
253. Ade, P.A.; Aghanim, N.; Armitage-Caplan, C.; Arnaud, M.; Ashdown, M.; Atrio-Barandela, F.; Aumont, J.; Baccigalupi, C.; Banday, A.J.; Barreiro, R.B.; et al. Planck 2013 results. XXV. Searches for cosmic strings and other topological defects. *Astron. Astrophys.* **2014**, *571*, A25. [CrossRef]
254. Vaskonen, V.; Veermäe, H. Lower bound on the primordial black hole merger rate. *Phys. Rev. D* **2020**, *101*, 043015. [CrossRef]
255. Carr, B.; Kohri, K.; Sendouda, Y.; Yokoyama, J. Constraints on Primordial Black Holes. *Rep. Prog. Phys.* **2021**, *84*, 116902. [CrossRef]
256. LIGO Scientific Collaboration; Virgo Collaboration; KAGRA Collaboration. Data Products and Supplemental Information for O3 Stochastic Directional Paper. 2021. Available online: https://dcc.ligo.org/LIGO-G2002165 (accessed on 1 November 2021).
257. Abbott, B.; Abbott, R.; Abbott, T.; Acernese, F.; Ackley, K.; Adams, C.; Adams, T.; Addesso, P.; Adhikari, R.; Adya, V.; et al. Search for gravitational waves from Scorpius X-1 in the first Advanced LIGO observing run with a hidden Markov model. *Phys. Rev. D* **2017**, *95*, 122003. [CrossRef]

258. Sun, L.; Melatos, A.; Lasky, P.D.; Chung, C.T.Y.; Darman, N.S. Cross-correlation search for continuous gravitational waves from a compact object in SNR 1987A in LIGO Science run 5. *Phys. Rev. D* **2016**, *94*, 082004. [CrossRef]
259. Aasi, J.; Abadie, J.; Abbott, B.P.; Abbott, R.; Abbott, T.; Abernathy, M.R.; Accadia, T.; Acernese, F.; Adams, C.; Adams, T.; et al. Directed search for continuous gravitational waves from the Galactic center. *Phys. Rev. D* **2013**, *88*, 102002. [CrossRef]
260. Abbott, R.; Abbott, T.D.; Acernese, F.; Ackley, K.; Adams, C.; Adhikari, N.; Adhikari, R.X.; Adya, V.B.; Affeldt, C.; Agarwal, D.; et al. All-sky, all-frequency directional search for persistent gravitational-waves from Advanced LIGO's and Advanced Virgo's first three observing runs. *arXiv* **2021**, arXiv:2110.09834.
261. Tenorio, R.; Keitel, D.; Sintes, A.M. Application of a hierarchical MCMC follow-up to Advanced LIGO continuous gravitational-wave candidates. *Phys. Rev. D* **2021**, *104*, 084012. [CrossRef]
262. Burke-Spolaor, S.; Taylor, S.R.; Charisi, M.; Dolch, T.; Hazboun, J.S.; Holgado, A.M.; Kelley, L.Z.; Lazio, T.J.W.; Madison, D.R.; McMann, N.; et al. The astrophysics of nanohertz gravitational waves. *A&A Rev.* **2019**, *27*, 5. [CrossRef]
263. Taylor, S.R. The Nanohertz Gravitational Wave Astronomer. *arXiv* **2021**, arXiv:2105.13270.
264. Sazhin, M.V. Opportunities for detecting ultralong gravitational waves. *Sov. Astron.* **1978**, *22*, 36–38.
265. Detweiler, S. Pulsar timing measurements and the search for gravitational waves. *ApJ* **1979**, *234*, 1100–1104. [CrossRef]
266. Siemens, X.; Ellis, J.; Jenet, F.; Romano, J.D. The stochastic background: Scaling laws and time to detection for pulsar timing arrays. *Class. Quantum Gravity* **2013**, *30*, 224015. [CrossRef]
267. Bailes, M.; Jameson, A.; Abbate, F.; Barr, E.D.; Bhat, N.D.R.; Bondonneau, L.; Burgay, M.; Buchner, S.J.; Camilo, F.; Champion, D.J.; et al. The MeerKAT telescope as a pulsar facility: System verification and early science results from MeerTime. *PASA* **2020**, *37*, e028. [CrossRef]
268. Jonas, J.L. MeerKAT - The South African Array With Composite Dishes and Wide-Band Single Pixel Feeds. *IEEE Proc.* **2009**, *97*, 1522–1530. [CrossRef]
269. Jenet, F.A.; Hobbs, G.B.; van Straten, W.; Manchester, R.N.; Bailes, M.; Verbiest, J.P.W.; Edwards, R.T.; Hotan, A.W.; Sarkissian, J.M.; Ord, S.M. Upper Bounds on the Low-Frequency Stochastic Gravitational Wave Background from Pulsar Timing Observations: Current Limits and Future Prospects. *ApJ* **2006**, *653*, 1571–1576. [CrossRef]
270. Demorest, P.B.; Ferdman, R.D.; Gonzalez, M.E.; Nice, D.; Ransom, S.; Stairs, I.H.; Arzoumanian, Z.; Brazier, A.; Burke-Spolaor, S.; Chamberlin, S.J.; et al. Limits on the Stochastic Gravitational Wave Background from the North American Nanohertz Observatory for Gravitational Waves. *ApJ* **2013**, *762*, 94. [CrossRef]
271. Shannon, R.M.; Ravi, V.; Coles, W.A.; Hobbs, G.; Keith, M.J.; Manchester, R.N.; Wyithe, J.S.B.; Bailes, M.; Bhat, N.D.R.; Burke-Spolaor, S.; et al. Gravitational-wave limits from pulsar timing constrain supermassive black hole evolution. *Science* **2013**, *342*, 334–337. [CrossRef]
272. Lentati, L.; Taylor, S.R.; Mingarelli, C.M.F.; Sesana, A.; Sanidas, S.A.; Vecchio, A.; Caballero, R.N.; Lee, K.J.; van Haasteren, R.; Babak, S.; et al. European Pulsar Timing Array limits on an isotropic stochastic gravitational-wave background. *MNRAS* **2015**, *453*, 2576–2598. [CrossRef]
273. NANOGrav Collaboration; Arzoumanian, Z.; Brazier, A.; Burke-Spolaor, S.; Chamberlin, S.; Chatterjee, S.; Christy, B.; Cordes, J.M.; Cornish, N.; Crowter, K.; et al. The NANOGrav Nine-year Data Set: Observations, Arrival Time Measurements, and Analysis of 37 Millisecond Pulsars. *ApJ* **2015**, *813*, 65. [CrossRef]
274. Shannon, R.M.; Ravi, V.; Lentati, L.T.; Lasky, P.D.; Hobbs, G.; Kerr, M.; Manchester, R.N.; Coles, W.A.; Levin, Y.; Bailes, M.; et al. Gravitational waves from binary supermassive black holes missing in pulsar observations. *Science* **2015**, *349*, 1522–1525. [CrossRef] [PubMed]
275. Chen, S.; Caballero, R.N.; Guo, Y.J.; Chalumeau, A.; Liu, K.; Shaifullah, G.; Lee, K.J.; Babak, S.; Desvignes, G.; Parthasarathy, A.; et al. Common-red-signal analysis with 24-yr high-precision timing of the European Pulsar Timing Array: Inferences in the stochastic gravitational-wave background search. *MNRAS* **2021**, *508*, 4970–4993. [CrossRef]
276. Antoniadis, J.; Arzoumanian, Z.; Babak, S.; Bailes, M.; Bak Nielsen, A.S.; Baker, P.T.; Bassa, C.G.; Bécsy, B.; Berthereau, A.; Bonetti, M.; et al. The International Pulsar Timing Array second data release: Search for an isotropic gravitational wave background. *MNRAS* **2022**, *510*, 4873–4887. [CrossRef]
277. Shannon, R.M.; Osłowski, S.; Dai, S.; Bailes, M.; Hobbs, G.; Manchester, R.N.; van Straten, W.; Raithel, C.A.; Ravi, V.; Toomey, L.; et al. Limitations in timing precision due to single-pulse shape variability in millisecond pulsars. *MNRAS* **2014**, *443*, 1463–1481. [CrossRef]
278. Lam, M.T.; McLaughlin, M.A.; Arzoumanian, Z.; Blumer, H.; Brook, P.R.; Cromartie, H.T.; Demorest, P.B.; DeCesar, M.E.; Dolch, T.; Ellis, J.A.; et al. The NANOGrav 12.5 yr Data Set: The Frequency Dependence of Pulse Jitter in Precision Millisecond Pulsars. *ApJ* **2019**, *872*, 193. [CrossRef]
279. Kerr, M.; Reardon, D.J.; Hobbs, G.; Shannon, R.M.; Manchester, R.N.; Dai, S.; Russell, C.J.; Zhang, S.; van Straten, W.; Osłowski, S.; et al. The Parkes Pulsar Timing Array project: Second data release. *PASA* **2020**, *37*, e020. [CrossRef]
280. Lentati, L.; Shannon, R.M.; Coles, W.A.; Verbiest, J.P.W.; van Haasteren, R.; Ellis, J.A.; Caballero, R.N.; Manchester, R.N.; Arzoumanian, Z.; Babak, S.; et al. From spin noise to systematics: Stochastic processes in the first International Pulsar Timing Array data release. *MNRAS* **2016**, *458*, 2161–2187. [CrossRef]
281. Goncharov, B.; Zhu, X.J.; Thrane, E. Is there a spectral turnover in the spin noise of millisecond pulsars? *MNRAS* **2020**, *497*, 3264–3272. [CrossRef]

282. Chalumeau, A.; Babak, S.; Petiteau, A.; Chen, S.; Samajdar, A.; Caballero, R.N.; Theureau, G.; Guillemot, L.; Desvignes, G.; Parthasarathy, A.; et al. Noise analysis in the European Pulsar Timing Array data release 2 and its implications on the gravitational-wave background search. *MNRAS* **2022**, *509*, 5538–5558. [CrossRef]
283. Haskell, B.; Melatos, A. Models of pulsar glitches. *Int. J. Mod. Phys. D* **2015**, *24*, 1530008. [CrossRef]
284. Hazboun, J.S.; Simon, J.; Siemens, X.; Romano, J.D. Model Dependence of Bayesian Gravitational-wave Background Statistics for Pulsar Timing Arrays. *ApJ* **2020**, *905*, L6. [CrossRef]
285. Goncharov, B.; Reardon, D.J.; Shannon, R.M.; Zhu, X.J.; Thrane, E.; Bailes, M.; Bhat, N.D.R.; Dai, S.; Hobbs, G.; Kerr, M.; et al. Identifying and mitigating noise sources in precision pulsar timing data sets. *MNRAS* **2021**, *502*, 478–493. [CrossRef]
286. Meyers, P.M.; O'Neill, N.J.; Melatos, A.; Evans, R.J. Rapid parameter estimation of a two-component neutron star model with spin wandering using a Kalman filter. *MNRAS* **2021**, *506*, 3349–3363. [CrossRef]
287. Tiburzi, C.; Hobbs, G.; Kerr, M.; Coles, W.A.; Dai, S.; Manchester, R.N.; Possenti, A.; Shannon, R.M.; You, X.P. A study of spatial correlations in pulsar timing array data. *MNRAS* **2016**, *455*, 4339–4350. [CrossRef]
288. Guo, Y.J.; Li, G.Y.; Lee, K.J.; Caballero, R.N. Studying the Solar system dynamics using pulsar timing arrays and the LINIMOSS dynamical model. *MNRAS* **2019**, *489*, 5573–5581. [CrossRef]
289. Vallisneri, M.; Taylor, S.R.; Simon, J.; Folkner, W.M.; Park, R.S.; Cutler, C.; Ellis, J.A.; Lazio, T.J.W.; Vigeland, S.J.; Aggarwal, K.; et al. Modeling the Uncertainties of Solar System Ephemerides for Robust Gravitational-wave Searches with Pulsar-timing Arrays. *ApJ* **2020**, *893*, 112. [CrossRef]
290. Hazboun, J.S.; Romano, J.D.; Smith, T.L. Realistic sensitivity curves for pulsar timing arrays. *PRD* **2019**, *100*, 104028. [CrossRef]
291. Hazboun, J.; Romano, J.; Smith, T. Hasasia: A Python package for Pulsar Timing Array Sensitivity Curves. *J. Open Source Softw.* **2019**, *4*, 1775. [CrossRef]
292. Verbiest, J.P.W.; Shaifullah, G.M. Measurement uncertainty in pulsar timing array experiments. *Class. Quantum Gravity* **2018**, *35*, 133001. [CrossRef]
293. Lommen, A.N. Pulsar timing arrays: The promise of gravitational wave detection. *Rep. Prog. Phys.* **2015**, *78*, 124901. [CrossRef] [PubMed]
294. Sesana, A.; Vecchio, A. Measuring the parameters of massive black hole binary systems with pulsar timing array observations of gravitational waves. *PRD* **2010**, *81*, 104008. [CrossRef]
295. Mingarelli, C.M.F.; Lazio, T.J.W.; Sesana, A.; Greene, J.E.; Ellis, J.A.; Ma, C.P.; Croft, S.; Burke-Spolaor, S.; Taylor, S.R. The local nanohertz gravitational-wave landscape from supermassive black hole binaries. *Nat. Astron.* **2017**, *1*, 886–892. [CrossRef]
296. Arzoumanian, Z.; Baker, P.T.; Blumer, H.; Bécsy, B.; Brazier, A.; Brook, P.R.; Burke-Spolaor, S.; Charisi, M.; Chatterjee, S.; Chen, S.; et al. Searching for Gravitational Waves from Cosmological Phase Transitions with the NANOGrav 12.5-Year Dataset. *PRL* **2021**, *127*, 251302. [CrossRef] [PubMed]
297. Xue, X.; Bian, L.; Shu, J.; Yuan, Q.; Zhu, X.; Bhat, N.D.R.; Dai, S.; Feng, Y.; Goncharov, B.; Hobbs, G.; et al. Constraining Cosmological Phase Transitions with the Parkes Pulsar Timing Array. *PRL* **2021**, *127*, 251303. [CrossRef] [PubMed]
298. Moore, C.J.; Vecchio, A. Ultra-low-frequency gravitational waves from cosmological and astrophysical processes. *Nat. Astron.* **2021**, *5*, 1268–1274. [CrossRef]
299. Chen, Z.C.; Yuan, C.; Huang, Q.G. Non-tensorial gravitational wave background in NANOGrav 12.5-year data set. *Sci. China Physics, Mech. Astron.* **2021**, *64*, 120412. [CrossRef]
300. Chen, Z.C.; Wu, Y.M.; Huang, Q.G. Searching for Isotropic Stochastic Gravitational-Wave Background in the International Pulsar Timing Array Second Data Release. *arXiv* **2021**, arXiv:2109.00296.
301. Wu, Y.M.; Chen, Z.C.; Huang, Q.G. Constraining the Polarization of Gravitational Waves with the Parkes Pulsar Timing Array Second Data Release. *arXiv* **2021**, arXiv:2108.10518.
302. Arzoumanian, Z.; Baker, P.T.; Blumer, H.; Bécsy, B.; Brazier, A.; Brook, P.R.; Burke-Spolaor, S.; Charisi, M.; Chatterjee, S.; Chen, S.; et al. The NANOGrav 12.5-year Data Set: Search for Non-Einsteinian Polarization Modes in the Gravitational-wave Background. *ApJ* **2021**, *923*, L22. [CrossRef]
303. Aggarwal, N.; Aguiar, O.D.; Bauswein, A.; Cella, G.; Clesse, S.; Cruise, A.M.; Domcke, V.; Figueroa, D.G.; Geraci, A.; Goryachev, M.; et al. Challenges and opportunities of gravitational-wave searches at MHz to GHz frequencies. *Living Rev. Relativ.* **2021**, *24*, 4. [CrossRef]
304. Weber, J. Detection and Generation of Gravitational Waves. *Phys. Rev.* **1960**, *117*, 306–313. [CrossRef]
305. Weber, J. Evidence for discovery of gravitational radiation. *Phys. Rev. Lett.* **1969**, *22*, 1320–1324. [CrossRef]
306. Aguiar, O.D. The Past, Present and Future of the Resonant-Mass Gravitational Wave Detectors. *Res. Astron. Astrophys.* **2011**, *11*, 1–42. [CrossRef]
307. Harms, J.; Ambrosino, F.; Angelini, L.; Braito, V.; Branchesi, M.; Brocato, E.; Cappellaro, E.; Coccia, E.; Coughlin, M.; Della Ceca, R.; et al. Lunar Gravitational-wave Antenna. *Astrophys. J.* **2021**, *910*, 1. [CrossRef]
308. Jani, K.; Loeb, A. Gravitational-Wave Lunar Observatory for Cosmology. *J. Cosmol. Astropart. Phys.* **2021**, *2021*, 044. [CrossRef]
309. Sesana, A.; Korsakova, N.; Sedda, M.A.; Baibhav, V.; Barausse, E.; Barke, S.; Berti, E.; Bonetti, M.; Capelo, P.R.; Caprini, C.; et al. Unveiling the gravitational universe at μ-Hz frequencies. *Exper. Astron.* **2021**, *51*, 1333–1383. [CrossRef]
310. Book, L.G.; Flanagan, E.E. Astrometric Effects of a Stochastic Gravitational Wave Background. *Phys. Rev. D* **2011**, *83*, 024024. [CrossRef]

311. Moore, C.J.; Mihaylov, D.P.; Lasenby, A.; Gilmore, G. Astrometric Search Method for Individually Resolvable Gravitational Wave Sources with Gaia. *Phys. Rev. Lett.* **2017**, *119*, 261102. [CrossRef]
312. Garcia-Bellido, J.; Murayama, H.; White, G. Exploring the Early Universe with Gaia and THEIA. *J. Cosmol. Astropart. Phys.* **2021**, *2021*, 023. [CrossRef]
313. Graham, P.W.; Hogan, J.M.; Kasevich, M.A.; Rajendran, S.; Romani, R.W. Mid-band gravitational wave detection with precision atomic sensors. *arXiv* **2017**, arXiv:1711.02225.
314. Abe, M.; Adamson, P.; Borcean, M.; Bortoletto, D.; Bridges, K.; Carman, S.P.; Chattopadhyay, S.; Coleman, J.; Curfman, N.M.; DeRose, K.; et al. Matter-wave Atomic Gradiometer Interferometric Sensor (MAGIS-100). *Quantum Sci. Technol.* **2021**, *6*, 044003. [CrossRef]
315. Vitale, S.; Farr, W.M.; Ng, K.K.Y.; Rodriguez, C.L. Measuring the Star Formation Rate with Gravitational Waves from Binary Black Holes. *ApJ* **2019**, *886*, L1. [CrossRef]
316. Regimbau, T.; Evans, M.; Christensen, N.; Katsavounidis, E.; Sathyaprakash, B.; Vitale, S. Digging deeper: Observing primordial gravitational waves below the binary black hole produced stochastic background. *Phys. Rev. Lett.* **2017**, *118*, 151105. [CrossRef] [PubMed]
317. Ackley, K.; Adya, V.B.; Agrawal, P.; Altin, P.; Ashton, G.; Bailes, M.; Baltinas, E.; Barbuio, A.; Beniwal, D.; Blair, C.; et al. Neutron Star Extreme Matter Observatory: A kilohertz-band gravitational-wave detector in the global network. *Publ. Astron. Soc. Austral.* **2020**, *37*, e047. [CrossRef]
318. Maggiore, M.; Van Den Broeck, C.; Bartolo, N.; Belgacem, E.; Bertacca, D.; Bizouard, M.A.; Branchesi, M.; Clesse, S.; Foffa, S.; García-Bellido, J.; et al. Science Case for the Einstein Telescope. *JCAP* **2020**, *03*, 050. [CrossRef]
319. Cutler, C.; Harms, J. BBO and the neutron-star-binary subtraction problem. *Phys. Rev. D* **2006**, *73*, 042001. [CrossRef]
320. Sachdev, S.; Regimbau, T.; Sathyaprakash, B.S. Subtracting compact binary foreground sources to reveal primordial gravitational-wave backgrounds. *PRD* **2020**, *102*, 024051. [CrossRef]
321. Sharma, A.; Harms, J. Searching for cosmological gravitational-wave backgrounds with third-generation detectors in the presence of an astrophysical foreground. *PRD* **2020**, *102*, 063009. [CrossRef]
322. Raidal, M.; Spethmann, C.; Vaskonen, V.; Veermäe, H. Formation and evolution of primordial black hole binaries in the early universe. *J. Cosmol. Astropart. Phys.* **2019**, *2019*, 018. [CrossRef]
323. Mandic, V.; Bird, S.; Cholis, I. Stochastic Gravitational-Wave Background due to Primordial Binary Black Hole Mergers. *Phys. Rev. Lett.* **2016**, *117*, 201102. [CrossRef] [PubMed]
324. Ali-Haïmoud, Y.; Kovetz, E.D.; Kamionkowski, M. Merger rate of primordial black-hole binaries. *Phys. Rev. D* **2017**, *96*, 123523. [CrossRef]
325. De Luca, V.; Franciolini, G.; Pani, P.; Riotto, A. The Minimum Testable Abundance of Primordial Black Holes at Future Gravitational-Wave Detectors. *J. Cosmol. Astropart. Phys.* **2021**, *2021*, 039. [CrossRef]
326. Ng, K.K.Y.; Chen, S.; Goncharov, B.; Dupletsa, U.; Borhanian, S.; Branchesi, M.; Harms, J.; Maggiore, M.; Sathyaprakash, B.S.; Vitale, S. On the single-event-based identification of primordial black hole mergers at cosmological distances. *arXiv* **2021**, arXiv:2108.07276.
327. Biscoveanu, S.; Talbot, C.; Thrane, E.; Smith, R. Measuring the primordial gravitational-wave background in the presence of astrophysical foregrounds. *Phys. Rev. Lett.* **2020**, *125*, 241101. [CrossRef] [PubMed]
328. Mukherjee, S.; Silk, J. Can we distinguish astrophysical from primordial black holes via the stochastic gravitational wave background? *Mon. Not. R. Astron. Soc.* **2021**, *506*, 3977–3985. [CrossRef]
329. Mukherjee, S.; Meinema, M.S.P.; Silk, J. Prospects of discovering sub-solar primordial black holes using the stochastic gravitational wave background from third-generation detectors. *arXiv* **2021**, arXiv:2107.02181.
330. Mukherjee, S.; Silk, J. Fundamental physics using the temporal gravitational wave background. *Phys. Rev. D* **2021**, *104*, 063518. [CrossRef]
331. Schumann, W.O. Über die strahlungslosen Eigenschwingungen einer leitenden Kugel, die von einer Luftschicht und einer Ionosphärenhülle umgeben ist. *Z. Naturforschung Teil A* **1952**, *7*, 149–154. [CrossRef]
332. Schumann, W.O.; König, H. Über die Beobachtung von "atmospherics" bei geringsten Frequenzen. *Naturwissenschaften* **1954**, *41*, 183–184. [CrossRef]
333. Christensen, N. Measuring the stochastic gravitational radiation background with laser interferometric antennas. *Phys. Rev. D* **1992**, *46*, 5250–5266. [CrossRef] [PubMed]
334. Thrane, E.; Christensen, N.; Schofield, R.M.S. Correlated magnetic noise in global networks of gravitational-wave detectors: Observations and implications. *PRD* **2013**, *87*, 123009. [CrossRef]
335. Thrane, E.; Christensen, N.; Schofield, R.M.S.; Effler, A. Correlated noise in networks of gravitational-wave detectors: Subtraction and mitigation. *PRD* **2014**, *90*, 023013. [CrossRef]
336. Coughlin, M.W.; Christensen, N.L.; De Rosa, R.; Fiori, I.; Gołkowski, M.; Guidry, M.; Harms, J.; Kubisz, J.; Kulak, A.; Mlynarczyk, J.; et al. Subtraction of correlated noise in global networks of gravitational-wave interferometers. *Class. Quantum Gravity* **2016**, *33*, 224003. [CrossRef]
337. Himemoto, Y.; Taruya, A. Impact of correlated magnetic noise on the detection of stochastic gravitational waves: Estimation based on a simple analytical model. *PRD* **2017**, *96*, 022004. [CrossRef]

338. Coughlin, M.W.; Cirone, A.; Meyers, P.; Atsuta, S.; Boschi, V.; Chincarini, A.; Christensen, N.L.; De Rosa, R.; Effler, A.; Fiori, I.; et al. Measurement and subtraction of Schumann resonances at gravitational-wave interferometers. *PRD* **2018**, *97*, 102007. [CrossRef]
339. Himemoto, Y.; Taruya, A. Correlated magnetic noise from anisotropic lightning sources and the detection of stochastic gravitational waves. *PRD* **2019**, *100*, 082001. [CrossRef]
340. Himemoto, Y.; Nishizawa, A.; Taruya, A. Impacts of overlapping gravitational-wave signals on the parameter estimation: Toward the search for cosmological backgrounds. *PRD* **2021**, *104*, 044010. [CrossRef]
341. Janssens, K.; Martinovic, K.; Christensen, N.; Meyers, P.M.; Sakellariadou, M. Impact of Schumann resonances on the Einstein Telescope and projections for the magnetic coupling function. *PRD* **2021**, *104*, 122006. [CrossRef]
342. Saulson, P.R. Terrestrial gravitational noise on a gravitational wave antenna. *PRD* **1984**, *30*, 732–736. [CrossRef]
343. Hughes, S.A.; Thorne, K.S. Seismic gravity-gradient noise in interferometric gravitational-wave detectors. *PRD* **1998**, *58*, 122002. [CrossRef]
344. Harms, J. Terrestrial gravity fluctuations. *Living Rev. Relativ.* **2019**, *22*, 6. [CrossRef]
345. Amann, F.; Bonsignorio, F.; Bulik, T.; Bulten, H.J.; Cuccuru, S.; Dassargues, A.; DeSalvo, R.; Fenyvesi, E.; Fidecaro, F.; Fiori, I.; et al. Site-selection criteria for the Einstein Telescope. *Rev. Sci. Instruments* **2020**, *91*, 094504. [CrossRef] [PubMed]
346. Driggers, J.C.; Harms, J.; Adhikari, R.X. Subtraction of Newtonian noise using optimized sensor arrays. *PRD* **2012**, *86*, 102001. [CrossRef]
347. Coughlin, M.; Harms, J.; Christensen, N.; Dergachev, V.; DeSalvo, R.; Kandhasamy, S.; Mandic, V. Wiener filtering with a seismic underground array at the Sanford Underground Research Facility. *Class. Quantum Gravity* **2014**, *31*, 215003. [CrossRef]
348. Coughlin, M.; Mukund, N.; Harms, J.; Driggers, J.; Adhikari, R.; Mitra, S. Towards a first design of a Newtonian-noise cancellation system for Advanced LIGO. *Class. Quantum Gravity* **2016**, *33*, 244001. [CrossRef]
349. Coughlin, M.W.; Harms, J.; Driggers, J.; McManus, D.J.; Mukund, N.; Ross, M.P.; Slagmolen, B.J.J.; Venkateswara, K. Implications of Dedicated Seismometer Measurements on Newtonian-Noise Cancellation for Advanced LIGO. *PRL* **2018**, *121*, 221104. [CrossRef]
350. Badaracco, F.; Harms, J.; Bertolini, A.; Bulik, T.; Fiori, I.; Idzkowski, B.; Kutynia, A.; Nikliborc, K.; Paoletti, F.; Paoli, A.; et al. Machine learning for gravitational-wave detection: Surrogate Wiener filtering for the prediction and optimized cancellation of Newtonian noise at Virgo. *Class. Quantum Gravity* **2020**, *37*, 195016. [CrossRef]
351. Harms, J.; Hild, S. Passive Newtonian noise suppression for gravitational-wave observatories based on shaping of the local topography. *Class. Quantum Gravity* **2014**, *31*, 185011. [CrossRef]
352. Badaracco, F.; Harms, J. Optimization of seismometer arrays for the cancellation of Newtonian noise from seismic body waves. *Class. Quantum Gravity* **2019**, *36*, 145006. [CrossRef]
353. Harms, J.; Venkateswara, K. Newtonian-noise cancellation in large-scale interferometric GW detectors using seismic tiltmeters. *Class. Quantum Gravity* **2016**, *33*, 234001. [CrossRef]
354. Creighton, T. Tumbleweeds and airborne gravitational noise sources for LIGO. *Class. Quantum Gravity* **2008**, *25*, 125011. [CrossRef]
355. Fiorucci, D.; Harms, J.; Barsuglia, M.; Fiori, I.; Paoletti, F. Impact of infrasound atmospheric noise on gravity detectors used for astrophysical and geophysical applications. *PRD* **2018**, *97*, 062003. [CrossRef]
356. Muratore, M.; Vetrugno, D.; Vitale, S. Revisitation of time delay interferometry combinations that suppress laser noise in LISA. *Class. Quantum Gravity* **2020**, *37*, 185019. [CrossRef]
357. Estabrook, F.B.; Tinto, M.; Armstrong, J.W. Time-delay analysis of LISA gravitational wave data: Elimination of spacecraft motion effects. *Phys. Rev. D* **2000**, *62*, 042002. [CrossRef]
358. Prince, T.A.; Tinto, M.; Larson, S.L.; Armstrong, J. The LISA optimal sensitivity. *Phys. Rev. D* **2002**, *66*, 122002. [CrossRef]
359. Sylvestre, J.; Tinto, M. Noise characterization for LISA. *Phys. Rev. D* **2003**, *68*, 102002. [CrossRef]
360. Crowder, J.; Cornish, N.J. LISA source confusion. *Phys. Rev. D* **2004**, *70*, 082004. [CrossRef]
361. Chen, Z.C.; Huang, F.; Huang, Q.G. Stochastic Gravitational-wave Background from Binary Black Holes and Binary Neutron Stars and Implications for LISA. *Astrophys. J.* **2019**, *871*, 97. [CrossRef]
362. Caprini, C.; Chala, M.; Dorsch, G.C.; Hindmarsh, M.; Huber, S.J.; Konstandin, T.; Kozaczuk, J.; Nardini, G.; No, J.M.; Rummukainen, K.; et al. Detecting gravitational waves from cosmological phase transitions with LISA: An update. *JCAP* **2020**, *03*, 024. [CrossRef]
363. Boileau, G.; Jenkins, A.C.; Sakellariadou, M.; Meyer, R.; Christensen, N. Ability of LISA to detect a gravitational-wave background of cosmological origin: The cosmic string case. *Phys. Rev. D* **2022**, *105*, 023510. [CrossRef]
364. Crowder, J.; Cornish, N. A Solution to the Galactic Foreground Problem for LISA. *Phys. Rev. D* **2007**, *75*, 043008. [CrossRef]
365. LISA Data Challenge Manual. Available online: https://lisa-ldc.lal.in2p3.fr/static/data/pdf/LDC-manual-Sangria.pdf (accessed on 1 November 2021).

MDPI
St. Alban-Anlage 66
4052 Basel
Switzerland
Tel. +41 61 683 77 34
Fax +41 61 302 89 18
www.mdpi.com

Galaxies Editorial Office
E-mail: galaxies@mdpi.com
www.mdpi.com/journal/galaxies